ANNUAL REVIEW OF PSYCHOLOGY

ANNUAL REVIEW OF PSYCHOLOGY

MARK R. ROSENZWEIG, *Editor*
University of California, Berkeley

LYMAN W. PORTER, *Editor*
University of California, Irvine

VOLUME 27

1976

ANNUAL REVIEWS INC.   4139 EL CAMINO WAY   PALO ALTO, CALIFORNIA 94306

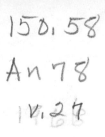

ANNUAL REVIEWS INC.
Palo Alto, California, USA

International Standard Book Number: 0–8243–0227–3
Library of Congress Catalog Card Number: 50–13143

REPRINTS

The conspicuous number aligned in the margin with the title of each article in this
volume is a key for use in ordering reprints. Available reprints are priced at the
uniform rate of $1 each postpaid. Effective January 1, 1975, the minimum acceptable
reprint order is 10 reprints and/or $10.00, prepaid. A quantity discount is available.

PRINTED AND BOUND IN THE UNITED STATES OF AMERICA

PREFACE

In 1975 the *Annual Review of Psychology* introduced an innovative feature, namely, two special review topics not covered in the Master Plan, but ones considered to be of especially timely interest. These articles were prepared on shorter deadlines than the other chapters so that they could include the most recent developments. This year we offer two more "current topic" chapters: "Psychology and the Law" and "Program Evaluation." Three such chapters are planned for 1977. Since this type of chapter is a new departure, the editors would be interested in receiving readers' comments regarding the inclusion of such articles in each volume.

Another kind of special chapter is also included in this volume. As has been done from time to time in the past, we present a review of developments in psychology in a specific country. This year the country is France, a particularly appropriate choice, we feel, because the 21st International Congress of Psychology will be held in Paris in July 1976.

Topics to be reviewed in successive volumes of the *Annual Review of Psychology* are selected according to a Master Plan, which was designed to serve as a guide rather than as a rigid prescription for chapter allocations. As further proof of its flexibility, the Plan is subject to review and modification at each of the annual meetings of the Editorial Committee. The current form of the Plan appears on the following pages.

The Editorial Committee considers its primary function to be that of nominating highly qualified authors, who are then given wide discretion, but limited space, for a selective survey of the literature and a critical analysis of the state of the area assigned. Authors frequently select a specialized subsection of the topic for intensive review. Thus any given volume may appear to emphasize some topics while slighting others, but a broader view over a span of several years shows a well-rounded portrayal of up-to-date developments in psychological research and theory.

Each year one member of the Editorial Committee completes a five-year term of service. The person rotating off the Committee at the close of 1975 was Leona Tyler. Her vast knowledge of a variety of areas of psychology and her wide acquaintance-ship with psychologists have contributed greatly to the work of the Committee. We are sorry to lose her, but welcome her replacement on the Committee.

L.W.P.

M.R.R.

MASTER PLAN

*The numbers represent the intervals in years between successive chapters. The Xs indicate only occasional appearance.

CHAPTERS PLANNED FOR NEXT
ANNUAL REVIEW OF PSYCHOLOGY

VOLUME 28 (1977)

CONTENTS

ANNUAL REVIEWS INC. is a nonprofit corporation established to promote the advancement of the sciences. Beginning in 1932 with the *Annual Review of Biochemistry,* the Company has pursued as its principal function the publication of high quality, reasonably priced Annual Review volumes. The volumes are organized by Editors and Editorial Committees who invite qualified authors to contribute critical articles reviewing significant developments within each major discipline.

Annual Reviews Inc. is administered by a Board of Directors whose members serve without compensation.

Annual Reviews are published in the following sciences: Anthropology, Astronomy and Astrophysics, Biochemistry, Biophysics and Bioengineering, Earth and Planetary Sciences, Ecology and Systematics, Energy, Entomology, Fluid Mechanics, Genetics, Materials Science, Medicine, Microbiology, Nuclear Science, Pharmacology and Toxicology, Physical Chemistry, Physiology, Phytopathology, Plant Physiology, Psychology, and Sociology. In addition, two special volumes have been published by Annual Reviews Inc.: *History of Entomology* (1973) and *The Excitement and Fascination of Science* (1965).

PERSONALITY ❖246

Lee Sechrest[1]
Department of Psychology, Florida State University, Tallahassee, Florida 32306

The task of reviewing the most recent year of work in personality is akin to the task of a wine buyer faced with the necessity of predicting what a newly processed batch of red Bordeaux is going to taste like in 8 or 10 years. The new product is raw, perhaps even unpleasant, and yet within it are the clues that will inform the discerning oenophile of its ultimate character and even how long it will take to get there. Would that the clues were a bit more evident in personality theory and research. Or else that this reviewer were more discerning.

Upon first undertaking the assignment of reviewing 1974's product, I thought to take a look at the work of 1965 (the first year of publication of the *Journal of Personality and Social Psychology*) in hope that there might be in the perspective of time some useful clues as to what is enduring and worth reviewing in personality. Unfortunately, that quick overview of *Personality 1965* did not offer much of any utility nor any basis for encouragement about 1974. I will not attempt here to give quantitative data, even where I have them, but I do want to convey two or three impressions which helped to condition my attitudes in undertaking this review.

First, the themes of research have changed somewhat. Hypnosis loomed larger in the literature of 1965, as did conformity and need for approval. Obesity was missing then and so was attribution theory and so largely was sex-role research. Research on aggression was only just beginning to pick up, and locus of control had not yet been the subject of a literature review. Now why have the themes changed? If it were because issues have been resolved, because important phenomena are now so well understood that they no longer merit attention, it would be cause for encouragement—rejoicing perhaps. Alas, one cannot escape the conclusion that investigators ran out of steam, that issues were abandoned, and that problems were never resolved. If that conclusion is not justified, then we badly need some articles

[1]The writer wishes to acknowledge the many stimulating discussions with his colleagues, Russell D. Clark III and Steven G. West, out of which this chapter grew. In addition, thanks must be extended to David Sofferin for bibliographic and other help.
Preparation of this chapter was supported by Research Grant No. HS01628.

1

explaining conformity, hypnosis, etc for those of us who do not yet understand them fully. Let me suggest here that far too often the innovative, motivated investigators who initiate a promising line of research tire of it after 5 years or so, letting it fall into the hands of the less talented, the desultory seekers of the dissertation topic, and the dilettantes, who have not the insight, the ability, and the drive to penetrate the methodological and conceptual obstacles that arise once the initial scientific debris is cleared. Where will our current "hot" topics be in 5 years when their progenitors have gone on to newer, more exciting things?

Second, the methods of studying personality have not changed much, and that is too bad. Correlation is still the method of choice for too many investigators, and experimental paradigms often have no counterpart outside the laboratory. Field experiments were rare in social psychology in 1965; they are frequent now. In personality they always have been and continue to be rare. Identical manipulations are often employed to produce purportedly different internal states, e.g. induced failure to produce "lowered self-esteem" and "anxiety." It would be an interesting experiment to mix up the methods sections of samples of 1965 and 1974 articles and then determine whether judges rating them on methodological adequacy would produce any indication of overall improvement over the 9 year span. I am forced to the conclusion that personality is not a sufficiently cumulative scientific field either with respect to content or method.

Third, most research—the *vast* proportion of research—in personality is inconsequential, trivial, and pointless even if it is well done. In the perspective of 9 years one can see that it matters not at all that most of it was ever done and published. In fact, as Garvey[2] and others have shown, we can also assume that even after publication most of the research was never even read by more than a handful of people. Now there are two things that can be said in this regard. All of science is wasteful, as indeed are most other processes of intellectual and creative production. Personality research probably is not worse in that regard, in its probability of survival, than patented inventions, copyrighted songs, published novels, works of art, and research in physical chemistry. Still it is saddening and discouraging to review in such a perspective literally thousands of pages from hundreds of published articles. A second point is that *some* of the work is of consequence. Some of it is seminal, heuristic, and fundamental to an important line of continuing thought and investigation. It is not easy, in the opinion of this reviewer, to tell in 1974 just what will have been demonstrated to have paid off 5 or 10 years later. Looking back on 1965 does not provide any very evident clues. One final, perhaps too personal, view on this matter: a great deal of what gets into our journals is of such little worth that surely it should be recognized for what it is at the time it is reviewed. Too much published work is methodologically so sloppy that its publication is an indictment of the editor and his referees, and too much other work is so evidently trivial in conception that no amount of methodological elegance makes it worth the attention

---

[2]Here and elsewhere in this chapter it is assumed that readers will be generally familiar with literature previous to 1974 and that specific citations can be safely omitted, thus conserving space for current citations.

it gets by its entombment in a journal.[3] We may not in fact have a genuine shortage of space in our journals.

But the 1965–1974 comparisons may not all be so discouraging. Two trends seemed noticeable. Research in personality may be growing in complexity, with the operation of more variables being considered simultaneously. (Curiously the use of the colon to punctuate within titles has also increased greatly, and more than in 1965, the colon in 1974 is used to suggest a paradox, a complication, or a juxtapositioning of argument and counter-argument.) Secondly, physiological concepts and measures are more and more involved in research in personality. Physiological measures used to supplement self-report measures not only point to the incompleteness or insufficiency of the latter, but they also lead to the discovery of other interesting processes involved in human functioning. Physiological and personality concepts are more often being interwoven in ways that may eventually provide a durable theoretical fabric with which to replace our tattered and outmoded remnants originally acquired in the early part of this century.

Personality theory is, in my estimation, in sad shape. When new textbooks come out, whether in personality or introductory psychology, the discussion of theory is almost invariably organized around presentations of Freud, Jung, Adler, the neo-Freudians, etc, with a usual bow toward the end in the direction of "social learning theory." In no other field purporting to be scientific are the current heroes of theory nearly all dead. And in every other field of science the current basic research is directed toward the testing of the theories being taught to students. Even in other areas of psychology things are nowhere near so bad as in personality. The theories of Pavlov, Watson, Tolman, and Hull are not taught because they are assumed to be correct, but rather for the historical perspective they afford in relation to current work. Why for so many psychologists in personality is the major theory one which was formulated more than a half century ago?

Current personality theorizing is modest in scope, perhaps overly so, with the result that research in personality is fragmentary and disconnected both within and across temporal units. Social learning theory does not seem to have provided enough integrating power to overcome the centrifugal forces that operate to keep lines of investigation separate and nonconverging. A case could be made for the notion that no special theory of personality is needed, and in fact much of social learning theory is simply the explication of those aspects of human behavior usually thought of as personality in terms of familiar concepts of learning and cognition. Still, some more generally integrating and rigorous theory would be welcome.

Readers will have concluded by now that I am not quite so optimistic about the field of personality as last year's reviewer, Rae Carlson. Perhaps part of the difference lies in our discrepant interests and orientations toward the field. I have focused my attention on the basic understanding of the nature and processes of personality and upon the legitimacy of our casual inferences. I am not so interested just now in research on the role of personality variables in marijuana smoking, success in

---

[3]By and large, this criticism does not apply to the *Journal of Personality and Social Psychology* and the *Journal of Personality,* although neither can be said to have an unblemished record for screening out the meretricious from among their published articles.

school, or recovery from cancer. Not that such research is of no value, but it scarcely ever contributes anything to our fundamental understanding of personality other than perhaps what we have suspected all along, that personality research is important and worth doing. Unfortunately, it is exacty in contribution to our understanding of the basic processes of personality that current research is weak and formless.

Ordinary definitions of personality put emphasis on individual differences in a way that has been, I think, detrimental to progress in theory and research. That emphasis is mistaken, but to too great an extent the field of personality has been dominated, at least in terms of salience, by psychologists pursuing the ubiquitous but elusive, and maybe chimerical, differences between persons. Paradoxically, these psychologists have operated more often than not from a theory that posits not differences but universals. Freud's developmental states, Adler's striving for superiority, Jung's animus-anima, Maslow's need hierarchy, and many other concepts were meant to apply to everyone everywhere, but psychologists became bogged down in studying differences in a way that has never been very productive. If anatomists had proceeded in the same way as personality psychologists, we would know a great deal about minor variations in the location of the heart without ever realizing that for just about everyone everywhere it is located in the chest just slightly to the left of center. The above is not to deny the importance of individual differences; but until we know more about basic processes of personality, it is difficult to know how to fit the differences in.

That this reviewer's somewhat negative and pessimistic view of the field of personality is not totally idiosyncratic is evidenced by a provocative article by Donald Fiske (36), in which he suggests that our current conceptions of personality and their associated research paradigms have led us about as far as we are going to go. Fiske believes that the field of personality needs restructuring in order to permit the development of better personality constructs and measures of them. Our current work suffers from three interrelated problems: "Most of the data are the products of complex interpretive judgmental processes within observers; the agreement between sets of observations is limited; the ties between observations and concepts are tenuous and inadequate" (36, p. 3).

THE IDENTITY CRISIS IN PERSONALITY

If there is such a thing as an identity crisis, the field of personality (especially research) has one, whether the crisis is being experienced or not. To begin with, there is not even a proper term by which the personality researcher can identify him/herself, there being no adjectival form for personality. "I am a personality psychologist," is awkward and maybe even egotistical in sound. The term "personologist" is not lexically correct as a descriptor for psychologists who study personality, and in any case it has been preempted by the "soft" methodologists who study "whole people." Winston Churchill once was supposed to have said that the proper spelling of Istanbul was Constantinople. Well, the proper spelling of personality today has two variants: "social" and "clinical."

It is very difficult to distinguish between social and personality psychology today, but clearly a large part of what might be, and probably even should be, personality is, by passive consensus, within and/or dominated by social psychology. Consider that the *Journal of Personality* was for many years edited by a social psychologist and that it has for many years published articles in the mainstream of social psychological theory. One recent lead article in that journal was on the contributions of the social psychologist William McDougall. The *Journal of Personality and Social Psychology* is heavily oriented toward social psychology. The study of emotions and other internal states is widely seen as "social" psychology because a social psychologist, Schachter, started the field. Edward Jones, another social psychologist, nabbed off attribution theory for social psychology, even though much of that theory is as relevant to personality as to social psychology. Leonard Berkowitz, social psychologist, has been the central figure in research on aggression and catharsis for the past 15 years or so. Sex-role research has been a topic of interest for social psychologists for the past 2 or 3 years. The list could go on, but just to give final substance to the notion that the study of personality really lies in large part in social psychology, along the way Schachter and his students added obesity and now smoking (Herman 50) to social psychology's domain.

To paint the picture more fairly it should be noted that social psychologists do clearly have legitimate interest in personality, and the reverse is true. They have extended themselves not out of imperialist tendencies but, in this reviewer's opinion, from the lack of imagination and leadership in the field of personality itself. In part the relative stagnation of personality study has arisen from the strong but stultifying identification of so much of personality with clinical psychology and its preoccupations and methods: individual differences, self-report "scales," abnormal behavior, correlational research, description, therapy. Take a look, for example, at the 1974 volume of *Progress in Experimental Personality Research,* edited by B. A. Maher. Two of the chapters deal with self-report scales, one for clinical screening for adjustment (Lanyon 74) and one for "sensation seeking" (Zuckerman 140). Another chapter has to do with Pavlovian inhibitory mechanisms in certain types of behavior therapy (Rizley & Reppucci 105). Still another is on schizophrenic performance decrement (Megaro 84). Finally, one chapter is a review of research on self-disclosure (Goodstein & Reinecker 41), much of which is correlational and very little of which is subjected to rigorous methodological scrutiny. Now all of these chapters are in a volume supposedly on *experimental* research and representing progress in *personality.* One can only sympathize with the editor. Where could he have found enough to fill a volume with experimental personality research? (Well, by going to Berkowitz, Jones, Schachter, and their students, one supposes.)

The close identification of so much of personality theory and research with clinical psychology has diluted almost every aspect of the field of personality to the point of loss of visibility and separate identity. There are few psychologists in personality and *not* in clinical psychology. Issues of theoretical interest, e.g. catharsis, become enmeshed in practical concerns, e.g. the relationship of TV viewing to violent aggression, to the detriment of methodology for studying them. Researchers are seduced into demonstrating the therapeutic consequences of their discoveries. I am by no means a purist in my views of psychology, but it seems to me that personality needs an identity of its own to live up to.

SUBJECT VARIABLES IN PERSONALITY RESEARCH

In their 1972 review article Sarason & Smith made a strong case for research incorporating both subject and experimental variables into the same design so that subject "times" treatment interactions could be studied. It is early to be assessing any trends in research designs subsequent to their recommendation, but one's impression is that more and more personality researchers who do experiments are utilizing personality measures in order to partition subjects according to their potentially different responses to the experimental treatment. Such a trend is to be commended, and hopefully it will be continued. We also hope the trend will be for inclusion of carefully chosen, theoretically meaningful subject variables and not simply for "throwing in" measures because they are currently in vogue, easy to collect, or routinely available. Which leads into the consideration of the study of demographic variables in relation to personality.

Such variables as sex, age, race, socioeconomic status, and education are tempting additions to personality studies because they are easy to obtain, of obvious social importance, and misleadingly objective in measurement. Unfortunately, they are not *psychological* variables, and they help very little in understanding most experimental outcomes; in fact, they present the danger of fostering erroneous interpretations and unjustified complacency. The problem with demographic variables in psychological studies is that they really end up being surrogate variables, but it is rarely possible to know for what real variables they are surrogates in any given case. Take sex as an example. When sex is included as a variable in personality research, the investigator is almost never interested in biological maleness or femaleness per se. Yet any given samples of males and females potentially differ in so many ways, e.g. in field-independence, aggressive tendencies, self-esteem, interests, ambitions, sex-role orientation, hairiness of chest—and on and on—that it is difficult, if not impossible, to know what specific characteristic might have been involved in a sex X treatment interaction. However tempting it may be for an investigator to interpret differences associated with demographic variables, it needs to be recognized that any given interpretation is usually highly arbitrary and likely in the long run to be wrong. To the extent that an investigator is willing to be confined to mere description, e.g. "males obtained higher scores than females—period," the study of demographic variables cannot be faulted except on grounds of triviality and failure to excite much interest.

It should be reiterated that demographic variables are scarcely ever likely to be of direct interest in psychology. It cannot be of any psychological interest that someone has indicated completion of 12 years of school. Rather, indication of completion of 12 years of school is taken as an index of social class, of intelligence, of motivation, or some other variable. That a respondent is male is in itself of little psychological import. What is of consequence are the patterns of attitudes or abilities or problems or interests that are presumed to go along with being male. It is important not to let the exactness and usual trustworthiness of measures of education or sex or marital status, or whatever, mislead us into exaggerating the value of such measures as surrogates. Twelve years of education will have rubbed off more on some people than others; some biological males will be more "feminine" in interests than many females; not all blacks will have been disadvantaged. Thus the demographic variable is certain to be highly fallible as a measure of anything of interest to the psychologist.

The solution would seem to lie in developing measures, or using those available, of the variables for which demographic variables are surrogates and which are those of interest in the first place. Thus if one is interested in field-independence, then a direct measure should be included in the study. In that way one not only has a more certain knowledge of just what variable is implicated in an interaction, but one can determine whether the interaction exists within sexes and hence is a genuine field-independence effect. If years of education is really to be interpreted as a surrogate for intelligence, then it is preferable to measure intelligence. While there are certainly limits on the ability of any one investigator to measure every variable which is of interest, even a relatively weak but unidimensional measure may be better than a complex surrogate for some set of unknown variables. When surrogates must be used, their interpretation should be undertaken with full knowledge of the hazards involved.

SOME NAGGING AND PERSISTENT METHODOLOGICAL PROBLEMS

Research in personality continues to be plagued by methodological or interpretive problems that should long since have been resolved and by others that perhaps we are only now discovering as the relative sophistication of our methods increases. It will serve no very useful purpose here to point to specific instances of deficiencies; they are widespread. This reviewer has encountered all of the following problems several times in the literature of 1974.

To begin with, Olweus (96) provides a good example of the principle that in interpreting data one should not attempt to have one's cake and eat it too. He notes specifically that those such as Mischel who argue for the weakness of self-report methods should be careful about using data obtained by those very methods when the data tend to support their case, e.g. on the importance of situational factors in behavior. To point to a few other examples of the kinds of biases in interpretation encountered recently by the reviewer, writers have argued in one place that laboratory evidence is irrelevant to "real life," and in other places they have cited laboratory work in support of a point they have wished to make; they have argued that Freud was wrong, outmoded, and untrustworthy and also that he was especially astute in agreeing with them; still others have suggested that certain data should be ignored because of the small and unrepresentative sample and have in the same article cited in a favorable way evidence from equally small and unrepresentative samples. The Law of Symmetry in Data Interpretation should prevail: what disqualifies research on one side of an argument disqualifies it on the other side too.

Personality as a research field is still too much dominated by correlational studies. While correlational studies will remain useful in years to come, more effort should be expended to implement experimental paradigms in personality research. There is a widespread *assumption* about what can and cannot be studied experimentally. What may limit us as much as anything is lack of motivation and imagination—and prior assumptions about the nature of the variables we are studying. For example, our assumptions about the nature of intelligence involve notions of immutability. But we can certainly imagine situations in which people might be made to *feel* more intelligent or *act* more intelligently than at other times. Those manipulations should be studied where intelligence is at issue in order to determine to what extent intelligence must be studied as a subject rather than an experimental variable and whether as a moderator of other performances it differs as an organic as opposed to an elicited variable. Gender, i.e. feeling of masculinity or femininity, locus of control, need for approval, hypnotic suggestibility, depression, and many other variables might profitably be studied as experimental variables rather than as subject variables as they usually are. There are many clues from the social psychological literature on such topics as congitive consistency, dissonance, attribution, the bogus pipeline, and the like that might suggest to imaginative researchers how important personality variables might be manipulated for purposes of experimental study.

There is a persisting tendency in personality research to ignore the differences between within-subject and between-subject experimental designs with the consequence that discrepant results from different studies are misinterpreted and supposed replications of studies are misdesigned. A similar occasion for misinterpretation arises when the nature of different samples is ignored in comparing results. Folklore, and some evidence, suggests that subject pools change in character from early to late in an academic term, and subjects get into pools in different ways that may make them less comparable than they ought to be. For example, male and female college students at the same university are not necessarily recruited from the same pool upon entry into college or enrollment into a particular class or as volunteers for a particular experiment. The widely discrepant results on the need to avoid success in college women and men (see below) is a good case in point for the notion that discrepant results may not mean anything more than that samples were recruited on a different basis. Cross-cultural research, ethnic and racial comparisons, sex-role research, and the like are all subject to the problems of differential sampling. Hyland & Foot (61) have outlined a method of analyzing indirectly for individual differences in a between-group design, and assuming that their method proves correct and robust, it should help considerably in comparing between- and within-subject designs.

It will often be the case that an experimenter will want to compare the explanatory power of two or more experimental variables and arrive at some such conclusion as "Variable (treatment) B accounts for approximately twice as much of the variance as variable A." Such a conclusion is rarely justified in any larger context than that of the immediate experiment in question if for no other reason than that we lack the capacity to scale the strength of an experimental treatment in any very convincing way. Two treatments for reducing aggression may differ in part because one is a very strong manipulation and one is very weak. For example, how would one ever decide how much opportunity for verbal expression of aggression should be offered to be equal to the opportunity to give ten shocks? It may be that one can at some times do something equivalent to a cost-effectiveness analysis, e.g. in comparing two therapies, and one can say that two treatments seem about representative of what would happen in a real life setting, but the ultimate inference about relative strengths should be made with greater caution than is characteristic of much of the literature.

Finally, this reviewer would make a strong plea for more representative experimental designs and more diverse paradigms. Far too large a proportion of what we know in personality, particularly in experimental personality, is not in any demonstrable way generalizable beyond some unknown universe of college and university students enrolled in psychology (mostly introductory) courses. Moreover, most of what we know is not generalizable beyond very specific and narrow representations of treatments and other experimental and subject variables. The "teacher-learner" paradigm employing the Buss Aggression Machine is *de rigeur* in the study of aggression; the Horner type story completion measure is virtually the sole representation of need to avoid success; the Rotter Locus of Control Scale is standard. Such specificity has its advantages, but there are also attendant dangers, and it is time personality researchers began to explore some of the latter.

REVIEW OF LITERATURE

The review of literature which follows has stemmed from ground rules set by the reviewer, a practice which seems to have become normal over the years of existence of the *Annual Review of Psychology*. The principal rules of interest to the reader are:
1. An annual review, even in an area so circumscribed as personality, cannot serve as a substitute for *Psychological Abstracts*. No pretense of breadth or depth of coverage is made here. The materials cited were chosen because they fit a topic or illustrate a point to be made.
2. In general an attempt has been made to include articles which contribute to basic understanding of personality.
3. Articles involving applications of personality to understanding of other problems such as response to therapy, drug use, and abnormal behavior have not been included.
4. Again in general, research involving experimental manipulations has been preferred over correlational studies.

Interaction in Personality

If there is a conceptual trend which is evident in current notions of personality, it is *interactionism,* the proposition that behavior is to be understood as the joint product of the individual and the situation in which he is operating. Yet Ekehammar (31) shows that interactionism is anything but new. Why has it taken us so long to incorporate it into our thinking? Like the weather which everyone discusses but nobody does anything about, situational influences on behavior have been discussed for a good long while without much progress in dealing with them.

A major deficiency in the doctrine of interactionism lies in our lack of a taxonomy of situations and suitable measurement procedures for classifying them. A number of investigators in recent years have attempted to determine the extent of situational as opposed to dispositional influences on behavior, but their choice of situations to be studied has been fairly arbitrary and largely unguided by theories concerning situational variables. Apparently we are not yet close to developing a system for classifying situations so that they might be systematically studied, but Price & Bouffard (101) have at least made a start in showing that on a self-report measure persons X situation interactions accounts for a good portion of the variance in appropriateness of behavior. What is of interest taxonomically is that situations seem to differ substantially in the constraints they impose on behavior, with some situations—e.g. church, an employment interview—constraining many behaviors and others—e.g. a picnic in a public park—constraining relatively few. Kanfer et al (66) has reported three experiments showing that situational factors are important in determining whether or not a subject will carry out a performance "contracted for" in an experimental setting. Such variables as fidelity of performance by the experimenter, likelihood of own responsibility for previous breaches of performance, and time relationship between making and carrying out the agreed upon contract operate to determine whether a subject will or will not ultimately agree to go through with an unpleasant task.

Other investigators have attempted to show that consistency of persons across situations may well be greater than early criticisms by Mischel and others have suggested to be the case. Olweus (96) makes a distinction between genotype and phenotype with respect to performances and indicates that there is probably considerably more consistency across situations than is usually reported for the expression of overt aggression; indeed, his data support his contention. Bem & Allen (9) argue that our intuitions tell us people *are* consistent in behavior, and they note that the fact that the literature tends so strongly to suggest that there are only a few and weak consistencies demands explanation. The explanation, they believe, may lie in the fact that the literature is based on nomothetic assumptions about individual differences; the traits studied are in the heads of the investigators, not in the heads of the subjects. Moreover, our nomothetic research procedures require the assumption that items are scalable in the same way for all subjects, e.g. a subject may appear "inconsistent" because an expected response is idiosyncratically either more difficult or more easy for him than for most persons. Bem & Allen (9) believe that our intuitions are more likely to operate on the basis of idiographic assumptions. They present data which show rather clearly that subjects differ in consistency of "friendliness" and "conscientiousness" across situations, with some people being far more consistent than others. Similar findings are reported by Campus (15), but she shows in addition that subjects who tend to be consistent can be characterized by one of two styles: (*a*) an active coping style, or (*b*) a passive coping style. Inconsistent persons tend to be high on a number of somewhat incompatible traits such as abasement, aggression, defendence, exhibitionism, and anxiety. Subsequent work will be needed to study the consistency of consistency.

Aggression

The topic of aggression was one of the most popular of 1974, with much of the work being of high quality from the standpoint of methodology but with far less than ideally representative design. There were a number of major theoretical and method-ological contributions during the year, some of which may go a long way to clearing up some of the confusion that reigns. Avis (4) reviews work on the neurophar-macology of aggression, suggesting that it may be desirable to differentiate different types of aggression, e.g. isolation-induced aggression and pain-induced aggression. Berkowitz (11) shows that impulsive aggression may result in part from mediated associations with reinforcements for aggression. For example, a subject who is anger-aroused and in the presence of stimuli previously associated with aggression may behave more aggressively than he normally would. Hokanson (53) shows that the "cathartic" effect of aggression may merely reflect prior conditioning and be reversible so that "friendly" responses to aggression can have a cathartic effect. Both Olweus (96) and Rath (103) point to the importance of moderator variables in research on aggression. The latter paper makes the point that while in some condi-tions the relationship of hostile and aggressive thematic content to aggressive behav-ior is direct, in the conditions most resembling the usual clinical assessment situation the relationship tends to be reversed. Turner & Simons (128) and Schuck & Pisor (111) both present evidence that demand characteristics may affect aggression ex-periments, and Turner & Simons conclude that only the most naive and unsophis-ticated subjects should be run in aggression experiments. It remains to be seen whether their advice will be taken.

Finally, in an influential paper that should demand response, Tedeschi, Smith & Brown (124) suggest a substantially complete reinterpretation of research on aggres-sion, centering on the concept of *coercive power*. They believe that the problems with aggression as a concept include: the lack of functional unity of responses labeled aggressive; that definitions depend on implicit value judgments of the experimenter rather than on outcomes or the character of the response; the notion of intent to do harm implies unjustifiability of the actor's plans from the standpoint of the norms or laws that regulate interactions between people and by that definition of illegiti-macy we almost never observe aggression in the laboratory. The concept of coercive action in terms of threat and punishment provides a "more discriminating, denota-tive, and value-free language with which to construct a theory of harm-doing actions" (124, p. 540).

The issue of intent continues to be raised in aggression research, and it is becom-ing increasingly clear that intent must somehow be taken into account in the study of aggression. Nickel (92) showed that when subjects are shocked, their counterag-gressions match the perceived intentions of the original aggressor rather than the amount of shock they received. Rule & Nesdale (107) even showed that insulted subjects would shock *less* if they thought that their shocks were helpful to the learning of the insulting person. Anchor & Cross (2) found that subjects with less developed moral perspectives as determined by interview were more likely than those with developed moral perspectives to engage in maladaptive, i.e. self-harmful, aggression, operationalized as self-loss in a prisoner's dilemma game.

Reactance effects from limitation of choice (Worchel 135) may be added to the variables which will instigate aggression. There were two studies which produced results suggesting that residual but irrelevant arousal effects could enhance expres-sions of aggression. Zillman & Bryant (138) found that a session of bike-riding prior to provocation to aggression would result in increased aggression, and Jaffe et al (62) found that arousal from reading erotic material would increase intensity of shocks administered, the latter finding holding without regard to sex of either subject or target of aggression. On the other hand, Baron (6) found that if erotic material is presented after provocation, aggression will be inhibited, and suggested that the arousal produced in part by aggression may have been perceived as sexual arousal. Baron also noted, however, that summation of sexual and aggressive arousal might produce a state making the resultant instigation to aggression seem inappropriately high and thus inhibitory. In another study, Baron (5) found that exposure to the pain cues of a victim tended to inhibit expression of aggression when the potential aggressor was not aroused to anger, but there was no inhibition when anger was aroused. Also, an aggressive model did not disinhibit aggression in the absence of anger arousal. Geen, Stonner & Kelley (39) also produced evidence of the importance of cognitive effects in understanding aggression, finding that subjects who have an anchor point for aggression that is relatively high will judge subsequent aggressive scenes to be less violent. Finally, in a study with a younger sample of boys, Perry & Perry (99) discovered that when boys high in aggressive tendencies were led to believe that their victim was not suffering, they escalated their level of attack whereas low aggressive boys did not. Previous anger arousal was not necessary for the effect to occur.

A number of subject variables were found to affect expression of aggression. Guilt over aggression (Knott, Lasater & Shuman 69) reduces aggression, while high MMPI Pd scores are associated with higher levels of aggression (Wilkins, Scharff & Schlottmann 132). Scarpetti (109) found male repressors and sensitizers to differ in tendencies toward aggression but in a complex way, with sensitizers being inclined to give more shocks, while repressors give more shock when provoked and without expectation of later meeting their victim. Physiological recordings indicated differential response to making of aggressive responses by sensitizers and repressors, with sensitizers generally recovering faster. Scarpetti also found it possible to reverse these relationships by conditioning, a finding utilized by Hokanson (53).

Finally, Leak (76) discovered that subjects who had a chance to experience a little hostile humor after being provoked to anger showed less subsequent hostility than subjects exposed to other types of humorous materials. And Pelton (98) tried to redress some of the imbalance of interests in aggression with an intriguing book entitled *The Psychology of Nonviolence,* surely a topic we should know more about.

Sex-Role Research

A second major area of research activity in personality for 1974 was research on sex roles and related topics. A major contribution to all sex-role researchers was the book by Maccoby & Jacklin (79), *The Psychology of Sex Differences.* This new book is a revision in a general way of Maccoby's 1966 volume but is expanded considerably. It contains a highly useful annotated bibliography along with the tabular presentation of findings familiar from her previous work. Yorburg (137) reviews the problems of sex roles from a sociological standpoint. Two new and potentially very useful questionnaires were published during 1974. Bem (10) reported on a measure of "psychological androgyny" which permits separate calculations of masculinity and femininity, with androgyny being the difference between those two scores, the lack of sex-typing. All three scores were shown to be internally consistent, and while both masculinity and femininity correlated with social desirability, androgyny did not. Spence, Helmreich & Stapp (121) developed the Personal Attributes Questionnaire, which is a measure of sex-role stereotypes and masculinity-femininity, and which also permits the assessment of masculinity and femininity separately for each sex. They note that the female-valued items on their questionnaire are primarily expressive, while male-valued items are primarily instrumental.

Concern for the need to avoid success, or alternatively the fear of success, in women continues to be a major topic. However, it now appears that concern about need to avoid success in males may have to increase, also. Hoffman (52) repeated Horner's original 1965 research in the same university and under the same conditions with the result that about the same fear of success was found for females in 1971 as in 1965, but fear of success in males increased over that time. Moreover, achievement motivation scores were lower generally in 1971 than in 1965. A clue to what may have been happening is found in the observation that the most common negative theme for women was affiliative loss as a consequence of success, while for males the most common negative theme was questioning the value of the achievement in the first place. Spence (120) also found a growing tendency for males to downgrade achievement, but she found a generally lower fear of success score in her sample than did Horner. Spence believes that the need to avoid success as usually measured is not a personality attribute but one of basic attitudes toward achievement in men and women. Other studies suggest the importance of cultural determinants of the fear of success motive (Feather & Raphelson 34; Monahan, Kuhn & Shaver 89). Puryear & Mednick (102) studied fear of success in black women and concluded that their achievement dynamics are similar to those for white women. Not altogether incidentally, Gallimore (38) found that achievement in Hawaiian children may be linked to affiliative rather than achievement motives, a possibility that needs exploration in female samples.

Two studies of behavioral consequences of fear of success produced consistent results. House (58) found that when females were in explicitly competitive situations, they expressed lower expectancies for their performances than did males, and males thought that females would have lower expectancies in competition. Somewhat unexpectedly the expectancies of females were lower in an all female than a mixed-sex context. Karabenik & Marshall (67) found that females high in fear of success improved less when placed in competition with males than did females low in fear of success. Females low in fear of failure improved more when in competition with males, and fear of success and fear of failure were shown to be orthogonal.

A more ambitious and especially intriguing study by Heilbrun, Kleemeier & Piccola (48) may eventually provide important keys to understanding the phenomena of sex-role identity and achievement. These investigators found that there are important differences between father-identified girls who have integrated their role performances successfully and those who are less consistent in reported behavior.

Specifically, the former girls show a preference for traditional female roles and performed much better in an all-girl competitive situation than the low role consistency girls. However, with boys present the latter girls improved markedly while the high role consistency girls declined somewhat in performance. The low role consistency, father-similar girls showed a strong preference for contemporary female roles and had higher positive achievement goals. The theoretical discussion of the authors cannot easily be summarized here, but it is stimulating and should foster additional research.

Three additional studies relate attributions of causality to sex roles. Midgley & Abrams (86) found that the motive to avoid success was associated with high external scores on the Locus of Control Scale in a sample of undergraduate women, thus indicating that such women do not feel a strong sense of personal control over their own fates. Neither may males think that women have much control over their fates. Deux & Emswiller (27) found that good performances by females are more likely to be attributed to luck than the same performances by males, and Feldman-Summers & Kiesler (35) got similar results in a study of attribution of occupational success, although in the latter study successful women were sometimes seen as having higher motivation, i.e. as a compensation for less ability.

It might be expected that attitudes toward success of women such as the above would be reflected in various aspects of occupational choice and performance by women, and O'Leary (95) reviewed the attitudinal barriers to occupational aspirations of women. Stewart & Winter (123) found evidence that even women with a strong career orientation are concerned by potential loss of affiliative satisfactions, i.e. becoming social outcasts, by choosing a career over marriage, a theme earlier noted in the work of Hoffman (52). Shaffer & Wegley (115) concluded that the competent woman who rejects traditional sex-role preferences, especially if oriented toward successful competition with males, is likely to be judged less attractive as a work partner or socially, although she may be judged quite favorably by an employer. There is a rather ugly possibility suggested by the work of Touhey (127) that one effect of the success of women in invading previously male-dominated professions may be a decrease in the prestige of those professions. It would be worse than ironic if just when women achieve success in high prestige occupations society decides it no longer values those occupations nor chooses to pay them so well.

There was a small but provocative set of studies of motivational differences between males and females that should be of interest in personality. Wilsnack (133) tested the effects of drinking alcohol on women's fantasy motives, previous investigators having found that males show an increase in power motive while under the influence. Wilsnack's results suggest that for at least some women drinking increases feelings of womanliness and does away with concerns about masculine power and aggressiveness. Along the latter lines Hottes & Kahn (57) found that in a prisoner's dilemma game males are more success oriented and play more opportunistically so that even cooperation occurs for the sake of maximizing gains. Women play more defensively. In a study involving a very different research paradigm, Mikula (87) found that men tended to take a larger share of available rewards than women, even when they were in an ostensibly weak position. Nevill

(91) found that females were more affected than males by a dependency manipulation when eye contact was the outcome measure.

It should be noted that even though the above studies are interesting, there is probably less to them than meets the eye because they suggest nothing about the origins, the mutability, or the future of male-female differences in motivation. They may be peculiar to particular samples or to our times. Some use of such measures as the Attitudes Toward Women Scale or the Androgyny Scale (Bem 10) might help in the future in explicating male-female differences.

In 1968 Donald Broverman and his colleagues discussed the roles of activation and inhibition processes in relation to sex differences in cognitive tasks. Morgan Worthy (136), in a book otherwise devoted to the relationship of eye color to performance, has indicated that women seem to differ from men on motor tasks in about the same way that dark-eyed men differ from light-eyed men, and the major difference seems to be that dark-eyed males and females are better on tasks that require speed and rapid reaction, while light-eyed males are better on tasks that require inhibition of movement and self-paced activity.

Locus of Control

The third major area of research in personality during 1974 was locus of control, nearly always in relation to Rotter's Internal-External Control Scale. There were, however, three new I-D scales published during the year. Mischel, Zeiss & Zeiss (88) published the Stanford Preschool Internal-External Control Scale, a 14 item forced-choice scale providing separate scores for sense of control over positive and negative events. Mischel et al found that persistence in working on tasks that are to be rewarded is related to I+ but not to I–, while persistence to avoid negative outcome is related to I–but not to I+. Gruen, Korte & Baum (45) presented the Gruen, Korte & Stephens I-E Scale, a cartoon format. The scale was given to 1100 heterogeneous children, and it was shown that both internal consistency and test-retest reliabilities are moderately high. Surprisingly, and surely a finding that deserves to be pursued, it was found that in this sample of children in grades 2, 4, and 6 girls were more internal than boys, a finding different from what is usually reported for adults. Finally, Nowicki & Duke (93) reported on a preschool and primary I-E scale, again with a cartoon format, and again with some evidence for internal consistency and construct validity. They note that now there is an I-E scale for every age level and that work on I-E can get under way. There is as yet no I-E infancy scale.

It used to be common for researchers in personality to do at least quasi-developmental research on various traits and attitudes, but that tradition seems to have faded, and there is still very little evidence concerning the origins of LOC, e.g. in child-rearing patterns, early childhood environment, etc. However, Nowicki & Segal (93a) studied a group of high school seniors and found that cross-sex nurturance as perceived by the subjects was associated with internality, and that parents are perceived as being similar to the subject in LOC.

Four studies are concerned with the multidimensionality of the Rotter I-E Scale but come to somewhat different conclusions. Collins (21) found four factors in the I-E scale, although not orthogonal factors. MacDonald & Tseng (80) and Viney

(131), the latter separately for male and female adolescents, found a sizeable first factor that accounted for a good part of the reliable variance among the items. Gootnick (42) did show that a separately constructed measure of "control over large-scale social and political events" correlated with first-time voter registration of students whereas the Rotter I-E did not. However, it should be added that the Rotter I-E scale correlated .46 with the former scale. The degree and meaning of multidimensionality of I-E remains to be elucidated.

Evidence continues to accrue showing that I-E relates to preferred styles of behavior or situations, but gradually more sophisticated and differential predictions are being made. Harvey et al (47) showed that Is believe themselves to have more choice in a choice situation, but that Es perceive themselves as having relatively greater choice when outcomes are negative rather than positive. The size of the difference between options is also related to perceived choice for Is but not for Es. Krovetz (71) and Gilmor & Minton (40) found that Internals tend more than Externals to attribute success to their own ability and failure to luck or whatever. In the Krovetz study, which involved an ESP type task, at the very highest levels of false feedback without success the Internals and Externals showed a crossover, with the Internals believing more in external factors and the Externals believing more in internal factors in performance. Krovetz speculates that at that very high level of performance the Internals no longer believed that they could be that skillful, and the Externals no longer believed they could be that lucky. Arkin et al (3) studied the situation of two participants in a simulated therapy session and found that the actors tended to think positive results were more attributable to their ability than negative results, while observers tended to attribute negative results more to the ability of the actor. I-E has an obvious tie-in with attribution processes, and Sosis (119) reports that after reading an account of an auto accident, Internals attributed more responsibility for the accident to the driver than did moderates or Externals. Internals can be hard on others as well as themselves.

Internals prefer positions of power in groups while Externals prefer to work in low power positions (Hrycenko & Minton 60), and Internals show greater reactance when freedom is limited than do Externals, although the latter show relatively more reactance when freedom is limited by impersonal means (Cherulnik & Citrin 20). Locus of control also makes a difference in task ability. Internals showed higher ability than Externals for both intentional performance and incidental learning (Wolk & DuCette 134). Also, Internals perform better when they are permitted to discover for themselves the rightness or wrongness of their response while Externals perform better when they are told whether they are right or wrong (Baron et al 7). These findings held for both preadolescent boys and college students. When Internals and Externals are threatened with or meet failure, they react in somewhat different ways. As indicated above, Internals tend to deny personal responsibility for failure (40, 71), but Externals prefer to work on tasks with a built-in rationalization for failure (Phares & Lamiell 100). Hochreich (51) suggests that there are two types of Externals, defensive and nondefensive, and finds that defensive external males react to failure with blame attribution more than do Internals and that they are lower in adjustment than other groups. Lefcourt, Sordoni & Sordoni (77) find that

Internals are particularly likely to respond to tension or threat with humor, especially with humor that implies a withdrawing from a previous stance of involvement and seriousness.

Cross-cultural studies show students in the United States to be more internal than those of most other countries and females generally to be more external than males (McGinnies, Nordholm & Ward 82; Parsons & Schneider 97). However, McGinnies & Ward (83), while confirming a previous finding that American Internals are equally influenced by high and low credibility sources of information but are generally less influenced than Externals, did not replicate the effect in three other national samples and found it reversed in one.

Anxiety

The topic of anxiety continues to be of interest. Shedletsky & Endler (116) present a well-reasoned and documented argument in favor of a person-situation interaction model of anxiety as opposed to Spielberger's state-trait model, which is seen as a special case of the interaction model. Ziv, Kruglanski & Schulman (139), in one of the rare "real life" anxiety studies, show that Israeli children exposed to the stress of enemy shelling do not differ in any remarkable way from children not so exposed, but they were higher in "locale patriotism," extrapunitiveness, and covert aggression, and their sociometric choices were determined to a greater degree by the trait of courage. Fugita (37) found that social anxiety aroused by situational context affects eye contact by decreasing visual interaction with a disapproving person. Teichman (125) reports that subjects high in trait anxiety prefer to be alone when highly aroused while low trait anxiety subjects prefer affiliation when aroused.

To conclude this brief resume of anxiety research, a prize for imaginative field experimentation should go to Dutton & Aron (30) for two studies of effects of anxiety on sexual attraction. Male passers-by on a high, narrow swinging bridge were approached by an attractive female for an interview in which they completed a questionnaire and wrote a TAT story. Using well-selected control subjects not on the bridge, Dutton & Aron found that subjects in the arousing condition produced more sexual content in their stories. Moreover, after the interview the female experimenter gave her name and phone number to the subjects so that they could call her later for more information about the study. Far more of the subjects in the fear-arousing condition called. To cap off their work, Dutton & Aron more or less replicated the study in the laboratory with consistent results.

In the nature of an epilogue, Greden (43) reports on a diagnostic problem: some cases of either state or trait anxiety may be attributable to caffeinism. The correct diagnosis may be essential.

Interpersonal Attraction

Sexual arousal can enhance attraction to another person as indicated by evaluated likability of a symbolic person by females (but not by males). This is also indicated by the fact that sexually aroused subjects (compared to nonaroused subjects) of both sexes attended visually more to opposite sex than to same sex targets (Griffitt, May & Veitch 44). Social traits as opposed to nonsocial traits are more important determiners of the likeability of a person and are more important for female than for male subjects (Diggins 29). One of the social traits that may determine likeability of a person is modesty, but not so much of it that it raises issues of credibility (Brickman & Seligman 13). And there was yet another demonstration that propinquity is a stronger determinant of friendship choice than almost any other variable (Segal 113).

Three additional studies indicate strongly that attractiveness is an important asset. Kleck, Richardson & Ronald (68) found that social acceptance in a camp situation was predictable from rated attractiveness of photos, but they also note that there is a distinct need for behavioral studies of attractive and unattractive subjects. Essays are rated more favorably when photos of attractive putative authors are attached than when unattractive authors are depicted, and the effect is most pronounced when the objective quality of the essay is poor (Landy & Sigall 75). Apparently male and female subjects subscribe to the same standards in rating attractiveness of males and females, but the meaning of attractiveness is somewhat different when males and females are being rated (Morse et al 90). Judging a female as attractive seems to imply friendliness while for a male it implies assertiveness. A finding of special interest is that women seen as assertive by males are also seen as lacking in sex appeal.

Self-Disclosure

The literature was reviewed by Goodstein & Reinecker (41), and additions show that intimate self-disclosure can be seen as inappropriate while failure to engage in self-disclosure may be inappropriate only under special circumstances (Chaikin & Derlega 17, 18), one of those circumstances being failure to reciprocate disclosure. Reciprocal disclosure produced more subsequent disclosure than did disclosure by a model (David & Skinner 26).

Cognitive Factors in Personality

An especially interesting set of independent but related studies shows the importance of cognitive aspects of personality and personality functioning. First, there were three studies which illustrated further the Bem & Allen (9) position recounted above that it may be important to define traits in the subject's own terms rather than in those of the experimenter. Shrauger & Patterson (117) gave subjects the opportunity to describe people they knew in their own terms and then to apply those terms to themselves. Descriptions of others tended to be in terms of dimensions regarded as highly relevant to the self, and subjects high in self-esteem had a greater correspondence between dimensions regarded as self-relevant and those on which they experienced self-satisfaction. Lemon & Warren (78) also found that self-relevant traits are more central and more salient, but they found that centrality and self-relevance of traits are fairly distinct. In a third study Jones, Sensenig & Haley (65) found that college student subjects asked to describe themselves tended to state their best traits first and to present themselves as completely nonthreatening. Evidently the imposition of a standard list of terms by an experimenter interested in trait attributions might produce some distortion of responses.

Four studies dealt with effects of inconsistency and type of integration achieved.

Crockett & Meisel (24) were interested in the ways in which impressions change as a function of the degree of connectedness of constructs elicited by a version of Kelly's Role Constructs Repertory Test. When central constructs were disconfirmed, change in impressions was extensive. In general it was concluded that when the connectedness of constructs is great, any change in one inference resulted in widespread change. Shaffer & Hendrick (114) found that subjects who were closed-minded and intolerant of ambiguity experienced greater discomfort from cognitive imbalance than did their opposite counterparts, but neither group found cognitive inconsistency easy to bear. The effects of dissonance produced by apparent deviation from life style was investigated by Cooper & Scalise (22), who found that extraverts changed their attitudes only when they had been led to believe that they were nonconforming while introverts experienced an attitude change only when they were led to believe that they were conforming with opinions of others. Scott (112) described four types of cognitive integration and found a general tendency for subjects to be consistent in the use of one or another of the four styles across four domains of cognition, e.g. acquaintances and self.

Four additional studies dealt in one way or another with the effects of preparatory messages or instructions on reactions of subjects in test situations. Vernon & Bigelow (130) found that hernia patients given specific information about their prospective surgery showed somewhat more positive responses to the surgery, but their data did not provide support for Janis's ideas about anticipatory fear or the "work of worry." That preparatory information can reduce stress was also shown by Johnson & Levanthal (63). They found that patients instructed about a somewhat difficult medical procedure they were to undergo showed less distress and greater compliance with instructions. One way in which preparation may reduce threat was discovered by Krupat (72). Subjects exposed to very threatening stimuli, in this case simulated driving experiences, showed reduced evaluation of threat compared to when they were exposed to moderate or nonthreatening stimuli. One additional study of interest involved instructions to focus on internal cues and induced stress as determinants of field independence (Reinking, Goldstein & Houston 104). Stress increased the natural tendencies of subjects to be either field dependent or independent, and instructions to focus on internal cues made subjects generally more field independent, which suggests that field independence may be at least partially a matter of preferred style rather than of ability.

Feedback Mechanisms in Personality

Several studies had to do in one way or another with the effect on behavior of feedback to the subject concerning his own or another's performance. Two studies had to do with humor. Laird (73) found that if subjects were induced to "smile" or "frown" under the guise of making muscle recordings, their ratings of cartoons were affected in the direction of their facial expression. Cupchik & Levanthal (25) found that cartoons produced more mirth responses if they were accompanied by canned laughter, and mirth was also increased when subjects were required to monitor their own mirth reactions. There were some complex differences, however. One of the new measures of the year was a self-monitoring of expression scale designed for measuring tendencies toward impression management (Snyder 118).

The scale appears to be independent of a number of other dimensions and some evidence of construct validity was produced. Schiffenbauer (110) aroused different emotional states in his subjects and found that their ratings of the emotional states of others were both more intense and colored by their own emotions. Two additional studies showed that subjects asked to role-play an "upset" reaction to electric shock later showed less pain response to shock than did subjects asked to role-play a "calm" reaction to shock (Kopel & Arkowitz 70), and that children who saw a model showing no response to an injection showed more pain response to a later injection than did children who saw a "realistic" model (Vernon 129).

Nonverbal Communication

That communication may occur without verbal context continues to be of interest. Although subjects *believed* that if they behaved deceptively, facial cues would give them away, body cues were actually better cues to both deception and honesty (Ekman & Friesen 32). Apparently there are individual differences in the degree to which people express their emotions. Buck, Miller & Caul (14) had subjects view a variety of emotionally arousing slides while being observed by judges who attempted to guess the subject's reaction and the nature of the slide. Females betrayed their emotions more faithfully than males, and the more accurate "senders" showed smaller skin conductance and heart rate response than did less accurate persons. Those subjects with relatively little outward expression showed lower self-esteem, greater introversion, and greater sensitization than did the outwardly expressive.

Judgments about filmed social interactions were affected by amount of eye contact between the persons portrayed, with more and more reciprocal contact indicating a longer relationship (Thayer & Schiff 126). Eye contact is also of apparent importance in mediating the teacher expectancy effect, but nodding, smiling, and leaning toward are also involved (Chaikin, Sigler & Derlega 19). Obviously one's eyes can give one away. Meskin & Singer (85) studied eye shifts during an interview and found that men who tend to shift their gaze to the left rather than to the right are more "inner-attentive."

Depth Psychology

The case for dynamic, depth-analytic psychology did not grow stronger during 1974. Holmes (54) reviewed a portion of the research literature on repression without being tempted to conclude more than that there is as yet no research evidence clearly interpretable as a demonstration of repression. Holmes (55) also found that the TAT is easily faked for achievement motivation and that subjects can clearly respond in such a way as to inhibit revealing responses; moreover, judges cannot identify subjects who are faking. Holmes & Houston (56) did show a much more cognitive and deliberate mechanism for coping with stress, and the possibility that cognitive reappraisal of a threatening situation can lessen stress (Houston & Holmes 59). A study of women's fantasies during sexual intercourse (Hariton & Singer 46) gave indication that such fantasies reflect a personality-cognitive disposition toward enrichment of experience through fantasy or an adaptive mechanism to an otherwise uncomfortable or unsatisfying situation. There was little reason to believe that such fantasies involve deep-lying conflicts and that they are compensatory in nature. The concepts of perceptual defense and vigilance also underwent a new examination (Erdeli 33) and a cognitive reinterpretation in terms of selectivity in processing of information, and the author concludes that several mechanisms are involved and that no one explanation will suffice. The one plus for psychoanalytic theory was a study showing that oral imagery from the Rorschach is related to accuracy of interpersonal perception and that subjects high in oral dependence imagery received better evaluations by a Peace Corps Assessment Board (Masling, Johnson & Saturansky 81).

Miscellany

Obesity is a current topic of interest, and Johnson (64) found as predicted that the prominence of food cues affects the amount of food that obese subjects will consume. On the other hand, Herman (50) found that heavy smokers are affected by internal cues, while light smokers are affected by both internal and external cues, hence resembling in some ways the obese. Rodin & Slochower (106) added to the stock of information indicating that obese individuals are more affected by external cues than are subjects of normal weight. In their study they found that obese subjects show better incidental learning when there is no distraction and poorer incidental learning when there is high distraction. In a second part of the study they found that when subjects are asked to comply with a request, obese subjects are more affected than normals by both the weight and manner of the person making the request.

As stated earlier, physiological measures are becoming more common in personality research, and a particularly interesting and promising report on heartrate variability was issued in 1974 (Offerhaus 94), it being found that high heartrate variability under stress induced by performance overload is related to a variety of other measures. Sales, Guydosh & Iacono (108) also produced a highly interesting and almost certain to be controversial paper based on the idea that individuals have an optimal level of received internal stimulation and that they will attempt to change input if it is either too large or too small. They further suggest that the optimum level of internal situation is the same for all persons, so that the difference between persons is attributable to tendencies either to augment or damp down objective inputs. They operationalize their concept in terms of auditory threshold and find that high auditory threshold is related to boredom in an experiment, coffee drinking, and an urban background. On the other hand, during a summer period, presumed to be dull, high threshold subjects were more likely to volunteer for an experiment and gave responses indicative of greater tolerance for interpersonal crowding. In an apparently unrelated paper Stelmack & Campbell (122) report a difference in auditory threshold between introverts and extraverts that is consistent with the Sales hypothesis, i.e. extraverts have a higher threshold.

In a study which is interesting in its own right and something of a model for developmental studies, Dien (28) reasoned that because high Mach mothers should be better able to manipulate their children, their children should tend to be low Mach. Conversely, low Mach mothers should produce high Mach children. Since these effects were expected to be diluted for later born children, Dien predicted only that first and only born children of low Mach mothers would cheat more in a skill-ball game. The hypothesis was confirmed for children 4-5 years old, and there was no effect for later born children. When both parents are high Mach, the suppressive effect on cheating is very strong.

Several new and potentially useful scales were published during the year (other than ones previously mentioned). We now have the Texas Social Behavior Inventory, an objective measure of self-esteem or social competence (Helmreich, Stapp & Ervin 49); a test of emotional styles (Allen & Hamsher 1); a pessimism or hopelessness scale (Beck et al 8), and a measure of addiction-proneness thought to be useful with alcoholics (Cowan, Auld & Be'gin 23).

New books of importance include Cartwright's (16) textbook on personality that is selective but far more than a rehashing of various theories and a review of miscellaneous research. Breger's (12) book on personality development should be of distinct theoretical interest because it represents a synthesis of Freud, Erikson, and Piaget and is both thoughtful and insightful.

CONCLUSIONS

This writer took the idea of doing a one year review of work in personality rather literally, in part out of curiosity. At this point, at the end of the review, it is evident, as probably it should have been from the beginning, that limiting one's perspective to the work published in a single year presents serious difficulties. Themes are obscured; trends cannot be seen; theories cannot be observed in the act of unfolding. Nonetheless, there are some advantages in the narrowness of a year's perspective, not the least of which is that that very narrowness probably makes some of the shortcomings of a field stand out a bit more clearly. Examining each study as a free-standing contribution forces more attention to its limitations, its methodology, and to its own wider implications.

From this writer's perspective the field of personality, at least the experimental study of personality, needs a tonic—several of them, in fact. It needs better methodology, more truly experimental work, and better and more integrating theory. It needs to divest itself of 50-year-old theories and 25-year-old measures and methods. The reader, along with this writer, may think that many of the 1974 studies are individually interesting. Many of the findings are fascinating, and some are bound to prove seminal to a series of fairly integrated efforts. But most are likely, however dazzling they may be, to have little longer life and impact than the rockets of the Fourth of July. The individual studies lack direction and staying power, and they suggest a status for the field of personality that puts one in mind of the apocryphal jet pilot who assured his passengers that while the plane was lost, it was at least making good time.

Literature Cited

1. Allen, J. G., Hamsher, J. H. 1974. The development and validation of a test of emotional styles. *J. Consult. Clin. Psychol.* 42:663–68
2. Anchor, K. N., Cross, H. J. 1974. Maladaptive aggression, moral perspective, and the socialization process. *J. Pers. Soc. Psychol.* 30:163–68
3. Arkin, R., Gleason, J. M., Harvey, J. H., Johnston, S. 1974. Effect of expected and observed outcome of an action on the differential causal attributions of actor and observer. *J. Pers.* 42:62–77
4. Avis, H. H. 1974. The neuropharmacology of aggression: a critical review. *Psychol. Bull.* 81:47–63
5. Baron, R. A. 1974. Aggression as a function of victim's pain cues, level of prior anger arousal, and exposure to an aggressive model. *J. Pers. Soc. Psychol.* 29:117–24
6. Ibid. The aggression-inhibiting influence of heightened sexual arousal. 30:318–22
7. Baron, R. M., Cowan, G., Ganz, R. L., McDonald, M. 1974. Interaction of locus of control and type of performance feedback: considerations of external validity. *J. Pers. Soc. Psychol.* 30:285–92
8. Beck, A. T., Weissman, A., Lester, D., Trexler, L. 1974. The measurement of pessimism: the Hopelessness Scale. *J. Consult. Clin. Psychol.* 42:861–65
9. Bem, D. J., Allen, A. 1974. On predicting some of the people some of the time: the search for cross-situational consistencies in behavior. *Psychol. Rev.* 81:506–20
10. Bem, S. L. 1974. The measurement of psychological androgyny. *J. Consult. Clin. Psychol.* 42:155–62
11. Berkowitz, L. 1974. Some determinants of impulsive aggression: role of mediated associations with reinforcements for aggression. *Psychol. Rev.* 81:165–76
12. Breger, L. 1974. *From Instinct to Identity: The Development of Personality.* Englewood Cliffs, NJ: Prentice-Hall
13. Brickman, P., Seligman, C. 1974. Effects of public and private expectancies on attributions of competence and interpersonal attraction. *J. Pers.* 42:558–68
14. Buck, R., Miller, R. E., Caul, W. F. 1974. Sex, personality, and physiological variables in the communication of affect via facial expression. *J. Pers. Soc. Psychol.* 30:587–96
15. Campus, N. 1974. Transitional consistency as a dimension of personality. *J. Pers. Soc. Psychol.* 29:593–600
16. Cartwright, D. S. 1974. *Introduction to Personality.* Chicago: Rand McNally
17. Chaikin, A. L., Derlega, V. J. 1974. Variables affecting the appropriateness of self-disclosure. *J. Consult. Clin. Psychol.* 42:588–93
18. Chaikin, A. L., Derlega, V. J. 1974. Liking for the normbreaker in self-disclosure. *J. Pers.* 42:117–29
19. Chaikin, A. L., Sigler, E., Derlega, V. J. 1974. Nonverbal mediators of teacher expectancy effects. *J. Pers. Soc. Psychol.* 30:144–49
20. Cherulnik, P. D., Citrin, M. M. 1974. Individual difference in psychological reactance: the interaction between locus of control and mode of elimination of freedom. *J. Pers. Soc. Psychol.* 29:398–404
21. Collins, B. E. 1974. Four components of the Rotter Internal-External Control Scale: belief in a difficult world, a just world, a predictable world, and a politically responsive world. *J. Pers. Soc. Psychol.* 29:381–91
22. Cooper, J., Scalise, C. J. 1974. Dissonance produced by deviations from life styles: the interaction of Jungian typology and conformity. *J. Pers. Soc. Psychol.* 29:566–71
23. Cowan, L., Auld, F., Be'gin, P. E. 1974. Evidence for distinctive personality traits in alcoholics. *Br. J. Addict.* 69:199–205
24. Crockett, W. H., Meisel, P. 1974. Construct connectedness, strength of disconfirmation and impression change. *J. Pers.* 42:290–99
25. Cupchik, G. C., Levanthal, H. 1974. Consistency between expressive behavior and the evaluation of humorous stimuli: the role of sex and self-observation. *J. Pers. Soc. Psychol.* 30:429–42
26. Davis, J. D., Skinner, A. E. G. 1974. Reciprocity of self-disclosure in interviews: modeling or social exchange. *J. Pers. Soc. Psychol.* 29:779–84
27. Deaux, K., Emswiller, T. 1974. Explanation of successful performance on sex-linked tasks: what is skill for the male is luck for the female. *J. Pers. Soc. Psychol.* 29:80–85
28. Dien, D. S. 1974. Parental Machiavellianism and children's cheating in Japan. *J. Cross-Cult. Psychol.* 5:259–70

29. Diggins, D. 1974. The role of social and nonsocial traits in interpersonal attraction. *J. Pers.* 345–59

30. Dutton, D. G., Aron, A. P. 1974. Some evidence for heightened sexual attraction under conditions of high anxiety. *J. Pers. Soc. Psychol.* 30:510–17

31. Ekehammar, B. 1974. Interactionism in personality from a historical perspective. *Psychol. Bull.* 81:1026–48

32. Ekman, P., Friesen, W. V. 1974. Detecting deception from the body or face. *J. Pers. Soc. Psychol.* 29:288–98

33. Erdeli, M. H. 1974. A new look at the New Look: perceptual defense and vigilance. *Psychol. Rev.* 81:1–25

34. Feather, N. T., Raphelson, A. C. 1974. Fear of success in Australian and American student groups: motive or sex-role stereotype? *J. Pers.* 42:190–201

35. Feldman-Summers, S., Kiesler, S. B. 1974. Those who are number two try harder: the effect of sex on attributions of causality. *J. Pers. Soc. Psychol.* 30:846–55

36. Fiske, D. W. 1974. The limits for the conventional science of personality. *J. Pers.* 42:1–10

37. Fugita, S. S. 1974. Effects of anxiety and approval on visual interaction. *J. Pers. Soc. Psychol.* 29:586–92

38. Gallimore, R. 1974. Affiliation motivation and Hawiian-American achievement. *J. Cross-Cult. Psychol.* 5:481–91

39. Geen, R. G., Stonner, D., Kelley, D. R. 1974. Aggression anxiety and cognitive appraisal of aggression-threat stimuli. *J. Pers. Soc. Psychol.* 29:196–200

40. Gilmor, T. M., Minton, H. L. 1974. Internal versus external attribution of task performance as a function of locus of control, initial confidence and success-failure outcome. *J. Pers.* 42:159–73

41. Goodstein, L. D., Reinecker, V. M. 1974. Factors affecting self-disclosure: a review of the literature. *Progr. Exp. Pers. Res.* 3:49–77

42. Gootnick, A. T. 1974. Locus of control and political participation of college students: a comparison of unidimensional and multidimensional approaches. *J. Consult. Clin. Psychol.* 47:54–58

43. Greden, J. F. 1974. Anxiety or caffeinism: a diagnostic dilemma. *Am. J. Psychiatry* 131:1089–92

44. Griffitt, W., May, J., Veitch, R. 1974, Sexual stimulation and interpersonal behavior: heterosexual evaluative responses, visual behavior, and physical proximity. *J. Pers. Soc. Psychol.* 30:368–77

45. Gruen, G. E., Korte, J. R., Baum, J. F. 1974. Group measure of locus of control. *Dev. Psychol.* 10:683–86

46. Hariton, B. E., Singer, J. L. 1974. Women's fantasies during sexual intercourse: normative and theoretical implications. *J. Consult. Clin. Psychol.* 42:313–22

47. Harvey, J. H., Barnes, R. D., Sperry, D. L., Harris, B. 1974. Perceived choice as a function of internal-external locus of control. *J. Pers.* 42:437–52

48. Heilbrun, A. B., Kleemeier, C., Piccola, G. 1974. Developmental and situational correlates of achievement behavior in college females. *J. Pers.* 42:420–36

49. Helmreich, R., Stapp, J., Ervin, C. 1974. The Texas Social Behavior Inventory (TSB): An objective measure of self-esteem or social competence. *JSAS Cat. Selec. Doc. Psychol.* 4:79

50. Herman, C. P. 1974. External and internal cues as determinants of the smoking behavior of light and heavy smokers. *J. Pers. Soc. Psychol.* 30:664–72

51. Hochreich, D. J. 1974. Defensive externality and attribution of responsibility. *J. Pers.* 42:543–57

52. Hoffman, L. W. 1974. Fear of success in males and females: 1965–1971. *J. Consult. Clin. Psychol.* 42:353–58

53. Hokanson, J. E. 1974. An escape-avoidance view of catharsis. *Crim. Justice Behav.* 1:195–223

54. Holmes, D. S. 1974. Investigations of repression: differential recall of material experimentally or naturally associated with ego threat. *Psychol. Bull.* 81:632–53

55. Holmes, D. S. 1974. The conscious control of thematic projection. *J. Consult. Clin. Psychol.* 42:323–29

56. Holmes, D. S., Houston, B. K. 1974. Effectiveness of situation redefinition and affective isolation in coping with stress. *J. Pers. Soc. Psychol.* 29:212–18

57. Hottes, J. H., Kahn, A. 1974. Sex differences in a mixed-motive conflict situation. *J. Pers.* 42:260–75

58. House, W. C. 1974. Actual and perceived differences in male and female expectancies and minimal goal levels as a function of competition. *J. Pers.* 42:493–509

59. Houston, B. K., Holmes, D. S. 1974. Effect of avoidant thinking and reappraisal for coping with threat involving temporal uncertainty. *J. Pers. Soc. Psychol.* 30:382–88

60. Hrycenko, I., Minton, H. L. 1974. Internal-external control, power position, and satisfaction in task-oriented groups. *J. Pers. Soc. Psychol.* 30:871–78
61. Hyland, M., Foot, H. 1974. Group data, individual behavior: a methodological note. *Br. J. Soc. Clin. Psychol.* 13:93–95
62. Jaffe, Y., Malamuth, N., Feingold, J., Feshbach, S. 1974. Sexual arousal and behavioral aggression. *J. Pers. Soc. Psychol.* 30:759–64
63. Johnson, J., Leventhal, H. 1974. Effects of accurate expectations and behavioral instructions on reactions during a noxious medical examination. *J. Pers. Soc. Psychol.* 29:710–18
64. Johnson, W. G. 1974. Effect of cue-prominence and subject weight on human food-directed performance. *J. Pers. Soc. Psychol.* 29:843–48
65. Jones, R. A., Sensenig, J., Haley, J. V. 1974. Self-descriptions: configurations of content and order effects. *J. Pers. Soc. Psychol.* 30:36–45.
66. Kanfer, F. H., Cox, L. E., Greiner, J. M., Karoly, P. 1974. Contracts, demand characteristics, and self control. *J. Pers. Soc. Psychol.* 30:605–19
67. Karabenik, S. A., Marshall, J. M. 1974. Performance of females as a function of fear of success, fear of failure, type of opponent and performance-contingent feedback. *J. Pers.* 42:219–37
68. Kleck, R. E., Richardson, S. A., Ronald, L. 1974. Physical appearance cues and interpersonal attraction in children. *Child Dev.* 45:305–10
69. Knott, P. D., Lasater, L., Shuman, R. 1974. Aggression-guilt and conditionability for aggressiveness. *J. Pers.* 42:332–44
70. Kopel, S. A., Arkowitz, H. S. 1974. Role playing as a source of self-observation and behavior change. *J. Pers. Soc. Psychol.* 29:677–86
71. Krovetz, M. L. 1974. Explaining success or failure as a function of one's locus of control. *J. Pers.* 42:175–89
72. Krupat, E. 1974. Context as a determinant of perceived threat. *J. Pers. Soc. Psychol.* 29:731–36
73. Laird, J. D. 1974. Self-attribution of emotion: the effects of expressive behavior on the quality of emotion experience. *J. Pers. Soc. Psychol.* 29:475–86
74. Lanyon, R. I. 1974. Technology of personality assessment: the Psychological Screening Inventory. *Progr. Exp. Pers. Res.* 7:2–48

75. Landy, D., Sigall, H. 1974. Beauty is talent: task evaluation as a function of the performer's physical attractiveness. *J. Pers. Soc. Psychol.* 29:299–304
76. Leak, G. K. 1974. Effects of hostility arousal and aggressive humor on catharsis and humor preference. *J. Pers. Soc. Psychol.* 30:736–40
77. Lefcourt, H. M., Sordoni, Carl, Sordoni, Carol 1974. Locus of control and the expression of humor. *J. Pers.* 42:130–43
78. Lemon, N., Warren, N. 1974. Salience, centrality and self-relevance of traits in construing others. *Br. J. Soc. Clin. Psychol.* 13:119–24
79. Maccoby, E. E., Jacklin, C. N. 1974. *The Psychology of Sex Differences.* Stanford Univ. Press
80. MacDonald, A. P., Tseng, M. S. 1974. Dimensions of internal versus external control revisited. *JSAS Cat. Select. Doc. Psychol.* 4:13
81. Masling, J., Johnson, C., Saturansky, C. 1974. Oral imagery, accuracy of perceiving others, and performance in Peace Corps training. *J. Pers. Soc. Psychol.* 30:414–19
82. McGinnies, E., Nordholm, L. A., Ward, C. D., Bhanthumnavin, D. L. 1974. Sex and cultural differences in perceived locus of control among students in five countries. *J. Consult. Clin. Psychol.* 42:451–55
83. McGinnies, E., Ward, C. D. 1974. Persuasibility as a function of source credibility and locus of control: five cross-cultural experiments. *J. Pers.* 42:360–71
84. Megaro, P. A. 1974. Theories of schizophrenic performance deficit: an integration theory synthesis. *Progr. Exp. Pers. Res.* 7:150–208
85. Meskin, B. B., Singer, J. L. 1974. Daydreaming, reflective thought, and laterality of eye movements. *J. Pers. Soc. Psychol.* 30:64–71
86. Midgley, N., Abrams, M. S. 1974. Fear of success and locus of control in young women. *J. Consult. Clin. Psychol.* 42:737
87. Mikula, G. 1974. Nationality, performance, and sex as determinants of reward allocation. *J. Pers. Soc. Psychol.* 29:435–40
88. Mischel, W., Zeiss, R., Zeiss, A. 1974. Internal-external control and persistence: validation and implications of the Stanford Preschool Internal-External Control Scale. *J. Pers. Soc. Psychol.* 29:265–78

26   SECHREST

89. Monahan, L., Kuhn, D., Shaver, P. 1974. Intrapsychic versus cultural explanations of the "fear of success" motive. *J. Pers. Soc. Psychol.* 29:60–64
90. Morse, S. J., Reis, H. T., Gruzen, J., Wolff, E. 1974. The "eye of the beholder": determinants of physical attractiveness judgments in the U.S. and South Africa. *J. Pers.* 42:528–42
91. Nevill, D. 1974. Experimental manipulation of dependency motivation and its effects. *J. Pers. Soc. Psychol.* 29:72–79
92. Nickel, T. W. 1974. The attribution of intention as a critical factor in the relation between frustration and aggression. *J. Pers.* 42:482–92
93. Nowicki, S. Jr., Duke, M. P. 1974. A preschool and primary internal-external control scale. *Dev. Psychol.* 10:874–80
93a. Nowicki, S. Jr., Segal, W. 1974. Perceived parental characteristics, locus of control orientation, and behavioral correlates of locus of control. *Dev. Psychol.* 10:33–37
94. Offerhaus, R. E. 1974. *Heartrate variability binary choice capacity in psychiatry.* Res. Rep. St. Bavo Psychiatric Center, Noordwijkerhout, Holland
95. O'Leary, V. E. 1974. Some attitudinal barriers to occupational aspirations in women. *Psychol. Bull.* 81:809–26
96. Olweus, D. 1974. Personality factors and aggression—with special reference to violence within the peer group. In *Aggression: Origins and Determinants,* ed. W. W. Hartup, J. deWit
97. Parsons, O. A., Schneider, J. M. 1974. Locus of control in university students from Eastern and Western societies. *J. Consult. Clin. Psychol.* 42:456–61
98. Pelton, L. H. 1974. *The Psychology of Nonviolence.* New York: Pergamon
99. Perry, D. G., Perry, L. C. 1974. Denial of suffering in the victim as a stimulus to violence in aggressive boys. *Child Dev.* 45:55–62
100. Phares, E. J., Lamiell, J. T. 1974. Relationship of internal-external control to defensive preferences. *J. Consult. Clin. Psychol.* 42:872–78
101. Price, R. H., Bouffard, D. L. 1974. Behavioral appropriateness and situational constraint and dimensions of social behavior. *J. Pers. Soc. Psychol.* 30:579–86
102. Puryear, G. R., Mednick, M. S. 1974. Black militancy, affective attachment, and the fear of success in black college women. *J. Consult. Clin. Psychol.* 42:263–66
103. Rath, F. H. Jr. 1974. Relationship of thematic content to aggressive behavior, aggressive inhibition, and stimulus variation. *JSAS Cat. Selec. Doc. Psychol.* 4:45
104. Reinking, R., Goldstein, G., Houston, B. K. 1974. Cognitive style, proprioceptive skills, task set, stress, and the Rod-and-Frame Test. *J. Pers. Soc. Psychol.* 30:807–11
105. Rizley, R., Reppucci, N. D. 1974. Pavlovian conditioned inhabitory processes in behavior therapy. *Progr. Exp. Pers. Res.* 7:209–63
106. Rodin, J., Slochower, J. 1974. Fat chance for a favor: obese-normal differences in compliance and incidental learning. *J. Pers. Soc. Psychol.* 29:557–65
107. Rule, B. G., Nesdale, A. R. 1974. Differing functions of aggression. *J. Pers.* 42:466–81
108. Sales, S. M., Guydosh, R. M., Iacono, W. 1974. Relationship between "strength of the nervous system" and the need for stimulation. *J. Pers. Soc. Psychol.* 29:16–22
109. Scarpetti, W. L. 1974. Autonomic concomitants of aggressive behavior in repressors and sensitizers: a social learning approach. *J. Pers. Soc. Psychol.* 30:772–81
110. Schiffenbauer, A. 1974. Effect of observer's emotional state on judgments of the emotional state of others. *J. Pers. Soc. Psychol.* 30:31–35
111. Schuck, J., Pisor, K. 1974. Evaluating an aggression experiment by the use of simulating subjects. *J. Pers. Soc. Psychol.* 29:181–86
112. Scott, W. A. 1974. Varieties of cognitive integration. *J. Pers. Soc. Psychol.* 30:563–78
113. Segal, M. W. 1974. Alphabet and attraction: an unobtrusive measure of the effect of propinquity in a field setting. *J. Pers. Soc. Psychol.* 30:654–57
114. Shaffer, D. R., Hendrick, C. 1974. Dogmatism and tolerance for ambiguity as determinants of differential reactions to cognitive inconsistency. *J. Pers. Soc. Psychol.* 29:601–8
115. Shaffer, D. R., Wegley, C. 1974. Success orientation and sex-role congruence as determinants of the attractiveness of competent women. *J. Pers.* 42:586–600
116. Shedletsky, R., Endler, N. S. 1974. Anxiety: the state-trait model and the interaction model. *J. Pers.* 42:511–27
117. Shrauger, J. S., Patterson, M. B. 1974. Self-evaluation and the selection of di-

mensions for evaluating others. *J. Pers.* 42:569–85

118. Snyder, M. 1974. Self-monitoring of expressive behavior. *J. Pers. Soc. Psychol.* 30:526–37

119. Sosis, R. H. 1974. Internal-external control and the perception of responsibility of another for an accident. *J. Pers. Soc. Psychol.* 30:393–99

120. Spence, J. T. 1974. The Thematic Apperception Test and attitudes toward achievement in women: a new look at the motive to avoid success and a new method of measurement. *J. Consult. Clin. Psychol.* 42:427–37

121. Spence, J. T., Helmreich, R., Stapp, J. 1974. The personal attributes questionnaire: a measure of sex role stereotypes and masculinity-femininity. *JSAS Cat. Selec. Doc. Psychol.* 4:43–44

122. Stelmack, R. M., Campbell, K. B. 1974. Extraversion and auditory sensitivity to high and low frequency. *Percept. Mot. Skills* 38:875–79

123. Stewart, A. J., Winter, D. G. 1974. Self-definition and social definition in women. *J. Pers.* 42:238–59

124. Tedeschi, J. T., Smith, R. B. III, Brown, R. C. Jr. 1974. A reinterpretation of research on aggression. *Psychol. Bull.* 81:540–62

125. Teichman, Y. 1974. Predisposition for anxiety and affiliation. *J. Pers. Soc. Psychol.* 29:405–10

126. Thayer, S., Schiff, W. 1974. Observer judgment of social interaction: eye contact and relationship inferences. *J. Pers. Soc. Psychol.* 30:110–14

127. Touhey, J. C. 1974. Effects of additional women professionals on ratings of occupational prestige and desirability. *J. Pers. Soc. Psychol.* 29:86–89

128. Turner, C. W., Simons, L. S. 1974. Effects of subject sophistication and evaluation apprehension on aggressive responses to weapons. *J. Pers. Soc. Psychol.* 30:341–48

129. Vernon, D. T. A. 1974. Modeling and birth order in responses to painful stimuli. *J. Pers. Soc. Psychol.* 29:794–99

130. Vernon, D. T. A., Bigelow, D. A. 1974. Effect of information about a potentially stressful situation on responses to stress impact. *J. Pers. Soc. Psychol.* 29:50–59

131. Viney, L. L. 1974. Multidimensionality of perceived locus of control: two replications. *J. Consult. Clin. Psychol.* 42:463–64

132. Wilkins, J. L., Scharff, W. H., Schlottmann, R. S. 1974. Personality type, reports of violence, and aggressive behavior. *J. Pers. Soc. Psychol.* 30:243–47

133. Wilsnack, S. C. 1974. The effects of social drinking on women's fantasy. *J. Pers.* 42:42–60

134. Wolk, S., DuCette, J. 1974. Intentional performance and incidental learning as a function of personality and task dimensions. *J. Pers. Soc. Psychol.* 29:90–101

135. Worchel, S. 1974. The effect of three types of arbitrary thwarting on the instigation to aggression. *J. Pers.* 42:300–18

136. Worthy, M. 1974. *Eye Color, Sex and Race: Keys to Human and Animal Behavior.* Anderson, S. C.: Droke House/Hallux

137. Yorburg, B. 1974. *Sexual Identity: Sex Roles and Social Change.* New York: Wiley

138. Zillman, D., Bryant, J. 1974. Effect of residual excitation on the emotional response to provocation and delayed aggressive behavior. *J. Pers. Soc. Psychol.* 30:782–91

139. Ziv, A., Kruglanski, A. W., Schulman, S. 1974. Children's psychological reactions to war-time stress. *J. Pers. Soc. Psychol.* 30:24–30

140. Zuckerman, M. 1974. The sensation seeking motive. *Progr. Exp. Pers. Res.* 7:80–148

COGNITIVE DEVELOPMENT ❖247

Herbert Ginsburg and Barbara Koslowski[1]
Department of Human Development, Cornell University, Ithaca, New York 14853

INTRODUCTION

This is the first chapter in the *Annual Review of Psychology* to be devoted entirely to cognitive development, so it seems appropriate to begin by identifying the field's main characteristics and placing it in historical perspective.

The field may be characterized in terms of its empirical focus and theoretical concerns. Cognitive development has as its empirical subject matter the growth of intellectual activities such as using and understanding language, remembering, thinking, and perceiving. The concern is with how the individual gets, creates, and uses knowledge about the physical and social worlds. The focus of study is extremely wide, potentially encompassing a large range of phenomena from the learning of distinctive features of letters to the perception of another's unconscious motivation. At this stage in the field's development, the focus changes as interesting problems emerge.

Although problems of this type have been approached from a variety of points of view, including behaviorist, the cognitive approach is characterized by a distinctive theoretical perspective involving two components: cognition and development. The cognitive component has several premises. The basic one is that intellectual activities (and many others as well) must be explained by reference to internal psychological processes of one kind or another (e.g. grammars, concrete operations, mental imagery, pick-up of distinctive features). A subsidiary premise is that these internal processes most often consist of hierarchical or other organizations (rather

[1]We wish to acknowledge the assistance of a number of colleagues who commented on earlier versions of this paper: Barbara Allardice, Arthur Baroody, Richard Boyd, Urie Bronfenbrenner, Janet Fritz, Eleanor Gibson, Kathy Hebbeler, Jane Knitzer, David Littman, Andrea Petitto, Jill Posner, Sylvia Scribner. Thanks also to Sandy Rightmyer and Elizabeth Swartwout for typing the manuscript and to Ada Weiskopf for putting the bibliography in order. Both authors participated equally in the preparation of this paper.

29

than chain-like associations). Today few question *whether* to accept some form of cognitive theory; the controversial questions are mainly technical, relating to *what kind* of cognitive theory best fits the available data in a given area of study.

There is less of a consensus on the concept of development. Many theorists now agree that development is an active process, that development and cognition have biological foundations and are species-specific, that simple reinforcement and other behaviorist principles are inadequate to explain development, and that a major influence on development is some kind of perceived conflict (e.g. Piaget's "equilibration" theory or E. J. Gibson's "reduction of uncertainty"). At the same time there is considerable disagreement within the field on these issues and on other problems, such as whether or not development involves a series of qualitatively different stages. In brief, the field seems to agree on the necessity for explanation in terms of cognitive processes but has not yet evolved a clear concept of what these processes are like or how they develop.

Cognitive developmental psychology has its roots in the cognitive tradition, as expressed in the work of such thinkers as Dewey (on the inadequacy of the concept of reflex arc), Wertheimer (on the holistic nature of perception), Tolman (on alternatives to a behaviorist account of learning), Lashley (on the necessity for central, hierarchical mechanisms to explain the serial order of behavior), Bartlett (on the organization of memory and thought), and even Freud (on the cognitive apparatus governing the dream work). These theorists were all concerned in one way or another with what is inside the "black box," and stressed the role of mental processes and activities, usually considered in a holistic and hierarchical fashion. In addition, the cognitive theorists exposed the fallacies inherent in atomism, associationism, and behaviorism.

Early in the twentieth century, the cognitive point of view exerted an influence on developmental psychology through the work of such figures as J. M. Baldwin, Buhler, Lewin, Piaget, and Werner. The most influential of these figures is perhaps Piaget, who for the past half century has made major contributions to the study of cognitive development.

From about 1930 to 1960, the contributions of the cognitive developmental theorists were largely ignored by certain influential segments of experimental psychology. Particularly in the area of learning, the cognitive view was overshadowed by developments in behavior theory and by (ultimately fruitless) controversies over such issues as latent learning in the rat. But around 1960 the time was ripe for major paradigm shifts within psychology. Behaviorism began to lose its popularity, partly because of its internal contradictions and sterility and partly because it could not explain basic psychological phenomena, especially in the area of language. But more importantly, there began to emerge several more interesting, vital, and productive lines of research and theory. Three of these in particular created a new field of cognitive development.

First, Piaget's work began to receive the attention it deserved. Interest in Piagetian problems has grown to the point where they are the subject matter for a significant proportion of all research in developmental psychology. Second, psycholinguistics, as developed by such theorists as G. A. Miller and deriving inspiration from Chomsky's work, became a major force within experimental psychology and provided a new and apparently rigorous framework for studying problems of "mind," its development, and its organization. Psycholinguistic theory provided a clear, concrete, and successful alternative to behaviorism in one area of study and thus conferred credibility on a cognitive approach in general. Third, E. J. Gibson raised many fundamental issues concerning the nature of perceptual learning and initiated an influential body of research on perceptual development.

Thus three forces—Piaget's theory, psycholinguistics, and the E. J. Gibson theory of perceptual development (strange bed-persons indeed!)—shaped the emerging field of cognitive development and produced an area of research and theory which is characterized by a great deal of excitement, accomplishment, and even practical implications.

The present review attempts to provide an overview of the current state of this field. We do not present a thorough bibliography of current research, since various journals and computers already do that. Further, our aim is not to provide an in-depth analysis of any one problem in the field, since such an effort, done properly, would limit us to a consideration of only one or two problems. Our purpose instead is to describe and comment on the main ideas and directions in the field of cognitive development.

Our method was first to perform an extensive search through the literature—both journal articles and books—published from approximately June 1973 through December 1974. Colleagues were kind enough to send suggestions and preprints. Second, we generally did not focus on behaviorist approaches or on infancy studies, since the latter are to be emphasized in the "Developmental Psychology" chapter scheduled for Volume 28. Third, we decided to include different topics for different reasons. Language, for example, was included because it is currently a very fertile and innovative field. Language, as well as memory, was also included for a second reason. Although many researchers have for a long time stressed the importance of the interaction between organism and environment, not nearly as many researchers have explicitly studied this interaction. Such study now constitutes an important part of the research efforts in both areas. Humor was reviewed because it exemplified a new approach to a recently neglected but potentially important topic. Piagetian work was reviewed because Piaget's theory is still the most comprehensive and influential one in the field, whether or not one agrees with it. Social cognition was included because work in this area attempts to provide a link between social and cognitive phenomena and to treat the child as an integrated person. Sections were included which covered research on cross-cultural differences, the IQ controversy, and education because it is becoming increasingly clear that the academic discipline of cognitive development is not carried out in isolation from the rest of the world. It is important to acknowledge openly this lack of isolation and to realize that grappling with such issues can have controversial if not significant consequences. Throughout the review we tried as much as possible to focus on work which goes beyond explaining how and why children behave in the laboratory. We preferentially included work which attempted to attain some degree of ecological validity. Finally, we should remark that our review places heavier emphasis than usual on books as opposed to journal articles. Books often present integrated accounts of research programs, whereas papers tend to constitute a more fragmentary approach.

LANGUAGE ACQUISITION

If research motivated by Piagetian approaches accounts for the largest proportion of work in cognitive development, then clearly work on language acquisition accounts for the second largest proportion. It is impossible to even list, let alone summarize, all of this work in the current chapter. Accordingly, we have limited the review to work which involves either new methodological or theoretical approaches or else which falls near the cognition end of the cognition-linguistics dimension.

Categories and Concepts

Two excellent papers, one by Nelson and one by Rosch, have dealt with category formation. Although Rosch used young adults in her study, we nevertheless report the results because of their potential applicability to category formation in children. Rosch (49) found that there are nonarbitrary, "natural" categories "composed of a 'core meaning' which consists of the 'clearest cases' (best examples) of the category, 'surrounded' by other category members of decreasing similarity to that core meaning" (p. 112). "Some colors to which English speakers apply the word 'red' are 'redder' than others. Some breeds of 'dog' (such as retriever) are more representative of the 'meaning' of 'dog' than others (such as Pekinese)" (p. 111). The clearest or most salient cases of a category are called "natural prototypes." "When category names are learned, they tend to become attached first to the salient stimuli (only later generalizing to other instances), and by this means 'natural prototypes' become foci of organization for categories" (p. 330).

Subjects in a study of natural color categories were members of the Dani tribe, who have only two color terms which divide the color space on the basis of brightness rather than hue. The task consisted of learning color names for various sets of color stimuli. Within a set the hue of the colors varied. In some sets, natural prototype colors were central; in some sets, peripheral. In spite of their color vocabulary, the Dani found it easier to learn the names for natural prototypes than for other stimuli, even if the natural prototypes were not the central members of categories. They also found it easier to learn concepts when natural prototypes were central members of these concepts than when they were not. And they chose the natural prototype as the most typical member of a category even when it was actually peripheral.

Using American undergraduates, Rosch next studied nonperceptual natural categories such as the natural semantic categories of vehicle, science, fruit, disease, etc. The results were similar to those for perceptual categories. There was high agreement among subjects in ranking the clearest instances of these categories. For example, murder was the clearest instance of crime, chemistry the clearest instance of science. Further, rankings of clearest instances were different from rankings of *preferred* instances of a category. Thus, even though these *nonperceptual* natural categories do not possess perceptually determined natural prototypes, they do seem to have artificial—presumably socially determined—prototypes.

We turn now from Rosch's work on concepts in adults to Nelson's (43) account of the concept acquisition which takes place even before the child learns to talk, and of the way in which these prelinguistic concepts are formed in order to fit the way in which available words are used by others. Nelson's account seems to be related to Rosch's work on natural categories in two ways. First, both authors agree that categories are not initially defined in terms of abstract attributes. Rosch suggests instead that categories may be initially defined in terms of clear cases or instances. Nelson makes a somewhat similar claim when she notes that " . . . analysis [of attributes common to the instances of concepts] is not the *prerequisite* to the synthesis of concepts." Second, both authors speak to the issue of how early instances of a category come to be grouped together. However, Rosch emphasizes the role of the perceptual characteristics and the "artificial" characteristics of the early instances of prototypes. Nelson stresses instead the functional relations into which early concept instances enter. It is not clear whether this difference between the two accounts can be resolved simply by noting that Nelson is discussing prelinguistic concepts while Rosch is discussing later concepts. It is also worth pointing out that at some level the distinction between perceptual attributes and functional relations is difficult, if not impossible, to make. A perceptual attribute of a ball—namely, its roundness—not only permits, but indeed is necessary for, the functional relation of rolling which the ball enters into.

Nelson (43) criticizes the traditional theory that concept formation is based on the abstraction of common elements or attributes by first pointing out that this theory presupposes what it is relevant to explain: "the principle by which common elements are abstracted *as* common." Why is it that certain elements are seen as common in the first place? Also, the theory equates concept formation with association of diverse elements with an "arbitrary response" rather than with "principled organization." Further, it attempts to account for identification of concept instances specified by the parent but not for concept selection and generation by the child. Nelson also criticizes semantic feature theory as being a "revised version of the abstraction of critical attributes, plus hypothesis testing," which allows the child to decide which attributes are the correct ones. As an alternative, Nelson postulates that there are two potentially separable aspects involved in learning concepts: (*a*) "distinguishing entities (objects, events, abstractions) on the basis of a set of currently useful roles or relationships"; and (*b*) "finding the stable characteristics of the set of entities grouped according to this principle and setting up an attribute hierarchy according to which new instances of the concept can be identified independently of knowledge about their participation in the defining relations." This distinction corresponds to that between concept generation and concept identification. If we view attributes as the products of analysis and concepts as the products of synthesis, then it becomes clear that abstraction theories assume that the analysis comes first. "However, analysis is not the *prerequisite* to the synthesis of concepts. Rather, a dual process is found to be at work—first categorizing according to some principle and then identifying common attributes. But if categorizing does not depend upon analysis, what is its basis?" "Whole elements . . . take on definitions as concepts in terms of the synthesis of their functional or dynamic *relations.*" For example, a ball rolls, is thrown, is held, bounces, is on the floor, etc. This first process is equivalent to the formation of what Piaget calls "action schemes." After concepts begin to be formed on the basis of the similarity of relations into which the concept instances enter, analysis of the concept instances themselves takes place. One result of this analysis is that the child learns which attributes (e.g. location of the ball) are irrelevant to the defining, functional core of the concept. This analysis also permits the child to specify the attributes which permit the identification of instances outside of their definitional contexts as well as to identify new instances of the concept.

Thus both Nelson and Rosch employ a notion of "core" or "natural" concepts, although they seem to define these concepts in somewhat different ways.

In both of the papers reviewed above, there is a fair amount of emphasis on the relationship between internal, cognitive processes on the one hand and the external, empirical world on the other. However, the discussion of this relationship focuses on general concept formation and structure. Katz et al (32) offer an example of the interaction between cognition and the external world in a more specific area of development, namely, the acquisition of the distinction between common and proper nouns. Common nouns refer to classes of objects, proper nouns to individuals. The authors' findings support their hypothesis that "children are able to learn the distinction between common and proper nouns and the syntactic marking of that distinction . . . [because] they have previously made the relevant distinction among the referents." "What children learn to begin with is that the individuals of certain classes are important as individuals." "One spoon, for example, is usually as good as another. But . . . it must be your own mother you go home with, not just any lady who happens to be about." Once the individuality among some classes of objects becomes salient, it serves as a clue to a distinction between two semantically different types of names: common nouns and proper nouns. "By bearing in mind the semantic distinction, the child is in a position to detect its syntactic markers, that is, among other things, presence or absence of the article 'a' or 'the.' "

Recall that one of the points Nelson makes about concept acquisition is that the child must eventually learn which attributes of early instances are irrelevant to the defining core of the concept. Maratsos (41) offers a specific example of how this learning takes place during semantic concept acquisition and suggests that a similar process is probably operating in other areas of cognitive development as well. Maratsos studied the way in which children learn the semantics of the term "big." He found that, with increasing age, "top point" acquires more influence as a defining characteristic of "high," "tall," and "big." ("Top point refers to the distance of an object's top from the baseline or ground." For young children, a child who is standing and whose head is thus higher than the head of an adult who is squatting will be judged to be bigger or taller than the adult.) For "tall" and "big," this increasing influence results in increasing inaccuracy, for although "top point" is correlated with bigness and tallness, the correlation is not perfect. Maratsos relates his results to Gelman's finding that lack of conservation of number results from attending to irrelevant cues. In her view, conservation judgments improve when children are trained to ignore irrelevant situational cues. He suggests that the acquisition of both semantic as well as cognitive concepts might involve learning "the importance of context in determining when individual components [of a concept] become determinative of usage . . ."

Language Comprehension

During the past year, a continuing theme in the work on language comprehension is that semantics plays at least as important a role as syntax in the understanding of sentences. Just as knowledge about the empirical world is important to concept formation, so also is knowledge of the empirical world important to the comprehension of language.

First, however, consider a study related to the child's acquisition of syntax. Starr (58) used a preference method to measure the discrimination of grammatical from ungrammatical sentences and tested children (18–30 months of age) who were only speaking in either one- or two-word utterances. Both groups of children discriminated the two kinds of sentences. Although this preference method suggested that even very young children could discriminate grammatical from ungrammatical sentences, Starr points out that comprehension involves more than a knowledge of syntax: it involves memory, context cues, and comprehension strategies as well.

The following two studies dealt with extra-syntactic cues from the environmental context and their role in language comprehension. Strohner & Nelson (59) examined the role of two types of cues: event probabilities (e.g. cats often chase mice) and the word order "actor-action-object" which occurs in active sentences. For 3- to 5-year-olds, sentences which were in the active voice and which referred to probable actor-action-object events elicited consistently correct performance. In contrast, 3-year-olds performed much more poorly than did 5-year-olds with two types of sentences: active sentences which referred to improbable events, and "reversible" passive sentences where the event probabilities are about equal for the sequences actor-action-object and object-action-actor (e.g. "Black cats are chased by white cats.") The authors conclude that ". . . if the child fails to extract explicit information about object and actor from syntactic structure, then the child usually does not guess randomly—instead, influenced in part by context, he applies extra-syntactic strategies such as the probable event strategy or the actor-action-object strategy."

Wetstone & Friedlander (65) also questioned the primacy of syntactic cues in sentence comprehension by directly examining the role of word-order. They presented 2- and 3-year-old children with simple questions and commands which were spoken in varying degrees of word-order distortion (e.g. "Show to clown the Mommy"; "Mommy clown to the show."). The children were required to act out the sentences with concrete objects. Although the fluent 3-year-old children responded more poorly to the scrambled than to the normal sentences, the nonfluent 2-year-old children responded appropriately to both kinds of sentences. The authors ask ". . . how are these (nonfluent) children able to understand what is said as well as they seem to when they don't have access to so many of the basic linguistic modes of establishing meaning, which are taken so much for granted by the experienced listener that their misuse seriously disrupts comprehension?" They suggest that for very young children, sentence "comprehension is confined to recognition of familiar words" and to "their ability to integrate the meaning of the familiar words they hear with the objects and events immediately before them."

Additional Contributions

Behaviorist accounts of language acquisition emphasize imitation as the process by which relatively passive learners acquire language. Imitation plays a role in cognitive accounts of language acquisition as well. However, research generated by this theoretical framework finds that the learner is so nonpassive that he imitates only after he has already learned something on his own.

Bloom et al (8) examined the way in which imitation of adult language affects language production. The authors focused on spontaneous speech that occurred during the period in which children progress from using only one word at a time to using two. First of all, there were marked differences in the extent to which children imitated. Secondly, there was evidence that the children already knew something about what they were imitating: ". . . it was almost always the case that when observed imitation exceeded expected imitation within a category or subcategory, there were spontaneous utterance types as well. . . ." ". . . children imitated only words and structures in the speech that they heard which they appeared to be in the process of learning. They tended not to imitate words and structures that they themselves either used spontaneously and so presumably knew, or did not use spontaneously at all and so presumably did not know."

A recurring theme in this chapter will be that there is often a discrepancy between what a child does in a laboratory situation and what that same child does in a more naturalistic situation. Blank (5) offered an explanation to account for discrepancies between language use in laboratories and language use which is spontaneous. She focused on three areas: concept formation, communication, and problem solving. She notes that

> . . . prelinguistic mastery in these functions is available through sensorimotor skills. Such skills, however, are geared to visual spatial information. . . . the child employs language and recognizes its power in those situations in which he finds that his other representational skills (e.g. imagery, gesture, etc.) are usless. . . . present experimental tasks, for the most part, do not assess such situations; instead the tasks are either ones in which the child can function with this nonverbal repertoire or ones that involve cognitive demands so complex as to preclude adequate performance by the child.

PIAGETIAN STUDIES

Research "on Piaget" proceeds with a ferocity which makes a comprehensive review impossible. Hence, we focus on the problem of development and on some new developments in Piaget-related work.

Development

Learning and maturation are usually considered the main contributors to ontogenetic development. Not so, according to Piaget. In his view, development is the prior concept, blending both "nature" and "nurture" and permitting learning to occur. Furth (18) provides an extensive theoretical elaboration of Piaget's position, with special reference to the nature-nurture controversy. According to Furth's account of Piaget, a species' evolution (or phylogenetic development) involves the acquisition of a hereditary endowment which provides the individual with physiological (e.g. the central nervous system) and behavioral structures (e.g. walking) which permit, regulate, and set limits on both ontogenetic development and learning. The interaction between the species' hereditary endowment and the environment which is common to all members of the species results in development which involves the formation of new structures for adaptation to the environment. Development is said to stem from "logico-mathematical experience" (the individual's learning about the results of his own actions on the world), and is controlled by internal self-regulating mechanisms. Development leads to the formation of general structures of knowledge which may be common to all members of the species. By contrast, learning is a function of the individual's interaction with particular (idiosyncratic) aspects of the environment. Learning involves reversible (in the sense of forgettable) acquisitions of a nongeneral sort, and depends heavily on "physical experience" (perceptual learning). Thus development might involve an infant's acquisition of object permanence which may derive from interaction with any objects, whereas learning might involve the infant's getting information about a unique red ball which must derive from experience with that object and that object only. There is a strong sense in which learning is dependent on development: the general structures acquired through development permit specific learning to occur. [A most lucid and brief account of his theory of development is given by Piaget (46).] Furth shows how systematic application of this framework may clarify some puzzles inherent in the nature-nurture controversy.

Piaget's theory of development addresses itself to issues other than the nature-nurture controversy; specifically, the theory proposes that development involves the acquisition of a series of stages, acquired through an equilibration process. Many investigators have attempted to test Piaget's theory by investigating the effects of various forms of training. Kuhn (35) provides an interesting analysis of two basic issues involved in training studies. One refers to the question of whether laboratory procedures can provide a fair test of Piaget's equilibration theory. As Kuhn interprets Piaget, "conservation reflects a reorganization of cognitive structure and it is not the attainment of any specific information or any single capacity, such as reversibility of operations, that leads the child to this reorganization in the natural (nonexperimental) situation" (35, p. 596). Kuhn goes on to show how many laboratory procedures intended to simulate this natural process fail to do so. For example, conflict producing methods may not produce *perceived* conflict in the child. Kuhn suggests that adequate laboratory tests of Piaget's theory have not been performed. A second issue is the criterion for conservation: how can one evaluate the success of a training study, whether its intent is to evaluate Piaget's theory or test an opposing view? Kuhn shows that many of the criteria for successful conservation usually used in research are ambiguous. The most serious ambiguity is in the area of generalization. On the one hand, if the child "really has" conservation it should generalize beyond the training situation. On the other hand, the phenomenon of décalage is well known: conservation does not generalize in all possible ways. Given both these situations, it is unclear as to how much generalization is required to infer successful conservation; hence, unambiguous evaluation of training is impossible. In brief, Kuhn argues that it is extremely difficult to simulate the equilibration process in the laboratory, and that ambiguities in the criteria for successful conservation make the training study an extremely limited technique. Kuhn goes on to suggest some improvements in the methodology of conservation studies: longitudinal designs and wide ranging assessments. These require further elaboration and empirical demonstration.

Brainerd (9) also provides a review of training studies, but sees in them less ambiguity than does Kuhn. Since his criteria for successful conservation are less stringent than Kuhn's, he concludes that many training studies are effective. Brainerd's criteria seem less adequate than Kuhn's, since the former's show an unfortunate tendency to use simple responses rather than explanations as the criterion for conservation.

Turiel (61) reports a theoretical analysis and empirical study of equilibration which seems to avoid many of the pitfalls described by Kuhn. The study examines development as it occurs naturally and deals not with conservation but with moral judgment, specifically the transition between Kohlberg's stages 4 and 5. Turiel offers a thoughtful analysis of equilibration theory and presents data which convincingly support the claim that "transition from one stage to the next involves a phase of conflict or disequilibrium during which the existing mode of thinking is reevaluated and a new mode is constructed" (p. 14).

Hollos & Cowan (28) attempted to examine Bruner's hypothesis that verbal stimulation and schooling play central roles in conceptual development (e.g. conservation). They investigated the effects of various social settings on the development of conservation, classification, and role taking. The social settings, all within Norway, differed primarily in the amount of verbal interaction that children have with peers and parents and in the amount of schooling. Thus the attempt is to take advantage of a "natural experiment" which presumably is more powerful than the manipulations one can perform in the laboratory. The danger, of course, is that the complexities of an ordinary environment hopelessly confound the natural experiment and make it uninterpretable. Hollos & Cowan found that language stimulation and schooling do not seem to exert major effects on conservation and classification, but do affect the development of role taking. Piaget's theory of development which stresses the role of logico-mathematical experience (learning about one's actions on objects in the absence of social or educational factors) in the development of conservation seems better able to account for these results than Bruner's.

West (64) elaborates on one aspect of the Hollos & Cowan study, namely, the role of social interaction in fostering role-taking skills. In a study comparing Israeli children reared in nuclear families versus communal settings on role taking tasks, West substantiates the Hollos & Cowan hypothesis that "the proper development of role-taking skill requires a basic minimum of early social interaction, but that beyond this, differences in the amount of such experience fail to contribute differentially to individual achievement" (p. 1121).

Research on development has often been unsuccessful and does not suggest clear directions which future efforts might take. As Kuhn points out, many laboratory studies are ambiguous. Yet there are reasons for optimism. Studies like Turiel's provide valuable theory and data on equilibration, and studies like Hollos & Cowan's attempt to employ novel methods for the study of development. Perhaps further progress will be made when two conditions are fulfilled: when investigators explore naturalistic and other techniques for the study of development; and when they become less concerned with studying Piaget's theory of development (especially the development of conservation) and more interested in the phenomena of development themselves. The field requires a broadening of both the theoretical framework and empirical concerns.

The Revisionist Movement

Our bias is that Piagetian orthodoxy is self-defeating and unworthy of Piaget's immense contribution. We believe that the productive approach is to go beyond Piaget, to use whatever is useful in his approach and whatever other ideas are necessary in an attempt to explain fundamental phenomena, including some (e.g. reading) which Piaget has not studied. Within this perspective, we applaud several recent attempts to produce neo-, pseudo-, or non-Piagetian theories. These revisionist attempts are too complex to describe in detail here; we merely mention their main features.

Klahr (33) attempts "to apply the theoretical and methodological approach of Newell and Simon to the complex problems raised by empirical work in the Piagetian tradition" (p. 141). He constructs computer program models for tasks like classification. This approach seems to have the advantage of providing for cognitive process explanations a concrete embodiment which may be subjected to empirical test. At the same time, we remain to be convinced that the computer program approach adds anything to our understanding of how children actually go about solving various problems. Rather, the computer program approach seems mainly to formalize what we already know about children. This may be useful, but one must place the effort in proper perspective.

Bryant (10) proposes a theory which will surely have the unique distinction of alienating both Piagetians and Gibsonians. He takes on the Piagetians by claiming to prove that children reason logically much earlier than Piaget proposes. He challenges the Gibsonians by resurrecting the Helmholtz approach to perception with a new twist: logical mechanisms of a sort different from those proposed by Helmholtz provide the basis for unconscious inference in perception. Bryant's program of research is intriguing and must be taken seriously by students of development.

Case (11) presents a comparison of Pascual-Leone's theory with Piaget's. Pascual-Leone's theory is intended to supplement Piaget's structural approach by providing a functional (performance) account, "that is, one which describes the devices or mechanisms by which human knowledge [cognitive structure] is actually acquired and utilized" (11, p. 544). While many of Pascual-Leone's theoretical notions are intriguing, the research they result in seems to involve mainly a lot of intercorrelations among measures like the WISC and Field Independence, and we wonder what kind of progress this represents.

MEMORY

Since Bartlett's (2) classic study of memory, it has been widely accepted that the organization of memory is too complicated to be described solely in terms of associationist principles. For Bartlett, acquired information is transformed and remembered in a form which makes it congruent with the rest of the person's remembered information. That is, Bartlett stressed the way in which empirical knowledge about the real world serves as the basis for transforming and organizing new information in memory. Piaget & Inhelder (47) postulate yet another determinant of memory organization. Instead of stressing congruence with empirical information, they focus on developing cognitive processes as the basis for organizing remembered information. They claim that the content of what is remembered is organized to make it congruent with the particular cognitive operations that characterize the child's thought at the time his memory is tested. This position leads to an apparently paradoxical prediction: memory may improve rather than deteriorate over time. For example, asked to seriate a set of sticks of ordered lengths, a preoperational child may arrange them in two piles, large and small. By contrast, a concrete operational child seriates a set of ordered sticks correctly. Shown a set of already seriated sticks, a preoperational child *remembers* only two piles, large and small, since he assimilates the sticks into his current cognitive structures. If this same child is tested later when he reaches the stage of concrete operations, he remembers the sticks as seriated; his memory has undergone an improvement since his thinking structures have changed.

Independent research on the Piaget-Inhelder theory is just beginning and much of it is rightfully concerned with replication, since the original work suffers from some methodological and reporting difficulties. Liben (39) maintains that sometimes in the Piaget-Inhelder research, change in children's intellectual status is not independently assessed but is instead inferred from observed changes in memory—a procedure which is plainly circular. Similarly, Furth, Ross & Youniss (19) omit separate measures of intellectual status. Using a methodology which remedies this situation, Liben obtains complex results which support the Piaget-Inhelder hypothesis to only a limited extent. Some children's memory does improve in apparent conjunction with intellectual development, as predicted by the theory. On the other hand, there are many regressions in memory as well, and not all improvements in memory can be related to development in the Piagetian stages. Samuels (50) finds a good deal of reconstruction in children's memory, but some of it has nothing to do with development of the Piagetian stages. According to Samuels, there may be reconstruction based on intellectual factors other than those Piaget describes. In brief, it seems that the Piaget-Inhelder theory may account for some aspects of memory change, but further research is required to isolate the precise manner in which Piagetian intellectual development affects memory and to investigate the possible ways in which non-Piagetian intellectual factors operate in reconstruction. These non-Piagetian factors may be the more commonly used in everyday life; how often does the child normally have to remember seriated sticks, tilted jars, and the like?

In addition to the Piagetian studies of memory, several investigators examined the ways in which linguistic principles affect the organization of memory. By and large, studies of this sort used material which was linguistically rather than visually presented. Several studies have demonstrated that semantic content, rather than syntactic cues, play a much greater role in memory organization than was hitherto thought.

For example, Paris & Carter (44) presented 7- to 11-year-olds with a number of sentences (e.g. The bird is inside the cage. The cage is under the table). They then tested the children's "recognition" memory by presenting them with a new set of sentences which were syntactically different from the original sentences. However, the semantic content of these new sentences was congruent with inferences that could be educed by relating the sentences to one another and integrating them in terms of semantic content rather than by treating the original sentences as units isolated from one another (e.g. The bird is under the table). The new sentences were "recognized" as having been previously presented. The children had synthesized semantic information not contained within the underlying structures of the individual sentences. The authors point out that their results support Bransford's claim that "People carry meanings, and linguistic inputs merely act as cues which people can use to recreate and modify their previous knowledge of the world."

Barclay & Reid (1) focused on one particular syntactic structure, the truncated passive sentence (e.g. The ball was hit), and obtained similar results. Truncated passive sentences were usually recalled verbatim "when the actors missing from their surface structures remained unspecified. However, when missing actors were introduced elsewhere in a story, verbatim recall of truncated passives decreased markedly, becoming no more frequent than conversions to actives." What is striking about both of these studies is that the individual sentence is not always the basic unit of memory. Rather, children implicitly construct semantic relationships among sentences and integrate these relationships in memory.

In addition to work on the semantic organization of memory, there has also been a continuation of work on what Flavell (17) has called the "planful" quality of memory—the conscious and deliberate processing of present data in such a way as to facilitate its future recall. Rogoff et al (48) studied the specific aspect of planning ability involved in "the tendency to adjust inspection times in accord with the length of time the child believes he will have to remember the pictures." While 8-year-olds adjusted their inspection times in such a fashion, 4- and 6-year-olds did not. The authors note that their finding is in accord with the previously observed emergence of planful mnemonic strategies at 6 to 7 years of age.

A study by von Wright (62) suggests that planfulness may facilitate memory only in some situations—those that involve recall rather than recognition, and immediate rather than delayed recall. Von Wright presented 5-year-old children with drawings of common objects. In the intentional learning condition, children were told to name the objects pictured and were told that they would later be asked to recall the object names. Successful performance on this task required planfulness. In the incidental learning condition, children were shown the pictures two at a time and asked to silently point to the one they preferred. A verbal recall and a visual recognition task followed, either immediately or after a 2-week interval. Intentional rather than incidental learning facilitated memory only in the verbal recall test that was administered immediately after training. However, the two learning conditions resulted in no differences for delayed recall or for either delayed or immediate recognition. The author suggests that the process of recognizing previously presented pictures of objects and the process of recalling the names of these objects involve two different and largely independent ways of "accessing" memory. Thus the planfulness which is presumably involved in intentional learning seems to facilitate only immediate recall.

HUMOR

For a long time, a widely accepted view of humor was that it was based on repressed aggression which was released at another person's expense. For those of us who were studying psychology during the heyday of elephant and grape jokes,[2] this view was not an especially flattering one, but, alas, there were few well-articulated alternatives. Fortunately, the past few years have seen a revival of interest in the role of cognitive processes in the development of humor. Part of this interest stemmed from the fact that the apprehension of incongruity, an activity important to the understanding of many humorous situations, has also been receiving increasing attention as a factor in producing cognitive conflict and subsequent cognitive development. Another source of this interest is the hypothesis that full appreciation of many humorous situations often involves an increase in arousal when the incongruity is apprehended, followed by a decrease in arousal when the incongruity is resolved or explained. This hypothesis means that once again the activities associated with understanding humorous situations can be viewed as specific instances of more general principles of development, such as those proposed by Berlyne (3).

Using verbal jokes, Shultz & Horibe (56) experimentally investigated a little-known facet of Freud's theory of humor. Freud proposed that processes involving incongruity and resolution appear in a developmental sequence. That is, children first respond to the incongruity involved in many humorous situations even if such

[2]From personal experience, H. G. points out that some of the more mature readers of this chapter may not be familiar with elephant and grape jokes. It seems appropriate, therefore, to offer two representative examples: How can you tell when an elephant has been in your refrigerator? You can see his footprints in the Jello. What is purple, weighs 2000 pounds, and swims in the ocean? Moby Grape.

It should be pointed out that in some circles these sorts of jokes reached profound levels of sophistication. Consider the following: What is purple and commutes? An Abelian grape. (Note that this last joke provides an additional bit of evidence for the view, discussed below, that humor involves "applied cognition.")

incongruity is merely nonsensical. At a later stage, children begin to prefer meaningful jokes—jokes which are based on an incongruity which children can resolve or explain.

Shultz & Horibe studied the development of both the apprehension and the resolution of incongruity. They presented 6- to 12-year-olds with a series of jokes of three different types: the original (e.g. Call me a cab. You're a cab.); resolution-removed or nonsensical (e.g. Call a cab for me. You're a cab.); and incongruity removed (Call me a cab. Yes ma'am.) Thus the resolution-removed form preserved incongruity, but a nonsense kind of incongruity for which there was no obvious explanation or resolution. The incongruity-removed form preserved neither resolvable nor nonsensical incongruity. For 6-year-olds, there was no difference in the original and resolution-removed (nonsense-preserving) forms of the jokes, and both forms were appreciated more than were the incongruity-removed jokes. For the 8- to 12-year-olds, the original jokes were funnier than the resolution-removed jokes, and these in turn were funnier than the incongruity-removed forms. Thus the 6-year-olds appreciated the incongruity structure but not the resolution structure of jokes, while the older children appreciated both types of structure. The authors view these findings as evidence for a developmental theory of humor: that children can appreciate pure incongruity (or nonsense) before they are able to resolve or explain this incongruity. The finding is perhaps related to the more general principle that much of cognitive development proceeds by the child's first noticing an incongruity (initial nonsense) and then resolving it by moving to a more advanced level of thinking (resolution).

Although 6-year-olds in the above study preferred the resolution-removed to the incongruity-removed forms of jokes, Shultz (55) found that 6-year-olds had no preference for resolution-removed as opposed to incongruity-removed forms of riddles. Shultz suggests that "riddles are posed as problems to be solved, whereas jokes . . . are not." Thus, "in the context of a joke, an unresolved incongruity may be experienced as enjoyable nonsense, whereas in the context of a problem, it may generate a relatively unpleasant state of cognitive tension." As Harter (27) suggests in a study of anagram problem solving, enjoyment of a problem may depend on the child's being able to solve it.

Humor may also be studied from a psycholinguistic point of view. In each of the Shultz experiments reported above, for example, the authors also found that the incongruity inherent in both jokes and riddles is often based upon some sort of linguistic ambiguity. Both studies found that, in general, phonological and lexical ambiguities are detected at an earlier age than are syntactic ambiguities. The authors relate this finding to the fact that in situations of nonhumorous linguistic ambiguity, phonological ambiguity is detected first, lexical ambiguity second, and surface (and deep) structure ambiguities last (57). The development of humor then reflects advances in the development of language. In this respect at least, the development of humor also seems to be similar to the development of memory. They both seem to involve what Flavell has called "applied cognition," in that they both seem to reflect changes in more general cognitive development. Just as the development of memory parallels the development of other cognitive processes, so also does the detection of *humorous* linguistic ambiguity parallel the detection of *general* linguistic ambiguity.

McGhee (42) studied children's ability to create as well as to detect the humorous relationships expressed in riddles. He found that "creating a joking relationship is more difficult than successfully identifying an already created one." This seems similar to Flavell's (16) finding that children can use various mnemonic devices when suggested, before they can spontaneously produce them. However, "some children as young as 7 or 8 are able to learn sufficiently from concrete examples of a given type of joking relationship to enable them, in some cases, to create an example of that relationship, even though they cannot verbalize the basis on which they created that relationship."

A study by Groch (26) brings us full circle to our original point that the enjoyment of elephant jokes may be quite unrelated to the base instinct of aggression. Groch (26) addressed the question of whether humor emerges as a single trait or as a cluster of related dimensions. She recorded the occurrence of three forms of humor in preschool children: responsive humor (a smile or laugh in the presence of unexpected stimuli); hostile productive humor; and nonhostile productive humor (silliness, teasing, deliberate violation of meaning). These three forms of humor were not significantly correlated, suggesting that humor has multiple aspects and is not a unitary trait of which children simply possess different quantities. Further, different forms of humor occurred in different circumstances.

We would like to suggest two reasons for the importance of the topic of humor. The first reason is that this topic attains a degree of ecological validity which is lacking in many other areas of research. In our nonlaboratory lives, few of us learn lists of paired-associates, but most of us enjoy jokes and riddles. The second reason is that sharing a humorous situation is an example of a very rewarding, though little studied, form of social communication and intimacy. Sharing a humorous situation with someone involves the exchange of some very complicated information in a nonexplicit way and leads to a feeling of camaraderie. In sharing a joke, each person understands why the other person is laughing. And even more important, each person realizes that the fact that he knows why the other person is laughing is known to the other person as well. And all of this complex information is communicated without putting any of it into words. The intimacy which results from this kind of nonverbal communication may well be a very basic, and thus particularly rewarding, form of social interaction.

Finally, there are a number of intriguing questions about humor which remain unanswered. For example, what makes satire funny? The incongruity involved in satire is less pronounced than it is in jokes and riddles and, if anything, simply consists of an exaggeration of what does happen. Why do people find puns funny? Why is understatement often humorous? And, lastly, how do children develop the ability to both appreciate and create different forms of humor?

SOCIAL COGNITION

The child employs his developing cognitive processes to adapt to the social world. Early in life he learns to perceive others' motives, to anticipate their behavior, to detect regularities in their action, and to understand the reasons for their conduct. Surely the cognitive processes producing social knowledge are as important for the child as those that provide the basis for adaptation to the physical world. While this is so, we possess few empirical data and little in the way of integrative theory concerning the development of social cognition.

Given this state of affairs, a theoretical paper by Flavell (15) is most welcome. Flavell begins by speculating that "social-cognitive skill" is a "cognitive-developmental universal," and hence of interest to the student of cognitive development. In other words, social knowledge is not present at birth, must be acquired in the course of development, and is eventually attained to a significant extent by all intact adults. In these respects social knowledge is similar to other cognitive processes such as language.

Flavell proposes a model of social cognition involving four components. The *Existence* component refers to the fact that the child must learn about the possible existence of psychological states and processes in others. Such learning is a prerequisite for perceiving a particular psychological state in a particular person. This is a controversial notion. Indeed, on the basis of principles of perceptual development, it seems more likely that exactly the reverse is true; children probably learn first to perceive specific psychological states in specific individuals and then later learn to make generalizations concerning these states' general "existence." Flavell goes on to propose that as a corollary, the child must learn that others' psychological processes (whatever they are) are not necessarily the same as his own in a given situation, although they often may be. In Piaget's terms, the child must abandon cognitive "egocentrism." There has been a fair amount of research on this problem.

A second component of Flavell's model refers to *Need*. Suppose the child has some knowledge of the *Existence* (component 1) of psychological states and has means for identifying them (component 3, to be described below). Given this competence, does he use it to cope with social problems? This is the question of *Need* (perhaps an unfortunate term). The general issue is whether the child spontaneously brings to bear on social problems (performance) the potential knowledge he possesses concerning psychological processes (competence).

A third component is *Inference* which refers to "somehow obtaining impressions about" (15, p. 66) the psychological states of others. *Inference* can mean any process by which one knows another in a given situation. Flavell proposes that the social psychology of person perception in adults provides an "elegant account of overall structure of this component" (p. 70). We do not altogether agree. It seems to us that while theorists like Tagiuri have made a useful start on the problem of *Inference*, much in the way of fundamental cognitive analysis of the problem remains to be accomplished—e.g. specifying what kind of information is involved in person perception.

The fourth component of the model refers to the question of the *Application* of knowledge. What does the child do with what he knows?

The Flavell model, despite its preliminary character, may serve a useful purpose if it is employed as a challenging framework with which to approach and conceptualize problems of social knowledge. For example, the notion of *Need* allows us to entertain the important possibility that the child's behavior on certain social knowledge tasks may not reflect the full extent of this knowledge. And the notion of *Inference* (interpreted broadly so as to refer to any process of knowing another) should lead to a detailed examination of such issues as the processes children use to pick up information concerning others.

Unfortunately, some contemporary research on social knowledge concentrates on very limited aspects of the problem. In fact, much of this research focuses on the *verbal* description of persons and therefore sheds little light on either the *Existence* or *Inference* components of Flavell's model. Secord & Peevers (53) obtained, from kindergarten through college students, verbal descriptions of friends, a disliked person, and the self. A content analysis of the data showed that children's verbal conceptualization of others proceeds from relatively specific and superficial characteristics like physical appearance ("She has red hair") to more abstract characterizations in terms of interests, psychological states, and other dispositional terms which have the power to explain behavior in a wide variety of circumstances. Livesley & Bromley (40) obtained similar results.

Studies like these must be evaluated with caution. On the one hand, they indicate that children's verbally expressed (through speech or writing) concepts of people become increasingly elaborate, differentiated, abstract, and psychological as development proceeds. This is perhaps not very surprising. On the other hand, one must place such data in proper perspective. They do not necessarily mean that in real situations young children fail to cognize others' psychological states in subtle ways. Children are able to perceive many things they cannot express well in words, especially when real objects (people) are present. In Flavell's terms, verbal performance may not reflect underlying competence.

Other studies deal more directly with processes of social knowledge. Livesley & Bromley asked children from 4 to 8 to describe "what is happening" in a silent motion picture film concerning a man going about his ordinary activities. The investigators found that young children could describe the action with more success than they could verbalize underlying processes. The possibility that the young child may be adept at perceiving and even predicting behavior deserves further research.

Kun, Parsons & Ruble (37) report an interesting study, based on Heider's theory, of children's use of various kinds of information to predict another's behavior. Children from 6 to 11 years of age were asked to predict how many puzzles another child would solve if he were characterized by one of three different levels of ability (e.g. very good at puzzles) in combination with one of three different levels of effort (e.g. didn't try at all). The results show that children at all ages made use of both types of information (ability and effort). At the same time, younger and older children reasoned about the information differently. The older children dealt with the interaction between ability and effort in subtle ways, realizing, for example, that "differences in ability have a greater effect on outcome when a person tries hard than when his efforts are only mediocre" (37, p. 720). Younger children use simpler forms of reasoning (although the report does not make clear what they are). The study thus attempts to specify the ways in which children use information and reason about it to reach a judgment concerning another person. The main weakness of the study is perhaps its use of hypothetical problems rather than more ecologically valid and informationally rich situations (like videotapes of real people).

Whiteman, Brook & Gordon (66) also used a verbal method and found that young children tend to base their judgments of another's intention more on the outcomes of an action than on its source, whereas older children take both factors into account. Thus the young child might say that an act was intended if it led to a good result, whether or not the individual initiated the act. This study is important because it is one of few dealing with the perception of intention, surely a fundamental aspect of person perception.

The area of social cognition does not seem to have made great leaps forward in recent years, if indeed it ever has. In our view, research in the area might profit from a focus on children's strengths in social cognition. It is necessary to explain why and how infants and very young children, and indeed retarded individuals, are enormously skilled at the perception and prediction of others' behavior, emotions, and intentions. These strengths are especially clear when we examine social interaction in natural settings, rather than mere verbal descriptions. Piaget shows, for example, that anticipation of others' behavior occurs early in infancy; clinicians' observations attest to the social skill of Mongoloids; recent studies of social interaction in young children demonstrate its successful, interactive nature (54). The problem is not to explain why young children do badly at social cognition. Rather the task is to describe the psychological processes involved in young children's generally successful and adaptive social cognition. In doing this, it may be useful to consider social cognition from a *perceptual* point of view and to raise questions like these: What is the stimulus information children employ to perceive emotions or intentions in others? How do children learn to detect and predict important aspects of behavior? What are the proper units of analysis for person perception—do children perceive details of behavior, acts, or sequences? Perhaps an approach of this sort may shed light on the child's early successes in social cognition and lead to fruitful analyses of its later complexities.

CROSS-CULTURAL STUDIES AND SOCIAL CLASS

Recent research into the relations between culture and cognitive development provides important insights into questions of both theory and method. The methodological implications are especially important, and should be seriously considered by researchers in all areas of cognitive development. We review two lines of work, the first involving culture and the second social class.

Cross-Cultural Studies

Cole & Scribner (12) have written an important book containing: an overview of published cross-cultural research on cognitive development; a report of many new studies by the investigators and their colleagues; and, most importantly, a theoretical framework for the consideration of cross-cultural issues. Since we cannot here summarize in detail their work, we describe one empirical study and some of the complexities to which it leads and then some general theoretical principles which one may derive from Cole & Scribner's research and review.

Cole & Scribner report a study (pp. 118–21) examining the effects of schooling on classification in the Kpelle, a West African tribe. The concern with this issue stems in part from Greenfield & Bruner's hypothesis (25) that Western schooling makes complex intellectual demands on the child and promotes advances in activities like classification. The research reported by Cole & Scribner examined Kpelle children and adults having varying degrees of contact with Western culture and schooling. Some of the results are as follows: Young children (6 to 8 years of age), whether or not they attended school, did not group objects on the basis of common categories (as defined by the Kpelle culture) and instead made idiosyncratic collections. Of the older children (10 to 14 years old), those who did not attend school also failed to group by category, whereas those in school began to use categories. This evidence implies that schooling accelerates the use of categories. Yet further aspects of the data show that almost all nonschooled Kpelle adults group quite well on the basis of categories which are conventional within the culture. Categorization may be a cognitive universal whose ultimate appearance is relatively unaffected by schooling. The study goes on to show that schooling nevertheless has some interesting effects. Those attending Western type schools were generally able to describe and otherwise talk about their categories more effectively than their nonschooled peers. While the schooled and nonschooled "were quite similar in their *practical* classifying activities, they were very dissimilar in the verbal explanations they gave for these activities" (12, p. 121). The Cole & Scribner research thus highlights an important complexity involved in the question of schooling.

Other investigators obtain similarly complex effects. Wagner (63) finds that some aspects of short-term memory may not develop without schooling [recall von Wright's study (62)], whereas schooling exerts relatively little influence on the selective attention involved in incidental memory tasks. Youniss (67) found that schooling and culture influence late concrete and formal operations in deaf Costa Rican children more heavily than the early concrete operations.

It is clear that there are multiple and perhaps interrelated effects of schooling; but are there any generalizations one may make about them? Scribner & Cole (51) offer some general principles. One is that schooling may promote verbalization about one's cognitive activities. A second is that "unschooled populations tended to solve individual problems singly, each as a new problem, whereas schooled populations tended to treat them as instances of a class of problems that could be solved by general rule" (p. 554). These proposals are interesting but extremely speculative. The second idea seems to overestimate the amount of rationality inculcated by schooling and to underestimate the amount of organization in nonschooled thought.

Consider now issues other than the effects of schooling. From their research and review of the literature, Cole & Scribner (12) draw some general conclusions concerning culture and the development of cognition. First, members of non-Western cultures do not think in basically different ways from Westerners. "Thus far there is no evidence for different *kinds* of reasoning processes such as the old classic theories alleged—we have no evidence for a 'primitive logic' " (p. 170). Many aspects of cognition may even be universal. Non-Western thought is not generally deficient, inadequate, different, or illogical. Second, while "there is no evidence . . . that any cultural group wholly lacks a basic process such as abstraction . . . sociocultural factors play an important role in influencing which possible alternative processes . . . are evoked in a given situation and what role they play in the total performance" (p. 193). Third, traditional tests using experimental methods may fail to tap intellectual competence. Experiment must be supplemented by observation and flexible methods of testing. More specifically, one must interpret the meaning of experiments in the light of general knowledge of the culture and everyday use of the intellectual activity in question.

The first of these conclusions receives support from a variety of sources. A number of studies suggest that primitive thought is basically similar to Western. They show that various forms of cognitive activity are widespread, if not universal, and may be found in many cultures. Tulkin & Konner (60) cite many examples of what are usually thought to be Western intellectual abilities—for example, a scientific approach to botany and to hunting—in primitive groups. Berry & Dasen (4) show that the Piagetian stage progressions are found in many non-Western cultures. Similarly, Feldman et al (14) report a study which attempts to determine whether in a non-Western culture the Piagetian stages follow one another in sequence as hypothesized. Data on Eskimos seem to support the notion of a Piagetian sequence (although it is not clear to us that Feldman's tasks measure the Piagetian operations they are intended to measure). Kagan & Klein (30) find that 11-year-old Indian children in isolated villages in Guatemala show cognitive skills comparable to those shown by American middle class children, even though infants in the Guatemalan setting appear to be somewhat slow in developing these skills. Thus, in agreement with Cole & Scribner's first principle, a good deal of contemporary research stresses basic competencies in non-Western thought. Unfortunately, little research has been conducted on Cole & Scribner's second principle—the notion of cultural differences in the application of underlying universals.

Social Class

Research on social class differences in intellect within Western societies is now beginning to take the same general direction as cross-cultural work and in the process is abandoning such ethnocentric theories as the "cultural deprivation" view. Much of this progress may be attributed to the pioneering work of Labov (38) on black language. In his volume, Labov summarizes many of his findings and discusses their implications for the cultural deprivation view and problems of methodology. His voluminous data on Black English Vernacular (BEV) show that it is based on a grammar which is as rich as, although somewhat different from, standard English. BEV "differs from other dialects in regular and rule-governed ways, so that it has equivalent ways of expressing the same logical content" (p. 238). BEV is not deficient, concrete, lacking in complexity, or unable to communicate logically. Labov's book may be consulted for details of his analysis of BEV; here we discuss basic aspects of his methodological approach.

Labov argues that ordinary methods for testing the language abilities of black children are inadequate. In the typical procedure, the black child is given a standard test in a school setting by a "large, friendly, white interviewer." The black child's usual response to this situation is inadequate speech: "We have here the same kind of defensive, monosyllabic behavior which is reported in Bereiter's work." The standard test gives an inaccurate view as to the child's competence with respect to language. Observation of the child in his natural environment and in other, nonstandard test situations show that his speech is far from deficient.

Labov proposes an approach to methodology—similar to Cole & Scribner's—which is radically different from the testing procedures ordinarily employed by most psychologists. There are several components to Labov's approach. He assumes that cognitive competencies in areas like language may manifest themselves in the child's interaction with his natural environment, whereas standard tests or the laboratory setting may fail to elicit them. Therefore, the researcher must become familiar with the child's ordinary activities in his natural environment. Labov assumes further that cognitive activities are complex and must be described in terms of "processes," "rule-systems," and the like. Therefore, the researcher should employ measurement techniques that are sensitive to process and not merely outcome. Labov also assumes that one must draw a distinction between the best a child can do (what we may call his "competence") and how he behaves in any given situation (his "performance"). The researcher must be cautious in drawing inferences concerning competence from a child's performance, especially in certain situations (e.g. a poor child's response to standard tests in a school setting).

These methodological principles may be used to evaluate the research of Jensen (29), who has proposed that blacks and poor people generally are weak in "Level II" abilities demanding "intelligence," "conceptualization," and the like, but are relatively adept at "Level I" abilities which consist of "rote learning" and "primary memory." To demonstrate propositions of this sort, Jensen's basic strategy is to investigate standard test performance in large numbers of blacks and whites. To measure Level I abilities Jensen employs such tests as digit span memory (subjects have to write down as many digits as they can remember from a spoken series); and to measure Level II abilities he uses such tests as the Lorge-Thorndike IQ. (For a discussion of the validity of the IQ test, see our section on Race and IQ, pp. 52–56.) The tests are given in the standard way in the school setting. The usual result is that whites do much better than blacks on Level II tests, whereas both groups score about the same (or whites only slightly better) on Level I tests. The general conclusion is that blacks are deficient in abstract thought.

Using Labov's methodological principles, we see that Jensen's research is deficient in several ways. First, the Jensen approach fails to take account of or dismisses the importance of black children's intellectual activities in their natural environment. Labov's data, as well as "ethnographies" like those of Cottle (13), show that black children have a rich intellectual life outside of school and standard test situations. Cottle gives a detailed account of two black children's insightful analysis of the political structure of American society. Cottle's intention is obviously not to claim that such sophistication is typical of all blacks, whites, or even college professors.

Rather he proves that in the natural environment blacks may exhibit powerful intellectual skills. Therefore, it is at his own peril that an investigator ignores the possibility that such phenomena are widespread, or that laboratory or standard test results indicating the contrary are simply wrong. Informal data like Cottle's are not, of course, the last word on the matter. But—as Labov and Cole & Scribner argue—general knowledge of the child's ordinary activities in his natural environment provides a kind of baseline for evaluation of research on black children or other "minority" cultural groups. Cole & Scribner describe how their initial experiments on Kpelle memory did not seem to yield results that reflected Kpelle competence as revealed in observed daily life activities or ethnographic accounts. In the face of this incongruity, Cole & Scribner modified their experimental techniques until these were suitable for the population under investigation. Glick (24) advocates a similar approach. In the same manner, Labov abandoned standard language tests because they did not reflect black children's true abilities which he was already familiar with through personal knowledge of their culture. According to Labov: "Like Bereiter and Englemann, Jensen is handicapped by his ignorance of the most basic facts about human language and the people who speak it" (38, p. 239). We may add that the Jensen approach is at least equally handicapped with respect to other aspects of human cognition. Hence Jensen does not have an appropriate conceptual framework with which to evaluate his test results.

Second, although Jensen attempts to describe deficiencies in cognitive processes, he describes the latter with great imprecision and measures them even more inadequately. Jensen is never very clear on what he means by "rote memory" or "conceptual thought" in the first place. Furthermore, he uses total number of correct responses on a test like the digit span or IQ to give an indication of *process.* This procedure is unacceptable. As Scribner & Cole (52) put it, Jensen's typical rote memory score "is completely noninformative as to the *processes* involved in the task" (p. 17). The same may be said of the Lorge-Thorndike IQ score.

Third, Jensen's test administration makes no sense from the point of view of the measurement of competence. Administration of the same items to diverse cultural groups fails to guarantee that the items are subjectively equivalent for all. Subjective equivalence demands nonstandard administration or different items for different groups. As Scribner & Cole put it: "the naive assumption still persists—especially in developmental research—that stimulus *identity* assures stimulus equivalence . . . [instead] . . . 'equivalence' is best approximated by use of culture-*specific* materials that are equivalent along critical dimensions but not carbon copies of each other" (52, pp. 9–10). Labov makes the same point.

Moreover, the methodological arguments just reviewed are not limited to cross-cultural studies or social-class research. The same logic applies, although with perhaps lesser urgency, to any research involving different age groups, even if all are white and middle class. This methodological approach demands that: (*a*) One must evaluate laboratory or test measures of cognitive skills by reference to cognitive activities in the natural setting. One cannot determine whether a task is "ecologically valid" unless one knows something of what happens in the natural ecology, and this is as true for white, middle-class 5-year-olds as it is for black children.

(*b*) One must employ subtle procedures to obtain descriptions of process. This often rules out tests of the paper-and-pencil variety and points in the direction of naturalistic observation, clinical interview, or carefully devised laboratory conditions. (*c*) One must attempt to measure competence. Again, this often points to "devious" (Chomsky's term) approaches to measurement. At the very least, this concern should make one suspicious of conclusions based on one-shot administration of standard tests in the school setting. Consideration of the points raised by Labov thus demands new approaches to methodology. The Jensen approach fails to do this and hence its conclusions, which have unfortunately received widespread publicity, are thoroughly misguided.

PUTATIVE RACIAL DIFFERENCES IN INTELLIGENCE

In terms of social implications, perhaps the most important research of the past year and a half concerns the question of group differences in, and the heritability of, IQ test scores. The view that IQ tests are valid measures of genetically determined group differences in intelligence has not been restricted to professional journals with a small circulation. On the contrary, this view has been (often uncritically) summarized in *Time, Newsweek, The New York Times,* etc, so that the audience has become expanded to include educators, social workers, health-care professionals—in short, a number of people who have daily contact with different racial groups and whose behavior vis à vis these people may well be influenced by beliefs about their genetic capabilities and limitations.

The issue of IQ tests and of what they measure is also of some interest (though perhaps in a less urgent way) to the field of cognitive development. The widespread use of and the importance attached to IQ tests can only be understood by realizing that (in spite of some disclaimers to the contrary) these tests are viewed as generally valid (although sometimes inaccurate) measures of intelligence. Assessments of intervention programs almost always include an IQ test as one of the measures. Indeed, level of cognitive development is often (operationally) defined in terms of a score on an IQ test. Such practices oversimplify and therefore obscure the issue of what constitutes intelligent activity as well as the issue of what constitutes cognitive development.

In spite of many criticisms of this research, the nagging feeling still persists that there must be something to the literature on group differences in intelligence—something that critics of this literature have not quite put their fingers on. During the past year, a number of excellent publications have tried to speak to the possible causes of this nagging feeling.

Kamin (31) has written an excellent book which traces the history of the IQ test and also assesses the empirical evidence for the claim that IQ test scores are heritable. First, the history. Kamin's contribution to this area is an important one because the belief that IQ tests are valid measures of group differences in intelligence has been accepted for a very long time, and long-term acceptance in itself tends to lend credibility to a belief. In the first part of his book, Kamin evaluates the historical evidence which might justify consideration of IQ as a valid measurement, and then he carefully documents the fact that the belief is not justified. He points out that historically the major translators and importers of Binet's test (the first influential IQ test) in this country "held in common some basic sociopolitical views . . . manifested by their enthusiastic memberships in various eugenic societies and organizations" (31, p. 6). They welcomed Binet's test as a way of providing statistical justification for a position they already held. "The early history of testing in America fixed upon the Binet test an apparently indelible genetic interpretation. The hereditarian interpretation (of the IQ test) shared by Terman, Goddard and Yerkes did not arise as a *consequence* of the collection of IQ data. Their involvement in the eugenics movement *predated* the collection of such data" (31, p. 10, italics added).

Thus the persistence over time of the belief that IQ tests are valid measures of group differences in intelligence is not necessarily based on sound scientific evidence. (See the discussion below of Kamin's review of the research on which current estimates of heritability are based.) Block & Dworkin (6) ask whether there exists new, sound evidence for this belief. They note that on the face of it there might appear to be two sources of such evidence. The first is that IQ test scores are correlated with various measures of success. The second is the sheer number of tests which find group differences in the same direction. Group differences on IQ tests have been found by many researchers using many tests. Surely consistency must count for something.

In an elaborate series of cogent arguments, Block & Dworkin show that the correlations of IQ with various measures of success are substantially artifactual. For example, they point out that the correlation between IQ scores and number of years in school is largely an artifact of two things: factors which themselves affect both IQ and (independently) years in school; and the fact that evaluations and advice of teachers, guidance counselors, etc probably are based to a large extent on their knowledge of the students' IQ (or achievement test) scores during his school years.

Block & Dworkin (6) point out that much of the correlation of IQ with occupational success rests on the (largely artifactual) correlation of IQ with years in school, and thus with the *credentials* necessary for occupational success. Within occupations, both IQ and grades in school fail to correlate well with occupational proficiency. One is forced to conclude that either intelligence is not very involved in occupational proficiency, or else neither IQ nor grades has much to do with intelligence. Thus neither the correlation of IQ with schooling, nor the correlations of IQ with occupational success, provide good scientific evidence for the claim that IQ is a valid measure of intelligence.

In light of the preceeding discussion, consider the sheer number of tests on which blacks score lower than whites. Since there seems to be little evidence that IQ tests are valid measures of intelligence, it is not clear what can be inferred from the black-white difference on these tests. One thing it indicates is that various IQ tests are explicitly set up to be correlated with one another. Indeed, Block & Dworkin document the claim that ". . . modern I.Q. tests do not differ in any essential scientific respect from Binet's tests" (p. 347). It is not surprising then that so many tests yield group differences in the same direction. The tests simply are not independent measures of the same trait!

The recent resurgence of interest in group differences on IQ tests has assigned an important role to putative measures of heritability in order to support the claim that group differences in IQ test scores are due to genetic rather than environmental factors. During the past year, there have been a number of excellent critiques of the use of the statistic of heritability (e.g. 7, 31). We can summarize these critiques in one sentence: In the research purporting to show genetically determined group differences in intelligence, the statistic of heritability has been misapplied.

The heritability of a characteristic in a population is "the proportion of the characteristic's variation in that population which is due to genetic differences . . . (it) is the variance caused by genetic differences divided by the total variance" (7, p. 40). Two characteristics of heritability are particularly important (and the tendency to ignore these characteristics when discussing group differences is a particularly important source of invalid argumentation). The statistic of heritability is a population statistic that can vary not only *among* populations but also *within* the same population over time. Thus estimates of the heritability of one population can be extrapolated to another population only in very special circumstances. What this means is that one cannot infer, as Jensen did, that if the heritability of intelligence among whites is .85, it is likely that the heritability of intelligence among blacks is also .85. Furthermore, even if we grant, for the sake of argument, that the heritability of IQ for both blacks and whites is .85, it does not follow that the much-cited 15 point IQ difference between blacks and whites is due to genetic variation. Indeed, it is quite likely that, given differential access to schooling, this difference is caused by environmental differences. Finally, even if the heritability of a characteristic within each of two populations is 1.0, it is still possible for the difference between the two populations to be environmentally caused.

In addition to current misapplications of the *statistic* of heritability, Kamin points out that the *empirical data* on which current estimates of heritability are based leave much to be desired. He concludes: "There exist no data which should lead a prudent man to accept the hypothesis that IQ test scores are in any degree heritable" (31, p. 1).

Kamin begins with the widely cited "studies" of Cyril Burt. The most charitable comment one can make about Burt's studies is that they represent brilliant examples of how to violate every accepted canon of scientific research. The testing situation as well as the tests themselves were anything but standardized. The test was never completely described in any publication. Rules for adjusting various assessments of IQ were inconsistently applied, often leading to circular arguments. Twins, who should have been raised in very different environments in order for Burt's conclusions to be valid, in fact were often raised in very similar environments. And perhaps most striking, internal evidence suggests that the data themselves are of doubtful reliability. For example, in spite of an alternately shrinking and growing sample size over an 11 year period, the correlations for monozygotic twins on Burt's "group tests" of intelligence remained *unchanged* to three decimal places!

Kamin also discusses other studies of identical twins reared apart, as well as of adopted children. None of the data from these studies is conclusive. Sometimes the environments of the members of a pair of twins were not significantly different. In other cases, the researchers preselected those pairs of twins who were very much alike in behavior and in general social situation to begin with. And in some of the studies the correlations may have been confounded by effects of age and of sex.

Thus, although there is what *appears* to be an impressive array of statistical evidence in support of a genetically based black-white IQ difference, the impressiveness of this evidence does not stand up under close examination. The particular statistic of heritability is misapplied, and even if it were not, the data on which it is based are questionable at best.

Given the lack of sound scientific evidence for the claim that IQ tests are a valid measure of group differences in intelligence, one is almost compelled to ask why this claim is so widely accepted. To answer this question, one must realize that scientific claims are accepted or rejected not only on the basis of experimental results or systematically collected data, but also because such claims provide explanations for some widely observed phenomena. For example, Kamin points out that during the 1920s and 1930s, the issue of group differences in intelligence centered on differences between immigrants and native-born Americans, rather than between blacks and whites. The assumption that the low IQ scores of these immigrant groups indicated a correspondingly low level of native intelligence provided a possible (although mistaken) explanation for the low socioeconomic status of these immigrant groups, as well as for the participation of their members in various forms of "labor unrest" ranging from "industrial inefficiency" to strikes. Similarly, the recent increase in the publicity accorded black-white IQ differences may well be related to the fact that such differences provide a possible (although mistaken) explanation for both the lower socioeconomic status of blacks as well as for their recent participation in various forms of social protest. In principle, there is nothing wrong with accepting claims on the basis of how well they seem to explain some widely observed phenomena. However, when this happens, it is imperative that one also consider alternative explanations better supported by the evidence. For example, an extremely plausible alternative explanation for the low socioeconomic status of blacks is racism, which in turn results in differential access to education and to jobs. An equally plausible alternative explanation for blacks' involvement in social protest is that this involvement is a natural (and often effective) response to oppression. As noted above, a similar failure to consider alternative explanations often occurs in the literature on cross-cultural and social-class differences.

In the face of a mass of negative information about what blacks do *not* do well, one of the points which Ginsburg (23) makes is especially well taken. He notes that assessments of intellectual functioning are often done in a context (either the laboratory or the school) which almost guarantees that many of the poor child's intellectual skills will not be tapped. He points out that in the few instances where researchers (e.g. Labov) have studied children in their natural surroundings, poor children, black and white, have been found to have abilities which they had previously been thought to not have. We know next to nothing about how these abilities are used or how they develop. For example, we understand very little, if anything, about toasting, playing the dozens, or the rules for the clapping game depicted in the film *Pizza-Pizza, Daddyo-o*. We can predict, however, with a fair amount of

56   GINSBURG & KOSLOWSKI
certainty that if the performance of blacks and whites was compared on tests which measured these skills, the direction of the difference would be reversed.

In concluding this section, we would like to suggest that IQ tests be placed in perspective. Intelligence includes a wide range of very sophisticated cognitive activities which develop via the *interaction* of phylogenetic predispositions and ontogenetic experiences. As was pointed out in the section on cross-cultural studies and social class, there is strong evidence that these cognitive activities are universal, and that they are used in different situational contexts by different groups of people. Furthermore, we hope that the above sections of this chapter have made it clear that the activities involved in language, social cognition, memory, etc are not yet completely and perfectly understood. Given this state of affairs, it seems ludicrous to suppose that a collection of items measuring a restricted set of cognitive activities in a restricted situation provide an adequate measure of native intelligence.

COGNITIVE DEVELOPMENT AND EDUCATION

What kind of contribution can the psychology of cognitive development make to the understanding of education? We focus on only two of the many approaches to this issue. One involves cognitive development as a *model* for education; the other, *basic research* into the educational process.

Kohlberg & Mayer (34) offer an extensive theoretical rationale for the first approach. They argue that according to the Piaget-Dewey "progressive" theory, the aim of education is to foster the child's development. The details of this development may be specified in the moral area by Kohlberg's stage theory and in the intellectual by Piaget's. Thus, according to Kohlberg & Mayer, the most important goal for education is to help children progress through the series of stages described by Piaget and by Kohlberg. One may ask how the traditional school subjects—e.g. the three Rs—fit into this scheme. According to Kohlberg & Mayer, these activities are valuable insofar as they help promote what is seen as the major emphasis of education: stimulation of development through the cognitive stages. All aspects of instruction are thus evaluated in terms of their potential to facilitate psychological growth, defined mainly in terms of Piaget's and Kohlberg's stages.

A rationale of this sort has prompted many workers to design curricula intended to promote the development of Piagetian stages. Kohlberg & Mayer cite with approval the work of Kamii, who has developed a "program of preschool intervention related to each of the chapter headings of Piaget's books: space, time, causality, number . . ." (34, p. 488). A similar venture is that of Furth & Wachs (20), whose aim was to put Piaget's theory into practice so as to create a "school for thinking," which operates chiefly through the medium of various "thinking games." Some of the games are clearly Piagetian in origin, for example, the "How would it look from there?" game (game No. 68, p. 147), which is essentially an adaptation of Piaget's mountains (egocentrism) task. Other games involve neither thinking nor Piaget: for example, the "See me clear" game (game No. 25, p. 114) encourages the child "to focus alternately on a target held close to his eyes and then on a target across the room."

In evaluating the Kohlberg-Mayer approach, we must distinguish between their goal of promoting the Piagetian stages and the various methods employed (e.g. Kamii's) for doing this. The methods—that is, the particular curricula—must be judged on the basis of empirical data concerning their effectiveness in promoting the Piagetian stages. Unfortunately, such data are often unavailable, as in the case of the Furth-Wachs program. But more fundamentally, one must examine the assumptions underlying the Kohlberg-Mayer approach. The main assumption is, of course, that education should facilitate development as defined either by Piaget or Kohlberg. Our view is that this assumption, which Kohlberg and Mayer attribute to Piaget, is highly suspect. (It is not at all clear that Piaget himself would endorse this "Piagetian" approach.) One objection is that it makes no sense to teach or otherwise facilitate the Piagetian stages, since they form a sequence of development which all children, at least in Western society, attain spontaneously without special environments and without instruction. Kohlberg & Mayer attempt to refute this objection by arguing that "natural or universal forms of development are not inevitable" (pp. 486–87). In support of this contention they cite a study by Kuhn et al (36), which seems to show that only about half the adults tested reach the stage of formal operations. Contrary to Kohlberg & Mayer's claim, this study does not demonstrate that half the adult population lacks formal operations; the subjects simply did not demonstrate formal operations on the particular test items emphasized in the study. These adults might readily demonstrate formal operations in other contexts, since as Piaget himself suggests (45), formal operations may be tied to occupational preferences. Indeed, Kuhn et al recognize this argument when they state: "Whether there are actually many normal adults who do not apply formal operations in *any* domain of their everyday reasoning is a question the present study is inadequate to answer" (p. 31). Thus the evidence does not presently support the Kohlberg-Mayer position that the Piagetian stages are not universal and therefore need to be taught.

But suppose that Piagetian stage development were in fact incomplete in some individuals. Would this then imply that education should be modeled after the Piagetian stages? Should Piaget's theory serve as a blueprint for the goals of education, or putting it another way, should one limit education to promoting the kinds of development defined by Piaget or by Kohlberg? We think not. Such a view represents a kind of psychological imperialism which ultimately impoverishes the educational enterprise. One reason for saying this is that education is fundamentally concerned with many aspects of intellectual growth on which Piaget's theory sheds little light—reading, the appreciation of literature, and creative writing are but a few obvious examples. Since Piaget's theory does not deal with these activities, the developmental progression he describes can hardly serve as a model for them. An attempt to fit education into a Piagetian mold—to make teaching of Piagetian stages a dominant aim of education—can be just as limiting as the attempt to conceive of education in Skinnerian terms.

An alternative approach is to use relevant concepts from cognitive developmental theory in an attempt to understand fundamental educational phenomena like reading or mathematical thinking. This approach assumes that no existing theory, including Piaget's, already explains these phenomena; they must be subjected to direct study and analysis. The aim of the alternative approach is to produce theory-based research which will explicate the intellectual processes involved in educational activities. This approach results in basic research on children's reading, mathematics, and the like. The aim is not to model education after some theory, but to develop a theory that can account for the kind of intellectual activities developed in school.

The most impressive work of this type has been done by Gibson & Levin (21, 22), who have conducted a program of basic research on reading, provided an integrative review of the literature, and proposed a general theoretical framework. The theory and results are too complex to summarize here, so we focus on a few main points. Gibson & Levin define reading as a process of extracting information from text, not decoding written symbols into sound. The investigators begin their account of reading's development by examining possible prereading skills. One is the ability to segment or analyze spoken words into component sounds—an activity which young children find difficult and which seems important for later reading. Another is scribbling and printing which seem to develop spontaneously during the preschool years and which may in part involve the perceptual analysis of letter features. Before schooling begins, children seem to know what letters are and can discriminate among them. There is little if any evidence demonstrating that reading readiness programs like the Frostig, emphasizing "perceptual" training, are either needed or valuable.

At the earliest stages of reading instruction, children attempt to preserve the meaning of a sentence even though they cannot read some individual words. They fail to attend to relevant graphic information. Gradually they discover that spoken words are determined by graphic text in regular ways. But the relation between the phonetic and graphic is not simple: "English spelling does not map to sound by way of single letters representing single phonemes . . . Nor can a spoken word often be spelled correctly by the use of a simple phonetic code. That is why we must speak of mapping rules which are often conditional and usually involve units larger than the letter and the single phoneme." To read, the child must therefore learn to pick up higher order structure in graphic material.

The Gibson-Levin theory, based heavily on notions derived from the study of perceptual development and psycholinguistics, goes on to consider such issues as the effects of grammatical constraints on reading, the nature of comprehension, and the process of skilled reading. According to this view, no one model of skilled reading is sufficient, because there are different processes of reading which have been developed to accomplish various purposes. The process of reading a novel is different from the process of reading an advertisement or scientific journal. Gibson & Levin illustrate this important point with fascinating introspective accounts.

The Gibson-Levin approach should serve as a model for one kind of contribution a psychology of cognitive development can make to education: the construction of a theory of the intellectual processes forming the heart of education.

CONCLUSIONS

We conclude with a few general comments concerning major themes running through the apparent diversity of research and theory in the area of cognitive development. First, the field has much more to say about *cognition* than *development*. Most research focuses on the explication of mental processes at various points in development rather than on developmental principles—the rules of transition. Second, the search for cognitive processes is obviously a fruitful enterprise, leading to important insights concerning phenomena as diverse as semantics, humor, memory, and reading. Third, the field is beginning to develop a common array of theoretical principles which seem useful in dealing with many of these diverse phenomena. Thus the pickup of information underlies reading, person-perception, and concept formation (semantics). Fourth, the field exhibits a concern with the relation between cognitive processes and the real world. Cognitive processes are anchored in the context of the child's interaction with objects and people in a complex environment. Fifth, as a result of this emphasis, there is a new concern with ecologically valid methods of research, including various kinds of observational methods. Finally, the field exhibits a concern with various implications of its basic ideas and "applied" problems, particularly educational issues.

Literature Cited

1. Barclay, J. R., Reid, M. 1974. Semantic integration in children's recall of discourse. *Dev. Psychol.* 10:277–81
2. Bartlett, F. C. 1932. *Remembering.* Cambridge Univ. Press
3. Berlyne, D. E. 1960. *Conflict, Arousal and Curiosity.* New York: McGraw-Hill
4. Berry, J. W., Dasen, P. R., Eds. 1974. *Culture and Cognition: Readings in Cross-Cultural Psychology.* New York: Barnes & Noble. 487 pp.
5. Blank, M. 1974. Cognitive functions of language in the preschool years. *Dev. Psychol.* 10:229–45
6. Block, N. J., Dworkin, G. 1974. I.Q.: heritability and inequality. *Philosophy and Public Affairs,* Part I, 3(4)
7. Ibid. Part II, 4(1)
8. Bloom, L., Hood, L., Lightbrown, D. 1974. Imitation in language development: If, when, and why. *Cogn. Psychol.* 6:380–420
9. Brainerd, C. J. 1973. Neo-Piagetian training experiments revisited: Is there any support for the cognitive-developmental stage hypothesis? *Cognition* 2:349–70
10. Bryant, P. 1974. *Perception and Understanding in Young Children: An Experimental Approach.* New York: Basic Books. 195 pp.
11. Case, R. 1974. Structures and strictures: some functional limitations on the course of cognitive growth. *Cogn. Psychol.* 6:544–73
12. Cole, M., Scribner, S. 1974. *Culture and Thought: A Psychological Introduction.* New York: Wiley. 227 pp.
13. Cottle, T. J. 1974. *Black Children, White Dreams.* Boston: Houghton Mifflin. 187 pp.
14. Feldman, C. F., Lee, B., McLean, J. D., Pillemer, D. B., Murray, J. R. 1974. *The Development of Adaptive Intelligence.* San Francisco: Jossey-Bass. 184 pp.
15. Flavell, J. H. 1974. The development of inferences about others. In *Understanding Other Persons,* ed. T. Mischel, 66–116. Totowa, NJ: Rowman & Littlefield. 266 pp.
16. Flavell, J. H. 1970. Developmental studies of mediated memory. *Adv. Child Dev. Behav.* 5:182–211
17. Flavell, J. H. 1970. What is memory development the development of? *Hum. Dev.* 14:272–80
18. Furth, H. G. 1974. Two aspects of experience in ontogeny: development and learning. *Adv. Child Dev. Behav.* 9:47–67
19. Furth, H. G., Ross, B. M., Youniss, J. 1974. Operative understanding in reproduction of drawings. *Child Dev.* 45:63–70
20. Furth, H. G., Wachs, H. 1974. *Piaget's Theory in Practice—Thinking Goes to School.* New York: Oxford Univ. Press. 228 pp.
21. Gibson, E. J. 1974. Trends in perceptual development: Implications for the reading process. In *Minn. Symp. Child Psychol.* 8:24–54

22. Gibson, E. J., Levin, H. 1975. *The Psychology of Reading.* Cambridge: MIT Press. 342 pp.
23. Ginsburg, H. 1972. *The Myth of the Deprived Child.* Englewood Cliffs, NJ: Prentice-Hall. 252 pp.
24. Glick, J. 1974. Culture and cognition: Some theoretical and methodological concerns. Unpublished
25. Greenfield, P. M., Bruner, J. S. 1969. Culture and cognitive growth. In *Handbook of Socialization Theory and Research,* ed. D. A. Goslin, 633–60. New York: Rand McNally. 1182 pp.
26. Groch, A. S. 1974. Joking and appreciation of humor in nursery school children. *Child Dev.* 45:1098–1102
27. Harter, S. 1974. Pleasure derived by children from cognitive challenge and mastery. *Child Dev.* 45:661–69
28. Hollos, M., Cowan, P. A. 1973. Social isolation and cognitive development: Logical operations and role-taking abilities in three Norwegian school settings. *Child Dev.* 44:630–41
29. Jensen, A. R. 1974. Interaction of level I and level II abilities with race and socioeconomic status. *J. Educ. Psychol.* 66:99–111
30. Kagan, J., Klein, R. E. 1973. Cross-cultural perspectives on early development. *Am. Psychol.* 28:947–61
31. Kamin, L. J. 1974. *The Science and Politics of I. Q.* Potomac, Md.: Erlbaum
32. Katz, N., Baker, E., Macnamara, J. 1974. What's in a name? A study of how children learn common and proper names. *Child Dev.* 45:469–73
33. Klahr, D. 1973. An information-processing approach to the study of cognitive development. *Minn. Symp. Child Psychol.* 7:141–77
34. Kohlberg, L., Mayer, R. 1972. Development as the aim of education. *Harvard Educ. Rev.* 42:449–96
35. Kuhn, D. 1974. Inducing development experimentally: comments on a research paradigm. *Dev. Psychol.* 10:590–600
36. Kuhn, D., Langer, J., Kohlberg, L., Haan, N.S. 1975. The development of formal operations in logical and moral judgment. *Genet. Psychol. Monogr.* In press
37. Kun, A., Parsons, J. E. 1974. Development of integration processes using ability and effort information to predict outcome. *Dev. Psychol.* 10: 721–32
38. Labov, W. 1972. *Language in the Inner City: Studies in Black English Vernacular.* Philadelphia: Univ. Pennsylvania Press. 412 pp.
39. Liben, L. 1974. Operative understanding of horizontality and its relation to long-term memory. *Child Dev.* 45:416–24
40. Livesley, W. J., Bromley, D. B. 1973. *Person Perception in Childhood and Adolescence.* New York: Wiley. 320 pp.
41. Maratsos, M. P. 1974. When is a high thing the big one? *Dev. Psychol.* 10:367–75
42. McGhee, P. E. 1974. Development of children's ability to create the joking relationship. *Child Dev.* 45:552–56
43. Nelson, K. 1974. Concept, word and sentence: interrelations in acquisition and development. *Psychol. Rev.* 81: 267–85
44. Paris, S. G., Carter, A. Y. 1973. Semantic and constructive aspects of sentence memory in children. *Dev. Psychol.* 9: 109–13
45. Piaget, J. 1972. Intellectual evolution from adolescence to adulthood. *Hum. Dev.* 15:1–12
46. Piaget, J. 1964. Development and learning. In *Piaget Rediscovered,* ed. R. E. Ripple, V. N. Rockcastle, 1–12. Ithaca: Cornell Univ. Press. 103 pp.
47. Piaget, J., Inhelder, B. 1973. *Memory and Intelligence.* New York: Basic Books. 414 pp.
48. Rogoff, B., Newcombe, N., Kagan, J. 1974. Planfulness and recognition memory. *Child Dev.* 45:972–77
49. Rosch, E. H. 1973. On the internal structure of perceptual and semantic categories. In *Cognitive Development and the Acquisition of Language,* ed. T. E. Moore. 111–44. New York: Academic
50. Samuels, M. T. 1974. *Children's long-term memory for events.* PhD thesis. Cornell Univ., Ithaca, NY. 144 pp.
51. Scribner, S., Cole, M. 1973. Cognitive consequences of formal and informal education. *Science* 182:553–59
52. Scribner, S., Cole, M. 1975. Studies of subcultural variation in semantic memory: Implications of cross-cultural research. *Can. J. Psychol.* In press
53. Secord, P. F., Peevers, B. H. 1974. The development and attribution of person concepts. In *Understanding other Persons,* ed. T. Mischel, 117–42. Totowa, NJ: Rowman & Littlefield. 266 pp.
54. Shatz, M., Gelman, R. 1973. The development of communication skills. *Monogr. Soc. Res. Child Dev.* 38: Serial No. 152. 38 pp.

55. Shultz, T. R. 1974. Development of the appreciation of riddles. *Child Dev.* 45:100–5
56. Shultz, T. R., Horibe, F. 1974. Development of the appreciation of verbal jokes. *Dev. Psychol.* 10:13–20
57. Shultz, T. R., Pilon, R. 1973. Development of the ability to detect linguistic ambiguity. *Child Dev.* 44:728–33
58. Starr, S. 1974. Discrimination of syntactical errors in children under two and one-half years. *Dev. Psychol.* 10:381–86
59. Strohner, H., Nelson, K. E. 1974. The young child's development of sentence comprehension: Influence of event probability, nonverbal context, syntactic form, and strategies. *Child Dev.* 45:567–76
60. Tulkin, S. R., Konner, M. J. 1973. Alternative conceptions of intellectual functioning. *Hum. Dev.* 16:33–52
61. Turiel, E. 1974. Conflict and transition in adolescent moral development. *Child Dev.* 45:14–29
62. von Wright, J. M. 1973. Relation between verbal recall and visual recognition of the same stimuli in young children. *J. Exp. Child Psychol.* 15:481–87
63. Wagner, D. A. 1974. The development of short-term and incidental memory: a cross-cultural study. *Child Dev.* 45: 389–96
64. West, H. 1974. Early peer-group interaction and role-taking skills: an investigation of Israeli children. *Child Dev.* 45:1118–21
65. Wetstone, H. S., Friedlander, B. Z. 1973. The effect of word order on young children's responses to simple questions and commands. *Child Dev.* 44:734–40
66. Whiteman, M., Brook, J. S., Gordon, A. S. 1974. Children's motivational perception as related to the instrumentality and effect of action. *Dev. Psychol.* 10: 929–35
67. Youniss, J. 1974. Operational development in deaf Costa Rican subjects. *Child Dev.* 45:212–16

COLOR VISION

❖248

Gerald H. Jacobs

Department of Psychology, University of California, Santa Barbara, California 93106

We have recently been admonished that "The trouble with colour vision is the mentality of those that write on it . . ." (141). For anyone seeking to read and review the literature on color vision, the "trouble" lies not so much with the mentality of the color vision writers as with their excessive energy. It might be thought that the recent surge of interest in the analysis of spatial vision would have detracted somewhat from the pursuit of truth about color vision. Not so! While the contemporary literature on color vision does indicate a growing concern with spatial variables, the traditional interests in color continue to be robustly represented. In the face of this flood of information, and with the severe limitation on space, this reviewer has opted to select rather stringently from among the current literature on color vision. Guilt generated by this procedure is alleviated by the knowledge that slights here are amply compensated for in the substantial range of other secondary sources currently being published on color vision topics. The bias in this review is toward those studies dealing with color vision mechanisms, and to those studies whose outcomes contain some implications about mechanisms.

GENERAL REFERENCES

There has been an impressive increase in the number of secondary sources on color vision during the past few years. The preeminent event is the appearance of several of the constituent volumes of the *Handbook of Sensory Physiology*. Much has already been written about the contents and the prices of these books—the former universally praised, the latter universally deplored. Each of the five parts which collectively make up Volume VII of this work contains chapters relevant to an interest in color. Many of these chapters contain exceptionally good literature reviews as well as new insights into the various problems of color vision. Some of these will be referred to individually below. It suffices to say here that no one with an interest in color vision can afford to be without access to these important books. Volumes of the *Handbook of Perception* (29) have also begun to appear, and although less central to the topic of this paper, they contain several reviews of quality and usefulness for an understanding of color vision.

The proceedings of several symposia dealing with color vision have been published. Both *Color Metrics* (172) and *Color 73* (76) deal heavily with color theory and the metrics of color space. The proceedings of the First and Second Symposia of the International Research Group on Colour Vision Deficiencies have been published (170, 171). A symposium conducted by the International Society of Clinical Electroretinography (7) contains some material on color vision, while a symposium sponsored by the National Research Council–National Academy of Science (117) has papers on color-defective vision and several other applied topics.

Several single-authored works have appeared which will also compete for space on the shelves of color vision scientists. These include attempts to deal with the complexities of color appearance by Beck (12) and by Evans (52) and the issuance of new editions of two well-known texts which contain standard material on color vision (37, 59). More specialized treatment is to be found in an impressive monograph entitled *The Vertebrate Retina,* written by Rodieck (138), and in a volume on the electroretinogram authored by Armington (8).

MECHANISMS

Ocular Filters

Because they condition spectral sensitivity and can serve to mold color vision in a nontrivial way, the various ocular filters have been a traditional topic of interest within color vision. All such filters tend to reduce the effectiveness of the short wavelengths as compared to the long wavelengths. Muntz (115) has recently reviewed from a comparative viewpoint the literature on the variety of forms these filters assume. The filters of concern for human vision are the lens and macular pigment. New deductions about human lens pigmentation have been made from psychophysical measurements (35, 122). Norren & Vos (122) provide a useful compilation of recent data on lens absorption and some new calculations of lens density based on the differences between the human scotopic spectral sensitivity function and the rhodopsin absorbance curve. Ruddock (139) argues that variation in foveal color matching is due to variation in the density of the macular pigment, and he raises the possibility that in some retinas the macular pigment is located behind the photoreceptors. Some calculations on the effects of chromatic aberration have been taken as arguments in favor of the old notion that the role of the macular pigment is to offset the deleterious effects of scatter of short wavelength radiation (132).

Structural Characteristics of the Photoreceptors

The whole question of developing criteria for distinguishing rods from cones in an unambiguous, across-species manner has still not been resolved. Although the issues cannot be developed here, and perhaps bear only tangentially on color vision, a superb treatment of the problem, produced by Cohen (33), is highly recommended.

Prior to the advent of photoreceptor microspectrophotometry (MSP) it was occasionally suggested that waveguide properties of the individual photoreceptors, not a multiplicity of photopigments, might serve as an initial stage of color signal processing. The MSP data demonstrating the presence of three primate cone photopigments, and the behavioral observation that monochromatic lights presented axially and transclerally match in hue, effectively laid such suggestions to rest. However, there is no denying that the dimensional characteristics of photoreceptors can condition the effectiveness of retinal irradiation, and recently Snyder and his colleagues (111, 157, 158) have examined some of the implications of photoreceptor structure. They show (158) that the physical dimensions of the receptor can influence importantly its measured spectral sensitivity. For example, the rhabdomeres in the eye of the fly fall into two classes according to their cross-sectional diameters. This difference in diameter is sufficient to cause the modal energy patterns in the two types of photoreceptors to differ. Thus, with the same photopigment in each of the two classes of rhabdomeres (having a λ_{max} of 515 nm), peak sensitivity may occur at either 515 or 478 nm depending on the dimensions of the rhabdomere in which the photopigment is placed. The point is that the dimensions of the photoreceptor could easily cause confusion about the correct spectrum for the photopigment contained within it. In another paper, Miller & Snyder (112) make the interesting suggestion that the well-known differences in the shapes of human foveal and peripheral cones may imply substantially different roles. The shape of the peripheral cone is such as to make it an efficient device for trapping incident light. However, because of its lower refractive index, and because the peripheral cone outer segment terminates near the base of the rod outer segment, the peripheral cone may serve to radiate substantial amounts of light to the surrounding rods. Thus the roles of the peripheral cone could include the enhancement of rod sensitivity at scotopic light levels. Receptor shape has been frequently used to attempt to account for the Stiles-Crawford effects. Several new models have been developed to explain these directional dependencies; they involve both the structural characteristics of the cones and some appeals to pigment self-screening (145, 159, 186).

Cone Photopigments

A decade ago, following the initial reports of successful measurements of primate cone pigments by MSP, there was wide expectation that very shortly most of the traditional questions about photopigment spectra and their retinal distributions would be rapidly and finally answered. This has not happened. Although useful MSP work on nonmammalian cones continues to appear, little new has been offered about those cones of greatest interest to most color vision workers. Liebman (95), one of the leading MSP practitioners, has reviewed the state of this art and pointed out the strengths and limitations of the technique. His sober conclusion that the current primate MSP data "cannot be regarded as accurate to better than 20–30 nm" makes it clear that these data are hardly the ones on which to build detailed models of color vision. For the time being we must continue to rely on other sources of information.

Some recent interest has been centered on the relationship between the spectra for extracted photopigments and those measured in situ (23, 24, 181). Bowmaker (24) specifically contends that the Dartnall nomogram for pigments in solution may not be applicable to pigments in intact retinas. Since there is considerable question about the adequacy of this nomogram for cone pigments anyway (see below), and since almost all cone pigments are still refractory to extraction procedures, these issues may not be very relevant to color vision at the moment.

The previous review in this series (176) pointed out that the absorption curves for the cone pigments are believed to be different in shape from that of the rods. This belief remains in force although it is not clear whether this difference obtains for all classes of cone pigments. LeGrand (94) maintains that the spectra for cones are always narrower than those for rods, while others (153, 166) claim that it depends on which cone pigments you are talking about. Thus, on the basis of color matching data, Stiles & Wyszecki (166) conclude that a cone pigment with a peak at 540 nm can be fit by the Dartnall nomogram, but Smith & Pokorny (153) argue that all cone pigments with a λ_{max} at 520 nm or less are fit by the Dartnall nomogram, whereas those peaking at longer wavelengths are not. The spectra for these latter pigments are well described by the Vos-Walraven G function (173).

Argument also continues about the optical densities of the cone pigments. Estimates derived from retinal densitometry (84, 85) and from psychophysical experiments (110, 154) on humans yield average densities of 0.4 to 0.6 for the long-wavelength photopigment and densities of 0.3 to 0.5 for the middle-wavelength photopigment. The range of density estimates for individual subjects is disturbingly large, enough to suggest that the question is still open and may indeed not be answered by psychophysical experiments (154).

Some information has been reported concerning the dynamics of cone pigment activity. Norren & Padmos (121) used intense chromatic preexposure to isolate the recovery of various chromatic components during dark adaptation. Predictably, they find a substantially faster recovery time for the red-green mechanisms than for the blue mechanism. In an extensive parametric study, Hollins & Alpern (71) have probed the limits of the Dowling-Rushton relationship between threshold and pigment regeneration. Using both densitometry and psychophysics, they found that the linear relationship between log threshold and fraction of unregenerated cone pigment holds over a wide range of experimental conditions. The exceptions involve recovery from brief saturating flashes of light (the Theta effect) and an immediate desensitization after weak bleaches which appears akin to what has been called neural adaptation in the rods.

Electrophysiology: Background

The electrophysiology of color vision, particularly of the responses of single cells at the level of the ganglion cells and beyond, has been the topic of three excellent review articles (1, 38, 43). Consequently, here I will comment specifically only on those sources of information appearing subsequent to the other papers. To recapitulate the basic facts briefly, over the past 15 years it has become generally accepted that the outputs from the cone pigments are transmitted as neural signals along two different types of channels. In one, the outputs are summed in some fashion so that the direction of the neural response is the same for all stimulus wavelengths; elements of this type are frequently called non-opponent. In the other type of channel, the outputs from different cone pigments are combined antagonistically so that the nature of the neural response depends on stimulus wavelength and on the spectral characteristics of the parent cone pigments. Elements of this latter type are usually called chromatic opponent. All species known to have color vision have cells show-ing these chromatic-opponent properties at some visual system locations, and thus a variety of specific suggestions have been made as to the ways in which the chromatic-opponent cells might be important for color vision. With the addition of spatial location as a stimulus variable, visual cells are also characterized in terms of their receptive-field properties. This has expanded substantially the number of potentially descriptive categories since cells may show either spectral or spatial antagonisms or both.

Receptor Potentials

It is now clear that an increase in the rate of quantal absorption of light by vertebrate photoreceptors leads to a slow hyperpolarizing response, generated, possibly, by a decrease in the conductance of ionic channels in the receptor outer segments. The big news is that several groups of investigators are busily engaged in putting ques-tions to single photoreceptors that have relevance to a variety of issues of visual interest. The current focus is on those retinas whose receptors are large enough to survive microelectrode impalement, primarily turtle and mudpuppy.

The oft-debated question of whether rods are more sensitive than cones has been answered in the affirmative (54, 120). Direct measurements on mudpuppy photore-ceptors, and some calculations on data from a variety of other species, indicate that individual rods are on the order of at least one log unit more sensitive than individual cones. This difference is apparently not due to differences in the density or the amount of pigment in these two types of photoreceptors (54). Similarly, some of the differ-ence in the temporal resolution of rod versus cone vision is now shown to be correlated with the differences in recovery time of the responses of these two types of photoreceptors—the cone potential returns to its voltage baseline following illu-mination much more rapidly than the rod potential (54, 120). The cones in the turtle retina are coupled together [by contacts between adjacent pedicles (93)] in a mutu-ally facilitatory manner so as to permit spatial summation over a region equivalent to the diameters of about five receptors. The turtle retina has three cone pigments, and it is particularly interesting to note that this receptor-to-receptor coupling is limited to cones containing the same type of photopigment (10, 57). Turtle cones are also affected by an antagonistic feedback from the horizontal cells. Since the horizontal cells themselves may be influenced by more than one class of cone, then the response of each cone, by virtue of this feedback, reflects both a direct response due to illumination of it and its neighbors and some modification through horizontal cell activation. Thus the cone response depends not only on the rate of quantal absorption in the photoreceptor, but also on the distribution of wavelengths in the light falling in the neighboring regions. That is, the so-called principle of univariance does not hold for the response of the individual photoreceptor (at least in the turtle) if one includes the possibility of modification of response by interaction with other elements (57, 137).

Moving outside of the photoreceptor, there have also been some studies of receptor electrophysiology as measured with extracellular electrodes. In previous years
the early receptor potential (ERP) attracted much attention. It no longer appears
to be a very active issue—the only contributions were a dispute as to how accurately
one can characterize cone pigment regeneration rates by using the ERP (14, 180)
and some measurements suggesting that the spectral response differs for the two
components of the human ERP (194). More common are investigations involving
the late receptor potential (LRP). Boynton & Whitten (22) have used chromatic
adaptation in an attempt to isolate the components of the monkey LRP. They find
that the waveform of the LRP response is different for the blue than for the red and
green cones, with the former showing a slower onset in response to a luminance step.
Evidence is also presented that the responses of the three different cone classes sum
linearly to produce the LRP in the primate eye, a situation obviously different from
any of the gross evoked potentials at more central locations in the visual system.
Several comparisons of the time courses of both rod and cone LRPs have also
appeared (150, 184, 185). The LRP response to temporal square waves reveals the
same differences in recovery rate for rods and cones as those noted above for
intrareceptor recordings.

S-Potentials

At least in the cat, it appears that S-potentials may reflect either pure rod or mixed
rod-cone input. Some argue (118) that the mixing of rod and cone signals at this
level is a mere superposition of potentials and that any antagonistic rod-cone interactions must occur more centrally. This would seem to contradict the results
from monkey LRP recording (185). However, it is worth emphasizing that species
differences in horizontal-cell morphology are great, and it is unreasonable to expect
that the physiological differences are going to be any less profound. Fuortes and his
co-workers (57, 58) have made a serious attempt to devise a wiring diagram to show
how signals are processed by turtle receptors and horizontal cells. Already noted
above are the feedback interactions between horizontal cells and cones. There are
two other points of interest. First, they find (58) that the L-type S-potential in the
turtle does show some wavelength-dependent changes in response and is thus potentially capable of transmitting color-relevant information. Since this is not generally
thought to be the case, it is possible that a reexamination of the conventional scheme
for color coding may be in order. A second important observation is that the
chromatic-opponent responses at this level, the C-potentials, arise primarily through
a direct cone input and modifying interactions. That is, the spectral antagonism of
these units is not established by directly antagonistic inputs from two classes of
cones. Again, this is somewhat more complicated than the earlier schemes suggested. Extending studies of S-potentials to those species whose color vision has been
intensively investigated by other methods will be technically challenging but of high
priority.

Inner Nuclear Layer

Not much is known about signal processing by the cells of the inner nuclear layer
and almost nothing about color information at this level. Kaneko (80) has recently

examined the receptive fields of bipolar and amacrine cells in the goldfish retina. He reports that over half of the bipolar cells in this trichromat show chromatic-opponent responses. The receptive fields of these cells give a center response due to input from the red cones with a spatially antagonistic surround driven by both the red and green cones. Some of the amacrine cells also show chromatic-opponent responses although there are no spatial antagonisms apparent in these cells. Comparison of spectral and spatial organizations suggests that the center responses of goldfish ganglion cells reflect inputs from the bipolar cells, whereas the surround responses seem to result from amacrine cell inputs.

Ganglion Cells

Our knowledge about the diversity of receptive-field organization of ganglion cells continues to grow. In the goldfish, ganglion cells examined at photopic levels of illumination can be classified into as many as 12 different groups according to their spectral sensitivity and spatial organization (160). The most common of these possibilities are the double-opponent cells which show a red-green spectral antagonism in the center region and a similar antagonism but of reversed sign in the surround region (11). In addition to all of the various types of goldfish ganglion cells having a typical center-surround arrangement, there are also a small number having more complex receptive-field organizations, including some which are both directionally sensitive and color coded (39). On the other hand, Reuter & Virtanen (136) have shown that the receptive field organization of frog ganglion cells can be viewed in a much more conventional way than has been done heretofore for that species. It is been regularly found that the ganglion cells in many species transmit signals from both rods and cones. In the goldfish the sign of the rod response (that is, excitatory or inhibitory) is invariably the same as that for the center red mechanism in the light-adapted retina (11, 131). The functional significance of this relationship is unknown. An attempt was made to develop an analogy between the spectral location at which the red-green cells in the goldfish transit from excitation to inhibition and the spectral location of unique yellow for the human observer (31). Given the photopigment differences between the two species the analogy seems uncompelling.

Abramov & Levine (2) have reminded us of the potential dangers of trying to infer normal neural organization from any particular physiological preparation. They show that in the excised-retina preparation of the goldfish, a modest change in the proportions of the gas perfusants can lead to drastic changes in the characteristics of the ganglion cell's response so that, for example, under some conditions one is much more likely to encounter chromatic-opponent responses than under others. This problem is unlikely to be less severe at other visual system locations; nor does it appear unique to the goldfish, as suggested by some rather similar results on the ground squirrel retina (67).

Marrocco (104) has examined the properties of optic-tract fibers in the monkey. The major outcome is that, although there are other important differences, the spectral properties of optic-tract fibers are very similar to those of cells in the lateral geniculate nucleus, suggesting that little if any chromatic processing is accomplished by the transfer of information from ganglion cell axons to lateral geniculate cells.

Although there has never been any physiological evidence for it, a common explanation for the Prevost-Fechner-Benham colors has been that color might be encoded by the temporal structure in action potential sequences. Kozak & Reitboeck (89) examined this proposition by recording spike train sequences from cat optic-tract fibers in response to diffuse retinal illuminations of different luminances and spectral distributions. They report finding wavelength-dependent differences in spike sequences and suggest this may reflect an additional mechanism for the coding of color information. This study can be criticized for the choice of species, the adequacy of the luminance equations for the chromatic stimuli, and for the lack of any positive attempt to rule out rod contribution. Nevertheless, the possibility that color-relevant information might be transmitted to the central visual system by the temporal sequences of spikes cannot be ruled out at this time.

Lateral Geniculate Nucleus

Some new information about the properties of cells in the lateral geniculate nucleus (LGN) of the monkey has appeared. De Valois & Marrocco (44) examined the response of such cells to a diffuse light stimulus which was abruptly shifted from achromatic to an equiluminant mixture of chromatic and achromatic light. In verification of earlier ideas it was found that the non-opponent cells do not detect such shifts. However, the chromatic-opponent cells do respond under such conditions, giving greater responses to those mixtures having higher purities. Determination of threshold purity increments for different wavelengths and types of chromatic-opponent cells yielded a function which closely matched the behaviorally determined, saturation-discrimination function for this species, suggesting that as a group the chromatic-opponent cells contain the information necessary for saturation discrimination. Identification of the photopigments providing input to the yellow-blue cells of the monkey LGN remains problematic (43). Apparently one of the inputs to these cells is from the 440-nm cone pigment (77), but it is not clear which of the other two pigments supply input to these cells. Perhaps both do.

The establishment of a distinction between phasic and tonic cells in the cat visual system represents one of the important advances in visual physiology over the past several years. A similar distinction has been reported for ganglion cells in the monkey visual system, with those cells having chromatic-opponent properties showing tonic responses (60). Since psychophysical models based on this distinction are beginning to appear (75), it is worth pointing out that the phasic-tonic distinction cannot be observed among the cells in the parvocellular layers of the monkey LGN (42).

Michael (109) has continued his exploration of the visual system of the ground squirrel, a dichromat having a cone-dominated retina. In the LGN of this species about 65% of all cells show chromatic-opponent properties. By far the most common among these are those cells having double-opponent receptive fields with inputs from the two cone pigments represented antagonistically in the center regions and also in the surround but with opposite signs in the two regions. Such cells are particularly interesting because they respond most strongly to stimuli having complementary hues in adjacent spatial regions. As noted above, cells of this kind are common at the level of the ganglion cell in the goldfish. They are not found in the retina or the LGN of the monkey, and the degree of their presence in visual cortex is not yet well established.

Cortex

Although several groups have now described recordings from single cells in the monkey visual cortex, there is still no consistent story of how this tissue processes information to produce color vision. One of the most puzzling aspects arising from Hubel & Wiesel's (73) pioneering study of the receptive fields of cells in macaque visual cortex was the finding that only a small proportion of cortical cells seemed to be involved in color processing. In the LGN of this species, a large majority of the cells have chromatic-opponent properties, but Hubel & Wiesel found less than 25% of the cortical cells to have similar specificities. Part of the reason for the discrepancy appears to be related to the fact that the Hubel-Wiesel results were for cells having parafoveal inputs. In five more recent studies, all directed specifically toward the foveal projection, the number of cells showing color-selective response properties is consistently higher, ranging from 30% (48) to 54% (60) of the total number of cells examined. These figures still seem low if one accepts the much higher percentage of color-selective cells reported as characteristic of the foveal projection regions of the macaque LGN (43).

Part of the difficulty may reside in the problem of defining what constitutes a color-specific response. The chromatic-opponent cells of the LGN are easily identified, but because of their much lower spontaneous activity rates, the inhibitory responses of cortical cells are difficult to see, and consequently some cells with opponent properties probably go undetected. De Valois (43) has made the additional suggestion that cortical cells might utilize color selective inputs in a generalizing manner; that is, to detect a form stimulus without regard to its color but only because the stimulus is colored. Presumably this situation could arise in a cortical cell receiving inputs from different types of chromatic-opponent cells.

Given these problems of definition, what kinds of responses are seen in monkey visual cortex? All the investigators have reported finding cells showing what appear to be the same types of chromatic-opponent responses as are seen in LGN. The percentage of cells showing chromatic-opponent properties seems to be inversely related to the complexity of the cell's spatial organization. Unlike the cat cortex, many of the cells in the foveal projection region of monkey cortex do not show orientational preferences—as many as 60–70% of these cells are chromatic-opponent (48, 61). Beyond that, the more complex the spatial characteristics of the cell's receptive field, the less likely is it to show a color-specific response (48, 49, 61). Thus Gouras (61) reports finding 12 of 16 simple cells to give color selective responses but no such selectivity among any of a total of 21 cells showing hypercomplex receptive fields. This led him to suggest that there are hierarchical channels in the visual system selective for either color or form. This issue clearly requires further investigation.

Two other points deserve mention. One is that the double-opponent receptive field arrangement, common at the level of the ganglion cells and the LGN of other species, appears in only a restricted number of cells in monkey striate cortex (49). The other noteworthy finding is that a small number of cells in monkey cortex apparently respond specifically only to rather compact spectral bands (193)—for example, from 600 to 650 nm. Cells of this latter type do not exist at levels peripheral to the cortex, or indeed at any other locations as far as is now known.

If the nature of color processing by striate cortex is still unclear, what happens at locations farther along the pathway is totally mysterious. Gross et al (66) report that some of the cells in monkey inferotemporal cortex respond specifically to colored stimuli. Much more exciting, however, is the finding by Zeki (195) that cells in visual Area IV of the monkey (a region receiving inputs from both Areas 18 and 19) all show color specificity. The nature of the receptive fields of these cells was varied: some cells showed little spatial specificity while others had those properties generally associated with complex and hypercomplex cells. All, however, gave differential responses to various spectral stimuli equated in luminance. The clear suggestion is that this may represent an area in which color processing is particularly emphasized, and thus it is an attractive and important target for further research.

Visually Evoked Cortical Potentials (VECPs)

Although quite informative about other aspects of vision, the VECP cannot be said to have yielded much new information about color vision. This is certainly not due to any lack of interest, as there are numerous studies that have explored wavelength as a parameter in the elicitation of VECP. Most of these studies either verify the presence of information in the VECP recording already predicted on other grounds, or they attempt to use this response as a descriptive measure—for example, to detect defective color vision or to measure spectral sensitivity.

The question of whether the waveform of the VECP is characteristically different as a function of stimulus wavelength and whether this reflects color vision differences continues unanswered. It has variously been contended that wavelength-unique responses do reliably occur in at least some observers (125), that there are no detectable differences associated with stimulus wavelength (187), and that there are no differences in waveform that reflect the presence or absence of color coding (3). The truth probably depends on the set of stimulus conditions and may at any rate not be very important if, as Kinney & McKay (87) suggest, there are wavelength-specific components in the VECP but the differences between them are often smaller than the normal variability for single stimulus conditions.

With regard to mechanisms influencing the VECP, the following points have been established. Krauskopf (90) has used a Stiles-type increment-threshold procedure to isolate the contributions of the various cone mechanisms to the VECP. As expected from a variety of other kinds of experiments, the implicit times generated by stimulation of the Π_1 mechanism are longer (by 50–75 msec) than those generated by stimulation of Π_4 or Π_5. Evidence that chromatic-opponent mechanisms must contribute to the VECP comes from the observation that under some sets of conditions the response is larger for chromatic stimulation than for any achromatic stimulation (62). Presence of these mechanisms also seems to be required by the finding that there are phase shifts in the VECPs generated by flickering stimulus patterns which cannot be nulled out by any adjustment of the relative luminances of the two chromatic components (133). It has also been reported that the latency of the VECP is longer for stimuli containing only hue differences than for similar stimuli containing luminance differences, implying thereby a more lengthy processing sequence for hue than for brightness (87).

It is well known that VECPs are more reliably elicited by stimuli containing some spatial structure. Consequently, a number of experimenters have utilized patterned stimuli which permit independent manipulation of wavelength and luminance among the components of the stimulus. With such arrays, a more systematic exploration of the relevant parameters can be carried out and results appear to be more clear-cut. For example, it seems that detection of differences in color vision capacity can be made quite reliably in this manner (87, 88, 134, 135), and thus these techniques appear to be the most promising ones for future work on the VECP.

BEHAVIOR

Rod-Cone Interactions

To the extent that rod signals interact with cone signals, one would like to be able to define the characteristics of the interactions, the importance of such interactions for color vision, and the locations in the visual system where such interactions occurs. A little progress has been made toward each of these goals.

Predictably, the nature of the interaction between rods and cones is found to depend on the situation used for examination, as the following results attest. First, manipulation of the timing of rod-activating and cone-activating inputs indicate that rod-cone interactions may be either inhibitory or facilitatory (56). Second, in a clever experiment, MacLeod (98) showed that under mesopic conditions a flickering light detected by the cones can be completely masked by concomitant periodic stimulation of the rods. This cancellation effect is apparently due to the latency differences in rod and cone systems. Third, utilizing differences in directional sensitivity between rods and cones, it was shown that excitation of the cones can cause a significant increase in the rod threshold (100). The direction of this interaction suggests that the widespread use of a red light to "isolate" the rods may in fact entail interaction effects not intended. Finally, rod-cone interactions are sufficient to lead to the production of Land-type induction effects (106). In sum, rod-cone interactions appear in a variety of circumstances—they may be bidirectional and either facilitatory or inhibitory.

The quality of the contribution of the rod signal to color vision has never been agreed on. It is still not. Opinion ranges over the ideas that the rods contribute an achromatic desaturant (161), or that they contribute a signal whose effect mimics that of the short-wavelength cones (5), or that the nature of the rod contribution is widely variable depending on the past history of chromatic stimulation (162, 163).

The visual system abounds with potential locations for significant rod-cone interactions. Some of these interactions, particularly those showing a suppressive effect of cones on rods, probably occur at the receptor level (185). Others (163) seem to demand a location where the chromatic-opponent interactions are well established, like the inner nuclear layer. Still others depend on the particular spatial characteristics of the stimuli and so may very well imply a cortical interaction site (167).

Component Mechanisms: Spectral, Distributional, and Latency Characteristics

Some comments have already been made about the spectra of the human cone pigments. From the viewpoint of psychophysics, most attempts to define the spectral characteristics of the component mechanisms involve threshold measurements on chromatically adapting backgrounds. Measurements of this kind, derived from the work of Stiles and his followers, have recently been critically evaluated in an interesting review by Enoch (50). His conclusion is that these components (the Stiles Π mechanisms) are neither direct representations of the cone pigments, nor are they free of interactions one with another. However, they are close enough on both of these scores to make them valuable as indices of the initial stages of processing.

During this review period, measurements of the spectra for the component mechanisms involved the utilization of several new techniques. These were usually accompanied by comparisons to previous measurement of the component spectra, typically either the Stiles Π mechanisms or estimates derived from the data on dichromatic observers. Thus the effects of intense chromatic adaptation on interocular brightness matching (183), on the radiance required for flicker fusion (102), on the pupillary reflex (9), and on the thresholds for photopic saturation (86) have all been reported. In each case the spectra for the derived mechanisms fit more or less well to the previous estimates. In addition, an anomaloscope-type measurement was adapted to allow the estimation of spectral sensitivity for the blue (72) and the green and red mechanisms (143).

The role of the short-wavelength mechanisms has often been disputed. Among other things, the lack of contribution by this mechanism to some types of spectral sensitivity functions has sometimes been taken as evidence that it contributes little or nothing to brightness. However, magnitude estimates of brightness produced by this mechanism (when isolated by chromatic adaptation) make it clear that it can mediate suprathreshold brightness information (101).

Some interesting new information on the retinal distribution of the component mechanisms has become available. Wooten & Wald (190) utilized a chromatic-adaptation procedure to assess the presence and the sensitivity of each of the three component mechanisms in a region extending from the fovea to 80° peripheral. They found that all three components are present throughout this range, although there are losses in sensitivity at the peripheral locations along with some apparent changes in the spectral sensitivity of the components. This suggests that the large qualitative changes in color vision associated with stimulation of the peripheral retina may be due to an alteration in neural connections. An evaluation of this idea could be made directly, but unfortunately no one has yet mapped the relative proportions of chromatic-opponent and non-opponent cells which receive their inputs from various retinal locations. Since the short-wavelength mechanism shows a particularly pronounced decline in sensitivity in the periphery, these results might be thought to raise the problem of how to explain the enhanced sensitivity to the short wavelengths that sometimes appears in spectral sensitivity functions (114). The answer may be that the peripheral retina does not in fact show such a short-wavelength enhancement (63, 188). The dichromacy of the central fovea has been reexamined (27, 140). Dichromatic color matches for stimuli imaged onto the central 16' of the fovea were found to be upset by chromatic adaptation of a surrounding area. This implies that the dichromacy of this region is due not to a loss of one photopigment but rather to some sort of postreceptor defect.

There is a substantial, but largely contradictory, literature bearing on the question of whether the different cone mechanisms respond with different latencies. Some allusions to these differences have already been made. Mollon & Krauskopf (113) pointed out that suprathreshold flashes presented on an achromatic background will excite a single cone mechanism only under restricted circumstances. To avoid this problem, they isolated the mechanisms individually with a Stiles-type procedure and then measured the reaction times supported by each mechanism. They found that the time constants of the chromatic mechanisms vary independently and that the reaction times mediated by the Π_1 mechanism were as much as 50 msec longer than those mediated by the long-wavelength mechanisms. Weingarten (182) has added the information that wavelength effects on latency are much more obvious if the situation is structured such that no luminance changes are introduced. Studies showing wavelength-related differences have typically reported shorter latencies for longer wavelengths; however, if the task is made more complex, for example by requiring the visual system to deal with some spatial aspects of the stimuli (169), this ordering may be completely reversed.

Component Mechanisms: Spatial and Temporal Characteristics

Sekuler (147) has provided a very useful review of the burgeoning literature on measurements of spatial contrast sensitivity. In this review he catalogs the descriptive and theoretical ends to which these measurements are directed. Although not yet extensively exploited in studies of color vision, some information on the contrast sensitivity of the component mechanisms has appeared. The paradigm typically used involves the measurement of sensitivity to spatial sine waves presented as chromatic stimuli on chromatic backgrounds. The blue mechanism so isolated shows fairly low contrast sensitivity with a peak centered at 1 to 2 cycles per degree (40, 65, 81). These results are in accord with much other data showing a lowered spatial resolution for this system. Not surprisingly, the green and red component mechanisms are more difficult to isolate by chromatic adaptation. When this is accomplished (81), the green mechanism is found to have a somewhat higher frequency peak than the isolated red mechanism and a somewhat higher overall contrast sensitivity. Relative to the blue mechanism, both of the other components are much more sensitive.

The presence of a decline in contrast sensitivity for the low spatial frequencies is usually taken as evidence for the presence of laterally interactive antagonistic processes. Thus it is of interest to note that each of the isolated chromatic mechanisms shows a low frequency falloff—that is, there must be lateral interaction within each component system. Additionally, Kelly (81) has found that the low frequency falloff is not as steep in the isolated red and green systems as in the contrast sensitivity function determined under neutral adaptation. This implies that there must be lateral interactions between the red and green component mechanisms as well as within them. In other experiments, spatial interactions between components of this kind were shown to occur in some situations (55) but not in others (13).

All of the measurements just referred to involved luminance modulation of the spectral stimuli, and thus it could be argued justifiably that these experiments provide valuable information about cone-fed systems but not necessarily about color vision. Indeed, the basic fact that cone signals are used for purposes other than color vision often seems to be forgotten. In an occasional study, including a recent one (64), spatial contrast sensitivity has been measured for chromaticity modulation (for example, a pattern that changes sinusoidally from a pure green to a pure red with luminance constant at each point in the waveform). This situation clearly speaks to the question of color vision mechanisms, and although the results of this manipulation have not been entirely consistent, it has usually been found that the contrast sensitivity functions for these pure hue changes show no low frequency falloff. A physiological correlate of this result may reside in the observation made by De Valois (42) that the receptive fields of chromatic-opponent cells in the LGN show center-surround antagonism when spatial stimuli containing luminance differences are presented but show no center-surround antagonism when spatial stimuli containing only hue changes are presented.

Some efforts are also underway to characterize the responses of isolated component mechanisms to various temporal waveforms, primarily sinusoids (51, 82, 103). As in the spatial case, the red and green component mechanisms show higher contrast sensitivity and peak at higher temporal frequencies than does the isolated blue mechanism. Kelly (82) has advanced the view that since there are significant spatiotemporal interactions in the responses of the component mechanisms to sinusoidal temporal and spatial waveforms, then it becomes necessary to consider these stimulus dimensions jointly. He has accomplished this task in an incisive paper (82) that is highly recommended. He points out that sine-wave thresholds for the component mechanisms can be considered to occupy a three-dimensional space with temporal and spatial frequency as the independent variables. As mentioned, there are substantial spatiotemporal interactions; for example, the low frequency ends of both spatial and temporal contrast sensitivity functions can be flattened by concurrent modulation in the other domain (as with flickering grating). One of the virtues of this line of thinking is that the various interactions can be taken to suggest the operation of particular pathways and connections. It seems inescapable that this sort of approach will gain increasing popularity.

Spectral Sensitivity and Wavelength Discrimination

It is no longer news that spectral sensitivity functions depend, among many other well-known factors, on the particular psychophysical method used to make the measurements. The reasons for these method-dependent differences are of interest, though still often obscure. New spectral sensitivity measurements have been made using flicker photometry, brightness matching, border minimization, and direct thresholds (69, 174). The border and flicker photometry methods yield functions very similar to the 1951 version of the CIE photopic spectral sensitivity function. On the other hand, brightness matching and threshold measurements yield sensitivity functions significantly broader in shape than do the other techniques. This difference is usually explained as reflecting the fact that the matching and threshold techniques utilize information in chromatic as well as in achromatic channels, the former having higher sensitivity toward the spectral extremes. Over the range from about 25–35 Hz, spectral sensitivity data obtained by determining flicker fusion also pretty well match the CIE function (19, 102). At higher flicker rates (40 Hz and above) the sensitivity function becomes significantly narrower. The reason for this change is not known but it probably involves interactions between the underlying component mechanisms. Direct magnitude estimates of brightness have also been used to determine a spectral sensitivity function (30). This function shows significantly heightened sensitivity to the short wavelengths. As if all these method dependencies were not enough, it has also been claimed that there may be significant systematic variations in the spectral sensitivity functions among normal trichromatic observers (32, 124).

Siegel & Siegel (149) have conducted an extensive study of the effects of luminance on wavelength discrimination. They find that as stimulus luminance is reduced from 10 to 0.1 foot Lamberts, the accompanying reduction in wavelength discrimination is much greater for the short than for the long wavelengths. Indeed, at the lowest luminance level the discrimination function shows only a single minimum at about 580 nm. Greater complication emerged when wavelength discrimination was examined with square-wave grating patterns variant in frequency and in the luminance contrast between the spectral stimuli. In this situation the effects of luminance contrast and spatial frequency were found to be interactive so that the spatial frequency leading to optimal wavelength discrimination depended on whether or not there was some luminance contrast between the spectral stimuli (70).

INTENSITY EFFECTS   A cornerstone for models developed to explain hue-luminance interactions (the Bezold-Brücke effect) is the presence of invariant points—wavelengths where hue does not change in the face of luminance changes. Recently, Savoie (146) has argued that there are no invariant points (at least in the region between 560 and 620 nm). His measurements suggest that the radiance-hue contours in this spectral range are nonmonotonic. These results are explained in a model as consequences of nonlinearities in the red and green color systems. Perhaps models of this kind are premature, as Larimer, Krantz & Cicerone (92) have reported a quite contrary result. Determination of unique hues (equilibrium hues in their terminology) shows that there are indeed hues which are invariant over reasonable luminance ranges. The substantial differences between subjects, as well as those differences probably dependent on the measurement situation, suggest that the issue is not yet ready for retirement.

TEMPORAL EFFECTS   The wide variety of changes in hue dependent on the temporal properties of the stimulus have intrigued scientists for many years. To this point most of the work has been descriptive in nature. Campenhausen (28) has recently postulated that the pattern-induced colors, like those of the Benham top, arise as a result of lateral interactions between adjacent regions in the retina with the horizontal cells identified as a likely locus. A parametric investigation of pulse rate and duration on the hue of monochromatic stimuli revealed a very complicated set of changes dependent on both wavelength and luminance (119). Thus at some luminance levels the flicker-induced hue shifts are similar in direction to those seen in the Bezold-Brücke hue shift, while at other luminance levels the hue shifts are quite different in both direction and extent.

Two explanatory mechanisms sometimes invoked to explain afterimages have been subjected to tests. Using dark adaptation thresholds, Wooten & Makous (189) showed that there is no spatial spread of desensitization in the vicinity of the region where an afterimage was formed. This result argues against Brindley's theory (25) that bleaching liberates a substance which diffuses laterally and desensitizes neighboring cones. Loomis (96) tested the proposition that the characteristics of a complementary afterimage could be explained on the basis of photopigment bleaching. Utilizing the production of Bidwell colors, he found that stimuli that yielded equal bleaching effects, but that were of quite different colors, produced afterimages clearly different in hue. Neural effects of the chromatic-opponent variety seem to be required to explain this result. Finally, Shiveley (148) has described a new afterimage effect appearing to involve simultaneous contrast during the adaptation phase.

SPATIAL EFFECTS   An experimental technique involving the adjustment of the relative luminances of two juxtaposed stimulus fields (different in chromaticity) so as to minimize the distinctness of the boundary between the two has been utilized in a variety of investigations (21, 174, 178, 179). Boynton (20) has clearly summarized these results in his Tillyer Medal address. When two such fields have been equated so as to produce a minimally distinct border (MDB) between the two, then the more saturated of the two fields appears distinctly brighter. As tested by MDB measurements, Abney's law holds perfectly, thus the mechanisms underlying this operation behave linearly. The theory developed to account for the MDB results posits chromatic and achromatic neural elements; both of these contribute to brightness but only the latter to whiteness. In this view, the MDB criterion is achieved when there are equal numbers of achromatic elements activated by the two halves of the field. Thus increment thresholds measured at various locations across a border between a white and a chromatic field show no change if the two fields are equated by MDB techniques (179), but they show a substantial change if the two fields are equated by traditional brightness matching (165).

A standard situation for examining spatial interactions involves a circular center region and an inducing annulus. A large and complex literature attests to the wide variety of ways in which spatial interactions between these two regions can be assessed and to the large number of variables which may have some importance in such situations. In general, lateral effects between the annulus and the center region may be due to neural interactions or to the presence of stray light from the annular region reaching the center. J. Walraven (175) examined several stimulus situations and found that chromatic induction effects could be explained completely by the presence of entoptically scattered light in a situation where the annulus was illuminated continuously, but lateral neural effects were required to account for cases where the annular field was flashed briefly. He adds the information that the lateral effects appear to build only over narrow spatial regions, suggesting that they are mediated by color-coded border mechanisms.

The question of whether lateral interactions are between or within cone types received considerable attention in the past. Two recent studies provide further evidence for a within-cone specificity in lateral interaction (68, 83). In an interesting paper, Guth (68) has pointed out that the interpretation of thresholds measured within a center region to assess the effects of an annular induction may be complicated by the fact that the threshold measuring light (the ΔI) is itself subject to lateral influences from the surround. He explores many of the implications of this possibility in his paper.

The search to determine the cues critical for stereoscopic vision included two attempts to see if chromatic contours alone constitute a sufficient condition. Lu & Fender (97) found it impossible to produce a depth effect from stimulus pairs of random dot patterns in which there were color but no luminance differences. On the other hand, Comerford (34) found equally clear evidence of stereopsis for test figures variant in color but equal in luminance. It appears that chromatic contours are sufficient to support some but not all stereoscopic processes. The so-called color stereoscopic effect, in which different colored objects lying in the same plane appear to lie in different planes, has now been attributed to variations in pupil size (168).

Defective Color Vision

It is hardly necessary to point out that defective color vision is a traditionally attractive target for research. Given all the new literature, little more can be done than to mention a few issues of particular concern. Fortunately, there are a large number of good, recent reviews of this topic. Particularly worthy of attention is a thoughtful treatment by Hurvich (74).

The true color blinds, the monochromats, present a series of fascinating puzzles. Clearly the place to seek enlightenment on these matters is now Alpern's Friedenwald lecture (4) in which he summarizes the literature on monochromacy and reports his own measurements on a large number of such subjects. To summarize drastically, two classes of so-called rod monochromats are identified—one class has a small number of cone receptors but only rhodopsin, the other class apparently has the normal complement of rod and cone photopigments coupled with what must be a severe postreceptor defect. There is also a bewildering variety of cone monochromats. Much recent attention has been directed toward the blue-cone monochromats, a group which appears to thrive in the state of Michigan. Their defect seems explainable as a simple loss of two classes of photopigments, although there are some indications that this group may not be entirely homogeneous (40, 65). For those who admire contradiction, Alpern (4) offers the case of an individual who apparently lacks a single class of photopigment but who also shows evidence of a neural defect that reduces his potentially dichromatic color vision to a monochromacy. Alpern's pithy conclusion as to whether the monochromacies involve pigment or neural defects is that, "Evidently, if it is not one or the other, then it is both together."

The mechanisms supporting anomalous trichromacy are only poorly understood. Several recent studies have been directed toward a determination of the spectra for the cone pigments in protanomalous and deuteranomalous subjects; despite some convergence of opinion, significant disagreements and uncertainties still remain. Of the four groups of investigators who have pursued this problem, all start from the assumption that the anomalies result from a simple shift of the pigment absorption curves along the wavelength scale. This is an assumption unlikely to account for the behavior of the full range of individuals classified as anomalous trichromats, as Hurvich & Jameson have so forcefully pointed out (74). The wide variation in color naming by deuteranomalous observers further supports this view (156). On the basis of analyses of literature data (99, 129) and some new measurements (126, 127, 144), it appears that protans and deutans each have two cone photopigments identical to those of the normal trichromats. However, neither the assumed peak locations nor the shapes of these normal pigment functions are the same in all of these studies. The spectra for the anomalous pigments in both deutans and protans were found to be shifted close to the locations of the other long-wavelength (normal) pigment, but again the peak location is not agreed on. The peak for the anomalous pigment in the protan ranged from 544 to 550 nm in these various studies, while that for the deutan ranged from 544 to 560 nm. One set of investigators concluded that the anomalous pigment is the same for both protan and deutan individuals (99), but this seems quite unlikely in the face of the other studies. In sum, the anomalies may be yielding to analysis but they have not yet surrendered.

Rushton, Powell & White (142) developed a new psychophysical technique to permit the measurement of cone pigment sensitivity. The technique involves the use of a stimulus field which is abruptly shifted from one radiance-wavelength complex to another. The radiance and wavelength values of the two components are selected such that the quantal catch for one photopigment system remains undisturbed, and thus any changes must reflect the intervention of a second photopigment. Utilizing this method, they measured the photopigments for deuteranopes and protanopes. The values derived were found to agree well with previous densitometry and behavioral results. The recurring issue of deuteranope luminosity functions was again considered by Pokorny & Smith (128). As determined by several measurement methods, deuteranopes were shown to have a sensitivity loss below about 570 nm. Elsewhere on the dichromatic front, a reassessment of tritanopic convergence points was published (177), and it was shown that dichromatic convergence points can be estimated by a subtractive color matching technique (16).

A dispute as to whether congenital tritanopia exists, or whether this condition is always secondary to ocular disease, seems to have been resolved in favor of the view that an inherited congenital tritanopic condition can be demonstrated unequivocally (152). Nevertheless, conditions of dominantly inherited optic nerve atrophy do produce much of the range of tritan symptoms, and so Smith & Pokorny (155) argued that the same genetic defect may be involved in both instances. The picture of the tritan defects was not made clearer by the observation that tritanopes and tritanomalous subjects show essentially indistinguishable color naming and hue discrimination (151). Other losses of cone function as a result of degenerative diseases were the subject of an extensive review by Krill et al (91).

Omissions

The reader's attention is drawn to some behavioral topics missing from this review. There has been significant activity in the area of color metrics and color theory. Both of these are extensively covered in the symposia referred to earlier. There has also been an explosion of experimental activity (about three dozen articles were seen) on the topic of color contingent aftereffects. Although interesting in other regards, these contingent aftereffects do not seem to have told us much yet about color vision. Unfortunately for the nonparticipant, this literature so far has not been subjected to critical review.

COMPARATIVE COLOR VISION

The rationales for studying color vision in species other than our own include, in addition to a straightforward curiosity about our fellow creatures (fortunately still a respectable motivation), an interest in providing a basis for evaluating physiological, biochemical, and anatomical information about color vision mechanisms. It is also often asserted that such comparative information might lead to an understanding of the contexts which led to the development of elaborate color vision in some species but not in others. The research published during this review period is sufficiently heterogeneous to allow little more than a capsulization of what has been accomplished.

Experts in color vision are frequently embarrassed to have to admit that there is little hard scientific fact about the nature of color vision in the young of our own species. Although there are indications that things are now changing, only quite crude assessments of infant color vision have been made in the past. Fagan (53) has recently used a stimulus-preference technique to assess the ability of infants from 4 to 6 months of age to discriminate hue. His conclusion that infants are capable of hue discrimination by this age is very likely correct, but the inadequacies of brightness control in this experiment make it impossible to draw any more informative conclusions. Bornstein(18) has produced an interesting review of the degree of variation in color naming among different human societies. He finds that the likelihood of confusion among the names for the short-wavelength stimuli (the blues and the greens) increases with increasing proximity to the equator and argues that the explanation for this may lie in increases in lens density caused by the presence of greater amounts of ultraviolet radiation.

With regard to nonhuman primates, new information became available on several species. The macaque monkey is widely used as a human surrogate because it is usually asserted or assumed that the visual systems and vision of these two are highly similar. Further support for this proposition comes from a study (46) showing that three species of macaques perform very much like man on tests of spectral sensitivity and color vision. The color vision tests included wavelength discrimination, purity discrimination, and the establishment of Rayleigh matches. In each case the macaque and human results are nearly identical. However, before everyone concludes that man and macaque monkey are interchangeable, it should be noted that the optic nerve of the macaque contains a significantly larger number of optic nerve fibers than that of man (130). If not in color vision, it seems inescapable that these two species differ in some visual capacities. In earlier experiments it has been concluded that a prototypical New World monkey, the squirrel monkey, is a protanomalous trichromat. New measurements of wavelength and purity discrimination in this species tend to support this conclusion (45). A prosimian having a rod-rich retina (*Lemur catta*) was found to show some color vision (107).

The history of the search for color vision in the domestic cat is well known. Despite a fair number of cones [26,000–27,000/mm^2 in the *area centralis* (164)], it has consistently required heroic efforts to demonstrate color vision in this animal. Brown et al (26) have added a study on color discrimination in the cat. After carefully matching four spectral stimuli in cat-brightness, they attempted to demonstrate discriminations between blue, green, yellow, and red stimuli. Of all possible pairings of these stimuli, only the green-yellow pair proved indiscriminable. On the basis of two presumptive photopigments peaking at 460 and 540 nm (41), it is not clear how the animals succeeded at the red-yellow discrimination but failed the green-yellow pair. Apparently not all has yet been learned about cat color vision. Just how comparatively easy it is for the psychophysicist working with human observers is indicated by the observation in this report that the unsuccessful attempts to demonstrate a yellow-green discrimination led to both a loss of enthusiasm and a loss of fur from the subject.

That favorite rodent of the psychologist, the rat, continues to receive attention. Messing (108) measured aversion thresholds for various monochromatic lights in albino rats, and despite presenting some data which appear to indicate the contrary, concluded these animals showed no Purkinje shift. Actually, differences in scotopic and photopic spectral sensitivity have regularly appeared in ERG studies done on this rodent and, in fact, another behavioral study showed that hooded rats have two photopically active mechanisms and thus the potential for some color vision (15).

Primarily because of their cone-rich retinas, a number of sciurid species have been investigated. The ground-dwelling sciurids have retinas containing only a very small number of rodlike photoreceptors, and consequently, vision under scotopic light levels is quite restricted in these species. All of the species from this group that have been examined (several species of ground squirrels and prairie dogs) have been found to have a dichromatic color vision somewhat similar in character to human protanopia (6, 36, 79). The tree squirrels have a greater number of rods, but they, too, have cone-dominated retinas. These animals give behavioral evidence of viable scotopic and photopic vision (47) and seem to have dichromatic color vision (78).

Although potentially very interesting from the point of view of color vision, only a few species of birds have yet received experimental attention. One that has is the pigeon. Two good studies of wavelength discrimination in this trichromatic species have been published. The spectral location of best discrimination is at about 600 nm with secondary minima at about 540 nm and perhaps 500 nm (17, 191). The pigeon eye contains multiple photopigments and several classes of colored oil droplets, and the question of how all these mechanisms combine to produce trichromacy remains unanswered. An almost totally nocturnal owl (*Strix aluco*) was also shown to have some color vision (105).

Only a limited amount of new information on color vision in fish has been published. In one study the effects of chromatic adaptation on saturation discrimination in the goldfish was measured (192). In another study Rayleigh matches were established for carp subjects (123). Although the demonstration of color mixing by this fish is not surprising, the fact that the red-green mix required to match a spectral yellow was the same as that for a human observer is surprising. Given the differences in photopigments in these two species, this similarity of outcome seems quite coincidental. Although not yet dealing with color vision, a research effort reported by Munz & McFarland (116) bears mention. In a large comparative study they tried to establish correlations between the characteristics of the retinal photopigments in a large number of fish species and their photic ecology. The potential for relating light environment and color vision capacities in this same context seems clear.

ACKNOWLEDGMENTS

Preparation of this review was facilitated by a grant from the National Eye Institute (EY-00105). A number of friends were kind enough to read a version of this paper and offer helpful comments. I thank them all.

Literature Cited

1. Abramov, I. 1972. Retinal mechanisms of colour vision. In *Physiology of Photoreceptor Organs,* ed. M. G. F. Fuortes, 567–607. Berlin: Springer. 765 pp.
2. Abramov, I., Levine, M. W. 1972. The effects of carbon dioxide on the excised goldfish retina. *Vision Res.* 21:1881–95
3. Adachi-Usami, E., Heck, J., Gavriysky, V., Kellermann, F.-J. 1974. Spectral sensitivity function determined by visually evoked cortical potential in several classes of colour deficiency (Cone monochromatism, Rod monochromatism, Protanopia, Deuteranopia). *Ophthalmic Res.* 6:273–90
4. Alpern, M. 1974. What is it that confines in a world without color? *Invest. Ophthalmol.* 13:648–74
5. Ambler, B. A. 1974. Hue discrimination in peripheral vision under conditions of dark and light adaptation. *Percept. Psychophys.* 15:586–90
6. Anderson, D. H., Jacobs, G. H. 1972. Color vision and visual sensitivity in the California ground squirrel (*Citellus beecheyi*). *Vision Res.* 12:1995–2004

7. Arden, G. B., Ed. 1972. *The Visual System: Neurophysiology, Biophysics and their Clinical Application.* New York: Plenum. 335 pp.
8. Armington, J. C. 1974. *The Electroretinogram.* New York: Academic. 478 pp.
9. Banks, M. S., Munsinger, H. 1974. Pupillometric measurement of difference spectra for three color receptors in an adult and a four-year-old. *Vision Res.* 14:813–17
10. Baylor, D. A. 1974. Lateral interaction between vertebrate photoreceptors. *Fed. Proc.* 33:1074–77
11. Beauchamp, R. D., Daw, N. W. 1972. Rod and cone input to single goldfish optic nerve fibers. *Vision Res.* 12:1201–12
12. Beck, J. 1972. *Surface Color Perception.* Ithaca: Cornell Univ. 206 pp.
13. Bender, B. G. 1973. Spatial interactions between the red- and green-sensitive colour mechanisms of the human visual system. *Vision Res.* 13:2205–18
14. Berson, E. L., Goldstein, E. B. 1972. Cone pigment regeneration, retinitis

pigmentosa, and light deprivation. *Vision Res.* 12:479–52

15. Birch, D., Jacobs, G. H. 1975. Behavioral measurements of rat spectral sensitivity. *Vision Res.* 15:687–91

16. Birch, J. 1973. Dichromatic convergence points obtained by subtractive colour matching. *Vision Res.* 13:1755–65

17. Blough, P. M. 1972. Wavelength generalization and discrimination in the pigeon. *Percept. Psychophys.* 12:342–48

18. Bornstein, M. H. 1973. Color vision and color naming: A psychophysiological hypothesis of cultural difference. *Psychol. Bull.* 80:257–85

19. Bornstein, M. H., Marks, L. E. 1972. Photopic luminosity measured by the method of critical frequency. *Vision Res.* 12:2023–33

20. Boynton, R. M. 1973. Implications of the minimally distinct border. *J. Opt. Soc. Am.* 63:1037–43

21. Boynton, R. M., Greenspon, T. S. 1972. The distinctness of borders formed between equally saturated, psychologically unique fields. *Vision Res.* 12:495–507

22. Boynton, R. M., Whitten, D. N. 1972. Selective chromatic adaptation in primate receptors. *Vision Res.* 12:855–74

23. Bowmaker, J. K. 1972. Kundt's rule: The spectral absorbance of visual pigments in situ and in solution. *Vision Res.* 12:529–48

24. Ibid 1973. Spectral sensitivity and visual pigment absorbance. 13:783–92

25. Brindley, G. S. 1962. Two new properties of foveal after-images and a photochemical hypothesis to explain them. *J. Physiol. London* 164:168–79

26. Brown, J. L., Shiveley, F. D., LaMotte, R. H., Sechzer, J. A. 1973. Color discrimination in the cat. *J. Comp. Physiol. Psychol.* 84:531–44

27. Burton, G. J., Ruddock, K. H. 1972. A lateral light adaptation effect in human vision. *Vision Res.* 12:347—52

28. Campenhausen, C. 1973. Detection of short time delays between photic stimuli by means of pattern induced flicker colors (PIFCs). *Vision Res.* 13:2261–72

29. Carterette, E. C., Friedman, M. P., Eds. 1973. *Handbook of Perception, Vol. 3: Biology of Perceptual Systems.* New York: Academic. 521 pp.

30. Cavonius, C. R., Hilz, R. 1973. Brightness of isolated colored lights. *J. Opt. Soc. Am.* 63:884–88

31. Cerf-Beare, A. 1973. Regions of response transition of color-coded retinal units and an attempted analogy to behavioral response transition. *Percept. Psychophys.* 13:541–47

32. Cobb, S. R. 1974. The luminosity curves for class I and class II color normals. *Vision Res.* 14:529–33

33. Cohen, A. I. 1972. Rods and cones. See Ref. 1, 63–110

34. Comerford, J. P. 1974. Stereopsis with chromatic contours. *Vision Res.* 14:975–82

35. Coren, S., Girgus, J. S. 1972. Density of human lens pigmentation: In vivo measures over an extended age range. *Vision Res.* 12:343–46

36. Crescitelli, F., Pollack, J. D. 1972. Dichromacy in the antelope ground squirrel. *Vision Res.* 12:1553–86

37. Davson, H. 1972. *The Physiology of the Eye.* New York: Academic. 643 pp.

38. Daw, N. W. 1973. Neurophysiology of color vision. *Physiol. Rev.* 53:571–611

39. Daw, N. W., Beauchamp, R. D. 1972. Unusual units in the goldfish optic nerve. *Vision Res.* 12:1849–56

40. Daw, N. W., Enoch, J. M. 1973. Contrast sensitivity, Westheimer function and Stiles-Crawford effect in blue cone monochromat. *Vision Res.* 13:1669–80

41. Daw, N. W., Pearlman, A. L. 1970. Cat colour vision: Evidence for more than one cone process. *J. Physiol. London* 211:125–37

42. De Valois, R. L. 1972. Processing of intensity and wavelength information by the visual system. *Invest. Ophthalmol.* 11:417–26

43. De Valois, R. L. 1973. Central mechanisms of color vision. In *Central Visual Information A,* ed. R. Jung, 209–53. Berlin: Springer. 775 pp.

44. De Valois, R. L., Marrocco, R. T. 1973. Single cell analysis of saturation discrimination in the macaque. *Vision Res.* 13:701–11

45. De Valois, R. L., Morgan, H. C. 1974. Psychophysical studies of monkey vision. II. Squirrel monkey wavelength and saturation discrimination. *Vision Res.* 14:69–73

46. De Valois, R. L., Morgan, H. C., Polson, M. C., Mead, W. R., Hull, E. M. 1974. Psychophysical studies of monkey vision. I. Macaque luminosity and color vision tests. *Vision Res.* 14:53–67

47. Dippner, R. 1974. Dark adaptation in the American red squirrel (*Tamiosciurus hudsonicus*). *J. Comp. Physiol. Psychol.* 87:62–72

48. Dow, B. M. 1974. Functional classes of cells and their laminar distribution in

monkey visual cortex. *J. Neurophysiol.* 37:927–46

49. Dow, B. M., Gouras, P. 1973. Color and spatial specificity of single units in the Rhesus monkey foveal striate cortex. *J. Neurophysiol.* 36:79–100

50. Enoch, J. M. 1972. The two-color threshold technique of Stiles and derived component mechanisms. In *Visual Psychophysics*, ed. D. Jameson, L. M. Hurvich, 537–67. Berlin: Springer. 812 pp.

51. Estevez, O., Spekreijse, H. 1974. A spectral compensation method for determining the flicker characteristics of the human colour mechanisms. *Vision Res.* 14:823–30

52. Evans, R. M. 1974. *The Perception of Color.* New York: Wiley. 248 pp.

53. Fagan, J. F. III 1974. Infant color perception. *Science* 183:973–75

54. Fain, G. L., Dowling, J. E. 1973. Intracellular recordings from single rods and cones in the mudpuppy retina. *Science* 180:1178–81

55. Foster, D. H., Idris, I. I. M. 1974. Spatio-temporal interaction between visual colour mechanisms. *Vision Res.* 14:35–39

56. Frumkes, T. E., Sekuler, M. D., Barris, M. C., Reiss, E. H., Chalupa, L. M. 1973. Rod-cone interaction in human scotopic vision. I. Temporal Analysis. *Vision Res.* 13:1269–82

57. Fuortes, M. G. F., Schwartz, E. A., Simon, E. J. 1973. Colour-dependence of cone responses in the turtle retina. *J. Physiol. London* 234:199–216

58. Fuortes, M. G. F., Simon, E. J. 1974. Interactions leading to horizontal cell responses in the turtle retina. *J. Physiol. London* 240:177–98

59. Geldard, F. A. 1972. *The Human Senses.* New York: Wiley. 584 pp.

60. Gouras, P. 1972. Color opponency from fovea to striate cortex. *Invest. Ophthalmol.* 11:427–34

61. Gouras, P. 1974. Opponent-colour cells in different layers of foveal striate cortex. *J. Physiol. London* 238:583–602

62. Gouras, P., Padmos, P. 1974. Identification of cone mechanisms in graded responses of foveal striate cortex. *J. Physiol. London* 238:583–602

63. Graham, B. V., Holland, B., Sparks, D. L. 1975. Relative spectral sensitivity to short wavelength light in the peripheral visual field. *Vision Res.* 15:313–16

64. Granger, E. M., Heurtley, J. C. 1973. Visual chromaticity-modulation transfer function. *J. Opt. Soc. Am.* 63:1173–74

65. Green, D. G. 1972. Visual acuity in the blue cone monochromat. *J. Physiol. London* 222:419–26

66. Gross, C. G., Rocha-Miranda, C. E., Bender, D. B. 1972. Visual properties of neurons in inferotemporal cortex of the macaque. *J. Neurophysiol.* 35:96–111

67. Gur, M., Purple, R. L. 1974. A new receptive field organization in the ground squirrel retina. *Physiologist* 17:236

68. Guth, S. L. 1973. On neural inhibition, contrast effects and visual sensitivity. *Vision Res.* 13:937–57

69. Guth, S. L., Lodge, H. R. 1973. Heterochromatic additivity, foveal spectral sensitivity, and a new color model. *J. Opt. Soc. Am.* 63:450–62

70. Hilz, R. L., Huppmann, G., Cavonius, C. R. 1974. Influence of luminance contrast on hue discrimination. *J. Opt. Soc. Am.* 64:763–66

71. Hollins, M., Alpern, M. 1973. Dark adaptation and visual pigment regeneration in human cones. *J. Gen. Physiol.* 62:430–47

72. Hollins, M., Montabana, D. J. 1973. Spectral sensitivity of the foveal blue-sensitive mechanism determined by color mixture. *Vision Res.* 13:1391–93

73. Hubel, D. H., Wiesel, T. N. 1968. Receptive fields and functional architecture of monkey striate cortex. *J. Physiol. London* 195:215–43

74. Hurvich, L. M. 1972. Color vision deficiencies. In *Visual Psychophysics*, ed. D. Jameson, L. M. Hurvich, 582–624. Berlin: Springer. 812 pp.

75. Ingling, C. R. Jr., Drum, B. A. 1973. Retinal receptive fields, correlations between psychophysics and electrophysiology. *Vision Res.* 13:1151–63

76. International Colour Association 1973. *Color 73.* New York: Wiley. 566 pp.

77. Jacobs, G. H. 1974. Spectral sensitivity of the short wavelength mechanism in the squirrel monkey visual system. *Vision Res.* 14:1271–73

78. Jacobs, G. H. 1974. Scotopic and photopic visual capacities of an arboreal squirrel (*Sciurus niger*). *Brain, Behav. Evol.* 10:307–21

79. Jacobs, G. H., Pulliam, K. A. 1973. Vision in the prairie dog: Spectral sensitivity and color vision. *J. Comp. Physiol. Psychol.* 84:240–45

80. Kaneko, A. 1973. Receptive field organization of bipolar and amacrine cells in

the goldfish retina. *J. Physiol. London* 235:133–53

81. Kelly, D. H. 1973. Lateral inhibition in human colour mechanisms. *J. Physiol. London* 228:55–72

82. Kelly, D. H. 1974. Spatio-temporal frequency characteristics of color-vision mechanisms. *J. Opt. Soc. Am.* 64:983–90

83. Kerr, L. 1974. Detection and identification of monochromatic stimuli under chromatic contrast. *Vision Res.* 14:1095–1105

84. King-Smith, P. E. 1973. The optical density of erythrolabe determined by retinal densitometry using the self-screening method. *J. Physiol. London* 230:535–49

85. Ibid. The optical density of erythrolabe determined by a new method, 551–60

86. King-Smith, P. E., Webb, J. R. 1974. The use of photopic saturation in determining the fundamental spectral sensitivity curves. *Vision Res.* 14:421–30

87. Kinney, J. A. S., McKay, C. L. 1974. Test of color-defective vision using the visual evoked response. *J. Opt. Soc. Am.* 64:1244–50

88. Kinney, J. A. S., McKay, C. L., Mensch, A. J., Luria, S. M. 1972. Techniques for analyzing differences in VERs: Colored and patterned stimuli. *Vision Res.* 12:1733–47

89. Kozak, W. M., Reitboeck, H. J. 1974. Color-dependent distribution of spikes in single optic tract fibers of the cat. *Vision Res.* 14:405–20

90. Krauskopf, J. 1973. Contributions of the primary chromatic mechanisms to the generation of visual evoked potentials. *Vision Res.* 13:2289–98

91. Krill, A. E., Deutman, A. F., Fishman, M. 1973. The cone degenerations. *Doc. Ophthalmol.* 35:1–80

92. Larimer, J., Krantz, D. H., Cicerone, C. M. 1974. Opponent-process additivity–I. Red/green equilibria. *Vision Res.* 14:1127–40

93. Lasansky, A. 1974. Synaptic actions on retinal photoreceptors: Structural aspects. *Fed. Proc.* 33:1069–73

94. LeGrand, Y. 1972. About the photopigments of colour vision. *Mod. Probl. Ophthalmol.* 11:186–92

95. Liebman, P. A. 1972. Microspectrophotometry of photoreceptors. In *Photochemistry of Vision*, ed. H. J. A. Dartnall, 481–528. Berlin: Springer. 810 pp.

96. Loomis, J. M. 1972. The photopigment bleaching hypothesis of complementary after-images: A psychophysical test. *Vision Res.* 12:1587–94

97. Lu, C., Fender, D. H. 1972. The interaction of color and luminance in stereoscopic vision. *Invest. Ophthalmol.* 11:482–90

98. MacLeod, D. I. A. 1972. Rods cancel cones in flicker. *Nature* 235:173–74

99. MacLeod, D. I. A., Hayhoe, M. 1974. Three pigments in normal and anomalous color vision. *J. Opt. Soc. Am.* 64:92–96

100. Makous, W., Boothe, R. 1974. Cones block signals from rods. *Vision Res.* 14:285–94

101. Marks, L. E. 1974. Blue-sensitive cones can mediate brightness. *Vision Res.* 14:1493–94

102. Marks, L. E., Bornstein, M. H. 1973. Spectral sensitivity by constant CFF: Effect of chromatic adaptation. *J. Opt. Soc. Am.* 63:220–26

103. Marks, L. E., Bornstein, M. H. 1974. Spectral sensitivity of the modulation-sensitive mechanism of vision. *Vision Res.* 14:665–69

104. Marrocco, R. T. 1972. Responses of monkey optic tract fibers to monochromatic lights. *Vision Res.* 12:1167–74

105. Martin, G. R. 1974. Color vision in the tawny owl (*Strix aluco*). *J. Comp. Physiol. Psychol.* 86:133–41

106. McCann, J. J. 1972. Rod-cone interactions: Different color sensations from identical stimuli. *Science* 176:1255–57

107. Mervis, R. F. 1974. Evidence of color vision in a diurnal prosimian, *Lemur catta. Anim. Learn. Behav.* 2:238–40

108. Messing, R. B. 1972. The sensitivity of albino rats to lights of different wavelength: A Behavioral assessment. *Vision Res.* 12:753–61

109. Michael, C. R. 1973. Opponent-color and opponent-contrast cells in lateral geniculate nucleus of the ground squirrel. *J. Neurophysiol.* 36:536–50

110. Miller, S. S. 1972. Psychophysical estimates of visual pigment densities in red-green dichromats. *J. Physiol. London* 223:89–107

111. Miller, W. H., Snyder, A. W. 1972. Optical functions of myoids. *Vision Res.* 12:1841–94

112. Ibid 1973. Optical function of human peripheral cones. 13:2185–94

113. Mollon, J. D., Krauskopf, J. 1973. Reaction time as a measure of the temporal response properties of individual colour mechanisms. *Vision Res.* 13:27–40

114. Moreland, J. D. 1972. Peripheral color vision. See Ref. 50, 517–36
115. Muntz, W. R. A. 1972. Inert absorbing and reflecting pigments. See Ref. 95, 529–65
116. Munz, F. W., McFarland, W. N. 1973. The significance of spectral position in the rhodopsins of tropical marine fishes. Vision Res. 13:1829–74
117. National Academy of Sciences 1973. Color Vision. Washington. 124 pp.
118. Niemeyer, G., Gouras, P. 1973. Rod and cone signals in S-potentials of the isolated perfused cat eye. Vision Res. 13:1603–12
119. Nilsson, T. H. 1972. Effects of pulse duration and pulse rate on hue of monochromatic stimuli. Vision Res. 12:1907–21
120. Normann, R. A., Werblin, F. S. 1974. Control of retinal sensitivity: I. Light and dark adaptation of vertebrate rods and cones. J. Gen. Physiol. 63:37–61
121. Norren, D., Padmos, P. 1974. Dark adaptation of separate cone systems studied with psychophysics and electroretinography. Vision Res. 14:677–86
122. Norren, D., Vos, J. J. 1974. Spectral transmission of the human ocular media. Vision Res. 14:1237–44
123. Oyama, T., Jitsumori, M. 1973. A behavioural study of color mixture in the carp. Vision Res. 13:2299–2308
124. Palmer, D. A. 1972. Two types of parafoveal spectral sensitivity. Vision Res. 12:1271–79
125. Perry, N. W. Jr., Childers, D. G., Dawson, W. W. 1972. Reliability of the monochromatic VER. Vision Res. 12:357–58
126. Piantanida, T. P., Sperling, H. G. 1973. Isolation of a third chromatic mechanism in the protanomalous observer. Vision Res. 13:2033–47
127. Ibid. Isolation of a third chromatic mechanism in the deuteranomalous observer, 2049–58
128. Pokorny, J., Smith, V. C. 1972. Luminosity and CFF in deuteranopes and protanopes. J. Opt. Soc. Am. 62:111–17
129. Pokorny, J., Smith, V. C., Katz, I. 1973. Derivation of the photopigment absorption spectra in anomalous trichromats. J. Opt. Soc. Am. 63:232–37
130. Potts, A. M., Hodges, D., Shelman, C. B., Fritz, K. J., Levy, N. S., Mangnall, Y. 1972. Morphology of the primate optic nerve. I. Method and total fiber count. Invest. Ophthalmol. 11:980–88

131. Raynauld, J. P. 1972. Goldfish retina: Sign of the rod input in opponent color ganglion cells. Science 177:84–85
132. Reading, V. M., Weale, R. A. 1974. Macular pigment and chromatic aberration. J. Opt. Soc. Am. 64:231–34
133. Regan, D. 1973. An evoked potential correlate of colour: Evoked potential findings and single-cell speculations. Vision Res. 13:1933–41
134. Ibid. Evoked potentials specific to spatial patterns of luminance and colour, 2381–2402
135. Regan, D., Spekreijse, H. 1974. Evoked potential indications of colour blindness. Vision Res. 14:89–95
136. Reuter, T., Virtanen, K. 1972. Border and colour-coding in the retina of the frog. Nature 239:260–63
137. Richter, A., Simon, E. J. 1974. Electrical responses of double cones in the turtle retina. J. Physiol. London 242:673–83
138. Rodieck, R. W. 1973. The Vertebrate Retina. San Francisco: Freeman. 1044 pp.
139. Ruddock, K. H. 1972. Observer variations in foveal colour vision responses. Vision Res. 12:145–49
140. Ruddock, K. H., Burton, G. J. 1972. The organization of human colour vision at the central fovea. Vision Res. 12:1763–69
141. Rushton, W. A. H. 1972. Pigments and signals in colour vision. J. Physiol. London 220:1–31
142. Rushton, W. A. H., Powell, D. S., White, K. D. 1973. Exchange thresholds in dichromats. Vision Res. 13:1993–2002
143. Ibid. The spectral sensitivity of "red" and "green" cones in the normal eye, 2003–15
144. Ibid. Pigments in anomalous trichromats, 2017–31
145. Sansbury, R., Zacks, J., Nachmias, J. 1974. The Stiles-Crawford effect: Two models evaluated. Vision Res. 14:803–12
146. Savoie, R. E. 1973. Bezold-Brücke effect and visual nonlinearity. J. Opt. Soc. Am. 63:1253–61
147. Sekuler, R. 1974. Spatial vision. Ann. Rev. Psychol. 25:195–232
148. Shiveley, F. 1973. A new afterimage (color contrast afterimage?). Percept. Psychophys. 13:525–26
149. Siegel, M. H., Siegel, A. B. 1972. Hue discrimination as a function of stimulus luminance. Percept. Psychophys. 12:295–99

150. Sillman, A. J. 1974. Rapid dark-adaptation in the frog cone. *Vision Res.* 14:1021–27

151. Smith, D. P. 1973. Color naming and hue discrimination in congenital tritanopia and tritanomaly. *Vision Res.* 13:209–18

152. Smith, D. P., Cole, B. L., Isaacs, A. 1973. Congenital tritanopia without neuroretinal disease. *Invest. Ophthalmol.* 12:608–17

153. Smith, V. C., Pokorny, J. 1972. Spectral sensitivity of color-blind observers and the cone photopigments. *Vision Res.* 12:2059–71

154. Ibid 1973. Psychophysical estimates of optical density in human cones. 13:1199–1202

155. Smith, V. C., Pokorny, J. 1974. Autosomal dominant tritanopia. *Invest. Ophthalmol.* 13:706–7

156. Smith, V. C., Pokorny, J., Swartley, R. 1973. Continuous hue estimation of brief flashes by deuteranomalous observers. *Am. J. Psychol.* 86:115–31

157. Snyder, A. W., Hamer, M. 1972. The light-capture area of a photoreceptor. *Vision Res.* 12:1749–53

158. Snyder, A. W., Miller, W. H. 1972. Fly colour vision. *Vision Res.* 12:1389–96

159. Snyder, A. W., Pask, C. 1973. The Stiles-Crawford effect—Explanation and consequences. *Vision Res.* 13:1115–37

160. Spekreijse, H., Wagner, H. G., Wolbarsht, M. L. 1972. Spectral and spatial coding of ganglion cell responses in goldfish retina. *J. Neurophysiol.* 35:73–86

161. Spillmann, L., Conlon, J. E. 1972. Photochromatic interval during dark adaptation and as a function of background luminance. *J. Opt. Soc. Am.* 62:182–85

162. Stabell, U., Stabell, B. 1973. Chromatic rod activity at mesopic intensities. *Vision Res.* 13:2255–60

163. Ibid 1974. Chromatic rod-cone interaction. 14:1389–92

164. Steinberg, R. H., Reid, M., Lacy, P. L. 1973. The distribution of rods and cones in the retina of the cat (*Felis domesticus*). *J. Comp. Neurol.* 148:229–48

165. Sternheim, C. E., Glass, R. A., Keller, J. V. 1972. Visual sensitivity in the region of chromatic borders. *Vision Res.* 12:1715–24

166. Stiles, W. S., Wyszecki, G. 1974. Colour-matching data and the spectral absorption curves of visual pigments. *Vision Res.* 14:195–207

167. Stromeyer, C. E. III 1974. Form-specific colour after effects. *Nature* 250:266–68

168. Sundet, J. M. 1972. The effect of pupil size variations on the colour stereoscopic phenomenon. *Vision Res.* 12:1027–32

169. Uttal, W. R. 1973. Chromatic and intensive effects in dot-pattern masking: Evidence for different time constants in color vision. *J. Opt. Soc. Am.* 63:1490–94

170. Verriest, G., Ed. 1972. *Acquired Colour Vision Deficiencies.* Basel: Karger. 230 pp.

171. Verriest, G., Ed. 1973. *Colour Vision Deficiencies II.* Basel: Karger. 380 pp.

172. Vos, J. J., Friele, L. F. C., Walraven, P. L., Eds. *Color Metrics.* Soesterberg: Institute for Perception, TNO. 389 pp.

173. Vos, J. J., Walraven, P. L. 1971. On the derivation of the foveal receptor primaries. *Vision Res.* 11:799–818

174. Wagner, G., Boynton, R. M. 1972. Comparison of four methods of heterochromatic photometry. *J. Opt. Soc. Am.* 62:1508–15

175. Walraven, J. 1973. Spatial characteristics of chromatic induction: The segregation of lateral effects from straylight artefacts. *Vision Res.* 13:1739–53

176. Walraven, P. L. 1972. Color vision. *Ann. Rev. Psychol.* 23:347–74

177. Walraven, P. L. 1974. A closer look at the tritanopic convergence point. *Vision Res.* 14:1339–43

178. Ward, F., Boynton, R. M. 1974. Scaling of large chromatic differences. *Vision Res.* 14:943–50

179. Ward, F., Tansley, B. W. 1974. Increment thresholds across minimally distinct borders. *J. Opt. Soc. Am.* 64:760–62

180. Weale, R. A. 1972. Cone pigment regeneration, retinitis pigmentosa and light deprivation. *Vision Res.* 12:747–49

181. Ibid 1973. Spectral sensitivity and visual pigment absorbance. 13:1797–98

182. Weingarten, F. S. 1972. Wavelength effect on visual latency. *Science* 176:692–94

183. Whittle, P. 1973. The brightness of coloured flashes on backgrounds of various colours and luminances. *Vision Res.* 13:621–38

184. Whitten, D. N., Brown, K. T. 1973. The time courses of late receptor potentials from monkey cones and rods. *Vision Res.* 13:107–35

185. Ibid. Photopic suppression of monkey's rod receptor potential, apparently

by a cone-initiated lateral inhibition, 1629–58

186. Wijngaard, W., Bouman, M. A., Budding, F. 1974. The Stiles-Crawford colour change. *Vision Res.* 14:951–58

187. Wooten, B. R. 1972. Photopic and scotopic contributions to the human visually evoked cortical potential. *Vision Res.* 12:1647–60

188. Wooten, B. R., Fuid, K., Spillmann, L. 1974. Photopic spectral sensitivity of the peripheral retina. *J. Opt. Soc. Am.* 65:334–42

189. Wooten, B. R., Makous, W. 1973. Test of Brindley's after-image hypothesis. *J. Opt. Soc. Am.* 63:1268–69

190. Wooten, B. R., Wald, G. 1973. Color-vision mechanisms in the peripheral retinas of normal and dichromatic observers. *J. Gen. Physiol.* 61:125–45

191. Wright, A. A. 1972. Psychometric and psychophysical hue discrimination functions for the pigeon. *Vision Res.* 12:1447–64

192. Yager, D. 1974. Effects of chromatic adaptation on saturation discrimination in goldfish. *Vision Res.* 14:1089–94

193. Yates, T. 1974. Chromatic information processing in the foveal projection (*area striata*) of unanesthetized primate. *Vision Res.* 14:163–73

194. Zanen, A., Debecker, J. 1975. Wavelength sensitivity of the two components of the early receptor potential (ERP) of the human eye. *Vision Res.* 15:107–12

195. Zeki, S. M. 1973. Colour coding in rhesus monkey prestriate cortex. *Brain Res.* 53:422–27

BIOCHEMISTRY AND BEHAVIOR: SOME CENTRAL ACTIONS OF AMPHETAMINE AND ANTIPSYCHOTIC DRUGS[1]

❖249

Philip M. Groves and George V. Rebec[2]
Department of Psychology, University of Colorado, Boulder, Colorado 80302

INTRODUCTION

This review is intended to provide the reader with an overview of current research on the biochemical, neurophysiological, and behavioral correlates of amphetamine administration. Within the past decade or so, research and theoretical speculation regarding the mechanisms of action of amphetamine and related drugs have proliferated enormously. This review is not exhaustive, although the authors have attempted to present a relatively broad coverage of the different levels of analysis of amphetamine actions. We have chosen to emphasize two prominent behavioral effects of amphetamine on spontaneous behavior, i.e. increased locomotor behavior and stereotyped behavior, and the biochemical and neurophysiological studies that relate primarily to these behavioral effects. One of the most interesting aspects of this emphasis will be the provocative effects of long-term amphetamine administration, which in experimental animals leads to a progressive augmentation of these behavioral effects, and which in humans produces the condition termed "amphetamine psychosis." Clinically the symptoms associated with this syndrome are difficult to distinguish from those characteristic of paranoid schizophrenia, and without a prior knowledge of the history of drug abuse, amphetamine psychosis has often been misdiagnosed as an idiopathic schizophrenic disorder. A large number of books and reviews on amphetamine and related drugs has been published within the past 5 years, many of which are cited in this review for the interested reader. However, this topic has not been treated previously in the *Annual Review of Psychology*. The literature search for this manuscript ended in March 1975.

[1]Preparation of this review was supported in part by grant MH 19515 and Research Scientist Development Award K02 MH 70706 from the National Institute of Mental Health to P.M.G.
[2]Current address: Department of Psychiatry, University of California at San Diego, La Jolla, California 92037.

NEUROTRANSMITTERS RELEASED BY AMPHETAMINE

One of the most prominent effects of amphetamine is to promote the release of catecholamines from peripheral and central catecholaminergic nerve terminals. Catecholamines released into the synaptic cleft can be inactivated metabolically by catechol-O-methyl transferase, which converts extracellular dopamine (DA) to 3-methoxytyramine and converts norepinephrine (NE) to normetanephrine (see reviews 26, 27). Another method of inactivation is by a saturable, energy-dependent reuptake process which returns the catecholamines into the presynaptic ending (see reviews 180, 189, 190, 221, 325). A central catecholamine releasing action of amphetamine was first suggested by the observation that administration of this compound to rats increased brain concentrations of 3-methoxytyramine and normetanephrine (15, 59, 157, 331), while reducing intraneuronal levels of DA and NE (66, 233, 234, 318). These alterations in catecholamine levels and metabolites may occur independently of reuptake blockade since benztropine and desipramine, potent inhibitors of the membrane pump in DA and NE neurons respectively (97, 138, 156), do not significantly increase the accumulation of O-methylated metabolites nor do they substantially alter intraneuronal catecholamine levels (300). Further, the release of catecholamines appears to be prepotent with respect to reuptake blockade since at doses too low to prevent the intraneuronal accumulation of intraventricularly administered amines in reserpine pretreated animals, d-amphetamine is still capable of depleting the extragranular stores of these exogenous catecholamines (141, 142).

Amphetamine-induced release of catecholamines has also been demonstrated by perfusion of brain areas believed to be rich in dopaminergic or noradrenergic nerve terminals. This drug enhanced the spontaneous release of tritiated DA endogenously synthesized from labeled tyrosine in the caudate nucleus in a series of in vitro (37, 40, 153) and in vivo (38, 39, 72) studies. Both the caudate nucleus and the putamen (collectively termed the neostriatum) are densely innervated by dopaminergic nerve terminals (10, 136, 137, 139) whose fibers originate from cell bodies in the ipsilateral substantia nigra pars compacta and its posteroventral extension in the brain stem [catecholaminergic nuclear groups A9 and A8, respectively, of Dahlström & Fuxe (105)]. Unilateral destruction of the nigro-neostriatal projection causes extensive terminal degeneration throughout the ipsilateral neostriatum (10, 183, 184, 261) accompanied by a marked reduction of DA (167, 272, 276, 333, 351, 352) and the enzymes necessary for its synthesis (254, 255, 261, 342). Stimulation of this ascending dopaminergic pathway potentiates amphetamine-induced DA release, while acute or chronic lesions of the nigro-neostriatal projection or the administration of α-methyl-para-tyrosine, which selectively inhibits catecholamine synthesis at the rate-limiting tyrosine hydroxylase step (90, 112, 122, 228, 327, 350), disrupts the release of DA by amphetamine (39, 70, 361). In conjunction with experiments demonstrating an amphetamine-induced release of NE from central noradrenergic nerve terminals in the cerebral cortex, hypothalamus, and amygdala (68, 71, 273, 379) and from peripheral adrenergic terminals (5, 26, 271, 287), these results imply that the release of catecholamines following amphetamine administration occurs at the expense of a functional or readily releasable catecholamine pool which is normally maintained by de novo biosynthesis (154, 155) and that this release process is, at least in part, dependent on nerve impulse flow (85, 361).

Interestingly, amphetamine is also capable of promoting the in vivo release of extragranular stores of serotonin from the serotonergic nerve terminals of the corpus striatum (141) and reducing the fluorescence intensity among the serotonergic cell bodies of the dorsal raphe nucleus (147), although only relatively large doses were able to produce these effects. Further, amphetamine increases brain levels of 5-hydroxyindole acetic acid, the major metabolite of this monoamine (301). High doses of amphetamine have also been shown to enhance the release of acetylcholine from the cerebral cortex in vivo, but in this case an influence of the drug on subcortical structures may be likely (109, 179).

The amphetamine-induced release of exogenous labeled monoamines has also been demonstrated in vitro from brain slices of corpus striatum, cerebral cortex, and medulla oblongata (28, 376). Although in vitro demonstrations of release may also reflect an uptake blockade effect of the drug (280), Rutledge, Azzaro & Ziance (298) reported a releasing action of amphetamine even in the presence of potent catecholamine uptake blockers, suggesting that the appearance of catecholamines in the incubation medium is not necessarily due to inhibition of neuronal uptake (376). The noradrenergic terminals of the cerebral cortex proved to be the most sensitive and serotonergic terminals least vulnerable to the releasing action of amphetamine (28).

AMPHETAMINE EFFECTS ON NEUROTRANSMITTER INACTIVATION

At higher doses than those required to demonstrate an in vivo catecholamine release, amphetamine gains the ability to block the uptake of exogenous catecholamines across the neuronal membrane (142, 158). In vitro studies dealing largely with striatal and cortical brain homogenates have confirmed the uptake blocking properties of amphetamine on dopaminergic and noradrenergic nerve terminals. Apparently, the *anti* conformation of the amphetamine molecule (with the isopropylamine side chain fully extended and the amino group above the plane of the phenyl ring) is most effective in blocking catecholamine uptake into brain synaptosomes (186), although the α-methyl group of this drug may also contribute to the uptake blocking effect (43, 55). Considerable controversy remains, however, regarding the relative potencies of the optical isomers of amphetamine in preventing catecholamine uptake. Several investigators (98, 191, 325) found that the uptake of catecholamines into dopaminergic nerve terminals was not stereospecific, and this was presumed to be a reflection of the fact that DA itself has no stereoisomers. Naturally occurring l-NE, on the other hand, had a greater affinity for the uptake system in noradrenergic nerve terminals than its *d*-enantiomer. Coyle & Snyder (98), relying on these observations, reported that *d*-amphetamine was ten times more effective than *l*-amphetamine in blocking catecholamine uptake in cortical synaptosomes, which they presumed to contain mostly noradrenergic terminals, but *d*-amphetamine was not significantly different from the *l*-isomer in blocking DA uptake in striatal homogenates. Other investigators, however, have proposed that the relative affinities of *d*- and *l*-amphetamine for the dopaminergic and noradrenergic uptake systems are unrelated to the steric nature of the catecholamines. Ferris, Tang & Maxwell (128) reported that the optical isomers of amphetamine were nearly equipotent in blocking uptake of catecholamines into crude synaptosomal preparations of rat cerebral cortex and hypothalamus, but in neostriatal tissue *d*-amphetamine was more effective in blocking catecholamine uptake than *l*-amphetamine. Harris & Baldessarini (176) similarly reported that *d*-amphetamine was approximately four times more potent than the *l*-enantiomer in inhibiting uptake of DA into synaptosomal preparations of rat corpus striatum, while they observed a less than twofold difference for inhibition of NE uptake into cortical homogenates. Finally, Thornburg & Moore (344) reported that the optical isomers of amphetamine were equipotent in inhibiting uptake of NE into telencephalic synaptosomes, whereas *d*-amphetamine was approximately five times as potent as *l*-amphetamine in blocking uptake of DA into striatal synaptosomes. These differences in potency obtained from different laboratories may be related to the experimental techniques used in each case (see, for example, 31, 323).

At concentrations of the drug still higher than those required to enhance release or block the uptake of catecholamines, amphetamine may also inhibit monoamine oxidase activity (158, 189, 376), the enzyme responsible for the oxidative deamination of unbound axoplasmic catecholamines (see reviews 75, 213, 264). Although amphetamine administration reduces brain levels of the deaminated metabolites of DA and NE (157, 158, 376), this effect may be secondary to its ability to prevent the reuptake of catecholamines (297) since amines recently taken up by the nerve ending are vulnerable to deamination (104).

AMPHETAMINE EFFECTS ON THE REGULATION OF MONOAMINE BIOSYNTHESIS

Because of its ability to potentiate catecholaminergic transmission, amphetamine may set in motion compensatory feedback processes that are presumably activated to overcome such an imbalance. Support for the notion that catecholaminergic neurons may be subject to some regulation has been derived from biochemical and neurophysiological evidence obtained from the nigro-neostriatal dopaminergic system demonstrating that a pharmacological blockade of central DA receptors enhances DA synthesis and neuronal activity of DA neurons, while drugs that stimulate these receptors reduce amine metabolism and dopaminergic nerve impulse flow (see reviews 1, 61, 63, 89, 366).

The antipsychotic phenothiazines and butyrophenones, which allegedly block DA receptors and, in some cases, NE receptors as well (4), generate an increased accumulation of catecholamine metabolites (12, 65, 106), accelerate the disappearance of catecholamines following AMPT pretreatment (8, 11, 85), and enhance the formation of catecholamines from their amino acid precursor tyrosine (143, 146, 197, 268, 270). Centrally acting catecholamine agonists such as apomorphine, a presumed DA receptor stimulant (123, 124), on the other hand, reduce these biochemical indices of catecholaminergic activity (6). Consistent with its role as DA agonist, amphetamine, like apomorphine, inhibits striatal tyrosine hydroxylase activity and this drug effect has been demonstrated both in vivo (41, 177, 197) and in vitro (41, 154). Although other workers demonstrated an increased turnover of striatal DA following amphetamine administration (87, 88), this result may be a reflection of the assumption that catecholamines contained in the nerve terminal are distributed in a single homogeneous pool (see 153, 358).

The work of Aghajanian, Bunney, their associates, and others has revealed a number of significant effects of dopaminergic agonists and antagonists on the activity of dopaminergic neurons in the substantia nigra, and these often parallel the effects of such drugs on firing rates of postsynaptic neurons in the caudate-putamen. Antipsychotic drugs that block dopaminergic receptors cause changes in neuronal activity that parallel their effects on DA turnover. Haloperidol increases the firing rate of neurons in the caudate nucleus (168); this is presumed to occur secondary to the release of striatal neurons from dopaminergic inhibition, since considerable evidence indicates that DA acts as an inhibitory transmitter in this region of the brain (see review 218). Both haloperidol and chlorpromazine also increase neuronal activity among the dopaminergic neurons of the substantia nigra pars compacta (54). Apomorphine and amphetamine, on the other hand, decrease firing rate in both these areas (53, 288, 289, 316, 356), and the depression of neuronal activity can be blocked by DA antagonists (51, 54, 168). In order to account for these changes in DA metabolism and impulse flow, pre- and postsynaptic compensatory feedback mechanisms have been proposed, the common purpose of which has been to reconcile the degree of catecholamine receptor stimulation with the extent of transmitter biosynthesis and release in catecholaminergic neurons (see reviews 1, 2, 296).

One negative feedback mechanism that has been proposed for the regulation of dopaminergic neuronal activity is a postsynaptic neuronal feedback loop presumed to project from the basal ganglia back to dopaminergic neurons in the substantia nigra (1, 65). Evidence in support of this concept shows that the amphetamine-induced depression of neuronal activity in the substantia nigra pars compacta is blocked by dopaminergic receptor blocking agents (see above) and is abolished by α-methyl-para-tyrosine pretreatment (53), illustrating that the depression of neuronal activity results from an indirect mechanism of action, presumably due to the release of dopamine from nigro-neostriatal terminals (see also 167); further evidence is that the depression of dopaminergic neuron activity by amphetamine is abolished following a diencephalic transection anterior to the substantia nigra which is presumed to sever the feedback pathway (1, 52). There is convincing anatomical evidence for a striato-nigral projection (e.g. 255) although the other elements presumed to be in the striato-nigral neuronal feedback loop have yet to be demonstrated. Additional evidence in support of the concept of a postsynaptic neuronal feedback loop that may regulate catecholaminergic transmission has come from the observation that chlorpromazine, an antipsychotic phenothiazine, no longer increases catecholamine turnover after lesions that disrupt the nigro-neostriatal projection (8, 269).

The reduction in striatal DA synthesis associated with amphetamine administration may reflect this drug's effect on nerve impulse flow in the nigro-neostriatal projection (177) since catecholamine biosynthesis appears to be directly related to neuronal activity (for reviews see 5, 26, 27, 62, 368, 369). It has already been reported that haloperidol produces an allosteric activation of striatal tyrosine hydroxylase, presumably because this drug increases the firing rate of dopaminergic neurons (383). Electrical stimulation of central noradrenergic pathways elicits a similar activation of this enzyme in noradrenergic nerve terminals (295).

The amphetamine-induced decrease in DA synthesis has also been attributed to an intraneuronal end-product feedback inhibition occurring at the tyrosine hydroxylase step (41). Tyrosine hydroxylase, the first enzyme involved in the conversion of tyrosine to catecholamines (for reviews see 264, 350), is subject to a competitive inhibition by DA and NE which compete with the pteridine cofactor for access to the enzyme (for reviews see 89, 239). Thus drugs which increase the normally low levels of intraneuronal catecholamines reduce tyrosine hydroxylase activity (90, 154, 196, 326, 368). Presumably amphetamine, by releasing DA from storage sites in the nerve terminal, increases cytoplasmic DA levels which are capable of initiating an inhibition of tyrosine hydroxylase activity (154). In support of this notion, Weiner et al (369) reported that the amphetamine-induced reduction of tyrosine hydroxylase activity in the intact mouse vas deferens preparation was partially overcome by adding reduced pteridine cofactor to the incubation medium.

Recent evidence, however, suggests a different feedback mechanism by which the regulation of DA biosynthesis could occur independently of the hypothetical postsynaptic neuronal feedback loop or by an intraneuronal biochemical process based on end-product inhibition (63). Following an acute blockade of impulse flow in the nigro-neostriatal projection, which may be achieved by surgical transection or by the administration of γ-butyrolactone, both intraneuronal DA levels and striatal tyrosine hydroxylase activity show a transient but significant increase (64, 207, 208, 306, 366, 367). Such an effect cannot be explained by end-product inhibition since DA biosynthesis increases even as the end-product continues to accumulate in the nerve terminal. The brief increase in tyrosine hydroxylase activity is reversed by administration of apomorphine or amphetamine (63, 64, 209, 367). Roth, Walters & Morgenroth (296) proposed that presynaptic DA receptors, when deprived of a suitable agonist in the synaptic cleft, cause an allosteric activation of the rate-limiting enzyme such that tyrosine hydroxylase increases its affinity for substrate and cofactor but reduces its affinity for the end-product inhibitor DA. According to this model, presynaptic receptors modulate calcium fluxes in the nerve terminal, which in turn regulate tyrosine hydroxylase activity. A disruption of impulse flow prevents the influx of calcium usually associated with depolarization (for review see 274), but apomorphine, by directly stimulating DA presynaptic receptors, or amphetamine, by releasing DA from the nerve terminal which may then act on presynaptic receptors, restores calcium fluxes in the nerve terminal and thereby reverses the enhanced tyrosine hydroxylase activity. Indeed, an inactivation of calcium fluxes in striatal slices produces the same allosteric activation of tyrosine hydroxylase as an acute blockade of impulse flow (296). The administration of haloperidol or other

DA receptor blockers can reverse the effects of DA agonists on DA synthesis following a transection of the nigro-neostriatal projection, further suggesting the importance of presynaptic DA receptors in altering tyrosine hydroxylase activity (73, 208, 209). Presynaptic receptors, by monitoring transmitter concentrations in the synaptic cleft, may also regulate transmitter release (see review 226).

Interestingly, the conversion of tyrosine to DA is not reduced in the substantia nigra (an area rich in DA cell bodies) following amphetamine administration (197). Different physical forms of tyrosine hydroxylase in the corpus striatum and substantia nigra, associated with different kinetic properties, have been demonstrated (220, 310). Methamphetamine administration induces a shift in striatal, but not midbrain, tyrosine hydroxylase from the soluble to the membrane-bound form (247).

Amphetamine produces different effects on the regulation of NE synthesis. The conversion of tyrosine to NE is enhanced following amphetamine administration according to both in vivo (154, 198) and in vitro (40, 153) results. However, the amphetamine-induced increase in NE turnover was observed only in the brain stem and not in the telencephalon-diencephalon. The significance of these regional differences in enzyme activity following amphetamine administration remains to be elucidated, although it has already been shown that noradrenergic nerve terminals in different regions are differentially sensitive to the release (28) and eventual depletion of brain NE (66) produced by amphetamine. Further, different forms of tyrosine hydroxylase may be differentially distributed in the brain (201). Interestingly, amphetamine administration causes a decrease in neuronal activity among the noradrenergic neurons of the locus coeruleus, and this has also been attributed to an amphetamine-induced activation of a compensatory feedback mechanism (163) which may exist among noradrenergic neurons (6, 85), although it has not been as well characterized as that associated with the dopaminergic nigro-neostriatal projection. Recently Stolk (330) reported that amphetamine may directly retard dopamine-β-hydroxylase activity, the enzyme responsible for the conversion of DA to NE in noradrenergic neurons (for reviews see 25, 205, 206, 264). Adrenal tyrosine hydroxylase activity appears to be accelerated by methamphetamine in rats (50) and by amphetamine administration to chickens (248).

Serotonin synthesis also shows regional differences in its susceptibility to amphetamine administration. Tryptophan hydroxylase activity, the first enzyme involved in the biosynthesis of serotonin from tryptophan, is inhibited by amphetamine in the lateral but not in the medial midbrain area (212). Further, some neurons in the raphe system have been shown to increase their firing rate following systemic administration of the drug (133).

AMPHETAMINE-INDUCED LOCOMOTOR AND STEREOTYPED BEHAVIOR

Amphetamine produces a variety of behavioral effects in humans and experimental animals which include marked sympathomimetic signs, hyperthermia, anorexia, and alterations in mood and motor behavior (see previous reviews 76, 329). In this section, attention is directed specifically to the prominent motor disturbances produced by amphetamine administration which recent evidence suggests are at least in part due to the effects of amphetamine on the ascending dopaminergic projections to the neostriatum.

In the rat, amphetamine produces an increase in locomotor activity and an induction of stereotyped behaviors which have been characterized as stereotyped licking, gnawing, biting, and sniffing (e.g. 117, 283, 284; see recent reviews 282, 285, 363). Such stereotyped behavior may include a variety of other abnormal postural positions, stereotyped rearing, and dyskinetic movements such as backward and/or jerky locomotion (e.g. 117). These prominent behavioral effects of amphetamine probably occur in all mammalian species as well as some avian groups, although the characteristics of the stereotypies may vary for different species (284, 363). Whereas in rats and mice a sniffing, licking, and/or biting response predominates following amphetamine administration (282–286), cats display some sniffing but may also display repetitive head turning and "searching behaviors" (364). In primates, eye-hand examination patterns develop along with a scanning of the visual field (144, 284), and in humans, perceptuo-motor compulsions may appear that have been characterized as meaningless investigative behaviors (e.g. 282).

The occurrence of locomotor activity and stereotyped behaviors following amphetamine administration is dose-dependent and sequentially patterned. At low doses amphetamine produces an increase in locomotion without pronounced stereotypies. At higher doses, both locomotor behavior and stereotyped behaviors may be produced (282–284). In those instances where multiple and quantitative measures of behavior have been used, the pattern of behavioral effects consists of an initial increase in locomotion and rearing, followed by an extended bout of stereotyped behaviors in the absence of normal, forward locomotion, followed by a second variable increase in locomotion and rearing behavior, and finally lethargy, depression, and/or sleep (117, 267, 304, 308). In view of the sequential and complex nature of the behavioral changes resulting from amphetamine intoxication [an increasingly obvious feature of long-term amphetamine administration (see below)], the importance of multiple and quantitative measures of behavior and standardization of rating scales used to assess these behavioral effects have been emphasized by several investigators (e.g. 117, 219). In some instances, amphetamine may produce a paradoxical drowsiness in humans or a decrease in exploratory behavior in experimental animals (e.g. 30, 340). In such cases, individuals may be predisposed to these paradoxical effects. Evidence for such predispositions has been deduced from experiments which demonstrate that the effects of amphetamine on spontaneous motor activity may be inversely related to the baseline rate of activity prior to drug administration (152), and the fact that amphetamine is effective to some degree in treating hyperkinesis (e.g. 22, 224, 227).

THE ROLE OF CENTRAL NEUROTRANSMITTERS IN THE BEHAVIORAL EFFECTS OF AMPHETAMINE

There is now substantial evidence suggesting that the behavioral effects of amphetamine are related in part to this drug's effects on monoaminergic neurons in the central nervous system. Pretreatment of mice, rats, and cats with α-methyl-para-tyrosine, which blocks catecholamine synthesis in central catecholaminergic neurons (see above), blocks the increased locomotor activity and stereotyped behavior produced by amphetamine (e.g. 32, 59, 111, 132, 185, 283, 294, 309, 332, 336, 345, 365, 374). This effect of blocking amphetamine-induced locomotion and stereotyped behavior may be overcome by administering L-dopa [which in rats and mice, if given peripherally, is usually accompanied by a peripheral decarboxylase inhibitor to overcome the decarboxylating enzymatic barrier in brain capillaries (e.g. 79, 225)], which bypasses tyrosine hydroxylation and allows the formation of DA and NE by dopa-decarboxylase and dopamine-β-hydroxylase respectively (e.g. 26). Furthermore, treatments that inhibit the degradation of catecholamines, such as monoamine oxidase inhibitors, enhance the behavioral effects of amphetamine (e.g. 282, 291, 299, 375, 379).

The fact that amphetamine-induced behaviors may persist after reserpine pretreatment has been interpreted by some investigators (e.g. 279, 318, 359) as an indication that amphetamine acts directly on catecholaminergic receptors. However, the effects of inhibiting biosynthesis of catecholamines suggest that the effects of amphetamine do not depend upon the absolute amount of catecholamines stored in the nerve terminal, but rather on a small readily releasable pool of catecholamines that is supplied by de novo synthesis (see above). Although reserpine reduces central catecholamine levels by interfering with the vesicular storage process (60, 62, 174, 240, 277, 370), catecholamine synthesis may continue, and amphetamine is capable of releasing catecholamines in reserpine pretreated animals (15, 236a, 281). Furthermore, during the period of maximal depletion of catecholamines by reserpine (3 to 6 hours after administration), amphetamine-induced behavioral effects are reduced (32, 33, 291); they begin to intensify when the drug is administered 8 to 12 hours after reserpine when the vesicular uptake mechanism begins to regain its functional integrity even though normal catecholamine levels may not be restored for days (240). The heightened behavioral response to amphetamine that develops in rats several hours after reserpine has been interpreted as a sign of developing supersensitivity of central catecholamine receptors (33, 290), although such a phenomenon has not been seen in cats (365). Fibiger, Trimbach & Campbell (130) proposed that the enhanced psychomotor stimulant effects of amphetamine observed in rats pretreated with reserpine is due to the weight loss associated with reserpinization, and Campbell & Fibiger (57) had reported that weight loss alone may increase the behavioral effects of amphetamine administration.

Pretreatment with compounds that act principally to inhibit NE biosynthesis has considerably less effect on amphetamine-induced locomotion and stereotyped behavior, although the evidence here is somewhat less consistent. In an early experiment, Randrup & Scheel-Krüger (286, 303), for example, found that diethyldithiocarbamate, which acts at least in part to inhibit dopamine-β-hydroxylase thus producing a fall in brain NE content, did not inhibit amphetamine-induced stereotyped behavior but did block the increase in locomotor activity, and they argued that the effects of amphetamine on dopaminergic systems may be more important for stereotyped behavior while its effects on adrenergic transmission may be more important for the increased locomotor behavior produced by amphetamine.

The notion that dopamine might be relatively more important for stereotyped behavior produced by amphetamine administration, while norepinephrine might bear the same more or less specific relationship to locomotor activity, was supported in a provocative series of papers by Coyle & Snyder (98) and Taylor & Snyder (337, 338). In their experiments, the optical isomers of amphetamine were compared, both with respect to their effects on stereotyped behavior and locomotion in rats, and with respect to their abilities to block reuptake of DA and NE into catecholaminergic nerve terminals. These investigators observed that in rats d-amphetamine was 10 times as potent as l-amphetamine in blocking reuptake of NE, while it was only 2 times as potent in blocking reuptake of DA into catecholamine nerve terminals (see above). Similarly, d-amphetamine was 10 times as potent as l-amphetamine in enhancing locomotor behavior, but only 2 times as potent in producing stereotyped behavior. In a subsequent paper, North, Harik & Snyder (266) supported these findings in cats. Despite the attractive correspondence of these ratios of potency, the differences between d-amphetamine and l-amphetamine on these variables may not be as dramatic as suggested by these data. We have noted previously that there is now a variety of less dramatic estimates of the differences in potency of the optical isomers of amphetamine in their ability to block the uptake of catecholamines into central nerve terminals. In comparing the behavioral and biochemical effects of these isomers, Scheel-Krüger (300) reported that d-amphetamine was approximately 10 times as potent as l-amphetamine in enhancing locomotor activity, although the isomers did not differ in their effects on NE metabolism, while d-amphetamine was 4–6 times as potent as the l-isomer in producing stereotyped behavior and was more potent on DA metabolism as well. Despite the conflicting evidence regarding the exact ratios of potency of the optical isomers of amphetamine on catecholaminergic transmission on the one hand and the behavioral effects of these isomers on the other, the evidence does point to a marked difference in potency, with l-amphetamine being considerably less potent than d-amphetamine with respect to their behavioral effects. Exact comparisons between processes such as blockade of uptake or release of catecholamines and the behavioral effects of amphetamine are complicated because of the lack of standardized, linearly related units of measure for such diverse dependent variables.

There is now substantial evidence to suggest that DA may be significantly related to both stereotypy and locomotor behavior produced by amphetamine, while the effects of amphetamine on noradrenergic transmission may influence locomotor behavior but not without some participation of dopaminergic systems. Thus in mice and rats pretreated with reserpine, or in nonpretreated animals, amphetamine-induced locomotor activity is effectively blocked by α-methyl-para-tyrosine but is only partially or not at all affected by the presumed dopamine-β-hydroxylase inhibitors FLA 63 or U-14, 624 (59, 86, 185, 336, 345), the latter being accompanied by a decline in endogenous brain NE content (e.g. 84, 335, 345). An analog of amphetamine, para-methoxyamphetamine, which is capable of releasing NE from cortical slices as effectively as d-amphetamine but has no measurable effect on brain DA (348), at high doses elicits hyperactivity but not stereotyped behavior in rats. However, at low doses para-methoxyamphetamine does not produce a marked increase in locomotor behavior but does so when combined with apomorphine (349), a presumed dopamine receptor stimulant (123, 124, 343). Maj et al (246) reported that clonidine, which acts principally to stimulate central noradrenergic receptors (7, 172), decreased locomotor activity in mice despite marked sympathomimetic signs, but it enhanced motor activity when combined with apomorphine in normal mice or in mice pretreated with reserpine, α-methyl-para-tyrosine, or FLA 63. Maj et al concluded that both central dopaminergic and noradrenergic mechanisms were involved in spontaneous locomotor activity in mice.

In general, the effects of presumed catecholamine receptor blocking agents support the conclusion that dopaminergic activity is significantly involved in the stereotyped behavior produced by amphetamine, while both DA and NE influence amphetamine-induced locomotion. Thus DA receptor blocking agents believed to have little effect on noradrenergic systems, such as haloperidol, spiroperidol, and pimozide (4), abolish the stereotyped and locomotor responses to amphetamine (293, 294), while noradrenergic blocking agents only partially antagonize locomotor behavior in response to amphetamine (32, 126, 294) with little effect on amphetamine-induced stereotyped behavior (302, 373; see review 363).

The role of catecholamines in the behavioral arousal and stereotyped behavior produced by amphetamine has also been emphasized by studies of the effects of amphetamine on neuronal firing rates in the reticular formation of the brain stem. Thus iontophoretically applied d-amphetamine mimics the excitatory and inhibitory effects of iontophoretic norepinephrine on brain stem neurons (44, 45). Further, Segal & Mandell (307) demonstrated that intraventricular infusion of norepinephrine produces increased locomotor activity and apparent behavioral arousal. Similar effects occur following intraventricular infusion of d-amphetamine (309). Similar but less marked effects were also obtained following intraventricular infusion of DA (148). Intraperitoneally administered d-amphetamine typically produces increased neuronal firing in reticular formation neurons and a marked depression of neuronal activity in the caudate-putamen (e.g. 167, 168, 288, 289, 364). At higher doses, this marked depression of neuronal firing is preceded by an initial brief potentiation of neuronal activity and may also be followed by a variable increase in neuronal activity, thus paralleling in a qualitative way the sequence of increased locomotor behavior and stereotyped behavior produced by such drug treatment.

We have emphasized the role of catecholamines in the mediation of the behavioral effects of amphetamine because of the relative emphasis placed on catecholamines in the research literature. Treatments that affect serotonergic systems, however, also affect the behavioral consequences of amphetamine administration. Green & Harvey (164), for example, reported an enhancement of amphetamine effects on variable interval operant responding in rats following large lesions of the medial forebrain bundle which resulted in a 60 to 80 percent decrease in telencephalic serotonin content. The administration of 5-hydroxytryptophan, the immediate amino acid precursor to serotonin, antagonized amphetamine-induced stereotypy, while methysergide, a presumed serotonin antagonist (but see 173), potentiated this amphetamine effect (159, 372). Similar effects have been reported for apomorphine-induced behavior (e.g. 159, 162, 371). Pretreatment of rats with para-chlorophenylalanine, which results in a substantial depletion of brain serotonin, enhanced the locomotor response to amphetamine and this effect was reversed by administration of 5-hydroxytryptophan (47, 244). However, PCPA did not affect this response to amphetamine in immature animals (243). Further, adult stereotyped behavior was unaffected by PCPA treatment (47).

The effects of amphetamine may also be altered by centrally acting cholinergic agonists and antagonists. Amphetamine-induced stereotyped behavior can be antagonized by such cholinergic agents as physostigmine, an anticholinesterase, while anticholinergic drugs such as the muscarinic receptor blocking agent scopolamine potentiate amphetamine-induced stereotypies (21, 282). DA agonists such as amphetamine produce an increase in striatal acetylcholine levels presumed to be secondary to the inhibitory effect of DA on the firing rates of cholinergic interneurons (77, 78, 222, 223, 256, 311–313) intrinsic to the corpus striatum (56, 241). Similarly, DA receptor blocking agents such as haloperidol and chlorpromazine reduce striatal acetylcholine levels and increase the release of acetylcholine as determined by superfusion of the ventricular surface of the caudate-putamen, effects presumed to be secondary to the increased firing of cholinergic interneurons released from dopaminergic inhibition (42, 170, 171, 256, 312, 313, 328). A dopamine-acetylcholine interaction in the corpus striatum has been postulated for many years on the basis of the clinical efficacy of anticholinergic drugs in the treatment of Parkinson's disease (113; see reviews 125, 237), which is associated in part with degeneration of the dopaminergic nigro-neostriatal projections (see below). Further, cholinergic agonists such as physostigmine exacerbate the condition of such patients (113).

DAMAGE TO THE NIGRO-NEOSTRIATAL SYSTEM PRIOR TO AMPHETAMINE ADMINISTRATION

Because of its relevance to a variety of extrapyramidal motor disorders, the effects of unilateral as well as bilateral destruction of the nigro-neostriatal system have been studied in some detail. Rats or mice with the nigro-neostriatal system on one side destroyed by electrolytic or 6-hydroxydopamine lesions, display an ipsilateral motor asymmetry and rotate vigorously toward the side with the lesion when given amphetamine. This ipsilateral turning syndrome is dose-related and is partially or totally abolished following inhibition of catecholamine synthesis or administration of dopaminergic blocking agents such as haloperidol or chlorpromazine (9, 13, 46, 74, 250, 262, 351, 353, 354, 362). This effect is interpreted by most authors to result from the release of DA from the nigro-neostriatal projections on the intact side which produces rotation toward the operated side. In an interesting extension of this work, Jerussi & Glick (199) found that amphetamine could produce rotation in normal rats, and Zimmerberg, Glick & Jerussi (382) reported that the side preference displayed by intact animals was correlated with a higher DA content in the contralateral striatum. A similar ipsilateral turning syndrome can be produced following unilateral lesions of the corpus striatum. In these experiments, amphetamine, apomorphine, or L-dopa administration produces turning toward the side of the lesion, and this effect is blocked by dopaminergic blocking agents (3, 169, 238).

While indirectly acting DA agonists such as amphetamine produced ipsilateral turning in animals with unilateral loss of striatal dopaminergic terminals, presumed direct DA agonists such as apomorphine, L-dopa, or ET 495 (piribedil) produce contralateral rotation, which has been interpreted to indicate an increased sensitivity of the denervated corpus striatum to DA receptor stimulants (e.g. 140, 343, 352, 362). Indeed, the ipsilateral versus contralateral rotation in animals with unilateral damage to the ascending dopaminergic projection from the substantia nigra has been proposed as a test for DA agonists which act indirectly or directly, respectively (e.g. 259). Interestingly, apomorphine may also cause unilateral rotation in normal rats; the direction preference may influence rotation subsequent to unilateral caudate lesions (200).

A wide variety of additional evidence bearing on the unilateral motor asymmetry produced by destruction of the substantia nigra or corpus striatum suggests that while dopaminergic activity is significant in producing such effects, a variety of other treatments, including different unilateral brain lesions as well as intrastriatal application of a wide variety of pharmacological agents, may also produce similar motor asymmetries. Unilateral removal of frontal cortex in rats, for example, results in ipsilateral rotation following amphetamine administration for a period of from 1–7 days following surgery, but contralateral turning 15–30 days after surgery (149). Lesions of the mesencephalic reticular formation unilaterally in rats produce a contralateral asymmetry which is potentiated by amphetamine injections (250). In the cat, Poirier, Langelier & Boucher (275) were unable to produce the asymmetry to amphetamine seen in rats following unilateral damage to the substantia nigra alone, but did see contralateral turning with L-dopa and apomorphine administration in animals with unilateral lesions of the ventral tegmental area including the posterior commissure.

High frequency electrical stimulation of the caudate nucleus or substantia nigra, as well as intrastriatal application of a variety of agents including DA, L-dopa, NE, apomorphine, and potassium chloride have been reported to produce contralateral motor asymmetries in several species (20, 80–83, 93, 355, 381), while intrastriatal applications of procaine and chlorpromazine have been reported to produce ipsilateral turning in rats and cats respectively (81, 82, 355). In many cases, the amounts of these substances injected directly into the caudate-putamen are extremely high and the mechanisms by which such asymmetries are produced are not well understood.

Bilateral damage to specific ascending monoaminergic projections has been associated with alterations in the behavioral effects of amphetamine in experimental animals as well as certain forms of pathology in humans. Parkinson's disease, for example, is associated in part with degeneration of the ascending nigro-neostriatal dopaminergic projection and a decrease in telencephalic catecholamine content (e.g. 36, 187). The current therapy of choice in the treatment of Parkinson's disease consists of a form of replacement therapy involving the administration of L-dopa (e.g. 36). The literature on Parkinson's disease is closely aligned to studies of amphetamine because of the involvement of the catecholamines and basal ganglia in both lines of investigation. Interestingly, amphetamine has been regarded as a valuable adjunctive therapy for some Parkinsonian patients (e.g. 257). In addition, L-dopa therapy can produce symptoms which are similar to those seen following long-term amphetamine abuse (e.g. 188, 251) (see below). In experimental animals L-dopa administration may produce stereotyped behavior similar to that seen following amphetamine administration (e.g. 187, 258, 365) as well as increased locomotor activity (e.g. 110, 175). Direct administration of L-dopa into the head of the caudate nucleus can also produce stereotyped behavior in rats (124). Along similar lines, L-dopa will reverse the akinesia produced by reserpine pretreatment (249), and we noted previously that L-dopa is effective in restoring the behavioral effects of amphetamine following inhibition of catecholamine synthesis.

Experiments on the effects of brain damage in experimental animals as they relate to the behavioral effects of amphetamine have emphasized the role of ascending dopaminergic projections, especially those from the pars compacta of the substantia nigra to the basal ganglia. There are, however, conflicting views in the literature which relate to the techniques that have been used to produce damage to this pathway. Thus bilateral destruction of the ascending nigro-neostriatal dopaminergic projection has been achieved by electrolytic lesions placed directly in the substantia nigra, or more commonly such lesions are placed at the level of the lateral hypothalamus just medial to the ventral portion of the internal capsule. At this point, the ascending dopaminergic fibers are assembled before passing into the basal ganglia. With lesions in the substantia nigra, Costall, Naylor & Olley (95) reported that bilateral lesions induced spontaneous stereotypy for 4–6 days postoperatively but only slightly reduced stereotypy induced by amphetamine after this initial period. Similarly, Simpson & Iversen (317) had observed spontaneous stereotyped behavior and some locomotion after bilateral electrolytic lesions of the substantia nigra, although amphetamine stereotypy was evident only for high doses of amphetamine. Iversen (192) had also noted the increased spontaneous stereotypy and motility after lesions of the substantia nigra and found that locomotion induced by amphetamine was potentiated in one group of damaged subjects but reduced in another. Costall & Naylor, in a subsequent paper (91), reported that following nigro-striatal bundle lesions the dose-dependent stereotypy produced by either d-amphetamine or l-amphetamine was unaffected. In contrast to these findings, Creese & Iversen (99–101), using intraventricular injections of 6-hydroxydopamine in neonatal rats, reported that in adulthood both locomotion and stereotyped behavior failed to occur in response to amphetamine but did occur in response to the direct dopamine receptor stimulants, apomorphine and ET495. Interestingly, they also noted that clonidine failed to stimulate locomotor activity, suggesting again that functional dopaminergic activity is necessary for adrenergic induction of locomotion. These same authors had reported previously that 6-hydroxydopamine lesions induced by direct injection into the substantia nigra in adult rats blocked amphetamine-induced stereotypy, although this was accompanied by increased locomotor activity (100). Low doses of 6-hydroxydopamine led to enhanced locomotor effects of amphetamine but higher doses did not. Evetts et al (127) reported a similar effect following intraventricular injections of 6-hydroxydopamine. That is, high doses of 6-hydroxydopamine had little effect on locomotion produced by amphetamine while low doses enhanced amphetamine-induced locomotor behavior. In a number of recent papers, 6-hydroxydopamine lesions of the ascending dopaminergic projections from the substantia nigra resulted in an abolition of amphetamine-induced stereotyped behavior but not apomorphine-induced stereotypy (23, 102, 193, 194, 278.) The findings that 6-hydroxydopamine lesions produced by injection into the terminal sites (caudate-putamen) or the origins (substantia nigra, pars compacta) of the ascending nigro-neostriatal dopaminergic projection will abolish amphetamine stereotypy in rats provides strong evidence that this pathway is important in amphetamine stereotypy. Further, the different routes used to produce damage suggest that the nonspecific toxic effects of 6-hydroxydopamine are probably not an essential correlate of these behavioral effects. The reports of a lack of effect following electrolytic lesions of the ascending nigrostriatal dopaminergic projections may be due to incomplete destruction of neostriatal dopaminergic innervation, as suggested by many investigators in this area. Price & Fibiger (278) have recently emphasized that in addition to careful histological analysis of brain damage, presumed depletions of neurotransmitters should be verified by biochemical or histoflourescence techniques. The degree of depletion in those studies utilizing 6-hydroxydopamine is usually verified by one of these methods (e.g. 23, 102, 278). Indeed, Asher & Aghajanian (23) did note that marked bilateral depletion of DA in the corpus striatum was essential to abolish amphetamine-induced stereotypy.

Consistent with the evidence that the ascending dopaminergic nigro-neostriatal system may be an important pathway for amphetamine-induced stereotypy, is evidence showing that destruction of the globus pallidus, which probably eliminates a substantial majority of efferents from the basal ganglia, also abolishes both amphetamine-induced stereotypy (265) and stereotyped behavior induced by methylphenidate (Ritalin) (92). Lesions of the globus pallidus may also lead to an increase in spontaneous locomotion (94) and an enhancement of amphetamine-induced locomotor activity (265).

While a number of early reports suggested that bilateral destruction of the caudate nucleus (265) or the caudate-putamen (131) reduced or abolished amphetamine-induced stereotypy in rats, Costall & Naylor reported that caudate-putamen lesions did not modify stereotypy induced by amphetamine or methylphenidate (91, 92). Along similar lines, Wolfarth (380) reported that destruction of the caudate-putamen bilaterally enhanced apomorphine-induced stereotypy. These conflicting results are as yet difficult to interpret. It is not difficult to imagine that even large lesions of the caudate-putamen bilaterally might leave some dopaminergic input intact and that this could be sufficient to produce stereotyped behavior in response to amphetamine administration. These speculations are consistent with the anatomy of the basal ganglia and the widespread distribution of nigro-neostriatal dopaminergic terminals in the caudate-putamen, and they could account for the apparently conflicting results of electrolytic versus 6-hydroxydopamine lesions of the nigro-neostriatal projection.

There is still some question regarding the role of mesolimbic dopaminergic projections in amphetamine-induced stereotyped behavior. Costall & Naylor, in a recent series of papers (e.g. 91), have reported that electrolytic lesions in areas of termination of mesolimbic dopaminergic projections, or in ascending fibers presumed to carry these projections, will modify some components of amphetamine stereotyped behavior, while Asher & Aghajanian (23) and Creese & Iversen (102) reported that following partial 6-hydroxydopamine lesions in the areas of termination of mesolimbic dopaminergic projections, amphetamine-induced stereotypy was unaffected.

An enhancement of the behavioral effects of amphetamine has been reported following lesions of the frontal cortex. Iversen (192) reported that bilateral aspiration of frontal cortex in rats produced an increase in spontaneous locomotor activity as well as a marked enhancement of the locomotor and stereotyped behavior induced by amphetamine. Glick & Marsanico (150, 151) similarly reported a shift to the left in the dose-response curve of amphetamine on locomotor behavior following frontal lesions (i.e. enhancement of the effects, especially at low doses of amphetamine). They observed a similar effect of hippocampal lesions, and relevant to the previous discussion of lesions of the caudate nuclei, bilateral but only partial removal of the caudate nuclei did affect locomotor activity in response to amphetamine 1 day after surgery, but the animals appeared normal after 1 month.

CORRELATES OF LONG-TERM AMPHETAMINE ADMINISTRATION

Long-term treatment with d-amphetamine results in a significant depletion of brain catecholamines even if the dose has no measurable effect on catechoamine levels following an acute injection (49, 229, 231, 235). NE levels are especially reduced among the nerve terminals in the reticular formation, hypothalamus, amygdala, olfactory bulb, and parts of the hippocampus, while telencephalic DA levels are also diminished (118, 119). Brain catecholamines are also reduced following the administration of high doses of l-amphetamine, but catecholamine levels may not remain depleted once l-amphetamine is eliminated from the tissue (49). It is unlikely that the loss of brain NE produced by d-amphetamine is due to the action of this drug alone since the persistence of NE depletion outlasts, by a considerable margin, the presence of d-amphetamine in the brain (87). This has suggested to some investigators (49, 87, 166, 235) that a unique metabolite of d-amphetamine, with a considerably longer half-life than the parent compound, may be responsible for the prolonged decrease of NE levels typically associated with chronic amphetamine treatment.

Consideration of the metabolic pathway of amphetamine reveals a long-lived metabolite that may play such a role. Amphetamine is first metabolized in the liver to form para-hydroxyamphetamine which may then be converted to para-hydroxynorephedrine by dopamine-β-hydroxylase (160, 166, 232, 234), an enzyme confined to adrenergic tissues, including the noradrenergic neurons of the central nervous system (292; see review 25). Only the d-isomer of the parent drug is capable of undergoing β-hydroxylation, whereas both isomers may be converted to para-hydroxyamphetamine. A systemic injection of either d-amphetamine or para-hydroxyamphetamine and an intraventricular injection of the latter compound but not the former results in an accumulation of para-hydroxynorephedrine in the brain, thus confirming this sequence of reactions (135). The half-life of para-hydroxynorephedrine in the brain is considerably longer than that of either amphetamine or its para-hydroxylated metabolite (87, 339), suggesting that this compound could be responsible, at least in part, for the sustained reduction of NE levels during chronic amphetamine intoxication (49). Indeed, there appears to be an approximate stoichiometric relationship between the persistence of NE depletion and the tissue concentration of para-hydroxynorephedrine (87, 234, 235). In addition, the intraventricular administration of the para-β-hydroxylated metabolite of amphetamine results in a significant reduction of brain NE levels (48, 339). The accumulation of para-hydroxynorephedrine in noradrenergic neurons has led to the suggestion that this amphetamine metabolite acts as a false transmitter (for reviews see 214, 215). Stimulation of the spleen following amphetamine administration results in release of para-hydroxynorephedrine, and both amphetamine and reserpine are capable of preferentially releasing this metabolite after its assimilation in noradrenergic neurons (48, 234, 341).

The formation of para-hydroxynorephedrine does not occur, however, in all species. In the rat, and to a lesser extent the dog, the amphetamine molecule is hydroxylated to a greater degree than in the guinea pig, rabbit, or man, although there are individual differences (320). In these latter species, amphetamine is primarily converted to benzoic acid by a sequence of deamination and oxidation reactions, after which it is excreted in the urine as hippuric acid (29, 320). Inhibitory substances in the liver appear to be responsible for preventing the enzymatic deamination of the drug in species that rely primarily on the hydroxylation of phenylisopropylamines (24). The deaminated metabolites of amphetamine have little effect on catecholamine levels since in the guinea pig even high doses of d-amphetamine do not result in a prolonged depletion of NE beyond the time that the drug is eliminated from the body (87).

Both hydroxylated metabolites of amphetamine, however, are capable of promoting the release and blocking the reuptake of catecholamines almost as efficiently as the parent compound (31, 176, 339, 376). In addition, para-hydroxyamphetamine and para-hydroxynorephedrine are capable of producing locomotor and stereotyped behaviors following their intraventricular injection in rats (339).

Despite the similar neurochemical and behavioral effects caused by the amphetamine hydroxylated metabolites and the parent compound, the amphetamine molecule need not first be hydroxylated to produce its characteristic pharmacological actions. Intraventricular administration of amphetamine, which for the most part bypasses the para-hydroxylation step in the liver, does not result in a significant formation and accumulation of para-hydroxynorephedrine in the brain (135), but it still produces pronounced and characteristic behavioral effects (309). Further, the administration of drugs that inhibit the enzymatic metabolism of amphetamine does not diminish its behavioral effects and may even potentiate them (134, 203, 230, 235, 334). Apparently the hydroxylated metabolites of amphetamine are primarily responsible for the sustained depletion of NE following amphetamine administration.

The ability of the amphetamine hydroxylated metabolites to alter brain DA levels is transient and in no case as severe as the effect on NE levels (234). The progressive depletion of brain DA associated with long-term amphetamine treatment is also unrelated to an altered accumulation of the drug in the brain since the tissue distribution of amphetamine is not substantially altered during repeated administration (204, 236). A reduction of DA synthesis, however, may be a contributing factor to the amphetamine-induced decline of brain DA. Chronic treatment with amphetamine or its analogs reduces the conversion of tyrosine to DA in the corpus striatum (50, 129, 308) but does not inhibit catecholamine synthesis in noradrenergic areas (129, 198), suggesting the existence in the neostriatum of a serious imbalance between the amphetamine-induced release of DA and transmitter biosynthesis which, with chronic amphetamine administration, results in a depletion of striatal DA. For reasons not yet explained, DA biosynthesis, and consequently DA levels, are severely reduced for several hours after the last chronic amphetamine injection (see 308) even at a time when the amphetamine concentration of the brain is very low (49, 233). Segal & Mandell (308) have suggested that perhaps the altered DA biosynthetic capacity in the corpus striatum reflects a compensatory adjustment of dopaminergic neurons to some chronic amphetamine-induced alteration in dopaminergic transmission. Lewander (233) proposed that the reduced DA levels associated with long-term amphetamine intoxication may be related to a diminished storage capacity of dopaminergic storage vesicles in the nerve terminal.

Little information is available regarding the effects of chronic amphetamine treatment on serotonergic systems. Measuring whole brain levels of serotonin in rats, Lewander (236) found only a slight reduction of this monoamine following chronic amphetamine administration, although a more substantial depletion of brain tryptophan and 5-hydroxyindole acetic acid levels was reported. Utena (357) reported a chronic methamphetamine-induced decline of striatal serotonin levels that was not evident in other areas of the brain.

The behavioral effects produced by amphetamine are not equally influenced by chronic treatment. The cardiovascular, hyperthermic, and anorexigenic properties of amphetamine show evidence of tolerance, while the amphetamine-induced psychomotor stimulation does not (16, 35b, 49, 96, 178, 216, 232, 242, 245, 346, 347). Attempts have been made to relate amphetamine tolerance to the formation of para-hydroxynorephedrine in adrenergic neurons, but these studies have not produced consistent results. Pretreatment with para-hydroxynorephedrine appears to protect against amphetamine-induced hyperthermia in male rats (49, 232) but not in female rats (314), although both sexes show tolerance to this effect of the drug. Amphetamine-induced anorexia is still evident following pretreatment with the hydroxylated metabolites of amphetamine (232), and the development of tolerance to this effect does not parallel the changes in brain NE levels produced by chronic amphetamine treatment (236). As noted above, the brain distribution of the drug does not change during prolonged intoxication (204, 233, 236). Further, the rate of amphetamine metabolism or elimination from the brain is not suggestive of tolerance (121, 181, 233, 245). Recently Shoeman, Sirtori & Azarnoff (315) reported an inhibition of tolerance to amphetamine-induced anorexia by concomitant treatment with propranolol which was associated with a decreased metabolism of amphetamine. Amphetamine-induced tolerance may also reflect a functional change in the mechanisms of catecholaminergic transmission rather than a change in drug metabolism per se (69, 245). Tolerance also develops to the disruptive effects of amphetamine on behaviors that are associated with reinforcement (216). This has been demonstrated on operant tasks and suggests that behavioral tolerance will develop only if the drug interferes with the response necessary to obtain reinforcement (58, 67, 305).

In animal subjects, long-term amphetamine administration produces a progressive augmentation of the hyperactivity and stereotypy that characterize its acute administration (116, 118, 119, 232, 242, 308, 360). In immature rats such treatment produces a progressive augmentation of exploratory behaviors (35b). The enhancement of these behaviors with chronic amphetamine treatment is not associated with a linear increase in response intensity but rather involves a sequential change in the pattern of locomotion and stereotypy which is dependent on the dose administered as well as the duration of treatment (120, 308). Such differences in the behavioral effects of long-term treatment may be characterized by differing degrees of augmentation of locomotion and stereotypy, as well as a progressive alteration in the components of the stereotyped behavior and the intensity with which different components are displayed. Segal & Mandell (308) observed that a low intraperitoneal dose (0.5 mg/kg) of d-amphetamine, which initially elicits clear locomotor responses, becomes more effective in increasing locomotor activity after repeated administration, while a dose (2.5 mg/kg) that produces some components of both stereotypy and locomotion after a single administration generates enhanced stereotyped behaviors which are then followed by an augmentation of the locomotor responses with long-term administration. The stereotypy syndrome, which has been extensively studied with higher doses of d-amphetamine and occasionally with a methylated analog of amphetamine, methamphetamine, initially appears to be characterized by purposeful investigative behaviors (i.e. sniffing and licking in macrosmatic animals; probing and visual scanning in primates) but gradually deteriorates with repeated injections until these responses gain an autonomy of their own and become restricted to certain elements in the environment (115, 116, 120, 144, 285). Animals develop an increasingly abnormal reaction to extraneous stimuli, and eventually, as the chronic administration continues, fear emerges along with postural asymmetries (116, 144, 357). Long-term administration of amphetamine may also produce conditioning of the behavioral effects of the drug (115, 346), although such conditioned effects are not considered sufficient to completely account for the dramatic augmentation of locomotion and stereotypy followed repeated injections over days or weeks (308).

Amphetamine Psychosis as a Heuristic Model for Schizophrenia

Chronic amphetamine intoxication in humans elicits a peculiar series of motor behaviors and thought disturbances which together constitute a clinical syndrome termed "amphetamine psychosis" (34, 35, 114, 165, 321, 324). Stereotyped behaviors, including bruxism, compulsive grooming, repetitive searching, scanning, and probing activities, may predominate among amphetamine abusers along with fear, suspiciousness, paranoid delusions, and auditory and visual hallucinations (120, 202, 217, 282, 319). During prolonged intoxication with the drug both the aberrant motor and cognitive patterns become increasingly constricted and repetitive, ultimately resulting in a breakdown of organized behavior (120, 165, 217). The striking similarities of these behavioral effects with those found in animals after chronic amphetamine administration have implicated drug-induced stereotyped behaviors as an animal model for human psychoses (e.g. 16a, 120, 285, 322, 363).

The symptoms associated with amphetamine psychosis are remarkably similar to those associated with paranoid schizophrenia such that in the absence of knowledge of the history of drug abuse, amphetamine psychosis has been often misdiagnosed as paranoid schizophrenia (see 34, 35, 321, 322). Interestingly, the administration of amphetamine or amphetamine-like compounds exacerbates schizophrenic signs (107, 195, 322, 377), while the antipsychotic phenothiazines and butyrophenones, which are potent DA antagonists, can antagonize amphetamine-induced stereotypy in animals (see above) and are used to treat amphetamine psychosis and paranoid schizophrenia in humans (17, 145, 322, 324). In addition to amphetamine, drugs that act as DA agonists, such as cocaine, L-dopa, or methylphenidate, can also elicit psychotic reactions, and both cocaine and methylphenidate produce psychotic symptoms that are indistinguishable from amphetamine psychosis (120, 322). Further, weakly acting antipsychotics which also have little effect on DA transmission (54, 252) are unreliable in treating schizophrenia (252, 253, 324). Taken together, this evidence has helped to promote the concept of amphetamine psychosis as a heuristic model for schizophrenia (210) which may be characterized by a serious functional alteration of central dopaminergic transmission (16a, 18, 252, 253, 321, 322).

Both the selective augmentation of motor behaviors in animals and the psychosis in humans associated with chronic amphetamine abuse may reflect a change in catecholaminergic receptor sensitivity. Ellinwood, Sudilovsky & Nelson (120) proposed that the substantial depletion of catecholamines that accompanies long-term amphetamine treatment allows certain central catecholamine receptors to become supersensitive, which may account for the heightened psychomotor stimulation produced by subsequent injections of amphetamine. Indeed, a prolonged depletion of brain DA or a long-term drug-induced disruption of DA transmission has been shown to produce an enhanced behavioral response to DA agonists (for reviews see 194, 260, 353). Klawans, Crossett & Dana (211) reported that in guinea pigs chronic amphetamine treatment produced a full-blown stereotypy in response to a subsequent injection of a subthreshold dose of apomorphine that had no effect on naive animals. Although it has been suggested that an excess dopaminergic stimulation, perhaps in the form of a DA receptor supersensitivity (144), may be involved in paranoid schizophrenia (16a, 252, 324), such a conclusion must be interpreted with caution since other possible psychological and physiological pathologies may contribute to this disorder (see reviews 19, 103, 107, 108, 161, 263, 378).

SUMMARY AND CONCLUSIONS

It seems clear from current literature that amphetamine acts, at least in large measure, by releasing and blocking the reuptake of catecholamines from peripheral and central catecholaminergic nerve terminals. At high doses, amphetamine may release serotonin and perhaps acetylcholine, although a firm conclusion concerning the release of the latter transmitter must await further analysis. In addition to these prominent effects, amphetamine results in changes in biosynthesis in catecholaminergic systems, as well as alterations in impulse flow in catecholaminergic neurons. Both presynaptic and postsynaptic regulatory feedback mechanisms have been proposed to account for the interrelationships between the changes in biosynthesis and neuronal activity that accompany amphetamine administration and its release and blockade of reuptake of catecholamines. The continuing analysis of the regulation of catecholamine biosynthesis, especially in response to amphetamine and related compounds, forms an exciting area of current research activity.

The effects of amphetamine on spontaneous motor behavior, i.e. locomotion and stereotypy, have been closely linked to its effects on catecholaminergic systems in the central nervous system. A compelling case for the involvement of the dopaminergic nigro-neostraital projection in the psychostimulant effects of amphetamine has come from pharmacological and surgical manipulations of this and other monoaminergic pathways. Yet a great deal remains to be learned about the nigro-neostraital system and its involvement in the expression of these behaviors, including an understanding of the efferent pathways involved in the production of such responses. Even more, however, remains to be known about the so-called mesolimbic dopaminergic projections which, as shown recently, may include projections to several regions of cerebral cortex (35a, 182, 340a), and have for several years been at the center of speculation concerning the disorders of mood and thought which appear with chronic amphetamine abuse (e.g. 253). The analysis of differential effects of antipsychotic drugs on these different dopaminergic systems may provide additional information of relevance in such functional speculations (e.g. 14).

Perhaps the most exciting aspect of current research on the mechanisms of action of amphetamine and related antipsychotic drugs is the close similarity between amphetamine psychosis and paranoid schizophrenia. Like so many others, the authors hope that understanding the mechanisms of action of acute and chronic amphetamine may help to unravel, at least in some small way, the biological substrates of this dramatic mental disorder. The wealth of information on brain function and behavior already derived from the study of amphetamine, however, demonstrates that the value of such efforts extend even beyond this significant human goal.

Literature Cited

1. Aghajanian, G. K., Bunney, B. S. 1974. Pre- and post-synaptic feedback mechanisms in central dopaminergic neurons. In *Frontiers in Neurology and Neuroscience Research 1974,* ed. P. Seeman, G. M. Brown, 4–11. Toronto: Neurosci. Inst., Univ. Toronto. 154 pp.
2. Andén, N.-E. 1974. Antipsychotic drugs and catecholamine synapses. *J. Psychiatr. Res.* 11:97–104
3. Andén, N.-E., Bedard, P. 1971. Influences of cholinergic mechanisms on the function and turnover of brain dopamine. *J. Pharm. Pharmacol.* 23:460–62
4. Andén, N.-E., Butcher, S. G., Corrodi, H., Fuxe, K., Ungerstedt, U. 1970. Receptor activity and turnover of dopamine and noradrenaline after neuroleptics. *Eur. J. Pharmacol.* 11:303–14
5. Andén, N.-E., Carlsson, A., Häggendal, J. 1969. Adrenergic mechanisms. *Ann. Rev. Pharmacol.* 9:119–34
6. Andén, N.-E., Corrodi, H., Fuxe, K., Hökfelt, T. 1967. Increased impulse flow in bulbospinal noradrenaline neurons produced by catecholamine receptor blocking agents. *Eur. J. Pharmacol.* 1:59–64
7. Andén, N.-E. et al 1970. Evidence for a central noradrenaline receptor stimulation by clonidine. *Life Sci.* 9:513–23
8. Andén, N.-E., Corrodi, H., Fuxe, K., Ungerstedt, U. 1971. Importance of nervous impulse flow for the neuroleptic induced increase in amine turnover in central dopamine neurons. *Eur. J. Pharmacol.* 15:193–99
9. Andén, N.-E., Dahlström, A., Fuxe, K., Larsson, K. 1966. Functional role of the nigro neostriatal dopamine neurons. *Acta Pharmacol. Toxicol.* 24:263–74
10. Andén, N.-E. et al 1966. Ascending monoamine neurons to the telencephalon and diencephalon. *Acta Physiol. Scand.* 67:313–26
11. Andén, N.-E., Fuxe, K., Hökfelt, T. 1967. Effect of some drugs on central monoamine nerve terminals lacking nerve impulse flow. *Eur. J. Pharmacol.* 1:226–32
12. Andén, N.-E., Roos, B.-E., Werdinius, B. 1964. Effects of chlorpromazine, haloperidol and reserpine on the levels of phenolic acids in rabbit corpus striatum. *Life Sci.* 3:149–58
13. Andén, N.-E., Rubenson, A., Fuxe, K., Hökfelt, T. 1967. Evidence for dopamine receptor stimulation by apomorphine. *J. Pharm. Pharmacol.* 19:627–29

14. Andén, N.-E., Stock, G. 1973. Effect of clozapine on the turnover of dopamine in the corpus striatum and in the limbic system. *J. Pharm. Pharmacol.* 25:345–48
15. Andén, N.-E., Svensson, T. H. 1973. Release of dopamine from central noradrenaline nerves after treatment with reserpine plus amphetamine. *J. Neural Transm.* 34:23–30
16. Anggard, E. 1970. Methodological aspects of studies on amphetamine dependence in man. In *Int. Symp. Amphetamines and Related Compounds. Proc. Mario Negri Inst. Pharmacol. Res., Milan, Italy,* ed. E. Costa, S. Garattini, 191–203. New York: Raven. 962 pp.
16a. Angrist, B., Gershon, S. 1974. Dopamine and psychotic states: Preliminary remarks. In *Neuropsychopharmacology of Monoamines and Their Regulatory Enzymes,* ed. E. Usdin, 211–19. New York: Raven. 462 pp.
17. Angrist, B., Lee, H. K., Gershon, S. 1974. The antagonism of amphetamine-induced symptomatology by a neuroleptic. *Am. J. Psychiatry* 131:817–19
18. Angrist, B. M., Shopsin, B., Gershon, S. 1971. Comparative psychotomimetic effects of stereoisomers of amphetamine. *Nature* 234:152–53
19. Antun, F. 1973. The biochemistry of psychosis. *Leb. Med. J.* 26:615–25
20. Arbuthnott, G. W., Crow, T. J., Fuxe, K., Ungerstedt, U. 1970. Behavioural effects of stimulation in the region of the substantia nigra. *J. Physiol.* 210:61–62P
21. Arnfred, T., Randrup, A. 1968. Cholinergic mechanisms in brain inhibiting amphetamine-induced stereotyped behaviour. *Acta Pharmacol. Toxicol.* 26:384–94
22. Arnold, L. E., Wender, P. H., McCloskey, K., Snyder, S. H. 1972. Levoamphetamine and dextroamphetamine: Comparative efficacy in the hyperkinetic syndrome. *Arch. Gen. Psychiatry* 27:816–22
23. Asher, I. M., Aghajanian, G. K. 1974. 6-hydroxydopamine lesions of olfactory tubercles and caudate nuclei: Effect on amphetamine-induced stereotyped behavior in rats. *Brain Res.* 82:1–12
24. Axelrod, J. 1970. Amphetamine: Metabolism, physiological disposition, and its effects on catecholamine storage. See Ref. 16, 207–16
25. Axelrod, J. 1972. Dopamine-β-hydroxylase: Regulation of its synthesis and

release from nerve terminals. *Pharmacol. Rev.* 24:233–43
26. Axelrod, J. 1971. Noradrenaline: Fate and control of its biosynthesis. *Science* 173:598–606
27. Axelrod, J. 1974. Regulation of the neurotransmitter norepinephrine. In *The Neurosciences: Third Study Program*, ed. F. O. Schmitt, F. G. Worden, 863–76. Cambridge, Mass.: MIT. 1107 pp.
28. Azzaro, A. J., Rutledge, C. O. 1973. Selectivity of release of norepinephrine, dopamine and 5-hydroxytryptamine by amphetamine in various regions of rat brain. *Biochem. Pharmacol.* 22:2801–13
29. Baggot, J. D., Davis, L. E. 1973. A comparative study of the pharmacokinetics of amphetamine. *Res. Vet. Sci.* 14:207–15
30. Bainbridge, J. G. 1970. The inhibitory effect of amphetamine on exploration in mice. *Psychopharmacologia* 18:314–19
31. Baldessarini, R. J., Harris, J. E. 1974. Effects of amphetamines on the metabolism of catecholamines in the rat brain. *J. Psychiatr. Res.* 11:41–43
32. Banerjee, U., Geh, S. L. 1973. On the mechanism of central action of amphetamine: The role of catecholamines. *Neuropharmacology* 12:917–31
33. Banerjee, U., Geh, S. L. 1973. Time-related interaction patterns of amphetamine with reserpine and other central depressants. *Res. Commun. Chem. Pathol. Pharmacol.* 6:104–22
34. Bell, D. S. 1965. Comparison of amphetamine psychosis and schizophrenia. *Int. J. Psychiatry* 111:701–7
35. Bell, D. S. 1973. The experimental reproduction of amphetamine psychosis. *Arch. Gen. Psychiatry* 29:35–40
35a. Berger, B., Tassin, J. P., Blanc, G., Moyne, M. A., Thierry, A. M. 1974. Histochemical confirmation for dopaminergic innervation of the rat cerebral cortex after destruction of the noradrenergic ascending pathways. *Brain Res.* 81:332–37
35b. Bennett, E. L., Rosenzweig, M. R., Wu, S.-Y. C. 1973. Excitant and depressant drugs modulate effects of environment on brain weight and cholinesterases. *Psychopharmacologia* 33:309–28
36. Bernheimer, H., Birkmayer, W., Hornykiewicz, O., Jellinger, K., Seitelberger, F. 1973. Brain dopamine and the syndromes of Parkinson and Huntington. Clinical, morphological, and neurochemical correlations. *J. Neurol. Sci.* 20:415–55
37. Besson, M.-J., Cheramy, A., Feltz, P., Glowinski, J. 1969. Release of newly synthesized dopamine from dopamine-containing terminals in the striatum of the rat. *Proc. Natl. Acad. Sci. USA* 62:741–48
38. Besson, M.-J., Cheramy, A., Feltz, P., Glowinski, J. 1971. Dopamine: Spontaneous and drug-induced release from the caudate nucleus in the cat. *Brain Res.* 32:407–24
39. Besson, M.-J., Cheramy, A., Gauchy, C., Glowinski, J. 1973. In vivo continuous estimation of ^{3}H-dopamine synthesis and release in the cat caudate nucleus. *Naunyn-Schmiedeberg's Arch. Pharmacol.* 278:101–5
40. Besson, M.-J., Cheramy, A., Glowinski, J. 1969. Effects of amphetamine and desmethylimipramine on amines synthesis and release in central catecholamine-containing neurons. *Eur. J. Pharmacol.* 7:111–14
41. Besson, M.-J., Cheramy, A., Glowinski, J. 1971. Effects of some psychotropic drugs on dopamine synthesis in the rat striatum. *J. Pharmacol. Exp. Ther.* 177:196–205
42. Bianchi, S., Consolo, S., Ladinsky, H. 1974. Dopaminergic-cholinergic antagonists. *Br. J. Pharmacol.* 52:428–29P
43. Biel, J. H. 1970. Structure-activity relationships of amphetamine and derivatives. See Ref. 16, 3–19
44. Boakes, R. J., Bradley, P. B., Candy, J. M. 1971. Abolition of the response of brain stem neurones to iontophoretically applied *d*-amphetamine by reserpine. *Nature* 229:496–98
45. Boakes, R. J., Bradley, P. B., Candy, J. M. 1972. A neuronal basis for the alerting action of (+)-amphetamine. *Br. J. Pharmacol.* 45:391–403
46. Boulu, R., Rapin, J. R., Lebas, M., Jacquot, C. 1972. Action centrale de l'amphétamine, de l'éphédrine et de leur dérivé *p*-hydroxyle, après lésion unilatérale du faisceau nigrostriatal chez le rat. *Psychopharmacologia* 26:54–61
47. Breese, G. R., Cooper, B. R., Mueller, R. A. 1974. Evidence for involvement of 5-hydroxytryptamine in the actions of amphetamine. *Br. J. Pharmacol.* 52:307–14
48. Breese, G. R., Kopin, I. J., Weise, V. K. 1970. Effects of amphetamine derivatives on brain dopamine and noradrenaline. *Br. J. Pharmacol.* 38:537–45

49. Brodie, B. B., Cho, A. K., Gessa, G. L. 1970. Possible role of *p*-hydroxynorephedrine in the depletion of norepinephrine induced by *d*-amphetamine and in tolerance to this drug. See Ref. 16, 217–30

50. Buening, M. K., Gibb, J. W. 1974. Influence of methamphetamine and neuroleptic drugs on tyrosine hydroxylase activity. *Eur. J. Pharmacol.* 26: 30–34

51. Bunney, B. S. 1974. Dopaminergic blocking effects of antipsychotic drugs. *J. Psychiatr. Res.* 11:72–73

52. Bunney, B. S., Aghajanian, G. K. 1973. Electrophysiological effects of amphetamine on dopaminergic neurons. In *Frontiers in Catecholamine Research*, ed. E. Usdin, S. H. Snyder, 957–62. New York: Pergamon. 1219 pp.

53. Bunney, B. S., Aghajanian, G. K., Roth, R. H. 1973. Comparison of effects of L-dopa, amphetamine and apomorphine on firing rate of rat dopaminergic neurones. *Nature New Biol.* 245:123–25

54. Bunney, B. S., Walters, J. R., Roth, R. H., Aghajanian, G. K. 1973. Dopaminergic neurons: Effect of antipsychotic drugs and amphetamine on single cell activity. *J. Pharmacol. Exp. Ther.* 185:560–71

55. Burgen, A. S. V., Iversen, L. L. 1965. The inhibition of noradrenaline uptake by sympathomimetic amines in the rat isolated heart. *Br. J. Pharmacol.* 25: 34–49

56. Butcher, S. G., Butcher, L. L. 1974. Origin and modulation of acetylcholine activity in the neostriatum. *Brain Res.* 71:167–71

57. Campbell, B. A., Fibiger, H. C. 1971. Potentiation of amphetamine-induced arousal by starvation. *Nature* 233: 424–25

58. Campbell, J. C., Seiden, L. S. 1973. Performance influence on the development of tolerance to amphetamine. *Pharmacol. Biochem. Behav.* 1:703–8

59. Carlsson, A. 1970. Amphetamine and brain catecholamines. See Ref. 16, 289–300

60. Carlsson, A. 1966. Morphologic and dynamic aspects of DA in the CNS. In *Biochemistry & Pharmacology of the Basal Ganglia*, ed. E. Costa, L. J. Cote, M. D. Yahr, 107–13. New York: Raven. 238 pp.

61. Carlsson, A. 1974. Pharmacological and biochemical aspects of striatal dopamine receptors. See Ref. 1, 1–3

62. Carlsson, A. 1967. Pharmacology of synaptic monoamine transmission. *Prog. Brain Res.* 31:53–60

63. Carlsson, A., Kehr, W., Lindqvist, M. 1974. Short-term control of tyrosine hydroxylase. See Ref. 16a, 135–42

64. Carlsson, A., Kehr, W., Lindqvist, M., Magnusson, T., Atack, C. V. 1972. Regulation of monoamine metabolism in the central nervous system. *Pharmacol. Rev.* 24:371–84

65. Carlsson, A., Lindqvist, M. 1963. Effect of chlorpromazine and haloperidol on formation of 3-methoxytyramine and normetanephrine in mouse brain. *Acta Pharmacol. Toxicol.* 20:140–44

66. Carlsson, A., Lindqvist, M., Dahlström, A., Fuxe, K., Masuoka, D. 1965. Effects of the amphetamine group in intraneuronal brain amines in vivo and in vitro. *J. Pharm. Pharmacol.* 17:521–23

67. Carlton, P. L., Wolgin, D. L. 1971. Contingent tolerance to the anorexigenic effects of amphetamine. *Physiol. Behav.* 7:221–23

68. Carr, L. A., Moore, K. E. 1969. Norepinephrine: Release from brain by *d*-amphetamine in vivo. *Science* 164: 322–32

69. Chiel, H., Yehuda, S., Wurtman, R. J. 1974. Development of tolerance in rats to the hypothermic effects of *d*-amphetamine and apomorphine. *Life Sci.* 14:483–88

70. Chiueh, C. C., Moore, K. E. 1974. Effects of α-methyltyrosine on *d*-amphetamine-induced release of endogenously synthesized and exogenously administered catecholamines from the cat brain in vivo. *J. Pharmacol. Exp. Ther.* 190:100–8

71. Chiueh, C. C., Moore, K. E. 1974. In vivo release of endogenously synthesized catecholamines from the cat brain evoked by electrical stimulation and by *d*-amphetamine. *J. Neurochem.* 23: 159–68

72. Chiueh, C. C., Moore, K. E. 1973. Release of endogenously synthesized catechols from the caudate nucleus by stimulation of the nigro-striatal pathway and by the administration of *d*-amphetamine. *Brain Res.* 50:221–25

73. Christiansen, J., Squires, R. F. 1974. Antagonistic effects of neuroleptics and apomorphine on synaptosomal tyrosine hydroxylase in vitro. *J. Pharm. Pharmacol.* 26:742–43

74. Christie, J. E., Crow, T. J. 1971. Turning behavior as an index of the action of amphetamines and ephedrines on cen-

tral dopamine-containing neurons. *Br. J. Pharmacol.* 43:658–67

75. Clarke, D. E., Sampath, S. S. 1973. Studies on the functional role of intraneuronal monoamine oxidase. *J. Pharmacol. Exp. Ther.* 187:539–49

76. Cole, S. O. 1967. Experimental effects of amphetamine: A review. *Psychol. Bull.* 68:81–90

77. Consolo, S. et al 1975. Dopaminergic-cholinergic interaction in the striatum: Studies with piribedil. In *Advances in Neurology*, Vol. 9, *Dopaminergic Mechanisms*, ed. D. B. Calne, T. N. Chase, A. Barbeau, 257–72. New York: Raven. 427 pp.

78. Consolo, S., Ladinsky, H., Garattini, S. 1974. Effect of several dopaminergic drugs and trihexyphenidyl on cholinergic parameters in the rat striatum. *J. Pharm. Pharmacol.* 26:275–77

79. Constantinidis, J., de la Torre, J. C., Tissot, R., Geissbuhler, F. 1969. La barrière capillaire pour la dopa dans le cerveau et les différents organes. *Psychopharmacologia* 15:75–87

80. Cools, A. R. 1973. Chemical and electrical stimulation of the caudate nucleus in freely moving cats: The role of dopamine. *Brain Res.* 58:437–51

81. Cools, A. R. 1971. The function of dopamine and its antagonism in the caudate nucleus of cats in relation to the stereotyped behaviour. *Arch. Int. Pharmacodyn. Ther.* 194:259–69

82. Cools, A. R., Janssen, H.-J. 1974. The nucleus linearis intermedius raphe and behaviour evoked by direct and indirect stimulation of dopamine-sensitive sites within the caudate nucleus of cats. *Eur. J. Pharmacol.* 28:266–75

83. Cools, A. R., Van Rossum, J. M. 1970. Caudate dopamine and stereotyped behaviour of cats. *Arch. Int. Pharmacodyn. Ther.* 187:163–73

84. Corrodi, H., Fuxe, K., Hamberger, B., Ljungdahl, A. 1970. Studies on central and peripheral noradrenaline neurons using a new dopamine-β-hydroxylase inhibitor. *Eur. J. Pharmacol.* 12:145–55

85. Corrodi, H., Fuxe, K., Hökfelt, T. 1967. The effect of some psychoactive drugs on central monoamine neurons. *Eur. J. Pharmacol.* 1:363–68

86. Corrodi, H., Fuxe, K., Ljungdahl, A., Ögren, S.-D. 1970. Studies on the action of some psychoactive drugs on central noradrenaline neurones after inhibition of dopamine-β-hydroxylase. *Brain Res.* 24:451–70

87. Costa, E., Groppetti, A. 1970. Biosynthesis and storage of catecholamines in tissues of rats injected with various doses of *d*-amphetamine. See Ref. 16, 231–55

88. Costa, E., Groppetti, A., Naimzada, M. K. 1972. Effects of amphetamine on the turnover rate of brain catecholamines and motor activity. *Br. J. Pharmacol.* 44:742–51

89. Costa, E., Meek, J. L. 1974. Regulation of biosynthesis of catecholamines and serotonin in the CNS. *Ann. Rev. Pharmacol.* 14:491–511

90. Costa, E., Neff, N. H. 1966. Isotopic and non-isotopic measurements of the rate of catecholamine biosynthesis. See Ref. 60, 141–55

91. Costall, B., Naylor, R. J. 1974. Extrapyramidal and mesolimbic involvement with the stereotypic activity of *d*- and *l*-amphetamine. *Eur. J. Pharmacol.* 25:121–29

92. Costall, B., Naylor, R. J. 1974. The involvement of dopaminergic systems with the stereotyped behaviour patterns induced by methylphenidate. *J. Pharm. Pharmacol.* 26:30–33

93. Costall, B., Naylor, R. J. 1974. Specific asymmetric behaviour induced by the direct chemical stimulation of neostriatal dopaminergic mechanisms. *Naunyn-Schmiedeberg's Arch. Pharmacol.* 285:83–98

94. Costall, B., Naylor, R. J., Olley, J. E. 1972. On the involvement of the caudate-putamen, globus pallidus and substantia nigra with neuroleptic and cholinergic modification of locomotor activity. *Neuropharmacology* 11:317–30

95. Costall, B., Naylor, R. J., Olley, J. E. 1972. The substantia nigra and stereotyped behaviour. *Eur. J. Pharmacol.* 18:95–106

96. Cowan, F. F., Cannon, C., Koppanyi, T., Maengwyn-Davies, G. D. 1961. Reversal of phenylalkylamine tachyphylaxis by norepinephrine. *Science* 134:1069–70

97. Coyle, J. T., Snyder, S. H. 1969. Antiparkinsonian drugs: Inhibition of dopamine uptake in the corpus striatum as a possible mechanism of action. *Science* 166:899–901

98. Coyle, J. T., Snyder, S. H. 1969. Catecholamine uptake by synaptosomes in homogenates of rat brain: Stereospecificity in different areas. *J. Pharmacol. Exp. Ther.* 170:221–31

99. Creese, I. 1974. Behavioural evidence of dopamine receptor stimulation by

piribedil (ET 495) and its metabolite S584. *Eur. J. Pharmacol.* 28:55–58
100. Creese, I., Iversen, S. D. 1972. Amphetamine response in rat after dopamine neuron destruction. *Nature New Biol.* 238:247–48
101. Creese, I., Iversen, S. D. 1973. Blockage of amphetamine induced motor stimulation and stereotypy in the adult rat following neonatal treatment with 6-hydroxydopamine. *Brain Res.* 55:369–82
102. Creese, I., Iversen, S. D. 1974. The role of forebrain dopamine systems in amphetamine-induced stereotyped behavior in the rat. *Psychopharmacologia* 39:345–57
103. Cromwell, R. L. 1975. Assessment of schizophrenia. *Ann. Rev. Psychol.* 26:593–619
104. Cubeddu, L. X., Barnes, E. M., Langer, S. Z., Weiner, N. 1974. Release of norepinephrine and dopamine-β-hydroxylase by nerve stimulation. I. Role of neuronal and extraneuronal uptake and of alpha presynaptic receptors. *J. Pharmacol. Exp. Ther.* 190:431–50
105. Dahlström, A., Fuxe, K. 1964. Evidence for the existence of monoamine-containing neurons in the central nervous system. I. Demonstration of monoamines in the cell bodies of brain stem neurons. *Acta Physiol. Scand.* (Suppl. 232) 62:1–55
106. DaPrada, M., Pletscher, A. 1966. On the mechanism of chlorpromazine-induced changes of cerebral homovanillic acid levels. *J. Pharm. Pharmacol.* 18:628–30
107. Davis, J. M. 1974. A two factor theory of schizophrenia. *J. Psychiatr. Res.* 11:25–29
108. Denber, H. C. B. 1970. Some current biochemical theories concerning schizophrenia. In *Biochemistry of Brain and Behavior*, ed. R. E. Bowman, S. P. Datta, 171–205. New York: Plenum
109. Deffenu, G., Bartolini, A., Pepeu, G. 1970. Effect of amphetamine on cholinergic systems of the cerebral cortex of the cat. See Ref. 16, 357–68
110. Derkach, P., Larochelle, L., Bieger, D., Hornykiewicz, O. 1974. L-dopa-chlorpromazine antagonism on running activity in mice. *Can. J. Physiol. Pharmacol.* 52:114–18
111. Dingell, J. V., Owens, M. L., Norvich, M. R., Sulser, F. 1967. On the role of norepinephrine biosynthesis in the central action of amphetamine. *Life Sci.* 6:1155–62
112. Dowson, J. H. 1973. Quantitative histochemical studies of striatal dopamine depletion following *dl*-α-methyl-*p*-tyrosine administration. *Neuropharmacology* 12:949–53
113. Duvoisin, R. C. 1967. Cholinergic-anticholinergic antagonism in Parkinsonism. *Arch. Neurol.* 17:124–36
114. Ellinwood, E. H. Jr. 1967. Amphetamine psychosis: I. Description of the individuals and process. *J. Nerv. Ment. Dis.* 144:273–83
115. Ellinwood, E. H. Jr. 1971. "Accidental conditioning" with chronic methamphetamine intoxication: Implications for a theory of drug habituation. *Psychopharmacologia* 21:131–38
116. Ellinwood, E. H. Jr. 1974. Behavioral and EEG changes in the amphetamine model of psychosis. See Ref. 16a, 281–97
117. Ellinwood, E. H. Jr., Balster, R. L. 1974. Rating the behavioral effects of amphetamine. *Eur. J. Pharmacol.* 28:35–41
118. Ellinwood, E. H. Jr., Escalante, O. 1970. Behavior and histopathological findings during chronic methedrine intoxication. *Biol. Psychiatry* 2:27–39
119. Ibid. Chronic amphetamine effect on the olfactory forebrain, 189–203
120. Ellinwood, E. H. Jr., Sudilovsky, A., Nelson, L. M. 1973. Evolving behavior in the clinical and experimental amphetamine (model) psychosis. *Am. J. Psychiatry* 130:1088–93
121. Ellison, T., Okun, R., Silverman, A., Siegel, M. 1971. Metabolic fate of amphetamine in the cat during development of tolerance. *Arch. Int. Pharmacodyn. Ther.* 190:135–49
122. Enna, S. J., Dorris, R. L., Shore, P. A. 1973. Specific inhibition by α-methyltyrosine of amphetamine-induced amine release from brain. *J. Pharmacol. Exp. Ther.* 184:576–82
123. Ernst, A. M. 1967. Mode of action of apomorphine and dexamphetamine on gnawing compulsion in rats. *Psychopharmacologia* 10:316–23
124. Ernst, A. M., Smelik, P. G. 1966. Site of action of dopamine and apomorphine on compulsive gnawing behaviour in rats. *Experientia* 22:837–38
125. Esplin, D. W. 1970. Centrally acting muscle relaxant: Drugs for Parkinson's disease. In *The Pharmacological Basis of Therapeutics*, ed. L. S. Goodman, A. Gilman, 226–36. New York: Macmillan. 1794 pp. 4th ed.

126. Estler, C.-J., Ammon, H. P. T. 1971. Modification by two beta-adrenergic blocking drugs of the effects of methamphetamine on behaviour and brain metabolism of mice. *J. Neurochem.* 18: 777–79

127. Evetts, K. D., Uretsky, N. J., Iversen, L. L., Iversen, S. D. 1970. Effects of 6-hydroxydopamine on CNS catecholamines, spontaneous motor activity and amphetamine induced hyperactivity in rats. *Nature* 225:961–62

128. Ferris, R. M., Tang, F. L. M., Maxwell, R. A. 1972. A comparison of the capacities of isomers of amphetamine, deoxypipradrol and methylphenidate to inhibit the uptake of tritiated catecholamines into rat cerebral cortex slices, synaptosomal preparations of rat cerebral cortex, hypothalamus and striatum and into adrenergic nerves of rabbit aorta. *J. Pharmacol. Exp. Ther.* 181: 407–16

129. Fibiger, H. C., McGeer, E. G. 1971. Effect of acute and chronic methamphetamine treatment of tyrosine hydroxylase activity in brain and adrenal medulla. *Eur. J. Pharmacol.* 16:176–80

130. Fibiger, H. C., Trimbach, C., Campbell, B. A. 1972. Enhanced stimulant properties of (+)-amphetamine after chronic reserpine treatment in the rat: Mediation by hypophagia and weight loss. *Neuropharmacology* 11:57–67

131. Fog, R., Pakkenberg, H. 1970. Lesions in corpus striatum and cortex of rat brains and the effect on pharmacologically induced stereotyped, aggressive and cataleptic behaviour. *Psychopharmacologia* 18:346–54

132. Fog, R. L., Randrup, A., Pakkenberg, H. 1967. Aminergic mechanisms in corpus striatum and amphetamine-induced stereotyped behaviour. *Psychopharmacologia* 11:179–83

133. Foote, W. E., Sheard, M. H., Aghajanian, G. K. 1969. Comparison of effects of LSD and amphetamine on midbrain raphe units. *Nature* 222: 567–69

134. Freeman, J. J., Sulser, F. 1972. Iprindole-amphetamine interactions in the rat: The role of aromatic hydroxylation of amphetamine in its mode of action. *J. Pharmacol. Exp. Ther.* 183:307–15

135. Freeman, J. J., Sulser, F. 1974. Formation of *p*-hydroxynorephedrine in brain following intraventricular administration of *p*-hydroxyamphetamine. *Neuropharmacology* 13:1187–90

136. Fuxe, K. 1965. Evidence for the existence of monoamine neurons in the central nervous system. III. The monoamine nerve terminal. *Z. Zellforsch.* 65:573–96

137. Fuxe, K. 1965. Evidence for the existence of monoamine neurons in the central nervous system. IV. Distribution of monoamine nerve terminals in the central nervous system. *Acta Physiol. Scand. Suppl.* 247:37–85

138. Fuxe, K., Goldstein, M., Ljungdahl, A. 1970. Antiparkinsonian drugs and central dopamine neurons. *Life Sci.* 9:811–24

139. Fuxe, K., Hökfelt, T., Ungerstedt, U. 1970. Morphological and functional aspects of central monoamine neurons. *Int. Rev. Neurobiol.* 13:93–126

140. Fuxe, K., Ungerstedt, U. 1974. Action of caffeine and theophyllamine on supersensitive dopamine receptors: Considerable enhancement of receptor response to treatment with dopa and dopamine receptor agonists. *Med. Biol.* 52:48–54

141. Fuxe, K., Ungerstedt, U. 1970. Histochemical, biochemical and functional studies on central monoamine neurons after acute and chronic amphetamine administration. See Ref. 16, 257–88

142. Fuxe, K., Ungerstedt, U. 1968. Histochemical studies on the effect of (+)-amphetamine, drugs of the imipramine group and tryptamine on central catecholamine and 5-hydroxytryptamine neurons after intraventricular injection of catecholamines and 5-hydroxytryptamine. *Eur. J. Pharmacol.* 4:135–44

143. Fyrö, B., Nybäck, H., Sedvall, G. 1972. Tyrosine hydroxylation in the rat striatum in vitro and in vivo after nigral lesion and chlorpromazine treatment. *Neuropharmacology* 11:531–37

144. Garver, D. L., Schlemmer, R. F. Jr., Maas, J. W., Davis, J. M. 1975. A schizophreniform behavioral psychosis mediated by dopamine. *Am. J. Psychiatry* 132:33–38

145. Gerlach, J., Koppelhus, P., Helweg, E., Monrad, A. 1974. Clozapine and haloperidol in a single-blind cross-over trial: Therapeutic and biochemical aspects in the treatment of schizophrenia. *Acta Psychiatr. Scand.* 50:410–24

146. Gey, K. F., Pletscher, A. 1968. Acceleration of turnover of 14C-catecholamines in rat brain by chlorpromazine. *Experientia* 24:335–36

147. Geyer, M. A., Dawsey, W. J., Mandell, A. J. 1975. Differential effects of caf-

feine, D-amphetamine and methylphenidate on individual raphe cell fluorescence: A microspectrofluorimetric demonstration. *Brain Res.* 85: 135–39

148. Geyer, M. A., Segal, D. S., Mandell, A. J. 1972. Effect of intraventricular infusion of dopamine and norepinephrine on motor activity. *Physiol. Behav.* 8:653–58

149. Glick, S. D., Greenstein, S. 1973. Possible modulating influence of frontal cortex on nigro-striatal function. *Br. J. Pharmacol.* 49:316–21

150. Glick, S. D., Marsanico, R. G. 1974. Comparative time-dependent changes in sensitivity to locomotor effects of *d*-amphetamine in mice with caudate, hippocampal or frontal cortical lesions. *Arch. Int. Pharmacodyn. Ther.* 209: 80–85

151. Glick. S. D., Marsanico, R. G. 1974. Shifting of the *d*-amphetamine dose-response curve in rats with frontal cortical ablations. *Psychopharmacologia* 36: 109–15

152. Glick, S. D., Milloy, S. 1973. Rate-dependent effects of *d*-amphetamine on locomotor activity in mice: Possible relationship to paradoxical amphetamine sedation in minimal brain dysfunction. *Eur. J. Pharmacol.* 24:266–68

153. Glowinski, J. 1970. Effects of amphetamine on various aspects of catecholamine metabolism in the central nervous system of the rat. See Ref. 16, 301–16

154. Glowinski, J. 1972. Some new facts about synthesis, storage, and release processes of monoamines in the central nervous system. In *Perspectives in Neuropharmacology: A Tribute to Julius Axelrod,* ed. S. H. Snyder, 349–404. New York: Oxford Univ. 404 pp.

155. Glowinski, J. 1973. Some characteristics of the "functional" and "main storage" compartments in central catecholaminergic neurons. *Brain Res.* 62:489–93

156. Glowinski, J. Axelrod, J. 1964. Inhibition of uptake of tritiated noradrenaline in the intact rat brain by imipramine and structurally related compounds. *Nature* 204:1318–19

157. Glowinski, J., Axelrod, J. 1965. Effect of drugs on the uptake, release, and metabolism of H^3-norepinephrine in the rat brain. *J. Pharmacol. Exp. Ther.* 149: 43–49

158. Glowinski, J., Axelrod, J., Iversen, L. L. 1966. Regional studies of catecholamines in the rat brain. IV. Effects of

drugs on the disposition and metabolism of ^3H-norepinephrine and ^3H-dopamine. *J. Pharmacol. Exp. Ther.* 153:30–41

159. Goetz, C., Klawans, H. L. 1974. Studies on the interaction of reserpine, *d*-amphetamine, apomorphine and 5-hydroxytryptophan. *Acta Pharmacol. Toxicol.* 34:119–130

160. Goldstein, M., Anagnoste, B. 1965. The conversion in vivo of D-amphetamine to (+)-*p*-hydroxynorephedrine. *Biochim. Biophys. Acta.* 107:166–68

161. Goldstein, M., Freedman, L. S., Ebstein, R. P., Park, D. H. 1974. Studies of dopamine-β-hydroxylase in mental disorders. *Arch. Gen. Psychiatry* 31: 205–10

162. Grabowska, M., Michaluk, J. 1974. On the role of serotonin in apomorphine-induced locomotor stimulation in rats. *Pharmacol. Biochem. Behav.* 2:263–66

163. Graham, A. W., Aghajanian, G. K. 1971. Effects of amphetamine on single cell activity in a catecholamine nucleus, the locus coeruleus. *Nature* 234:100–2

164. Green, T. K., Harvey, J. A. 1974. Enhancement of amphetamine action after interruption of ascending serotonergic pathways. *J. Pharmacol. Exp. Ther.* 190:109–17

165. Griffith, J. D., Cavanaugh, J. H., Held, J., Oates, J. A. 1970. Experimental psychosis induced by the administration of *d*-amphetamine. See Ref. 16, 897–904

166. Groppetti, A., Costa, E. 1969. Tissue concentrations of *p*-hydroxynorephedrine in rats injected with *d*-amphetamine: Effect of pretreatment with desipramine. *Life Sci.* 8:653–65

167. Groves, P. M., Rebec, G. V., Harvey, J. A. 1975. Alteration of the effects of (+)-amphetamine on neuronal activity in the striatum following lesions of the nigrostriatal bundle. *Neuropharmacology* 14:369–76

168. Groves, P. M., Rebec, G. V., Segal, D. S. 1974. The action of *d*-amphetamine on spontaneous activity in the caudate nucleus and reticular formation of the rat. *Behav. Biol.* 11:33–47

169. Guilleux, H., Peterfalvi, M. 1974. Le comportement de rotation après lésion unilatérale du striatum analysé à l'aide d'un rotomètre. *J. Pharmacol.* 5:63–74

170. Guyenet, P. G. et al 1975. Effects of dopaminergic receptor agonists and antagonists on the activity of the neo-striatal cholinergic system. *Brain Res.* 84:227–44

171. Guyenet, P. G., Javoy, F., Agid, Y., Beaujouan, J. C., Glowinski, J. 1975. Dopamine receptors and cholinergic neurons in the rat neostriatum. See Ref. 77, 43–51
172. Haeusler, G. 1974. Clonidine-induced inhibition of sympathetic nerve activity: No indication for a central presynaptic or an indirect sympathomimetic mode of action. *Naunyn-Schmiedeberg's Arch. Pharmacol.* 286:97–111
173. Haigler, H. J., Aghajanian, G. K. 1974. Peripheral serotonin antagonists: Failure to antagonize serotonin in brain areas receiving a prominent serotonergic input. *J. Neural Transm.* 35:257–73
174. Hamberger, B. 1967. Reserpine-resistant uptake of catecholamines in isolated tissues of the rat: A histochemical study. *Acta Physiol. Scand. Suppl.* 295:1–64
175. Harik, S. I., Morris, P. L. 1973. The effects of lesions in the head of the caudate nucleus on spontaneous and L-dopa induced activity in the cat. *Brain Res.* 62:279–85
176. Harris, J. E., Baldessarini, R. J. 1973. Uptake of (^{3}H)-catecholamines by homogenates of rat corpus striatum and cerebral cortex: Effects of amphetamine analogues. *Neuropharmacology* 12:669–79
177. Harris, J. E., Baldessarini, R. J. 1973. Amphetamine-induced inhibition of tyrosine hydroxylation in homogenates of rat corpus striatum. *J. Pharm. Pharmacol.* 25:755–57
178. Harrisson, J. W. E., Ambrus, C. M., Ambrus, J. L. 1952. Tolerance of rats toward amphetamine and methamphetamine. *J. Am. Pharm. Assoc.* 41:539–41
179. Hemsworth, B. A., Neal, M. J. 1968. The effect of stimulant drugs on the release of acetylcholine from the cerebral cortex. *Br. J. Pharmacol.* 32:416–17P
180. Hertting, G., Suko, J. 1972. Influence of neuronal and extraneuronal uptake on disposition, metabolism, and potency of catecholamines. See Ref. 154, 267–300
181. Hitzemann, R. J., Loh, H. H., Craves, F. B., Domino, E. F. 1973. The use of *d*-amphetamine pellet implantation as a model for *d*-amphetamine tolerance in the mouse. *Psychopharmacologia* 30:227–40
182. Hökfelt, T., Ljungdahl, A., Fuxe, K., Johansson, O. 1974. Dopamine nerve terminals in the rat limbic cortex: Aspects of the dopamine hypothesis of schizophrenia. *Science* 184:177–79
183. Hökfelt, T., Ungerstedt, U. 1969. Electron and fluorescence microscopical studies on the nucleus caudatus putamen of the rat after unilateral lesions of ascending nigro-neostriatal DA neurons. *Acta Physiol. Scand.* 76:415–26
184. Hökfelt, T., Ungerstedt. U. 1973. Specificity of 6-hydroxydopamine induced degeneration of central monoamine neurones: An electron and fluorescence microscopic study with special reference to intracerebral injection on the nigro-striatal dopamine system. *Brain Res.* 69:269–97
185. Hollister, A. S., Breese, G. R., Cooper, B. R. 1974. Comparison of tyrosine hydroxylase and dopamine-β-hydroxylase inhibition with the effects of various 6-hydroxydopamine treatments on *d*-amphetamine induced motor activity. *Psychopharmacologia* 36:1–16
186. Horn, A. S., Snyder, S. H. 1972. Steric requirements for catecholamine uptake by rat brain synaptosomes: Studies with rigid analogs of amphetamine. *J. Pharmacol. Exp. Ther.* 180:523–30
187. Hornykiewicz, O. 1966. Dopamine (3-hydroxytyramine) and brain function. *Pharmacol. Rev.* 18:925–64
188. Horvath, T. B., Meares, R. A. 1974. L-dopa and arousal. *J. Neurol. Neurosurg. Psychiatry* 37:416–21
189. Iversen, L. L. 1967. *The Uptake and Storage of Noradrenaline in Sympathetic Nerves.* Cambridge Univ. 253 pp.
190. Iversen, L. L. 1968. Role of noradrenaline uptake in adrenergic neurotransmission. In *Adrenergic Neurotransmission,* ed. G. E. W. Wolstenholme, M. O'Connor, 44–56. Boston: Little, Brown. 107 pp.
191. Iversen, L. L., Jarrot, B., Simmonds, M. A. 1971. Differences in the uptake, storage and metabolism of (+)- and (−)-noradrenaline. *Br. J. Pharmacol.* 43:845–55
192. Iversen, S. D. 1971. The effect of surgical lesions to frontal cortex and substantia nigra on amphetamine responses in rats. *Brain Res.* 31:295–311
193. Iversen, S. D. 1974. 6-hydroxydopamine: A chemical lesion technique for studying the role of amine neurotransmitters in behavior. See Ref. 27, 705–11
194. Iversen, S. D., Creese, I. 1975. Behavioral correlates of dopaminergic supersensitivity. See Ref. 77, 81–92
195. Janowsky, D. S., Davis, J. M. 1974. Dopamine, psychomotor stimulants, and schizophrenia: Effects of methylphenidate and the stereoisomers of am-

phetamine in schizophrenics. See Ref. 16a, 317–24

196. Javoy, F., Agid, Y., Bouvet, D., Glowinski, J. 1972. Feedback control of DA synthesis in dopaminergic terminals of the rat striatum. *J. Pharmacol. Exp. Ther.* 182:454–63

197. Javoy, F., Hamon, M., Glowinski, J. 1970. Disposition of newly synthesized amines in cell bodies and terminals of central catechol aminergic neurons. (1) Effect of amphetamine and thioproperazine on the metabolism of CA in the caudate nucleus, the substantia nigra and the ventromedial nucleus of the hypothalamus. *Eur. J. Pharmacol.* 10:178–88

198. Javoy, F., Thierry, A. M., Kety, S. S., Glowinski, J. 1968. The effect of amphetamine on the turnover of brain norepinephrine in normal and stressed rats. *Commun. Behav. Biol.* (A) 1:43–48

199. Jerussi, T. P., Glick, S. D. 1974. Amphetamine-induced rotation in rats without lesions. *Neuropharmacology* 13:283–86

200. Jerussi, T. P., Glick, S. D. 1975. Apomorphine-induced rotation in normal rats and interaction with unilateral caudate lesions. *Psychopharmacologia* 40:329–34

201. Joh, T. H., Reis, D. J. 1975. Different forms of tyrosine hydroxylase in central dopaminergic and noradrenergic neurons and sympathetic ganglia. *Brain Res.* 85:146–51

202. Jonsson, L.-E., Gunne, L.-M. 1970. Clinical studies of amphetamine psychosis. See Ref. 16, 929–36

203. Jonsson, J., Lewander, T. 1974. Effects of the dopamine-β-hydroxylase inhibitor FLA 63 on the kinetics of elimination of amphetamine in the rat. *J. Pharm. Pharmacol.* 26:907–9

204. Kalant, H., LeBlanc, A. E., Gibbons, R. J. 1971. Tolerance to, and dependence on, some non-opiate psychotropic drugs. *Pharmacol. Rev.* 23:135–91

205. Kaufman, S. 1974. Dopamine-β-hydroxylase. *J. Psychiat. Res.* 11:135–91

206. Kaufman, S., Friedman, S. 1965. Dopamine-β-hydroxylase. *Pharmacol. Rev.* 17:71–100

207. Kehr, W. 1974. Temporal changes in catecholamine synthesis of rat forebrain structures after axotomy. *J. Neural Transm.* 35:307–17

208. Kehr, W., Carlsson, A., Lindqvist, M.

1975. Biochemical aspects of dopamine agonists. See Ref. 77, 185–96

209. Kehr, W., Carlsson, A., Lindqvist, M., Magnusson, T., Atack, C. 1972. Evidence for a receptor-mediated feedback control of striatal tyrosine hydroxylase activity. *J. Pharm. Pharmacol.* 24:744–47

210. Kety, S. S. 1972. Toward hypotheses for a biochemical component in the vulnerability to schizophrenia. *Semin. Psychiatry* 4:233–38

211. Klawans, H. L. Jr., Crossett, P., Dana, N. 1975. Effect of chronic amphetamine exposure on stereotyped behavior: Implications for pathogenesis of L-dopa-induced dyskinesias. See Ref. 77, 105–12

212. Knapp, S., Mandell, A. J., Geyer, M. A. 1974. Effects of amphetamines on regional tryptophan hydroxylase activity and synaptosomal conversion of tryptophan to 5-hydroxytryptamine in rat brain. *J. Pharmacol. Exp. Ther.* 189:676–89

213. Kopin, I. J. 1964. Storage and metabolism of catecholamines: The role of monoamine oxidase. *Pharmacol. Rev.* 16:179–91

214. Kopin, I. J. 1968. False adrenergic transmitters. *Ann. Rev. Pharmacol.* 8:377–94

215. Kopin, I. J. 1972. False aminergic transmitters. See Ref. 154, 339–48

216. Kosman, M. E., Unna, K. R. 1968. Effects of chronic administration of the amphetamines and other stimulants on behavior. *Clin. Pharmacol. Ther.* 9:240–54

217. Kramer, J. C. 1967. Amphetamine abuse: Pattern and effects of high doses taken intravenously. *J. Am. Med. Assoc.* 201:305–9

218. Krnjevic, K. 1975. Electrophysiology of dopamine receptors. See Ref. 77, 13–24

219. Krsiak, M., Borgesova, M. 1972. Drugs and spontaneous behaviour: Why are detailed studies still so rare? *Act. Nerv. Super.* 14:285–93

220. Kuczenski, R. T., Mandell, A. J. 1972. Regulatory properties of soluble and particulate rat brain tyrosine hydroxylase. *J. Biol. Chem.* 247:3114–22

221. Kuhar, M. J. 1973. Neurotransmitter uptake: A tool in identifying neurotransmitter-specific pathways. *Life Sci.* 13:1623–34

222. Ladinsky, H., Consolo, S., Garattini, S. 1974. Increase in striatal acetylcholine levels in vivo by piribedil, a new dopa-

mine receptor stimulant. *Life Sci.* 14:1251–60

223. Landisky, S., Consolo, S., Bianchi, S., Somanin, R., Ghezzi, D. 1975. Cholinergic-dopaminergic interaction in the striatum: The effect of 6-hydroxydopamine or pimozide treatment on the increased striatal acetylcholine levels induced by apomorphine, piribedil and D-amphetamine. *Brain Res.* 84:221–26

224. Ladisich, W., Volbehr, H., Matussek, N. 1970. Paradoxical effect of amphetamine on hyperactive states in correlation with catecholamine metabolism in brain. See Ref. 16, 487–92

225. Langelier, P., Parent, A., Poirier, L. J. 1972. Decarboxylase activity of the brain capillary walls and parenchyma in the rat, cat and monkey. *Brain Res.* 45:622–29

226. Langer, S. Z. 1974. Presynaptic regulation of catecholamine release. *Biochem. Pharmacol.* 23:1793–1800

227. Lasagna, L., Epstein, L. C. 1970. The use of amphetamines in the treatment of hyperkinetic children. See Ref. 16, 849–64

228. Levitt, M., Spector, S., Sjoerdsma, A., Udenfriend, S. 1965. Elucidation of the rate-limiting step in norepinephrine biosynthesis in the perfused guinea-pig heart. *J. Pharmacol. Exp. Ther.* 148: 1–8

229. Lewander, T. 1968. Urinary excretion and tissue levels of catecholamines during chronic amphetamine intoxication. *Psychopharmacologia* 13:394–402

230. Lewander, T. 1969. Influence of various psychoactive drugs on the in vivo metabolism of *d*-amphetamine in the rat. *Eur. J. Pharmacol.* 6:38–44

231. Lewander, T. 1970. Catecholamine turnover studies in chronic amphetamine intoxication. See Ref. 16, 317–30

232. Lewander, T. 1971. A mechanism for the development of tolerance to amphetamine in rats. *Psychopharmacologia* 21:17–31

233. Lewander, T. 1971. Effects of chronic amphetamine intoxication on the accumulation in the rat brain of labelled catecholamines synthesized from circulating tyrosine-^{14}C and dopa-^{3}H. *Naunyn-Schmiedeberg's Arch. Pharmacol.* 271:211–33

234. Lewander, T. 1971. Displacement of brain and heart noradrenaline by *p*-hydroxynorephedrine after administration of *p*-hydroxyamphetamine. *Acta Pharmacol. Toxicol.* 29:20–32

235. Ibid. On the presence of *p*-hydroxynorephedrine in the rat brain and heart in relation to changes in catecholamine levels after administration of amphetamine, 33–48

236. Lewander, T. 1974. Effect of chronic treatment with central stimulants on brain monoamines and some behavioral and physiological functions in rats, guinea pigs, and rabbits. See Ref. 16a, 221–40

236a. Lindbrink, P., Gösta, J., Fuxe, K. 1974. Selective reserpine-resistant accumulation of catecholamines in central dopamine neurones after DOPA administration. *Brain Res.* 67:439–56

237. Lloyd, K. G., Hornykiewicz, O. 1974. Dopamine and other monoamines in the basal ganglia: Relation to brain dysfunctions. See Ref. 1, 26–35

238. Lotti, V. J. 1971. Action of various centrally acting agents in mice with unilateral caudate brain lesions. *Life Sci.* 10:781–89

239. Lovenberg, W., Victor, S. J. 1974. Regulation of tryptophan and tyrosine hydroxylase. *Life Sci.* 14:2337–53

240. Lundborg, P. 1967. Studies on the uptake and subcellular distribution of catecholamines and their alpha-methylated analogues. *Acta Physiol. Scand. Suppl.* 302:1–34

241. Lynch, G. S., Lucas, P. A., Deadwyler, S. A. 1972. The demonstration of acetylcholinesterase containing neurons within the caudate nucleus of the rat. *Brain Res.* 45:617–21

242. Lyon, M., Randrup, A. 1972. The dose-response effect of amphetamine upon avoidance behavior in the rat seen as a function of increasing stereotypy. *Psychopharmacologia* 23:334–47

243. Mabry, P. D., Campbell, B. A. 1974. Ontogeny of serotonergic inhibition of behavioral arousal in the rat. *J. Comp. Physiol. Psychol.* 86:193–201

244. Mabry, P. D., Campbell, B. A. 1973. Serotonergic inhibition of catecholamine-induced behavioral arousal. *Brain Res.* 49:381–91

245. Magour, S., Coper, H., Fähndrich, C. H. 1974. The effects of chronic treatment with *d*-amphetamine on food intake, body weight, locomotor activity and subcellular distribution of the drug in rat brain. *Psychopharmacologia* 34:45–54

246. Maj, J., Sowinska, H., Baran, L., Kapturkiewicz, Z. 1972. The effect of clonidine on locomotor activity in mice. *Life Sci.* 11:483–91

247. Mandell, A. J., Knapp, S., Kuczenski, R. T., Segal, D. S. 1972. A methamphetamine induced alteration in the physical state of rat caudate tyrosine hydroxylase. *Biochem. Pharmacol.* 21: 2737–50

248. Mandell, A. J., Morgan, M. 1970. Amphetamine induced increase in tyrosine hydroxylase activity. *Nature* 227:75–76

249. Marsden, C. D., Dolphin, A., Duvoisin, R. C., Jenner, P., Tarsy, D. 1974. Role of noradrenaline in levodopa reversal of reserpine akinesia. *Brain Res.* 77: 521–25

250. Marsden, C. A., Guldberg, H. C. 1973. The role of monoamines in rotation induced or potentiated by amphetamine after nigral, raphé and mesencephalic reticular lesions in the rat brain. *Neuropharmacology* 12:195–211

251. Marsh, G. G., Markham, C. H. 1973. Does levodopa alter depression and psychopathology in Parkinsonism patients? *J. Neurol. Neurosur. Psychiatry* 36: 925–35

252. Matthysse, S. 1974. Schizophrenia: Relationships to dopamine transmission, motor control, and feature extraction. See Ref. 27, 733–37

253. Matthysse, S. 1974. Implications of catecholamine systems of the brain in schizophrenia. In *Brain Dysfunction in Metabolic Disorders, Res. Publ. Assoc. Nerv. Ment. Dis.,* ed. F. Plum, 53:305–15. New York: Raven

254. McGeer, E. G., Fibiger, H. C., McGeer, P. L., Brooke, S. 1973. Temporal changes in amine synthesizing enzymes of rat extrapyramidal structures after hemitransections or 6-hydroxydopamine administration. *Brain Res.* 52: 289–300

255. McGeer, P. L. et al 1974. Biochemical neuroanatomy of the basal ganglia. *Adv. Behav. Biol.* 10:27–47

256. McGeer, P. L., Grewaal, D. S., McGeer, E. G. 1974. Influence of noncholinergic drugs on rat striatal acetylcholine levels. *Brain Res.* 80:211–17

257. Miller, E., Nieburg, H. A. 1973. Amphetamines: Valuable adjunct in treatment of Parkinsonism. *NY State J. Med.* 73:2657–61

258. Molander, L., Randrup, A. 1974. Investigation of the mechanism by which L-dopa induces gnawing in mice. *Acta Pharmacol. Toxicol.* 34:312–24

259. Moore, K. E. 1974. Behavioral effects of direct- and indirect-acting dopaminergic agonists. See Ref. 16a, 403–14

260. Moore, K. E., Thornburg, J. E. 1975. Drug-induced dopaminergic supersensitivity. See Ref. 77, 93–104

261. Moore, R. Y., Bhatnager, R. K., Heller, A. 1971. Anatomical and chemical studies of a nigro-neostriatal projection in the cat. *Brain Res.* 30:119–35

262. Muller, P., Seeman, P. 1974. Neuroleptics: Relation between cataleptic and anti-turning actions, and role of the cholinergic system. *J. Pharm. Pharmacol.* 26:981–84

263. Murphy, D. L., Belmakel, R., Wyatt, R. J. 1974. Monoamine oxidase in schizophrenia and other behavioral disorders. *J. Psychiatr. Res.* 11:221–47

264. Nagatsu, T. 1973. *Biochemistry of Catecholamines.* Baltimore: Univ. Park. 362 pp.

265. Naylor, R. J., Olley, J. E. 1972. Modification of the behavioural changes induced by amphetamine in the rat by lesions in the caudate nucleus, the caudate-putamen and globus pallidus. *Neuropharmacology* 11:91–99

266. North, R. B., Harik, S. I., Snyder, S. H. 1974. Amphetamine isomers: Influences on locomotor and stereotyped behavior of cats. *Pharmacol. Biochem. Behav.* 2:115–18

267. Norton, S. 1973. Amphetamine as a model for hyperactivity in the rat. *Physiol. Behav.* 11:181–86

268. Nybäck, H., Sedvall, G. 1968. Effect of chlorpromazine on acculamation and disappearance of catecholamines formed from tyrosine-C[14] in brain. *J. Pharmacol. Exp. Ther.* 162:294–301

269. Nybäck, H., Sedvall, G. 1971. Effect of nigral lesion on chlorpromazine-induced acceleration of dopamine synthesis from ^{14}C-tyrosine. *J. Pharm. Pharmacol.* 23:322–26

270. Nybäck, H., Sedvall, G., Kopin, I. J. 1967. Accelerated synthesis of dopamine-^{14}C in rat brain after chlorpromazine. *Life Sci.* 6:2307–12

271. Obianwu, H. O. 1969. Possible functional differentiation between the stores from which adrenergic nerve stimulation, tyramine and amphetamine release noradrenaline. *Acta Physiol. Scand.* 75:92–101

272. Oltmans, G. A., Harvey, J. A. 1972. LH syndrome and brain catecholamine levels after lesions of the nigrostriatal bundle. *Physiol. Behav.* 8:69–78

273. Philippu, A., Glowinski, J., Besson, M.-J. 1974. In vivo release of newly synthesized catecholamines from the hypothalamus by amphetamine. *Naunyn-*

Schmiedeberg's Arch. Pharmacol. 282:1–8

274. Phillis, J. W. 1974. The role of calcium in the central effects of biogenic amines. *Life Sci.* 14:1189–1201

275. Poirier, L. J., Langelier, P., Boucher, R. 1973. Spontaneous and L-dopa induced circus movements in cats with brain stem lesions. *J. Physiol.* 66:735–54

276. Poirier, L. J., Sourkes, T. L. 1965. Influence of the substantia nigra on the catecholamine content of the striatum. *Brain* 88:181–92

277. Potter, L. T., Axelrod, J. 1963. Studies on the storage of norepinephrine and the effect of drugs. *J. Pharmacol. Exp. Ther.* 140:199–206

278. Price, M. T. C., Fibiger, H. C. 1974. Apomorphine and amphetamine stereotypy after 6-hydroxydopamine lesions of the substantia nigra. *Eur. J. Pharmacol.* 29:249–52

279. Proctor, C. D., Kirby, J., Wood, M. H., Wade, L. H., King, P. K. 1974 Comparison of the effects of d-amphetamine and l-amphetamine in reversing depression of mouse locomotor activity caused by reserpine. *Arch. Int. Pharmacodyn. Ther.* 212:108–15

280. Raiteri, M., Levi, G., Federico, R. 1974. D-amphetamine and the release of ^{3}H-norepinephrine from synaptosomes. *Eur. J. Pharmacol.* 28:237–40

281. Randrup, A., Jonas, W. 1967. Brain dopamine and the amphetamine-reserpine interaction. *J. Pharm. Pharmacol.* 19:483–84

282. Randrup, A., Munkvad, I. 1970. Biochemical, anatomical and psychological investigations of stereotyped behavior induced by amphetamines. See Ref. 16, 695–714

283. Randrup, A., Munkvad, I. 1966. Role of catecholamines in the amphetamine excitatory response. *Nature* 211:540

284. Randrup, A., Munkvad, I. 1967. Stereotyped activities produced by amphetamine in several animal species and man. *Psychopharmacologia* 1:300–10

285. Randrup, A., Munkvad, I. 1974. Pharmacology and physiology of stereotyped behavior. *J. Psychiatr. Res.* 11:1–10

286. Randrup, A., Scheel-Krüger, J. 1966. Diethyldithiocarbamate and amphetamine stereotype behaviour. *J. Pharm. Pharmacol.* 18:752–53

287. Rapin, J., Jacquot, C., Hamar, C., Cohen, Y. 1973. Etude in vitro du mécanisme d'action noradrénergique de

l'amphétamine et de ses métabolites p. hydroxylés. *J. Pharmacol.* 4:519–26

288. Rebec, G. V., Groves, P. M. 1975. Differential effects of the optical isomers of amphetamine on neuronal activity in the reticular formation and caudate nucleus of the rat. *Brain Res.* 83:301–18

289. Rebec, G. V., Groves, P. M. 1975. Apparent feedback from the caudate nucleus to the substantia nigra following amphetamine administration. *Neuropharmacology* 14:275–82

290. Rech, R. H. 1964. Antagonism of reserpine behavioral depression by d-amphetamine. *J. Pharmacol. Exp. Ther.* 146:369–76

291. Rech, R. H., Stolk, J. M. 1970. Amphetamine-drug interactions that relate brain catecholamines to behavior. See Ref. 16, 385–413

292. Reis, D. J., Molinoff, P. B. 1972. Brain dopamine-β-hydroxylase: Regional distribution and effects of lesions and 6-hydroxydopamine on activity. *J. Neurochem.* 19:195–204

293. Rolinski, Z. 1973. Analysis of aggressiveness-stereotypy complex induced in mice by amphetamine or nialamide and L-DOPA. *Pol. J. Pharmacol. Pharm.* 25:551–56

294. Rolinski, Z., Scheel-Krüger, J. 1973. The effect of dopamine and noradrenaline antagonists on amphetamine induced locomotor activity in mice and rats. *Acta Pharmacol. Toxicol.* 33: 385–99

295. Roth, R. H., Salzman, P. M., Morgenroth, V. H. III, 1974. Noradrenergic neurons: Allosteric activation of hippocampal tyrosine hydroxylase by stimulation of the locus coeruleus. *Biochem. Pharmacol.* 23:2779–84

296. Roth, R. H., Walters, J. R., Morgenroth, V. H. III, 1974. Effects of alterations in impulse flow on transmitter metabolism in central dopaminergic neurons. See Ref. 16a, 369–84

297. Rutledge, C. O. 1970. The mechanisms by which amphetamine inhibits oxidative deamination of norepinephrine in brain. *J. Pharmacol. Exp. Ther.* 171: 188–95

298. Rutledge, C. O., Azzaro, A. J., Ziance, R. J. 1972. The importance of neuronal uptake for the release of ^{3}H-norepinephrine by d-amphetamine. *Fed. Proc.* 31:601

299. Sayers, A. C., Handley, S. L. 1974. Catalepsy induced by α-methyl-p-tyrosine and d-amphetamine: The role of

catecholamine metabolism. *Psychopharmacologia* 34:325–34

300. Scheel-Krüger, J. 1972. Behavioural and biochemical comparison of amphetamine derivatives, cocaine, benztropine and tricyclic anti-depressant drugs. *Eur. J. Pharmacol.* 18:63–73

301. Scheel-Krüger, J., Hasselager, E. 1974. Studies of various amphetamines, apomorphine and clonidine on body temperature and brain 5-hydroxytryptamine metabolism in rats. *Psychopharmacologia* 36:189–202

302. Scheel-Krüger, J., Jonas, W. 1973. Pharmacological studies on tetrabenazine-induced excited behaviour of rats pretreated with amphetamine or nialamide. *Arch. Int. Pharmacodyn. Ther.* 206:47–64

303. Scheel-Krüger, J., Randrup, A. 1967. Stereotype hyperactive behaviour produced by dopamine in the absence of noradrenaline. *Life Sci.* 6:1389–98

304. Schiorring, E. 1971. Amphetamine induced selective stimulation of certain behaviour items with concurrent inhibition of others in an open-field test with rats. *Behaviour* 39:1–17

305. Schuster, C. R., Dockens, W. S., Woods, J. H. 1966. Behavioral variables affecting the development of amphetamine tolerance. *Psychopharmacologia* 9:170–82

306. Sedvall, G., Fryö, B., Nybäck, H., Wiesel, F. A. 1975. Actions of dopaminergic antagonists in the striatum. See Ref. 77, 131–40

307. Segal, D. S., Mandell, A. J. 1970. Behavioral activation of rats during intraventricular infusion of norepinephrine. *Proc. Natl. Acad. Sci. USA* 66:289–93

308. Segal, D. S., Mandell, A. J. 1974. Long-term administration of d-amphetamine: Progressive augmentation of motor activity and stereotypy. *Pharmacol. Biochem. Behav.* 2:249–55

309. Segal, D. S., McAllister, C., Geyer, M. 1974. Ventricular infusion of norepinephrine and amphetamine: Direct versus indirect action. *Pharmacol. Biochem. Behav.* 2:79–86

310. Segal, D. S., Kuczenski, R. 1974. Tyrosine hydroxylase activity: Regional and subcellular distribution in brain. *Brain Res.* 68:261–66

311. Sethy, V. H., Van Woert, M. H. 1973. Effect of L-DOPA on brain acetylcholine and choline in rats. *Neuropharmacology* 12:27–31

312. Sethy, V. H., Van Woert, M. H. 1974. Modification of striatal acetylcholine concentration by dopamine receptor agonists and antagonists. *Res. Commun. Chem. Pathol. Pharmacol.* 8:13–28

313. Sethy, V. H., Van Woert, M. H. 1974. Regulation of striatal acetylcholine concentration by dopamine receptors. *Nature* 251:529–30

314. Sever, P. S., Caldwell, J., Williams, R. T. 1974. Evidence against the involvement of false neurotransmitters in tolerance to amphetamine-induced hyperthermia in the rat. *J. Pharm. Pharmacol.* 26:823–26

315. Shoeman, D. W., Sirtori, C. R., Azarnoff, D. C. 1974. Inhibition of amphetamine tolerance and metabolism by propranolol. *J. Pharmacol. Exp. Ther.* 191:68–71

316. Siggins, G. R., Hoffer, B. J., Ungerstedt, U. 1974. Electrophysiological evidence for involvement of cyclic adenosine monophosphate in dopamine responses of caudate neurons. *Life Sci.* 15:779–92

317. Simpson, B., Iversen, S. D. 1971. Effects of substantia nigra lesions on the locomotor and stereotypy responses to amphetamine. *Nature* 230:30–32

318. Smith, C. B. 1965. Effects of d-amphetamine upon brain amine content and locomotor activity in mice. *J. Pharmacol. Exp. Ther.* 147:96–102

319. Smith, D. E. 1969. Physical vs. psychological dependence and tolerance in high-dose methamphetamine abuse. *Clin. Toxicol.* 2:99–103

320. Smith, R. L., Dring, L. G. 1970. Patterns of metabolism of β-phenylisopropylamines in man and other species. See Ref. 16, 121–39

321. Snyder, S. H. 1973. Amphetamine psychosis: A "model" schizophrenia mediated by catecholamines. *Am. J. Psychiatry* 130:61–67

322. Snyder, S. H. 1974. Catecholamines as mediators of drug effects in schizophrenia. See Ref. 27, 721–32

323. Snyder, S. H. 1974. Stereoselective features of catecholamine disposition and their behavioral implications. *J. Psychiatr. Res.* 11:31–39

324. Snyder, S. H., Banerjee, S. P., Yamamura, H. I., Greenberg, D. 1974. Drugs, neurotransmitters, and schizophrenia. *Science* 184:1243–53

325. Snyder, S. H., Kuhar, M. J., Green, A. I., Coyle, J. T., Shaskan, E. G. 1970. Uptake and subcellular localization of

neurotransmitters in the brain. *Int. Rev. Neurobiol.* 13:127–58
326. Spector, S., Gordon, R., Sjoerdsma, A., Udenfriend, S. 1967. End-product inhibition of tyrosine-hydroxylase as a possible mechanism for regulation of norepinephrine synthesis. *Mol. Pharmacol.* 3:549–55
327. Spector, S., Sjoerdsma, A., Udenfriend, S. 1965. Blockade of endogenous norepinephrine synthesis by α-methyltyrosine, an inhibitor of tyrosine hydroxylase. *J. Pharmacol. Exp. Ther.* 147:86–95
328. Stadler, H., Lloyd, K. G., Gadea-Ciria, M., Bartholini, G. 1973. Enhanced striatal acetylcholine release by chlorpromazine and its reversal by apomorphine. *Brain Res.* 55:476–80
329. Stein, L. 1964. Self-stimulation of the brain and the central stimulant action of amphetamine. *Fed. Proc.* 23:836–50
330. Stolk, J. M. 1975. Evidence for reversible inhibition of brain dopamine-β-hydroxylase activity in vivo by amphetamine analogues. *J. Neurochem.* 24:135–42
331. Stolk, J. M., Barchas, J. D., Goldstein, M., Boggan, W. O., Freedman, D. X. 1974. A comparison of psychotomimetic drug effects on rat brain norepinephrine metabolism. *J. Pharmacol. Exp. Ther.* 189:42–50
332. Stolk, J. M., Rech, R. H. 1970. Antagonism of *d*-amphetamine by alpha-methyl-l-tyrosine: Behavioral evidence for the participation of catecholamine stores and synthesis in the amphetamine stimulant response. *Neuropharmacology* 9:249–63
333. Stricker, E. M., Zigmond, M. J. 1974. Effects on homeostasis of intraventricular injections of 6-hydroxydopamine in rats. *J. Comp. Physiol. Psychol.* 86:973–94
334. Sulser, F., Owens, M. L., Dingell, J. V. 1966. On the mechanism of amphetamine potentiation by desipramine. *Life Sci.* 5:2005–10
335. Svensson, T. H. 1971. On the role of central noradrenaline in the regulation of motor activity and body temperature in the mouse. *Naunyn-Schmiedeberg's Arch. Pharmacol.* 271:111–20
336. Svensson, T. H. 1970. The effect of inhibition of catecholamine synthesis on dexamphetamine induced central stimulation. *Eur. J. Pharmacol.* 12:161–66
337. Taylor, K. M., Snyder, S. H. 1970. Amphetamine: Differentiation by *d*- and

l-isomers of behavior involving brain norepinephrine or dopamine. *Science* 168:1487–89
338. Taylor, K. M., Snyder, S. H. 1971. Differential effects of D- and L-amphetamine on behavior and on catecholamine disposition in dopamine and norepinephrine containing neurons of rat brain. *Brain Res.* 28:295–309
339. Taylor, W. A., Sulser, F. 1973. Effects of amphetamine and its hydroxylated metabolites on central noradrenergic mechanisms. *J. Pharmacol. Exp. Ther.* 185:620–32
340. Tecce, J. J., Cole, J. O. 1974. Amphetamine effects in man: Paradoxical drowsiness and lowered electrical brain activity (CNV). *Science* 185:451–53
340a. Thierry, A. M., Hirsch, J. C., Tassin, J. P., Blanc, G., Glowinski, J. 1974. Presence of dopaminergic terminals and absence of dopaminergic cell bodies in the cerebral cortex of the cat. *Brain Res.* 79:77–88
341. Thoenen, H., Hurlimann, A., Gey, K. F., Haefely, W. 1966. Liberation of *p*-hydroxynorephedrine from cat spleen by sympathetic nerve stimulation after pretreatment with amphetamine. *Life Sci.* 5:1715–22
342. Thoenen, H., Tranzer, J. P. 1973. The pharmacology of 6-hydroxydopamine. *Ann. Rev. Pharmacol.* 13:169–80
343. Thornburg, J. E., Moore, K. E. 1974. A comparison of effects of apomorphine and ET 495 on locomotor activity and circling behaviour in mice. *Neuropharmacology* 13:189–97
344. Thornburg, J. E., Moore, K. E. 1973. Dopamine and norepinephrine uptake by rat brain synaptosomes: Relative inhibitory potencies of *l*- and *d*-amphetamine and amantadine. *Res. Commun. Chem. Pathol. Pharmacol.* 5:81–89
345. Thornburg, J. E., Moore, K. E. 1973. The relative importance of dopaminergic and noradrenergic neuronal systems for the stimulation of locomotor activity induced by amphetamine and other drugs. *Neuropharmacology* 12:853–66
346. Tilson, H. A., Rech, R. H. 1973. Conditioned drug effects and absence of tolerance to *d*-amphetamine induced motor activity. *Pharmacol. Biochem. Behav.* 1:149–53
347. Tormey, J., Lasagna, L. 1960. Relation of thyroid function to acute and chronic effects of amphetamine in the rat. *J. Pharmacol. Exp. Ther.* 128:201–9
348. Tseng, L. F., Hitzemann, R. J., Loh, H. H. 1974. Comparative effects of *dl-p*

-methoxyamphetamine and d-amphetamine on catecholamine release and reuptake in vitro. *J. Pharmacol. Exp. Ther.* 189:708–16

349. Tseng, L. F., Loh, H. H. 1974. Significance of dopamine receptor activity in dl-p-methoxyamphetamine- and d-amphetamine-induced locomotor activity. *J. Pharmacol. Exp. Ther.* 189:717–24

350. Udenfriend, S. 1966. Tyrosine hydroxylase. *Pharmacol. Rev.* 18:43–51

351. Ungerstedt, U. 1971. Striatal dopamine release after amphetamine or nerve degeneration revealed by rotational behaviour. *Acta Physiol. Scand. Suppl.* 367:49–68

352. Ibid. Postsynaptic supersensitivity after 6-hydroxydopamine induced degeneration of the nigro-striatal dopamine system, 69–73

353. Ungerstedt, U. 1974. Brain dopamine neurons and behavior. See Ref. 27, 695–703

354. Ungerstedt, U., Arbuthnott, G. W. 1970. Quantitative recording of rotational behavior in rats after 6-hydroxydopamine lesions of the nigrostriatal dopamine system. *Brain Res.* 24:485–93

355. Ungerstedt, U., Butcher, L. L., Butcher, S. G., Anden, N.-E., Fuxe, K. 1969. Direct chemical stimulation of dopaminergic mechanisms in the neostriatum of the rat. *Brain Res.* 14:461–71

356. Ungerstedt, U., Ljungberg, T., Hoffer, B., Siggins, G. 1975. Dopaminergic supersensitivity in the striatum. See Ref. 77, 57–66

357. Utena, H. 1966. Behavioral aberrations in methamphetamine-intoxicated animals and chemical correlates in the brain. *Prog. Brain Res.* 21:192–207

358. Vaatstra, W. J., Eigeman, L. 1974. Dopamine turnover in the rat corpus striatum: In vivo and in vitro studies of the action of amantadine. *Eur. J. Pharmacol.* 25:185–90

359. Van Rossum, J. M., Van Der Schoot, J. B., Hurkmans, J. A. Th. M. 1962. Mechanisms of action of cocaine and amphetamine in the brain. *Experientia* 18:229–31

360. Vizi, E. S. 1972. Amphetamines-disturbances of spontaneous behaviour and tolerance. *Act. Nerv. Super.* 14:297

361. Von Voightlander, P. F., Moore, K. E. 1973. Involvement of nigro-striatal neurons in the in vivo release of dopamine by amphetamine, amantadine, and tyramine. *J. Pharmacol. Exp. Ther.* 184:542–52

362. Von Voightlander, P. F., Moore, K. E. 1973. Turning behavior of mice with unilateral 6-hydroxydopamine lesions in the striatum: Effects of apomorphine, L-dopa, amantadine, amphetamine and other psychomotor stimulants. *Neuropharmacology* 12:451–62

363. Wallach, M. B. 1974. Drug-induced stereotyped behavior: Similarities and differences. See Ref. 16a, 241–60

364. Wallach, M. B., Gershon, S. 1971. A neuropsychopharmacological comparison of d-amphetamine, L-DOPA and cocaine. *Neuropharmacology* 10:743–52

365. Wallach, M. B., Gershon, S. 1972. The induction and antagonism of central nervous system stimulant-induced stereotyped behavior in the cat. *Eur. J. Pharmacol.* 18:22–26

366. Walters, J. R., Bunney, B. S., Roth, R. H. 1975. Piribedil and apomorphine: Pre- and postsynaptic effects on dopamine synthesis and neuronal activity. See Ref. 77, 273–84

367. Walters, J. R., Roth, R. H. 1974. Dopaminergic neurons: Drug-induced antagonism of the increase in tyrosine hydroxylase activity produced by cessation of impulse flow. *J. Pharmacol. Exp. Ther.* 191:82–91

368. Weiner, N. 1970. Regulation of norepinephrine biosynthesis. *Ann. Rev. Pharmacol.* 10:273–90

369. Weiner, N., Cloutier, G., Bjur, R., Pfeffer, R. I. 1972. Modification of norepinephrine synthesis in intact tissue by drugs and during short-term adrenergic nerve stimulation. *Pharmacol. Rev.* 24:203–21

370. Weiner, N., Rutledge, C. O. 1966. The actions of reserpine on the biosynthesis and storage of catecholamines. In *Mechanisms of Release of Biogenic Amines*, ed. U. S. Von Euler, S. Rosell, B. Uvnas, 307–18. Oxford: Pergamon. 482 pp.

371. Weiner, W. J., Goetz, C., Klawans, H. L. Jr. 1975. Serotonergic and antiserotonergic influences on apomorphine-induced stereotyped behaviour. *Acta Pharmacol. Toxicol.* 36:155–60

372. Weiner, W. J., Goetz, C., Westheimer, R., Klawans, H. L. Jr. 1973. Serotonergic and antiserotonergic influences on amphetamine-induced stereotyped behavior. *J. Neurol. Sci.* 20:373–79

373. Weinstock, M., Speiser, Z. 1974. Modification by propranolol and related compounds of motor activity and

stereotype behaviour induced in the rat by amphetamine. *Eur. J. Pharmacol.* 25:29–35

374. Weissman, A., Koe, B. K., Tenen, S. S. 1966. Antiamphetamine effects following inhibition of tyrosine hydroxylase. *J. Pharmacol. Exp. Ther.* 151:339–52

375. Welch, B. L., Welch, A. S. 1970. Control of brain catecholamines and serotonin during acute stress and after *d*-amphetamine by natural inhibition of monoamine oxidase: An hypothesis. See Ref. 16, 415–45

376. Wenger, G. R., Rutledge, C. O. 1974. A comparison of the effects of amphetamine and its metabolites, *p*-hydroxyamphetamine and *p*-hydroxynorephedrine, on uptake, release and catabolism of ³H-norepinephrine in cerebral cortex of rat brain. *J. Pharmacol. Exp. Ther.* 189:725–32

377. West, A. P. 1974. Interaction of low-dose amphetamine use with schizophrenia in outpatients: Three case reports. *Am. J. Psychiatry* 131:321–23

378. Wise, C. D., Bad᾽ n, M. M., Stein, L.

1974. Post-mortem measurement of enzymes in human brain: Evidence of a central noradrenergic deficit in schizophrenia. *J. Psychiatr. Res.* 11:185–98

379. Wise, C. D., Stein, L. 1970. Amphetamines: Facilitation of behavior by augmented release of norepinephrine from the medial forebrain bundle. See Ref. 16, 463–85

380. Wolfarth, S. 1974. Reactions to apomorphine and spiroperidol of rats with striatal lesions: The relevance of kind and size of lesion. *Pharmacol. Biochem. Behav.* 2:181–86

381. York, D. H. 1973. Motor responses induced by stimulation of the substantia nigra. *Exp. Neurol.* 41:323–30

382. Zimmerberg, B., Glick, S. D., Jerussi, T. P. 1974. Neurochemical correlate of a spatial preference in rats. *Science* 185:623–25

383. Zivkovic, B., Guidotti, A., Costa, E. 1974. Effects of neuroleptics on striatal tyrosine hydroxylase: Changes in affinity for pteridine cofactor. *Mol. Pharmacol.* 10:727–35

ETHOLOGY AND COMPARATIVE PSYCHOLOGY

♦250

William A. Mason

Psychology Department, California Primate Research Center, University of California, Davis, California 95616

Dale F. Lott

Division of Wildlife and Fisheries Biology, Psychology Department, University of California, Davis, California 95616

Scientific disciplines cannot stand still. They gain or lose adherents, their methods and resources change, and their hopes and visions prosper or diminish with the passing of time. As with organic evolution, this historical process occasionally results in a fundamental transformation, bringing with it a new order of possibilities, a higher level of organization, and the emergence of fresh and largely unforeseen prospects for future growth. As we see it, this is precisely what is happening in the field of animal behavior. Beginning as a set of discrete inquiries, directed toward highly restricted questions, and carried forward chiefly by a few workers within psychology and zoology—most of whom were unknown to each other and unconcerned with the larger implications of their research—the field has grown steadily in scope and vigor.

A chapter in the *Annual Review of Psychology* provides an occasion to consider the recent history of these developments and to take a brief look ahead. We propose to make use of both viewpoints here since the emerging orientation toward animal behavior is so much broader in scope and richer in ideas and content than anything that has gone before that it requires this somewhat enlarged perspective.

We need not look back very far to appreciate that the changes have been broad and rapid. Less than 20 years ago, Karl Lashley summed up the existing situation as follows:

> The study of animal behavior during the present century has developed along two distinct lines, the products of professional psychologists in America and zoologists in Europe. In America the prevailing interest has been in the phenomenon of learning ... In Europe the comparative study of behavior has been chiefly in the hands of zoologists whose interests were in taxonomy, evolution and ecology rather than in learning theory (54).

129

This appeared in 1957, in a preface to one of the first books to offer English-speaking readers an introduction to the original scientific writings of the founding fathers of ethology. Lashley, who as a young man had worked with John B. Watson on the natural history of terns, was sympathetic with the ethological approach and no doubt believed that a synthesis was overdue. In fact, it was on its way. The formal announcement that it had taken place appeared less than a decade later, in 1966, with the publication of Robert Hinde's *Animal Behaviour: A Synthesis of Ethology and Comparative Psychology* (44).

Much has changed even within the relatively brief period since this masterful compendium was produced. Many of the questions that are being posed today involve so much more than was foreseen in the original programs of either ethology or comparative psychology that new names seem called for. And suggestions have not been wanting: Behavioral Biology (58), Sociobiology (95), Social Ethology (23), and Evolutionary-Behavioral Biology (11) are some of the more recent candidates.

Whatever it is called, it is clear that a new synthesis is emerging that draws heavily on biological sources and that promises to change our whole approach to behavior —to influence the kinds of questions we ask, our research strategies, our methods, and our long-range goals. The reasons for this change are many. Foremost among them is the fact that behavior is now seen as a major evolutionary achievement, which for most animal species is the principal vehicle mediating between the organism and its environment. A fundamental activity of the organism as a whole, behavior plays a central role in day-to-day adjustments, with obvious consequences for individual survival and evolutionary success. With a fuller realization of the implications of this fact, attitudes towards the place of behavioral studies in the biological sciences have undergone a fundamental change (3). For the same reasons, behavioral research is becoming increasingly informed by biological thought. These changes are still very much in the making, but they add up to a new orientation toward animal behavior whose major outlines are already clear. Our aim in this chapter is to describe the common elements in this orientation and to consider certain aspects of the comparative approach as they relate to the general problems of homology and analogy and to specific strategies and issues in studies of social behavior and learning.

THE COMMON GROUND

The major unifying theme in the current perspective is, of course, the synthetic theory of organic evolution. Within this framework there are a number of generally agreed upon principles and assumptions. Most prominent among these is that animal species are the products of natural selection, that genes are the foundation of all traits, structural and behavioral, and that selection favors those animals whose genes interact with the environment in such a fashion as to produce successful phenotypic outcomes, defined ultimately (and theoretically) in terms of reproductive success.

It is also generally recognized that natural selection operates directly on the phenotype—on the organism as a whole—and only indirectly on the genotype.[1] Behavior is one aspect of a larger organizational pattern that permits the animal to function with some degree of success within its natural environment. It follows, therefore, that the relation between the organism and its environment is the central question for behavioral inquiries, as it is for all biology. The "environment" in this case is not the environment in the nature-nurture issue. It is the environment in the ecological sense, including all those circumstances of habitat, predation, and social life with which organisms must cope. The study of behavior is thus focused on the diverse means through which organisms are able to adjust to their life circumstances and the ways in which these modes of coping have been achieved. Owing to this emphasis, natural history research has gained a new respectability. In addition to the traditional scientific goals of prediction and control, the animal behaviorist is now concerned with the "... integration of materials from different levels and sources into a pattern which illuminates and explains the behavior while maintaining an appreciation of the diversity of the processes involved, and of the diversity of the lives and natures of different animals" (56).

The elements required for such a broad synthesis depend upon a scientific division of labor, of course, which is based partly on the level of inquiry (e.g. physiological mechanisms, behavioral processes, ecological relations) and partly upon the kinds of questions that are asked. The four principal questions about any biological phenomenon, including behavior, have to do with *causation* (what makes it work, what is the mechanism?), *function* (how does it benefit the individual, contribute to "genetic" survival?), *ontogeny* (how does the mechanism develop in the individual?), and *evolution* (what course has it followed through time, what are the causes of its historical development?) (81, 86). A complete explanation of any biological phenomenon requires that attention be given to each of these questions and to the relations between them. To be sure, no one expects one person to have the time, the talent, or the inclination to develop the highly specialized knowledge and skills required to do creative work in all of these areas, but it is not unreasonable to expect that whatever his special line of research he will be aware of how it fits within the broader framework.

That this awareness is increasing is evident in recent textbooks (2, 10, 29, 92). These books make clear that the study of animal behavior is no longer tied to a handful of species, nor restricted to a single set of questions or method of approach. Analyses of mechanisms, functions, adaptation, and evolution have a necessary place in the animal behavior enterprise, and they require a diversity of specimens and procedures.

The growing concern with the integration of information from multiple levels and sources, with the different kinds of questions that must be considered, and with the diverse ways that animals have evolved for coping with their environments, has gone hand in hand with the development of what is sometimes called the *systems point*

[1]It is genetic selection, of course, which is critical for evolutionary change.

of view (1, 12, 19, 91). The major virtue of the systems orientation is heuristic, in that it provides a generalized set of carefully defined terms and explicit concepts for dealing with the organization and behavior of complex biological entities (functional part-systems, individuals, social groups, populations) within their environments.

The apology that animals are convenient and useful stand-ins for man in the investigation of complex psychological processes—which was never entirely persuasive—is being met with increasing skepticism in the general scientific community (76). Although this change reflects a more realistic and sophisticated understanding of the nature and limitations of comparative research, it could produce an unwarranted sharpening of the distinction between studies of animal behavior and research focused specifically on man.

Any animal behaviorist is bound to view the strengthening of this dichotomy as pernicious and fundamentally incompatible with a unified biological perspective toward behavior. Human behavior, after all, is also the result of natural selection. In spite of its unique features, it shares many commonalities with the behavior of nonhuman animals. An informed and critical evaluation of the origin and nature of these commonalities, as well as the attributes peculiar to man, requires an enlarged perspective toward behavior. The main source of ambivalence on the part of animal behaviorists toward such popular social commentaries as *The Territorial Imperative, On Aggression, The Naked Ape,* and *Beyond Freedom and Dignity* is that these works assert the commonalities while neglecting the differences that are equally important to a complete comparative approach to human behavior, the aim of which is neither to exalt nor diminish the human species, but to see it in the contexts of its origins and its relations to its environment and to the other creatures of the earth.

THE PROBLEM OF COMPARISONS

The comparative method, applied to a description of similarities and differences among animal species, is at the very heart of the animal behavior enterprise. Everyone agrees that the appropriate application of this method can lead toward a general understanding of animal behavior. Such understanding may take the form of deducing or reconstructing the evolution of a particular functional pattern (7), providing a broader perspective on how part-processes operate within the total life history of a species or group of species (57), discovering the "rules" and "strategies" of the evolutionary process (50), arriving at a general statement of mechanisms or principles governing behavior (74), or clarifying the selective consequences of a given behavior pattern (61, 94).

It is also accepted virtually as axiomatic that the most significant and profitable behaviors for study are those that can be presumed to play some useful role in the survival of the individual or the species (61, 74, 82). Functionally defined behaviors are likely to hang together, to be components of "natural" systems (and thus more amenable to causal analysis). Moreover, similar functional patterns in different species very often appear to have identical survival value, thereby offering clues as to how similar selection pressures give rise to similar behavioral outcomes (parallel or convergent evolution).

Within these broad areas of agreement many possibilities exist for uncertainty, confusion, and differences of opinion. One problem concerns selection of the appropriate organizational level for interspecies comparison. Should we focus on broad life-history patterns, on particular systems identified by functional criteria, or on specific part-processes within such systems? The difficulties here seem easily resolved. Clearly, the appropriate level for comparison will depend upon the kind of questions that are asked, as will the choice of methods and the kinds of generalizations that may be expected to come out of the data (97). No given level is appropriate to all questions. Studies focused on more proximate causes will most often deal with part-processes within some broader functionally defined system—for example, the effects of specific hormones on maternal behavior. Descriptive studies or studies directed toward establishing correlations between ecological factors and social organization will most often be concerned with total life-history patterns.

A more difficult and convoluted issue revolves around the status and relative merits of interspecies comparisons based on homologous behaviors (that is, behaviors similar by reason of common descent) and on functional analogies (that is, similar patterns that are not based on similarities in the genotype). It is commonly suggested that homologous behaviors should occupy a central place in comparative research, and (because similarities in distantly related species are likely to be analogous) that the most useful comparisons will be within restricted taxonomic levels (7–9, 58). Such claims need to be examined critically.

Two aspects of the problem can be readily distinguished. First, what is the special value of homologies in the comparative approach? If one is interested in reconstructing the evolution of a given pattern or trait within a taxonomic series, or in drawing inferences about phyletic relatedness, a focus on homologous behaviors is plainly desirable, if not essential (85). Apart from rather specialized concerns of this sort, however, there are no compelling reasons for advocating that interspecies comparisons be limited to homologous behaviors. In fact, Ratner (74) has described a comparative approach to animal behavior in which the concept of homology has no place.

A second question is whether one can in fact identify behavioral homologies with some degree of confidence. Here opinions vary, owing in large part to the ambiguities inherent in the concept of homology. The concept has its roots in comparative morphology, and originally referred to similarities in structural organization between different types of organisms, without regard to evolutionary origins. It was only later that similar structural arrangements in closely related species came to be thought of as reflecting common genetic mechanisms (9, 38).

As DeBeer (27) points out, however, the connection between genotype and phenotype is infinitely complex, even when one is dealing with relatively simple morphological characters. Since natural selection operates directly on the phenotype, it is entirely possible that within a given phyletic series a character controlled by one set of genes may in the course of time come under the control of a different set. For example, comparative embryological studies indicate that quite similar structures in related species may be formed from different embryological tissues, or result from different developmental mechanisms (27). It is clearly the phenotypic outcome that is critical, and one cannot discount the possibility that similar characters, even in closely related species, may be the result of parallel adaptations or convergent evolutionary processes. In spite of these problems, DeBeer advocates retaining the concept of homology in comparative morphology because of its unique value in relating structures of organisms to their phylogenetic histories.

The possibility that motor patterns could be homologized in the same sense as anatomical patterns played a seminal role in the early development of comparative ethology. Indeed, Lorenz has recently remarked that he regards the discovery that the concepts of analogy and homology are as applicable to characters of behavior as to morphological characters as his most important scientific contribution (61). Notwithstanding the historical significance of this discovery, it is now generally recognized that the establishment of behavioral homologies poses more difficult problems than does the recognition of structural homologies, particularly when the behavioral characters involve more than relatively simple stereotyped motor patterns.

Opinions vary on the severity of the difficulties. The traditional ethological position, presented in recent papers by Lorenz (61) and Wickler (94), continues to see broad application for the concept of homology. Wickler, for example, believes that the concept is potentially relevant to all behavior characters, from insect courtship to human cultural traditions (see also Lorenz for a similar view). It is noteworthy, however, that the papers by both Lorenz and Wickler are primarily concerned with clarifying the meaning and utility of the concept of analogy. Wickler goes so far as to urge "... the need to study convergencies instead of homologies, which have been favored in the past" (94, p. 68).

Beer is more cautious. Although he recognizes that the concept of homology "... lacks the precision and rigor that one is accustomed to in science ...," he maintains that it is of central importance to comparative ethology. He believes that, applied to closely related species and pursued with proper methodological sophistication, the concept of homology can lead to plausible accounts of behavioral evolution (8). Atz (6) takes a more uncompromising position, arguing that homology, an essentially morphological concept, can seldom be meaningfully applied to behavior in our present state of knowledge because the structural correlates of specific behavior patterns have not been worked out. Klopfer (50) is also pessimistic. The difficulties in establishing behavioral homologies are so serious, he believes, that all attempts to reconstruct the evolutionary history of a particular behavior pattern are on shaky ground, and extrapolations from one species to another are likely to prove of little value, possibly even in those instances in which independent evidence of ancestry exists.

Although we believe that the concept of behavioral homology has a necessary place in comparative research, it seems destined to play a much more restricted and specialized role in the immediate future than it has in the recent past. Because of the serious difficulties in identifying homologous behavioral characters with confidence, and the likelihood that seemingly homologous patterns are the result of convergent evolution, it must be presumed that most interspecies comparisons refer to analogous traits or processes. Moreover, it is clear that the concept of homology will not be useful in approaching questions of behavioral adaptation to differing ecological conditions, and thus will play little part in one of the current major themes in the study of animal behavior. The concept of analogy, on the other hand, is ideally suited to present needs and interests. Increased reliance on this concept should result in a more sophisticated and deliberate approach to the treatment of analogical comparisons.

Such a change is bound to be beneficial. Much of the current confusion and debate over the scientific status of comparative statements reflects a failure to make the necessary distinction between homology and analogy, and to recognize the nature and limitations of inferences based on analogical comparisons. In contrast to the concept of homology, the concept of analogy, even in its pre-Darwinian beginnings, referred to function (38, 67). In modern usage analogs are functional similarities, not related by community of descent. Presumably they are often a response to similar environmental demands (80).

The important point is that as a matter of practice behavioral similarities between species are characteristically established (at least initially) using purely functional criteria—for example, feeding behavior, mating behavior, filial behavior, aggressive behavior, learned behavior, etc—that is, on the basis of analogy. There is inevitably an element of personal or consensual judgment in this process. The observer identifies (more strictly speaking, hypothesizes) a function or set of functions around which various behaviors appear to be organized. Apart from such common functions, the nature and number of additional points of similarity are empirical matters. One cannot assume a priori that similar functions are necessarily making the same contribution to survival, or that they are responses to similar selection pressures. Nor can one assume that similar functions are dependent upon similar mechanisms. Behaviors that seem to serve the same function may differ in form, in their relation to physiological variables, to eliciting stimuli, and to developmental history (61, 67, 94).

Inasmuch as the majority of comparative statements must be presumed to be based on perceived analogies, the disciplined use of analogical reasoning becomes an important part of the logic of the comparative method. Lorenz claims that there are no "false" analogies. Perhaps this is correct—analogies, after all, are in the mind of the analogizer. He adds, however, that analogies can be more or less detailed and hence more or less informative (61). True, but a more useful distinction, we believe, is between strong and weak analogies. To make such a distinction requires a clear statement of the level(s) at which the analogy applies (e.g. physiological mechanism, spatiotemporal organization of specific behaviors, patterns of social interaction, social systems), and a balanced and systematic assessment of interspecies similarities and differences at the relevant level(s) (67). The strength of an analogy increases as a function of the number of significant resemblances at a given level and the number of levels at which similarities occur. Indeed, strong analogies, coupled with independent evidence of phyletic relatedness, provide an excellent base for establishing behavioral homologies.

Analogous comparisons, it should be noted, imply the development of conceptual models, in which the structure (i.e. elements of the model and relations among elements) worked out on one species is expected to show partial but not complete isomorphism, with a similar structure worked out on a different species. Relations between analogous models or between models and the natural phenomena to which they refer can be evaluated in terms of "goodness of fit." The accepted functions of such models are to put together diverse facts or observations within a coherent framework, to broaden the base for generalizations, lead to new questions, and to generate predictions, based on assumptions implied in the model. The choice of domain to which models are addressed depends entirely on theoretical considerations. Thus we find models based on analogous comparisons of the causal basis for the development of filial bonds in birds and primates (46), of patterns of social structure in relation to ecology (24, 32), and of learned performance in various species (14).

Misunderstandings arise chiefly when analogical comparisons are confused with comparisons based on homology—a shortcoming to which comparative psychologists are sometimes prone—or when the analogies are *weak* (vague with respect to specification of levels and of characters or traits) or *strained* (similarities at one level are made a basis for claiming similarities at quite different levels)—shortcomings evident in the popular writings of the ethologists. B. F. Skinner provides the best-known example of an approach that does not distinguish clearly between comparisons based on analogy and homology. Skinner clearly recognizes the existence of phylogenetic differences in behavior. In his search for universals of learning, however, he chooses to disregard them. This is accomplished by designing learning situations and measures of learned performance that eliminate species differences. By judicious selection of stimuli, responses, and reinforcers " . . . species differences in sensory equipment, in effector systems, in susceptibility to reinforcement, and in possible disruptive repertoires are minimized. The data then show an extraordinary uniformity over a wide range of species" (82, p. 1210). The analogies are strong at the selected level (that is, rate of responding, as a function of manipulated stimulus and reinforcement variables) but narrow, since they apply only within a rather circumscribed domain, defined by specific experimental arrangements and procedures. Outside this operationally specified domain the case for interspecies generality and uniformity in learned performance is seriously weakened (16, 45, 93). Unlike many psychologists, the ethologists have generally been aware of the importance of distinguishing between homology and analogy, but analogies have often been weak and strained, particularly in popular accounts (67, 90). Once more, we draw our examples from a notable contributor. Konrad Lorenz (60) refers to the "aggressive instinct" in such species as stickleback fish, geese, and man—which not only implies that the mechanism for aggression is unitary [for contrary evidence, see Moyer (70)], but also that the same mechanism is responsible for aggressive behavior in these diverse species. Lorenz is plainly aware that this is not the case, and leaves no doubt that his comparisons of distant species are based on functional analogies. At the same time, however, his analogies are frequently vague with respect to levels and points of comparison; similarities are emphasized rather than differences; and the analogies are often strained. These characteristic shortcomings can be seen in the following excerpts fi ɔm a discussion of pair bonds in goose and man:

> If, in the Greylag Goose and in man, highly complex norms of behavior, such as falling in love, strife for ranking order, jealousy, grieving, etc., are not only similar but down to the most absurd details the same, we can be sure that every one of these instincts has a very special survival value, in each case almost or quite the same in the Greylag and in man (60, p. 218).

And later in the same section: "In all these points this bond is analogous with those human functions that go hand in hand with the emotions of love and friendship in their purest and noblest form" (p. 219).

THE PROBLEM OF SOCIAL BEHAVIOR

For many years the biological study of social behavior was primarily concerned with the evolution and function of social signals, generally from the standpoint of homologous comparisons. Darwin's *The Expression of the Emotions in Animals and Man* (26), often cited as a cornerstone of ethology (51, 59), unequivocally expressed the homologist's faith:

> With mankind some expressions, such as the bristling of hair under the influence of extreme terror, or the uncovering of the teeth under that of furious rage, can hardly be understood, except on the belief that man once existed in a much lower and animal-like condition. The community of certain expressions in distinct though allied species, as in the movements of the same facial muscles during laughter by the man and by various monkeys, is rendered somewhat more intelligible, if we believe in their descent from a common progenitor. He who admits on general grounds that the structure and habits of all animals have been gradually evolved, will look at the whole subject of Expression in a new and interesting light (26, p. 12).

Darwin's position was that a single set of emotions extended throughout a large number of vertebrate taxa and that their expression was a conservative trait, firmly established by natural selection during eons of evolution, and usually modified only by the special circumstances of changed morphology of the expressive organs. Andrew's (5) analysis of the evolution of facial expression is a recent example of the Darwinian approach and assumptions.

From the Darwinian thesis that social motivations (emotions) and their expression are widely shared (at least in mammals), it is but a short step to conceptualizing the resulting social relationships also as homologous processes. Thus the social behavior of one species can be viewed as based on the same mechanisms and controlled by the same causal factors as that of a related species.

In comparative psychology, behavior and social relationships presumed to be homologous to those of man are often studied by establishing conditions similar to those in which humans characteristically live or might be expected to encounter.

Perhaps the strongest development of this approach is found in the work of Harlow and his associates on rhesus monkeys (43). The patent concern with using nonhuman primates as a means of investigating distinctively human problems is a specialized application of the comparative approach, and it presents some unusual interpretive difficulties.

The use of rhesus monkeys (or whatever nonhuman primate) in such research is justified chiefly on the grounds of phyletic relatedness. It is assumed that strong parallels exist between monkey and man in the organization of social behavior. An experimental analog of some human social situation is established for the monkey —such as providing a behaviorally deviant monkey with a conspecific "psychotherapist" or raising it as a member of a monogamous "nuclear family"—in the apparent expectation that the monkey's responses are either homologs or functional analogs to those that man would make to the same situation. With specific reference to animal models in psychiatry, McKinney and Bunney (68, 69) indicate four criteria that, in generalized form, apply to the evaluation of all such research. The criteria refer to the degree of similarity between the animal "preparation" and the human condition in (a) the situation, (b) behavioral responses to the situation, (c) underlying mechanisms, and (d) the organism's responses to systematic manipulation of the independent variable(s). Although each of these criteria presents problems, they are for the most part similar to those already considered in our earlier general discussion of the comparative approach. The criterion of situational similarity, however, raises new questions that stand much in need of clarification.

In the examples of rhesus psychotherapists and nuclear families, the concern is plainly with human situations that have no apparent counterpart in the normal social life of these nonhuman primates. Indeed, no claim is made that they do. Even though it is clear that the reference situation is human, however, the specific assumptions and expections behind the animal analogy need to be examined. Two rather different emphases can be distinguished.

On the one hand, the experimental situation may aim to *simulate* (that is provide a literal copy of) actual elements in the natural habitat—as is implied in the use of such terms as "psychotherapists" or "nuclear families." It is evident that laboratory simulations of human environments for nonhuman subjects are likely to lack fidelity. The best examples of faithful simulations are the chimpanzee rearing experiments as in the research by Kohts, the Kelloggs, the Hayses, and the Gardners, in which the subject is actually brought up within a human household. On the other hand, the laboratory situation may aim to create a *model* which bears only a schematic or structural resemblance to variables encountered in the natural environment. That is, rather than striving to achieve ecological fidelity, this approach aims for structural isomorphism between the elements of the model and certain events or attributes of the natural environment.

Investigators are not likely to consider whether they are dealing with simulated environments or structural models. A clearer awareness of the distinction, however, will lead to more effective experimental research and fewer interpretive difficulties. With few exceptions meaningful simulations are best carried out within a framework of within-species comparisons in which the focal concern is either with improving the quality of normative data or with examining the consequences of variations in the natural environment.

Simulations are thus continuous with so-called experiments of nature in which the same species is available to observation in contrasting environments. A simulation presupposes only that a reasonably complete description of the natural environment is available. Models, however, have the additional requirement that a structural analysis of the environment is completed before the model is established. A model lends itself more readily than does a simulation to between-species comparisons and to the identification of effective variables, but it is necessarily more restricted in scope and several steps further removed from the natural environment. Although active manipulation of independent variables is often associated with a modeling approach to the environment, this is not a necessary feature. For example, in Mason & Epple's (66) comparative study of social organization in titi monkeys and squirrel monkeys, groups of both species were observed in an enclosure containing elevated pathways, widely dispersed food stations and shelters, and a relatively low population density—all of which corresponded (however imperfectly) to certain structural attributes of the natural environment. In no sense, however, could this situation be considered a faithful simulation of the actual habitat of either species.

The distinction between the two approaches to studying the environment as a determinant of behavior is fundamental. As J. Altmann (4) points out in a very useful discussion of observational methods, models (our term) often rank high in internal validity (i.e. reliability of statements about the sample) and low on external validity (i.e. reliability of generalizations from the sample to other situations and populations), whereas simulations, like field studies, are most successful in maximizing external validity. Although one can always try to maximize both kinds of validity, this ideal is never fully achieved in practice. The analytic precision that a model provides can only be attained at some cost in external validity, whereas to the extent that a simulation approaches the richness of the real-life situation it multiplies the number of alternative hypotheses that may account for the data.

Both the richness and the ambiguity are clearly illustrated in the approach to social organization as an adaptation to ecological circumstances. This perspective was being developed at about the same time that experimental investigations of social behavior were going forward, and it raises a new set of interpretive problems. It also focused on comparisons of related species, but with a view to understanding how behavior provided the means for successful radiation into new habitats or life styles. Rather than stressing the conservative nature of social traits and similarities across species, however, the emphasis here was on evolutionary divergence from a common ("ancestral") pattern in response to different environmental demands or opportunities.

A classic example of such divergence is the dash for cover in the threatened young of the beach nesting herring gull, as compared with the stationary appeasement signaling of threatened young in the related cliff-nesting kittiwake (whose life circumstances make any dash suicidal) (25). Such studies pointed up the niche-specificity of behavior patterns and their sensitivity to specific selection pressures.

Social Organization and Ecological Constraints

The same line of reasoning was soon extended to entire social systems, viewed as sets of co-adapted behaviors. Variations in social organization among closely related species were approached as adaptive radiations from some prototypic pattern in response to specific selection pressures and environmental opportunities (22, 75).

This development coincided with the exponential growth of field studies of social organization during the 1950s and 1960s, and the results of such studies were interpreted within this framework (24, 30, 31).

Perhaps the best known of these analyses is the one advanced to explain the troop composition of Anubis baboons (28). These savannah vegetation eaters exploit an environment containing a reasonably lush plant community, which they share with a number of herbivores, mostly various species of antelope. This dense population of large herbivores supports a sizable and varied population of big carnivores. The carnivores also pose a threat to the rather slow and small savannah baboons. Baboon exploitation of the savannah plant community is presumed to require a social system which contains a number of vigorous and cooperative adult and subadult males, essentially as antipredator devices. Strong sexual dimorphism and tolerance and cooperation among males were presumably the "optimum" solution available to these animals in response to the particular conditions of relative dense food supplies and strong predation pressure that prevail on the African savannah.

The Anubis social organization has been contrasted with that of a close relative, the desert dwelling Hamadryas baboon. The Hamadryas lives in an environment that lacks the plant base necessary to support a large population of herbivores, hence heavy predation pressure from big carnivores is not a serious problem (53). However, the scarcity of plants also means that large foraging groups of baboons cannot find enough food to go around. The increased demand for smaller foraging units, and relaxation of predator pressure requiring cooperation among mature males, are considered the basis for a behavioral radiation from the Anubis ancestral pattern to one in which the basic social unit is a single male and his jealously guarded group of females. [It may be noted here that the importance of predation pressure in the evolution of these and other social systems is usually inferred rather than determined empirically. The observed frequency of predation may be quite rare, though this can be a poor indication of its biological significance, especially in long-lived, slowly reproducing species. The impact of predation can be evaluated more accurately by systematic observations of the predator, rather than the prey (52).]

As an outgrowth of this approach, it seems reasonable to analyze social systems in terms of "goodness of fit" between the system and the requirements of the environment (24). Although comparisons are generally based on closely related species, there is an implicit assumption of generality. Given certain ecological pressures or constraints, it is assumed that the prototypic pattern of social organization will be modified in predictable ways, the outcome of which is the improvement, if not optimization, of evolutionary success. Thus an entire social system can be viewed as an adaptive unit, and the principle that analogous functions have the same survival value is thereby extended from individual organisms to social organization.

Recent efforts to test the idea that patterns of social organization are closely tied to ecological constraints have not been completely successful. For example, when Moynihan applied the theory worked out on Old World primates to the monkeys of the New World, he concluded that it had little predictive power. In fact, there seemed to be almost no end to the kinds of social organization that were effective in successfully exploiting any given ecological situation (71).

In a similar undertaking, Estes (33) analyzed the social systems of 70 species of African bovids (mostly antelopes) as a function of their ecological circumstances. He suggests that the ancestral pattern was that of a solitary forest dweller, whose radiation into the remarkably diverse forms of plains antelope communities was aided and accompanied by an increase in the size of social groups and the complexity of social systems. Exceptions were found, and it is noteworthy that in dealing with them Estes does not rely on arguments based on special environmental circumstances. Instead he notes that the bulk of the exceptions occur in the subfamily bovinae, thus invoking phylogenetic history as an important determinant of social organization.

Kaufman (48) attempted to apply ecologic arguments similar to those developed by Estates to the prediction of social organization in kangaroos. This is clearly an appropriate extension. Kangaroos and African bovids are subject to similar selection pressures and fill similar ecological roles. They are both the major large grazers and browsers in the plains and woodland plant communities of their respective continents. At the most general level the arguments had some predictive power, but even here it was, as Kaufman says, "modest." In particular the degree of social complexity that Estes found to be typical of open country grazers is not really approached by any of the 45 species of the macropodidae. Kaufman interprets this lack of correspondence between bovid and macropodid patterns on a phylogenetic basis, arguing that the levels of social complexity achieved by the African bovids cannot be expressed by kangaroos under similar circumstances because they lack the requisite behavioral resources.

From the standpoint of interspecies comparisons of social systems, the Estes-Kaufman studies arrive at a kind of halfway house. On the one hand, comparisons are based on similar ecological circumstances, and the observed similarities in social outcomes between different species are interpreted on the basis of functional analogies (convergent evolution). On the other hand, both men are inclined to attribute discrepancies from the theoretically expected outcome to the intrusion of phylogenetic constraints, presumably shared by all species within a larger taxonomic unit (20).

That such constraints exist is not surprising, of course, but to fall back on them as an ad hoc explanation of deviations from theoretical expectancy does not take us very far toward understanding the evolution of social systems. What is required is a causal analysis at the level of the individual animals that are the products and producers of the social systems. The limits of complexity of social organization, the range of adaptability, and the sources of stability and change must be sought in events occurring within the system—which is to say at the level of interbehaving individuals. This does not imply that each member of a social species carries a "blueprint" of the species-typical pattern of social organization; nor does it suggest a return to simple dyadic encounters as the method of choice in studies of social behavior. Rather, the intent is to emphasize the need in discussions of between- and within-species variations in social organization to consider such matters as patterns and sources of attraction and repulsion, abilities to deal with various kinds and amounts of social information, and the potential for achieving different forms and levels of social skill. Such questions—which define social systems research, one of the three components in Crook's (23) programmatic statement of social ethology— are only beginning to be investigated within a comparative framework (53, 65).

The hypothesis that entire social systems are adaptive units has dominated field research for more than a decade. It is easy to appreciate why this should be so. It reinforces the general view that social organization, like individual behavior, is tested at the ecological level, and it seems to account for otherwise inexplicable variations in social organization by invoking established evolutionary principles. It remains an hypothesis, however, and its major value will not be found in its explanatory power, but in the kinds of questions to which it has directed attention.

Altruistic Behavior and Kinship Selection Theory

The emphasis on the whole social system operating as an adaptive unit contained an apparent paradox. In field research the behavior of individuals was often described and analyzed in terms of its contribution to the welfare of the group. It was sometimes implied that individuals occasionally behaved in ways that benefited the group as a whole without deriving any advantage themselves; often, in fact, such behavior entailed a personal risk. Whether or not such an idea is emotionally appealing depends upon one's politics. But intellectually it strikes at the very foundation of the theory of natural selection. It implies that a trait that *decreases* the reproductive rate of an individual (and hence his contribution to the next generation's gene pool) can be preserved by selection. The concept of group selection, advocated by Wynne-Edwards (96), can account for the loss of breeding potential by some individuals on the grounds that it is "good for the group." But contemporary evolutionary thought gives little if any credence to the idea that natural selection will preserve traits that do not in some fashion yield a net genetic gain to the individual actor.

The validity of some of the phenomena that seemed to Wynne-Edwards to require the concept of group selection is questionable (e.g. "epideictic displays," leading to voluntary withdrawal from reproductive activity). Yet there remain certain classes of behavior that seem to confound the theory that natural selection operates on individuals. Among the most salient of these is "altruistic" behavior. By definition, such behavior confers no apparent or direct reproductive advantage on the actor, while providing tangible benefits to other individuals who are not its direct descendants. For example, the alarmed pronghorn flashes conspicuous rump patches that seemingly alert other pronghorns to danger (49). But if other pronghorns are warned of the presence of a predator, the individual spreading the alarm has obviously made himself more visible and hence more vulnerable. How can natural selection preserve such behavior?

The repertoire of those struggling with this sort of issue has been enlarged by the advance of kinship selection theory (41, 42). Hamilton calls attention to the fact that while most individuals are unique collections of genes, they hold varying numbers of those genes in common with other members of their species, the number of shared genes being predictable on the average from the degree of consanguinity. An individual's parent or its full sibling share half that individual's genes (with certainty in a parent's case, and on the average in a sibling's case), so two offspring from parents or siblings carry as many of that individual's genes into the next generation as one of its own offspring. Thus natural selection will preserve any behavior that favors the survival of relatives so long as the number of shared genes being transmitted by them outweighs the reduction in one's own reproductive success. Altruism can develop only when the genetic gain to the altruist exceeds the genetic cost.

The arithmetic virtually assures cooperative relationships among individuals, varying as a predictable function of two things: first, the average degree of genetic relationship, and second, the balance between the positive influence one can have on a relative's reproductive success, and the reduction in one's own reproductive success. The quantification of these positive and negative effects in any given instance may be a laborious and uncertain task, but this has no bearing on the logic of the argument. If individuals vary in a way that produces a net gain in the numerical representation of their own genes in the next generation through helping others, and the basis for such variation is hereditary, then kinship selection is at work. Thus kinship selection theory demonstrates that altruism is only a special case of natural selection.

The value of this idea is that it directs attention to the costs and benefits of social acts and of social life in general (21). The theory of kin selection predicts relationships, not in terms of their form, but in terms of their outcome.

The analysis is essentially economic and is based on the postulate that each individual must behave in such a manner that in the long run the (genetic) benefits it derives from group life exceed its costs. Thus a theoretical basis is supplied for formulating optimal strategies that can be compared against the actual patterns of social relations at each stage of a social animal's life cycle.

The basic argument of "genetic self-interest" advanced to explain altruistic behavior has been recently extended to include sexual selection, parental investment, parent/offspring conflict, mutual aid between unrelated individuals (reciprocal altruism), and certain aspects of social status (87–89; Popp & DeVore, personal communication). The task of testing these theoretical notions against the social dynamics of complex "multi-purpose" groups has scarcely begun. Certainly it presents formidable difficulties; indeed, there are no assurances at this point that it can be accomplished on a broad scale. Even so, the heuristic value of the approach is enormous. Many questions have been raised that in the recent past were obscured by the tacit assumption that natural selection operates at the level of the social system, irrespective of (or at the expense of) the genetic success of particular individuals. The questions are founded on analogy, with the difference, of course, that in this case the analogies concern the arithmetical balance between the benefits and costs (measured by the frequency with which one's genes are represented in the next generation's gene pool) that derive from the sum total of the individual's participation in group life.

E. O. Wilson has remarked that the "... formulation of theory of sociobiology offers one of the great manageable tasks of biology for the next twenty or so years" (95). Such a theory, as Wilson sees it, will transcend the particularities of homology and phylogenetic history and aim to encompass all social species: "When the same parameters and quantitative theory are used to analyze both termite colonies and troops of rhesus macaques, we will have a unified science of sociobiology" (p. 400).

The prospect of an integrative theory of such sweep and grandeur is bound to enliven the field for generations to come. We feel that the approach Wilson outlines will properly constitute one of the major directions that studies of animal social behavior will follow. Yet it would be unfortunate if it became our only guide. While an evolutionary perspective must provide the basic conceptual framework, an evolutionary *explanation* of social behavior is necessarily incomplete. One thing that is missing is an understanding of the complex machinery of social behavior, the many ways of being and becoming a functioning member of a viable and ongoing social system.

Even if the behavior of termites and rhesus should lead to some functionally identical social outcome, the developmental and social processes by which individuals of these species establish and maintain their social systems are clearly quite different in many ways. Sex roles have different hormonal bases; group membership is determined by radically different mechanisms; and experience, one of the major determinants of behavior, plays a profoundly different part. To ignore these essential contrasts would be a fatal error.

We do not suppose this specter is before us. Interest in the organization and causation of behavior shows no sign of fading. The study of learning, for example, has taken on a new vitality, a reflection in part of the same intellectual trends that we have noted in the area of social behavior.

THE PROBLEM OF LEARNING

Man views himself as the learner par excellence. He also recognizes, of course, that the ability to learn is widely distributed throughout the animal kingdom, and he has long assumed that the efficiency, amount, and variety of learning increases in direct proportion to a species' relatedness to man. What could be more appropriate, therefore, than to investigate how such an ability evolves progressively into its human form, and to discover the general laws that govern this biologically important function? Perhaps no one ever wholly embraced this commonsensical view, but for many years comparative research on learning was conducted as though guided by such a theme.

With few exceptions scientists concerned with the evolution of learning were also interested in the role of the brain in learned performance. Most research assumed a rather small number of basic abilities that could be determined adequately by measuring performance in standard tests, and that each such ability was a function of some identifiable structure or process occupying a definite location within the central nervous system. Homologous structures in different species were presumed to serve homologous functions. Again we oversimplify perhaps, but unless some like assumption is made it is difficult to see how such techniques as selective ablation, local anesthesia, or recording from specific brain sites in rats or cats or monkeys (which essentially exhausts the species roster in these studies) could be expected to yield results of more than limited generality.

The approach of M. E. Bitterman—one which has produced some of the most systematic data on comparative aspects of learning—was developed within this general tradition (13–15). There were several significant departures, however. First, as an alternative to surgical intervention as a means of determining relations between brain and learning, he chose to study intact animals representing species with different brains. Second, he rejected the assumption that the laws of learning were the same for all animals in favor of the hypothesis that differences in brain structure produce qualitative differences in learning. Third, he advocated comparison based on functional relations rather than numerical scores. Fourth, to minimize the confounding effects of sensory, motor, or motivational factors, he devised the method of control by systematic variations (13, 14).

In spite of such innovations, however, the search for meaningful correlations between learning ability and taxonomic standing has not been rewarded. The current situation is summed up by Warren (93):

> Comparisons of vertebrate species in terms of their performances on standard laboratory tests of learning yield no convincing support for the notions that animals can be characterized in terms of a general ability to learn and that the distribution of this trait is correlated with taxonomic rank. A given species may learn as well as, or better or worse than, a second species, depending upon the nature of the task and the conditions of testing.

That the classical approach to the comparative psychology of learning was based on faulty ideas of the nature of homology and the action of natural selection is now generally recognized. Many authors are urging greater attention to the specific requirements an animal faces in its natural habitat, and comparisons between closely related species confronting different ecological demands, or between unrelated species confronting similar demands. The emphasis thus shifts from variations in homologous processes (the now discredited traditional approach) to the study of divergence and functional analogies.

The idea that behavioral plasticity (or the lack of it) should be approached from the ecological perspective is not new. It has long been advocated by people attempting to understand the behavior of animals in their natural surroundings. For example, Tinbergen (84) and Lehrman (55) note that what animals need to learn may be determined by particular aspects of their habitat and life style, and that the kinds of behavioral plasticity that characterize a given species are often closely correlated with specific ecological demands. A hunting wasp, for example, must use local landmarks to find the tunnel she has dug in the sand when she returns to it with food for her young. She can acquire such information in a reconnaissance flight of a few seconds; yet she is implacably stupid in most ways (84). Similarly, Lehrman (55) points out that

... the ability of red-winged blackbirds to select birds of the same species as mates depends to some extent on their experience. In the cowbird, which is fairly closely related to the blackbird, no such effect is possible since cowbirds are brood parasites, in which all individuals are reared by foster parents of other species and then must find fellow members of their own species when all their early experience has been with birds of other species.

The use of demonstrated or suspected ecological demand to interpret species differences in learning characterizes what Seligman & Hager (78) call the "new comparative psychology," samples of which can be found in Shettleworth (79), Hinde & Stevenson-Hinde (45), as well as in Seligman & Hager. There is currently a sense that conceptualization of the role of experience in behavior has just taken a quantum step forward. Not only are old processes (e.g. imitation, observational learning, perceptual learning, etc) being revived and old paradigms revisited, but new paradigms are being devised to accommodate a spate of new and qualitatively different data.

We have no intention of reviewing these developments in detail. The few topics we have chosen serve to illustrate some of the achievements and interpretive problems resulting from the current ecological emphasis on learning. The central issue, as we see it, revolves around the generality of the learning process. Admittedly, learning is at all points influenced by species-typical constraints. Nevertheless, it seems obvious that some forms of learning are closely tied to quite specific ecological requirements—often at certain phases of the life cycle (as in imprinting)—whereas other forms of learning are to some extent "emancipated" from the particularities of the environment and thus become major contributors to adaptability. We realize that the distinction is one of degree, but with the increasing emphasis on ecological influences, it is essential to bear in mind that the evolutionary process can result in radical changes in adaptive "strategies," of which reliance on learning seems to be one of singular importance.

Acquisition of Bird Song

The acquisition of bird song provides an excellent illustration of how learning can relate in highly specific ways to the particular life-history requirements of a species. In a number of birds, full development of the male courtship song depends on the opportunity to hear the adult song of the species at specific stages during development (72, 73, 83). Such birds reared in acoustical isolation generally produce a song that bears a definite structural resemblance to the adult song but lacks its richness (62). If the basic song has local dialects, dialectical peculiarities are, of course, missing.

The degree to which the male courtship song is open to modification by experience varies widely across species. The parasitic cowbird, whose courtship song is a unique, unmelodic squawk (39), lays its eggs in the nests of a variety of host species, so that its young are exposed to a range of adult songs during development. Nevertheless, as adults they display the species-typical song. The reproductive advantages of the cowbird's resistance to experiential influences on song development are obvious, for adult birds must be able to locate and identify conspecifics, no matter which species serve as its foster parents.

White crowned sparrows display a species-typical courtship song with regional dialects, and young male white crowns are predisposed to learn the species-typical song (62). Isolated young males exposed to two songs, one which is typical of the species and another which is not, will sing the species song as adults (64). Some learning is clearly involved, however, for they acquire whichever white crown dialect they are exposed to. This means that local dialects could accomplish reproductive isolation of locally adapted races, thus contributing to the adaptation of the species to a range of local conditions (62).

As in some interpretations of social systems, this analysis opposes the adaptive and the phylogenetic bases for the response to experience. Marler (62) compares the predictive value of phylogenetic history with that of adaptation, noting that in the taxonomic group from which white crown sparrows are drawn, very closely related species differ greatly in the degree to which the male courtship song can be modified by experience, and that such differences are adaptively correlated with habitat characteristics. Thus ecological demand, in this instance, is a better predictor of how experience will influence behavior than is phylogenetic history.

The experimental analysis of bird song development has remained firmly tied to parameters directly relevant to the natural environment. Sounds have been selected from the bird's real world (with the exception of "unnatural" control stimuli), and interpretations have been closely tied to significant life-history events. The result has been an exemplary demonstration of the ways in which specific predispositions interact with certain experiences, at certain times in the life cycle, to produce an important adaptive outcome.

This is a substantial and worthwhile accomplishment. The discovery of an important phenomenon, however, is usually accompanied by the temptation, or (depending upon your point of view) the obligation, to extend its generality. With respect to the findings on bird song, Marler has suggested certain developmental parallels with the acquisition of human language, such as dependence on imitation, presence of critical periods, dialects, importance of auditory feedback, and lateralization of neural control (63). In this case, the intent is heuristic. No claim is made for a close functional analogy between bird song and human speech. Instead, the data are used to support the view that speech development, like song development, is modifiable only within well-defined biological limits.

This is a rather modest claim, and few would care to dispute it. At the same time, however, one somehow misses the sweeping statements that were the style in a brasher era. This is more than mere nostalgia for a period when ignorance gave license to flights of fancy. How does one attempt to maximize the generality of his findings? We have no answer, but it will be instructive to consider another approach to the problem of constraints on learning. In contrast to the study of song development, which had its roots firmly in the naturalistic tradition of ethology, this development originated in an "accidental" discovery in the experimental learning laboratory.

Acquisition of Food Aversion

Garcia and his co-workers discovered two rather remarkable facts about learning in the rat. First, they found that when a toxic agent (such as irradiation) is paired with ingestion of substances having a particular taste quality, the taste quickly acquires the property of inhibiting drinking or eating of the substance it identifies. In contrast, a visual or auditory stimulus paired with the same toxic stimulus does not acquire this inhibitory effect (36). Secondly, they found that an association between the taste quality and the toxic agent will occur even when the delay between ingestion and the aversive condition is more than an hour (34) (in contrast to the fraction of a second to which such effects are normally limited with arbitrarily chosen UCS, UCR, and CS combinations).

These findings are often cited as a demonstration of the situation-specific character of learning, and are interpreted within a general framework based on the concept of ecological demand. The specific hypothesis states that it is highly advantageous for rats to learn to reject foods that cause illness. The sensory mode best fitted to screen possible illness-inducing materials being ingested by the rat is taste. Therefore, natural selection has resulted in a predisposition ("preparedness") to associate taste with the occurrence of digestive distress. This talent can only be used to full advantage, however, if the association between the taste and subsequent digestive distress can take place over an extended period because rats are not likely to become ill immediately after eating bad foods. Hence they have evolved the ability of forming an association between two events (taste and illness) that are widely separated in time.

Although this research, like the study of bird song, is interpreted within the framework of the adaptive requirements of the subject species, it is actually quite different in its methodology and in the kind of claims that are made for its findings. Consider the independent variables. Both aspects of the Garcia effect were demonstrated in studies using irradiation as the means of inducing illness in rats (37). It was assumed that the specific nature of the noxious stimulus was irrelevant so long as it resulted in nausea, and this assumption has been pretty well confirmed in subsequent studies using a variety of toxic agents (35). Nevertheless, it is noteworthy that none of these substances is likely to be encountered by the rat in its natural environment—they simply represent a broad class of stimuli that are presumed to produce a common psychosomatic effect. Similarly, the arrangements for measuring experimental effects and the choice of responses do not closely approximate the circumstances of feeding activity in free-ranging rats.

It is appropriate to repeat here a distinction made earlier in the context of research on social behavior. The approach to bird song development was conceived as a simulation procedure in which actual relevant elements of the natural environment were brought into the laboratory in the interests of experimental convenience and control. The behavioral outcome was likewise restricted to a species-typical response. The food aversion studies have been conceived and carried out on the presumption that certain broad classes of events (i.e. those resulting in illness or pain) and certain broad classes of behavioral functions (e.g. approach, ingestion, avoidance) correspond to significant structural dimensions of the rat's "real" behavioral world. This approach was characterized earlier as a modeling procedure.

The results in this case are used to support the claim that we are dealing with a class of functional relations of some generality, at least for the rat. A reasonable next step would be to hypothesize that similar relationships will be found in other species that are similarly dependent upon a varied and changing diet. In fact, the acquisition of aversions has been investigated in species quite remote from the rat, namely, the coyote (40) and man (77). Although there are surely many contrasts between these organisms in the details of their feeding behavior and their responses to food poisoning, such differences are not stressed. The theoretical thrust of Garcia's approach, in fact, does not emphasize the species-specificity of learning so much as it does the basic difference between adaptation to the external environment (where information comes from telereceptors, and effective time and space are measured in milliseconds and millimeters) and regulation of the milieu interne (where information comes from internal receptors, effective time is measured in hours, and space is essentially irrelevant) (35).

Evolutionary Convergence in Behavioral Modifiability

Our final example is hardly new. In fact, it was among the first to dramatize the serious inadequacies in the traditional omnibus approach to animal learning. We have selected it because it points toward certain aspects of the comparative psychology of learning that remain essentially unexplored.

It will be recalled that in 1961 the Brelands described their tribulations with the application of operant conditioning principles to training animals for commercial exhibits. A well-known example concerns the use of a wooden coin that had to be inserted into a bank to trigger the release of a bit of food. Both pigs and racoons quickly acquired this trick, but in time their performance deteriorated, the pig beginning to root the coins, and the racoon starting to "wash" them (17). The Brelands' enterprise was strictly an applied venture in which the tasks they set were determined by commercial considerations. As technicians (and erstwhile Skinnerians) they were not concerned with a refined analysis of learning as a hypothetical process, but with the practical question of how performance might be modified in response to certain environmental demands.

We believe that current approaches to animal learning will profit from a more "practical" interest in the modification of behavior of the sort the Brelands exemplify, but with the important distinction that problems will be sought in the animal's natural habitat, rather than in the human market place. This does not mean that learning studies will be conducted in the field (although in a limited way this is possible), but that the design of environmental models will place greater emphasis on problems and achievements that are representative of those an animal can be expected to encounter. Rather than assuming, as is now the case, that all forms of learning are adaptive and therefore equally in need of study, the focus will shift to the environment and to sources of adaptedness and adaptability: Under what circumstances, to what extent, and in what ways is performance on a given problem modified in response to changing conditions?

There are definite suggestions that the Brelands anticipated this approach, although they did not develop it. In their search for a plausible account of their findings, they turned to the model of ecological demand (18). When it became impossible to get a cow to run for a food reward, the failure was interpreted as the result of cows having evolved to subsist on food sources producing "energy packets" too small to warrant a response entailing a high energy cost to obtain them. A cat's failure to extinguish an operant after a long period of reinforcement was interpreted as an adaptation to the very large energy packet that a cat can capture, thus making a long wait worthwhile. Note that in contrast to most other approaches which emphasize qualitative differences in the species-specificity of learning, the Brelands stressed that animals show adaptive specializations not only in what they do or do not learn, but also in the rates at which they change performances that are within the repertoire of a vast number of species.

The Brelands imply that regularities across species in learned performance might become more apparent if the problem was approached in terms of general niche characteristics (e.g. browsers, grazers, predators, marine mammals, etc), rather than in terms of taxonomic status. Thus a new source of generalizations is suggested, based on broad functional analogies across species occupying similar niches. Such an approach, which might be described as the study of evolutionary convergence in behavioral modifiability, would be quite similar to one that is currently taken toward social systems. It would complement the search for generality in studies based on niche divergence among closely related species [as in research on the acquisition and extinction in carnivorous and herbivorous mice (47)], and in studies based on comparisons of widely divergent species representing broadly different adaptive radiations (14).

It is evident that we are advocating a strategy that precludes a monolithic approach to the comparative psychology of learning. The first question—and the last —is: What part does learned behavior play in total life-history patterns? This is primarily a question of adaptedness and adaptability. Problems of phylogeny, of interspecies commonalities and contrasts, and of intraspecies predispositions and constraints—which have an obvious and necessary place in the total enterprise— will plainly require a broad spectrum of specimens and procedures. The experiments they generate will likewise differ broadly in generality and scope. Experiments that presuppose a high degree of species-specifity in learned performance are likely to find it, just as those that presuppose unbounded generality, if carried far enough, are certain to be wrong. It is necessary and proper that both kinds of research be done, for the one demonstrates the adaptedness of learning in fitting species to particular niche requirements, while the other establishes the limits of adaptability that learning can achieve.

CONCLUSION

For many years urgent calls have been made for the rapprochement of Ethology and Comparative Psychology. Today it appears that the synthesis is essentially complete. This has not come about simply because workers trained in the two traditions have combined their approaches to old problems, but because they share a common concern with new issues centering around the lively development of the concepts of adaptation and ecological demand.

The naturalistic field study, characterized by a new breadth, sophistication, and rigor, has become the touchstone for this new development. To be sure, research will continue to be carried out within the familiar settings of the experimental surgery, the Skinner Box, the Wisconsin General Test Apparatus, the field cage, and the like. These devices have not outlived their usefulness. We do not anticipate any diminution in the amount or quality of experimental research.

The point, rather, is that the questions selected for study and the answers that will be considered intellectually satisfying will further understanding of the behavior of animals in the settings in which they normally function. We have noted some of the conceptual and methodological problems that are raised or sharpened by this development, among them the need for a careful approach to comparative statements (particularly the treatment of functional analogies) and for more sophisticated concepts of the effective environment and of adaptedness and adaptability. These are not questions that will be resolved once and for all so much as recurrent problems inherent in the new comparative view of behavior. Instead of the rather casual way they have been handled in the past, such questions need to be considered deliberately in the formulation of research plans, the analysis of data, and the interpretation of findings.

Diversity of questions and approaches is a necessary feature of this enlarged view of behavior. Contention and debate will continue, of course, but these can be conducted within a framework of shared assumptions and common aims as vital accompaniments of healthy scientific growth. The unifying perspective that is emerging seems destined to abide, and we believe that it will guide and stimulate research for many years to come.

ACKNOWLEDGMENTS

Preparation of this review was aided by grants HD 06367 and RR 00169 from the National Institutes of Health to William A. Mason.

Literature Cited

1. Ackoff, R. L., Emery, F. E. 1972. *On Purposeful Systems.* Chicago: Aldine-Atherton. 288 pp.
2. Alcock, J. 1975. *Animal Behavior: An Evolutionary Approach.* Sunderland, Mass.: Sinauer. 547 pp.
3. Alexander, R. D. 1974. The evolution of social behavior. *Ann. Rev. Ecol. Syst.* 5:325–83
4. Altmann, J. 1974. Observational study of behavior: Sampling methods. *Behaviour* 49:227–68
5. Andrew, R. J. 1963. The origin and evolution of the calls and facial expressions of the primates. *Behaviour* 20:1–109
6. Atz, J. W. 1970. The application of the idea of homology to behavior. In *Development and Evolution of Behavior,* ed. L. R. Aronson, E. Tobach, D. S. Lehrman, J. S. Rosenblatt, 53–74. San Francisco: Freeman. 656 pp.
7. Baerends, G. P. 1958. Comparative methods and the concept of homology in the study of behaviour. *Extr. Arch. Neer. Zool.* 8:401–17
8. Beer, C. G. 1973. Species-typical behavior and ethology. See Ref. 29, 21–71
9. Beer, C. G. 1974. Comparative ethology and the evolution of behaviour. In *Ethology and Psychiatry,* ed. N. F. White, 173–81. Univ. Toronto Press. 264 pp.
10. Bermant, G., Ed. 1973. *Perspectives on Animal Behavior: A First Course.* Glenview, Ill.: Scott, Foresman. 400 pp.
11. Bermant, G., Alcock, J. 1973. Perspectives on animal behavior. See Ref. 10, 1–47
12. Berrien, F. K. 1968. *General and Social Systems.* New Brunswick: Rutgers Univ. 231 pp.
13. Bitterman, M. E. 1960. Toward a comparative psychology of learning. *Am. Psychol.* 15:704–12
14. Ibid 1965. Phyletic differences in learning. 20:396–410

15. Bitterman, M. E. 1968. Comparative studies of learning in the fish. In *The Central Nervous System and Fish Behavior*, ed. D. Ingle, 257–70. Univ. Chicago Press. 272 pp.

16. Bolles, R. C. 1973. The comparative psychology of learning: The selective association principle and some problems with "general" laws of learning. See Ref. 10, 280–306

17. Breland, K., Breland, M. 1961. The misbehavior of organisms. *Am Psychol.* 16:681–84

18. Breland, K., Breland, M. 1966. *Animal Behavior.* New York: McMillan. 210 pp.

19. Buckley, W. 1967. *Sociology and Modern Systems Theory.* Englewood Cliffs, NJ: Prentice-Hall. 227 pp.

20. Clutton-Brock, T. H. 1974. Primate social organisation and ecology. *Nature* 250:539–42

21. Cody, M. L. 1974. Optimization in ecology. *Science* 183:1156–64

22. Crook, J. H. 1965. The adaptive significance of avian social organizations. *Symp. Zool. Soc. London* 14:181–218

23. Crook, J. H. 1970. Social organization and the environment: Aspects of contemporary social ethology. *Anim. Behav.* 18:197–209

24. Crook, J. H., Gartlan, J. S. 1966. Evolution of primate societies. *Nature* 210:1200–3

25. Cullen, E. 1957. Adaptations in the kittiwake to cliff-nesting. *Ibis* 99:275–302

26. Darwin, C. 1873. *The Expression of the Emotions in Animals and Man.* New York: Appleton. 372 pp.

27. DeBeer, G. 1958. *Embryos and Ancestors.* Oxford: Clarendon. 197 pp. 3rd ed.

28. DeVore, I. 1963. Comparative ecology and behavior of monkeys and apes. In *Classification and Human Evolution*, ed. S. L. Washburn, 301–9. Chicago: Aldine. 371 pp.

29. Dewsbury, D. A., Rethlingshafer, D. A., Eds. 1973. *Comparative Psychology: A Modern Survey.* New York: McGraw-Hill. 625 pp.

30. Eisenberg, J. F. 1962. Studies on the behavior of *Peromyscus maniculatus gambelii* and *Peromyscus californicus parasiticus. Behaviour* 19:177–207

31. Eisenberg, J. F., McKay, G. M. 1974. Comparison of ungulate adaptations in the new world and the old world tropical rain forests with special reference to Ceylon and the rain forests of central America. In *The Behaviour of Ungulates and Its Relation to Management,* ed. V. Geist, F. Walther, 585–602. IUCN publications new series No. 24. 2 vols. 940 pp.

32. Eisenberg, J. F., Muckenhirn, N. A., Rudran, R. 1972. The relation between ecology and social structure in primates. *Science* 176:863–74

33. Estes, R. D. 1974. Social organization of the African bovidae. See Ref. 31, 166–205

34. Garcia, J., Ervin, F., Koelling, R. A. 1966. Learning with prolonged delay of reinforcement. *Psychon. Sci.* 5:121–22

35. Garcia, J., Hawkins, W. G., Rusiniak, K. W. 1974. Behavioral regulation of the milieu interne in man and rat. *Science* 185:824–31

36. Garcia, J., Koelling, R. A. 1966. Relation of cue to consequence in avoidance learning. *Psychon. Sci.* 4:123–24

37. Garcia, J., McGowan, B. K., Green, K. F. 1972. Biological constraints on conditioning. See Ref. 78, 21–43

38. Gray, P. H. 1973. Comparative psychology and ethology: A saga of twins reared apart. *Ann. NY Acad. Sci.* 223:49–53

39. Greenewalt, C. H. 1969. How birds sing. *Sci. Am.* 221:126–39

40. Gustavson, C. R., Garcia, J., Hawkins, W. G., Rusiniak, K. W. 1974. Coyote predation control by aversive conditioning. *Science* 184:583–85

41. Hamilton, W. D. 1964. The genetical evolution of social behaviour. I. *J. Theor. Biol.* 7:1–16

42. Ibid. The genetical evolution of social behaviour. II, 17–52

43. Harlow, H. F., Harlow, M. K., Suomi, S. J. 1971. From thought to therapy: Lessons from a primate laboratory. *Am. Sci.* 59:538–49

44. Hinde, R. A. 1966. *Animal Behaviour: A Synthesis of Ethology and Comparative Psychology.* New York: McGraw-Hill. 534 pp. 2nd ed. 1970

45. Hinde, R. A., Stevenson-Hinde, J., Eds. 1973. *Constraints on Learning.* New York: Academic. 488 pp.

46. Hoffman, H. S., Ratner, A. M. 1973. A reinforcement model of imprinting: Implications for socialization in monkeys and men. *Psychol. Rev.* 80:527–44

47. Hopwood, J. H., Lott, D. F. 1971. *Differences in acquisition and extinction in two species of desert mice occupying different ecological niches.* Presented at Anim. Behav. Soc. Meet., Logan, Utah

48. Kaufman, J. H. 1974. The ecology and evolution of social organization in the

kangaroo family (*Macropodidae*). *Am. Zool.* 14:51–62

49. Kitchen, D. 1974. Social behavior and ecology of the pronghorn. *Wildlife Monogr. No. 38.* 96 pp.

50. Klopfer, P. H. 1973. Does behavior evolve? *Ann. NY Acad. Sci.* 223:113–19

51. Klopfer, P. H., Hailman, J. P. 1967. *An Introduction to Animal Behavior: Ethology's First Century.* Englewood Cliffs, NJ: Prentice-Hall. 297 pp.

52. Kruuk, H. 1972. *The Spotted Hyena: A Study of Predation and Social Behavior.* Univ. Chicago Press. 335 pp.

53. Kummer, H. 1971. *Primate Societies.* Chicago: Aldine-Atherton. 160 pp.

54. Lashley, K. S. 1957. Introduction. In *Instinctive Behavior: The Development of a Modern Concept,* ed. C. H. Schiller, ix–xii. New York: Int. Univ. Press. 328 pp.

55. Lehrman, D. S. 1962. Varieties of learning and memory in animals. In *Macromolecular Specificity and Biological Memory,* ed. F. O. Schmitt, 108–10. Cambridge, Mass: MIT Press

56. Lehrman, D. S. 1971. Behavioral science, engineering, and poetry. In *The Biopsychology of Development,* ed. E. Tobach, L. R. Aronson, E. Shaw, 459–71. New York: Academic. 593 pp.

57. Lehrman, D. S. 1974. Can psychiatrists use ethology? See Ref. 9, 187–96

58. Lockard, R. B. 1971. Reflections of the fall of comparative psychology: Is there a message for us all? *Am. Psychol.* 26:168–80

59. Lorenz, K. Z. 1965. Preface. In *The Expression of Emotions in Man and Animals,* ed. C. Darwin, ix–xiii. Univ. Chicago Press. 372 pp. (Originally published 1873)

60. Lorenz, K. Z. 1966. *On Aggression.* New York: Harcourt, Brace & World. 306 pp.

61. Lorenz, K. Z. 1974. Analogy as a source of knowledge. *Science* 185:229–34

62. Marler, P. 1970. A comparative approach to vocal learning: Song development in white-crowned sparrows. *J. Comp. Physiol. Psychol. Monogr.* 71(No. 2, Part 2):1–25

63. Marler, P. 1970. Bird song and speech development: Could there be parallels? *Am. Sci.* 58:669–73

64. Marler, P., Tamura, M. 1964. Culturally transmitted patterns of vocal behavior in sparrows. *Science* 146:1483–86

65. Mason, W. A. 1971. Field and laboratory studies of social organization in *Saimiri* and *Callicebus. Primate Behav.* 2:107–37

66. Mason, W. A., Epple, G. 1969. Social organization in experimental groups of *Saimiri* and *Callicebus. Proc. 2nd Int. Congr. Primatol.* 1:59–65

67. Masters, R. D. 1973. Functional approaches to analogical comparison between species. *Soc. Sci. Inform.* 12:7–28

68. McKinney, W. T. Jr. 1974. Animal models in psychiatry. *Perspect. Biol. Med.* 17:529–41

69. McKinney, W. T. Jr., Bunney, W. E. Jr. 1969. Animal model of depression. I. Review of evidence: Implications for research. *Arch. Gen. Psychiatry* 21:240–48

70. Moyer, K. E. 1968. Kinds of aggression and their physiological basis. *Commun. Behav. Biol.* 2:65–87

71. Moynihan, M. 1973. The evolution of behavior and the role of behavior in evolution. *Brevoria* 415:1–29

72. Nicolai, J. 1959. Familiertradition in der Gesangsentwicklung des Gimpels (*Pyrrhula pyrrhula L.*). *J. Ornithol.* 100:39–46

73. Poulsen, H. 1951. Inheritance and learning in the song of the Chaffinch, *Fringilla coelebs L. Behaviour* 3:216–28

74. Ratner, S. C. 1972. Comparative psychology: Some distinctions from animal behavior. *Psychol. Rec.* 22:433–40

75. Schaller, G. B., Emlen, J. T. Jr. 1963. Observations on the ecology and social behavior of the mountain gorilla. In *African Ecology and Human Evolution,* ed. F. C. Howell, F. Bourliere, 368–84. Chicago: Aldine. 666 pp.

76. Seay, B., Gottfried, N. W. 1975. A phylogenetic perspective for social behavior in primates. *J. Gen. Psychol.* 92:5–17

77. Seligman, M. E. P. 1972. Editorial comment. See Ref. 78, 8–9

78. Seligman, M. E. P., Hager, J. L., Eds. 1972. *Biological Boundaries of Learning.* New York: Appleton-Century-Crofts. 480 pp.

79. Shettleworth, S. J. 1972. Constraints on learning. *Study Behav.* 4:1–62

80. Simpson, G. G. 1961. *Principles of Animal Taxonomy.* New York: Columbia Univ. Press. 247 pp.

81. Simpson, G. G. 1962. The status of the study of organisms. *Am. Sci.* 50:36–45

82. Skinner, B. F. 1966. The phylogeny and ontogeny of behavior. *Science* 153:1205–13

83. Thorpe, W. H. 1961. *Bird Song: The Biology of Vocal Communication and Expression in Birds.* Cambridge, England: Cambridge Univ. Press, 142 pp.
84. Tinbergen, N. 1951. *The Study of Instinct.* New York: Oxford Univ. Press. 228 pp.
85. Tinbergen, N. 1960. Behaviour, systematics, and natural selection. In *Evolution After Darwin. Vol. 1. The Evolution of Life,* ed. S. Tax, 595–613. Univ. Chicago Press. 629 pp.
86. Tinbergen, N. 1968. On war and peace in animals and man. *Science* 160:1411–18
87. Trivers, R. L. 1971. The evolution of reciprocal altruism. *Quart. Rev. Biol.* 46:34–57
88. Trivers, R. L. 1972. Parental investment and sexual selection. In *Sexual Selection and the Descent of Man: 1871–1971,* ed. B. Campbell, 136–79. Chicago: Aldine. 378 pp.

89. Trivers, R. L. 1974. Parent-offspring conflict. *Am. Zool.* 14:249–64
90. Vine, I. 1973. Social spacing in animals and man. *Soc. Sci. Inform.* 12:7–50
91. Von Bertalanffy, L. 1968. *General System Theory.* New York: Braziller. 289 pp.
92. Wallace, R. A. 1973. *The Ecology and Evolution of Animal Behavior.* Pacific Palisades, Calif.: Goodyear. 342 pp.
93. Warren, J. M. 1973. Learning in vertebrates. See Ref. 29, 471–508
94. Wickler, W. 1973. Ethological analysis of convergent adaptation. *Ann. NY Acad. Sci.* 223:65–69
95. Wilson, E. O. 1971. The prospects for a unified sociobiology. *Am. Sci.* 59:400–3
96. Wynne-Edwards, V. C. 1963. Intergroup selection in the evolution of social systems. *Nature* 200:623–26
97. Zeigler, H. P. 1973. The problem of comparison in comparative psychology. *Ann. NY Acad. Sci.* 223:126–34

MODELS OF LEARNING ♦251

John W. Cotton[1]
Departments of Education and Psychology, University of California, Santa Barbara,
California 93106

This review centers on mathematical models of learning and their empirical tests.[2] Trends noted by Greeno & Bjork (77) have continued and accelerated: mathematical learning theory has become more cognitive in terminology, learning models have made even greater use of trees or networks to represent process and structure, and material learned in the laboratory has born increasing similarity, if not identity, to real world knowledge. Extension of these trends raises a question whether practice effects or tasks requiring extensive practice during acquisition are a central aspect of learning. Indeed it could be argued that one of the finest learning models available, that of Norman, Rumelhart, and the LNR group[3] (140), discusses learning only peripherally as a side issue to the treatment of memory storage, question answering, and problem solving.

Greeno & Bjork's (77) implicit definition of learning as the new storage of information in memory or the modification of a structure of knowledge forms a basis for identifying studies to be cited here. The range of studies from which selection is to

[1]Part of this review was prepared in the Center for Human Information Processing, University of California, San Diego. The hospitality of the Director, George Mandler, is gratefully acknowledged, as is secretarial assistance provided at UCSD and support provided by the UCSB Committee on Research and the UCSB Bureau of Educational Research and Development. I thank the following readers of a draft of this chapter for their helpful suggestions: J. Block, R. Bortnick, L. Gregg, J. Helland, R. Klatzky, E. Lovejoy, S. Marshall, and M. McClure. Richard Houang rendered valuable bibliographic assistance.

[2]This chapter is a sequel to Greeno & Bjork's (77) "Mathematical Learning Theory and the New Mental Forestry," published in the 1973 *Annual Review of Psychology;* it emphasizes developments in the period from January 1, 1972 through December 31, 1974. Three recent *Annual Review* chapters (Johnson-Laird 94, Neimark & Santa 133, Postman 154) treat empirical evidence related to the present chapter but give little attention to mathematical models per se.

[3]LNR group stands for Lindsay, Norman, and Rumelhart and their associates; when pronounced, LNR becomes ELINOR, an early name for their model.

155

be made has grown; Greeno (75) doubts that a rigorous distinction can be made between learning and comprehension. Accordingly, this review reports on some experiments or models emphasizing comprehension or other cognitive tasks, mentioning practice effects when present [e.g. changes in strategies for proving theorems of logic (136, pp. 593–96) and changes in transition probabilities for calculus problem-solving states (100)].

One model (Anderson & Bower 9) out of several reflecting this combining of performance and learning theories is partially described early in this review to indicate the sort of theorizing which has been especially important in the past 3 years.

COMMENT ON CHANGES IN THE TYPES OF MATHEMATICS USED IN LEARNING MODELS   As psychologists develop rigorous descriptions of the structured behavior mentioned above, they find it necessary to use mathematical tools which are new to them. The substantial importance of Markov techniques to learning theory in general and stimulus sampling theory in particular has been noted by Greeno (76) and Estes & Suppes (62). But networks and automaton devices, previously more relevant to computer science and linguistics (36), are increasingly used by learning theorists. Terms such as "pushdown automaton" and its linguistic counterpart, "context-free grammar," appear without definition in this review. Relatively informal introductions to such topics are available in books on learning theory (9, 140). Technical discussions may also be found easily (36, 57).

ANDERSON & BOWER'S "HUMAN ASSOCIATIVE MEMORY" (HAM)—A REFERENCE POINT AMONG THEORIES

Processes and Structures Assumed by HAM

This is a theory (9) of human associative memory (HAM) combining a so-called strategy-free component of memory and an interface system. The strategy-free component of HAM deals with three languages (input, probe, and output), one set of structures (the memory structures), and two fundamental processes (encoding or learning and decoding or output generation). The interface system connects the outside world to the organism, with stimulus input, for example, being external and input being organismic. The interface system also controls reasoning processes.

The Strategy-Free Component of HAM

INPUT   Stimulus input for HAM is typically in English sentences placed first in acoustic and visual buffers. The linguistic parser (part of the interface system) accepts these sentences and converts them to base structure, binary tree structures (input) somewhat like old-fashioned sentence diagrams.

PROBES   Probes are also tree structures. They come from "yes-no" questions or "wh"-questions (who, what, which, etc), with the former having the same parsing as stimulus input and the latter having a similar parsing but with an empty terminal node (i.e. endpoint) to be filled in with the desired answer.

OUTPUT   Output is in trees leading by the interface system to sentences or to implicit sentences.

MEMORY STRUCTURES   The memory structure is the set of propositions or partial propositions currently stored in memory. It is larger than input and has an inverse relation as well as an original relation (labeled arc) between each connected pair of nodes, thus facilitating responding.

ENCODING   One form of encoding is learning, a probabilistic conversion of terminal nodes in an input tree into memory nodes. If full learning of the tree occurs, it will all be included in the memory structure.

DECODING WITH THE MATCH PROCESS   To test for recognition, MATCH takes an input tree from the parser and seeks to match the nodes and labeled arcs of that tree to a set of nodes and labeled arcs in memory. If a perfect match is found, the "person" outputs that he "recognizes" the input. Otherwise he uses statistical decision theory processes to decide which output (recognition or nonrecognition) to make. Fact retrieval (recall) uses MATCH in a manner comparable to recognition.

The Interface System

In addition to converting stimulus input to input and output to overt responses, the interface system controls the search procedure involved in general question answering (as distinguished from fact retrieval). Note that fact retrieval answers questions for which the MATCH process alone is sufficient, whereas general question answering requires at least one step of inference, as in inferring that Fido is a canine from "Fido is a dog" and "dog is a synonym for canine."

Mathematical Properties of HAM

Stimulus input sentences must conform to a particular surface grammar which can be generated by a pushdown automaton. The deep structure form used by input, probes, and output also appears generable by such an automaton. The memory structure is a finite labeled graph. Except for nodes existing at birth which have not yet been connected to other nodes, each node of the graph has at least one other node with which it is linked by a pair of symmetric relations.

HAM assumes that an exponential distribution of times is required for an association of a node pair and relation to occur in working memory before it is encoded into the memory structure. With the further assumption that n such links exist in working memory, it is possible to derive that the number of associations formed in time t is binomially distributed. Further theorizing leads to the probability of forming an association in t sec and to such predictions as probability of recalling sentences with certain structures.

PROCESSES OF LEARNING

Hereafter the abbreviations STM (short-term memory) and LTM (long-term memory) will be used for memory occurring within a short or long time after stimulus presentation. When a supposed locus of memory is mentioned, it will be called STS (short-term store) or LTS (long-term store).

Encoding—Transformation of Perceptions into Storable Elements

STIMULUS SAMPLING THEORY   Estes (59) has incorporated the following encoding notions into his theory: If a word such as "bet" is to be memorized, associations must be formed between a control element C and each letter in the word rather than simply between successive letters of "bet." Since another word such as "boy" is learned by association with some other control element, interference of the two words via the Bs in them is unlikely. Probabilistic losses of phase in reverberations between C and each element connected to it produce errors in STM recall of the stimuli in proper order. LTM recall of order information depends upon appropriate excitation and inhibition of successive elements. The total number of such required connections determines the difficulty for a given grouping, such as six items in one chunk.

Bower's (27) version of encoding in stimulus sampling theory assumes that for a given external stimulus such as *XQH,* there are N coding operators. Exactly s operators will be applied, the s being selected randomly. These s operators yield s encodings of the original stimulus. Each is stored in STS, and each is further encoded by a *list label* so that retrieval for the appropriate list may be possible. Standard assumptions about stimulus fluctuation ensure that different encodings will occur on different presentations of the stimulus, causing difficulty in recognition of stimuli previously presented unless the number of list-markers in common between newly encoded and previously encoded stimuli is large.

LINGUISTIC TRANSFORMATION OF INPUT   We have already seen that Anderson & Bower (9) parse their input sentences into base structure form, connecting the result to existing memory where possible. Rumelhart, Lindsay & Norman (161) and related models (137, 139, 140, 162) use a different linguistic representation of propositions, going even farther than Anderson & Bower in making memory an organized set of propositions learned by the individual. The mathematical structure of the labeled directed graph employed is that of an augmented recursive transition network which may also be viewed as a computer program with subroutines or as a context-sensitive grammar (98, 203).

Rumelhart, Lindsay & Norman (161) code items in STS by their category if two or more members of the category have been stored (STS entries of "dog" and "cat" are replaced by a single entry such as "pet"). Permanent entries in LTS include a tag or marker indicating when or in which list they were presented.

Atkinson & Juola (16) stand at the junction between an encoding by environmental category theory and a linguistic transformation model for encoding. Every word in the learner's vocabulary occupies a specific location or node in the lexical store section of LTS. Other nodes represent concepts such as "to the left of." When a word is presented as an external stimulus, it is encoded with relevant auditory, pictorial, and graphemic representations and mapped onto a lexical store node.

Kintsch (101, 103), in models reminiscent of the LNR group, has been even more formal in describing the structure of memory. Collins & Quillian (41) have developed a computer simulation for semantic memory with a hierarchical organization of concepts and with contextual connections to clarify meanings but with little other encoding of input words.

ENCODING BY ENVIRONMENTAL CATEGORY OF STIMULI   Newell (134) presents a computer simulation of human encoding of a series of visually displayed bottles of different colors pointing up or down or right or left, the encoding being intended to facilitate a series completion task in which the human predicts from the present display what future additions to it should be. It may be seen from a later part of this review that some encodings of stimulus lists in series completion tasks are so complete as to constitute the solution to the task (173).

Newell's simulations show some encodings without obvious psychological importance. His simulations of appropriate memorization of a paired-associate item with variable sizes of chunks, in a response such as X QKF H (see also 93), use "productions" (135) to shift positions of chunks in STS in a way which may be called rehearsal but that does not have the usual stigmata of rehearsal (duplication of items, intensification of items, etc). During STS processing, decoding may be followed by re-encoding, as in a case where output is desired to be in successive letter pairs, regardless of whether the input was so presented.

Short-Term Memory Events

SINGLE-STAGE THEORY   Murdock (128), denying that different processes or structures underlie STM and LTM, has applied the following Markov model to STM and LTM data: There are two states for an item, accessible (A) and not accessible (N). The initial vector has P_0 as the probability of an item's being in A already. The transition matrix has probabilities α of moving from A to N and β of moving from N to A on presentation of a new item or testing of an old item. Murdock hypothesized that each correct recall of a paired-associate item decreases α and each repetition of an item increases β. Paired-associate acquisition data have been successfully described by a Monte Carlo simulation of this model. Conventional curve fits have shown adequate prediction of recall probabilities in single-trial, paired-associate probe experiments and dependence of parameter values on specific experimental variables, e.g. serial position trends in free recall as a function of modality of item presentation (66).

TWO-TRACE STRENGTH THEORY   Wickelgren (197) assumes that item presentation yields a short and a long trace, each with a property (strength) determining recognition and recall probabilities. Each additional learning trial increases the strength of each trace. The two trace strengths are additive. The short trace decays with the passage of time but also has a short-term maintenance parameter. Estimates of memory strength for recognition memory data for single letters at different rates of presentation conform to this model, showing a decline in the maintenance parameter with increased presentation rate.

TWO-STAGE THEORY Greeno (76) has recommended that Markov learning models assuming separate STS and LTS states be used only as approximations to more detailed and accurate theories. One such detailed two-stage model (16) is used for describing recognition memory. Glanzer (73) has presented a minimodel relevant to a phenomenon which Greeno sees as needing explanation, i.e. the smaller improvement on an item when presented twice in succession than when presented twice but with several other items intervening. Glanzer assumes that an item currently in STS has a $.5^j$ probability of remaining there after j other items have been presented. If d is the time from item presentation to item presentation, a geometric series argument yields an average of $2d$ units in which the item is in STS and has a chance of being transferred to LTS. Glanzer assumes that one item cannot appear twice in STS at one time; therefore a second presentation of an item resets its probability of remaining to $.5^{j'}$, where j' is a new index on other items. Immediate re-presentation of the item yields a total of $3d$ units of time for transfer to LTS; a long delay between successive presentations yields $4d$ units and thus a greater probability of that transfer and consequent permanent learning.

A computer simulation of Kintsch's free recall model (101) ensures that when a word is presented, phonetic features from sensory encoding plus a sample from the description list in LTS for the word are jointly tagged with a list marker. Also, the executive makes STS scan its contents looking for a way to generate a proposition from those contents. The proposition implied by the surface structure, "The girl eats an apple," may result in this sentence then being stored with the property lists for both "girl" and "apple"; "girl" and "apple" are both found in STS.

J. R. Anderson's (6) Free Recall Associative Network (FRAN) (see also 8, 26, 89) has up to five items in STS plus any item currently being processed. Given study time T immediately following item presentation, there is a probability of $1-a^T$ that an item in STS will be tagged with a list identification. A search for associations to an STS word may bring list members from LTS to STS for another chance to be tagged. FRAN also has an *entryset* of three words which were tagged while in STS and then placed in LTS as a point of entry for LTS search for list members. The learning process is undirected because no principles are available to predict which associative links to a given word in STS are likely to lead to other list members.

The Rumelhart, Lindsay & Norman (161) model also treats STS as a list of items. Until STS is full, each item presented is placed on the top of STS. Once STS is full, the encoding process begins, with class names such as "animal" replacing member names such as "dog" and "cat" to make more room for new items. Retrieval processes call forth a series of member names from LTS, thus leading to recall which is segregated by category, a well-known phenomenon of organized list learning.

In their discussion of concept identification models, Millward & Wickens (125) classify hypotheses currently under consideration as a kind of STM and all other stored information as part of LTM. These models, like Theios' (178) use of yoked or parallel STS and LTS processes in a reaction time model, illustrate an emphasis upon a response generation function in memory storage.

TWO-STAGE SEMANTIC THEORY   The LNR group (161) also has a reconstruction model of memory with directed storage and retrieval. In this model, a semantic discrimination net, the items in STS are concepts that are needed to cue retrieval of those portions of LTS necessary to reconstruct the input list. Typically there will be one item in STS for every connected structure in LTS that must be retrieved, with each such structure having one or more items reconstructable from it.

HAM (9) is more complex than its parent FRAN, storing propositions and having three kinds of STS: *(a)* sensory buffers to hold representations of words in memory while they are being parsed; *(b)* a holding tank or push-down stack for keeping track of the parser's progress through a sentence; and *(c)* a working memory (really a currently active part of LTS), which holds partial tree structures during parsing and complete tree structures while they are being learned, i.e. transferred to LTS. Use of HAM to simulate learning of individual items uses all the linguistic structure previously mentioned as handling learning of propositions. Lists of nonsense *n*-grams, paired associates, or words to be memorized are placed in STS as groups of propositions, with the size of working memory controlling how many memory nodes can simultaneously be accessed and held available during development of the parsing tree. HAM is clearly an associative model, but its propositional storage of information permits directed search for associates. It also can employ reconstruction of memory items since recall of a portion of a proposition may suggest likely ways to complete the proposition.

Long-Term Memory Events

STRENGTH THEORY   Wickelgren (196, 197) assumes that the strength of a long-term trace develops to some level by the end of training and decays with the passage of time t, despite growth with time of "trace resistance" to protect very old learning. In Atkinson & Juola's (15, 16) model of recognition memory with well-learned target words, information relevant to responding is stored in two places: the lexical store of LTS contains familiarity values for words stored there; and the event-knowledge (E/K) store of LTS contains a listing of all target words learned for the experiment, the familiarity value decaying with time since last use of the mode for an item.

ALL-OR-NONE ITEM STORAGE IN LTS   Greeno (76) has reviewed a number of experimental and theoretical papers suggesting that movement in a Markov chain from the first to the second stage of learning corresponds to movement from storage of an item to capability to recall the item. The storage process involves both STS and LTS in this case, with recall depending on LTS. FRAN (6) contains 262 nouns in its LTS, connected by two-way links whenever one word is used in the definition of another. Recall of nouns in a specific list may occur for three reasons: (*a*) they are identified by a tag for that list; (*b*) they appear in STS; or (*c*) they are a member of *entryset*. During study time t for any word, $5 + t$ of its associates in LTS are examined to see if they can be identified as list members. Any list member not previously tagged is given a probabilistic opportunity to be tagged at the time another item replaces it in STS.

STORAGE OF PROPOSITIONS IN LTS   Kintsch's (101, 103) models define all entries in their lexicon by propositions. The list of propositions about a word forms a structured description list available for use in question answering, for example. Nouns and verbs are organized in two separate systems. A system of inference rules is used to generate information not directly stored in LTS.

Familiarity tags on propositions associated with words recalled and already in STS are examined during free recall tests, with high familiarity values on individual words from these description lists indicating that those words should be recalled (101). We have already seen that HAM (9) stores propositions in LTS in such a way that syllable, word, sentence, or idea recall is feasible. Nodes and adjacent relations in the memory structure have continuously updated GET-lists showing, in order of recency of mention, the nodes that have been linked to the original nodes and relations. Thus GET (dog, ϵ^{-1}) would list the particular dog you have most recently encoded in memory, then the next most recent dog, etc.

Kintsch (103) used encoding biases to make episode memory show context-specific effects, an item learned in one episode having different encoding than the same item in another episode. Rumelhart, Lindsay & Norman (161) employed a semantic discrimination net in which the first entry to STS would be given a label in STS and stored in LTS with some propositions forming a partially defining graph. If the second entry to STS had no properties in common with the stored graph for the first entry, it would receive a new label to be stored separately in STS. Otherwise the two original concepts would be subdivided to permit specification of their common parts, forming two unique concepts and one common concept such that the propositions for representing the original concepts would be easy to restate. Then the STS list would include enough concept identifiers to lead to either original concept as desired.

Disappearance of STS vs LTS Distinctions

Postman (154) has warned against reifying STS and LTS or the distinction between them. Kiss (105) has also argued that LTS and STS are not structures, i.e. physically distinct systems for handling different kinds of processes. Accordingly, he gives a programmatic description of the verbal memory system as an automaton with a large number of subautomata for different processes. STM and LTM events are processes controlled by the automata rather than being automata themselves.

Several authors cited above have been moving in this direction, for example, by asserting that working memory is part of LTS rather than a separate structure (9). Norman, Rumelhart & the LNR group (140) seem also to practice what Kiss advocates. However, they treat so little learning data that it is difficult to know whether the Rumelhart, Lindsay & Norman (161) approach to STS will be used with the later system. Their current computer simulation (MEMOD) consists of three major component systems: interpreter, parser, and nodespace. The parser, with help from the interpreter and information from the nodespace, converts verbal input into propositional form appropriate for storage in the nodespace. During this conversion period, information is stored in the parser, which could be a useful basis for explaining STM phenomena. Nodes in the nodespace are quite complex, with the most important features being the word for that node, together with a listing of each node to which that word is linked and the relation by which the link is made. The nodespace developed by the LNR group serves the role of an LTS.

Decoding and Response Generation—Specific Tasks

RECOGNITION MEMORY   For Atkinson & Juola (16) short-term recognition memory depends upon storage of the immediately previous set of stimulus items in STS. If this list is short, a recognition (called "Yes" here) or nonrecognition ("No") decision can be made most easily by taking a representation of the test stimulus from the lexical store in LTS and scanning STS serially to seek a matching item. With long lists scanning would take longer and so STS is bypassed if a judgment can be reasonably based on familiarity values. Reaction times for correct judgments are predicted from one of six models tested, taking into account such variables as time required for encoding and familiarity retrieval and time required for a decision based on familiarity alone. The model correctly predicts greater mean latencies for distractor items than for target items presented as tests and a linear increase in latency as target set size increases.

Shevell & Atkinson (172) have developed eight list-scanning models crossing the three factors of serial vs parallel processing, self-terminating vs complete processing of target list, and self-terminating vs complete processing of features of an item on that list. The target list analyzed employed K features for each of N nonidentical items. The positive test item duplicated all K features of one target item whereas the negative item duplicated up to $K-1$. Parallel processing did not multiply the number of features examined per second by a constant; rather it provided for examination of the Kth feature of each item (unless termination was dictated for an item or list) before examination of the kth+1 feature of any item. Subject to this slight idiosyncracy in the definition of parallel search, the authors found equivalent implications of the two serial and parallel models with complete processing of an item and also for the two such models with self-terminating processing of an item, so long as complete processing of the list was assumed. If errorless processing was also assumed, linear increases in number of required feature comparisons were predicted as a function of N for all models; slight nonlinearities were predicted otherwise.

The Atkinson & Juola model for long-term recognition memory (16, see also 14, 15) differs from their short-term model only in that search of STS replaces search of the E/K store. Data from a study of list length and number of test repetitions (96) were successfully fitted by this model. A combined model for short- and long-term recognition memory was presented (16), using a hypothesis of parallel search of STS and the E/K store in order to accommodate findings (126, 194) that reaction time to positive test stimuli from the LT set does not depend on ST set size.

The various Atkinson & Juola papers present a combined model accounting for both a strong serial position effect on reaction time in short-term recognition, supporting a strength model over a scanning model (43), and clearly linear reaction time trends as a function of target list length, as predicted by a scanning model (44). Strength theory also must deal with Murdock & Dufty (130), who find generally higher standard deviations of latencies for false recognitions than true ones and generally higher standard deviations of latencies for "No" to old items than for "No" to new items (a result alleged to be the reverse of that predicted from strength theory and the fact that latencies peak near the cutoff strength that divides "Yes" from "No" responses, declining on either side). Unfortunately, Murdock & Dufty's proof assumes a truncated normal distribution of latencies for each subpopulation of responses (which cannot follow exactly from the normal distribution of strengths unless the latency curve peaks precisely at the cutoff point, which is usually not true in these data) and assumes that the decline in latency is a linear function of change in strength (only approximately true).

The Murdock & Dufty topic need not concern Atkinson & Juola because they assume a normal distribution of underlying strengths but do not generate memory operating characteristic (MOC) curves or assume anything about the distribution of latencies other than its mean. Recent studies by Wickelgren (196, 197) do the former; earlier research (141) also made MOC curves for latencies, thus making the Murdock & Dufty issue worthy of further examination.

Whereas Atkinson & Juola's recognition memory studies ensured high probabilities of correct judgments and predicted their latencies, the Wickelgren research varies retention time in order to predict declines in probability of correct recognition. The empirical measure typically used in curve-fitting is d_a, an unbiased, low variance estimate of d', the standard signal detection theory measure of subject sensitivity. A d_a value is generated from an MOC and is then plotted as a function of retention time, the best fitting equation for these data being called the relation between memory strength and retention time. Exponential decay of the strength of short trace is confirmed by curve-fitting (197) of probe-recognition data (195) for retention intervals from 0 to 13 sec. Exponential power decay of the long trace has been confirmed by similar fits reported (196) for several experiments with various retention intervals ranging up to 2 years. Note that procedural differences between investigators and different explanatory mechanisms are such that Wickelgren's short trace data (so called because they came from short retention intervals) employ stimuli much like Atkinson & Juola's long-term set (so called because those stimuli have been used and reused in the experiment). For this reason Wickelgren (197) emphasized that the assumed additivity of short and long trace strengths caused no problems, with long traces having no effect on the resulting memory strength curve because equal long traces for positive and negative stimuli canceled each other out in their contribution to recognition behavior.

Perhaps the most notable confirmation of Wickelgren's (196) long-term memory model, other than fitting the general form of the decay function for strength, was his (Fig. 8) finding of greater memory strength after two trials of training with 10 min spacing than with lesser spacing. This supports the assumption that resistance is determined completely by the length of time since training began.

Anderson & Bower (9) have generated a new model for recognition judgments. That model, a part of the large model FRAN, generates binomial approximations to the normal distributions of detection theory from the assumption that when an identification tag (the List n marker) is attached to a word in a list, there is a fixed probability θ for each of k elements in that list's population to be associated with that list marker. The number x of elements so associated is called the amount of List n evidence and is obviously binomial in distribution. Generalizations between list contexts generates another distribution of x, with lower mean, for a word from another list or for a word from this list which did not have a List n marker attached to it. When the probability of such an attachment is not unity, a mixture distribution of x goes with the word, thus combining two binomial distributions and possibly producing a bimodal curve of x for a particular List n member. Note that although x could be called memory strength, Bernbach's (21) precursor of this model has been called a finite state model, not a strength model.

Anderson & Bower (9) found list-by-list declines in ability to recognize which words had appeared in the most recent list. Fitting of recognition data to their FRAN model showed that these declines could be interpreted as the consequence of declines in the probability of tying a List n marker to a word in that list, a manifestation of negative transfer with presentation of the same words in many lists. There was also some indication of a decline in μ_m, the mean of the xs for words which had such list n markers.

The model just described is unable to account for reductions in recognition latency in double-word displays (where S must say whether neither, one, or both words is an old item) when both items come from a preexisting category or from a category defined by earlier pairing during the experiment (83, 122). The investigators of this phenomenon advocate postulation of two storage systems in LTS, as used by Atkinson & Juola (16). Naus, Glucksberg & Ornstein (132) have investigated two scanning models for recognition of organized items. They found that a "random entry" model satisfactorily describes their own data in which the slope of the reaction time function with increased target set size is only three-fourths as large when items from two categories appear as when all items come from the same category. With this model the category scanned first is selected at random; if the probe stimulus is in that category (regardless of whether it is positive or negative), search concludes at the end of that category's target listing in memory. Otherwise the other category is also searched. The random entry model and Estes' (59) control element model seem related.

Klatzky & Smith (107) have studied the effect of telling subjects that a particular target set stimulus has a given probability of presentation as a recognition probe if the next probe is a positive one. For probabilities greater than $1/s$, this procedure lowered the linear reaction time vs s (set size) function by 46 msec compared to the relevant function without such instructions. The investigators concluded that this procedure either increased the speed of encoding the high-probability probe or speeded the decision stage. They advocated parallel decision and comparison (scanning) processes, with the former fast process sometimes leading to a response before scanning was complete.

Theios et al (179) also showed faster recognition responses with increased probability of probe (even a negative probe, in their case). The most parsimonious of their models assumes a self-terminating search of positive and negative stimuli in an STS stack.

These and other Theios data (178), as well as some discrimination reaction time data, have been fitted by J. A. Anderson (5) to his 4-parameter interactive filter model. This model compares the feature strength vector for an input stimulus to the weighted average strength vector for the positive set of stimuli in memory (or for the negative set) after correction for any coupling effect between the positive and negative filters. Estes (60) has said that his control elements at the feature level, the letter level, or the word level may be considered an interactive filter. Note that this model produces an approximately linear increase in reaction times as a function of size of the positive set but does so without assuming a search process.

RECALL   Bernbach (21) combined a recall theory with his finite state, signal detection approach to recognition memory generating the prediction of no effect of serial position or amount of practice upon d'', the mean difference in strength parameters of old and new items. Early evidence seemed to support that implication, but controversy followed (22, 86). Bamber (18) points out that Bernbach & Kupchak (23) gave up an original assumption and prediction in trying to extend Bernbach's theory. This seems to eliminate a major prediction formerly used to differentiate the finite state model from more general strength models (also see 8).

Both Glanzer (73) and Murdock (128) interpret the bowed serial position curve for free recall as evidence of STM for the last items presented and of extra rehearsal for the first item presented. Murdock's Markov model fitted such data once one further assumed that all recently presented items which were in the available (A) state would be outputted as a single chunk, after which all other available items would be outputted with some fixed probability. Murdock gives an alternate fit of the primary memory process aspect of these same data, using the Waugh & Norman (193) conversion from probability of recall to probability $P(i)$ of being in primary memory (STM). This assumes that the flat bottom of the serial position curve for free recall yields the probability of being in secondary memory (LTM). This fit yields a double exponential Gompertz function relating $P(i)$ to item position i.

Anderson & Bower (9, p. 447) are doubtful of the capacity of HAM or FRAN to show organizational effects in free recall by outputting items in clusters corresponding to categories of input stimuli. They suggest that use of category names as members of *entryset* in FRAN might be useful for this purpose. The simulation of organizational effects in Kintsch's (101) free recall model is much like a combination of the two LNR methods described earlier under the headings Two-Stage Theory and Two-Stage Semantic Theory except that a description list for an item in STS will consist of a proposition generated for mnemonic purposes and will be searched for other items to be remembered, rather than using only characteristics of the concept.

Rundus (163) has interpreted clustering in free recall as the result of a hierarchical memory structure with list identification at the top, retrieval cues directly below, and a cluster of items below each retrieval cue, with a specific item. The computer model employed successfully predicted that the probability of retrieval of a specific item from a given category would be a declining function of the number of items in the category that were shown to the subject just before testing for recall of the others.

In a recall study somewhat like Naus, Glucksberg & Ornstein's (132) study of recognition of categorized items, Seamon (169) found a linear increase in mean reaction time with increased size of category such as names of cities. His findings of increased latency as number of categories increased from three to five and a decline for a further increase to six is not consistent with the random entry strategy, which can be shown to predict a linear increase with number of categories. Seamon further found that over two-thirds of the responses in his study were reported to be automatic (giving the first word which came to mind rather than searching through the list for a category until the desired item position was found) rather than nonautomatic.

The high speed of the automatic responses just discussed may prove interpretable by a model somewhat like that developed by Forrin & Cunningham (67) to explain serial position effects in recognition tests. They assumed that in addition to the commonly assumed serial exhaustive scanning of the target list, there is a physical identity comparison which can be performed almost immediately for any items in a rapid-access state. The number of items in this state is assumed to be independent of target list sizes but to decline with increased retention time, giving certain serial positions an advantage over others in their use of the rapid access state. This model accounts for several features of recognition performance; to handle Seamon's data, it would have to incorporate a small effect of s upon the rapid-access comparison.

Collins & Quillian (40, 41) also take a semantic approach to retrieval. For them, an important part of retrieval is like the evaluation which takes place as persons try to comprehend something which has been told to them. The theory provides for checks of compatibility between statements made or questions asked of a person and his previously stored knowledge. Each concept involved in a question has one or more paths leading from it; a tag is left at each concept to indicate that a search is moving from that concept. When such a search leads to a meeting of searches from two concepts, a proposition relating the two concepts is implied. If relevant to the question asked, that proposition is converted to a sentence and stated overtly. A wide variety of answers might prove suitable in a semantic theory. Thus D. Norman (137) discusses various answers to the question "Where is the Empire State Building?" as depending on the place and situation in which one is asked the question.

MEMORIZATION OF PROSE   Anderson & Bower's (7; 9, pp. 337–41) analysis of crossover cues raises problems for Gestalt theory. These authors present experimental evidence that study of pairs of sentences such as "The child hit the landlord," and "The minister praised the landlord," by a subject leads to responding "landlord" to both "The child hit the _____" and "The child praised the _____." This response to the second query is counterintuitive, and yet was found, as predicted from a semantic association assumption, to be more frequent than the same response to the first. The instructions used by Anderson & Bower (7) seem to bias subjects in favor of this result.

Using letters and digits as elements (ideas) in a marginal approximation to a Bransford & Franks (29) task, Reitman & Bower (155) showed that recognition confidence increased with number of elements in the test item for obvious concepts; they subsequently presented a pair of probabilistic models to predict that phenomenon. The better of the two models presumes that presentation of a string such as 123 causes tagging of the string and of all adjacent subunits such as 12. The probability that the number of tags for a string or substring of length i will exceed threshold strength during the experiment is a declining function of i. As a consequence, recognition confidence (dependent on frequency of tags exceeding a given threshold) will increase with string length where substrings have been presented separately and with exposure of the total string.

Anderson & Bower's (9) model has been pitted against Rumelhart, Lindsay & Norman's (161) model in a study of recognition of previously learned sentences as a function of overlap in sentences' subjects, verbs, and objects (183). For Anderson & Bower the base structure is binary with access to LTM possible at any terminal node in a test sentence. For a sentence in Rumelhart, Lindsay & Norman's model, the corresponding base structure is a node for a predicate (verb) with n arguments (agent, object, . . .); access apparently comes through the verb. Recognition testing which uses verb access should speed recognition of several sentences with constant subjects and objects but different verbs, compared to sentences with different objects but the same subjects and verbs. Access through any member should cause no difference in recognition times between those two conditions. Thorndyke & Bower (183) found latencies most like those predicted for access through any idea node, supporting the Anderson & Bower model. Note that this study casts more doubt on Rumelhart, Lindsay & Norman's implied accessing of information through the predicate [made explicit in (140)] than on their use, or Kintsch's (103) use, of n-ary rather than binary branching in LTM.

COMPREHENSION OF PROSE   Hayes & Simon's (81) *Understand* program begins with "language" processes for converting instructions into deep structure. "Construction" processes follow as needed to convert the deep structure into acceptable input for a problem solving program. Moore & Newell (127) have systematically examined issues to be faced in designing a system such as *Understand*. Their own *Merlin* emphasizes an assimilation criterion—finding ways for the internal structure of a computer model to make contact with the external structure to be understood. Two kinds of internal structure, (*a*) a Gestalt perceptual algorithm and (*b*) an analytic algorithm, are shown by Hunt (88) to solve some (*a*) or all (*b*) of a set of Raven's Progressive Matrices problems. Hunt distinguishes the two algorithms on the basis of cognitive style, not IQ. Two major models not previously mentioned are Winograd's (200) extensive computer simulation permitting two-way communication about a world of geometric objects to be manipulated and Schank's (168) conceptually based (language-independent) theory of natural language acquisition.

More experimentally oriented theorizing includes Kintsch & Keenan's (104) use of a Poisson variable to predict percent recall as a function of number of propositions per sentence, stemming from an observed linear relation between mean reading time and the number of propositions in a sentence of fixed length.

Kintsch (102, 103) has presented a model of episodic memory which assumes common encoding and storage operations for list learning and for text learning. Text learning also involves extensive syntactic and semantic processing. Passages of text are converted to a "text base" or series of related propositions in case frames. Recognition of an old word or passage occurs if a pattern match of the test item and some stored memory episode is perfect or nearly so.

Kintsch (103) has reported on a series of experiments by himself and his students which show longer latencies for confirming implicitly than explicitly presented propositions. This latency difference disappears with 15 min or more delay between reading a paragraph and being tested on it; supporting a Kintsch hypothesis that explicit propositions have lexical and linguistic traces as well as sensory and propositional traces, the former traces decaying more rapidly in time than the propositional traces common to explicit and implicit propositions.

MODELS OF THE QUESTION-ANSWERING PROCESS   Fiksel (65) has described a question-answering network of finite automata with parallel search techniques. Question-asking consists of presenting a list of two automata and a path or ordered sequence of relations. If such a path exists between the two automata, "Yes" is answered. For example, there may be a path from *robin* to *feathers* by way of the relations "subset of" and "has-as-parts," in that order, those two relations constituting the path. Then the question: "(*robin*, subset of, has-as-parts, *feathers*)," read in English as "does *robin* have a path 'subset of' followed by 'has-as-parts' leading to *feathers*?", would be answered affirmatively. Like Collins & Quillian (40, 41), Fiksel generates predictions of reaction latencies to test questions as a function of the maximum number of arcs to be searched in looking for a given path between nodes.

D. Norman's (137, 140) nodespace seems to be the same as Fiksel's in its ultimate elements but can be considerably more differentiated by virtue of the way its interconnections are structured. For example, use of primitives such as "poss" (for possess) as part of several verbs such as *received, took, had, kept,* and *bought*—and separate organization of linguistic types and tokens make Norman's model much more human in responding to questions.

Kintsch (103) has questioned the necessity to decompose lexical items for storage. Phenomena such as understanding paraphrases or showing interference in sentence recall between related verbs such as "received" and "borrowed" (140, chap. 9) can be predicted either with a decomposability assumption or by adding meaning postulates to LTM. Kintsch performed a series of experiments showing that generating a sentence from a word, sentence comprehension, and memory are all unimpaired if a key word is complex (and thus decomposable) rather than simple. However, even simple words such as "announce" used by Kintsch appear more complex than words such as "put" and "kill" which have been decomposed elsewhere (140, 161).

Carbonell & Collins (31) and Collins, Carbonell & Warnock (39) detail the operation of *Scholar,* a semantic network instructional system capable of asking questions, answering questions whose answers are directly retrievable, and generating plausible answers which must be inferred from information stored, sometimes without being implied logically. Kintsch's (101, pp. 292–99) question-answering mechanism is closer to Fiksel's in emphasizing pattern matching and strictly logical inference.

Freedle (69) has presented a simple question-answering model to handle subjects' accuracy in making "all," "some," or "none" judgments about items in a story read to them. Anderson & Hastie (4) used HAM to predict shorter verification latencies for a sentence such as "James Bartlett caused the accident," knowing that (*a*) James Bartlett is the lawyer and (*b*) the lawyer caused the accident, if (*a*) was learned before (*b*) rather than the reverse.

RULE GOVERNED BEHAVIOR

Concept Identification

SURVEYS   Millward & Wickens (125) have surveyed various hypothesis models of concept identification, classifying axioms such as those pertaining to time of sampling hypotheses, sampling probabilities, and hypothesis elimination and replacement. This paper and a critique of it by Falmagne (64) and related chapters in (110) are very useful as an integration of theoretical work. Brown (30) has summarized much of the empirical evidence on variants of hypothesis theory.

SEQUENCE-SPECIFIC EFFECTS   Cotton (46) has investigated a one-hypothesis-at-a-time, win-stay lose-shift model (156) for affirmative problems (those using a single dimension to define the solution). Given a local consistency assumption, this model implies a high presolution probability of correct responding for certain stimuli such that a large number of hypotheses are consistent with feedback on adjacent trials. Cotton also showed that a similar "congruence effect" is implied by the corresponding Chumbley (37) all-hypotheses-at-a-time model. Paranjpe (148) has compared four Markov models (without free parameters) for sequence-specific behavior in three-category affirmative problems.

PROBES FOR IDENTIFYING HYPOTHESES   Aiken, Santa & Ruskin (2) have replicated earlier findings of a similarity effect closely related to the congruence effect just discussed, as well as confirming the predictions of several theorists [and the results of a later study by Coltheart (42)] that blank trials do not affect hypothesis behavior in affirmative, nonredundant concept tasks. Levison & Restle (120) report that with certain differences between the types of stimuli presented on feedback and on blank trials of redundant relevant cues problems, new information is presented on blank trials, thus reducing the number of solvers of two or more dimensions as implied by Restle's model.

Millward & Spoehr (124) used a single-cue-at-a-time blank trial procedure with several such blank trials permitted between feedback trials. Results supported a focusing assumption but not a sampling with replacement assumption. Sampling may also be systematic, not random (see also 87 and 199). Berger's (20) study using both single-cue and multiple-cue tracking of hypotheses gave results suggesting a random reversal of hypothesis assumption. There is a small probability of loss or reversal of information from the stimulus, the feedback, or the processing done immediately after feedback. Cotton (47) found similar processing errors to those of Berger; a passive state modification of the Restle model eliminated some inconsistencies between theory and data.

Gholson, Levine & Phillips (72) distinguished between two systems of hypotheses ("strategies" such as focusing and dimension checking and "stereotypes" such as stimulus preference and position preference), showing that kindergarten children almost always used stereotypes and that the proportion of strategies increased with age, with focusing and dimension checking being the most common methods of college students.

MULTIPLE-LOOK MODELS AND ONE-LOOK MODELS PRODUCING MULTIPLE-CUE SOLUTIONS   Levison & Restle (119) compared two, three, and four redundant relevant cue (RRC) problems. They concluded that Trabasso & Bower's (189) earlier theoretical and empirical work on the first of these three types of problems holds for all of them except that the number of elements originally in the focus sample was often very large and fluctuated from person to person. Cotton (45) has noted mathematical and empirical problems with Trabasso & Bower's predictions. Two articles (99, 171) have presented a one-look model which predicts possible learning of more than one cue in an RRC problem by random variation in the cue selected on different trials.

MEDIATION   Polson & Dunham (152) provided a Markov hypothesis model and a transfer model [see also M. Levine's (117) transfer hypothesis] to explain such phenomena as faster learning of intradimensional and reversal shifts than extradimensional shifts by adults. Kajita (97) hypothesized that superiority of adults, as opposed to children, in reversal shifts follows from children's inability to form a set theoretic description of the positive stimuli in training in order to facilitate later reversal learning. Norman & Levine (143) reported successful use of two Markov models for mediation of an A–C verbal relation after training of an A–B verbal association and a B–C verbal relation. Ellis (56) found no evidence that kindergarten children classified as concept users on a three-dimensional optional shift task were more likely than nonconcept users to have previously demonstrated initial learning describable as hypothesis learning rather than independent subproblem learning. Each tenable hypothesis after one reversal trial was equally likely to be chosen; there was no preference for within-dimensional shifts. Tighe (185) used "stat-rats" to simulate single-link theory reversal shift and extradimensional shift learning by animals, finding much but not all of his own data to fit that theory. Tighe's closely related studies with children from about 3 to 11 years of age pose problems for single-link theory, mediation theory, and attention theory alike.

Wilson (199) found that a hierarchical sampling rule for selecting new hypotheses would work better than mediation theory in explaining observed trials to attain shift criteria for different reversal conditions in conjunctive concept performance with adults.

OTHER HYPOTHESIS THEORY ISSUES   K. Norman (142) has studied a distance-combining task interpretable as concept identification with a continuously variable response, modeling asymptotic performance only. Falmagne (63) found increased confidence ratings for specific hypotheses with increased numbers of successive precriterion confirmations of them, supporting her previous theoretical work. Wickens & Zax (198) reported failures of the additivity of cues assumption for two out of six conditions where learning rate predictions were made from that assumption and other groups' data, explaining the discrepancies in terms of specific properties of the stimuli involved. Cotton & Harris (48) showed that the Bower & Trabasso (28) and Restle models (156) imply generation of substantial individual differences as a consequence of practice. Polson (150) reported an extensive theoretical and experimental comparison of learning successive paired-associate lists, with and without each item on List i having the same response as that in List i-1 for a corresponding item mediated by a concept rule or sense impression. A two-stage theory (with subjects either holding an incorrect hypothesis about relationships between successive lists or behaving according to a cue selection process which permits retention of the correct cue from one list to another) proved necessary to predict the degree of transfer within the concept groups. Nonconcept groups' behavior was predicted with the cue selection process alone.

Theories of Rule and Attribute Learning for Complex Problems

Sawyer (165) has assumed that naive subjects compare the stimulus for a trial to a previous comparison stimulus and feedback, with respect to a randomly selected dimension, copying the feedback for the comparison stimulus if the two stimuli are alike on the selected dimension. Otherwise the subject copies that feedback with probability 0.16 and shifts to the opposite response with probability 0.84. This model is successful in predicting the observed order of difficulty of the following rule-learning problems, the most difficult being listed first: biconditional, conditional, disjunctive, and conjunctive.

Bourne (25) and Salatas & Bourne (164) presented a less quantitatively explicit model to deal with rules complementary to the four studied by Sawyer. Salatas & Bourne assume, on the basis of previous research, that sophisticated subjects are less likely to show an initial bias in favor of a conjunctive solution and more likely, when told the "true-true" instance definition, to code all stimuli according to their truth value.

Haygood, Fishbein & Pinzka (82) showed the implications of a holist strategy of concept identification appropriate to affirmative problems (with or without redundant relevant dimensions) or to any conjunctive concept combining two or more dimensions in the conjunction. Perfect memory for positive instances required in future comparisons permits exclusion of irrelevant dimensions as soon as logically possible. These assumptions, plus a presolution response rule, permit exact predictions for perfect processors. Indow, Dewa & Tadokoro (90) performed simulations of holist and one-element models for affirmative and conjunctive problems, obtaining good fits to data of those subjects whose trial-by-trial verbal reports indicated use of those strategies. The proportion of persons using holist strategies or holist strategies with occasional processing errors was high, presumably because of the large number of problems learned by each subject. Such strategies have also been examined with affirmative concepts (91, 92).

Laughlin (116) computed means and standard deviations of a number of possible solutions searched before solution of a four- to six-dimensional conjunctive concept task with two, three, or four relevant, nonredundant dimension values under perfect processing assumptions for successive scanning, conservative focusing, and focus sampling strategies. Laughlin (115) verified experimentally that instructions to use a focusing strategy on every trial led to greater focusing than other instruction and to faster learning of conjunctive concepts. Neither this study nor one by Miller (123) found a significant effect of number of values per dimension, confirming Miller's theoretical predictions for ideal focusers.

Chumbley's (38) duoprocess theory of concept learning, separating learning into selection of relevant dimensions and assignment of responses to values of those dimensions, received general confirmation from Chumbley's own examples. Thomson (181) obtained mixed evidence about the theory's applicability to a four- to six-response conjunctive task.

Aiken (1) predicted simple reaction times at the asymptote of learning for several complex concept rules, using decision tree structures. Egan & Greeno (55) consider tree structures central to performance of a wide class of rule induction problems such as concept identification and problem solving. Whereas they emphasize the differences in structure for different problems, Simon & Lea (174) have developed a single General Rule Induction (GRI) executive program. Application of the GRI to concept identification requires both a problem space for rules to be followed and for instances to test the rules against, whereas problem solving needs only the problem space for rules.

Other Inference Problems

Erickson (58) has developed and tested three probabilistic models of Aristotelian deduction, including one model which generates the well-known atmosphere effect. Huesmann & Cheng (87) have modeled subjects' search for a simple algebraic expression to imply Y as a function of A and B when all three values are given for six examples. They assume several pools of solution classes of increasing complexity plus a systematic search order within pools.

Frederiksen (68) developed and tested a multivariate response model of learning and comprehension, hypothesizing the combination of three nonstationary Markov simplex growth processes. The first such process is the learning of directly presented (veridical) relations, the second of inferrable relations, and the third of elaborated relations in a story presented several times. Good fits of the data to the model resulted, with a striking finding being this: to maximize amounts of inferred and elaborated relations learned per veridical item learned, one should instruct subjects to develop solutions to problems described in the story, rather than to memorize relations.

PROBABILITY LEARNING   Estes (61) used observation of simulated opinion polling results as a probability learning input, concluding that the learning of probabilities is much faster than formerly believed. He showed good fits of much probability learning data to a model for encoding information about the relative frequencies of winning and total trials for each possible winner in a fixed set. Thomas (180) has generated probability matching using a combined signal detection and learning model with a shift in decision criterion only after incorrect responses. M.V. Levine (118) has shown that data from a single subject can be used to estimate the generalization function associated with responses to a probability learning task using continuous response and reinforcement variables. Work by Herrnstein (84) and others (3, 49, 186) supports variants of the probability-matching hypothesis in operant behavior. Relations between this hypothesis and the Luce choice axiom are sometimes evident (89).

A variation on the Trabasso & Bower (188) four-choice concept identification model based on conjunctions of values of two binary dimensions has been employed (192) to describe concept performance with 100%, 84.4%, or 68.8% correct feedback. Assumptions of response reversal, resampling with replacement, and resampling with delayed replacement were equally effective in accomodating inconsistent feedback. In a two-choice task Edgell & Castellan (54) combined probabilistic reinforcement for affirmative responses on one or both stimulus dimensions with probabilistic reinforcement for conjunctive responses using both dimensions. Their subjects proved sensitive to reinforcement with conjunctive contingencies, thus supporting their earlier (33) configural hypothesis generation model for probabilistic multiple-cue tasks.

SERIAL PATTERN LEARNING   Simon (173) found that in data presented by earlier investigators (190) there was a correlation of 0.70 to 0.98 between pairs of measures from the triad: information-theoretic measures of sequence complexity, subjectively rated sequence complexity, and the length of the code used by those authors to describe a given sequence. Simon also compared a variety of coding schemes. He concluded that using a push-down list notation tended to increase the number of symbols required to characterize complex sequences but to minimize STM requirements of persons learning the sequence with that notation. Kotovsky & Simon (109) replicated an earlier study of acquisition of 14 Thurstone letter-series-completion tasks, finding three ways in which their earlier computer model for the task should be revised.

Egan & Greeno (55) have shown the mathematical structure of several serial patterns; for example, 12124654 can be generated by a finite automaton whereas

2645979 . . . requires a pushdown automaton. Greeno & Simon (78) have focused upon the problem of generating serial patterns from storage using three kinds of devices. The pushdown interpreter is intermediate with respect to five criteria, the recompute interpreter is high in such things as the number of operations and low in terms of STS space requirements, and the doubling interpreter is approximately the reverse of the recompute interpreter in efficiency.

Restle (157) has shown that speed of presentation of serial patterns in a preview does not affect later learning by the anticipation method. However, increasing the number of previews is beneficial to later learning, as is the use of good phrasing (increasing the temporal gaps at logical shift points in the sequence). Increasing these gaps at inappropriate points is worse than using even spacing throughout. Restle & Burnside (159) studied very rapid tracking, rather than anticipation of serial patterns. This series of experiments confirmed the principal phenomena obtained with the earlier method, notably the greater incidence of errors at decision points in the tree for the problem, with more errors occurring at higher levels of the tree. Restle (158) found inconsistent effects of different kinds of shifts in structure. Estes (59) has indicated that his hierarchically organized control element mechanism for stimulus encoding will account for grouping effects in serial pattern learning.

Two experiments by Jones (95) on prediction and/or recall of 24-item serial lists of numbers gave support to Vitz & Todd's (190) theory that sequence difficulty depends upon the amount of information in the code required to summarize a sequence and to a dimensional organization hypothesis of Ebenholtz (52).

INSTRUCTIONAL MODELS

Optimization Procedures in Computer-Assisted Instruction (CAI)

Optimization procedures have been applied recently to CAI sequencing of items or allotment of computer instructional time for students of spelling (17), reading (11, 13), and foreign languages (11, 12, 17, 114). Atkinson (11) recommends the goal of maximizing average percent correct, $P_i(t)$ at posttesting, subject to the condition that the variance of this average be no larger than if CAI had not been employed.

Allotment of computer time to individual students of beginning reading was based on an instructional objective plus an assumption that $P_i(t)$ was an exponential growth function of alloted time t for each individual, with the parameters for this function being fitted separately for each individual (11, 13). Sequencing of items presentation in second-language vocabulary instruction attempted to maximize average percent correct at posttesting, with the sequencing implied for the linear model or for the trial-dependent Markov model. The latter model yielded a much more effective sequencing procedure, especially when different parameter estimates were obtained for each item being learned (11, 12). Student self-selection of items yielded superior performance to all groups except that for the trial-dependent model with different parameter estimates. This may be because student's naive tendency to study items they have been failing recently is quite like the strategy implied by an all-or-none model. Atkinson & Paulson (17) found that the all-or-none strategy yields higher mean posttest spelling performance than the strategy for the linear model. These authors also compared a strategy based on the all-or-none model to a strategy based on the random-trial increments model plus an assumption of an individual differences parameter for each learner and an item parameter for each item, showing that the latter strategy yielded a higher mean posttest performance in learning Swahili vocabulary. Laubsch & Chiang's (114) comparison of linear model and general forgetting theory strategies in sequencing Chinese characters whose meaning was to be learned yielded similar results. However, adding individual differences and item parameters did not facilitate posttest performance.

CAI curricula typically involve several strands or subcurricula. For example, a beginning reading curriculum may include a *readiness strand* (teaching the student to use a teletype and to perform skills preliminary to reading) and a *letter strand* (to provide experience in recognition and recall of letters of the alphabet), among other strands. Chant & Atkinson (34) presented the control theory necessary to allocate relative amounts of instructional time to two strands known to interact, with learning rate (x_1) on Strand 1 declining and learning rate (x_2) on Strand 2 increasing when x_1-x_2 is large and positive. An estimate of the (x_1, x_2) vector for each student is obtained at the end of each day, with the subsequent day's relative allocation being selected to move him toward, or keep him on, what is called a turnpike path. This yields an approximation to optimality, with a final period occurring near the end of training being devoted wholly to one strand in order to maximize overall learning.

Chant & Luenberger (35) used a generalization of Thurstone's (184) learning model as a basis for a model of instruction from which optimization procedures could be generated. Given a performance index dependent on the probability of correct response and a loss function based on intensity of instruction and cost to the learner, then the optimal amount of instruction, rate of presentation of information, etc are derived for individuals and groups as a function of ability and homogeneity of ability.

A Structural Approach to Teaching

Scandura (166, 167) and Durnin & Scandura (51) showed that a given algorithm for a problem class such as column subtraction may be decomposed into component acts required to perform that algorithm. Unless the learner has a second, nonequivalent algorithm available for that class of problems, one can predict from the list of component rules he knows what subsets of the problem class he can and cannot solve. Correspondingly one can predict from the subsets (equivalence classes with respect to rules required in solution) he can solve, which rules he knows. Higher order rules, such as rules for inferring parameters of a linear equation from observed values, are hypothesized to be invoked when lower order rules capable of solving the problem are not available to the learner. This view bears some similarity to Huesmann & Cheng's (87) ordering of pools of solution classes.

Scandura (166, pp. 177, 185) has assumed (*a*) that if a subject has an available rule that can lead him to his goal, he will use it; and (*b*) if the rules of an algorithm all act in atomic fashion, then if and only if a subject can solve one problem in an equivalence class, he can solve all problems in that class. These assumptions have led to good predictive success in a variety of mathematical tasks. Note that (*a*) is a fairly weak psychological assumption and that (*b*) looks suspiciously like a theorem from (*a*) plus the properties of equivalence classes. Scandura believes that studying behavior under memory-free conditions reduces the need for probabilistic theories to describe it. "Memory-free conditions" presumably means little demand is placed on STM; LTM is still important.

Other Instructional Models

In using an information structured CAI approach to tutoring in integral calculus, Kimball (100) developed and tested an impressive model of problem solving learning and performance. Students are assumed to be in a state characterizable as a problem description state or as a failure state associated with a particular problem description. The transition probability for moving from one state (s_i) to another (s_k) depends on the probabilities (t_{ij}) of applying technique j to s_i and the probabilities of moving from one state to another, given that j is applied. Solution of certain problems can occur with a fixed t_{ij} matrix. Learning occurs when t_{ij} changes in value, typically after a failure of technique j in state i. Contrary to theory, there was a noticeable spread of success and failure effects over the five most recently previously applied techniques and the five next applied techniques.

Groen & Parkman (79) have shown that children's addition of pairs of single digits have reaction times which are linear functions of the smaller members of the pair, supporting the hypothesis of counting to obtain the sum. These first grade children are presumed to begin with the minimum and count upward as many steps as required by the larger addend. Pairs of identical members behave as if their lesser member were zero; adults act like children except that the slopes of their linear functions reduce twentyfold to 20 msec per item, about the same as Atkinson & Juola's (16) slope for recognition latency in an STM study as a function of memory-set size. Groen & Poll (80) found a linear relation between reaction time of elementary school children in solving for u in sentences of the form $x + u = y$ (and sometimes in $u + x = y$) as a function of the minimum of x and y–x. Parkman (149) found that college students exhibited linear reaction times in single-digit pair multiplication as a function of the smaller member of the pair. A complex model implying a linear function as a function of the log of the sum-plus-the-product of the pair members received even more support from these data.

Suppes (175) and Suppes & Morningstar (177) presented a finite automaton model for column addition which employs two states ("carry" and "no-carry") and three parameters, one the probability of making an error by not carrying when it is necessary, one the probability of making an error by carrying when it is undesirable, and one the probability of outputting the wrong digit for a column. Offir (147) refined this model. A more advanced mechanism, Suppes' (175) register machine model, is based on machines developed by Shepherdson & Sturgis (170) but which employ more perceptual mechanisms than necessary for the earlier, linguistically oriented work.

Such register machines have instruction sets comparable to assembly language computer programs, together with subroutines for certain processes. A register machine is a very general form of automaton, being able to compute all computable (partial recursive) functions and thus being equivalent to Turing machines (170). It is a performance system, not a learning system. However, Suppes (175) has suggested for single-column addition with an indefinite number of rows, a classification of the instruction set into four parts to be learned separately, indicating two models of learning the four parts. One model assumes independence of the parts. The other is hierarchical, requiring that all lower levels be learned before a higher level part can be learned. Wollmer (201) examined a slightly different hierarchical model in which successful performance of a task at one level increases the average probability of being correct at the next level. Dynamic programming was used to find an instructional sequence of levels to be passed (and number of times each should be passed) to minimize the expected time to complete a course on a topic such as Kirchoff's laws of electricity.

Norman, Gentner & Stevens (139) discuss schemata which when stored by the learner facilitate or retard learning of specific tasks. Gentner (71) reported on the development in childhood of understanding of verbs of possession such as "give" and "take," together with a computer representation of their knowledge structures and associated schemata. D. Norman (138) has advocated a still vague procedure of *web teaching* rather than step-by-step teaching in logical order (linear teaching), justifying it by asserting that integration of new material requires building a supporting structure by learning an outline of the material, then a more detailed overview, and then more and more detailed structures. This view is congruent with earlier comments of a painter friend of Virginia Woolf's (19, p. 106) objecting to linear constraints in writing and suggesting that a word's effects could be represented "by placing the word in the middle of a page and surrounding it radially with associated ideas."

Carroll (32) tested his own theory of school learning with a massive cross-sectional data set. After some post hoc rescaling of each variable, aptitude (STAA Memory Test scores) proved an approximately linear function of school grade level (t) for groups of students with growth rate α. Achievement (CAT Arithmetic Total scores) proved approximately equal to a constant plus αt.

In an important Russian book now available in English, Landa (113) presented a mathematico-logical method of analyzing tasks such as grammar. Indicative features comparable to dimension values in rule learning problems are used to identify such units as compound sentences. Optimization procedures order decision points on the basis of the probability of a given indicative feature and the time necessary to identify it. There is experimental evidence of high efficiency of instruction with such procedures.

Suppes, Fletcher & Zanotti (176) obtained the function $y = bt^k + c$ where y is grade placement in a subject, t is the number of sessions of instruction, and b, c, and k are individually estimated for each student. They show good fits of this equation to achievement in elementary mathematics by hearing-impaired students, with almost as good estimation occurring with a fixed k value for all individuals.

Discrimination Learning and Partial Reinforcement Models

Robbins (160) found that existing and new variants of stimulus sampling theory can account for successive discrimination learning and transfer. M. Norman (145) has developed a Markov attentional model for a variety of discrimination phenomena. Koteskey (108) explained several partial reinforcement phenomena by using stimulus sampling theory together with an assumption that the number of stimulus elements sampled immediately after a nonreinforcement is an exponentially increasing function of the number of successive nonreinforcements. Frey & Colliver (70) developed their own sensitivity and response bias measures for applying signal detection theory to differential eyelid conditioning in rabbits as a function of cue similarity. Eckerman, McGourty & Shonfeld (53) found partial success of the Luce model in predicting stimulus generalization by pigeons.

Other Models

Polson (151) has generated conditional mean latency functions and presolution choice functions for Markov models. Wolter & Earl (202) found the Audley-Jonckheere urn model superior to the linear model, Luce model, or Spence model for predicting asymptotic choice behavior of rats given 100% reinforcement regardless of T-maze choice, with a modified Bush-Mosteller model proving superior in the 0% reinforcement case. Arnold (10) has made a further extension of the classical urn model.

STATISTICAL CONSIDERATIONS WITH REGARD TO LEARNING MODELS

Identifiability

Nahinsky (131) has shown that for outcome-contingent models, being in a learned state must still permit rare response errors if a model is to be identifiable. Townsend (187) showed that mathematical models of serial and parallel scanning have special cases in which the two kinds of processes are equivalent. Wandell, Greeno & Egan (191) proved how a Markov model in matrix form could be changed into another Markov model with the same likelihood function but possibly with fewer states. Polson & Huizinga (153) have shown that if a model is not identifiable, it will have a flat spot or connected area of parameter values with constant likelihood. This theorem should be relatable to Dorfman's (50) statement of the conditions under which an additive learning model will have a strictly concave likelihood function and his proof that it will therefore have a unique global maximum.

Estimation

Bogartz (24) has compared guessing probabilities estimated when responses to one stimulus are independent of those to another and when assignment of a correct response to one stimulus excludes it from assignment to any other stimulus. Use of the former method when the experimental procedure of the latter case applies leads to systematic overestimation of the probability that an item is in the learned state.

Thomson (182) developed least squares parameter estimates for a model of three-trial object-discrimination learning-set performance with some missing data. Fisher (65a), dealing with the same model, performed stat-subject analyses of a case in which an active hypothesis was omitted from the set identified by the investigator. When a nonorthogonal hypothesis is overlooked, the estimated probabilities of some other hypotheses can easily be negative. Assuming that the strengths of estimated hypotheses sum to 1 or less than 1 allows appropriate estimates to be obtained by linear programming. Offir (146) showed that the fit of models to certain data was improved by assuming different parameters for each learner.

Statistical Tests

Grams & van Belle (74) have provided a test of the adequacy of a particular grouping of experimental subjects into a set of "macrosubjects," showing whether the angular transformation of data from these macrosubjects has corrected for failure of binomial assumptions and whether regrouping is desirable before further analysis.

TEXTBOOKS

Two textbooks appropriate to mathematical psychology courses (Laming 112, M. Norman 144) have appeared recently. The former gives primary emphasis in its learning sections to stimulus sampling theory, Markov models, discrimination learning, avoidance learning, and probability learning. The latter, which deals exclusively with Markov models, presupposes competence in integration, metric topology, functional analysis, and theory of probability. Mathematical models of learning receive emphasis in an outstanding memory text by Murdock (129); most of these models are described verbally by Klatzky (106). Restle (158a) has written a somewhat mathematical textbook which integrates material in cognitive psychology, learning theory, and animal behavior. Lindsay & Norman (121) survey much relevant material. A two-volume series entitled *Contemporary Developments in Mathematical Psychology* (110, 111) is well described by its title. Chapters on mathematical learning theory and information-processing theories appear in the new edition of *Theories of Learning* by Hilgard & Bower (85).

CONCLUSION

Taken as a whole, recent research on models of learning exhibits both methodological and topical changes. Earlier mathematical tools have been supplemented, but not supplanted, by increasing use of semantic theory, of the theory of computational machines, and of computer simulation techniques. There is an increased study of such topics as natural language behavior, e.g. the comprehension or memorizing of stories and factual writings.

These changes may make it possible to relate certain subfields of psychology more closely. For example, Norman, Rumelhart, and the LNR group (140, pp. 77–87) have emphasized "conversational postulates," conventions and presuppositions persons have concerning the understandings they and their listeners share about acceptable conversational procedures and about specific topics being discussed. Since the idea of conversational postulates has origins in both linguistics and sociology, use of this idea can readily be an intersection point for theories of learning, psycholinguistics, and social psychology. Such innovations make learning theory more of a social science than was true a decade ago, but enough ties to the biological sciences remain to satisfy many of us who were trained in a reductionist tradition. Hopefully interest will continue in both biological and social determinants of learning.

Literature Cited

1. Aiken, J. O. 1972. *Choice reaction times for complex concepts*. PhD thesis. Brown Univ., Providence, RI. 127 pp.
2. Aiken, L. S., Santa, J. L., Rushkin, A. B. 1972. Nonreinforced trials in concept identification: Presolution statistics and local consistency. *J. Exp. Psychol.* 93:100–4
3. Ambler, S. 1973. A mathematical model of learning under schedules of interresponse time reinforcement. *J. Math. Psychol.* 10:364–86
4. Anderson, J., Hastie, R. 1974. Individuation and reference in memory: Proper names and definite descriptions. *Cogn. Psychol.* 6:495–514
5. Anderson, J. A. 1973. A theory for the recognition of items from short memorized lists. *Psychol. Rev.* 80:417–38
6. Anderson, J. R. 1972. FRAN: A simulation model of free recall. In *The Psychology of Learning and Motivation*, ed. G. H. Bower, 5:315–78. New York: Academic. 388 pp.
7. Anderson, J. R., Bower, G. H. 1972. Configural properties in sentence memory. *J. Verb. Learn. Verb. Behav.* 11:594–605
8. Anderson, J. R., Bower, G. H. 1972. Recognition and retrieval processes in free recall. *Psychol. Rev.* 79:97–123
9. Anderson, J. R., Bower, G. H. 1973. *Human Associative Memory*. Washington, D.C.: Winston. 524 pp.
10. Arnold, B. C. 1973. Response distributions for a generalized urn scheme under noncontingent reinforcement. *J. Math. Psychol.* 10:232–39
11. Atkinson, R. C. 1972. Ingredients for a theory of instruction. *Am. Psychol.* 27:925–31
12. Atkinson, R. C. 1972. Optimizing learning a second vocabulary. *J. Exp. Psychol.* 96:124–29
13. Atkinson, R. C. 1974. Teaching children to read by computer. *Am. Psychol.* 29:169–78
14. Atkinson, R. C., Herrmann, D. J., Wescourt, K. T. 1974. Search processes in recognition memory. In *Theories in Cognitive Psychology*, ed. R. L. Solso, 101–46. Potomac, Md.: Erlbaum. 386 pp.
15. Atkinson, R. C., Juola, J. R. 1973. Factors influencing speed and accuracy in word recognition. In *Attention and Performance*, ed. S. Kornblum, 4:583–612. New York: Academic. 771 pp.
16. Atkinson, R. C., Juola, J. F. 1974. Search and decision processes in recognition memory. See Ref. 110, 243–93
17. Atkinson, R. C., Paulson, J. A. 1972. An approach to the psychology of instruction. *Psychol. Bull.* 78:49–61
18. Bamber, D. 1974. Comment on Bernbach's prediction of the variance of type 2 d' in confidence-rated recall. *J. Math. Psychol.* 11:33–41
19. Bell, Q. 1972. *Virginia Woolf. A Biography*. New York: Harcourt-Brace-Jovanovich. 314 pp.
20. Berger, D. E. 1974. Measures of information processing in concept identification. *J. Exp. Psychol.* 102:384–92
21. Bernbach, H. A. 1967. Decision processes in memory. *Psychol. Rev.* 74:462–80
22. Ibid 1972. Confidence ratings for individual items in recall. 79:536–37
23. Bernbach, H. A., Kupchak, P. G. 1972. Recognition and recall in short-term memory. *J. Math. Psychol.* 9:237–42
24. Bogartz, W. 1974. Note on guessing probabilities. *J. Math. Psychol.* 11:328–33
25. Bourne, L. E. Jr. 1974. An inference model for conceptual rule learning. See Ref. 14, 231–56
26. Bower, G. H. 1972. A selective review of organizational factors in memory. In *Organization of Memory*, ed. E. Tulving, W. Donaldson, 93–137. New York: Academic. 423 pp.

27. Bower, G. H. 1972. Stimulus-sampling theory of encoding variability. In *Coding Processes in Human Memory*, ed. A. W. Melton, E. Martin, 85–123. Washington, D.C.: Winston. 448 pp.

28. Bower, G. H., Trabasso, T. R. 1964. Concept identification. In *Studies in Mathematical Psychology*, ed. R. C. Atkinson, 32–94. Stanford Univ. Press. 414 pp.

29. Bransford, J. D., Franks, J. J. 1972. The abstraction of linguistic ideas: A review. *Cognition* 1:211–49

30. Brown, A. S. 1974. Examination of hypothesis-sampling theory. *Psychol. Bull.* 81:773–90

31. Carbonell, J. R., Collins, A. M. 1973. Natural semantics in artificial intelligence. *Proc. 3rd Int. Joint Conf. Artif. Intel.*, Stanford Univ., 344–51

32. Carroll, J. B. 1974. Fitting a model of school learning to aptitude and achievement data over grade levels. In *The Aptitude-Achievement Distinction*, ed. D. Green. New York: McGraw-Hill

33. Castellan, N. J. Jr., Edgell, S. E. 1973. An hypothesis generation model for judgment in nonmetric multiple-cue probability learning. *J. Math. Psychol.* 10:204–22

34. Chant, V. G., Atkinson, R. C. 1973. Optimal allocation of instructional effort to inter-related strands. *J. Math. Psychol.* 10:1–25

35. Chant, V. G., Luenberger, D. G. 1974. A mathematical theory of instruction: instructor/learner interaction and instruction pacing. *J. Math. Psychol.* 11:132–58

36. Chomsky, N. 1963. Formal properties of grammars. In *Handbook of Mathematical Psychology*, ed. R. D. Luce, R. R. Bush, E. Galanter, 2:323–418. New York: Wiley. 606 pp.

37. Chumbley, J. I. 1969. Hypothesis memory in concept learning. *J. Math. Psychol.* 6:528–40

38. Ibid 1972. A duoprocess theory of concept learning. 9:17–35

39. Collins, A. M., Carbonell, J. R., Warnock, D. H. Semantic inferential processing by computer. In *Advances in Cybernetics and Systems*, ed. J. Rose. London: Gordon & Breach. In press

40. Collins, A. M., Quillian, M. R. 1972. Experiments on semantic memory and language. In *Cognition in Learning and Memory*, ed. L. W. Gregg, 117–37. New York: Wiley. 263 pp.

41. Collins, A. M., Quillian, M. R. 1972. How to make a language user. See Ref. 26, 310–51

42. Coltheart, V. 1973. Concept identification with and without blank trials. *Quart. J. Exp. Psychol.* 25:1–9

43. Corballis, M. C., Kirby, J., Miller, A. 1972. Access to elements of a memorized list. *J. Exp. Psychol.* 94:185–90

44. Corballis, M. C., Miller, A. 1973. Scanning and decision processes in recognition memory. *J. Exp. Psychol.* 98:379–86

45. Cotton, J. W. 1972. Mathematical analysis of a multiple-look concept identification model. *Br. J. Math. Stat. Psychol.* 25:257–73

46. Cotton, J. W. 1974. Implications of two local consistency strategy selection models. *J. Math. Psychol.* 11:364–90

47. Cotton, J. W. 1975. Effects of stimulus congruence on hypotheses held in a concept identification task. *Psychol. Res.* 37:229–43

48. Cotton, J. W., Harris, C. W. 1973. Reliability coefficients as a function of individual differences induced by a learning process assuming identical organisms. *J. Math. Psychol.* 10:387–420

49. de Villiers, P. A. 1972. Reinforcement and response rate interaction in multiple random-interval avoidance schedules. *J. Exp. Anal. Behav.* 18:499–507

50. Dorfman, D. D. 1973. The likelihood of additive learning models: Sufficient conditions for strict log-concavity and uniqueness of maximum. *J. Math. Psychol.* 10:73–85

51. Durnin, J., Scandura, J. M. 1973. An algorithmic approach to assessing behavior potential: comparison with item forms and hierarchical technologies. *J. Educ. Psychol.* 65:262–72

52. Ebenholtz, S. M. 1972. Serial learning and dimensional organization. See Ref. 6, 267–314

53. Eckerman, D. A., McGourty, D. P., Shonfeld, R. E. 1972. A comparison of models relating successive to simultaneous measures of stimulus control. *Learn. Motiv.* 3:223–36

54. Edgell, S. E., Castellan, N. J. Jr. 1973. Configural effect in multiple-cue probability learning. *J. Exp. Psychol.* 100:310–14

55. Egan, D. E., Greeno, J. G. 1974. Theory of rule induction: knowledge acquired in concept learning, serial pattern learning, and problem solving. In *Knowledge and Cognition*, ed. L. W. Gregg, 43–103. Potomac, Md.: Erlbaum. 321 pp.

56. Ellis, R. H. 1974. *Conceptual and nonconceptual processes in the concept-shift behavior of kindergarten children.* PhD thesis. Univ. California, Santa Barbara. 117 pp.
57. Engeler, E. 1973. *Introduction to the Theory of Computation.* New York: Academic. 231 pp.
58. Erickson, J. R. 1974. A set analysis theory of behavior in formal syllogistic reasoning tasks. See Ref. 14, 305–29
59. Estes, W. K. 1972. An associative basis for coding and organization in memory. See Ref. 27, 161–90
60. Estes, W. K. 1974. *Memory, perception, and decision in letter identification.* Presented at Loyola Symp. Cogn. Psychol., Chicago
61. Estes, W. K. 1974. *The cognitive side of probability learning.* Presented at Midwest. Psychol. Assoc., Chicago
62. Estes, W. K., Suppes, P. 1974. Foundations of stimulus sampling theory. See Ref. 110, 163–83
63. Falmagne, R. J. 1972. Memory process in concept identification. *J. Exp. Psychol.* 92:33–42
64. Falmagne, R. J. 1974. Mathematical psychology and cognitive phenomena: Comments on preceding chapters. See Ref. 110, 145–61
65. Fiksel, J. 1973. A network-of-automata model for question-answering in semantic memory. *Stanford Univ. Inst. Math. Stud. Soc. Sci. Tech. Rep. 218.* 84 pp.
65a. Fisher, M. A. 1974. Estimating hypothesis strengths. *Behav. Res. Meth. Instrum.* 6:309–11
66. Flade, A., Wender, K. F. 1974. Der Einfluss der Darbietungsmodalität auf das kurzfristige Behalten. *Psychol. Res.* 37:125–42
67. Forrin, B., Cunningham, K. 1973. Recognition time and serial position of probed item in short-term memory. *J. Exp. Psychol.* 99:272–79
68. Frederiksen, C. H. 1972. Effects of task-induced cognitive operations on comprehension and memory processes. In *Language Comprehension and the Acquisition of Knowledge,* ed. J. B. Carroll, R. O Freedle, 211–45. Washington, D.C.: Winston. 380 pp.
69. Freedle, R. 1972. Language users as fallible information processors: Implications for measuring and modeling comprehension. See Ref. 68, 169–209
70. Frey, P. W., Colliver, J. A. 1973. Sensitivity and responsivity measures for discrimination learning. *Learn. Motiv.* 4:327–42

71. Gentner, D. 1975. Evidence for the psychological reality of semantic components: the verbs of possession. See Ref. 140, 211–46
72. Gholson, B., Levine, M., Phillips, S. 1972. Hypotheses, strategies, and stereotypes in discrimination learning. *J. Exp. Child Psychol.* 13:423–46
73. Glanzer, M. 1972. Storage mechanisms in recall. See Ref. 6, 129–93
74. Grams, W., van Belle, G. 1972. Departures from binomial assumptions in short-term memory models. *Psychometrika* 37:137–41
75. Greeno, J. G. 1974. Processes of learning and comprehension. See Ref. 55, 17–28
76. Greeno, J. G. 1974. Representation of learning as discrete transition in a finite state space. See Ref. 110, 1–43
77. Greeno, J. G., Bjork, R. A. 1973. Mathematical learning theory and the new "mental forestry". *Ann. Rev. Psychol.* 24:81–116
78. Greeno, J. G., Simon, H. A. 1974. Processes for sequence production. *Psychol. Rev.* 81:187–98
79. Groen, G. J., Parkman, J. M. 1972. A chronometric analysis of simple addition. *Psychol. Rev.* 79:329–43
80. Groen, G. J., Poll, M. 1973. Subtraction and the solution of open sentence problems. *J. Exp. Child Psychol.* 16:292–302
81. Hayes, J. R., Simon, H. A. 1974. Understanding written problem instructions. See Ref. 55, 167–200
82. Haygood, R. C., Fishbein, H. D., Pinzka, C. F. 1972. A mathematical model for the wholist strategy in concept identification. *Psychon. Sci.* 27: 321–24
83. Herrmann, D. J., McLaughlin, J. P. 1973. Effects of experimental and preexperimental organization on recognition: Evidence for two storage systems in long-term memory. *J. Exp. Psychol.* 99:174–79
84. Herrnstein, R. J. 1974. Formal properties of the matching law. *J. Exp. Anal. Behav.* 21:159–64
85. Hilgard, E. R., Bower, G. H. 1975. *Theories of Learning.* Englewood Cliffs, NJ: Prentice-Hall. 698 pp. 4th ed.
86. Hintzman, D. L. 1972. Confidence ratings in recall: A reanalysis. *Psychol. Rev.* 79:531–35
87. Huesmann, L. R., Cheng, C. 1973. A theory for the induction of mathematical functions. *Psychol. Rev.* 80:126–38
88. Hunt, E. 1974. Quote the Raven? Nevermore! See Ref. 55, 129–57

89. Hursh, S. R., Fantino, E. 1973. Relative delay of reinforcement and choice. *J. Exp. Anal. Behav.* 19:437–50

90. Indow, T., Dewa, S., Tadokoro, M. 1974. Strategies in attaining conjunctive concept: Experiment and simulation. *Jap. Psychol. Res.* 16:132–42

91. Indow, T., Suzuki, S. 1972. Strategies in concept identification: Stochastic model and computer simulation I. *Jap. Psychol. Res.* 14:168–75

92. Ibid 1973. Strategies in concept identification: Stochastic model and computer simulation II. 15:1–9

93. Johnson, N. F. 1972. Organization and the concept of a memory code. See Ref. 27, 125–59

94. Johnson-Laird, P. N. 1974. Experimental psycholinguistics. *Ann. Rev. Psychol.* 25:135–60

95. Jones, M. R. 1973. Higher order organization in serial recall of digits. *J. Exp. Psychol.* 99:106–19

96. Juola, J. F., Fischler, I., Wood, C. T., Atkinson, R. C. 1971. Recognition time for information stored in long-term memory. *Percept. Psychophys.* 10:8–14

97. Kajita, M. 1972. Mediational models in reversal and nonreversal shift learning. *Jap. Psychol. Res.* 14:1–7

98. Kaplan, R. M. 1972. Augmented transition networks as psychological models of sentence comprehension. *Artif. Intel.* 3:77–100

99. Kemler, D. G., Anderson, D. R. 1972. The breadth of attention in learning: A new one-look model. *Br. J. Math. Stat. Psychol.* 25:131–50

100. Kimball, R. B. 1973. Self-optimizing computer-assisted tutoring: theory and practice. *Stanford Univ. Inst. Math. Stud. Soc. Sci. Tech. Rep. 206.* 132 pp.

101. Kintsch, W. 1972. Notes on the structure of semantic memory. See Ref. 21, 247–308

102. Kintsch, W. 1974. *Memory Representations of Text.* Presented at Loyola Symp. Cogn. Psychol., Chicago

103. Kintsch, W. 1974. *The Representation of Meaning in Memory.* Hillsdale, NJ: Erlbaum. 279 pp.

104. Kintsch, W., Keenan, J. 1973. Reading rate and retention as a function of the number of propositions in the base structure of sentences. *Cogn. Psychol.* 5:257–74

105. Kiss, G. R. 1972. Long-term memory: A state-space approach. *Br. J. Psychol.* 63:327–41

106. Klatzky, R. L. 1975. *Human Memory: Structures and Processes.* San Francisco: Freeman

107. Klatzky, R. L., Smith, E. E. 1972. Stimulus expectancy and retrieval from short-term memory. *J. Exp. Psychol.* 94:101–7

108. Koteskey, R. L. 1972. A stimulus-sampling model of the partial reinforcement effect. *Psychol. Rev.* 79:161–71

109. Kotovsky, K., Simon, H. A. 1973. Empirical tests of a theory of human acquisition of concepts for sequential patterns. *Cogn. Psychol.* 4:399–424

110. Krantz, D. H., Atkinson, R. C., Luce, R. D., Suppes, P., Eds. 1974. *Contemporary Developments in Mathematical Psychology Vol. I: Learning, Memory, and Thinking.* San Francisco: Freeman. 299 pp.

111. Krantz, D. H., Atkinson, R. C., Luce, R. D., Suppes, P., Eds. 1974. *Contemporary Developments in Mathematical Psychology Vol. II: Measurement, Psychophysics, and Neural Information Processing.* San Francisco: Freeman. 468 pp.

112. Laming, D. 1973. *Mathematical Psychology.* New York: Academic. 388 pp.

113. Landa, L. N. 1974. *Algorithmization in Learning and Instruction.* Englewood Cliffs, NJ: Educ. Technol. Publ. 713 pp.

114. Laubsch, J. H., Chiang, A. 1974. *Proc. Int. Comput. Symp.* 1973:481–87

115. Laughlin, P. R. 1973. Focusing strategy in concept attainment as a function of instructions and task complexity. *J. Exp. Psychol.* 98:320–27

116. Laughlin, P. R. 1973. Selection strategies in concept attainment. In *Contemporary Issues in Cognitive Psychology: The Loyola Symposium,* ed. R. L. Solso, 277–311. Washington, D.C.: Winston. 348 pp.

117. Levine, M. V. 1974. A transfer hypothesis, whereby learning-to-learn, Einstellung, the pree, reversal-nonreversal shifts, and other curiosities are elucidated. See Ref. 14, 289–303

118. Levine, M. V. 1974. The generalization function is determined by one subject's probability learning data. *J. Math. Psychol.* 11:245–58

119. Levison, M. J., Restle, F. 1972. *Ind. Univ. Math. Psychol. Prog. Rep. 72–3.* 27 pp.

120. Levison, M. J., Restle, F. 1973. Effects of blank-trial probes on concept-identification problems with redundant relevant cue solutions. *J. Exp. Psychol.* 98:368–74

121. Lindsay, P. H., Norman, D. A. 1972. *Human Information Processing.* New York: Academic. 737 pp.
122. McLaughlin, J. P., Herrmann, D. J. 1972. Recognition of a categorized list. *J. Exp. Psychol.* 96:235–36
123. Miller, L. A. 1974. Conjunctive concept learning as affected by prior relevance information and other informational variables. *J. Exp. Psychol.* 103:1220–22
124. Millward, R. B., Spoehr, K. T. 1973. The direct measurement of hypothesis-sampling strategies. *Cogn. Psychol.* 4:1–38
125. Millward, R. B., Wickens, T. D. 1974. Concept-identification. See Ref. 110, 45–100
126. Mohs, R. C., Wescourt, K. T., Atkinson, R. C. 1973. Effects of short-term memory contents on short- and long-term memory searches. *Mem. Cogn.* 1:443–48
127. Moore, J., Newell, A. 1974. How can MERLIN understand? See Ref. 55, 201–52
128. Murdock, B. B. Jr. 1972. Short-term memory. See Ref. 6, 67–127
129. Murdock, B. B. Jr. 1974. *Human Memory: Theory and Data.* Potomac, Md.: Erlbaum. 362 pp.
130. Murdock, B. B. Jr., Dufty, P. O. 1972. Strength theory and recognition memory. *J. Exp. Psychol.* 94:284–90
131. Nahinsky, I. D. 1973. Identifiability of a class of theories with states not directly observed over trials. *J. Math. Psychol.* 10:296–325
132. Naus, M. J., Glucksberg, S., Ornstein, P. A. 1972. Taxonomic word categories and memory search. *Cogn. Psychol.* 3:643–54
133. Neimark, E. D., Santa, J. L. 1975. Thinking and concept attainment. *Ann. Rev. Psychol.* 26:173–205
134. Newell, A. 1972. A theoretical exploration of mechanisms for coding the stimulus. See Ref. 27, 373–434
135. Newell, A. 1973. Production systems: models of control structures. *Visual Information Processing,* ed. W. G. Chase. New York: Academic. 555 pp.
136. Newell, A., Simon, H. A. 1972. *Human Problem Solving.* Englewood Cliffs, NJ: Prentice-Hall. 920 pp.
137. Norman, D. A. 1973. Memory, knowledge, and the answering of questions. See Ref. 116, 135–65
138. Norman, D. A. 1975. Cognitive organization and learning. In *Attention and Performance,* ed. P.M.A. Rabbitt, S.

Dornic, 5:530–46. London: Academic. 750 pp.
139. Norman, D. A., Gentner, D. R., Stevens, A. L. 1975. Comments on learning: Schemata and memory representation. In *Cognitive Approaches to Education,* ed. D. Klahr. Potomac, Md.: Erlbaum
140. Norman, D. A., Rumelhart, D. E., LNR research group 1975. *Explorations in Cognition.* San Francisco: Freeman
141. Norman, D. A., Wickelgren, W. A. 1969. Strength theory of decision rules and latency in retrieval from short-term memory. *J. Math. Psychol.* 6:192–208
142. Norman, K. L. 1974. Rule learning in a stimulus integration task. *J. Exp. Psychol.* 103:941–47
143. Norman, K. L., Levin, I. P. 1972. Tests on an all-or-none model of verbal mediated responding. *J. Exp. Psychol.* 96:247–54
144. Norman, M. F. 1972. *Markov Processes and Learning Models.* New York: Academic. 274 pp.
145. Norman, M. F. 1974. Effects of overtraining, problem shifts, and probabilistic reinforcement in discrimination learning: Predictions of an attentional model. See Ref. 110, 185–208
146. Offir, J. D. 1972. Stochastic learning models with distributions of parameters. *J. Math. Psychol.* 9:404–17
147. Offir, J. D. 1973. Automaton models of performance. *J. Math. Psychol.* 10: 353–63
148. Paranjpe, A. V. 1974. *A sequence-specific model for multiple-category concept identification.* PhD thesis. New York Univ., New York. 77 pp.
149. Parkman, J. M. 1972. Temporal aspects of simple multiplication and comparison. *J. Exp. Psychol.* 95:437–44
150. Polson, P. G. 1972. A quantitative theory of the concept identification processes in the Hull paradigm. *J. Math. Psychol.* 9:141–67
151. Polson, P. G. 1972. Presolution performance functions for Markov models. *Psychometrika* 37:453–59
152. Polson, P. G., Dunham, J. L. 1972. *Stud. Math. Learn. Theory Psycholing.* Boulder: Univ. Colo. Quant. Psychol. Program Comput. Lab. Instr. Psychol. Res. 38 pp.
153. Polson, P. G., Huizinga, D. 1974. Statistical methods for absorbing Markov-chain models for learning: Estimation and identification. *Psychometrika* 39: 3–22

154. Postman, L. 1975. Verbal learning and memory. *Ann. Rev. Psychol.* 26:291–335
155. Reitman, J. S., Bower, G. H. 1973. Storage and later recognition of examplars of concepts. *Cogn. Psychol.* 4:194–206
156. Restle, F. 1962. The selection of strategies in cue learning. *Psychol. Rev.* 69:329–43
157. Restle, F. 1972. Serial patterns: The role of phrasing. *J. Exp. Psychol.* 92:385–90
158. Ibid 1973. Serial pattern learning: Higher order transitions. 99:61–69
158a. Restle, F. 1975. *Learning: Animal Behavior and Cognition.* New York: McGraw-Hill. 317 pp.
159. Restle, F., Burnside, B. L. 1972. Tracking of serial patterns. *J. Exp. Psychol.* 95:299–307
160. Robbins, D. 1972. Some models for successive discrimination learning and transfer. *Br. J. Math. Stat. Psychol.* 25:151–67
161. Rumelhart, D. E., Lindsay, P. H., Norman, D. A. 1972. A process model for long-term memory. See Ref. 26, 198–246
162. Rumelhart, D. E., Norman, D. A. 1973. *Univ. Calif. San Diego Cent. Hum. Inform. Process. Rep. 33.* 10 pp.
163. Rundus, D. 1973. Negative effects of using list items as recall cues. *J. Verb. Learn. Verb. Behav.* 12:43–50
164. Salatas, H., Bourne, L. E. Jr. 1974. Learning conceptual rules: III. Processes contributing to rule difficulty. *Mem. Cogn.* 2:549–53
165. Sawyer, C. R. 1972. *A concept learning model.* PhD thesis. Univ. New Mexico, Albuquerque. 114 pp.
166. Scandura, J. M. 1973. *Structural Learning I. Theory and Research.* New York: Gordon & Breach. 367 pp.
167. Scandura, J. M. 1974. Role of higher order rules in problem solving. *J. Exp. Psychol.* 102:984–91
168. Schank, R. C. 1972. Conceptual dependency: A theory of natural language understanding. *Cogn. Psychol.* 3:552–631
169. Seamon, J. G. 1973. Retrieval processes for organized long-term storage. *J. Exp. Psychol.* 98:170–76
170. Shepherdson, J. C., Sturgis, H. E. 1963. The computability of partial recursive functions. *J. Assoc. Comput. Mach.* 10:217–55
171. Shepp, B. E., Kemler, D. G., Anderson, D. R. 1972. Selective attention and the breadth of learning: An extension of the one-look model. *Psychol. Rev.* 79:317–28
172. Shevell, S., Atkinson, R. C. 1974. A theoretical comparison of list scanning models. *J. Math. Psychol.* 11:79–106
173. Simon, H. A. 1972. Complexity and the representation of patterned sequences of symbols. *Psychol. Rev.* 79:369–82
174. Simon, H. A., Lea, G. 1974. Problem solving and rule induction: A unified view. See Ref. 55, 105–27
175. Suppes, P. 1973. Facts and fantasies of education. In *Changing Education. Alternatives from Educational Research,* ed. M. C. Wittrock, 6–45. Englewood Cliffs, NJ: Prentice-Hall. 184 pp.
176. Suppes, P., Fletcher, J. D., Zanotti, M. 1973. Models of individual trajectories in computer-assisted instruction for deaf students. *Stanford Univ. Inst. Math. Stud. Soc. Sci. Tech. Rep. 214.* 33 pp.
177. Suppes, P., Morningstar, M. 1972. *Computer-Assisted Instruction at Stanford, 1966–68.* New York: Academic. 533 pp.
178. Theios, J. 1973. Reaction time measurements in the study of memory processes: Theory and data. In *The Psychology of Learning and Motivation,* ed. G. H. Bower, 7:44–85. New York: Academic. 370 pp.
179. Theios, J., Smith, P. G., Haviland, S. E., Traupmann, J., Moy, M. C. 1973. Memory scanning as a serial self-terminating process. *J. Exp. Psychol.* 97:323–36
180. Thomas, E. A. C. 1973. On a class of additive learning models: Error-correcting and probability matching. *J. Math. Psychol.* 10:241–64
181. Thomson, W. J. 1972. Effect of number of response categories on dimension selection, paired-associate learning, and complete learning in a conjunctive concept identification task. *J. Exp. Psychol.* 93:95–99
182. Thomson, W. J. 1972. Least squares application of Levine's hypothesis model to missing reward sequence situations. *Psychol. Bull.* 77:356–60
183. Thorndyke, P. W., Bower, G. H. 1974. Storage and retrieval processes in sentence memory. *Cogn. Psychol.* 6:515–43
184. Thurstone, L. L. 1930. The learning function. *J. Gen. Psychol.* 3:469–93
185. Tighe, T. 1973. Subproblem analysis of discrimination learning. See Ref. 178, 183–226
186. Todorov, J. C. 1973. Interaction of frequency and magnitude of reinforcement

on concurrent performances. *J. Exp. Anal. Behav.* 19:451–58

187. Townsend, J. T. 1972. Some results concerning the identifiability of parallel and serial processes. *Br. J. Math. Stat. Psychol.* 25:168–99

188. Trabasso, T., Bower, G. H. 1964. Component learning in the four-category concept problem. *J. Math. Psychol.* 1:143–69

189. Trabasso, T., Bower, G. H. 1968. *Attention in Learning: Theory and Research.* New York: Wiley. 253 pp.

190. Vitz, P. C., Todd, T. C. 1969. A coded element model of the perceptual processing of sequential stimuli. *Psychol. Rev.* 76:433–49

191. Wandell, B. A., Greeno, J. G., Egan, D. E. 1974. Equivalence classes of functions of finite Markov chains. *J. Math. Psychol.* 11:391–403

192. Wandmacher, J., Vorberg, D. 1974. Application of the Bower and Trabasso theory to four-category concept learning with probabilistic feedback. *Acta Psychol.* 38:215–33

193. Waugh, N. C., Norman, D. A. 1965. Primary memory. *Psychol. Rev.* 72:89–104

194. Wescourt, K., Atkinson, R. C. 1973. Scanning for information in long-term and short-term memory, *J. Exp. Psychol.* 98:95–101

195. Wickelgren, W. A. 1970. Time, interference, and rate of presentation in short-term recognition memory for items. *J. Math. Psychol.* 7:219–35

196. Ibid 1972. Trace resistance and the decay of long-term memory. 9:418–55

197. Wickelgren, W. A. 1974. Strength/resistance theory of the dynamics of memory storage. See Ref. 110, 209–42

198. Wickens, T. D., Zax, B. 1973. Asymmetric attribute interaction in concept identification. *J. Exp. Psychol.* 98: 335–38

199. Wilson, A. 1973. The mediational model and shift behavior in a complex concept-attainment paradigm. *Can. J. Psychol.* 27:39–45

200. Winograd, T. 1972. Understanding natural language. *Cogn. Psychol.* 3:1–191

201. Wollmer, R. D. 1973. A Markov decision model for computer-aided instruction. *Univ. S. Calif. Dep. Psychol. Tech. Rep. 72.* 30 pp.

202. Wolter, D. G., Earl, R. W. 1972. The asymptotic distribution of response probabilities in the Audley-Jonckheere learning model. *Psychometrika* 37: 167–77

203. Woods, W. A. 1970. Transition network grammar for natural language analysis. *Commun. ACM* 13:591–606

NEUROLOGICAL AND PHYSIOLOGICAL BASES OF PSYCHOPATHOLOGY

Ralph M. Reitan

Departments of Psychology and Neurological Surgery, University of Washington, Seattle, Washington 98195

The biological bases of adverse psychological functions represent an area entirely too extensive to deal with satisfactorily in a review chapter. The present paper attempts to provide an overview of the area, highlighting interesting recent contributions and citing earlier references in some instances to help identify emerging trends of research. In addition to reviewing some of the aberrant biological findings associated with the major psychoses, consideration is given to psychological deficits resulting from known structural cerebral lesions in adults and children as well as those related to minimal brain dysfunction and learning disabilities.

PATHOLOGICAL FINDINGS IN SCHIZOPHRENIA

In his review of this area, Mirsky (93) considered in some detail various EEG studies in schizophrenic and comparison samples. He discussed some of the general results obtained through quantitative EEG analysis, drug activation of the EEG, sleep studies, and sensory-evoked responses. He concluded that there is a considerable degree of variation from study to study, although in general schizophrenics tend to show certain abnormalities that are not seen in normal subjects. Mirsky emphasized that it is scarcely acceptable in research on schizophrenia to label the group only as schizophrenic without providing more detailed diagnostic information. Almost certainly the term schizophrenia is used differently in various parts of the world, but nevertheless some resolution of the potential problem implicit in the use by researchers of quite different populations under the same heading may be achieved by providing a complete description of the characteristics of the group. In addition to age, sex, and length of hospitalization, which are commonly reported, a detailed statement of the duration of the illness, the types of behavioral manifestations, and the pharmacological history of the subjects should be provided. Mirsky pointed out

189

the findings of Cochin & Kornetsky (15), who demonstrated the long-term effects of a single dose of morphine in rats and cited the definite possibility that one compound might modify the subsequent neuropsychopharmacological response to compounds later administered.

Mirsky (93) reviewed briefly several papers which indicate the presence of positive neuropathological findings in schizophrenic patients. He indicated that the test of any theory of an organic etiology of schizophrenia ultimately requires the demonstration of clear-cut changes in brain tissue. He also indicated the difficulty in obtaining this kind of evidence, particularly in consideration of the fact that schizophrenia does not necessarily shorten life span and that direct evidence of a histopathological nature is difficult to obtain. While additional neurological diagnostic procedures may be used, these methods may reflect neuropathology which is not specific to the disease, or very possibly may be related only incidentally. He cited Kury & Cobbs' report (67a) of a 75-year-old epileptic schizophrenic woman who was described as having pathological brain changes. She was characterized clinically as being confused, demented, aggressive, and in poor contact. In addition, however, she had many prior episodes suggestive of possible traumatic and infectious injury of the brain. Mirsky also cited a paper in which Borreguero & Iñiguez de Onzoño (10) described a man who died at the age of 30, had a psychosis from his 17th year of age, and had both EEG and structural (gross and histological) changes involving his brain.

The problem with these cases is that there is no guarantee of immunity from brain damage as a result of having schizophrenia or the converse. Thus individual cases do little to answer the question. More systematic and intensive investigations are required in order to determine whether biological brain changes are consistently more frequent in schizophrenic than normal subjects.

A very significant study that does more to answer the question was published by Haug (47). Haug reported pneumoencephalographic and clinical findings in a series of 278 mental patients. Diagnoses resulting from evaluation of these patients on admission were classified into three principal groups: (a) nonorganic mental disorders, (b) schizophrenia, and (c) organic mental disorders. Of 67 patients with organic mental disorders, 72% presented a definitely abnormal encephalogram. Only 49% of 70 cases with nonorganic mental disorders follow this categorization. This difference was significant beyond the .01 level. Among the schizophrenic subjects, 61% of 137 patients showed an abnormal encephalogram. Comparison of the schizophrenics and the nonorganic mental disorders indicated that the mean size of the various parts of the ventricular system was larger in the schizophrenic than in the nonorganic group, although the largest mean sizes were recorded in the group with organic mental disorders. In the latter group the pneumoencephalographic evidence of enlargement was usually diffuse, while in the nonorganic group a purely focal dilatation usually was present, most often involving one temporal horn. About two-thirds of all schizophrenic patients with abnormal pneumoencephalograms had diffuse organic cerebral changes.

Haug presented a detailed description of the groups used in this study, emphasizing that they represented patients with a long history of illness in most cases and patients who had been rather resistive to various forms of therapy. In considering the difficulties in establishing a reliable and comparable diagnosis of schizophrenia or mental illness, it is clear that generalization of the results should be done cautiously. However, it does seem that the pneumoencephalographic findings in these patients are entirely reliable and reflective of actual and definite cerebral changes.

Haug presented detailed information regarding his criteria for classification of pneumoencephalograms, particularly differentiating normal from deviant X rays. Although few pneumoencephalographic studies in the area of mental disease have been published, he indicated that an unexpectedly high rate of abnormal findings have been reported in the so-called "functional" mental disorders. A number of investigators have reported that a slight degree of cerebral atrophy was present in a majority of their cases. Schimmelpenning (126) concluded that there was hardly a more common manifestation of cerebral disorder in patients with mental illness than cerebral atrophy as revealed by pneumoencephalography. Hermann (50) suggested that the diffuse representation of cerebral atrophy might be a factor contributing to the emergence of psychiatric symptoms. Jacobi & Winkler (57) were the first to report pneumoencephalographic abnormalities in schizophrenic subjects, but a number of subsequent investigators have indicated that a majority of schizophrenic patients show evidence of mild to moderate cerebral atrophy (29, 39a, 55, 68, 95). Prior to Haug's study, Huber's analysis represented the largest number that had been studied. Among his 190 schizophrenic subjects admitted to a psychiatric clinic, he found that atrophic changes were present in two-thirds of the patients and that there was good correlation between degree of mental deterioration and pneumoencephalographic abnormality. Others who have investigated the possibility of degenerative cerebral disease in other types of mental disorders have also found a high frequency of cerebral atrophy. Wigert (136) reported such findings in "constitutional psychopathics," whereas Bredmose & Munch-Petersen (11) have reported evidence of cerebral atrophy in neurotic subjects. Similar reports on heterogeneous groups of mental patients have been made by Eitinger (31), Haugen & Hove (48), Laane et al (67b), Moore et al (96), and Wagner (135). Such studies have not been done recently, probably because there is no specific indication that performing these studies is in the patient's own clinical interest. As Haug indicated, he found relatively few cases of specific cerebral lesions or of conditions that were subject to any form of direct treatment.

Among Haug's 137 schizophrenic patients, he omitted 36 from the complete analysis because he was able to identify various complicating disorders such as head trauma, alcoholism, prior leukotomy, or advanced age. Among the remaining 101 schizophrenics, all below the age of 60 years and representing the various types of schizophrenia, he found abnormal pneumoencephalograms in 58%. Forty-three of these patients showed enlargement of the ventricles, whereas only slight enlargement was present for 21; only one patient showed marked cortical atrophy. Mean ventricular size was significantly larger than found in the group of "nonorganic" mental patients, but the significance was only at the .05 level for comparisons of the size of the third ventricle and the right cella media. No differences in abnormality rates were found among hebephrenic, catatonic, and paranoid schizophrenics. Some evidence was found to indicate that the degree of mental deterioration correlated with the degree of ventricular enlargement. Of 46 highly defective schizophrenics, only 9 (20%) had normal pneumoencephalograms. The results were highly consistent when related to comparisons among groups or with relation to progression of symptomatology. In 28 cases who had been identified as showing marked mental reduction within a period of 2 years following the initial symptoms, only 2 (7%) had normal pneumoencephalograms.

An effort was made to determine the reliability of pneumoencephalographic results by performing repeat pneumoencephalograms on 24 schizophrenic patients at periods ranging from 7 to 4½ years after the original examination. In no case did the repeated examination show evidence of an improved status. In 16 cases judged to be stationary or improved from a clinical point of view, the pneumoencephalogram was unchanged, whereas in 8 cases who had shown clinical progression, 4 showed pneumoencephalograms with increased abnormality. Thus the findings suggest that morphological changes as shown by pneumoencephalograms of the brains of schizophrenics may be associated with progression of clinical deterioration. One might interpret this evidence as suggesting that cerebral atrophy is a structural correlate of the conditions that may represent the pathogenesis of the disorder, although this type of evidence does not permit any definite inference with respect to etiology. Of course, cerebral atrophy also occurs in many persons who are not schizophrenic. Thus the evidence of atrophy by itself obviously does not necessarily imply that atrophy produces a psychosis of a schizophrenic nature.

Findings such as those reported by Haug definitely suggest that deterioration of brain functions may be a contributory factor with respect to the presence of schizophrenic disorders. Certainly cerebral atrophy, as studied with neuropsychological methods, is associated with a substantial degree of deterioration of basic adaptive skills and may serve to undercut the stability of the individual or serve to interact with other factors in producing psychosis.

ELECTROENCEPHALOGRAPHIC AND EVOKED POTENTIAL STUDIES

Shagass (129) has recently presented an extensive and detailed review of electroencephalography and evoked potentials in psychotic patients. In addition to reviewing technical problems concerned with recording electrophysiological brain responses, he has summarized the major findings in affective psychoses as compared with schizophrenia. These findings have been summarized under separate headings of EEG and evoked responses. While he finds many statistically significant electrophysiological differences between patients and normals, as well as between patients in these two categories, he concludes that any rapid progress in terms of relating electrophysiological responses of the brain to psychotic disorders is probably unrealistic. Although both electroencephalographic and evoked response measures are quite stable over time (Shagass 127, 128; Itil et al 56), variability, particularly in EEG, is substantial from one patient to the next. Genetically oriented studies have indicated that factors deriving from this source exert a considerable degree of control on EEG findings. Lennox, Gibbs & Gibbs (69) have shown a considerable degree of concurrence in EEG measurements in twins, and evoked responses also have been found to support this contention (Dustman & Beck 30).

A significant component of genetic determination of both EEG and evoked response findings has been reported (Buchsbaum 12). Dustman & Beck (30) found a median correlation of 0.88 between wave shapes of monozygotic twins, whereas the median correlation was only 0.37 for dizygotic twins. Shagass (129) concludes that possibly more than half of the individual differences in EEG and evoked response characteristics may be genetically determined, and an additional substantial proportion of the remaining variability may be due to uncontrolled or "noise" factors. Thus, when the genetic and "noise" factors are considered, the remaining differences due to clinical differentiation among groups may be relatively small. However, if genetic factors are related to expression of illness, which is a definite possibility, the differences between diagnostic groups could be enlarged. In addition, if illness or psychopathological factors are of such magnitude that they override genetic and "noise" determinants, the differences also could be large. However, Shagass points out that psychiatric electrophysiology is still at an early stage of development, and computer methodology, which might have a valuable potential effect, so far has been realized only to a minimal extent. The question of interhemispheric relationships poses an interesting question of functional behavioral significance, but a major technical problem still exists in developing adequate methods for quantifying topographic and relationship data. Thus, while both schizophrenic and affective psychoses appear to differ from normal in a number of EEG and evoked response characteristics, little is available in the literature to indicate any diagnostic specificity.

SKELETAL MUSCLE AND MOTORNEURON ABNORMALITIES IN PSYCHOSIS

Meltzer (84) has been involved for a number of years in studies concerned with skeletal muscle and subterminal motorneuron abnormalities in patients with schizophrenia and affective psychoses. He has produced exciting work which indicates that the majority of patients with these psychoses demonstrate abnormalities including (a) increased activity in serum of skeletal muscle-type creatine phosphokinase (CPK) and aldolase activity (80–83, 88, 89, 91, 92); (b) abnormal extrafusal muscle fibers in skeletal muscle biopsies (32, 82, 90); and (c) abnormalities of subterminal motor nerves (85, 86). He has investigated these measurements of serum enzymes as well as the morphology of subterminal motor nerves in a number of groups, including patients with acute and chronic schizophrenia, unipolar and bipolar affective psychoses, nonpsychotic psychiatric patients, and normal controls. His results, indicating increased serum CPK activity in psychotic patients, are quite impressive. They were demonstrated in samples taken at various intervals (including admission and discharge) in 75.9% of 187 institutionalized psychotics. At admission only 88 of 187 patients (47.1%) showed increased CPK activity.

Meltzer has noted no significant differences among psychotic patients grouped according to type, in the incidence of increased serum CPK activity. However, in 25% of the psychotic patients, the peak increase was equal to or greater than five times the upper limit of normal. It should be noted, however, that only the skeletal muscle isozyme of CPK was present in the serum.

Increases in serum CPK activity were related to a number of factors that seem to give additional validity to the observation. Serum CPK activity at admission was significantly greater for those patients whose gross psychotic symptoms began one to seven days prior to admission than for those whose symptoms began eight or more days prior to admission. Some types of psychopathology were more intense or more frequently present in patients with increased serum CPK activity at admission—all of which suggest that acute psychotic behavior may be associated with elevated CPK levels. Meltzer studied detailed ratings of psychopathology in these patients and found that patients with increased serum CPK activity at any time during hospitalization had significantly greater mean ratings for some types of psychopathology, had longer mean hospitalization stays, and required higher doses of medication than patients who never had such increases. In studying first degree relatives of these psychotic patients, 103 of 337 (30.6%) also had slightly increased serum CPK activity. A significantly greater proportion of these relatives with slight elevations were related to patients who had elevated serum CPK activity. Meltzer notes that the characteristics of increased serum CPK levels in patients with psychoses are similar to each other and also to increases present in patients with a variety of acute brain disease. He postulates that there might be a common mechanism which produces increased efflux of CPK from skeletal muscle or decreased clearance of CPK from serum. These various findings, which relate serum CPK levels to psychotic disorders as well as to acute manifestations of symptomatology, and also to somewhat increased levels in relatives of the psychotic patients with increased CPK activity, all present a rather convincing picture to the effect that increased CPK levels may be of definite significance in psychotic manifestations.

Rowland (124), in a very knowledgeable discussion of Meltzer's findings, indicated that increased serum CPK levels occur in many neuromuscular as well as nervous system disorders, and he concludes that increase in serum CPK in acute psychoses is at this point an unanswered problem, representing one addition to a long list of unanswered questions relating to serum enzyme activity in health and disease. Nevertheless, as Rowland indicated, Meltzer has been meticulous in using controls and in seeking quantitative and objective expression of his results, and one can hardly quibble with the actual findings he has reported. The possibility exists that these serum enzyme changes reflect some neuropathic or myopathic disorder directly related to cerebral abnormality which causes, or directly influences, psychotic behavior. An explanation of the mechanisms involved is not available, but this research promises to be of great interest as it unfolds in the future.

In addition to serum enzyme studies, Meltzer and his associates recently have investigated and summarized muscle pathology in patients with major mental illnesses (87). Having demonstrated release of creatine phosphokinase (CPK) and other enzymes from skeletal muscle of most but not all psychotic patients, they proceeded next to examine skeletal muscle specimens taken by biopsy from psychotic patients, first-degree relatives of psychotic patients, nonpsychotic psychiatric patients, and normal controls. Five of 34 specimens from control subjects were considered abnormal as was one from 19 nonpsychotic patients. Differences between these control groups did not reach statistical significance. Among 166 psychotic patients, 115 (69.3%) had abnormal biopsies. All groups of psychotic patients showed marked differences from the controls, although they did not show differences among themselves. However, there was a tendency for the incidence of abnormal muscle specimens in chronic schizophrenic patients (30 of 36 patients) to be slightly greater than that of the combined group of patients with remitting psychoses (the acute schizophrenics and the patients with affective psychoses) in whom 85 of 130 (65.4%) had abnormal skeletal muscle. It is especially interesting to note that 13 of 26 first-degree relatives of psychotic patients also had abnormal muscle. This frequency differs significantly from the incidence found among control subjects but was not significantly less than that of the psychotic patients.

Recognizing that abnormalities of the motor nerve rather than intrinsic pathology of the muscle fiber itself might be the primary cause for the various abnormal muscle fibers found in specimens from psychotic patients, Meltzer & Crayton (87) decided to examine the subterminal motor axon and the subneural apparatus using the supravital staining method of Cöers & Woolf (16) as modified by Evans and his co-workers (33). They found that 54% of all psychotic patients showed abnormalities as did 63% of the first degree relatives of psychotic patients. Meltzer & Crayton (87) were careful to point out that a variety of pathophysiological mechanisms could be involved in the observation of abnormality of motor neurons among psychotic patients. Thus the possible significance of these abnormalities is an intriguing question. Impaired psychomotor performances among schizophrenics has been demonstrated for many years (Holzman 53), and abnormalities of motor nerves might have a definite adverse effect on many critical fine motor processes. Thus the various reports over the years of impaired motor functions among schizophrenic subjects might well be related to these observations of muscle fiber and subterminal motor nerve abnormalities.

BIOLOGICAL FACTORS IN PATIENTS WITH OTHER "EMOTIONAL" DISORDERS

Slater & Glithero (133) identified 99 patients who, 7 to 11 years earlier, had been diagnosed as having hysterical reactions. Follow-up information was obtained on 85 of these patients. Four had committed suicide and 8 had died of various organic illnesses which probably were present when the initial diagnosis of hysteria was made. Of the 73 living patients, 19 had received diagnoses of organic illness along with the original diagnosis of hysteria, 22 had developed organic illnesses that probably were present but undetected when the diagnosis of hysteria was originally made, and 32 patients showed no development of organic disease. The authors conclude that the presence of organic disease, even though unrecognized, probably predisposes toward a diagnosis of hysteria. First, the symptoms in the early stages may possibly be so subtle that they cannot be demonstrated as evidence of a physical basis for the patient's complaints. Secondly, the authors believe that organic disease may bring about a general disturbance of personality adjustment which may in turn cause affective lability, hypochondriasis, attention-seeking, self-concern, suggestibility, and variability of symptoms. All of these factors may contribute to the initial diagnosis of hysteria. In another paper, Slater (131) proposes that the diagnosis of hysteria is essentially a statement that none of the symptoms of the patient is caused by disease or that the probability that the patient is suffering from any physical illness is negligible. Slater proposes that under these conditions one must find the cause of the "hysterical" reaction. If this is not done, he feels that the patient has been left undiagnosed. He points out that his various follow-up studies indicate organic illness or a specific lesion, usually involving the nervous system, exists in approximately 60% of the patients who were initially diagnosed as having hysteria.

Slater reports that he and his colleagues were able to study 69 patients who had both epilepsy and a schizophrenic-like disorder. He indicates that in the past there has been a tendency to dissociate these diagnoses, devaluing either the epilepsy or the schizophrenia so as to maintain a unitary diagnosis. He feels that this is not possible and that in fact epilepsy and schizophrenia are associated more commonly than would be expected on the basis of chance probability. He indicated that in each of these 69 subjects the diagnosis of schizophrenia would have been required, on the basis of the patient's symptomatology and behavioral manifestations, even if epilepsy had not been present. In following these patients, however, he found that there were changes that were not entirely typical for schizophrenics. For example, the patients demonstrated a rather episodic or fluctuating onset of psychotic behavior, they often retained a warmth of personality that is not usually seen among schizophrenics, and in time a picture developed that was characterized more by organic personality impairment rather than a typical schizophrenic end-state. With respect to the basis for epilepsy, most of the patients had focal brain involvement, with EEG evidence particularly pointing to a large preponderance of temporal lobe foci. Clinical neurological findings were generally negative, but air encephalography showed normal results in only 17 of 56 patients.

While Slater and his colleagues have been searching for patients who represent the coincidence of schizophrenia-like psychoses and epilepsy, other studies have inquired regarding the frequency of psychotic behavior in patients who have sustained specific brain lesions. During World War II, Aita & Reitan (1) reviewed 500 consecutive brain-injured soldiers and found that only 4 showed definite, unequivocal evidence of psychotic behavior in the intermediate recovery period (2–9 months). A search of preinjury data on these subjects indicated that each of them showed strong tendencies toward psychopathic behavior prior to the injury. Although the psychotic-like manifestations of each of these subjects were quite varied, in each instance the psychotic behavior was an elaboration of the preexisting behavior pattern of the subject. For example, the subject who as a college student had been secretive and suspicious (often would eat only in his own home and would spend weekends locked in his room) showed strong paranoid tendencies after his brain injury. Such results suggest that there very probably is some relationship between injury or impairment of organic brain functions and psychopathological manifestations. Slater (132) indicates that he and his colleagues were unable to confirm the suggestion that patients who develop schizophrenia-like symptoms do so as a result of the stress of an organic insult or have some genetic predisposition to psychotic behavior. The results of Aita & Reitan, on the other hand, suggest that such stress or insult can be a contributing factor. While Slater and his colleagues argue that epilepsy may be inherently related to schizophrenia-like manifestations, other results point toward an interaction of factors that may be relatively independent as contrasted with a unitary process.

This brief review of biological factors in mental illness obviously is far from complete. Space limitations preclude, for example, a review of an excellent recently published volume by Kietzman, Sutton & Zubin (60) that is concerned with experimental approaches to psychopathology. This volume is organized into sections entitled arousal, attention, learning, and methodological issues. The content ranges from psychophysiological indicators of neurosis and early psychosis (14) to a number of presentations concerned with psychoses (3, 137, 140). There are theoretical formulations concerned with neurophysiological models in psychopathology (51) and specific behavioral data correlated with mental disorders (61). This volume presents a great deal of valuable information concerning biological factors as related to psychopathology.

Further examples of the many recent contributions regarding the biological bases of mental disorders are hardly necessary, but specific mention should be made of the many excellent contributions in the forthcoming volume of the Association for Research in Nervous and Mental Diseases, edited by Freedman (38). It includes a number of fascinating papers on drug effects (21, 41, 42, 45, 62), as well as papers on evoked responses (13) and biological antecedents of psychosis in children (35).

PSYCHOLOGICAL EFFECTS OF CEREBRAL LESIONS IN ADULTS

A detailed review of individual studies in the area of adult brain-behavior relationships related to the presence of cerebral lesions does not seem necessary considering the fact that Reitan & Davison (114) recently published a rather extensive volume in this area. This book has a definite practical orientation. In addition to providing a review of the literature, concentrating on Halstead's tests and related ones, many of the research results are related to clinical application through presentation of case examples. The volume is intended as an assessment of the current state of affairs in the clinical neuropsychology of both children and adults as well as to present a consideration of major issues and avenues for progress in the future. Reitan (111) considers methodological problems in the area of clinical neuropsychology but also presents a chapter on the effects of cerebral lesions in children of early school age (112). Boll (7) reviews the literature and presents experimental findings in children aged 9 through 14 years. Benton (4) reviews briefly the clinical neuropsychology of childhood and identifies principal problems in the area and directions of future research. Klove (65) reviews current knowledge in the area of adult clinical neuropsychology, and Klove & Matthews (67) have prepared a similar review of neuropsychological studies of patients with epilepsy. Meier's chapter (78) on challenges for clinical neuropsychology represents a particularly comprehensive review of the literature together with an assessment of the problems and prospects in the clinical neuropsychology of adulthood. Davison, in addition to providing an introductory chapter (22), wrote an overview of the book (23) coordinating the presentations of the various authors as well as presenting a resolution, insofar as possible, of many of the problems which are cited. Finally, this volume contains an appendix which gives a description of all of the testing procedures that are referred to in the book, including Halstead's Neuropsychological Test Battery for Adults, Halstead's Neuropsychological Test Battery for Children, The Reitan-Indiana Neuropsychological Test Battery for Children, the Klove-Matthews Motor Steadiness Battery, and a number of additional specialized neuropsychological test batteries as well as individual tests.

Matarazzo (73) recently published an extensive and scholarly manual that reviewed research on Wechsler's tests. One of the chapters in this volume was explicitly devoted to brain-behavior relationships as expressed in the Wechsler scales. Matarazzo began this review by citing the status of research and clinical application that existed at the time of World War II and traced the developments up to the present time. Because of the recency of Matarazzo's review, it is not necessary to repeat it at this point. However, it is clear that a great deal of reliable data is currently present which relates results obtained on the Wechsler scale to lateralization of cerebral damage; localization in some areas of cerebral lesions; type of cerebral damage; duration of cerebral damage; and differential results obtained in studying adults and children. It is fair to point out that the Wechsler scales were not developed specifically as instruments for evaluation of brain functions and in general are not as sensitive to the condition of the brain as, for example, the Halstead Impairment Index (Reitan 105), but the published reports make it quite clear that the Wechsler scales, in a clinical sense, provide a very useful procedure in conjunction with other methods. This is particularly significant in consideration of the widespread use of the Wechsler scales and the possibility of using these results not only for assessing general intelligence but also for evaluating brain functions. Reitan & Davison (114) provide examples of how results on the Wechsler scale can be used in conjunction with other data for drawing conclusions regarding brain-behavior relationships for individual subjects.

It should be noted that Luria (71) has added another impressive volume to his extensive series of works in the area of human brain-behavior relationships. In this volume he offers a review not only of the types of deficits associated with lesions in various areas of the brain, but also an overview of his concept of the functional organization of "mental activity" and the role and organization of cerebral processes in developing complex psychological functions such as attention, perception, memory, speech, and thinking. Luria explicitly states that the purpose of this book is to lay the foundations of a method of approach—". . . an analysis of the internal structure of psychological processes by use of neuropsychological methods." These methods begin with a detailed analysis of the changes arising in psychological processes with local brain lesions, after which an attempt is made to show how complexes or symptoms of psychological processes are disturbed by these lesions.

This method, according to Luria, provides an approach to the analysis of the internal structure of psychological processes and of the interconnections which unite the various psychological processes.

It is apparent that Luria has had a good deal of experience in personal examination and evaluation of patients with cerebral lesions. However, in spite of his apparent insight and understanding, his reports essentially represent evaluations of "critical cases" based upon his own observations, conclusions, and statements of significance. There is little doubt that much of what Luria has to say about the psychological effects of brain lesions is accurate and insightful, concurring with observations of others who have carefully studied individual patients with cerebral lesions. Nevertheless, his procedure seems to be entirely permissive regarding the data obtained in each case as a basis for drawing conclusions and offering generalizations. His testing procedures appear to have been devised at the moment for the particular patient in accordance with the insights and expectations of the person asking the questions (in this case, Luria). This approach, of course, is in direct opposition to the development and use of standardized procedures which offer quantitative results. In the opinion of many psychologists in the area of human brain-behavior relationships, the insights and understanding of a particular psychologist, based upon the questions he happens to think of or procedures he decides to use at the moment in evaluating a patient with a brain lesion, are hardly adequate for generalization. This type of approach, in brief, shows little respect for the difficulties implicit in devising an experiment which would be of general significance. The particular deficiencies shown by an individual patient might, because of procedural considerations, not be shown by another patient. In spite of these criticisms of the methods used by Luria, there is no question that his insights have a good deal of general meaning and that his proposals regarding the "principal" functional units of the brain, as well as types of losses sustained by various patients, are stimulating in their effects. Had Luria used procedures which were devised to produce quantitative scores reflecting the actual performances of the individual rather than Luria's impressions of the performances, one might have had more confidence in the validity of the results. As things stand, one has to take Luria's word for it when he says things such as, "I have listed only the chief components of the structure of the complex speech process" (71, p. 309). Speaking in the personal tense, he makes it clear throughout this book that the conclusions represent personal judgments based upon personal observations. One can conclude that Luria's methods represent the ultimate in disregard of the time-honored concept of cross-validation inasmuch as Luria's method itself precludes the prospect of objective cross-validation. Nevertheless, as mentioned above, there is no doubt in my mind that many of Luria's observations are quite accurate and his theoretical proposals, based on these observations, are of definite interest. Had Luria demonstrated that these observations would serve validly for *prediction* of the neurological variables with which he associated them, his case would have been very substantially strengthened. Instead, the association between areas of involvement and the dissolution or alteration of quite simple and complex functions seems entirely to be represented by Luria's personal analysis.

PSYCHOLOGICAL EFFECTS OF CEREBRAL LESIONS IN CHILDREN

In their review of psychological deficit with cerebral lesions, Zimet & Fishman (138) effected a differentiation of studies of brain damage in adults as compared with children. They indicated that their reviews of the literature concerning adults revealed that nearly all studies have been done on subjects who had "achieved full psychological development before deterioration of cerebral functioning took place." In children, conversely, they point out that normal psychological development is considerably retarded when cerebral lesions occur. They pointed out further that while studies of deficits (or losses) as a result of structural brain damage are largely limited to adults, the work on children is principally concerned with "minimal brain dysfunction."

Differences between persons who sustain brain injury in adulthood and in childhood have been demonstrated. Reed & Fitzhugh (101) studied adults who had sustained injury in adulthood as compared with those who had sustained injury early in life. Their findings indicated that when brain injury was sustained in childhood, the consequences in adulthood are represented by more severe impairment in a generalized sense. Fitzhugh & Fitzhugh (36), comparing groups who differed with respect to when the cerebral damage occurred (prior to age 10 and after age 12), found that those persons who had sustained early damage were generally more impaired. These studies, considered in combination, suggest that the nature of psychological deficit is different when brain damage is sustained early in life as compared to adulthood. The major differences include more generalized impairment, lack of specific deficits, and more serious impairment in terms of level of performance. In addition, among adults who sustained brain damage in childhood, there is evidence of more impairment on measures of stored memory than on tests of immediate problem-solving abilities, whereas the reverse is true for adults who sustained brain damage in adulthood.

In spite of the professed interest in the psychological correlates of brain damage in children, most of the studies in this area have been done either on children with ill-defined brain lesions (cerebral palsy) or with learning disabilities that might possibly be attributable to cerebral dysfunction (138). There has been a paucity of studies on children with known cerebral lesions. Of the studies of this kind that have been done, one of the first (102) reported quite striking differences across a broad battery of psychological tests when brain-damaged were compared with normal children. Particularly notable were the results of tests showing that the major deficits were quite different from those obtained with adult subjects. In the main, measures from the Wechsler scale showed the principal impairment in brain-damaged children, whereas measures concerned with immediate adaptive abilities, reflected principally by Halstead's tests, registered as significantly impaired, though not as strikingly as measures from the Wechsler scales. Boll (7) performed essentially a replication of this study and found very similar results. Boll & Reitan (8) studied motor and tactile-perceptual deficits in children with definite brain lesions and found that these children were quite seriously impaired in this area.

In another study, Boll & Reitan (9) evaluated ability interrelationships in brain-damaged and normal children by computing coefficients of correlation among various tests and comparing the results obtained in each group. The basic aim of this study was to explore among children the fundamental nature of psychological changes resulting from brain damage. Some years previously Reitan (104) had used this approach to determine whether or not relationships among a variety of measures were essentially the same in adult brain-damaged and control subjects, using the procedure to test whether or not there were basic changes in *kind* as contrasted with changes in *degree* as a result of cerebral damage. While Reitan had not found significant differences in correlational matrices among brain-damaged and control subjects, Boll & Reitan (9), using the same method with children, found differences that went beyond expected chance variations.

In a study pointed toward determining the types of deficits that are most pronounced in brain-damaged children, Boll (5) inquired as to the degree of deficit in conceptual vs perceptual vs motor functions. Even though children having impaired brain functions are often identified as being "perceptually handicapped," his results indicated that conceptual deficiencies were most prominent, followed by tactile-perceptual and motor deficits. Among younger children (age 5 through 8 years), Reitan (108) found sensory-motor functions to be significantly impaired in brain-damaged as compared with control children and also found complex motor functions of the preferred and nonpreferred hands, as expressed by name-writing speed, to show significant differences in these two groups (109). Reitan (110) also reported definite impairment of brain-damaged children on the Trail Making Test even though in both groups of normal and brain-damaged children there was a definite age-related developmental progression in achievement of skills on this test.

These various studies were reviewed and integrated by Boll (7) and Reitan (112). The volume edited by Reitan & Davison (114) included a very considerable amount of information on the effects of cerebral lesions in children. In addition to the studies cited above, Klonoff & Low (63) presented detailed results concerned with correlation of neuropsychological measurements and electroencephalographic tracings in children as well as a detailed study of neuropsychological and neurological residual effects of acute head injuries in children (64). In the same volume, Matthews (74) presented details of his neuropsychological investigations of mentally retarded subjects, and Benton (4) presented an overview of the clinical neuropsychology of childhood, addressing himself to the current status of the area and an assessment of significant current problems as well as approaches that are likely to be profitable for future pursuit.

Boll (6) investigated age-of-onset of cerebral damage with respect to later intellectual and cognitive development. He used a comprehensive test battery including the Wechsler Intelligence Scale for Children and the Reitan-Indiana Neuropsychological Test Battery (114) administered to three groups of children in whom cerebral damage was sustained at birth, between 2 and 4 years of age, and between 5 and 7 years of age. All three groups were examined at approximately 7 years of age. Boll found more impairment in the children with earlier age of onset. The extensive battery of tests used made it possible to offer some preliminary assessments of areas that were particularly affected by early age of onset. His results suggested higher-level cognitive functions were more adversely affected than were levels of performance on a number of motor proficiency measures. This finding is of particular interest in consideration of some of the animal work (58, 59) which suggests that damage sustained by the immature brain may be compensated for, through additional plasticity of brain functions, more effectively than damage sustained by the mature brain. However, in the animal work the principal measures of deficit have related to motor proficiency.

A similar study was performed by Dikmen, Matthews & Harley (26). These investigators studied two groups of adult subjects, each of whom had evidence of major motor epilepsy, but in one group the onset occurred between the time of birth and 5 years of age, whereas in the other group the onset occurred between 17 and 50 years of age. For comparative purposes, two additional similar groups were composed of persons with definitely established cerebral lesions but without epilepsy. Again, measures of higher level intellectual and cognitive functions were used with data being obtained from the Wechsler Adult Intelligence Scale and the Halstead Neuropsychological Test Battery. In each instance the groups with early onset earned poorer scores on an extensive battery of psychological tests. Thus, in general, the findings indicated an adverse association between early onset of cerebral damage and dysfunction, regardless of whether or not major motor seizures were present. The subjects with early onset of major motor seizures tended to have the poorest scores of any group. These various studies seem to support a generalization to the effect that the longer the human being has to develop with a normal brain during the early part of his life, the better the end result. Obviously there may be individual exceptions depending upon the type of cerebral damage involved, possibly upon the areas involved, and perhaps with relation to the extent of cerebral damage.

PSYCHOLOGICAL CORRELATES OF THALAMIC FUNCTIONS

Investigation of thalamic functions with relation to higher level language activities have been under way for a number of years, being performed particularly on human beings who have been candidates for surgically induced thalamic lesions intended to improve movement disorders. Much of this work has been summarized recently in an issue of *Brain and Language* for which George A. Ojemann (97) was the guest editor. Riklan and his associates have performed psychometric studies on such patients for at least the last 15 years. Most of the patients studied were ones with Parkinson's disease who underwent ventrolateral thalamectomy for the relief of tremor and rigidity, but more recently patients with movement disorders, including spasticity or pain secondary to stroke, have also been assessed before and after pulvinar surgery (17). As indicated in the general review by Riklan & Cooper (116), in most instances the psychological studies involved pre- and postoperative administration of standardized psychological tests. These studies suggest that thalamic nuclei, particularly the ventrolateral nuclei, and pulvinar play a role in verbal functions most specifically involving verbal fluency. The left thalamus seems to be more closely involved in language functions than the right thalamus, but Riklan &

Cooper believe that this is a quantitative rather than qualitative difference and more in the nature of a continuum than a dichotomy. They believe that the thalamus interacts with cortical, brain stem, basal ganglia, and possibly limbic systems in these functions as well as participating in specific sensorimotor functions which underlie verbal behavior and also participate in the alerting or arousal aspects of such behavior. The integrative competence represented by the brain before operation is also felt to be a significant variable in determining whether or not postoperative verbal changes occur and their degree. Long-lasting alterations in verbal functions following surgical intervention ordinarily are not observed, apparently because of compensatory mechanisms of the brain.

Darley, Brown & Swenson (20) summarized results of tests on 123 patients with Parkinson's disease and other movement disorders. They found that approximately one-fourth of these patients showed changes after thalamotomy, pallidectomy, and mixed pallidectomy-thalamotomy. The incidence of language changes was higher in cases of left thalamotomy, multiple thalamotomies, and mixed procedures. These investigators did not feel that generalized intellectual impairment in these patients was a sufficient basis for explaining the language impairment following surgery. Mohr, Watters & Duncan (94) reported on four carefully selected autopsied cases (derived from a 15-year retrospective review of 16,000 autopsies) and two living patients who had suffered left thalamic hemorrhage. They report that these patients frequently lapsed into a state of paraphasia almost resembling delerium, even though when fairly alert they appeared fully intact in language functions. Mohr and associates considered the language manifestations of these patients sufficiently unusual to warrant differentiation from traditional aphasic syndromes.

Van Buren (134), on the basis of his experience and critical review of the literature involving primary intrathalamic lesions as well as thalamic stimulation, suggests caution in assigning to the left thalamus more than a minor role in the speech mechanism. Schaltenbrand (125), who has had very extensive experience with stereotactic surgery for relief of movement disorders, pain, and epilepsy, considerably generalizes the loci which may have an effect on speech and language. Schaltenbrand indicates that various effects on speech are frequently observed, including silencing of speech with involvement of the anterior part of the corpus callosum, interruption of speech due to confusion of thinking with stimulation of the posterior part of the corpus callosum, and interruption of speech or compulsory speech as well as alterations in articulation during stimulation of the ventro-oral and posterior part of the thalamus. When compulsory speech occurred, usually associated with the left side of the brain, other behavioral changes also were present which had the character of a psychomotor attack with hallucinations and motor responses. Schaltenbrand feels that the occurrence of speech changes during stimulation of the thalamus serves as a warning against producing larger lesions in the thalamus because of the possible consequences for speech impairment.

Ojemann & Fedio (99) and Ojemann, Fedio & Van Buren (100) began experimentally oriented studies of the effect of stimulation of the thalamus. Ojemann, in summarizing his work (98), reported results obtained with a standard test of object naming and mental arithmetic for recall of short-term memory. Testing was performed during stimulation of the ventrolateral thalamus at the time of stereotactic thalamotomy and 2 days after the operation. Object naming was altered during stimulation of the left side of the thalamus although no such deficit was observed with right thalamic stimulation. Ojemann believes that repetition of the wrong verbal response was evoked from the anterolateral ventrolateral nucleus, while perseveration and naming difficulties were more frequently evoked from central portions of the ventrolateral nucleus. Ojemann believes that his data support an interpretation to the effect that left thalamic stimulation evokes a "specific alerting response" that directs attention to information in the external environment while simultaneously blocking the retrieval from memory. This alerting response seems to affect both short and long-term memory, and in Ojemann's observations, is closely correlated with the degree of postoperative naming difficulty. Fedio & Van Buren (34) emphasized the differences in effects of stimulation of the left and right pulvinar nuclei. Stimulation of the left pulvinar nucleus induced transient dysphasia and a retrograde loss in recent memory for verbal material. In contrast, their results point toward a failure of right pulvinar stimulation to disrupt verbal behavior, but on the other hand, stimulation on the right side did impair discrimination and recognition of complex visual patterns. Their findings suggest asymmetry in the functional organization of language and nonlanguage abilities even at the level of the lateral thalamus.

These various studies suggest that there is a differentiation of function of the two sides of the thalamus in higher-level activities, essentially similar to the differentiation that occurs at the level of the cerebral cortex. However, the findings certainly suggest that the role of the thalamus is not as predominant as is the role of the cortex, even though the thalamus does seem to be involved. As pointed out by Ojemann (97), there is no general agreement on the nature of the specific role of the thalamus in language or nonlanguage functions. Several investigators have identified aspects of arousal, alerting, activation, and attention, possibly involving interaction with memory mechanisms; others have suggested timing mechanisms and the specific thalamic contribution to language functions; and other proposals have included the role of the thalamus in initiation and modulation of speech. It is apparent from our present information that the role of the thalamus and its interaction with other structures, in terms of overall aspects of brain functions, is still in need of further investigation. However, this work has been stimulating in terms of the attempt to reach more complete conceptualizations of brain functions as related to higher-level abilities.

MMPI STUDIES IN BRAIN DAMAGE

The Minnesota Multiphasic Personality Inventory has been studied in various ways with respect to its value in identifying the effects of cerebral damage. Hovey (54), in an item analysis, found that five MMPI items discriminated between patients with and without central nervous system damage who were drawn from a neurology service. All of the items involved physical symptoms, and positive responses to these items were associated with brain damage. Zimmerman (139) found that these five items were effective in identifying patients with severe brain damage but ineffective when the damage was of lesser degree.

This type of empirical approach, in which the presumption is made that a meaningful insight may be obtained from the answers to a few simple questions, does little justice to the complexity of brain damage. Shaw & Matthews (130) compared MMPI results of patients with definitely established cerebral lesions as contrasted with patients who had been admitted to a neurological ward but who, after extensive neurological evaluations, were not found to have cerebral lesions. They found 17 MMPI items that differentiated the two groups, but in this instance the presence of physical symptoms was associated with the pseudo-neurologic group rather than the group with actual brain lesions. It is apparent that a chance selection of a few items that happen to differentiate two samples cannot be a very effective method, considering the total number of items that are compared. A more meaningful approach is represented by prior selection of independent variables, all of which are included in analysis of the results. Matthews, Shaw & Klove (76a) performed such a study using tests from the Wechsler Adult Intelligence Scale as well as Halstead's Battery. They found that the patients with identified cerebral lesions, based on neurological evaluation, performed quite poorly on these tests in contrast with the "pseudo-neurologic" patients. Thus, when cerebral lesions are independently established through neurological evaluation, the test results showed definite deficiencies.

Meier (77) has reviewed MMPI studies and assessed the degree to which differential results are related to the location of cerebral lesions. Interestingly, of the 56 references used by Meier in this review, only 9 include MMPI data and 6 of these 9 were published from 1949–1952. The interest in differential MMPI results related to localization of cerebral damage apparently stemmed initially from observations by Andersen & Hanvik (2) and an unpublished study by Friedman (39). It is somewhat curious that a continuing interest persists in this topic, especially considering the fact that there have been only a few investigations and these were done many years ago.

Meier & French (79) have published interesting work on the personality correlates of unilateral and bilateral EEG abnormalities in psychomotor epileptics, but this is a rather different type of problem. It is not surprising in Meier's review (77) that his section on conclusions and implications of his research relating localization of cerebral lesions to MMPI results rather lacks substance. He cites various technical problems relating to the nature of brain disorders, the difficulties they present in reaching generalizations, and concludes that such difficulties ". . . detract from the evidence provided by these findings for the regional localization hypothesis." Results, in brief, were not very convincing with respect to anterior-posterior differences nor with respect to right cerebral vs left cerebral differences. Nevertheless, Meier feels that investigation of ". . . the vertically organized limbic system in the generation of motivation-emotional behavior disturbances in man would seem worthy of continued investigation" (77, p. 258).

Detailed investigations related to cerebral localization have, in fact, recently been done. Dikmen & Reitan (27) have published the most extensive investigation of MMPI correlates of localized cerebral lesions yet done. The lesions were classified according to laterality and caudality dimensions. Fifty-nine subjects with lateralized lesions principally involving anterior or posterior cerebral areas were tested. Although the group with anterior cerebral lesions and the group with posterior cerebral lesions both showed evidence of some degree of emotional disturbance characterized particularly by neurotic-like manifestations [confirming results previously reported by Reitan (103)], no significant differential findings emerged in association with the caudality dimension. Similar results were obtained in comparing patients with right vs left cerebral lesions. These were the largest groups of patients with localized cerebral lesions yet reported, the criteria for group composition were based strictly upon pathoanatomical information, and various types of cerebral lesions were presented in each group. Thus these findings rather definitely suggest that localization of cerebral damage is not a significant variable as reflected by MMPI results.

It should be noted that a number of clinical studies have reported relationships between lesion location and types of personality disturbances (37, 49, 52, 70). These various clinical studies were selective with respect to the types of patients used in each study as contrasted with inclusion of various types of lesions. In addition, clinically oriented studies based upon interview procedures obviously might differ considerably in terms of results obtained as compared with studies based only upon MMPI results.

Dikmen (25) and Dikmen & Reitan (28) also pursued the relationship of MMPI results in brain-damaged subjects to areas of psychological deficit as contrasted with location of lesions in the brain. In one study (25) groups were composed with respect to adequacy of function in verbal and performance intelligence, concept formation abilities, and sensory-perceptual and motor skills. These results were assessed in 129 subjects with definite evidence of cerebral lesions. Patients with greater impairment of abilities showed higher elevations on the MMPI variables, suggesting the presence of increased emotional difficulties. While the previous study had indicated that MMPI variables were not closely related to lesion-localization data based upon pathoanatomical findings, the relationship was somewhat closer with regard to impairment of intellectual and cognitive skills. The results, especially for verbal skills, were fairly definite.

Additional investigation of impaired language functions with relation to MMPI results was effected through study of patients with brain damage and dysphasia (Dikmen & Reitan 28). Two groups of brain-damaged subjects were selected, one of which was definitely dysphasic but the other having no evidence of organic language difficulties. In addition to requiring completion of the MMPI by each subject, the profiles were individually inspected for validity by three experienced psychologists, and only valid scales, according to consensus, were selected. The groups were matched on the basis of sex, age, education, and lesion type, but not on location of cerebral lesion. A significant overall difference on the nine clinical scales combined was shown by multivariate analysis, with the higher scores being obtained by the dysphasic subjects. Further univariate analysis showed significantly higher scores for the dysphasic groups on the Psychopathic Deviate and Schizophrenia Scales. These results also indicated that areas of deficit associated with brain damage may have fairly specific adverse influences on MMPI results, whereas localization of lesion seems to have no such effect or only a secondary influence. It should also be noted, however, that uncritical transference of MMPI findings based on initial validation with psychiatric patients to patients with central nervous system lesions might lead to misinterpretation. It is entirely possible that a particular positive response by a person with brain damage may have quite different implications than the same response by a psychiatric patient. Thus there probably is a need for validation studies investigating social-behavioral correlates of MMPI results in persons with cerebral lesions in an effort to determine anew the particular significance of individual responses. Very probably entirely new items should also be added in assessing and differentiating the neurologically based complaints of persons with cerebral lesions as compared with manifestations of their emotional or affective disturbances.

Still another investigation of MMPI results in persons with major motor epilepsy was reported by Matthews, Dikmen & Harley (75). This study was directed toward investigating MMPI findings with relation to age of onset, duration of brain dysfunction, and degree of impairment of intellectual functions. Prior work (Matthews & Klove 76) had indicated that differential MMPI profiles do not appear to be closely associated with specific classifications of seizure disorders. These investigators had compared groups of patients having major motor, psychomotor, or mixed seizure disorders with patients having seizures of unknown etiology, and found essentially no MMPI profile differences. Guerrant et al (44) also found no systematic MMPI differences between groups of patients with psychomotor and major motor epilepsy. As additional background research, Klove & Doehring (66) studied five groups of patients (epilepsy of unknown etiology, symptomatic epilepsy, brain damage without epilepsy, primary affective disturbances, and general medical problems without cerebral involvement) and failed to find any particular MMPI differences. Meier & French (79), however, had noted that the presence of bitemporal independent spike foci implied greater chronicity of the pathophysiological process and thus longer exposure to any secondary environmental stress associated with clinical manifestations. Such patients showed evidence of greater MMPI disturbances than groups with either unilateral or bilateral temporal lobe foci. In the study by Matthews, Dikmen & Harley (75), groups of patients were separated according to evidence of major motor epilepsy and of brain damage but without past or present epilepsy. The variables studied represented age of onset, duration of brain dysfunction, and adequacy of intellectual functions. The results indicated that MMPI indices of emotional disturbance were more closely associated with the degree of psychometric and cognitive impairment than they were with age of onset or duration of brain dysfunction. This finding appeared both in groups of patients with major motor epilepsy and in nonepileptic brain-damaged subjects. Interestingly, whereas intellectual and cognitive functions showed a relationship to the age of onset, in another study (26) MMPI results supposedly reflecting the emotional status of the patient showed no such relationship. It would appear that these various studies support a conclusion that emotional stress factors may well be related to MMPI results in neurological patients but that neurological criteria per se are not closely related. In the context of these findings, it is interesting to note recent postulates by Gazzaniga (40) and Flor-Henry (37) that the right cerebral hemisphere is the "emotional hemisphere" of the brain. However, there is no evidence from any of the studies based on MMPI results that any such differentiation is valid. It may well be that we have not yet learned to ask the correct questions of the right cerebral hemisphere, and, considering our strong verbal orientation as psychologists as well as our general commitment to verbal abilities, it may be some time before we do learn to explore experimentally right cerebral capabilities!

As an example of an effort to determine the usefulness of MMPI evaluation of patients with cerebral lesions, Green & Reitan (43) have recently investigated MMPI results in subjects with rapidly growing as compared with more slowly growing cerebral neoplasms. Two groups were comprised so that laterality, locus, and size of lesion in the cerebral hemisphere, as far as could be determined, were closely matched. Age, sex, and education variables were also closely comparable. Control groups consisted of psychiatric patients and normals also matched on the basis of the foregoing variables. Several differences were found in level of performance on MMPI scales, resulting in configural differences for the groups. The results seemed to be meaningful in terms of the underlying nature of the lesion—gradual onset, with possible compensation, of symptoms in slowly growing tumors, and the precipitous onset of symptoms in fast-growing tumors.

LEARNING DISABILITIES AND "MINIMAL BRAIN DYSFUNCTION"

The following investigations have laid something of a groundwork with regard to psychological deficits among children with definite proved cerebral lesions—the type of information that seems to be imperative if we are going to evaluate learning disabilities and other types of disorders which can only be presumed to have some possible cerebral basis. The incidence of learning disabilities is variously estimated but clearly involves many children. The prevalence of "minimal brain dysfunction" also is substantial, approximately equaling that of epilepsy among children. Rose et al (117) performed an epidemiological study of the incidence of epilepsy and minimal brain dysfunction among third-grade students in Washington County, Maryland. Of 2042 families to whom a questionnaire was mailed, final responses were obtained from 1866 families. The investigators used procedures for estimating the minimal, reasonable, and maximum prevalence rates, with validation of the questionnaire being based upon 200 children selected for their variety of responses to the questionnaire. Recognizing the difficulties implicit in a definitive diagnosis of either condition, they estimated exactly identical reasonable prevalence rates for both epilepsy and minimal brain dysfunction—18.6 persons per 1000.

In the area of learning disabilities a number of interesting contributions have been made recently. Hallahan & Cruickshank (46) devote a considerable section of their book to a review of etiological factors, omitting neurological determinants because, as they point out, this area has been fairly well represented in the literature. They concentrate on nutritional deficiencies as related to brain development and to impaired learning. Citing the work of Cravioto (18, 19) particularly, the authors conclude (not entirely convincingly) from their review of the literature that nutritional deficiencies are very likely to have a direct causal link to impaired learning. These investigators go on to consider and review the evidence related to cultural deprivation as an etiological factor in mental retardation and learning disabilities. They also review the approaches of major contributors in the area, discuss historical trends in the literature, and summarize psychological deficiencies of children with learning impairment under various categories of performance.

An interesting research program that seems to be producing results of considerable value in the area of learning disabilities is being conducted by Rourke and his associates at the University of Windsor. Rourke's basic approach (118) has involved testing the assumption that cerebral dysfunction is a contributing factor in the etiology of learning disabilities. Essentially the question has been whether the results obtained with children who have learning disabilities are similar, according to specified criteria, to results shown by groups with known cerebral damage. He has been using a model of brain-behavior relationships described by Reitan (107) as a basis for employing strategies in his research. The approaches Rourke has used in defining his various studies have concerned the level of performance, specific deficits or pathognomonic signs, differential scores or patterns of results, and comparative performances on the two sides of the body.

Using a design representing specific deficits or the pathognomonic sign approach, MacDonald & Rourke (72) studied behavioral correlates of different patterns of habituation of the cortical arousal response to auditory stimulation. They found that children with learning disabilities, who differed in type and rate of habituation of the cortical arousal response, also differed in highly significant ways with respect to performances on motor, perceptual, language, and cognitive tasks.

Rourke et al (122) studied the effect of lateralized motor deficits, determined by performances on the Grooved Pegboard Test, with relation to other deficits. They found that the pattern of higher-level deficits for children with learning disabilities was strikingly similar, depending upon the side of the lateralized deficit (presumably contralateral to the dysfunctional cerebral hemisphere), to patterns of performance previously reported in adults with well-documented cerebral lesions.

Rourke and his students also have explored the relationships of verbal and performance IQ results in a series of studies (119, 121, 123). Using as criterion a 10-point discrepancy between these two IQ values, the investigators demonstrated that older children with learning disabilities performed essentially as would have been expected from persons with lateralized cerebral lesions on a broad range of behavioral measures that included motor, psychomotor, auditory, and visual perceptual tasks, as well as verbal abilities, cognitive abilities, etc. When the same design was tested with younger children, the results were definitely not as clear cut. Rourke & Finlayson (120) studied differential patterns of performance in children with learning disabilities on the Wide Range Achievement Test and the Trail Making Test with relation to neuropsychological patterns. They compared groups of older children who were (a) relatively adept at reading and spelling and poor at arithmetic; (b) relatively poor at reading and spelling and arithmetic; and (c) relatively adept at arithmetic and poor at reading and spelling. When compared on 25 neuropsychological test variables, the children in the first group performed as if they had a relatively dysfunctional right cerebral hemisphere and the children in the other two groups performed as if they had relatively dysfunctional left cerebral hemispheres. Thus the children used in this investigation simulated the results obtained by Reitan & Tarshes (115), especially in terms of patterns of results obtained on Part A and Part B of the Trail Making Test. Considering the similarity in results obtained with relation to patterns of abilities shown in groups with known brain lesions, these various studies rather clearly identify the role of impaired brain functions in learning disability. The relevance of neuropsychological studies in persons with proved brain lesions can thus be generalized to groups of children or even adults with possibly impaired brain functions but in whom neurological evaluation procedures produce negative or equivocal results.

A volume that must be taken seriously by any investigator in the area of impaired brain functions and learning disabilities was recently published under the auspices of the New York Academy of Sciences (de la Cruz, Fox & Roberts 24). This volume is the printed expression of a three-day conference held on minimal brain dysfunction. The contents range from conceptual models of this disorder (which are, in fact, quite poorly defined) to treatment procedures. Sections of the volume included presentations of experimental data, epidemiological information, environmental and hereditary factors in the development of minimal brain dysfunction, criteria for diagnosis of the condition (an area which produced a considerable degree of diversity of opinion), and finally two sections on drug and nondrug treatment. This volume is probably the definitive current statement in the area of minimal brain dysfunction and is entirely too extensive to review in the present context. However, Reitan & Boll (113) contributed a chapter concerned with clinical neuropsychological evaluation of children with minimal brain dysfunction. They compared such children with normals and with children having definite structural damage of the cerebral hemispheres. The results indicated that in terms of level of performance the children with minimal brain dysfunction were generally somewhat more similar to the controls than to children with definite cerebral lesions, although they usually performed somewhat more poorly than the control subjects. Recognizing that an analysis concerned with individual tests can produce possible confounding of results, the investigators also performed another analysis that evaluated individual subjects, taking all of the test results for each individual into consideration at the same time. Using this latter method, they classified children with respect to estimated cerebral dysfunction into three categories: normal, some degree of neuropsychological abnormality of brain functions, and definite brain damage. Nearly all of the children with structural brain lesions were classified on the basis of their test results alone into the latter category, and the great majority of the normal children fell in the category of normal brain functions. It would appear that for the individual child, interrelationships among test results had special meaning with respect to the minimal brain dysfunction as contrasted with level of performance considered alone. As Reitan (106) suggested some years ago, brain-behavior relationships do not seem to lend themselves adequately to our usual conceptual models of statistical analysis, and very probably as much or more may be concealed than is revealed when using such models for research purposes. The intraindividual variations shown by both adults and children with impaired brain functions seem to carry the principal information of significance, and we still are in need of adequate rigorous methods for evaluating patterns and relationships of this kind with regard to their full significance.

CONCLUDING COMMENTS

A remarkably strong interest seems to have emerged in the last few years in human brain functions with regard to behavior. Earlier clinicians had been interested particularly from a diagnostic point of view, and human experimental and physiological psychologists were curious especially regarding localization of abilities. The differential functions of the two cerebral hemispheres have now prompted a great interest, with students being seriously curious about the role of the brain in many perceptual functions and even in questions as to which cerebral hemisphere relates to transcendental meditation! These interests prompt the prediction that the next decade will see a strong effort to apply knowledge of brain-behavior relationships to many aspects of human behavior, probably including such things as vocational guidance to personality differences. While the brain as the organ of behavior is undoubtedly relevant across these broad areas—and it is gratifying to see these interests develop—it is equally clear that the approaches often taken will naively oversimplify the problems of human brain-behavior relationships. Already the literature is being filled with such suggestions as that the direction in which one glances is an indication of his brainedness, or that the left side of the face reflects the fundamental characteristics of the right cerebral hemisphere whereas the right side expresses left cerebral functions! One might wish that the problem were that simple. Those of us who have studied damaged brains, where one might presume that the impaired functions would be more easily determined than functions of the normal brain, know the many individual differences that exist and the frequent difficulty in identifying even a seriously damaged cerebral hemisphere. Thus we need to continue to study the areas of deficit that accompany brain lesions and to learn sufficiently well that we can predict accurately, in the individual case, the status of the two cerebral hemispheres and areas within them. When we have reached this point, the methods that have proved to be valid (as contrasted with the easy presumptions currently being made by many experimenters) may be applied in assessing normal brain functions and the significance of the human brain in activities of daily living.

Literature Cited

1. Aita, J. A., Reitan, R. M. 1948. Psychotic reactions in the late recovery period following brain injuries. *Am. J. Psychiatry* 105:161–69
2. Andersen, A. L., Hanvik, L. J. 1950. The psychometric localization of brain lesions: the differential effect of frontal and parietal lesions on MMPI profiles. *J. Clin. Psychol.* 6:177–80
3. Ax, A. F. 1975. Emotional learning deficiency in schizophrenia. See Ref. 60, 255–68
4. Benton, A. L. 1974. Clinical neuropsychology of childhood: An overview. See Ref. 114, 47–52
5. Boll, T. J. 1972. Conceptual vs. perceptual vs. motor deficits in brain-damaged children. *J. Clin. Psychol.* 28:157–59
6. Boll, T. J. 1973. *The effect of age at onset on brain damage and adaptive abilities in children.* Presented at APA, Montreal, Quebec
7. Boll, T. J. 1974. Behavioral correlates of cerebral damage in children aged 9 through 14. See Ref. 114, 91–120
8. Boll, T. J., Reitan, R. M. 1972. Motor and tactile-perceptual deficits in brain-damaged children. *Percept. Mot. Skills* 34:343–50
9. Boll, T. J., Reitan, R. M. 1972. Comparative ability relationships in brain-damaged and normal children. *J. Clin. Psychol.* 28:152–56
10. Borreguero, A. D., Iñiguez de Onzoño, A. 1965. Estudio clinico, electropneumoencefalográfico seriado y antompathológico. Un caso de esquizofrenia. *Arch. Neurobiol. (Madrid)* 28:414–39
11. Bredmose, G. V., Munch-Petersen, C. J. 1941. Encephalographier hos Patienter med Neuroser og neurotisk praegede Sygdomsbilleder. *Nord. Med.* 10:1367–74
12. Buchsbaum, M. 1974. Average evoked responses and stimulus intensity in identical and fraternal twins. *J. Physiol. Psychol.* 2:365–70
13. Buchsbaum, M. 1975. Average evoked responses augmenting/reducing in schizophrenia and affective disorders. See Ref. 38
14. Claridge, G. S. 1975. Psychophysiological indicators of neurosis and early psychosis. See Ref. 60, 89–107
15. Cochin, J., Kornetsky, C. 1964. Development and loss of tolerance of morphine in the rat after single and multiple injections. *J. Pharmacol. Exp. Ther.* 145:1–10
16. Cöers, C., Woolf, A. L. 1959. *The Innervation of Muscle.* Oxford: Blackwell. 42 pp.
17. Cooper, I. S., Amin, I., Chandra, R., Waltz, J. M. 1973. A surgical investigation of clinical physiology of the pulvinar complex in man. *J. Neurol. Sci.* 18:89–110
18. Cravioto, J. 1958. Protein metabolism in chronic infantile malnutrition (kwashiorkor). *Am. J. Clin. Nutr.* 6:495
19. Cravioto, J. 1972. Nutrition and learning in children. In *Nutrition and Mental Retardation,* ed. N. S. Springer, 25–44. Ann Arbor: Inst. Study Ment. Retard. and Related Disab.
20. Darley, F. L., Brown, J. R., Swenson, W. M. 1975. Language changes after neurosurgery for parkinsonism. *Brain Lang.* 2:65–69
21. Davis, J. M. 1975. Critique of single amine theories: Evidence of a cholinergic influence on the major mental illnesses. See Ref. 38
22. Davison, L. A. 1974. Introduction. See Ref. 114, 1–18
23. Ibid. Current status of clinical neuropsychology, 325–61
24. de la Cruz, F. F., Fox, B. H., Roberts, R. H., Eds. 1973. *Minimal Brain Dysfunction.* New York: Ann. NY Acad. Sci., Vol. 205. 396 pp.
25. Dikmen, S. 1973. *Minnesota Multiphasic Personality Inventory correlates of structural and functional cerebral deficits in patients with brain lesions.* PhD thesis. Univ. Washington, Seattle. 89 pp.
26. Dikmen, S., Matthews, C. G., Harley, J. P. 1975. The effect of early vs. late onset of major motor epilepsy upon cognitive intellectual performances. *Epilepsia* 16:73–81
27. Dikmen, S., Reitan, R. M. 1974. MMPI correlates of localized cerebral lesions. *Percept. Mot. Skills* 39:831–40
28. Dikmen, S., Reitan, R. M. 1974. MMPI correlates of dysphasic language disturbances. *J. Abnorm. Psychol.* 83:675–79
29. Donovan, J. F., Galbraith, A. J., Jackson, J. 1949. Some observations on leucotomy and investigations by pneumoencephalography. *J. Ment. Sci.* 95:655–66
30. Dustman, R. E., Beck, E. C. 1965. The visual evoked potential in twins. *Elec-*

troencephalogr. Clin. Neurophysiol. 19: 570–75
31. Eitinger, L. 1959. Hjerneatrofiens betydning ved psykiatriske sykdomsbilleder. *Nord. Med.* 61:301–3
32. Engel, W. K., Meltzer, H. 1970. Histochemical abnormalities of skeletal muscle in patients with acute psychoses. Part I. *Science* 168:273–76
33. Evans, R. H., Haynes, J., Morris, C. J., Woolf, A. L. 1970. In vitro staining of intramuscular endings. *J. Neurol. Neurosurg. Psychiatry* 33:783–85
34. Fedio, P., VanBuren, J. M. 1975. Memory and perceptual deficits during electrical stimulation in the left and right thalamus and parietal subcortex. *Brain Lang.* 2:78–100
35. Fish, B. 1975. Biological antecedents of psychosis in children. See Ref. 38
36. Fitzhugh, K. B., Fitzhugh, L. C. 1965. Effects of early and later onset of cerebral dysfunction upon psychological test performance. *Percept. Mot. Skills* 20:1099–1100
37. Flor-Henry, P. 1969. Schizophrenic reactions and psychoses associated with temporal lobe epilepsy: Etiological factors. *Am J. Psychiatry* 126:148–52
38. Freedman, D. X., Ed. 1975. *The Biology of the Major Psychoses: A Comparative Analysis.* Proc. Assoc. Res. Nerv. Ment. Dis. In press
39. Friedman, S. H. 1950. *Psychometric effects of frontal and parietal lobe brain damage.* PhD thesis. Univ. Minnesota, Minneapolis, Minn.
39a. Froshaug, H., Retterstöl, N. 1956. Clinical and pneumoencephalographic studies on cerebral atrophies of middle age. *Acta Psychiat. Scand. Suppl.* 106:83–102
40. Gazzaniga, M. S. 1970. *The Bisected Brain.* New York: Appleton-Century-Crofts
41. Gershon, S., Angrist, B., Shopsin, B. 1975. Drugs, diagnosis, and disease. See Ref. 38
42. Glowinski, J. 1975. Effects of neuroleptics on the nigro neostriatal and mesocortical dopaminergic systems. See Ref. 38
43. Green, T. K., Reitan, R. M. 1975. *Effect of the rate of lesion development on behavioral adaptations in intracranial neoplasms.* Presented at Soc. Neurosci., Bethesda. In press
44. Guerrant, J. et al 1962. *Personality in Epilepsy.* Springfield: Thomas
45. Halaris, A. E., Freedman, D. X. 1975. Psychotropic drugs and dopamine uptake inhibition. See Ref. 38
46. Hallahan, D. P., Cruickshank, W. M. 1973. *Psychoeducational Foundations of Learning Disability.* Englewood Cliffs, NJ: Prentice-Hall. 317 pp.
47. Haug, J. O. 1962. Pneumoencephalographic studies in mental disease. *Acta Psychiat. Neurol. Scand. Suppl.* 165, 38:1–104
48. Haugen, A., Hove, J. 1948. Encephalographic investigations of psychiatric patients. *Acta Psychiat. Scand.* 23:79–93
49. Hécaen, H. 1964. Mental symptoms associated with tumors of the frontal lobe. In *The Frontal Granular Cortex and Behavior,* ed. J. M. Warren, K. Akert, 335–52. New York: McGraw-Hill
50. Hermann, K. 1951. Atrophia cerebri: Some remarks on the clinic of atrophy of the brain. *Acta Psychiat. Scand. Suppl.* 74:165–74
51. Hernández-Péon, R. 1975. Some neurophysiological models in psychopathology. See Ref. 60, 15–37
52. Hillbom, E. 1960. Aftereffects of brain injuries. *Acta Psychiat. Scand. Suppl.* 142
53. Holzman, P. S. 1972. Assessment of perceptual functioning in schizophrenia. *Psychopharmacologia* 24:29–41
54. Hovey, H. B. 1964. Brain lesions and five MMPI items. *J. Consult. Psychol.* 28:78–79
55. Huber, G. 1957. Pneumoencephalographische und psychopathologische Bilder bei endogenen. *Psychosen.* Berlin: Springer
56. Itil, T. M., Saletu, B., Davis, S., Allen, M. 1974. Stability studies in schizophrenics using computer-analyzed EEG. *Biol. Psychiatry* 8:321–35
57. Jacobi, W., Winkler, H. 1927. Encephalographische Studien an chronisch Schizophrenen. *Arch. Psychiat.* 81:299–332
58. Kennard, M. A. 1938. Reorganization of motor function in the cerebral cortex of monkeys deprived of motor and premotor areas in infancy. *J. Neurophysiol.* 1:477–96
59. Kennard, M. A. 1942. Cortical reorganization of motor functions: Studies on series of monkeys of various ages from infancy to maturity. *Arch. Neurol. Psychiat.* 48:227–40
60. Kietzman, M. L., Sutton, S., Zubin, J., Eds. 1975. *Experimental Approaches to Psychopathology.* New York: Academic, 448 pp.

61. King, H. E. 1975. Psychomotor correlates of behavior disorder. See Ref. 60, 421–50
62. Klawans, H. L. 1975. Amine precursors in neurological disorders and the psychoses. See Ref. 38
63. Klonoff, H., Low, M. 1974. Disordered brain function in young children and early adolescents: Neuropsychological and electroencephalographic correlates. See Ref. 114, 121–78
64. Klonoff, H., Paris, R. 1974. Immediate, short-term, and residual effects of acute head injuries in children: Neuropsychological and neurological correlates. See Ref. 114, 179–210
65. Klove, H. 1974. Validation studies in adult clinical neuropsychology. See Ref. 114, 211–35
66. Klove, H., Doehring, D. 1962. MMPI in epileptic groups with differential etiology. J. Clin. Psychol. 18:149–53
67. Klove, H., Matthews, C. G. 1974. Neuropsychological studies of patients with epilepsy. See Ref. 114, 237–65
67a. Kury, G., Cobb, S. 1964. Epileptic dementia resembling schizophrenia: Clinical pathological report of a case. J. Nerv. Ment. Dis. 138:340–47
67b. Laane, C. L., Solheim, T., Straand, A. 1957. Luftencephalografiens og andre undersøkelsesmetoders verdi for diagnosen av organiske hjernesykdommer. Tidsskr. Nor. Lægeforen. 77:107–12
68. Lemke, R. 1935. Untersuchungen uber die soziale Prognose der Schizophrenie unter besonderer Berucksichtingung des encephalographischen Befundes. Arch. Psychiat. Nervenkr. 104:89–136
69. Lennox, W. G., Gibbs, F. A., Gibbs, E. L. 1942. Twins, brain waves and epilepsy. Arch. Neurol. Psychiat. 47: 702–6
70. Lishman, W. A. 1968. Brain damage in relation to psychiatric disability after head injury. Br. J. Psychiatry 114:373–410
71. Luria, A. R. 1973. The Working Brain: Introduction to Neuropsychology. New York: Basic Books. 398 pp.
72. MacDonald, G. W., Rourke, B. P. 1974. Neuropsychological significance of differences in the rate of habituation of the cortical arousal response. Presented at CPA, Windsor, Ontario
73. Matarazzo, J. D. 1972. Wechsler's Measurement and Appraisal of Adult Intelligence. Baltimore: Wilkins. 572 pp.
74. Matthews, C. G. 1974. Applications of neuropsychological test methods in mentally retarded subjects. See Ref. 114, 267–88
75. Matthews, C. G., Dikmen, S., Harley, J. P. 1975. Age of onset and psychometric correlates of MMPI profiles in major motor epilepsy. Dis. Nerv. Syst. In press
76. Matthews, C. G., Klove, H. 1963. MMPI performances in major motor, psychomotor and mixed seizure classifications of known and unknown etiology. Epilepsia 9:43–53
76a. Matthews, C. G., Shaw, D. J., Klove, H. 1966. Psychological test performances in neurologic and "pseudoneurologic" subjects. Cortex 2:244–53
77. Meier, M. J. 1969. The regional localization hypothesis and personality changes associated with focal cerebral lesions and ablations. In MMPI: Research Developments and Clinical Applications, ed. J. N. Butcher, 243–61. New York: McGraw-Hill. 402 pp.
78. Meier, M. J. 1974. Some challenges for clinical neuropsychology. See Ref. 114, 289–323
79. Meier, M. J., French, L. A. 1965. Some personality correlates of unilateral and bilateral EEG abnormalities in psychomotor epileptics. J. Clin. Psychol. 21:3–9
80. Meltzer, H. Y. 1968. Creatine kinase and aldolase in serum; abnormality common to acute psychoses. Science 159:1368–70
81. Meltzer, H. Y. 1969. Muscle enzyme release in the acute psychoses. Arch. Gen. Psychiatry 21:102–12
82. Meltzer, H. Y. 1973. Skeletal muscle abnormalities in patients with affective disorders. J. Psychiat. Res. 10:43–57
83. Meltzer, H. Y. 1974. Serum creatine phosphokinase and serum aldolase levels in acutely psychotic patients. In Enzymology in the Practice of Laboratory Medicine, ed. P. Blume, E. F. Freier, 251–379. New York: Academic
84. Meltzer, H. Y. 1975. Neuromuscular abnormalities in the major mental illnesses. I. Serum enzyme studies. See Ref. 38
85. Meltzer, H. Y., Crayton, J. W. 1974. Subterminal motor nerve abnormalities in psychotic patients. Nature 249: 373–75
86. Meltzer, H. Y., Crayton, J. W. 1974. Muscle abnormalities in psychotic patients. II. Serum CPK activity, fiber abnormalities and branching and sprouting of subterminal nerves. Biol. Psychiatry 8:191–208

87. Meltzer, H. Y., Crayton, J. W. 1975. Neuromuscular abnormalities in the major mental illnesses. II. Muscle fiber and subterminal motor nerve abnormalities. See Ref. 38
88. Meltzer, H. Y., Elkun, L., Moline, R. 1969. Serum enzyme changes in newly admitted psychiatric patients. *Arch. Gen. Psychiatry* 21:731–38
89. Meltzer, H. Y., Grinspoon, L., Shader, R. 1970. Serum creatine phosphokinase and aldolase activities in acute schizophrenic patients and their relatives. *Compr. Psychiatry* 11:552–58
90. Meltzer, H. Y., McBride, E., Poppei, R. W. 1973. Rod (memaline) bodies in the skeletal muscle of an acute schizophrenic patient. *Neurology* 23:769–80
91. Meltzer, H. Y., Moline, R. 1970. Muscle abnormalities in acute psychoses. *Arch. Gen. Psychiatry* 23:481–91
92. Meltzer, H. Y., Nankin, R., Raftery, J. 1971. Serum creatine phosphokinase activity in newly admitted psychiatric patients. II. *Arch. Gen. Psychiatry* 24:568–72
93. Mirsky, A. F. 1969. Neuropsychological bases of schizophrenia. *Ann. Rev. Psychol.* 20:321–48
94. Mohr, J. P., Watters, W. C., Duncan, G. W. 1975. Thalamic hemorrhage and aphasia. *Brain Lang.* 2:3–17
95. Moore, M., Nathan, D., Elliot, A. R., Laubach, C. 1933. Encephalographic studies in schizophrenia (Dementia praecox). *Am. J. Psychiatry* 89:801–10
96. Ibid 1935. Encephalographic studies in mental disease. 92:43–67
97. Ojemann, G. A., Ed. 1975. *Brain and Language,* 2:1–2
98. Ibid. Language and the thalamus: Object naming and recall during and after thalamic stimulation, 101–20
99. Ojemann, G. A., Fedio, P. 1968. Effect of stimulation of the human thalamus and parietal and temporal white matter on short-term memory. *J. Neurosurg.* 29:51–59
100. Ojemann, G. A., Fedio, P., VanBuren, J. M. 1968. Anomia from pulvinar and subcortical parietal stimulation. *Brain* 91:99–116
101. Reed, H. B. C., Fitzhugh, K. B. 1966. Patterns of deficit in relation to severity of cerebral dysfunction in children and adults. *J. Consult. Psychol.* 30:98–102
102. Reed, H. B. C., Reitan, R. M., Klove, H. 1965. The influence of cerebral lesions on psychological test performances of older children. *J. Consult. Psychol.* 29:247–51
103. Reitan, R. M. 1955. Affective disturbances in brain-damaged patients: Measurements with the Minnesota Multiphasic Personality Inventory. *Arch. Neurol. Psychiat.* 73:530–32
104. Reitan, R. M. 1958. Qualitative versus quantitative mental changes following brain damage. *J. Psychol.* 46:339–46
105. Reitan, R. M. 1959. The comparative effects of brain damage on the Halstead Impairment Index and the Wechsler-Bellevue Scale. *J. Clin. Psychol.* 15:281–85
106. Reitan, R. M. 1964. Psychological deficits resulting from cerebral lesions in man. See Ref. 49, 295–312
107. Reitan, R. M. 1966. A research program on the psychological effects of brain lesions in human beings. In *International Review of Research in Mental Retardation,* ed. N. R. Ellis, 1:195–218. New York: Academic. 306 pp.
108. Reitan, R. M. 1971. Sensorimotor functions in brain-damaged and normal subjects of early school age. *Percept. Mot. Skills* 33:655–64
109. Ibid. Complex motor functions of the preferred and nonpreferred hands in brain-damaged and normal children, 671–75.
110. Ibid. Trail Making Test results for normal and brain-damaged children, 575–81
111. Reitan, R. M. 1974. Methodological problems in clinical neuropsychology. See Ref. 114, 19–46
112. Ibid. Psychological effects of cerebral lesions in children of early school age, 53–89
113. Reitan, R. M., Boll, T. J. 1973. Neuropsychological correlates of minimal brain dysfunction. See Ref. 24, 65–88
114. Reitan, R. M., Davison, L. A., Eds. 1974. *Clinical Neuropsychology: Current Status and Applications.* Washington: Winston. 417 pp.
115. Reitan, R. M., Tarshes, E. L. 1959. Differential effects of lateralized brain lesions on the Trail Making Test. *J. Nerv. Ment. Dis.* 129:257–62
116. Riklan, M., Cooper, I. S. 1975. Psychometric studies of verbal functions following thalamic lesions in humans. *Brain Lang.* 2:45–64
117. Rose, S. W., Penry, J. K., Markush, R. E., Radloff, L. A., Putnam, P. L. 1973. Prevalence of epilepsy in children. *Epilepsia* (AMST) 14:133–52
118. Rourke, B. P. 1974. *Brain-behaviour relationships in children with learning dis-*

abilities: A research programme. Presented at APA, New Orleans

119. Rourke, B. P., Dietrich, D. M., Young, G. C. 1973. Significance of WISC verbal-performance discrepancies for younger children with learning disabilities. *Percept. Mot. Skills* 36:275–82

120. Rourke, B. P., Finlayson, M. A. J. 1974. *Neuropsychological significance of variations in reading, spelling, and arithmetic achievement for older children with learning disabilities.* Presented at Int. Neuropsychol. Soc., Boston

121. Rourke, B. P., Telegdy, G. A. 1971. Lateralizing significance of WISC verbal-performance discrepancies for children with learning disabilities. *Percept. Mot. Skills* 33:875–83

122. Rourke, B. P., Yanni, D. W., MacDonald, G. W., Young, G. C. 1973. Neuropsychological significance of lateralized deficits on the Grooved Pegboard Test for older children with learning disabilities. *J. Consult. Clin. Psychol.* 41:128–34

123. Rourke, B. P., Young, G. C., Flewelling, R. W. 1971. The relationships between WISC verbal-performance discrepancies and selected verbal, auditory-perceptual, visual-perceptual, and problem-solving abilities in children with learning disabilities. *J. Clin. Psychol.* 27:475–79

124. Rowland, L. P. 1975. Discussion of Meltzer's paper, "Neuromuscular abnormalities in the major mental illnesses. See Ref. 38

125. Schaltenbrand, G. 1975. The effects of speech and language of stereotactical stimulation in thalamus and corpus callosum. *Brain Lang.* 2:70–77

126. Schimmelpenning, G. W. 1958. Zur psychopathologischen Abgrenzung von hirnatrophischen Hypochondrien und Körperschizophrenien. *Arch. Psychiat. Nervenkr.* 197:463–83

127. Shagass, C. 1972. Electrical activity of the brain. In *Handbook of Psychophysiology,* ed. N. S. Greenfield, R. Sternbach, 262–328. New York: Holt, Reinhart & Winston

128. Shagass, C. 1972. *Evoked Brain Potentials in Psychiatry.* New York: Plenum

129. Shagass, C. 1975. EEG and evoked potentials in the psychoses. See Ref. 38

130. Shaw, D. J., Matthews, C. G. 1965. Differential MMPI performance of brain-damaged vs. pseudo-neurologic groups. *J. Clin. Psychol.* 21:405–8

131. Slater, E. 1965. Diagnosis of "hysteria." *Br. Med. J.* 29:1395–98

132. Slater, E. 1969. The schizophrenia-like illnesses of epilepsy. In *Current Problems in Neuropsychiatry, Schizophrenia, Epilepsy, and the Temporal Lobe,* ed. R. N. Herrington. London: Headly. 184 pp.

133. Slater, E. T. O., Glithero, E. 1965. A follow-up of patients diagnosed as suffering from "hysteria." *J. Psychosom. Res.* 9:9–13

134. Van Buren, J. M. 1975. Question of thalamic participation in speech mechanisms. *Brain Lang.* 2:31–44

135. Wagner, F. 1951. Brain atrophy in a psychiatric clinic diagnosed by pneumoencephalography. *Acta Psychiat. Scand. Suppl.* 74:212–15

136. Wigert, V. 1938. Enzephalographische Befunde bei sog "Psychoneurosen." *Acta Psychiat. Scand.* 13:401–15

137. Zahn, T. P. 1975. Psychophysiological concomitants of task performance in schizophrenia. See Ref. 60, 109–31

138. Zimet, C. N., Fishman, D. B. 1970. Psychological deficit in schizophrenia and brain damage. *Ann. Rev. Psychol.* 21: 113–54

139. Zimmerman, I. L. 1965. Residual effects of brain damage and five MMPI items. *J. Consult. Psychol.* 29:394

140. Zubin, J. 1975. Problem of attention in schizophrenia. See Ref. 60, 139–66

CHANGE INDUCTION IN SMALL GROUPS[1]   ❖253

Morton A. Lieberman[2]

Departments of Behavioral Science (Human Development) and Psychiatry, University of Chicago, Chicago, Illinois 60637

INTRODUCTION

Almost every conceivable arrangement used for almost every conceivable end with almost every conceivable type of person can define the small face-to-face group whose function is to effect change or psychological repair. A fair reading of the literature suggests that no single technique, type of group, or theoretical orientation succeeds for the majority of group participants. On the other hand, one cannot find a technique, type of group, or orientation that does not work with at least one other person. The focus of this review lies between these poles.

Although the specific focus is the use of groups in meeting mental health goals, the more general area considered is group-based changed induction. The survey is of group psychotherapy, experiential groups (variously labeled sensitivity training or encounter groups), consciousness-raising activities, and self-help groups. This inclusiveness is justified by observations that the processes of these various groups are

---

[1]The following abbreviations are used throughout text and in Table 1 of this article.

CPI	California Psychological Inventory
EPI	Eysenck Personality Inventory
FIRO	Fundamental Interpersonal Relations Orientation
HIM	Hill Interaction Matrix
HSR	Meninger Health Sickness Rating
LIC	Leary Interpersonal Checklist
PAS	Problem Appraisal Scale
16 PF	Cattell Sixteen Factor Personality Test
POI	Personal Orientation Inventory
Rotter I-E	Rotter Internal-External Scale
TAT	Thematic Apperception Test
TSCS	Tennessee Self-Concept Scale

[2]This chapter was written while the author was supported by a Research Scientist Award 1 KO5-MH20342 from the National Institute of Mental Health.

217

sufficiently related, their goals are frequently identical, and their client populations highly overlapping. Boundaries often reflect professional narrowness and language systems more than substantive differences.

This review will address the classic questions: does it work? how well? for whom? how can we improve it? what is it about what we do that works? and—for those with somewhat more intellectual curiosity—why does it work if it does?

I have chosen to be extensive rather than intensive, particularly with regard to the initial question, does it work? Outcome studies in the 1973 and 1974 literature (June 1973 through December 1974) are numerous. An examination of the effectiveness of groups for change induction leads immediately to the standard comments about psychotherapy research. Reading the classic works on the problems in psychotherapy research, such as Bergin & Garfield (12), will serve the reader better than their repetition. This is not to imply that a few of the studies reviewed have not been responsive to the classic criticisms and suggestions. There is a trend towards increasing sophistication in selecting control conditions, usually cleverly designed "placebo treatment situations" or reasonably potent designs of contrasting treatments. Most, however, fail to specify with any degree of precision (homogeneity) the patient populations, or perhaps even more serious, to specify the nature of the treatment. To use such labels as psychoanalytic psychotherapy, T-group, etc as substitutes for treatment specifications is unsatisfactory. This is particularly true if one tries to chart the past 20 years or so of research in this area; for example, the T-group of the 1950s is probably not the T-group of the 1970s. There is reason to believe that during the past 20 years not only have clients changed (both in terms of the goals that they bring to sensitivity training and in their degree of sophistication about change and learning in small groups) but also that leaders have altered their assumptions about the function and operation of such groups (68).

OUTCOME STUDIES

Over 50 published articles and dissertations appeared in 1973–74 addressed either to the simple question, does it work? or to the more complex question, which works better? An equal number of published reports were concerned with more specific questions about the process of change induction. These studies are reviewed in a later section.

Does it work and how well? Of the 47 studies shown in Table 1, one-third were concerned with ostensibly normative college populations, another 8 with adult "normals," and the remaining 22 with individuals of concern to mental health. Of these 22, 9 involved the neurotic problems of college-age and adult-age populations, and only 2 involved psychotic populations. Ten focused on various forms of deviant behavior—primarily alcoholism and drug abuse—but did include other forms of abuse (such as overeating). An occasional study reported on the use of groups for other problems such as community relationships (police/delinquents). Studies not shown in Table 1 were omitted because they did not contain specific measures of outcome. Many of these reported on other targeted populations and problems, i.e. those physically ill, schizophrenic patients, parents of disturbed children, and those in correction institutions. It is difficult to find a societal problem that has not, in some setting, been treated by use of group methods.

Some General Trends in Design of Outcome Studies

Two-thirds of the studies surveyed used some form of control with the majority providing active alternative treatment or simulation of treatment rather than "inert" or "nonactive" control groups. Many of the controls chosen were based on sophisticated research strategies and creative design, using active or alternate treatment methods and often involving true random assignment. In contrast, some of the inert control groups were primitively chosen and represented no more than a nodding afterthought to research design.

The range of measures was broad, as were the populations and conditions of treatment. Some studies relied totally on one self-report scale while others used a multimethod approach. None met the more stringent requirements for excellence in design. The most popular measure of outcome was the POI; 20% of the studies used this instrument. However, this turned out to be problematic. Recall that a majority of the studies surveyed are those of the encounter group/sensitivity training variety, in which values of self-development, openness, honesty, etc are intrinsic to the method itself. The POI closely matches the value systems portrayed in such groups; consequently, it is difficult to distinguish this measure from the overt values of the change-induction system itself. Other frequently used measurement devices were testimony reports, standard personality inventories such as the MMPI or the CPI, measures of state or trait anxiety, symptomatology, and various standard and "home-brewed" indices of self-acceptance and self-ideal congruity. A few studies used peer measures of change; surprisingly few used leader judgments of change. Only one used third-party measurement. Other favorites included the FIRO, the Hill Interaction Matrix, and the Rotter. Some studies relied on situation type tests —frequently little more than standard replication of the change induction system itself, such as self-disclosing behavior to a stranger—as an index of how well this particular behavior was learned. Eight of the 47 studies used one form or another of behavioral index ranging from measures of attendance to assessments of alcohol consumption or weight loss.

Table 1, which contains brief summaries of outcome studies, is divided into two main parts: Part 1 surveys outcome studies in which the investigators contrast treatment conditions against inert control groups (or no control at all); Part 2 scans those studies which emphasize comparative treatment modalities.

Simple Outcome Studies

Of the 31 studies reported in Part 1, 14 are directed toward college students. All but 2 of the 14 reported positive results—lower anxiety, increased internal locus of control, increased social interaction, increased self-esteem, value changes, and decreased discrepancy between self and ideal. The two studies of college samples showing negative results—Kaye's (50) on academic failures and Lunceford's (71) on black female undergraduates—involved populations that ordinarily may have values incongruous with sensitivity training/encounter groups. Although less nu-

Table 1   Studies of outcome

PART 1 Outcome of Treatment versus Inert Control Group or No Control			
Author	Sample	Method	Finding
Arbes & Hubbell (5)	16 male, 14 female self-referred undergraduates	Random assignment to one of two experimental groups. 2½ hr/7 wk or a control group. FIRO–B, Concept Specific Anxiety and Interpersonal Relationship Rating Scale pre-post	Ss improved on almost all scales of Concept Specific Anxiety Scale & Interpersonal Relationship Scale. FIRO–B (expressed affects) subscale used
Barrett-Lennard et al (8)	62 mental health professionals	2 wk encounter group workshop. Open-ended Qs 6 mo after participation. Change ratings (77% rates agreement)	Change in level of self-regard, interpersonal behavior, and attitudes for majority of Ss
Battle & Zwier (9)	8 male chronic hospital elopers	21 weekly therapy sessions	Group effective in reducing absences
Brown (19)	54 chronically mentally ill patients under medication	Assigned to 3 groups: 1. using tokens to reinforce comments and reports about community adjustment; 2. nontoken group stressing support for community adjustment; 3. medication supervision only	Observed no differences between treatment conditions
Cooper (22)	30 members of helping profession	1 wk sensitivity group. Neuroticism scale of EPI and a behavior change Q by participants, friends, and family members	Increase in neuroticism on EPI, not "confirmed" by family and friends 2 wk later
Deleppo (26)	Drug addicts in self-help treatment and methadone maintenance	Comparison between the effects of peer-directed psychotherapy and methadone on MMPI scores	Self-help group scored significantly lower on Depression and Psychopathic Scales
Diamond (27)	Phase I: 39 grad students; Phase II: 44 equivalent Ss	Investigated effects of encounter group on locus of control (Rotter). Phase I: 3 groups led by supervised grad students and 1 no-treatment control group; Phase II: 4 encounter groups	Increases in internal locus of control
Dies & Sadowsky (28)	Women in dormitory living on 3 separate floors; women on 2 other floors were control group	Experimental Ss provided with group experience. Semantic differential ratings of atmosphere and self-reported number of acquaintances	Improvement in semantic differential ratings and increase in number of acquaintances
Felton & Davidson (32)	61 high school low achievers	57 sessions, 3/wk and nontreatment control. Rotter I–E pre-post	Increase in internality
Foulds (34)	14 undergraduates who had signed up for encounter group	Six 4-hr sessions/wk. Ss rated themselves and others on 29 semantic differential scales pre-post. 14 control undergrads from waiting list	Increases in positive rating of self and others
Fromme et al (36)	A "conservative population" of 91 county extension agents	One wk T-group. CPI and TSCS pre-post	10 of 18 CPI scales showed Ss becoming more cautious, inhibited, defensive, disorganized, and emotionally upset. TSCS less conclusive. 2 scales (Personality Interpretation and Ethical Self-Concept Scale) showed decline and 3 improved (physical self-concepts)
Gilligan (38)	50 T-group volunteers, college students	24 hr in a weekend, compared to a nontreatment group of 55 student volunteers. POI pre-post and 6 wk followup	Post-test, Ss improved on 6 of 12 scales. 6 wk, Inner Direction, Self-Regard and Acceptance of Aggression significant

Table 1 (Continued)

Author	Sample	Method	Finding
Herz et al (46)	144 aftercare patients	Randomly assigned to group or individual therapy with first year psychiatric residents. Therapist rating after 1 yr on PAS and HSR, patient self-report	No differences. Therapists preferred groups. Group patients more enthusiastic
Kaye (50)	27 academically unsuccessful undergrads	In 2 T-groups for 18 sessions/10 days. Control groups: (a) balloted out of T-group participation; (b) refused the invitation; (c) academically successful students. HIM–B, FIRO–B, and LIC pre-post and 8 mo later	HIM–B initially increased on post-test but decreased 8 mo later. No other changes
Kilmann (52)	9 university students	10 hr marathon group on state and trait anxiety pre-post	Anxiety state showed decline; anxiety trait was unchanged
Kilmann & Auerbach (53)	84 institutionalized female narcotic drug addicts	Randomly assigned to (a) a marathon (23 hr) directive group following defined and planned exercises; (b) nondirective marathon group where therapist relinquished responsibility	Ss in nondirective therapy declined in anxiety trait; directive therapy Ss showed increase, controls stayed same
Kleeman (56)	Undergrads from 25 colleges: 188 participants and 140 control non-participants, of whom 141 of former and 89 of latter were involved in original experiment and replication; follow-up involved 97 Ss and 89 controls	Wrightman's Philosophy of Human Nature Scale and a self-report of self-determining and motivating behavior pre-post. Ss participated for 29–40 hr during an academic term	Positive changes on Philosophy of Human Nature Scales
Klingberg (57)	48 male seminary students	POI, Frankl's Purpose in Life Test, and Broen's Religious Attitude Inventory given pre-post in professionally and self-directed (leaderless) T-groups	No consistent differences
LaCalle (61)	Mexican American and non-Mexican American drug addicts on methadone	Assigned to four groups: 1. Mexican Americans on methadone only; 2. on methadone with group therapy; 3. non-Mexican Americans on methadone only; 4. non-Mexican Americans on methadone with group therapy. A behavioral Q and CPI	Methadone treatment Ss improved in observable behavior; no improvement in the methadone plus group therapy Ss
Lunceford (71)	Black female undergrads	Weekend encounter group; non-participant control group. TSCS pre-post	Only one significant subscale difference: Ss increased in category of personal self
Margulies (72)	40 middle management employees	One T-group and one control group. POI given pre-post	Positive changes in self-actualization
Martin & Fischer (73)	38 Ss aged 17–45	One weekend (30 hr) encounter group. Ss named 38 persons like selves for control group. Adjective Checklist given pre-post	4 of 13 Adjective Checklist Scales improved: 1 self-concept and 3 social skills
McIntire (78)	17 randomly assigned Ss aged 22 to late 50s	Met 5 hr/wk for 6 wk. POI given pre-post and a year later	2 days after, Inner Directed and Self-Acceptance POI scales increased. Still significant at year

Table 1 (Continued)

Author	Sample	Method	Finding
Posthuma & Posthuma (92)	73 Unitarian Church members	Ss met in encounter group for one 12-hr session followed by 10 weekly 2-hr sessions; Placebo control group met for 10 content oriented, 3-hr sessions; nontreatment control group. Self-reports on Behavioral Change Index used to assess casualties post- and at 6 months	Negative indices undifferentiated among three groups by 6-mo followup
Reddy (93)	36 YMCA administrators	Met in three 10-day residential sensivity groups. POI given pre-post and at one year. Multiple Affect Adjective Checklist given daily to measure anxiety. No control group	All three groups reported changes. Variance on 9 of 12 POI subscales. Correlations of pre-post to post-followup negative, suggesting "late bloomers." Anxiety scores positively related to POI scores in one group over followup year.
Redfering (94)	18 female delinquents who had participated in previous study	Received group counseling during year following previous study in which Ss had given significantly more positive connotative meanings to concepts of father, mother, self, and peers. One year followup tested these effects	Positive effects were still present on all concepts except those of peers as measured by the Semantic Differential Technique
Romano & Quary (96)	68 undergrads, former encounter group participants.	Responded to followup Q on harmful effects of their group experience (25% of original group did not respond)	67 reported that they had not been harmed by the groups
Vicino et al (107)	96 undergraduate volunteers	Ss took set of self-administered exercises. Outcome measures by "Who am I," peer-ratings, and Bills, Rokeach & Marlowe Crowne personality inventories. Eight experimental and 4 control (delayed treatment) groups	Reduction in discrepancy between self and ideal. Other indices not different. Despite positive change, member satisfaction with groups was low
Walton (108)	25 undergraduates	Met in two encounter groups, 14 1-hr sessions. Control group of 9 undergrads enrolled in seminar on counseling concepts and procedures for increasing self-acutalization. POI and 16 PF, pre-post	Gains on Inner Direction and Spontaneity scales of POI and Adventuresome and Creative Personality prediction scales of the 16 PF. Controls increase on POI Nature of Man
White (110)	85 undergrads; control group of 75 undergrads	Met in human potential lab for 2½ hr/wk for 12 wk. POI pre-post. Control group of 75 undergrads matched for sex and age	Ss increased on Self-Actualizing, Reactivity, Spontaneity, and Nature of Man subscales
PART 2 Comparative Treatment A. Specific techniques			
Archer & Kagan (6)	Undergraduates in T-groups	Compared Ss led by undergraduate paraprofessionals using videotape feedbacks with limited structure encounter group model and nontreatment control. Empathy test, POI, and peer relationship ratings	Participants in interpersonal process recall video feedback groups score higher than unstructured encounter and control group
Bolan (14)	College student volunteers	"Experimental" group and "standard" encounter group. Compared differences resulting from two approaches to encounter groups: experimental group used nonverbal and verbal activities. POI and FIRO-B.	Experimental Ss showed more gain on Time Competence, Inner Directed, and Self-Acceptance scales-POI

Table 1 (Continued)

Author	Sample	Method	Finding
Bornstein & Sipprelle (17)	40 obese male and female volunteers	Four groups: 1. nontreatment control group; 2. therapy, relaxation group; 3. therapy; 4. induced anxiety therapy. Weight loss assessed post-test, 3 mo and 6 mo later	No significant differences posttest. Significant differences in weight loss favored induced anxiety group compared to others at 3 and 6 mo followup
Dye (29)	56 associate degree nursing freshmen	Five groups: 1. encountertape group; 2. affect-oriented T-group; 3. cognitively oriented group using verbal and nonverbal interactions; 4. placebo group maintaining journal of critical life events; 5. nontreatment group. TSCS, Manifest Anxiety Scale, State-Trait Anxiety Inventory, and Affect Adjective Checklist, HIM-B pre-post, and 1 month post-test	No significant differences between the groups were found
Hagen (41)	54 obese female undergraduates	Three conditions: 1. group therapy; 2. use of written manual (bibliotherapy); 3. group therapy and bibliotherapy combined. Weight loss was outcome measure	All treatment groups showed more weight loss than controls. Ss reported group treatments significantly more helpful than manual only. Changes in eating habits but not in physical activity were different across groups
Hand et al (42)	25 adult patients with agoraphobia	Each patient received 12 hr exposure (flooding) in vivo for 3 days, 4 hr/day. 3 groups structured to increase social cohesion during exposure; other 3 unstructured to expose members to minimal group influence. Behavioral tests and phobic anxiety measured	Structured groups improved more than unstructured groups 3 and 6 mo later
McCardel & Murray (77)	47 Ss recruited from campus ad	Three weekend groups whose methods varied from highly structured, exercise-oriented techniques to nonstructured. At-home and on-site controls, the latter led to believe that they were also in encounter group but given only recreational activities. POI, Marlow-Crowne Scale, Rokeach Dogmatism Scale, and peer rankings given pre-post and at 10 wk	Significant differences on 7 of 12 POI scales. On-site control group and 3 encounter groups did not differ on any measure. Followup confirmed these findings
McLeish & Park (82)	94 teacher trainees	Two types of human relations training: self-analytic treatment (SAT) or direct communications treatment (DCT) for two types of observer groups: Bales O group and clinical (nontrained) O group. 15 sessions. Park Matheson Human Relations Videotape Test, Park Matheson Group Process Analysis Test, Cambridge Survey of Education Opinions, and Rokeach Dogmatism Tests given pre-post	No changes found on personality and attitude measures, but DCT participants and Os were higher on measures of empathetic understanding
Rimm et al (95)	13 male college students responding to newspaper ad to join T-group for help in controlling anger	Ss randomly assigned to assertive training group or placebo group. Controls talked about anger. Lawrence Assertive Inventory, Rotter I-E, ratings of Ss responses to situations	No treatment effects on Rotter or Lawrence Inventory. Ss showed improvement on rated responses to situations

Table 1 (Continued)

Author	Sample	Method	Finding
PART 2 Comparative Treatments			
B. Peer versus leader			
Conyne (21)	48 Ss enrolled in counselor education course	3 facilitator-directed sensitivity training group experiences and 3 self-directed experiences on development of intrapersonal perceptions of congruency and disclosure. Congruency assessed by group semantic differential and disclosure assessed by Johari window	No differences between treatments found. All groups increased in self-congruency and self-disclosure. 4 mo followup showed self-disclosure scores stable, but not self-congruency scores
Hurst et al (47)	40 university students in counseling center	Professionally led group met 2 hr/wk for 8 wk; 1 encountertape group met 3 hr/wk for 5 wk; another had an active member; third had an active member and met for a weekend. 5 controls were on waiting list at counseling center. Miskimins Self, Goal, Other Discrepancy Scale given pre-post	Only Ss in encountertape group with no active member decreased their discrepancy between present and desired self-concept
Kroeker et al (60)	60 inner city youths (15–21 yr) and 48 Rochester policemen	Human relations program. Ss randomly assigned to 1 of 3 workshops or 1 of 3 control groups. Youths attended an average of 4.5 workshops, policemen 3.5. Alienation Index Inventory and a TAT of police-black youth potential conflict situations	Pretesting effects far outweighed experimental effects. No significant differences between Ss and controls
PART 2 Comparative Treatments			
C. Comparative Modes			
Miller et al (83)	30 male alcoholics	Compared 3 types of treatment: electrical aversion conditioning; group therapy (confrontational psychotherapy); control conditioning. All Ss given instructions designed to produce high expectancy for therapeutic success. Pre-post measures of alcohol consumption and attitudes toward alcohol obtained using an analog "taste test" assessment	No differences found among groups
Newcomer & Morrison (85)	Institutionalized retarded children	3 groups: individual play therapy; group therapy; or nontreatment control group. Denver Developmental Screening Test given pretest and after 3 10-session blocks of therapy	Nontreatment group did not change while scores for individual and group therapy groups increased across sessions. No differences between group and individual therapy
PART 2 Comparative Treatments			
D. Time			
King et al (54)	57 undergraduates	Studied changes in self-acceptance measured before and after participation in a marathon or a prolonged encounter group. Six groups: 3 met 24 hr each (marathon); 3 prolonged encounter groups met 3 or 4 hr/wk for 14 weeks; also control group and nontreatment control. Lesser Self-Acceptance and Smith Social Approval scales pre-post	Both treatment conditions increased self-acceptance, but marathon group members were significantly lower than others in self-acceptance both pre- and post-test. Self-acceptance scores not associated with need for social approval

Table 1   (Continued)

Author	Sample	Method	Finding
Ross et al (98)	12 female narcotic addicts	Compared treatment of 6 Ss in a 17-hr marathon and 6 in group therapy in daily 2-hr sessions for 2 weeks. Lexington Personality Inventory	Both treatments reduced scores on neurotic triad of MMPI. Marathon also showed more change toward internal control

merous, studies reporting the effects of encounter or sensitivity training on adults echo similar themes. Educated middle class adults who participate in sensitivity training groups show the same pattern of positive results as do college students. When studies using similar group settings were directed at populations probably not value-congruent with the particular group, such as that by Fromme et al (36) on a conservative population (fundamentalist background), they showed converse results—in this instance, an increase in emotional disturbance. Although having different goals and using different measures, the study reported by Kroeker et al (60) on attitude shifts for ghetto-dwelling adolescents and police demonstrates the limitations of such groups for particular populations. Studies of addict populations are inconsistent. Some reported positive results, while others—and again, this seems to relate to populations that may be more value incongruent with the particular group —found negative results.

The positive results from most reported studies on the effects of groups cannot be explained away on the basis of inadequate controls. Nevertheless, these 31 studies do not measurably increase our knowledge about change-induction groups. Too many rely upon change measures that offer little more than attitude-change evidence. More important, the particular change conditions are usually unspecified. They range, with similar outcomes, from peer-controlled groups with sets of tasks to accomplish, to groups led by sophisticated leaders. In addition, the fact that such groups work best with "volunteer subjects," i.e. people who seek such settings, ordinarily with positive expectations of change, leads one to question the robustness of these findings. The fact that individuals less likely to be changed are also those whose values are less congruent with the particular set espoused by such groups casts doubt on the meaningfulness of the findings. Too, the slice of human behavior considered appropriate outcome in most studies is relatively narrow. In sum, this reviewer is less than enthusiastic about this set of research reports.

Comparative Treatment Studies

Part 2 of Table 1 reports on studies that involved some form of comparative treatment. They range from relatively informal designs in which specific directions were given to leaders on their leadership role to highly distinct leadership conditions —such as group versus individual context, token versus nontoken environment, peer-controlled versus leader-led groups—to indirect learning conditions, such as groups of students observing other groups of students as they experience intensive face-to-face groups. As a rule this set of research reports was more tightly designed than the first set, though the outcome criteria were for the most part similar.

Four major types of research are apparent: 1. comparative treatments—various forms of group treatment, usually sharing theoretical underpinnings but emphasizing variations in technique, content focus, or mode of communication (see Part 2A of Table 1); 2. some variant of comparison of groups—again groups within the same theoretical tradition but distinguished on the basis of leader-led or peer-controlled groups (see Part 2B of Table 1 and its discussion in the section on boundaries); 3. research reports comparing types of treatment, individual treatment, and group treatment, or comparing different forms of groups, behavioral and "talk" therapy (see Part 2C of Table 1); and 4. studies which report on alterations of time arrangements, usually time-extended versus time-concentrated situations (see Part 2D of Table 1).

COMPARATIVE TECHNIQUES   Overall, studies of structured techniques or learning devices produced results favoring the particular technique which interested the investigator. Ten studies examined comparative treatments in which one of the treatments emphasized greater structure or specific technical interventions. Six of these produced results affirming the investigators' hypotheses that groups using each particular technical "advantage" examined—video feedback, nonverbal emphasis, induced anxiety, structured groups, assertiveness training versus talk, etc—derived greater benefit than comparable groups not using these techniques. Several studies of this genre produced negative results: no differences were found between particular treatment conditions. Included here were the failure to find the effectiveness of token reinforcement for physically ill patients, the failure to find distinctions between affect-oriented and cognitively oriented T-groups, the ambiguous results reported on obese women in regard to group therapy versus a manual for controlling eating. (In this last, some differences were found with regard to eating habits and attitudes, but not with regard to weight loss.)

Two studies (77, 81) were of particular interest to this reviewer. Both contained unusual "placebo" groups, and both produced results which suggest that nonspecific therapeutic factors may be responsible for the major effects reported in many of the outcome studies reviewed in Part 1. McCardel & Murray (77) utilized an on-site control group. Subjects had expected to participate in change-induction groups, but instead they were exposed only to recreational activities and relatively nonintense interactive events. Nevertheless, this condition produced high changes comparable to the other treatment conditions—structured and unstructured sensitivity training. McLeish & Park (81) studied various group treatment forms as well as two conditions for groups of observers. Increases in empathy, the only positive finding for the treatment conditions, occurred just as strongly among the observers.

The core question—to what degree do the comparative treatments transcend nonspecific treatment conditions—remains open. On balance, the studies reported favor specific directed interventions over less directed interventions (structure versus unstructure). But the possibility of the enthusiasm and bias of the experimenter affecting the results cannot be ignored. Furthermore, the fact that the structured formats appear more effective may be less a result of the particular intervention system than of the influence of structure on the purveyor. Most of the groups were conducted by relatively inexperienced leaders "trained in particular methods." It is quite likely that "knowing what to do," a powerful anxiety reducer, may have been the more significant active ingredient than the particular form of intervention itself. Without increased knowledge on the particular mechanisms of change, that chain of events between the input and output variables, it is difficult to make generalizations from these studies. Finally, it is difficult to evaluate two sets of conflicting results, i.e. that *(a)* structured intervention techniques are better, or *(b)* peer-controlled groups are as good as or occasionally better than leader-led groups. This is especially true when leaders use many of the specific intervention systems tested in the research reports just described.

COMPARATIVE TREATMENTS   Studies which compared treatment modalities generally reported no differences. The question may again be one of general or nonspecific treatment conditions. However, it is also likely that the indices used to measure outcome are relatively insensitive to the potentialities of different treatment contexts such as group and individual psychotherapy.

TIME ARRANGEMENTS   Several studies on time alterations show evidence indicating greater effectiveness of time-intensive groups. Although the findings point in this direction, the conceptual underpinnings of time arrangements in therapy are so indeterminate that, without some knowledge about the underlying mechanism, it is difficult to build from the results.

BOUNDARIES—INTEGRATION, DIFFERENTIATION

Evidence is plentiful that groups are capable of producing change in participants. Perhaps all too evident, studies on the effects of such groups report findings from populations as diverse as is our society. The diversity of methods and populations which has been caught up in our review of outcomes signals what appears to be the major intellectual issue within the field: the development of a parsimonious set of constructs that will encompass such diversity and yet not move too far into a sterile reductionism. This issue is often expressed in terms of integration/differentiation, general systems theory, or boundary concerns.

Distinctions are currently based on different theoretical perspectives purporting to have the same goal for the same population. These distinctions are analogous to schools of psychotherapy which define themselves as being relevant to groups of individuals called patients. Boundary concern is also expressed through goals such as repair versus growth. Boundary issues are defined, too, by purveyors of group change activities—disciplines, demidisciplines, professional versus nonprofessional, peer control. How meaningful are these boundary issues? Or perhaps more specifically, which ones are useful for patterning the field and which ones should be discarded?

Schools of Group Psychotherapy

The issues mirror the history of psychotherapy. With few exceptions, theories and practice orientation in group psychotherapy grew out of their counterparts in individual psychotherapy. Language systems used to describe therapeutic procedures are highly distinctive. However, there is only poor correspondence between theoretical positions and actual leader or member behavior. Lieberman et al (70) report that experienced therapists sharing identical theoretical orientations neither behaved similarly with comparable populations, nor did they achieve similar success (or failure) rates. Furthermore, observed behavioral and symbolic differences among leaders did not correspond to their theoretical orientation, a finding that echoes the psychotherapy literature of the 1960s. This does not mean that various theoretical perspectives are similar; their assumptions about the nature of man and the goals of learning are distinct. Empirical data do not exist for assessing the effects of such perspectives on outcome.

Evidence does not suggest that all group leaders act alike. Instead it suggests that their theoretical positions do not predict their behavior. Thus we are not saying that everyone is doing the same thing, and that productive therapists act the same way and unproductive therapists act differently. Rather, because of the poor correspondence between theoretical orientation and behavior, it is difficult to evaluate realistically similarities and differences among the various theoretical positions.

Clients

Differences in client populations have underscored differences among the various forms and types of group endeavors. In its simplest form, the issue has been joined as "repair" versus "growth." Historically, this theme appeared in the late 1950s under the rubric "therapy for normals" as the sensitivity training movement, begun as an educational endeavor, then slowly altered its processes in the direction of what we today term "encounter groups." The influence of humanistic psychology, particularly the thinking of Maslow and Rogers during the 1960s, strongly colored the goal orientation of the burgeoning human potential movement and its most visible form, the encounter group. Not only were sharp boundaries drawn between the objectives of psychotherapy and those of encounter groups, but the often implicit, at times explicit, distinction between populations was emphasized: individuals go to psychotherapists for "repair," to encounter groups for "growth." Several recent studies on who volunteers for sensitivity training suggest that such distinctions are probably not realistic. Evidence (69) indicates that those who choose activities under the rubric of the human potential movement resemble psychiatric clinic populations. Most growth center attenders had scores comparable to psychiatric clinic populations on symptoms, life stress, and help-seeking motivations. In fact, eight out of ten participants in growth centers had previous or current psychotherapeutic experience. Other research on those who volunteer for encounter or sensitivity training (86) further underscores the overlap between these populations and those entering psychotherapy. Some current work (M. A. Lieberman, University of Chicago, and D. Kravetz, University of Wisconsin at Madison) on Consciousness-Raising Groups suggests similar results. Despite wide ideological differences between psychotherapy, human potential movements, and consciousness-raising groups, individuals enter all these systems with degrees of psychological distress and motivational goals that are indistinguishable. Kirsh (55) made a similar point in her portrayal of consciousness-raising groups as therapy for women. It seems to be an exercise in futility to create boundaries based on theoretical objectives which are unrecognized by the client populations. Thus, although it appears reasonable to establish differentiated systems in order to provide sharply different goal objectives for the participants, to do so makes little sense until the problem of client perceptions has been dealt with on a practical level.

Leadership

Perhaps no other single issue generates more interest, controversy, and trivia than the question of who shall lead change-induction groups. Historically this issue began as an intense but relatively quiet interdisciplinary warfare among mental health professionals. It has progressed through the passionate debate surrounding the appearance of para- or semiprofessionals, and has recently begun to emerge as a question of whether or not the leader exerts any significant influence at all on the change process itself. A number of forces have contributed to these cycles. Overall, it seems that boundaries based on the traditional characterization of leaders have been breached so that they are no longer viable or meaningful. Obviously other forces in society have contributed to the rapid fluctuations and controversy surrounding the question of who should provide psychotherapeutic service. However, because of some of the special characteristics of small groups, the issue has become especially sharpened and highlighted.

Empirical research reflecting on this issue usually takes one of two forms. Over the years, a steady trickle of reports comparing experienced and untrained therapists has appeared. The study reported by Poser (91) typifies such research. More or less, such studies have suggested no differences in output (not necessarily behavior) of experienced compared to inexperienced therapists. Unfortunately, such studies rarely reflect sophisitcated research methodology, especially with regard to controls and outcome measures. Thus it becomes difficult to draw more than speculative conclusions. Another view might be provided by a survey across outcome studies comparing level of leader experience. Unfortunately, the vast majority of research reports indicates that the individuals conducting groups are at the junior end (the proverbial resident in group psychotherapy or the graduate student in counseling). Examination of Table 1 amply demonstrates why, at the current level of published research, it is well-nigh impossible to determine the correlation between the level of the leader's skill (measured by years of experience) and outcome.

Another strategy is to focus upon specific definitions of leader skill whereby variations in leader behavior along the lines of some model can be assessed. Truax & Carkhuff (105), offering perhaps the best example of such inquiry, strongly indicate that particular therapist-fostered conditions in psychotherapy are associated with productivity for the client. However, similar measures by Truax on group leaders are ambiguous. Thus the utility of this particular model of leader skill with regard to the group field remains indeterminate.

Generally, definition of leader skill is based upon theoretical statements about specific change mechanisms. The sections in this chapter on the Role of Leadership and on Change Mechanisms suggest that an attack on the issue of skill from a theoretical standpoint will prove inconclusive. Perhaps some research inroads could be made by combining strategies so that, for example, studies would not only assess contrasts between experienced and inexperienced therapists, but also would concern themselves with particular operations that distinguish the skilled from the unskilled. Type, frequency, and timing in relation to group conditions are some possible initial candidates for empirical examination. It is likely, however, that this complex issue will remain unresolved for quite some time.

Skill issues have been superceded by increasing discussions about leader role and contribution to the change process. Change groups that rely on peer direction originating in the self-help and consciousness-raising movements have served to exacerbate this issue. The implicit (and often explicit) goals of such groups are identical to those of psychotherapy. Shifting societal values, expressed as egalitarian trends, which tend to demystify the mental health specialists and minimize their special skills, have probably served to highlight this issue. A number of studies in the current literature reflect this theme.

Conyne (21) compared the effectiveness of leader-directed sensitivity groups with self-directed groups on the development of interpersonal perception, congruency, and self-disclosure. As is typical in this type of research, Conyne provided some structure for the "peer-directed" groups by using tape-recorded instructions for a portion of the time they met. These structured inputs were used at one out of every five meetings in both the leaderless and the leader-directed groups. No significant difference between conditions was found, although both groups showed pre-post changes. These results were stable as measured four months after the end of the experiment.

Dye (29) compared four treatment conditions: 1. Bell & Howell encountertapes; 2. sensitivity training with a leader; 3. a leader-directed, communication-oriented group; and 4. nontreatment conditions. The TSCS, Manifest Anxiety Indices, adjective checklists, and the HIM were administered pre-post and one month post-test; data presented by Dye reports greater changes in the HIM for the leaderless groups. Overall, data indicate that the active treatment modalities and the "placebo treatment" were undifferentiated, including no differences between leader-led and leaderless groups. Hurst et al (47) compared professional encounter leaders and encountertape-led groups with both regular membership (naive) and an "active" member group. Changes in self-concept were assessed (self/ideal). Only the leaderless groups with no active member showed significant pre-post change.

Vicino et al (107) used a set of self-administered exercises and found that these leaderless structured groups produced positive changes, reductions in self-ideal discrepancy, and greater congruence between peer- and self-ratings of behavior as compared to randomly assigned control group nontreatment situations.

McLaughlin et al (80), in an extensive examination of various treatment modalities, compared leader-led groups with tape conditions on both outcome measures and process measures within the group. Five measures were used: Semantic Differential Rating Scales, Training Group Rating Scale, Wayland's Group Rating Category System, the FIRO, and a videotape of cognitive-effective competence in knowledge of group process. The investigators' results were complex. They found differences between specific groups on a number of process scales, but not on outcome scales. The general sweep of their conclusions certainly suggests that leaderless conditions, i.e. the use of structured tape exercises, is in no demonstrable way inferior to leader-led situations.

Ficht (33) compared leader-led with encountertape-led groups in a black and a white college population. Among the whites using analysis-of-feeling statements, no significant differences were produced between the two treatment conditions. Among the blacks, however, counselor-led groups were more productive.

In a study by Lieberman et al (70) on various types of professional encounter leaders, two tape-led groups were also studied. The tape groups were more successful on a variety of outcome measures than three-quarters of the professionally led groups. Similar to the finding of Vicino, tape-led groups were rated by the members as being less liked than those led by leaders, even though the actual outcome results proved to be superior.

Ample evidence suggests that a rather simple arrangement of individuals, whether peer-controlled or aided by some external structuring mechanism, produced results that are undifferentiated from groups led by either untrained or trained leaders. It should be emphasized that most of these studies examined situations of relatively short duration and none involved clinic populations. Collectively, the studies are no better (or worse) than other investigations of the effects of groups conducted by leaders, and they appear to produce about the same range of positive results. It can be argued that groups structured from the outside by tapes or by assignments are not leaderless. But such groups certainly do not contain behaviors usually associated with leader-interventions described by most theoretical orientations. Lieberman et al (70) suggest that these minimally structured groups have distinct normative systems. Analyses of change mechanisms suggest that peer-controlled groups are likely to provide experience of the same order as leader-led groups. Such results provide sufficient data to raise questions about the role and contribution of a leader to the change-induction process in small groups.

It seems that if such sterile, quasi-experimental settings can accomplish the same range of effects as leader-led groups, then the ideologically oriented self-help and consciousness-raising movements, which thrive on peer control, should be considered potentially powerful change-induction systems. Unfortunately, we are only beginning to see empirical studies on the effects of some of these movements. They are difficult to research; like most social movements at their onset, they tend to produce results desired by investigators ideologically committed to their growth and survival.

Theoretical Proposals for Boundaries

Efforts to draw meaningful distinctions among change-induction groups based upon empirical studies of psychotherapy schools, specification of the client system, or descriptions of leader role, have led neither to viable differentiation nor robust constructs leading towards integration. During the past year, three publications have addressed the issues of reorganizing the field of group-based change systems. Schaffer & Galinsky (99) carefully analyzed 11 theoretical orientations to professionally led groups. Their work provided hypotheses based upon potential differences that grew out of their theoretical analysis. They suggest that basic distinctions among these 11 theoretical positions rest on: *(a)* concerns with the group as a social system compared to an interpersonal relationship model between the therapist and individuals within the group; *(b)* goal orientation, the hoped-for outcomes; *(c)* the degree to which the process of change is predicated on need gratification versus need frustration within the group; and *(d)* degree of structuring.

Singer et al (102) examined group activities directed towards change, therapy, and education. Their work emphasizes boundaries more than integration. Toward this end they provide a framework for distinguishing among groups on the basis of task and relevant psychological level—group process, interpersonal and intrapersonal. Implications of this framework are examined for the effects on contracts between participants and leaders, the relationship of the temporary small change-induction group to its institutional context, and role of the leader.

Lieberman (67) proposed a framework for examining a variety of change-induction groups—group psychotherapy, groups originating out of the human potential movement, self-help groups, and consciousness-raising groups. The model is based upon structural characteristics thought to maximize differences within the system and considered central to the change-induction process. Its five characteristics are: 1. level of psychological distance between participant and leader; 2. the attribution system with regard to the cause, source, and cure of psychological misery; 3. the extent to which the principles of change involve the group as a social microcosm; 4. the degree to which dominant organizational principles among members is based upon differentiation as opposed to similarity; and 5. the relationship between the two main axes of leader behavior and modes of learning—cognitive-expressive.

All three proposals for reorganizing and restructuring conceptions about small change-induction groups emphasize groups extending far beyond the traditional treatment groups that have been the concern of the mental health professional and researcher. The last section of this chapter, Prospectus, draws on some implications of such perspectives for future research.

ROLE OF LEADERSHIP IN CHANGE INDUCTION

Theories of personal change in groups emphasize the relationship of the leader to participants. Like theories of individual therapy, they underscore the central importance of the therapist. Through his actions or abstinence from action, change processes are initiated and set in the right (or wrong) direction. Theories are maximally distinguishable by the particular dimensions of the leader/client relationship they emphasize. For some the core concepts emphasize the interpersonal conditions the leader creates between himself and each participant, such as positive regard and genuineness. Some stress the leader's symbolic properties, such as the specific transference relationship between each individual patient and the leader, and some stress the symbolic relationship of the leader to the group as a whole. Others, although emphasizing the unique relationship of each patient to the leader, accentuate the negative rather than positive interaction through such devices as the "hot seat," in which the group acts as a Greek chorus or background to this primary relationship. Despite such fundamentally different conclusions about what leader "inputs" are crucial, all these theories agree on the centrality of the leader to the change process. It is he who sets up the learning experience, who makes the interpretations or analyzes resistance, who establishes norms, who is the "model," and so forth. The specific content of the leader's actions and responsibilities may vary, but the underlying assumption is that the central factor in changing people is what the leader does or how he expresses himself.

It is possible, however, that the behavior, personality, and skill level of the leader has taken on mythic proportions as a basic force for successful personal change in groups. Several obvious factors in the history and development of the use of groups for people-changing may have contributed to this view. Theories of group change of individuals naturally have given great prominence to the role of the leader; most theories have been developed by leaders who have also been highly charismatic individuals. Clinicians who have developed what little theory there is on changing people through groups could easily be pardoned if they have been somewhat myopic in overestimating the contribution of the leader (themselves) to the curative process. Thus it is understandable that we find assumptions of leader centrality in most theories.

But what about "transference"? Could anyone who has ever worked with a people-changing group realistically ignore the magical expectations, distortions, and overestimations that are directed toward the person of the leader? No matter what one labels the feelings and thoughts of members toward their leader, they are unmistakably central phenomena common to all people-changing groups. Whether or not transference is a universal product of psychotherapeutic contact, its existence cannot be denied. The fact that supercharged feeling towards the leader is usually generated in a group therapeutic context does not, in and of itself, demonstrate that the leader is central to the curative process or that transference is intrinsically a curative factor in the group context. The evidence that leaders usually become objects of intense feelings colored by unusual perceptions does not demonstrate their contribution to change.

Several other conditions may account for the strong belief that the leader is central. Professionalization, length of time invested in training, sharp boundaries surrounding the help-giving professions, distinctive languages, fee structures, etc all tend to emphasize the centrality, prominence, and indispensability in the curative process of the leader's role. It seems reasonable that to the degree that an activity in our society becomes professionalized, the professional's role will be enhanced in the minds of both the professional and the layman. Furthermore, it is natural that theories of group personal change, as a latter day development, should have been influenced by images of the obvious influence and control therapists exercise in dyadic therapy. This historical fact is probably another reason we assume that the person and behavior of the leader are critical in group personal change.

Thus many forces exist for creating a mythology surrounding the person of the leader. Journals and professional meetings endlessly encourage debates that support the "prominence" of the therapist or leader—what he is, how he does it, when he does it, how he feels, what his hangups are, how aware he is, what his theory is, whether he works alone or with a co-therapist, whether "he" is he or she, black or white, kindly or hostile, and so forth.

Consider for a moment the full implications of discovering that what helps patients most in groups is not directly related to the behavior and person of the leader but rather stems from the relationships members have to one another and to processes that are only tangentially related to the leader. Such a view would in all certainty make questions about how much, if any, professionalization is necessary very important. What data then can the field bring to bear on this issue—not whether groups help people, but whether what the therapist or leader does is central in the help-giving process, and if not, what precisely can be specified as essential leader contributions?

Empirical Studies of Leadership

Despite the prominence that the therapist or leader is accorded in theoretical propositions about effecting change in groups, empirical studies addressing this issue are relatively sparse. For convenience, they may be grouped under three general categories: 1. experimental studies that compare particular aspects of leader style; 2. reports on the relationship of leader traits or qualities associated with the participants' liking for or dislike of the leader; and 3. studies directing their attention to the matching of client personalities, attitudes, or orientations to therapist or leader orientations, attitudes, or personalities.

LEADERSHIP STYLE   Four studies examined effects of different leader styles. Schubert (100) examined the effects of two models of sensitivity training on level of experiencing measured one month following a weekend sensitivity workshop. No differences were found. Kilmann (52) investigated "direct" and nondirect therapist behavior on locus of control, measured by Rotter's instrument, using 84 female narcotic addicts. No differences were found between the two different leader styles. Abramowitz & Jackson (2) compared interpretations styles ("then and there" and "here and now") in insight production on college student clients. There were no salient differences.

Lieberman et al (70) studied 16 experienced leaders from a variety of theoretical orientations—NTL, Gestalt, transactional analysis, Esalen eclectic, personal growth, Synanon, psychodrama, marathon, and psychoanalytic—who conducted randomly assigned college undergraduates in encounter groups. Observer ratings of leader behaviors, leader styles, and leader focus, as well as measures on the symbolic value of the leader, yielded four basic leadership parameters: emotional stimulation, caring, meaning attribution, and executive functions. Typologies based on these four dimensions suggest three basic leader styles: 1. Energizers, charismatic leaders who emphasized stimulation; 2. Providers, who exhibited high levels of meaning attribution (cognitive behavior) and caring; and 3. Social Engineers, who emphasized management of the group as a social system and meaning attribution. Three other styles—Impersonals, Laissez-Faire, and Managers—were variants of the initial three.

Leader profiles showed little similarity between leaders of identical theoretical position. But there did exist a close correspondence between particular styles and outcome. Measures were based on a series of perspectives and instruments—self-rating of change, leader estimation of change, third party measures, social network, peer-ratings of change, various attitude measures, tests of coping behavior, self-concept and self/ideal discrepancy, as well as perceptions of significant others and measures of behavior external to the group. These measures were assessed pre-post and 8 months subsequent to the termination of the groups. Outcome is highly associated to these particular leader styles, ranging from a high of 57% change for the Providers to 0% change for the Managers. Conversely, each of these styles carried its own level of risk, measured by psychiatric casualty, negative change, and dropout. The Energizers and Impersonals (both of whom use high levels of stimulation) showed the highest risk factor, and the Providers the lowest.

LEADER ATTRACTION   Several studies reported on the relationship between leader behavior and member attitudes. May & Thompson (75) found a correlation between seeing leaders as high in self-disclosure and perceiving them as mentally healthy and helpful. Bolman (15) reported on the relationship between leader traits of affection, conceptual input, conditionality, congruence/empathy, dominance, and openness as perceived by members, and member liking of leaders and improvement (self- and peer-ratings). Affection and congruence/empathy were positively related to liking. However, Bolman failed to replicate his previous findings in which liking and improvement were associated.

LEADER-CLIENT MATCHING   Leader-participant match was investigated in several studies. McLachlan (79) reported a study of 94 alcoholic inpatients in which patients and therapists were matched for conceptual level ratings based on Hunt's Paragraph Completion Test. Matched therapist/patient pairs were positively associated to outcome as evaluated by staff ratings 12–16 months later on drinking behavior. Beutler et al (13) investigated the effects of patient-therapist matching on attitudes. Similarity was associated with self-rated improvement (although some degrees of attitude dissimilarity did produce more attitude change in patients). Abramowitz & Abramowitz (1) studied insight orientation match to therapeutic conditions among 26 undergraduates who volunteered for "interpersonal adjustment groups." Students having greater psychological sophistication (as measured by the Toler & Resnikkoff Insight Test) made more psychosocial strides in insight-grounded group experience compared to similar students in noninsight-grounded group experience.

Some Implications of the Research on Leader Behavior

Research on leader behavior in groups is open to many of the same shibboleths encountered in the psychotherapy literature. Several studies used highly experienced professionals, but most relied upon leaders who had only a modicum of training and experience. The crude comparison of school of orientation studies (Bethel vs Tavistock, direct vs nondirect) leads basically to the same conclusion reflected in the general psychotherapy literature. Findings (70) on the lack of relationship between theoretical position and behavior underscore the problem. The range of outcome measures in these studies makes it difficult to generate any higher order of abstraction than the studies themselves report. Studies of member perception fall heir to the charge of vacuous attitude research. This charge is reinforced by several studies which strongly suggest that, although liking for the leader or therapist is associated with certain leader traits and behavior, the correlation between liking and improvement often hovers around zero (15, 70). The most hopeful direction is the relatively consistent finding on client-therapist matching. As yet, few replication studies exist. The history of replication studies of client-therapist matching for individual therapy warrants caution.

Research on leadership styles using generalized leadership variables such as directive/nondirective or theoretical orientation comparisons appear to this reviewer to be primitive returns to an era long passed in social psychology of small groups and psychotherapy research. Even research geared toward specific leader behavior rather than generalized inputs needs careful scrutiny, for the chain of relationships between leader behavior and outcome is long and complex.

Effects of leader behavior were tested (70) in relation to a set of group characteristics such as group norms, cohesiveness, and climate, as well as to member position or status in the group and salient "change mechanisms." A chain of events forms between leader behavior and social system characteristics, as well as member role within the social system, and particular events hypothesized to be therapeutic. To ignore the chain can only produce relatively weak relationships between leader behavior and outcome, no matter how elegant the measure of leadership. For example, in the aforementioned study, although some correspondence was found between specific types of leader behavior and normative characteristics of groups, this correspondence could not be demonstrated to be a cause-effect relationship. In fact, two subsequent studies (11, 16) demonstrated that member expectation was of greater significance in establishing normative characteristics of groups than was leader behavior. Thus, without understanding the events that occur between leader behavior and the product, outcome, research on therapist style can only produce weak relationships.

Does this suggest that small studies looking at single variables are likely to be without benefit to the growth of our field? This reviewer concludes that progress is unlikely to be made through the addition of many small research efforts. Problems concerning the complexity of outcome measures and the heterogeneity of participants (with consequent multiple goals necessitating even more complex outcome assessment) lead one to this conclusion. What is required is admittedly difficult, namely approaches which undertake with sufficiently large populations the teasing out of a complex set of intervening variables between leader behavior and the final product, outcome. Thus the role of research on leader variables in the group area is clouded. Unlike individual psychotherapy where progress has been made by studying therapist-fostered conditions of the psychotherapeutic procedure, change groups create a social system in which the therapist or leader is only one influence among many; this situation adds considerable complexity and doubt to the fate of research on leader or therapist variables. The previous section in this chapter describing current findings on peer-led groups underscores the question of how much variation in leader behavior can account for outcome and client group behavior.

THERAPEUTIC PROCESSES

Clinical Applications

A review such as this must reflect the numerous and diverse contributions concerned with application. More often than not they reflect programmatic attempts to apply group procedures to particular populations, i.e. the obese, the alcohol or drug abuser, the physically ill or relatives of the physically ill, schizophrenics, parents of disturbed or physically ill children, "minority populations" such as blacks, the aged, women, the mentally retarded, etc. At other times the focus is on the use of group methods for change under specific institutional arrangements such as prisons.

A review of the specific content of this vast literature is not likely to serve a useful function; instead, the themes underlying the various "clinical publications" will be appraised. Practitioners, as reflected in their published writings, are wrestling with two general issues. One concern is with applying clinical skills and approach to out-of-the-ordinary client populations. For example, several studies describe treatment situations involving alcoholic patients: a treatment program based on behavior modification (3); a reality therapy model used with adolescent alcoholics emphasizing the problems involved in therapist closeness (18); using marital group therapy in the treatment of alcoholism (20); a group decision-making model of treatment (39); an interpersonally oriented approach to group therapy (111). Such reports reflect a growing interest of practitioners to apply their methods to new situations making different demands and the required modifications of technique. These "adjustments" in technique will not lead to major theoretical revisions. Rather they point toward technological considerations that therapists believe are required. Alterations in fundamental assumptions about the nature of the small group as a change-producing context will not necessarily follow.

The second major theme concerns practitioners' chronic struggle to improve their batting average. Universally, clinicians assume that certain rates of verbal behavior or certain levels of emotional intensity are necessary for the therapeutic process. A variety of devices or arrangements designed to increase stimulation of verbal activity, emotional intensity, or a particular type of content are described. The use of structured "exercises," proscriptive activities set out by leaders (89), is one common practice. Varying the patient composition within a group, i.e. intergenerationally composed groups, is another method. Such arrangements attempt to induce discussion of different content than would occur in randomly assigned or less structured groups. Videotape feedback (74), another popular modality, is intended to stimulate intense feelings and to provide a mechanism for the exploration of productive content. Other devices include artificially creating subgroupings within a group to generate both feelings of cohesiveness and feelings of anger and competition, or altering the power relations in groups to encourage alternate therapeutic techniques such as the assumption of a therapeutic role by patients (51). Some studies explore alternate time arrangements such as a marathon (87) or patient preparation (44, 45). These are ways to increase intensity and to alter content. The impetus for such work has, in part, been therapist experience with populations not accustomed to verbal psychotherapy.

Although the specifics are wide-ranging, the various arrangements and structures provided by the therapist are based on the common assumption that increased verbal behavior, increased emotional intensity, and specific content areas are productive, that is, they lead to change. The literature reflects wide use of these variegated improved techniques, but empirical literature reviewed in the following section does not strongly substantiate their efficiency.

Empirical Studies of Therapeutic Processes

Inquiry into the conditions and processes by which small groups function to enhance individuals is closely tied to attempts to improve the efficiency of practice. This section examines studies on therapeutic processes. The topics to be discussed include: (a) patient characteristics; and (b) mechanisms of change, specific member experiences hypothesized to be change inducing. The two most widely examined are self-disclosure and feedback. Generally, investigators examine the conditions or procedures which increase the frequency of such events as self-disclosure or feedback; very few have asked whether such experiences are facilitative, and still fewer, under what conditions they are or are not facilitative.

Most studies addressed questions about patient characteristics associated with productive or counterproductive utilization of the group, for example, who drops out, who self-discloses more, etc. Other studies of this type ask the question, are certain features characteristic of individuals who come into the various group contexts?

Group process (aspects of the social system), once a dominant force in the small-group field, produced fewer studies than might be anticipated from past history. Increasingly prevalent, however, were studies on patient expectations. (This is both a theoretical issue and a strong pragmatic one.) These studies attempt to demonstrate that therapeutic qualities of group settings can be enhanced by specific manipulation of expectational sets, i.e. "preparation."

PATIENT CHARACTERISTICS ASSOCIATED WITH PRODUCTIVE AND COUN-TERPRODUCTIVE BEHAVIOR AND OUTCOME   Concern with characteristics of "early terminators"—clients who break off the therapeutic relationship prematurely (from the point of view of the service provider)—has long been fashionable in psychotherapy research. The form and structure of this branch of research in the group area is similar in kind and in quality to what one finds in psychotherapy. Koran & Costell (59) demonstrated that patients who fail to fill out questionnaires on feeling, personality, and projective group behavior will terminate with a relatively high level of predictability. Unfortunately, they failed to specify the particular group conditions (compatibility, cohesiveness, etc) associated with termination. The small sample size makes this a study of little more than passing interest. A more comprehensive study by Rosensweig (97) investigated personality characteristics of patients and demographic variables, as well as therapists' impressions. The findings suggested that the patient's attraction towards a therapist (based upon the indirect evidence of therapists' impressions) was highly associated with educational level. This was the single most important determinant for remaining in therapy (beyond 16 weeks). These investigators, nevertheless, were unable to isolate the particular personality characteristics of the terminators.

Noticeably absent were studies of particular group conditions which led to termination. Were they aversive climates? Did the patients show good sense by leaving the situation? Lieberman et al (70) found that early termination was prevalent under particular sets of group conditions that proved harmful for other participants. Would the patients be better off in other treatment modalities or other group settings? It is probably fair to say that few generalizations can be made in the group area concerning characteristics of terminators. Occasional studies in the past have produced personality qualities that seem to be associated with termination, but these have failed to find replication in later studies by other investigators. Nothing in the few studies that have appeared in this area suggests that the traits or characteristics of the patients who failed to complete the proscribed regime of treatment are different from those characteristics of patients who have been isolated as premature terminators in individual psychotherapy. This lack of distinction between these two vastly different treatment conditions may point to the investigators' failure to identify correctly relevant personality characteristics. Required are sensitive indicators of the psychological fit between a particular treatment modality and a person rather than concluding, on the basis of such findings, that they are similar in both circumstances. Without more precisely defined characteristics of the conditions of treatment (the nature of the group), it is unlikely that such a research strategy will yield important results. The lack of replication suggests that the factors may be highly specific to particular sets of circumstances, rather than general characteristics of a client population.

Some studies examined the patients' characteristics responsive to particular conditions or specific group types. McCall (76) found a relationship between deviant MMPI profiles in short-term group therapy oriented toward development of self-control techniques for weight reduction and positive results. Hargreaves (43), studying 366 persons randomly assigned to individual therapy, weekly group therapy, or daily nonappointment groups, found that shy and distressed Ss best accepted nonappointment groups. Articulate and outgoing clients responded best to more traditional individual and group therapy. Pattison & Rhodes (88) reported a pilot study on correlations between the NOYSE-30 Scale and effective group psychotherapy participation. McLachlan (79) found that alcoholic inpatients who described themselves and others as being more socially competent were more likely to improve in group therapy. Lewis & Glaser (66) described different life styles among heroin users and suggested that particular life styles are specifically related to the ability to use group treatment successfully. Poland & Jones (90) examined orientations prior to student participation in T-groups and found that those oriented to interaction—as opposed to self or task—were more likely to benefit from the group process. As in the previous article, however, the relationship of predispositional set or personality to outcome measures is often tainted; so, for example, in Poland's study, the outcome measure was peer nomination. Perhaps those who are more interactionally oriented do behave this way in T-groups and are so judged because they are consonant with the value of the particular group type. Without some external evidence about outcome, it is difficult to evaluate such research.

D'Augelli (25), in a study of the effects of leaderless groups on state and trait anxiety, found that Ss with higher levels of interpersonal skills showed significantly more decrease in state anxiety. Anchor et al (4), in a study of A-trait schizophrenics, reported on the relationship of personality characteristics to self-disclosure. Seldman et al (101) found that encounter group participants with high dependency needs (Edwards Personality Preference Schedule) produced significantly more positive estimates of leader functioning than did low dependency participants.

The conceptual issues in this area remain large. Some of the obvious problems mirror those raised in the extensive literature on research and client variables in psychotherapy. Most predictive studies of client variables are made to a relatively unknown situation, i.e. treatment. Although several generalizations appear in therapy literature concerning aspects of group participants that are likely to lead to termination, they all too frequently can be reduced to social class parameters. To some extent, the research reviewed reflects a crass empiricism, an understandable outcome of a practical orientation in which the issue the investigator attempts to isolate is the most powerful predictor. Such findings offer little surplus meaning to help clarify why these personal characteristics make a difference. Because some studies differentiate between those who terminate early and those who remain, while others examine output regarding benefit (or risk), it is obviously difficult to formulate reasonable generalizations. Variations in outcome measures are so great that each individual study is difficult to link with any other. Those studies beginning to examine personal characteristics related to particular form, kind, or frequency of behavior in the group may eventually unravel this complex issue. Knowing that certain kinds of individuals are less likely to self-disclose, hear feedback, etc would help in understanding the relationship between personal characteristic and outcome. Unfortunately, the studies mentioned in the review have not closed the circle. They have not related the particular behavior to outcome.

CHANGE MECHANISMS All systems concerned with changing individuals in groups implicitly or explicitly assume that patients experience certain events that are central in inducing change. These events or experiences in most theories are proximally associated to change itself. In 1955, Corsini & Rosenberg (23) first gave formal expression to change mechanisms by abstracting "change" events from about 300 group therapy articles. Although changes in style have, to some extent, altered labels and emphasis, most of the mechanisms have remained intact in the theories of group therapy over the past 20 years. Yalom's explication of change mechanisms in groups (111) offers the most extensive theory of such events. He hypothesizes 12 core experiences leading to change: interpersonal input, catharsis, cohesiveness, insight, interpersonal output, existential awareness, universality, installation of hope, altruism, family reenactment, guidance, and identification. Much of the current group therapy research makes assumptions about such events and is addressed to conditions that increase or decrease their frequency. The literature of the past several years places most emphasis on self-disclosure, receiving feedback and expressing and experiencing intense emotions. Research strategies range from (a) phenomenologically based inquiries which ask participants to reflect on their group experiences and describe those that they found most helpful, useful, or productive to (b) experimentally designed studies in which particular mechanisms are related to process or outcome measures.

Phenomenological studies   In the most extensive study of this type, Lieberman et al (70) investigated a series of mechanisms which included experiencing and expressing strong emotions, self-disclosure, feedback, cognitive learning, communion, altruism, spectatorism, discovery of similarity, active involvement, modeling, receiving advice, and experiencing the group as the symbolic representation of primary family. In contrast to the usual methods in which lists of items are provided, Lieberman and his colleagues used a critical incident technique. At the end of each group session, members were asked to answer in paragraph format the question, "What was the most important event for you personally in the group today and why was it important?" Each of the 210 Ss was classified as learner, unchanged, or negative outcome. The major mechanisms distinguishing learners from the unchanged were cognitive ones. Expressing anger, experiencing profound emotions, receiving feedback, self-disclosing, etc appeared not to differ markedly between those who learned and those who remained unchanged. The negative outcomes and the unchanged showed greater differences in mechanisms. Although as active as those who changed or remained unchanged, those who wrought negative benefits were less able to use cognitive devices to structure their more frequent experience of negative emotions. They could not take advantage of the variety of mechanisms available to others—spectatorism, altruism, etc.

Similar to the Yalom study (111), members were also asked to rank order at the end of the experience what events were most useful in their learning. Not surprisingly, the events listed by members of encounter groups differed from those listed by group psychotherapy patients. Although in both systems interpersonal input or feedback was seen as the single most important experience associated with learning, encounter participants placed less value on cohesiveness and existential awareness and more emphasis on advice-getting and experiencing universality. Comparing participants' perceptions of salient experiences provides information about the character of the system, but does not provide an indication of their function in learning. Participants universally saw receiving feedback as the salient mechanism when asked to compare various mechanisms one to another (70). Yet the frequency of reported feedback was comparable for those who learned and those who remained unchanged.

Weiner (109), in a followup of Yalom's study (111), questions using such an instrument and presents information suggesting that particular systems produce different ordering of material. Although this finding is not surprising, neither study presents evidence that participants' perceptions of the mechanisms of learning are related to the frequency with which they occur or to their utility in the learning cycle.

Experimental research on mechanisms of change   Studies of feedback were most frequent. Freeland (35) analyzed the interaction in two professionally led marathon groups for graduate students. He coded interaction for type and amount of feedback. The results showed no relation between number of units or type of feedback received and outcome assessed by self-ideal discrepancy scores. In a study of hospitalized schizophrenics randomly assigned to ongoing videotape replay or verbal feedback group therapy sessions, Ennis (31) found no differences in behavioral change index and self-rating scores between the two different feedback conditions. In a study comparing self-other discrepancies in 38 psychiatric patients in short-term group therapy (48), no differences were found between patients trained in feedback and those untrained.

Jacobs et al (49) studied 48 undergraduates in six programmed sensitivity training groups. Feedback categories were coded on the basis of behavioral, emotional, combined behavioral-emotional, as well as positive and negative valence. Credibility was assoicated with positive feedback; negative behavioral feedback was perceived as more credible than negative emotional feedback.

Overview of mechanism research   Research on feedback parallels research on self-disclosure. Despite the long history of both dating back to the early work of Kurt Levin, available research does not clearly indicate whether they make specific contributions in the learning process. Findings certainly underscore the significance that group participants place on receiving feedback and, to some extent, in self-disclosing. Most current research is directed towards specifying particular characteristics of this experience hypothesized as facilitative—emotional balance, the form such information takes, and method of display. Findings are ambiguous on increasing the facility of feedback by training participants to engage in such behavior. Studies that examine the form or content of the information presented suggest that such factors do influence the credibility of the information. Overall the effects of mode of display, particularly the utilization of mechanical devices such as videotape, are inconsistent, although the current crop of research studies tends to discount videotape's effects.

Such inconsistent findings as these on feedback are the rule for change mechanism research. Perhaps the central question is whether studies of change mechanisms—either examined in vivo, in quasi-experimental studies, or through analog research—can isolate specific mechanisms from other factors or conditions of the learning environment itself. Illustrating this attempt, the study by Lieberman et al (70), which examined self-disclosure in detail, showed that absolute frequency of such behavior was unrelated to outcome, that self-disclosure produced at later group stages was more likely to be productive than when it was produced early, and that self-disclosure was primarily a social act in a particular context. Self-disclosure took on salience to outcome if some cognitive structure was constructed by the participant around it or the meaning it had to him. Thus, despite findings that the quality of such events can be enhanced or changed by various input variables (10), studies which isolate them as a specific mechanism have not borne the expected fruit given the long practical and theoretical interest in them. There is no strong direct evidence that mechanisms such as self-disclosure and feedback are central to the change process, in and of themselves. Their importance may rest instead on the role they play in the maintenance and development of any person-changing group. Their absence would suggest an environment that is inimical to change, but their presence has not been directly tied to learning. More likely, these mechanisms bear some relation to outcome. However, without more precise research exploring context, relationship to other events, and individual differences, it will be hard to develop strong evidence for their utility.

USE OF SMALL GROUPS FOR TRAINING AND EDUCATION

The predicaments portrayed in theory building, evaluation, and analysis of the use of groups for change are more than matched by these published reports on the use of "experiential" small face-to-face groups for education and training. They reflect three major themes: 1. training leaders to conduct such groups; 2. what might be called "therapy for therapists"; and 3. use of groups by the helping professions, not to acquire professional skills to conduct groups, but to assume specific roles within their professions.

Studies on the training of therapists emphasize the use of "experiential education," providing small face-to-face intense experiences as a major educational context. Research attempts in this area are still at a primitive level. Eiben & Clack (30) compared didactic courses with encounter groups composed of students in counseling training. Those in the experience groups increased significantly more on 11 of the 12 POI scales. The crude assumption that self-actualizing leaders are more effective lacks any empirical base. Stimpson (104) found that T-group participants among students learning counseling increased congruity between what they wanted and what was given in a helping relationship. Again, the relationship of this finding to therapeutic skill is unclear. Other reports describe the specific methods educators use in training: a theme-centered method for training paraprofessionals (63); experiential models for training group counselors (64) and for teaching group psychotherapy in an undergraduate curriculum (103); various models of group psychotherapy supervision (40). The complex task of educating group leaders or therapists is little advanced theoretically or empirically by such research. Changing conditions have created a need to train large groups of individuals for leadership roles, but the field has not yet succeeded in revising traditional styles of education. Traditional styles involve cognitive inputs reflecting a particular theoretical view and a primary emphasis on an apprentice-type relationship. These styles do not suit new populations; however, substitution of "group experiences " for traditional educational methods has not, in this reviewer's view, borne fruit.

The problems described in a previous section of this paper regarding leadership should alert us to the pitfalls in educational design. Findings on leadership behavior (70) show that even successful leaders have little knowledge of their operations that lead to success. Consequently, experienced group leaders may teach theoretical concepts that have little to do with their actual behavior. Most reports of experiential education for leadership training implicitly assume that what occurs is behavior modeling. However, without the model's explication of relevant behavior, modeling may be an inefficient procedure. Inability of leaders to articulate those operations shown empirically to be related successfully to outcome makes using such an approach to training problematic. Clearly, specific analyses of skills are required. Probably we need to create particular conditions or settings to train specific skill areas. Without such an approach, the lengthy, often wasteful, apprenticeship model or the hasty shortcuts epitomized by experiential groups as a substitute for education are likely to continue.

Boundaries are blurred between the training of therapists and the use of groups to provide personal outlets for those in the therapeutic profession. The use of such techniques has been studied for teachers (84) and for mental health workers for attitude change, personal involvement, and the development of specific clinical skills (7). Van Ostenberg (106) described the "development of an educational didactic seminar into a psychotherapeutic group."

Related to these are a plethora of other reports on the use of such "educational techniques" for mental health personnel dealing with dying patients (58), for student nurses rotating through psychiatric services (62), for medical students (24), and for nurses (37). Common to all was the creation of a temporary system that legitimized discussing areas about self not sanctioned in the particular institutional context. These groups provided an institutional format for communication which may be carried on at informal levels in other systems. They reflect a concern of many institutional structures in our society to provide legitimized personal experience or safety valves for the participants in such systems. These compelling groups appeal directly to both participants and purveyors. In all likelihood, but as yet undemonstrated, they serve a useful purpose, for they probably create a more functional equilibrium between the person and a specific social structure.

PROSPECTUS

The degree of confidence this reviewer has in predicting the future direction of practice, in contrast to inquiry, is a good index of the state of the science. We can safely assume that in the next several years we shall see a greater proliferation of group-based change modalities. The labels may change. In fact, they are almost certain to change, and the activities may on the surface look different from what is currently practiced. Boundaries will increasingly become blurred between traditional mental health practices using groups for change and practices originating outside the traditional disciplines. More than likely, innovative technology initiated by newer, "nonprofessional" purveyors will come to be the major influence on professional practice in group psychotherapy, and not the reverse. Despite profound distinctions among such groups based upon assumptions about what ails man and what he must do to exorcise his problem, practice will become increasingly similar. To cite one example, dynamic group psychotherapy places its emphasis on locating the source of difficulty within the person and views change in terms of mastery when intrapsychic characteristics are realigned and rearranged. Women's consciousness-raising groups, in contrast, see the source and cause of problems as the product of societal structures. Closely bound to such fundamentally different views regarding the source of personal difficulties are conceptions of how a small face-to-face group functions in the change process. Dynamic group psychotherapy views the group as a social microcosm. Changes are assumed to be contingent on the simulation of important personal areas. Consciousness-raising groups eschew the social microcosm aspect of the group, and do not view this group property as a primary mechanism of change. Nevertheless, blurring of boundaries along technical lines and the continuous incorporation of seemingly effective leader behavior and devices across various perspectives will continue to close the distance between various forms and types of groups.

It is also likely that the near future will experience stronger influence from clients. Although clients have always exerted an impact on practice, that impact will not only increase but assume a new form. Heretofore traditional sources of client influence could be seen in terms of sanctions; client dissatisfaction certainly has been a major factor in shaping activities. Withdrawal of client support creates a profound cataclysm. This, perhaps more than any other force, induces those who provide the activities to alter what they do. The range of alternative systems now available for clients with similar needs and goals obviously will increase the possibility of sanctions. More importantly, based on experience in other related activities, clients bring increasingly sophisticated knowledge and expectations to groups. It is likely that more clients will be coming to change-induction systems with already tested notions of what is productive or comforting for them.

The change toward therapist transparency is one illustration of this trend. Although usually treated by purveyors as a major theoretical controversy, it is probable that client expectations have changed to such a degree that it is impossible for the classical "blank screen" of dynamic psychotherapies to be effective. Clients simply will not tolerate it. They expect considerably more exchange between therapists and patients in the change process than has heretofore been theoretically considered relevant. It is probably this expectation rather than theoretical considerations which has introduced such topics into the therapeutic literature. Another source of such influence is based on research on norm formation in groups (11, 16). These studies suggest that client expectations prior to actual entrance into the group account for more of the variance of norms than does leader behavior. These illustrations underscore a major factor that will probably influence the practice and form of groups in the future.

Charting the form and spread of group-based change systems provides little information about the shape of future research. Notoriously absent in this review were citations of theoretical contributions of the past year and a half. To this reviewer the reasons are self-evident, but worth mentioning. It is difficult to find major sets of ideas that have altered the field over the past 2 years. The idea systems used to describe the variety of group activities directed toward change are not new. They stem from seminal works about the nature of social systems long associated with the classics in group therapy, or from the slowly accrued theories of many practitioners about critical events associated with change induction, or on the other hand, they stem from ideas about personal influence growing out of the large body of experimental social psychology. These ideas, in combination with the numerous language systems represented by specific theoretical orientation indistinguishable from psychotherapy, form the loosely interrelated notions that make up theory in this area. It is difficult to find a cutting edge that is likely in the near future to produce major reorganizations of these sets of ideas. The trend in group therapy to anchor ideas on general systems theory appears, to this reviewer, as too premature for evaluation. As yet it seems to represent little more than the translation from one language system to another. Others proposing to utilize experimental analysis of behavior (27) give little cause for expecting a major breakthrough. Social learning theory as currently constituted contains crucial weaknesses. For example, it cannot specify social system properties such as the circumstances under which the group becomes a reinforcing agent or the operations by which the group determines what behavior to reinforce.

More than likely, future developments in articulating the specific processes and mechanisms involved in change induction in small groups will stem from two types of current research activity. The growing recognition that society contains a large variety of group-based activities having similar or at least overlapping goals, processes, and client populations that extend beyond the boundaries of traditional group psychotherapy offers the raw material for the development of empirically grounded theories of group change. For those investigators who eschew the experimental social-psychological approach, these "naturally occurring variations" offer an alternative to laboratory-grounded experimentation. The existence of a wide range of change systems offers wide variations that can be addressed to some of the major "pay-off variables" in group research. Variations among these systems provide a basis for comparative research on critical variables. Research could look at systematic differences in such parameters as psychological distance between member and leader, differences in emphasis on cognitive and emotional aspects of group life, the disparities in degree to which the group as a social microcosm forms the basis of change, different emphasis on such qualities as relevant content, appropriate interrelationships among members, and specific time perspectives, as well as the attribution system inherent in each of these groups as to the source and cause of disability. Such characteristics provide a matrix for meaningful empirical inquiry and offer a setting in which differences can be organized along theoretically relevant variables that may have large effects on group participants. Ongoing work of Lieberman at Chicago and Levy (65) at Indiana, who study comparative systems, shows promise of eventually producing an empirically grounded theory of group change.

The contrasting work of some investigators using pathways provided by experimental social psychology also shows promise. Analog research can specify and manipulate such variables as expectational sets (10). Both approaches may generate the middle-level abstractions that we need so desperately to fill in a reasonable theory of using groups to change people. These two approaches obviously are quite distinctive. It is much too early to tell whether they will produce comparable or at least consistent information. The usual problems inherent in analog research, so exquisitely demonstrated in experimental social psychology, certainly will plague this approach. Comparing systems by taking advantage of "natural experiments" presents major methodological dilemmas: comparability of populations and appropriate outcome measures make such research feasible but technically difficult. Both approaches, however, share a distinct advantage. They move out of a relatively narrow context and destroy, once and for all, the artificial boundaries that separate the various systems of group change induction. Both research strategies bypass the ecological restraints that have limited the salience of current research findings.

Literature Cited

1. Abramowitz, S. I., Abramowitz, C. V. 1974. Psychological-mindedness and benefit from insight-oriented group therapy. *Arch. Gen. Psychiatry* 30: 610–15
2. Abramowitz, S. I., Jackson, C. 1974. Comparative effectiveness of there-and-then versus here-and-now therapist interpretations in group psychotherapy. *J. Couns. Psychol.* 21:288–93
3. Allman, L. R. 1973. Group drinking during stress: Effects on alcohol intake and group process. *Int. J. Addict.* 8:475–88
4. Anchor, K. N., Vojtisek, J. E., Patterson, R. L. 1973. Trait anxiety, initial structuring and self-disclosure in groups of schizophrenic patients. *Psychother. Theory Res. Pract.* 10:155–59
5. Arbes, B. H., Hubbell, R. N. 1973. Packaged impact: A structured communications skills workshop. *J. Couns. Psychol.* 20:332–37
6. Archer, J., Kagan, N. 1973. Teaching interpersonal relationship skills on campus: A pyramid approach. *J. Couns. Psychol.* 20:535–40
7. Barber, W. H., Lurie, H. J. 1973. Designing an experientially based continuing education program. *Am. J. Psychiatry* 130:1148–50
8. Barrett-Lennard, G. T., Kwasnik, T. P., Wilkinson, G. R. 1973–74. Some effects of participation in encounter group workshops: An analysis of written follow-up reports. *Interpers. Dev.* 4:35–41
9. Battle, E., Zwier, M. 1973. Efficacy of small group process with intractable neuropsychiatric patients. *Newslett. Res. Ment. Health Behav. Sci.* 15:15–17
10. Bednar, R. L. et al 1974. Empirical guidelines for group therapy: Pretraining, cohesion, and modeling. *J. Appl. Behav. Sci.* 10:149–65
11. Beismeier, P. 1974. *The relationship of leader influence to norm development in small groups.* PhD thesis. Univ. Chicago, Chicago, Ill.
12. Bergin, A. E., Garfield, S. L., Eds. 1971.

Handbook of Psychotherapy and Behavior Change. New York: Wiley
13. Beutler, L. E., Jobe, A. M., Elkins, D. 1974. Outcomes in group psychotherapy: Using persuasion theory to increase treatment efficiency. *J. Consult. Clin. Psychol.* 42:547–53
14. Bolan, S. L. 1973. *A study exploring two different approaches to encounter groups: The combination of verbal encounter and designed nonverbal activity versus emphasis upon verbal activity only.* PhD thesis. Diss. Abstr. Int., Ann Arbor, Mich: Univ. M-Films No. 73–14390
15. Bolman, L. 1973. Some effects of trainers on their groups: A partial replication. *J. Appl. Behav. Sci.* 9:534–39
16. Bond, G. 1975. *Norm formation in therapy groups.* PhD thesis. Univ. Chicago, Chicago, Ill.
17. Bornstein, P. H., Sipprelle, C. N. 1973. Group treatment of obesity by induced anxiety. *Behav. Res. Ther.* 11:339–41
18. Bratter, T. E. 1974. Reality therapy: A group psychotherapeutic approach with adolescent alcoholics. *Ann. NY Acad. Sci.* 233:104–14
19. Brown, T. R. 1973. Evaluation of a group centered aftercare system. *NIMH Grant MH-21975 Rep.* 5 pp.
20. Cadogan, D. A. 1973. Marital group therapy in the treatment of alcoholism. *Quart. J. Stud. Alc.* 34:1187–94
21. Conyne, R. K. 1974. Effects of facilitator-directed and self-directed group experiences. *Couns. Educ. Superv.* 13: 184–89
22. Cooper, C. L. 1974. Psychological disturbance following T-groups: Relationship between the Eysenck Personality Inventory and family/friends perceptions. *Br. J. Soc. Work* 4:39–49
23. Corsini, R., Rosenberg, B. 1955. Mechanisms of group psychotherapy: Processes and dynamics. *J. Abnorm. Soc. Psychol.* 51:406–11
24. Dashef, S. S., Espey, W., Lazarus, J. A. 1974. Time-limited sensitivity groups

for medical students. *Am. J. Psychiatry* 131:287–92

25. D'Augelli, A. R. 1974. Changes in self-reported anxiety during a small group experience. *J. Couns. Psychol.* 21:202–5

26. Deleppo, J. D. 1973. *Assessment of personality changes of drug addicts under two types of treatment modalities.* EdD thesis. Diss. Abstr. Int., Ann Arbor, Mich: Univ. M-Films No. 73–23545

27. Diamond, M. J. 1974. From Skinner to Satori? Toward a social learning analysis of encounter group behavior change. *J. Appl. Behav. Sci.* 10:133–48

28. Dies, R. R., Sadowsky, R. 1974. A brief encounter group experience and social relationships in a dormitory. *J. Couns. Psychol.* 21:112–15

29. Dye, C. A. 1974. Self-concept, anxiety, and group participation as affected by human relations training. *Nurs. Res.* 23:301–6

30. Eiben, R., Clack, R. J. 1973. Impact of a participatory group experience on counselors in training. *Small Group Behav.* 4:486–95

31. Ennis, D. L. 1973. *The effects of video-tape feedback versus verbal feedback on the behavior of schizophrenics on group psychotherapy.* PhD thesis. Diss. Abstr. Int., Ann Arbor, Mich: Univ. M-Films No. 73–28657. 94 pp.

32. Felton, G. S., Davidson, H. R. 1973. Group counseling can work in the classroom. *Acad. Ther.* 8:461–68

33. Ficht, J. C. 1973. *Social perceptions and verbal interactions in tape-directed and counselor-directed encounter groups.* EdD thesis. Diss. Abstr. Int., Ann Arbor, Mich: Univ. M-Films No. 73–22722. 99 pp.

34. Foulds, M. L. 1973. Effects of a personal growth on ratings of self and others. *Small Group Behav.* 4:508–12

35. Freeland, R. C. 1973. *Some effects of verbal feedback on perceptions of members in two marathon encounter groups.* EdD thesis. Diss. Abstr. Int., Ann Arbor, Mich: Univ. M-Films No. 73–25510. 197 pp.

36. Fromme, D. K., Jones, W. H., Davis, J. O. 1974. Experimental group training with conservative populations: A potential for negative effects. *J. Clin. Psychol.* 30:290–96

37. George, J. A., Gowell, E. C. 1973. Transactional analysis in sensitivity groups for students of nursing. *Nurs. Forum* 12:82–95

38. Gilligan, J. F. 1974. Sensitivity training and self-actualization. *Psychol. Rep.* 34:319–25

39. Goldman, M. S., Taylor, H. A., Carruth, M. L., Nathan, P. E. 1973. Effects of group decision-making on group drinking by alcoholics. *Quart. J. Stud. Alc.* 34:807–22

40. Grossman, W. K., Karmiol, E. 1973. Group psychotherapy supervision and its effects on resident training. *Am. J. Psychiatry* 130:920–21

41. Hagen, R. L. 1974. Group therapy versus bibliotherapy in weight reduction. *Behav. Ther.* 5:222–34

42. Hand, L., Lamontagne, Y., Marks, I. M. 1974. Group exposure (flooding) in vivo for agoraphobics. *Br. J. Psychiatry* 124:588–602

43. Hargreaves, W. A. et al 1974. Treatment acceptance following intake assignment to individual therapy, group therapy, or contact group. *Arch. Gen. Psychiatry* 31:343–49

44. Heitler, J. B. 1973. Preparation of lower-class patients for expressive group psychotherapy. *J. Consult. Clin. Psychol.* 41:251–60

45. Heitler, J. B. 1974. Clinical impressions of an experimental attempt to prepare lower-class patients for expressive group psychotherapy. *Int. J. Group Psychother.* 24:308–22

46. Herz, M. I., Spitzer, R. L., Gibbon, M., Greenspan, K., Reibel, S. 1974. Individual versus group aftercare treatment. *Am. J. Psychiatry* 131:808–12

47. Hurst, J. C., Delworth, U., Garriott, R. 1973. Encountertapes: Evaluation of a leaderless group procedure. *Small Group Behav.* 4:476–85

48. Jacobs, M., Gatz, M., Truck, O. 1974. Structured versus unstructured feedback in training patients to be more effective participants in group treatment. *J. Couns. Psychol.* 20:528–30

49. Jacobs, M., Jacobs, A., Feldman, G., Cayior, N. 1973. Feedback. II. The "credibility gap": Delivery of positive and negative and emotional and behavioral feedback in groups. *J. Consult. Clin. Psychol.* 41:215–23

50. Kaye, J. D. 1973. Group interaction and interpersonal learning. *Small Group Behav.* 4:424–48

51. Ketai, R. 1973. Peer-observed psychotherapy with institutionalized narcotic addicts. *Arch. Gen. Psychiatry* 29:51–53

52. Kilmann, P. R. 1974. Anxiety reactions to marathon group therapy. *J. Clin. Psychol.* 30:267–68

53. Kilmann, P. R., Auerbach, S. M. 1974. Effects of marathon group therapy on trait and state anxiety. *J. Consult. Clin. Psychol.* 42:607–12

54. King, M., Payne, D. C., McIntire, W. G. 1973. The impact of marathon and prolonged sensitivity training on self-acceptance. *Small Group Behav.* 4:414–23

55. Kirsh, B. 1974. Consciousness-raising groups as therapy for women. *Women in Therapy*, ed. V. Franks, V. Burtle, Chap 15. New York: Brunner/Mazel

56. Kleeman, J. L. 1974. The Kendall College Human Potential Seminar model: Research. *J. Coll. Stud. Personnel* 15:89–95

57. Klingberg, H. E. 1973. An evaluation of sensitivity training effects on self-actualization, purpose in life, and religious attitudes of theological students. *J. Psychol. Theology* 1:31–39

58. Kopel, K., O'Connell, W., Paris, J., Girardin, P. 1973. A didactic-experiential death and dying lab. *Newslett. Res. Ment. Health Behav. Sci.* 15:1–2

59. Koran, L. M., Costell, R. M. 1973. Early termination from group psychotherapy. *Int. J. Group Psychother.* 23:346–59

60. Kroeker, L. L., Forsyth, D. R., Haase, R. F. 1974. Evaluation of a police-youth human relations program. *Prof. Psychol.* 5:140–54

61. LaCalle, J. J. 1973. *Group psychotherapy with Mexican-American drug addicts.* PhD thesis. Diss. Abstr. Int., Ann Arbor, Mich.: Univ. M-Films No. 73-22675

62. LaCoursiere, R. 1974. A group method to facilitate learning during the stages of a psychiatric affiliation. *Int. J. Group Psychother.* 24:342–51

63. Lederman, S. 1974. Some ideas and gains in training paraprofessionals as group therapists. *J. Bronx State Hosp.* 2:86–95

64. Lee, J. L. 1974. *The Counselor's Handbook*, ed. G. F. Farwell, N. R. Gamsky, F. Mathiew-Coughlan. New York: Intext. 530 pp.

65. Levy, L. 1975. *Mental health oriented self-help groups: Twelve untested hypotheses concerning their function.* Presented at Conf. Exper. Small Group Res., Univ. Indiana, Bloomington

66. Lewis, V., Glaser, D. 1974. Lifestyle among heroin users. *Fed. Probation* 38:21–28

67. Lieberman, M. A. 1975. People-changing groups: The new and not so new.

68. Lieberman, M. A. 1975. Some limits to research on T-groups. *J. Appl. Behav. Sci.* 11:241–49

69. Lieberman, M. A., Gardner, J. 1975. Institutional alternatives to psychotherapy: A study of growth center users. *Arch. Gen. Psychiatry.* In press

70. Lieberman, M. A., Yalom, I. D., Miles, M. B. 1973. *Encounter Groups: First Facts.* New York: Basic Books

71. Lunceford, R. D. 1973. *Self-concept change of black college females as a result of a weekend black experience encounter workshop.* PhD thesis. Diss. Abstr. Int., Ann Arbor, Mich.: Univ. M-Films No. 73-22678.

72. Margulies, N. 1973. The effects of an organization sensitivity training program on a measure of self-actualization. *Stud. Personnel Psychol.* 5:67–74

73. Martin, R. D., Fischer, D. G. 1974. Encounter group experience and personality change. *Psychol. Rep.* 35:91

74. Marvit, R. C., Lind, J., McLaughlin, D. G. 1974. Use of videotape to induce attitude change in delinquent adolescents. *Am. J. Psychiatry* 131:996–99

75. May, O. P., Thompson, C. L. 1973. Perceived levels of self-disclosure, mental health, and helpfulness of group leaders. *J. Couns. Psychol.* 20:349–52

76. McCall, R. J. 1974. Group therapy with obese women of varying MMPI profiles. *J. Clin. Psychol.* 30:466–70

77. McCardel, J., Murray, E. J. 1974. Nonspecific factors in weekend encounter groups. *J. Consult. Clin. Psychol.* 42:337–45

78. McIntire, W. G. 1973. The impact of T-group experience on level of self-actualization. *Small Group Behav.* 4:459–65

79. McLachlan, J. F. 1974. Therapy strategies, personality orientation and recovery from alcoholism. *Can. Psychiat. Assoc. J.* 19:25–30

80. McLaughlin, F. E., White, E., Byfield, B. 1974. Modes of interpersonal feedback and leadership structure in six small groups. *Nurs. Res.* 23:307–18

81. McLeish, J., Park, J. 1973. Outcomes associated with direct and vicarious experience in training groups: II. Attitudes, dogmatism. *Br. J. Soc. Clin. Psychol.* 12:353–58

82. Ibid. Outcomes associated with direct and vicarious experience in training groups: III. Intended learning outcomes, 359–73

83. Miller, P. M., Hersen, M., Eisler, R. M., Hemphill, D. P. 1973. Electrical aversion therapy with alcoholics: An analogue study. *Behav. Res. Ther.* 11: 491–97

84. Nagy, T. F., Boyd, R. E. 1973. Experiential groups for teachers. *Pupil Personnel Serv. J.* 2:36–42

85. Newcomer, B. L., Morrison, T. L. 1974. Play therapy with institutionalized mentally retarded children. *Am. J. Ment. Defic.* 78:727–33

86. Noll, G. A., Watkins, J. T. 1974. Differences between persons seeking encounter group experiences and others on the Personal Orientation Inventory. *J. Coun. Psychol.* 21:206–9

87. Paradis, A. P. 1973. *Brief out-patient group psychotherapy with older patients in the treatment of age-related problems.* PhD thesis. Diss. Abstr. Int., Ann Arbor, Mich.: Univ. M-Films No. 73-31401. 107 pp.

88. Pattison, E. M., Rhodes, R. J. 1974. Clinical prediction with the N-30 Scale. *J. Clin. Psychol.* 30:200-1

89. Payn, S. B. 1974. Reaching chronic schizophrenic patients with group pharmacotherapy. *Int. J. Group Psychother.* 24:25–31

90. Poland, W. D., Jones, J. E. 1973. Personal orientations and perceived benefit from a human relations laboratory. *Small Group Behav.* 4:496–502

91. Poser, E. G. 1966. The effect of therapists' training on group therapeutic outcome. *J. Consult. Psychol.* 30:283–89

92. Posthuma, A. B., Posthuma, B. W. 1973. Some observations on encounter group casualties. *J. Appl. Behav. Sci.* 9:595–608

93. Reddy, W. B. 1973. The impact of sensitivity training on self-actualization: A one-year follow-up. *Small Group Behav.* 4:407–13

94. Redfering, D. L. 1973. Durability of effects of group counseling with institutionalized delinquent females. *J. Abnorm. Psychol.* 82:85–86

95. Rimm, D. C., Hill, G. A., Brown, N. N., Stuart, J. E. 1974. Group-assertive training in treatment of expression of inappropriate anger. *Psychol. Rep.* 34:791–98

96. Romano, J. L., Quary, A. T. 1974. Follow-up of community college C-group participants. *J. Coll. Stud. Personnel* 15:278–83

97. Rosenzweig, S. P., Folman, R. 1974. Patient and therapist variables affecting premature termination on group therapy. *Psychother. Theory Res. Pract.* 11:76–79

98. Ross, W. F., McReynolds, W. T., Berzins, J. I. 1974. Effectiveness of marathon group psychotherapy with hospitalized female narcotics addicts. *Psychol. Rep.* 34:611–16

99. Schaffer, J. B. P., Galinsky, M. D. 1974. *Models of Group Therapy and Sensitivity Training.* New Jersey: Prentice-Hall

100. Schubert, M. L. 1973. *A comparison of the effects of two models of sensitivity-training on "level of experiencing."* PhD thesis. Diss. Abstr. Int., Ann Arbor, Mich.: Univ. M-Films No. 73-20159. 235 pp.

101. Seldman, M. L., McBrearty, J. F., Seldman, S. L. 1974. Deification of marathon encounter group leaders. *Small Group Behav.* 5:80–91

102. Singer, D. L., Astrahan, B. M., Gould, L. J., Klein, E. B. 1975. Boundary management in psychological work with groups. *J. Appl. Behav. Sci.* 11:137–76

103. Smith, E. F. 1973. Teaching group therapy in an undergraduate curriculum. *Perspect. Psychiat. Care* 11: 70–74

104. Stimpson, D. V. 1975. T-group counseling to improve counseling skills. *J. Psychol.* 89:89–94

105. Truax, C., Carkhuff, R. R. 1967. *Towards Effective Counseling and Psychotherapy.* Chicago: Aldine

106. Van Ostenberg, D. L. 1973. Therapy groups for staff and interns. *Hosp. Community Psychiatry* 24:474–75

107. Vicino, F., Crusall, J., Bass, B., Deci, E., Landi, D. 1973. The impact of process: Self-administered exercises for personal and interpersonal development. *J. Appl. Behav. Sci.* 9:737–56

108. Walton, D. R. 1973. Effects of personal growth groups on self-actualization and creative personality. *J. Coll. Stud. Personnel* 14:490–94

109. Weiner, M. F. 1973. Termination of group psychotherapy. *Group Process* 5:85–96

110. White, J. 1974. The human potential laboratory in the community college. *J. Coll. Stud. Personnel* 15:96–100

111. Yalom, I. D. 1974. Group therapy and alcoholism. *Ann. NY Acad. Sci.* 233:85–103

TEST THEORY[1]

♦254

James Lumsden

Department of Psychology, University of Western Australia, Nedlands, 6009, Australia

Test theory has had few major ideas. I can list only five:

1. the decomposition of obtained scores into true and error components (20, 32, 66, 81, 90);
2. the duality of psychophysics and psychometrics (16, 72, 73, 88, 91);
3. the notion of unidimensionality (33, 34, 51, 68);
4. the conception of test validity as theoretical equivalence, usually called construct validity (21);
5. the scaling ideas derived from various item characteristic curve models (3, 4, 54, 75, 91, 93).

Apart from the first, these ideas have been hesitatingly and unconfidently applied.

As both an effect and a cause, there has been a general atmosphere of melancholia and lassitude among latter-day test theorists. Bock & Wood (7) point out that the uncritical use of tests gives test theorists little incentive to improve them, and this may account for the discouragement. There is, I believe, a more important reason. The shreds of theory that have been developed and the time-worn true score models are not rich sources of ideas about testing, and the ideas that are generated seem to relate mainly to the internal workings of the models.

A VULGAR ANALOGY—THE FLOGGING WALL TEST

What test theory needs is a tool for thought experiments. I have constructed a test for test theorists which illustrates, and at times illuminates, many of the problems of test theory. Along a long wall at widespread intervals flexible canes are attached at various heights. These canes flog slowly and independently up and down at varying amplitudes. Subjects stand on a cart which is drawn quickly along near the wall. A subject's score is the number of canes which touch him. The scores represent a mapping of the attribute of height into the number system. This follows from the fundamental theorem of axiomatic approaches to measurement:

$$a \in M \text{ iff } a \in O M$$

[1] This essay covers, very roughly, the period from 1904–1974. More detailed attention is given to the events, mainly unfortunate, of the period 1970–1974.

which may be translated: *a* is a legitimate mapping if, and only if, *a* is an obviously legitimate mapping.

How could we make the flogging wall test more reliable? One way would be to make it longer, to use more items. Another would be to reduce the amplitude of the flogging, that is, to make the items more reliable. Suppose that we stopped the flog so that the canes were static. The test would be perfectly reliable and the obtained scores would be identical with the platonic true scores. The platonic true score is respectable. It represents the scores obtained when the most popular item selection procedure is carried to the limit.

When we stop the canes the test is obviously perfectly reliable. What method of estimating reliability would show it to be so? The problem is more difficult than it seems. I will consider only the test-retest method and leave the reader to work out the difficulties with other methods. The test-retest method will yield a reliability coefficient of one if there is no practice effect. But suppose that we send a sample of test theorists through the test and that because their heads are unbowed they become bloody. Let us suppose further that soon after, not during, the test all their heads swell by exactly 3 inches. (The relationship between within-testing practice effects and between-testing effects appears not to have been investigated.) Notice that this is an attribute effect and is extremely unlikely. Long Louis hits many more canes than Big Louis, who is 6 inches shorter, and Short Sam hits only one or two. Will, however unlikely, uniform practice effect on the attribute yield a perfect reliability estimate? Not at all, because the effect in score terms will be different. Suppose that there are three canes within less than an inch around 5 feet and the next is at 5 feet 6 inches. A subject whose height at first testing was just under 5 feet would have his score increased by three, while a subject whose height at first

testing was just above 5 feet would remain at the same score on second testing. What is required to produce a perfect reliability coefficient is that each *score* will be increased by exactly the same amount. It requires a very watchful and kindly providence to stretch all subjects by precisely the different attribute amounts necessary for this to happen. Yet this is the assumption made by test-retest and parallel form estimates of reliability. It is hard to believe that any test theorist could believe it.

Does a perfectly reliable test perfectly reflect the attribute? No, because in the case we have just discussed subjects who differ in height by almost 6 inches (in the region of 5'0" to 5'6") will have the same score, while subjects in other regions who differ in height by only an inch may differ in score by three or more. Subjects with the same score may have widely different attribute values and subjects with different scores may have very similar (never identical) attribute values. The reader may wonder whether the perfectly reliable test is all that he had been led to expect. If we allow the canes to flog, the probability now is that subjects near 5'6" in height will have higher scores than subjects near 5'0", and so on for other positions. If the gaps are large, it may be necessary to have a large amplitude of flog and to make up for the heavy loss of reliability by increasing the number of items. The consequence of this will be that the obtained scores, now somewhat unreliable, will represent the attribute more accurately and that, therefore, the correlation between the scores and any criterion for which height is relevant will increase. In other words, validity will increase when reliability decreases.

Anyone for attenuation? The attenuation paradox has been noted many times (10, 52, 53, 92). It is significant that the attenuation paradox is mentioned in Lord & Novick (66, p. 344) almost 300 pages after an uncritical advocacy of the correction and that nowhere do they state that the correction almost always produces an overestimate. The attenuation paradox has been attributed by Cronbach and associates (20) to a narrowing of the universe, i.e. to a decrease in the variety of item types included in the test. The example quoted above shows that this is not necessarily the case.

Someone may object that the rather eccentric distribution of item difficulties given in the paradox example is untypical of psychological tests. That is true, but many test constructors attempt to peak difficulties around the 0.50 level and have few easy or difficult items. The result with highly reliable items is a breakdown in discrimination at the high and low levels.

The attenuation paradox cannot occur if the item difficulties have a distribution which is adequately and uniformly dense across the range of attribute values to be assessed. Lord & Novick (66, p. 465) seem to agree. Adequate density means that subjects falling in a given interval between items, in attribute terms, will be treated as having the same attribute value for all relevant purposes. What constitutes adequate density will depend on circumstances.

Distribution of item difficulties has another advantage. Recall the second of our major ideas in test theory: the duality of psychophysics and psychometrics. If there is an item characteristic curve, then there must exist a person characteristic curve. If items need two (maybe three) parameters, then persons do so too. The person characteristic curve is the plot for a particular individual of proportion passed for items of different difficulty. Two persons with the same location value may have different slopes. Bill, a careful worker, may get all easy items right but no hard ones. Joe gets some easy ones wrong but some hard ones right. Whether we should take this into account is a matter for empirical determination. Certainly there seems no theoretical ground for not taking a look. Thorndike (85) and Furneaux (29) have adopted this procedure. The advocacy of peaked tests seems to have arisen from a preoccupation of test theorists with obtaining the most efficient estimation of the location parameter. The third parameter? Well, Guilford (31, p. 139), in a discussion of the constant methods, suggests that proportion of "doubtful" judgments (unwillingness to guess) may be an important personality characteristic. Swineford (84) and Ziller (102) have made similar suggestions.

The flogging wall is a powerful tool for thought experiments. Some may object that computer simulations of various mathematical models of items do much the same thing more elegantly. The alternatives are not vulgar enough. They do not have a highly visible, distinctive attribute. Even more importantly, the distinction between attribute values and scores is not made palpably obvious. The flogging wall test together with some elementary statistics is almost a test theory in its own right, and we shall see demonstrations of its power throughout this essay.

A MUSEUM FOR MODEL T

The most highly regarded notion in all test theory, and the only one to be seriously developed, has been the venerable: $O = T + E$. I term this Model T for polemical purposes. The idea has been stated and restated and variously applied and interpreted. Legend has it that it began with Udny Yule, who told Spearman (81). The idea was perpetuated and elaborated by a royal line which included Thurstone (90) and Gulliksen (32) and achieved a memorial in a grand mausoleum constructed by Lord & Novick (66). In the period under review Cronbach et al (20) have made a gallant attempt to boost the sales of the old Tin Lizzie but the color remains black. The decomposition of obtained scores into true scores and error scores is unfruitful. When true score is defined as an ideal (platonic) score stripped of error, the result is a contradiction. When true score is defined in other ways so as to avoid the contradiction, then the resultant statistics have no useful application.

Consider an eight-item completion test in which items are scored dichotomously. The obtained scores can only take integral values from 0–8. Suppose that we define a true score as an obtained score stripped of error, that is, when both the items and the persons are perfectly reliable. The platonic true scores also can only take on integral values from 0–8. Consider a subject whose true score is 8. His obtained score can never exceed this value so that his error score can only be zero or negative. Similarly, a person whose true score is zero can only have error scores which are zero or positive. For other true scores both positive and negative error scores are possible. Error score is not independent of true score, and in most situations it would appear that $r_{TE} < 0$, which is a contradiction of the Model T assumption that $r_{TE} = 0$. In the face of this it is necessary to abandon either Model T or the platonic true score definition. Most test theorists have taken the latter course, agreeing with the Bock & Wood (7, p. 198) statement: "There seems little to be gained from further prolonging the life of the platonic true score as a concept in test theory." There is some curious fear of the platonic true score as representing an "eye-of-God-reality" (20, p. 19). Stanley (82) and Thorndike (86) seem to be similarly troubled when they say that true score is not recorded in the book of heaven. Yet the very same writers will freely admit that estimates of true score may be in error, i.e. differ from some really true score. If not recorded in the book of heaven, one wonders in what demonic book the Lord & Novick expectations or the Cronbach et al universe scores are recorded.

There is, however, no joy for Model T pushers in other definitions of true score. Lord & Novick (66) define true score as the expected value of the obtained score over replications. Definitions in terms of limits (Gulliksen 32) amount to the same thing. The contradiction is now avoided since the only way that maximum or minimum true scores can be obtained is by the occurrence of invariant maximum or minimum obtained scores over replications. The expected value of the error score can now be zero for all values of true score, and the assertion $r_{TE} = 0$ is not contradicted. But there remains a problem. Error score is not completely independent of true score. While the expected value of the error score is constant (zero) for all values of T, the variance of error scores is not constant but clearly zero at the maximum and minimum scores and rising to a maximum at some middling value of T. It should be noted also that the distribution of error scores is likely to be highly skewed for extreme values of true score because of the bounds on obtained score. The breakdown in homoscedasticity for the bivariate distribution of true and error scores has been demonstrated by Lord (53).

It is clear that in the Lord & Novick model the regression of obtained score on true score is linear. A little reflection on the results for a short test will show that the regression of true scores on obtained scores is not linear. Lord & Novick (66) state that the conditions for linearity for the true score on obtained score regression are that the errors should be normally distributed around true scores and that the distribution of the true scores should be normal. The first of these conditions is impossible and the second not very likely. In a a later section Lord & Novick concede that generally the regression is not linear.

The major purpose of the Model T decomposition is to provide a rationale for the reliability coefficient. Why do we need the reliability coefficient? Three major reasons have been suggested: 1. to guide test selection, 2. to support inferences about test scores based on regression estimates of true scores and the standard error of measurement, and 3. to support inferences about the validity of perfectly reliable tests (correction for attenuation). The first of these need not concern us. For most purposes there are better guides (Cronbach 17), and we have already seen that the reliability guide may be misleading. The second reason does not apply. Linear regression estimates of true score may be quite misleading if regression is not linear. Setting up confidence limits using the standard error of measurement will also be misleading since the standard deviation of error scores is not independent of true scores. It is not good enough to scrub around this latter problem as is often done in other contexts by asserting that the standard error of measurement represents in an average sense the standard deviation of the error arrays and that departures from homogeneity may be tolerated. The departures are systematic and may be too large to be tolerated. A different line of attack on this problem will be presented in the consideration of recent work on reliability where it will be shown that even if the problems of nonlinearity and heteroscedasticity are solved, the true score concept remains useless.

There remains the third reason: the use of reliability estimates in the correction for attenuation. This is regarded by Lord & Novick (66, p. 71) as one of the best justifications of reliability theory. Cronbach et al (20) also strongly advocate the correction. The correction should never be used. It too often produces corrected correlations which are greater than one, and it is not sufficient to pass these occasions off with an embarrassed smile and some mutterings about unreliability of estimates. The problem is simple and unsolvable, at least by classical methods. All estimates of the reliability coefficient (with the possible exception under certain conditions of the test-retest estimate) are underestimates, sometimes gross underestimates, of reliability as classically defined. Since the correction for attenuation requires division by the square roots of the reliability coefficients, it follows that the correction produces estimates which are overestimates, sometimes gross overestimates. Note, too, that the attenuation paradox makes nonsense of the correction.

What has gone wrong? The Yule suggestion that $O = T + E$ was probably made, unless it was a cruel joke, in the belief that we were dealing with something like length measures where the t's and e's are continuous and essentially unbounded. In this case the assumptions of Model T can hold without contradiction and the inferences will generally be sound, but now they will refer to attribute values.

A technical criticism of theories based on the true score model and a sketch of an attribute based model, Model A, may be found in Ross & Lumsden (80). In this paper it is suggested that test theory followed a will o' the wisp when it set out on the false trail of true score. Whenever a procedure is set up which estimates the attribute value, it will be unnecessary and misleading to think of an ideal value of the estimator.

1970–1974

Few valuable contributions to test theory have appeared during the review period. There seems to be a degree of desperation among test theorists as if they are groping for suitable topics to write about. Many papers are of very slight merit and, though this may simply be a case of reviewer's jaundice, there seem to be more technical errors than in previous review periods. The standards set by editors and article reviewers are low, and many papers could be greatly improved by some criticism. It is appropriate here to suggest that *Educational and Psychological Measurement* should review its policy of not publishing comments. These, if prompt and hot, can have a salutory effect. A battered author and a reviewer who has had to say an abject mea culpa will be likely to be more careful next time. And so will others.

This review follows Bock & Wood (7) in restricting consideration largely to test theory as concerned with itemized tests of ability and achievement. It is the reviewer's belief that if progress in test theory is to be made at all, and there is not much evidence of it yet, it will be made first in this area. The review is organized under traditional topic titles with the addition of a section on dimensionality. This is partly because your reviewer is conservative, but mainly because it is important to reveal what has not been done as well as what has been done. There are some alarming holes.

Reliability

As usual, there have been many papers in this area. Generally the authors uncritically adopt one form or another of the true score model and reveal little understanding of the problems which the model was designed to solve. There is, with one exception, no imaginative approach to any of the problems but simply a grinding of mathematical symbols (with fantastic assumptions when things get tough) to produce nothing of any worth. It is extraordinary that gifted mathematicians should constantly fail to realize that the obtained scores can do exactly the same task as the estimated true scores. Rarely do they see that the reliability problem is best conceived as part of a wider question: how well does the test represent the attribute? When this question is posed and understood it becomes clear that the true score and the reliability coefficient can play no part in providing an answer and should be abandoned.

What will almost certainly come to be considered the outstanding contribution of the period is the book by Cronbach, Gleser, Nanda & Rajaratnam (20), which is the culmination of a decade of work on reliability seen as generalizability. Cronbach et al treat the obtained score as a sample from a universe of admissible observations. It is the responsibility of a test publisher to state what he considers to be this universe. The statement will consist of specifications of a number of facets or dimensions and of permitted levels of them. Thus he may state that all forms (or only one form) of a particular test are to be considered as equivalent, and in the universe of admissible observations, various examiners trained or certified in certain ways may be used, other conditions such as time and place may vary within certain defined limits. A particular person's score is obtained from one form of the test, with a particular examiner, in a certain place and on a certain occasion. This obtained score will normally differ from his universe score which is defined as the expected score over all admissible observations. The universe score is perfectly analogous to the true score of classical reliability theory.

After defining the universe of admissible observations, Cronbach et al say that the publisher should carry out a G (generalizability) study, which will permit variance components to be estimated for persons, forms, examiners, occasions, and for the interaction terms. Ideally the G study should be completely crossed, but it is recognized that some nesting (e.g. with occasion) is inevitable and that economics, subject fatigue, etc will often require further nesting. From the variance components it is possible to estimate the coefficient of generalizability defined as the ratio of universe score variance to expected observed score variance. The estimate is made by calculating an intra class correlation from the ratio of person variance to the sum of the person variance and the variance components for person interactions, and the residual variance. The coefficient of generalizability is perfectly analogous to the classical reliability coefficient. It is recognized that different test users may have different acceptable modes of forming the universe of admissible observations and that therefore a particular test may have many coefficients of generalizability. These may often be calculated from the publisher's G study by fixing one facet at a particular level and making the appropriate changes in the variance components for the intra class correlation.

The coefficient of generalizability obtained in the G study may be used in a D (decision) study to estimate the universe score from a subject's obtained score. The universe score is said by Cronbach et al (20, p. 15) to be the "ideal datum on which to base. . . . decision" (s).

The book is in many respects a considerable achievement. It bites firmly on the sour apple of Guttman's (35) critique of Gulliksen (32), where he points out that a test will have as many reliabilities as there are acceptable bases for forming parallel tests. It makes concrete sense of the sampling model (in many places at least) and points out the importance of often disregarded facets such as examiners. The book provides the foundation and much of the superstructure of the unified treatment of reliability via the intra class correlation that was requested by Bock & Wood (7). A detailed examination with numerous examples is given of the various experimental designs that may be used for G and D studies. Cronbach et al are frank about the problems, e.g. with estimation of variance components, and I have no doubt that the next decade will see many papers attempting to solve these problems (101). Wiggin's textbook (100) already has an accurate account of the generalizability approach, and one can confidently predict that many others soon will be attempting to do the same.

In a D study with test theorists as raters, I am sure the Cronbach et al contribution would receive a very high universe score. But here we are concerned with its value on the attributes of logical correctness and fruitfulness. On this basis the book is—unfortunate. The great expertise so often displayed and the highly professional care in exposition only make things worse. The book shows all the poverty of imagination and all the elementary logical and even mathematical errors so characteristic of reliability theory. I have several reasons for these strong remarks. The general ones are set out in the introductory sections of this essay. The occasion demands, however, a more specific rebuttal.

In all their designs Cronbach et al advocate repeated measures without emphasizing the obvious dangers that main effects and interactions with persons are inextricably confounded with sequence effects and their interactions. This may matter more in some cases than others, but it is clear that for parallel forms or test-retest procedures the occurrence of differential practice effects cannot be ruled out and cannot be considered as properly included, for example, within the between-form effect or the person-by-form interaction. Much that is of value in the generalizability approach can be obtained without repeated measures; for example, by simple fully randomized designs main effects for form or for examiners can be readily estimated. I hesitate to suggest it in case someone does it, but some very powerful and efficient designs can be worked out using parallel persons. I am fascinated by the thought that ETS should employ 100 sets of identical twins, all reared together, who do tests all morning and are used for other experiments in the afternoon.

Cronbach et al properly point out that the common practice of setting up confidence limits around the obtained score is not correct. They recommend that universe scores should be estimated via linear regression and confidence limits set out around them using an equivalent of the standard error of measurement. They realize that if all scores are regressed toward the population mean, then the universe score estimates will be perfectly correlated with observed scores and little will be gained. But if there exist subgroups of persons with different means and the regression estimates are toward the subgroup means, then the correlation will not be perfect and the universe score estimates will reflect important information not obtainable from the obtained score alone. This approach can be criticized on several grounds. As we have seen previously, it it is known that the regression of true scores (universe scores) on obtained scores is nonlinear. It is true that if the reliability estimate is high, then the departures from linearity cannot be great. But in this case the regression estimate of the universe score will differ only trivially from the obtained score. (Recall, too, that estimates of unreliability are typically understimates.) When the reliability is not high, then the departures from linearity may be substantial. It follows that when the reliability is high the linear regression estimate is not worth making, and when it is low the linear regression estimate may be misleading. We have already seen that the standard error of measurement is not constant for all values of true score and is, therefore, a dubious base for the formation of confidence limits. But even if by some mathematical magic these problems can be overcome, the approach remains inappropriate. We do not need the true score!

Cronbach et al (20, p. 14) state that measuring procedures are to be used as the basis for decisions about classifications, course success, etc, and that "the accuracy of measurement must in principle be examined separately for each application of the procedure." In the light of this very wise statement, why not simply examine the scatter diagram relating criterion performance to test performance? For any given obtained score we can observe the scatter of criterion scores and from this obtain the expected criterion score and the required confidence limits. For different subgroups we can if necessary set up different scatter diagrams. Why do we need the estimates of universe scores? But suppose we were foolish enough to calculate the regressed scores as recommended. Would we not, in principle, still need to consult the scatter diagrams in order to arrive at a sensible decision? And wouldn't these be exactly the same scatter diagrams with the numbers shifted a bit on one axis?

Let me make this matter painfully obvious with some brilliant mathematics. Suppose that you were unhappily calculating x from y using some complicated function such as $x = ay + b$ and that someone told you that a better procedure was to calculate x from z using the function $x = cz + d$. You inquire how to find the z's and are told that you can estimate these accurately enough from y using the function $z = ey + f$. Would you tell this drongo[2] to go jump in a polykay, nick himself with a jackknife, or lose himself in a Bayesian convolution?

Cronbach et al go further and recommend that profiles be plotted in universe scores with all the information from all the tests used to yield a multiple regression estimate (linear of course) of the universe scores. This is consistent with the recommendation for a single test score. Subjects with similar scores on several of the tests are treated in effect as a subgroup, and the score obtained in a particular test is regressed toward the mean of that group. The advocated procedure amounts to bad, indeed dangerous, practice. Consider the case of a boy who is referred with high scores on an intelligence and an arithmetic test and with a low score on a reading test. We are interested precisely because we expect superior reading performance from high performers on intelligence and arithmetic tests. Now any psychologist worth his salt knows that test scores are not completely reliable and that differences between scores may be misleading. So we take no action until we check the results in some way. We ask the teacher, who says that Joe seems bright, is good at arithmetic, but poor at reading. We proceed with inquiries into Joe's reading problems. Suppose that after regressing to the universe scores Joe's reading score was within the normal range. Would Cronbach et al tell Joe's teacher to quit worrying about Joe's reading? Of course they would do nothing so crass because the information from the teacher would be taken into account. But often information arrives at different times and may be passed through several hands. How can we protect against possible gross misinterpretation? Finally there is the gruesome thought, which may be termed the erosion nightmare, that through inadvertence or incompetence a profile might be regressed several times. Let us stick to the old-fashioned percentile ranks and a little common sense.

Cronbach et al (20, p. 309) give as part of the justification of their advocacy of universe score profiles this statement: "The scientist is concerned with relations among constructs which are always universe scores or functions of universe scores." This presumably is also a justification of their advocacy of the correction for attenuation. The first part of the quoted sentence is false and the second misleading. Constructs (in measurement theory) are attributes, traits, latent abilities, etc, and should be sharply distinguished from obtained scores, true scores, or universe scores. If constructs are functions of universe scores (estimated), then they will be the same kind of function of obtained scores. The quoted statement should be compared with Cronbach's (18) well-argued defense of surplus meaning of constructs against ultraoperationists.

But let's look again at the correction for attenuation. If the regression estimates of true score are any good, then if we calculate them for x and then for y the correlation between these estimates should approach the correlation between x and y corrected for attenuation. Would anyone like to bet on the result of this foolish experiment? Why hasn't it been done?

[2]Drongo: an extinct Australian bird that slept with its eyes open and flew with its eyes shut.

As a final example of the looseness of thinking that Model T, by some rule of perversity, seems so often to engender, consider the following statement: "The distribution of μ_p (universe scores) is unknown. The most plausible approximation available is a normal distribution with mean $\hat{u}$ and variance σ^2 (p)" (20, pp. 146–47). Suppose that we select two very large samples randomly from a given population and that one sample does an easy and the other a difficult arithmetic test. Will the frequency distributions of the obtained scores have the same shape? It would be very strange if they did. The most likely result is that for the easy test the score would be negatively skewed and for the hard test positively skewed. What would be the distribution shapes of the universe scores for the two tests? From the assumptions of Cronbach et al, they would be almost exactly the same. After all, they go to considerable lengths to try to convince us that linear regression provides a reasonable estimate of universe scores. There is no "plausible assumption" that can be made a priori about the shape of the distribution of universe scores. The distribution of obtained scores and of universe scores is a complex function of the distribution of attribute values for the sample and of the item characteristics of the test.

Let us pause to consider what has been revealed by this tedious critique of Cronbach et al. Simply that Model T in either its classical form or in generalizability trim cannot perform the task for which it was designed. The reliability coefficient and statistics calculated from it have no useful application. They should not be used to select tests, to estimate true scores, to estimate confidence limits for scores either true or obtained, in the correction for attenuation, or for anything else. More fortunately it has been shown that this does not matter. The problems for which these devices were alleged to be the solution can be handled more simply, more sensibly, more fruitfully, though perhaps (to some) less elegantly by the application of simple regression methodology, i.e. by best validity practice.

Lest I have made an accidental friend, it should be made clear that I regard most of the criticisms as applying to reliability theory as a whole. The book by Cronbach et al received special attention because it is the latest, and by all odds one of the greatest, in the Model T tradition. But all reliability theorists from Spearman on have been about equally mistaken.

Stanley (82), in his chapter on reliability, gives an insightful account of the sources of variance in test scores and goes on to a highly technical consideration of recent work. The rule of perversity still operates. Stanley manages to produce this gem:

> Differences in test reliability among several tests or different ways of scoring tests frequently appear negligible unless expressed in signal-to-noise ratios. An improvement of only .01 in a high reliability coefficient is equivalent to the increase in reliability obtained by lengthening the test 10 per cent or more. One can readily appreciate the practical significance of the improvement in these terms (82, p. 375).

I have news for Professor Stanley. The practical significance of an increase in a reliability coefficient of .01 is negligible whether it represents an increase of 10, 100, or even 1000 per cent in the length of the less reliable test. Reflect on what use might be made of the reliability coefficient. The signal-to-noise ratio is as useless as any other reliability statistic. Another example of the rule is provided by Cureton (23), who calculates what he calls a coefficient of stability by correcting a between-forms correlation for attenuation using KR_{20} reliability estimates. The KR_{20} estimates are directly affected by the dispersion of item difficulties and by item heterogeneity. The between-forms correlation is not so affected. The correction seems likely to produce in many cases a gross overestimate. Cureton obligingly provides one example where the resultant correlation is greater than 1.0. There is only one word to describe coefficients like this. The word is: Baloney! (Cureton 22).

Cureton and five others (24) compare the standard errors of measurement for six tests (one each?) and find confirmation for Lord's (55, 56) assertion that tests of the same length have the same standard error of measurement. The Lord assertion is based on the consideration that when the item intercorrelations increase the reliability increases but so does the test variance, and these effects compensate to give a constant standard error of measurement. Consideration of a flogging wall with static canes or very little flog will show that the effect is not general across the possible range of item intercorrelations. The Cureton et al study considers only tests where the mean item intercorrelations are very similar, and therefore it is not a very interesting confirmation.

Loyal members of the Model T club will find some pretty algebra in Kristoff's (46, 48) papers on the reliability of reliability estimates. Joreskog (44) continues his saga of the statistical treatment of congeneric tests. Zimmerman (103) gives the umpteenth rederivation of KR_{20} with "relaxed" assumptions. The derivation is extremely rigorous but, as always, it turns out that the only feasible way that the relaxed assumptions can be met is if the original (49) stringent ones are met. Kristoff (47) shows that for tests differing only in length signal-to-noise ratios are additive. Lord (63) considers partial correlations corrected for attenuation. He finds, sadly, that the sampling error is "overwhelming" but gives a more powerful test of the hypothesis that the sign of the partial is positive or negative! Ebel (28) gives a very neat demonstration of why a longer test is usually more reliable than a shorter test. Bay (2) shows that the sampling distributions and standard errors of reliability estimates under an analysis of variance model are substantially affected if the distribution of true scores is not normal. Jackson (40) attempts to estimate true score variance and error variance. In order to keep the algebra tractable, or for some other reason about which he does not care to inform us, Jackson assumes that true scores are normally distributed and that the scores for repeated measures on parallel forms are independently and identically distributed.

A different and promising approach to the problems of reliability (and some others as well) is given by the information measure developed by Birnbaum (4). This measure $I(\theta,x)$ is considered by Birnbaum to be a kind of index of precision which for a given test and scoring formula reflects the information provided by the test in the vicinity of a given value of the attribute θ. It should be noted that this measure is not based on any of the Model T assumptions. This is why it is described as promising. Birnbaum provides a formula for this which is based on the slope of the score on ability regression line in the vicinity of a particular value of θ. A little

reflection on a flogging wall test with static canes will provide an intuitive justification of the procedure and illustrate some of the determinants of the measure. The
flogging wall test will give much information at ability levels where the canes are
dense and little information where there are few canes. It is clear that the slope of
score on ability will be steep at points where the canes are dense and that at these
points $I(\theta,x)$ will be large; where the slope is flat (few canes) $I(\theta,x)$ will be small.
When the canes flog, nothing much will be changed except that it will not simply
be the local density of the canes that will determine the slope of score on ability.

Birnbaum[3] gives a mathematical justification of his information measure by demonstrating that it is inversely proportional to the width of the confidence interval
we would construct in estimating ability θ from test score x. This demonstration
requires three highly questionable assumptions about $F(x/\theta)$, the cumulative distribution function of the test scores. These assumptions are: 1. $F(x/\theta)$ is normal;
2. $F(x/\theta)$ can be approximated by $1\frac{1}{2}$ terms of a Taylor expansion; and 3. $F(x/\theta)$
is . . . "continuously strictly increasing in x and decreasing in θ" (4, pp. 417–18).

The first assumption is palpably false for any test unless we avoid the edges of
the test. It may be false elsewhere if the attenuation paradox region is approached.
Consider a flogging wall test with little flog where items are irregularly dispersed
in difficulty. Birnbaum stops the Taylor expansion and rejects terms involving the
derivative of the variance, justifying this by assuming that changes in the mean with
respect to θ dominate changes in the conditional variance:

$$\frac{du(x/\theta)}{d\theta} \qquad \frac{dV(x/\theta)}{d\theta}$$

For many tests this second assumption is grossly violated (Ross 79). Consider a
flogging wall test as we pass from a region of high density. The mean will change
slowly but the variance will decrease sharply and then bounce back as we exit the
region of low density.

The third assumption is used to define the estimates of the upper and lower
bounds of the confidence interval. Following Birnbaum (4, p. 409), we will consider
the case for the lower bound; the case for the upper bound is the same. Birnbaum
defines the lower α-level estimator of θ based on the test score x*, t(x*) as that value
of θ for which $F(x^*/\theta) = \alpha$ and calls this value θ^*. In order for t to be well defined
there must be only one value θ^* which fulfils this condition for each x* and
Birnbaum's assumption is sufficient to guarantee this. This assumption is also sufficient to guarantee that if x < y then t(x) < t(y). That the estimator is monotonic
with test score allows Birnbaum to relate the distribution of estimators to the
distribution of test scores and so define the confidence interval. Note that it is not
sufficient to guarantee the existence of a bound.

The third assumption is sufficient to permit definition of the confidence limits if
the bounds exist. It turns out to be much more restrictive than appears on the
surface. If, for example, $F(x/\theta)$ takes the form of the logistic (not very different from

[3]I am indebted to Dan Milech, University of Western Australia, for the mathematical
argument to follow.

the normal), it can be shown that the assumption implies that the mean test score $\mu(x/\theta)$ is strictly increasing in θ and that the variance $V(x/\theta)$ is strictly nondecreasing in θ. This latter restriction is likely to be violated in many tests (79) and in particular cannot be met by a peaked test. For other distribution functions the restriction on variance may not be so simply describable but seems likely to be equally severe.

It is possible that the assumptions of the information measure can be met, at least approximately, by a test with items of equivalent discriminatory power dispersed uniformly across an ability range that is not too broad. In this case the slope of score on ability will be approximately constant and it will be sufficient to take as the information measure the inverse of the conditional variance $V(x/\theta)$. It is not known just what effect violation of the assumptions will have on the Birnbaum information measure. The measure should be used cautiously or not at all until this matter has been investigated.

Lord (65) considers the Birnbaum relative efficiency index defined as: $RE(x, y) = I(\theta, x)/I(\theta, y)$ and shows that by rescaling θ to true score values for x and then for y, $RE(x, y)$ is equal to the ratio of the variance of obtained scores on the two tests for fixed corresponding true scores multiplied by a scaling factor which varies with θ, the attribute value. Thus Lord very cleverly makes the slopes constant at unity but pays for this with the variable scaling factor. The scaling factor requires the computation of the density functions of the distribution of true scores for the two tests and the formation of the ratio of the ordinates at corresponding (equipercentile) points. Lord finds good agreement with relative efficiencies computed by the Birnbaum method and at a considerable saving of computer time. Granted the shaky Birnbaum foundation, the Lord derivation is a mathematical tour de force, but one wonders whether the scaling factor ratios will always be as well behaved as they appear to have been in the study. With tests of unequal difficulty, for example, a small change in true score for one test may correspond to a large change in true score for another and the ratio of the ordinates may be unstable.

It is a little puzzling that test theorists have neglected the other regression line, the regression of ability on score. If the scatter diagram can be formed, it would be simple and very informative to examine the variance of ability for particular values of the score. An information measure based on the inverse of the conditional variance would seem to do everything useful that the Birnbaum measure does and to require no elaborate justification. The required scatter diagram can be computed from the conditional variance of score on ability if we are willing to make an assumption about the distribution of ability. This would be mild compared with the assumptions of the Birnbaum argument and, in any case, could always be perfectly met with the artificial data so frequently used for scaling studies. A statistic of this type would have many advantages over the reliability statistics currently misused. In the first place, the statistic is attribute based and gives a direct answer to an important question: how well does the test score represent the attribute? In the second place, it will often vary with score and be known to vary. Finally, it is not a regression coefficient and test theorists will be less likely to attempt foolish things with it. The measure will be affected not only by noise (item flog) but also by item difficulty dispersion. For most practical purposes it will be unnecessary to attempt to separate the components (Ross & Lumsden 80).

I can find only three propositions about reliability worth remembering by test users or constructors:

1. Test scores are unreliable.

2. All other things being equal (item type, dispersion of item difficulties, item correlations) and up to a certain point a longer test is better than a shorter test. By "better" it is meant that the test score represents the attribute more accurately. The "certain point" is a function of subject fatigue or boredom.

3. All other things being equal (item type, dispersion of item difficulties, test length) and up to a certain point a test with higher item intercorrelations is better than a test with lower item intercorrelations. The certain point is reached when the item intercorrelations become high enough for the attenuation paradox to occur. The attenuation paradox will not occur if the item difficulties are adequately dispersed.

It should be noted that these propositions do not relate only to problems of reliability and that all can be derived from a contemplation of the flogging wall test without using the concept of true score. Yule's evil suggestion has yielded a meager fruit and has devoured the energy and skill of some of the finest minds in psychology. It is tempting to believe that this is an illustration of the Nimzovitch dictum: "When there is no good move a botch will come along to fill the breach." But there has always been a better move, and wise test users—some of them, curiously, Model T buffs—have often played it. Thus they have chosen tests in terms of their superior validity. They have advocated the use of expectancy tables (e.g. 1, 18) and have derived their expectations and confidence limit information directly from these rather than indirectly and uncertainly from reliability theory statistics.

The conclusion is obvious but I will state it anyway. Reliability theory in its present form should be abandoned. To echo Bock & Wood (7), there seems no point in further prolonging the lives of the true score or the reliability coefficient, classically defined, as concepts in test theory. The problems of reliability should be assimilated into validity and scaling theory where they have already been partly solved. Nothing in this recommendation should be taken as advising students of practice, transfer, or training effects on test scores against calculating test-retest or between form coefficients. These coefficients should not, in my opinion, be called reliability coefficients, but if they are, care should be taken that they are not confused with reliability coefficients as classically defined.

> Macbeth: "............. this is a tale
> Told by an idiot, full of sound and fury,
> Signifying nothing."

Unidimensionality

The topic of unidimensionality continues to be neglected. Most of the articles considered in the section on test scores pay lip service to the notion, usually in the form of a bland statement about the assumption of local independence, a single latent trait or the like. Nowhere in the period under review is there any evidence of a serious attempt to construct a unidimensional test, and there is only one attempt (38) to suitably test an assumption of unidimensionality. Yet it is clear that most of test theory, not merely esoteric scaling procedures, depends vitally on the assumption. A simple example is the much admired KR_{20} which may be a gross underestimate of reliability unless the test is unidimensional.

The importance of unidimensionality does not depend only on its function as a quasi-mathematical assumption for reliability and scaling theory. The whole conception of psychological testing as measurement depends on it. This has never been more clearly put than in an early, and much neglected, paper by McNemar (71, p. 268):

> Measurement implies that one characteristic at a time is being quantified. The scores on an attitude scale are most meaningful when it is known that only one continuum is involved. Only then can it be claimed that two individuals with the same score or rank can be quantitatively and, within limits, qualitatively similar in their attitude towards a given issue. As an example suppose a test of liberalism consists of two general sorts of items, one concerned with economic and the other with religious issues. Two individuals could thus arrive at the same numerical score by quite different routes. Now it may be true that economic and religious liberalism are correlated but unless highly correlated the meaning of scores based on such a composite is questionable.

Jones (43) makes it clear that measurement is always of an attribute or property of an object or event. He goes on to state that: "no attribute can be observed unless man has arrived at some concept of it" (p. 337). We may paraphrase this as: *the beginning of measurement is the conception of the measurable attribute.* How can we make any claims to measure if our measuring instrument has a number of different sorts of items based presumably on different attribute conceptions? Jones (pp. 350–57) makes clear his support for the use of unidimensional tests in a statement that echoes (with some irritating imprecisions) McNemar's.

Foolish things continue to be said about unidimensionality by people who should know better. Thus Guttman (36) asserts that unidimensional scales should be discovered not constructed, and that item culling procedures to obtain a unidimensional set are illegitimate, representing an unworthy capitalization on chance and item diversity. Guttman is right only if the test constructor fails to repeat his work with other samples and if he fails to write a specification for the items and to test that by constructing new items that fit the specifications. Item culling procedures will always be necessary because any specification is likely to be incomplete and because of human imperfections in carrying out the specifications. Suppose that a set of 20 items was constructed and that 19 of them were perfectly scalable and the other was a maverick. Most test constructors would arrange a stealthy murder of the culprit and burn all the records of its birth. What would you do, Professor Guttman? Cronbach (18), in an otherwise excellent paper on validity, asserts that a test constructor should not attempt to maximize item intercorrelations because this may mean that important criterion relevant items will be omitted. Cronbach et al (20) make the same point when they suggest that narrowing of the universe may lead to a reduction of validity. But nowhere have the advocates of unidimensionality suggested that only one unidimensional test should be constructed in a given area or for a particular purpose.

There seems to be, despite Jones' remarks, a popular belief that the construction of unidimensional tests is difficult. Hambleton & Traub (38) assert that construction of a unidimensional test is very difficult and that the factor analytic procedure is dubious because of difficulty factors. With modern computers there should be no problem. The factor analytic procedure (27, 68) usually converges rapidly if the items are constructed according to a strict specification. Lumsden (Unpublished Masters thesis, University of Western Australia, 1959) found that with four number series tests item rejections were few and with one test a Guttman coup was achieved, all items being retained. Normally it should not be necessary to use tetrachorics. McDonald & Ahlawat (70) have shown that difficulty factors will not arise with phi-coefficients if regression is linear and that generally difficulty factors will be negligible unless item difficulties are widely different or the item discriminatory power is high. For these latter cases it usually should be sufficient to carry out what may be termed cascade analysis. Thus we could divide the items into three difficulty levels and analyze each level in turn, starting with the easiest and passing the more difficult selected items from each analysis into the analysis for the next level.

It is possible that the worry about the difficulty of constructing unidimensional tests arises from a confusion between unidimensionality and theoretical singularity. A unidimensional test does have a single attribute but the attribute is complex. Consider the following sample item:

$$1 \quad 2 \quad 4 \quad 7 \quad 11 \quad \text{..} \quad \text{..}$$

A test with items of this sort is unidimensional and maps the ability of the subject to do items like that (see the validity section for a specification of these items). The ability is complex, involving number and reasoning abilities and probably others as well. It does not reflect a single theoretical attribute or construct in the Cronbach & Meehl (21) terminology. It may be thought of as a compound with constructs as elements. The construction of theoretically singular tests is probably impossible (69).

Special problems in constructing unidimensional tests are likely to be encountered in the personality domain. Vernon (97), in a very early paper which may have been the first to use the term "unidimensional," pointed out that it is usually not feasible to ask the same question many times. This has not deterred all test constructors. Jackson (39) discusses his attempts to produce unidimensional tests of personality by maximizing item-test correlations. He employs an additional constraint that social desirability correlations should be low for each item. The method is not the most effective and in most of the cases reported does not appear to have succeeded very well. Neill & Jackson (74) examine different item selection techniques in the development of an Evaluation Sensitivity test. They found that different methods of selecting items produced tests with about the same K-R$_{20}$ values (n = 40 KR$_{20}$ = 93). The method of forming the item pool from a detailed specification is admirable, but the item culling procedures are not as effective as the residual minimization procedure (68).

Kirkham (University of Western Australia, personal communication) made the interesting observation that groups of second year university students were remarkably accurate at estimating the relative difficulty of items from a unidimensional number series test. Both paired comparison and magnitude estimates were used, and the correlations of judged difficulty with proportion passing for a large sample of children were of the order of 0.9. This finding is important because it could lead to a useful saving of time in item tryouts.

Validity

Most test theorists have fled from the field of validity, apparently considering that it is adequately handled by regression procedures or that it is too difficult for simple model makers. On the first consideration they are partly, and on the second wholly, justified. Validity theory has been kept alive by the efforts of Cronbach and various associates.

Cronbach's (18) chapter gives a comprehensive statement of what has been achieved in validity theory. The concentration throughout is on validation as a process of coming to some understanding of the meaning of test scores for various applications of the test procedure. All the standard approaches to validation and the relationships between them are discussed and illustrated. There is a great deal of practical wisdom in the chapter, no doubt derived from Cronbach's concern with problems of using tests in educational settings. I could find only two flaws worth remarking. His advice on test construction should not be accepted blindly. His treatment of his own work on utility interpretations of validity is trenchantly brief and quite unsatisfactory.

Cronbach & Gleser (19) performed a great service in incorporating predictive validity into the general area of decision processes and in emphasizing the benefits to be derived from sequential procedures. The book is not the easiest to read, and it is good that simpler but adequate descriptions of the approach are beginning to be incorporated in textbooks (100). It is curious that no chapter in Thorndike's edition of *Educational Measurement* (87) makes more than a glancing reference to sequential procedures. Test users should not be too much dismayed by the formidable problems of estimating utilities. It is true that absolute utilities are usually difficult and sometimes impossible to estimate. Relative utilities are usually much simpler to estimate and are adequate to support rational choice of procedures.

Test publishers could assist greatly in the application of the Cronbach & Gleser procedures by including suggestions for sequential strategies in their manuals. It would also be helpful if they would adopt suggestions (e.g. 1, 18) to provide validity evidence in the form of scatter diagrams (expectancy tables) rather than via the usual correlation coefficients. Inferences concerning the effect, for example, of changing cutting points can be made more directly and more quickly than by the use of Taylor-Russell tables or the like. Where validity data are available for only a relatively small sample, as is often the case for quite legitimate reasons, a theoretical expectancy table should be constructed from the correlation coefficient and the usual assumptions. But the generating scatter diagram should be given too so that the test user can add his cases as they arise, eventually correcting any errors in the original estimate. This procedure has the additional merit of allowing for any local variations in the testing or criterion estimation situation.

An interesting approach to the solution of the Cronbach & Gleser equations for the two-stage selection process is given by Rock, Barone & Boldt (76). They ignore costs and propose that the number of applicants undergoing second stage testing should be proportional to the ratio of the squared part correlation of the second stage test with the criterion to the squared zero order correlation of the first stage with the criterion. They justify this with the argument that if the second stage contributes nothing additional to the first stage, then nobody should do it. This is unexceptionable, but they go on to argue that if the second stage adds as much (or more) as the contribution of the first stage, then everyone should do the second stage. But in this case it would normally mean that the second stage would have a higher zero order correlation with the criterion than the first stage. Then surely the test of the second stage should be given first; and it would be unless the first stage test was very much cheaper than the second stage test. But this would mean that fewer subjects should be given the second stage test. It seems that no rational solution to the Cronbach & Gleser problem can be obtained without taking some account of costs.

Sequential testing, where after each item a decision is made to accept, reject, or continue testing, was examined by Linn, Rock & Cleary (50). They compared sequential and conventional short tests on accuracy of assignment to high and low groups on full College Board College Level Examination Program tests. They found that sequential tests required only about half the number of items as conventional tests for the same accuracy of classification.

A comparison of predictor selection techniques using Monte Carlo methods was provided by Rock et al (77). They found, not unexpectedly, that criterion-dependent methods were superior to criterion-independent methods. They also found that forward selection methods were superior to backward elimination methods. Campbell & Ignizio (12) used linear programming methods for predicting student performance and found the prediction less biased for extreme cases than the least squares procedure. Jackson & Novick (41) examined the problem of optimizing the time allocation between various battery components in order to maximize battery validity with a fixed total testing time. They worked out an example but provided no test of the efficacy of the procedure.

Two papers (13, 14) discuss the problems of suppressor variables and conclude that the search for suppressor variables probably had better be suppressed. There is usually more to be gained from finding a predictor for unaccounted criterion variance than in attempting to suppress irrelevant predictor variance. Conger considers the charming possibility of mutual suppression where two variables each have positive correlations with the criterion and negative correlations with each other. Such pairs are likely to be as rare as unicorns.

A number of papers consider the multi-trait multi-method approach of Campbell & Fiske (11), a procedure that is an elaboration of congruent validity. There are considerable practical and theoretical problems in its application. It places great strain on the art of the test constructor to produce tests of the same trait with different methods. The problems are analogous to those of parallel form reliability where a test is held to be reliable only if it has an identical twin. The multi-trait multi-method procedure seems to require that a test have an identical twin of the opposite sex. Krause (45) points out that convergent confirmations may simply reflect unconscious bias in test construction by the inclusion of some common sources of variance not related to the trait in question or to the method. Similarly discriminant confirmations may represent a failure of test construction rather than trait divergence. There are problems of additivity of method and trait variance, and with factor analytic procedures the possibility of correlation between content and method factors must be considered (8, 9). Fair agreement was found in two cases between analysis of variance, factor analytic, and inspectional procedures. It is clear that the multi-trait multi-method approach should not be employed mechanically. The production of 9 X 9 matrices with little thought given to the selection of traits and methods should cease. It seems likely, however, that where great care has been given to test construction, where much is known a priori about traits, methods, and the relationship between them, the validation procedure will more and more resemble construct validation and the explicit setting up of the multi-trait multi-method matrix will be rare. It is clear that the method is not worth using badly. Is it worth the trouble of using it well?

Lumsden & Ross (69) examine the construct validation program of Cronbach & Meehl (21). They argue that the program requires: (*a*) test unidimensionality and theoretical singularity, (*b*) operational criteria for all the theoretical terms used to describe tests, and (*c*) multiple theoretical linkages for the terms. They point out that individual difference measures based on performance are intractably complex and that theories of individual differences are not sufficiently developed to meet the third requirement. Construct validation of tests is, therefore, impossible. It is possible that a refutation of this argument, or a way out of the difficulties, will be discovered. It does seem very unlikely, however, that in any foreseeable time psychology will be able to construct and validate the equivalent of 100 or more thermometers.

A lower keyed approach to the validity problem seems necessary. One possibility is via an extension of some content validity notions. The suggested procedure is not my creation. For reasons of delicacy I withhold the mother's name, but possible fathers of the idea are Ebel, Guttman, Guilford, and Cronbach. We begin by constructing a unidimensional test of, say, 20 items. We characterize the test by saying that it measures the ability to do items *like that,* pointing to any item of the set. Notice that it is impossible to do this with a heterogeneous test since no single item can be considered as characteristic of the set. We now attempt to write specification sentences for the item set. Suppose that the items in the set are all number series where the subject is required to write the next two numbers in the series and that they are all of this type:

$$1 \quad 2 \quad 4 \quad 7 \quad 11 \quad \cdot\cdot \quad \cdot\cdot$$

The specification sentences for the items might be as follows:
1. They are increasing number series.
2. The differences are in increasing A.P.
3. The first difference is greater than zero.
4. The numbers in the series are all positive integers less than 100.

Suppose that we now write many items from the specifications and find that they all meet the unidimensionality criterion with the original set. We now have confidence that we know what we are doing and can make judgments about set membership without empirical evidence. In the language of automata theory (Rogers 78), the original set was *recursively enumerable* but is now also *recursive*. If counterexamples occur during the testing of the items generated from the specifications, then the specifications will be altered. Of course our confidence in the specifications can never be absolutely complete since there remains always the possibility of a counterexample appearing. It is a species of theory confirmation: a hundred or even a thousand confirmations cannot produce logical certainty, but most of us will proceed as if it did.

So far this is simply content analysis carried out rather carefully under conditions which permit confirmation or disconfirmation of the specifications. Suppose we now ask the questions: are the specifications too stringent? Are there other types of items which belong in the set? We can treat each specification in turn as a facet for possible variation. Will letter series (with appropriate variations to specifications 2 and 4) be found to belong in the set? Will decreasing number series (i.e. reversals of original items) belong in the set? If the answer is yes to any of these questions, then the specification can be broadened. If the answer is no, then the next question is: do the new set of items themselves form a unidimensional set? If not can a sizable group of items which meet a unidimensionality criterion be found in the set? Proceeding in this fashion it seems likely that a well-constructed test will frequently give rise to a family of tests differing only in one or two clearly described facets. We can now look at the intercorrelations between tests in the family and even more importantly at the correlations with exterior measures. From these results and with a mode of thinking characteristic of factor analysts we may come to some understanding of the meaning in ability terms of the facets and the exterior measures.

The approach is low keyed and does not pretend to meet the challenge posed by Cronbach & Meehl. It does seem appropriate for factor analysts who wish to have some basis for factor naming and in any event provides some guide for test constructors. The method seems far superior to the much trouble much muddle procedures currently in vogue.

Test Scoring

Test scoring or scaling is a topic close to the heart of the problems of test theory. How can we best use the information given us by the item performances of our subjects? How well do the test scores represent the attribute? These are central questions for test theory. It is pleasing to be able to note that test scaling and related problems have been the subject of some of the most energetic work of the period. There are a number of interesting papers; none are inspired but some are elegant and a few even suggest procedures that may be usable. Most of the papers on scaling use forms of the relatively well developed logistic models. This is, I believe, wise. Unfortunately, all papers which do not rely on simulated data continue a scaling tradition of using inappropriate test material. If the model requres a unidimensional test, then a unidimensional test, or a near facsimile of one, should be found or constructed. It is useless, and bad publicity, to run a Cadillac scaling method on paraffin item sets.

Most studies using real data make no serious attempt to evaluate the worth of the suggested procedures. What can it mean to say that one scaling method is better than another? The only answer that makes any sense is to say that it means that one method gives a more accurate representation of the attribute values than the other. If this is the case, then the better method will have higher correlations with any criterion for which the attribute is relevant. This test is sure fire and should be completely convincing to a potential user of the method. The correlation test should be carried out routinely, pitting the new procedure against alternatives, one of which should always be that old trouper the normalized standard score. The test has been used many times (83, 98), particularly in the 1920–1940 period, and the results have usually shown that differential weighting of item scores made no appreciable difference to either the reliability or the validity of the test. I have found no instance of the use of this test on real data during the review period. Why?

Goodness-of-fit procedures have been employed (6, 38) and several writers (5, 37, 59–62, 65) have used forms of the Birnbaum information measure whose possible deficiencies have already been noted. But even if the procedures were not objectionable, they can never be as convincing or as direct as the correlation test, particularly when plausible alternatives are not considered. And in any case the test user is left wondering what it all means. Should he spend his dollars on fancy scoring or on more testing? Users of goodness-of-fit tests should ponder Torgerson's (91) discussion of the trading relation between assumptions which sometimes yield good fits when the assumptions have been clearly violated. It is worthy of note, and to his honor, that Rasch (75) was concerned when the fit was too good.

Lord (58) attempts a direct confrontation of the Birnbaum logistic model by attempting to estimate the form of the item characteristic curve by plotting proportion passing against true score. He finds excellent agreement between item characteristic curves for SAT verbal items obtained by this method and those obtained by Lord (57), under the assumption that all were three parameter logistic curves. Lord finds these results impressive. So they are—but not for the reasons given by Lord. In support of his procedure, Lord (58, p. 42) presents the following argument: "Now the true score on a test and the latent trait measured by the test are precisely the same thing, except for a possible monotonic transformation of the scale of measurement. Thus the regression of item score on true score is a characteristic curve of the item."

This argument is absurd in two ways. Recall that the true scores have to be estimated—only the Devil has access to the book in which the expectations are recorded. If *estimated* true score is a monotonic transformation of the latent trait, then so is the obtained score. Lord could have saved himself a lot of trouble by simply plotting proportion passing against normalized obtained score. Ross (79) did exactly this and found excellent fit for the logistic. Secondly, Lord is mistaken in thinking that monotonic transformations, even if strictly increasing, make no difference to the form of the item characteristic curve. Try this simple experiment. Draw two normal ogive item characteristic curves with different location values but the same slope. Now apply some monotonic transformations to the score scale. You will find that the shapes of the curves will differ a great deal from the originals. They will also often differ from each other.

A maximum likelihood solution for the normal ogive model is supplied by Bock & Lieberman (6). They find a good fit between theoretical and empirical score distributions for one section of the Law School Admission Test and a not-so-good fit for another. They suggest that the difference may be the result of the greater heterogeneity of items in the second section. They note that proportion passing and item test correlations give excellent estimates of the maximum likelihood solutions for location and slope parameters. Urry (96) gives a graphical procedure for estimating item parameters. Jensema (42) found, for the three-parameter logistic model, a high correlation between the Urry graphical estimates and maximum likelihood estimates, and suggests that with further development the expensive maximum likelihood process may no longer be needed.

The one-parameter Rasch model is compared with two- and three-parameter logistic models by Hambleton & Traub (37). Using simulated data generated by a three-parameter model, they compare the three models using information curves and relative efficiency estimates. Not unexpectedly they find the three-parameter model best when guessing is a factor but only at the lower levels of ability. Where guessing is unimportant and the range of slope parameters is not great the Rasch model is quite efficient. Hambleton & Traub fail to emphasize one of their most important findings. The Rasch one-parameter model is remarkably efficient except at the very lowest ability level when guessing was important ($C = 0.20$) or when the range of slope parameters (0.19–0.99) was far beyond that conceivably tolerable in a test alleged to be of a single trait. In the Rasch model the simple number right score is a sufficient statistic for estimating the attribute, so there is still a lot of life left in unit weight scoring.

Hambleton & Traub (38) proceed with a comparison of one- and two-parameter logistic models using data from the SAT Mathematics and Verbal Test. This study would be a model of what not to do except that some others are worse. Remarkably, they do a sensible test of undimensionality by factorizing the items. The test fails; more than one factor is required to account for the item intercorrelations. But they proceed anyway! They use fit between theoretical and empirical score distributions as the criterion and find that the two-parameter model does somewhat better than the one-parameter Rasch model. The difference is greater with the shorter test, which is consistent with Birnbaum's (4) observation that with long tests weighting items makes little difference.

Bock (5) points out that in multiple choice items some wrong answers are better than others. He outlines a very elegant maximum likelihood procedure for weighting the various responses whether right or wrong to obtain an estimate of ability. The computational problems are very formidable for any large number of items. Bock, using a 20-item vocabulary test, compares the procedure with a procedure using dichotomous scoring and finds a moderate increase in information as measured by the Birnbaum index. No external criterion is used and no comparison is made with the Guttman (33) suggestion that the response options be weighted by the criterion scores of subjects giving a particular option. Dalrymple-Alford (25) tackles the problem of wrong answers in multiple choice tests by requiring the subject to continue giving answers until he is correct. He then calculates an average uncertainty measure for each subject. A useful way of collecting the data for this would be to require the subject to order the options in terms of his preference for them as answers. This procedure is simpler and quicker than the De Finetti (26) procedure of asking the subject to assign probabilities of correctness to the option. It would be interesting if, for example, on an easy item best discrimination was given by the second rather than the first choice.

Lord (64) considers the nasty problem of omitted responses and suggests a method which assumes that if subjects were obliged to respond to omitted items, they would choose randomly. This assumption is probably incorrect but must be closer to reality than the usual assumption that the subject would always choose wrongly. Bock (5), in the paper discussed above, simply treats "no response" as another option. There is a problem here in that "no response" is often given a higher weight than some of the incorrect options. If this became known after the test was published, the proportion of omissions might increase and the weights require drastic modification.

Angoff (1) gives a very clear account of the various types of derived scores and norms commonly used in education. His nonmathematical description of the item characteristic curve approach to scaling is very lucid but unwontedly brief. He goes on to a technical consideration of methods of establishing norms and equating scores. Angoff (1, p. 522) resurrects an old notion of Thurstone's (89) and suggests that mental age norms could just as logically be developed by finding the mean age of children who get a certain score, i.e. by using the age on score regression line rather than the score on age regression line. This is incorrect. The age on score regression line is the appropriate one if we wish to estimate a subject's chronological age from his score. But we already know his chronological age. The Angoff suggestion could lead to the situation where a 10-year-old boy who had the average score for his age could be described as bright or dull (67). Cooley (15) looks at techniques for considering multiple measurements. He points out difficulties involved in staring at the parallel stalks of the usual profiles and then goes on to discuss with admirable clarity and a simple example the trait-space model. He illustrates the use of centours, a chi square test for profile conformity, discriminant analysis, multiple regression, and canonical correlation. There is a problem with profiles that is not considered by Cooley and is not completely solved by the centour approach. The problem is that the profile of averages for chemists may not represent the average chemist or indeed any chemist. There is an exactly parallel problem in the determination of learning curves. For this Tucker (94, 95) developed the Eckhart-Young procedure which analyzes the results into families of learning curves, each characteristic of some learners but not others. There seems no reason why this approach could not be applied to profiles.

There are a number of important papers on tailored testing. Lord (59–62) considers the problem first as a computer application and then, with an eye to practicality, ways of approximating tailored testing with paper and pencil tests. Lord (61) points out that shrinking step size procedures are impracticable because they require an impossibly large number of items even for modest test length. Fixed step size up and down procedures are about as good as the shrinking step size procedure Hybrid procedures which begin with a few large steps and then continue with small fixed steps appear an attractive compromise, analogous to artillery ranging, but in the Lord simulation were no more effective than simple fixed step size. It should be noted that in these studies Lord assumed a rather low value for the slope parameter (Ag = 0.5) and that some of his conclusions may need to be amended with more discriminating items. Lord (59) considers two-stage testing and concludes that with no guessing two-stage procedures may be about as effective for all but extreme ability levels as the best up and down technique. With guessing possible 20% of the time, up and down procedures were clearly superior. Again Lord only considers peaked tests with rather low item slope parameters. The flexilevel test (62) is another attempt to provide tailored testing with paper and pencil presentation. In flexilevel tests the subject knows whether he was correct or not on each item. Subject answers first an item of median difficulty. If correct he moves to the easiest item of above median difficulty; if incorrect he moves to the hardest item of below median difficulty. The examinee attempts only $(N+1)/2$ items in the set, which has a rectangular distribution of item difficulty, and it turns out that even though examinees do different items of different difficulties, the number right score is an excellent estimate of ability. Using a form of information measure, Lord found that near the middle of the range for which the test was designed a flexilevel test is slightly less effective than a conventional peaked test. At other points in the ability range the flexilevel test was better. It should be noted that the flexilevel test is after a point an increasing step size up and down procedure and should be inferior to other types of tailored tests. All of the work described above was done with computer simulated data, and Lord was able to test a very large variety of tailored procedures. He points out that his own feet-on-the-desk intuitions about suitable procedures were often shown to be wrong. Lord's results in this series of studies should be accepted only tentatively since they depend on a possibly inappropriate information measure.

Waters & Bayroff (99) compared various fixed step size up-down procedures with conventional tests either peaked or with normal or rectangular distributions of difficulty. All tests were computer simulated, and the criterion was the correlation between score and ability. It was found that a peaked conventional test was best at low item biserials ($r_{it} = 0.30$) but various branching tests did better, but not much better, when item biserials were higher. Jensema (42), using computer simulation and some real data where tailoring was simulated by selection of results, examined Bayesian procedures for estimating ability. He suggests that tailoring is likely to be most beneficial when the item discriminating power is fairly high (Ag > 0.8). He found that the use of prior information did not lead to a substantial reduction in the number of items required for a given precision or increase in the correlation between estimated ability and true ability. There is some gain from the prior information when the correlation between prior estimate and ability equals 0.9. With a prior like that the posterior can be given the boot. Test something else instead.

With some trepidation, considering Lord's experience, I suggest that a useful two-stage procedure would be to give a short test with items peaked at 0.25 and 0.75 difficulty levels for the population concerned. On the basis of the pretest assign subjects to three groups to do different tests with items distributed uniformly in difficulty: (a) from 0.99 to 0.50, (b) from 0.75 to 0.25, and (c) from 0.50 to 0.01. This procedure with item slopes greater than 1.0 should give excellent discrimination across the range and permit, if required, the formation of the person characteristic curve. It is probable, however, that it will prove more useful in practice to assimilate tailored testing into the sequential procedures discussed in the validity section (Green 30). Thus on the basis of a relatively short test, accept or reject decisions can be made for some of the subjects and the remainder can then be tested adequately by a test with items in the range 0.75–0.25 or even by a peaked test.

It is necessary to reconsider the whole approach to test scoring problems. The item characteristic curve approaches and various estimation procedures are reasonably well developed, and problems with the information measures probably will be solved fairly soon. Yet nothing much seems to be happening except that those obedient monsters, the computers, are now doing almost as many tests as the disobedient ones. There is need for a more rational and more determined approach to item writing and item selection. The construction of unidimensional tests seems possible in many areas, and it is likely that high values of the slope parameter may often be obtainable (Ross 79). This would make tailored and sequential testing more attractive. It would make conventional testing with dispersed item difficulties very attractive too because there will be no need to use tests of more than 15–20 items. It is important that test theorists should attempt to help themselves here. The tacit acceptance, amounting at times to advocacy, of poor tests should cease. It is preposterous that test scaling should be the only branch of experimental psychology where the experimenter does not set up the apparatus and does not care how his data are collected.

CONCLUSION

The picture revealed is grim. Little of any consequence has been achieved during the review period; nor can we look with any great pride at the cumulative result for this century. It is only slightly unfair to say that test theory has failed as theory. In most areas it does not act as a set of propositions which generates testable propositions in the content area of interest. It fails in the minimal demand which can be made of a theory: that it act as an aide memoire. We have seen that reliability theory has been dominated by an inappropriate and unfruitful model. Other aspects of test theory have been generally little developed and rarely applied. This is partly because the problems are difficult and partly because of the obsession of test theorists with reliability theory.

The popular view is tha. test theorists sit in corners playing with their t's and e's and minding their p's and q's. It is further believed that they speak seldom, except to each other, and that what they have to say has no or little practical application. The popular view is substantially correct, but I hope that it will not continue to be so. We must change. We need a new kind of test theorist. The new test theorists (happily, some of the old transformed) will be primarily test constructors and validity people who attempt to realize their dreams. They will not accept the current state of the art in testing as the datum but will try to elevate the art. They will not test a new model with a few items from the SAT files (or from a computer), find a mediocre fit to some dubiously relevant criterion, and then go on to the next. Rather they will set out the requirements for the application of the model and sweat to meet those requirements, testing the model against a user-for-blood standard of efficiency. They will not seek salvation in the epicene elegance of elevated algebras but will prefer vulgar analogies. They will not behave like British gentlemen, as if they had been trained not to notice unpleasant things and never to mention them if they do. They will criticize one another incessantly, zestfully, and, I hope, gleefully. But who will train them?

And so let me end it. "I have supped my fill of horrors."

Literature Cited

1. Angoff, W. H. 1971. Scales, norms and equivalent scores. See Ref. 87, 508–600
2. Bay, K. S. 1973. The effect of non-normality on the sampling distribution and standard error of reliability coefficient estimates under an analysis of variance model. *Br. J. Math. Statist. Psychol.* 26:45–57
3. Birnbaum, A. 1957. Efficient design and use of tests of mental ability for various decision making problems. *Sch. Aviat. Med. USAF Rep. No. 58*
4. Birnbaum, A. 1968. Some latent trait models and their use in inferring an examinee's ability. See Ref. 66, 397–472
5. Bock, R. D. 1972. Estimating item parameters and latent ability when responses are scored in two or more nominal categories. *Psychometrika* 37:39–51
6. Bock, R. D., Lieberman, M. 1970. Fitting a response model for *n* dichotomously scored items. *Psychometrika* 35:179–97
7. Bock, R. D., Wood, R. 1971. Test theory. *Ann. Rev. Psychol.* 22:193–224
8. Boruch, R. F., Larkin, J. D., Wolins, L., MacKinney, A. C. 1970. Alternative methods of analysis: multi-trait multi-method data. *Educ. Psychol. Meas.* 30:833–55
9. Boruch, R. F., Wolins, L. 1970. A procedure for estimation of trait, method and error variance attributable to a measure. *Educ. Psychol. Meas.* 30: 547–74
10. Brogden, H. 1946. Variation in test validity with variation in the distribution of item difficulties, number of items and degree of their intercorrelations. *Psychometrika* 11:197–214
11. Campbell, D. T., Fiske, D. W. 1959. Convergent and discriminant validation by the multi-trait multi-method matrix. *Psychol. Bull.* 56:81–105
12. Campbell, H. G., Ignizio, J. P. 1972. Using linear programming for predicting student performance. *Educ. Psychol. Meas.* 32:397–401
13. Conger, A. J. 1974. A revised definition of suppressed variables: a guide to their identification and interpretation. *Educ. Psychol. Meas.* 34:35–46
14. Conger, A. J., Jackson, D. N. 1972. Suppressor variables, prediction and the interpretation of psychological relationships. *Educ. Psychol. Meas.* 32:579–99
15. Cooley, W. W. 1971. Techniques for considering multiple measurements. See Ref. 87, 601–22
16. Coombs, C. H. 1952. A theory of psychological scaling. *Eng. Res. Bull. No. 34.* Ann Arbor: Univ. Michigan Press
17. Cronbach, L. J. 1970. *Essentials of Psychological Testing.* New York: Harper & Row. 3rd ed.

18. Cronbach, L. J. 1971. Test validation. See Ref. 87, 443–507
19. Cronbach, L. J., Gleser, G. C. 1965. *Psychological Tests and Personnel Decisions.* Urbana: Univ. Illinois Press. 2nd ed.
20. Cronbach, L. J., Gleser, G. C., Nanda, H., Rajaratnam, N. 1972. *The Dependability of Behavioral Measurements: Theory of Generalizability for Scores and Profiles.* New York: Wiley
21. Cronbach, L. J., Meehl, P. E. 1955. Construct validity in psychological tests. *Psychol. Bull.* 52:281–302
22. Cureton, E. E. 1950. Validity, reliability and baloney. *Educ. Psychol. Meas.* 10:94–96
23. Ibid 1971. The stability coefficient. 31:45–53
24. Cureton, E. E. et al 1973. Length of test and standard error of measurement. *Educ. Psychol. Meas.* 33:63–68
25. Dalrymple-Alford, E. C. 1970. A model for assessing multiple-choice test performance. *Br. J. Math. Statist. Psychol.* 23:199–203
26. De Finetti, B. 1965. Methods for discriminating levels of partial knowledge concerning a test item. *Br. J. Math. Statist. Psychol.* 18:87–123
27. Du Bois, P. H. 1970. Varieties of psychological test homogeneity. *Am. Psychol.* 25:532–36
28. Ebel, R. H. 1972. Why a longer test is usually a more reliable test. *Educ. Psychol. Meas.* 32:249–53
29. Furneaux, W. D. 1956. *Nufferno Tests of Speed and Level.* Nat. Found. Educ. Res.
30. Green, B. F. 1970. Comments on tailored testing. In *Computer-assisted Instruction, Testing, and Guidance,* ed. W. H. Holtzman. New York: Harper & Row
31. Guilford, J. P. 1954. *Psychometric Methods.* New York: McGraw-Hill. 2nd ed.
32. Gulliksen, H. 1950. *Theory of Mental Tests.* New York: Wiley
33. Guttman, L. 1941. The quantification of a class of attributes: a theory and method of scale construction. In *The Prediction of Personal Adjustment,* ed. P. Horst. New York: Soc. Sci. Res. Counc.
34. Guttman, L. 1944. A basis for scaling qualitative data. *Am. Sociol. Rev.* 9:139–50
35. Guttman, L. 1953. A special review of Harold Gulliksen's *Theory of Mental Tests. Psychometrika* 18:123–30
36. Ibid 1971. Measurement as structural theory. 36:329–47
37. Hambleton, R. K., Traub, R. E. 1971. Information curves and efficiency of three logistic test models *Br. J. Math. Statist. Psychol.* 24:273–81
38. Ibid 1973. Analysis of empirical data using two logistic latent trait models. 26:195–211
39. Jackson, D. N. 1971. The dynamics of structured personality tests. *Psychol. Rev.* 78:229–48
40. Jackson, P. H. 1973. The estimation of the true score variance and error variance in the classical test theory model. *Psychometrika* 38:183–201
41. Jackson, P. H., Novick, M. R. 1970. Maximizing the validity of a unit weight composite as a function of relative component length with a fixed total testing time. *Psychometrika* 35:333–47
42. Jensema, C. J. 1974. An application of latent trait mental test theory. *Br. J. Math. Statist. Psychol.* 27:29–48
43. Jones, L. V. 1971. The nature of measurement. See Ref. 87, 335–55
44. Joreskog, K. G. 1971. Statistical analysis of sets of congeneric tests. *Psychometrika* 36:109–33
45. Krause, M. S. 1972. The implications of convergent and discriminant validity data for instrument validation. *Psychometrika* 37:179–86
46. Kristoff, W. 1970. On the sampling theory of reliability estimates. *J. Math. Psychol.* 7:371–77
47. Kristoff, W. 1971. On the theory of a set of tests which differ only in length. *Psychometrika* 36:207–25
48. Ibid 1974. On accuracy in reliability estimation. 39:23–29
49. Kuder, G. F., Richardson, M. W. 1937. The theory of the estimation of test reliability. *Psychometrika* 2:151–60
50. Linn, R. L., Rock, D. A., Cleary, T. A. 1972. Sequential testing for dichotomous decisions. *Educ. Psychol. Meas.* 32:85–95
51. Loevinger, J. 1948. The technic of homogeneous tests compared with some aspects of 'scale analysis' and factor analysis. *Psychol Bull.* 45:507–30
52. Ibid 1954. The attenuation paradox in test theory. 51:493–504
53. Lord, F. M. 1952. A theory of test scores. *Psychometric Mongr. No. 7*
54. Lord, F. M. 1953. An application of confidence intervals and of maximum likelihood to the estimation of an examinee's ability. *Psychometrika* 18:57–77

55. Lord, F. M. 1957. Do tests of the same length have the same standard errors of measurement? *Educ. Psychol. Meas.* 17:511–21

56. Ibid 1959. Tests of the same length do have the same standard errors of measurement 19:233–39

57. Ibid 1968. An analysis of the verbal scholastic aptitude test using Birnbaum's three parameter logistic model. 28:989–1020

58. Lord, F. M. 1970. Item characteristic curves as estimated without knowledge of their mathematical form–a confrontation of Birnbaum's logistical model. *Psychometrika* 35:43–50

59. Lord, F. M. 1970. Some test theory for tailored testing. See Ref. 30

60. Lord, F. M. 1971. A theoretical study of two stage testing. *Psychometrika* 36:227–42

61. Lord, F. M. 1971. Robbins-Monro procedures for tailored testing. *Educ. Psychol. Meas.* 31:5–31

62. Ibid. A theoretical study of the measurement effectiveness of flexilevel tests, 805–13

63. Ibid 1974. Significance test for a partial correlation corrected for attenuation. 34:211–20

64. Lord, F. M. 1974. Estimation of latent ability and item parameters when there are omitted responses. *Psychometrika* 39:247–64

65. Ibid. The relative efficiency of two tests as a function of ability level, 351–58

66. Lord, F. M., Novick, M. R. 1968. *Statistical Theories of Mental Test Scores.* Reading: Addison-Wesley

67. Lumsden, J. 1956. Classical and standard I.Q's. *The Educand* 3:38–42

68. Lumsden, J. 1961. The construction of unidimensional tests. *Psychol. Bull.* 58:122–31

69. Lumsden, J., Ross, J. 1973. Validity as theoretical equivalence. *Aust. J. Psychol.* 25:191–97

70. McDonald, R. P., Ahlawat, K. S. 1974. Difficulty factors in binary data. *Br. J. Math. Statist. Psychol.* 27:82–99

71. McNemar, Q. 1946. Opinion - attitude methodology. *Psychol. Bull.* 43:289–374

72. Mosier, C. I. 1940. Psychophysics and mental test theory. Fundamental postulates and elementary theorems. *Psychol. Rev.* 47:355–66

73. Ibid 1941. Psychophysics and mental test theory II. The constant process. 48:235–49

74. Neill, J. A., Jackson, D. N. An evaluation of item selection strategies in personality scale construction. *Educ. Psychol. Meas.* 30:647–61

75. Rasch, G. 1960. *Probabilistic Models for Some Intelligence and Educational Tests.* Copenhagen: Danish Inst. Educ. Res.

76. Rock, D. A., Barone, J. L., Boldt, R. F. 1972. A two stage decision approach to the selection problem. *Br. J. Math. Statist. Psychol.* 25:274–82

77. Rock, D. A., Linn, R. L., Evans, F. R., Patrick, C. 1970. A comparison of predictor selection techniques using Monte Carlo methods. *Educ. Psychol. Meas.* 30:873–84

78. Rogers, H. 1967. *Theory of Recursive Functions and Effective Computability.* New York: McGraw-Hill

79. Ross, J. 1966. An empirical study of a logistic mental test model. *Psychometrika* 31:325–40

80. Ross, J., Lumsden, J. 1968. Attribute and reliability. *Br. J. Math. Statist. Psychol.* 21:251–63

81. Spearman, C. 1910. Correlation calculated from faulty data. *Br. J. Psychol.* 3:271–95

82. Stanley, J. C. 1971. Reliability. See Ref. 87, 356–442

83. Stanley, J. C., Wang, M. D. 1970. Weighting test items and test-item options, an overview of the analytic and empirical literature. *Educ. Psychol. Meas.* 30:21–35

84. Swineford, F. 1941. The measurement of a personality trait. *J. Educ. Psychol.* 32:438–44

85. Thorndike, E. L., Bregman, E. O., Cobb, M. V., Woodyard, E. 1927. *The Measurement of Intelligence.* New York: Columbia Univ. Teachers' Coll. Bur. Publ.

86. Thorndike, R. L. 1951. Reliability. In *Educational Measurement,* ed. E. F. Lindquist. Washington: Am. Counc. Educ.

87. Thorndike, R. L., Ed. 1971. *Educational Measurement.* Washington: Am. Counc. Educ. 2nd ed.

88. Thurstone, L. L. 1925. A method of scaling psychological and educational tests. *J. Educ. Psychol.* 16:433–51

89. Thurstone, L. L. 1926. The mental age concept. *Psychol. Rev.* 33:268–78

90. Thurstone, L. L. 1931. *The Reliability and Validity of Tests.* Ann Arbor: Edwards Bros.

91. Torgerson, W. S. 1958. *Theory and Methods of Scaling.* New York: Wiley

92. Tucker, L. R. 1946. Maximum validity of a test with equivalent items. *Psychometrika* 11:1–13
93. Tucker, L. R. 1952. A level of proficiency scale for a unidimensional skill. *Am. Psychol.* 7:408
94. Tucker, L. R. 1958. Determination of parameters of a functional relationship by factor analysis. *Psychometrika* 23:19–23
95. Tucker, L. R. 1960. *Determination of generalized learning curves by factor analysis.* Tech. Rep. Educ. Test. Serv.
96. Urry, V. W. 1974. Approximation to item parameters of mental test models and their use. *Educ. Psychol. Meas.* 34:253–69
97. Vernon, P. E. 1938. The assessment of psychological scales by verbal methods. *Natl. Res. Counc. Ind. Health Res. Board Rep. No. 58*
98. Wang, M. D., Stanley, J. C. 1970. Differential weighting, a survey of methods and empirical studies. *Rev. Educ. Res.* 40:663–705
99. Waters, C. W., Bayroff, A. G. 1971. A comparison of computer-simulated conventional and branching tests. *Educ. Psychol. Meas.* 31:125–36
100. Wiggins, J. S. 1973. *Personality and Prediction: Principles of Personality Assessment.* Reading: Addison-Wesley
101. Woodward, J. A., Joe, G. W. 1973. Maximizing the coefficient of generalizability in multi-facet decision studies. *Psychometrika* 38:173–81
102. Ziller, R. P. A. 1957. A measure of the gambling response set in objective tests. *Psychometrika* 22:289–92
103. Zimmerman, D. W. 1972. Test reliability and the Kuder-Richardson formulas: derivation from probability theory. *Educ. Psychol. Meas.* 32:939–54

SCIENTIFIC PSYCHOLOGY IN FRANCE[1]

Robert Francès

Laboratoire de Psychologie Expérimentale et Différentielle, Université de Paris X, 92001 Nanterre, France

This review was prepared with certain limitations that should be made explicit. By scientific psychology we mean work where the experimental method is employed, whether in the laboratory or in the field. It is certain that this method, even if it is the best for testing hypotheses, is not the only one that French psychologists use. But it is the only one in which the author has some competence and, therefore, is able to select material for an international public. Within this limitation we will nevertheless treat many of the main areas of psychology—perception, learning, language, differential, personality, developmental, social, and industrial psychology. For the same reason of personal competence, we have had to eliminate the areas of physiological psychology and animal psychology, even though these are particularly active in France. A further limitation comes from the necessity of presenting a somewhat coherent review focused on a small number of themes; in order to satisfy this requirement we have selected only work touching on problems treated by at least two or three investigators, in some cases adding other studies that have an indirect but clear relation to these.

Having decided upon these limitations, we have also added two other "filters" that seemed necessary to satisfy an international public. We have given priority to original research rather than to synthesizing reviews, and we are restricting this review almost entirely to already published research because of its greater availability than unpublished research.

It is hoped that non-French readers will keep in mind all of these limitations and will realize that the following pages give only a partial review of psychological research in France.

[1]This review is based on research published from 1967 through 1975. Preparation of this chapter was greatly aided by the collaboration of the following colleagues from the University of Paris X and C.N.R.S.: Yvonne Bernard, Michel Denis, Michèle Carlier, and François Molnar. The review was translated into English by Janine and Mark Rosenzweig; Susan Ervin-Tripp helped to translate the section on psycholinguistics.

281

GENERAL PSYCHOLOGY

By this heading we mean the study of psychological functions and of their mechanisms without consideration of individual differences as such. Subject variables such as age are not considered except to bring out the role played by a mechanism in the function in general.

Perception

IDENTIFICATION, MEANING, DISCRIMINATION   Perceptual identification was studied by Noizet & Giniaux (145). In their first experiment they employed stimuli of maximal ambiguity using graded double-ended scales whose poles served as indices. When the indices were meaningful, the thresholds of identification were lower and first responses were more frequent than when they were not meaningful. In a second experiment they trained the subjects with indices that appeared more or less often. On further testing it was found that identification was facilitated by the frequent occurrence of the indices during the training. This indicates that the selection of factors determining identification is regulated by the availability of a model for assimilation. The operational characteristics that determine identification and differential discrimination were studied by Francès (69). He showed, especially in the perception of words, the existence of positive transfer of training of discrimination of letters on identification of words and a negative transfer of identification on discrimination. These relations between tasks were then used in an experiment on learning of spelling where teaching children to discriminate letters during a small number of sessions led to marked progress (70).

Noizet & Flament (144) found that in a task of discrimination of visual length, the performance of subjects varied according to whether their response was focused on the stimulus (the subject giving his judgment directly) or on the subject himself (the subject expressing the degree of certainty that he attached to his response). The distinction between these two situations was illustrated in another psychophysical study on the absolute threshold done by Noizet & Petit (146). The task focused on the stimulus is a forced choice discrimination, whereas the subjective task of evaluating the subject's impression is derived from the constant method. The difference may be interpreted by considering either input, the gathering of information, or output, the cost of the response.

The genetic development of perceptual differentiation shows that, even independently of the insufficiency of their visual exploration, 4-year-old children do not discriminate between two objects offered for their comparison and having between 0 and 4 differences. This result was established by Berthoud & Vurpillot (13). At later ages the judgments vary as a function of the relative number of differences. By the age of 5 years many children adopt the adult criteria, as shown by Vurpillot & Moal (186). There is in fact an evolution of the criteria of identity. The first stage is that the two figures have an equal number of significant parts. Next is the requirement that these parts be identical, and finally is the requirement of identity of location of the parts. This evolution was found by Vurpillot & Moal (186) to occur between the ages of 3 years 10 months and 6 years 8 months. In testing with changes of location and permutations of the parts, Vurpillot & Moal showed that at all ages the most frequent erroneous identifications were due to permutations that involved mirror images.

PERCEPTION OF MOVEMENT, TIME, AND RHYTHM   The perception of movement has been the subject of experiments conducted by Bonnet with various collaborators, and we will note a few of their results. In studying the threshold of detection of movement, Bonnet (15) showed that, in the range of duration of the stimulus between 50 and 700 milliseconds, the product of speed and duration is constant. In consecutive perception, a figural movement effect was demonstrated, resulting from an interaction between two perceptual systems, each of which furnishes specific information. One system holds for those aspects of movement that are spatially defined, while the other holds for spatial relations within the visual field (16).

The perception of rhythm is a special problem because, according to Fraisse (68), perceived rhythm has both muscular and motor accompaniments. It is true both that the characteristics of our perception of successive events (grouping, accentuation, etc) influence our repetitive movements and that these same characteristics in our movement influence our perception. Fraisse (67) showed in experiments on synchronization of motor responses to auditory rhythms that the most important cues coming from the subject's responses are, in order of importance, tactile, kinesthetic, and auditory. The results and the many implications of studies on rhythm in biology and in art are brought out in the recent book by Fraisse (68).

NEW TECHNIQUES IN THE STUDY OF PERCEPTION   Visual perception has been studied by several French investigators who have recorded oculomotor responses made during inspection of the visual field. An evaluation of what may be achieved by these methods to determine the hierarchy of parameters of visual exploration has been provided by Vurpillot (185) for stimulus variables and by Molnar (131) for subject variables. The former has used this method especially from a developmental perspective. The latter has employed it in situations where a variable, such as hue, is set in opposition to spatial variables, or is employed in perceptual situations as complex as paintings (132). The reliability of the ocular movement strategy is less satisfying when one compares it to that of the verbal responses that describe a perception. Lévy-Schoen (115) showed this in a task of localization involving a judgment of position after masking or when "unexpected" information appeared after stabilization of the trajectory of gaze (181). Lévy-Schoen (116) studied a case of conflict among several homogeneous symbols (letters of the alphabet) that were more or less distant from the point of fixation and found that letters close to the fixation point had an important advantage.

Learning Processes

PARAMETRIC STUDIES OF RETENTION   Memory has been studied as a function of parameters such as (a) the materials to be learned, and (b) the sensory modalities employed. Fraisse (66) studied memory for drawings or words indicating the same objects. After a single presentation to 8-year-old children, the drawings are always recalled more frequently than the corresponding verbal stimuli. Verbalization by the subjects of the content of the drawings when they are presented does not facilitate retention except when the drawing is rather complex. The same two kinds of material were used by Denis (49) to study retroactive interference in memorization of sentences. If the sentences are concrete, an equal degree of interference is produced by the interpolated presentation of either drawings or concrete verbal material, whether in immediate recall or in recall after a delay of 2 days. If the sentences are abstract, there is no interference when the interpolated material is concrete, but interpolation of abstract sentences does produce interference. These results are explained by hypothesizing that the encoding of concrete sentences involves the production of mental images which are disturbed by interpolation of concrete material whether this be words or drawings. This kind of comparison was done previously by Sasson & Fraisse (170). Denis (50) then studied the ability of children to recall a sequence of information previously presented either in a motion picture or in verbal form. The degree of recall was lower in the case of the movie than for the verbal material, but the responses to the movie showed less dispersion and greater accuracy than responses to the verbal material (51).

Using auditory or visual presentation of letters, Oléron & Charles (152) did not find different response functions according to the interval elapsing between presentation and response. The stimuli were presented by groups of five and the subjects could pronounce them either separately or by forming syllables or paralogs. The time taken to pronounce the response was longer for auditory than for visual presentation.

SELF-PACED LEARNING   This type of learning enriches our understanding of the laws of retention. In this procedure, the subject can terminate his trials when he believes he has mastered the task. In many cases he can also determine the rhythm and speed of practice. Le Ny, Denhière & Le Taillanter (103, 104) showed that under these conditions, practice takes more time if the series of stimuli (here pairs of numbers) is homogeneous than if it is not. The number of errors is also greater for homogeneous material. These authors also found that the time taken by subjects varied as a function of the informational content of the material. In the case of sentences, the time devoted to learning is longer if they are composed of specific terms than of general terms. Thus study time is a good index of difficulty of retention. But the adjustment of study time to effective retention is more precise when the subjects are able to insert recall trials among cycles of study. This procedure permits a better evaluation of the learning accomplished, but according to Martins (124) it requires more time. Tiberghien (178) reported that the assurance with which the subject gives responses is greater when the response occurs later in the process of learning, and the degree of certainty with regard to an intrusion is greater the more its similarity to the corresponding correct response.

The latency of responses is also a measure used to test hypotheses about the mechanisms of learning. Gauzinille (77), utilizing this measure, found that in a task of identification of concepts, the pool from which the subject drew a sample of hypotheses to test diminished during the trials as certain hypotheses could be eliminated by the information supplied.

The type of test to be used can modify selectively the time that a student uses in studying a text. Furthermore, Tiberghien (179) found that no matter what the form of the test, the student spends less time reading supplementary material than definitions.

MEDIATING PROCESSES INFLUENCING MEMORY   A new tendency is to define memory as an organized functional system which serves as the basis for many activities of the person. "Semantic memory" is defined as an organized system of complex mental structures including conceptual structures (what is signified) and verbal structures (which signify). Research in this area has developed in three principal directions.

1. Ehrlich (63) has studied the general properties of the semantic system which is acquired by the subject during development and which possesses certain structural and functional properties whose nature and role can be determined.

2. Bramaud du Boucheron (20, 21) made a developmental study of vocabulary and its transformations in children 3 to 11 years of age and prepared a developmental dictionary of meanings.

3. Several studies have been concerned with the utilization of semantic systems during learning tasks. Champagnol (28, 29) investigated this with regard to acquisition of foreign languages, Esperet & Ricateau (65) with regard to learning to employ logical connections, and Mariaux (123) concerning learning mathematics. Ehrlich (62, 64) has found that the processes of organization and structuring determined the learning of meaningful verbal material.

The study of imagery in cognitive representation was undertaken by Denis (52) in a general investigation of effects of imagery on memorization. This investigation concerns the relative effectiveness of two forms of imagery, the one resulting from the activation of schemas belonging to the personal repertory of the individual, and the other coming from utilization by the subject of figural material imposed by the experimental situation (drawings). This study, while bringing out the facilitation related to imagery, nevertheless also shows certain limits to its effectiveness.

In studies of verbal learning, George (78) found that the response is determined either locally by a differentiated search or in a more global manner by regulation of the whole. These results, which can be affected by many factors, cannot be interpreted by the classic laws of reinforcement. The elaboration of the response by the aid of mediating processes has also been studied by Richard (167). This investigator proposes a model of acquisition involving, on the one hand, selective attention and, on the other hand, association which permits the items selected to be connected to the responses supplied. This model has been tested by computer simulation, and the predictions obtained were in accord with the results of experimentation. De Schonen (173) has studied the relations between the properties of items of information during the perception and comprehension of an event, on the one hand, and the properties of the information remembered, on the other.

Psychology of Language

RETENTION AND PRODUCTION   Linguistic relations are often tested through memory tasks, especially recall. Thus Ségui (174) showed that in the recall of pairs composed of a noun and an adjective, the major variables were the order of the components and their semantic congruence, and these effects were additive. In the recall of sentences cued by one of the words, Ségui & Dachet (175) found that the cue value is greater when the word is the subject than if the word occupying the same place in the sentence is an adverb. The retention of isolated verbs that are either intransitive or deletable-object transitive is superior to that of object-required transitive verbs. When verbs of these categories are placed in complex sentences, the same differences are found in regard to memory (176).

The light that linguistics throws on the learning of verbal material organized in sentences is just as useful for the knowledge of laws of learning as is the light shed on psycholinguistics by variations in retention. Dubois (58) has studied memorization of simple statements in this regard. In general the results have shown that the factors of position, word frequency, and instructions are not the most important determinants of recall, whereas the grammatical functions of the words are.

The different types of linguistic relations are not equally available among subjects of a given age. Thus Noizet & Pichevin (147) showed in a verbal association task that around the age of 11, paradigmatic and classificatory relations dominate over syntagmatic relations.

Noizet, Deyts & Deyts (143) compared the performances of children and adults in producing sentences that involve a relative transformation. Productions were based on pairs of kernel sentences (noun phrase$_1$ + verb + noun phrase$_2$) containing a noun phrase common to both. The frequency distribution of types that were produced displays clear divergences according to the types of embedding and the kind of relative pronoun. The dominant strategy is a search for the most available kind of production, and this is followed with more inflexibility by adults than by children. The acquisition and the scope of negation, as a syntactic operator as well as in lexical negation, have been studied by de Boysson-Bardies (17–19). Mehler et al (128) have shown that in the case of comparative sentences, such as "the elephant is bigger than _____," the choice of the second noun is highly restricted.

PERCEPTION AND ANALYSIS OF LANGUAGE   Taking the estimation of time of presentation as an index of the syntactic complexity of sentences, Noizet, Bleuchot & Henry (142) showed that as far as reading is concerned, the factors that favor discovery of structure in the sentences are determinant, and that these are not always the factors that aid in production. From the first stages of perception (detection) a strategy is brought into play and is utilized until the sentence is identified. Furthermore, it has been found that the main strategy of subjects consists in discovering which of the words are transformational markers. This strategy makes it possible to show the influence of the type of transformation on the perception of words in the sentence.

Starting with concern for content analysis, which is current in social psychology,

Pêcheux (156) came to conceive a method for automatic analysis of discourse. The directing principle of this method is the following: Analysis of discourse requires linguistics to the extent that it cannot rely upon the linear appearance of the surface of the discourse but requires a "delinearization" of the surface for which a syntactic theory is the necessary if not sufficient condition. Starting with a group of texts considered to have been produced under homogeneous conditions and examined simultaneously, the investigators constructed a comparator which superimposed the delinearized texts upon each other, element by element. The method for automatic analysis of discourse was realized in the form of programs in several computer languages (157).

DIFFERENTIAL PSYCHOLOGY

Personality

Whether extroversion-introversion is a single factor or multifactorial was studied by Demangeon (48) by means of factor analysis. At first three factors were found—a general factor corresponding to Cattell's factor of surgency and two independent factors, sociability and impulsivity. Later all items indicating value were eliminated, and the multifactorial structure disappeared; a substantially homogeneous dimension appeared, more homogeneous for boys than for girls. Extroversion is a dimension of temperament which correlated with expansiveness of gestures. This was shown by Bruchon (26), who found a general factor loading tests of arm movement, locomotion, and posture as well as group factors (expansiveness in writing, in arm posture, and locomotion). Furthermore, she demonstrated correlations between most of these factors and Guilford's measures of introversion (25).

Among temperamental variables, anxiety has been the subject of careful research. Thus Demangeon (48) measured the trait of anxiety among boys and girls at the end of their primary schooling; some of them were going to secondary school whereas others, because of scholastic difficulties, were not. Students at the beginning of secondary school were also tested. The results indicated that we should distinguish a phobic aspect of anxiety which diminishes with age among the boys but not among the girls and also a situational aspect; the latter is related to the school environment and does not replace the phobic aspects but develops later under the pressure of school demands.

Interests and Cognitive Capacities

The progressive differentiation of interests and their relation to academic success have been studied by Larcebeau & Bourdeyre (99). The data concerning interests were gathered in 1964 and in a follow-up study 3 years later. From the ninth grade interests are different and correspond to the different specializations the students have chosen for the baccalaureate. Furthermore, interests help to predict success, independently of level of general intelligence. In the case of discrepancy between intelligence and rank in class, interests play a more important role than do specific aptitudes (98). The choice of a profession or of artistic training depends on a constellation of personal variables among which interests are an essential element. But this pattern of variables does not determine the choice of an artistic career unless it is joined by certain favorable situational variables—especially a high professional status of the head of the family (97).

Leisure artistic interests of students have been studied by Francès, Roubertoux & Denis (72). Three factors were found from the analysis of responses to a questionnaire of 100 items given to more than 400 subjects and confirmed in a second sample. In general they reflect either behavior related to one or several artistic domains or behaviors appropriate to or opposed to several domains (for example, consumption vs creation).

The interaction between personality and socioeconomic class has been demonstrated in relation to continuation of studies after secondary education. The unused pool of talent made up of young people who do not continue their studies although capable of doing so has been investigated by Bacher et al (3). For equal intelligence, one finds a difference in the percentage of students continuing studies according to socioeconomic class, but with little difference in chance of success among those who continue. Factors determining the giving up of studies by good students are also social and economic (4).

The differential method clarifies certain aspects of developmental psychology such as logical thought. Thus Hornemann (89) compared the age at which the stage of formal logic was reached by students showing regular school progress and those who had been held back. In the regular classes factorial analysis revealed a general factor, whereas in the other classes the first factor is related to the content of the test items (amount of illustrational material and kind of situation examined). The same problems were presented either symbolically or in terms of test objects. The analysis of variance showed an interaction between groups and type of presentation.

The relationship between general psychology of intelligence and differential psychology was shown by Longeot, who constructed intelligence tests based on formal operations (117). These tests include tests of combinatorial logic, logic of proportions and of probabilities. They are considered to measure the degree to which the subject has attained the stage of formal logic, moving from the stage of concrete operations.

Hornemann & Longeot (90) showed that school achievement of children of this age, in general subjects as well as in mathematics, was predicted as precisely (but not more) by tests inspired by the theory of Piaget as by factorial tests of intelligence. Learning of serial rules in problem-solving tasks was used by Bajard (5) to differentiate subjects. A special index allowed this to be done and appeared useful in tests in which the number of trials is constant.

The explanation of individual differences in terms of processes or mechanisms established in general psychology was done by Carlier (27) in relation to flexibility considered as a modality in creativity. After having established the existence of a general factor of flexibility (and of group factors of verbal, written, and ideational flexibility), Carlier linked it to the existence of systems of nonhierarchical reinforcement.

PSYCHOLOGY OF DEVELOPMENT

Psychomotor and Psychological Development

Research on psychomotor development has been conducted with special emphasis on mechanisms of regulation and control behaviors. Thus in the studies of Merlet-Vigier (130) and Zazzo (196) the relation of speed to accuracy in a test of cancellation of two letters in a text provided operational definitions of three types of control, on the basis of which these investigators have systematically studied indices of deficiencies of regulation.

Nadel (135, 136), using a test of static work with a dynamometer, studied the development of muscular persistence in children from 7 to 12. The results indicate that the development occurs on two different levels between 7 and 9, where it is related to development of muscular persistence to attain a goal. The study of relations between performance and electromyographic indices during prolonged muscular activity reveals the appearance in older subjects (13 to 14 years) of an organization of muscular activity which permits both more accurate performance (transition from global functioning of the limb to selective activation of only certain muscles) and also more economical performance (achieved by alteration in contraction of groups of muscles) (137).

Finally, Chiva et al (33) attempted to study certain control mechanisms and adaptive behaviors by means of the Rorschach test and of several tests of drawing.

Motor activity of the young in both drawing and writing has been studied by Lurçat (118–122). The first rectilinear strokes—vertical, horizontal, and oblique—are initiated by arm movements at the level of the shoulder which extend along the vertical and horizontal axes. Between 4 and 5 years the drawing of the child shows two kinds of progress—representational (progressive realism of manifest representation) and nonrepresentational (progressive complication of form). Study of development in the copying of letters and words shows different stages between 3 and 6 years, the major barriers to correct copying being motor and perceptuo-spatial.

Netchine (140) has prepared a review of cerebral electrical activity in the child. He furnishes an overall description of the characteristics of this activity in the normal school-age child, studied from developmental and typological perspectives. Netchine (141) also presents a factor analysis of the EEG and an overview of the choice of variables and the structural approach in the study of development of the EEG and in investigation of relations between EEG and psychological data, especially from a developmental perspective.

Language and Intellectual Cognitive Activity

The study of language in children has been taken up from the viewpoint of verbal perception and comprehension. Oléron (149) showed the role of letters with vertical strokes and of different parts of the word in identification of words. Coslin (37) indicated the role of critical locations and of partial information in the identification of words.

The most notable advance has occurred in research in children's language in relation to intellectual and cognitive activities. In this field Oléron (150) has presented a review of the role of language in mental development. Language is held to be less important in furnishing instruments of thought (as is held by the theory of verbal mediation, for example) than in its indirect effects due to training, among which are attitudes and personal detachment with regard to perception and action.

Bresson (24) and Frankel & Le Rouzo (73) have studied some linguistic subsystems which perform semantic and referential functions: quantifiers and articles, aspects and tenses, spatial references, etc. These studies in production and comprehension do not proceed from syntactic forms, but on the contrary, concern the evolution of these subsystems of operators and of the syntactic forms in which they are carried out through language acquisition. The authors also show relations between the development of these performances and cognitive development.

Certain more specific researches have emphasized the role of language in reasoning and problem-solving, whether in terms of verbal habits studied by Dufoyer (60), verbal communication among children studied by Beaudichon et al (7, 8), or of soliloquy studied by Beaudichon & Melot (9, 10). In sensorimotor tasks and in problem-solving, it was reported by Beaudichon, Legros & Oléron (6) that subjects perform better when they are required to speak than during silent activity. Bresson has proposed a theoretical reformulation of the development of perception (23) and of the way in which infants discover the properties of objects (22). In this work he has emphasized the role of the subject's movements. A new subject has been explored by Piéraut-Le Bonniec (163): the development of modal thinking and its function in reasoning in children from 3 to 7 years old. The same author has also provided more precise information regarding the development of classification operations in children (162), and Maury & Rogalski (125) have shown how the development of the operations of cartesian product and of complementation are highly correlated. Mehler has proposed a new theory of cognitive development that involves both learning and unlearning and that stresses the growing loss of flexibility (126, 127).

The development of capacity to perceive musical expression (acculturation) has been studied carefully by Zenatti (199–201). She also studied relations between these capacities and certain forms of discrimination, for example, of consonance.

Under the heading of intellectual and cognitive activities, we must point out an important group of researches devoted to the use of schemas and their role in the assimilation of knowledge. A schematic pictorial symbolism, to the extent that it does not adhere too closely to the material to be learned, promotes both the learning and its transfer to new facts, according to Vézin (182). Also, concrete schemas were found to be more effective, and the use of examples facilitated the putting into relationship of verbal statements and schemas (183). A related direction of research concerns the roles of summaries and repetitions in learning. Vézin (184) showed that a summary that follows a text allows a better level of generality of response than a summary placed before the text; repetition leads to better memorization of statements than a summary, but repetition tends to lessen the level of generality of the response. In a study of development of perception of pictures by children, de Schonen (172) has shown that the status of pictures changes and that perception of perspective becomes progressively better organized up to the age of 5.

Nguyen Xuan, Lemaire & Rousseau (148) studied strategies of selection of information in the construction of a series by children of 9 to 11. Analysis of the responses showed an evolution from random selection toward selection of items according to a plan. Furthermore, many children of these ages do not distinguish between sufficient and necessary information for construction of a series, and this suggests that those subjects form the series without utilizing transitive inferences.

Effects of categorizing material on memory have been investigated by Melot (129), Ricateau (165), Winnykamen & Bonnin (190), and Winnykamen & Dhenin (191). In an important experimental study, Winnykamen (189) examined two types of activity of subjects during complex learning: on the one hand, responding to questions during learning and on the other hand, mental reorganization of the items learned. The results indicate greater efficiency of a form of questioning that promotes seeking comparison and finding relations among concepts.

Emotional and Personal Development

Bloch & Gratiot-Alphandéry (14) presented a major review of emotional and moral development of children. Coslin, Denis-Pradet & Selosse (38) studied differential aspects of moral judgment and actual behavior of delinquent and nondelinquent adolescents. The results showed that the two groups did not differ at the level of moral judgment but at the level of behavior and that in the delinquents there was a strong disparity between moral judgment and behavior.

The topic of self-images and identification in the development of personality has been studied in several ways. B. Zazzo (194, 195) made an original study of what he called "evolving dynamism" concerning children of school age. It was found that the self-image is formed in relation to the preferential perception that the child has of his own age in contrast to other ages. Several stages were distinguished, and the influence of the family milieu was brought out by comparison of groups of children from clearly different sociocultural levels. Perron (160) has also made an important study on self-image of the child. This study brought out the existence of a real stereotype of personal values in our society and its progressive appearance in children between the ages of 8 and 14. This investigation stressed that the model of values that society proposes can, in certain social and interpersonal conditions, lead to alienation. But in more favorable cases it appears to be necessary to personal development and to autonomy. Rodriguez-Tomé (168) presented a synthesis on social self-image, based on a study of 800 adolescents. His work showed the integration and organization of opinions of others in consciousness of oneself.

Finally, the question of self-image has been examined through the study of body image. Garelli (74) and Garelli, Lepage & Misteli (75) employed a battery of original tests with normal children and children with cerebral motor handicaps. The body image developed in specialized ways among the handicapped children as dictated by their bodily experience and in close relation with their difficulties of spatial organization.

A set of studies on anxiety were conducted by Zlotowicz (202, 203), using questionnaires and physiological measures made while the subjects were answering the questionnaire. The physiological measures provided indices of the intensity of certain anxieties and worries concerning parents, fear of certain animals, fear of the dark and being alone. The study of intensity was then related to a study of meaning of anxieties, conducted by means of factorial analysis of verbal responses (205).

Other approaches to fears among school-age children, preadolescents, and adolescents have involved thematic and morphological analyses of nightmares, conducted by Rodriguez-Tomé & Zlotowicz (169) and Zlotowicz (203, 204).

Studies Concerning the School Environment

Gilly (80) has made a study of factors involved in success or failure in primary schools, emphasizing three kinds of factors: (*a*) somatophysiological conditions; (*b*) "processes of mobilization," that is, factors related to energy and regulatory mechanisms governing the efficient use of intellectual potentialities; (*c*) the educational climate of the family. The results bring out in particular the influence of somatophysiological factors on the processes of mobilization and indicate by what mechanisms they can affect school work. The same investigator has also done research on the influence of degree of scholastic success on self-image (82) and on the image the teacher has of the student (81).

From another point of view, Léon (105) has studied how adolescents imagine the future; this is linked to the perception of difficulties in the school situation. He has also shown the importance of certain aspects of the school (type of school, nature of the trade learned) on the development of motivations (106).

Adjustment of children to nursery school has been the subject of many studies. Gratiot-Alphandéry (84) has emphasized the process of socialization. B. Zazzo (196), on the basis of sociometric tests, questionnaires, and direct observation of behavior both at work and at play, was able to find a relation between adjustment to the peer group and adjustment to demands of the school (discipline and group work). This finding led Zazzo to hypothesize a general factor of adaptability, at least for the age she studied (5 to 6 years).

Danset, Danset-Léger & Winnykamen (45) made a French adaptation of the American Devereux Elementary School Behavior Rating Scale. They and others (177) also participated in an intercultural study which permitted them to specify relations between school success and certain aspects of classroom behavior and also to define the differences between what French and American teachers expect of children in regard to level of activity and degree of attention.

Abnormal Psychology

R. Zazzo (197) edited a book on retardation. In his introduction, Zazzo proposed a multidimensional definition of retardation, distinguishing causes or etiologies (biological, cultural, emotional), and social criteria (criteria related to social demands, requirements that vary from one society to another and from one age to another). Among the original studies published in this volume, those of Chiva (30) and Chiva & Rutschmann (34) emphasized the relation between etiology and the psychological characteristics of the retardates. This topic has also been treated in another work by Chiva (32). Also, Netchine (138, 139) has offered several critical analyses of the concept of retardation. Perron (158) has investigated self-image in the adolescent retardate; he has found that the types of self-image vary greatly as a function of both the level of retardation and the degree of social success.

Capacities for cognitive learning among retarded children have been studied in several investigations. Thus Hurtig (91) has shown that, while the retardates differ little from normal children of the same mental age in their comprehension and degree of transfer among intellectual tasks, there are differences in the degree of resistance to learning but not in the learning itself. Also Dufoyer & Lhuillier (61), from their examination of organization of spatial perception in retarded children, found, in addition to retardation, certain peculiarities of reasoning based on intensive but nonstructured utilization of perceptual indices.

The deaf child has been studied from a number of points of view. Several investigations have concerned his perceptual activity. Oléron (151) has studied how deaf children grasp perceptual differences under several conditions of stimulus presentation. Colin & Vurpillot (36) have shown that in a task of finding hidden figures, the differences between deaf and hearing children are quantitative rather than qualitative; this suggests that the laws of perceptual organization are identical in the two groups. Finally, the development of sociability in deaf and hearing children has been studied in a test of cooperative behavior by Herren & Colin (86). The results showed that behavioral integration of schemas of behavior corresponding to cooperation increases with age and that there is retardation in this development among deaf children starting at age 10.

We should also note some studies made by Colin & Ritaine (35) and Herren et al (87) of mental development in children with motor handicaps.

Perron-Borelli & Perron (161) prepared a general treatment of psychological examination of children. In it they have reevaluated the procedures used by the clinical psychologist who examines children in a medical-psychological context. Perron (159) has also published an original projective test, while Beizmann (11) has presented an important synthesis on the Rorschach test.

Specific problems of psychometric examination of handicaps has been the object of studies by Chiva (31) and Zazzo (198). The question of measuring mental level in the case of cerebral motor disorders has also been examined by Dague & Garelli (44) and Garelli & Martins (76).

SOCIAL PSYCHOLOGY

Basic Mechanisms of Social Interaction

Apfelbaum (1), using experimental games, has studied the development of attitudes in regard to each other by subjects whose powers are equal and shared; cooperative and competitive attitudes were emphasized. The behavior of the subjects was determined less by their initial attitudes than by the styles of behavior that they attributed to their partner. Cooperative behavior developed when a subject perceived the actions of his partner as responses to his own (2). Similarity, whether perceived or supposed, increased positive and cooperative exchanges whereas perceived heterogeneity favored competitive exchanges (independently of the initial attitudes which had been established outside the test situation). The perception of the other could be modified by the expectation of future interaction with him. The longer the interaction, the more likely it was that the representation of the partner would be detailed and would include a greater number and more favorable evaluative aspects. These results were obtained by Lesage de la Haye (113, 114) both in a school setting and in the laboratory.

The variables that determine influence in social interaction have been studied both in a natural setting, with subjects who have known each other for a long time, and in the laboratory. In the former case, Desportes & Dequeker (53) have used ambiguous perceptual situations with highly variable responses (the autokinetic phenomenon). The assimilation of responses of a subject to those of the group depend both on cohesiveness of the group (measured by a sociometric questionnaire) and on the hierarchical structure. The patterns of interaction of daily life play a considerable role in construction of reality when information is insufficient. In a laboratory situation, Lemaine & Guimelchain (101) used a perceptual task related to the preceding one but more reliable in regard to intrasubject responses. Here social influence is brought to bear on a naïve subject by another subject who is actually an accomplice of the experimenter; the attitudes of the accomplice were made to vary in social and political respects (the attitude of the subject having been measured previously). The results showed that similarity between subject and accomplice favored the movement of judgments of the former toward those of the latter when the original judgments were quite different. Dissimilarity, on the contrary, caused the judgments to depart from each other even when they agreed at the start.

But the desire to assert one's own identity can in certain conditions be a tendency as strong as the desire to assimilate to others. Kaisersztein & Lemaine (92), going from the study of self-assertion to that of aggression, have raised doubts, in a series of experiments, about the theory linking aggression simply to frustration of the subject. According to them, one must add the concept of attribution, indicating the willful character of the frustrating action in the eyes of the victim. This character is linked to cognitive operations associating the frequency and the sequential constraint of the frustrations suffered. The result of these operations depends on the emotional state of the subjects, determined by the number of frustrations suffered in the immediate past. This kind of problem was also studied by Da Gloria (42) and Da Gloria & De Ridder (43).

Estimation of Chance and Risk-Taking in Groups

The comparative study of individual choices before group consensus and of the corresponding group choice shows, according to Lambert (93, 94), that the majority opinion, if it is taken right at the start, carries the decision to an extreme position. In the opposite case, the decision appears difficult to predict, sometimes being more risky and sometimes less risky than the mean of the individual opinions before consensus. This majority model is applicable both to real and to imaginary situations, and it is modulated by personality factors or by mental illness (95, 96).

When one varies both expectation and amount of reward, the results are different according to whether decisions are individual or collective. When the stakes are relatively low, the level of risk taken by groups is significantly higher than the mean of individual decisions; when the stakes are relatively high, the group risk is equal to or less than the individual mean (192). Zaleska (193) found that in a group discussion before arriving at a decision, the arguments in favor of risk taking are more frequent and judged to be more convincing than arguments in favor of caution.

In a game situation Plon (164) found that when choices conflict, situations that are equivalent from a logical point of view but different in content produce different choices of the subject. Doise (55) reported that in game situations, provisional assignment to two conflicting groups (for example, to two different nationalities) favors discrimination of each group against the other (46).

Influence Processes

The influence of point of view and of theoretical or ideological systems on cognitive performances has been studied experimentally by Pêcheux & Haroche (157). In a previous study on perception, Pêcheux had shown that denial of a suprathreshold perception could be obtained overwhelmingly among adult subjects who had been taught an epistemological trap (a pseudotheory concerning subliminal perception). These subjects, when given suprathreshold stimuli, did not identify these stimuli because they held to the theory. Pêcheux & Haroche then obtained a similar result with a logical test of variable content. The influential social viewpoints here were of ideological-political nature: the fact that the subjects belonged to a particular social class, making them participate in a particular ideological system, prevented them from solving a puzzle. Deconchy (46, 47) has studied a similar influence—that of religious orthodoxy defined as a system holding sway over logical thought. Religious ideology was conceived of as a process regulating thought and which checks access to new information, especially scientific information, and protects already acquired information; it makes up for the weakness from a rational point of view of its information (effectively an intuitive cluster of beliefs) by the strength of social regulation. Deconchy showed that the orthodox subject, when faced with a presentation criticizing rational information, attributes greater informative value to symbolic material (esthetic, gestural, mystic) than he would have otherwise.

Esthetic norms, cultural models, and their influences on art appreciation have been studied both in the laboratory and in the field and with both stimuli prepared for this study (drawings, patterns, forms) and works of art (reproductions of paintings). In a field study Bernard (12) showed that, among psychological determinants of choice of paintings, the accuracy of representation varying according to the modernism of the works had the greatest influence on preferences, and this influence was in direct relation with the educational level of the subjects who were all adults. A similar result was found by Francès (71) in experiments done with drawings or photographs. He varied six collative variables, among which were incongruity and incongruous juxtaposition (which represent lowered accuracy of representation). Incongruity is mainly rejected by adults with only an elementary level of education whereas it is accepted by students. A similar difference holds for irregularity of figures which may be considered as a case of cultural strangeness.

PRESENCE OF OTHERS AND ECOLOGICAL SOCIAL PSYCHOLOGY   The effects of presence of others are an elementary form of social influence (see Duflos, Desportes & Zaleska 59). Desportes & Dequeker (53) studied the effect of passive presence of spectators. The simple presence of spectators induces in a normal subject a feeling of being evaluated, which involves him in the experimental tasks and raises the level of his performance. Among anxious subjects, this involvement provokes anxiety and increases the probability of irrelevant responses which reduces the level of performance. Instructions calling for comparison with another person have similar effects even if the other person is absent. The task used in this study was a subtest of the Wechsler-Bellevue intelligence scale, and anxiety was measured by Taylor's Manifest Anxiety Scale. It should be noted that in the adults as in the child, the passive presence of peers is not an unconditional stimulus; it is effective only if certain relations or communications have been established among the subjects. An analogous establishment of relationships in animals is seen in the relation of dominance in the mouse (54).

The complex effect of presence of others has long been neglected in experimental psychology. Nevertheless, laboratory situations, the administration of questionnaires in surveys, or of tests in psychological examinations all imply presence of others, and it is hard to believe that this factor is without effect either in the subject or in the psychologist. Lemaine, after having studied this problem in the specific case of verbal conditioning (101), treated it in all its aspects in a general review (100). In particular he showed that in the dyad of the laboratory, survey, or examination, the influence of the psychologist cannot be considered as an artifact but is an integral aspect of the situation.

In the performance of tasks, the functional aspect of the cooperation demanded of another has rarely been taken into consideration. Gineste (83) has shown that choosing a partner is more frequent (in relation to not choosing one) when the subject is uncertain of his own performance. But among the possible partners the choice usually falls on a partner believed to be similar, whether or not one has information about his performance. Thus social comparison comes in when it is necessary to seek the help of a partner.

Ghiglione & Beauvois (79) analyzed studies concerning individual performance and group performance in problem solving. They concluded that contradictions concerning the superiority of one or the other condition are not attributable to the complexity of the topic but to the use of different statistical models. Some have tested weak hypotheses while others have tested strong hypotheses.

Subjects having no power may nevertheless attempt to exert influence. Moscovici showed that if the behavior of a minority is consistent, its impact on the majority is greatest (133). The source of influence may be absent and nevertheless be effective (134). The image of the minority, elaborated during negotiation, is essential to the influence exercised by that minority. The influence of a person with deviant opinion was studied by Doise & Moscovici (57). They found that the "late" statement of a deviant opinion was often followed by the others, especially if the group was not very cohesive, whereas precocious divergence provoked avoidance which was stronger in groups of low cohesion. From another point of view, Doise (56) showed that collective judgments are clearer and less variable than individual judgments.

INDUSTRIAL PSYCHOLOGY

The current development of industrial psychology shows the desire to consider it as a branch of general psychology oriented to the analysis of behavior revealed in the work situation. It usually favors the study of complex behavior and does not necessarily imply a goal of short-term application. From this point of view, the study of the genesis of behavior, that is to say the development of apparently acquired cognitive modalities, occupies a major place. The studies of Pailhous (153–155) afford good illustrations of this tendency. Analyzing the mechanisms shown by subjects moving in an unfamiliar urban space, this investigator, after having stressed the functional role of spatial images, studied the processes of construction and utilization of these images. The same tendency is to be found in the work of Cuny (39, 40). Other research on perceptual discrimination in tasks of inspection has helped to formalize a hypothesis concerning the mechanism that determines discrimination. Leplat (107) used computer simulation to evaluate sequential statistics for this purpose and to construct a stochastic model of inspection.

Modern technological systems bring about many situations in which operators must use more or less complex plans in order to program their activities. The genesis and nature of the plans and their use during the task to achieve the final objective also constitute an important topic of research by Leplat (108, 109, 111).

The situation in which learning occurs has been interpreted as a rupture of the equilibrium between a subject and his environment, and the process of learning has been seen as a process of reequilibration which gives psychologists the opportunity of studying the microgenesis of a new behavior (112). A study of learning to read mechanical drawings has revealed different levels of performance, according to Weill-Fassina (187). The use of a complex apparatus (cathode ray oscilloscope) by adults during a training program brought out the processes of transitory loss of equilibrium that had been hypothesized (188). A study of the cognitive processes shown in the analysis of problems to program them for a computer takes up the problem of schemata in a new way. Considering the activity as hypothetico-deductive, Hoc (88) found it necessary to construct a model that would take account of the alteration of different systems of representation arriving simultaneously during the task of the subject.

Keeping in mind the perspective of relating industrial psychology to major questions of general psychology, the analysis of a concrete situation of group work was studied from the perspective of problem-solving in a group. The results showed a major disparity between psychosociological research on groups and the behavior of a real work group. Since each worker was primarily responsible for completing his own task, the interaction within the team was quite dependent on the individual cognitive activities; this problem was investigated by Leplat (110) and Savoyant (171). The major dimension of psychological climate in organizations was studied by Cuny (41).

This survey, which cannot be considered complete, has shown that a continually greater number of relations is growing in France between the different branches and sectors of experimental psychology; discoveries made in one area illuminate problems raised in another. We have seen this, for example, in the reciprocal relations between general and differential psychology, developmental and general psychology, social and developmental psychology, etc. This difficult progression toward integration is a favorable sign that augurs well for the evolution of scientific psychology.

Literature Cited

1. Apfelbaum, E. 1969. *Interdépendance, renforcement social et réactivité: analyse de la dynamique des interactions dans le cadre de "jeux expérimentaux."* PhD thesis. Univ. Paris, France. 254 pp.
2. Apfelbaum, E. 1969. "Reactivity" and cooperation in dyadic interaction. *Experimental Social Psychology*, 243–84. Prague: Inst. Psychol., Czech. Acad. Sci.
3. Bacher, F., Abramson, C., Martin, M. H., Norguet, T. 1971. Réserves d'aptitudes et démocratisation de l'enseignement. *Bull. Inst. Nat. Orient. Profess.* 27 (special number): 7–29
4. Bacher, F., Archambaud, N. 1972. La poursuite des études à la fin du premier cycle secondaire: problèmes posés par les élèves bien doués qui abandonnent. *Orient. Scol. Profess.* 1:317–37
5. Bajard, G. 1970. Apprentissage et lois de séries. *Psychol. Fr.* 15:61–68
6. Beaudichon, J., Legros, S., Oléron, P. 1973. Les débuts de l'auto-régulation verbale du comportement. Nouveau contrôle expérimentale des thèses de A. R. Luria. *Neuropsychologia* 11:337–41
7. Beaudichon, J., Levasseur, J. 1972. Procédés et contenus de la communication entre enfants lors de la résolution d'un problème. *J. Psychol. Norm. Pathol.* 69:69–82
8. Beaudichon, J., Melot, A. M. 1972. The influence of interindividual communication on problem solving. *Determinants of Behavioral Development.* London: Academic
9. Beaudichon, J., Melot, A. M. 1972. Emergence et fonction du soliloque. *Psychol. Fr.* 17:33–42
10. Beaudichon, J., Melot, A. M. 1973. Nature and instrumental function of private speech in problem solving situations. *Merrill-Palmer Q.* 4:117–36
11. Beizmann, C. 1974. *Le Rorschach de l'Enfant à l'Adulte.* Neuchâtel: Delachaux et Niestlé. 296 pp.
12. Bernard, Y. 1973. *Psychosociologie du Goût en Matière de Peinture.* Paris: C.N.R.S. 138 pp.
13. Berthoud, M., Vurpillot, E. 1970. Influence du nombre de différences sur les réponses "pas pareil" chez l'enfant d'âge pré-scolaire. *Enfance* 23:23–30
14. Bloch, M. A., Gratiot-Alphandéry, H. 1970. Le développement affectif et moral. In *Traité de Psychologie de l'Enfant*, ed. H. Gratiot-Alphandéry, R. Zazzo, Vol. 4. Paris: P.U.F. 201 pp.
15. Bonnet, C. 1972. Movement detection thresholds and stimulus duration. *Percept. Psychophys.* 12:269–72
16. Bonnet, C., Pouthas, U. 1972. Interactions between spatial and kinetic dimensions in movement aftereffects. *Percept. Psychophys.* 12:193–200
17. Boysson-Bardies, B. de 1969. Négation syntaxique et négation chez le jeune enfant. *Langages* 16:111–18
18. Boysson-Bardies, B. de 1970. Syntax and semantics in memorization of negation. In *Advances in Psycholinguistics*, ed. G. B. Flores d'Arcais, W. J. M. Levelt, 237–46. Amsterdam, London: North Holland. 454 pp.
19. Boysson-Bardies, B. de, Carey, P. 1974. What is the scope of the negation? In *Current Problems in Psycholinguistics*, ed. F. Bresson, J. Mehler, 449–62. Paris: C.N.R.S. 524 pp.
20. Bramaud du Boucheron, G. 1972. *L'Apprentissage Verbal chez l'Enfant.* Paris: C.N.R.S. 138 pp.
21. Bramaud du Boucheron, G., Champagnol, R., Coirier, P., Ehrlich, M. F., Ehrlich, S. 1970. *Le Comportement Verbal.* Paris: Dunod. 273 pp.
22. Bresson, F. 1971. La genèse des propriétés des objets. *J. Psychol. Norm. Pathol.* 68:143–68
23. Bresson, F. 1972. Aspects génétiques de la perception. In *Neuropsychologie de la Perception*, ed. H. Hécaen, 168–84. Paris: Masson
24. Bresson, F. 1974. Remarks on genetic psycholinguistics: the acquisition of the article system in French. See Ref. 19, 67–72
25. Bruchon, M. L. 1969–70. L'amplitude gestuelle et la personnalité. *Bull. Psychol.* 23:426–27
26. Bruchon, M. L. 1974. L'expansivité gestuelle, étude dimensionnelle. *Rev. Int. Psychol. Appl.* 23:3–15
27. Carlier, M. 1973. *Etude Différentielle*

d'une Modalité de la Créativité: la Flexibilité. Paris: C.N.R.S. 105 pp.

28. Champagnol, R. 1972. L'efficience de l'enseignement des langues dans le secondaire: deux points de vue. *Langues Mod.* 66:765–77

29. Champagnol, R. 1974. Association verbale, structuration et rappel libre bilingue. *Psychol. Fr.* 19:83–100

30. Chiva, M. 1969. Tableaux psychologiques différentiels de la débilité mentale selon l'étiologie. In *Les Débilités Mentales,* ed. R. Zazzo, 251–87. Paris: Colin. 500 pp.

31. Chiva, M. 1970. L'évaluation psychométrique de la débilité. In *Psychiatrie et Médecine Scolaire,* ed. G. Daumezon, 90–95. Paris: Doin

32. Chiva, M. 1973. *Débiles Normaux, Débiles Pathologiques.* Neuchâtel: Delachaux et Niestlé. 225 pp.

33. Chiva, M., Fontaine, A. M., Babinet, M. A., Santucci, H. 1970. Les mécanismes de contrôle chez l'enfant au test de Rorschach et dans des activités psychomotrices. *Enfance* 23:47–54

34. Chiva, M., Rutschmann, Y. 1969. L'étiologie de la débilité mentale. See Ref. 30, 108–65

35. Colin, D., Ritaine, M. 1972. Etude du niveau de développement mental chez des enfants handicapés des membres supérieures. *Rev. Neuropsychiat. Infant. Hyg. Ment. Enf.* 20:357–66

36. Colin, D., Vurpillot, E. 1971–72. Influence de la surdité sur l'organisation perceptive visuelle chez les enfants d'âge préscolaire. *Bull. Psychol.* 25:882–87

37. Coslin, P. G. 1972–73. Rôle des "places sensibles" et de l'information lacunaire dans l'identification des mots mutilés. *Bull. Psychol.* 26:412–17

38. Coslin, P. G., Denis-Pradet, M., Selosse, J. 1972. Etude différentielle du jugement moral et de la conduite sur un échantillon de délinquants juvéniles. *Ann. Vaucresson* 10:225–45

39. Cuny, X. A. 1972. Eléments de formalisation par l'analyse psychologique d'un travail de contrôle. *Trav. Hum.* 35:1–16

40. Ibid 1973. Dimensions et mesure de l'implication dans le travail. Une analyse longitudinale. 36:361–74

41. Cuny, X. A. 1974. L'analyse psychologique des organisations. Le climat et ses dimensions. *Année Psychol.* 74:269–93

42. Da Gloria, J. 1975. La fréquence d'un acte d'autrui comme indice pour un sujet de son caractère volontaire. *Psychol. Fr.* In press

43. Da Gloria, J., De Ridder, R. 1974. Aggression in dyadic interaction. *Eur. J. Soc. Psychol.* In press

44. Dague, P., Garelli, M. 1969. Recherches sur l'échelle de Maturité Mentale de Columbia. Etude sur la validité génétique de l'échelle (contribution à l'étude de l'évolution de la pensée catégorielle chez l'enfant de 5 à 11 ans). *Rev. Psychol. Appl.* 19:155–94

45. Danset, A., Danset-Léger, J., Winnykamen, F. 1974. Application d'une échelle d'étude des conduites en classe à 1325 écoliers parisiens (Le DESB, version française). *Rev. Psychol. Appl.* 24:87–102

46. Deconchy, J. P. 1971. *L'Orthodoxie Religieuse. Essai de Logique Psychosociale.* Paris: Ed. Ouvrières. 378 pp.

47. Deconchy, J. P. 1975. *Sciences Humaines et Orthodoxie Religieuse.* PhD thesis. Univ. Paris X, Nanterre. 372 pp.

48. Demangeon, M. 1973. Etude différentielle de l'anxiété. *Orient. Scol. Profess.* 2:363–85

49. Denis, M. 1971. La mémoire d'un message filmique comparée à celle d'un message verbal chez des enfants d'âge scolaire. *J. Psychol. Norm. Pathol.* 68:69–87

50. Denis, M. 1973. Stabilité comparée de l'apprentissage d'un matériel imagé et d'un matériel verbal. *Psychol. Fr.* 18:47–59

51. Denis, M. 1974. Rappel d'un matériel complexe filmique ou verbal par l'enfant:dispersion et originalité des réponses en fonction de l'âge et du matériel. *Enfance* 27:131–42

52. Denis, M. 1975. *Représentation Imagée et Activité de Mémorisation.* Paris: C.N.R.S. In press

53. Desportes, J. P., Dequeker, A. 1971. Effets de la présence de l'expérimentateur sur la performance en fonction de l'anxiété des sujets et de la structure de la tâche. *Bull. Cent. Etud. Rech. Psychotech.* 20:93–98

54. Desportes, J. P., Duflos, A., Provansal, B. 1973. Effet de la présence d'un congénère "spectateur" sur l'apprentissage d'un parcours simple en fonction des positions hiérarchiques du sujet "acteur" et du sujet "spectateur" chez la souris mâle C57Bl6. *Rev. Comport. Anim.* 7:259–71

55. Doise, W. 1969. Les stratégies de jeu à l'intérieur entre groupes de nationalité différente. *Bull. Cent. Etud. Rech. Psychotech.* 18:13–26

56. Doise, W. 1970. L'importance d'une dimension principale dans les jugements collectifs. *Année Psychol.* 70:151–57
57. Doise, W., Moscovici, S. 1969–70. Approche et évitement du déviant dans des groupes de cohésion différente. *Bull. Psychol.* 23:522–25
58. Dubois, D. 1971. *Rappel et Reconnaissance d'Enoncés, Aspects Syntaxiques et Sémantiques.* Paris:C.N.R.S.
59. Duflos, A., Desportes, J. P., Zaleska, M. 1972. L'étude des effets de la présence physique des congénères chez l'homme: modes d'approche et perspectives de recherche. *Modèles Animaux du Comportement Humain.* Paris: C.N.R.S. 287–302
60. Dufoyer, J. P. 1969–70. Rôle de certaines habitudes verbales dans la conduite du raisonnement chez des adolescents et des adultes. *Bull. Psychol.* 23:526–32
61. Dufoyer, J. P., Lhuillier, G. 1974. Contribution à l'étude de la représentation de l'espace chez l'enfant déficient mental. *Rev. Neuropsychiat. Infant. Hyg. Ment. Enf.* 22:75–86
62. Ehrlich, S. 1970. Structuration and destructuration of responses in free recall learning. *J. Verb. Learn. Verb. Behav.* 9:282–86
63. Ehrlich, S. 1972. *La Capacité d'Appréhension Verbale.* Paris: P.U.F. 216 pp.
64. Ehrlich, S., Ricateau, M. 1970. Le rôle de la structuration dans la rétention verbale, *Année Psychol.* 70:95–108
65. Esperet, E., Ricateau, M. 1972. L'utilisation des connecteurs logiques et niveau opératoire formel. *Psychol. Pédag.* 6:13–29
66. Fraisse, P. 1970. La verbalisation d'un dessin par l'enfant facilite-t-elle son évocation? *Année Psychol.* 70:109–22
67. Fraisse, P. 1974. Cues in sensori-motor synchronization. In *Chronibiology,* ed. L. E. Scheving, F. Halberg, J. E. Pauly, 517–22. Tokyo: Igaky Shon
68. Fraisse, P. 1974. *Psychologie du Rythme.* Paris: P.U.F. 244 pp.
69. Francès, R. 1967. Identification et distinction différentielle. Deux mécanismes perceptifs et leurs relations réciproques. *Psychol. Fr.* 12:91–100
70. Francès, R. 1969–70. Apprentissage perceptif et apprentissage de l'orthographe. *Bull. Psychol.* 23:416–21
71. Francès, R. 1975. Comparative effects of six collative variables on interest and preference in adults of different educational levels. I. Experiment on design;

II. Experiment using photographs. *J. Pers. Soc. Psychol.* In press
72. Francès, R., Roubertoux, P., Denis, M. 1975. *Intérêts Artistiques et Instruction Supérieure. La Structure des Intérêts Artistiques de Loisirs chez les Etudiants.* Paris: Mouton. In press
73. Frankel, J., Le Rouzo, M. L. 1974. Psycholinguistique et enseignement du français à l'école primaire. *Langue Fr.* 22:107–19
74. Garelli, M. 1970. Le schéma corporel chez les enfants I.M.C. Impuissance corporelle et images de soi. *Enfance* 23:343–63
75. Garelli, M., Lepage, A., Misteli, E. 1973–74. L'enfant I.M.C. et son corps. Contribution à l'étude de la genèse du corps représenté et du corps vécu. *Bull. Psychol.* 27:362–84
76. Garelli, M., Martins, C. 1969. L'appréciation du niveau mental dans l'infirmité motrice cérébrale. *Rev. Prat.* 19:1551–63
77. Gauzinille, E. 1972. Analyse, à l'aide d'indicateurs temporels de quelques mécanismes d'apprentissage mis en jeu dans des tâches d'identification de concept. *Année Psychol.* 72:443–62
78. George, C., 1971. *Choix et Apprentissage en Situation Aléatoire.* Paris: C.N.R.S. 212 pp.
79. Ghiglione, R., Beauvois, J. L. 1972. Performance individuelle et performance de groupe dans des tâches de résolution de problèmes. *Année Psychol.* 72:519–45
80. Gilly, M. 1969. *Bon Elève, Mauvais Elève: Recherche sur les Déterminants des Différences de Réussite Scolaire à Conditions Egales d'Intelligence et de Milieu Social.* Paris: Colin. 253 pp.
81. Gilly, M. 1974. La représentation de l'élève par le maître à l'école primaire: aspects liés au sexe de l'élève et au sexe de l'enseignant. *Psychol. Fr.* 19:127–50
82. Gilly, M., Lacour, M., Meyer, R. 1971–72. Image propre, images sociales et statut scolaire: étude comparative chez des élèves de CM2. *Bull. Psychol.* 25:792–806
83. Gineste, M. D. 1973. Incertitude sur la performance et choix d'un partenaire de travail. *Année Psychol.* 73:555–64
84. Gratiot-Alphandéry, H. 1970. *Initiation à la Vie Sociale. Les Moins de 4 Ans à l'Ecole Maternelle.* Paris: Colin. 263 pp.
85. Haroche, C., Pêcheux, M. 1972. Facteurs socio-métriques et résolution de

problèmes. *Bull. Cent. Etud. Rech. Psychotech.* 21:101–17
86. Herren, H., Colin, D. 1972. Langage implicite et coopération chez l'enfant:étude comparative de sourds et d'entendants dans une tâche à deux. *Enfance* 25:325–47
87. Herren, H., Colin, D., Goddet, F., Alchenberger, N. 1972. Etude de niveau de développement mental chez les paraplégiques d'âge scolaire à spina-bifida. *Rev. Neuropsychiat. Infant. Hyg. Ment. Enf.* 20:681–700
88. Hoc, J. M. 1972. Représentation mentale et modèles cognitifs de traitement de l'information. *Trav. Hum.* 35:17–36
89. Hornemann, J. 1972. Classes de transition et classes terminales pratiques. *Doc. Psychol. Différentielle,* 2. Mimeo
90. Hornemann, J., Longeot, F. 1973. La validité prédictive des tests d'opérations formelles (T.O.F.) *Orient. Scol. Profess.* 2:245–59
91. Hurtig, M. 1969. Une expérience d'apprentissage cognitif chez le débile. See Ref. 30, 317–33
92. Kaiserszttein, J., Lemaine, G. 1971. *Recherches sur l'originalité sociale.* Lab. Psychol. Soc., Univ. Paris. 23 pp. Mimeo
93. Lambert, R. 1969. Extrémisation du comportement de prise de risque et modèle majoritaire. *Psychol. Fr.* 14:113–25
94. Ibid. Le comportment de prise de risque, 83–85
95. Lambert, R. 1970–71. Prise de risque en situation réelle ou imaginaire et facteurs de personnalité. *Bull. Psychol.* 24:105–10
96. Lambert, R. 1970. Extrémisation du comportement de prise de risque en groupe chez des malades mentales. *Encéphale* 59:499–514
97. Larcebeau, S. 1971. *Les intérêts artistiques: évaluation et signification.* Presented at 17th Congr. Int. Assoc. Psychol. Appl., Liège
98. Larcebeau, S. 1973. Intérêts, orientation et réussite scolaire. *Orient. Scol. Profess.* 2:45–60
99. Larcebeau, S., Bourdeyre, R. 1971. Intérêts et choix d'un type d'études *Bull. Inst. Nat. Orient. Profess.* 27 (special number):65–95
100. Lemaine, J. M. 1975. *Le Facteur Humain dans l'Expérience de Psychologie.* PhD thesis. Univ. Paris X, Nanterre, France
101. Lemaine, J. M., Guimelchain, M. 1971. Conditionnement verbal et problèmes

cognitifs (1954–69). *Année Psychol.* 71:209–34, 583–602
102. Lemaine, G., Lash, E., Ricateau, P. 1971–72. L'influence sociale et les systèmes d'action: les effets d'attraction et de répulsion dans une expérience de normalisation avec l'"allocinétique". *Bull. Psychol.* 25:482–93
103. Le Ny, J. F., Denhière, G., Le Taillanter, D. 1972. Regulation of study time and interstimulus similarity in self-paced learning conditions. *Acta Psychol.* 36:280–89
104. Ibid 1973. Study time of sentences as a function of their specificity and of semantic exploration. 37:43–53
105. Léon, A. 1969–70. Relation pédagogique et représentation de l'avenir chez des adolescents de l'enseignement technique. *Bull. Psychol.* 23:1069–81
106. Léon, A. 1972. La motivation chez les élèves de l'Enseignement Technique. *Psychol. Scol.* 9:69–79
107. Leplat, J. 1971. La psychologie du travail dans le monde. In *Traité de Psychologie Appliquée,* ed. M. Reuchlin, 1:105–60. Paris: P.U.F.
108. Leplat, J. 1971–72. Planification de l'action et régulation d'un système complexe. *Bull. Psychol.* 25:533–39
109. Leplat, J. 1974. Diagnostic et résolution de problèmes dans le travail. Rapport introductif à un symposium. *Actes 17th Congr. Int. Assoc. Psychol. Appl.,* Bruxelles, 129–39
110. Leplat, J., Chesnais, M., Gulian, E. 1971. Etude d'un modèle stochastique pour une tâche d'inspection. *Trav. Hum.* 34:265–76
111. Leplat, J., Pailhous, J. 1972–73. L'activité intellectuelle dans le travail sur instruments. *Bull. Psychol.* 26:673–80
112. Leplat, J., Pailhous, J., Vermersch, P. 1974–75. L'acquisition d'un système de représentation est-il rationalisable? Communication au Colloque Franco-Soviétique sur l'enseignement programmé. *Bull. Psychol.* 28:398–409
113. Lesage de la Haye, A. M. 1970. Effets de la durée future d'une interaction sur les évaluations réciproques des partenaires. *Psychol. Fr.* 15:147–56
114. Lesage de la Haye, A. M. 1972. Effet de l'intéraction anticipée sur la représentation d'autrui. *Bull Cent. Etud. Rech. Psychotech.* 21:103–20
115. Lévy-Schoen, A. 1973. Une expérience sur petit ordinateur concernant la perception visuelle et l'activité oculomotrice. *Lille Méd.* 18:729–32

116. Lévy-Schoen, A. 1974. Le champ d'activité du regard. Données expérimentales. *Année Psychol.* 74:43–66
117. Longeot, F. 1969. *Psychologie Différentielle de l'Intelligence.* Paris: Dunod. 191 pp.
118. Lurçat, L. 1968. Evolution du graphisme entre quatre et cinq ans: les figurations. *J. Physchol. Norm. Pathol.* 65:433–48
119. Ibid 1969. Genèse des liaisons visuographiques. 66:71–82
120. Lurçat, L. 1970. L'activité graphique des deux mains: contrôle visuel et contrôle kinesthésique. *Rev. Psychol. Appl.* 20:164–79
121. Ibid 1971. Espace et latéralité. 21:31–43
122. Lurçat, L., Kostin, I. 1970. Study of graphical abilities in children. *Percept. Mot. Skills* 30:615–30
123. Mariaux, J. 1971. Le rôle des contre-exemples dans l'acquisition des concepts d'application. *Psychol. Pédag.* 1–8
124. Martins, D. 1973. L'influence de rappels répétés sur la performance finale. *Année Psychol.* 73:101–13
125. Maury, L., Rogalski, J. 1970. Produit cartésien et complément. Etude génétique. *Année Psychol.* 70:53–71
126. Mehler, J. 1974. Connaître par désapprentissage. In l' *Unité de l'Homme,* ed. M. Piatelli, E. Morin, 287–99. Paris: Le Seuil
127. Ibid. A propos du développement cognitif, 300–11
128. Mehler, J., Barrière, M., Ruwet, N., Segui, J. 1974. Comparing comparatives. See Ref. 19, 431–48
129. Melot, A. M. 1972–73. Effet de la catégorisation du matériel sur la reconnaissance d'une liste de mots en fonction de l'âge et du type de reconnaissance. *Bull. Psychol.* 26:464–70
130. Merlet-Vigier, L., Zazzo, R. 1971–72. Le test des deux barrages et la théorie du contrôle. *Bull. Psychol.* 25:910–21
131. Molnar, F. 1970. Influence de la chromie sur le déclenchement du réflexe de fixation. *Année Psychol.* 70:7–18
132. Molnar, F. 1975. *La Perception Visuelle de l'Unité.* PhD thesis. Univ. Paris X, Nanterre. 544 pp.
133. Moscovici, S., Lage, E., Naffrechoux, M. 1969. Influence of a consistent minority on the response of a majority in a color perception task. *Sociometry* 32:365–80
134. Moscovici, S., Nève, P. 1971. Studies in social influence I. Those absent are in the right. *Eur. J. Soc. Psychol.* 1:201–14
135. Nadel, J. 1969. La ténacité musculaire en travail statique chez l'enfant de 7 à 12 ans. *Enfance* 22:165–82
136. Ibid 1971. Moments-clé d'une activité musculaire prolongée chez l'enfant de 7 à 12 ans. 24:49–77
137. Nadel, J., Netchine, S. 1975. Changements de réponse et changements de mode d'obtention de la réponse: une approche ontogénétique. *J. Psychol. Norm. Pathol.* In press
138. Netchine, G. 1970–71. La représentation psychologique de la déficience mentale, de Descartes à Binet. *Bull. Psychol.* 24:403–14
139. Netchine, G. 1972. Définition unitaire des déficiences mentales et définition unitaire de l'intelligence à la fin du XIXe siècle. *Enfance* 25:94–97
140. Netchine, S. 1969. *L'activité électrique cérébrale chez l'enfant normal de 6 à 10 ans.* Paris: P.U.F. 248 pp.
141. Netchine, S. 1969 Introduction à l'étude de l'activité électrique cérébrale chez l'enfant normal. In *Des Garçons de 6 a 12 Ans,* ed. R. Zazzo, Chap. 5, 205–17. Paris: P.U.F.
142. Noizet, G., Bleuchot, S., Henry, R. 1972. Complexité syntaxique des phrases et stratégies de leur décodage perceptif. *Aix-en-Provence, Labo. Psycho. Exp.* 91 pp. Mimeo
143. Noizet, G., Deyts, J. P., Deyts, F. 1972. Producing complex sentences by applying relative transformations: a comparative study. *Linguistics* 89:49–67
144. Noizet, G., Flament, C. 1970. Influence du système de réponse sur la discrimination perceptive. *Cah. Psychol.* 14:3–15
145. Noizet, G., Giniaux, F. 1970. Influence de la fréquence de marqueurs sur la perception d'un stimulus ambigu. *Psychol. Fr.* 15:85–96
146. Noizet, G., Petit, A. M. 1970. Système de réponse centré sur le sujet et système de réponse centré sur l'objet: comparaison de leurs effets dans une mesure de seuils absolus. *Cah. Psychol.* 13:53–68
147. Noizet, G., Pichevin, C. 1962. Etude génétique de la structure linguistique de l'association verbale. *Année Psychol.* 68:391–408
148. Nguyen Xuan, Lemaire, F., Rousseau, J. 1974. La sélection des informations dans la résolution du problème de série à trois termes. *J. Psychol. Norm. Pathol.* 71:297–317
149. Oléron, P. 1970. Sur les stratégies dans l'identification des mots. *J. Psychol. Norm. Pathol.* 67:313–23

150. Oléron, P. 1972. *Langage et Développement Mental.* Bruxelles: Dessart. 299 pp.
151. Oléron, P. 1972. Obnarujenie glukhimi det'mi razlistii mejdu visual'nymi ob'ektami pri ikh simul'tannom i suktsessivnom pred'yavleniyakh (Perception of differences by deaf children with simultaneous or successive presentation). *Defectologia,* 18–23
152. Oléron, G., Charles, A. 1971. Rapidité de codage verbal et modalité sensorielle de réception. *Année Psychol.* 71:87–98
153. Pailhous, J. 1971. Elaboration d'images spatiales et de règles de déplacements. *Trav. Hum.* 34:299–324
154. Ibid 1972. Influence de l'ordre de présentation des données sur la constitution de l'image spatiale. 35:68–84
155. Pailhous, J. 1974. Espace et formalisation. *Congrès de l'A.P.S.L.F. Espace Corporel à l'Espace Ecologique,* 325–32. Paris: P.U.F.
156. Pêcheux, M. 1969. *Analyse Automatique du Discours.* Paris: Dunod. 140 pp.
157. Pêcheux, M., Haroche, C. 1971. *Manuel pour l'Utilisation de la Méthode d'Analyse Automatique du Discours,* 24:93–106. Lab. Psychol. Soc., Univ. Paris VII
158. Perron, R. 1969. Déficience mentale et représentation de soi. In *Les Débilités Mentales,* 424–88. Paris: Colin
159. Perron, R. 1969. *Dynamique Personnelle et Images. Épreuve Projective Thématique. Manuel.* Paris: Ed. Cent. Psychol. Appl. 16 pp.
160. Perron, R. 1971. *Modèles d'Enfants, Enfants Modèles.* Paris: P.U.F. 252 pp.
161. Perron-Borelli, M., Perron, R. 1970. *L'Examen Psychologique de l'Enfant.* Paris: P.U.F. 240 pp.
162. Piéraut-Le Bonniec, G. 1972. Recherche sur l'évolution génétique des opérations de classification. *Arch. Psychol.* 162:89–117
163. Piéraut-Le Bonniec, G. 1974. *Le Raisonnement Modal, Etude Génétique.* Paris, La Haye: Mouton. 288 pp
164. Plon, M. 1968. Observations théoriques et expérimentales sur le rôle des représentations dans des situations de choix conflictuels. *Bull. Cent. Etud. Rech. Psychotech.* 17:205–44
165. Ricateau, P. 1970–71. Processus de catégorisation d'autrui et mécanismes d'influence sociale. *Bull. Psychol.* 24: 909–19
166. Rey, B. 1972–73. La mémorisation des mots catégorisés et non catégorisés.

Etude génétique. *Bull. Psychol.* 26: 458–63
167. Richard, J. F. 1974. *Attention et Apprentissage en Situation Aléatoire.* Paris: C.N.R.S. 230 pp.
168. Rodriguez-Tomé, H. 1972. *Le Moi et l'Autre dans la Conscience et l'Adolescent.* Neuchâtel: Delauchaux et Niestlé. 200 pp.
169. Rodriguez-Tomé, H., Zlotowicz, M. 1972. Peur et angoisse dans l'enfance et à l'adolescence. *Enfance* 25:167–74
170. Sasson, R. Y., Fraisse, P. 1972. Images in memory for concrete and abstract sentences. *J. Exp. Psychol.* 94:149–55
171. Savoyant, A. 1974. Eléments pour la définition d'un cadre d'analyse, des situations de résolution de problème en groupe. *Année Psychol.* 74:219–38
172. Schonen, S. de 1974. Etude de la lecture des représentations bidimensionnelles statiques de l'espace en perspective projective chez des enfants de 2:6 à 4:6 ans. *Arch. Psychol.* 16:287–310
173. Schonen, S. de 1974. *La Mémoire, Connaissance Active du Passé.* Paris, La Haye: Mouton. 335 pp.
174. Ségui, J. 1970. Rétention de paires de mots en fonction de certaines variables linguistiques. *Année Psychol.* 70: 123–30
175. Ségui, J., Dachet, F. 1970. Structure de la phrase et valeur syntactique des éléments de la phrase dans le rappel. *Année Psychol.* 70:461–66
176. Ségui, J., Kail, M. 1970. Rôle des caractéristiques lexicales du verbe dans le rétention d'énoncés. *Année Psychol.* 72:117–30
177. Swift, M. S., Spivack, G., Danset, A., Danset-Léger, J., Winnykamen, F. 1972. Classroom behaviour and academic success of French and American elementary school children. *Int. Rev. Appl. Psychol.* 21:1–11
178. Tiberghien, G. 1968. Etude de la certitude du rappel au cours d'un apprentissage verbal. *Année Psychol.* 68:357–72
179. Tiberghien, G. 1974. Contrôle des connaissances et contrôle de l'activité d'étude. *Rev. Fr. Pédag.* 28:5–10
180. Vermersch, P. 1972. Quelques aspects des comportements algorithmiques. *Trav. Hum.* 35:117–30
181. Verchuren, M., Levy-Schoen, A. 1973. Information inattendue et stratégies d'exploration oculaire. *Année Psychol.* 73:51–65
182. Vézin, J. F. 1970. Procédés de démonstration chez des enfants de 10 à 12 ans. *J. Psychol. Norm. Pathol.* 67:71–87

304   FRANCÈS

183. Vézin, J. F. 1974. Etude comparée de schémas plus ou moins concrets et d'énoncés verbaux: mise en correspondance et rôle dans l'apprentissage en fonction de l'âge. *Enfance* 27:21–44
184. Vézin, J. F., Berge, O., Mavrellis, P. 1973–74. Rôle du résumé et de la répétition en fonction de leur place par rapport au texte. *Bull. Psychol.* 27:163–67
185. Vurpillot, E. 1969. Activité oculomotrice et activités cognitives. *Bull. Psychol.* 22:660–68
186. Vurpillot, E., Moal, A. 1970. Evolution des critères d'identité chez des enfants d'âge pré-scolaire dans une tâche de différenciation perceptive. *Année Psychol.* 70:391–406
187. Weill-Fassina, A. 1973. La lecture du dessin industriel. Perspectives d'études. *Trav. Hum.* 36:121–39
188. Weill-Fassina, A. 1973. Difficultés de l'apprentissage de la lecture du dessin technique. *Bull. Liaison Pédag. Enseign. Technol. Form. Profess.*
189. Winnykamen, F. 1973. *Modalités de l'Activité du Sujet dans l'Acquisition de Connaissances.* Paris:C.N.R.S.
190. Winnykamen, F., Bonnin, M. C. 1972–73. Etude de l'entraînement de la catégorisation et de son évolution avec l'âge. *Bull. Psychol.* 26:968–73
191. Winnykamen, F., Dhenin, N. 1973–74. Evolution génétique de la catégorisation d'une liste de mots. Effet de la nature des listes (mots abstraits ou mots concrets). *Bull. Psychol.* 27:48–55
192. Zaleska, M. 1969. Prise de risque pour soi et pour autrui par des individus et par des groupes. *Psychol. Fr.* 14:97–112

193. Zaleska, M. 1972. *Comparaison des Décisions Individuelles et Collectives dans des Situations de Choix avec Risque.* PhD thesis. Univ. Paris V
194. Zazzo, B. 1969. Le dynamisme évolutif: la genèse des valeurs du moi chez l'enfant, étudiée à travers ses représentations de l'évolution. See Ref. 141
195. Zazzo, B. 1969. L'image de soi chez l'enfant de 6 à 12 ans. *Rev. Neuropsychiat. Infant. Hyg. Ment. Enf.* 17:479–86
196. Zazzo, B. 1971–72. Quelques aspects de l'adaptation de l'enfant à l'école maternelle. *Bull. Psychol.* 25:778–91
197. Zazzo, R., Ed. 1969. See Ref. 30
198. Zazzo, R. 1972. L'examen des débiles mentaux. In *Les Enfants et les Adolescents Inadaptés.* Paris: Colin. 284 pp.
199. Zenatti, A. 1969. *Le Développement Génétique de la Perception Musicale.* Paris: C.N.R.S. 111 pp.
200. Zenatti, A. 1973. Etude de l'acculturation musicale chez l'enfant dans une épreuve d'identification mélodique. *J. Psychol. Norm. Pathol.* 70:453–63
201. Zenatti, A. 1974. Perception et appréciation de la consonance musicale par l'enfant entre 4 et 10 ans. *Sci. Art. Sci. Aesth.* 9:47–61
202. Zlotowicz, M. 1969. L'anxiété à l'âge scolaire: aperçu génétique. See Ref. 141, 301–16
203. Zlotowicz, M. 1971–72. Essai d'interprétation des peurs enfantines. *Bull. Psychol.* 25:336–43
204. Ibid 1972–73 Sur l'analyse du cauchemar enfantin. 26:615–21
205. Zlotowicz, M. 1974. *Les Peurs Enfantines.* Paris: P.U.F. 186 pp.

ENGINEERING PSYCHOLOGY AND HUMAN PERFORMANCE[1]

♦256

Earl A. Alluisi and Ben B. Morgan, Jr.[2]
Performance Assessment Laboratory, Department of Psychology,
Old Dominion University, Norfolk, Virginia 23508

INTRODUCTION

There have been four previous chapters on "Engineering Psychology" in the 27-year history of the *Annual Review of Psychology*. The first, by the late Paul M. Fitts (74), appeared in Volume 9 (1958) and covered the literature from January 1956 to May 1957. This was followed 2 years later (Volume 11) by the chapter by Arthur W. Melton and the late George E. Briggs (153), which surveyed the literature from June 1957 through May 1959. The third chapter, by Alphonse Chapanis (39), appeared in Volume 14 (1963) and extended the survey of the literature to April 1962. E. C. Poulton's (172) review was published in Volume 17 (1966) and was based on literature surveyed to April 1965.

The present chapter, for which a 10-year span of literature has been surveyed, has the two terms in its title, "Engineering Psychology and Human Performance." It is meant to provide a transition from the reviews of engineering psychology that appeared every two or three years between 1958 and 1966, to the reviews of human performance that are being planned to appear at 4–year intervals hereafter [see the master plan listed in the preface of Volume 26, 1975 (181)].

The Changing World of Engineering Psychologists

The transition in review titles from "engineering psychology" to "human performance" is justified primarily by the transition in review topics that would be neces-

[1]The survey of literature pertaining to this review extended from January 1965 through December 1974.

[2]The preparation of this paper was supported in part by the Old Dominion University Research Foundation, the US Army Research Institute for the Behavioral and Social Sciences under Contract No. DA HC19-74-G-0018, "Sustained Performance During Continuous Operations," and the National Aeronautics and Space Administration under Grant No. NSG–1092, "A Review and Preliminary Evaluation of Methodological Factors in Performance Assessments of Time-Varying Aircraft Noise Effects." The authors wish to acknowledge the helpful assistance of G. D. Coates, H. G. Luhring III, and M. J. Alluisi.

305

sary to cover adequately the range of activities of engineering psychologists over the past decade. When Paul Fitts (74) described the professional and scientific aspects of engineering psychology in 1958, he correctly reported that the professional aspect involved ". . . the application of psychological knowledge to the design of human tasks, man-operated equipment, and man-machine systems, usually in collaboration with engineers . . ." (74, p. 267). The emphasis was clearly and pointedly on man-machine systems, and especially on their design or redesign.

The next review (153), while claiming no change in emphasis, explicitly extended the coverage beyond the design of man-machine systems to include ". . . the determination of operational procedures and work environments for the human operator . . ." (153, p. 71). Three years later, Chapanis's review (39), admittedly influenced by the successes of the earliest manned space flights in 1961 and 1962 and by the challenges implicit to the Apollo projeċ s goal of sending astronauts to the moon (and bringing them safely back to earth), carefully defined engineering psychology as the psychological component of the broader field of human factors engineering; other components included anthropometry, biology, industrial engineering, medicine, physiology, and toxicology. Then, in addition to covering the "traditional" areas such as visual displays, controls, tracking studies, and tactual communication, he included a major section on environmental problems (noise, illumination, stress, G-forces, etc), another on automation, and another on successful applications of engineering psychology in diverse settings around the world. Poulton (172) broadened the definition of engineering psychology still further in 1966 when he wrote of it as ". . . the experimental psychology of man in the complex technology of the mid-twentieth century . . ." (172, p. 178).

The trend evidenced in this brief recapitulation of the definitions employed in the earlier reviews of this topic has continued during the past decade. Indeed, during 1974 the Society of Engineering Psychologists—Division 21 of the American Psychological Association—voted to change the stated purpose of their organization in order to remove from the Bylaws what had come to be viewed as an overemphasis on the man-machine aspects of their field as it had evolved into the mid-1970s. The newly adopted statement of purpose commits the organization of engineering psychologists ". . . to promote research, development, application, and evaluation of psychological principles relating human behavior to the characteristics, design, and use of the environments and systems within which human beings work and live. . . ."

Thus the professional aspects of engineering psychology have broadened from their early emphasis as the psychological component of human factors engineering of man-machine systems to their current employment as the human factors or human resources applications of the data, methods, theories, and philosophies of experimental psychology in the design, maintenance, operation, and improvement of all kinds of operating systems in which humans are components. Such systems include the narrowly defined man-machine systems of the past and their engineering, as well as the more broadly defined environmental, social, and governmental systems of present concern and their management. They include as well all the mixed operating systems between the narrow and broad ends of the dimension of system complexity.

In short, on the professional side, the field would now be better described by the title or name that was first used for it, *applied experimental psychology* (43), because its former emphasis on "engineering" has been replaced by its broader current employment.

Human Performance: The Scientific Aspects of Engineering Psychology

The scientific side of engineering psychology was for Fitts mainly the ". . . conventional areas of experimental psychology, such as vision, hearing, perception, and learning . . ." (74, p. 267), but in the sense of relevant human performance functions applicable in the domain of the field's professional aspects (cf 153, p. 71; 172, pp. 177–78).

If this view is still held, and if it is recognized that the professional aspects of the field have been extended beyond the engineering of man-machine systems as indicated above, then the relevant human performance functions encompass just about all of that part of experimental psychology that deals with human performance. This is the sense in which it appears quite proper for this review, at this point in time, to serve as the transition from the past reviews of "engineering psychology" to the future reviews of "human performance."

This shift in nomenclature has the potential advantage of helping to keep conceptually distinct the two aspects of the field, the professional and the scientific. As Howell & Goldstein (112) point out, the distinction has not always been made clear, and the attempt to have "engineering psychology" stand for the scientific aspect, with "human factors engineering" or "human engineering" used to represent the professional aspects has generally failed. We are proposing that the name "engineering psychology" be used to represent that field which is embedded on the professional side in applied experimental psychology, human factors, or human resources applications, and on the scientific side in human performance research. This proposal appears to be consistent with the development of the field over the last decade, as argued above, and with the historical perspectives presented by Grether (94) for engineering psychology in the United States and by Murrell (164) for ergonomics research in the United Kingdom.

METHOD OF LITERATURE SURVEY

For this review, we have personally surveyed a 10-year span (January 1965 through December 1974) of 12 selected journals: *American Psychologist, Ergonomics, Human Factors, Journal of Applied Psychology, Journal of Experimental Psychology, Journal of Motor Behavior, Journal Supplement Abstract Service (JSAS), Catalog of Selected Documents in Psychology, Organizational Behavior and Human Performance, Perception & Psychophysics, Perceptual and Motor Skills, Psychological Bulletin, and Psychological Review.* There are many additional journals that we would have liked to survey directly (e.g. *American Journal of Psychology, Applied Ergonomics, British Journal of Psychology, Canadian Journal of Psychology, Quarterly Journal of Experimental Psychology,* etc), but time and resources are not without limits, so the relevant papers in these other journals were identified through two different approaches: (*a*) we surveyed selected topical areas of *Ergonomics Abstracts* and *Psychological Abstracts* for the same 10-year span, and (*b*) we made use of the *Psychological Abstracts Search and Retrieval Services* (PASAR) of the American Psychological Association. This last source, which included materials only from 1967 to the present, provided an additional 355 titles and abstracts not previously acquired through our other procedures. Finally, the senior author received numerous papers and reports in response to requests that had been published in the *Bulletin* of the Human Factors Society and the *Newsletter* of the Society of Engineering Psychologists.

Excluded Areas

Three broad areas have been excluded from this review, although each has sufficient worth and new information to warrant consideration for specific review in the future. They were the areas of research and applications in (*a*) personnel and training; (*b*) cybernetics, computers, and simulation; and (*c*) biotechnology, kinesiology, work physiology, and sport psychology.

Favored Items

The number of items in the remaining areas identified as candidates for inclusion was slightly in excess of 3000. Space limitations demanded that no more than about 5% of these be cited, so selections had to be made. The decision rules for the selections favored (*a*) published over private or institutional reports; (*b*) consolidations of several studies or groups of papers on a given topic over isolated papers or single experiments; (*c*) new areas of application and new phenomena over older ones that were judged more widely known; and (*d*) predictors of future trends over indicators of past trends.

Many of the items that have appeared in the literature of engineering psychology and human performance during the past decade are truly of exceptionally high quality, deal with important and interesting issues, represent significant contributions to the advancement of the field, and yet have escaped citation in this review. We regret this because we should have liked to include them. On the other hand, we are happy that the items of worth *cannot* be reduced to a relatively small fraction of the 3000 identified. We apologize for any errors in judgment that may seem apparent in our selections to different readers, but we offer no defense. We admit that a few vital signs may be insufficient to show the full state of good health in this field.

APPLICATIONS: ERGONOMICS AND HUMAN FACTORS ENGINEERING

Handbooks and Texts

If conceptual stability is demonstrated for a field by the existence of handbooks and specialized texts, then engineering psychology's growth to maturity has been amply established during the past decade. The second edition of Woodson & Conover's (226) handbook had just become available at the beginning of the period (1964), the year following the appearance of the long-awaited *Human Engineering Guide to*

Equipment Design (158). A revised, expanded, and improved edition of this latter appeared under the editorship of Van Cott & Kinkade (213) in 1972 and stands now as the latest, most authoritative sourcebook in the field. Data, principles, and design practice are presented for use in making human factors engineering decisions about equipment design and use. The data are arranged in ways that permit application to a broad array of systems, and the principles and recommendations included are presented in forms that permit interpretation and translation for application to specific systems in light of the operational and environmental properties of those systems. The revised *Guide* does not include information regarding the general areas of life support and environmental control, but those areas are covered in the second edition of the *Bioastronautics Data Book* edited by Parker & West (167). Together, these two books (167, 213) serve three functions: (*a*) guides for general system conceptualization; (*b*) handbooks for data, principles, and design practices to be applied in system design; and (*c*) texts or supplements for the acquisition of skill in human factors engineering.

McCormick's texts (146–148) have dominated the field in the United States for nearly a score of years—in part because they have presented a coherence that is difficult to obtain in anything other than the well-integrated work of a single author. Contributing to their success has been the basic soundness of McCormick's approach and presentation, the high quality of his scholarship, and the timeliness with which his revisions have kept the work current.

Several other books that could serve well as texts or supplements (depending on the class characteristics) have appeared during the review period. Chapanis's paperback (41) emphasizes methodology and the problems of testing people in experiments and on the job. Murrell's text (162), the English counterpart (163) of which was the first British textbook of ergonomics, presents research and theory in the first part and applications in the second; it contains, in addition to the traditional coverage, a final chapter on age in relation to industrial work—a topic that we predict will be of increasing importance to the field during the next decade.

Meister's book (151), organized like Murrell's with theory in the first part and practice in the second, is otherwise characteristically American with an aerospace industry flavor. It does an excellent job of presenting a picture of the human factors aspects of systems development, and because of this is one of the best available texts to start a student's thinking along the lines of the systems sciences. The papers collected and edited by Howell & Goldstein (113) could serve this purpose also, but more in the sense of supplementary readings that show something of the current breadth of engineering psychology.

Among the brief introductory booklets that have appeared are four of mixed merit but potential utility (again depending upon the characteristics of the audience). There is Chapanis's booklet (40) with a rather "classical" approach (but one chapter that is still successful in explaining the systems approach to human factors in a way that college sophomores seem to understand). There is Fitts & Posner's *Human Performance* booklet (75), which is more like a very clearly written scholarly review of research than an introductory work. There is the Singleton introduction (193), sponsored by the World Health Organization, intended for use as a teaching aid in the developing countries, which could be used in any classroom to present a brief but well-balanced review of the current state of the field; and finally there is the booklet edited by Shackel (188), which in spite of its title is more an introduction than a "handbook" and which suffers in its class only from the usual ills of similar collections of previously published papers by different authors.

While considering collections of readings, three sections of Fleishman's 1967 edition (77) are quite relevant and useful. The sections on fatigue, monotony, and working conditions, accidents and safety, and engineering psychology total 200 pages on which are reproduced 20 papers representing as good a coverage of the breadth of interests and applications in the area as we believe possible. The newer third edition (78) attempts to cover the same ground in just two sections totaling 113 pages and presenting 11 papers, representing a 44% reduction in the number of pages (the text's total pages were also reduced, but by only about 24%). As could be expected, the reduced coverage in the newer edition results in a less useful volume for the special purposes of engineering psychology.

Some of the major contributions of engineering psychology, such as the systems approach, the conceptualization of man as an information processing system, and the identification of human performance as an area of psychological research separate from the traditional areas (sensation and perception, learning, motivation), have been assimilated into the apperceptive mass of general psychology. One indication of this is the appearance of a few introductory psychology textbooks with strong emphasis in one or more of these approaches. For example, Heimstra & Ellingstad (107) employ the systems approach and present traditional topics in terms of the human behavioral system and interacting subsystems; abnormal psychology appears under "System Malfunctions." Lindsay & Norman (138) stress the information-processing and decision-making models in their introductory text and provide a creditable, but less than compelling, presentation of many of the traditional areas. We judge an emphasis on human performance, combined with a functional or "dimensional" approach to the kinds of things humans can do, as being the approach of potential greatest utility at the introductory psychology level; this was precisely the design of the Gagne & Fleishman textbook (87) which first appeared in 1959. The text and its approach would be most welcome in an updated version, and we hope a revision is currently under way or being considered.

Industrial Work and Production

There has been a trend towards increased applications of human factors engineering in industrial work and production, although proportionally the trend in the United States has lagged behind that in Europe, especially Britain. The spread of areas to which application has been made is broader there than in the United States, where the applications appear to have been dominated by the aerospace industry and the requirements established by military equipment procurement regulations.

A survey of human factors concerns in industrial systems is given in an issue of *Human Factors* specially edited by Harris (103). The diversity of topics is both informative and illustrative of the growing breadth of human factors applications —from work physiology and a mathematical model of hand-motion paths, through piecework production in a British factory and the manufacturing of microelectronic devices in the United States, to employee motivation and the training of personnel in remote locations. Twelve papers by different authors are included in the special issue.

More recently, another special survey of human factors in industry was edited by Davis (59, 60) for two numbers of the same journal. The 14 papers included were aimed at showing the new opportunities that exist for human factors engineering beyond the military weapons systems and aerospace industries in which it has been concentrated in the United States. The papers run the gamut of topics from the design of manufacturing systems and an ergonomic study of large offices to presentations on human factors and safety, work place design and posture, and the evaluation of user interaction with computerized management information systems.

Among the texts that have appeared, Swain's (207) is aimed at increasing the quality of industrial production and reducing human errors. The topics covered include selection, training, motivation, work-situation design, error identification and analysis, prediction of errors, and error-cause removal programs. Johnsen & Corliss (120) have written a text suitable for the engineer and general professional reader on human factors applications in teleoperator design and operation. Guidelines for the development and implementation of a maintenance engineering program for electrical systems have been prepared by Cunningham & Cox (55). Their chapters are collated with reference to the Military Standard Maintainability Program Requirements for Systems and Equipment (US MIL-STD-470), but many of their recommended practices are applicable to the design of equipment for commercial and domestic markets.

Quality assurance and industrial inspection have received considerable attention during the last decade. A good introduction to the topic and survey of methods available can be found in Harris & Chaney's book (104). Among the papers of note that have appeared, Jamieson's (116) was a field study of inspection problems in the telecommunications industry in Britain, and included an assessment of the effects of age on inspection performance. He reported that where performance differences existed, they favored the older inspectors, and that visual inspection was improved when isolated from production. Teel, Springer & Sadler (210) found that human performance in the assembly and inspection of microelectronic devices was improved with the use of special tools specifically designed to reduce human error. One design characteristic for microminiature inspection is the magnification provided, and Smith & Adams (196) have reported that time per correct inspection will be minimized when the visual angle subtended by the magnified defect is between 9.0 and 12.0 minutes of arc. Although they found essentially no influence due to ambient illumination where the inspection was made with use of a binocular microscope, other findings continue to favor the use of fluorescent over tungsten lighting for more general inspection tasks (139).

The applicability of theoretical models of behavior to the inspection task has been studied from at least two perspectives. First, Badalamente & Ayoub (12) have demonstrated that the detection of defectives in an assembly-line inspection of products can serve as reinforcements for observing behavior. The implication that rather precise control can be exerted by the environment (or contingent probabilities of the work situation) over the worker's inspections (or observing behaviors) should be surprising to neither Skinnerians nor engineering psychologists—it is the former's theoretical position and the latter's reason for existing as members of a distinctive field of research and applications. More recently, Drury & Addison (62) used a signal-detection theory approach to analyze the performances of on-line inspectors and concluded that on the whole the inspectors followed the theoretical predictions; also, they found that effective detectability of faults was significantly increased when more rapid feedback of performance was provided to the inspectors.

As we have indicated previously, ergonomics and human factors engineering abroad have been applied across a wider range of industries than has been the case in this country. Among the published examples of such applications are papers dealing with the automation of meat handling on the London docks (189), the design of tasks in a tea blending plant (136) and in the catering industry (56, 203), the ergonomics research needs in maritime operations (215), human factors aspects of materials handling tasks such as fork-lift truck operations (63, 64) and of textile handling (228), and the evaluation of two jobs in an iron foundry (98).

In the last cited report, which relates work conducted in Italy, the measures employed for the evaluations were heart rate, energy cost, and vertical vibrations that had to be endured in the two jobs. This tendency for European work to be oriented towards the use of psychophysiological criterion measures, while American work is oriented more towards the use of behavioral measures (with the British between the two), is clearly noted in a book edited by Singleton, Fox & Whitfield (194). The book consists of 27 papers based on presentations made during a symposium held in Amsterdam in September 1969 under the sponsorship of the International Ergonomics Association and at the instigation of Professor A. Chapanis. The papers are excellent "state-of-the-art" reports of various research programs that in the main emphasize atypical rather than "normal" jobs and situations (e.g. piloting rather than driving, stress rather than typical work, and limited rather than general populations of workers). One of the healthier trends of the past decade has been the tendency to move away from an overemphasis on the atypical, and the data being collected in studies such as those cited in the preceding paragraph are adding to the field's store of baseline data regarding human performance under varieties of normal working conditions.

Health and Safety

The area of occupational health and safety has expanded greatly during the last decade, with ergonomics and human factors engineering contributing their part to the expansion. The two-volume *Encyclopedia of Occupational Health and Safety* (67) has appeared under the sponsorship of the International Labor Office to claim the distinction of the definitive work in the area of health, safety, and the well-being of people at work. It is written by specialists from 70 different countries and consists of about 900 papers. Sleight & Cook's (195) less ambitious review of selected physical and psychological factors in occupational health and safety may be of greater direct utility to the researcher on the engineering psychology side of the problem. That the proper application of human factors considerations can improve safety and reduce typical accidents is illustrated by Winsemius's (225) case study of certain types of punching machine operations in a stationery factory. Also, Turbiaux's review (211) may be of use to those who are searching for European references on accidents and safety on the job.

Midway through the past decade there was a movement to explicate the role(s) that psychology and human factors applications could play in the further development of health delivery systems (176, 187). Although the practice of medicine itself appears not to have been touched, several related areas have received some attention. For example, Ronco's paper (180) seeks to bring consideration of the needs of the patient into hospital design. A job analysis method devised for the health-related professions was tested by Dumas & Muthard (65), who reported that use of the method permitted reliable reports over an extended period of time of the detailed characteristics of the tasks in a physical therapy service.

Human factors applications both in dentistry (127) and dental education (142) have received general consideration, and studies have been published on the design and evaluation of dental hand instruments (70) as well as on the visual interpretation of dental radiographs (91, 92).

Human factors applications to the design and evaluation of prosthetic devices for amputees, as well as assessments of the use of crutches as a temporary ambulatory device, have been studied by Ganguli (88) and his colleagues in India; only the latest of several publications has been cited and references to their other work can be found therein.

Researchers at Nottingham have been interested in road accidents involving child pedestrians and the development of measures of children's exposure to risk as pedestrians (111, 182, 183). The three investigations recently reported provide, in addition to the findings, a useful illustration of logical progression in the study of a problem. The findings indicate that children slightly under-report their actual exposure, that there is no difference in exposure between boys and girls, and that there is a highly significant increase in exposure with age of child. In the United States, Cross & de Mille (53) studied some of the human factors in bicycle-motor vehicle accidents and then recommended a combination of remedial programs that they concluded would result in a significant reduction in bicycle accidents.

Behavioral toxicology and the behavioral monitoring and detection of occupational hazards probably will be an area of increasing research and applications activities during the next decade. A state-of-the-art report in the form of the proceedings of a workshop on the topic has recently been published (227). The papers indicate formal concern with, and research on, worker exposure to occupational hazards such as solvents, pesticides, metals, toxic gases, irritants, odors, alcohol, and the interactive effects of drugs. Further, it is our judgment that behavioral monitoring may prove to provide more sensitive indicators of such hazards in occupational settings than environmental, clinical, or biochemical monitoring. It is an area of increasing importance, and one to which engineering psychology can contribute.

Automotive and Other Transportation Systems

The border between parts of the preceding area and this one has always been a bit fuzzy; we have elected to put pedestrian and bicycle safety (and accidents) there and highway traffic safety and automotive accidents here. The division may seem arbitrary, but in the past it has seemed justified on the basis of the greater emphasis on vehicular systems design on this side of the border. The appearance of the Environmental Protection Agency during the past decade and the greater concern for environmental pollution by automotive and other transportation systems again cloud the clarity of the distinction. In some future review it might seem more appropriate to have this section combined with the preceding one on health and safety. Clearly, this has been the trend over the decade.

Forbes (80) has edited into a single volume a collection of papers by authorities in the area of highway safety. Topics covered include driving simulation for testing and research; biographical and medical characteristics of drivers; visibility and legibility of highway signs; driver information systems; human factors in vehicle design, in driver training and education, and in control and modification of driving behavior by the legal system; and the effects of fatigue, alcohol, drugs, and psychosocial factors on driving behaviors and accidents.

Among the many advantages of the *JSAS Catalog of Selected Documents in Psychology* is that it makes generally available reports that would otherwise have been classified as private institutional publications. Five such reports from the General Motors Research Laboratories (90) appeared in one issue of the *Catalog* in 1972. The topics covered in these five papers range from the general (public transportation and human factors engineering; analysis of consumer preferences for a public transportation system) to the specific (three papers dealing with case studies and user preferences for a demand-responsive transportation system). Elsewhere, Melsa & Cohn (152) describe the development and use of a computer-based model of consumer attitudes regarding transportation systems (e.g. with travel time, perceived cost, and social status factors).

These studies illustrate a trend in human factors engineering to attend to attitude measurement as well as "hard" experimental measurements of human or system performance. Nor is the trend limited to the United States or to the automotive field as shown by a questionnaire study of British railway carriages of five types based on a stratified sample of some 1500 passengers (221). Experimental tests are still being conducted, as in Brown's report (33) of evaluations of motor vehicle occupant restraint systems, and we hope the trend to greater use of attitude measurements represents an attempt at achieving a more comprehensive evaluation (consumer acceptance has always been an important goal of human factors engineering) and not a tendency towards substitution of attitude data for performance data. We would caution researchers to keep conceptually distinct the differences among attitudes, expressions of attitudes, and the correlations of these with performance and behavior.

In a related vein, human factors considerations were emphasized in the design and development of the passenger vehicle as well as the train attendant's pod for the Bay

Area Rapid Transit (BART) system developed for the San Francisco Bay Area (205). With the system now in operation, it would be useful and perhaps even extremely valuable to assess the results. Information regarding both successes and failures (or oversights) should have implications for methodology and future applications.

Driving and highway safety research has grown worldwide. The Forbes text (80), previously cited, concentrates on work in the United States. Likewise, Hahn's (101) recommendations of more than a score of specific research programs (or program modules) are aimed at the development of a comprehensive research program on highway traffic safety in this country. The British have long been interested in research on the topics of driving and highway safety (e.g. 27, 29) as well as driver training (26, 28), as have other Western Europeans (see the Michon & Fairbank paper in 194, pp. 203–11; see also 7).

Subsequent to his successful demonstration with Poulton of the applicability of the subsidiary task technique for measuring the loading of the car driver, Brown (29) has employed that technique with others in studying fatigue in car drivers (24, 30, 32). The findings with the various measures have not always been consistent, and Brown, Tickner & Simmonds (32) have been led to the conclusion that fatigue effects are assessed better with subjective than with objective techniques. In Sweden, researchers found the use of a subsidiary reaction-time task better than psychophysiological measures (heart and respiration rates) in studying the effects on driving performance of 3 hr continuous driving (140). Direct measures of driving performances were employed by Sussman & Morris (206) in their study of driver alertness, and they found, for example, that during long-duration low-event driving, there was a linear increase in road position error.

The results of two studies (25, 131) suggest that driving performance can benefit from the presence of background music. However, telephoning appears to interfere with driving, minimally on the more automated driving skills, but more so on the perceptual and decision-making components of driving that might even be impaired critically by switching between visual and auditory inputs (31).

An impressive program of human factors research on vehicle handling variables and distance field of view as related to driver steering control and performance has been conducted at Melbourne by researchers Hoffmann, Joubert, McLean, and Sweatman (109, 149, 150, 208). In general, their results show that driver performance in steering is not greatly affected over a fairly broad range of vehicle characteristics, and their research should lead to clear specification of the range over which optimum performance can be expected. Related research has been reported by Olson & Thompson (166), who found that variable ratio steering gears may improve steering performance significantly in tasks such as parallel parking, and by Hindle (108) and by Weir & McRuer (220).

Eye movements and visual search patterns in driving have been studied directly by Mourant & Rockwell (159, 160), who found the visual search and scan patterns of novice drivers an indication that their visual information acquisition process was unskilled and overloaded. Information on vision test performance and other characteristics of nearly 18,000 California drivers has been reported by Burg (35). Dynamic visual acuity was found to be most closely related to driving record (accidents and convictions for traffic citations), followed by static visual acuity, visual field, and night vision.

Davies & Watts (57) have studied the nonoptimality of the positional relations of brake and accelerator pedals in contemporary automobiles, and Richter & Hyman (178) report significantly shorter response times for hand-operated trigger-actuated brakes than for the normal foot controls. Normative data on the brake reaction times of drivers who have to brake suddenly and unexpectedly in traffic situations were collected in Sweden by Johansson & Rumar (119); they report a median of 0.9 sec, and a third quartile of 1.2 sec. Regarding the importance of such reaction times, however, Smith & Kaplan (197) report that steering visual feedback delays of 0.2 and 0.4 sec result in severely impaired driving accuracy and learning in a simulated driving situation; they interpret their findings as indicating that delayed steering feedback, rather than the reaction time of the driver, is a primary factor in loss of control in emergency and difficult driving situations.

Along with the trend to attend to a greater degree to the situational factors that can contribute to highway safety, some attention has been given to the design of highway or road signs. In Sweden, Johansson conducted two studies, one reported in 1966 with Rumar (118) and the other in 1970 with Backlund (117). The results of the studies are disturbingly compelling in demonstrating that there is a human factors problem—on the average, drivers notice fewer than 50% of the road signs they drive past, the probability of detection of different kinds of signs ranging on the average from about 25% to 75%. Fortunately, the more urgent the information carried by the sign, the higher the percentage of drivers who report having seen it. Forbes & Gervais (81) have provided an excellent illustration of a combination of laboratory and field studies of symbol effectiveness for lane controls on the highway.

The lighting of automotive vehicles, both for driver performance in that vehicle and for the operators of other cars, has received some attention. Kao & Nagamachi (124) report that by increasing visual operational feedback through illumination of certain points on the hood of a car, safety and accuracy of driving performance at night could be enhanced. Plummer & King (171) report a laboratory study of perception of left-turn indicators of different designs, and Voevodsky (214) reports on the effectiveness of a deceleration warning light (an amber light mounted on the rear) in reducing rear-end collisions. The development of a novel kinesthetic-tactile display of intervehicular spacing, and the improvement in car-following performance achieved with its use, have been reported by Fenton & Montano (72).

Thus, in the automotive transportation field, we find that human factors considerations are being treated with more than the rhetorical interest that characterized the field prior to the past decade. We attribute this in part to demonstrations of the cost effectiveness of good human factors applications [as in the Voevodsky study (214)], and in part to the maturity of human factors engineering. We have simply amassed enough data, refined our methodologies sufficiently, and demonstrated the effectiveness of successful applications adequately to claim credibility in a very "hard-nosed" arena. Continued development of mathematical and theoretical formulations that can be validly applied, such as Forbes's (79) corrections of traffic flow theory with human factors considerations, will serve to establish the utility of human factors engineering and ergonomics even more solidly, and such developments are to be encouraged.

A great deal of work has been devoted to further human factors engineering of air traffic control (ATC) systems during the past decade. This has been one of the classical areas of engineering psychology [cf the paper by Fitts and his colleagues as reproduced in the 1967 edition of Fleishman's book of readings, previously cited (77, pp. 676–92)]. Of the many reports that have been produced on this topic during the decade, we shall cite only three.

The first is a booklet by Peters (169), part of a module of the British Open University course on "Systems Behaviour." The booklet is an easy-to-read introduction to the principles and British procedures in air traffic control.

The second citation is a special issue of *Ergonomics,* edited by Rohmert (179). It consists of 15 papers presented at an international symposium on the objective assessment of work load in ATC tasks. Of the 15 papers, 8 are from Germany, 4 from the Netherlands, 2 from France, and 1 from Britain. Thus they provide a survey of the ATC-human factors work in Western Europe.

The third citation is a report by Buckley, O'Connor & Beebe (34) of a simulation study conducted at the National Aviation Facilities Experimental Center (NAFEC) in Atlantic City. ATC simulators have come a long way since their early use in the Laboratory of Aviation Psychology at Ohio State University (cf paper by Fitts et al in 77, pp. 676–92)! With the capability has come also a great deal of research, and NAFEC publishes an impressive listing of reports.

Urban and Environmental Systems

"Human Factors and the Law" is the topic of a special issue of *Human Factors* edited by Chubb (47). The issue consists of a preface and six papers by different authors; they deal with issues such as the human factors engineer becoming the advocate of the consumer, experiences of a human factors engineer in providing expert testimony in court, his roles as expert witness or consultant with discussion of potential liability, and legal and ethical aspects of using human subjects in research. The emphasis of concern for legal matters as they might affect the working professional was the *Zeitgeist* of the late 1960s and the early 1970s; let us hope that now we can return to a balanced view such as that thoughtfully presented in the cited papers.

Human factors engineering reflected the national concern for law enforcement during the latter half of the past decade, and there were numerous specific studies dealing with such matters as: (*a*) the design of police patrol vehicles (48); (*b*) the selection of police patrol beats (155); (*c*) computer aiding in the identification of criminal suspects (184); and (*d*) human factors in command-and-control (communications) systems (102, in this case within a fire department).

Parsons (168) edited a special issue of *Human Factors* devoted to "Environmental Design." The seven papers included considerations from a human factors viewpoint of home, office, hospital, and museum environments. A survey of human factors applications suitable for problems of urban housing, with 47 references, has been presented by Carson (38), and a similar overview of human factors engineering as it could be applied to offices has been given by Fucigna (86). Taylor (209) has described a graduate program in architectural psychology, and with that we can conclude that engineering psychology has indeed been extended from the man-machine system to include at least urban and environmental systems.

The human factors engineering of the home has received long-overdue attention during the decade. Steidl & Bratton's book (201) deals exhaustively with every aspect of housework, as does the translation of Grandjean's analysis (93) of Western European ergonomics research applicable to the home, including a chapter on the special needs of the old and the handicapped. The kitchen (100, 216, 217), bathroom (130), and bedroom (168, pp. 421–50) have received special attention. This trend is both promising and exciting for two reasons: (*a*) we judge home design to have lagged behind other areas in the adoption of human factors considerations; and (*b*) the marketplace—the number of people whose lives can be somewhat improved —is very great. We hope the trend continues and expands.

RESEARCH: HUMAN PERFORMANCE

Methodology

At the beginning of our review decade, the mood was one of questioning the relevance of laboratory research and the capability of its findings being generalized and implemented in practical situations. Chapanis (42) stated the questions, and reflected the mood; the majority of the papers in the report of the 1969 Amsterdam conference previously cited (194) dealt with the methodology and techniques of measuring man at work both in the laboratory and in the field.

A grouping of seven papers, specially edited by Chiles (44) for *Human Factors,* resulted from an Aerospace Medical Research Laboratories conference and an American Psychological Association symposium on "Methodology in the Assessment of Complex Performance." The papers covered questions of methodology and techniques in field research, full-scale mission simulation, factor anlaytically derived test batteries, and the synthetic work methodology. The most important problems were identified as those related to (*a*) the criterion problem, (*b*) task taxonomies, (*c*) the reliability of measures, and (*d*) the role of face validity in the design of research equipment for measuring complex performances.

Papers have appeared on specific test batteries and methodologies (e.g. 156, 192), and Uhlaner (212) has drawn attention to the need for converging the selection, training, and job design areas to develop an optimum methodology for studying the effectiveness of human performance (and for human factors applications). Considerable attention has been given the development of a taxonomy of human performance tasks (e.g. 19, 76, 154), with major efforts devoted to this topic by different researchers at the American Institutes for Research (4, 5). Williges (224) edited five invited papers for a special issue of *Human Factors* on the subject of "Response Surface Methodology" in human factors research—a methodology that promises to permit efficient development of functional relations between human performance and other experimental variables through use of multivariate data-collection techniques and multiple-regression prediction equations. "Field Testing" was the topic of another special issue of *Human Factors,* edited by Baker & Johnson (13).

Temporal Influences on Human Performance

Colquhoun (50, 51) has edited two books dealing with temporal influences on human performance. Both books consist of papers prepared by the currently active researchers in the areas covered, and thereby serve well as state-of-the-art reports. The seven chapters in the earlier book, *Biological Rhythms and Human Performance* (50), deal with topics such as the nature of biological rhythms, circadian rhythms and their effects on mental efficiency, periodicities in sleep behavior and in perception, the menstrual cycle, and industrial work rhythms.

The second book (51) is subtitled, *Diurnal Rhythm and Loss of Sleep;* it represents the proceedings of a NATO-sponsored conference held at Strasbourg in 1970. There were 45 invited participants: 13 from Britain, 11 from France, 6 from West Germany, 4 from Sweden and the United States, 2 from Belgium and the Netherlands, and 1 each from Canada, Luxembourg, and Portugal. There are 22 papers in the text: 4 on general problems in the area, 8 on the performance effects of sleep deprivation, 4 on the effects of transzonal flights, and six on interactions of performance with circadian rhythms.

Considerable additional research on human performance effects of sleep (and sleep loss) has appeared (e.g. 15, 84, 105, 157, 165), as well as research on shift-work and work-rest cycles both in the laboratory (e.g. 45, 52) and in industrial settings (e.g. 8, 115). Although we have not attempted to cover it, research on fatigue is closely related to that of temporal influences on human performance. Two rather comprehensive references will be noted: the first is a book edited by Hashimoto, Kogi & Grandjean (106), based on a symposium on fatigue methodology held in Kyoto, and the second is a special number of *Ergonomics* (69) devoted to research on fatigue.

Environmental Influences on Human Performance

We have more items (well over 500) categorized in this section than in any of the others of this review. The effects of environmental factors such as noise, vibration, and illumination has been, and evidently continues to be, one of the basic research areas of engineering psychology. The trends during the decade have been (*a*) consolidations of data in major areas such as noise (e.g. 135), and (*b*) a shifting of emphasis from industrial application goals (as in the search for optimum illumination conditions) to goals of environmental design and control for protection of the consumer and public (as in raising the quality of life by avoidance of unpleasant vibrations or noise "pollution").

Poulton's book (173), *Environment and Human Efficiency,* represents a major consolidation of data on the adverse conditions endured by man, and includes not only adverse environmental effects such as heat, cold, vibration, and noise, but also other adverse conditions such as personal threat, drugs and poisons, and old age. This book could serve as a handbook for the researcher and as a textbook for the serious student in this area.

Aulciems (10) reports a rather comprehensive study of the effects of both indoor and outdoor climatic conditions (air temperature, humidity, radiation, air movement, atmospheric pressure) on the comfort and performances of secondary school boys and girls engaged in concentrated mental work. The importance of dealing with combinations of environmental stresses is pointed to by Grether (95), and Wilkinson (223) makes the point that not only do individuals differ in their responses to environmental stresses, but also that comfort and working efficiency are not necessarily equated.

Kryter's monumental monograph (135), *The Effects of Noise on Man,* will dominate this area for some time to come. He does point, however, to the general paucity of data, and the lack of clarity of findings even where data are available, concerning the effects of noise on human performance. The same point is made by Grether (96), who reports that overall the research data on noise and performance (reaction time, vigilance, time estimation, tracking, mental work, and industrial task performances) are rather contradictory and inconsistent. It may be that additional order can be brought to the area by use of the subsidiary task method, as suggested by Finkelman & Glass (73). The interaction of performance and noise effects should be an area of growing research interest, and Burns's book (36) may prove to be of some help to the researcher in this area; its final chapters present rather complete reviews of aircraft and impulse noise and of high intensity noise and sonic boom.

Two critical reviews of environmental temperature effects on human performance have appeared during the decade: Fox's review (83) dealt with human performance in the cold, and Jones's (123) dealt with the effects of high thermal stress. Experimental studies of heat stress (e.g. 11, 175) and body cooling (e.g. 128, 141) on human performance continue, as do studies of performance and thermal comfort (e.g. 71, 99). This area could benefit from a major consolidation of data, and Fanger's book (71) may provide a reasonable start and stimulus in this direction.

In the area of effects of vibration on human performance, we have four reviews of note (49, 97, 110, 191). Hornick & Lefritz's review (110) is combined with a report of a study they conducted to measure the effects of long-duration random vibration on human performance (as well as certain physiological, biodynamic, and tolerance responses). Shoenberger's paper (191) covers both subjective judgments of vibration intensity and the effects of vibration on human performance, and Collins (49) covers decrements in performance on tracking and visual acuity tasks during vibrations in terms of frequency, acceleration, and direction of the vibration. Grether (97) concludes that the lowest tolerance level for vibration occurs at about 5 Hz in terms of subjective discomfort, that visual acuity is severely impaired by vibrations in the range of 10–25 Hz and manual tracking performances by vibrations below 5 Hz. He points out that centrally mediated tasks such as reaction time, monitoring, and pattern recognition are highly resistant to the effects of vibration.

Although there are numerous other publications, especially in the areas of ambient illumination, underwater environments, reduced gravity environments, and special requirements (and applications) for space-flight environments, their coverage in prior reviews and in sections of the more general texts and handbooks previously cited herein justifies, we feel, our decision to devote no further space to them here.

Organismic Influences on Human Performance

There was very little work in this area prior to the review decade, and although work has increased during the decade it remains one of the under-researched areas that we predict will grow in the future. Programmatic research on the behavioral effects of illness (with infectious disease) was conducted and completed during the decade. A comprehensive review of the literature by Warm & Alluisi (219) had indicated in 1967 that there were essentially no prior studies of the effects of infectious disease on human performance. A summary of the research findings has appeared in the medical literature (3): decrements in synthetic work performance (156) first appeared in coincidence with onset of illness and became maximal when symptoms were greatest. Patterns of decrements were similar in bacterial (tularemia) and viral (Sandfly fever) illnesses, but the degree was greater on the average with the more severe tularemia (drops to 69% and 80% of baseline, respectively). Individual differences were essentially maximal in range; even with as few as 16 subjects who were equally febrile, some showed no decrements in performance whereas others were unable to work at all during peak illness. In a subsequent study (18), symptomatic therapy was employed in a viral illness, and performance was found to be essentially unaffected by the illness. It would appear that human performance in a work situation will vary as a function of the subjective symptoms rather than the objective indicators of illness.

There have been numerous studies of the effects of different drugs such as alcohol (46), caffeine (14), chlorpromazine (177), marihuana (37), and tobacco (122), on various aspects of human performance, but the research area can be characterized currently as fractionated and lacking direction. There is simply insufficient activity to cover all drugs on all aspects of human performance, and unless the overall level of activity increases, the field would be better served with more studies being concentrated in fewer areas.

Displays, Controls, and Information Processing

During the past decade, research on displays and controls has continued along now classic lines as evidenced by the several rather comprehensive reviews that have appeared on human operator performance in manual control (218), foot operation of controls (134), keyboard design and operation (2), design of electronic displays (161), and sampled imagery displays (21), as well as a special number of *Ergonomics* devoted to the subject of "seating" (68). Specialized books have appeared combining human factors and other branches of engineering on such topics as *Perception of Displayed Information* (20), *Information, Control and Decision Models of Human Performance* (190), and *Visual Search and Image Quality* (199).

An important trend during the past decade appears to be increased research efforts on the use of new methodologies in equipment and work-space design, e.g. computer algorithms (16), linear programming (85), biokinematic models (129), and an emphasis on the design for maintainability (54). We predict an increase in emphasis on research to provide methods for designing for trainability during the next decade.

As indicated at the end of an earlier section on handbooks and texts, the concept of man as an information processing system has been assimilated into psychology generally; at least one introductory textbook of psychology has been designed around this model (138), and chapters of other books have appeared with sections showing the use of information and uncertainty metrics in human performance research (61, pp. 171–206). Needless to say, a great number of studies have been published, but we shall cite only Johnson's (121) bibliography of 942 studies that have used information theory concepts or metrics in psychological research. Among the major consolidations of information theory applications in psychological research on human performance are Staniland's (200), which deals with perception and cognitive abilities, Laming's (137), which deals with choice reaction times, and the updated presentation of Garner's (89) formulations of information and structure. In all, information theory is less a model of human behavior than the source of useful metrics and concepts.

Skilled Performance and Vigilance

We have elected to include vigilance in this category because we tend to view it as skilled choice-reaction performance where the stimulus or signal has high temporal uncertainty relative to its spatial and stimulus uncertainty (cf 198). The blending of vigilance with information theory concepts, with research on attention and performance, and with quality control and industrial inspection on the applications side, has been a phenomenon of the past decade. Little of this was predicted, although some of the trends can be inferred from certain of the eight papers that made up the special issue of *Human Factors* on "Vigilance," edited by Adams (1).

Of the several notable texts, those by Mackworth (144, 145) and Stroh (204) relate vigilance to habituation and attention, whereas that by Davies & Tune (58) emphasizes more the performance aspects. The topic is related to complex monitoring by Howell, Johnston & Goldstein (114), while the applicability of vigilance research with low-probability signals is nicely illustrated in Fox & Haslegrave's (82) study of efficiency in industrial inspection (quality control tasks). Wiener (222) has extended Kelley's (126) ideas regarding adaptive controls to the measurement of vigilance decrements in a discerning way that may prove to be quite worthy.

The four volumes on *Attention and Performance* (132, 133, 185, 186), the first and third edited by Sanders (185, 186), the second by Koster (133), and the fourth by Kornblum (132), contain numerous papers by researchers from many different countries. Their reading should be mandatory for researchers who want to be aware of activities in this field on a worldwide basis.

Bilodeau's book (22) on *Acquisition of Skill*, with ten chapters and comments based on a conference held during 1965, formed the basis of a later volume edited by both the Bilodeaus (23) on the same topic. The earlier volume will still be of use to the researcher and advanced student, but the later one will serve better as a textbook in intermediate and advanced classes. Poulton's (174) recently published book on *Tracking Skill and Manual Control* gives promise of becoming a classic in the field. The Ammons's have summarized their more than 20 years of work on decremental processes in skilled performance (6), and concluded that there are many data capable of meaningful integration within a formal theory, but they are not yet so integrated. Among the new methods and theories of skilled performance that show promise are those of adaptive tracking, control, and training advanced by Kelley (125, 126), process-oriented theory (170), and intermittent control (17). Perhaps a new comprehensive theory is just around the corner; perhaps Poulton (174) is already showing us the way to it!

EPILOGUE

As we look back at what we have produced, we note that we have devoted about twice as many pages to a review of the applications as we have to the research. This does not accurately reflect the literature surveyed, for the research publications outnumbered those on applications easily by odds of 10:1 or more. There were literally dozens, and in some cases scores, of worthy papers on the same or similar research topic for each cited reference. But we did not attempt to reflect the distribution of published reports; rather, we chose to emphasize the applications. We believe that it is in the application that one finds the touchstone of validity of research findings and theory. And unlike the commonly held notion that research findings typically lead to fruitful implementation, we find that research needs to be translated into applications (cf 143). More often than not, it is the application that gives impetus and direction to future research by showing areas of informational and conceptual need. Thus the road map for the next decade of human performance research is to be found in the current applications of human factors engineering and ergonomics.

We note also that the great majority of items cited in the section on applications came from two journals, *Ergonomics* and *Human Factors,* that were well represented among the items cited in the section on research, too. Their editors are to be complimented on their encouragement of publication of high quality studies of human factors applications and research, especially in the form of longer papers representing consolidations of several studies and in special issues given over to several papers about a specific topic.

The past decade can be characterized as having produced (*a*) consolidations of data regarding both research and applications, and (*b*) extensions of engineering psychology at both its research and applications ends—applications moving from equipment design in man-machine systems to all aspects of design and use of all kinds of systems in which man has an involvement, and research moving from the man-machine interface to all aspects of human performance. The field is less "engineering psychology" today than it is "applied experimental psychology" (as noted in our introduction) or even "systems psychology" [as suggested by DeGreene (61)]. We predict continuation of the trends noted, but with fruition along two lines in the future.

First, we predict a growth in the consolidations of data combined from research and implementation areas; an example, too new to have been included otherwise in our survey period, is the review edited by Sticht (202) of the HumRRO research program on literacy in relation to job performance.

Secondly, we predict a formalization of recognition of the extension from human *factors engineering* to human *resources* applications, as was suggested 8 years ago by Eckstrand, Askren & Snyder (66). And, as a timely confirmation of our prediction, the first issue of *Human Factors* beyond our survey period is a special issue edited by Askren (9) on this very topic!

There is a potential danger in all this, and we would be remiss were we to close this chapter without calling attention to it. The extensions of engineering psychology on both the research (human performance) and the applications sides (human resources engineering) has the potential of posing a crisis of identity. Fitts's (74) definition was clear, but the successes of the field have carried it far beyond the man-machine interface. Let us hope that its new identity will emerge with clarity during the next decade.

Literature Cited

1. Adams, J. A., Special Ed. 1965. Vigilance. *Hum. Factors* 7:91–180
2. Alden, D. G., Daniels, R. W., Kanarick, A. F. 1972. Keyboard design and operation: a review of the major issues. *Hum. Factors* 14:275–93
3. Alluisi, E. A., Beisel, W. R., Bartelloni, P. J., Coates, G. D. 1973. Behavioral effects of tularemia and Sandfly fever in man. *J. Infect. Dis.* 128:710–17
4. American Institutes for Research 1972. Development of a taxonomy of human performance (3 papers). *JSAS Cat. Selec. Doc. Psychol.* 2:39–41
5. Ibid 1973. Development of a taxonomy of human performance (12 papers). 3:22–30
6. Ammons, R. B., Ammons, C. H. 1970. Decremental and related processes in skilled performance. In *Proceedings of CIC Symposium on Psychology of Motor Learning*, ed. L. E. Smith, 205–38. Chicago: Athletic Inst. 376 pp.
7. Anonymous 1968. Activities of the Traffic Psychology Institute of Vienna. *Rev. Psichol. Gen. Apl.* 23:553–62
8. Aseev, V. G., Mishin, Y. T. 1971. Work-rest schedule in performing a particularly monotonous task. *Vopr. Psikhol.* 17:110–20
9. Askren, W. B., Special Ed. 1975. Human resources as criteria for system design and organizational planning. *Hum. Factors* 17:2–70
10. Aulciems, A. 1972. *The Atmospheric Environment: A Study of Comfort and Performance*. Univ. Toronto Press. 166 pp.
11. Azer, N. Z., McNall, P. E., Leung, H. C. 1972. Effects of heat stress on performance. *Ergonomics* 15:681–91
12. Badalamente, R. V., Ayoub, M. M. 1969. A behavioral analysis of an assembly line inspection task. *Hum. Factors* 11:339–52
13. Baker, J. D., Johnson, E. M., Special Eds. 1974. Field testing. *Hum. Factors* 16:199–252
14. Baker, W. J., Theologus, G. C. 1972. Effects of caffeine on visual monitoring. *J. Appl. Psychol.* 56:422–27
15. Barrett, T. R., Ekstrand, B. R. 1972. Effect of sleep on memory: III; controlling for time-of-day effects. *J. Exp. Psychol.* 96:321–27
16. Bartlett, M. W., Smith, L. A. 1973. Design of control and display panels using computer algorithms. *Hum. Factors* 15:1–7
17. Beggs, W. D. A., Sakstein, R., Howarth, C. I. 1974. The generality of a theory of the intermittent control of accurate movements. *Ergonomics* 17:757–68
18. Beisel, W. R., Morgan, B. B. Jr., Bartelloni, P. J., Coates, G. D., DeRubertis, F. R., Alluisi, E. A. 1974. Symptomatic therapy in viral illness: a controlled study of effects on work performance. *J. Am. Med. Assoc.* 228:581–84
19. Bennett, C. A. 1971. Toward empirical, practicable, comprehensive task taxonomy. *Hum. Factors* 13:229–35
20. Biberman, L. M., Ed. 1973. *Perception of Displayed Information*. New York: Plenum. 345 pp.
21. Biberman, L. M. 1974. Fallacy and fact of sampled imagery displays. *Hum. Factors* 16:286–99
22. Bilodeau, E. A., Ed. 1966. *Acquisition of Skill*. New York: Academic. 539 pp.
23. Bilodeau, E. A., Bilodeau, I. McD., Eds. 1969. *Principles of Skill Acquisition*. New York: Academic. 386 pp.
24. Brown, I. D. 1965. Comparison of two subsidiary tasks used to measure fatigue in car drivers. *Ergonomics* 8:467–73

25. Ibid. Effect of a car radio on driving in traffic, 475–79
26. Ibid 1966. Subjective and objective comparisons of successful and unsuccessful trainee drivers. 9:49–56
27. Brown, I. D. 1967. Car driving and fatigue. *Triangle* 8:131–37
28. Brown, I. D. 1968. Some alternative methods of predicting performance among professional drivers in training. *Ergonomics* 11:13–21
29. Brown, I. D., Poulton, E. C. 1961. Measuring the spare 'mental capacity' of car drivers by a subsidiary task. *Ergonomics* 4:35–40
30. Brown, I. D., Simmonds, D. C. V., Tickner, A. H. 1967. Measurement cf control skills, vigilance, and performance on a subsidiary task during 12 hours of car driving. *Ergonomics* 10:665–73
31. Brown, I. D., Tickner, A. H., Simmonds, D. C. V. 1969. Interference between concurrent tasks of driving and telephoning. *J. Appl. Psychol.* 53:419–24
32. Brown, I. D., Tickner, A. H., Simmonds, D. C. V. 1970. Effect of prolonged driving on overtaking criteria. *Ergonomics* 13:239–42
33. Brown, P. J. 1968. Human factors research in motor vehicle occupant restraint systems. *IEEE Trans. Man-Machine Syst.* 9:88–89
34. Buckley, E. P., O'Connor, W. F., Beebe, T. 1969. A comparative analysis of individual and system performance indices for the air traffic control system. *Fed. Aviat. Admin. NAFEC Rep. No. RD-69-50.* 348 pp.
35. Burg, A. 1971. Vision and driving: a report on research. *Hum. Factors* 13:79–87
36. Burns, W. 1968. *Noise and Man.* London: Murray. 336 pp.
37. Caldwell, D. F., Myers, S. A., Domino, E. F., Merriam. P. E. 1969. Auditory and visual threshold effects of marihuana in man. *Percept. Mot. Skills* 29:755–59
38. Carson, D. H. 1969. Human factors in urban housing. *Consult. Eng.* 32:158–64
39. Chapanis, A. 1963. Engineering psychology. *Ann. Rev. Psychol.* 14:285–318
40. Chapanis, A. 1965. *Man-Machine Engineering.* Belmont, Calif: Wadsworth. 134 pp.
41. Chapanis, A. 1965. *Research Techniques in Human Engineering.* Baltimore: Johns Hopkins Press. 316 pp.

42. Chapanis, A. 1967. The relevance of laboratory studies to practical situations. *Ergonomics* 10:557–77
43. Chapanis, A., Garner, W. R., Morgan, C. T. 1949. *Applied Experimental Psychology.* New York: Wiley. 434 pp.
44. Chiles, W. D., Special Ed. 1967. Methodology in the assessment of complex performance. *Hum. Factors* 9:325–92
45. Chiles, W. D., Alluisi, E. A., Adams, O. S. 1968. Work schedules and performance during confinement. *Hum. Factors* 10:143–96
46. Chiles, W. D., Jennings, A. E. 1970. Effects of alcohol on complex performance. *Hum. Factors* 12:605–12
47. Chubb, G. P., Special Ed. 1972. Human factors and the law. *Hum. Factors* 14:1–40
48. Clark, G. E., Ludwig, H. G. 1970. Police patrol vehicles. *Hum. Factors* 12:69–74
49. Collins, A. M. 1973. Decrements in tracking and visual performance during vibration. *Hum. Factors* 15:379–93
50. Colquhoun, W. P., Ed. 1971. *Biological Rhythms and Human Performance.* New York: Academic. 283 pp.
51. Colquhoun, W. P., Ed. 1972. *Aspects of Human Efficiency.* London: English Univ. Press. 344 pp.
52. Colquhoun, W. P., Blake, M. J. F., Edwards, R. S. 1969. Experimental studies of shift-work III: stabilized 12-hour shift systems. *Ergonomics* 12:865–82 (see also 11:431–53, 517–46)
53. Cross, K. D., de Mille, R. 1974. Human factors in bicycle-motor vehicle accidents. *JSAS Cat. Selec. Doc. Psychol.* 4:158
54. Cunningham, C. E., Special Ed. 1970. Maintenance and maintainability. *Hum. Factors* 12:239–96
55. Cunningham, C. E., Cox, W. 1972. *Applied Maintainability Engineering.* New York: Wiley. 414 pp.
56. Cutcliffe, G., Strank, D. 1971. *Analysing Catering Operations.* London: Edward Arnold Luncheon Voucher Catering Educ. Res. Inst. 99 pp.
57. Davies, B. T., Watts, J. M. Jr. 1970. Further investigations of movement time between brake and accelerator pedals in automobiles. *Hum. Factors* 12:559–61
58. Davies, D. R., Tune, G. S. 1969. *Human Vigilance Performance.* New York: American Elsevier. 291 pp.
59. Davis, H. L., Special Ed. 1973. Human factors in industry—I. *Hum. Factors* 15:103–77

60. Ibid. Human factors in industry—II, 195–268
61. DeGreene, K. B., Ed. 1971. *Systems Psychology.* New York: McGraw-Hill. 593 pp.
62. Drury, C. G., Addison, J. L. 1973. An industrial study of the effects of feedback and fault density on inspection performance. *Ergonomics* 16:159–69
63. Drury, C. G., Cardwell, M. C., Easterby, R. S. 1974. Effects of depth perception on performance of simulated materials handling tasks. *Ergonomics* 17:677–90
64. Drury, C. G., Dawson, P. 1974. Human factors limitations in fork-lift truck performance. *Ergonomics* 17:447–56
65. Dumas, N. S., Muthard, J. E. 1971. Job analysis method for health-related professions: a pilot study of physical therapists. *J. Appl. Psychol.* 55:458–65
66. Eckstrand, G. A., Askren, W. B., Snyder, M. T. 1967. Human resources engineering: a new challenge. *Hum. Factors* 9:517–20
67. *Encyclopedia of Occupational Health and Safety* 1971: Geneva: Int. Labor Off. Vol. I, 753 pp.; Vol. II, 800 pp.
68. *Ergonomics* 1969. Special number on seating. 12(2):132–337
69. *Ergonomics* 1971. Special number on fatigue. 14(1):1–186
70. Evans, T. E. Jr., Lucaccini, L. F., Hazell, J. W., Lucas, R. J. 1973. Evaluation of dental hand instruments. *Hum. Factors* 15:401–6
71. Fanger, P. O. 1970. *Thermal Comfort: Analysis and Application in Environmental Engineering.* Copenhagen: Danish Technical Press. 244 pp.
72. Fenton, R. E., Montano, W. B. 1968. An intervehicular spacing display for improved car-following performance. *IEEE Trans. Man-Machine Syst.* 9: 20–35
73. Finkelman, J. M., Glass, D. C. 1970. Reappraisal of the relationship between noise and human performance by means of a subsidiary task measure. *J. Appl. Psychol.* 54:211–13
74. Fitts, P. M. 1958. Engineering psychology. *Ann. Rev. Psychol.* 9:267–94
75. Fitts, P. M., Posner, M. I. 1967. *Human Performance.* Belmont, Calif: Brooks/Cole. 162 pp.
76. Fleishman, E. A. 1967. Development of a behavior taxonomy for describing human tasks: a correlational-experimental approach. *J. Appl. Psychol.* 51:1–10
77. Fleishman, E. A., Ed. 1967. *Studies in Personnel and Industrial Psychology.* Homewood, Ill: Dorsey. 821 pp. Revised ed.
78. Fleishman, E. A., Bass, A. R., Eds. 1974. *Studies in Personnel and Industrial Psychology.* Homewood, Ill: Dorsey. 623 pp. 3rd ed.
79. Forbes, T. W. 1963. Human factor considerations in traffic flow theory. *Highway Res. Rec. No. 15,* NAS-NRC Publ. 1112:60–66
80. Forbes, T. W., Ed. 1972. *Human Factors in Highway Traffic Safety Research.* New York: Wiley. 419 pp.
81. Forbes, T. W., Gervais, E. 1972. Effectiveness of symbols for lane control signals. *Proc. Int. Conf. Highway Sign Symbology,* 92–105. Int. Road Fed. & Fed. Highway Admin., US Dep. Transp.
82. Fox, J. G., Haslegrave, C. M. 1969. Industrial inspection efficiency and the probability of a defect occurring. *Ergonomics* 12:713–21
83. Fox, W. F. 1967. Human performance in the cold. *Hum. Factors* 9:203–20
84. Freemon, F. R. 1972. *Sleep Research: A Critical Review.* Springfield, Ill: Thomas. 205 pp.
85. Freund, L. E., Sadosky, T. L. 1967. Linear programming applied to optimization of instrument panel and workplace layout. *Hum. Factors* 9:295–300
86. Fucigna, J. T. 1967. The ergonomics of offices. *Ergonomics* 10:589–604
87. Gagne, R. M., Fleishman, E. A. 1959. *Psychology and Human Performance.* New York: Holt. 493 pp.
88. Ganguli, S., Bose, K. S., Datta, S. R., Chatterjee, B. B., Roy, B. N. 1974. Biomechanical approach to the functional assessment of the use of crutches for ambulation. *Ergonomics* 17:365–74
89. Garner, W. R. 1974. *The Processing of Information and Structure.* Potomac, Md: Halstead. 203 pp.
90. General Motors Research Laboratories 1972. Five papers on human factors aspects of public transportation systems. *JSAS Cat. Selec. Doc. Psychol.* 2:43–45
91. Goldstein, I. L., Mobley, W. H. 1971. Error and variability in the visual processing of dental radiographs. *J. Appl. Psychol.* 55:549–53
92. Goldstein, I. L., Mobley, W. H., Chellemi, S. J. 1971. The observer process in the visual interpretation of radiographs. *J. Dent. Educ.* 35:485–91
93. Grandjean, E. 1973. *Ergonomics of the Home.* Transl. H. Oldroyd. London: Taylor & Francis. 344 pp.

94. Grether, W. F. 1968. Engineering psychology in the United States. *Am. Psychol.* 23:743–51
95. Grether, W. F. 1970. Effects on human performance of combined environmental stresses. *USAF AMRL Tech. Rep. No. 70-68.* 15 pp.
96. Grether, W. F. 1971. Noise and human performance. *USAF WADC Tech. Rep. No. 70-29.* 48 pp.
97. Grether, W. F. 1971. Vibration and human performance. *Hum. Factors* 13:203–16
98. Grieco, A., Sartorelli, E., Talamo, L. 1968. The ergonomic evaluation of two jobs in an iron foundry. *Ergonomics* 11:467–72
99. Griffiths, I. D., Boyce, P. R. 1971. Performance and thermal comfort. *Ergonomics* 14:457–68
100. Guilford, J. S. 1973. Prediction of accidents in a standardized home environment. *J. Appl. Psychol.* 57:306–13
101. Hahn, C. P. 1968. *Recommendations for a Research Program to Investigate the Human Factors Aspects of Driving and Highway Safety.* Washington DC: Am. Inst. Res. Rep. No. R68-4. 304 pp.
102. Harper, W. R. 1974. Human factors in command and control of the Los Angeles Fire Department. *Appl. Ergon.* 5:26–35
103. Harris, D. H., Special Ed. 1969. Human factors in industrial systems. *Hum. Factors* 11:99–196
104. Harris, D. H., Chaney, F. B. 1969. *Human Factors in Quality Assurance.* New York: Wiley. 234 pp.
105. Hartmann, E. L. 1973. *The Functions of Sleep.* New Haven: Yale Univ. Press. 198 pp.
106. Hashimoto, K., Kogi, K., Grandjean, E., Eds. 1971. *Methodology in Human Fatigue Assessment.* London: Taylor & Francis. 200 pp.
107. Heimstra, N. W., Ellingstad, V. S. 1972. *Human Behavior: A Systems Approach.* Monterey, Calif: Brooks/Cole. 563 pp.
108. Hindle, A. 1967. Motor vehicle handling properties and driver control. *Ergonomics* 10:675–82
109. Hoffmann, E. R., Joubert, P. N. 1966. The effect of changes in some vehicle handling variables on driver steering performance. *Hum. Factors* 8:245–64
110. Hornick, R. J., Lefritz, N. M. 1966. A study and review of human response to prolonged random vibration. *Hum. Factors* 8:481–92
111. Howarth, C. I., Routledge, D. A., Repetto-Wright, R. 1974. An analysis of road accidents involving child pedestrians. *Ergonomics* 17:319–30
112. Howell, W. C., Goldstein, I. L. 1970. Engineering psychology today: some observations from the ivory tower. *Organ. Behav. Hum. Perform.* 5:159–69
113. Howell, W. C., Goldstein, I. L., Eds. 1971. *Engineering Psychology: Current Perspectives in Research.* New York: Appleton-Century-Crofts. 648 pp.
114. Howell, W. C., Johnston, W. A., Goldstein, I. L. 1966. Complex monitoring and its relation to the classical problem of vigilance. *Organ. Behav. Hum. Perform.* 1:129–50
115. Ivancevich, J. M. 1974. Effects of the shorter workweek on selected satisfaction and performance measures. *J. Appl. Psychol.* 59:717–21
116. Jamieson, G. H. 1966. Inspection in the telecommunications industry: a field study of age and other performance variables. *Ergonomics* 9:297–303
117. Johansson, G., Backlund, F. 1970. Drivers and road signs. *Ergonomics* 13:749–59
118. Johansson, G., Rumar, K. 1966. Drivers and road signs: a preliminary investigation of the capacity of car drivers to get information from road signs. *Ergonomics* 9:57–62
119. Johansson, G., Rumar, K. 1971. Drivers' brake reaction times. *Hum. Factors* 13:23–27
120. Johnsen, E. G., Corliss, W. R. 1971. *Human Factors: Applications in Teleoperator Design and Operation.* New York: Wiley. 252 pp.
121. Johnson, E. M. 1972. A bibliography on the use of information theory in psychology, 1948–1966, and addendum. *JSAS Cat. Selec. Doc. Psychol.* 2:131
122. Johnston, D. M. 1966. Effect of smoking on visual search performance. *Percept. Mot. Skills* 22:619–22
123. Jones, R. D. 1970. Effects of thermal stress on human performance: a review and critique of existing methodology. *USA HEL Tech. Memo. No. 11-70.* 71 pp.
124. Kao, H. S. R., Nagamachi, M. 1969. Visual operational feedback and design of vehicle front-end illumination for night driving performance. *Percept. Mot. Skills* 28:243–46
125. Kelley, C. R. 1969. The measurement of tracking proficiency. *Hum. Factors* 11:43–64
126. Ibid. What is adaptive training? 547–56
127. Khalil, T. M. 1974. Dentistry: a grow-

ing domain for ergonomics. *Ergonomics* 17:75–86

128. Kiess, H. O., Lockhart, J. M. 1970. Effects of level and rate of body surface cooling on psychomotor performance. *J. Appl. Psychol.* 54:386–92

129. Kilpatrick, K. E. 1972. A biokinematic model for workplace design. *Hum. Factors* 14:237–47

130. Kira, A. 1966. *The Bathroom: Criteria for Design.* Ithaca, NY: Cornell Univ. Center for Housing & Environmental Studies. 116 pp.

131. Konz, S., McDougal, D. 1968. The effect of background music on the control activity of an automobile driver. *Hum. Factors* 10:233–44

132. Kornblum, S., Ed. 1973. *Attention and Performance IV.* New York: Academic. 771 pp.

133. Koster, W. G., Ed. 1969. *Attention and Performance II.* Amsterdam: North Holland. 449 pp.

134. Kroemer, K. H. E. 1971. Foot operation of controls. *Ergonomics* 14:333–61

135. Kryter, K. D. 1970. *The Effects of Noise on Man.* New York: Academic. 633 pp.

136. Lacy, B. A. 1967. The design of the operators' tasks in a tea blending plant. *Ergonomics* 10:266–70

137. Laming, D. R. J. 1968. *Information Theory of Choice Reaction Times.* New York: Academic. 172 pp.

138. Lindsay, P. H., Norman, D. A. 1972. *Human Information Processing.* New York: Academic. 737 pp.

139. Lion, J. S., Richardson, E., Browne, R. C. 1968. A study of the performance of industrial inspectors under two kinds of lighting. *Ergonomics* 11:23–34

140. Lisper, H. O., Laurell, H., Stening, G. 1973. Effects of experience of the driver on heart-rate, respiration-rate, and subsidiary reaction time in a three hours continuous driving task. *Ergonomics* 16:501–6

141. Lockhart, J. M. 1968. Extreme body cooling and psychomotor performance. *Ergonomics* 11:249–60

142. Lucaccini, L. F., Podshadley, D. W., Kreit, L. H. 1970. The role of human factors in dental education. *Hum. Factors* 12:39–46

143. Mackie, R. R., Christensen, P. R. 1967. *Translation and Application of Psychological Research.* Goleta, Calif: Hum. Factors Res. 142 pp.

144. Mackworth, J. F. 1969. *Vigilance and Habituation.* Harmondsworth, England: Penguin. 237 pp.

145. Mackworth, J. F. 1970. *Vigilance and Attention.* Harmondsworth, England: Penguin. 189 pp.

146. McCormick, E. J. 1957. *Human Engineering.* New York: McGraw-Hill. 467 pp.

147. McCormick, E. J. 1964. *Human Factors Engineering.* New York: McGraw-Hill. 653 pp.

148. McCormick, E. J. 1970. *Human Factors Engineering.* New York: McGraw-Hill. 639 pp. 3rd ed.

149. McLean, J. R., Hoffmann, E. R. 1971. Analysis of drivers' control movements. *Hum. Factors* 13:407–18

150. Ibid. 1973. The effects of restricted preview on driver steering control and performance. 15:421–30

151. Meister, D. 1971. *Human Factors: Theory and Practice.* New York: Wiley. 415 pp.

152. Melsa, J. L., Cohn, D. L. 1973. A computer-based model of attitudes in multimodal transportation. *IEEE Trans. Syst. Man Cybern.* 3:521–26

153. Melton, A. W., Briggs, G. E. 1960. Engineering psychology. *Ann. Rev. Psychol.* 11:71–98

154. Miller, R. B. 1967. Task taxonomy: science or technology? *Ergonomics* 10:167–76

155. Mitchell, P. S. 1972. Optimal selection of police patrol beats. *J. Crim. Law, Criminol. Police Sci.* 63:577–84

156. Morgan, B. B. Jr., Alluisi, E. A. 1972. Synthetic work: methodology for assessment of human performance. *Percept. Mot. Skills* 35:835–45

157. Morgan, B. B. Jr., Brown, B. R., Alluisi, E. A. 1974. Effects on sustained performance of 48 hours of continuous work and sleep loss. *Hum. Factors* 16:406–14

158. Morgan, C. T., Cook, J. S. III, Chapanis, A., Lund, M. W., Eds. 1963. *Human Engineering Guide to Equipment Design.* New York: McGraw-Hill. 615 pp.

159. Mourant, R. R., Rockwell, T. H. 1970. Mapping eye-movement patterns to the visual scene in driving: an exploratory study. *Hum. Factors* 12:81–87

160. Ibid. 1972. Strategies of visual search by novice and experienced drivers. 14:325–35

161. Munns, M. 1972. Recent research applicable to the design of electronic displays. *Percept. Mot. Skills* 34:638–90

162. Murrell, K. F. H. 1965. *Human Performance in Industry.* New York: Reinhold. 496 pp.

163. Murrell, K. F. H. 1965. *Ergonomics: Man in His Working Environment.* London: Chapman & Hall. 496 pp.
164. Murrell, K. F. H. 1969. Beyond the panel. *Ergonomics* 12:691–700
165. Naitoh, P. 1969. Sleep loss and its effects on performance. *USN MNRU Rep. No. 68–3.* 51 pp.
166. Olson, P. L., Thompson, R. R. 1970. The effect of variable-ratio steering gears on driver preference and performance. *Hum. Factors* 12:553–58
167. Parker, J. F., West, V. R., Eds. 1973. *Bioastronautics Data Book.* Washington DC: GPO (NASA SP 3006). 930 pp.
168. Parsons, H. McI, Special Ed. 1972. Environmental design. *Hum. Factors* 14:369–482
169. Peters, G. 1973. *Air Traffic Control: A Man-Machine System.* London: Open Univ. Press/Milton Keynes. 104 pp.
170. Pew, R. W. 1970. Toward a process-oriented theory of human skilled performance. *J. Mot. Behav.* 1:8–24
171. Plummer, R. W., King, L. E. 1974. A laboratory investigation of signal indications for protected left turns. *Hum Factors* 16:37–45
172. Poulton, E. C. 1966. Engineering psychology. *Ann. Rev. Psychol.* 17:177–200
173. Poulton, E. C. 1970. *Environment and Human Efficiency.* Springfield, Ill: Thomas. 328 pp.
174. Poulton, E. C. 1974. *Tracking Skill and Manual Control.* New York: Academic. 427 pp.
175. Provins, K. A., Bell, C. R. 1970. Effects of heat stress on the performance of two tasks running concurrently. *J. Exp. Psychol.* 85:40–44
176. Rappaport, M. 1970. Human factors applications in medicine. *Hum. Factors* 12:25–35
177. Rappaport, M., Hopkins, H. K. 1971. Signal detection and chlorpromazine. *Hum. Factors* 13:387–90
178. Richter, R. L., Hayman, W. A. 1974. Research note: driver's brake reaction times with adaptive controls. *Hum. Factors* 16:87–88
179. Rohmert, W., Special Ed. 1971. An international symposium on objective assessment of work load in air traffic control tasks. *Ergonomics* 14:545–672
180. Ronco, P. G. 1972. Human factors applied to hospital patient care. *Hum. Factors* 14:461–70
181. Rosenzweig, M. R., Porter, L. W., Eds. 1975. *Annual Review of Psychology,* Vol. 26, Palo Alto, Calif.: Ann. Rev. 731 pp.
182. Routledge, D. A., Repetto-Wright, R., Howarth, C. I. 1974. A comparison of interviews and observations to obtain measures of children's exposure to risk as pedestrians. *Ergonomics* 17:623–38
183. Ibid. The exposure of young children to accident risk as pedestrians, 457–80
184. Rudov, M. H., Zavala, A., Okonski, E. S. 1971. Computer aiding in the human identification of criminal suspects. *JSAS Cat. Selec. Doc. Psychol.* 1:2–3
185. Sanders, A. F., Ed. 1967. *Attention and Performance.* Amsterdam: North Holland. 452 pp.
186. Sanders, A. F., Ed. 1970. *Attention and Performance III.* Amsterdam: North Holland. 442 pp.
187. Schofield, W. 1969. The role of psychology in the delivery of health services. *Am. Psychol.* 24:565–84
188. Shackel, B., Ed. 1974. *Applied Ergonomics Handbook.* Guildford, Surrey: IPC Business Press. 122 pp.
189. Shackel, B., Beevis, D., Anderson, D. M. 1967. Ergonomics in the automation of meat handling in the London docks. *Ergonomics* 10:251–65
190. Sheridan, T. B., Ferrell, W. R. 1974. *Man-Machine Systems.* Cambridge, Mass: MIT Press. 452 pp.
191. Shoenberger, R. W. 1972. Human response to whole-body vibration. *Percept. Mot. Skills* 34:127–60
192. Siegel, A. I., Lanterman, R. S. 1968. A portable test battery for comparatively evaluating operator performance in full-pressure suit assemblies. *USAF AMRL Tech. Rep. No. 68–74.* 75 pp.
193. Singleton, W. T. 1972. *Introduction to Ergonomics.* Geneva: World Health Organ. 148 pp.
194. Singleton, W. T., Fox, J. G., Whitfield, D., Eds. 1971. *Measurement of Man at Work.* London: Taylor & Francis. 267 pp.
195. Sleight, R. B., Cook, K. G. 1974. Problems in occupational health and safety: a critical review of select worker physical and psychological factors, Vol. 1. *HEW NIOSH Rep. No. 75–124.* 422 pp.
196. Smith, G. L., Adams, S. K. 1971. Magnification and microminiature inspection. *Hum. Factors* 13:247–54
197. Smith, K. U., Kaplan, R. 1970. Effects of visual feedback delay on simulated automobile steering. *J. Mot. Behav.* 2:25–36
198. Smith, R. P., Warm, J. S., Alluisi, E. A. 1966. Effects of temporal uncertainty on

watchkeeping performance. *Percept. Psychophys.* 1:293–99
199. Snyder, H. L., Keesee, R., Beamon, W. S., Aschenbach, J. R. 1974. Visual search and image quality. *USAF AMRL Tech. Rep. No. 73–114.* 120 pp.
200. Staniland, A. C. 1966. *Patterns of Redundancy: A Psychological Study.* London: Cambridge Univ. Press. 216 pp.
201. Steidl, R. E., Bratton, E. C. 1968. *Work in the Home.* New York: Wiley. 419 pp.
202. Sticht, T. G., Ed. 1975, *Reading for Working.* Alexandria, Va: HumRRO. 186 pp.
203. Strank, R. H. D. 1971. *Ergonomics: Functional Design for the Catering Industry.* London: Edward Arnold Luncheon Voucher Catering Educ. Res. Inst. 56 pp.
204. Stroh, C. M. 1971. *Vigilance: The Problem of Sustained Attention.* Oxford, England: Pergamon. 106 pp.
205. Sundberg, C. W., Ferar, M. 1966. Design of rapid transit equipment for the San Francisco Bay Area Rapid Transit System. *Hum. Factors* 8:339–46
206. Sussman, E. D., Morris, D. F. 1971. Investigation of factors affecting driver alertness. *JSAS Cat. Selec. Doc. Psychol.* 1:30
207. Swain, A. D. 1972. *Design Techniques for Improving Human Performance in Production.* London: Ind. Commer. Tech. 140 pp.
208. Sweatman, P., Joubert, P. N. 1974. Detection of changes in automobile steering sensitivity. *Hum. Factors* 16:29–36
209. Taylor, C. W. 1969. A new psychology for urban design. *Consult. Eng.* 32:152–57
210. Teel, K. S., Springer, R. M., Sadler, E. E. 1968. Assembly and inspection of microelectronic systems. *Hum. Factors* 10:217–24
211. Turbiaux, M. 1970. The human factors in accidents on the job. *Bull. Psychol.* 24:952–60
212. Uhlaner, J. E. 1972. Human performance effectiveness and the systems measurement bed. *J. Appl. Psychol.* 56:202–10
213. Van Cott, H. P., Kinkade, R. G., Eds. 1972. *Human Engineering Guide to Equipment Design.* Washington: GPO. 752 pp. Revised ed.
214. Voevodsky, J. 1974. Evaluation of a deceleration warning light for reducing rear-end automobile collisions. *J. Appl. Psychol.* 59:270–73
215. Walraven, P. L. 1967. Future research needs in maritime operations. *Ergonomics* 10:607–9
216. Ward, J. S. 1974. Critical ergonomics factors in domestic kitchen design. *Ergonomics* 17:233–40
217. Ward, J. S., Kirk, N. S. 1970. The relation between some anthropometric dimensions and preferred working surface heights in the kitchen. *Ergonomics* 13:783–97
218. Wargo, M. J. 1967. Human operator response speed, frequency, and flexibility: a review and analysis. *Hum. Factors* 9:221–38
219. Warm, J. S., Alluisi, E. A. 1967. Behavioral reactions to infection: review of the psychological literature. *Percept. Mot. Skills* 24:755–83
220. Weir, D. H., McRuer, D. T. 1973. Measurement and interpretation of driver/vehicle system dynamic response. *Hum. Factors* 15:367–78
221. West, A., Ramagge, F., West, J., Jones, H. 1973. The quality of railway carriage environments. *Appl. Ergon.* 4:194–98
222. Wiener, E. L. 1973. Adaptive measurement of vigilance decrement. *Ergonomics* 16:353–63
223. Wilkinson, R. T. 1974. Individual differences in response to the environment. *Ergonomics* 17:745–56
224. Williges, R. C., Special Ed. 1973. Response surface methodology. *Hum. Factors* 15:293–354
225. Winsemius, W. 1965. Some ergonomic aspects of safety. *Ergonomics* 8:151–62
226. Woodson, W. E., Conover, D. W., Eds. 1964. *Human Engineering Guide for Equipment Designers.* Berkeley: Univ. California Press. 473 pp. 2nd ed.
227. Xintaras, C., Johnson, B. L., de Groot, I., Eds. 1974. Behavioral toxicology: early detection of occupational hazards. *HEW NIOSH Rep. No. 74–126.* 507 pp.
228. Yoshida, M. 1968. A psychometric analysis of textile handling. *Psychol. Res.* 10:1–12

CONSUMER PSYCHOLOGY: AN OCTENNIUM

Jacob Jacoby[1]

Department of Psychological Sciences, Purdue University, West Lafayette, Indiana 47907

The previous article on consumer psychology in the *Annual Review of Psychology* appeared in 1968 (310) and covered a 3 year span since its predecessor (415). During the intervening 8 years, consumer research has witnessed an information explosion. In their second edition of the leading marketing-oriented consumer behavior text, Engel et al write: "Between 1968 and 1972 there has been more published research than during *all* years prior to 1968. In revising [just] one of the [26] chapters in this text, the authors reviewed 125 studies and 10 monographs, all published since 1968" (122, p. 662; italics added). This writer estimates that 7,000 to 10,000 directly relevant papers have been published since the end of 1967. Keeping abreast of this literature is made difficult by the fact that only a small fraction of these articles (approximately 50 per year) are cited in *Psychological Abstracts.*

Accordingly, we see our function primarily as one of guiding the unfamiliar reader to and through some of this literature, not as providing rigorous and detailed evaluations on a study-by-study or even topic-by-topic basis. Actually, much consumer behavior research is at the relatively primitive level of identifying variables and relationships. We are still mapping the terrain; detailed criticism of most research areas would be premature. For these reasons, this paper adopts an excursion rather than an evaluation orientation.

Still, delimitation rules are necessary. We have chosen to confine attention to articles appearing in the *Journal of Consumer Research* and *Journal of Marketing Research* in particular, and also in the *Journal of Advertising Research, Journal of Applied Psychology,* and *Journal of Marketing.* The published conference proceedings of the Association for Consumer Research (141, 421, 426), American Psychological Association (Division 23), and American Marketing Association are also covered. Thus much relevant material in *Public Opinion Quarterly, Journal of Consumer Affairs, Journal of Business, FDA Reports,* etc is neglected, as are relevant articles sporadically appearing in other APA publications (e.g. 118). This strategy

[1]Preparation of this chapter was facilitated in part by a grant from the National Science Foundation (GI–43687). The substantial assistance of R. W. Chestnut and R. F. Silva in preparing abstracts of many of the cited articles is also gratefully acknowledged.

should result in our covering highly representative, although not always the "best" work. A final delimitation tactic has been to focus on "content issues" and ignore the wealth of generally excellent material on quantitative models (e.g. 153, 175) and multivariate statistics and designs [(cf 371) and the stream of publications on multivariate statistics by Green and his colleagues (e.g. 152)], all of which have exerted considerable impact on the field.

Consumer Behavior and Consumer Psychology

The distinction between consumer psychology and consumer behavior has been discussed at length elsewhere (194, 195). Suffice it to say that *consumer behavior* may be defined as the acquisition, consumption, and disposition of goods, services, time, and ideas by decision making units. *Consumer psychology* is defined as the utilization of distinctively psychological concepts and methods to understand (explain and predict) the dynamics underlying, influencing, and determining consumer behavior. Thus one need not be a psychologist and/or publish in psychology journals in order to engage in consumer psychological research. Much of the research discussed below is of this variety.

Trends

Several clearly discernible trends have emerged during this octennium. Of greatest impact is the attempt to begin working at levels of abstraction and the development of theory. The five most influential pre-1968 works in this regard have been March & Simon's classic *Organizations* (251), the Lavidge & Steiner article on advertising effects (243), Rogers' work on the *Diffusion of Innovations* (347), Nicosia's *Consumer Decision Processes* (289), and the volume on perceived risk edited by Cox (94). All have exerted considerable impact on Engel, Kollat & Blackwell (121, 122) and Howard & Sheth (182), who have published the two most influential treatises during our octennium. Reliance upon theory is also reflected in books by Hansen (167), Haines (161), Robertson, (342), Rogers & Shoemaker (348), and Ward & Robertson (425).

A second trend has been the shift from a focus on macro relationships, as influenced by Katona (cf 217, 218, 266), to the study of micro and intraconsumer factors. Four of the better anthologies clearly indicate this trend (84, 125, 178, 216).

Both of these developments have facilitated the development of a series of other trends. In particular, a third major trend is the shift from the simple identification and description of variables and relationships toward explanatory research and the search for cause-effect relationships. This has been aided by the development of a field and lab experimentation research tradition which is increasingly being applied to test theoretically derived propositions.

A fourth trend has been the rapid and substantial increases in behavioral science sophistication in regard to both concepts and methods. This trend is particularly true with respect to the incorporation of social psychological concepts and methods —a fifth trend. Moreover, there are signs of reciprocation on the part of social psychology. Reasons why social psychology will benefit from such an infusion are discussed elsewhere (194).

Sixth has been to move from a simplistic consideration of basic psychological constructs (e.g. motives, personality, attitudes) in relative isolation to a highly cognitive, information processing, decision making perspective. While the majority of the work being published is still of the isolated construct variety, stirrings toward studying consumer behavior from an information processing perspective were already in evidence in 1968, and the approach started to gather momentum circa 1972–73. This shift reflects a natural move to encompass and integrate more of the determinant influences on behavior and to do so with terms and concepts more meaningful and directly applicable to the consumer context. An emerging offshoot of this trend is the use of "process" methodologies (cf 37, 38, 47, 48, 205, 456) in an attempt to capture consumer information processing and decision making as an ongoing, dynamic phenomenon. This represents an improvement over three relatively static approaches that have been dominant for so long, namely: (a) large scale survey work, often of a longitudinal-panel nature and utilizing diary entries as the data of primary interest; (b) use of verbal report data collected post hoc, principally through recall; and (c) verbal report data derived by asking the consumer how he thinks he would behave or feel if and when confronted with certain (sometimes hypothetical) situations.

A seventh trend is the strong shift toward an interdisciplinary orientation. It has become obvious that serious scholars studying aspects of consumer behavior are harbored in a wide variety of disciplines and professional environments, and no single discipline is likely to solve major problems or come close to approximating the "truth" in isolation. One manifestation of this trend was the formation of the Association for Consumer Research in 1969. Although now moving into new spheres (e.g. the publication of special topic monographs), its basic contribution has been to enable consumer behavior researchers from more than a score of source disciplines (e.g. psychology, agricultural economics, architecture, law, medicine, marketing, etc) and operating within a variety of academic, governmental, and industrial contexts to interact on issues of mutual concern at its annual conferences. The proceedings of these conferences (141, 421, 426) amply reflect the multifaceted interdisciplinary nature of consumer research. Another manifestation of the interdisciplinary orientation is the *Journal of Consumer Research.* Cosponsored by ten different organizations—American Association for Public Opinion Research, American Council on Consumer Interests, American Economic Association, American Home Economic Association, American Marketing Association, American Psychological Association (Division of Consumer Psychology), American Sociological Association, American Statistical Association, Association for Consumer Research, and The Institute of Management Sciences—*Journal of Consumer Research* started with 4500 subscribers for its first issue in June 1974.

The eighth trend is an emerging concern with social issues. While stimulated by government (particularly the Federal Trade Commission and the Food and Drug Administration) and consumer activist efforts, this trend had already surfaced as a function of the burgeoning interdisciplinary diversity within the consumer research community itself. Traditionally there were three research questions of overriding importance: (a) How do you get the consumer to try a new product (the subject of innovators and innovations)? (*b*) How do you get consumers to buy the product on a more or less regular basis once they have tried it (the subject of brand loyalty)? (*c*) What is the effect of advertising on all this? Other meaningful research questions, many reflecting a concern with social issues, are now also being addressed. An excellent case in point is the Sheth & Wright volume (380) which covers, among other things, the subjects of health care, birth control, environmental problems, and public policy issues in the consumer realm. Also noteworthy are *Consumerism,* edited by Aaker & Day (1), *Advertising and the Public Interest,* edited by Divita (108), and the work of Friedman (132–134).

A final trend is one toward scientific respectability and legitimacy. To a certain extent, such legitimacy is conferred in psychology when recognized scholars such as William McGuire, Martin Fishbein, and Paul Slovic become involved in consumer behavior activities and research. To a very great extent, instant legitimization was bestowed when the National Science Foundation, through its Research Applied to National Needs program, began awarding grants for consumer research in 1973.

Cumulatively these trends indicate that consumer psychology is entering a more mature, scientific-scholarly phase. No longer are consumer psychologists interested only in the consumer qua purchaser, i.e. as a buyer of goods and services. Rather, the focus has shifted to an examination of the consumer qua consumer and to considering consumer behavior as a domain meriting scholarly and scientific attention in its own right.

Notwithstanding the fact that consumer behavior may simply be a stochastic process (26), the overwhelming amount of effort is directed toward demonstrating that it is not. We turn now to what of necessity is a highly selective review of this literature, first considering studies with a basic psychological construct orientation, and second considering studies which fall easily into a decision process/choice behavior mold.

CHARACTERISTICS OF THE CONSUMER: SELECTED PSYCHOLOGICAL CONSTRUCTS

Sensory Processes

Few studies were published which were primarily physiological or sensory in nature. Examples include Kohan's (231) article on skin resistance (GSR), Moskowitz's (278) research on scaling and the sensory dimensions of foods, Morrison & Dainoff's (277) study on looking time, and Bruvold's (67, 68, 70) work on the taste and flavor assessment of water. Somewhat related is the human factors work of Poulton (322, 323), whose findings suggest that the minimum type size necessary for reading food ingredients on packages be 6 pt. Univers and the minimum letter to background contrast ratio by 60%.

Perception

Perception touches upon many aspects of consumer behavior. Advertising and packaging provide numerous examples. Page constraints force us to delimit attention to three topics historically considered under this rubric: image research (which is probably more attitudinal than perceptual), perceived risk, and pricing and the price/perceived quality relationship (more accurately considered a judgmental rather than perceptual process).

IMAGE RESEARCH   Image research relates to a variety of image objects, including the following examples: products—tea vs coffee; brands—Coke vs Pepsi; corporations, i.e. manufacturers (cf 338, 406); stores, i.e. retail outlets; media—broadcast vs print; industries—the oil industry, the advertising industry; countries—"Made in Japan" (cf 124); and persons—an insurance salesman (cf 317), a celebrity doing a commercial, a politician (cf 265). Published research, however, seems to be concentrated on store image (11, 14, 235, 246, 294, 391, 405), product image (165, 211, 226, 276) and brand image.

Bird, Channon & Ehrenberg (49), noting that the real usefulness of brand image data depends on the extent to which it can explain differences in buying or usage behavior, describe the mathematics of relating brand image to purchase and usage behavior. Rao (327) examined brand images which developed when brand name was the only cue available, and Jacoby, Olson & Haddock (201) examined the impact of brand name image on quality judgments. Woodside (448) notes that beer brand images arise primarily through marketing efforts. Spence & Engel (388) found that preferred brand names are recognized faster than nonpreferred brand names. Kanungo found better recall (209) and awareness (210) for "fitting" brand names (i.e. those which sounded like the most frequent word association to the generic product), and describes the associative learning process played by fittingness and meaningfulness in brand awareness. Others have focused on related issues (cf 267, 268, 320).

PERCEIVED RISK   Bauer's (29) seminal statement on consumer behavior as risk taking behavior, coupled with the Cox (94) volume which summarized much of the work conducted from 1960 to 1967, gave impetus to widespread use of and research on the concept of perceived risk. Although not always clear in some of the early studies, a distinction can be made among perceived risk as associated with a product, as part of the purchasing environment, and as a characteristic of the consumer. Regardless of its locus, perceived risk is assumed to have motivational properties which usually direct the consumer toward risk reduction.

Five different types of perceived risk were identified and related to each other and to overall perceived risk (197) and later cross-validated (212). A variety of risk reduction strategies (e.g. buy only high priced brands, be brand loyal) have been studied, usually as they relate to the specific types of risk (cf 236, 242, 249, 293, 313, 350, 463). A number of studies have found that new product offerings typically are higher in perceived risk (112, 259, 304, 340, 360) and have examined the impact of such "higher risk" new products on consumer behavior. Particularly noteworthy in this regard is the rare application of experimental manipulation by Sheth & Venkatesan (379).

There have been several investigations bearing on the personality characteristics of high and low risk perceivers (cf 92, 176, 253, 463) and two studies which investigated the provocative issue of risk enhancement strategies (92, 106). Woodside has explored the possibility of a risky shift in consumer behavior (332, 447, 451). Environmental risk has been studied in relation to store selection and purchasing from catalogs (176, 334, 389).

Bettman has conceptualized perceived risk in terms of an information processing perspective (45) and has distinguished between "inherent" and "handled" risk (41). These latter two concepts seem useful but require conceptual and empirical clarification, perhaps evolving into a tripartite system of inherent, handled, and residual perceived risk. Bettman (42) has also proposed a theoretical model and measurement system for perceived risk and its components, and Taylor (410) has erected a scaffold for a theory of risk taking in consumer behavior.

PRICE PERCEPTION AND PERCEIVED QUALITY   Products may be conceived of as bundles of information cues (e.g. price, package, brand name, etc) which the consumer selectively attends to and uses in arriving at product evaluations and purchase decision. Given its nearly ubiquitous presence, considerable attention has understandably been devoted to examining the effect of price on consumer behavior. Two broad streams of work have resulted. One raises the question: What is the impact of price on the perception of quality? The second raises a logically prior set of questions: To what extent are consumers aware of and knowledgeable regarding prices?

Price perception   Monroe's (273) review suggests that there is a general lack of awareness of prices paid for recent purchases. Brown (62) noted that the validity of price perceptions varied markedly across communities but could find no other variables strongly associated with valid price perception (63). Granger & Billson (149) found that while prices were of clear importance in determining package size selection, consumers had no idea of relative value, according to some index such as cents per pound. Bettman (43) posits a relationship between the information properties of price and uncertainty. Monroe (271) describes psychophysical experiments for determining price thresholds and notes that buyers have ranges of acceptable purchase prices and tend to reject brands priced above or below this range. Bitta & Monroe (55) found that price perceptions are anchored by prices presented first in a series of price stimuli. Kamen & Toman (207) developed and tested a "fair price" theory which seemingly contradicts Weber's Law and stimulated some controversy (139, 208, 272, 392) and subsequent research (107).

Price and perceived quality   The price/perceived quality relationship has spawned more laboratory-experimental research during the review period .han probably any other topic in the field. Not surprisingly, studies which utilized price as the only independent variable (261, 262, 316, 452) generally found a significant main effect to confirm that price is used as an indicant of product quality. Interestingly, the price/quality relationship even seems to exist when subjects are not provided with price information but must supply their own (285). Evaluation of subjects who had already made selection decisions (237, 242) also provides evidence for a price/quality relationship. Multi-cue studies provide a much more complex picture. Several provide evidence of a price-quality relationship (13, 14, 81, 391, 417, 418). Others have found price to exert an inconsequential impact on quality judgments, particularly when cues normally available to the consumer are taken into account (142, 201, 325, 326, 405). Rao (326) and Olson & Jacoby (299) provide explanations for these negative findings, and evidence has been adduced in support of these explanations (326, 405). Some evidence exists to suggest that price reliance may be determined by consumer characteristics to a large degree (368), particularly consumer expertise (391, 418). An excellent unpublished critical review of the price/quality literature has been prepared by Olson (297) and is available as Paper No. 20, Working Series in Marketing Research, The Pennsylvania State University, 1974.

Learning

As with perception, learning has many interfaces with consumer behavior, only a tiny fraction of which is noted here. Association learning with respect to brand names has been studied (209, 210) as has semantic generalization (349). Several studies have examined semantic satiation in advertising ("ad wear out": 15, 150, 151, 443), and a published review on the subject exists (154). The Zeigarnik (172) and Von Restorf (177) effects have also been studied. Frequency effects have been considered (247, 264, 330) and attention also given to developmental (424) and sociological-situational (12) factors as these relate to learning. An excellent overview has been provided by Ray (329), and the volume by Haines (161) is also worth examining.

Attitudes

No other single psychological construct has permeated consumer research as has the construct of attitude. It would require more than all the allotted space to simply list the references to all the consumer research articles published between 1968 and 1975 which consider the subject of attitudes. Here we can only provide some idea of what has transpired.

COGNITIVE DISSONANCE   The flurry of dissonance studies which began in the early 1960s continued until 1972, and has dramatically tapered off since then. A review of the pre-1968 work is provided by Engel & Light (123). Since then, post-decision dissonance has been studied (87, 115, 145, 186, 369, 372, 440). The relationship of dissonance to brand loyalty was examined by Cohen & Houston (89) and Mittelstaedt (269). The relationship of dissonance to smoking behavior (296), to saving and spending (163), to the effectiveness of "hard" vs "soft" personal selling techniques (333), to increases in sales as a function of modifying introductory sales prices (118), and to disconfirmed expectations (8, 9, 295, 449) has also been studied. Cognitive dissonance as applied in consumer research has not been without its critics (300–302) and champions (170, 373). Venkatesan (422) has provided an insightful treatment of cognitive consistency and novelty seeking in relation to consumer behavior.

BELIEF-EXPECTANCY MODELS   While dissonance research has declined, expectancy-valence models of the Rosenberg (351, 352) and Fishbein (130) variety were introduced in 1969 (27, 53, 166) and have been a rapidly ascending fad[2] ever since. Although they have been used to directly predict choice behavior (166, 167, 438), they are more often used to predict attitudes/preferences. The effect of using only the most important predictors (166) and just how to identify them (5) has been considered. Controversy exists over whether the full scale model (27, 28, 32, 168, 248, 428) or a portion thereof (58, 80, 85, 270, 284, 376, 378) is the better predictor. Fishbein has argued that the purported tests of the Fishbein model were not tests of the pure model, but of hybrid variants (86), and replies (25, 375, 407) have provided interesting perspectives on the purpose of value-expectancy models in consumer research. Additional hybrids have emerged and been supplied with empirical support (19, 195, 200). The Hughes & Ray (184) volume contains additional relevant literature.

Insightful constructive criticism has been provided by many (see 59, 168). The most detailed, scholarly review of the issues and complexities involved was provided by Wilkie & Pessemier (435). Perhaps the most telling point, however, was made by Bettman (44, p. 299) when he noted that these models "may have predictive value, but research aimed at *understanding* how consumers make choices may be emphasizing the wrong approach in concentrating on these models alone" (italics supplied).

ATTITUDES AND BEHAVIOR   The relationships existing between attitudes and attitude change and behavior and behavior change have been explored in many studies (e.g. 18, 145, 174, 234, 279, 312, 436). A now classic paper is that by Axelrod (21) which presents data on the sensitivity, reliability, and validity of several attitude measuring techniques employed in advertising research. Perhaps the three most interesting studies are those by Aaker & Day (2), O'Brien (291), and Perry (312), because they examine the effect of attitudes, along with awareness and intentions, on each other and on behavior. Also worthy of attention is Sandell's (356) work on situational influences and Myers & Alpert's (281) paper on identifying "determinant" attitudes.

INTENTIONS   Verbally reported intentions, considered to intervene between attitudes and behavior (cf 243), are often studied in conjunction with, and sometimes subsumed under the rubric of attitudes (e.g. 59, 95, 279, 292, 296, 312, 386, 405). Often they provide the primary or sole focus of attention (e.g. 3, 16, 82, 119, 241, 408, 409). Two types of scales are typically used to collect intentions data, and the superiority of one is described by Gruber (159).

MISCELLANEOUS ATTITUDE RESEARCH   Several other noteworthy streams of attitude research have surfaced. Attribution theory (220) serves as the focal point for one such stream (72, 345, 346, 364, 366). Another is concerned with various

[2]For example, more than half the March 1975 issue of the *Journal of Consumer Research* (published after this review was completed) is devoted to these models.

aspects of the communication message, including fear appeals (331, 387, 394, 395, 419, 431, 433), distraction effects (50, 140, 172, 177, 393, 423), and immunization characteristics (52, 357, 403). A series of studies have been addressed to the impact of integrated advertising on black and white attitudes and purchase intentions (23, 24, 73, 74, 79, 110, 148, 160, 213, 214, 280, 362, 390, 404, 406, 413, 432). The results seem consistently to indicate virtually no effect on white attitudes but major effects on black attitudes. Attitudes toward numerous objects and events have been measured, including such wide ranging items as seat belts (129), playground equipment (315), skyjacking (91), usage of reclaimed water (69), and inner city transportation (248, 307). The effect of prior attitudes on the perception and effect of advertising messages has been considered in several studies (e.g. 147, 230, 257, 382, 437, 439, 455), as has the effect of corrective advertising (185) and the attitudinal profiles of different media audiences (225). The effects of heredity (311), scarcity (136), and government prohibitions (258) on attitudes have been examined as has the relationship between political attitudes and store patronage (116). Finally, the work of Day (102, 103) and the methods described by Hughes & Guerrero (183) are deserving of attention. Having scratched but the surface of an enormous iceberg, we take leave of the work on attitude and consumer behavior.

Personality

Although not as prevalent as attitudes, the construct of personality has also had widespread application in consumer research. The reader is directed to reviews (215, 429) for more comprehensive coverage. Most of the early research tended to be of the atheoretical, correlational, shotgun variety (i.e. let's take an easy-to-administer personality inventory, apply it, and see what we get); some of the more recent work has adopted theoretical and/or experimental orientations. With few exceptions, studies which utilized broad scale personality inventories such as the Edwards Personal Preference Schedule (e.g. 61, 131), the California Psychological Inventory (343; see critique 64 and rejoinder 344), the Jackson Personality Research Form, or some combination of these and other scales (e.g. 4, 51, 137) generally found weak-to-nonexistent relationships with consumer behavior when bivariate statistics were used, but moderate relationships when multivariate statistics (e.g. canonical correlation, cluster analysis) were employed (cf 6, 155, 221, 228, 385, 453). Arguments against the shotgun application of general personality scales in consumer research were made in an unpublished working paper[3] which has been liberally quoted in several subsequent evaluations of the personality-consumer behavior literature (e.g. 215, p. 416; 122, pp. 652–53). A critique delimited to consideration of only the EPPS in consumer research has also been supplied (180).

Much of the more recent work has focused on the relationship of specific personality characteristics to specific aspects of consumer behavior. Some of the personality dimensions studied are need for achievement (143, 172, 239, 240), category width (113, 114, 306), self-concept (109, 157, 158, 241), self-actualization (164), self-

[3]Jacoby, J. 1969. Personality and consumer behavior: How *NOT* to find relationships. *Purdue Papers in Consumer Psychology* No. 102.

confidence (22, 30, 54, 303, 381, 420), inner- vs other-directedness (111, 117, 367, 446), and dogmatism (10, 56, 90, 96, 187, 260, 414). Other traits examined include empathy (20), intolerance of ambiguity (57), uniqueness motivation (135), general dissatisfaction with interpersonal relationships (358), and compliance-aggressiveness-detachment (222).

Sometimes (e.g. 122, 429) considered along with the subject of personality inventories in consumer research is a set of studies variously termed "life style," "psychographic," or "AIO" (for *a*ctivities, *i*nterests, and *o*pinions) research. Representative studies include (66, 314, 318, 321, 430, 462). Applications of the Strong Vocational Interest Blank have also been reported (308, 319).

CHARACTERISTICS OF CONSUMER DECISION MAKING AND THE CHOICE BEHAVIOR CONTEXT

All major conceptualizations of consumer behavior (e.g. 121, 122, 182, 243, 289, 342, 348) are in agreement that consumer behavior is a dynamic, ongoing process subsuming several subprocesses of varying importance and temporal duration. The central notion common to all of these models is that man, qua consumer, is an information processor having information storage capacity in long-term memory and is capable of storing and using information via feedback loops and recall mechanisms. While the terminology and specific details may differ, most view consumer behavior as a series of sub stages (or sub processes) which move in sequence from awareness or problem recognition, to interest, to a recursive search and evaluation stage, to purchase, to post-purchase experiences and behavior. Not all stages are present in every acquisition-consumption situation, nor does the onset of any prior stage necessarily lead to any subsequent stage. The interested reader is referred back to the original sources for the richness of detail and elaboration which cannot be presented here. To a certain extent, earlier cited work which concurrently considers the interrelationship of awareness, attitudes, and intentions to each other and to overt behavior (2, 291, 312) is relevant here. Probably more directly relevant are (39, 40, 47, 48, 83, 219, 290, 324, 328, 354, 384, 454) and those contributions in (184) which focus on models and strategies of consumer information processing.

Pre-Acquisition Processes

NATURE AND EXTENT OF SEARCH   Field and laboratory evidence exists to show that the amount of information sought is typically small relative to the amount of information available (205, 286, 299). Information search is a negative function of time pressure (457), of the number of prior reinforcing experiences (36, 255), and declines when costs are imposed (401), when a satisficing rather than optimizing set is employed (400), and when past performance exceeds expectations (401). Information seeking declines when one learns to choose by brand name (205, 400). Under time pressures, consumers tend to accentuate negative evidence in search (457). Decision makers tend to engage in more flexible and extensive search than non-decision makers (256). Consumers use more information sources under conditions of high perceived performance risk, while perceived social risk appears to exert no influence on search behavior (249). Distinct types of risk perceivers tend to exhibit distinct types of search behavior (92). Government efforts to reduce financial risk through Truth-in-Lending legislation seem to have had no effect on the extent of information search (105, 132). Ratchford & Andreasen (328, p. 335) propose that "the breadth of information actually sought for any given decision is a function of the *demand* for information across respondents and the supply of information typically available for that type of decision." Pre-1968 findings are covered in *Consumer Behavior* (122, Chap. 16–18), and time-related aspects of search are treated in a special issue of the *Journal of Consumer Research* (204).

SOCIODEMOGRAPHICS AND INFORMATION SEARCH   In general, higher educated, higher income consumers are more likely to engage in search (293, 411), and search strategy seems to differ for males vs females (293, 402). Husband and wife influence varies at different stages in the decision process (99, 128, 450). The limits of bivariate demographic research has been discussed by Brandt & Day (60).

INFORMATION SOURCES   Consumer sources of information are both internal (i.e. memory as a function of past experience) and external. Little attention has been devoted to internal storage, except as related to the elderly (359) and in cases where the consumer has prior brand information (444). External sources are typically classified as marketer dominated (e.g. advertising, packaging, salespeople, etc), consumer dominated (i.e. informal word-of-mouth communication), or "neutral" (e.g. government reports, *Consumer Reports,* etc). Given our page constraints, almost none of the 1000 plus studies on advertising, packaging, and salesperson effects, or the smaller but growing literature on neutral sources, will be noted here.

Word-of-mouth   Word-of-mouth communication refers to the flow of information and influence between and among consumers. The substantial impact of interpersonal influence on consumer behavior is well documented (88, 335, 337, 383, 427, 441, 442). Most studies comparing the two find that word-of-mouth influence is considerably more potent than information obtained via advertising (17, 34, 75, 101, 292). Consumers tend to actively seek word-of-mouth information (287), and this influence seems to have greater impact under conditions of high risk (313). Conflicting evidence exists on whether neutral sources are more effective than word-of-mouth or advertising sources (227, 445).

Opinion leadership   Substantial evidence exists to indicate that some people are more influential than others; they are referred to as opinion leaders. Numerous investigations have attempted to identify the sociodemographic and psychological characteristics of opinion leaders (e.g. 93, 97, 127, 223, 229, 282, 336, 361, 396). Several studies have found a low positive relationship between opinion leadership and the tendency to be an innovator (191, 341, 397). The question of whether opinion leadership overlaps across different spheres of influence has also been addressed (156, 193, 224, 275, 282), with most results seeming to indicate that the closer the content of the spheres in question, the greater the likelihood and degree of overlap. Only two studies seem to have addressed the measurement issues of opinion leadership reliability (283) and validity (193). One interesting study (250) sought to "create" opinion leaders. Reviews of the word-of-mouth and opinion leadership literature, particularly as these sources of influence relate to the adoption of new products, are to be found in several recent works (122, 342, 348), and the application of these concepts to intraorganizational communication are discussed in a chapter by Jacoby (195).

Acquisition Processes

DECISION CRITERIA   Numerous aspects of the product, the purchase environment, and other circumstances can and do serve as decision criteria for consumers. Most major conceptualizations of consumer behavior (122, 167, 182, 289) devote considerable attention to the development and utilization of evaluative criteria into the decision process and a consideration of several specific decision criteria can be found in *Consumer Behavior* (122). Recent studies have examined color (309), warranty information (245), ecologically relevant information (173), and driving time (65) as decision criteria. Much attention has also been directed toward the use of unit pricing, open dating, and nutrient labeling information (133, 134, 144, 181, 254, 274). An excellent review of these investigations and related literature is forthcoming (104).

INFORMATION PROCESSING AND COMPARISON PROCESSES   Considerable work is now in evidence and in progress in the consumer sphere under this rubric. As examination of Hugh & Ray's recent book (184) indicates, much of the work on expectancy-valence attribute models is considered to fall into this category. A multiattribute, 0-1 threshold model for combining criteria to arrive at satisfaction decisions has been proposed (46) as has a similar threshold model for arriving at purchase decision (219).

The subject of the amount of information to be processed has received some attention. Haines (162) has proposed a Principle of Information Processing Parsimony according to which "consumers seek to process as little data as is necessary in order to make decisions." Although consumers seem rarely to limit themselves to one brand (363), they do tend to perceive more brands to exist than they would "ideally" like to have (365).

Information load   For any given product class in a purchase situation, information load for the consumer will be a function of many things, including the number of brands, the number of information dimensions available per brand, and the extent of articulation along each dimension (cf 192). Jacoby and colleagues (198, 202, 203) postulated a series of information overload effects between amount of information (defined in terms of number of brands X number of information dimensions per brand) and choice accuracy, decision time, and a series of subjective states (e.g. satisfaction with the decision) and provided evidence in apparent support of these relationships. These findings brought forth a series of critical commentaries (355,

399, 434); one rejoinder is in press (202a) and another has been submitted for publication.[4] Subsequent studies appear to confirm the overload effect (cf 204), and an overview of this research program has recently appeared (196). Consonant with Haines' Principles of Information Parsimony, evidence exists to indicate that consumers will confine attention to limited numbers of brands, variously termed their "evoked set" (182) or acceptance region (188), and limited amounts of information (196, 299).[5] In terms of expectancy-valence formulations, evidence exists to show that choice behavior can be predicted just as well from knowledge of the three most important attributes as from ratings on all available attributes (166).

Purchase strategies It is often argued that much purchase behavior is unplanned and done on impulse, and strategies are not involved. Kollat & Willett (233) note many problems with the notion of impulse purchasing and question its utility. Wright (458) provides interesting data regarding how consumers feel after using a maximizing vs satisficing choice strategy (cf March & Simon 251), while Ross (353, p. 46) summarizes the work of others in support of the predominance of a satisficing strategy. Roselius (350) examined strategies employed to handle perceived risk and found brand loyalty most consistently reported as the dominant strategy, while buying the most expensive alternative was the least often used. However, several studies have found that, particularly where the available brands are perceived to vary considerably in quality, there is a tendency for consumers to adopt a price-related purchasing strategy (236, 237, 242). Carman (76) suggests that what may be a "good" shopping strategy for one product category may not be good for another.

Brand loyalty Well over 100 articles have appeared on this subject since January 1968—and nearly as many different operationalizations! A proprietary monograph prepared by the author (and R. W. Chestnut) in September 1974 for Proctor & Gamble identified 40 specific operational measures of brand loyalty, 18 of which were first published during our review period (e.g. 35, p. 42; also 7, 71, 77, 100, 138, 188, 252, 288, 370). Unfortunately, rarely is more than one index employed in a given study or are the validities and/or reliabilities of the individual measures examined (two notable exceptions being 252 and 298). Only recently have comprehensive conceptualizations been developed to serve as a basis for deriving operational definitions (cf 122, 189, 199, 377) and the distinction made between brand consistent behavior and brand loyalty (cf 100, 189, 199, 206, 377). There appears to be a discernible shift in focus from the development of quantitative models of brand loyalty based solely upon overt purchase behavior to approaches which combine cognitive and affective factors with overt behavior. Occasional experimental work is in evidence (199, 263, 269), and interesting attempts to study brand loyalty through brand switching patterns also exist (78, 244). However, until the

---

[4]Available from the author as *Purdue Papers in Consumer Psychology* No. 144.
[5]Several studies in progress by the author under NSF Grant No. GI-43687 consistently show that, under conditions of *ad libitum* information acquisition, most consumers acquire substantially less than 10% of the information available.

turbid state of brand loyalty measures is clarified, no conclusion regarding brand loyalty findings seems justified. The problems with much of the early research are detailed most explicitly in two useful sources (122, 199). Relatedly, there have been several investigations directed toward the subject of store loyalty (e.g. 51, 77, 246).

Innovations and Innovators: The Case of New Products

For a variety of reasons, considerable attention has been devoted to studying consumer reaction to new products and services. Fortuitously, the knowledge and principles derived in the commercial context can often be applied in other socially beneficial contexts (cf 459).

Attention has been devoted to conceptually defining what constitutes an innovation and innovator. Probably the best treatment of these issues is found in the work of Robertson (342), Rogers (348), and Zaltman (461), all of whom have written extensively on the subject. Because of the potentially great applied value accruing to valid and reliable findings on this subject, considerable empirical attention has been devoted to identifying the sociodemographic and personal characteristics of innovators (e.g. 31, 56, 57, 98, 111, 112, 114, 117, 126, 135, 146, 187, 304–306, 412, 416) and how they acquire and use information about the innovation (e.g. 33, 37, 120, 179, 238, 339, 340, 374, 398). It has been argued that categorizing a consumer as an innovator because of a single new product purchase provides an insufficient basis for drawing conclusions regarding innovators "in general" (190). Crude attempts to assess the interrelationship among different operational measures of innovativeness are described by Kohn & Jacoby (232). Several experimental studies have been conducted (cf 135, 145), as has an investigation using one of the new process methodologies (37).

Before one can have an innovator, one must first be able to define what constitutes an innovation, and several writers have addressed this issue (e.g. 112, 113, 122, 169, 342, 348, 460, 461). The general trend has been to move away from using the marketer's or investigator's arbitrary assertion that a product is "new" to employing definitions based upon the respondent's perceptions of the object. Evidence exists to suggest that perceptual variables are more effective predictors of purchase than are the respondent's personal characteristics. It also appears as if the perception of recency, in contrast to perceptions of novelty and scarcity, account for the major proportion of variance in perceptions of "newness" (169).

CONCLUSION

We estimate that our perforce selective overview of what has transpired in consumer psychology during the elapsed octennium has touched upon substantially less than 10% of the available material. Discernible trends were noted at the outset. Major problems and future directions are briefly noted here.

The rudimentary task of ascertaining the validity, reliability, and sensitivity of the measures being employed, and their interrelationship to other indices which purportedly measure the same phenomenon, has generally been ignored (cf 171). Many investigators seem to be totally unaware of the vital necessity for such measure assessment research *prior to* using said measures in attempts to identify relationships, particularly cause-effect relationships. Unfortunately, the amount of such research conducted in regard to central constructs such as brand loyalty (252, 298), innovation proneness (232), opinion leadership (193, 283), and attitude measures that predict purchase (21, 159) is relatively meager. A weeding out of unsatisfactory measures is urgently needed. Relatedly, there is a need for research which moves from simplistic dependent variables toward employing multiple measures of the same dependent variable (e.g. 199), and to multiple dependent measures (e.g. 202). Too often conclusions are accepted on the basis of only a single test of the relationship in question, and opportunities for enhancing understanding through the inclusion of a variety of dependent variables are generally ignored. Additionally, there is need for greater conceptual specificity and clarity, especially in regard to definitions of terms and constructs. There is all too little programmatic research and too little replication and cross-validation of findings (e.g. 212). The fledgling trends toward incorporation of theory, use of an information processing framework, process research as opposed to terrain mapping and nose counting, examining a wider context of problems and issues (e.g. housing, energy, urban transportation, the elderly, the world food problem, etc) and experimental research (in both field and laboratory) should all be promoted. Finally, the disproportionate weighting given to studying the acquisition phase of consumer behavior should be counterbalanced by an increased effort devoted to studying both actual consumption (i.e. the post-purchase interaction between the product and the consumer of that product) and disposition. Automobiles, homes, and especially stock market securities would seem to offer particularly good opportunities for studying disposition although, particularly in these times of resource constriction, the intermediate and final disposition of all products (from toothbrushes to candy bars and candy bar wrappers to old bicycles etc) should be studied. As things stand now, we are considering only a fraction of the process of consumption. As a consequence, our resultant knowledge cannot help but be incomplete.

In our opinion, perhaps as much as 85% of what had been published under the rubric of consumer psychology prior to 1968 was rather low level and of questionable worth. At most, probably only 50% of the 1975 crop of articles belongs in this category. The amount of truly "good" work (as assessed in terms of psychology's historically rigorous criteria for behavioral science research) is certainly increasing. Surely the next octennium will witness even greater strides.

Literature Cited[1]

1. Aaker, D. A., Day, G. S., Eds. 1974. *Consumerism: Search for the Consumer Interest.* New York: Free Press. 2nd ed.
2. Aaker, D. A., Day, G. S. 1974. A dynamic model of relationships among advertising, consumer awareness, attitudes, and behavior. *JAP* 59:281–86
3. Abrams, J. 1969. Reducing the risk of new product marketing strategies testing. *JMR* 6:216–20
4. Ahmed, S. 1972. Prediction of cigarette consumption level with personality and socioeconomic variables. *JAP* 56:437–38
5. Alpert, M. L. 1971. Identification of determinant attributes: A comparison of methods. *JMR* 8(2):184–91
6. Ibid 1972. Personality and the determinants of product choice. 9(1):89–92
7. Anderson, E. E. 1974. The measurement of buyer brand preference and indifference under changing terms of trade. *Am. J. Agric. Econ.* 56:122–28
8. Anderson, R. E. 1972. Consumerism, consumer expectations, and perceived product performance. See Ref. 421, 67–79
9. Anderson, R. E. 1973. Consumer dissatisfaction: The effect of disconfirmed expectancy on perceived product importance. *JMR* 10(1):38–44
10. Anderson, W. T., Cunningham, W. H. 1972. The socially conscious consumer. *JM* 36(3):23–31
11. Andreasen, A. R., Alexis, M., Haines, G. H., Simon, L. S. 1971. Comparison of consumer and store manager attitudes: The case of racial effects in inner city retailing. See Ref. 141, 56–75
12. Andreasen, A. R., Durdson, P. G. 1968. Market learning of new residents. *JMR* 5(2):166–76
13. Andrews, I. R., Valenzi, E. R. 1970. The relationship between price and blind-rated quality for margarines and butters. *JMR* 7(3):393–95
14. Andrews, I. R., Valenzi, E. R. 1971. Combining price, brand, and store cues to form an impression of product quality. *Proc. APA* 6:649–50
15. Appel, V. 1971. On advertising wear out. *JAR* 11(1):11–13
16. Armstrong, J. S., Overton, T. 1971. Brief vs. comprehensive descriptions in measuring intentions to purchase. *JMR* 8(1):114–17
17. Arndt, J. 1968. Selective processes in word of mouth. *JAR* 8(3):19–22
18. Assael, H., Day, G. S. 1968. Attitudes and awareness as predictors of market share. *JAR* 8(4):3–10
19. Athola, O. T. 1975. The Vector Model of Preferences: An alternative to the Fishbein model. *JMR* 12(1):52–59
20. Auer, E. 1971. Innovative consumers—high empathics? See Ref. 141, 289–96
21. Axelrod, J. N. 1968. Attitude measures that predict purchase. *JAR* 8(1):3–17
22. Barach, J. A. 1969. Advertising effectiveness and risk in the consumer decision process. *JMR* 6(3):314–20
23. Barban, A. M. 1969. The dilemma of integrated advertising. *J. Bus.* 42:447–96
24. Barry, T. E., Hansen, R. W. 1973. How race affects children's TV commericals. *JAR* 13(5):63–67
25. Bass, F. M. 1972. Fishbein and brand preference: A reply. *JMR* 9(4):461
26. Ibid 1974. The theory of stochastic preference and brand switching. 11(1):1–20
27. Bass, F. M., Talarzyk, W. W. 1969. A study of attitude theory and brand preference. *Proc. AMA,* 272–79
28. Bass, F. M., Talarzyk, W. W. 1972. An attitude model for the study of brand preference. *JMR* 9(1):93–96
29. Bauer, R. A. 1960. Consumer behavior as risk taking. *Proc. AMA,* 389–98
30. Bauer, R. A. 1970. Self-confidence and persuasibility: One more time. *JMR* 7(2):256–58
31. Baumgarten, S. A. 1975. The innovative communicator in the diffusion process. *JMR* 12(1):12–18
32. Beckwith, N. E., Lehmann, D. R. 1973. The importance of differential weights in multiple attribute models of consumer attitude. *JMR* 10(2):141–45
33. Belk, R. W., Ross, I. 1971. An investigation of the nature of word of mouth communication across adoption catego-

[1]To conserve space, frequently cited sources have been abbreviated as follows: *JAP* (*Journal of Applied Psychology*); *JAR* (*Journal of Advertising Research*); *JCR* (*Journal of Consumer Research*); *JM* (*Journal of Marketing*); *JMR* (*Journal of Marketing Research*); *Proc. AMA* (*Proceedings of the American Marketing Association*); *Proc. APA* (*Proceedings of the American Psychological Association*).

ries for a food innovation. See Ref. 141, 470–75

34. Bell, J. E. 1969. Mobiles—a neglected market segment. *JM* 33(2):37–44

35. Bennett, P. D., Kassarjian, H. H. 1972. *Consumer Behavior.* Englewood Cliffs, NJ: Prentice-Hall

36. Bennett, P. D., Mandell, R. M. 1969. Prepurchase information seeking behavior of new car purchasers—The learning hypothesis. *JMR* 6(4):430–33

37. Berning, C. K., Jacoby, J. 1974. Patterns of information acquisition in new product purchases. *JCR* 1(2):18–22

38. Bettman, J. R. 1970. Information processing models of consumer behavior. *JMR* 7(3):370–76

39. Ibid 1971. The structure of consumer choice processes. 8(4):465–71

40. Bettman, J. R. 1971. Methods for analyzing consumer information processing models. See Ref. 141, 197–207

41. Bettman, J. R. 1972. Perceived risk: A measurement methodology and preliminary findings. See Ref. 421, 394–403

42. Bettman, J. R. 1973. Perceived risk and its components: A model and empirical test. *JMR* 10(2):184–90

43. Ibid. Perceived price and product perceptual variables. 10(1):100–2

44. Bettman, J. R. 1974. To add importance or not to add importance: That is the question. See Ref. 426, 291–301

45. Bettman, J. R. 1974. Relationship of information-processing attitude structures to private brand attitudes. *JAP* 59:79–83

46. Bettman, J. R. 1974. A threshold model of attribute satisfaction decisions. *JCR* 1(2):30–35

47. Ibid. Toward a statistics for consumer decision net models. 1(1):71–80

48. Bettman, J. R. 1974. Decision net models of buyer information processing and choice: Findings, problems, and prospects. See Ref. 184, 59–74

49. Bird, M., Channon, C., Ehrenberg, A. S. C. 1970. Brand image and brand usage. *JMR* 7(3):307–14

50. Bither, S. W. 1972. Effects of distraction and commitment on the persuasiveness of television advertising. *JMR* 9(1):1–5

51. Bither, S. W., Dolich, I. J. 1972. Personality as a determinant factor in store choice. See Ref. 421, 9–19

52. Bither, S. W., Dolich, I. J., Nell, E. B. 1971. The application of attitude immunization techniques in marketing. *JMR* 8(1):56–61

53. Bither, S. W., Miller, S. J. 1969. A cog-

nitive theory view of brand preference. *Proc. AMA,* 280–86

54. Bither, S. W., Wright, P. L. 1973. The self-confidence advertising response relationship: A function of situational distraction. *JMR* 10(2):146–52

55. Bitta, A. J. D., Monroe, K. B. 1974. The influence of adaptation levels on subjective price perceptions. See Ref. 426, 359–69

56. Blake, B. F., Perloff, R., Heslin, R. 1970. Dogmatism and acceptance of new products. *JMR* 7(4):483–86

57. Blake, B. F., Perloff, R., Zenhausern, R., Heslin, R. 1973. The effect of intolerance of ambiguity upon product perceptions. *JAP* 58:239–43

58. Bluestein, A., Capon, N., Farley, J. U., Howard, J. A. 1973. The structure of attitude: An empirical investigation. *Proc. AMA* 35:231–35

59. Bonfield, E. H. 1974. Attitude, social influence, personal norm, and intention interactions as related to brand purchase behavior. *JMR* 11(4):379–89

60. Brandt, W. K., Day, G. S. 1971. Decision processes for major durables: An empirical view. *Proc. AMA* 33:381–85

61. Brody, R. P., Cunningham, S. M. 1968. Personality variables and the consumer decision process. *JMR* 5(1):50–57

62. Brown, F. E. 1969. Price image versus price reality. *JMR* 6(2):185–91

63. Ibid 1971. Who perceives supermarket prices most validly? 8(1):110–13

64. Bruce, G. D., Witt, R. E. 1970. Personality correlates of innovative buying behavior. *JMR* 7(2):259–60

65. Brunner, J. A., Mason, J. L. 1968. The influence of driving time upon shopping center preference. *JM* 32(2):57–61

66. Bruno, A. V., Pessemier, E. A. 1972. An empirical investigation of the validity of selected attitude and activity measures. See Ref. 421, 456–74

67. Bruvold, W. H. 1968. Scales for rating the taste of water. *JAP* 52(3):245–53

68. Ibid 1970. Laboratory panel estimation of consumer assessments of taste and flavor. 54(4):326–30

69. Ibid 1971. Affective response toward uses of reclaimed water. 55:28–33

70. Bruvold, W. H., Gaffey, W. R. 1969. Rated acceptability of mineral taste in water: II. Combinatorial effects of ions on quality and action tendency ratings. *JAP* 53(4):317–21

71. Burford, R. L., Enis, B. M., Paul, G. W. 1971. An index for the measurement of consumer loyalty. *Decision Sci.* 2:17–24

72. Burnkrant, R. E. 1972. Beliefs about others as determinants of purchase behavior. See Ref. 421, 807–11

73. Bush, R. F., Gwinner, R. F., Solomon, P. J. 1974. White consumer sales response to black models. *JM* 38(2): 25–29

74. Cagley, J. W., Cardozo, R. N. 1970. White response to integrated advertising. *JAR* 10(2):35–39

75. Callahan, F. X. 1974. Advertising's influence on consumers. *JAR* 14(3):45–48

76. Carman, J. R. 1969. Some insights into reasonable grocery shopping strategies. *JM* 33(4):69–72

77. Carman, J. M. 1970. Correlates of brand loyalty: Some positive results. *JMR* 7(1):67–76

78. Chance, W. A., French, N. D. 1972. An exploratory investigation of brand switching, *JMR* 9(2):226–29

79. Choudhury, P. D., Schmid, L. S. 1974. Black models in advertising to blacks. *JAR* 14(3):19–22

80. Churchill, G. A. Jr. 1972. Linear attitude models: A study of predictive ability. *JMR* 9(4):423–26

81. Cimbalo, R. S., Webdale, A. M. 1973. Effects of price information on consumer-rated quality. *Proc. APA* 8:831–32

82. Clancy, K. J., Garsen, R. 1970. Why some scaling techniques work better. *JAR* 10(5):33–38

83. Clayton, J. D., Fry, J. N., Portis, B. 1974. A taxonomy of prepurchase information gathering patterns. *JCR* 1(3): 35–42

84. Cohen, J. B., Ed. 1972. *Behavioral Science Foundations of Consumer Behavior.* New York: Free Press

85. Cohen, J. B., Ahtola, O. T. 1971. An expectancy X value analysis of the relationship between consumer attitudes and behavior. See Ref. 141, 344–64

86. Cohen, J. B., Fishbein, M., Ahtola, O. T. 1972. The nature and uses of expectancy-value models in consumer attitude research. *JMR* 9(4):456–60

87. Cohen, J. B., Goldberg, M. E. 1970. The dissonance model in post-decision product evaluation. *JMR* 7(3):315–21

88. Cohen, J. B., Golden, E. 1972. Informational social influence and product evaluation. *JAP* 56:54–59

89. Cohen, J. B., Houston, M. J. 1972. Cognitive consequences of brand loyalty. *JMR* 9(1):97–99

90. Coney, K. A. 1972. Dogmatism and innovation: A replication. *JMR* 9(4): 453–55

91. Cooper, M. R., Boltwood, C. E., Wherry, R. J. 1974. A factor analysis of air passenger reactions to skyjacking and airport security measures as related to personal characteristics and alternatives to flying. *JAP* 59:365–68

92. Copley, T. P., Callom, F. L. 1971. Industrial search behavior and perceived risk. See Ref. 141, 208–31

93. Corey, L. G. 1971. People who claim to be opinion leaders: Identifying their characteristics by self-report. *JM* 35(4): 48–53

94. Cox, D. F., Ed. 1967. *Risk Taking and Information Handling in Consumer Behavior.* Cambridge, Mass: Harvard Univ. Press

95. Craig, C. S., Engel, J. F., Talarzyk, W. W. 1971. Consumer decision-making: On the importance of price. See Ref. 141, 243–55

96. Cunningham, W. H., Crissy, W. J. E. 1972. Market segmentation by motivation and attitude. *JMR* 9(1):100–2

97. Darden, W. R., Reynolds, F. D. 1972. Predicting opinion leadership for men's apparel fashions. *JMR* 9(3):324–28

98. Ibid 1974. Backward profiling of male innovators. 11(1):79–85

99. Davis, H., Rigaux, B. P. 1974. Perception of marital roles in decision process. *JCR* 1(1):51–62

100. Day, G. S. 1969. A two-dimensional concept of brand loyalty. *JAR* 9(3): 29–35

101. Ibid 1971. Attitude change, media, and word of mouth. 11(6):31–40

102. Day, G. S. 1972. Evaluating models of attitude structure. *JMR* 9(3):279–86

103. Day, G. S. 1973. Theories of attitude structure and change. See Ref. 425, 303–53

104. Day, G. S. 1976. Assessing the effects of information disclosure requirements. *JM* 40. In press

105. Day, G. S., Brandt, W. K. 1974. Consumer research and the evaluation of information disclosure requirements: The case of truth in lending. *JCR* 1(1): 21–32

106. Deering, B. J., Jacoby, J. 1972. Risk enhancement and risk reduction as strategies for handling perceived risk. See Ref. 421, 404–15

107. Ibid. Price intervals and individual price limits as determinants of product evaluation and selection, 145–66

108. Divita, S. F., Ed. 1974. *Advertising and the Public Interest.* Chicago: AMA

109. Dolich, I. J. 1969. Congruence relation-

ships between self images and product brands. *JMR* 6(1):80–84
110. Dominick, J. R., Greenberg, B. S. 1970. Three seasons of blacks on television. *JAR* 10:21–27
111. Donnelly, J. H. Jr. 1970. Social character and acceptance of new products. *JMR* 7(1):111–13
112. Donnelly, J. H. Jr., Etzel, M. J. 1973. Degrees of product newness and early trial. *JMR* 10(3):295–300
113. Donnelly, J. H., Etzel, M. J. 1974. Attempting to operationalize product newness: A reply to Ostlund and Tellefsen. *JAP* 59:761–63
114. Donnelly, J. H., Etzel, M. J., Roeth, S. 1973. The relationship between consumers' category width and trial of new products. *JAP* 57:335–38
115. Donnelly, J. H. Jr., Ivancevich, J. M. 1970. Post-purchase reinforcement and back-out behavior. *JMR* 7(3):399–400
116. Donnelly, J. H., Ivancevich, J. M. 1970. Study of consumer political orientations and store patronage. *JAP* 54(5):470–72
117. Donnelly, J. H. Jr., Ivancevich, J. M. 1974. A methodology for identifying innovator characteristics of new brand purchasers. *JMR* 11(3):331–34
118. Doob, A. N., Carlsmith, J. M., Freedman, J., Landauer, T. K., Tom, S. 1969. Effect of initial selling price on subsequent sales. *J. Pers. Soc. Psychol.* 11:345–50
119. Douglas, S. P., Wind, Y. 1971. Intentions to buy as predictors of buying behavior. See Ref. 141, 331–43
120. Engel, J. F., Blackwell, R. D., Kegerreis, R. J. 1969. How information is used to adopt an innovation. *JAR* 9(4):3–8
121. Engel, J. F., Kollat, D. T., Blackwell, R. D. 1968. *Consumer Behavior.* New York: Holt, Rinehart & Winston
122. Ibid 1973. 2nd ed.
123. Engel, J. F., Light, M. L. 1968. The role of psychological commitment in consumer behavior: An evaluation of the theory of cognitive dissonance. In *Applications of the Sciences in Marketing Management*, ed. F. M. Bass, C. W. King, E. A. Pessemier. New York: Wiley
124. Etzel, M. J., Walker, B. J. 1974. Advertising strategy for foreign products. *JAR* 14(3):41–44
125. Farley, J. U., Howard, J. A., Ring, L. W., Eds. 1974. *Consumer Behavior: Theory and Application.* Boston: Allyn & Bacon

126. Feldman, L. P., Armstrong, G. M. 1975. Identifying buyers of a major automotive innovation. *JM* 39(1):47–53
127. Fenton, J. S., Leggett, T. R. 1971. A new way to find opinion leaders. *JAR* 11(2):21–25
128. Ferber, R., Lee, L. C. 1974. Husband-wife influence in family purchasing behavior. *JCR* 1(1):43–50
129. Fhaner, G., Han, M. 1974. Seat belts: Relations between beliefs, attitude, and use. *JAP* 59:472–82
130. Fishbein, M. 1967. Attitude and the prediction of behavior. In *Readings in Attitude Theory and Measurement*, ed. M. Fishbein, 477–92. New York: Wiley
131. Frank, R. E., Massy, W. F., Lodahl, T. M. 1969. Purchasing behavior and personal attributes. *JAR* 9(4):15–24
132. Friedman, M. P. 1970. Using simulation techniques to predict the behavioral effects of new laws: The case of truth-in-lending legislation and the consumer. *JAP* 54(4):297–301
133. Ibid 1972. Consumer price comparisons of retail products: The role of packaging and pricing practices and the implications for consumer legislation. 56:439–46
134. Friedman, M. P. 1972. Consumer responses to unit pricing, open dating, and nutrient labeling. See Ref. 421, 361–69
135. Fromkin, H. L. 1971. A social psychological analysis of the adoption and diffusion of new products and practices from a uniqueness motivation perspective. See Ref. 141, 464–69
136. Fromkin, H. L., Olson, J. C., Dipboye, R. L., Barnaby, D. 1971. A commodity theory analysis of consumer preferences for scarce products. *Proc. APA* 6:653–54
137. Fry, J. N. 1971. Personality variables and cigarette brand choice. *JMR* 8(3):298–304
138. Fry, J. N., Shaw, D. C., Von Lanzenaver, C. H., Dipchand, C. R. 1973. Customer loyalty to banks: A longitudinal study. *J. Bus.* 46:517–25
139. Gabor, A., Granger, C. W. J., Sowter, A. P. 1971. Comments on "Psychophysics of Prices." *JMR* 8(2):251–52
140. Gardner, D. M. 1970. The distraction hypothesis in marketing. *JAR* 10(6):25–30
141. Gardner, D. M., Ed. 1971. *Proceedings, 2nd Annual Conference, Association for Consumer Research.* College Park: Univ. Maryland

350   JACOBY

142. Gardner, D. M. 1971. Is there a generalized price-quality relationship? *JMR* 8(2):241–43
143. Gardner, D. M. 1972. An exploratory investigation of achievement motivation effects on consumer behavior. See Ref. 421, 20–33
144. Gatewood, R. D., Perloff, R. 1973. An experimental investigation of three methods of providing weight and price information to consumers. *JAP* 57: 81–85
145. Ginter, J. L. 1974. An experimental investigation of attitude change and choice of a new brand. *JMR* 11(1): 30–40
146. Goldberg, M. E. 1971. A cognitive model of innovative behavior: The interaction of product and self-attitudes. See Ref. 141, 313–30
147. Goldberg, M. E., Gorn, G. J. 1974. Children's reactions to television advertising: An experimental approach. *JCR* 1(2):69–75
148. Gould, J. W., Sigband, N. B., Zoerner, C. E. 1970. Black consumer reactions to "integrated" advertising: An exploratory study. *JM* 34(3):20–26
149. Granger, C. W. J., Billson, A. 1972. Consumers' attitudes toward package size and price. *JMR* 9(3):239–48
150. Grass, R. C., Wallace, W. H. 1969. Satiation effects of TV commercials. *JAR* 9(3):3–8
151. Grass, R. C., Winters, L. C., Wallace, W. H. 1969. Generation and satiation of attention during an advertising campaign. *Proc. APA* 4:785–86
152. Green, P. E., Carmone, F. J. 1970. *Multidimensional Scaling and Related Techniques in Marketing Analysis.* Boston: Allyn & Bacon
153. Green, P. E., Devita, M. T. 1974. A complementary model of consumer utility for item collections. *JCR* 1(3):56–67
154. Greenberg, A., Sutton, C. 1973. Television commercial wearout. *JAR* 13(5): 47–54
155. Greeno, D. W., Sommers, M. S., Kernan, J. B. 1973. Personality and implicit behavior patterns. *JMR* 10(1):63–69
156. Gross, E. J. 1969. Support for a generalized marketing leadership theory. *JAR* 9(3):49–52
157. Grubb, E. L., Hupp, G. 1968. Perception of self, generalized stereotypes, and brand selection. *JMR* 5(1):58–63
158. Grubb, E. L., Stern, B. L. 1971. Self-concept and significant others. *JMR* 8(3):382–85
159. Gruber, A. 1970. Purchase intent and purchase probability. *JAR* 10(1):23–27
160. Guest, L. 1970. How negro models affect company image. *JAR* 19(2): 29–33
161. Haines, G. H. 1969. *Consumer Behavior: Learning Models of Purchasing.* New York: Free Press
162. Haines, G. H. Jr. 1974. Process models of consumer decision making. See Ref. 184, 89–107
163. Hamburger, C. D., Holmes, R. T., Mukai, R. S. 1968. Experimental study of the cognitive dissonance effect on saving and spending. *Proc. APA* 3: 665–66
164. Hamm, B. C., Cundiff, E. W. 1969. Self-actualization and product perception. *JMR* 6(4):470–72
165. Hamm, B. C., Perry, M., Wynn, H. F. 1969. The effect of a free sample on image and attitude. *JAR* 9(4):35–37
166. Hansen, F. 1969. Consumer choice behavior: An experimental approach. *JMR* 6(4):436–43
167. Hansen, F. 1972. *Consumer Choice Behavior: A Cognitive Theory.* New York: Free Press
168. Harrell, G. D., Bennett, P. D. 1974. An evaluation of the expectancy value model of attitude measurement for physician prescribing behavior. *JMR* 11(3): 269–78
169. Hart, E. W. Jr., Jacoby, J. 1973. Novelty, recency, and scarcity as predictors of perceived newness. *Proc. APA* 8:839–40
170. Hawkins, D. I. 1972. Reported cognitive dissonance and anxiety: Some additional findings. *JM* 36(3):63–66
171. Heeler, R. M., Ray, M. L. 1972. Measure validation in marketing. *JMR* 9:361–70
172. Heimbach, J. T., Jacoby, J. 1972. The Zeigarnik effect in advertising. See Ref. 421, 746–58
173. Henion, K. E. 1972. The effect of ecologically relevant information on detergent sales. *JMR* 9(1):10–14
174. Herberger, R. A. Jr., Buchanan, D. I. 1971. The impact of concern for ecological factors on consumer attitudes and buying behavior. *Proc. AMA* 33:644–46
175. Herniter, J. D. 1974. A comparison of the entropy model and the Hendry model. *JMR* 11(1):21–29
176. Hisrich, R. D., Dornoff, F. J., Kernan, J. B. 1972. Perceived risk in store selection. *JMR* 9(4):435–39
177. Hollander, S. W., Jacoby, J. 1973. Re-

call of crazy, mixed-up TV commercials. *JAR* 13(3):39–42
178. Holloway, F. J., Mittelstaedt, R. A., Venkatesan, M. 1971. Consumer Behavior: *Contemporary Research in Action*. Boston: Houghton-Mifflin
179. Holmes, J. H. 1971. Communication patterns and the diffusion of a consumer innovation: Preliminary findings. See Ref. 141, 459–63
180. Horton, R. L. 1974. The Edwards Personal Preference Schedule and consumer personality research. *JMR* 11(3): 335–37
181. Houston, M. J. 1972. The effect of unit-pricing on choices of brand and size in economic shopping. *JM* 36(3):51–54
182. Howard, J. A., Sheth, J. N. 1969. *The Theory of Buyer Behavior*. New York: Wiley
183. Hughes, G. D., Guerrero, J. L. 1971. Testing cognitive models through computer-controlled experiments. *JMR* 8(3):291–97
184. Hughes, G. D., Ray M. L., Eds. 1974. *Buyer/Consumer Information Processing*. Chapel Hill: Univ. North Carolina Press
185. Hunt, H. K. 1973. Effects of corrective advertising. *JAR* 13(5):15–22
186. Hunt, S. D. 1970. Post-transaction communications and dissonance reduction. *JM* 34(3):46–51
187. Jacoby, J. 1971. Personality and innovation proneness. *JMR* 8(2):244–47
188. Jacoby, J. 1971. A model of multi-brand loyalty. *JAR* 11(3):25–31
189. Jacoby, J. 1971. Brand loyalty: A conceptual definition. *Proc. APA* 6:655–56
190. Jacoby, J. 1971. Multiple-indicant approach for studying new product adopters. *JAP* 55:384–88
191. Jacoby, J. 1972. Opinion leadership and innovativeness: Overlap and validity. See Ref. 421, 632–49
192. Jacoby, J. 1974. Consumer reaction to information displays: Packaging and advertising. See Ref. 108, 101–18
193. Jacoby, J. 1974. The construct validity of opinion leadership. *Public Opin. Q.* 38(1):81–89
194. Jacoby, J. 1975. Consumer psychology as a social psychological sphere of action. *Am. Psychol.* 30(10):977–87
195. Jacoby, J. 1975. Consumer and industrial psychology: Prospects for theory corroboration and mutual contribution. In *The Handbook of Industrial and Organizational Psychology*, ed. M. D. Dunnette. Chicago: Rand McNally

196. Jacoby, J. 1975. Perspectives on a consumer information processing research program. *Comm. Res.* 2:203–15
197. Jacoby, J., Kaplan, L. B. 1972. The components of perceived risk. See Ref. 421, 382–93
198. Jacoby, J., Kohn, C. A., Speller, D. E. 1973. Time spent acquiring product information as a function of information load and organization. *Proc. APA* 9: 813–14
199. Jacoby, J., Kyner, D. B. 1973. Brand loyalty vs. repeat purchasing behavior. *JMR* 10(1):1–9
200. Jacoby, J., Olson, J. C. 1974. An extended expectancy model of consumer comparison process. See Ref. 426, 319–33
201. Jacoby, J., Olson, J. C., Haddock, F. A. 1971. Price, brand name, and product composition characteristics as determinants of perceived quality. *JAP* 55: 570–79
202. Jacoby, J., Speller, D. E., Berning, C. K. 1974. Brand choice behavior as a function of information load: Replication and extension. *JCR* 1(1):33–42
202a. Jacoby, J., Speller, D. E., Berning, C. K. 1975. Constructive criticism and programmatic research: reply to Russo. *JCR* 2(2):154–56
203. Jacoby, J., Speller, D. E., Kohn, C. A. 1974. Brand choice behavior as a function of information load. *JMR* 11(1): 63–69
204. Jacoby, J., Szybillo, G. J., Berning, C. A. K. 1976. Time and consumer behavior: An interdisciplinary review. *JCR* special issue, ed. R. Ferber, 2(4)
205. Jacoby, J., Szybillo, G. J., Busato-Schach, J. 1975. Information acquisition behavior in brand choice situations. *JCR.* In press
206. Kallick, M., Nearby, J., Shaffer, J. 1974. The dimensions of brand consistent behavior. See Ref. 426, 460–62
207. Kamen, J. M., Toman, R. J. 1970 Psychophysics of prices. *JMR* 7(1): 27–35
208. Ibid 1971. "Psychophysics of Prices": A reaffirmation. 8(2):252–57
209. Kanungo, R. N. 1968. Brand awareness: Effect of fittingness, meaningfulness, and product utility. *JAP* 52(4): 290–95
210. Ibid 1969. Brand awareness: Differential roles of fittingness and meaningfulness of brand names. 53(2):140–46
211. Kanungo, R. N., Pang, S. 1973. Effects of human models on perceived product quality. *JAP* 57:172–78

212. Kaplan, L. B., Szybillo, G. J., Jacoby, J. 1974. Components of perceived risk in product purchase: A cross-validation. *JAP* 59:287–91

213. Kassarjian, H. H. 1969. The Negro and American advertising 1946–1965. *JMR* 6:29–30

214. Kassarjian, H. H. 1971. Blacks in advertising: A further comment. *JMR* 8:392–93

215. Ibid. Personality and consumer behavior: A review, 409–18

216. Kassarjian, H. H., Robertson, R. S., Eds. 1973. *Perspectives in Consumer Behavior.* Glenview, Ill: Scott, Foresman

217. Katona, G. 1960. *The Powerful Consumer.* New York: McGraw-Hill

218. Katona, G. 1963. The relationship between psychology and economics. In *Psychology: A Study of Science,* ed. S. Koch, 639–76. New York: McGraw-Hill

219. Kau, P., Hill, L. 1972. A threshold model of purchasing decisions. *JMR* 9(3):264–70

220. Kelley, H. H. 1967. Attribution theory in social psychology. In *Nebraska Symposium on Motivation,* ed. D. Levine, 192–238. Lincoln: Univ. Nebraska Press

221. Kernan, J. B. 1968. Choice criteria, decision behavior, and personality. *JMR* 5(2):155–64

222. Kernan, J. B. 1971. The CAD instrument in behavioral diagnosis. See Ref. 141, 307–12

223. King, C. W., Sproles, G. B. 1973. Predictive efficacy of psychopersonality characteristics in fashion change-agent identification. *Proc. APA* 8:841–42

224. King, C. W., Summers, J. O. 1970. Overlap of opinion leadership across consumer product categories. *JMR* 7(1):43–50

225. King, C. W., Summers, J. O. 1971. Attitudes and media exposure. *JAR* 11(1):26–32

226. Kinnear, T. C., Taylor, J. R. 1973. The effect of ecological concern on brand perceptions. *JMR* 19(2):191–97

227. Kinnear, T. C., Taylor, J. R. 1973. The role of information sources in learning about ecological aspects of products. *Proc. AMA* 35:293–97

228. Kinnear, T. C., Taylor, J. R., Ahmed, S. A. 1972. Socioeconomic and personality characteristics as they relate to ecologically-constructive purchasing behavior. See Ref. 421, 34–60

229. Kirchner, D. F. 1971. Personal influ-ence, ordinal position and purchasing behavior. See Ref. 141, 82–98

230. Klippel, R. E., Bither, S. W. 1972. Attitude data in allocation models. *JAR* 12(2):20–24

231. Kohan, X. 1968. A physiological measure of commercial effectiveness. *JAR* 8(4):46–48

232. Kohn, C. A., Jacoby, J. 1973. Operationally defining the consumer innovator. *Proc. APA* 8:837–38

233. Kollat, D. T., Willett, R. P. 1969. Is impulse purchasing really a useful concept for marketing decisions? *JM* 33(1):79–83

234. Kraft, F. B., Granbois, D. H., Summers, J. O. 1973. Brand evaluation and brand choice: A longitudinal study. *JMR* 10(3):235–41

235. Kunkel, H. J., Berry, L. L. 1968. A behavioral conception of retail image. *JM* 32(4):21–27

236. Lambert, Z. V. 1970. Product perception: An important variable in price strategy. *JM* 34(4):68–71

237. Lambert, Z. V. 1972. Price and choice behavior. *JMR* 9(1):35–40

238. Ibid. Perceptual patterns, information handling and innovativeness. 9(4):427–31

239. Landon, E. L. Jr. 1972. A sex-role explanation of purchase intention differences of consumers who are high and low in need for achievement. See Ref. 421, 1–8

240. Landon, E. L. Jr. 1972. Role of need for achievement in the perception of products. *Proc. APA* 7:741–42

241. Landon, E. L. Jr. 1974. Self concept, ideal self concept and consumer purchase intentions. *JCR* 1(2):44–51

242. LaPlaca, P. J. 1974. The effect of unit pricing on product demand and perceived product satisfaction. See Ref. 426, 9–16

243. Lavidge, F. J., Steiner, G. A. 1961. A model for the predictive measurement of advertising effectiveness. *JM* 25:59–62

244. Lawrence, R. J. 1969. Patterns of buyer behavior: Time for a new approach? *JMR* 6(2):137–44

245. Lehmann, D. R., Ostlund, L. E. 1974. Consumer perceptions of product warranties: An exploratory study. See Ref. 426, 51–56

246. Lessig, V. P. 1973. Consumer store images and store loyalties. *JM* 37(4):72–74

247. LoSciuto, L. A. 1968. Effects of advertising frequency and product usage on

recall: A laboratory simulation. *Proc. APA* 3:679–80

248. Lutz, R. J. 1972. Investigating the feasibility of personalized rapid transit: An experimental approach. See Ref. 421, 800–6

249. Lutz, R. J., Reilly, P. J. 1974. An exploration of the effects of perceived social and performance risk on consumer information acquisition. See Ref. 426, 393–405

250. Mancuso, J. R. 1969. Why not create opinion leaders for new product introduction. *JM* 33(3):20–25

251. March, J. G., Simon, H. A. 1958. *Organizations.* New York: Wiley

252. Massy, W. F., Frank, R. E., Lodahl, T. 1968. *Purchasing Behavior and Personal Attributes.* Philadelphia: Univ. Pennsylvania Press

253. Mathews, H. L., Slocum, J. W., Woodside, A. G. 1971. Perceived risk, individual differences, and shopping orientations. See Ref. 141, 299–306

254. Mathews, H. L., Wilson, D. T., Tau, C. T., Sweeney, T. 1974. An exploratory study of the effects of unit pricing and nutritional labeling upon supermarket choice. See Ref. 426, 17–28

255. May, F. E. 1969. Adaptive behavior in automobile brand choices. *JMR* 6(1): 62–65

256. Mazis, M. B. 1972. Decision-making role and information processing. *JMR* 9(4):447–50

257. Mazis, M. B., Beuttenmuller, M. 1972. Attitudes toward women's liberation and perception of advertisements. See Ref. 421, 428–35

258. Mazis, M. B., Settle, R. B., Leslie, D. C. 1973. Elimination of phosphate detergents and psychological reactance. *JMR* 19(4):390–95

259. Mazis, M. B., Sweeney, T. W. 1972. Novelty and personality with risk as a moderating variable. *Proc. AMA* 34: 406–11

260. McClure, J. M., Andrews, I. R. 1974. A consumer profile analysis of the self-service gasoline customer. *JAP* 59:119–21

261. McConnell, J. D. 1968. The price-quality relationship in an experimental setting. *JMR* 5(3):300–3

262. McConnell, J. D. 1968. Effect of pricing on perception of product quality. *JAP* 52(4):331–34

263. McConnell, J. D. 1968. The development of brand loyalty: An experimental study. *JMR* 5(3):13–19

264. McConnell, J. D. 1970. Do media vary in effectiveness? *JAR* 19(5):19–22

265. McGinnis, J. 1969. *The Selling of the President.* New York: Trident

266. McNeil, J. 1974. Federal programs to measure consumer purchase expectations, 1946–1973: A post mortem. *JCR* 1(3):1–9

267. Miller, S. J., Mazis, M. B., Wright, P. L. 1971. The influence of brand ambiguity on brand attitude development. *JMR* 8(4):455–59

268. Misra, S., Jain, S. 1971. Effect of fittingness, type of goods, and type of slogan on brand awareness. *JAP* 55:580–85

269. Mittelstaedt, R. 1969. A dissonance approach to repeat purchasing behavior. *JMR* 6(4):444–46

270. Moinpour, R., Maclachlan, D. L. 1971. The relations among attribute and importance components of Rosenberg-Fishbein type attitude model: An empirical investigation. See Ref. 141, 365–75

271. Monroe, K. B. 1971. Measuring price thresholds by psychophysics and latitudes of acceptance. *JMR* 8(4):460–64

272. Ibid. "Psychophysics of Prices": A reappraisal. 8(2):248–57

273. Ibid 1973. Buyers' subjective perceptions of price. 10(1):70–80

274. Monroe, K. B., LaPlaca, P. J. 1972. What are the benefits of unit pricing? *JM* 36(3):16–22

275. Montogomery, D. B., Silk, A. J. 1971. Clusters of consumer interests and opinion leaders' spheres of influence. *JMR* 8(3):317–21

276. Morris, G. P., Cundiff, E. W. 1971. Acceptance by males of feminine products. *JMR* 8(3):372–74

277. Morrison, B. J., Dainoff, M. J. 1972. Advertisement complexity and looking time. *JMR* 9(4):396–400

278. Moskowitz, H. R. 1972. Subjective ideals and sensory optimization in evaluating perceptual dimensions in food. *JAP* 56:60–66

279. Murray, J. A. 1969. Canadian consumer expectational data: An evaluation. *JMR* 6(1):54–61

280. Muse, W. V. 1971. Product-related response to use of black models in advertising. *JMR* 8(1):107–9

281. Myers, J. H., Alpert, M. I. 1968. Determinant buying attitudes: Meaning and measurement. *JM* 32:13–20

282. Myers, J. H., Robertson, T. S. 1972. Dimensions of opinion leadership. *JMR* 9(1):41–46

283. Myers, J. H., Robertson, T. S. 1974. Stability of self-designated opinion leadership. See Ref. 426, 417–26

284. Nakanishi, M., Bettman, J. R. 1974. Attitude models revisited: An individual level analysis. *JCR* 1(3):16–21
285. Newman, D. Z., Becknell, J. C. 1970. The price-quality relationship as a tool in consumer research. *Proc. APA* 5: 729–30
286. Newman, J. W., Staelin, R. 1972. Prepurchase information seeking for new cars and major household appliances. *JMR* 9(3):249–57
287. Newman, J. W., Staelin, R. 1973. Information sources of durable goods. *JAR* 13(2):19–29
288. Newman, J. W., Werbel, R. A. 1973. Multivariate analysis of brand loyalty for major household appliances. *JMR* 10(4):404–9
289. Nicosia, F. M. 1966. *Consumer Decision Processes*. Englewood Cliffs, NJ: Prentice-Hall
290. Norman, K. L., Louviere, J. J. 1974. Integration of attributes in bus transportation: Two modeling approaches. *JAP* 59:753–58
291. O'Brien, T. V. 1971. Stages of consumer decision making. *JMR* 8(3):283–89
292. O'Brien, T. V. 1971. Tracking consumer decision making. *JM* 35(1): 35–40
293. O'Brien, T. V. 1972. Information use in consumer decisions. *Proc. APA* 7: 733–34
294. Olshavsky, R. W., Mackay, D. B., Sentall, G. 1975. Perceptual maps of supermarket locations. *JAP* 60:80–86
295. Olshavsky, R. W., Miller, J. A. 1972. Consumer expectations, product performance and perceived product quality. *JMR* 9(1):19–21
296. Olshavsky, R. W., Summers, J. O. 1974. A study of the role of beliefs and intentions in consistency restoration. *JCR* 1(1):63–70
297. Olson, J. C. 1973. *Cue properties of price: Literature review and theoretical considerations*. Presented at 81st Ann. Conv. APA, Montreal
298. Olson, J. C., Jacoby, J. 1971. Construct validation study of brand loyalty. *Proc. APA* 6:657–58
299. Olson, J. C., Jacoby, J. 1972. Cue utilization in the quality perception process. See Ref. 421, 167–79
300. Oshikawa, S. 1969. Can cognitive dissonance theory explain consumer behavior? *JM* 33(4):44–49
301. Oshikawa, S. 1971. Dissonance reduction or artifact? *JMR* 8(4):514–17
302. Oshikawa, S. 1972. The measurement of cognitive dissonance: Some experimental findings. *JM* 36(1):64–67
303. Ostlund, L. E. 1971. The interaction of self confidence variables in the context of innovative behavior. *Proc. AMA* 33:351–57
304. Ostlund, L. E. 1972. Identifying early buyers. *JAR* 12(2):25–30
305. Ostlund, L. E. Perceived innovation attributes as predictors of innovativeness. *JCR* 1(2):23–29
306. Ostlund, L. E., Tellefsen, B. 1974. Relationship between consumers' category width and trial of new products: A reappraisal. *JAP* 59:759–60
307. Paine, F. T., Nash, A. N., Hille, S. J. 1969. Consumer attitudes towards auto versus public transport alternatives. *JAP* 53(6):472–80
308. Pennington, A. L., Peterson, R. A. 1969. Interest patterns and product preferences: An exploratory analysis. *JMR* 6(3):284–90
309. Percy, L. 1974. Determining the influence of color on a product cognitive structure: A multidimensional scaling application. See Ref. 426, 218–27
310. Perloff, R. 1968. Consumer analysis. *Ann. Rev. Psychol.* 19:437–66
311. Perry, A. 1973. The effect of heredity on attitudes toward alcohol, cigarettes, and coffee. *JAP* 58:275–77
312. Perry, M. 1969. Discriminant analysis of relations between consumers' attitudes, behavior, and intentions. *JAR* 9(2):36–39
313. Perry, M., Hamm, B. C. 1969. Canonical analysis of relations between socioeconomic risk and personal influence in purchase decisions. *JMR* 6(3):351–54
314. Pessemier, E. 1971. An empirical investigation of the reliability and stability of selected activity and attitude measures. See Ref. 141, 389–403
315. Peterson, G. L., Bishop, R. L., Michaels, R. M., Gustave, J. R. 1973. Children's choice of playground equipment: Development of methodology for integrating user preferences into environmental engineering. *JAP* 58:233–38
316. Peterson, R. A. 1970. The price-perceived quality relationship: Experimental evidence. *JMR* 7(4):525–28
317. Peterson, R. A. 1972. Ratings of salespersons by male customers: 1971. *JAP* 56:433
318. Peterson, R. A. 1972. Psychographics and media exposure. *JAR* 12(3):17–20
319. Peterson, R. A., Pennington, A. L. 1969. SVIB interests and product preferences. *JAP* 53(4):304–8

320. Peterson, R. A., Ross, I. 1972. How to name new brands. *JAR* 12(6):29–34
321. Plummer, J. T. 1974. The concept and application of life style segmentation. *JM* 38(1):33–38
322. Poulton, E. C. 1969. Skimming lists of food ingredients printed in different sizes. *JAP* 53(1):55–58
323. Ibid. Skimming lists of food ingredients printed in different brightness contrasts. 53(6):498–500
324. Rao, T. R. 1969. Consumer's purchase decision process: Stochastic models. *JMR* 6(3):321–29
325. Rao, V. R. 1971. Salience of price in the perception of product quality: A multidimensional measurement approach. *Proc. AMA* 33:571–77
326. Rao, V. R. 1972. Marginal salience of price in brand evaluations. See Ref. 421, 125–44
327. Rao, V. R. 1972. Changes in explicit information and brand perceptions. *JMR* 9(2):209–13
328. Ratchford, B. T., Andreasen, A. A. 1974. A study of consumer perceptions of decisions. See Ref. 426, 334–45
329. Ray, M. L. 1973. Psychological theories and interpretations of learning. See Ref. 425, 45–117
330. Ray, M. L., Sawyer, A. G., Strong, E. C. 1971. Frequency effects revisited. *JAR* 11(1):14–20
331. Ray, M. L., Wilkie, W. L. 1970. Fear: The potential of an appeal neglected by marketing. *JM* 34(1):54–62
332. Reingen, P. H. 1974. Comment on Woodside. *JMR* 11(2):223–24
333. Reizenstein, R. C. 1971. A dissonance approach to measuring the effectiveness of two personal selling techniques through decision reversal. *Proc. AMA* 33:176–80
334. Reynolds, F. D. 1974. An analysis of catalog buying behavior. *JM* 38(3):47–51
335. Reynolds, F. D., Darden, W. R. 1971. Mutually adaptive effects of interpersonal communication *JMR* 8(4):449–54
336. Reynolds, F. D., Darden, W. R. 1972. Predicting opinion leadership for women's clothing fashions. *Proc. AMA* 34:434–38
337. Reynolds, F. D., Darden, W. R. 1972. Why the midi failed. *JAR* 12(4):39–44
338. Roach, D. E. 1969. Dimensions of the corporate image of multiline insurance companies. *Proc. APA* 4:791–92
339. Robertson, T. S. 1968. Purchase sequence responses: Innovators vs. non-innovators. *JAR* 8(1):47–52
340. Robertson, T. S. 1968. The effect of the informal group upon member innovative behavior. *Proc. AMA* 28:334–40
341. Robertson, T. S. 1970. *Consumer Behavior.* Glenview, Ill: Scott Foresman
342. Robertson, T. S. 1971. *Innovative Behavior and Communication.* New York: Holt, Rinehart & Winston
343. Robertson, T. S., Myers, J. H. 1969. Personality correlates of opinion leadership and innovative buying behavior. *JMR* 6(2):164–68
344. Ibid 1970. Personality correlates of innovative buying behavior: A reply. 7(2):260–61
345. Robertson, T. S., Rossiter, J. R. 1974. Children and commercial persuasion: An attribution theory analysis. *JCR* 1(1):13–20
346. Robertson, T. S., Rossiter, J. R. 1974. Children's attributions of intent in television commercials. See Ref. 426, 118–19
347. Rogers, E. M. 1962. *Diffusion of Innovations.* New York: Free Press
348. Rogers, E. M., Shoemaker, F. F. 1971. *Communication of Innovations.* New York: Free Press
349. Roman, H. S. 1969. Semantic generalization in formation of consumer attitudes. *JMR* 6(3):369–73
350. Roselius, T. 1971. Consumer rankings of risk reduction methods. *JM* 35(1):56–61
351. Rosenberg, M. J. 1956. Cognitive structure and attitudinal affect. *J. Abnorm. Soc. Psychol.* 53:367–72
352. Rosenberg, M. J. 1960. A structural theory of attitude dynamics. *Public Opin. Q.* 24:319–40
353. Ross, I. 1974. Applications of consumer information to public policy decisions. See Ref. 380, 42–76
354. Russ, F. A. 1971. Evaluation process models and the prediction of preference. See Ref. 141, 256–61
355. Russo, J. E. 1974. More information is better: A reevaluation of Jacoby, Speller, and Kohn. *JCR* 1(3):68–72
356. Sandell, R. G. 1968. Effects of attitudinal and situational factors on reported choice behavior. *JMR* 5(4):405–8
357. Sawyer, A. G. 1973. The effects of repetition of refutational and supportive advertising appeals. *JMR* 19(1):23–33
358. Scherf, G. W. H. 1974. Consumer dissatisfaction as a function of dissatisfaction with interpersonal relationships. *JAP* 59:465–71
359. Schiffman, L. G. 1971. Sources of information for the elderly. *JAR* 11(5):33–37

360. Schiffman, L. G. 1972. Perceived risk in new product trial by elderly consumers. *JMR* 9(1):106–8

361. Schiffman, L. G., Gaccione, V. 1974. Opinion leaders in institutional markets. *JM* 38(2):49–53

362. Schlinger, M. J., Plummer, J. T. 1972. Advertising in black and white. *JMR* 9(2):149–53

363. Seggev, E. 1970. Brand assortment and consumer brand choice. *JM* 34(4): 18–24

364. Settle, R. B., Faricy, J. H., Warren, G. T. 1971. Consumer information processing: Attributing affects to causes. See Ref. 141, 278–88

365. Settle, R. B., Golden, L. L. 1974. Consumer perceptions: Overchoice in the market place. See Ref. 426, 29–37

366. Settle, R. B., Golden, L. L. 1974. Attribution theory and advertiser credibility. *JMR* 11(2):181–85

367. Settle, R. B., Mizerski, R. 1973. Differential response to objective and social information in advertisements. *Proc. AMA* 35:250–55

368. Shapiro, B. P. 1973. Price reliance: Existence and sources. *JMR* 10(3):286–94

369. Sheth, J. N. 1968. Cognitive dissonance, brand preference, and product familiarity. In *Insights into Consumer Behavior*, ed. J. Arndt. Boston: Allyn and Bacon

370. Sheth, J. N. 1968. A factor analytic model of brand loyalty. *JMR* 5:395–404

371. Sheth, J. N. 1970. Multivariate analyses in marketing. *JAR* 10(1):29–39

372. Sheth, J. N. 1970. Are there differences in dissonance reduction behavior between students and housewives? *JMR* 7(2):243–45

373. Ibid 1971. Dissonance reduction or artifact? A reply. 8(4):516–17

374. Sheth, J. N. 1971. Word-of-mouth in low-risk innovations. *JAR* 11(3):15–18

375. Sheth, J. N. 1972. Reply to comments on the nature and uses of expectancy-value models in consumer attitude research. *JMR* 9(4):462–65

376. Sheth, J. N. 1973. Brand profiles from beliefs and importances. *JAR* 13(1): 37–42

377. Sheth, J. N., Park, C. W. 1973. A theory of multidimensional brand loyalty. See Ref. 421, 449–59

378. Sheth, J. N., Talarzyk, W. W. 1972. Perceived instrumentality and value importance as determinants of attitudes. *JMR* 9(1):6–9

379. Sheth, J. N., Venkatesen, M. 1968. Risk-reduction processes in repetitive consumer behavior. *JMR* 5(3):307–10

380. Sheth, J. N., Wright, P. L., Eds. 1974. *Marketing Analysis for Societal Problems.* Urbana-Champaign: Univ. Illinois Press

381. Shuchman, A., Perry, M. 1969. Self-confidence and persuasibility in marketing: A reappraisal. *JMR* 6(2):146–54

382. Simon, M. F. 1970. Influence of brand names on attitudes. *JAR* 10(3):28–30

383. Sims, J. T. 1971. Comparison of consumer behavior conformity and independence between blacks and whites: An exploratory study. See Ref. 141, 76–81

384. Slovic, P. 1969. Analyzing the expert judge: A descriptive study of a stockbroker's decision processes. *JAP* 53(4): 255–63

385. Sparks, D. L., Tucker, W. T. 1971. A multivariate analysis of personality and product use. *JMR* 8(1):67–70

386. Speller, D. E. 1973. Attitudes and intentions as predictors of purchase: A cross-validation. *Proc. APA* 8:825–26

387. Spence, H. E. 1972. Fear appeals in marketing—A social perspective. *JM* 36(3):39–43

388. Spence, H. E., Engel, J. F. 1969. The impact of brand preference on the perception of brand names: A laboratory analysis. *Proc. AMA* Ser. 30:267–71

389. Spence, H. E., Engel, J. F., Blackwell, R. D. 1970. Perceived risk in mail-order and retail store buying. *JMR* 7(3): 364–69

390. Stafford, J. E., Birdwell, A. E., Van Tassel, C. E. 1970. Integrated advertising—white backlash? *JAR* 10(2):15–20

391. Stafford, J. E., Enis, B. M. 1969. The price-quality relationship: An extension. *JMR* 6(4):456–58

392. Stapel, J. 1972. "Fair" or "Psychological" pricing? *JMR* 9(1):109–10

393. Sternthal, B., Craig, C. S. 1973. Humor in advertising. *JM* 37(4):12–18

394. Sternthal, B., Craig, C. S. 1974. Fear appeals: Revisited and revised. *JCR* 1(3):22–34

395. Stuteville, J. R. 1970. Psychic defenses against high fear appeals: A key marketing variable. *JM* 34(2):39–45

396. Summers, J. O. 1970. The identity of women's clothing fashion opinion leaders. *JMR* 7(2):178–85

397. Ibid 1971. Generalized change agents and innovativeness. 8(3):313–16

398. Summers, J. O. 1972. Media exposure patterns of consumer innovators. *JM* 36(1):43–49

399. Summers, J. O. 1974. Less information is better? *JMR* 11(4):467–68
400. Swan, J. E. 1969. Experimental analysis of predecision information seeking. *JMR* 6(2):192–97
401. Swan, J. E. 1972. Search behavior related to expectations concerning brand performance. *JAP* 56:332–35
402. Swanson, C. E. 1968. Anxiety and the consumer: Model and method applied to fears of air travel. *Proc. APA* 3:671–72
403. Szybillo, G. J., Heslin, R. 1973. Resistance to persuasion: Inoculation theory in a marketing context. *JMR* 10(4): 396–403
404. Szybillo, G. J., Jacoby, J. 1974. Effects of different levels of integration on advertising preference and intention to purchase. *JAP* 59:274–80
405. Ibid. Intrinsic versus extrinsic cues as determinants of perceived product quality. 74–78
406. Szybillo, G. J., Jacoby, J., Busato, J. 1973. Effects of integrated advertising on perceived corporate hiring policy. *Proc. APA* 8:815–16
407. Talarzyk, W. W. 1972. A reply to the response to Bass, Talarzyk, and Sheth. *JMR* 9(4):465–67
408. Tauber, E. M. 1972. What is measured by concept testing? *JAR* 12(6):35–37
409. Tauber, E. M. 1973. Reduce new product failures: Measure needs as well as purchase intent. *JM* 37(3):61–70
410. Taylor, J. W. 1974. The role of risk in consumer behavior. *JM* 38(2):54–60
411. Thorelli, H. B. 1971. Concentration of information power among consumers. *JMR* 8(4):427–32
412. Tigert, D. J., Arnold, S. J. 1971. Profiling self-designated opinion leaders and self-designated innovators through life style research. See Ref. 141, 425–45
413. Tolley, B. S., Goett, J. J. 1971. Reactions to blacks in newspaper ads. *JAR* 11(2):11–17
414. Tongberg, R. C. 1973. An empirical study of the relationships between dogmatism and attitudes toward foreign products. *Proc. AMA* 35:87–91
415. Twedt, D. W. 1965. Consumer psychology. *Ann. Rev. Psychol.* 16:265–94
416. Uhl, K., Andrus, R., Poulsen, L. 1970. How are laggards different: An empirical inquiry. *JMR* 7(1):51–54
417. Valenzi, E. R., Andrews, I. R. 1971. Effect of price information on product quality ratings. *JAP* 55:87–91
418. Valenzi, E. R., Eldridge, L. 1973. Effect of price information, composition differences, expertise, and rating scales on product-quality rating. *Proc. APA* 8:829–30
419. Vavra, R. G., Winn, P. R. 1971. Fear appeals in advertising: An investigation of the influence of order, anxiety and involvement. *Proc. AMA* 33:444–49
420. Venkatesan, M. 1968. Personality and persuasibility in consumer decision making. *JAR* 8(1):39–45
421. Venkatesan, M., Ed. 1972. *Proceedings, 3rd Annual Conference, Association for Consumer Research.* Iowa City: Univ. Iowa Press. Lib. Congr. Cat. Card No. 72-97997
422. Venkatesan, M. 1973. Cognitive consistency and novelty seeking. See Ref. 425, 354–84
423. Venkatesan, M., Haaland, G. A. 1968. Divided attention and television commercials: An experimental study. *JMR* 5(2):203–5
424. Ward, S. 1974. Consumer socialization. *JCR* 1(2):1–13
425. Ward, S., Robertson, T. S., Eds. 1973. *Consumer Behavior: Theoretical Sources.* Englewood Cliffs, NJ: Prentice-Hall
426. Ward, S., Wright, P. L., Eds. 1973. *Advances in Consumer Research.* Vol. 1. Urbana, Ill: ACR Lib. Congr. Cat. Card No. 74-76437
427. Weber, J. E., Hansen, R. W. 1972. The majority effect and brand choice. *JMR* 9(3):320–23
428. Weddle, D. E., Bettman, J. R. 1974. Marketing underground: An investigation of Fishbein's behavioral intention model. See Ref. 426, 310–18
429. Wells, W. D., Beard, A. D. 1973. Personality and consumer behavior. See Ref. 425, 141–99
430. Wells, W. D., Tigert, D. J. 1971. Activities, interests, and opinions. *JAR* 11(4): 27–35
431. Wheatley, J. J. 1971. Marketing and the use of fear or anxiety-arousing appeals. *JM* 35(2):62–64
432. Wheatley, J. J. 1971. The use of black models in advertising. *JMR* 8:390–92
433. Wheatley, J. J., Oshikawa, S. 1970. The relationship between anxiety and positive and negative advertising appeals. *JMR* 7(1):85–89
434. Wilkie, W. L. 1974. Analysis of effects of information load. *JMR* 11(4):462–66
435. Wilkie, W. L., Pessemier, E. A. 1973. Issues in marketing's use of multiattribute attitude models. *JMR* 10(4): 428–41

436. Willenborg, J. F. 1971. Determining the durable product needs of households. See Ref. 141, 108–18
437. Willenborg, J. F. 1972. A study of the relationship between social values and attitudes toward advertising. See Ref. 421, 783–90
438. Wilson, D. T., Mathews, H. L., Monoky, J. F. 1972. Attitude as a predictor of behavior in a buyer-seller bargaining situation: An experimental approach. *Proc. AMA* 34:390–95
439. Winter, F. W. 1973. A laboratory experiment of individual attitude response to advertising. *JMR* 10(2):130–40
440. Ibid 1974. The effect of purchase characteristics on postdecision product reevaluation. 11(2):164–71
441. Witt, R. E. 1969. Informal social group influence on consumer brand choice. *JMR* 6(4):473–76
442. Witt, R. E., Bruce, G. D. 1972. Group influence and brand choice congruence. *JMR* 9(4):440–43
443. Wolf, A., Newman, D. Z., Winters, L. C. 1969. Operant measures of interest as related to ad lib readership. *JAR* 9(2):40–45
444. Woodruff, R. B. 1972. Measurement of consumer's prior brand information. *JMR* 9(3):258–63
445. Ibid. Brand information sources, opinion change, and uncertainty. 9(4):414–18
446. Woodside, A. G. 1968. Social character, product use and advertising appeals. *JAR* 8(4):31–35
447. Woodside, A. G. 1972. Informal group influence on risk taking. *JMR* 9(2):223–25
448. Woodside, A. G. 1972. A shopping list experiment of beer brand images. *JAP* 56:512–13
449. Woodside, A. G. 1972. Positive disconfirmation of expectation and the effect of effort on evaluation. *Proc. APA* 7:743–44
450. Woodside, A. G. 1972. Dominance and conflict in family purchasing decisions. See Ref. 421, 650–59
451. Woodside, A. G. 1974. Is there a generalized risky shift phenomenon in consumer behavior? *JMR* 11(2):225–26
452. Woodside, A. G. 1974. Relation of price to perception of quality of new products. *JAP* 59:116–18
453. Worthing, P. M., Venkatesan, M., Smith, S. 1973. Personality and product use revisisted: An exploration with the Personality Research Form. *JAP* 57:179–83
454. Wright, P. L. 1972. Consumer judgement strategies: Beyond the compensatory assumption. See Ref. 421, 316–24
455. Wright, P. L. 1973. The cognitive processes mediating acceptance of advertising. *JMR* 10(1):53–62
456. Wright, P. L. 1974. On the direct monitoring of cognitive responses to advertising. See Ref. 184, 220–48
457. Wright, P. 1974. The harassed decision maker: Time pressures, distractions, and the use of evidence. *JAP* 59:555–61
458. Wright, P. 1975. Consumer choice strategies: Simplifying vs. optimizing. *JMR* 12(1):60–67
459. Zaltman, G. 1974. Strategies for diffusing innovations. See Ref. 380, 78–100
460. Zaltman, G., Dubois, B. 1971. New conceptual approaches in the study of innovation. See Ref. 141, 417–24
461. Zaltman, G., Stiff, R. 1973. Theories of diffusion. See Ref. 425, 416–68
462. Ziff, R. 1971. Psychographics for market segmentation. *JAR* 11(2):3–9
463. Zikmund, W. G., Scott, J. E. 1974. A multivariate analysis of perceived risk, self-confidence, and information sources. See Ref. 426, 406–16

PSYCHOLOGY AND THE LAW: AN OVERTURE[1]

258

June Louin Tapp[2]

Institute of Child Development and Department of Criminal Justice Studies, University of Minnesota, Minneapolis, Minnesota 55455

INTRODUCTION

1976 is an auspicious birth year for the first chapter on the state of the psychology/ law interface. Although it has not been 200 years since these two fields—concerned with the rules of and for human behavior—initiated collaboration, the history of psychology and law dates back to the first decade of the twentieth century. While Freud in 1906 in Vienna (42) was lecturing judges on the practicality of psychology, others in the United States circa 1910 were also connecting the classroom (psychological laboratory) with the courtroom (law). In 1908, Munsterberg of Harvard University's psychological laboratory attempted in his book, *On the Witness Stand,* to apply psychology to legal problems by demonstrating that the psychological processes of perception and memory must be considered in evaluating courtroom testimony (128). In 1909, Healy established in Chicago the first psychological clinic to be attached to a juvenile court—a first also for law; in 1915, he wrote *Honesty:*

[1]The collection of literature and materials pertinent to this chapter, stressing current but selected topics, was concluded in July 1975. For historical and critical reasons other germinal works published in the decade preceding 1975, which is also generally under review, are mentioned as are several still in press. Some of the ideas herein were presented in preliminary form at a plenary session entitled "Law and Society: Progress of A Decade" at the Law and Society Association's First Research Colloquium, June 5–7, 1975, at the State University of New York, Faculty of Law and Jurisprudence.

[2]The author wishes to express deep appreciation to those individuals whose supportive services and intellectual interests aided in the preparation of this manuscript: to Gary Engstrand and William Hafling, graduate students in psychology and law, for continuing efforts in the critical search for significant materials; to graduate students John Drozdal, Ann Juergens, and Christine Kegler and undergraduate Elizabeth Irby, whose seminar questions and papers fed my ever-growing pile of ideas and references; to undergraduate research assistant Patricia Smolka for devoted ministrations in the manuscript's preparation; to my secretary, Kay Adams, for supportive services beyond typing; and to Felice J. Levine, critic and colleague in matters regarding psychology and law.

A Study of the Causes and Treatment of Dishonesty among Children (67). By 1913, Watson, expressing his dissatisfaction with psychology, suggested that jurists could utilize data in a practical way as soon as psychologists could obtain them (191).

Discussion of a rapprochement between psychology and the law among psychologists in the United States is thus old and recurrent (e.g. 9, 24, 35, 111, 118, 142, 151, 172, 174, 183, 184, 194). The task of this chapter is to trace the nature of this relationship, especially over the past 10 years. To this end, several tacks are employed:

(*a*) A brief description of historical trends.

(*b*) An examination of current indicators from the past decade, covering conferences, patterns of research publication, organizational responses, academic programs, and educational materials.

(*c*) A selective survey of research, focusing on these topics: legal socialization, including cross-cultural and developmental dimensions and issues in children's rights; the judicial process, including decision making in the adversary system, eyewitness identification, the jury decision process, and the role of psychologists in jury selection; the criminal justice process, with perspectives on the roles of psychologists and alternative models for justice.

(*d*) Along with the survey of research, consideration is given to issues and recommendations concerning both research and reform.

The usual disclaimers made by contributors to the *Annual Review of Psychology* about the selection bias of the author, the enormity of the field (in this case, the fields), the incompleteness of the coverage, the press of time and timeliness are all in order. Given the problems of breadth and interpretation in defining the psychology/law interface, the author adds to these the criterion of attending only to those empirical events and research endeavors by psychologists working alone or in concert with lawyers that revealed an interest in law and legal instititions. Although many psychologists are investigating areas or processes that have implications for the law, for purposes of this initial report intensive analysis was given primarily to those efforts that were explicitly psychology-and-law directed in terms of the design of the endeavor (experiment) or the discussion of the results. I hope this chapter can serve as the overture inviting further consideration of the issues and area. Only psychologists and lawyers together can provide the orchestration.

HISTORICAL CONTEXT

In his perceptive and comprehensive book of 1961, *Legal and Criminal Psychology,* Toch defined legal psychology as a "science" that "*studies* the process whereby justice is arrived at, examines the people who take part in this process, and looks into their purposes, motives, thoughts, and feelings" (184, pp. 3–4). Inevitably analysts of the relationship of psychology and law, regardless of the school of psychology or law, highlight the union as promoting and understanding justice in or out of formal legal settings. Certainly even before 1910 with the classic experiments relating testimony and evidence to perception and memory by Stern (170), Munsterberg (128), and Whipple (193), law was acknowledged as a fit concern for psychology and vice versa. But examinations of the relationship between psychology and law in potential areas of study or collaboration indicate that after the first flirtation little happened through the mid-1960s.

The scattered attempts during the 1920s, 1930s, 1940s, and 1950s by psychologists or lawyers (e.g. 23, 41, 82, 113, 127, 146) reflected little progress in the rapprochement between psychology and law. The major empirical work on law in the 1940s, 1950s, and early 1960s was heavily anthropological, sociological, or psychiatric (30, 88, 107, 171). There were few calls for advancing a legal psychology, despite psychologist Clark's contribution to the historical 1954 *Brown vs Board of Education* case. The psychological input was primarily as an expert witness or in other forensic capacities. Even Toch's generally comprehensive volume, using then current work, sought to "spell out and define" the status of the field "without benefit of interaction" (184, pp. ix, vii). Beyond Marshall's *Law and Psychology in Conflict* (111) that reported experiments by lawyer Marshall and psychologist Mansson on the vagaries of evidence, recall, and courtroom behavior, there was little demand for a legal psychology. Not until the late 1960s and early 1970s was the exchange between psychologists and lawyers on matters of justice and law anything more than sparse and sporadic.

It is difficult to pinpoint the variables that relate to contemporary change. Have social/political crises, modernization, and the press for relevance accounted for the burgeoning and renewed interest of psychologists in the law or the reverse? Is it perhaps the recognition that individuals *and* institutions have rights, roles, and responsibilities? Perhaps it is the recognition that not only education but the law as well is an important mobility belt for the rights-deprived. Perhaps recent efforts toward mutual research and reform by psychologists and lawyers signal an increased awareness of their role and responsibility in working with "subjects" or "clients" as patients or prisoners—pressing for rights and legitimate claims in and outside of institutions. Or perhaps the present interest parallels a general concern about the rising crime rates and violence patterns. For psychologists this trend may reflect a desire to extend knowledge about human behavior and consider "how legal policies and institutions could be employed to decrease the appalling level of violence in our society" (L. Berkowitz, personal communication, 1975). For lawyers it may reflect the view that "the pressure of our present predicament pushes us—as we have not been pushed for a long time—toward an effort at comprehension. We must come to perceive and understand the moral and psychological forces that underlie law generally and give it efficacy in human affairs" (45, p. 1).

While commentators increasingly are mindful that psychology's unique contribution is its brands of empiricism, they also acknowledge that frequently psychological insights are directed uncritically and too quickly to the basic problems of justice and the legal process (e.g. 32, 53, 77, 103, 118, 166, 172; G. Bermant and J. Davis, personal communications, 1975). Therefore, as psychologists begin to elaborate their commitments to law, they must be cognizant of and clear about the nature of their limitations. For these and other reasons, Campbell's creative approach to methodology and policy (research and reform) is persuasive. In reviewing Campbell's application of psychological methods for introducing and assessing changes brought about by legal events (24), Meehl cogently depicted the strengths of this approach:

> There is need for a change in the political atmosphere . . . toward a more open recognition that we do not know exactly how to proceed. . . . The mandate should not be to stamp out crime (or poverty, or discrimination, or inflation) but the mandate should be to embark, wholeheartedly but skeptically, upon the social experiment to see whether or not it works. . . . Only in such a political [legal] atmosphere can the psychologist reach the full potential of his contribution to the amelioration of social problems (117, pp. 29–30).

The present chapter aims to review the rapprochement between law and psychology building upon the principles of Campbell's counsel—both methodological and conceptual (e.g. 24–26, 151).

CURRENT INDICATORS: EMPIRICAL EVIDENCE

There are two terms, interstitial and interfacial, that describe the possible relationship between two bodies of matter—in this instance, law and psychology. The history of the relationship between psychology and law over the first half-century indicates communication more in the mode of two separate and distinct parts of a body divided by space (i.e. interstitial). In contrast, the events of the past 5 to 10 years reveal movement toward the creation of a common boundary (i.e. interfacial). Slowly the disciplines of psychology and law have grown to view their relationship and respective responses to understanding human behavior as complementary, interlocked, and coincident. As both fields increasingly address fundamental problems and assumptions of law, justice, and the individual in society, the potential of mutual, interfacial exchange is evident.

Conferences

At the Law & Society Association's First Research Colloquium in June 1975, a psychologist joined ranks with a political scientist, anthropologist, sociologist, and lawyer to compose the panel for the plenary session entitled, "Law and Society: Progress of a Decade." Of the 100 workshop panelists on the program, only 4 were psychologists (2 of whom were also lawyers), and the others were lawyers (about 40) and social scientists (primarily sociologists and political scientists). But 10 years ago at such a research colloquium the "psychological" representatives both presenting and attending would have been psychiatrists or, if psychologists, probably clinicians with forensic expertise. In 1975 the forensic psychologist is but one of several specialists active at the psychology/law interface. Social, experimental, and child psychologists frequently function as expert witnesses and equally importantly are contributing research on fundamental assumptions about legal phenomena. They are indeed "empiricizing" by scientific research the study of law (e.g. 32, 62, 124, 150, 151, 172, 181, 183, 189; also 174, pp. 2–4)—advancing the possibility for more productive and systematic *questions* and *answers* to traditional conceptual debates.

The Law & Society Research Colloquium is particularly encouraging when it is juxtaposed to the National Science Foundation's (NSF) Assessment Conference on "Developments in Law and Social Sciences Research," held 2 years earlier, April 1973. Of 20 participants at that conference, only two were psychologists and one presented psycholegal research funded by this agency (129). But perhaps anticipating future trends, law professor Friedman, one of 13 lawyers, called for increased law and psychology efforts:

> [A] couple of areas, so far neglected, will enjoy . . . something of a minor boom. One is psychology and law. This is long overdue. There has been some interest in psychiatry or psychoanalysis and law, but this has diminished. As far as psychology itself is concerned, . . . [i]n recent years . . . a few scholars have turned to problems of attitude and behavior rather than perception: compliance and deviance, the relative efficacy of rewards and punishments, application of learning theory to law, and so on. Some of these interests are not absolutely new, but they have gotten a new lease on life. At present, no more than two or three law schools have given joint appointments in psychology and law. There is bound to be more action in the future (129, p. 1070).

While the preceding 5 to 10 years were characterized by a paucity of research colloquia or assessment conferences involving psychologists, the proliferation during the 1974–1975 period is indicated by at least three other events. The First Annual Convention of the American Psychology-Law Society (APLS) occurred in June 1974. A year later in June 1975, the Battelle Institute convened a conference on "Psychological Factors in Legal Processes," and in October that same year, the First Bi-Annual Law-Psychology Conference was held at the University of Nebraska. Unlike other or earlier conferences, the latter three meetings focused on psychology and were populated by practitioners and academicians drawn from child, experimental, and social psychology as well as from law. In addition to these conferences, the coming-of-age of the psychology/law movement from an interstitial to interfacial position is also illustrated by the psychology "establishment's" decision for this chapter—a first—in the *Annual Review of Psychology* series.

Patterns of Research Publication

The major difficulty encountered in researching the state of the law/psychology interface is the lack of adequate indexing systems in both law and psychology. As Caplan & Nelson noted (27, p. 205), *Psychological Abstracts* (*PA*) are virtually useless in assessing an interdisciplinary or untraditional relationship. Because of the bias in indexing ("labeling"), the areas of crime, juvenile delinquency, and drug addiction are grouped under the subheading of Behavior Disorder within the division of Clinical Psychology. There are now such headings as justice, rights, or punishment. However, a 10-year count of entries under descriptors generally related to law (e.g. crime, criminals, law, government, prisons, prisoner-inmates, and courts) provides some perspective on the extent and nature of the interface. For example, in 1965, 111 articles (excluding 8 in the courts category) were identified; in 1968, 493 items were indexed; in 1971, 592; and in 1972, 718 made *PA*.[3] Even with the limited *PA* system, growing interest in problems relating psychology and the legal process is evident. In 1973, *PA* changed its method of indexing the annual volume. Based on a new search system with some 70 descriptors drawn and created from the *PA* thesaurus (e.g. criminal law, legal decisionmaking, compliance, fairness, jury or forensic), 2221 articles were identified on both title and abstract contents for the period from January 1967 to December 1972 and 1771 for the period from January 1973 to May 1975. Comparing the earlier 6-year span to the most recent 2½ years revealed a significant and further increase since 1972 in the magnitude of research devoted to topics at the psychology/law interface.

A search of the *Index to Legal Periodicals* from September 1964 to August 1974 evidenced an analogous increase in the number of entries for three psychologically related categories. For the categories "psychology" and "mental health," there were approximately as many entries (36 and 63 respectively) for the 1-year period, September 1973 to August 1974, as there were for any preceeding 3-year period (1970–73, 1967–70, 1964–67). The most dramatic increase in 1973–74 was under the "psychiatry" listing. For that 1-year period, 129 entries were identified in contrast to 49, 60, and 14 during prior 3-year periods. Overall for the three categories, the total entries during the 1964 to 1974 period were: psychology, 157; mental health, 276; psychiatry, 252. (The precipitating issues for the disproportionate "psychiatry" increment seem to be involuntary commitment, patients' rights, and predictions of dangerousness.) But beyond the currency of these topics, the 1973–74 data suggested a general trend toward greater attention to psychological considerations in legal periodicals. If anything, this pattern is understated—since some literature placed elsewhere by the *Index* editors would have been categorized under "psychology" by this author.

Another informative indicator could be found in the programs for meetings of the American Psychological Association (APA). Although the Central Office had no archival data or listing of presentations "relating to the interface of psychology and law during the last ten years" (C. Won, personal communication, 1975), an inspection of annual programs from 1965 to 1975 disclosed a remarkable increase in symposia, workshops, paper sessions, and invitational addresses by psychologists and lawyers. While in 1965 there was only a single presentation, by 1974 and 1975 the numbers jumped to 28 and 33 respectively, not including those dealing with alcoholism, drugs, or juvenile delinquency. Also in 1975, the APLS, which previously had co-sponsored its program with relevant APA divisions, convened eight independent sessions at APA including four symposia, two paper sessions, and two

[3]The category "courts" was dropped by *PA* after 1967. A frequency distribution for all categories from 1965 to 1972 is available from the author. Counts are not available after 1972 because *PA* switched its method of indexing. Brodsky reported analogous patterns related to crime. In calculating the number of publications reported in the *PA,* he found that until 1950 such articles constituted less than 2.5% of the total publications while in the "1966–1970 period, for the first time, the rate of increase of publications in this area kept pace with the overall increase in American psychology" (21, p. 9).

workshops. Additionally in 1975, two major APA addresses (28, 137) dealt directly with psychology/law issues.

Organizational Responses

Increasingly over the past decade, psychologists have been engaged in research or in providing services at the psychology/law interface within and beyond psychological organizations. In 1972, Brodsky reported that:

> Between the American Psychology-Law Society, the International Academy of Forensic Psychology, and the American Association of Correctional Psychologists, about 800 psychologist-members identify themselves as having substantial interest in law, justice, or corrections. Since 1967, APA has had a Task Force on Crime, Delinquency, and Social Disorders and, since 1970, a Task Force on Standards for Service Facilities. The APA Division of Psychological Aspects of Disability has an ad hoc Committee on the Public Offender. Division 9, the Society for the Psychological Study of Social Issues (SPSSI), has several active committees, and probably represents the highest level of organized interest in the APA (21, p. 10).

SPSSI continues to be the most active division in the law and justice area. In 1974 it sought through its Justice and Law Coordinating Committee to integrate the activities of the five Committees on Law and Crime, Socialization and the Law, Police, Courts, and Corrections, while also maintaining the Committees on Privacy and Rights of Children.

The expanding interest of other divisions in matters of law and justice is also evident. For example, the December 1972 Division 8 Newsletter featured an article on social science and law (29). A perusal of the 1975 APA annual program showed that beyond 8 and 9 at least seven other divisions were reporting or supporting some type of activity of a psycholegal nature. While in 1975 Division 9 still maintained the highest level of organized interest in the APA, Divisions 8, 12, 13, 14, 18, 22, 25, and 27 were all running close behind.

Similarly APA's Board of Social and Ethical Responsibility for Psychology (BSERP) in 1973–75, alone and in concert with other APA boards (e.g. Board of Scientific Affairs, Board of Professional Affairs), accelerated attention to issues related to the criminal justice system and the areas of human rights, privacy, and confidentiality. In addition to BSERP's Task Force on the Role of Mental Health Workers in the Criminal Justice System (1975), the Task Force on Children's Rights (1975), the Task Force on Privacy and Confidentiality (1975), and the Commission on Behavior Modification (1974), the Board of Scientific Affairs recently initiated efforts for a Task Force on Law and Psychology (H. Pick, personal communication, 1973; E. Loftus, personal communication, 1975). The contemplated Task Force would identify research programs of potential value in assessing and improving the legal system and promote further activity while maintaining concern about the possible misuse of psychological findings, methods, or theories.

Another indicator of institutionalized professional interest is reflected in the APA's official journal, the *American Psychologist.* Increasingly from 1973 to 1975, articles on law-related topics appeared. While many dealt with applied issues such as the rights and kinds of treatment for offenders, the utilization and training of psychologists for the criminal justice system, and law enforcement, others considered the problems of scientific method in psychological research, compliance, attitudes toward law, and legal socialization (e.g. 55, 75, 80, 103, 144, 147, 165, 166).

Beyond the undertakings mentioned thus far, there are other worthy psychology/ law efforts outside of the traditional framework of APA. By 1975, APLS had expanded its membership drawn from psychologists and lawyers to over 500, a substantial growth pattern from its inception in 1968 after an APA symposium entitled "Psychology and the Law." The basic aim of APLS is "to promote exchanges between the disciplines of psychology and law in regard to areas of mutual interest such as teaching, research, administration of justice, jurisprudence, as well as other matters at the psychology-law interface" (81, p. 8). In its August 1975 Newsletter, APLS initiated a column entitled "Law-Psychology Update."

From the legal profession too efforts toward rapprochement have been forthcoming. By 1976 one social psychologist will have been a research social scientist for 10 years at the American Bar Foundation, the research affiliate of the American Bar Association (ABA). By 1975 the ABA had invited a number of psychologists to join interdisciplinary commissions that function to advise ABA committees and councils. For example, three psychologists sit on the Advisory Commission for the ABA's Special Committee on Youth Education for Citizenship and two sit on the Commission on the Mentally Disabled. Further, in October 1974, the ABA's Institute of Judicial Administration sponsored, as part of its Juvenile Justice Standards Project, a conference of about 60 participants on "Moral Development and Juvenile Justice" to which 10 psychologists were invited, with 2 presenting position papers. In concert with lawyers, judges, economists, sociologists, philosophers, and journalists, this group sought to evolve an adequate justice model and an ethical treatment mode.

Beyond activity under way in professional organizations, the extent of support provided to research by the federal funding agencies is an important index of interest.[4] Government is another organizational system that both influences and reflects research priorities. Therefore, the pattern of involvement by the "feds" should likewise by considered. (Local or state patterns are not reviewed.)

Initially the National Institute of Mental Health (NIMH), especially through its Center for Studies in Crime and Delinquency, provided funds for research, training grants, and fellowships. Accordingly, using information provided by Shah, Chief of the Center, Brodsky reported:

> Just under half of the research grants active in fiscal year (FY) 1972 had psychologists as principal investigators. The majority of the remaining principal investigators were sociologists. Only 2 of 52 training grants went to psychologists. . . . most NIMH support

[4]Although there are private sources for funding, they are typically less substantial than the federal government grants and are more inclined to support lawyers and sociologists—traditional partners in research. On occasion the Russell Sage Foundation and the Ford Foundation have departed from this pattern, but overall private organizations have not substantially advanced psycholegal research to date.

for psychology graduate programs not necessarily in psychology and law comes from another branch of NIMH. Overall, 28% [47 out of 171] of the recipients were psychologists, a figure that corresponds closely to the proportion of crime and law enforcement dissertations written by psychologists (21, p. 10).

In 1975 Shah indicated that probably the majority of projects in the law and mental health area were covered by the Center after 1968 (personal communication, 1975). An examination of the Center's active research grants from June 1967 to December 1976 revealed an increase in the number of psychologist-directed projects to about 40%. Equally important, the projects were becoming broader in scope and greater in variety (e.g. differential treatment for delinquents, interpersonal relationships of prisoners, effects of film or television violence, personality factors in aggressive and antisocial behavior, empirical and legal bases for dangerousness, criteria for adequacy of treatment, information integration in juror judgments, gene-environment interactions and criminality, abnormal mother-infant behavior, and child abuse). These studies were directed as much to basic as to applied problems, to children as to adults, and to civil as to criminal justice systems.

Less actively but significantly, NSF through its law and social science section has supported several well-known projects co-directed by psychologists (e.g. Free Press-Fair Trial, Human Behavior and the Legal Process). Funds also available through NSF-RANN (Research Applied to National Needs) auspices indicate interest in psychologically oriented legal research.

It is the Law Enforcement Assistance Administration (LEAA) that seems to have had the most profound impact on law-related research directed by psychologists in the mid-1970s. Perhaps because of the general community apprehension regarding crime since the late 1960s, funds have been made available through LEAA, the Department of Justice, and the Youth Development and Delinquency Prevention Administration. New legislation regarding child abuse affords another source for training and research grants. However, psychologists may have to be as wary of "justice" ("crime") monies in the 1970s as they should have been of "poverty" monies in the 1960s. Regardless of the source of their support, psychologists must continuously evaluate their efforts to provide methodologically and ethically sound research that facilitates understanding the human capacity to function in and create a just legal order.

Academic Programs

Over the past 10 years and particularly the last 5, another institutional system—education—has also indicated its support of rapprochement between psychology and law through academic programs in law and social science at the undergraduate and graduate levels as well as in law schools. Ladinsky's 1975 report provides a comprehensive, current, and useful description. Noting "a substantial development over the past 12 years" (98, p. 1), Ladinsky described the 1950s as the birthtime of "genuine cross-disciplinary research efforts" citing Cohen, Robson & Bates' *Parental Authority: The Community and the Law* (30) and Zeisel, Kalven & Buckholz's

Delay in the Court (198) as key indicators of this trend. He also reported that "the amount of formal teaching remained insignificant" (p. 6). In essence, the picture has changed for research and teaching in law and social science and even in law and psychology, but not overwhelmingly.

The 1960s brought the Russell Sage (RS) Foundation's cross-disciplinary programs in law and social science, primarily in sociology, political science, and anthropology, to the University of California at Berkeley, Northwestern University, University of Wisconsin at Madison, and the University of Denver. While small grants, usually fellowships, were made elsewhere, it was not until 1972 that RS launched a law and psychology program at Stanford University, the last of its law-social science projects. Further, within the past 5 years, several RS Law and Social Science Fellows in the Yale University program have been psychologists who contributed visibly to psychology as well. The "vital breakthrough generally in the law and social science partnership" is evident by the continuation of such programs with and without Russell Sage or other agency funds (98, pp. 5–6).

Sorely lacking in most of these programs or their offspring is the presence of psychologists in substantial numbers. To the best of this author's knowledge, beyond Stanford University and the University of Denver (with one psychologist each on the law faculty), only the University of Nebraska at Lincoln by 1975 had officially inaugurated a jointly administered law/psychology studies program leading to a JD (Juris Doctor) and PhD in psychology (i.e. Experimental, Social-Personality, Community-Clinical). Students at Northwestern may enter the joint-degree program in law and psychology and at other universities (e.g. Minnesota, Harvard, Chicago) may devise two-degree programs, but only Nebraska has a program that specifically aims "to produce lawyer-psychologists whose training will provide all the necessary skills to do basic and applied research and writing on issues and problems in our legal system, in general, and the criminal and correctional system in particular" (Program Description 1975, p. 1).

Furthermore, the criminal justice/correctional system direction in the Nebraska program is noted as well in programs at other graduate and undergraduate centers. The University of Alabama, the John Jay College of Criminal Justice, and the School of Criminal Justice at State University of New York at Albany have programs at both the graduate and undergraduate levels with substantial psychological input. Other examples of universities with undergraduate and master's degree programs and psychologists on their faculties include the University of California at Irvine, University of Illinois, University of Washington, and University of Minnesota. An increasingly important center for undergraduate training in social science and law with some psychological orientation is the Five College Legal Studies Program—Amherst, Mount Holyoke, Smith, Hampshire, and the University of Massachusetts. Apparently law and society, crime and society, and/or criminal justice studies majors, housed in colleges of liberal arts, provide alternatives to majors in sociology, political science, psychology, or economics. And psychologists are likely to be participating in such programs. As Gormally & Brodsky observed (55, p. 928), "the 40-year trend toward diminished involvement of psychologists in justice work seems . . . reversed."

Educational Materials

With typical course titles like "Law, Justice and the Individual in Society," "Legal and Psychological Aspects of Moral and Altruistic Behavior," "Legal Socialization: Impact of Legal and Criminal Justice Systems," "Rights of Children," "Law and Society," "Psychology and the Criminal Law," and plain old "Psychology and Law," the problem of materials for classroom and research purposes is primary. While "output in research articles, monographs, and textbooks in American social science and law has been very extensive over the past 12 years" (98, p. 20), an up-to-date textbook or reader does not exist for the psychology/law field. Previously published books emphasize law and anthropology, sociology, psychiatry, or political science rather than psychology (cf 44). Ladinsky's bibliography of materials through the 1960s and the early 1970s corroborates that, while some sources are interdisciplinary, they are usually inclusive of social sciences other than psychology. Thus, for the most part, those in teaching or research at the interface of psychology and law have had to develop their own materials, drawing from original research contributions and selecting from texts, readers, and casebooks in the broad field of law and the social sciences. Except for efforts in the 1930s, the best, if not only, psycholegal textbook in the 1960s was a 14-chapter volume edited by Toch (184). Marshall's book (111), a research monograph, is a conceptual and empirical document on the problem of eyewitness identification, thus providing a powerful, although somewhat specialized, pedagogical frame.

Despite the general paucity, more recently some specific efforts have been made in terms of research and teaching needs. Since 1969 a number of special journal editions have been published both in psychology and law. The February 1969 issue of *Psychology Today* on the theme "Does the Law Work for You?" included articles by psychologists, psychiatrists, prisoners, and lawyers. In May 1970, the Law & Society Association's *Review* published a special issue on "Compliance and the Law" with contributions primarily from psychologists. According to Editor Galanter, however, the number of articles in the *Review* by psychologists or about psycholegal issues remains negligible: Only 3.5% of the total manuscripts submitted during 1972–74 were in the psychology/psychiatry category. Another example of journal interest was the 1971 issue of the *Journal of Social Issues* (*JSI*) on "Socialization, the Law, and Society" (174). That 13-chapter offering edited by Tapp was an interdisciplinary effort of both psychologists and lawyers. More recently, the *Stanford Law Review* devoted the June 1974 issue to a symposium on "Law and Psychology" and continued its dual commitment to this area in the next issue where the lead article was on legal socialization (181).

Among the books with an interdisciplinary format is an expanded version of the *JSI* symposium to 26 chapters, edited by Tapp & Levine and forthcoming as a SPSSI-sponsored volume entitled *Law, Justice, and the Individual in Society* (182). Partially published in psychology journals and law reviews during the early 1970s, the jointly authored book by psychologist Thibaut and lawyer Walker, *Procedural Justice: A Psychological Analysis* (183), is likely to be as monumental and controversial an empirical study as Kalven & Zeisel's *The American Jury* was in 1966 (88).

And, as one might expect, two further examples of psycholegal offerings are in the criminal justice area. Brodsky's edited book *Psychologists in the Criminal Justice System* (21) contains 14 chapters, and Monahan's edited volume *Community Mental Health and the Criminal Justice System* (125) includes 21.

In addition to these materials available for teaching and research, two new journals are specifically oriented to the dual perspectives of psychology and law: *Criminal Justice and Behavior*, published since 1974, and the *Journal of Law and Human Behavior*, planned for 1976–77. As these new efforts further suggest, even in the space of 5 years the coterminal interests and colloborative efforts of psychologists and lawyers are on the increase. Selected books and research reports, available and forthcoming, are reviewed in the subsequent section.

SELECTED THEMES

The topic "psychology and the law" shares the complexities of a symphony or opera: It is difficult to hum all the tunes simultaneously or to say that all the solos are equally salient or important. The overture provides a sampling of the entire piece, and, in like manner, this chapter reviews several motifs. To this composer there are currently three key areas of the interface of psychology and the law. They include (*a*) the legal socialization process, (*b*) the judicial process, and (*c*) the criminal justice process. Within this triadic framework the basic issue for psychology and the law—the acquisition and administration of justice and the corollary issues of rules, rights, and responsibilities vis-à-vis individuals and institutions—can be examined, drawing upon both empirical efforts and commonsense experiences of psychologists and lawyers.

In choosing these three themes, which embrace the community, courtroom, and corrections, I aim to characterize the growing attention paid by developmental, social, and clinical psychologists to the roles of the law and to their roles in the law. The range of issues at the nexus of psychology and law serves to underscore the fact that the law is not simply a system of social control nor the product or possession of one institution. No longer are the problems of law and order, justice and society —or their investigation and treatment—solely the domain of the legal theoretician or clinician. The corpus of materials relevant to the legal process appearing during the past several years in the psychological literature attests to the contrary. In the 1970s the phrase "psychology and law" means more than forensic psychologist. It means that more than one species of psychologist, solely or in concert, is working with more than one species of lawyer at the interface. It means, too, that communication and collaboration between and within both disciplines are occuring across levels (e.g. practitioner and researcher) and fields (cf 172).

Topics of traditional interest to the psychologist such as socialization, decision-making, information processing, perception, memory, cognition, attitudes, group dynamics, and interpersonal relations all have relevance for various aspects of the legal system. Further, psychologists are more actively translating traditional legal terms into behavioral constructs and also examining them by systematic empirical designs. In pursuing this work, psychologists and lawyers alike must be receptive not only to viewing research and reforms as experiments, but also to accepting the innovative, inferential, and interactive aspects of both the scientific and social enterprise. As my review of the selected solos commences, the cautions addressed by Judge David Bazelon at a conference of correctional psychologists serve as a reminder:

> Regretfully, I must tell you that the papers prepared for this conference . . . do nothing to allay my increasing doubts and uncertainties about what it is that psychologists or any other behavioralists can offer. . . . The issue is not whether psychology is good, but what it is good at. . . . Why should we even consider fundamental social changes of massive income redistribution if the entire problem can be solved by having scientists teach the criminal class—like a group of laboratory rats—to march successfully through the maze of our society? In short, before you respond with enthusiasm to our plea for help, you must ask yourselves whether your help is really needed, or whether you are merely engaged as magicians to perform an intriguing side-show so that the spectators will not notice the crisis in the center ring. In considering our motives for offering you a role, I think you would do well to consider how much less expensive it is to hire a thousand psychologists than to make even a miniscule change in the social and economic structure. . . . The critical issue . . . is whether the fundamental postulates of your discipline make it impossible for you to reach the central problem. . . . (13, pp. 149–50, 152).

The Legal Socialization Process

Legal socialization is a construct of the 1970s. It refers to the process of dealing with the emergence of legal attitudes and behaviors and describes the development of individual standards for making sociolegal judgments and for using the law and legal systems for problem solving. While the 1960s and to some degree the 1950s yielded extensive work, first in political socialization from political scientists and psychologists (e.g. 3, 4, 34, 59, 68, 69, 83, 84, 121, 122, 159, 160) and then in moral development primarily from psychologists of both a cognitive-developmental and social learning persuasion (e.g. 10, 11, 14, 61, 71, 93, 94, 110, 136, 149, 187), it was not until the 1970s that the term "legal socialization" came into being (172; 174, pp 4–5; 178). The transition period commenced in approximately 1968, and by 1974 the field had received sufficient legitimation to yield a SPSSI Committee on Socialization and the Law (1970), a special issue of *JSI* (174), APA symposia in both 1973 and 1974 (see e.g. 6, 7), and reference in a major personality and culture book (104) as well as in an *Annual Reviews* chapter (79).

To some degree, legal socialization—emerging from political socialization and moral development—overlaps these two research traditions. In fact, it is likely to be categorized frequently under political socialization or moral development research in textbooks or reviews. There are, however, important differences among these three realms of ideological socialization with regard to contexts of learning and expression, indicators of authority, and topics of research. Although all three focus on the growth of ideas especially in youth and increasingly into adulthood, the moral development research in the tradition of moral psychology and moral philosophy emphasizes general "valuation" processes, and the political development literature primarily provides descriptive information on attitudes and opinions relevant to political-legal settings. There are many excellent reviews of political socialization and moral development research that trace the development, dimensions, and differences within and between these areas (e.g. 40, 70, 91, 92, 94, 97, 110, 159, 160, 168, 196). Thus the task herein is primarily to consider the emergence of legal socialization and legal development as an identifiable research and reform area, not to review either political socialization or moral development.

CROSS-CULTURAL/DEVELOPMENT DIMENSIONS Tapp's idea for the legal socialization approach germinated during her involvement in a six-country, seven-culture study [Denmark, Greece, Italy, India, Japan, US (black & white)] of some 5000 urban preadolescents in grades 4, 6, and 8. This study, known as the Compliance Project (CP), had as its overall focus children's perspectives on authority, rules, and aggression. Secondary themes were dimensions of children's socialization into various compliance systems (family, school, religion, local or national government, friendship circle) and their judgments of aggressive confrontations, reported respectively in Parts I and II (68, 122).[5] Among the first cross-national psychologically oriented studies in political socialization of children, CP was directed by an interdisciplinary team of an educational psychologist (Hess), an anthropological psychologist (Minturn), and a social-political psychologist (Tapp)—all of whom shared developmental interests. In addition to the influence of a previous US political socialization study (34, 69), the CP was significantly affected by the interdisciplinary makeup of the six national teams in both the development of instruments and the ultimate research design. Typical of political socialization research in the 1960s, this effort is best described as an empirical survey with four instruments and minimal or mixed theoretical orientations.

The range of potential inferences from the CP for "rule systems" suggested the demarcation of legal socialization and legal development as distinct from political and moral. As initially constructed by Tapp and developed with Levine, this conceptualization was not intended to imply a restrictive focus on the institution of law (101, 172–182). Rather these terms characterized an approach to understanding the processes and products of reasoning about "legal" norms in a multiplicity of legal or "rule" systems—from church to community, government to games. Almost simultaneously Hogan & Henley (77) advanced a broad rule-oriented perspective for analyzing the process of rule acquisition, justice orientations, and compliance modes. These psychological models and others that have emerged in jurisprudence (15, 45–47, 140) are consistent with the assumptions of a rule-guided or law-consciousness sense (e.g. 77, 123).

From a "developmental" perspective, Tapp's initial work in legal socialization described children's legal values and assessed the effect especially of age-related changes while attending as well to sex, social class, and national differences (173, 175, 178, 180). This work, derived in part from the CP, considered the utility of

[5]Hess, Minturn & Tapp conducted this cooperative, cross-cultural study along with European and Asian field teams under the direction of S. Skyum-Nielsen (Denmark), V. Vassiliou (Greece), B. Kuppuswamy (India), M. Cesa-Bianchi (Italy), and A. Hoshino (Japan).

cognitive developmental and social learning assumptions for interpreting cross-cultural and developmental data. Various samples were included in analyses primarily of open-ended interviews but also of group-administered instruments: (*a*) 406 middle school boys and girls of high and low socioeconomic status (SES) in seven cultures; (*b*) 124 US black and white children of both low and high SES in grades 4, 6, and 8; and (*c*) 115 high SES, US white children from kindergarten through college.

The data from these samples revealed commonalities across cultures and the saliency of the age or developmental variable. With few exceptions black and white US preadolescents, like children in the other six cultures, were astonishingly similar in viewing human nature and the need for rules, the justice of rules, the legitimacy of rule-breaking, the power of enforcement, and the justice of punishment. Above all, developmental processes affected children's conceptions of justice and the role of law. The kindergarten to college data permitted further elaboration of these developmental patterns. Questions on the function of rules, the dynamics of legal compliance, the changeability and breakability of rules, and the nature of justice elicited parallel changes from kindergarten to college in youth's defining their role relationships to law. For example, most middle school children (73%) maintained that rule-breaking was permissible if the rule was less important than the reason for breaking it, but by college such circumstantial rationales (35%) were superseded by concerns about the morality of the rule (53%). Such data on the "legal value" system of middle class US youth indicated the utility of the cognitive developmental frame and also the value of attending to modeling, role portrayals, and reinforcements by adult socializing agents.

In the search for a theoretical and methodological framework, Tapp & Levine found that both the cognitive developmental, stage theory (93, 94, 138, 139) and the social learning models (10, 11, 14, 70, 71, 149) offered useful perspectives for work in legal development. As Maccoby cautioned in a review of moral development research, "both formulations will turn out to be right to a degree" (110, p. 253). Thus, although to these investigators a cognitive theory of legal development provided "a set of working hypotheses useful in attempting to clarify and describe the legal worlds of individuals and institutions" (181, p. 19; see also 176), Tapp & Levine's legal socialization research was directed at illuminating the "natural" and "social" ethic underlying modes of legal reasoning. In this work, the cognitive developmental theories introduced by Piaget (138, 139) and advanced by Kohlberg (94) had substantial impact. Also integrating jurisprudential notions of Rawls (140) and Fuller (45, 46), Tapp & Levine articulated a model of legal reasoning that classifies empirically derived interview categories according to three cognitive developmental levels (101, 175–177, 179, 181). From the theoretical vantage of this model, legal levels denote "a person's basic problem-solving strategies and conceptual framework [toward] law" (181, p. 2).

While Tapp & Levine adapted both Piaget and Kohlberg's sequencing notions to the realm of law, they characterized legal levels in Kohlberg's terminology—preconventional, conventional, postconventional. To illustrate the continuities between cognitive moral development and the development of one's legal reasoning capacity,

Tapp & Kohlberg (177), in an initial exercise crossing theories and methods, demonstrated the utility of a cognitive framework for studying legal development. The findings presented therein and the more detailed analyses by Tapp & Levine are consistent with other research using a stage-sequence approach (e.g. 39, 56, 61, 121, 148). While the data disclosed a shift in conceptualization from a preconventional law-obeying, to a conventional law-maintaining, to a postconventional law-making orientation, overall the conventional law-and-order-maintaining perspective was modal in the US and cross-culturally. Apparently individuals had the cognitive ability to reach "higher" levels of legal reasoning, but the question remained whether the socializing settings and figures accelerate, retard, or fixate legal development.

In a comprehensive and integrative article on "Legal Socialization: Strategies for Achieving an Ethical Legality" (181), Tapp & Levine considered the role of socializing agents and institutions. Adopting a biosocial interactive model, they emphasized evaluating the "match" (or "mismatch") between social inputs and the individual's natural capacity. To assess this relationship, they attended to adult data on graduating law students, elementary and high school teachers, incarcerated prisoners, as well as to the cross-cultural preadolescent and US developmental data. Basically for adult groups, like the college sample, the characteristic mode of reasoning was conventional. Further, the commonalities between the adult and child data suggested that crystallization occurs during the adolescent years and that substantial consistency is demonstrated during adulthood.

In addition to comparing youth and adults, Tapp & Levine considered the potential of select legal institutions in the US and cross-culturally for stimulating individual legal development. Based on published data and field reports on the US, Latin America, Asia, and Africa, they determined legal levels (i.e. "leveled") various approaches to the delivery of legal services to the "poor"—the "rights-deprived." A historical analysis indicated a shift from a preconventional level to a conventional level provision of legal services; further, the conventional level presently prevailed. If this work or the research on the moral structure of a prison (96, 153) and on the Stanford prison experiment (63, 64) are indicative, agents in conventional or preconventional rule systems, who themselves reason at such cognitive levels, are unlikely to accept conventional reasoning or stimulate postconventional thought. To foster the development of both the individual and institution, Tapp & Levine recommended four legal socialization strategies (acquisition of legal knowledge, mismatch and conflict, participation, and legal continuity) for community and school. In concluding, these investigators argued that various types of theories, empirical evidence, methods, and data are necessary in order to examine their contentions. Much as Thibaut & Walker noted one year later (cf 183, Chap. 11 & 12), Tapp & Levine stipulated that both their "social-scientific, interdisciplinary, problem-solving perspective" and the legal socialization recommendations would be contrary to a postconventional legality unless guided by principles of fairness and justice and "built upon" experimentation from the dual perspectives of law and psychology (181, p. 71).

The research of Tapp and colleagues in legal socialization and at the psychology and law interface continues in projects designed to ascertain further the validity of a levels theory of legality. For example, in 1972 Levine (101) commenced a preliminary study on dimensions of legal reasoning using approximately 90 children from grades 5, 10, and 11. This research tests directly the relationship between an individual's legal and moral reasoning, assesses the relationship between legal reasoning and self/other acceptance, and evaluates if an individual's legal level predicts behaviors and conception of rights, roles, and rules. Likewise, since late 1973 Tapp and her students have been engaged in five pilot projects dealing with the relationship of legality to personality, ethnicity, and socializing experiences. Participation in a jury selection project provided a naturalistic setting for aspects of the initial pilots. Follow-up field studies were undertaken with impanelled and challenged jurors and their kin as well as with adult/child and parent/child (N = 100) respondents drawn from jury wheels and a related community survey. The aim of these studies in legal socialization is to consider the biosocial variables affecting the development of legal reasoning in individuals. Therefore, in addition to assessing the relationship between age, personality styles, and sociality for legal level, Tapp throughout this work focuses on the "match" and interaction of parent/adult/child to legal reasoning, assessing such variables as self/other acceptance and authoritarianism.

Also in the 1970s three illustrative applications of the Tapp-Levine legal reasoning model were undertaken. Each piece of research took as one point of departure the Tapp & Kohlberg article that appeared in the initial 1971 *JSI* symposium on "legal socialization." Two of the efforts, one by Bloom (18) and the other by Fields (38), were cross-cultural projects: The Bloom study sought to demonstrate that social principledness and social humanism—aspects of moral and legal forms of thought—were underlying and independent dimensions of politico-moral reasoning "rather than merely culture-specific ranges of attitudinal clustering" (p. 13). In the contexts of primarily university students in Hong Kong, France, and the US (N = 120, 76, and 52 respectively), Bloom identified these factors and delineated behavior-relevant correlates. His effort constituted one of the first to connect social psychological and cognitive developmental theories cross-culturally. The Fields' study, yielding direct evidence for the legal levels construct, was a particularly intriguing investigation. Administering TAT cards and replicating the questions presented in Tapp & Kohlberg in an interview with Protestant and Catholic children from Belfast and Dublin (N = 44), Fields reported that the Belfast sample remained at the lowest level of reasoning while the Dublin children demonstrated the same developmental trends evident among US youth. It is precisely this difference that undergirds the view (96, 160, 175–179, 181, 199) that the "experience" (the legal level of the social system or socializer) does affect the "natural" level of legal or moral development.

This interest in the role of socializers and "social input" led also to the third study by Simpson (167) of 784 teachers, 65 of whom were interviewed on the legal reasoning questions. Simpson's goal in part was to examine the Tapp & Kohlberg assertion that "the role of the educator or socializer is to stimulate and facilitate youth to higher cognitive positions" (177, p. 85). She found that the majority of teachers' attitudes, values, and beliefs could be described in terms of (*a*) the nature of authority and justice vis-à-vis norms, rules, and laws; (*b*) the nature of individual self or personality as related to society; and (*c*) the school as an arena for studying law and the development of teachers. Simpson reported that over two-thirds of the sample valued procedures protecting individual rights (p. 6), but—with more years of teaching—they were more likely to rank *equality* and *freedom* low and *responsibility* high (p. 9). Furthermore, congruent with Tapp & Levine's findings on adults generally and teachers in particular (181), conventional reasoning strongly predominated—though instances of preconventional and postconventional responses among young and older adults appeared.

As indicated by the direction of these studies, various samples and methods are being employed for refining an approach to analyzing legally relevant cognitions. Ultimately the value of such projects rests on answering questions about the limits of law and the psychological limits of the human capacity—how far can individual reasoning go, especially as affected by the institution of law. These are the central concerns and questions of others as well working on socialization questions at the interface of psychology and law.

Although Hogan does not consider the age variable, he represents one departure from the cognitive-structural-stage model that is particularly relevant to understanding legal development. With Henley (77), he reminded psychologists interested in problems of law, justice, and compliance that a paradigm viewing humans as rule-guided potentially encourages a more comprehensive study of behavior. Thus his primary efforts have been directed toward the construction of an interdisciplinary model that can be described in terms of five dimensions: moral knowledge, socialization, empathy, autonomy, and a dimension of moral judgment ("ethics of personal conscience" and "ethics of personal responsibility"). All five concepts are basic to the structure of an individual's moral conduct. Over the past 5 years, Hogan and colleagues have operationalized these dimensions (72–74, 76) and considered interrelationships and antecedents.

While there are other psychologists whose work bears relevance to legal socialization, Hogan's contributions are particularly pertinent because they raise questions about rule acquisition modes, suggest an alternative multidimensional framework of compliance, and stimulate critiques of various approaches to understanding the relationship between moral development and moral thought and conduct. In Hogan's view, a major problem in US society and psychology is a stress on individualism and an ambivalence toward modes of compliance (75). Noting four modes of individualism (romantic, egocentric, ideological, alienated), Hogan—in the jurisprudential tradition of Hart (65)—maintained that "[b]ecause most historically sanctioned institutions express or satisfy man's need for social attention, regularity and aggression, these institutions, far from being necessary evils (as in an individualistic perspective), often give form and meaning to individual lives" (75, p. 537). Attributing problems of individualism to cognitive theories of moral development (cf 92), Hogan posed a role-theoretical perspective. Yet he draws upon the same mentors (i.e. 114, 116) whom Kohlberg (94) integrated in his theory and upon whom Tapp & Levine (176, 181) also drew in further articulating a cognitive legal model. Although Hogan and colleagues specify points of departure worthy of attention between their perspective and that of the cognitive developmental, social psychological frame, the question remains whether these distinctions are more apparent than real.

Hogan's views on the limitations of cognitive developmental theory are part of a more general concern voiced during the mid-1970s. Particularly the Kohlbergian model, as distinct from the Piagetian, has been under attack or critical review by both supporters (e.g. 78, 145, 181, 188) and nonsupporters (e.g. 12, 75, 97, 168) as culturally biased, empirically limited, insufficiently interactive, rigidly invariant, or inadequate methodologically. These viewpoints cannot, however, dismiss the primacy of the finding in Kohlberg's and others' work that age trends are more persuasive than sex, social class, or national differences. Generally this finding seems to be consistent even with researchers using other instruments and in other countries (e.g. 1, 3, 48, 50, 51, 58, 60, 121).

Since the late 1960s and early 1970s the age variable has been the *dominant* component in the work of psychodynamically oriented Adelson and his colleagues (1–4, 48, 50, 51). In these studies, such topics as the growth of the idea of law, legal guarantees for individual freedom, individual rights and the public good were investigated by probing, in-depth interviews about the formation of a political order and legal system in a new Pacific society. The data base was approximately 450 male and female adolescents, aged 11 to 18 years, in the US, West Germany, and Great Britain (with 50 youths comprising a longitudinal sample interviewed at either 13 and 15 or 15 and 18).

The primary result in this set of studies, for example in Gallatin & Adelson (50, 51) and Adelson's integrative piece on "The Political Imagination of the Young Adolescent" (1), was that the years from 12 to 16 are a "watershed" for political thought on matters of government and law. In response to traditional philosophical or jurisprudential questions on the purpose of law, the action to be taken when law is violated and hard to enforce, the nature of crime and justice, and the reciprocal obligations of the citizen and the state, the major effect was age. Sex did not account for differences in youth's ideas, and social class effects were variable. Like other work in legal socialization, moral development, and political socialization, the overall potency of developmental trends was the most striking finding.

Work by Gallatin (48) further underscored the impact of development on changing conceptions. In 1970 with Adelson & O'Neil, Gallatin undertook a study of the "process by which political [law, government] thinking itself evolves" (48, p. 2). The sample for the study was comprised of 463 black and white children in grades 6, 8, 10, and 12, primarily from lower class backgrounds. In addition to the questionnaire originally constructed for the 1963 Adelson et al studies, items were added on five "contemporary problems": crime and delinquency, police-community relations, poverty and unemployment, class distinctions and discriminations, the political process and dissent (p. 70). Again analysis of the questionnaire responses revealed a distinctively developmental pattern—by grade 12 children were typically well equipped to handle their franchise. Of particular interest to this review are the explicit findings related to psychology and the law:

> [Increasingly with age] teenagers ... become less inclined to offer punitive solutions for youth law-breaking and more likely to favor rehabilitative programs (p. 83). ... [W]hat seems to develop during adolescence is the perception that government is a kind of social contract. ... [The] community is perceived as having certain collective rights ... like "public welfare" and "national security." But the individual citizen is seen as having guaranteed certain reciprocal rights as well ... "privacy," "freedom of speech" and so forth (48, pp. 83, 128).

ISSUES IN CHILDREN'S RIGHTS   Friedman's articulation of the idea of right as a social and legal concept invited psychologists and lawyers alike to examine the acquisition of a rights consciousness (43). From the framework of a cognitive interactional model of development (181), how individuals come to view law and legal institutions and develop a conception of their roles in legal systems is significantly affected not only by the content of what they are taught but by the process of teaching as well. The treatment that children and youth experience, the operational definitions they receive about their *own* rights and roles, and the nature of their interactions with peers and adults (e.g. parents, police, judge) are the social inputs that relate to legal development. Beyond then the independent significance of the treatment of children, the issue of children's rights is important as a statement about society and its legal socializers. Therefore, in this section I review contemporary activity in children's rights as a case in point to explore the research and reform possibilities for psychology/law collaboration.

Over the past 5 years attention to the rights of children has increased dramatically. The 1973 book, *Beyond the Best Interests of the Child,* by lawyer-psychoanalyst Goldstein and psychoanalysts Freud & Solnit (54), is an index of contemporary ferment about the rights and relationships of the young. In a controversial reconceptualization of child welfare law, Goldstein et al called for a reordering of the criteria of children's rights and children's services. Essentially this psychoanalytic triad adopted "the least detrimental alternative" because the courts have inadequate knowledge of the psychological needs of the child and are incompetent to supervise human development adequately. To some degree, past performance of the court generally, and the juvenile and family (social) courts particularly, tends to support that assumption. However, in this psychiatric-legal effort to confront the problems of the abused and/or neglected child, the result was embarrassingly devoid of extensive or "hard" evidence and impressively rich with proposed guidelines based primarily on singular cases from professional experience.

As observed in the critique by Katkin, Bullington & Levine (89), *Beyond the Best Interests of the Child* by all standards is an "intellectual event" whose value is diminished by the absence of systematic empirically based analysis of the problems and by a distinct psychoanalytic orientation. In essence, these reviewers concluded that the book is the "wrong way to employ social science to solve problems of social policy" (89, p. 669). Given the research and reform perspective that guides this chapter. I can only underscore that, while this volume was presumably psychologically oriented, the model for "evidence" was primarily psychoanalytic documentation. Thus the Goldstein et al book raises for the psychological sciences basic questions about the nature of the proposed reforms and the proper transformation of social science knowledge into the form and forums of law.

The *Harvard Educational Review's* (*HER*) 1973–74 special issue on "The Rights of Children" (66) left many of the same questions unanswered. Intended to "restructure the inquiry to take into account the standpoint of the child" (p. v), this volume dealt with conceptions of children's rights, advocacy for children, and social policy for children. The stress was on the importance of competence and choice, the problematic role of control by the court, and the difference between children's rights and needs. Further, the contributors to this symposium (e.g. Judge Polier) emphasized that, although some legal attention has been directed toward safeguarding the rights of children accused of being "delinquent," far less activity has occurred related to the rights of nondelinquent children. Unfortunately, while the pages of this excellent "call-for-action" were populated by experts in law, education, sociology, philosophy, psychiatry, and criminology, there was no psychologist—social, developmental, or clinical—evident. This omission was an oversight both on the part of *HER* and of psychologists.

The essential paucity of data or research in the area of children's rights and the meaning of rights generally is awesome, especially in light of the general press for rights by children and parents, patients and prisoners, "subjects" and students. The policy statements in *HER*—proposed, for example, respectively by Rodham, Mnookin, Mondale, Worsfold, and Edelman—require research or experimental reforms of various sorts. Similarly, a key issue for research work by psychologists is one totally missed in *HER*'s special issue on children's rights: how children themselves understand the concept. The research to be reviewed herein covers attitudes toward children's rights, privacy, child abuse, and child custody. As this array of topics suggests, despite calls for action and concerns of psychologists, particularly developmental ones, there has been little research on children's rights and less on children's concepts of them. In fact, a large proportion of the literature from both the legal and/or psychological realms is heavier on rhetoric than research.

Wrightsman and colleagues, in a series of working papers (197), responded to the complex issues, definitions, and examples used by the advocates of children's rights —from nutrition needs to legal rights. Seeking clarification on "what is thought of as a right," these investigators aimed to measure "attitudes regarding children's rights" (197, p. 1). Guided initially by Webster's dictionary definition of a right and based on a reading of various reform and research statements (e.g. SPSSI Committee on Children's Rights), Wrightsman et al considered rights in terms of three aspects: potential vs actual rights, conceptions of rights as nurturance vs self-determination, and five content areas.

Recently these researchers constructed a Children's Rights Attitude (CRA) Scale of 150 Likert-type statements in the areas of health, education/information, economic, safety/care, and legal/judicial/political. The conceptualization of ten subscales (the two orientations X five areas) has been administered to samples of high school students, teachers and undergraduate majors in education. Importantly, Wrightsman & colleagues recognized that people's attitudes toward children's rights may be affected by their perceptions of children's age. Therefore, items on alternative forms of CRA dealt with four age groups from "up to 6 years of age" to "15–18," and respondents were instructed to envision a specific age level. From a legal socialization perspective, this aspect of the research is valuable because it addresses the relationship between attribution of rights to children and notions about child development.

The Wrightsman et al pilot studies focus on measuring the attitudes of adolescents and adults about children's rights. Such items as "contracts with children should *not* be binding unless the children's parents also sign" probably could not be administered to elementary or junior high school samples. In contrast to the work of Wrightsman's group, there are studies of children's general "rights" conceptions. The strength of the latter work is that it directly considers children's *own* views— although as yet, not specifically about children's rights. Several investigations, recently completed or currently under way, fall into this camp.

For example, Zellman & Sears (199), studying attitudes toward freedom of dissent among 1384 children in grades 5 through 9, found that the right of free speech was more readily accepted as an abstract slogan than applied in concrete situations. This pattern held comparatively with adults. While children 12–14 years old were generally more tolerant of free speech than those 9–11 years old, even by age 11 most children acknowledged the existence of such a right, and tolerance did not markedly increase with age. The single most important determinant of endorsing the free speech right was self-esteem—suggesting that socialization experiences that encourage tolerance for others and incorporate tolerance from others would effectuate greater acceptance of rights in real-life contexts.

Likewise, Gallatin's research in the 1970s reflects an interest in the development of the concept of rights. The Gallatin & Adelson cross-cultural, developmental study (50, 51) emphasized legal infringements on liberty and legal guarantees of individual freedom. Similarly, the research (48) based on 1970 black and white samples revealed that older children were more capable of weighing one set of rights and interests (individual) against another (community). Thus, in the 1963 study 12% of the 11-year-olds and 65% of the 18-year-olds thought that laws about individual freedoms (e.g. speech, religion) should be permanent; in the 1970 research, 7% of the children at grade 6 and 74% of the children at grade 12 expressed this view (48, 51). Gallatin (49) posited two types of rights: negative rights that are rights to noninterference (e.g. speech) and positive rights that are guarantees of opportunities (e.g. education). These two concepts are generally analogous to the self-determination and nurturance orientations discussed by Wrightsman et al (197). Overall, Gallatin found that developmentally a similar orientation to both concepts of rights emerged for blacks and whites and across national groups.

In the early 1970s, Tapp & Levine also modified their measure and model of legal reasoning to incorporate conceptions of rights. Additional questions have been administered to samples of adults and children by both investigators regionally.

Preliminary empirical codes suggested a progression in reasoning modes from an egoistic to an interpersonal to a societal and ultimately to a rights-consciousness perspective. Beyond including the rights questions as a dimension of legal reasoning, Tapp and investigators are also considering the content of responses. For example, paralleling Gallatin's negative and positive rights notions, the two major definitional dimensions being examined are "absence of restraint" and "equality of opportunity." Furthermore, since the sample in Tapp's studies is in part comprised of actual jurors, those data permit testing a problem at the core of legal socialization—the interaction as modulated by experience between conceptions of individual rights and institutional expectations (e.g. perceptions of the role of courts, judge, and jury).

Using completely different tacks, Wolfe & Laufer (195) and Parke & Sawin (135) considered the concept of privacy rights. Wolfe & Laufer focused on "the developmental aspects of the problem of human privacy" (195, p. 1). Parke & Sawin attended to developmental and situational factors related to children's use of privacy rules (e.g. knocking on doors) and markers (e.g. closing doors) in regulating family members' access to personal space areas. Based on an open-ended interview data from 287 volunteer school children aged 5–17, Wolfe & Laufer reported that the ability to define privacy is a function of age, first occurring between ages 5 and 7 and then increasing in complexity between ages 11 and 13. At all ages the four meanings of privacy most frequently used were: being alone, controlling access to information, no one bothering me, and controlling access to spaces. Two factors influencing the meanings of privacy were age and own room versus shared room. The latter—the use and meaning of access to space especially bedrooms—had a substantial effect on privacy conceptions in both studies.

Methodologically Parke & Sawin differed from Wolfe & Laufer, who used individual interviews and viewed the decrease in volunteer response rate with age as an unobtrusive measure of privacy (response rate was lowest, 60%, for ages 15–17). Parke & Sawin mailed a questionnaire to parents of 112 middle class children, ages 2–17, who were participating in the Fels Longitudinal Study. The instruction to parents stated that the project was concerned with ways in which space is typically organized and used at home. These investigators obtained a return rate of 85%, but since the study was not explicitly about privacy, this higher rate does not contradict Wolfe & Laufer's point about response as an unobtrusive measure.

Zeroing in on rules regarding use of bathrooms and bedrooms and the resultant definitions of privacy, Parke & Sawin also found that privacy is a developmental variable—with "the most dramatic shift in privacy behavior [occurring] during adolescence" (135, p. 10). In addition, size of home was a determinant of privacy —less privacy with fewer facilities. On balance, both studies (135, 195) reached distinctly similar conclusions: privacy behaviors and concepts follow a clear developmental pattern; privacy is a mechanism of social interaction management tied to familial patterns of socialization; the manifestation and conceptualization of privacy is affeoted by an ecological space perspective; and the study of social behaviors is best pursued in naturalistic settings with multimethods. These two studies with different theoretical and empirical traditions provide excellent examples of "the importance of considering the interactions of developmental, situational, ecological, and child-rearing variables in the development of children's social behavior" (135, p. 12). This approach is especially necessary when data may be used to make or support policy decisions.

A related issue—research on assuring confidentiality and privacy with regard to social and behavioral research data—is still in the formulative stage. While not reviewed in detail, work is under way or anticipated by psychologists that delineates problems and strategies for (a) eliciting, maintaining, merging, and disseminating confidential social research data; and (b) assuring access to archival data without jeopardizing individual privacy. The reader is referred to Boruch's materials for an excellent synthesis of the issues as well as reports and models addressing the problem of related costs, benefits, and legal implications of social research (e.g. 19, 26). Trachtman, considering the effects of invasion of privacy on children in schools, heralded efforts "focused on protection of children, not psychologists" (185, p. 45). The Appendix to the 1971 Brief for Respondents in *Laird vs Tatum* (No. 71–288) on "Chilling Effect: A View from the Social Sciences" serves also as a reminder that privacy and confidentiality are two "rights" requiring attention. For psychologists interested in the psychology/law interface, this is an area for systematic research pregnant with possibilities because civil and criminal as well as public and private assumptions are much in dispute.

Child abuse is a further topic in children's rights that critically relates to the process of socialization generally and legal socialization particularly. As yet there is no research on children's conceptions of abuse or abusive situations. In two integrative pieces, psychologist Parke reviewed the problem of child abuse (133, 134). His national and cross-cultural analysis with Collmer (134) considered the scope and definition of the problem, alternative theoretical models (i.e. psychiatric, sociological, social-situational), parent and child roles, and research-based recommendations on abuse control. The authors pressed for rigorous evaluation and assessment of all facets of the child abuse problem and unobtrusive, action-oriented but "carefully designed field intervention experiments" (134, p. 83; see also Campbell 24). Considering the social psychology of child abuse, Parke (133) also assessed the implications of the "abuse" label, reviewed the interaction of cultural, familial, and community roles, and analyzed the possible resocialization of abusive families using, for example, the legal system and societal-community control. In this piece Parke argued that "the socialization of families into abusive patterns is a multiply-determined [modifiable] process" (133, p. 27). Basic to his approach is the view that child abuse is both a socio-psychological and a legal problem (p. 29). Therefore, in an evident shift from a strictly social-learning paradigm and in an apparent effort to conceptualize a multifaceted problem from a more integrative and interdisciplinary perspective, Parke incorporated legal-judicial (e.g. 66, 140) and other psychological perspectives (e.g. 177, 181) relevant to child-rearing and children's rights.

These psychological and developmental approaches to the notions of privacy and abuse illustrate the difficulty and necessity of researching complex problems in real-life settings. Moreover, they emphasize the problems in transmitting what is *known* or translating what is *knowable* to the legal system. Perhaps then it is fitting that this section end with a review of an interdisciplinary team that demonstrated the potential of empirically oriented psychology joined with law.

The psychology/law effort by Ellsworth & Levy (35) applied selected social science data to legislative reform of child custody adjudication. They reported research studies on deviant and neglected groups and in a methodological analysis described the difficulties in scientific research. But it is the research review on divorce, broken homes, father separation and absence, remarriage and step-parenthood, and parental deprivation, along with suggestive hypotheses for future research, that are most valuable. Despite a paucity of specifically relevant psychological data in 1969 (and little more can be reported at this date), Ellsworth & Levy constructed a critical review of present and/or obtainable data of direct relevance to judges and legislators and of indirect utility for breaking the barriers between law and psychology. In contrast to the book by Goldstein et al (54) with which I began this section, these investigators argued for the importance of psychological criteria, stressed empirical studies, considered the psychological effects of courtroom decisionmaking, and suggested a paradigm "to test the law's hypotheses, while profiting from the methodological rigor possible with a scientific approach" (35, p. 215). Their work strikes a delicate balance between behavioral science findings and suggestions for formulating legal policy. Like the other research described thus far, there is evidence of increased use of an interdisciplinary paradigm in the systematic formulation and investigation of issues that are "empirical" or "factual" in psychology and law.

The Judicial Process

A key issue uniting law and psychology is justice and the role of law for achieving a just social order. A scan of newspapers or research literature reveals much concern about crime and about law enforcement security (e.g. 9, 52, 57, 80, 103, 166). Ignoring white collar crime, in the US alone "crime" is up 18% in 1975 over 1974, and 45% of Americans fear walking at night (Gallup Poll in *Minneapolis Tribune,* July 28, 1975, pp. 1, 4). Because our concern should be as much for justice and law as for order and law enforcement, in this review I address both issues. This section focuses on research analyses of the judicial process specifically: (*a*) decisionmaking in the adversary systems; (*b*) eyewitness identification and evidence; and (*c*) juries and jurors. The next major section emphasizes the criminal justice process.

DECISIONMAKING IN THE ADVERSARY SYSTEM   The 1970s brought major theoretical and methodological constructs from moral philosophy (140) and jurisprudence (e.g. 46, 65) to various psychologists interested in procedural justice. (See the earlier section on "Legal Socialization Process" for other applications of these constructs by Fuller, Hart, and Rawls.)

Many in law and psychology have considered the conditions of fairness in the adversary system in and out of the courtroom, but few have approached this topic with as much novelty, ingenuity, and comprehensiveness as psychologist Thibaut and lawyer Walker. Between 1971 and 1975 they conducted their simulated laboratory studies on the ubiquitous student (undergraduate and law in US and non-US locales) and integrated their findings into a book that concentrated on the nature and impact of procedures in adversary and inquisitorial legal systems (183).[6] In their work Thibaut & Walker's topical decisions were influenced in part by the general absence of such social science research and by the lack of integrative, analytic concepts from legal scholars. Their efforts were guided by the view that the principal formal device for dispute settlement—courts—has "much potential for creating widespread justice or injustice" (pp. 1–2). Thus the *fundamental question* for these investigators and their colleagues was: What procedures are just? Their *special concern* was in litigation procedures in developed societies; the *basic variable* for assessing the justice of all forms of dispute resolution was the distribution of control; the *major finding* was the superiority of the adversary system and trial procedures for attaining justice; and the *key requirement* for procedural justice was optimal control distribution among role participants.

Building upon both social psychological (e.g. 90, 190) and jurisprudential legal constructs (46, 140), the authors proffered findings and field applications to stimulate "communication" and "best facilitate the adoption of just procedures" (183, p. 5). For example, to study the effect of third-party control in prelegal settings on disputants (134 undergraduates and 97 law students), the authors considered the relationships among five dispute-resolution procedures and eight dimensions of preference (e.g. attractive or aversive). In this and their other studies, Thibaut & Walker evaluated (*a*) the impact of determinative procedures and procedural requirements in the disputants' social environments on justice views, and (*b*) the impact of internal or external biases on justice attainment (e.g. presentation mode and order, sampling error in discovered facts, locus of control, role relationships, and information processing). After appraising various procedures for dispensing justice, they finally analyzed the normative standards of justice as fairness by utilizing a "veil of ignorance" paradigm (140).

From the analyses of their experiments, Thibaut & Walker concluded that the adversary legal process was judged by all subjects as the most preferable, fairest, satisfactory, and beneficial regardless of culture (140, pp. 81, 114–15). In *all* experimental conditions decisionmaker control decreased steadily while satisfaction and perceived fairness of the evidence increased as the method moved from inquisitorial to adversary (pp. 94, 106). All roles preferred minimizing decisionmaker control and maximizing self-control (p. 110). The simulation of the original position sufficiently incorporated the essentials of Rawls' "veil" construct to confirm that "Behind the veil of ignorance is created that conception of procedural justice that uniquely implies the adversary system" (p. 116).

[6]Collaborators on Thibaut & Walker's studies include V. Andreoli, B. Erickson, N. Freidland, R. Frey, C. L. Gruder, J. Holmes, P. Houlden, S. LaTour, and E. A. Lind, whose reports appear in psychological and legal periodicals. These reports and additional ones in press or preparation are variously listed in Thibaut & Walker's book, *Procedural Justice: A Psychological Analysis.*

To Thibaut, Walker and colleagues, the high degree of control by the disputants and the high degree of regulated contentiousness between the disputants are basic to the efficacy of the adversary system. Therefore they advocate the use of this model in, for example, litigating the controversial arena of welfare law, due process and the achievement of rights, and consideration of shifting control to the judge. Although this research may be a byproduct of what Hogan (75) called America's problem of overemphasizing "individualism," it certainly is evidence for the importance of participation and conflict, skepticism and information exchange as basic to institutional forms that increase capacities for self-control, choice, and competence (e.g. 61, 64, 160, 174, 181). On balance, this psycholegal analysis of procedural justice may prove both an irritant and provocateur to lawyer and psychologist alike. To those persuaded by the legal-philosophical models of Fuller and Rawls, this interdisciplinary effort will be cheered; to those who decry laboratory experiments, there will be the questions about reality and respondents; to those who seek an action research strategy, there will be recognition of an intellectual and empirical attempt to demonstrate congruent constructs basic to an experimenting society. Finally, Thibaut & Walker in acknowledging their biases (i.e. sample, setting) underscored that research about individual humans or human institutions cannot be value-free. While psychologists must be cautious about their techniques *and* findings, they must also investigate legal behaviors cognizant of ideological implications *and* concerned about evolving ethical and scientifically sound measures. The efforts by Thibaut & Walker et al generate a kind of intellectual and ideological excitement that can only further sensitize scientific and social experimentation.

The orchestration of the Thibaut-Walker group accentuates the controversy in both law and psychology about the adversary and inquisitorial systems. Some lawyers (e.g. 31, 99, 100) using social psychological findings especially on persuasion and communication continue to ferret out results defending the adversary system. Costopoulos's (31) review of psychological research, while broader than Lawson's (99), reached the same conclusions regarding the order of arguments, primacy-recency effects and jury decisionmaking—although earlier Lawson conceded that experimental work on order effects was conducted in settings too dissimilar from the courtroom. In contrast to those who applaud the adversary system, many distrust it. Long-time activist in the courtroom, clinical psychologist Redmount (141–143) represents that group. Basically Redmount concluded that juries are not trained or practiced in evidence or argument evaluation. He argued too that data presentation in the adversary system (e.g. fragmentary and disjointed evidence procedures, dramatic partisan revelations) militates against a reasoned and reasonable conclusion. Since to Redmount "Judgmental decision is more correctly a product of the adjudicators, the means of persuasion and the focal issues, and certain events and circumstances" (143, p. 254), he would use skilled adjudicators to get at truth fairly. The work of psychologist Haggard and lawyer Mentschikoff on arbitrated decisionmaking (62, 120) suggested a similar conclusion.

According to Haggard & Mentschikoff, "decisionmaking" has multiple meanings and is used in many contexts from executive, legislative, and judicial levels of government to an array of nongovernmental "legal" or norm settings (e.g. dissertation committees, funding agencies, or baseball umpires). In a unique in situ approach, this lawyer and psychologist team (62, 120) addressed the problem and scope of "responsible decisionmaking" (i.e. decisions by third parties with the authority to affect others, from one person to an entire society). The Haggard-Mentschikoff research on institutionalized commercial arbitration (based on observations and simulated experiments at the American Arbitration Association) provides an interesting counterpoint to data reported by Thibaut & Walker (in simulated laboratory settings). Such comparisons should help sort the pros and cons for the adversarial vs inquisitorial systems as well as the effects of third parties in formal and informal "legal" settings.

Psychologist Haggard reported (62) on how 60 individual arbitrators in 20 panels made decisions and how groups achieved decision consensus after they heard tapes on a business contract cancellation and deliberated until they settled the dispute. The psychological data (e.g. questions on predeliberation and postdeliberation awards, measures of arbitrators' views of the central issues and evaluations of the parties, content analysis of the deliberations) provided a backdrop for lawyer Mentschikoff's formulating a model of the rules that guide arbitrators in dispute settlement. Although nonrational factors (e.g. private views, sense of affinity, or idiosyncratic aspects of deliberations) emerged, Haggard found that decisions were predominately "rational." As hypothesized, arbitrators' choice of the central issue in the dispute and how evidence was perceived were primary in their decisionmaking. Mentschikoff (120) further explored the role of the normative standards used to judge the parties' conduct during the dispute and at the hearing as well as to regulate the arbitrators' behavior at hearings and during subsequent deliberations. She identified substantive norms and fact-finding norms operative during the dispute; procedural norms, role norms, and status norms functioned during the arbitration. Noting that the "potential range [of] norms is theoretically infinite," Mentschikoff reported that in practice arbitrators' norms in commercial cases like many in civil courts are "relatively few and recurrent" (pp. 3–4). Affinity and communication are the two major personal interactional factors operative in identifying and endorsing norms. While "the absence of institutional pressure" may minimize "the problems in reaching consensus," Mentschikoff opined that "responsible decisionmaking in a context of adversary proceedings is predominantly a normative matter" (pp. 26, 31) where the expertise and prior experience of the arbitrator remains the single most important factor in both decisional and consensual processes.

Both the Thibaut & Walker and Haggard & Mentschikoff projects showed that a dispassionate search for ideal procedures is as complicated as the debate between advocates of the adversary and inquisitorial systems. Fortunately, psychologists and lawyers have pressed to study decisionmaking despite the systematic flaws in both disciplines and precisely because problems can be ameliorated only by understanding the nature of the "flaws" in the individual, the institution and their interaction. That much research is categorized under the topic of decisionmaking seems to be a phenomenon of the 1970s. This becomes apparent again in research on the jury and juror.

EYEWITNESS IDENTIFICATION AND EVIDENCE   Lawyer Hutchins, recalling his 1929 work with psychologist Slesinger (82) noted, "as far as the searching of Law of Evidence is concerned, it was affected only incidentally. We hoped it would be affected ultimately by what we were trying to do" (37, p. 22). Some 45 years later, and almost 70 years since the initial efforts (see "Historical Context"), psychologists and lawyers still confront the problems of eyewitness evidence, but most law classrooms remain unaffected by the accrued knowledge on mediating psychological processes.

Prompted by the diminished judicial concern (*Kirby vs Illinois,* 406 US 682, 1972) after court attempts to confront the inherent dangers in eyewitness identification (e.g. *US vs Wade,* 388 US 218, 1967), Levine & Tapp (102) reviewed psychological research basic to illuminating problems of fallibility and suggestibility. Perhaps one of the most comprehensive reviews to date on the psychological aspects of identification, their survey and critical analysis is bolstered by recommendations for future research and pre- and in-court procedures. To demonstrate the use of systematically synthesized psychological evidence, they chose a specific area related to eyewitness evidence—pretrial confrontation.

By undertaking an observational-interview field study, Levine & Tapp sought to bring empirical clarity to the problem of faulty witness or victim identification at lineups. In addition, they examined the traditional forensic literature, the research on processes that limit valid identification (e.g. perception, memory, perceptual selectivity, differences in mnemonic abilities), and the studies on social influences that modulate sensory processes (e.g. emotional state, motivation, stereotypes, prejudice). In distinguishing among factors that affect perception or memory of a criminal event and the psychological (social structural) variables operative during an actual identification proceeding, Levine & Tapp depicted the dimensions (e.g. group pressure, role conceptions, expectancy) that potentially affect decisionmaking processes and data-gathering validity. Like Thibaut & Walker's research (183) and Haggard & Mentschikoff's (62, 120), Levine & Tapp aimed to unravel complex phenomena by specifying identifiable relationships. Although many questions are left unanswered, their article provides those interested in this problem of the judicial process with an informed base to advance research and reform.

The recent research and reviews of Loftus (108, 109) and Buckhout (22) complement the analytic and descriptive reports of Levine & Tapp (102) as well as Marshall and associates (111, 112). The studies of Loftus and of Buckhout, done respectively in laboratory and field settings, reiterated the long known and psychologically verified findings on the inaccuracy of eyewitness evidence. For example, Loftus found that in simulated settings with over 100 student "jurors" the structure of written questions (e.g. the use of *a* vs *the*) or the event descriptors (e.g. smashed vs collided) significantly affected responses related to time, speed, and distance. These results are coincident with the general finding that eyewitness testimony is notoriously variable and consistently inaccurate. Furthermore, like Marshall et al (112), Loftus found that mode of interrogation had less effect on accuracy than timing. The questions asked immediately of 490 respondents introduced new, but not necessarily correct, data, and this was found to alter the recollection (109).

Mindful of the repeated point that simulated contexts are less stressful and partisan than normally encountered by real witnesses, Buckhout tried in situ settings to reduce potential artifacts and bias (22). He videotaped a staged assault on a professor witnessed by 141 students: 60% of the witnesses—including the attacked professor—chose the wrong man!

Regardless of time or technique then, most sets of data indicated that valid recall is altered by variables such as psychological processes of perception or motivation that mediate reconstruction of a remembered event. Perhaps more discouraging is the evidence that the essential finding on the unreliability of eyewitness testimony was made by Munsterberg nearly 70 years ago. Yet although numerous experiments have verified eyewitness error-proneness, such evidence is still deemed more reliable than other kinds of evidence (e.g. circumstantial). Despite repeated research and educational efforts, psychologists have had little impact on the law's unwarranted reliance on eyewitness reports.

JURIES AND JURORS   Creation of a setting consistent and conducive to just decisionmaking is paramount in any legal system, but particularly in an adversary one where the "verdict" reflects the "judgment" of one's peers. Among psychologists concerned with social behavior perhaps the oldest, best known, and continuous work has been in jury research. That the dynamics of the jury process have caught and maintained the imagination and ire of both citizens and scientist is intriguing, given that less than 3% to 5% of all US crimes ever come to trial! However, in the present social and scientific renaissance the concern is not that so few conflicts come to court but with the procedures by which judgments are processed. At least in the US in the 1970s "trial by jury" seems to be a test of the larger society's commitment to a just legal order for all. The role of psychologist in several trials of national prominence evoked much debate on the ethical, legal, theoretical, and practical aspects of such psycholegal cooperation. In this section two motifs that recently have captured the time and attention of psychologists in and out of real courtrooms are described: the jury decisionmaking process and the jury selection process.

The jury decision process   Research on decision processes in juries conducted over the past decade are well presented in the recent, critical, and comprehensive chapter by Davis, Bray & Holt (32). Therefore, I do not reiterate the details of those studies or several others that due to publication dates and space limitations cannot be specifically covered (e.g. 16, 20, 130). In addition to building a model of the decisionmaking process, Davis et al responded to a strong psychology/law research trend and aimed to examine jury research in terms of the theories that may be tested or developed from empirical findings. Explicitly psychological in approach, excluding legal/philosophical or small group research, Davis et al reported a "bewildering" and "disorderly" array of studies that produced many findings but little systematic theory. In their critical review they found more efforts devoted to *juror* than *jury* behavior—a pertinent division of past jury research. As a result of analyses of both types of jury research, the Davis group (32), unlike Thibaut & Walker (183), argued that few legal prescriptions can or should be drawn directly on a one-to-one basis from empirical studies (p. 2).

Grouping the juror research by content themes (e.g. attitudes, values, and guilt; effects of judicial instructions; "just world" hypothesis), Davis et al uncovered many differences, especially in dependent variables (e.g. sentence length, parole eligibility, damage awards). The results seemed problematic too because of the stimulus materials (e.g. case summaries), heavy reliance on student or mock jurors, and instances of influence not necessarily representative of jury functioning as so often implied (32, p. 34). For example, Davis et al found no generally "good" predictor from demographic variables; pretrial publicity data were equivocal; arguments for order-effects were ambiguous; and authoritarianism seen in punitive sentencing seemed unrelated to frequency of guilt judgments or initial guilt determinations. Such varied, inconclusive, or equivocal findings warrant skepticism and criticism of research or theory that primarily uses individual "jurors" rather than interacting "juries"—even mock ones.

Davis et al grouped the jury research in this manner: *deliberation* before verdict emphasizing interaction; *verdict* under various deliberation conditions; and *sample surveys*. The latter group tended to use actual cases (e.g. polling real jurors); the former two used mock or simulated cases. Critical of methodological flaws here too, Davis et al nonetheless detected some orderly findings. For example, demographic variables still offered lawyers a means to control decision outcome; jury size (i.e. 6 vs 12) was largely irrelevant to outcome; and the jury foreman was usually a white, high SES male. Evidence that the judge's instructions about the law decidedly affected verdicts supports Kadish & Kadish's interpretation of the impact of judicial role on jurors' perceptions of the legitimacy of rule departure (85).

In reviewing the juror and jury research, Davis, Bray & Holt found no theory specifically designed for juror decisionmaking and many serious methodological difficulties ranging from obtaining empirical data (e.g. courtroom access, "real" stress) to dealing with legal/ethical constraints (e.g. changing legal procedures, privacy, and confidentiality rights). As a result they recommended a social decision scheme (SDS) model, further substantiated by recent experimental results (p. 58) and devoid of the difficulties inherent in individually oriented, social psychological theories (e.g. attribution theory, cognitive dissonance). Advantages of the approach include (*a*) using a logical, mathematically deduced model of jury verdict behavior when it is impossible, uneconomical, or unethical to obtain relevant empirical data (32, pp. 59–60); and (*b*) detecting extent of change not as readily identified by gathered empirical data (p. 61). To Davis et al, the SDS model is less likely to oversimplify and more likely to provide a simple, convenient way to deduce specific outcomes about juries for normative or descriptive use. For example, in a traditional study to determine the effect of jury size (6 vs 12), in order for the largest difference of 0.08 to be significant at the 0.05 level, 1116 persons would be needed (p. 55); in contrast, the SDS permits detecting small but real differences, yet is also capable of exploring decision outcomes of juries (p. 56, e.g. two-thirds or three-fourths majority).

In sum then, Davis et al begin to answer the call for badly needed supplemental theory to analyze juror or jury decisionmaking processes, attending to individual and group levels of behavior and to interacting members of a jury. The search for validity across theories, methods, and fields is a necessary orientation for psychology/

law research, found increasingly in the 1970s. There is again a kind of experimental and social excitement generated by the critique and by the SDS model proffered by Davis et al. Clearly the battle to watch is between the advocates of experimental social psychological models and those who advocate in situ social research. As important is the attempt by both sets of researchers to develop formal theories. What either thinks about the model's acronym—SDS—is a moot point.

Jury selection: Psychologist as expert or advocate?   Whether the psychologist in the courtroom, acting as expert during the voir dire examination, advances the cause of justice has been a matter of intense debate in the 1970s, despite the fact that judges and lawyers have long used the "profile" technique and "experts" to justify decisions or selections (e.g. 33). The fervor of the recent debate is especially noteworthy since social scientists have participated in less than a dozen trials in the past 10 years (e.g. Camden 28, Gainesville, Ellsberg-Russo, Mitchell-Stans, Wounded Knee, Attica) and "there are perhaps 150,000 jury trials in the United States every year" (163, p. 1071). What is the reason for both the controversy and attraction to this aspect of the judicial process? Perhaps it is the symbolic representation of this society's commitment to obtain legal and social justice.

Critics argue that social science techniques threaten jury's impartiality (36) or produce stacked panels (86, 163). Advocates argue that, given the empirical battles over jury size and verdicts or eyewitness evidence, social science techniques protect the jury system—the only place for public participation in the judicial process (87). Proponents suggest that scientific analysis of demographic and personality data (e.g. religion, sex, education, authoritarianism, attitudes to capital punishment), used to develop profiles in the critical voir dire stage, aid judge and counsel in selecting a less biased jury, if not of one's peers (32, 87, 132, 150, 154, 155). Christie's unpublished "Probability vs precedence: The social psychology of jury selection" adds to the general point (see also 29), but still does not resolve the "fair" issue posed for both scientist and citizen (17).

Observers remind all sides concerned that the real questions are broader. They include whether social scientists are really manipulating juries; whether psychologists should get involved in social action research at all or only to test the relevance of their theories and findings to social problems; or whether selection of a fair, unbiased jury is analogous to a research problem and therefore a challenging opportunity to do research in the real world (e.g. 17, 24, 25, 29, 57, 80, 105, 115, 118, 150, 163; cf Christie's "Probability"). Others hint that instead of stacking the deck, social scientists working with juries have been finding out "how inequitable the much-vaunted American jury system is," and thus "the real boon" may be that their activities have encouraged both fairer jury selection procedures (163, pp. 1071, 1033) and reexamination of the administration of justice.

On the basis of their Black Panther trial experience, Rokeach & Vidmar concluded "that substantial bodies of social science findings obtained in other contexts for other purposes can at least sometimes be translated into applications that have real, palpable consequences in everyday life" (150, p. 27). However, there are only a few other reports that specifically describe data use from surveys, jurors' ratings, reputational measures, evaluation of jury interactional potential, and follow-up studies relevant to the voir dire aspect of the jury selection process (29, 87, 154, 155). Another exception is the experiment of Padawer-Singer, Singer & Singer (132) using lawyers. They compared voir dire selected juries to those selected randomly and found significant demographic differences. Participation by both defense and prosecution led to the most "impartial" jury; also the lawyer voir dire created greater commitment from "actual" jurors (in a rigged courtroom) to the law and to their role. Overall, voir dire seems to be an essential safeguard in the administration of justice, whether observed in situ or in simulated settings (17, 32, 87, 131, 132, 150; cf Christie's "Probability").

Whatever the reasons for or results of psychology in an adversary system, the advocates of research have demonstrated that, beyond the voir dire problem, there are substantive gaps in psycholegal knowledge and a need for more systematic theory and research [e.g. on ideology or attitude toward punishment, see (124, 189)]. While a major difficulty in "natural" research settings is absence of control, perhaps a major asset is that each research experience demands a review or reorganization of theory and technique, policy and procedure—both psychological and legal. Participation in jury selection or research on jurors—both mock and real—has apparently had some effect if only to encourage debate on the utility of the techniques and findings. But, except for the publicized "success" of the "conspiracy" trials on which psychologists worked, there is little conclusive evidence or systematic evaluation of the results for either research setting. The question remains: What keeps the psychologist in the courtroom? One answer may be that while psychologists cannot "experiment" on a societal scale, they can add to their and society's knowledge by systematically documenting events. Another answer may be that they recognize the participatory, interactive component of social science and society. A third may be that research on decisionmaking in the judicial process provides psychologists with an opportunity to review and research the dilemma of their role and responsibility. As the next section reveals, the criminal justice process also allows psychologists to address the issue of the rights of individuals and institutions with forensic fervor.

The Criminal Justice Process

Despite the fact that the mental health and criminal justice systems in theory are distinct, they are often interrelated in confusing and contradictory ways. In 1972 psychologist Shah said, "It is not very clear how one set of societal processes for defining and dealing with deviant behavior (the concept of mental disease and mental health handling) are to be related to another set of societal processes for dealing with social deviance (the concept of crime and the criminal justice system)" (161, p. 97). In 1974 he commented again on their long, complex but undistinguished interaction: "[T]he voluminous literature that has accumulated on the topic . . . reveals something close to the syncopated chaos that one associates with the Tower of Babel" (162, p. 676). In 1976 lawyer/psychologist Shuman, reflecting also on the numerous contesting views, observed:

> Given the present state of knowledge even in biology and genetics, let alone in sociology and psychology . . . we are unable to state with sufficient specificity the basic "objectives"

or "goals" about the prevention or suppression of criminal deviance. . . . The dearth of research is not due to lack of interest, nor to ignorance about alternatives to incarceration [for] we would not know what to do if it is convincingly demonstrated that institutionalization, in fact, is counterproductive (164, pp. 9, 16).

Because of these concerns and the preponderance of rhetoric over research, in this section I limit my attention to the role of psychology in the criminal justice system. My emphasis is not on the role of criminal law, but rather on that of the psychologist vis-à-vis criminals and prison settings.

PERSPECTIVES ON THE ROLE OF PSYCHOLOGISTS   By the mid-'70s, the 200-year-old experiment in prison reform begun by the Quakers had clearly failed. Evidence from both lawyers and psychologists indicated that the type of rehabilitative treatment made little difference in recidivism rates. The question being asked by psychologists and lawyers as well as prisoners and recidivists was whether the legal or psychological systems served justice or merely delivered punishment (e.g. 5, 8, 158, 164, 169, 171, 186, 186a, 192; S. Brodsky, P. Meehl, personal communications, 1975). Simultaneously over the past decade, as the efficacy of the rehabilitative —or resocialization—ideal was challenged, criticisms were advanced about the medical model of treatment; the validity or utility of predictions of dangerousness or violence; the role of psychologists in the criminal justice system; and the ethical and legal rights of prisoners in psychological treatment (e.g. 21, 53, 55, 64, 96, 100a, 106, 119, 125, 126, 147, 152, 161, 162, 165, 186, 186a). Doubts about the efficacy of the rehabilitative role, traditional therapies, and nonconsensual treatment caused many psychologists to review their place in the criminal justice system. A series of landmark decisions in the 1960s and 1970s from "right to treatment" to "right to due process" supported constitutional guarantees of equal protection and immunity from cruel and unusual punishment (e.g. *Rouse vs Cameron,* 373 F. 2d 451, D. C. Cir. 1966; *Wyatt vs Stickney,* 325 F. Supp. 781, M. D. Ala. 1971; *Inmate of Boys' Training School vs Affleck,* 346 F. Supp. 1345, D. R. I. 1972). These decisions moved psychologists of all persuasions to reconsider if their methods threatened the rights of individuals and distorted further the role of penal institutions. The central questions are how, who, and what achieves justice and health best in "correctional" settings? As some mental health professionals in prison institutions had already learned (e.g. 186, 186a): in the name of care, civil liberties may be restricted; in the name of competence, coercion may ensue; and finally in the name of choice, indeterminate escapes to or from freedom may be offered—and justice muted.

Despite the confusion—both public and professional—surrounding psychology's place and purpose and the assertion that perhaps examination of value-ethical questions had been ignored heretofore because treatment had been minimally successful, a number of critical analyses and constructive reviews have been forwarded recently by both psychologists and lawyers (e.g. 21, 53, 117, 126, 147, 156, 158, 162, 164, 165, 192). While this array reveals fundamental philosophical and psychological differences about the nature of humankind, it also yielded several innovative paradigms for psychologists working with the incarcerated for "rehabilitative" (i.e. resocialization) or "therapeutic" (e.g. alcoholism) purposes. The major battles being waged in the literature are over the applications of behaviorism, the right and role of choice in the therapeutic relationship, and the responsibility of psychologists both to the reality of the prison and to the person requiring the help. These issues are basic to understanding the emergence of both the community approach to corrections (e.g. 125) and the contractual or justice models (e.g. 53, 95, 158).

One basic descriptive overview of the problems and potentialities at the psychology/law interface came as an edited report (21) of a 1972 conference at which the participants discussed such issues as the application of psychological principles to corrections and courts, the impact of action research on policy, and an adequate education for correctional psychologists. At that meeting, Brodsky distinguished between "system-professionals" (traditional, within system workers) and "system-challengers" (advocacy, outside system workers). This distinction deserves attention because it offers psychologists a vehicle for interpreting and defining viable roles in the systems of psychology and penology.

Of value to both system-professionals and system-challengers is Monahan's critical, updated review of conceptual and empirical efforts to predict or prevent violence (126). Indeed, his review only underscored Megargee's earlier effort—and failure—to find any test to predict violence adequately: "None has been developed which will adequately *post*dict, let alone *pre*dict, violent behavior" (119, p. 145). Drawing heavily upon the work of others, Monahan vividly portrayed the confused definitions of violence and dangerousness; he reported, for example, that between 54% and 99% of those predicted "dangerous" are false positives. Culling a variety of empirical studies, he consistently found overpredictions. For Monahan, the key question is deterrence: How many false positives need be sacrificed to gain protection from one violent individual? After reviewing the psychological factors involved in overprediction, he concluded that since violent behavior is partially situation-determined, an ecological analysis is most compatible with a community mental health orientation. Various other contributions to Monahan's edited volume described the multifaceted model *in extenso* (125). Basically system-centered, the move is away from a medical (blame the individual) approach to one that emphasizes modalities of social and community support (e.g. diversion programs, training police in family crisis intervention).

The contributions of both Silber and Shah in Monahan's community based, ecologically oriented volume portrayed the ambivalence of psychologists regarding their role in prisons and in the community. Silber wryly concluded that "it is one of life's little ironies that treatment is attacked because it does not help prisoners . . . when in fact the prisoner's chance of receiving treatment is almost zero [and] [t]herapy has not been given the chance to work" (165, p. 242). He stressed that the most effective contribution is made when the mental health worker functions as a therapist and stays on the periphery. In contrast, Shah viewed many mental health concepts as inadequate and was attracted to a system-challenger's role that seeks legal safeguards in handling social deviance. Subsequently he formulated well the conflict facing contemporary correctional psychologists:

To intervene coercively in the life of an individual on the assumption, or even very real expectation, that he might in the future display dangerous behavior, raises very serious constitutional issues and appears to run afoul of very basic societal values pertaining to the primary importance of personal liberty and the general prohibition against preventive detention (162, p. 702).

This ambivalence about role and attraction to legal or judicial rationales was insightfully presented earlier in the 1968 interdisciplinary discussion by Livermore, Malmquist & Meehl (106).

The current debate on the most "just" and "right" mode of treatment for obtaining mental health and social justice is as often ⌐n the docket of lawyers as psychologists. A recent impressive analysis of the rel⌐.tionship between therapy—in this case behavior modification—and the law was undertaken by lawyer Wexler in 1973. He focused on the assent-dissent issues for individuals in situations of total institutional control, whether a hospital or a prison (192). Wexler's review of a spate of court decisions suggested that many activities emerging as absolute rights are the very activities that the behavioral psychologists would employ as reinforcers (i.e. contingent rights). His arguments emphasized that while there is no inherent set of "rights" implied by determinism (or probably any other type of therapy used to modify behavior), the principles underlying the "right to treatment" and traditional civil liberties may conflict. As Wexler duly noted, "In the psychologist's view it would surely be an ironic tragedy if, in the name of an illusory ideal such as freedom, the law were to deny the therapist the only effective tools he has to restore the chronic psychotic to his health—and his place in the community" (192, p. 17).

Taking a decidedly different stance toward the role of psychologists, lawyer/psychologist Shuman maintained that in our "state of knowledge about punishment and resocialization, except for extremely brief emergency confinement, incarceration as currently practiced is almost guaranteed to be dysfunctional. . . . Whether institutionalizing people under compulsory restraint is necessarily antithetical to resocialization is an open question" (164, p. 15). Hardly persuaded by the Skinnerian view that the more humane way to deal with individuals is to absolve them from the responsibility of being free, Shuman rejected the notion that unhealthy deviance is sufficient basis for involuntary or indeterminate therapy in the name of health and justice. After analyzing several solutions to deviance—institutionalization, conditioning, and biological reconstruction—Shuman suggested that the criminal law system may be "more expensive than it is worth" (164, p. 21) and perhaps ought be replaced by a law of torts framework. He proposed that we speculate carefully what life would be like if only tort remedies were available for deviant conduct. Shuman concluded with this observation: "A society without criminal law would necessarily be one where the price for real, universal freedom is never too high. In such a society, witches would not be burned, and even objectionable people would not be compelled to accept the 'benefits' of incarceration, conditioning, or corrective social surgery" (164, p. 25).

THE JUSTICE MODEL   Bearing in mind these criticisms of both criminal law and correctional methods, I now examine some proposals of contractual-consensual and justice models. Though these efforts have various origins from clinicians in hospitals to developmentalists in prisons, they have mutual applicability because of the captive quality of the populations and the total nature of the institutional settings. The notions of both a contractual-consensual relationship and the justice model emerged noticeably in the 1970s. In part, they were products of the collapse of the medical model, the reaction to various techniques of behavior modification from psychoanalysis to behaviorism, the methodological criticism of predictions of violence and dangerousness, the debate over indeterminate sentencing, the controversy over the discretionary powers of the prison officials including psychologists, the concern over the purposes of institutionalization, and the conflict between psychological therapies and constitutional rights.

Among the more interesting and impressive suggestions to ameliorate the knotty psychological, legal, and ethical problems were those from behaviorally inclined psychologists Meehl (106, 117), Goldiamond (53), and lawyer/psychologist Schwitzgebel (157, 158). In 1970 Meehl reminded lawyers that only the first of four aims of the criminal law—isolation of the offender—was being met; the other three—rehabilitation, general deterrence, and retribution—had remained unattained. Aware of the limited success of psychologists in prison settings, he cautioned lawyers about the primitive state of personality assessment and commended Skinner's behavior modification approach. He argued that most other therapy techniques do not "know how to rehabilitate criminals. . . . So you might as well let a zealous Skinnerian try *his* hand at it, because the available evidence shows that we are not accomplishing much of anything with the present conventional methods" (117, p. 22). In 1975 he maintained that same position and underscored the theoretical and practical sense of behavior modification as well as the individual's right to treatment for an emotional problem (e.g. schizophrenia) regardless of setting (P. Meehl, personal communication, 1975). So defined, the role of the psychologist is one principally accountable to the person, not the prison—the individual, not the institution. It is precisely this orientation that has moved both psychologists and penologists to review the nature of their relationship and responsibility to the individual and to the institution.

Elaborating these issues further, Goldiamond (53), in a truly perceptive and instructive paper on ethical and constitutional issues raised by applied behavior analysis, outlined a constructional approach whereby during the "custody" of a patient or criminal, any additional activity required should be *with* him and not *to* him. He emphasized that "Experimental and applied analysts of behavior have reason to be concerned, as people, regarding the possibilities for individual damage or ineffectiveness which may ensue; as citizens, regarding the constitutional issues involved; and as professionals whose discipline and opportunities may be affected" (p. 4). Goldiamond then attempted to define the psychologist's role as both researcher and practitioner in an institutional setting. While his contractual construction leaves some unanswered questions (e.g. what is "voluntary consent" in an institution restraining freedom?), he introduced an approach for use in total institutional settings that is thoroughly consistent with "(a) the constitutional requirements of mutual contracting and limitation of power, (b) other ethical obligations which the Constitution exemplifies, (c) the therapeutic needs of the patient (or other consumer), and (d) the investigative and analytic requirements of behavior analysis" (p. 14). Duly noting behavior modification's movement toward explicit contracts as part of its scientific rationale, Goldiamond importantly stressed the necessity of constitutional requirements rather than redefining the humanity of the clients

(p. 45)—whether prisoners, mental patients, or other subjects of institutional control.

Psychologist-lawyer Schwitzgebel, who in other work in behavioral electronics proposed using implanted devices to monitor parolees (e.g. 156), also realized the ethical and constitutional questions raised by such techniques (157, 158). Recently he readdressed the issue of patients' rights and liabilities (and psychologists' too) through an explicit consideration of treatment contracts (158). Ever sensitive to the responsibility that demonstrating the "benefit" falls upon the institution, not upon the patients who "pay" for treatment ineffectiveness with their freedom, Schwitzgebel articulated a contractual model based on informed consent that optimally would increase the opportunities for choice and self-determination and protect patients from unwarranted intrusions upon their persons or personalities. Schwitzgebel described the basic characteristics, advantages, and disadvantages of the consensual model, emphasizing that treatment procedures become increasingly effective as the contracts become more specific. He noted too that the accountability of the psychologists is increased, not lessened, by this "tort" model because of the often complicated therapeutic relationships.

Schwitzgebel, like Goldiamond and Meehl, persuasively argued that the best defense against coercive or imposed treatment in the name of justice or health are conditions that encourage choice and mutual exchange. The results of the Stanford University prison experiment underlined too the difficulty of establishing such conditions in "correctional" contexts without explicit contractual understandings. In a simulated experiment designed to study interpersonal dynamics, individuals while role-playing *unknowingly* became socialized into criminality, be they prisoners or guards (63, 64). Both "prisoners" and "guards" were observed continuously for behavioral manifestations using multiple, social psychological measures (e.g. videotaping, verbal interactions, sociometric ratings, authoritarianism measures). Within six days, the behavior of 21 stable, representative, middle-class Caucasian males became pathological and antisocial. The experimenters assessed the emergence of these patterns not as the product of deviant personalities but as the result of a pathological situation that rechanneled and distorted the behavior of normal individuals.

Beyond reporting the experiment in traditional terms, Haney & Zimbardo (64) vividly conveyed the power of prison situations to socialize individuals into dehumanizing roles. Using four scenarios to describe the experiences of two guards and two prisoners—one each from real and simulated prison settings—Haney & Zimbardo dramatized the impact of social-situational variables in controlling behavior and the lack of individual consistency across situations. In addition to considering the process of institutional socialization, they analyzed as well the phenomenology of imprisonment and the professional's difficulty in not perpetrating dehumanization. In sum, Haney & Zimbardo saw the psychologist's role in social institutions to be "a critical one in order to humanize impersonal structures and neutralize the harm" (64, p. 2).

An appealing but controversial paradigm for handling such problems as dehumanization is the just community approach to corrections, proposed by developmental psychologist Kohlberg and colleagues working within prison settings and in concert with prison staff (95). Their goal is to facilitate individual and institutional movement to more ethical and humane levels of interaction. The investigators examined the "moral"—not "moralistic"—atmosphere of two prison settings in part to test Kohlberg's 20-year-old theory of moral development. Their justice model of prison intervention was variously explicated in the mid-1970s (95, 96, 153).

Using interviews and participant observations, they asked whether the justice structure of a prison could be conceptualized in terms of stages of moral development and how perceptions of the justice practices of the inmates were ordered by the moral atmosphere of the prison. The in situ research team found that the Cheshire inmates operated basically on standards of fixed rule and/or manipulation of rules —a pattern consistent with other reported prison research. As importantly they found "Inmates tended to reason at lower levels on dilemmas placed within the prison context. Even 'conventionally reasoning inmates' . . . reverted. . . . *Independent* of stage, inmates perceived justice practices of the institution in Stage 1 (punishment and obedience) or Stage 2 (instrumental exchange) terms" (96, p. 7). The power of the situation was as evident here as in the simulated Stanford setting (63, 64). While some minor movement in moral stages occurred using the traditional methods of group discussions, "the low stage 'moral atmosphere' of the reformatory placed a 'ceiling' " on expected moral maturing (96, p. 7). Likewise, the prison's authority system supported punishment-oriented compliance, and the rigid structuring of roles blocked role-playing or shifts in perspectives. Although a cognitive theory of moral development marked their approach, there were social-situational variables lurking in this model.

Based on this in situ experiment, Kohlberg and his colleagues defined a just correctional community, trained an intervention staff, and tested the justice model at the Niantic State Farm for Women. Using justice strategies as a treatment (i.e. stressing community process and moral justice to represent "treatment" rather than phrasing "treatment" in psychological terms), they aimed to "stimulate the development of the offender's values and moral judgment to a higher level, and to stimulate correspondence of judgment and action" (p. 12). Details of their training procedures are described elsewhere (95). Of great interest in evaluating the potential of a justice model are the reports on the emergence of a self-governing prison structure where inmates were "disciplined" by their own board, where 90% of meetings were called by inmates, and where both staff and inmates had a single vote. Although the long-term results of the just community approach to "rehabilitation" await further testing and follow-up work, in 1974 only 5 of 33 inmates had returned to prison (153). The notion of justice as treatment emphasizing participation, exchange, choice, and shared community responsibility is consistent with the "official morality" of the US Constitution. If this method continued to work in US correctional contexts, then there would be further evidence that a "major force for change in small-group rehabilitation is the *moral pressure* of the group on its members and the *moral evaluation* of the individual by the staff and other members of the group" (96, p. 13).

What is fascinating about this psychology/law interface is the commitment across various psychological orientations to assure a relationship between prisoner (patient) and psychologist of choice and cooperation, not coercion and control. Although each psychologist stressed different variables, the concern for social exchange between "equals" was explicit and implicit (e.g. constructional contracts, just communities). Doubtless it may be difficult to put into effect justice models or rehabilitation treatments based on consensual contracts. But evidently psychologists of different persuasions (e.g. Meehl, Goldiamond, Schwitzgebel, Kohlberg, Zimbardo) are incorporating concepts of mutuality and reciprocity, participation and consent, exchange and choice in their therapy and research. As psychologists begin to denote the dimensions of a "just" or "constitutional" or "ethical" relationship between psychologist and patient, they can assume a pivotal role in altering the major behavior control systems—criminal justice and mental health. After all, the question of who and whether individuals become victims of these systems is as much a psychological as legal problem.

CODA

My subtitle, "An Overture," was a musical metaphor as well as a recognition of the selective and initial quality of this new *Annual Review* topic. Since I was guided also by the idea that a union of psychology and law promotes both science and justice, how could I revert to a conventional coda merely recapitulating themes? Like a complex concerto, work at the psychology/law interface has several movements, each with themes and subthemes. I chose to sketch three basic themes—the legal socialization, judicial, and criminal justice processes—because they seemed representative of the movement of the individual through the legal system as well as the shift from an interstitial to an interfacial mood in psychology and law—patent in the scoring of discordances. The potentiality and poignancy of these and other themes at the psychology/law interface seem to chasten the putative purities of our mutual theories, but the evidence of recent interdisciplinary and empirical work bodes well for both research and reform. While it is evident that the intertwining of psychology and law, like science and justice, is a difficult orchestration, such a possibility seems greater, though no less difficult or discordant, in the 1970s than it did in the 1900s. The difference may be that we compose with greater systematic sophistication—and in concert.

Literature Cited

1. Adelson, J. 1971. The political imagination of the young adolescent. *Daedulus* 100:1013–50
2. Adelson, J., Beall, L. 1970. Adolescent perspectives on law and government. *Law Soc. Rev.* 4:495–504
3. Adelson, J., Green, B., O'Neil, R. 1969. The growth of the idea of law in adolescence. *Dev. Psychol.* 1:327–32
4. Adelson, J., O'Neil, R. 1966. The development of political thought in adolescence: The sense of community. *J. Pers. Soc. Psychol.* 4:295–306
5. Allen, F. A. 1959. Criminal justice, legal values and the rehabilitative ideal.

J. Crim. Law, Criminol. Police Sci. 50:226–32
6. American Psychological Association 1973. *Symposium on Legal Socialization,* chair. J. L. Tapp. 81st Ann. Conv. APA, Montreal
7. Ibid 1974. *Legal Socialization: Theory and Practice,* chair. D. Levine. 82nd Ann. Conv. APA, New Orleans
8. Andenaes, J. 1975. General prevention revisited: Research and policy implications. *J. Crim. Law Criminol.* In press
9. Anderson, D. C., Whitman, T. L. 1972. The control of behavior through law:

Theory and practice. *Notre Dame Lawyer* 47:815–52

10. Aronfreed, J. 1968. *Conduct and Conscience: The Socialization of Internalized Control Over Behavior.* New York: Academic. 405 pp.

11. Bandura, A., McDonald, F. J. 1963. Influence of social reinforcement and the behavior of models in shaping children's moral judgments. *J. Abnorm. Soc. Psychol.* 67:274–81

12. Baumrind, D. 1975. It neither is nor ought to be: A reply to Wallwork. In *Human Rights and Psychological Research: A Debate on Psychology and Ethics,* ed. E. Kennedy, 83–102. New York: Crowell. 144 pp.

13. Bazelon, D. L. 1972. Psychologists in corrections—Are they doing good for the offender or well for themselves? See Ref. 21, 149–54

14. Berkowitz, L. 1964. *The Development of Motives and Values in the Child.* New York: Basic Books. 114 pp.

15. Berman, H. 1976. The use of law to guide people to virtue: A comparison of Soviet and American perspectives. See Ref. 182

16. Bermant, G., Jacoubovitch, M. D. 1975. Fish out of water: A brief overview of social and psychological concerns about videotaped trials. *Hastings Law J.* 26:999–1011

17. Bermant, G., Tapp, J. L. 1975. The notion of conspiracy is not tasty to Americans. *Psychol. Today* 9:60–63, 65–67

18. Bloom, A. H. 1974. *Social principledness and social humanism: A cross-cultural investigation into dimensions of politico-moral reasoning.* PhD thesis. Harvard Univ., Cambridge. 128 pp.

19. Boruch, R. F. 1974. *Costs, Benefits and Legal Implications in Social Research.* Evanston: Northwestern Univ. Press. 46 pp.

20. Brigham Young University Law Review 1975. *The Use of Videotape in the Courtroom.* Provo, Utah: Brigham Young Univ. Law Rev. (whole issue)

21. Brodsky, S. L., Ed. 1972. *Psychologists in the Criminal Justice System.* Carbondale: Am. Assoc. Correctional Psychol. 183 pp.

22. Buckhout, R. 1974. Eyewitness testimony. *Sci Am.* 231 (Dec.):23–31

23. Burtt, M. E. 1931. *Legal Psychology.* Englewood Cliffs: Prentice-Hall. 467 pp.

24. Campbell, D. T. 1969. Reforms as experiments. *Am. Psychol.* 24:409–577

25. Campbell, D. T. 1971. *Methods for the experimenting society.* Presented at 79th Ann. Conv. APA, Washington DC

26. Campbell, D. T., Boruch, R. F., Schwartz, R. D., Steinberg, J. 1975. Confidentiality preserving modes of access to files and to interfile exchange for useful statistical analysis. In *Protecting Individual Privacy in Evaluation Research,* ed. A. M. Rivlin et al, A1-A25. Washington DC: Rep. Comm. Fed. Agency Eval. Res., Natl. Acad. Sci. Natl. Res. Counc. 132 pp.

27. Caplan, N., Nelson, S. 1973. On being useful: The nature and consequences of psychological research on social problems. *Am. Psychol.* 28:199–211

28. Chein, I. 1975. *There ought to be a law—but why?* Presented at 83rd Ann. Conv. APA, Chicago

29. Christie, R. 1972. Some reflections on social science and the law: The Harrisburg conspiracy trial as an example. *Div. 8 Newslett.* APA 12:1–3

30. Cohen, J., Robson, R. A., Bates, A. 1958. *Parental Authority: The Community and the Law.* New Brunswick: Rutgers Univ. Press. 301 pp.

31. Costopoulos, W. C. 1972. Persuasion in the courtroom. *Duquesne Law Rev.* 10:384–409

32. Davis, J. H., Bray, R. M., Holt, R. W. 1976. The empirical study of social decision processes in juries. See Ref. 182

33. Diamond, S., Zeisel, H. 1974. *A courtroom experiment on juror selection and decisionmaking.* Presented at 82nd Ann. Conv. APA, New Orleans

34. Easton, D., Dennis, J. 1969. *Children in the Political System.* New York: McGraw-Hill. 440 pp.

35. Ellsworth, P. C., Levy, R. J. 1969. Legislative reform of child custody adjudication: An effort to rely on social science data in formulating legal policies. *Law Soc. Rev.* 4:167–233

36. Etzioni, A. 1974. Science threatens jury system. In *St. Paul Sunday Pioneer Press* June 2:1, 5 (Reprinted from *Washington Post*)

37. Fadiman, C., Hutchins, R. M. 1975. Get ready for anything. *Cent. Rep.* 8:20–24

38. Fields, R. 1973. Conversations with children under siege: 1972. See Ref. 91, 413–37

39. Fishkin, J., Keniston, K., MacKinnon, C. 1973. Moral reasoning and political ideology. *J. Pers. Soc. Psychol.* 27:109–19

40. Flavell, J. H. 1968. *The Development of Role-taking and Communication Skills in Children.* New York: Wiley. 239 pp.
41. Frank, J. 1930. *Law and the Modern Mind.* New York: Brentano's. 362 pp.
42. Freud, S. 1906. Psycho-analysis and the ascertaining of truth in courts of law. In *Clinical Papers and Papers on Technique, Collected Papers* (1959), 2:13–24. New York: Basic Books. 5 vols. 2274 pp.
43. Friedman, L. M. 1971. The idea of right as a social and legal concept. *J. Soc. Issues* 27:189–98
44. Friedman, L. M., Macaulay, S. 1969. *Law and the Behavioral Sciences.* Indianapolis: Bobbs-Merrill. 1059 pp.
45. Fuller, L. L. 1969. Human interaction and the law. *Am. Jurisprudence* 14:1–36
46. Fuller, L. L. 1969. *The Morality of Law.* New Haven: Yale Univ. Press. 202 pp.
47. Fuller, L. L. 1976. Some presuppositions shaping the concept of "socialization." See Ref. 182
48. Gallatin, J. 1972. *The Development of Political Thinking in Urban Adolescents.* Washington DC: US Dep. HEW
49. Gallatin, J. 1975. The conceptualization of rights: Psychological development and cross-national perspectives. In *Comparative Human Rights,* ed. R. Claude. In press
50. Gallatin, J., Adelson, J. 1970. Individual rights and the public good: A cross-national study of adolescence. *Comp. Polit. Stud.* 2:226–44
51. Gallatin, J., Adelson, J. 1971. Legal guarantees of individual freedom: A cross-national study of the development of political thought. *J. Soc. Issues* 27:93–108
52. Geis, G., Monahan, J. 1975. The social ecology of violence. In *Man and Morality,* ed. T. Lickona. New York: Holt, Rinehart & Winston. In press
53. Goldiamond, I. 1974. Toward a constructional approach to social problems: Ethical and constitutional issues raised by applied behavior analysis. *Behaviorism* 2:1–84
54. Goldstein, J., Freud, A., Solnit, A. J. 1973. *Beyond the Best Interests of the Child.* New York: Free Press. 170 pp.
55. Gormally, J., Brodsky, S. L. 1973. Utilization and training of psychologists in the criminal system. *Am. Psychol.* 28:926–28
56. Gorsuch, R., Barnes, M. 1973. Stages of ethical reasoning and moral norms of Carib youths. *J. Cross-Cult. Psychol.* 4:283–301

57. Gottfredson, D. M. 1972. Five challenges. *J. Res. Crime Delinquency* 9:68–86
58. Greenberg, E. S. 1970. Children and government: A comparison across racial lines. *Midwest. J. Polit. Sci.* 14:249–75
59. Greenstein, F. I. 1965. *Children and Politics.* New Haven: Yale Univ. Press. 199 pp.
60. Greenstein, F. I., Tarrow, S. 1970. *Political Orientations of Children: The Use of a Semi-Projective Technique in Three Nations.* Sage Prof. Pap. 01–009, Comp. Polit. Ser. 1:479–558. Beverly Hills: Sage Publ.
61. Haan, N., Smith, M., Block, J. 1968. Moral reasoning of young adults: Political-social behavior, family background, and personality correlates. *J. Pers. Soc. Psychol.* 10:183–201
62. Haggard, E. 1976. Making decisions that affect others. See Ref. 182
63. Haney, C., Banks, C., Zimbardo, P. G. 1973. Interpersonal dynamics in a simulated prison. *Int. J. Criminol. Penol.* 1:69–97
64. Haney, C., Zimbardo, P. G. 1976. The socialization into criminality: On becoming a prisoner and a guard. See Ref. 182
65. Hart, H. L. A. 1961. *The Concept of Law.* Oxford: Clarendon. 263 pp.
66. Harvard Educational Review 1973–74. *The Rights of Children.* Cambridge: Harv. Educ. Rev. 391 pp.
67. Healy, W. 1915. *Honesty: A Study of the Causes and Treatment of Dishonesty Among Children.* Indianapolis: Bobbs-Merrill. 220 pp.
68. Hess, R. D., Tapp, J. L. 1969. *Authority, Rules, and Aggression: A Cross-National Study of the Socialization of Children into Compliance Systems—Part I.* Washington DC: US Dep. HEW
69. Hess, R. D., Torney, J. V. 1967. *The Development of Political Attitudes in Children.* Chicago: Aldine. 288 pp.
70. Hoffman, M. 1970. Moral development. In *Carmichael's Manual of Child Psychology,* ed. P. H. Mussen. New York: Wiley. 2 vols. 1391 pp.
71. Hoffman, M., Saltzstein, H. D. 1967. Parent discipline and the children's moral development. *J. Pers. Soc. Psychol.* 5:45–57
72. Hogan, R. 1970. A dimension of moral judgment. *J. Couns. Clin. Psychol.* 35:205–12
73. Hogan, R. 1973. Moral conduct and

moral character: A psychological perspective. *Psychol. Bull.* 79:217–32

74. Hogan, R. 1975. The structure of moral character and the explanation of moral action. *J. Youth Adolescence* 4:1–15

75. Hogan, R. 1975. Theoretical egocentrism and the problem of compliance. *Am. Psychol.* 30:533–40

76. Hogan, R., Dickstein, E. 1972. Moral judgment and the perceptions of injustice. *J. Pers. Soc. Psychol.* 23:409–13

77. Hogan, R., Henley, N. 1970. Nomotics: The science of human rule systems. *Law Soc. Rev.* 5:135–65

78. Holstein, C. 1973. *Irreversible, stepwise sequence in the development of moral judgment: A longitudinal study.* Presented at Soc. Res. Child Dev., Philadelphia

79. Holzman, P. S. 1974. Personality. *Ann. Rev. Psychol.* 25:247–76

80. Howard, J. W. 1974. Law enforcement in an urban society. *Am. Psychol.* 29:223–32

81. Howell, R. 1975. The origins of the American Psychology-Law Society: A synopsis. *AP-LS Newslett.* 8:7–8

82. Hutchins, R. M., Slesinger, D. 1929. Legal psychology. *Psychol. Rev.* 36: 13–26

83. Hyman, H. 1959. *Political Socialization: A Study in the Psychology of Political Behavior.* Glencoe, Ill.: Free Press. 175 pp.

84. Jennings, M. K., Niemi, R. 1968. The transmission of political values from parent to child. *Am. Polit. Sci. Rev.* 62:169–84

85. Kadish, M. R., Kadish, S. H. 1971. The institutionalization of conflict: Jury acquittals. *J. Soc. Issues* 27:199–217

86. Kahn, J. 1974. Social scientists' role in selection of juries sparks legal debate. *Wall St. J.* Aug. 12:1, 13

87. Kairys, D., Schulman, J., Harring, S., Eds. 1975. *The Jury System: New Methods for Reducing Prejudice. A Manual for Lawyers, Legal Workers, and Social Scientists.* Philadelphia: Nat. Jury Proj. Nat. Lawyers Guild. 82 pp.

88. Kalven, H., Zeisel, H. 1966. *The American Jury.* Boston: Little, Brown. 559 pp.

89. Katkin, D., Bullington, B., Levine, M. 1974. Above and beyond the best interests of the child: An inquiry into the relationship between social science and social action. *Law Soc. Rev.* 8:669–87

90. Kelley, H. H., Thibaut, J. 1969. Group problem solving. In *The Handbook of Social Psychology,* ed. G. Lindzey, E.

Aronson, 4:1–101. Reading, Mass.: Addison Wesley. 2nd ed. 5 vols. 4180 pp.

91. Knutson, J. N., Ed. 1973. *Handbook of Political Psychology.* San Francisco: Jossey-Bass. 542 pp.

92. Koeppen, S. R. 1970. Children and compliance: A comparative analysis of socialization studies. *Law Soc. Rev.* 4:545–64

93. Kohlberg, L. 1963. Moral development and identification. In *Child Psychology 62nd Yearbook National Society for the Study of Education, Part 1,* ed. H. W. Stevenson, 277–332. Univ. Chicago Press, 554 pp.

94. Kohlberg, L. 1969. Stage and sequence: The cognitive-developmental approach to socialization. In *Handbook of Socialization Theory and Research,* ed. D. Goslin, 347–480. Chicago: Rand McNally. 1182 pp.

95. Kohlberg, L., Kauffman, K., Scharf, P., Hickey, J. 1974. *The Just Community Approach to Corrections: A Manual Part I.* Cambridge: Moral Educ. Rec. Found., Harvard Univ.

96. Kohlberg, L., Scharf, P., Hickey, J. 1971. Justice structure of the prison. *Prison J.* 51:3–14

97. Kurtines, W., Grief, E. B. 1974. The development of moral thought: Review and evaluation of Kohlberg's approach. *Psychol. Bull.* 81:453–70

98. Ladinsky, J. 1975. *The teaching of law and social science courses in the United States.* Work Pap. No. 11, Cent. Law Behav. Sci., Univ. Wis., Madison. 29 pp.

99. Lawson, R. G. 1968. Order of presentation as a factor in jury persuasion. *Kent Law J.* 56:523–55

100. Lawson, R. G. 1970. Experimental research on the organization of persuasive arguments: An application to courtroom communications. *Law Soc. Order* 1970:579–608

100a. Levine, D. 1976. Crime, mental illness, and political dissent. See Ref. 182

101. Levine, F. J. 1972. *The Legal Reasoning of Children: Dimensions and Correlates.* PhD thesis. Univ. Chicago. 39 pp.

102. Levine, F. J., Tapp, J. L. 1973. The psychology of criminal identification: The gap from *Wade* to *Kirby. Univ. Pa. Law Rev.* 121:1079–1131

103. Levine, M. 1974. Scientific method and the adversary model: Some preliminary thoughts. *Am. Psychol.* 29:661–67

104. Levine, R. A. 1973. *Culture, Behavior, and Personality.* Chicago: Aldine. 319 pp.

105. Lewin, K. 1948. *Resolving Social Conflicts: Selected Papers on Group Dynamics.* New York: Harper. 230 pp.
106. Livermore, J. M., Malmquist, C., Meehl, P. E. 1968. On the justifications for civil commitment. *Univ. Pa. Law Rev.* 117:75–96
107. Llewellyn, K. N., Hoebel, E. A. 1941. *The Cheyenne Way: Conflict and Case Law in Primitive Jurisprudence.* Norman: Univ. Okla. Press. 360 pp.
108. Loftus, E. 1974. Incredible eyewitness. *Psychol. Today* 8:117–19
109. Loftus, E. 1975. Leading questions and the eyewitness report. *Cogn. Psychol.* In press
110. Maccoby, E. E. 1968. The development of moral values and behavior in childhood. In *Socialization and Society*, ed. J. Clausen, 227–69. Boston: Little, Brown. 400 pp.
111. Marshall, J. 1966. *Law and Psychology in Conflict.* New York: Bobbs-Merrill. 119 pp.
112. Marshall, J., Marquis, K. H., Oskamp, S. 1971. Effects of kind of question and atmosphere of interrogation on accuracy and completeness of testimony. *Harv. Law Rev.* 84:1620–43
113. McCarty, D. G. 1929. *Psychology for the Lawyer.* New York: Prentice-Hall. 723 pp.
114. McDougall, W. 1908. *An Introduction to Social Psychology.* London: Methuen. 523 pp.
115. McGuire, W. 1973. The yin and yang of progress in social psychology: Seven koan. *J. Pers. Soc Psychol.* 26:446–56
116. Mead, G. H. 1934. *Mind, Self and Society: From the Standpoint of a Social Behaviorist.* Univ. Chicago Press. 400 pp.
117. Meehl, P. E. 1970. Psychology and the criminal law. *Univ. Richmond Law Rev.* 5:1–30
118. Meehl, P. E. 1971. Law and the fireside induction. *J. Soc. Issues* 27: 65–100
119. Megargee, E. I. 1970. The prediction of violence with psychological tests. In *Current Topics in Clinical and Community Psychology*, ed. C. Speilberger, 98–156. New York: Academic. 264 pp.
120. Mentschikoff, S. 1976. Decisionmaking and decision consensus in commercial arbitration. See Ref. 182
121. Merelman, R. M. 1969. The development of political ideology: A framework for the analysis of political socialization. *Am. Polit. Sci. Rev.* 63:750–67
122. Minturn, L., Tapp, J. L. 1970. *Authority, Rules, and Aggression: A Cross-National Study of Children's Judgments of the Justice of Aggressive Confrontations—Part II.* Washington DC: US Dep. HEW
123. Mischel, T. 1964. Personal constructs, rules, and the logic of clinical activity. *Psychol. Rev.* 21:180–92
124. Mitchell, H. E., Byrne, P. 1973. The defendant's dilemma: Effects of jurors' attitudes and authoritarianism on judicial decisions. *J. Pers. Soc. Psychol.* 25:123–29
125. Monahan, J., Ed. 1975. *Community Mental Health and the Criminal Justice System.* New York: Pergamon. 322 pp.
126. Ibid. The prevention of violence, 13–34
127. Moore, U., Callahan, C. 1943. *Law and Learning Theory: A Study in Legal Control.* New Haven: Yale Law. 136 pp.
128. Munsterberg, H. 1908. *On the Witness Stand: Essays on Psychology and Crime.* New York: Clark, Boardman. 269 pp.
129. North Carolina Law Review 1974. *Developments in Law and Social Sciences Research.* Chapel Hill, NC: North Carolina Law Review (whole issue)
130. Padawer-Singer, A. M., Barton, A. H. 1975. *Interim report: Experimental study of decision-making in the 12- versus 6-man jury under unanimous versus non-unanimous decisions.* New York: Columbia Univ. Bur. Appl. Soc. Res. 132 pp.
131. Padawer-Singer, A. M., Barton, A. H. 1975. *The Jury System: A Critical Analysis*, ed. R. Simon. Beverly Hills: Sage Publ. In press
132. Padawer-Singer, A. M., Singer, A., Singer, R. 1974. Voir dire by two lawyers: An essential safeguard. *Judicature* 57:386–91
133. Parke, R. 1976. 1976. Socialization into child abuse: A social interactional perspective. See Ref. 182
134. Parke, R., Collmer, C. 1975. Child abuse: An interdisciplinary analysis. In *Review of Child Development Research*, ed. E. M. Hetherington, 5:507–87. Univ. Chicago Press. In press
135. Parke, R., Sawin, D. B. 1975. *Children's privacy in the home: Developmental, ecological and child-rearing determinants.* Presented at Int. Soc. Study Behav. Dev., Bien. Conf., Guilford, England
136. Peck, R. F., Havighurst, R. J. 1960. *The Psychology of Character Development.* New York: Wiley. 267 pp.
137. Pepitone, A. 1975. *Social psychological perspectives in crime and punishment.* Presented at 83rd Ann. Conv. APA, Chicago

138. Piaget, J. 1932. *The Moral Development of the Child.* Glencoe, Ill: Free Press, 418 pp.

139. Piaget, J. 1967. *Six Psychological Studies.* New York: Random House. 169 pp.

140. Rawls, J. 1971. *A Theory of Justice.* Cambridge: Belknap. 607 pp.

141. Redmount, R. S. 1959. The psychological basis of evidence practices: Memory. *J. Crim. Law, Criminol. Police Sci.* 50:249–64

142. Redmount, R. S. 1961. Psychology and law. See Ref. 184, 22–50

143. Redmount, R. S. 1971. Persuasion, rules of evidence and the process of trial. *Loyola Univ. Law Rev.* 4:253–78

144. Reppucci, N. D., Saunders, J. L. 1974. Social psychology of behavior modification: Problems of implementation in natural settings. *Am. Psychol.* 29: 649–60

145. Rest, J., Cooper, D., Coder, R., Masanz, J., Anderson, D. 1974. Judging the important issues in moral dilemmas —An objective measure of development. *Dev. Psychol.* 10:491–501

146. Riesman, D. 1951. Some observations on law and psychology. *Univ. Chicago Law Rev.* 19:30–44

147. Robinson, D. N. 1974. Harm, offense, and nuisance: Some first steps in the establishment of an ethics of treatment. *Am. Psychol.* 29:233–38

148. Rodgers, H. R., Taylor, G. 1970. Preadult attitudes toward legal compliance and the law. *Soc. Sci. Q.* 51:539–51

149. Rodgers, R., Bronfenbrenner, U., Devereaux, E. 1968. Standards of social behavior among school children in four cultures. *Int. J. Psychol.* 3:31–41

150. Rokeach, M., Vidmar, N. 1973. Testimony concerning possible jury bias in a Black Panther murder trial. *J. Appl. Soc. Psychol.* 3:19–29

151. Ross, H. L., Campbell, D. T., Glass, G. V. 1970. Determining the social effects of a legal reform: The British "breathalyser" crackdown of 1967. *Am. Behav. Sci.* 13:493–509

152. Sarbin, T. 1967. The dangerous individual: An outcome of social identity transformation. *Br. J. Criminol.* 7:285–95

153. Scharf, P., Kohlberg, L. 1974. *The inmate's perception of institutional rules and legal norms: A developmental perspective.* Presented at 80th Ann. Conv. APA, New Orleans

154. Schulman, J., Kairys, D., Harring, S., Bonora, B., Christie, R. 1975. Systematic jury selection. In *The Jury System: New Methods for Reducing Prejudice. A Manual for Lawyers, Legal Workers, and Social Scientists,* ed. D. Kairys, J. Schulman, S. Harring. Philadelphia: Nat. Jury Proj., Natl. Lawyers Guild. 82 pp.

155. Schulman, J., Shaver, P., Colman, R., Emrich, B., Christie, R. 1973. Recipe for a jury. *Psychol. Today* 7:37–44, 77–84

156. Schwitzgebel, R. K. 1968. Electronic alternatives to imprisonment. *Lex Sci.* 5:99–104

157. Schwitzgebel, R. K. 1970. Ethical and legal aspects of behavioral instrumentation. *Behav. Ther.* 1:498–509

158. Schwitzgebel, R. K. 1975. A contractual model for the protection of the rights of institutionalized patients. *Am. Psychol.* 30:815–20

159. Sears, D. O. 1969. Political behavior. See Ref. 90, 5:315–458

160. Sears, D. O. 1974. Political socialization: Part I: Attachment to the system. In *Handbook of Political Science: Theoretical Aspects of Micropolitics,* ed. F. I. Greenstein, N. W. Polsby. Reading, Mass: Addison-Wesley. 8 vols. In press

161. Shah, S. A. 1972. The criminal justice system. In *Handbook of Community Mental Health,* ed. S. E. Golann, C. Eisdorfer, 73–105. New York: Appleton-Century-Crofts. 982 pp.

162. Shah, S. A. 1974. Some interactions of law and mental health in the handling of social deviance. *Cathol. Univ. Law Rev.* 23:674–719

163. Shapley, D. 1974. Jury selection: Social scientists gamble in an already loaded game. *Science* 185:1033–34, 1071

164. Shuman, S. 1976. Why criminal law?: Parameters for evaluating objectives and response alternatives. See Ref. 182

165. Silber, D. E. 1974. Controversy concerning the criminal justice system and its implication for the role of mental health workers. *Am. Psychol.* 29: 239–44

166. Silverman, I. 1975. Nonreactive methods and the law. *Am. Psychol.* 30: 764–69

167. Simpson, E. 1973. *Teachers of justice: A preliminary report of politico-legal socialization.* Presented at 79th Ann. Conv. APA, Montreal

168. Simpson, E. 1974. Moral development research: A case study of scientific cultural bias. *Hum. Dev.* 17:81–106

169. Singer, B. F. 1970. Psychological studies of punishment. *Calif. Law Rev.* 58:405–43

170. Stern, W. 1903. *Beiträge Zur Psychologie der Aussage.* Leipzig: Verlag Barth. 2 vols. 1155 pp.

171. Szasz, T. S. 1963. *Law, Liberty, and Psychiatry: An Inquiry Into the Social Uses of Mental Health Practices.* New York: Macmillan. 281 pp.

172. Tapp. J. L. 1969. Psychology and the law: The dilemma. *Psychol. Today* 2:16–22

173. Ibid 1970. A child's garden of law and order. 4:29–31

174. Tapp, J. L., Ed. 1971. Socialization, the law, and society. *J. Soc. Issues* 27(2) (whole issue)

175. Tapp, J. L. 1973. *Cross-cultural and Developmental Dimensions of a Jurisprudence of Youth.* Work. Pap. No. 5, Law & Soc. Cent., Univ. Calif., Berkeley. 28 pp.

176. Tapp, J. L. 1974. The psychological limits of legality. In *The Limits of Law, Nomos XV,* ed. J. R. Pennock, J. W. Chapman, 46–75. New York: Atherton. 276 pp.

177. Tapp, J. L., Kohlberg, L. 1971. Developing senses of law and legal justice. *J. Soc. Issues* 27:65–91

178. Tapp, J. L., Levine, F. J. 1970. Persuasion to virtue: A preliminary statement. *Law Soc. Rev.* 4:565–82

179. Tapp, J. L., Levine, F. J. 1971. *The Jurisprudence of Youth.* Chicago: Am. Bar Found. 186 pp.

180. Tapp, J. L., Levine, F. J. 1972. Compliance from kindergarten to college: A speculative research note. *J. Youth Adolescence* 1:233–49

181. Tapp, J. L., Levine, F. J. 1974. Legal socialization: Strategies for an ethical legality. *Stanford Law Rev.* 27:1–72

182. Tapp, J. L., Levine, F. J., Eds. 1976. *Law, Justice and the Individual in Society.* New York: Holt, Rinehart & Winston. In press

183. Thibaut, J., Walker, L. 1975. *Procedural Justice: A Psychological Analysis.* Hillsdale, NJ: 145 pp.

184. Toch, H., Ed. 1961. *Legal and Criminal Psychology.* New York: Holt, Rinehart & Winston. 426 pp.

185. Trachtman, G. M. 1972. Pupils, parents, privacy, and the school psychologist. *Am. Psychol.* 27:37–45

186. Trotter, S. 1975. Token economy program perverted by prison officials. *APA Mon.* 6:10

186a. Ibid. Patuxent: 'Therapeutic' prison faces test, pp. 1, 4, 12

187. Turiel, E. 1966. An experimental test of the sequentiality of developmental stages in the child's moral judgments. *J. Pers. Soc. Psychol.* 3:611–18

188. Turiel, E. 1974. Conflict and transition in adolescent moral development. *Child Dev.* 45:14–29

189. Vidmar, N., Ellsworth, P. 1974. Public opinion and the death penalty. *Stanford Law Rev.* 26:1245–70

190. Walster, E., Berscheid, E. S., Walster, G. W. 1973. New directions in equity research. *J. Pers. Soc. Psychol.* 25: 151–76

191. Watson, J. B. 1913. Psychology as the behaviorist views it. *Psychol. Rev.* 20:158–77

192. Wexler, D. B. 1973. Token and taboo. Behavior modification, token economies, and the law. *Behaviorism* 1:1–24. Reprinted from *Calif. Law. Rev.* 61:81–109

193. Whipple, G. M. 1909. The observer as reporter: A survey of the "psychology of testimony." *Psychol. Bull.* 6:153–70

194. Winick, C. 1963. A primer of psychological theories holding implications for legal work. *Am. Behav. Sci.* 7:45–47

195. Wolfe, M., Laufer, R. 1974. *The concept of privacy in childhood and adolescence.* Presented at Environ. Design Res. Assoc. Conf., Washington DC

196. Wright, D. 1971. *The Psychology of Moral Behavior.* Baltimore: Penguin. 288 pp.

197. Wrightsman, L., Rogers, C., Percy, J. 1975. *Conceptualization and measurement of children's rights.* Presented at 83rd Ann. Conv. APA, Chicago

198. Zeisel, H., Kalven, H., Buckholz, B. 1959. *Delay in the Court.* Boston: Little, Brown. 313 pp.

199. Zellman, G. L., Sears, D. O. 1971. Childhood origins of tolerance for dissent. *J. Soc. Issues* 27:109–36

PERSONNEL AND HUMAN RESOURCES DEVELOPMENT

259

Frank A. Heller and Alfred W. Clark[1]

Tavistock Institute of Human Relations, London NW3 5BA, England

"For four wicked centuries the world has dreamed this foolish dream of efficiency."

George Bernard Shaw

INTRODUCTION

In order to organize this chapter, an open systems model is put forward that views the personnel function as located on the boundary between the organization and the external environment. The inputs from the environment that the personnel function needs to mediate include uncertainty, changing values, rising expectations, and the emergence of new power groups in society. They also include increased concern for minority groups, whether based on enlightened self-interest or more humane considerations.

The review will present a critical discussion of certain aspects of our subject area and an assessment of changing trends since about 1970. Personal interests have influenced the choice of particular topics, but in addition an attempt has been made to guess which of the current trends and problems are likely to stay with us for some time. We have also been influenced by recent chapters in the *Annual Review of Psychology,* particularly those by Campbell (24), Back (6) and Friedlander & Brown (60), who between them have covered a very considerable range of research relevant to our field.

The literature and our own experience on several continents suggest that the role of psychology within what is broadly called the personnel area in modern organizations is now under critical review from a number of directions. We shall see that several eminent psychologists are dissatisfied with the development of our subject, and other social scientists, particularly sociologists, are covering crucial aspects of the personnel field. Even managers, who it is alleged psychologists are always trying to please, are sometimes bewildered by our reluctance to move into new areas of

---

[1]Now at La Trobe University, Melbourne, Australia. We are grateful to Don Bryant for helpful suggestions.

research which happen to be of great interest to them. Potential clients of organizational psychology, including governments, are concerned with problems of change, organizational design, the effect of uncertainty and turbulence in the environment, the changing balance of power, ethical valuations, and the effect of cultural differences in multinational organizations.

The ongoing discussion on what are appropriate areas for scientific research has been fanned by the increasingly bitter debate on research methods and the problem of the researcher's own values. In choosing areas for review, attention has been paid to these problems.

The personnel function is heavily involved in the responsibility of developing adaptive organizational responses to various inputs from the outside world (149). Consequently it must develop some conceptual apparatus for scanning them and assessing their implications for internal organizational processes. In a sense then the personnel function is dual. First, it must learn to interact with external groupings, such as government, unions, employers' federations, and grass roots movements; second, it must attend to its internal functions of selection, training, appraisal, salary negotiation, and the development of a general facilitating and motivating climate (131). In linking the microenvironment to the macroenvironment, a critical function is that of manpower planning.

Implicit in the systems approach is an increased appreciation both of the interdependence of internal parts of the organization and the connectedness of external parts that have traditionally been treated separately (52, 94, 127).

The question of who represents and/or influences the personnel function in organizations is an unsolved problem. From the point of view of this chapter, we have decided that many different groups, in addition to line management and the personnel department, make legitimate contributions to this area. There is the academic teaching and research community, the external consultants and, in some countries, the government and trade union movement.[2]

It is astonishing that the role of the personnel function in relation to other interest groups inside companies has hardly been questioned, either through research or public debate. Heller (83) has put forward the view that there might be considerable advantages to an organization if the personnel function were to be taken out of its traditional position as part and parcel of management and given a more neutral and professional role.

Looking at the purpose of the internal personnel function, it seems that traditionally it focuses on two concerns: the development of the person as such and the development of task related skills. In view of the rapidly accumulating research evidence that situations (including tasks, technology, and organizational structure) have at least as much effect on behavior as personality, a third focus may seem appropriate. It will be concerned with contingency theory and an understanding of the situational variables that affect behavior at work (84, 112, 176, 188).

---

[2]We have in mind, for instance, recent government and trade union involvement in the field of quality of working life in the United States (190), Germany (107), and the United Kingdom (187).

As far as personnel training and development is concerned, the traditional focus is on a precise specification of what is to be learned, how it is to be taught, and how it is to be evaluated. While some of the literature covering this area will be reviewed in the third section of this chapter, the emphasis will be on broader appreciation of values and style that characterize an organization, stressing the considerable element of situational learning, and avoiding specification of a given amount of material to be learned for narrowly defined tasks.

It seems reasonable to assume that organizations have an obligation to develop and use their human resources once they have recruited them. Discharging this obligation makes good sense both in terms of achieving organizational objectives and in terms of humanistic values. In the long term, the two go together. It is also assumed that the individual has a reciprocal obligation to further his own development.

The review is organized in three parts.

1. *Conditions for future developments:* By this we mean the trends that relate psychology to the personnel function—changing satisfactions, expectations, and environmental factors; we have also included comments on the current debate on research methodology and a paragraph on action research, since these topics are likely to determine the psychological findings used by the personnel function.
2. *Current research issues:* We have picked on subjects that have not received adequate attention, or which have changed as a result of recent research.
3. *Development of manpower resources:* This part contains less critical discussion than the previous two sections, presenting a series of quick reviews of the considerable current literature.

CONDITIONS FOR FUTURE DEVELOPMENTS

Job Dissatisfaction and Rising Expectations

On the basis of three separate national surveys in the United States, Sheppard & Herrick (157) conclude that dissatisfaction with work is increasing. The dissatisfaction is greatest among the younger, the more educated, and the less authoritarian workers. Trist (173) suggests that developing values stress joy and immediate gratification rather than resignation and delayed gratification. The volume *Work in America* (190) highlights the increasing disenchantment with work. Despite rising unemployment, the reaction against the dehumanization of work appears to be growing in most industrialized countries (45, 191).

Unfortunately, the concept of job satisfaction is multidimensional and several of the component parts do not correlate very well (4). If workers are simply asked to say how satisfied they are with their work, the majority report themselves satisfied. Strauss (168a) makes a case for the view that on the basis of some findings "the extent of worker dissatisfaction has been over-stated." He quotes in support of his argument a variety of American studies and suggests that recent negative factors such as reduced productivity, labor turnover, absenteeism, and strikes are due to economic factors.

However, we believe that on balance improved education and rising rates of expectations are major contributory factors to dissatisfaction and the widespread feelings of alienation (170). While these indices differ from country to country, we believe the position is deteriorating.

In some respects less developed countries may be in a better position. At least they have a wider choice. They can preserve their craft traditions and use small-scale or intermediate modern technology to complement it. Alternatively they can go all out for large-scale technology and scientific management, perhaps repeating the mistakes made by countries that industrialized earlier.

Sociotechnology at Macro and Micro Levels

The intermediate technology movement will have accelerated repercussions on managerial thinking because of the rising costs of energy. Intermediate technology, which began many years ago, summarized recently by Schumacher (155), sets out to devise methods of producing commodities in conditions of plentiful labor supply. It recommends that the technology chosen by a country for each industry should be adjusted to financial possibilities on the one hand and the supply and skill of labor on the other. It also considers the difficulties of servicing and maintaining complex advanced technology in a particular setting. Intermediate technology fits into a sociotechnical way of thinking but extends it to a more general economic planning level. In this sense the trend relates to the whole area of job design, particularly to the emphasis given to it in Scandinavia (55) and the well-known examples of work in Volvo and Saab, at Shell UK (88), and the American work at General Foods (180).

Even at an advanced technological level there has to be some kind of fit between the choice of a particular design of a machine and the environment, including the labor market and workers' expectations and skills. It is necessary to consider the requirements of skills and training in relation to the choice of any particular technology. Under conditions of intermediate technology and the job designs pioneered in Scandinavia, it is likely that the range and levels of skill will increase rather than decrease.

As productivity and work become less highly valued, not only youth but all groups will increasingly look for different satisfactions in their work life (61). Again, this will make demands on the personnel function. It will have to collaborate, possibly with external consultants, in attempting to bring people together to arrive at new organizational and work designs to meet these emergent and often poorly articulated needs (29).

A significant part of the reaction comes from women and minority groups such as the blacks in the United States and migrants. These groups provide cheap labor typically used to do the more routine and manual jobs. Women have been difficult to unionize, but there are growing signs of increasing militancy as reflected, for example, in the women's liberation movement (44).

Overall, people seem to be demanding more from their jobs as well as from life, and work will need to be restructured within organizations based on new design principles (34, 85). The sociotechnical requirements leading to a demand for design changes seem to coincide with a movement towards greater participation and industrial democracy (17, 93). This trend is particularly strong in the Scandinavian countries and is now spreading outward to the rest of Europe. In this context it is important to distinguish between job enrichment schemes designed by specialists and introduced by them (118) and the schemes which require worker participation in the job design changes. The latter are the ones to which we have referred earlier (55, 85, 88). The trade union movement has not remained indifferent to this choice of alternatives. It seems that in many countries imposed job design changes are seen as simple management productivity exercises, while autonomous work groups are not (92).

New Values and Turbulence

It is no more than a truism that modern organizations constantly have to adjust to changing circumstances. One thinks of changing economic conditions, technological innovation, and, as we have seen, changing expectations and satisfactions. While social scientists have always known about these problems, it is only recently that they have been given theoretical backing, and even more recently that a few empirical studies have used measures of turbulence and uncertainty (39, 53, 121, 122, 166).

Psychologists have of course been interested in the immediate physical environment as in ergonomics and in the cultural environment in cross-cultural studies, to some of which we refer later. Barker (7), however, started an important tradition in ecological psychology which has not been followed up in the field with which we are concerned here. The need is growing for an assessment of objective as well as subjective uncertainties and interorganizational pressures leading to turbulence. To some extent contingency theory is pushing researchers into this area of work. By contingency theory we mean the assessment of variables like organization structure or turbulence on which a particular outcome is contingent (38, 82, 89, 112, 176, 188). We will deal with these theories in greater detail in the section on leadership.

New values can create uncertainty. Managers in general have not shared the doubt expressed by Bernard Shaw's quotation at the beginning of this chapter, but recently some psychologists and economists have begun to question the meaning of efficiency, productivity, and economic growth. It probably started with Simon's (159) famous observation that managers do not in fact try to optimize their efficiency, but choose less perfect and less rational solutions. Questioning the basic rules of the game has been taken further by Cohen & March (33) and Leavitt (113). Argyris (4), making his attack from a different angle, questions the organizational psychologists' time-honored criterion of efficiency, and Child (27) demonstrates how difficult it is to measure organizational performance.

Another recent shift in emphasis questions the desirability of economic growth as a self-evident good. From the psychological point of view economic growth and success do not guarantee social harmony (80). The increasingly sophisticated discussions on the postindustrial society introduce a range of new values (53), including the notion that small is beautiful (155).

There are at least two further examples of new values which are causing organizations and the personnel function to experience turbulence. They are also good examples of the importance of an open systems framework. One is the growth of consumerism and the related cry for social as well as economic audits (13). A recent investigation shows that two-thirds of the companies surveyed had made organizational changes specifically because of new social pressures (76). Social responsibility was being taken seriously, despite stringent trading conditions and economic crises. The rapidly growing movement for greater worker representation on various consultative and executive bodies is our last example. It is mainly a European movement, although it has spread into a number of Third World countries. We will review this movement in the section on current research issues.

Viable Research Methodology

CHANGES IN ATTITUDES TO SCIENTIFIC METHOD   We come now to the debate on scientific method and its implications for the personnel field. The best known and most persistent critic of the "scientific rigor" school is Chris Argyris. In a series of hard-hitting essays (2, 4), he challenges the basic narrow framework of the conventional research methodology—the demands, for instance, that variables be defined to overlap minimally and to be so clearly observable that even graduate students can achieve a high degree of reliability. He argues that human behavior shows endless overlap, has redundancies, does not optimize as it is supposed to, and is sloppy. If we want to understand human behavior, we have to take it as we find it. He suggests that "pure" research designs have a number of unintended negative consequences, such as psychological withdrawal and even overt hostility, which will creep into the results and distort them. He also puts down a hard line of ethics; he is against deception in laboratory and field studies and accuses many modern psychologists of having the values shared with the early lumber kings who consumed trees without worrying very much about the future supply. More recently he has begun to question the appropriateness of the conventional criterion variables of production, quality, absenteeism, etc, suggesting that they are based on considerations and values which were useful in the past but are now substantially out of date (4).

If Argyris were a single voice in the wilderness, it would not justify lengthy comment in an *Annual Review* chapter, but over the last few years there have been other eminent psychologists who have either made substantial critical evaluations themselves or have shown themselves to be very ill at ease with the present state of the art. Harold Leavitt (113) is concerned about the quality of training managers get in the best business schools. He starts off a very carefully reasoned assessment with the words "Over the last couple of years a certain disenchantment has arisen with the hard-nosed, number-oriented emphasis. . . ." Leavitt agrees that the disenchantment is healthy. In a recent Edwin A. Henry Memorial Address, Bass (10) argues against premature theorizing, mechanistic models, aping the physical sciences, and continuing to use the classical Pearson-Neyman statistics instead of, for instance, a Bayesian approach. Heller identified four problem areas which threaten to hold up the progress of psychology in organizations:[3] academic boundary disputes (with sociology for instance), scientism, excessive reliance on causality in our models, and a morbid fear of subjectivity.

In some European countries there is evidence of an incipient revolt against certain aspects of the so-called hard-nosed methodology. For sociology this was recently analyzed by Goldthorpe (69), for psychology by Warr (181), Broadbent (18), and Joynson (102). The change is very noticeable in some countries like Sweden, where the emphasis has changed in a few years from sophisticated statistical work to case studies and phenomenology.

The methodological disputes have a direct effect on the nature of the work carried out. We can assume that training will always remain important. Selection is a little more doubtful although it has recently received more attention because of the burning political issues surrounding underprivileged groups. However, other areas of traditional personnel work such as attitude surveys, computer simulation, individual difference measurement, and even motivation are less likely to be favored by personnel specialists who sympathize with Argyris. At least the method of approach will be different. Furthermore, the dispute on methodology imperceptibly merges with the field of ethics.

ETHICS AND THE PERSONNEL FUNCTION   While hard and soft methodologies have fought each other since the dawn of social science, the deliberate evaluation of alternative values and ethical behavior has not always found an obvious lodging place in personnel departments.

In the last few years, however, large corporations in many of the developed countries have found themselves under increasing pressure from social scientists and others to examine their values. Psychologists were challenged on the assumptions supporting their various selection tests and even training procedures for minority or underprivileged groups (24, 50a). A few people seem to have produced findings of cultural homogeneity (150) while others show evidence that the values of the strong are imposed on the weak (25).

Modern organizations speak of social responsibility rather than the old fashioned work "ethics," but the area is wide. For instance, there is the question whether loyalty should be "created" deliberately. Campbell, in his chapter in the 1971 *Annual Review of Psychology* (24), cites two articles which suggest that "certain elements in the training program serendipitously increased loyalty and commitment to the organization." Trade unionists have been known to take a poor view of such a procedure. They tend to argue that loyalty for one group may be alienation from another. The main arguments will be joined on whether business's social responsibility can be achieved voluntarily, for instance by "social audit" (which we mentioned earlier), or whether the state will have to take a hand (25, 115, 175). The most thorough-going documentation of recent arguments surrounding the business ethic

---

[3]Chairman's address to the British Psychological Society's Occupational Psychology section. Tavistock Institute of Human Relations, 1974. Mimeographed.

in the United States has been assembled by Perrow (134). We will have further occasion to refer to the problem of values later.

ACTION RESEARCH   A victim of the struggle between the hard and soft methodologies, action research is usually accused of being strong on action and weak on research; occasionally the accusation goes the other way around (60).

Action research sets out both to make scientific discoveries and to engage in the important practical affairs of men (3, 29, 30a, 81). This is done by establishing the conditions for field experiments in such a way that members of the focal organization and its significant environment are drawn in as full collaborators in the process. Theoretical clarification and development, experimental design, implementation of the treatment, data collection and analysis, and report writing can be done jointly, respecting the rights of all parties and gaining privileged access to settings and information that are often closed to conventional academic research. The process points towards the solution of shared problems, not simply that of the experimenter in isolation. It becomes clear that people are prepared to collaborate on problems only if they are significant and relevant to them. This provides a corrective against trivial research, particularly as the participants are enmeshed in organizations that are attempting to cope with increasingly complex and rapidly changing environments.

Such an action research approach would integrate the macro and micro levels of analysis that are so critical to the personnel function. The process of collaboration among a range of groups located inside and outside the organization would get social science over the hump of boundary marking and demarcation disputes between disciplines. It would also provide a middle ground in the conflict about method. Methods are developed to cope with complex field situations, often generalized from inadequately understood traditions in the physical sciences. If methods became too sloppy, there would be a corrective when actions were based on the results and found to be ineffective. The repeated action research cycle of appreciation, theory building, change, and evaluation of intended and unintended consequences would, in addition, avoid the gap between theory building and research and between discovery and application. Through action research man is encouraged and given the means to shape his own future rather than waiting passively for events to unfold. To achieve this, however, it is necessary to return to the unity of research and action, drawing into complementary and collaborative relations such people as planners, policymakers, administrators, managers, and trade unionists, as well as social scientists (29).

A human resources development program sits happily in such a framework;[4] it sits unhappily in a framework of mechanistic packages. The advantages of action research include the following: (a) It preserves the best aspects of the scientific model. (b) It is tuned to real life situations, appreciating fully their uncertainties,

---

[4]Jyiji Misumi. "Action Research on the Development of Leadership in a Japanese Shipyard." Paper presented to 18th International Congress of Applied Psychology, July 1974. Mimeographed.

complexities and dynamic properties. In particular it stresses the interdependence between subsystems and systems that are usually treated as being independent of one another. (c) It allows us to move in the middle ground between so-called fundamental research and applied research. In connecting these usually disparate activities, it allows the social scientist to contribute to policy formulation and implementation. (d) It makes sense to the external world. It is not too theoretical nor too simplistic. It is beyond the narrowly practical and allows for the dissemination and diffusion of the results through other systems. (e) It makes a clear connection with policy formulation, providing a normative base and a proactive stance as well as an emphasis on continuous learning.

The link with policy planning and implementation assumes that all policy comes to be treated as a guiding hypothesis. Action research allows these guides to action to be subject to revision in terms of continuous evaluation and learning. In this way it follows Popper's (138) idea that all social administration should be conducted as experimentation.

It must be admitted, however, that a fair amount of work labeled action research turns out, on closer inspection, to have nothing to do with research. It is often little more than an implementation of a simple consultancy job.

SOME CURRENT RESEARCH ISSUES

Comparison Between Countries and Cultures

There are two main areas in which comparisons between countries affect the personnel function. One is the position of multinational companies or organizations with export businesses, the other is the special case of relationships with underdeveloped regions of the world.

So-called cross-cultural research is fraught with enormous methodological difficulties which are not easily overcome. In a very detailed review of this research field, Roberts (148) finds that the variable "culture" is inadequately conceptualized. Psychologists "view culture as a vague entity, cast it as their independent variable and forget it." Culture is too often seen as a phenotypical rather than a genotypical variable, and in any case it is likely that other factors like technology produce structural conditions that simply overwhelm "cultural" variations. Roberts concludes that what is needed is research seen in systems terms and using modern multivariate statistical procedures.

One interesting recent research set out to test the possible advantages of having overseas workers systematically trained for the "culture" of the country to which they were to be sent (132). They used programmed instructions for volunteers sent from the United States to Central America and compared them with a closely matched group of volunteers who had received no such training. The criterion variables were productivity in community development work and in clinical operations. Both trained and untrained volunteers were also divided into experienced (if they had worked in Central America before) or inexperienced categories. The results suggest that both experienced and inexperienced culture-trained teams did better than the control group.

Values and Culture

Triandis and collaborators have studied values and cognitive structures of students in Illinois, Athens, Bangalore, and Tokyo (172). As many of these students will later work in organizations, a study of their attitudes is relevant. Using concepts like "freedom," "power," and "wealth," they obtained judgments about their "antecendents" as well as their "consequences." This particular set of concepts is important for a psychological understanding of organizational dynamics.

They found that "freedom" is valued in all four countries, but more highly in Greece and Japan than in the USA and India. The "consequences" of freedom are conceptualized in an individualistic framework by American and Japanese students (joy, happiness, responsibility), but more in sociopolitical terms by Greek and Indian students (democracy, civilization, growth of civilization). "Power" has stronger values in the two Western than in the two Eastern countries. Similarly "wealth" is a strong value in America and Japan but less so in Greece and India. For American students the antecedents of wealth are drive, happiness, and success. For Greek students they are intelligence, patience, inquiring mind, and hard work.

For some time there has been a considerable interest in the comparative analysis of attitudes and behavior in industrialized and less industrialized countries. Researchers have looked for the elixir of economic success. Pioneering work in this field was done in the 1960s and again more recently (96, 110, 172).

The interest of business organizations in comparative studies is increasing. IBM saw the practical advantages for its own personnel function of having up-to-date information about staff attitudes and has continued with quite extensive survey-type research for many years (110, 161). At one time Philips in Holland was a pioneer in conducting quite sophisticated field work in its own companies in different countries (87).

It is likely that comparative studies will become more important during the next decade. Differences between managerial practices in different countries are beginning to be well documented (47, 48, 130, 170). A question that eventually will have to be answered is whether differences should be tolerated or reduced. What happens if differences in beliefs or styles of work are too great to be absorbed even in flexible organizations, or if people demand change? Who or what should give way? In the past, psychologists have tended to emphasize the use of training, selection, and change programs to adjust people to circumstances.

With the more recent emphasis on the interaction between the environment and people (7, 97, 112, 114), the possibility of changing certain aspects of organization structure becomes an alternative psychologists will have to consider. This question is raised in a recent psychological work on cognitive styles in non-Western countries. The research used well-established tests measuring "field articulation" with a scale varying from global homogeneous to specialized complex thinking (26). Field global people find it very difficult to impose a structure on unstructured fields, but what are called articulated thinkers find it quite easy to do this. The question raised by Gruenfeld & MacEachron (73a) is whether there is a relationship between successful economic development and people's cognitive style. Using a sample of over 300 managers and technicians from 21 non-Western countries in various stages of economic development, they found a significant relationship between six indices of economic development and articulated thinking. The possibility of selecting people by means of these tests obviously exists, but Gruenfeld & MacEachron also develop the more unusual possibility of deliberately designing organizations to adjust to the cultural predisposition of different countries.

The Successful Manager in Different Countries

Several recent researchers have pointed to the type of manager who becomes successful in modern organizations. Rapoport (143) studied 570 British managers who had attended a senior management development program and had been back on their job for varying lengths of time. The dependent variable was the respondent's post-course development. Using McQuitty's hierarchical analysis, Rapoport obtained three main clusters. The *metamorphic* manager was creative, ambitious, and venturesome but restless, hard-driving, and full of conflict. The *incremental* manager was uncritical but fulfilled having a happy personal and family life and a slow orderly progress at work. By contrast, the *tangential* manager was not primarily interested in the organization in which he worked. He was alienated or rebellious and his major interests were usually in the wider environment. While all three types were represented in a sample of successful managers, there is some indication that the metamorphic type may be more successful than the other two. This conclusion also emerges from a study in Royal Dutch Shell (126a). Upwardly mobile managers who have what has been called helicopter quality prefer to operate in a dynamic-active, possibly stressful environment. The less successful managers feel more at home in a static environment and give high priority to friendship, social values, and security.

Bass and his collaborators have used a series of standardized role-playing exercises in many countries. Some of these give us information on ethical preferences. The samples are large and subjects can be divided into "more" or "less" successful by using age and salary indicators. Young managers earning high salaries are called accelerated. They value wealth, pleasure, and self-realization; the less successful managers value security, service, duty, expertness, and social goals. However, these patterns are not uniform in each country (12). Using "exercise objectives," managers have to decide how much money they can spend on a variety of alternative decisions, for instance whether to clean up a polluted stream. In 10 out of 15 countries, successful managers were more pragmatic and less idealistic than less successful managers; for example, they would spend significantly less money on pollution (11).

England and his colleagues have done a considerable amount of research on personal value systems. In one study, they found—as predicted—that union leaders had moralistic while managers had pragmatic orientations. Employee and social welfare are important values for union leaders, but weak ones for managers. Managers valued the traditional goals of productivity, organizational growth, industrial leadership, and efficiency. They thought highly of ambition, ability, and skill. Union leaders, however, give their high rating to loyalty, honor, and trust (56).

The interpretation of these findings presents difficulties. One view is that people have different values and carry them over into work activity, but the opposite inference is almost equally plausible. It could be hypothesized that successful managers operate in a social and economic environment which rewards these values despite original preferences, while unsuccessful managers may start off with competitive values but change their preferences when their efforts go unrewarded. As soon as a person becomes aware that other people are more successful than himself, failure has to be rationalized. In such circumstances it makes less sense to believe in aggressiveness, ambition, competition, and risk-taking. One may settle for cooperation, loyalty, trust, and tolerance. Aspects of the organizational environment, including the existing leadership, plus the extant literature on economics and business management, may act as midwife to a competitive value orientation.

Value orientations appear to be remarkably stable over time; only 4 out of 66 concepts varied by 10 percent or more over a period of 6 years (72). At the same time there is evidence that personal values vary with the size of the organization. In large firms with over 5000 employees, objectives like profit maximization, growth, efficiency, productivity, and sound leadership are much more important than in firms with 500 to 4999 employees. These goals are least important in the small firm with up to 500 employees (57).

This relationship between size and ethical judgments was equally valid for samples from America, Japan, and Korea. However, some of the other findings on values seem to be more susceptible to national climates, and this is potentially of great importance for multinational companies.

Taking the decision to spend money on eliminating pollution, for instance, we find that 30 percent or less of successful managers in France, Britain, and Sweden are willing to spend money for this purpose, while as much as 50 to 60 percent of successful Swiss, Italian, Danish, and Japanese managers are willing to do so. Similar differences appear in managers' attitudes to major objectives or life goals (11, 72).

Leadership and Decision-Making

In recent years there has been a shift of emphasis in leadership studies. After World War II, and particularly in the 1950s, some psychologists began to recognize the limitation of personality variables and the measurement of individual differences in leadership studies. Gradually it became fashionable to talk about "situational" factors, but no clear theoretical framework emerged and few empirical studies treated this factor as anything other than an afterthought. In 1966 it was still necessary for a reviewer of the literature to conclude "what is needed. . . . is not just recognition of this factor of 'situational determinants' but rather a systematic conceptualization of situational variance as it might relate to leadership behavior" (109).

Since that time there has been an increase in studies which systematically tested situational variables (38, 59, 82, 89, 176, 188). Only Fiedler has developed a clear contingency theory. It has received wide recognition in spite of the continuing lack of clarity surrounding the measurement unit (5).

The new approach to the study of leadership and decision-making is of considerable importance to the personnel function. It has repercussions for selection, training, and promotion procedures, and is critical for the choice of an appropriate sociotechnology of organizational development. Basically the alternatives are between schemes that make "generalistic" assumptions and advocate a particular preferred style of behavior and schemes that distinguish between different situations. The latter approach is opposed to a "one best solution" or to the advocacy of simple principles enshrined in a two-dimensional grid.

The difference between the two alternatives can be summed up in this way:
Generalistic statement:

"Evidence on the relationship between leadership style and organizational effectiveness suggests that democratic or participatory styles are in general superior to autocratic methods."

Contingency statement:

"Evidence on the relationship between leadership style and certain measures of effectiveness suggests that under conditions a, b, c . . . styles m, n, o . . . respectively are appropriate."

Several recent research contributions appear to support a contingency model of leadership. One methodologically sophisticated research was designed to test a normative decision tree model incorporating eight contingencies and five alternative leadership styles. The findings with several quite large samples of American managers suggest that personality accounts for only 10 percent of the variation of styles, while the situation accounts for 30 percent (176). Managers used participatory methods when: (a) the quality of the decision was important; (b) when it was important that subordinates accepted the decision and it was unlikely that they would do so if they were not allowed to take part in it; (c) when subordinates could be trusted to pay attention to the goals of the organization rather than simply to their own preferences.

Another research (82, 84) used five decision styles almost identical to Vroom's but with a different set of contingencies, different samples in several countries, and two closely interrelated boss-subordinate groups of managers. Findings include the following: (a) managers use different decision styles on different task situations; (b) participative styles are used when the decisions are important to subordinates rather than to the company, and when managers see little difference in skill between their own jobs and the jobs of those with whom they work.

These results fully confirm the belief that it makes "at least as much sense to talk about autocratic and participative situations as it does to talk about autocratic and participative mangers" (176). The implications of these convergent findings for training and organization development will need to be explored by the personnel function.

The findings are also relevant to the current and fashionable arguments about "participation." Most of the literature assumes that the full range of alternatives can be adequately compressed into two extremes, democracy and autocracy, but this is a completely misleading assumption. Moreover, the research literature has sometimes given rise to the simplistic conclusion that participation is the solution to most organizational ills.

According to a contingency theory, one would expect different forms of participative decision-making to be associated with known and defined circumstances. Training situations should enable staff at all levels to examine the complexity of their tasks, the nature of the decisions they make, the skills and expectations of their subordinates, and the amount of information available.

The research we have reviewed here is relevant to the current and controversial discussion in most European countries about democracy and participation through formally constituted works councils.

Participation and Industrial Democracy

Participation can mean many things to different people. The lack of clarity in the concept was recognized early by Strauss (168) but has remained with us in spite of careful reviews of the literature (177). To add to the confusion, the idea of having worker participation on boards of directors of private companies has introduced a political dimension to the controversy, at least in Europe (177). From the point of view of the role played by the personnel function, the notion of legitimacy is more important than politics. For instance, can one give people a *feeling* of participating in a decision-making activity without giving them influence? Many people have been misled into believing that deception is as good as the real thing since it is the "feeling" that counts more than the activity.

Many years ago, even March & Simon defended pseudo-participation on the ground that successful deception has the same practical consequences as real participation (120, p. 54). Most psychologists today would reject such a notion on ethical grounds, but unfortunately the research evidence is not clear and as a consequence personnel advisers are often confused. The "how to be successful by reading my book" argument goes like this: participation increases commitment; commitment heightens motivation, which in turn makes people work harder, leading to increased productivity and greater prosperity.[5] Can all this be achieved by pseudo-participation? It now seems unlikely. Furthermore, one has come to suspect a nonlinear relationship between participative methods and effectiveness, however defined (104, 146). Kay & Warr (104) have argued that the usual research design and correlational analysis do not easily reveal the point of no return when increasing amount of participation will yield diminishing or negative results.

Participation is sometimes advocated on ideological grounds as a way of reducing power differences between groups of people. This, too, has been challenged on the basis of laboratory as well as field work. Mulder (126) has produced evidence that the effect of participation depends on the real differences in skill between members of the group. When differences in skill are great, participative practices will increase power differences instead of decreasing them. It now seems that neither structural consequences of participation (power equalization) nor functional consequences (improved productivity) can be taken for granted (111) and the grounds for legitimacy have to be further explored (151).

Considering that the issue of worker participation has become one of the major issues in the personnel field in all European countries, the dearth of research in this field is quite striking. There have been good theoretical contributions but very little

---

[5]Such a train of thought was proposed in a pamphlet produced by the American Management Association in 1966. It is quoted in Wickens (185).

empirical work (31, 50). In Europe, worker participation started very formally by legislation even before World War II and quite extensively after 1950, yet the only detailed field research we have relates to the self-management movement in Yugo-slavia,[6] although extensive descriptive material on the European and non-European experiments is available (21).

A recent comparative study in five countries may help us to bridge the gap between the extensive psychological literature on participation and the European initiated structural-legal schemes of participatory democracy (170). The researchers deliberately chose a group of countries in which two had what they call *formal* participation (Israel's kibbutz and Yugoslavia's self-management system) while the industries in three other countries relied almost entirely on *informal* methods (the United States, Italy, and Austria).

The research covered over 50 individual plants. In the kibbutz and Yugoslav plants power was fairly widely distributed. Participation, measured by Likert's system, was also high. At the other extreme were Italian plants with limited power distribution and low participation.

Favorable attitudes of workers and staff and an open climate of communication do not always flourish under formal systems of power-sharing, and job satisfaction is surprisingly low under the Yugoslav systems, but it is even lower in the Italian plants.

It seems that formal power equalization measures do not have a clear one-to-one relationship with psychological indicators of satisfaction, adjustment, or alienation. They may, however, reduce the negative effect of the hierarchical system of author-ity (170). There is also some evidence that informal interpersonal participation mediated through styles of leadership are somewhat independent of the formal legal systems of industrial democracy. Participative styles of leadership are very exten-sively used in the United States, where the psychological and management literature has advocated such methods for many years, reinforced by a variety of interpersonal training programs (15, 16, 145).

While most European countries have some legally based schemes of participation, England, despite imminent legislation, is closer to the United States in relying on informal and voluntary joint consultative schemes (31, 129), some of which have pioneered democratic procedures and survived for a long time (19).

The United States is involved in the European developments with respect to all multinational companies and overseas subsidiaries of US firms. Current plans in Germany are to extend the codetermination law so that German and foreign compa-nies operating in Germany may have a 50 percent worker-trade union representa-tion on the top policy-making body (Supervisory Board). Up to now the representation was one-third. The American business community is fighting the new measures very strenuously (183).

In any case, it seems that the personnel function in most parts of the industrialized world should be aware of these developments and the meager but important socio-

[6]See the six volumes of *Participation and Self Management,* published 1972–1973 by the Institute for Social Research, University of Zagreb, Zagreb, Yugoslavia.

psychological investigations in this area. One important question that cannot be answered on the basis of cross-sectional research is whether formal legal provisions help or hinder the development of informal decentralized participation or the development of semiautonomous work groups on the Tavistock-Norwegian pattern (55). What is needed is a before-and-after study coinciding with the advent of a formal participative scheme.

One finding of considerable importance has now received support from several of the studies we have reviewed. It concerns the relationship between human skills or formal educational qualifications on the one hand, and the use of power-sharing methods on the other. Two of the studies we have reviewed are quite specific on this point (82, 84, 176). When the quality of decision-making is relatively unimportant, participative behavior is less relevant. Participative behavior among American, British, and German managers is significantly correlated with the existence of skills among their subordinates; it is still more clearly related to perceived skills and perceived skill differentials. When superior-subordinate skill differences are great, authoritarian styles of decision-making result. When skill differences are small, participative decision-making is more usual. This finding is corroborated by the judgments and behavioral descriptions of both superior and subordinate levels (84).

We have already referred to the laboratory and field research findings which show that participative behavior is counterproductive when skill differences are great (126). Field studies support this finding (170). The kibbutz had the most even distribution of power of the five sample countries. and kibbutz members were also the only group which had a high and completely even distribution of educational experience. Tannenbaum et al (170) say that "education . . . is among the conditions that reduce the feeling of alienation, the sense of powerlessness and meaninglessness in socialist systems as in capitalist systems."

From the point of view of the personnel function, this relationship between skill and participative leadership behavior links up two classical subjects in the domain of applied psychology which have tended to be treated separately in the past. There is now strong empirical support for the view that participative behavior without due consideration to such contingencies as the availability of skill could result in manipulative behavior. The development of skill in organizations is the subject of the final section in this chapter.

DEVELOPMENT OF MANPOWER RESOURCES

In this section we will make a rapid survey of some of the relevant literature on the development of manpower skills. This is a traditional but important area for the personnel function, and the volume of writing is considerable. In the available space we have not been able to review the whole field. Even so, the citations are so numerous that we l.ave departed from the relatively leisurely and detailed review of the first two sections of this chapter.

Rapidly changing environments and rising expectations mean that organizations must be designed to develop their human resources so that they have the skills and flexibility to cope with change and to be proactive in shaping the social and physical environment.

Complementary Relationship of Training and Organizational Development

The model of man linked with this conception is that of complex man, not economic or rational man. He is unlikely to be developed in hierarchically arranged superior-subordinate pyramidal organizations (159). He is more likely to be developed in matrix organizations (105) within semiautonomous groups (85). Hill (88) provides a useful case study of an attempt to introduce a management philosophy pointing towards the joint optimization of social and technical resources. Although it is not couched in terms of training and personnel development, the process may well be seen as a model of a program of human resources development.

Many organizational development and action research schemes (29, 32, 70, 81) are essentially training programs, but at the moment change is a more glamorous concept than training. Consequently it often happens that people caught up in the threatening turmoil of change are left to train themselves to work in new ways without systematic help. A recent study of 240 Indian managers supports this point (14). It found that when management training is done outside the work setting, innovations are introduced in the back-home job settings only when the organizational climate is supportive. To achieve this the authors suggest that a large-scale organizational development effort must be concurrent with management training. It is likely that separate training departments within a particular organization face a similar problem when their trainees return to their home departments. An appreciation of the interdependence between training and production and possibly between these and the scheduling, inspection, costing, and sales departments is necessary before the training department can be effective. This analysis highlights the systems properties of organizations; it points to the hypothesis that the training and development of employees at any level will be successful to the extent that the organization operates as an effective system rather than as separate subsystems.

Teaching Methods and Materials

Development and training, even at the simplest psychomotor skill level, raises the question of the relationship between the trainer and the trainee. It also raises the question of method, both in teaching and evaluation. The problem area again reflects the emerging schism in social sciences between the advocates of scientific method, based largely on the physical sciences (51, 162), and the advocates of methods more appropriate to human beings and social processes (4, 136). Put another way, people can be processed as objects or taught as people. The first approach implies an objective and distant relationship and methodology; the second, a more subjective and closer relationship, an understanding of the person and his phenomenological world gained through collaboration of equals rather than through the investigation of subjects by an expert. Working *with* rather than *on* sums up the difference between the approaches.

Silvern (158) argues that an engineering systems model assumes that the material to be trained is inert. He advocates a chemical processing model that stresses the dynamic properties of the material: as the material varies so should mixes and processing. The US Instructional System Development (174) includes analysis of systems requirements; a block diagram shows feedback and interaction loops. It is likely that such a model can be used mechanically or with intuition. So, too, could programmed courses for operatives or sales courses and skills analysis training (91, 167).

Glaser (67) provides a useful discussion of changing educational models and their implications for evaluation. Abercrombie (1) discusses group teaching; Klein & Astrachan (106) look at team teaching, and Pitfield & Rees (137) compare study groups and T-groups. Rackham (141) suggests a new technique for training which he calls mixing. Crane (37) stresses involvement techniques, while Gregory (73) describes a training factory. Sorcher & Goldstein (165) describe a behavior modeling approach in training. Culbert (40) provides a phase progression model for accelerating learning in interpersonal relations. The stages are: development of a climate of trust, exposure of individual differences, exchange of perceptions of others, individual problem-solving, group problem-solving, and reconnaissance and perception of personal learning.

Pfeiffer & Jones (135) continue to provide structured exercises for human relations training, T-groups, team building sessions, and communications workshop. Engel (54) provides a book on the development and use of case studies, role playing, and related materials for training; it is carefully set out and very useful for the beginner. Kalt & Barrett (103) show how learning from a technical manual can be facilitated. Inbar & Stoll (95) and Gibbs (64) discuss games and simulation exercises. Cummins (43) attempts to develop rules for course development and provides an evaluation scale. O'Reilly (133) shows that four-fifths of supervisors of clerical workers in a public institution misreported what their subordinates were required to do in their jobs. When both parties agreed that a task was performed, they disagreed in over two-thirds of the cases on the level of skill or knowledge required to perform it satisfactorily.

These findings are in line with Heller's (81), who shows that these gaps may be reduced by group feedback analysis in which an independent outsider collects systematic data from the parties and feeds it back to them for discussion.

Job Design and Assumption about Human Capability

Davis & Taylor (46) bring together a number of papers on job design. This book could well be used as a manual for the design of training programs, as well as providing the basis for incremental organizational change by modifying key variables in the social and technical systems. When green sites are available, it provides useful design principles. Most of the papers are based on systems thinking. This contrasts with the philosophy of training that is prevalent in many large multinational companies. Modular training systems, for example, break a job into its components and also teach what is absolutely necessary. The assumption is that error will be reduced by such simplification and routinization. The chances are, however, that not using human capacity for judgment and discretion increased errors. In addition, it probably lowers motivation.

The trainer is often tempted to undertrain people for complex jobs and overtrain them for simple jobs. Work design and restructuring (45, 46) would resolve this by creating jobs that are optimum in complexity for people who are assumed to have needs, abilities, and potentialities similar to course developers, superiors, and social scientists.

Such an assumption clashes with many personnel managers' experiences with unskilled workers, particularly women and disadvantaged minority groups. For a sample of 38,452 job applicants, Wonderlic & Associates (189) show that Caucasian test performance is consistently higher than Negro performance on the omnibus Wonderlic Personnel Test, the difference amounting to one standard deviation. The authors point out that at least norms are now available for the conduct of affirmative action programs (23). The strategy for their use will depend on the values of the employer and his ability to meet minority hiring goals as well as the costs and risks associated with prediction errors. In a study of hard-core unemployed people, Gavin & Toole (62) found no association, however, between measures of verbal and arithmetic skills and job performance ratings. After an 8 week training program in basic skills, high scorers were more prone to be absent, late, or to leave than low scorers. The researchers interpret this as avoidance behavior. They suggest that the consideration they are shown in the training area and the boost they receive to their self-esteem compares unfavorably with their low level jobs, especially as about 90 percent of their sample came from minority groups, 76 percent blacks and 15 percent Puerto Ricans. The lesson is to present job opportunities that match developing skills and rising expectations.

Goodman, Salipante & Paransky (71) review 192 articles on training the hard-core unemployed. They consider that the hard-core unemployed operate in a complex and extended social system which affects expectancies about work and the rewards it offers. Their behavior is a product of expectancies about how behavior leads or does not lead to desired rewards. The design of a program involves decision about type of training, counseling, and pay.

Miner (123) defends testing programs against the charge of being discriminatory. He says that employers stopped testing programs because they were afraid of violating legislation being enforced by the US Equal Employment Opportunity Commission and the Office of Federal Contract Compliance. The American Telephone and Telegraph Company's testing program was exonerated, but $12 to $15 million is to be paid as compensation to women and minority group employees who have been victims of discrimination in promotions, transfers, and salary. Miner tries to identify what is fair practice rather than discriminatory practice. He says that the AT & T testing program is one of the few that has been cleared by the authorities. He points to a considerable number of studies to show that the program gives valid results in predicting training, post-training, and performance criteria. AT & T is able to show that imbalance in its work force in terms of sex, race, color, national origin, or religious group is job related rather than discriminatory.

It seems that individual differences will not disappear because of gestures towards equality (Cronbach 37a). It seems unwise to give up the use of measuring instruments rather than using them with a professional understanding of their strengths and weaknesses. Test fairness should be looked at rather than the pseudo-problem of racial differences in test validity (154).

The Status of Training, Manpower Planning, and Development

Judging from the paucity of studies reported in the more prestigious journals, training seems to have low status in academia. It may be ironic that, by contrast, macro studies of manpower enjoy prestige among academic model builders. Manpower planning occupies a middle position (8, 20).

Burack & Walker (22) have edited a useful collection of 36 articles highlighting the need to develop managerial skill against a decreasing lead time. Methods are outlined to determine future organizational requirements for people and to assess the ability of present resources to meet these demands. There is a recurrent theme that short-term profit objectives and the dearth of measures of effective manpower utilization act against the constructive development of key employees. Yet the efficient utilization of human resources may well be the most important determinant of success in the business world in the coming decade.

Doré & Meacham (49) draw on Super's theory of career development as the process of implementing a self-concept. They show that job satisfaction correlates significantly with the match between the self-concept favored by the individual and the self-concept required by the job. This implies that training and counseling efforts should aim at a match between these variables. However, unless one is aware of this, training could increase the gap between the self-concepts.

Ghiselli (63) puts forward his Self Description Inventory as a means of identifying and measuring managerial talent. Harrell & Harrell (77) found that Stanford Master of Business Administration graduates who reached general management earlier had stronger and more ambitious personalities than those who remained specialist managers. For instance, on the Guilford-Zimmerman Temperament Survey they were higher on general activity and ascendance. They were also higher on the scales of the Ghiselli Self Description Inventory.

Morris & Burgoyne (125) stress concepts and attitudes rather than techniques in the development of what they call resourceful managers. They say that when an organization focuses on the individual's skills and talents for a particular task, it thinks in terms of resourceful humans rather than human resources.

Appraisal and Performance

A number of writers are raising doubts about appraisal. For example, how far do promotion and salary issues reduce the chances of an exchange of information between superiors, subordinates, and personnel officers, and how happily do counseling and plans for future training and development fit into asymmetrical power relations? One can approach these problems by separating reward reviews, performance reviews, and potential reviews (142). If appraisals are done mechanically, however, even with the best intentions they may become another organizational ritual with neutral or even boomerang effects. Pym (140) attacks the politics of appraisals; whereas Farnworth (58) defends appraisals, describing how in Minnesota Mining & Metals the company links management by objectives as a way of life with self-appraisal. Wilson (186) also views appraisals more positively, focusing on the question of how appraisals can be done. Cummings & Schwab (41) present a rare example of the use of a theoretical model in writing a book for practitioners. They approach performance and appraisal through expectancy and instrumentality theory (139). In this model work performance is seen as a function of the workers' abilities and motivations as well as the environmental context in which work occurs.

Some years ago Bray and Grant described the use of the assessment center in the measurement of potential for business management. A recent report describes the results of a survey of current appraisal practice, including the use of assessment centers, in 360 organizations in the United Kingdom (65). A central finding is that only half the companies recognize the importance of training line managers in appraisal interviewing. The authors feel that there has been little specification of the conditions under which line managers or assessment centers achieve better forecasting. It seems in keeping with the changing spirit of the age to challenge the commodity theory of labor which regards labor's input as a cost rather than as an investment (179). Many consequences follow from a change of definition. For instance, it has been argued that status and pay could be arranged by age to combat divisive disputes and that natural teams could be arranged around task assignments leading to a relaxed social climate (179). Our Western industrial society gives out contradictory messages. Team work is extolled; individual self-seeking is rewarded.

Hardy (75) points out that the way managers are developed must be appropriate to the organization in which they are embedded. On the basis of Harrison's (78) classification of organizational ideologies or cultures, he specifies the modes of management development that match different organizations. Apprenticeship and modeling match a power culture, rational planning and absorption a role culture, open market and discovery a task culture, and happenstance and immersion a person culture. Development strategies must also be related to managers' needs and expectations about their satisfaction (28).

Task Specification, Training, and Criteria

It is clearly difficult to train somebody for an ill-defined task with unknown pathways towards its achievement. Clark & McCabe (30) showed that managers were in conflict because they believed that the individual's capacity for initiative and leadership is limited, while at the same time believing in democracy and the worth of the individual. A related issue is raised in group problem-solving situations. Should a manager allow free ranging discussion or should he structure it more? Maier (119) shows that a developmental discussion method in which the leader introduces structure into the process by making the coverage of the problem systematic and by holding participants to the same issues at the same time, leads to more high quality decisions than a free discussion method. When members made decisions prior to the discussion, however, neither method produced a pronounced change in the quality of decisions.

Rusmore (152) uses Hemphill's ten dimensions of executive positions in an empirical study of promotion. Cummins & King (42) look at the interaction of group size and task structure to focus on decision verifiability, goal clarity, goal path multiplicity, and solution specificity. They showed that group size is positively related to both productivity and leader-member relations for structured tasks. Thus a supervisor of a structured task is likely to have a better performing group and more cooperation if he is unable to pay close attention to each individual member. In relatively less structured tasks, no significant relationship was shown between size and both productivity and leader-member relations. This suggests that in this situation the assistance of the supervisor is not particularly important.

The problem of task specification is bound up with the issue of criteria of job success. James & Ellison (101) list the major issues inherent in the criterion problem: (a) what to use as criteria and subsequently what procedures to use for measurement; (b) the ultimate versus multiple criterion debate; (c) how differentially to weight criteria to form a composite; (d) degrees of relevance (or conversely, contamination and deficiency); (e) reliability of the criterion measures; (f) the use of global rather than behaviorally relevant job performance measures; (g) the effects of situational or organizational variables on criteria; (h) the construct validity of criteria; (j) the predictability of a criterion.

James & Ellison then focus on the ultimate versus multiple criterion debate. They look at three criteria which are assumed to be related conceptually to an ultimate criterion of creative scientific and engineering job performance. The criteria are number of publications, number of patents, and a global supervisory rating on creativity. The composites are viewed as representing a middle-ground approach between the usual ultimate criterion approach of overall success and a multiple criterion approach where criteria have generally been examined individually or by means of factor scores.

Career Choices and Development

This review began by saying that the organization has an obligation to develop its human resources. But the focal individual also must play a part in his own development and fortunately many do, particularly when they think in terms of career choice and development. Glueck (68) shows that undergraduates who make choices about organizations fall into three decision patterns: maximizer or would-be maximizer, validator, and satisficer. Each of these had displayed typical search and choice behavior. Past experience was shown to be a major determinant; for example, the greater the amount of past job experience, the more likely the student was to be a maximizer. Maximizers were generally satisfied with their choice; validators were uneasy, thinking they should have searched more thoroughly; satisficers, especially if forced because of restriction of choice, were generally dissatisfied.

Soelberg (163) shows that the decision maker develops a set of expectations of the ideal organization in which he would like to work. He does not accept the first satisfactory offer but waits for a comparison offer. Of these two, the nonfavored offer is subjected to perceptual and interpretational distortion to its detriment. Goal weights are shifted to fit the favorite, and the decision is made when a Pareto dominant decision rule has been constructed or when time runs out.

Salemi & Monahan (153) describe the finding about students' preferences for organizational climates in potential employers. Singer (160) shows that male and female college seniors desire autonomy in work more than freshmen. This attitude was correlated with a positive attitude towards the Women's Liberation Movement.

A number of theoretical schemas for career entry and development have been put forward (66, 124, 147). Midcareer development has become almost a separate subject of study (143, 164). Rapoport suggests that people who will not accept bureaucratic organizations deflect their energies from organizational goals; they become tangentials (143).

In looking at career development, Rusmore (152) puts forward the management advancement quotient. This was determined by dividing each management age by his chronological age and multiplying by 100, where management age was the mean age of managers at the subject's organizational level. An Achievement Index was determined by dividing the subject's chronological age by the point value, from a job-evaluation study of the subject's position and subtracting from 100. Rusmore found that positions have varying advancement characteristics. Long-range planning pays off in advancement whereas social and community relations do not. This supports the findings we quoted earlier in the section on the successful manager in different countries. In comparing rate of progress, advancement characteristics should be taken into account and, in addition, an assessment should be made of how the incumbent has modified the position by emphasizing some tasks against others. Wallace (178) discusses the wasteland of potential managerial talent. Livingston (116) examines the myth of the well-educated manager, while Scott (156) views management as a creative act in his discussion of the arts side of business education. Lynch (117) located and interviewed 90 women holding high-level executive positions. They claimed to have achieved career success without sacrificing their femininity or their roles as wives and mothers.

Increasing attention is being paid to the careers of aging workers, particularly as they approach the *rite de passage* of retirement. Jacobson (99) shows that females are less likely to be positively oriented towards retirement than are males. For both sexes, reluctance to retire is associated with expected deprivations of a primarily extrinsic nature. However, among women work-based social ties emerge as the chief correlate of the wish to go on working. It is suggested that females' preretirement attitudes are, in part, an extension of their degree of satisfaction with social attributes of the work situation. Their comparatively stronger inclination to remain employed may be affected by a changing life style which becomes less decisively centered on the home and its diminishing range of social options.

Jaffe (100) discusses the retirement dilemma as well as the way women in their middle years who return to work prop the economy of many countries. Streib & Schneider (169) in the United States and Hearnshaw (79) in the United Kingdom have produced books on the occupational aspects of aging and retirement.

Evaluation

If work is increasingly organized in semiautonomous groups, evaluation and training will need to match its requirements. It may need a collective rather than individualistic stance from both leaders and members of the group. At the same time it requires an appreciation of interdependence with related groups as well as strong loyalty to the in-group. Multigroup or overlapping group membership may be a fruitful approach to this problem. This parallels Blau's (17) analysis of the integration problem at a societal level. A very interesting schema of a total cycle of evaluation is put forward by Hamblin (74). He distinguishes between a scientific and heuristic approach, showing that the latter is much more effective.

In 1967 Bass concluded that "With a few interesting exceptions in small group and large organizations, the task-oriented person is up-graded by observers, peers and supervisors. He is more tolerant of deviant opinion, conflicting ideas and directive supervision, although he does better himself as a permissive superior . . . The interaction-oriented person is downgraded generally. . . ." (9). Ray (144) challenges this typology, especially the distinction between a task-oriented person and interaction-oriented person. He argues that the results are a function of the scoring method used. Ray uses Likert scales to show that task and interaction orientation are not opposed. A person may be high on both. He also shows, contrary to the previous findings, that interaction-orientation people are more tolerant of deviance than task-oriented people, and also less authoritarian.

Kohn (108) has compiled a bibliography on the evaluation of management training and development programs. Warr, Bird & Rackham (182), Hamblin (74), Whitelaw (184), and Hesseling (86) have produced books on evaluation of management training. Murray (128) and Holder (90) evaluate the effectiveness of in-company training programs and Cowell (36) of management courses. Couch & Strother (35) provide a critical incident evaluation of supervisory training. Jackson & Thompson (98) evaluate supervisory training in relation to organizational change. There is, to our knowledge, little in the literature to guide the design of training schemes and their evaluation for people working in decentralized organizations or semiautonomous groups (171).

CONCLUSION

The literature relevant to the personnel function reflects a diversity of approaches, but the unit of study is characteristically the individual, particularly in the well-accepted specialist personnel functions. More studies, however, are broadening their focus to include group and organizational levels of analysis; it is suggested that this trend might profitably be extended. It may be difficult for members of any one discipline to cope with this task. As a first move towards an interdisciplinary approach, it would be desirable to make more use of established middle range theories, such as balance theory, role theory, conflict theory, and theories of intergroup relations. These theories edge towards a more general systems approach that links macro and micro levels of analysis.

Our review of the psychologist's contribution to this field was cast in a multinational perspective. It stressed the interaction between people and their environment, giving special attention to recent preoccupations with justice and values. With the space available we chose to concentrate on a relatively small number of topics and are conscious of having omitted others, like payment systems and human resources accounting, which are equally important. The number of problem areas to which the psychologist could direct his skills is expanding rapidly, but increased opportunities are not always matched by a corresponding willingness to enter new fields and experiment.

Recent critics of the traditional approach have pointed out that the reluctance to take on new areas of work has been interpreted as supporting the status quo and being unduly influenced by top management: "In some cases the industrial psychologist may be seen as a genuine link to the top. In other cases, they are seen as the Gestapo" (4). The same critic points out that unions often mistrust psychologists and believe that they use their skills to give a scientific gloss to managerial policies, however ill-conceived.

It can now be argued that the personnel function and those who do research in this area must be more imaginative, more daring, and more neutral. One recent suggestion is to encourage relaxed behavior by what is called "organizational playfulness" (114). The game is to "abrogate organizational rules and constraints for certain of their members so that those members can 'play' and by playing perhaps discover not only new ways of approaching old problems, but new goals, new interests, new objectives" (114). It is thought that such relatively artificial methods may be justified if they induce people to reexamine their past objectives and standards of judgment. The next step is to ask "some underlying questions about what it is all for; what's the meaning of things, what are the really important things the organization might try to do" (113).

Psychological work in organizations has been fairly well sheltered from controversy for many years. Our review has drawn attention to the possibility that uncertainty and turbulence are not simply academic constructs we apply to others; they may also affect our own discipline and its relationship with the public on whose behalf we do research.

Literature Cited

1. Abercrombie, M. L. J. 1970. *Aims and Techniques of Group Teaching.* London: Soc. Res. Higher Educ.
2. Argyris, C. 1968. Some unintended consequences of rigorous research. *Psychol. Bull.* 70:185–97
3. Argyris, C. 1970. *Intervention Theory and Method: A Behavioral Science View.* Reading, Mass: Addison-Wesley
4. Argyris, C. 1976. Problems and new directions in industrial psychology. In *Handbook of Industrial and Organizational Psychology,* ed. M. D. Dunnette. Chicago: Rand McNally
5. Ashour, A. S. 1973. The contingency model of leadership effectiveness: An evaluation. *Organ. Behav. Hum. Perform.* 9:339–55
6. Back, K. W. 1974. Intervention techniques: Small groups. *Ann. Rev. Psychol.* 25:367–87

7. Barker, R. G. 1968. *Ecological Psychology: Concepts and Methods for Studying the Environment of Human Behaviour.* Stanford Univ. Press
8. Bartholomew, D. J. 1971. The statistical approach to manpower planning. *J. Inst. Stat.* 20
9. Bass, B. M. 1967. Social behaviour and the orientation inventory: A review. *Psychol. Bull.* 68:260–92
10. Bass, B. M. 1974. The substance and the shadow. *Am. Psychol.* 29:870–86
11. Bass, B. M., Eldridge, L. D. 1973. Accelerated managers' objectives in twelve countries. *Ind. Relat.* 12:158–71
12. Bass, B. M., Franke, R. 1972. Societal influences on student perceptions of how to succeed in organizations: A cross-national analysis. *J. Appl. Psychol.* 56:312–18
13. Bauer, R. A., Fenn, D. H. Jr. 1972. *The*

Corporate Social Audit. New York: Sage Found.

14. Baumgartel, H., Jeanpierre, F. 1972. Applying new knowledge in the back-home setting: A study of Indian managers' adoptive efforts. *J. Appl. Behav. Sci.* 8:674–94

15. Beckhard, R. 1969. *Organization Development Strategies and Models.* Reading, Mass: Addison-Wesley

16. Blake, R., Mouton, J. 1968. *Corporate Excellence through Grid Development.* Houston: Gulf

17. Blau, P. M. 1974. Parameters of social structure. Presidential address. *Am. Sociol. Rev.* 39:615–35

18. Broadbent, D. E. 1971. Relation between theory and application in psychology. In *Psychology at Work,* ed. P. B. Warr. Harmondsworth, Middlesex: Penguin

19. Brown, W. 1960. *Explorations in Management.* London: Heinemann

20. Bryant, D. T. 1972. Recent developments in manpower research. *Personnel Rev.* 1:14–31

21. Bulletin, International Institute of Labour Studies, Geneva, Switzerland. See particularly Vols. 2–9, 1967–1972

22. Burack, E. H., Walker, J. W., Eds. 1972. *Manpower Planning and Programming.* Boston: Allyn & Bacon

23. Bureau of National Affairs 1973. *Fair Employment Practices.* Washington, DC: B. N. A.

24. Campbell, J. 1971. Personnel training and development. *Ann. Rev. Psychol.* 22:565–602

25. Carr, A. Z. 1970. Can executives afford a conscience? *Harv. Bus. Rev.* July-August:58–64

26. Cattell, R. B. 1971. *Abilities: Structure, Growth and Action.* Boston: Houghton Mifflin

27. Child, J. 1975. Managerial and organizational factors associated with company performance. Part II. *J. Manage. Stud.* 12:12–27

28. Clark, A. W. 1972. The motivation and satisfaction of Australian managers. *Personnel Psychol.* 25:625–38

29. Clark, A. W., Ed. 1976. *Experimenting with Organizational Life: The Action Research Approach.* New York: Plenum. In press

30. Clark, A. W., McCabe, S. 1970. Leadership beliefs of Australian managers. *J. Appl. Psychol.* 54:1–6

30a. Clark, P. 1972. *Organizational Design.* London: Tavistock

31. Clarke, R. O., Fatchett, D. J., Roberts, B. C. 1972. *Workers' Participation in Management in Britain.* London: Heinemann

32. Coffee, D. 1972. Organizational development and training. *Train. Dev. J.* May:12–15

33. Cohen, M. D., March, J. G. 1974. *Leadership and Ambiguity.* New York:McGraw-Hill

34. Cotgrove, S. 1972. Alienation and automation. *Br. J. Sociol.* 23:437–51

35. Couch, P. D., Strother, G. B. 1971. A critical incident evaluation of supervisory training. *Train. Dev. J.* September:6–11

36. Cowell, D. W. 1972. Evaluating the effectiveness of management courses. *Eur. Train.* Spring:55–64

37. Crane, D. P. 1972. Involvement techniques for manager training. *Train. Dev. J.* May:26–29

37a. Cronbach, L. J. 1975. Five decades of public controversy over mental testing. *Am. Psychol.* 30:1–14

38. Crowe, B., Bochner, S., Clark, A. W. 1972. The effects of subordinates' behaviour on managerial style. *Hum. Relat.* 25:215–37

39. Crozier, M. 1972. The relationship between micro and macro sociology. *Hum. Relat.* 25:239–51

40. Culbert, S. 1970. Accelerating laboratory learning through a phase progression model for trainer intervention. *J. Appl. Behav. Sci.* 6:21–38

41. Cummings, L. L., Schwab, D. P. 1973. *Performance in Organizations: Determinants and Appraisal.* Glenview, Ill: Scott, Foresman

42. Cummins, R. C., King, D. C. 1973. The interaction of group size and task structure in an industrial organization. *Personnel Psychol.* 26:87–94

43. Cummins, R. J. 1968. Removing intuition from course development. *Train. Dev. J.* 22:18–30

44. Dahlstrom, E., Ed. 1971. *The Changing Roles of Men and Women.* Boston: Beacon

45. Davis, L. E., Cherns, A., Eds. 1975. *Quality of Working Life: Problems, Prospects and State of the Art,* Vol. 1. New York: Free Press

46. Davis, L. E., Taylor, J. C. 1972. *Design of Jobs: Selected Readings.* Harmondsworth, Middlesex: Penguin

47. Davis, S. M. 1971. *Comparative Management: Organizational and Cultural Perspectives.* New Jersey: Prentice-Hall

48. Doré, R. 1973. *British Factory—Japanese Factory: The Origins of National Diversity in Industrial Relations.* London: Unwin
49. Doré, R., Meacham, M. 1973. Self-concept and interests related to job satisfaction of managers. *Personnel Psychol.* 26:49–59
50. Drenth, P. J. D. 1969. The works' council in The Netherlands. In *Industrial Democracy in The Netherlands.* Meppel, Holland: Boom
50a. Drenth, P. J. D. 1975. La contestation des tests. *Int. Rev. Appl. Psychol.* 24: 17–34
51. Dubin, R. 1969. *Theory Building.* New York: Free Press; Collier Macmillan
52. Dunnette, M. D., Ed. 1973. *Work and Non-work in the Year 2001.* Monterey, Calif: Brooks/Cole
53. Emery, F. E., Trist, E. L. 1973. *Towards a Social Ecology.* London, New York: Plenum
54. Engel, H. M. 1973. *Handbook of Creative Learning Exercises.* Houston: Gulf
55. Engelstad, P. H. 1972. Socio-technical approach to problems of process control. In *Job Design,* ed. L. E. Davis, J. C. Taylor. Harmondsworth, Middlesex: Penguin
56. England, G. W., Agarwal, N. C., Trerise, R. E. 1971. Union leaders and managers: A comparison of value systems. *Ind. Relat.* 10:211–14
57. England, G. W., Lee, R. 1973. Organization size as an influence on perceived organizational goals: A comparative study among American, Japanese and Korean managers. *Organ. Behav. Hum. Perform.* 9:48–58
58. Farnworth, T. 1974. Appraising the appraisals. *Manage. Today,* November: 103, 108, 112
59. Fiedler, F. E. 1967. *A Theory of Leadership Effectiveness.* New York: McGraw-Hill
60. Friedlander, F., Brown, L. D. 1974. Organization development. *Ann. Rev. Psychol.* 25:313–41
61. Gardell, B. 1971. Technology, alienation and mental health in the modern industrial environment. In *Society, Stress and Disease,* Vol. 1, ed. L. Levi. London: Oxford Univ. Press
62. Gavin, J. F., Toole, D. L. 1973. Validity of aptitude tests for "hardcore unemployed." *Personnel Psychol.* 26:139–46
63. Ghiselli, E. E. 1971. *Explorations in Managerial Talent.* Pacific Palisades, Calif: Goodyear
64. Gibbs, G. I., Ed. 1974. *Handbook of Games and Simulation Exercises.* London: Spon
65. Gill, D., Ungerson, B., Thakur, M. 1974. *Performance Appraisal in Perspective: A Survey of Current Practice.* London: Inst. Personnel Manage.
66. Glaser, R. 1968. *Organizational Careers: A Source Book for Theory.* Chicago: Aldine
67. Glaser, R. 1970. Evaluation of instruction and changing educational models. In *The Evaluation of Instruction,* ed. M. Wittrock, D. Wiley. New York: Holt, Rinehart & Winston
68. Glueck, W. F. 1974. Decision making: Organization choice. *Personnel Psychol.* 27:77–93
69. Goldthorpe, J. 1973. A revolution in sociology. *Sociology* 7:449–62
70. Golembiewski, R. T. et al 1971. Changing climate in a complex organization: Interaction between a learning design and an environment. *Acad. Manage. J.* 22:465–81
71. Goodman, P. S., Salipante, P., Paransky, H. 1973. Hiring, training and retaining the hard-core unemployed. *J. Appl. Psychol.* 58:23–33
72. Graves, D., Ed. 1973. *Management Research: A Cross-cultural Perspective.* London: Elsevier
73. Gregory, J. 1972. The training factory. *Ind. Train. Int.* May: 158–60
73a. Gruenfeld, L. W., MacEachron, A. 1975. A cross-national study of cognitive style among managers and technicians. *Int. J. Psychol.* 10:27–54
74. Hamblin, A. C. 1974. *Evaluation and Control of Training.* New York: McGraw-Hill
75. Hardy, C. 1974. Pitfalls of management development. *Personnel Manage.* 6:2, 20–25
76. Harmon, F., Humble, J. 1974. Europe's first social audit. *Profile: ITT in Eur.* 2, Winter:3–5
77. Harrell, T. W., Harrell, M. S. 1973. The personality of MBA's who reach general management early. *Personnel Psychol.* 26:127–34
78. Harrison, R. 1972. How to describe your organization. *Harv. Bus. Rev.* May/June:119–28
79. Hearnshaw, L. S. 1971. *The Psychological and Occupational Aspects of Aging.* Liverpool: Med. Res. Counc.
80. Heilbroner, R. L. 1972. The future of capitalism: The future of industrial organization. *World* 9.12.72

432   HELLER & CLARK

81. Heller, F. A. 1970. Group feed-back analysis as a change agent. *Hum. Relat.* 23:319–33
82. Heller, F. A. 1971. *Managerial Decision-making: A Study of Leadership Styles and Power Sharing among Senior Managers.* London: Tavistock
83. Heller, F. A. 1971. An evaluation of the personnel management function. In *Personnel Management,* ed. D. E. McFarland. Harmondsworth, Middlesex: Penguin
84. Heller, F. A. 1976. The decision process: An analysis of power-sharing at senior organizational levels. In *Handbook of Work, Organization and Society,* ed. R. Dubin. Chicago: Rand McNally
85. Herbst, P. G. 1974. *Sociotechnical Design: Strategies in Multidisciplinary Research.* London: Tavistock
86. Hesseling, P. 1966. *Strategy of Evaluation Research in the Field of Supervisory and Management Training.* Assen, The Netherlands: Van Gorcum
87. Hesseling, P. 1973. Testing a strategy of comparative organization research. See Ref. 72, 261–82
88. Hill, C. P. 1971. *Towards a New Philosophy of Management.* London: Gower
89. Hill, W., Hughes, D. 1974. Variations in leader behavior as a function of task type. *Organ. Behav. Hum. Perform.* 11:83–96
90. Holder, J. J. 1972. Evaluation of an in-company management training programme. *Train. Dev. J.* April:24–27
91. Holzman, I. L., Carpenter, W. A. 1972. The confrontation method in sales training. *Train. Dev. J.* July:6–7
92. Hughes, J., Gregory, D. 1974. Richer jobs for workers. *New Society,* Feb. 14
93. Hunnius, G., Garson, G. D., Case, J., Eds. 1973. *Workers' Control: A Reader on Labor and Social Change.* New York: Random House, Vintage Books
94. Hunt, J. 1972. *The Restless Organization.* Sydney: Wiley
95. Inbar, M., Stoll, C. 1972. *Simulation and Gaming in Social Science.* New York: Free Press
96. Inkeles, A. 1973. A model of modern man: Theoretical and methodological issues. In *Social Science and the New Societies,* ed. N. Hammond. East Lansing, Mich.: Soc. Sci. Res. Bur., Mich. State Univ.
97. Inkson, J. H. K., Payne, R. L., Pugh, D. S. 1967. Extending the occupational environment. *Occup. Psychol.* 41:33–47
98. Jackson, P., Thompson, M. 1972. An evaluation of supervisory training and

organizational change. *Manage. Educ. Dev.* January: 142–48
99. Jacobson, D. 1974. Rejection of the retiree role: A study of female industrial workers in their 50's. *Hum. Relat.* 27:477–92
100. Jaffe, A. J. 1972. The retirement dilemma. *Ind. Gerontol.* 14:1–89
101. James, L. R., Ellison, R. L. 1973. Criterion composites for scientific creativity. *Personnel Psychol.* 26:147–61
102. Joynson, R. B. 1970. The breakdown of modern psychology. *Bull. Br. Psychol. Soc.* 23:261–69
103. Kalt, N. C., Barrett, K. M. 1973. Facilitation of learning from a technical manual. *J. Appl. Psychol.* 58:357–61
104. Kay, H., Warr, P. 1970. Some future developments in occupational psychology. *Occup. Psychol.* 44:293–302
105. Kingdon, D. R. 1973. *Matrix Organizations: Managing Information Technologies.* London: Tavistock
106. Klein, E. B., Astrachan, B. M. 1971. Learning in groups: A comparison of study groups and T-groups. *J. Appl. Behav. Sci.* November/December: 659–83
107. Klein, L. 1974. *New Forms of Work Organization.* Report to the German Institute for Industrial and Social Change. London: Tavistock Inst. Hum. Relat. Doc. SFP 2949, February. To be published in German, 1975
108. Kohn, V. 1970. *Selected Bibliography on Evaluation of Management Training and Development Programs.* New York: Am. Found. Manage. Res.
109. Korman, A. K. 1966. Consideration, initiating structure and organizational criteria: A review. *Personnel Psychol.* 19:349–61
110. Kraut, A. 1975. Cross-national management research. *Acad. Manage. J.* In press
111. Lammers, C. 1973. Two conceptions of democratization in organisations. In *Participation and Self Management,* Vol. 4. Univ. Zagreb, Inst. Soc. Res.
112. Lawrence, P. R., Lorsch, J. W. 1969. *Organization and Environment.* Homewood, Ill: Irwin
113. Leavitt, H. J. 1975. Beyond the analytic manager. *Calif. Manage. Rev.* May/-June
114. Leavitt, H. J., Pinfield, L., Webb, E., Eds. 1974. *Organizations of the Future: Interactions with the External Environment.* New York: Praeger
115. Levitt, T. 1970. The morality of adver-

tising. *Harv. Bus. Rev.* July/August: 84–92
116. Livingston, J. S. 1972. Myth of the well-educated manager. *McKinsey Q.* Summer:33–49
117. Lynch, E. M. 1973. *The Executive Suite —Feminine Style.* New York: Amacom, Div. Am. Manage. Assoc.
118. Maher, J. R. 1971. *New Perspectives in Job Enrichment.* New York: Van Nostrand-Reinhold
119. Maier, N. R. F. 1973. Prior commitment as a deterrent to group problem solving. *Personnel Psychol.* 26:117–26
120. March, J. G., Simon, H. A. 1958. *Organizations.* New York: Wiley
121. Metcalfe, J. L. 1974. Systems models, economic models and the causal texture of organizational environments. *Hum. Relat.* 27:639–63
122. Miles, R. E., Snow, C. C., Pfeffer, J. 1974. Organization-environment: Concepts and issues. *Ind. Relat.* 13:244–64
123. Miner, J. B. 1974. Psychological testing and fair employment practices: A testing program that does not discriminate. *Personnel Psychol.* 27:49–62
124. Moment, D. 1967. Career development: A future oriented historical approach for research and action. *Personnel Admin.* 30:6–12
125. Morris, J., Burgoyne, J. G. 1973. *Developing Resourceful Managers.* London: Inst. Personnel Manage.
126. Mulder, M. 1971. Power equalization through participation. *Admin. Sci. Q.* 16:31–38
126a. Muller, H. 1970. *The search for the qualities essential to advancement in a large industrial group: An exploratory study.* The Hague: Royal Dutch Shell
127. Murray, H., Spink, P. K., Welchman, R., Drake, R. I., Griffiths, J. T. 1972. *Location of Government Review: Human Aspect of Dispersal.* London: Tavistock Inst. Hum. Relat. Doc. No. HRC 794
128. Murray, P. E. 1971. Training BOAC secretaries: evaluation. *Ind. Commer. Train.* July:311–15
129. National Institute of Industrial Psychology 1952. *Joint Consultation in British Industry.* London: Staples
130. Negandhi, A., Prasad, B. 1971. *Comparative Management.* New York: Appleton-Century-Crofts
131. Nelson, C. W., Smith, E. V. 1975. Identification, change and evaluation of system states. *Hum. Relat.* 28. In press
132. O'Brien, G., Fiedler, F., Hewett, T. 1971. The effect of programmed culture

training upon performance of volunteer medical teams in Central America. *Hum. Relat.* 24:209–31
133. O'Reilly, A. P. 1973. Skill requirements: Supervisor-subordinate conflict. *Personnel Psychol.* 26:75–80
134. Perrow, C. 1972. *The Radical Attack on Business: A Critical Analysis.* New York: Harcourt-Brace-Jovanovich
135. Pfeiffer, J. W., Jones, J. E. 1973. *A Handbook of Structured Experiences for Human Relations Training,* Vol. 4, Iowa City: Univ. Assoc.
136. Phillip, D. L. 1973. *Abandoning Method.* San Francisco: Jossey Bass
137. Pitfield, M., Rees, F. M. 1972. Team-teaching—can it aid the integration of management education? *Manage. Educ. Dev.* August:98–106
138. Popper, K. R. 1945. *The Open Society and its Enemies.* London: Routledge & Kegan Paul
139. Porter, L. W., Lawler, E. E. 1968. *Managerial Attitudes and Performance.* Homewood, Ill: Irwin
140. Pym, D. 1973. The politics and ritual of appraisals. *Occup. Psychol.* 47:231–35
141. Rackham, N. 1971. Mixing: A new technique in training. *Ind. Commer. Train.* August:360–68
142. Randell, D. A., Packard, M. P. A., Shaw, R. L., Slater, A. J. 1974. *Staff Appraisal.* London: Inst. Personnel Manage.
143. Rapoport, R. N. 1970. *Mid-career Development.* London: Tavistock
144. Ray, J. J. 1973. Task orientation and interaction orientation scales. *Personnel Psychol.* 26:61–73
145. Reddin, W. 1970. *Managerial Effectiveness.* New York: McGraw-Hill
146. Ritchie, J. B. 1974. Supervision. See Ref. 168a
147. Roberts, K. 1967. The entry into employment: An approach towards a general theory. *Sociol. Rev.* 5:165–83
148. Roberts, K. 1970. On looking at an elephant: An evaluation of cross-cultural research related to organizations. *Psychol. Bull.* 74:327–50
149. Roeber, R. J. C. 1973. *The Organization in a Changing Environment.* Reading, Mass: Addison-Wesley
150. Rokeach, M. 1973. *The Nature of Human Values.* London: Cassell, Collier-Macmillan
151. Rus, V. 1972. The limits of organized participation. In *Participation and Self Management,* Vol. 2. Univ. Zagreb, Inst. Soc. Res.

152. Rusmore, J. T. 1973. Position description factors and executive promotion. *Personnel Psychol.* 26:135–38

153. Salemi, E. C., Monahan, J. B. 1970. The psychological contract of employment. *Personnel J.* 49:986–93

154. Schmidt, F. L., Berner, J. G., Hunter, J. E. 1973. Racial differences in validity of employment tests: reality or illusion. *J. Appl. Psychol.* 58:5–9

155. Schumacher, E. F. 1974. *Small is Beautiful.* London: Sphere Books, Abacus

156. Scott, D. J. R. 1972. Creative management: The arts side of business education. *Manage. Educ. Dev.* August: 113–24

157. Sheppard, H. L., Herrick, N. Q. 1972. *Where Have All the Robots Gone? Worker Dissatisfaction in the '70s.* New York: Free Press

158. Silvern, L. C. 1972. *Systems Engineering Applied to Training.* Houston: Gulf

159. Simon, H. 1960. *Models of Man.* New York: Harper

160. Singer, E. J. 1974. *Effective Management Coaching.* London: Inst. Personnel Manage.

161. Sirota, D., Greenwood, M. 1971. Understand your overseas workforce. *Harv. Bus. Rev.* January/February: 53–60

162. Skinner, B. F. 1975. The steep and thorny way to a science of behavior. *Am. Psychol.* 30:42–49

163. Soelberg, P. 1967. Unprogrammed decision making: Job choice. *Ind. Manage. Rev.* 1–12

164. Sofer, C. 1970. *Men in Mid-Career.* London: Cambridge Univ. Press

165. Sorcher, M., Goldstein, A. P. 1972. A behavior modeling approach in training. *Personnel Admin.* March/April: 35–41

166. Starbuck, W. H. 1975. Organizations and their environments. See Ref. 4

167. Strachan, I. 1971. *The Training and Development of Salesmen.* London: Kogan Page

168. Strauss, G. 1963. Some notes on power equalization. In *The Social Science of Organizations,* ed. H. J. Leavitt. Englewood Cliffs, NJ: Prentice-Hall

168a. Strauss, G. 1974. Job satisfaction, motivation and job design. In *Organizational Behavior: Research Issues,* ed. G. Strauss, R. Miles, C. Snow, A. Tannenbaum. Madison: Univ. Wisconsin. Ind. Relat. Res. Assoc. Ser.

169. Streib, G. F., Schneider, C. J. 1971. *Retirement in American Society: Impact and Process.* Ithaca, N.Y.: Cornell Univ. Press

170. Tannenbaum, A., Kavcic, B., Rosner, M., Vianello, M., Wieser, G. 1974. *Hierarchy in Organizations.* San Francisco: Jossey-Bass

171. Thurley, K., Wirdenius, H. 1973. *Supervision: A Reappraisal.* London: Heineman

172. Triandis, H. 1972. *The Analysis of Subjective Culture.* New York: Wiley, Interscience

173. Trist, E. L. 1976. Action research and adaptive planning. See Ref. 29

174. United States Air Force Manual 50–2, 1970. *US Instructional System Development*

175. Vickers, G. 1972. *Freedom in a Rocking Boat: Changing Values in an Unstable Society.* Harmondsworth, Middlesex: Penguin

176. Vroom, V., Yetton, P. 1973. *Leadership and Decision Making.* Univ. Pittsburgh Press

177. Walker, K. 1974. Workers' participation in management—problems, practice and prospects. *Int. Inst. Labour Stud. Bull.* 12:3–35

178. Wallace, H. 1972. A wasteland of potential managerial talent. *Rydges* September:18–22

179. Wallace, W. M. 1974. Where productivity slumps. *Manage. Today* November:62–65

180. Walton, R. D. 1974. Innovative restructuring of work. In *The Worker and the Job,* ed. J. W. Rosow. Englewood Cliffs, NJ: Prentice-Hall

181. Warr, P. 1973. Towards a more human psychology. *Bull. Br. Psychol. Soc.* 26:1–7

182. Warr, P., Bird, M., Rackham, N. 1970. *Evaluation of Management Training: A Practical Framework, with Cases, for Evaluating Training Needs and Results.* London: Gower

183. Wengler, W. 1974. A legal opinion concerning the admissibility under international law of applying the proposed German co-determination law to American investments in the Federal Republic of Germany. Publ. by American Chamber of Commerce in Germany

184. Whitelaw, M. 1972. *The Evaluation of Management Training: A Review.* London: Inst. Personnel Manage.

185. Wickens, J. D. 1968. Management by objectives: An appraisal. *J. Manage. Stud.* 5:365–79

186. Wilson, A. T. M. 1972. How to ap-

praise. *Manage. Today* December: 99–100, 104, 108

187. Wilson, N. A. B. 1973. *On the Quality of Working Life. Manpower Paper No. 7,* Dep. Employment. London: Her Majesty's Stationery Off.

188. Wofford, J. C. 1971. Managerial behaviour, situational factors, and productivity and morale. *Admin. Sci. Q.* 16:10–17

189. Wonderlic, E. F. & Associates 1972. *Negro Norms: A Study of 38,452 Job Applicants for Affirmative Action Programs.* Northfield, Ill: Wonderlic

190. *Work in America. Report of a Special Task Force to the Secretary of Health, Education and Welfare.* 1973. Cambridge, Mass: MIT Press

191. Yankelovich, D. 1974. The meaning of work. See Ref. 180, 19–47

HUMAN ABILITIES: A REVIEW OF RESEARCH AND THEORY IN THE EARLY 1970s

260

John L. Horn[1]

Department of Psychology, University of Denver, Denver, Colorado 80210

INTRODUCTION

Okay, so what are they saying in the study of human abilities? Granted that the "they" in this question is a 100-headed Hydra, is there any concert in the movements of this body such that we can make sense out of where it has been and where it is likely to meander tomorrow? Without in the least presuming to have discerned such harmony (if it exists) in the body of published material which has been presented since about 1971 in this area, the effort here nevertheless has been one of listening intently for any unification of thinking that is likely to carry forth into noteworthy clarifications. As in previous reviews of this area by Leona Tyler in 1972, Edwin Fleishman in 1969, and George Ferguson in 1965, the focus has been on substantively based theory development, critical evaluations, and research results derived mainly from study of individual differences, rather than on logical analyses, methods of measurement, tests, techniques of data analysis, description of norms, and textbook treatments of the subjects. Inevitably, of course, one will find spillover of the latter into the former: at least what looks to be critical evaluation, say, to the reviewer will be seen by some others as preoccupation with techniques for data analysis or with textbook treatment. So be it. In this respect also it must be acknowledged that the review is highly selective. The aim has been to develop a few major points adequately, rather than touch only briefly on a larger number of the important issues. Entire areas (e.g. physiological correlates) are thus omitted. The references cited are in many cases only illustrative, not the full list upon which the review evaluation is based. A larger, more fully documented draft of the review can be obtained from the author on request. In sum the aim has been to detect major trends rather than provide a full catalog of specific findings, to interpret history rather than to record it.

[1]Prepared under support from the National Science Foundation, GB-41452, and the Army Research Institute, DACH19-74-G-0012. I acknowledge valuable comment and criticism made by my colleagues, G. Donaldson, J. Pisarowicz, J. Undheim, C. Ward, and J. Loehlin.

437

ORGANIZATION AND DIFFERENTIATION

A major issue in this area continued to be one of specifying the basic cognitive processes, identifying the primary abilities, describing the essential functions (call it what you will) of intellectual performances. This is the task of finding a good way to talk about the ways in which humans process information, form concepts, solve problems, acquire and express knowledge, use language, etc. It is, in part, a problem of finding useful systems for simplifying. The human's intellectual capacities are so immensely varied, the sheer complexity of the variety overwhelms the human's capacity to comprehend. The variety of systems proposed to deal with this complexity is also imposing.

One may roughly classify this variety of systems in terms of two broad kinds of observational approaches and associated theories: (a) systems derived primarily from analyses of (observations of) interrelationships among samples of different performances. The systems based upon factor analyses of test behavior are examples here; (b) systems derived from analyses of behaviors appearing at, and being in some sense characteristic of, different ages in development. Piagetian systems are the most popular current exemplars in this category. The two kinds of systems need not be regarded as in competition. Indeed, to a considerable extent each should be complementary of and enhance the other. Unfortunately the two approaches often are carried forth in separate and somewhat opposed camps of workers. In the review period, however, there were a few signs of cross-fertilization between these two camps. These signs will be identified primarily in sections on development. These follow the section immediately below, in which the focus is on systems based upon psychometric analyses of broad collections of intellectual behaviors.

Concomitant Variational Systems

In the camps concerned primarily with interrelationships among ability performances, the factor analytic machines were busy. There were no fewer than 50 such studies (I got tired of counting them). These represent a great variety of tests, administered in a considerable variety of samples of subjects, and factored in a substantial variety of ways to suggest a rather bewildering variety of primary-level, second-level, and tertiary-level factors and concepts. Indeed, there was even some factoring of items within tests to suggest what might have to be regarded as subprimary factors and concepts (112). It is difficult to communicate the sense of all this work. The effort here will be to integrate findings using concepts of primary abilities and broad abilities.

There is, of course, no sure consensus as to what constitutes a primary-level or secondary-level or tertiary-level concept adumbrated by factor analytic (or other) research on human abilities. Depending on the sampling of variables and subjects and methods, for example, the results from a factor analytic study may indicate G, the general intelligence dimension, as a first-order, second-order, third-order (or higher-order) factor. This makes it very awkward to integrate findings from different studies in terms of whether or not they replicate primary or second-order findings. Nevertheless there is a bit of convention growing up in the field such that investigators are likely to use the terms "primary abilities" or "primary factors" when they have reference to factors of relatively narrow scope, factors of the kind represented in the French-Ekstrom-Price (FEP) kit of reference tests or in the structure-of-intellect (SI) model, and to use terms such as "broad abilities," or "second-order dimensions" when the reference is to rather highly variegated factors and concepts, such as are indicated by dimensions among primary factors. For example, if a battery comprised of one test per factor from the FEP kit is factored, the results are likely to be interpreted in accordance with theories pertaining to second-order abilities—fluid intelligence (Gf) and crystallized intelligence (Gc)—even though the factors, technically speaking, are defined at the first order of analysis. Similarly, the factors among the Wechsler scales are usually interpreted as representing broad dimensions involving several distinct processes, as in theories of verbal-educational (v:ed) and practical-mechanical-spatial (m:k) achievements. A major problem with trying to use this rather loose convention is that it is by no means always observed, with the result that factors which in one study are regarded as "primaries" are elsewhere regarded as second-order factors. And there are other problems. Nevertheless, in an overview summary of the kind attempted here, it has seemed useful to work with such consensus as does exist in specifying primary and second-order abilities.

PRIMARY ABILITIES

Structure   There were at least half a dozen studies verifying in one way or another —as across different cultures, different age levels, etc—that indeed the factors indicating primary abilities can be replicated if an investigator is moderately conscientious about obtaining good marker tests, administering them well in samples of sufficient size, and doing the factoring in a reasonable way. A study by Hakstian & Cattell (66) provides a particularly definitive example of this kind of demonstration. In a sample of 343 young adults, they used targeted rotation with three marker variables per factor to identify the abilities known as Verbal Comprehension (V), Induction (I), Number (N), Spatial Orientation (S), Perceptual (Clerical) Speed (P), Flexibility of Closure (Cf), Speed of Closure (Cs), Span Memory (Ms), Meaningful Memory (Mm), Associative Memory (Ma), Mechanical Knowledge (Mk), Aiming (Ai), Ideational Fluency (Fi), Word Fluency (Fw), Originality (O), Divergent Production of Semantic Classes (DMC), and Spelling (Sp). Each of these factors had been indicated in previous work, but not all in any one previous study. There had been doubts, therefore, as to whether the factors represented distinctly independent (within-sample) abilities. This study doesn't lay all of these doubts to rest. One would like to see the data analyzed with nontargeted rotation, for example, and to know how the squared multiple correlations of each factor with the others compares with the factor internal consistencies. But the study is helpful in indicating the kinds of elementary abilities one can use to help describe human intellect. Hakstian and Cattell also produced evidence for abilities that had not been well indicated (as factors) in previous work, namely, Esthetic Judgment (E), and Representational Drawing (Rd).

In other developments along these lines Flores & Evans (54) provided evidence that V, I, N, S, and Ma appear in samples as diverse as Filipino and Canadian children of about the same age, and in England a test representing the V, I, N, S, Ma, and Fi primaries was developed and standardized on a sample of 13,000 children (193).

There were a number of studies of this kind to suggest that by the criterion of judgment that loading patterns are similar, there is replication stability for many of the primary abilities factors which, according to the FEP review and several more recent reviews (80, 141, 158), had been indicated by previous research. This work can be seen to be part of a broad effort to establish confidence in findings by demonstrating replication and hardiness over different samples, different laboratories, different periods of history, etc. Such demonstrations need not be denigrated but they do have a number of limitations. Some of these limitations pertain to the fact that factoring procedures and judgments that replication has or has not occurred are subjective in several notable ways. A study by Harris & Harris (68) represents one of a number of efforts designed to reduce subjectivity in demonstration of the existence and independence of primary abilities.

Harris & Harris developed a method of comparable common factors (CCF) to help avoid errors of inference. In this method, analyses with several different but well-accepted factoring procedures are conducted on a given set of data. The factors which replicate, as it were, over these different analyses meet the CCF criterion. If results meet this test in addition to the traditional test—that factors be hardy across notable variations in sample, as in, say, samples of boys and samples of girls—then the claim that they represent stable phenomena is further enhanced. Harris & Harris found the abilities referred to as V, I, Ma, P, and Fw were thus stable for substantial samples of fifth grade boys and girls. This finding may not surprise anyone who believed the FEP summaries, but it may reassure them. It speaks also to questions about how early in development the distinctions among primary abilities can be reliably made. Perhaps not so reassuring, or else questioning the utility of the CFF criterion, were findings that: (a) Number Facility (N) met the criterion in the sample of boys, but not in the sample of girls, and (b) a factor which had some of the qualities of Spatial Orientation (S) and/or Flexibility of Closure (Cf) did not meet the criterion in either of the gender subsamples. Thus there is suggestion that CCF sets a stringent test, perhaps overly or wrongly stringent.

In the usual cross-laboratory and cross-occasion study, a factor is regarded as a replication of another if the two appear to represent the same kind of psychological function. The judgmental criterion in this respect usually permits somewhat different variables to be interpreted as representing similar functions. However, a criterion of replication can require that variables derived from the same measurement operations (i.e. the same tests) have precisely the same pattern of nonzero and zero factor coefficients in both (or more) studies. When the criterion is regarded in this way, the problem can be referred to as one of factor invariance. There were attacks from this vantage point on questions pertaining to the sampling stability of primary-level abilities.

Bechtoldt (9), building upon his previous analyses of data gathered by the Thurstones in the 1940s, used the confirmatory and cross-sample comparison procedures developed by Jöreskog (105) to test the stability of V, I, S, N, Ma, and Fw. An hypothesis that each variable was salient in one and only one factor would have to be rejected in these data. Invariance was indicated, however, when the tests were run in respect to hypotheses based upon a previously determined oblique simple-structure in which about one-half of the variables had nonhyperplane loadings on two factors. Moreover, ". . . the results of the simultaneous two-sample analyses indicated not only stability of a first-order unique simple-structure solution but also some degree of invariance of the second-order structure" (105, p. 324).

The Jöreskog procedures were used also by McGaw & Jöreskog (128) with four samples of subjects (each of very substantial sample size, N) selected from Project Talent data by dichotomizing SES and G and cross-classifying to get the Hi-Hi, Hi-Lo, Lo-Hi, and Lo-Lo combinations. The results in this case indicated that a common solution with the same pattern of factor loadings on the same number of common factors could be obtained for all samples. As in the work of Bloxom (14) and the Jöreskog and Bechtoldt studies cited above, it was noted that the question of factor invariance could be considered in respect to invariance of variable uniquenesses, factor variances, and factor intercorrelations, as well as in respect to factor loadings. As might well be expected from considerations of effects likely to be produced by the particular sampling of subjects in this experiment, McGaw & Jöreskog found differences when they looked at the question of invariance within this more demanding framework. The conclusion for purposes here, however, is that this study established invariance and independence at the primary level for V, P, a factor representing skill in the mechanics of English writing (punctuation, spelling, etc), hereafter referred to as Ve, and a factor which probably would line up with either Visualization (Vz) or Mechanical Comprehension (Mk), most likely the former.

Subjectivity of a different kind was considered in the work of Bratfisch (24) and his co-workers. They completed a series of studies suggesting that the stability and independence of factors is partly a reflection of, or at least is reflected in, the way people (subjects and experimenters) classify—i.e. perceive—ability tests problems. Multidimensional scaling analyses were used on similarity judgments (about quality rather than difficulty) of pairs of items drawn from different primary factor tests. The resulting subjective dimensions were found to correspond to the V, R, S, N, and P factors indicated by the usual analyses of individual differences in performances (i.e. the objective factors).

Guilford & Hoepfner (64) presented a definitive reanalysis of research designed to provide support for the structure-of-intellect (SI) theory of organization among primary abilities. This theory continued to be under attack, however, principally on grounds that the methods of proof used in the supportive research have been overly subjective (29, 69, 83, 84). Subjectivity in this instance refers to overfactoring to assure as many factors as desired, and targeted rotation to assure maximum correspondence between results and the desired factor pattern. It was demonstrated that when subjectivity comparable to that employed in SI studies was used on the data of these studies, but with randomly determined hypotheses, the pseudo-support obtained for the random hypotheses was very nearly as good as that claimed for SI hypotheses in the original studies (83, 84). Such findings led to a conclusion that much of the evidence presented in support of SI theory is not compelling.

As criticisms of SI theory flourished (32, 51, 125, as well as above), so also did the idea that a faceted organizational system might be useful for comprehending the stable findings of primary ability factors and for indicating the outlines of an adequate theory of cognitive functioning. Guttman (65), for example, modified his previous statements of such a system. The result is a 3 X 3 model in which contents or "languages of communication" (verbal, numerical, pictorial) are crossed with types of tasks (rule-inferring, rule-applying, achievement) to suggest a nine-factor system. Harris & Harris (70) suggested a 7 by 3 by 2 system in which the contents are Verbal-semantic, Pictorial-semantic, Number-semantic, Figural, Number-symbolic, Letter-symbolic, and Word-form, the types of tasks are Classifying, Excluding, and Naming, and a "Nature-of-exemplars" dimension is added, the two categories of this being Relations and Things. But perhaps the most ambitious of such systems was developed by Carroll (31). This was derived in part from Hunt's distributive memory model and Newell's ideas about production systems. In very general terms the theory supposes that in some measure individual differences in intellectual performances can be accounted for in terms of differences in sensory buffer systems (visual, auditory, etc), three kinds of memory (short term, intermediate term and long term, STM, ITM, and LTM respectively), several kinds of contents of LTM (e.g. visual representational, lexicosemantic, quantity), and several kinds of control processes or operations or strategies (e.g. address LTM to store or to retrieve, address attention to visual or auditory modality). To illustrate application of the theory Carroll classified the 24 replicated primary abilities of the FEP summary.

As with the Guilford SI model, there are notable problems in specifying the detailed empirical implications of Carroll's theory. It seems, however, that the theory has value relative to the many ad hoc theories which abound in this area. It represents a very serious effort to relate individual differences in performance to a unified theory of cognitive processes, as indicated not only by study of individual differences but also by the long history of controlled manipulative research on such processes as memory, learning, problem solving, strategies, concept formation, and language use. It should be interesting to see the research generated by considerations of Carroll's theory in the future.

Differentiation   Reinert (145) provided a review of research on the developmental differentiation of primary abilities, and there was empirical work pertaining to questions in this area. It would not be correct to say that major issues were resolved by either of these kinds of efforts, but some suggestive findings were produced, some possibly useful questions were raised, and some interesting approaches to solutions of the problems were tried out. An example of the empirical work is a study by Fitzgerald, Nesselroade & Baltes (53). These investigators used targeted rotation (but with careful attention to factor intercorrelations) to demonstrate that V, I, N, and S are distinguishable no later in development than about age 12–13 and remain clearly separable at ages 14–15 and 16–18. Khan (110) took a similar approach but used nontargeted (namely, varimax) rotations. He found that whereas all three marker variables per factor were appropriately salient and indicated independent V, N, S, and P factors at age about 17–18, and V and N were similarly clear and separate at ages 15–16 and 13–14, only two of three markers were appropriately salient in S and P at these last-mentioned age levels. The differences between the Khan results and those of Fitzgerald et al are not striking, but they are sufficient to suggest that one should remain alert to the fact that apparent consistencies or inconsistencies in findings can represent mainly agreement or disagreements in the rotational philosophies of investigators, rather than information about childhood development. This caution should be applied also in considerations of similarities or differences in findings involving ethnic group differences or other differences in sampling of subjects.

Nishikawa (139) looked at the age-differentiation hypothesis in the traditional way by considering the variance on G (the first principal component) at different age levels, but he introduced a few interesting twists. For example, he factored in adjacent age subgroups, and in these factorings he tried out different sets of items chosen on the basis of different rationales. His results suggest that one should use the same items in adjacent-age comparisons if he wants his results to support the age-differentiation hypothesis, but one should use different (but age-appropriate) items in adjacent-age comparisons if the aim is to refute the hypothesis. Pursuing this conception of the problem, the results of Ross (154) suggest that those seeking support for the age-differentiation hypothesis should choose samples of upper social-economic status (SES), while if the aim is to refute, samples should be chosen of lower SESs. This finding is not necessarily consistent with those obtained prior to the review period (see 145). We see then that the age-differentiation hypothesis remains a bone of contention.

BROAD ABILITIES

Creativity, verbal productive thinking, and intelligence   At the level of specifying abilities of a more pervasive nature than the primaries, many of the efforts in the review period can be classified in one of two ways: (*a*) as demonstrating useful ways in which general intelligence, G, can be analyzed in terms of distinct, but still broad, component abilities having different construct validities; or (*b*) demonstrating important abilities that are independent of intelligence as this is most often conceived. The first emphasis is represented by efforts to develop a verified theory of fluid and crystallized intelligence. It is represented also in work on Jensen's ideas about two levels of intelligence. The second emphasis is exemplified by efforts to define a creativity dimension or dimensions that is (are) quite different from intelligence.

In some respects, both of these lines of research are little more than restatements of the findings and the theories, developed at what was regarded as the primary level, and in hierarchical analyses, in a much earlier period of history. For example, the Gc dimension is in some respects only a swollen V, Gf is only a swollen R, and the memory factor identified in Thurstone's pioneering studies is at the core of, if it is not the essence of, Jensen's level I intelligence. Yet the second-order analyses may be helpful in showing the breadth of concepts adumbrated at the primary level (often treated as little more than parts in a catalog). Also, relative to much of the earlier work on primary abilities, the research on broad abilities is directed more surely at issues of development, at implications for understanding information processing generally, and at improving practical applications (as in diagnosis). Thus while it is useful to remain aware that old ground is being retreaded in much of the work on broad abilities, nevertheless there seem to be some important new developments represented by this work.

It has been known for years that various verbal fluency primary factors—e.g. Fi, Fw, Expressional Fluency (Fe), Associational Fluency (Fa)—are only lowly correlated ($\approx$0.30) with other verbal skills which are accepted as measures of G—skills such as those represented in V, Ve, General Reasoning, R (as in Word Problems) and Formal Reasoning, Rs (as in syllogisms or critical reading tasks). It has been known, too, that the fluency factors are lowly correlated with the primaries representing reasoning with figures or non-word symbols (Vz, S, I)—i.e. other major indicants of G. Since the early 1960s, however, when fluency primaries and other verbal productive thinking (VPT) tasks came under the label creativity measures, much has been made of this independence in arguments that creativity either is or is not independent of intelligence. There were several good reviews of this research (113, 135, 189–191) and some new integrative empirical analyses. The upshot of this work is to indicate that we now know with substantial confidence what we knew before—that verbal fluency is largely independent of, although positively correlated with, that which most commonly passes for intelligence.

The work demonstrating the distinction between VPT and G is perhaps best represented by the dissertation research of Murphy (135). His was a reanalysis of the data of Ward, Fee, Cropley & Maslany, Guilford and his co-workers, Wallach & Kogan, Wallach & Wing, and Getzels & Jackson, as well as analysis of data which Murphy himself gathered on a sample of high school students. P. E. Vernon (189–191) also completed an extensive series of studies bearing on the question of independence, and there were a number of other somewhat similar contributions (39, 56, 61, 156). To summarize briefly this entire batch of research is to ensure that several notable distinctions will be sloughed over, but nevertheless a general conclusion is that the following sets of measures stand apart in broad correlational clusters or factors and thus represent relatively independent, but broad, abilities or classes of achievements:

VPT: Verbal Productive Thinking.   Facility is producing verbal responses in tests such as those which require one to list similarities, improvements, or alternate uses of common objects, write about consequences or problems associated with unusual events, write interpretations of lines or simple figures or topics, or provide multiple definitions of a given word. This dimension is referred to as indicating creativity in the writings of Cropley, Kogan, Murphy, Torrance, Wallach, and others who have done the major work in this area. To help avoid begging questions to be considered later, the dimension here is labeled Verbal Productive Thinking.

Gc: Crystallized Intelligence.   Awareness of concepts and terms pertaining to a broad variety of topics, as measured in general information and vocabulary tests and in tests which measure knowledge in science, mechanics, social studies, English literature, mathematics, and a variety of other areas. It is also manifested in the Information, Vocabulary, Comprehension, Similarities and, to a lesser extent. Arithmetic subtests of the Wechsler scales (34, 75, 125, 144). This is the dimension most likely to be referred to as indicating intelligence. In much of the British work it is labeled verbal-educational (v:ed) intelligence.

Gf: Fluid Intelligence.   Facility in reasoning, particularly in figural and non-word symbolic materials, as indicated in tests such as letter series, matrices, mazes, figure classifications, and word groupings, as well as the block designs, picture arrangements, object assembly, and picture completion subtests of the Wechsler scales. This dimension also is likely to be referred to as indicating intelligence. Some characterize it as nonverbal intelligence (although verbal tests can measure it) or performance IQ. In the British work it is known as spatial-perceptual-practical intelligence (k:m).

In some of the research on VPT all three of these dimensions were distinguished. Other work was directed at demonstrating only the distinction between a VPT dimension and a combined Gf-Gc dimension. As Kogan (113) noted in one review of this area, the distinction between a VPT dimension and intelligence (usually $G = Gf + Gc$ in childhood studies) has been demonstrated all along the childhood development period from about kindergarten level into young adulthood. Other work (61, 169) suggested that the distinction is less clear in the lower ranges of ability than at higher levels. Often the VPT dimension was distinguished from Gf and Gc in studies that were not particularly focused upon making the distinction. In general the distinction appears to be hardy.

The reliability and particularly the validity of measurement of the VPT dimension is probably facilitated by generating a playful, relaxed atmosphere in the testing situation, as Wallach and Kogan had stressed when the issues about the independence of creativity and G first began to be debated. However, it is now reasonably clear that it is by no means necessary to go to special lengths to ensure a playful testing situation in order to demonstrate the independence noted above (at least this is true in samples of older children and young adults: with preschool children it may be advisable to attend carefully to the Wallach-Kogan cautions). P. E. Vernon (188) showed, however, that scores obtained under relaxed conditions had somewhat larger variances and correlations with other variables, particularly variables relating to creativity, than comparable scored obtained under "formal" testing conditions. Thus it can be said that the variables obtained under the relaxed conditions are more valid than those obtained under "formal" conditions. In part, however, this finding may represent the fact that reliability and validity tend to increase with the amount of time spent, and data gathered, in measurement (the relaxed administration required more time and produced more responses than the formal task presentation). In other work on the situational stability of measures of VPT, Ward, Kogan & Pankove (195) demonstrated that while incentives such as rewards of money increase ideational productivity, they do so uniformly for most subjects and therefore the rank order of subjects is not changed very much by introducing special rewards in the (standardized) testing situation (cf 67).

There were indications also (135, 181, 189) that a useful and stable distinction can be made between VPT in producing unusual and appropriate (satisfying to the receiver) responses on the one hand and simply producing many responses on the other hand. If tests allow both high productivity per se, and productivity of only distinct, original, unusual exemplars, and if scoring is carefully done to distinguish between these two forms of responses, then the VPT dimension can be split apart into two factors, each of which has higher internal consistency than the correlation between the two. The first of these factors is perhaps equivalent to the primary ability labeled Originality (O) in the FEP system. The second factor might be labeled simply Fluency (F). Originality is more closely linked to theory about creativity than is either the VPT dimension or the F factor. Whether or not it better represents the construct in actual measurement is a question which has yet to be clearly answered by empirical research (see 182).

There were also some indications that it may be useful to distinguish between what Murphy referred to as figural and verbal subfactors of the VPT. The usefulness of such a distinction was suggested not only by Murphy's findings indicating psychometric independence, but also by results of another study (157) indicating that verbal VPT correlated significantly with Torrance biographical measures of creativity in composition writing, dramatics, and the life sciences, but figural VPT did not correlate significantly with these or other biographical indicants of creativity.

In this context figural VPT does *not* refer to tests in which one must make drawings out of a few lines, or remove lines to make specified figures, or make aesthetic judgments about designs and drawings, as in creativity tests such as those of Meier and Barron or the Figural divergent production (DFP) tasks of Guilford's laboratory. Instead the figural VPT tasks are those in which one writes about figural materials, as in the Wallach-Kogan Lines test. It is clear from a number of studies that the DFP tasks are not a component of the VPT dimension (64, 80, 156, 190, 191). The Circles test of the Torrance battery, for example, in which the respondent draws a few lines to make a circle look like something else (e.g. a baseball), has only very low correlations with VPT tests (39, 64, 181, 182, 191). DFP may be indicative of creativity as measured in biographical questionnaires, however (182, 183).

While the evidence is compelling in indicating that VPT is largely independent of major dimensions of intelligence, it does not speak so clearly to the question of whether or not VPT should be regarded as a principal indicant of creativity. There is doubt that the dimension is any more related to what is commonly believed to be creativity in real life than are the dimensions of intelligence or other factors. Since G and VPT are positively correlated, one can easily get into discussions about whether it is mainly G or mainly an aspect of creativity-independent-of-G which accounts for a correlation between a VPT measure and an outcome which is readily accepted as indicating creativity. But how does one ask the important questions here in ways that permit of reasonable and compelling answers?

One way to deal with these issues is to ask that VPT show a different pattern of predictions than is shown by measures of intelligence, a pattern that specifies a meaningful and useful distinction between being creative and being intelligent in real life. P. E. Vernon (189) approached the issues in this way by asking what are the correlations between various VPT measures and a variety of achievement and adaptation measures after G (with emphasis on Gc) has been partialled out? His results suggest that in an age range of from 13 to 15 years the answer to this question may be rather different for boys than for girls,[2] but that in either case VPT does not provide very much independent variance in prediction of teachers' ratings (grades) in most school subjects, teachers' ratings of imagination and originality, or peer sociometric evaluations. Notable exceptions to this generalization were predictions for the quality of essay and story writing, particularly macabre story writing. Here the VPT measures added substantially (partial r's of 0.30) to the prediction obtained with Gc. Even in this case, however, teacher ratings of the stories and essays for imagination and creativity had only very small residual correlations with VPT after Gc had been partialled out.

Vernon's results are generally consistent with short-term (1 week to 9 months) and long-term predictions found in other work in which VPT generally was not pitted against Gf or Gc or G (39, 115, 156, 181). All in all, findings of several studies suggest that: (a) VPT correlates about as highly with school grades as it correlates with Gc (≈ 0.30); (b) it correlates somewhat more highly (perhaps 0.40 to 0.50) with composite biographical measures of creative achievements; (c) perhaps most of this latter correlation represents a relationship between writing achievements and VPT; (d) these validity coefficients are about the same for *quality* measures of achievements as for *quantity* measures; and (e) the predictions from Originality and Fluency subscores of VPT are about the same on an average over several studies and several criteria, although they fluctuate considerably. When the emphasis in prediction is on achievement as such, as when tests of literary comprehension or critical reading are used as criteria, then a stepwise multiple regression which starts with the best predictors is likely to begin with Gc, pick up a bit with Gf, and leave little or no significant prediction for VPT (177, 189). This generalization needs to be tried out in a wider array of circumstances than were represented by the research reviewed here, however, before it can be accepted as really well established. When teacher and peer ratings for creativity and intelligence are treated as the criteria to be predicted, the results suggest that VPT predicts creativity a bit better than it predicts intelligence, while the reverse is true for measures of G or Gf or Gc (156, 191). The differences of this kind were found to be very small, however.

One of the problems with this last-mentioned kind of research is that raters often have difficulty in separating their judgments about creativity and intelligence. Confusion or overlap in such judgments probably exists partly within subjects (the same characteristic being accepted as indicative of both attributes) and partly between subjects (what one judge calls creativity another calls intelligence). To the extent that such confusion exists in the criteria, there is bound to be difficulty in demonstrating convergent-discriminant validity. A study by Rossman & Gollob (155)

---

[2]Incidentally, girls and women consistently score higher in VPT than boys and men in most studies.

provided some help in dealing with this problem. They demonstrated that in order to maximize the judgmental distinction, one should provide the judges with, and get them to focus on, diverse kinds of information, some of which clearly represents intelligence and some of which clearly represents creativity conceived of as independent of intelligence. At a more general level the Rossman-Gollob findings remind us that convergent-discriminant validity for predictors can be only as good as the discriminations made in the criteria. This seems obvious enough, logically; yet it is probably more difficult to assure in the practice of research than many believe, with the result that creativity and intelligence criteria tend to be poorly distinguished.

This review only scratches the surface of interesting work done on creativity during the review period. It seems likely that this will continue to be a major line of research on intellectual processes.

Visualization and field independence   In work on what is known as field independence (identified by others names, too), the construct has been made operational with tasks such as embedded figures (EFT), rod-and-frame (RFT) and tilting-room-and-chair (TRC). The EFT is a version of the Gottschaldt figures tests which appeared as a principal marker for the Flexibility of Closure (Cf) primary ability in the early work of Thurstone and Thurstone on perceptual abilities. Several studies since the work of the Thurstones have established that Cf can be distinguished at the primary level from S, Vz, Cs, and perhaps other spatial abilities, as well as from the factors which are most readily accepted as indicants of intelligence. When analyses pertain to concepts more general than the primary abilities, the various spatial tasks of Cf, Cs, S, and Vz tend to hang together in what can be referred to as a general visualization (Gv) dimension which seems to be at least somewhat distinct from the Gf, and is clearly distinct from Gc and VPT. The distinction of Gv from G and VPT was shown convincingly in a study by P. E. Vernon (192) in which the focus was on the measurement basis for the concept of field independence.[3]

Vernon's analyses indicated that the major portion of the reliable variance of Witkin's EFT and Thurstone's concealed figures (each measuring the Cf primary) is in a Gv (or Gf) dimension, but that RFT tasks may involve a visuokinesthetic function that is largely independent of Gv, G, and VPT. This finding thus conforms with earlier results indicating that RFT, TRC, and body adjustment measures have only low correlations with Cf markers (EFT, etc). This had been the indication in Witkin's studies as well as in work of investigators who are less enamored than Witkin with the concept of field independence.

Vernon's analyses suggested also that RFT has different construct validity correlations than do EFT and Gv. When G was held constant and various Gv markers were taken as indicants of field independence,[4] the correlations with body sophistica-

---

[3]The Vernon paper also included a useful interpretive review of research on field independence.

[4]Because these measure one factor and they represent a connotatively richer representation of the concept at the level of operational definition.

tion measures and, in boys, with science activities suggested "... some, but rather little, confirmation of Witkin's claims regarding the characteristics of perceptually independent adolescents ..." (192, p. 384). But the results for RFT under these conditions provided a somewhat different picture, and there were notable differences between the residual correlations for boys and girls. For example, the residual correlations between RFT and body sophistication measures were significant for girls but not for boys.

These findings thus add to the previous evidence suggesting that it is unwise to assume that EFT and other indicants of Gv provide measure of the same attribute as is indicated by the RFT, TRC, and body adjustment measurements which first excited interest in the concept of field independence. The question then arises as to whether EFT (i.e. Cf) and/or Gv should be thought of as representing field independence, or a similar conceptual style, or as representing abilities which have rather different origins than are implied by the perceptual style theories.

A major problem in this respect is one of proper interpretation of the gender differences[5] (including both sex role and biological sex variance) associated with Gv and its components. There are low but reasonably consistent associations between these variables (gender, Gv, EFT) and various personality, child-rearing, SES and vocational-educational-avocational variables. In particular the visualization skills are associated with choice of, and performance in, "masculine" areas of study and work such as engineering, the physical and biological sciences, and mathematics (198). Some of the problems in interpreting such correlations result from the fact that Gv (EFT, etc) is correlated with G, which is not controlled even statistically in most studies, and yet G is correlated with the variables mentioned. To what extent are the observed relationships due to G? In a study by Erginel (48) it was found that a broadly valid and reliable measure of the Cf (i.e. EFT) factor did not add to the multiple prediction of academic achievement when measures of G were also allowed to be predictors. On the basis of these and similar results Erginel concluded that when G is taken into account, results do not support Witkin's claims that field independence represents a pervasive influence throughout cognitive behavior.

Added to these kinds of problems with the field independence formulation is the fact that it is by no means obvious that the "masculine" educational-occupation-avocational choices and performances indicate independent thinking as such, particularly if G is controlled. Work on creativity, for example, suggests that there is "task-boundess" in some forms of "masculine" thinking (that associated with being in engineering), and this is in some ways the antithesis of independent thinking (156). Girls and women in our culture tend to score higher on the VPT tasks which define (operationally) relative absence of this "task-boundness," but they tend to score lower on EFT and other measures of Gv. Girls and women in our culture also tend to enter relatively less often, and perhaps relatively less enthusiastically, into

[5]In one study in the review period the results suggested that when field independence is measured by the rod-and-frame test, rather than with EFT, there may be no notable differences associated with gender (159), thus again pointing to the differences in the construct validities of the original field independence measures and EFT.

the "masculine" areas of study and work which, according to Witkin, encourage and demand field independence. Black and low SES males also tend to eschew these latter fields of endeavor and they, too, tend to score lower on EFT tests. But again there is reason to suppose that this does not hold up when G is taken into account.

The circularity in all this is thus rather notable. Is the theory in this area saying mainly that if at a relatively early stage of development Gv (or perhaps GF) is developed to a high point relative to VPT (or perhaps Gc or simply V), then this condition favors a tendency to develop more skills with these kinds of concepts, whereas if the opposite (high VPT at the expense of Gv) is promoted by various child-rearing, intraperson and cultural influences, one tends to move in a direction away from developing visualization skills and toward developing skills in use of language (i.e. nonmathematical language) and perhaps skills of interpersonal relations? The value connotations associated with the concept of field independence probably do more to obfuscate than to clarify these kinds of ideas. For this reason, as well as because EFT appears to have little reliable variance independent of Gv, it seems wise to drop the theory "field independence" when the measure of this is EFT, and to direct research along the lines of identifying and distinguishing correlates and determinants of Gv. Moreover, the wide variety of tasks which specify the operational definition of Gv provide a more variegated behavioral concept (initial definition) than is indicated by EFT. (Indeed Gv may represent a broader concept than that indicated by the combination of EFT, RFT and TRC.)

In other work on spatial-visualization abilities, Eliot & Salkind (47) provided a comprehensive bibliography of research in this area. In comparisons of Eskimo and white Canadian adolescents, MacArthur (122) found that the smallest differences between the two groups were in respect to Gv abilities (the Eskimos scored higher on some of the Gv tasks), the largest differences were for Gc abilities (measured in English language and culture) and the differences for Gf abilities were intermediate. There were a number of studies investigating relationships between Gv abilities and school performances at various educational levels. This work supported the hypotheses that Gv is predictive of early school achievement in activities as diverse as reading and arithmetic. This was found to be true even when the predictor measurements were obtained in the first years of school and the criterion measurements were obtained 4, 5, or 6 years later (46, 131, 133, 179). Whether or not the relationship holds after G (or GF) is partialled out was not made clear, however. The generalization needs to be qualified also by recognition that gender differences in Gv probably exist even at grade-school level (63) and are associated with academic achievement. The somewhat better prediction of mathematical ability with Gv tasks, for example, may mainly reflect gender differences in both kinds of performance. Possibly also related to gender differences were findings of Stafford (174) indicating a rather consistent pattern of near-zero-to-negative correlations between Gv abilities and achievement in foreign language courses at the university level. These correlations (≈ -0.06 to -0.25) are striking partly because the Ns were substantial and partly because the correlations with performance in engineering courses (in which mainly only males are involved) were significant and positive ($r \approx 0.25$ to 0.30). Also of relevance in this context were findings which add to the evidence indicating an association between Gv abilities and a recessive sex-linked gene of intermediate frequency (15).

In sum then, pervasive Gv abilities appear to represent an important quality of thinking that is distinct from Gc and Gf, and this distinction has a number of theoretical and practical implications.

Memory   At least since the time of the pioneering work of Woodrow in the 1930s it has been known (by some) that there is only a low relationship ($r \approx 0.35$) between commonly accepted measures of intelligence and short-term acquistion of the kind measured in span memory, recognition memory, paired-associates learning, and serial learning tasks. In Thurstone's famous 1938 study the memory primary was identified with two recognition-memory and three one-trial paired-associates learning tasks, and the highest correlation this factor had with any of the other factors was 0.393 (with V). When the various memory primaries are considered in second-order analyses, a broad memory factor can be found to stand apart from Gf, Gc, Gv, and VPT. In the recent period this independence of short-term acquisition functions (SAF) and other functions of intelligence has been made the basis for theories that SAF represents another form of intelligence. Arthur Jensen in particular has sponsored the notion that there is an intelligence I (SAF) in which lower SES and ethnic minority groups score nearly as well as higher SES and majority groups, and there is an intelligence II (either Gf or Gc or G, depending on the context) which is (on the average) low for low SES and minority groups relative to high SES and majority groups. According to the theory, these different distributions come about in spite of the fact that the variances of both I and II are produced primarily by genetic factors; the differences result because upward social and economic mobility is dependent primarily on II rather than I, and racial differences are associated primarily with the genes producing II rather than those producing I. The theory states also that II is built upon I, that development of I is a necessary but not sufficient condition for development of II.

As Tyler noted in the previous review in this area, Humphreys & Dachler (89a) took issue with these ideas of Jensen, and he in turn argued against their criticisms. This controversy continued in the present review period (e.g. 89b, 96, 99, 102).

Jensen had originally rested his argument upon results from analyses in which he divided and cross-classified his samples with respect to IQ and SES to ensure equal (or nearly equal) Ns in the four resulting cells (hiIQ-hiSES, hiIQ-loSES, loIQ-hiSES, loIQ-loSES). He treated the SAF scores of these cells to analysis of variance just as if IQ and SES were independent treatments of an orthogonal two-by-two design, and interpreted the results, particularly the interactions, in accordance with his hypotheses. His principal hypothesis stipulates that among those selected for low IQ (low level II), those who are also of low SES will obtain higher SAF scores than those of high SES, while among those selected for high IQ, the reverse will be true or the differences will be negligible. Humphreys & Dachler had pointed out that IQ and SES are sampled variables correlated about 0.40 (rather than controlled variables in a truly orthogonal design) and that if the theory implied that one should generalize results to a population in which such correlation exists (as seems likely), then sample sizes in the cells of the 2-by-2 layout should be proportional to population Ns in these cells, and analyses and generalizations should proceed accordingly. Using the large and representative Project Talent data source, and analyzing a number of tests besides memory tests in accordance with this reasoning, Humphreys and Dachler found that the interactions for all variables were small relative to the main effects for both IQ and SES, and that the interactions called for in the theory were very small for the SAF abilities—in general, smaller for these hypothesized level I abilities than for other abilities which Jensen had not classified as indicating level I intelligence and in some cases had classified as indicating level II intelligence. On this basis, then, it could be maintained that unbiased data provided no support for either the interaction provisions of the theory or for the notion that level I abilities stand in a necessary-but-not-sufficient relationship to level II abilities.

In his most recent reply to these criticisms, Jensen in effect acknowledged this last point: "There appears to be only a slight degree of such dependence of Level II upon Level I . . ." (100). But he claimed support for a reformulation of the interaction hypothesis. This reformulation specifies that the slope for the regression of SAF on G should be larger for high than for low SES groups and for white as compared to black racial (ethnic) groups. His results are based upon analyses of Lorge-Thorndike (verbal and nonverbal) intelligence and span memory scores obtained in a large sample of 4th-, 5th-, and 6th-grade students from the Berkeley school system. These results can be roughly summarized as follows (considering only the racial group comparisons, which were emphasized in the Jensen report and lead to essentially the same conclusions as analyses for SES, as such).

1. The white sample appears to have been rather highly selected for IQ relative to national norms. The mean IQ for this group on the Lorge-Thorndike (LT) test was approximately 120. Relative to these same national norms the black sample appears to have been less highly selected for IQ, the mean for this group (≈ 95) being closer to the norm mean of 100. As would be expected, given this sampling and the assumption that LT items cut near the 0.50 difficulty level in the population, the raw-score LT standard deviation (sigma) was notably smaller for the white group than for the black group (approximately 11.8 as compared with 15.7).

2. On the memory test the sigma for the white group was somewhat smaller than that for the black group (15.6 as compared with 16.8), but the difference in this case was less than for the LT scores. This, too, is not unexpected for any of many variables that are only lowly correlated with IQ or with the factors which produced the selection of the high IQ sample.

3. The correlation between LT scores and memory in the white group ($r \approx 0.45$) was somewhat larger than the comparable correlation in the black group ($r \approx 0.40$). This is in accordance with Jensen's hypothesis, although it is consistent with other hypotheses as well. Moreover, even with the large samples at hand ($N_w = 1489$; $N_b = 1123$)[6] the difference between the two correlations was at only a borderline level of significance (yes at 0.05 but no at 0.01).

[6]The subscripts b and w are used to designate the black and white subsamples respectively in these symbols and others to follow.

4. When the slope values were calculated for the regression of memory on LT scores, the varying sigmas entered into the calculations, thus

$$m_w \approx 0.45\frac{(15.6)}{11.8} \approx 0.58$$

$$m_b \approx 0.40\frac{(16.8)}{15.7} \approx 0.42$$

The difference between the two slopes was found to be significant at a low p-value in accordance with hypothesis.

Thus, while these results are indeed consistent with an hypothesis of the two-level theory, as Jensen claimed, they can hardly be said to be less subject to bias or more convincing than the results which Humphreys & Dachler had earlier criticized as biased and unconvincing. It is not typical for the sigma of IQ to be smaller in samples of whites than in samples of blacks, and a sample having a mean which is 20 points above the norm of IQ is not notably less extreme, or less likely to be affected by influences associated with this extremity, than the low IQ groups that Jensen had used in the studies which Humphreys & Dachler faulted. More important, perhaps, Jensen's one-hypothesis answer is not a convincing reply to the Humphreys-Dachler arguments and demonstrations suggesting that many ability variables, not just those of memory, have somewhat different regression on G. As suggested above, regression slopes depend upon variable standard deviations and reliabilities, which in turn depend upon the difficulty levels, variances, and the extent of homogeneity of the particular item samples involved, all parameters that relate as much to whims of test construction as they do to levels of an ability I or ability II. This is not to argue that convincing evidence in support of Jensen's theory cannot be obtained; rather it is to argue that this is the kind of theory for which one needs comparisons for several measures of the relevant abilities. There is need for results for Level I measures and for several variables which supposedly do not measure Level I abilities. Had it been demonstrated, for example, that the $m_w > m_b$ relationship noted above was true *only* for Level I tasks and not for a good sampling of the many other abilities (Level II?) which are associated with G (of which G is comprised), one could be more convinced by Jensen's arguments even in spite of problems associated with sampling. The Humphreys-Dachler results suggest that without drastic modification the theory would not fare well by this test, however.

There was a considerable amount of other work pertaining to the relationships between various kinds of learning and various kinds of abilities. Some of this will be considered at later points in this review, particularly in the section on adulthood development. Several attempts to integrate this kind of research were produced in the review period (e.g. 3, 7, 21, 32, 71, 82, 125).

Auditory abilities   Most well-known theories about organization of human abilities include some reference to distinctions between visual, auditory, tactile, and other sensory input modalities. There is a body of research on musical abilities and on measurement of abilities in the deaf (18). But there is very little evidence to indicate the links between the organizational structures among auditory and visual abilities. There were a few studies in the review period which add to the small body of literature in this area, however. In one study which may be taken as illustrative (81), efforts were made to construct auditory-input tests which paralleled (in terms of the intellectual operations seemingly involved) visual test markers for established primary abilities. These auditory tests were factored in company with the musical ability measures of the Seashore, Wing and Drake batteries. The results indicated six primary-level abilities of the auditory realm: Auditory Reasoning (Ra), Temporal Reordering (Tr), Nonsymbolic Recognition Memory (Mr), Detection of Distorted Speech (DDS), Masked Speech Comprehension (MSC), and Rhythm (Ry). The Mr factor could be distinguished from span memory as usually measured, but the intercorrelations were high enough to suggest that Mr would probably line up with SAF at a second-order level if the sampling of variables was designed to reveal this. When the auditory primary factors were analyzed in company with visual primary markers to reveal second-order influences, there was indication of a broad auditory function (Ga) involving the major portion of variance of most of the auditory primaries and independent of Gv, Gf and Gc. However, several of the auditory primaries had notably nonzero correlations with Gf and Gc, as well as with Ga.

A second study in this area was directed mainly at indicating ways in which primary abilities are related to learning at different points in the learning process (197). The learning task was one of comprehending sounds in order to identify different categories of ships, as in sonar detection. The Seashore battery was used along with visual tests representing five established primary abilities. As in the study cited just previously, most of the auditory tasks defined a broad Ga dimension that was clearly independent of the visual factors. The results from projecting the visual and auditory factors onto the learning variables were rather different from previous findings in this kind of study. In contrast to the earlier findings of Fleishman & Zimmerman, for example, in which several primary abilities were found to be notably related to learning, and different abilities were involved at different stages of learning, here only the Ga factor had noteworthy correlations with parameters of the learning task, and the larger correlations indicated ability to cope with background noise and signal duration rather than stages of learning. The correlations of Ga with learning did increase systematically from early to late trials, however.

In general, the evidence accumulated in the review period suggests that there is considerable independence between abilities measured through the auditory modality and abilities measured through visual input. It suggests also that the independent variance of auditory abilities is related in noteworthy ways not only to auditory criteria, as in the study outlined above, but also to a variety of skills which have been described and predicted mainly in terms of the visual tasks of Gf, Gc, VPT, and Gv. In the Morency & Wepman (133) study mentioned earlier, for example, an auditory discrimination measure taken at first grade level had higher (significant) correlations with academic achievement in grades four and five than did memory and Gv measures. There was suggestion of support also for the commonly heard belief that conditions associated with loss of sight tend to promote development of auditory abilities (199).

Childhood Development

The major recent influence in theories about childhood development of intellectual abilities continued to come most directly for Piagetian formulations. This orientation is usually fairly well (if often uncritically) represented in other review papers, such as those on development generally, so it may not be necessary even to try fully to represent the influence here. Whether or not such is necessary or desirable, it can't be done: the literature in this area is too massive and too complex (too contradictory) to comprehend and summarize in the available space. Hence, while the tremendous importance of the Piagetian revolution in our thinking about human abilities is acknowledged, the treatment here must nevertheless only barely touch upon a few aspects of this work.

Stage theories (such as those stemming from Piaget) rest initially on the notion that if a hierarchy is logical and if a sequence exists in average age of acquisition, then this constitutes support for hypotheses about a developmental hierarchy of stages. The interpretations which are most popular in such theories, however, are those which imply that one stage is a psychologically necessary prerequisite (within *all* individuals) of every stage which has a larger average age on onset. This kind of interpretation implies that there can be no genuine discontinuities such that an individual is found at a later stage who has not been at a previous stage (all such apparent anomalies being explainable in terms of unreliabilities of observations, horizontal décalage *within* stages, etc). Call this the necessary relationship between stages (NRBS). Evidence of sequence of average age of acquisition, and logic, do not speak directly to the question of whether or not there is NRBS. Yet most of the evidence presented in support of Piagetian theory is of this type. More important, perhaps, the existing evidence usually has not indicated clearly that what might be an NRBS is also indicative of unitary process and that transition from what appears to be one stage to what appears to be another is accompanied by only those features which (according to theory) distinguish stages.

One may present what seems to be evidence for an NRBS by displaying a relationship between two dichotomous (pass-fail) tasks in which there are no (only random numbers of) subjects who pass the task of the more advanced (by hypothesis) stage but fail the task of the less advanced (by hypothesis) stage. But this need not be terribly convincing because there are several ways to get this kind of result even when the theory is not valid. For example, it is easy to show by this test that foot length (longer than X versus shorter than X) is a necessary precursor of conservation of fluids: a proper choice of X and an appropriate sampling of children can ensure that no children with feet shorter than X will pass a conservation task. To some extent this kind of problem is dealt with by demonstrating that the hypothesized NRBS hold for several adjacent stages. At least this kind of evidence becomes somewhat convincing if it is reasonable to suppose that the developmental periods are close together. But the evidence becomes truly convincing only when the tasks or the behaviors of different stages have many features in common but differ in only the one salient feature with defines transition from one stage to the other. Such evidence is particularly convincing if it is not predicted by other theory (or commonly known observations) and if the parts in common of the tasks or behaviors of the different stages clearly indicate parts of the same process.

It is important in evaluating evidence for Piagetian theory to ensure also that the salient feature which defines transition from one stage to another is indeed the feature specified in Piagetian theory and not simply degree of difficulty. It is a fairly easy matter to demonstrate NRBS for items or tests measuring the same factor if one properly selects them for degree of difficulty. For example, two multichotomous (continuous) tests of Gf can be dichotomized in such a way that only a few people meet a given pass-criterion for one and many people meet a pass-criterion for the other, whence the two-by-two relationship for the two tasks will indicate that those who fail to meet the easy pass-criterion will rarely or never meet the more difficult pass-criterion. Such a difficulty hierarchy is quite legitimate support for a stage theory, but it is not the kind of hierarchy called for in Piagetian theory. This theory requires a reorganization of thinking at one stage relative to another, not merely (or even necessarily) a capacity to solve more difficult problems.

Such then are some of the important problems for Piagetian theory. Hardly anyone who has looked at the evidence on infant and early childhood development doubts that in most cases the achievements of sensorimotor alertness precede the achievements which define the intellectual abilities of the preschool and early school years; demonstrations of the aging sequences for these tasks are thus not very compelling support for Piagetian or any other stage theory. But there is serious doubt that the sensorimotor abilities are of the same process as are represented by the abilities of later childhood. Similarly, it is clear that most children at one age fail to solve problems which most of them solve at an older age, but it is by no means always clear that this is indicative of a reorganization of the kind specified in Piagetian theory and is not just as parsimoniously interpreted as representing difficulty, as specified in other theories. In respect to such problems the evidence of the review period continued to be most unconvincing. While Piagetian theory flourished, and stages were divided and subdivided again to imply ever finer discriminations (90), most of the evidence presented in support of stage theories did not meet the conditions outlined above. Rather slavish obeisance to Piagetian formulations continued to be prevalent. Interesting results and issues of relevance for stage theories were considered, however; some of the following are representative.

INFANCY   Prior to the review period a considerable amount of evidence had accumulated to indicate that the infant tests which are most often believed to measure important aspects of intellectual development do not measure what is called intelligence at older ages.[7] The poor long-term predictive validity of infant tests is not well accounted for by supposing that the tests are unreliable; they have been

---

[7]It is being understood in this context that infant scales do measure gross retardation, even as do observation techniques that are less elaborate than infant scales.

found to have adequate internal consistency and short-period retest reliability. Relatedly, there had been other indications (often soto voce) that precocity, particularly in infancy but perhaps in later childhood as well, is not necessarily a favorable sign of subsequent level or asymptotic level of development. Noteworthy evidence in support of these positions was added during the review period. Lewis & McGurk (119), for example, with particular reference to the Mental Development Index, the object permanence measures of Escalona and Corman, and the Bayley Scales of Infant Development (BSID), delivered a spirited and rather scathing indictment of the whole enterprise of infant assessment aimed at diagnosing later IQ: infant test measurements (of the first 18 to 24 months) are neither unitary nor stable, they said, and the concept of general intelligence is inapplicable in this period. Pease, Wolins & Stockdale (142) echoed this refrain in reference to the Gesell, Cattell, California Motor Development, and (to a lesser degree) BSID scales.

In a somewhat more restrained variation on this theme, McCall, Hogarty & Hurlburt (127) provided an insightful review and some provocative results from analyses of Fels Institute data. The conclusion from their review is essentially the same as that stated in the previous paragraph, but with a few qualifiers deriving principally from their data analyses. One qualifier is that infant tests may contain subsets of items which are predictive of adjacent stages in what may be a single process even as the earliest stages are not predictive of remote stages. They used empirical grouping methods to form subsets of behaviors at each of several ages in infancy and then intercorrelated subset scores of different ages. The results suggest a major sequence for both boys and girls and a couple of less pervasive sequences mainly associated with gender.

At the youngest ages (up to 6 months), the major sequence appears to be manifested in manipulative exploration of objects that produce perceptual contingencies. Such manipulative behavior predicts behaviors involving imitation of fine motor and elementary verbal behavior in a social context in the range between 6 and 12 months of age. It is correlated at a lower degree with the verbal labeling and comprehension which characterize the 12–18 month "stage." This latter, in turn, is predicted by the second stage development and is itself predictive of the verbal fluency and grammatical maturity which defines the major component of behavior of the final 6 months of the first 2 years of life. Each stage was found to be correlated with the adjacent stage, but developmental level in only the last two stages for girls and the last stage for boys was indicative of WISC or SB intelligence measured in early or late childhood. These findings are thus consistent with earlier results suggesting that only as measurements at early ages involve skills mediated through verbal behavior and thus overlap (or measure similar) skills at later age levels do the earlier measurements predict the later measurements. More than most previous results these show an empirical link between, on the one hand, sensorimotor accomplishments that are not themselves predictive of G in later life and, on the other hand, accomplishments (perhaps best called conceptual rather than perceptual) that are at least somewhat predictive of later level of G (or Gc or Gf). Given these findings, it would seem desirable to design research to demonstrate operationally the relationships (if any) between the "stages" of McCall et al (127), particularly the second stage noted above, and processes which are suggested by Piaget's notions about assimilation and accommodation.

It may be useful also to look at these stages in terms of recent work on the concept of activation hypothesis, as developed by Kagan and his co-workers (106, 107). In this work the suggestion is that prior to about 8–12 months of age much of the infant's cognitive behavior can be described as primarily assimilative. From about this point on in development, however, more and more of the child's behavior involves inquiry, a checking to see if new information fits with past experience, with expectations, with patterns, etc. Kagan cites the U-shaped relationship between age and duration of attention (the trough in the U coming in the 9–11 month period) as one indicant of this shift in cognitive function. Data on cardiac response to notable changes in stimulus surround is also cited in support of the idea of the shift. The work of Lacey, Van Hoover, and others is taken to indicate that cardiac acceleration implies sustained "mental work" (e.g. problem solving) in respect to a change in stimulus surround. Prior to about 8–12 months of age the characteristic response to such change is cardiac deceleration, but at about this age and thereafter it becomes more and more likely that the response will be cardiac acceleration. The general suggestion is that the upturn one-half of the U-shaped attentional and cardiac response curves is predictive of later G development.

One of the less general behavioral sequences identified by McCall et al is mainly applicable for girls. It is reminiscent, at least, of the Gv dimension mentioned earlier in the present review. Some of the identifying behaviors of the sequence are those of coping with block building, paper folding, and form-board tasks. As noted earlier, by late adolescence males tend to cope with the Gv tasks somewhat better than females. Yet the analyses of McCall et al suggest that mainly for girls, but not for boys, performance with perceptual-figural tasks in the second year of life are predictive of verbal and performance IQ at age 7 and beyond with validities of the order of 0.3 to 0.6. The other sequence identified by McCall et al suggests that for boys, but not for girls, level of playful, spontaneous sensorimotor behavior is *contraindicative* of later IQ, the correlations in this case being of the order of minus 0.20 to minus 0.50.

In a somewhat different context but dealing with some of the same problems, Kagan & Klein (107) observed that various infant measures of lack of attentiveness and memory—tests of the kind often interpreted as indicating delayed development at this age—are not necessarily indicative of low or delayed development at later ages. Indeed, moving beyond infancy, the analyses of Kagan & Klein suggest that precocity in the ages between 5 and 12 is not really indicative of level of development at later ages. Results somewhat supportive of these ideas were produced by others (5, 19).

Some of the efforts in the study of infant abilities were concerned primarily with refinements in observational and measurement methods. Hunt (90), for example, proposed a revision of the idea of six stages of sensorimotor development. The revision is a more detailed set of observations about the kinds of infant behaviors that seem to appear sequentially. The work of Hunt and his co-workers also suggested particular kinds of stimulations (mainly verbal) which may bring on early mastery of sensorimotor skills. A question of the future will be to see if this kind of precocity is predictive of favorable intellectual development at older ages. Bruner & Koslowski (26) also proposed a rather detailed observational analysis of visual-motor coordination in the infant.

CHILDHOOD   There were notable efforts to relate findings and theory derived from Piagetian orientations to results and theory developed from other positions. Some of the moves in this direction were efforts to modify the *methode clinique* to provide for more objectivity in measurement and to permit better analyses to indicate reliability and relationships between variables. The scale developments of Ward (193) and Tuddenham (185) are representative.

In the Tuddenham work some 40 separate tasks were translated fairly directly from the *methode clinique* and tried out with a substantial sample of children. For the tasks designed to measure conservation of quantity (clay, water), conservation of volume, reversal perspective, simple seriation, and transitivity, there were orderly transitions with age in the average number of children passing the task, thus suggesting that the tasks were working as desired. The correlations between tasks at the same level were not high, however, or, to put the matter another way, horizontal décalage was common. Some of the specificity seemed to be due to factors other than those producing unreliability. There was a suggestion that conservation, classification, and perhaps seriation tasks would form separate group factors. The overall score, indicating the extent of transition from preoperational (PO) to operational (OP) thinking, correlated 0.6 with Matrices and only 0.21 with Vocabulary. It would seem, therefore, that development from PO to OP is more closely related to Gf than to Gc. There were, however, gender differences favoring the boys on most of the tasks. This suggests that the relationships with Matrices may be reflecting Gv variance in this latter and in the Piaget-task composite, rather than a link between Gf and PO-to-OP transition.

There were, however, other studies suggesting that Piagetian measures below the level of formal operations have relatively low correlations with Gc and V and somewhat higher correlations with Gf and/or Gv (42, 104, 129). Still other work suggested that PO and OP tasks may define a broad factor that is largely distinct from Gf, Gc, and Gv (109, 175). Attainment of formal operations appears to be more closely related to Gc than to Gf (72).

Ward's (193) work was part of a general effort (mentioned earlier) to construct a new British Intelligence Scale (BIS) incorporating some of the concepts and tests of the FEP primary abilities as well as some of the ideas from the Piagetian school. The Piagetian test is presented as a game in which two cartoon-character crooks, Butch and Slim, are associated with various statements pertaining to whether or not one or both did or did not rob a bank, and the subject's task is to indicate which of four pictures represents the logical possibilities of a particular statement. Items are derived from Piaget's combinational analysis of adolescent thinking, as set forth in *Traite de Logique*. This specifies what are called the 16 binary propositions of p and q. Each of the 16 propositions is represented by statements in which one of the crooks (Butch) is telling the truth and an equal number of propositions in which Butch is not telling the truth—a total of 32 items in all. The homogeneity reliability of the item set was quite good (≈0.90). The test correlated substantially with Watson-Glaser critical thinking and with the total score derived from the primary abilities measured in BIS. The items represented different logical operations such as conjunction, nonimplication, conjunctive negation, implication, and disjunction, but there was little evidence to suggest a developmental trend in such operations. There was some age transition in the items, however. Gender differences were not notable.

In further work with this kind of test, Ward & Pearson (194) found that manipulation of the content of the logical game situation produced substantial variability for items supposedly measuring the same logical operations. Analyses of these findings led the investigators to conclude that they ". . . now share considerable misgivings over the operations of formal logic as a behavioral universe and as a source of stable discriminative items" (194, p. 395).

Heron (73) pulled together results from a number of studies to suggest that the stage of concrete operations is not unitary, that ". . . it may be more productive to view it as a set of structures without necessary interdependence" (p. 8), a possibility that had been entertained earlier by Flavell and Wohlwill. In support of this position were results showing that in an age range from roughly 9 to 15 years, children from several cultures (Zambia, Papua, Hong Kong, Yugoslavia) who failed conservation of weight and volume tasks nevertheless demonstrated competencies in multiple classification tasks, other operational tasks, and intelligence tasks (Matrices) which clearly indicated that they were at the level of concrete operations or beyond. Of possible relevance here are results from a 2-year longitudinal study by Dudek & Dyer (45). In tasks extending over operational and causal thinking, these investigators found that only 9 of 65 children showed no regression to an earlier mode of thinking, 16 showed three or more regressions, and 40 had one or two regressions. Moreover, contrary to their expectations, the level of intellectual maturity, measured by the WISC and the Piagetian tasks, was higher for the children who regressed considerably than for the children who didn't regress or regressed very little. In this connection also, Dasen & Christie (41) first found, then replicated, then noted that others had found evidence that the percentages of children demonstrating conservation of weight increased fairly regularly from ages 5 to 10, but dropped for ages 10 and 11, and increased thereafter. They suggested that the child moving into use of formal operations confuses the concepts of weight and density (or perhaps the child assumes that the E is testing for awareness of the latter rather than the former). It may be that some such explanation will help to rationalize Heron's findings. Or it could be that there are correctable defects in the procedures whereby children were required to demonstrate conservation in the studies in question and if these defects are corrected, the problem to which Heron points may be solved. As of this writing, however, it seems that conservation tasks may not hang together as would be expected if they indicated a unitary process that is independent of that of formal operations.

In other detractions from Piagetian theory, Coie & Dorval (35) found no support for an hypothesis (derived by Flavell) that Piagetian spatial perspective-taking ability better predicts social role-taking behavior (giving and receiving information in social interaction) than does the matrices task. In a second study based on 6–11 year old Greek migrant children in Australia, it was found that 25 percent of those who passed English language pretests and failed to conserve length and number when the tasks were presented in English showed conservation when the tasks were given in Greek, but again failed to conserve when posttested in English (109a). Such findings seemingly are not in conformance with the Piagetian notion that level of cognitive development at a given point is not dependent upon level of concurrent language development. Mackay, Brazendale & Wilson (123) showed that one could demonstrate that representation of the horizontal preceded or followed representation of the vertical, depending on the tasks selected. Siegler, Liebert & Liebert (171) replicated Inhelder and Piaget's findings that 10–11 year olds do not often solve the pendulum problem without aid, but results did not support the Inhelder-Piaget hypothesis that the cognitive development of children who could not do the task was not advanced enough to permit them to learn to cope with such tasks. And there were other disconfirmations of Piagetian propositions, large and small (e.g. 52, 55).

Need it be added that there were also many bits of evidence submitted in support of Piagetian theory, some bearing on the very points that were disputed in the researches cited above (25, 90, 104, 143, 201)? For example, in work that wasn't designed specifically in accordance with Piagetian theory, M. Vernon (187) presented evidence that would seem to support the Piagetian claims for independence of cognitive and language development. In marshalling this case Vernon used the results from a number of studies of the deaf and partially deaf to show that conceptual development can be advanced when language development is primative, and that conceptual development can proceed to a high level with little or no verbal mediation.

There was a considerable amount of work in the review period to suggest that time-on-task and time-in-learning are variables which will be discussed considerably in coming years (e.g. 13, 30; see also the Eysenck, Furneaux, and White papers in 51a). As concerns childhood development, one principal thrust of this work was to reconsider the relationship which theoretically should exist between ability measurements taken at one age and achievement at a later age. Without trying to go into this work in detail, we can note that one basic idea is that some ability measures can be expected to predict primarily only time-in-acquisition in such massive learning as is represented by education (or still more broadly, acculturation). Only insofar as time-in-acquisition tends to be, or must be, related to asymptotic level of achievement should one expect ability measurements taken at one age to be predictive of the achievement at later ages. Carroll's (30) study was a particularly impressive demonstration of the complexities involved in attempting to work with such hypotheses in the study of school learning. It also provided some clear indications of the importance of considering time to acquisition. The work on time-on-task is perhaps best discussed in the next section (on adulthood development).

Development in Adulthood

There emerged in the review period a movement which may herald a major shift in emphasis in the entire field of psychology, particularly in the study of human abilities. This was a movement toward specifying a life-span orientation to research and theory building. We are still too close to this development to discern accurately its principal features, but it seems that one important part of it involves efforts to comprehend normal adulthood development as distinct from childhood development, gerontology, and psychopathology. To a considerable extent the movement was generated by people who found that in studying old age they either were studying, or they needed to study, development prior to old age. There were many conferences, articles, and books attesting to this transformation. Perhaps the more notable of these are well represented by a three-volume set of readings on life-span developmental psychology put together by Goulet & Baltes (60), Nesselroade & Reese (137), and Baltes & Schaie (8). A review of adulthood development in the 1975 *Annual Review of Psychology* also attests to the rise of interest in this area (162).

MACROLEVEL ABILITIES   Prior to the review period a considerable amount of evidence had accumulated to suggest that intelligence developed to a peak in the late teens or early twenties, perhaps stayed at this level for two or three decades, or perhaps declined even in this period, but in either case declined in late adulthood, perhaps at an accelerating rate as age 60 was approached and passed. There was evidence also to suggest that there is little or no important decline, and perhaps even notable improvement, in intelligence throughout most of the adulthood period.

It has been argued many times that the evidence for intellectual decline in adulthood is based upon cross-sectional studies, while results indicating no decline or improvement are based upon longitudinal designs. This is a misleading oversimplification: there are notable differences between the longitudinal and cross-sectional studies in addition to differences intrinsic to subject-sampling, and both kinds of studies have provided some of the evidence indicating both kinds of results—decline and no decline—although it probably is accurate to say that a larger proportion of the results from cross-sectional studies indicate decline than is true of longitudinal investigations. Nevertheless, it is clear that some of the important questions which must be considered in evaluating the data on aging and intelligence do indeed pertain to subject sampling (172). Other important questions pertain to the sampling of the abilities (tests) assumed to indicate intelligence. In the review period investigators who focused on one or the other of these two sets of questions sometimes seemed to arrive at somewhat different conclusions about intellectual development in adulthood. Schaie (161, p. 802), for example, claimed that the idea of intellectual decline is a "myth, . . . a methodological artifact . . . a misunderstanding of the relation between individual development and sociocultural change," while elsewhere (82) it was suggested that the weight of the evidence is on the side of hypotheses stipulating that there is adulthood decline in at least some of the important functions of intellectual behavior.

The conclusion that there is decline was based primarily on theory and results indicating that G is a mixture of different capacities, some of which are likely (in a probabilistic sense) to improve with age in adulthood, while others are likely to degenerate. The improvements result from increased learning, consolidation of knowledge in improved concepts, and generalized problem-solving techniques and increased opportunities for facilitation, positive transfer, and similar benefits of learning. Abilities which are enhanced in these ways define a form of intelligence (Gc) which is said to be indicated also in second-order analyses of interrelationships among abilities. Intellectual decline can be traced to such things as negative transfer and related "rigidities" produced by accumulated learning, and to loss and degeneration of the physiological (particularly neurological) substratum, as produced either by (or both by) catabolic maturational changes or (and) irreversible damage brought on by illnesses and injuries. The abilities most sensitive to these kinds of influences define a second form of intelligence (Gf) also expected to be indicated as a second-order factor. In most cases where results pertaining to intellectual decline in adulthood appear to be contradictory, it is because the measures have involved rather different mixtures of Gf and Gc; when the Gf-Gc distinction is made the contradictions are largely eliminated. Reviews and results lending support to this formulation were presented by several investigators during the review period (e.g. 32, 76, 78–82, 138, 170).

The conclusion that adulthood intellectual decline is myth derives in part from criticisms of both cross-sectional and longitudinal studies and in part from results obtained from time-sequential analyses. As is well known, cross-sectional designs are weak because results may indicate only differences between generational subcultures in the opportunities and experiences of relevance for performing on the measurement tasks. Longitudinal analyses also have a number of limitations, one of which is that any change they indicate may reflect only influences operating over a specific time period between test and retest, not ontogenetic development characteristics of other time periods. In time-sequential analyses the aim is to get around these difficulties by measuring the same generational cohorts at several different times. The measures are cross-classified according to age and year of testing. Thus a mean for a given age grouping is based upon people born at different times, and a main effect for this factor represents differences which persist despite within-age generational differences. In cross-sequential analyses on the same kind of data the scores are cross-classified according to year of birth and time of testing, and analyses are directed at indicating cohort differences that persist despite variation over time of testing. Schaie cites the results from several time-sequential analyses to support the above-mentioned claim that the idea of adulthood intellectual decline is myth (7, 163, 164).

The various studies Schaie cites are all based upon the same data source— volunteers (members of an insurance plan) tested in 1956, 1963, and 1970, some retested on each occasion, some merely age cohorts of those tested at earlier and later times. The cross-sequential results indicate little or no decline until beyond age 50 for V, N, and Fw, but nearly linear decline beginning in early adulthood for I, S, and indicants of flexibility (absence of rigidity). Such results are in agreement with those from a number of cross-sectional studies. They are quite consistent with explanations in terms of a Gf-Gc separation of abilities, V, N, and Fw being markers for Gc; I, S, and flexibility being indicative of Gf. The time-sequential results do not greatly alter the conclusions for Gc abilities, but they suggest that there is little or no decline in I and S until after age 40. The results do indicate decline in these abilities, however. It seems, therefore, that the major conclusion called for by these analyses is not that there is no adulthood decline in intellectual abilities, but that decline may occur later in life and perhaps is less severe than had been supposed from previous study. More specifically, the results suggest that in a population represented by samples of people who remain alive and volunteer for testing at various ages, there may be no intellectual decline indicated by group averages until the 40s, and then only in Gf abilities, and there may be no decline in Gc abilities until the 50s or 60s. Such a conclusion is not inconsistent with the Gf-Gc hypothesis that some abilities are affected more and earlier by influences associated with aging then are other abilities. The results are also compatible with the Gf-Gc notion that intellectual decline need not reflect inevitable catabolic maturation, but may result from extrinsic influences the cumulative effect of which, or the cumulative probability of which, increases for groups of individuals as age increases.

These conclusions need to be tempered by realization that the study designs, whether time-sequential or one of the others, are concomitant-variational, not controlled-manipulative or truly experimental. No amount of analysis of variance transforms the former into the latter. In addition to ontogenetic influences, there are all manner of selection and other nonrandom influences affecting the outcomes of both time-sequential and cross-sectional analyses. Thus the results do not provide a strong inference base for any particular theory about intellectual decline or lack of decline. The theories containing such hypotheses should be regarded as plausibility arguments. In this respect they are rather more similar to cases presented in a case of law than they are to the grand theories of physics. Similar views were developed rather fully by Baltes (6).

Some of the influences which should be considered in evaluating the conclusions drawn above are those associated with sample attrition and volunteer bias at different ages. Problems in this respect were examined by several investigators. Reigel's (147, 148) analyses were particularly insightful. The tenor of the evidence suggests that at all ages in adulthood those who resist testing and retesting tend to score lower on ability tests than those who cooperate, and the tendencies for low-scorers to resist and for high-scorers to cooperate increases with age. Similarly the less able tend to die at an earlier age than the more able, particularly before the age of about 60. The net effect of these sampling influences is to produce what can be called positive bias in both time-sequential (longitudinal) and cross-sequential (cross-sectional) analyses: the samples taken to represent older cohorts tend to be from higher portions of the cohort distribution than the samples drawn to represent younger cohorts. Related to these effects are scattered (by no means conclusive) results suggesting that persons initially high in SES and/or in G may improve their abilities over a longer developmental period, may thus show decline later and may decline at a slower rate than those initially low in G and/or SES.

Also complicating the matter are results suggesting that intellectual decline frequently may occur just a short time prior to death (92, 151, 153). It seems that if one compares (e.g. over 5 year intervals) the first test and retest average scores of those who do and those who do not survive for another 5 years, there is notable decline from first test to retest for nonsurvivors of all ages (the death-drop Ss), some decline for older survivors, and very little decline for younger survivors. The death-drop Ss are cooperators in the retest and would be expected to be volunteers in cross-sectional studies. Since relatively more of an older cohort than of a younger cohort can be expected to die within any given span of time, samples from among older cooperators can be expected to contain relatively more death-drop Ss than samples from among younger cooperators. Thus, considering only this influence, the mean scores for older cohort samples can be depressed relatively more as a result of the death-drop effect than means for younger cohort samples. The net effects in this case can be said to produce negative bias.

Just how the various negative bias and positive bias influences work out in any particular study is very difficult to estimate. The fact that such influences have not been estimated or controlled in studies of adulthood intellectual development means that our existing data base for inferring decline and improvements is far from solid. In such circumstances there is much to commend research strategies of comparing several abilities with the aim of describing decline and improvement in one kind of ability relative to another. In such circumstances it seems desirable also to consider the results from rather detailed analyses of the performances of younger and older persons, the aim being in this case to examine many pieces of the puzzle in hopes of finding some that will fit together to suggest the overall picture.

MICROLEVEL ABILITIES   The abilities referred to in the previous section are of the kind measured with more or less typical psychometric devices. Usually in this kind of data gathering the investigator does not have a high degree of control over, or detailed awareness of, the behavior of his subjects. Different subjects may use different strategies to obtain the same score on a given test, for example, and factoring or other similar analyses may not help much to indicate the nature of the different strategies. To obtain insights about such narrower processes one may need to increase the time the investigator spends in observing each subject, as in individual testing. This usually means loss in size and representativeness of subject samples and loss in the number of variables which may be studied simultaneously. Often, too, in this work the contrast between "younger" and "older" is between quite dissimilar subjects, as, for example, a group of 20-year-olds and a group of septuagenarians. It is hazardous to generalize from such contrasts that aging trends occur all across adulthood, as has been pointed out (167). The death-drop idea adds another dimension to this caution. Nevertheless, the findings from this kind of research can be useful.

The present review will focus on storage and retrieval processes. At this point in history quite a bit is known about these processes and there is a prima facia case for supposing that they relate in important ways to broader abilities of conceptual organization. This work has some interesting implications for understanding intellectual decline and improvement in adulthood. It doesn't speak too kindly to the hope that all intellectual decline is myth.

A carefully performed study by Waugh and associates (196) raised some interesting questions about choice reaction time (CRT) differences between younger and older adult subjects. It is fairly well documented that in cross-sectional analyses at least, CRT increases with age, the differences between older and younger adults becoming more pronounced as the number of choices increases beyond the simple one-choice task. Waugh et al used a two-choice task. Their results indicate notable difference between the oldest (median age 68) and the youngest (median age 33) of their subjects, and a main effect which includes this, but insignificant (by Tukey's conservative test) differences in the multiple comparisons involving the other sub-groups (one of median age 45, the other of median age 55). More surprising, differences for the group variances (sigmas) and for the within-subject sigmas (over 38 trials) were not significant. The Ns for the subsamples were quite sufficient to establish significance (65, 57, 62, and 18 for the youngest to the oldest subgroups respectively). The results are interesting partly because findings from a number of previous studies had been widely accepted as indicating that there are differences in the CRT variabilities within adult groups of different ages and differences in the within-subject variabilities for subjects of different ages (the older Ss being more variable in each case). Typically interpretations have suggested that the decision process becomes more unreliable with advancing age. The results of Waugh et al may call this interpretation into question. It is well to keep in mind, however, the fact that only a two-choice CRT task was considered in this study. The most convincing data suggesting CRT differences between older and younger adults have involved tasks in which the subject must maintain more than two things in immediate awareness (79).

Waugh et al (196) also developed an interesting gamma-distribution model to suggest a possible explanation for the CRT differences between the oldest and youngest subsamples of their data. In this model one assumes that a CRT decision involves a number of steps n, each step requiring a given amount of time a and an initiating time k to set the stepping process in action. When the model was fitted over subjects (rather than over trials within each subject), an excellent fit was obtained for different age groups. Most interesting was a finding that the n and the a parameters were not appreciably different for age groups, and therefore the difference in CRT was accounted for primarily by the parameter indicating time to initiate the process of responding.

Although Waugh et al (196) interpret this finding very cautiously, it is consistent with a fairly substantial body of data suggesting aging (in adulthood) decrements in (a) ability to transform stimuli (messages) into the terms (e.g. symbols) an individual uses in cognitive work, or (b) ability to call into awareness (retrieve) elements that have been transformed, or (c) both of these.

The work of Anders, Fozard & Lillyquist (2) and Anders & Fozard (1) is illustrative of some of the kinds of issues raised in considering these possibilities. The Anders-Fozard-Lillyquist study demonstrated that reacton time (RT) in immediate (after a few seconds) yes-no (Y-N) recognition of low-association items (letters, numbers) presented in short lists (e.g. three or five letters) is shorter for younger than for older adults. This was interpreted as indicating that the retrieval time from primary memory increases with age. In the Anders-Fozard study the task was the same as that described above except that the short list of, say, five items had been overlearned to the point where it could be recalled perfectly, rather as if it were one's own telephone number. Again the RT to recognize whether or not an item was of this list was considerably longer for older adults than for younger subjects, particularly so as lists were increased from three to five items. This was interpreted as indicating that retrieval time from secondary memory increases with age in adulthood. In both the primary and secondary memory tasks there were no significant differences between age groupings in the number of errors committed. Thus it seems that older persons were not slower simply because they were more careful not to misidentify a symbol. This is consistent with a variety of other results suggesting that in simple recognition memory tasks older Ss perform about as accurately (make as few errors) as younger Ss.

Other major reviews of the evidence in this area (3, 20, 21, 37) suggested, however, that neither rate of retrieval from primary memory nor the storage (up to about 30 seconds) of primary memory account for much of the variance in complex mental processes and thus are not likely to account for much of any decline in intellectual abilities. On the other hand, several lines of study suggest that secondary memory may be notably implicated in some of the problems of intellectual functioning which develop in adulthood. More precisely, recognizing that the distinction between primary and secondary memory very likely represents a continuum, it seems that as tasks are shifted from those exemplifying primary memory to those exemplifying secondary memory (and beyond; for example, to tasks indicating memory for prose), meaningful association looms ever larger as a determiner of whether or not material is retained and retrieved, and age decrements are more likely to be in evidence. It seems that the older the adult, the fewer the meaningful associations generated among elements (stimuli, symbols, signs, words, phrases, sentences, etc) for which the interrelationships are somewhat obscure (3, 58, 116).

In comprehending verbal material in which there is the potential for meaningful organization, the adult does indeed organize the material in ways which facilitate delayed recognition and recall (e.g. 94). It is this organization which seems to be mainly implicated in measures of intelligence. For example, Labouvie et al (117) demonstrated that the correlations between delayed recall and reasoning aspects of intelligence (S, I, and N) increased as the trial number increased. Correlations between recall and prior tests of memory (involving, in part, primary memory) decreased from early to late trials. These results are consistent with earlier findings, such as those coming from Fleishman's laboratory. Similarly, reviews of the literature reasserted earlier indications that it is primarily only extended learning, learning in which mediation is prominent, the kind of learning described under the rubric of massed practice and other such "meaningful" learning that is notably related to G or Gf or Gc (22, 130). "Meaningful" in this context translates, at least roughly, into emphasis on organization. This does not mean that the learner is necessarily highly conscious of the fact that he is imposing organization on the stimulus materials. Indeed, there is some suggestion that intelligence is mainly implicated when this organization is done spontaneously or incidentally, rather than under strong conscious "push" (124).

Thus it seems that primarily when organizational comprehension is emphasized in perception, retrieval, and learning, do adulthood age decrements appear and pertain to genuine decrement in important intellectual abilities. In other work related to this suggestion it was shown that when people are free to group words (concepts) in any way they wish in free association and historical recall, the responses of older as compared to younger adults involve a higher proportion of discrete elements and less classification in terms of logical and grammatical categories (44, 116). In part this may be due to the older person's poorer organization in the initial learning of material recently learned. That is, a major portion of what is most available to a person of any age is that which was learned in the fairly recent past (150). If the older adult organizes this material less well and less completely in acquisition, he may for this reason have poorer organization in recall. The older adult's retrieval may be less adequate also because in working on the part of the material which he does retrieve, he educes fewer of the possibly relevant correlates for any given element (word concept), thus perceives the element in a less adequate organizational scheme; hence he fails to comprehend the gap, so to speak, in which a retrieved element might fit, and therefore fails to look for an element to fit into the gap.

Of direct relevance here are findings from research using the reversal-nonreversal optimal shift paradigm and building upon the Kendlers' studies of the role of mediation and hypothesis testing in discrimination learning. As is well known, with age increase in childhood there is shift in such learning from predominantly single-unit associations to multiple-unit learning which appears to be mediated by perception of relationships and guided by hypothesis testing. In the review period there were several studies (e.g. 136, 200) suggesting that with age increase in adulthood there is reversal of the childhood shift. Adult learning becomes mediationally deficient and less guided by perception of relationships and eduction of correlates (i.e. hypothesis testing).

Some of the work on the effects of speed and pacing in adulthood learning can be comprehended within this framework. Botwinick (21) and Arenberg (3) provided reviews of evidence to indicate that under self-paced conditions the older person (relative to the younger person) tends to increase time to assimilate (e.g. time to inspect and/or time to anticipate) and time to produce response in learning tasks. Also, the older person's performance improves relatively more than the younger person's when time restrictions (related to the above-mentioned parameters) are relaxed. Several results in support of these observations and interpretations were produced (111, 132). In line with the results cited previously, the suggestion is that increases in time required in various learning tasks reflect an increasing problem the person has in perceiving relationships which are essential for efficient hypotheses-guided learning. It thus appears that as we become older we perform less well in novel learning tasks not so much because of slowing of elementary processes of sensing and responding, but because of decreased ability to perceive relationships and educe consequents. This produces an increase in time to direct the learning process in a meaningful way (it being implied, of course, that meaningful learning, in contrast to rote learning, is a principal characteristic of human intellectual function).

Results indicating distinctions between performance in recall and recognition tasks also are relevant in this context (cf 167). In general these results indicate relatively less aging deficit for recognition than for recall tasks (85). The suggestion is that elements (words, etc) which might be needed in intellectual tasks, or called for in memory tasks, are recorded as units by the older person nearly as well as by the younger person, and in this sense they are nearly equally available to both the young and the old person. When an association prompt is provided in a recognition task, the older person displays awareness of an element (i.e. matches) nearly as well as the younger person. Thus again it seems that adulthood age decrements in intellectual performances are not so much due to lack of awareness of elements of relevance for a task at hand as they are due to lack of internally generated associations and possible interpretations (hypotheses) for elements of which one is aware.

The results of Denny & Denny (43) point to another aspect of declining ability to direct intellectual processes in accordance with hypotheses derived from perception of relationships. The task in this study was to "guess" which of several pictures then in view E was thinking about. S was to inform his "guess" by asking any questions he cared to ask (the 20-questions game). The principal differences between the performances of older (mean age 82) and younger (mean age 38) groups could be comprehended in terms of the kinds of questions asked—namely, in terms of what were called constraint-seeking and redundant questions. A question was classified as constraint-seeking if the answer would enable one to deduce whether the picture belonged to one or another of several categories. The mean proportion of such questions was much smaller for older than for the younger persons. This effect was considerably more pronounced than that indicating that older subjects asked proportionately more redundant questions. In general the older person asked less relevant questions and thus required considerably more questions to reach a solution than the younger person (32 as compared with 18). Similar results were found by others (160).

Some of the data of this kind can be understood in terms of an hypothesis that older persons tend to perceive more, rather than fewer, relationships than are perceived by younger persons. The argument in this case is that the older person comprehends too much. By comprehending more he makes some tasks more difficult than they would otherwise be. He thus tries to solve more difficult problems than the younger person even as both are ostensibly working on the same task. This shows up in what appears to be, but isn't (by hypothesis), poor performance for older as compared to younger persons.

One rather commonly employed way to look at this hypothesis is in terms of interference. By virtue of having lived longer than younger persons, older persons tend to have been exposed to more opportunities to learn and therefore presumably (on the average) would have learned and stored more than younger persons. Thus it is not unreasonable to suppose that learning and memory deficits associated with age are, at least in part, a result of interference of one form or another. When a task calls for learning a relationship which contradicts a relationship previously learned, for example, it can be expected that because of a larger number of reinforcements, greater opportunities for the effects of intermittant reinforcement to operate, etc, the number of trials to unlearn the previous, and to learn the new, would be greater for older than for younger persons. This might be called the long-stored interference effect (LIE). A number of studies have provided some support for this kind of hypothesis (202).

It might seem, therefore, that LIE is the major factor operating when the older persons fail to learn and retrieve as well as younger persons. However, Traxler & Britton (184) presented results which inspire caution in moving to this conclusion. They demonstrated that interference associated with aging can be introduced over a very short period of time, as when a subject learns an association which may be symbolized as A $\longrightarrow$ B and then a few minutes later learns an association of the form A $\longrightarrow$ C. A serial learning study (85) may indicate the same thing. The task in this case was to first learn one list of 30 lowly associated words and then learn a second list of 30 different words. Relative to the younger subjects, the older adults tended to persist in recalling words from the previously learned list, particularly in the early learning trials. Thus in both cases the results suggest that part of any interference effect implicated in aging decrements is due to inability to unlearn material learned just a short time before. This might be referred to as the short-stored interference effect (SIE).

In general then, the findings suggest that if one lives long enough, he will experience difficulties, relative to his skills at an earlier age, in organizational thinking, perceiving relationships, forming hypotheses, making integrations, and shifting from one learning or thinking task to another. This will reflect in fewer elements comprehended in awareness that extends longer than 30 seconds, and therefore fewer possibilities for realizing adaptive, correct interpretations of tasks in which previously worked conceptions are of relatively little value. Such would seem to be the processes of fluid intelligence. But some intellectual changes with age in adulthood reflect changes in styles of thinking which are not indicative of decreased abilities to cope but instead indicate increased capacities. At a broad level such capacities are indicated in Gc. Some of the more specific aspects of these abilities may be adumbrated by studies such as that of Kogan (114) on styles of categorization.

Kogan used the Gardner object-sorting task and a photo-sorting task with college students (age about 21) and members of a gerontological club (age about 72). The amount of formal education in both subsamples was above the respective cohort averages. The older subjects classified relatively less frequently by grouping exemplars of a concept (e.g. kitchen utensils) and by grouping in terms of similar properties of objects (e.g. having handles), but they classified relatively more frequently by considering functional relationships (e.g. matches and pipe). Of the three modes of classification the latter was viewed by Kogan as the most subtle and as indicating the more imaginative, less conventional approach to the Gardner materials. One could question this interpretation, of course. In support of it, however, Kogan cited Wallach and Kogan results indicating that children who performed relatively better on divergent than on convergent thinking tasks (and thus were "creative" in this sense) also tended to classify in terms of functional relations, relative to children who performed better on the convergent than on the divergent tasks. Kogan's results also suggested that older adults tend to use somewhat fewer categories (roughly nine as compared with ten for 50 objects) and consequently had more examplars per category. (There were no notable age differences in number of objects or pictures left unclassified—i.e. singles—although females left fewer singles than males). It was argued that in this respect, too, the older person's behavior could be viewed as more adequate, as indicative of a higher developmental stage, than the behavior of the younger adults.

Riegel (149, 152) put the oft-expressed viewpoint that intelligence tests do not measure adult intelligence in a novel form which may help to generate interesting research. His criticism in this respect was directed at Piagetian theory viewed as an explanatory basis for understanding adult intellectual functioning. He argued that this theory is weak (for this purpose) in two principal respects: (a) the final stage of formal operations does not provide an adequate basis for understanding adult thinking and thus a fifth stage, one of dialectic operations, is needed; and (b) adult behavior is not well accounted for by supposing (as is implied particularly in the Piagetian notion of equilibrium) that one does not, should not, within a short span of time operate at different developmental levels.

In developing his arguments along these lines, Riegel characterized Piagetian stages as cognitive changes to deal with contradictions. For example, an aspect of the change from preoperational to concrete operational thinking can be regarded as an outcome of becoming aware of, and resolving, contradictions associated with conservation—of having to suppose that an amount of water increases, say, in being poured from one beaker to another. If a person at one stage realizes contradictions in his cognitions, then he searches for noncontradictory conceptualizations; if he finds these at the next level of thinking, this produces an entire reorganization of his thinking processes to establish equilibrium. Thus he fixates (equilibrates) at this next level. In this way a person must, if he can (i.e. if he can become aware of the fundamental contradictions), move inexorably from the sensorimotor stage to the level of formal operations, always away from the contradictions of phenomenologically veridicial thinking.

Riegel's views in this regard are the jumping-off point for emphasizing that to "equilibrate" at the level of formal operations simply isn't a good way to characterize adult thinking.

A cognitive theory of development which is not limited to a description of thought in infancy, childhood, and puberty, but aims at interpreting maturity, must realize that an individual has to overcome thinking as a form of cognitive alienation ... has to return to a concrete dialectic mode of operation ... has to accept contradiction as a fundamental ingredient of action and thought and not as an insufficiency which has to be denied ... (152, p. 480).

Moreover, partly because a mature person tolerates and accepts contradictions

... he can operate at different developmental levels at the same time. Indeed, such multilevel synchronicity is necessary and, thus, desirable for appropriate performance in different situations. Undoubtedly, a scientist has often to operate at the formal operations level; however, when he comes home and fixes the roof he proceeds at a level of concrete operations ... [and] even the individual as a scientist would be lost in endless "ifs" and "whens" generated through formal permutations unless he preserves or regains a creative disregard to alternative possibilities, unless he commits himself to dialectic contradictions . . . This . . . revives the most basic property of thought, its creative power (152, p. 481).

Riegel cites numerous examples to illustrate that logically people do indeed effectively think with contradictions, and to suggest that such thinking could be at a higher level. Empirical evidence for such a stage theory (or indeed for any stage theory) in psychological (in distinction from logical) adulthood development is lacking, however.

There is probably some mischaracterization of Piagetian theory in Riegel's analysis (cf 77). For example, it is not clear that Piagetian theory implies that because one can think at the level of formal operations, he necessarily fixates in that kind of thinking and thus cannot, or does not, employ the operations of earlier stages. Nevertheless, it is provocative to consider contradiction as a fundamental aspect of good thinking, rather than as a bad symptom to be eradicated if at all possible. One is reminded of William James's dictum to the effect that consistency is the hobgoblin of small minds.

Rather complex findings were presented in respect to hypotheses that there is a regression in Piagetian stage development in adulthood. Graves (62), in support of earlier findings, found that many (indeed, most) adults in their 20s, 30s, and 40s do not demonstrate conservation of volume. Most of his subjects were poorly educated. Papalia (140) found that conservation of volume dropped sharply over the span from below to above age 65, but in roughly the same age range Storck, Looft & Hooper (176) found no notable decline in volume conservation. Hawley & Kelly (72) helped to clarify these apparently contradictory findings. They showed that a variety of formal operations tasks are substantially correlated with crystallized intelligence (rather than Gf) and not substantially (negatively) correlated with age over a range from the 20s through the 60s ($r = -0.19$). Looking back then at Papalia's results, they found that the older Ss in this study were unrepresentatively lower in educational level than the younger Ss and thus could be inferred to be unrepresentatively low in crystallized intelligence. Putting this finding together with Graves' results (indicating that many poorly educated adults do not demonstrate conservation), it was reasoned that Papalia's findings mainly indicated selection of older adults who would never have demonstrated conservation even at earlier ages, in contrast to younger adults who had acquired conservation.

The general conclusion this reviewer draws from the data (not only those of the review period but much which went before) is that adulthood development of human abilities is not all on the positive side—that beliefs in decrement theories are not simply (or mainly) obeisance to myth—but that such development is not all on the negative side either—that beliefs in notable adulthood improvement in intellectual abilities are not simply (or mainly) wishful thinking. Neither of these extreme views of the matter seems to be maximally conducive to producing better study in this area. It may be, however, that the emphasis for too long has been with decrement theories and that what is most needed in the near future is more, and more creative, research in the service of increment theories.

CONTROVERSY OVER THE NATURE-NURTURE OF INTELLIGENCE

Tyler had noted in the previous review that the perennial (if often dormant) interest in the heritability of intellectual abilities was revived near the end of the decade of the "activist 60s" by the wide dissemination of a Harvard Educational Review (HER) article written by Jensen (95). This interest flourished in the period of the present review. The Jensen article and debate concerning it has been discussed in every *Annual Review of Psychology* since 1970. In large part the controversy centered around the question of whether or not the mean differences between whites and blacks on measures of intellectual achievement are indicative of innate differences between these ethnic groups. To a lesser extent the issues concerned social class differences. Much of the published work pertaining to these questions was argument and reanalysis (both conceptual and empirical) of extant data, rather than production of new data designed to help resolve long-standing differences in interpretations of established findings. There seemed to be a kind of pushing and shoving, as it were, to get into the limelight on one side or the other (or all sides) of the controversy. Much of the work seemed to be rather hastily done or done by amateurs. The major output of books on human abilities was in this area, there being no fewer than 11 such rushes to judgment. Eysenck (50, 51) and Jensen (97, 99) each contributed two volumes; Herrnstein (74) expanded his popular and controversial Atlantic article into a book. Volumes opposed to the Eysenck-Jensen-Herrnstein positions were put together by Brace, Gamble & Bond (23), Kamin (108), Richardson, Spears & Richards (146), and Senna (168). Cancro (28) organized an evenly balanced volume of edited papers, although the contributions (prepared expressly for the book) by Eckland, Ginsburg, Hirsch, Humphreys, Hunt, Jensen, and Vandenberg were not, in general, the best representations of the major points these investigators had made on questions about ethnic and social class differences. Somewhat related also were reanalyses of the Coleman report data by Mosteller & Moynihan (134) and Mayeske et al (126), and a scholarly treatment of the concept of inequality by Jencks et al (93). An Oxford zoologist (4) produced a comprehensive treatise on the races of mankind in which roughly 20–25 percent of the space is devoted to intelligence and achievement differences of different races. He thus joined an affray already involving a Harvard astronomer (Layzar) and a Stanford physicist (Shockley), as well as anthropologists (Brace & Livingston), educationalists and educational psychologists (Gage, Scarr-Salapatek), geneticists (Bodmer, Cavalli-Sforza, Dobzhansky), journalists (M. Hunt, Rice), philosophers (Scriven), sociologists (Eckland, Leggett), and, of course, psychologists. As I say, there seemed to be some pushing and shoving to get in on this one.

And what did this flurry of activity produce for posterity? More heat than light? Probably. Surely there was no dearth of polite name-calling and there was no absence of innuendo to suggest that those on the other side of the controversy were ignorant, pig-headed, closed-minded, unfair, ethically obtuse, or, at the very least, unconscionably unaware of their emotional commitment to an irrational position. Among advocates there was little frank acknowledgment of the permissibility of the theory championed by the opposition. Yet some cool heads did manage to step between the stalwarts. Individuals such as Biesheuvel (12), Bereiter (10), Bodmer (16), Gottesman (59), Humphreys (88), Sowell (173), and Thoday & Gibson (178), for example, managed to make the point that while existing results probably are not entirely nonsense and do have some important practical and theoretical implications, nevertheless the evidence is equivocal and far from from adequate to provide a convincing case for either a mainly genetical or a mainly environmental interpretation. Moreover, although the epistemological issues in respect to these questions were not themselves vigorously attacked, cool heads did at least reopen questions about whether or not heritability and the heritability of racial differences in intellectual capacities can be scientific hypotheses. These reflections, as well as some of the exchanges between advocates, also provided more precise specifications of concepts such as heritability and reaction range and more precise statements of the hazards in drawing inferences about between-group differences from only the results of within-group analyses. Indeed, an optimist (such as the reviewer) could detect noteworthy general advance in understanding of the problems of making valid nature-nurture inferences on the basis of research conducted with humans.

A very constructive bit of work was provided by Loehlin, Lindzey & Spuhler (121), for example. Their readable book contains carefully reasoned, judiciously balanced, and well-informed analyses of several important sets of data and reasoned arguments advanced in support of and in opposition to the race differences hypothesis. There is little doubt that this book will serve for several years as a major jumping-off point for serious study in this area.

Also illustrative of a basis for optimism is some important work coming from what has become known as the "Birmingham group"—Broadhurst, Eaves, Fulker, Jinks, Mather (and probably others).[8] In one article Jinks & Fulker (103) provided a clear statement of a number of the basic design and statistical requirements which studies must meet if they are to yield convincing indications of the extent of within-group and between-group genetic and environmental influences. This paper did not, of course, solve the intractable problems occasioned by the fact that natural and societal factors do not simulate the conditions of random assignment of related persons to available environments, but it did take us some distance along the path toward understanding the basic assumptions in genetical analyses on samples of human subjects.

It seems likely also that future generations will find that some of the work supporting and opposing the racial differences hypothesis is of value as such, rather than merely as stimulus for the development of better scientific methods, as was suggested above. In this respect Jensen's *Educability and Group Differences* (99) will furnish nourishing food for thought for several years. This book constitutes probably the best case yet made for the claim that there are notable racial differences, genetically determined, in important intellectual abilities. On the other side of this argument serious thought will have to be given to Kamin's (108) vigorous demoli-

[8]A review of behavioral genetics by Broadhurst, Fulker & Wilcock appeared in Volume 25 (1974) of the *Annual Review of Psychology*.

tion job on the foundations of the research advanced in support for the racial differences hypothesis. Whereas it is generally accepted that some shoddy research and shoddy thinking will always exist in any scientific field and thus hamper the surge toward better understanding, Kamin's polemics suggest that in the study of the heritability and racial differences of intelligence such research and thinking has been the rule rather than the exception, and worse, has been used for maleficent purposes. These are strong words, but they are not baseless.

Ironically, perhaps the most devastating attack on the evidential basis for the heritability hypothesis was made by, of all people, Jensen (101). The occasion for the attack, which is perhaps better characterized as an apologia, was a review of several anomalous features of the kinship data reported by Burt over the last 30-odd years. In some claims these data have been allowed the major influence in analyses upon which estimates of the heritability of intelligence have been based. Yet Jensen found a number of serious problems with these data. (These problems constituted a major part of Kamin's case mentioned above.) For example, it appears from Burt's reports that for some mysterious reason the sample of dizygotic twins decreased from 172 in 1955 to 127 in 1966 and yet the correlations for several variables remained identical to the third decimal place despite the change in sample size! Such a result could reflect the fact of missing data in respect to some variables, of course, but then one must wonder why this fact, if it is a fact, wasn't mentioned in the reports. Kamin was considerably less sympathetic (and less conflicted) than Jensen in his analysis of these findings. He concluded that "The numbers left behind by Professor Burt are simply not worthy of our current scientific attention" (108, p. 47). Considering the sheer number of implausibilities which were identified in Burt's data, one is hard pressed to escape Kamin's conclusion. More than this, one is led to question how Burt's reports got into refereed journals and were so widely and uncritically accepted elsewhere when, in fact, the difficulties to which Jensen and Kamin allude were there to be corrected 10 and even 20 years ago. When one then realizes that in 1972, almost at the time he was writing his disclosure article, Jensen (98) was also called upon to write the *Psychometrika* obituary and eulogy for Burt, the whole dreadful matter takes on the aspects of a Greek tragedy!

Several lessons can be learned from the study in this period of the heritability of intelligence. Perhaps the main lessons are those indicating the conditions which data, analyses, and interpretive discussions should in the future be required to meet before results will be accepted into serious scientific discourse having noteworthy social implications. Had these lessons been better learned, a considerable amount of patch-up work referred to above could have gone for other, more constructive purposes.

UNFAIRNESS IN THE USE OF ABILITY MEASUREMENTS

Almost as hot as the issues on nature-nurture and race differences were questions pertaining to whether or not, or to what extent, ability test measurements are valid and fair when used to aid selection and promotion decisions. Here, too, the questions were asked mainly in respect to the possibilities for unfairness to blacks, although there was some consideration given to possible unfairness to other ethnic groups and to women. Attention was given also to general problems of test bias in decision-making (36, 40, 87, 166, 180).

By the end of the 1960s the broadly disseminated reports of Clark and Plotkin, Kirkpatrick, and Cooper and Sabel had greatly strengthened the already widely held belief that while abilities tests might possibly be valid for use with the majority group (and of course many have never accepted this claim), they were not valid for use in minority groups. Much public policy was premised upon this belief. The principal opposition to this view was mounted by Cleary, Thomas, and Stanley and a few others just prior to the review period. The major thrust of the counterattack was based upon results indicating that the predictive regression lines in samples of blacks are nearly parallel to the lines for whites and are not above the latter. Indeed, the suggestion was that the regression lines for blacks were more often than not below the comparable lines for whites, thus indicating what came to be known as overprediction. The idea that use of tests is fair if the regression lines for a minority and the majority groups are not significantly different came to be referred to as the "Cleary definition," although surely many had learned this definition, as had the reviewer (from Humphreys), many years before Cleary's paper appeared. Results in the review period continued, in general, to support previous findings indicating that the use of intellectual ability tests in educational and vocational selection and promotion in young adulthood usually is, by the Cleary definition, fair to the minority group or unfair to the majority group (e.g. 17, 27, 57, 165). In the main this was the conclusion of the special study of these issues requested by the APA's Board of Scientific Affairs (33). In studies in which the Ns were small, and/or the criterion measures were complex, subjective, and different for the groups compared, and/or the predictor measures were short and narrow, the findings tended to be equivocal and thus suggestive of the possibility that different regression equations would obtain for different ethnic groups (e.g. 118). As Bray & Moses noted in the 1972 *Annual Review of Psychology,* the more nearly studies approached an ideal of having adequate N, reliable criterion measures that were comparable in both groups, and reliable predictor measures of fairly broad intellectual abilities, the better were the indications of fairness in accordance with the Cleary definition. In this respect Humphreys observed that:

> The lack of empirical support for big differences in either intercepts or slopes of regression lines should not be surprising. There was never any good theoretical expectation that such differences would be found. The assumption of cultural deprivation does not itself constitute a theory. When one starts with that as a premise and develops the intervening steps in the reasoning in order to form a theory, the expectation is that deprivation will depress the scores on both the predictor test and the criterion measure, but not the correlation between the two. Approximate identity of regressions for minority and majority groups is the result anticipated (86, p. 60).

The idea that selection with tests is fair to minority groups was vigorously opposed by Jackson (91), speaking from the chair of the Association of Black Psychologists. The main argument in this opposition is that the entire culture, and hence the tests and the criteria of the culture, are biased against the black. Thus to define test fairness in terms of biased criteria is virtually to assure an answer in conformance with racist prejudgment. This position is thus not dissimilar from Humphreys' position cited immediately above. On a somewhat softer key Bernal (11) also suggested that problem in test bias is primarily in the definition of what is important in both the tests and that which the tests are called upon to predict.

Perhaps the most interesting issues which developed in respect to test fairness grew out of a budding recognition that the Cleary definition was by no means the only definition of fair use of tests. Thorndike (180) brought the matter to attention. He pointed out that even when the regression lines for two groups were the same but the groups differed on mean predictor score (and hence on mean criterion measures), what is fair by the Cleary definition is not fair if one defines this as selection in which the qualifying scores on a test are set at levels that will qualify applicants in the two groups in proportion to the fraction of the two groups reaching a specified level of criterion performance (180, p. 63). Darlington (40) independently developed this definition and considered also some other possible definitions of fair test use. Linn & Werts (120), Cole (36), Humphreys (88), and Schmidt & Hunter (166) developed these ideas still further.

Several interesting implications came out of this work. For example, Schmidt & Hunter demonstrated with data that the Cleary and Thorndike definitions usually will lead to quite different conclusions about whether or not tests have been used fairly. Darlington showed that using the Cleary definition and assuming a constant correlation between the criterion and ethnic group differences, the lower the validity of a predictor, the higher it could correlate with ethnic differences and still be considered fair. This presented the interesting possibility of shifting from relatively valid to relatively invalid tests in order to meet a criterion of fair test use. As Schmidt & Hunter pointed out, this also implied that as the validity of a predictor decreased, the probability of acceptance for minority group persons would approach zero even as the test could be judged to be fair by the Cleary definition. This, they allowed, " . . . might plausibly be argued to be unfair." Linn pointed out that application of the Cleary definition also led to the interesting possibility that one could change the judgment that a test was fair to a judgment that it was unfair by simply increasing its reliability, and of course this direction of change could even more easily be reversed. In much the same way Linn pointed out that two tests which were judged fair when considered individually could be found to be unfair when combined to yield a more reliable and valid composite. Yet, as Schmidt and Hunter emphasized, application of the Cleary definition will, relative to the Thorndike definition, lead to higher levels of performance, better individual-occupational role fit, and greater benefit to the individual and to the society because of this better role fit. They pointed out that "use of the Thorndike definitions means that certain majority applicants will be rejected in favor of minority applicants with lower probabilities of success on the criterion—a situation that would be considered reverse discrimination by many." And they indicated that if only a very few groups were to demand equal treatment under the provisions of the Thorndike definition, " . . . much if not most of the societal benefit accruing from the use of valid selection procedures would be lost." And to move from tests to other kinds of selection procedures was seen to be in no way a solution to the basic problems. As Humphreys put it, "moves to abolish tests are more ostrich-like than human-like. The problem will simply not go away."

In sum, although there was no clear resolution of the social problems, the psychometric solution seemed to be on the side of the Cleary rather than the Thorndike definition of unfairness in test use. The denouement has yet to be recited in the courts, however.

OMISSIONS

Those who have suffered through the previous pages of this review will no doubt be anticipating more, for there was much more work on human abilities in the review period than has been touched upon in previous sections. And yet this review must end now. What can be said about the omitted research? One thing for sure, it is not less worthy as a mass than that which was included. There are piles of articles the reviewer has read (not to mention the bigger piles unread) which deal with many important issues. Each pile represents an area which could be as important as any included in the review. Failure to mention the work of any one of these piles mainly represents the reviewer's preferences, his inability to obtain a view of what the pile was all about, and time and space constraints, rather than lack of good stuff in the pile. My apologies to those whose work was thus slighted.

CONCLUDING REMARKS

However many heads the Hydra of study of human abilities may have, the beast is alive and moving. Here we have considered mainly only where it has been. Perhaps its heads are looking to see where it might best go? Is there a grand theory emerging from all this? Some of the signs are there. Cognitive development is merging with traditional learning theory. Memory theory is becoming part of theory of intellect. Psycholinguists are talking as if they were serial learning specialists, and vice versa. The concepts derived from study of individual differences are getting crossed with those derived from research in which individual differences are anathema. Cronbach's (38) ideas about education-ability interaction are exerting considerable influence. Underwood (186) and Estes (49) have "discovered" individual differences and intelligence. Physiologists and geneticists are in on the act, and computer simulators, and physicists, and opticians, and anthropologists, and so on and so forth. No fewer than 10 books on general theory about human abilities appeared during the short span of the review period [the contributions of Cattell (32) and Matarazzo (125) being perhaps most notable]. Thus here is where the action is. Perhaps the contemplation will get there, too, and the next reviewer will be able to report on the grand theory?

Literature Cited

1. Anders, T. R., Fozard, J. L. 1973. Effects of age upon retrieval from primary and secondary memory. *Dev. Psychol.* 9:411–15
2. Anders, T. R., Fozard, J. L., Lillyquist, T. D. 1972. Effects of age upon retrieval from short-term memory. *Dev. Psychol.* 6:214–17
3. Arenberg, D. 1973. Cognition and aging: verbal learning, memory, and problem solving. In *The Psychology of Adult Development and Aging*, ed. C. Eisdorfer, M. P. Lawton, 74–97. Washington DC: Am. Psychol. Assoc. 718 pp.
4. Baker, J. R. 1974. *Race.* New York: Oxford Univ. Press. 656 pp.
5. Bakker, D. J. 1972. *Temporal Order in Disturbed Reading.* Rotterdam Univ. Press
6. Baltes, P. B. 1973. Life-span models of psychological aging: A white elephant? *Gerontologist* 13:458–92
7. Baltes, P. B., Labouvie, G. V. 1973. Adult development of intellectual performance: Description, explanation, and modification. See Ref. 3, 157–219
8. Baltes, P. B., Schaie, K. W., Eds. 1973. *Life-span Developmental Psychology: Personality and Socialization.* New York: Academic. 452 pp.
9. Bechtoldt, H. P. 1974. A confirmatory analysis of the factor stability hypothesis. *Psychometrika* 39:319–26
10. Bereiter, C. 1972. The relation of social class and educational aptitude. *Can. Psychol.* 13:329–40
11. Bernal, E. M. Jr. 1975. A response to "Educational Uses of Tests and Disadvantaged Subjects." *Am. Psychol.* 30:93–95
12. Biesheuvel, S. 1972. An examination of Jensen's theory concerning educability, heritability and population differences. *Psychol. Afr.* 14:87–94
13. Bloom, B. S. 1974. Time and learning. *Am. Psychol.* 29:682–88
14. Bloxom, B. 1972. Alternative approaches to factorial invariance. *Psychometrika* 37:425–40
15. Bock, R. D., Kolakowski, D. 1973. Further evidence of sex-linked major-gene influence on human spatial visualizing ability. *Am. J. Hum. Genet.* 25:1–14
16. Bodmer, W. F. 1972. Race and IQ: the genetic background. See Ref. 146, 83–113
17. Boehm, V. R. 1972. Negro-white differences in validity of employment and training selection procedures: Summary of recent evidence. *J. Appl. Psychol.* 56:33–39
18. Bolton, B. 1972. Factor analytic studies of communication skills, intelligence and other psychological abilities of young deaf persons. *Rehabil. Psychol.* 19:71–79
19. Bosco, J. 1972. The visual information processing speed of lower middle class children. *Child Dev.* 43:1418–22
20. Botwinick, J. 1973. *Aging and Behavior.* New York: Springer
21. Botwinick, J., Storandt, M. 1974. *Memory, Related Functions and Age.* Springfield, Ill: Thomas. 198 pp.
22. Bourne, L. E., Ekstrand, B. R., Dominowski, R. L. 1971. *The Psychology of Thinking.* Englewood Cliffs, NJ: Prentice-Hall
23. Brace, C. L., Gamble, G. R., Bond, J. T., Eds. 1971. *Race and Intelligence.* Washington DC: Am. Anthropol. Assoc.
24. Bratfisch, O. 1971. *A further study on subjective and objective intelligence factors.* Rep. No. 20, Inst. Appl. Psychol., Univ. Stockholm
25. Briggs, C., Elkind, D. 1973. Cognitive development in early readers. *Dev. Psychol.* 9:279–80
26. Bruner, J. S., Koslowski, B. 1972. Visually preadapted constituents of manipulatory action. *Perception* 1:3–14
27. Campbell, J. T. 1973. Tests are valid for minority groups too. *Publ. Personnel Manage.* 2:70–73
28. Cancro, R., Ed. 1971. *Intelligence: Genetic and Environmental Influences.* New York: Grune & Stratton
29. Carroll, J. B. 1972. Stalking the wayward factors. *Contemp. Psychol.* 17:321–24
30. Carroll, J. B. 1974. Fitting a model of school learning to aptitude and achievement data over grade levels. In *The Aptitude-Achievement Distinction*, ed. D. R. Green, 53–78. Monterey, Ca: CTB/McGraw-Hill
31. Carroll, J. B. 1975. Psychometric tests as cognitive tasks: A new "structure of intellect." In *The Nature of Intelligence*, ed. L. Resnick. Erlbaum
32. Cattell, R. B. 1971. *Abilities: Their Structure, Growth and Action.* Boston: Houghton-Mifflin. 583 pp.
33. Cleary, T. A., Humphreys, L. G., Kendrick, S. A., Wesman, A. 1975. Educa-

tional uses of tests with disadvantaged students. *Am. Psychol.* 30:15–41

34. Coates, S., Bromberg, P. M. 1973. Factorial structure of the Wechsler preschool and primary scale of intelligence between the ages of 4 and 6½. *J. Consult. Clin. Psychol.* 40:365–70

35. Coie, J. D., Dorval, B. 1973. Sex differences in the intellectual structure of social interaction skills. *Dev. Psychol.* 8:261–67

36. Cole, N. S. 1972. *Bias in selection.* Res. Rep. 51. Iowa City: Am. Coll. Test. Serv.

37. Craik, F. I. M. 1971. Age differences in recognition memory. *Q. J. Exp. Psychol.* 23:316–23

38. Cronbach, L. J. 1975. Beyond the two disciplines of scientific psychology. *Am. Psychol.* 30:116–27

39. Cropley, A. J. 1972. A five-year longitudinal study of the validity of creativity tests. *Dev. Psychol.* 6:119–24

40. Darlington, R. B. 1971. Another look at "cultural fairness." *J. Educ. Meas.* 8:71–82

41. Dasen, P. R., Christie, R. D. 1972. A regression phenomenon in the conservation of weight. *Arch. Psychol.* 41:145–52

42. DeLacey, P. R. 1971. Verbal intelligence, operational thinking and environment in part-Aboriginal children. *Aust. J. Psychol.* 23:145–49

43. Denney, D. R., Denney, N. W. 1973. The use of classification for problem solving: a comparison of middle and old age. *Dev. Psychol.* 9:275–78

44. Denney, N. W., Lennon, M. L. 1972. Classification: a comparison of middle and old age. *Dev. Psychol.* 7:210–13

45. Dudek, S. Z., Dyer, G. B. 1972. A longitudinal study of Piaget's developmental stages and the concept of regression: II. *J. Pers. Assess.* 36:468–78

46. Duffy, O. B., Clair, T. N., Egeland, B., Dinello, M. 1972. Relationship of intelligence, visual-motor skills, and psycholinguistic abilities with achievement in the third, fourth and fifth grades. *J. Educ. Psychol.* 63:358–62

47. Eliot, J., Salkind, N. 1973. *Spatial Abilities and Children's Spatial Development.* College Park, Md: Inst. Child Study, 91 pp.

48. Erginel, A. 1972. The relation of cognitive style and intelligence to achievement and errors in thinking. *Hacettepe Bull. Soc. Sci. Hum.* 4:8–20

49. Estes, W. K. 1974. Learning theory and intelligence. *Am. Psychol.* 29:740–49

50. Eysenck, H. J. 1971. *The IQ Argument: Race, Intelligence and Education.* London: Temple-Smith. 155 pp.

51. Eysenck, H. J. 1973. *The Inequality of Man.* London: Temple-Smith. 288 pp.

51a. Eysenck, H. J., Ed. 1973. *The Measurement of Intelligence.* Baltimore: Williams & Wilkins. 488 pp.

52. Feldman, S. S. 1972. Children's understanding of negation as a logical operation. *Genet. Psychol. Monogr.* 85:3–49

53. Fitzgerald, J. M., Nesselroade, J. R., Baltes, P. B. 1973. Emergence of adult intellectual structure: prior to or during adolescence. *Dev. Psychol.* 9:114–19

54. Flores, M. B., Evans, G. T. 1972. Some differences in cognitive abilities between selected Canadian and Filipino students. *Multivar. Behav. Res.* 7:175–91

55. Freeman, N. H. 1972. Process and product in children's drawing. *Perception* 1:123–40

56. Fulgosi, A., Guilford, J. P. 1972. Factor structures with divergent- and convergent-production abilities in groups of American and Yugoslavian adolescents. *J. Gen. Psychol.* 87:169–80

57. Gael, S., Grant, D. L. 1972. Employment test validation for minority and nonminority telephone company service representatives. *J. Appl. Psychol.* 56:135–39

58. Gilberg, J. G., Levee, R. F. 1971. Patterns of declining memory. *J. Gerontol.* 26:70–75

59. Gottesman, I. I. 1972. Testimony submitted to United States Senate Select Committee on Equal Education Opportunity, Feb. 24.

60. Goulet, L. R., Baltes, P. B., Eds. 1970. *Life Span Developmental Psychology: Research and Theory.* New York: Academic. 591 pp.

61. Gowan, J. 1971. The relationship between creativity and giftedness. *Gifted Child Q.* 15:239–43

62. Graves, A. J. 1972. Attainment of conservation of mass, weight and volume in minimally educated adults. *Dev. Psychol.* 7:223

63. Gray, J. A., Buffrey, A. W. H. 1971. Sex differences in emotional and cognitive behavior in mammals including man: adaptive and neural bases. *Acta Psychol.* 35:89–111

64. Guilford, J. P., Hoepfner, R. 1971. *The Analysis of Intelligence.* New York: McGraw-Hill

65. Guttman, L. 1970. Integration of test design and analysis. *Proc. 1969 Invit. Conf. Test. Probl.* Princeton, NJ: ETS

66. Hakstian, A. R., Cattell, R. B. 1974. The checking of primary ability structure on a broader basis of performance. *Br. J. Educ. Psychol.* 44:140–54

67. Halpin, G., Halpin, G. 1973. The effect of motivation on creative thinking abilities. *J. Creative Behav.* 7:51–53

68. Harris, M. L., Harris, C. W. 1971. *Analysis of dimensions of a battery of reference tests for cognitive abilities: fifth grade boys and girls.* Tech. Rep. No. 192, A Structure of Concept Attainment Abilities, Univ. Wisconsin

69. Harris, M. L., Harris, C. W. 1971. A factor analytic interpretation strategy. *Educ. Psychol. Meas.* 31:589–606

70. Harris, M. L., Harris, C. W. 1971. *Three systems of classifying cognitive abilities as bases for reference tests.* Theor. Pap. 33, A Structure of Concept Attainment Abilities, Univ. Wisconsin

71. Harwood, E., Naylor, G. F. K. 1971. Changes in the constitution of the WAIS intelligence pattern with advancing age. *Aust. J. Psychol.* 23:297–303

72. Hawley, I., Kelly, F. J. 1973. *Formal operations among adults as a function of age, education, and fluid and crystalized intelligence.* Presented at Gerontological Soc., Miami, Fla.

73. Heron, A. 1973. Cultural determinants of concrete operational behavior. *Proc. 1st Conf. Int. Assoc. Cross-Cult. Psychol.* Hong Kong Univ. Press

74. Herrnstein, R. J. 1973. *IQ in the Meritocracy.* Boston: Little, Brown. 235 pp.

75. Hollenbeck, G. P., Kaufman, A. S. 1973. Factor analysis of the Wechsler Preschool and Primary Scale of Intelligence (WPPSI). *J. Clin. Psychol.* 29:41–45

76. Hooper, F. H. 1972. An evaluation of logical operations instruction in the preschool. In *The Preschool in Action: Exploring Early Childhood Programs,* ed. R. K. Parker, 134–86. Boston: Allyn & Bacon

77. Hooper, F. H. 1976. Life-span analyses of Piagetian concept tasks: The search for nontrivial qualitative change. In *The Developing Individual in a Changing World; General and Historical Issues,* ed. K. Riegel, J. Meacam. The Hague: Mouton

78. Hooper, F. H., Fitzgerald, J., Papalia, D. 1971. Piagetian theory and the aging process: extensions and speculations. *Aging Hum. Dev.* 2:3–20

79. Horn, J. L. 1970. Organization of data on life-span development of human abilities. See Ref. 60

80. Horn, J. L. 1972. The structure of intellect; primary abilities. In *Multivariate Personality Research,* ed. R. H. Dreger, 451–55. Baton Rouge, La.: Claitor

81. Horn, J. L. 1973. Theory of functions represented among auditory and visual test performances. See Ref. 158

82. Horn, J. L. 1975. Psychometric studies of aging and intelligence. In *Geriatric Psychopharmacology: The Scene Today,* ed. S. Gershon, A. Raskin. New York: Raven

83. Horn, J. L., Knapp, J. R. 1973. On the subjective character of the empirical base of Guilford's Structure-of-Intellect model. *Psychol. Bull.* 80:33–43

84. Horn, J. L., Knapp, J. R. 1974. Thirty wrongs do not make a right: a reply to Guilford. *Psychol. Bull.* 81:502–4

85. Hultsch, D. F. 1971. Adult age differences in free classification and free recall. *Dev. Psychol.* 4:338–42

86. Humphreys, L. G. 1973. Implications of group differences for test interpretation. *1972 Invit. Conf. Test. Probl.* Princeton, NJ: ETS

87. Humphreys, L. G. 1973. Statistical definitions of test validity for minority groups. *J. Appl. Psychol.* 58:1–4

88. Humphreys, L. G. 1975. Race and sex differences and their implications for educational and occupational equality. In *Culture, Child and School,* ed. M. C. Maehr, W. M. Stallings. Belmont, Calif: Brooks/Cole. In press

89a. Humphreys, L. G., Dachler, H. P. 1969. Jensen's theory of intelligence. *J. Educ. Psychol.* 60:419–26, 432–33

89b. Humphreys, L. G., Fleishman, A. 1974. Pseudo-orthogonal and other analysis of variance designs involving individual-differences variables. *J. Educ. Psychol.* 66:464–72

90. Hunt, J. McV. 1972. *Sequential order and plasticity in early psychological development.* Presented at Jean Piaget Soc. 2nd Ann. Symp., Temple Univ., Philadelphia, Pa.

91. Jackson, G. D. 1975. On the report of the ad hoc committee on educational uses of tests with disadvantaged students. *Am. Psychol.* 30:88–92

92. Jarvik, L. F., Blum, J. E. 1971. Cognitive declines as predictors of mortality in discordant twin pairs—a twenty-year longitudinal study. In *Prediction of Life Span,* ed. E. Palmore, F. C. Jeffers, 199–211. Lexington, Mass: Heath Lexington Books

93. Jencks, C. et al 1972. *Inequality: A Reassessment of the Effect of Family*

Schooling in America. New York: Basic Books

94. Jenkins, J. J. 1974. Remember that old theory of memory? Well, forget it! *Am. Psychol.* 29:785–95
95. Jensen, A. R. 1969. How much can we boost IQ and scholastic achievement? *Harv. Educ. Rev.* 39:1–123
96. Jensen, A. R. 1971. A two-factor theory of familiar mental retardation. *Proc. 4th Int. Congr. Hum. Genet.,* 263–71. Amsterdam: Excerpta Medica
97. Jensen, A. R. 1972. *Genetics and Education.* London: Methuen
98. Jensen, A. R. 1972. Sir Cyril Burt. *Psychometrika* 37:115–17
99. Jensen, A. R. 1973. *Educability and Group Differences.* New York: Harper & Row. 407 pp.
100. Jensen, A. R. 1974. Interaction of Level I and Level II abilities with race and socioeconomic status. *J. Educ. Psychol.* 66:99–111
101. Jensen, A. R. 1974. Kinship correlations reported by Sir Cyril Burt. *Behav. Genet.* 4:10–35
102. Jensen, A. R., Frederiksen, J. 1973. Free recall of categorized and uncategorized lists: a test of the Jensen hypothesis. *J. Educ. Psychol.* 65:304–12
103. Jinks, J. L., Fulker, D. W. 1970. Comparison of the biometrical, genetical, MAVA, and classical approaches to the analysis of human behavior. *Psychol. Bull.* 73:311–49
104. Jones, P. A. 1972. Formal operational reasoning and the use of tentative statements. *Cogn. Psychol.* 3:467–71
105. Jöreskog, K. G. 1971. Simultaneous factor analysis in several populations. *Psychometrika* 36:409–26
106. Kagan, J. 1972. Do infants think? *Sci. Am.* 226:74–82
107. Kagan, J., Klein, R. E. 1973. Cross-cultural perspectives on early development. *Am. Psychol.* 28:947–61
108. Kamin, L. J. 1974. *The Science and Politics of IQ.* New York: Wiley. 183 pp.
109. Kaufman, A. 1971. Piaget and Gesell: A psychometric analysis of tests built from their tasks. *Child Dev.* 42:1341–60
109a. Kelly, M., Tenezakis, M., Huntsman, R. 1973. Some unusual conservation behavior in children exposed to two cultures. *Br. J. Educ. Psychol.* 43:181–82
110. Khan, S. B. 1970. Development of mental abilities: an investigation of the "differentiation hypothesis." *Can. J. Psychol./Rev. Can. Psychol.* 24:199–202
111. Kinsbourne, M., Berryhill, J. L. 1972. The nature of the interaction between

pacing and age decrement in learning. *J. Gerontol.* 27:471–77
112. Klinger, D. E., Saunders, D. R. 1975. A factor analysis of items for nine subtests of the WAIS. *Multivar. Behav. Res.* 10:131–54
113. Kogan, N. 1971. A clarification of Cropley and Maslany's analysis of the Wallach-Kogan creativity tests. *Br. J. Psychol.* 62:113–17
114. Kogan, N. 1973. Categorizing and conceptualizing styles in younger and older adults, RB-73. Princeton, NJ: ETS
115. Kogan, N., Pankove, E. 1972. Creative ability over a five-year span. *Child Dev.* 43:427–42
116. Krizmanic, M. 1971. Conformity of free associations of young and old subjects. *Rev. Psichol.* 2:17–21
117. Labouvie, G. V., Frohring, W. R., Baltes, P. B., Goulet, L. R. 1973. Changing relationship between recall performance and abilities as a function of stage of learning and timing of recall. *J. Educ. Psychol.* 64:191–98
118. Lefkowitz, J. 1972. Differential validity: ethnic group as a moderator in predicting tenure. *Personnel Psychol.* 25: 223–40
119. Lewis, M., McGurk, H. 1972. Evaluation of infant intelligence: Infant intelligence scores—true or false? *Science* 178:1174–77
120. Linn, R. L., Werts, C. E. 1971. Considerations for studies of test bias. *J. Educ. Meas.* 8:1–4
121. Loehlin, J. C., Lindzey, G., Spuhler, J. 1975. *Race Differences in Intelligence.* San Francisco: Freeman. 380 pp.
122. MacArthur, R. S. 1973. *Cognitive strengths of Central Canadian and Northwest Greenland Eskimo children.* Victoria, B.C.: Can. Psychol. Assoc.
123. Mackay, C. K., Brazendale, A. H., Wilson, L. F. 1972. Concepts of horizontal and vertical: a methodological note. *Dev. Psychol.* 7:232–37
124. Marx, D. J. 1970. Intentional and incidental concept formation as a function of conceptual complexity, intelligence and task complexity. *J. Educ. Psychol.* 61:297–304
125. Matarazzo, J. D. 1972. *Wechsler's Measurement and Appraisal of Adult Intelligence.* Baltimore: Williams and Wilkins. 572 pp. 5th ed.
126. Mayeske, G. W. et al 1973. *A study of the achievement of our nation's students.* Washington DC: GPO
127. McCall, R. B., Hogarty, P. S., Hurlburt, N. 1972. Transitions in infant sen-

sorimotor development and the prediction of childhood IQ. *Am. Psychol.* 27:728–48

128. McGaw, B., Jöreskog, K. G. 1971. Factorial invariance of ability measures in groups differing in intelligence and socioeconomic status. *Br. J. Math. Stat. Psychol.* 24:154–68

129. Meyers, C. E., Orpet, R. E. 1972. Conservation of fluid predicted from structure of intellect and conceptual style. *Multivar. Behav. Res.* 7:135–46

130. Millman, J., Jacobson, L., Berger, S. E. 1971. Effects of intelligence, information processing and mediation conditions on conceptual learning. *J. Educ. Psychol.* 62:293–99

131. Mlodnosky, L. B. 1972. The Bender Gestalt and the Frostig as predictors of first-grade reading achievement among economically deprived children. *Psychol. Sch.* 9:25–30

132. Monge, R. H., Hultsch, D. F. 1971. Paired-associate learning as a function of adult age and the length of the anticipation and inspection intervals. *J. Gerontol.* 26:157–62

133. Morency, A., Wepman, J. M. 1973. Early perceptual ability and later school achievement. *Elem. Sch. J.* 73:323–27

134. Mosteller, F., Moynihan, D. P., Eds. 1972. *On Equality of Educational Opportunity.* New York: Vintage Books

135. Murphy, R. T. 1973. *Investigations of a creativity dimension,* RB-73-12. Princeton, NJ: ETS

136. Nehrke, M. F. 1973. Age and sex differences in discrimination learning and transfer of training. *J. Gerontol.* 28:320–27

137. Nesselroade, J. R., Reese, H. W., Eds. 1973. *Life-Span Developmental Psychology: Methodological Issues.* New York: Academic. 364 pp.

138. Nesselroade, J. R., Schaie, K. W., Baltes, P. B. 1972. Ontogenetic and generational components of structural and quantitative change in adult behavior. *J. Gerontol.* 27:222–28

139. Nishikawa, K. 1971. Longitudinal study of intellectual differentation. *Jpn. J. Psychol.* 42:217–20

140. Papalia, D. E. 1972. The status of several conservation abilities across the life-span. *Hum. Dev.* 15:229–43

141. Pawlik, K. 1971. *Dimensionen des Verhaltens.* Bern Stuttgart Wein: Huber. 561 pp.

142. Pease, D., Wolins, L., Stockdale, D. F. 1973. Relationship and prediction of infant tests. *J. Genet. Psychol.* 122:31–35

143. Piaget, J. 1973. *The Child and Reality: Problems of Genetic Psychology.* New York: Grossman. 182 pp.

144. Quereshi, M. Y. 1973. Patterns of intellectual development during childhood and adolescence. *Genet. Psychol. Monogr.* 87:313–44

145. Reinert, G. 1970. Comparative factor analytic studies of intelligence throughout the human life span. See Ref. 60a, 465–85

146. Richardson, K., Spears, D., Richards, M., Eds. 1972. *Race and Intelligence: The Fallacies Behind the Race-IQ Controversy.* Baltimore: Penguin. 205 pp.

147. Riegel, K. F. 1971. The prediction of death and longevity in longitudinal research. See Ref. 92, 139–52

148. Riegel, K. F. 1972. The changing individual in the changing society. Reprinted from *Determinants of Behavioral Development,* 239–57. New York: Academic

149. Riegel, K. F. 1973. Language and cognition: some life-span developmental issues. *Gerontologist* 13:478–82

150. Riegel, K. F. 1973. The recall of historical events. *Behav. Sci.* 8:354–363

151. Riegel, K. F., Ed. 1973. *Structure, Transformation, Interaction: Developmental and Historical Aspects.* Basel: Karger

152. Riegel, K. F. 1973. *Dialectic operations: the final period of cognitive development.* Princeton, NJ: ETS

153. Riegel, K. F., Riegel, R. M. 1972. Development, drop and death. *Dev. Psychol.* 6:306–19

154. Ross, J. E. 1970. Simplification of human abilities with age in four social class groups. *Proc. 78th Ann. Conv. APA*

155. Rossman, B. B., Gollob, H. F. 1975. Comparison of social judgments of creativity and intelligence. *J. Pers. Soc. Psychol.* 31:371–81

156. Rossman, B. B., Horn, J. L. 1972. Cognitive, motivational and temperamental indicants of creativity and intelligence. *J. Educ. Meas.* 9:265–86

157. Rotter, D. M., Langland, L., Berger, D. 1971. The validity of tests of creative thinking in seven-year-old children. *Gifted Child Q.* 15:273–78

158. Royce, J. R. 1973. The conceptual framework for a multi-factor theory of individuality. In *Contributions of Multivariate Analysis to Psychological Theory,* ed. J. R. Royce. London: Academic

159. Ruble, D. N., Nakamura, C. Y. 1972. Task orientation versus social orientation in young children and their atten-

tion to relevant social cues. *Child Dev.* 43:471–80

160. Sanford, A. J., Maule, A. J. 1973. The concept of general experience: Age and strategies in guessing future events. *J. Gerontol.* 28:81–88

161. Schaie, K. W. 1974. Translations in gerontology—from lab to life. *Am. Psychol.* 29:802–7

162. Schaie, K. W., Gribbin, K. 1975. Adult development and aging. *Ann. Rev. Psychol.* 26:65–96

163. Schaie, K. W., Labouvie-Vief, G. 1974. Generational versus ontogenetic components of change in adult cognitive behavior: A fourteen-year cross-sequential study. *Dev. Psychol.* 10:305–20

164. Schaie, K. W., Labouvie, G. V., Buech, B. U. 1973. Generational and cohort-specific differences in adult cognitive functioning: A fourteen-year study of independent samples. *Dev. Psychol.* 9: 151–66

165. Schmidt, F. L., Berner, J. G., Hunter, J. E. 1973. Racial differences in validity of employment tests. *J. Appl. Psychol.* 58:5–9

166. Schmidt, F. L., Hunter, J. E. 1974. Racial and ethnic bias in psychological tests. *Am. Psychol.* 29:1–8

167. Schonfield, D. 1972. Theoretical nuances and practical old questions: the psychology of aging. *Can. Psychol.* 13: 252–66

168. Senna, C., Ed. 1973. *The Fallacy of IQ.* New York: Third Press. 184 pp.

169. Shubert, D. S. 1973. Intelligence as necessary but not sufficient for creativity. *J. Genet. Psychol.* 122:45–47

170. Shucard, D. W., Horn, J. L. 1972. Cortical evoked potentials and measurement of human abilities. *J. Comp. Physiol. Psychol.* 78:59–68

171. Siegler, R. S., Liebert, D. E., Liebert, R. M. 1973. Inhelder and Piaget's pendulum problem: teaching preadolescents to act as scientists. *Dev. Psychol.* 9:97–101

172. Sontag, L. W. 1971. The history of longitudinal research implications for the future. *Child Dev.* 42:987–1002

173. Sowell, T. 1973. The great IQ controversy. *Change* 5:33–37

174. Stafford, R. E. 1972. Negative relationships between ability to visualize space and grades in specific courses. *J. Learn. Disabil.* 5:42–44

175. Stephens, B., McLaughlin, J. A., Miller, C. K., Glass, G. V. 1972. Factorial structure of selected psycho-educa-tional measures and Piagetian reasoning assessments. *Dev. Psychol.* 6:343–48

176. Storck, P. A., Looft, W. R., Hooper, F. H. 1972. Interrelationships among Piagetian tasks and traditional measures of cognitive abilities in mature and aged adults. *J. Gerontol.* 27:461–65

177. Sullivan, J. 1973. The relationship of creative and convergent thinking to literal and critical reading ability of children in the upper grades. *J. Educ. Res.* 66:374–77

178. Thoday, J. M., Gibson, J. B. 1970. Environmental and genetical contributions to class differences: a model experiment. *Science* 167:990–92

179. Thomas, J. R., Chissom, B. S. 1973. An investigation of the combination of a perceptual-motor test and a cognitive ability test for the purpose of classifying first-grade children into reading groups. *Psychol. Sch.* 10:185–89

180. Thorndike, R. L. 1971. Concepts of culture-fairness. *J. Educ. Meas.* 8:63–70

181. Torrance, E. P. 1972. Tendency to produce unusual visual perspective as a predictor of creative achievement. *Percept. Mot. Skills* 34:911–15

182. Torrance, E. P. 1972. Predictive validity of the Torrance tests of creative thinking. *J. Creative Behav.* 6:236–52

183. Torrance, E. P. 1972. Predictive validity of "bonus" scoring for combinations on repeated figures tests of creative thinking. *J. Psychol.* 81:167–71

184. Traxler, A. J., Britton, J. H. 1970. Age differences in retroaction as a function of anticipation interval and transfer paradigm. *Proc. 78th Ann. Conv. APA* 5:683–84

185. Tuddenham, R. 1970. A Piagetian test of cognitive development. In *On Intelligence,* ed. B. Dockrell. London: Methuen

186. Underwood, B. J. 1975. Individual differences as a crucible in theory construction. *Am. Psychol.* 30:128–34

187. Vernon, M. 1972. Language development's relationship to cognition, affectivity and intelligence. *Can. Psychol.* 13:360–74

188. Vernon, P. E. 1971. Effects of administration and scoring on divergent thinking tests. *Br. J. Educ. Psychol.* 41: 245–57

189. Vernon, P. E. 1972. The validity of divergent thinking tests. *Alberta J. Educ. Res.* 18:249–58

190. Vernon, P. E. 1972. The usefulness of 'creativity tests.' *Sch. Guid. Worker* 27:30–35

191. Vernon, P. E. 1972. Sex differences in personality structure at age 14. *Can. J. Behav. Sci.* 4:283–97

192. Vernon, P. E. 1972. The distinctiveness of field independence. *J. Pers.* 40: 366–91

193. Ward, J. 1972. The saga of Butch and Slim. *Bri. J. Educ. Psychol.* 42:267–89

194. Ward, J., Pearson, L. 1973. A comparison of two methods of testing logical thinking. *Can. J. Behav. Sci./Rev. Can. Sci. Comp.* 5:385–98

195. Ward, W. C., Kogan, N., Pankove, E. 1972. Incentive effects in children's creativity. *Child Dev.* 43:669–76

196. Waugh, N. C., Fozard, J. L., Talland, G. A., Erwin, D. E. 1973. Effects of age and stimulus repetition on two-choice reaction time. *J. Gerontol.* 28:466–70

197. Wheaton, G. R., Shaffer, E. J., Mirabella, A., Fleishman, E. A. 1973. *Methods for predicting job-ability requirements: 1. Ability requirements as a function of changes in the characteristics of an auditory signal identification task.* Res. Rep. Am. Inst. Res., Washington DC

198. Witkin, H. A. 1973. *The role of cognitive style in academic performance and in teacher-student relations,* RB-73-11. Princeton, NJ:ETS

199. Witkin, H. A., Oltman, P. K., Chase, J. B., Friedman, F. 1971. Cognitive patterning in the blind. In *Cognitive Studies, Vol. 2: Deficits in Cognition,* ed. J. Hellmuth, 16–46. New York: Brunner/Mazel

200. Witte, K. L. 1971. Optimal shift behavior in children and young and elderly adults. *Psychon. Sci.* 25:329–30

201. Youniss, J., Furth, H. G. 1973. Reasoning and Piaget. *Nature* 244:314–15

202. Zaretsky, H., Halberstam, J. 1968. Age differences in paired-associate learning. *J. Gerontol.* 23:165–68

ANALYSIS OF QUALITATIVE DATA ❖261

J. E. Keith Smith

Department of Psychology, University of Michigan, Ann Arbor, Michigan 48104

INTRODUCTION

Historically, psychological statistics texts, and indeed most other statistics texts, have emphasized the analysis of measurement data. The books from which we learned our data analysis and have continued to use as professional references seldom devote 10% of their space to the questions of how to treat data based on counts of the number of times a particular event has occurred rather than on how big or how long a response was. Even the more advanced books have concentrated on measurement data rather than qualitative or categorical data. The book on experimental design most used in psychology, written by Winer (69), relegates its only discussion of the analysis of contingency data to an appendix. For the most part, discussion of qualitative data is limited to description of the test of total independence in a two-way contingency table with perhaps a brief section on the McNemar test of correlated proportions. The primary effort instead has been to transform frequency data into a form which is at least approximately suitable for analysis by conventional measurement methods.

The main reason for this wildly disproportionate emphasis on measurement statistics has not been insensitivity on the part of textbook writers but rather the lack of well-documented and convenient qualitative methods. In the past 10 years or so this lack has been largely overcome, and it is the purpose of this review to acquaint psychologists with the very rich set of tools now available in the statistical literature for analyzing qualitative data as qualitative data, in terms of parameters natural to that data. There remain gaps in this sort of analysis so that some data still must be treated by conventional (arc-sin) methods, but even these gaps are likely to be filled in the near future.

Earlier authors in this series—Binder (4), Sitgreaves (65), Aitkin (1), and Meredith, Fredricksen & McLaughlin (53)—have noted briefly the developments discussed here, but with the publication of Haberman's book (35) and that of Bishop, Feinberg & Holland (7), it seems appropriate to discuss the area at some length.

The major portion of this review will be devoted to the new developments just mentioned. However, the first section will review recent publications relevant to older classical problems.

NEW WORK ON OLD PROBLEMS

Sample Size and Chi-Square

It is well known that the Pearsonian measure of goodness of fit of categorical data, $X^2 = \Sigma$ (O-E)/E, has approximately a chi-square distribution when a number of conditions are met. First, the sample size should be large. Second, the observed values should follow a multinomial distribution, or a product of multinomial distributions. Third, the expected values, if estimated, should be estimated in an asymptotically efficient way. Failure of any of these conditions will lead to problems. The major problem discussed in the literature is determining when a sample size is large enough. The trend has been downward. Older literature suggests that the minimum expected value should be at least 10, later cut to 5, and Yarnold (70) gives a rather simple rule suggesting that expected values even less than 1 may be acceptable under certain conditions. Zahn & Roberts (71) find the Coleman test, which has *all* cells with expected values of 1, to be satisfactory if there are enough cells in the table. On the other hand, Tate & Hyer (67) believe that even the older prescriptions may not be strong enough.

The principal problem seems to be that the criterion for good enough is quite ill defined. Tate and Hyer find that the X^2 test does not yield probabilities near enough those generated by the multinomial test, but whether this is a fault of X^2 or the multinomial test [see also Chapanis (12)] is an open question. To illustrate the multinomial test let us consider a bridge hand with (3, 3, 3, 4) distribution. What evidence does this hand give with respect to the null hypothesis of equal probability? The multinomial test would answer the question by ordering all possible distributions (there are 39 of them) by their multinomial probabilities under the null hypothesis and then summing the least probable until the observed one is reached. In the example the (3, 3, 3, 4) distribution is the fifth most likely. In fact (4, 4, 3, 2) is more than twice as likely, the reason being that there are three times as many *ways* of getting that particular distribution. This reviewer feels that it is the responsibility of the data analyst to identify those possible outcomes that are more discrepant than his own. The X^2 test differs from the multinomial test for small or moderately large samples because it has a different critical region. This is not to say that the X^2 test orders outcomes appropriately either. One might require, however, that if one sample is at least as close to the null hypothesis as another in each category, and closer in at least one, it should count as being more concordant with the hypothesis. The X^2 test does have the property that data matching the null hypothesis exactly are viewed as most supportive of it.

Even the "Fisher exact" test has been called into question as a criterion against which to compare X^2 with small samples. Pirie & Hamdan (62) point out that the usual justification for making the Yates correction in the 2X2 analysis is to improve the agreement between X^2—derived probabilities and those stemming from the exact test. The "exact" test, however, is exact only for a sampling model not usually appropriate, i.e. the model in which all marginal frequencies are experimentally fixed. If the row margins only are fixed, say, and two binomial populations with equal probabilities are sampled, then the use of the Yates correction seriously overcorrects. They suggest a correction of 1/2N rather than 1/2.

Conventionally, analysts are advised to collapse categories to avoid having cells with expected values less than required by whatever criterion. This has the disadvantage of losing distinctions being made elsewhere in that category which may be important. An interesting alternative might be to use Feinberg's (18) concept of quasi-independence, i.e. testing for independence, *except* in those cells having too small an expectation.

Sampling Assumptions

The second assumption, that of multinomial sampling, is a critical one. Nothing much on this topic has appeared in the literature beyond the now classic "Use and Misuse of Chi-Square" of the late 1940s. Goodman's paper (31) on the analysis of marginal contingency tables derived from multidimensional tables, to be discussed later, is highly relevant, however, since many violations of the assumption come from uncritically collapsing classifications.

In what may be a very important development, Kleinman (38) reports a study of extraneous variance in binomial data. The usual chi-square tests all assume that the variance of a cell frequency follows the binomial law. If cell frequencies are even slightly more variable than that, especially in tests with many degrees of freedom, the obtained chi-square values can be seriously inflated. The extraneous variation may come from combining dissimilar cells in collapsing across categories, or, in the case that Kleinman studies, it may be inherent in the materials. All other work reported in this review depends on finding binomial variation at some level of analysis.

Efficient Estimation

The null distribution of X^2 depends heavily on the appropriate estimation of expected values. Chase (13) studies the effect on the X^2 measure of estimating expected values from a different sample than that under test. This is frequently done in psychological research, for example, by using "baseline" data to estimate probabilities and then using these estimates to test data from an experimental condition. The effect is to inflate the X^2 value found, severely if the baseline data do not come from a large sample. The more appropriate procedure, of course, is to estimate expected values from both sets of data and test deviations in both sets.

The stricture to use efficient estimates is not extremely limiting, however. Four standard methods exist, of which three currently compete. These are minimum chi-square, modified minimum chi-square, minimum distance information, and maximum likelihood. All have advantages and disadvantages, and much of the variation of methods in the later section of this review comes from different evaluations of these advantages.

Minimum chi-square estimates are almost self-explanatory; they minimize the usual form of chi-square. Aside from this simplicity they have no advantages over the others and have the major disadvantage of being difficult to compute.

One way of overcoming the computational difficulty is to replace the expected value in the denominator of the X^2 statistic with the observed value. The solution of this system leads to estimates of cell expected values. If these estimates are then used in the denominator, a new set of estimates is obtained, and if this process is iterated, the minimum chi-square will be reached in most cases. However, there is little large sample advantage to the iteration, and if the estimates at the end of the first cycle are used, this is called modified minimum chi-square. If the observed value in a cell is zero, this causes difficulty, and such observed values are usually replaced by a conventional small number such as one-half.

Kullback (46) defined an information statistic, I, measuring the "distance" between two statistical distributions. If one estimates parameters to minimize the distance so defined between the empirical distribution and the null hypothesis distribution with those parameters, 2I will have approximately a chi-square distribution if the null hypothesis is true.

Finally, parameters may be chosen to maximize the likelihood of the obtained data. These parameters in many of the most frequently occurring tests will be the same as those obtained using Kullback's procedure.

Each of these procedures optimizes an index, and that index for any one problem will have an approximate chi-square distribution under the null hypothesis, and in general the tests will have the same power. Other considerations such as small sample behavior and calculational convenience should dictate the choice.

Misclassification

All the sophisticated statistical treatment in the world cannot overcome the effects of misclassification. Promised increases in precision with larger samples may not be delivered if larger samples are less carefully classified. Fleiss (22) has an excellent discussion of the effects of misclassification. He shows that misclassification need not lead only to underestimates of association. Bryson (9) discusses how limits on the effects of misclassification may be obtained, using two classifiers, and his work is extended by Krishnaswami & Nath (43). McCarthy (52) discusses the possible advantages of deleting cases which may be doubtfully classified, primarily because they lie near a classification boundary.

Miscellaneous

Hewett & Tsutakawa (36) report a two-stage chi-square test in which a small sample is used. If the obtained chi-square is small, the null hypothesis is accepted, if large it is rejected, and if intermediate a further sample is drawn. Tables of sample sizes to obtain appropriate power are given.

Several papers growing out of Bayesian considerations have appeared on the estimation of multinomial probabilities. If action is to be taken on such estimates, one can easily imagine circumstances in which acting as if a cell probability were zero would not be wise even though the appropriate event had not occurred in a sample. Leonard (47) and Feinberg & Holland (21) consider estimates which "smooth" such probability estimates.

Neter & Maynes (58) consider problems associated with correlating a binary variable with a continuous one. Morrison (56) discusses the same problem in connection with validating probabilistic predictions in which the event predicted either did or did not occur. He notes that this validity cannot be 1 unless all probability assessments are either 0 or 1, in which case they really are deterministic predictions.

He suggests comparing the obtained correlation with its maximum. A rejoinder by Goldberger points out that Morrison's index would not discriminate between two probabilistic predictors, one of whom estimated half for the probability of heads on each toss while the other estimated 0.8 half the time, 0.2 the other half, and was right 68% of the time.

Moore (55) and Krishnan (42) discuss the use of binary variables in discriminant analysis. Krishnan derives a binary discriminant based on the theory of switching functions and obtains somewhat better discrimination than that obtained through the direct application of Fisher's linear discriminant. Moore compares a number of methods including Fisher's linear and quadratic discriminant functions. He finds that the linear discriminant of Fisher holds up remarkably well unless there is a "likelihood reversal," i.e. when (0,0) and (1,1) observations favor one class while (0,1) and (1,0) observations favor the other. He points out that such reversals may be removed by recoding the offending variables. He does not consider how this might effect likelihood reversals with other predictors. It would be useful to study how a whole set of binary predictors might be recoded to provide a set with minimal "likelihood reversal." He also noted the difficulty in using full multinomial prediction, classifying each unknown as the more frequently occurring class, given that exact pattern. Krishnan's work included no discussion of statistical properties.

In a fascinating paper, Blyth (8; with discussion) discusses the problem posed by Simpson's paradox for contingency table analysts. Simpson (64) pointed out that it is quite possible for variable A to be positively associated wih variable B when factor C is present, and also when it is absent, and yet for the association between A and B to be negative when factor C is ignored. In probabilistic terms

$$P\,(A\,|\,B,\,C) > P\,(A\,|\,\bar{B},C)$$
$$P\,(A\,|\,B,\,\bar{C}) > P\,(A\,|\,\bar{B},\,C)$$

and yet $\qquad\qquad P\,(A\,|\,B) < P\,(A\,|\,\bar{B}).$

The paradox is puzzling as it stands, of course, but it is really distressing when one considers the number of "C" factors unknown to the analyst which might yield just such an anomaly. It is easy to prove that the paradox cannot occur if C is independent of either A or B. Lest it be thought that the paradox is a mathematical oddity, a real example can be found in Cohen & Nagel (14). Peacock (61) remarks also on the difficulties in interpreting marginal contingency, and several of the papers reviewed in the second section of this review are also relevant. As noted, the real problem for social scientists is that almost every table is marginal.

Light & Margolin (48) develop a very easy to use test for comparing parameters across a number of binomial samples. It compares well with contingency tests in power and with small samples. Margolin & Light (51) point out that the likelihood ratio test statistic (or Kullback's 2I) is always larger than the Pearson X^2 in 2XC tables with the binary marginal totals equal; it can be as much as 40% larger. Although this is a rather restricted case, it is not uncommon. It would be particularly troublesome in the small sample cases they study, but less so in large samples since the extreme difference is attained only when both measures take on their maximum values.

Miettinen (54) presents a statistic for comparing a sample of propositi, each with multiple controls and all-or-none responses. The solution corresponds to a randomized block analysis.

LOG-LINEAR MODELS

With the publication of books by Haberman (35) and Bishop, Feinberg & Holland (7) a major advance in data analysis is nearing completion. The Haberman book lays out the mathematical foundations of log-linear models clearly and relatively succintly, while the book by Bishop et al addresses itself to the problems of data analysis. Unquestionably a number of major problems in the analysis of qualitative or frequency data remain, but it now seems clear that the log-linear approach should be tried first. This review will concentrate on the maximum likelihood methods as described by Haberman and Bishop et al, but references will continually be made to parallel work on modified minimum chi-square techniques such as those of Grizzle, Starmer & Koch (34), and the minimum discrimination information work of Kullback and associates. As yet there seems to be no overriding theoretical reason to choose one or another of these techniques, but the generality and clarity of the books noted above provide considerable attraction for the techniques they describe.

Hierarchical Analysis of Contingency Tables

The basic paper on hierarchical analysis (Goodman 29) is difficult to read because it introduces a number of new concepts and discusses them in great generality. Goodman defines a class of hypotheses concerning relationships observable in a multidimensional contingency table. This class is very similar to the class of hypotheses for analysis of variance, except that they are inherently hierarchical in the sense that the assertion of an interaction of whatever order entails the assertion of all included interactions and main effects. For example, if an ABC interaction is assumed in the model, then the model necessarily asserts AB, AC, BC, A, B, C effects as well. Put another way, one cannot test for the AB interaction assuming the presence of an ABC interaction. This does not imply that such an hypothesis is impossible as a log-linear model, but rather that the iterative scaling procedure used is not suitable for that model. It is interesting that such models in analysis of variance settings, those asserting an interaction without the contained main effects, are often difficult to understand.

It is probably useful at this point to present a brief account of the iterative scaling scheme mentioned. The maximum likelihood solution for the parameters of a log-linear model has the property that cell expected values satisfy a set of linear equations also satisfied by cell observed values. The set is determined by the model being used, and in hierarchical models these equations all correspond to certain marginal sums. As an example, the hypothesis of "no three-factor interaction" in a three-way table leads to the constraints that all two-factor marginals of the expected value table should equal the corresponding two-factor marginals of the data table. The iterative scaling procedure starts with any table not having a three-factor interaction (for example, a table with "1's" in every cell). Then each cell in, say, the first row and column is multiplied by a constant such that the sum in that row and column is the same as that in the data table. When this has been done for all row-column combinations, the AB marginals have been adjusted. Then the AC and BC marginals are adjusted. In the example the latter adjustments will have disturbed the AB totals so that these totals are again adjusted, then BC again, iteratively until all three marginal tables agree with those of the data. Since the original table has no triple interaction and the adjustments affected only two-factor interactions, the final table will have none and it can be proved that that table is unique. Parameter estimates can then be solved for from the table of expected values.

The family of hierarchical models, all models pertaining to some sort of independence among the classifications involved, are further described as "elementary" and nonelementary, the elementary models being those statable in terms of equiprobability, independence, and conditional independence. With three or more classes, some of the models—those asserting second or higher-order interactions—have no such simple probability interpretation. In addition, the estimation of expected values under these models cannot be done without iteration. These are the nonelementary models. In a later paper, Goodman (31) expands and elaborates on these distinctions. Also included are methods for testing particular contrasts. A more detailed discussion of this system than is appropriate here is given by Shaffer (63).

What this system does is to provide a nearly complete analog in contingency analysis of the multifactorial analysis of variance. The difference is that the dependent variable is treated formally like the independent or design variables. What it does even further, however, is to allow the use of a number of dependent variables, and in the limit it becomes similar to a correlational analysis when all factors are considered dependent variables.

Very similar analyses are reported by Grizzle, Starmer & Koch (34) and by Ku, Varner & Kullback (45). The Ku, Varner & Kullback approach is based on minimum discrimination information statistics. It arrives at essentially the same measures as does Goodman's. The Grizzle-Starmer-Koch approach uses a weighted least-squares approach, arriving at modified minimum chi-square estimates. There seems to be little agreement on which approach is simpler, either computationally or conceptually. The computations by Ku, Varner & Kullback and Goodman involve simple routines applied iteratively, while the Grizzle, Starmer & Koch approach leads to complex matrix operations done once. The Goodman approach is specific to log-linear hypotheses, while the others are in principle applicable to other families of models [see, for example, Forthofer & Koch (23)].

A great deal of attention has also been paid to finding most parsimonious submodels. Goodman (30, 32), Koch, Johnson & Tolley (40), and Ku & Kullback (44) use their various methods to build up models which attempt to describe the data with a minimum number of parameters. These can either be "step-up" procedures which add parameters until no more are needed or "step-down" procedures which delete parameters until the remaining ones are necessary.

Goodman (30) suggests a preliminary analysis based on a simple calculation of log-odds ratios with their standard errors (Lindley 49) for all parameters in the saturated model. This yields a quick notion of which parameters are likely to be necessary. Goodman also recommends using a simultaneous test procedure based on the Bonferronni inequality for testing various interesting log-linear contrasts. Gabriel (25) gives a more comprehensive simultaneous test procedure similar to the Scheffé system for measurement data. The theory for Gabriel's procedure is based on the use of the log-likelihood measure rather than the Pearson index, and primarily for this reason as well as the additivity properties it has, this reviewer agrees with him and Goodman that the log-likelihood index should replace the classical Pearson index. Berkson (3) and others have argued against this position on the basis of slightly better fits between the Pearson measure and tabular chi-square.

One of the most pervasive problems confronting analysts of multivariate contingency tables is that there are seldom enough observations to permit inferences concerning the finer cross-tabulations. Another common problem is that of interpreting the data in a sample when certain characteristics of the sample data are not consistent with known population values. Mosteller (57) suggests using the methods discussed above in an inverse way to help with these problems. By fitting lower order interactions which are adequately sampled and assuming the absence of higher order interactions the methods above will provide expected values for the relevant cells in the table. If the high order interactions are nil, these estimates will be more precise than those obtained using the saturated model. Using the same procedures, marginal frequencies of an existing table may be adjusted to match known population frequencies without disturbing estimates of those interactions known only from the sample table.

Analysis of Incomplete or Truncated Tables

An exceptionally rich collection of techniques was introduced by Goodman (28) and expanded on by Bishop & Feinberg (6), Feinberg (18, 19), Grizzle & Williams (33) and Koch, Imrey & Reinfurt (39). Several examples of possible uses in psychological research were discussed by Smith (66).

Goodman (28) describes a number of data sets which can be seen as incomplete contingency tables. For example, a table relating birth order and family size to a dependent categorical variable could not be rectangular since a birth order larger than the family size is impossible. That is, certain combinations of levels of independent variables may be impossible, or certain cells may be missing or mistrusted, or certain information may not have been obtained in all samples. In any case the question arises, can the remainder of the table be analyzed? Goodman describes tests of quasi-independence, i.e. tests of the log-linear model on the remaining cells. Feinberg (19) extends these methods to multiway tables, and discusses difficulties that arise in determining appropriate degrees of freedom for the tests. Gail (27) extends the methods to permit fitting different quasi-independent models to subsets of cells in the same contingency table. Indeed, the orthogonal partitioning of chi-square (Gabriel 25) is an example of the use of quasi-independence. Feinberg (20) applies this methodology to the estimation of population size from multiple recapture data. If a closed population is sampled K times and sampled elements are identified, the data can be tabulated in a 2^K table corresponding to presence or absence of the elements in each of the K samples. The cell corresponding to absence in all K samples is of course empty. The log-linear methodology allows estimation of the entry in that cell without assuming independence of the K samples. Indeed, account can be taken of interactions up to $(K-1)^{st}$ order.

An unusual application of quasi-independence is the estimation of parameters for various scaling models. The Bradley-Terry model for paired comparison data (also known as the Bradley-Terry-Luce model) has a maximum likelihood solution (David 15). Rearranging the data in the form of a contingency table with a row for each pair and a column for each stimulus yields an incomplete contingency table with entries associated only with the choices which by the BTL theory is quasi-independent, and the analysis is simply done using the Goodman algorithm. Whether this method is simpler than the previously published one is unclear. It is useful in any case to be able to employ existing computer programs.

Luce's (50) biased choice model is a somewhat more complicated example. This model, as applied to identification experiments, is a log-linear model, not identifiably different from Caussinus's (11) model of "quasi-symmetry" (see also Ireland, Ku & Kullback 37). Since the linear constraints implied by the maximum likelihood solution are equivalent to those imposed by the BTL model on pairwise choice, that model can be fit in the same manner except that the entries in each row (i,j) consist of the number of errors "i" instead of "j" and "j" instead of "i" respectively. Bishop et al (7) suggest an alternative but equivalent procedure.

Davidson's (16) generalization of the BTL model can be treated similarly, using an extension of the marginal adjustment to be discussed below.

These all point up Feinberg's comment (19) concerning the value in attempting to arrange frequency data in contingency table form. Indeed, there may be several possible ways, one which may be much more revealing than another.

Log-Linear Models with Complex Constraints

All of the models discussed so far have led to simple constraints on cell expected values. They are simple in that each constraint has been on the sum of a set of cell expected values. The models so far have been rather general or canonical, asserting some form of independence or lack of it. As the models get more specific and detailed, the need arises for constraints on weighted sums. A most important paper by Darroch & Ratcliff (17) presents an iterative procedure which produces estimates for general positive-weight linear constraints. In this reviewer's opinion the importance of the paper lies in the proof that a scheme always exists, though not necessarily in the particular procedure proposed. There are always a number of schemes which will work, and research is needed on the problem of finding constraint systems which converge rapidly.

The psychophysical method of constant stimuli generates a RX2 contingency table, stimulus by response Yes-No, and has been analyzed by methods of biometry called probit analysis. Usually it has been assumed that "percent detection" follows a normal ogive and that the problem is to estimate the mean and variance of that curve. If the ogive is logistic (Bush 10, Ogilvie & Creelman 59), and Williams & Grizzle (68) instead of normal, the log odds of the successive rows are a linear function of the stimulus values and the model is log-linear. The linear constraint is now given by the appropriate orthogonal contrast.

Similarly, when one or more of the independent variables corresponds to an interval scale, linear, quadratic, and higher order effects may be extracted, and in general orthogonal contrasts may be extracted whatever the interpretation of the independent variable. As in the analysis of variance case, these really correspond to a re-parametrization of the original linear model.

Collapsed Contingency Tables

It is quite impossible in social science research to avoid analyzing marginal or collapsed tables, so the advice not to collapse over subjects or over sessions or whatever is not very helpful. Goodman (31) discusses the problems of analyzing marginal contingency tables in the context of log-linear models. Bishop (5) points out that collapsing over (ignoring) a variable is legitimate unless the collapsed variate is correlated with each component of the interaction being tested. Clearly if a variate is totally independent of the remainder, it can and should be collapsed, because more data are then available for testing for other relations. Bishop's and Goodman's discussions permit more refined consideration of whether and how much to collapse.

Peacock (61) and Fliess (22) also discuss this problem in the context of comparing contingency results across different studies.

Repeated Measures and Correlated Proportions

The analysis of repeated measures is not straightforward even in the measurement area. Winer (69) discusses the problem at some length. With only two repeated measures there is little problem since analysis of the differences is appropriate. With more than two repeated measures, however, the standard analysis requires the assumption that the covariance matrix of the measures exhibits compound symmetry. Along with the null hypothesis and the assumed normality of the measures, this implies that the repeated measures are interchangeable. This means that under the null hypothesis all permutations of any response pattern have equal likelihood. The usual test then actually tests interchangeability. Winer suggests a conservative test when these assumptions are questionable which assigns fewer degrees of freedom to each sum of squares involved. As a last resort he recommends Hotelling's T test which assumes only that the repeated measures, as a vector, have a multinormal distribution, but requires estimation of the entire covariance matrix.

The situation seems strikingly similar when the repeated measures are categorical. A simple analogous situation arises when the data consist of a number of binary variables which must be assumed correlated. When there are two variables, McNemar's test is used; when there are more, Cochran's Q test has been proposed. Berger & Gold (2) point out that Cochran's Q test will be biased toward rejection of equality unless the correlations of variables are equal, and indeed that the X^2 measure used may really have, with three variables, the distribution of $2X^2$. A conservative test would require comparing $X^2/2$ with the table. Alternatively they suggest that the null hypothesis be changed to the hypothesis of interchangeability, but then Cochran's test is not consistent. Berger & Gold then describe a test of interchangeability which is consistent and which tests for equal frequencies of permutations of the possible response patterns.

Ireland, Ku & Kullback (37), Gabrielsson & Seeger (26), Patil (60), and Koch & Reinfurt (41) also discuss the problem. Gabrielsson & Seeger, using Monte Carlo methods, find that applying the standard F statistics to the binary data is somewhat preferable to using Cochran's Q. Ireland, Ku & Kullback define marginal homogeneity in the relation between two categorical measures when their marginal distributions are equal, and Koch & Reinfurt use this concept to test equality. Patil derives the exact distribution of Cochran's Q under permutation.

The problem of what marginal homogeneity means in the absence of exchangeability is still open, and this area of analysis needs a great deal of further research.

Remaining Problems

Two major problems in the analysis of contingency data seem clear. The problem of what to do with correlated proportions has just been discussed. The most difficult problem, however, is the dependence of these methods on an underlying multinomial distribution. Unlike analysis of variance techniques, these provide no direct measure of variability of cell frequencies aside from that provided by the multinomial assumption. Kleinman's paper (38) opens a possibility, but in any event variability estimates will need to be obtained. Kleinman assumes the beta-binomial distribution which is attractive in that the variance-covariance matrices used by Grizzle and his co-workers would merely need to be multiplied by a heterogeneity factor. It is not at all clear how the Goodman approach would be modified since beta-binomial likelihoods are not amenable to simple treatment. Perhaps, as Gabriel (24) suggested, when heterogeneity problems are present a retreat to analysis of variance of transformed proportions may be necessary. The elegance of log-linear analysis would be sorely missed.

Literature Cited

1. Aitken, M. 1971. Statistical theory. *Ann. Rev. Psychol.* 22:225–50
2. Berger, A., Gold, R. Z. 1973. Note on Cochran's Q-test for the comparison of correlated proportions. *J. Am. Stat. Assoc.* 68:989–93
3. Berkson, J. 1972. Minimum discrimination information, the 'no interaction' problem, and the logistic function. *Biometrics* 28:443–68
4. Binder, A. 1964. Statistical theory. *Ann. Rev. Psychol.* 15:277–310
5. Bishop, Y. M. M. 1971. Effects of collapsing multidimensional contingency tables. *Biometrics* 27:545–62
6. Bishop, Y. M. M., Feinberg, S. E. 1969.

Incomplete two-dimensional tables. *Biometrics* 25:119–28
7. Bishop, Y. M. M., Feinberg, S. E., Holland, P. W. 1975. *Discrete Multivariate Analysis: Theory and Practice.* Cambridge: MIT Press. 557 pp.
8. Blyth, C. R. 1972. On Simpson's paradox and the sure-thing principle. *J. Am. Stat. Assoc.* 67:364–66; and comments, pp. 366–81
9. Bryson, M. R. 1965. Errors of classification in a binomial population. *J. Am. Stat. Assoc.* 60:217–24
10. Bush, R. R. 1963. Estimation and evaluation. In *Handbook of Mathematical Psychology,* ed. R. D. Luce, R. R. Bush. New York: Wiley

498   SMITH

11. Caussinus, H. 1965. Contribution à l'analyse statistique des tableaux de corrélation, *Ann. Fac. Sci. Univ. Toulouse* 29:77–182
12. Chapanis, A. 1969. An exact multinomial one-sample test of significance. *Psychol. Bull.* 59:306–10
13. Chase, G. R. 1972. On the chi-square test when the parameters are estimated independently of the data. *J. Am. Stat. Assoc.* 67:609–11
14. Cohen, M. R., Nagel, E. 1934. *An Introduction to Logic and Scientific Method.* New York: Harcourt, Brace. Problem 6, p. 449
15. David, H. A. 1963. *The Method of Paired Comparisons.* New York: Hafner. 124 pp.
16. Davidson, R. R. 1970. On extending the Bradley-Terry model to accomodate ties in paired comparison experiments. *J. Am. Stat. Assoc.* 65:317–28
17. Darroch, J. N., Ratcliff, D. 1972. Generalized iterative scaling for log-linear models. *Am. Math. Stat.* 43:1470–80
18. Feinberg, S. E. 1970. Quasi-independence and maximum likelihood estimation in incomplete contingency tables. *J. Am. Stat. Assoc.* 65:1610–16
19. Feinberg, S. E. 1972. The analysis of incomplete multi-way contingency tables. *Biometrics* 28:177–202
20. Feinberg, S. E. 1972. The multiple recapture census for closed populations and incomplete 2^K contingency tables. *Biometrics* 28:591–603
21. Feinberg, S. E., Holland, P. W. 1973. Simultaneous estimation of multinomial cell probabilities. *J. Am. Stat. Assoc.* 68:683–91
22. Fleiss, J. L. 1973. *Statistical Methods for Rates and Proportions.* New York: Wiley. 223 pp.
23. Forthofer, R. N., Koch, G. G. 1973. An analysis for compounded functions of categorical data. *Biometrics* 29:143–58
24. Gabriel, K. R. 1963. Analysis of variance of proportions with unequal frequencies. *J. Am. Stat. Assoc.* 58:1133–57
25. Gabriel, K. R. 1966. Simultaneous test procedures for multiple comparisons of categorical data. *J. Am. Stat. Assoc.* 61:1081–96
26. Gabrielsson, A., Seeger, P. 1971. Tests of significance in two-way designs (mixed model) with dichotomous data. *Br. J. Math. Stat. Psychol.* 24:111–16
27. Gail, M. H. 1972. Mixed quasi-independent models for categorical data. *Biometrics* 28:703–12

28. Goodman, L. A. 1968. The analysis of cross-classified data: independence, quasi-independence, and interactions in contingency tables with or without missing entries. *J. Am. Stat. Assoc.* 63:1091–1131
29. Goodman, L. A. 1970. The multivariate analysis of qualitative data: interactions among multiple classifications. *J. Am. Stat. Assoc.* 65:226–56
30. Goodman, L. A. 1971. The analysis of multidimensional contingency tables: stepwise procedures and direct estimation methods for building models for multiple classifications. *Technometrics* 13:33–61
31. Goodman, L. A. 1971. Partitioning of chi-square, analysis of marginal contingency tables, and estimation of expected frequencies in multi-dimensional contingency tables. *J. Am. Stat. Assoc.* 66:339–44
32. Goodman, L. A. 1973. Guided and unguided methods for the selection of models for a set of T multi-dimensional contingency tables. *J. Am. Stat. Assoc.* 68:165–75
33. Grizzle, J. E., Williams, O. D. 1972. Log-linear models and tests of independence for contingency tables. *Biometrics* 28:137–56
34. Grizzle, J. E., Starmer, C. F., Koch, G. G. 1969. Analysis of categorical data by linear models. *Biometrics* 25:489–504
35. Haberman, S. J. 1974. *The Analysis of Frequency Data.* Univ. Chicago Press. 419 pp.
36. Hewett, J. E., Tsutakawa, R. K. 1972. Two-stage chi-square goodness-of-fit test. *J. Am. Stat. Assoc.* 67:395–401
37. Ireland, C. T., Ku, H. H., Kullback, S. 1969. Symmetry and marginal homogeneity of an rxr contingency table. *J. Am. Stat. Assoc.* 64:1323–41
38. Kleinman, J. C. 1973. Proportions with extraneous variance: single and independent samples. *J. Am. Stat. Assoc.* 68:46–54
39. Koch, G. G., Imrey, P. B., Reinfurt, D. W. 1972. Linear model analysis of categorical data with incomplete response vectors. *Biometrics* 28:663–92
40. Koch, G. G., Johnson, W. D., Tolley, H. D. 1972. A linear models approach to the analysis of survival and extent of disease in multi-dimensional contingency tables. *J. Am. Stat. Assoc.* 67:783–96
41. Koch, G. G., Reinfurt, D. W. 1971. The

analysis of categorical data from mixed models. *Biometrics* 27:157–73
42. Krishnan, T. 1973. On linear combinations of binary item scores. *Psychometrika* 38:291–304
43. Krishnaswami, P., Nath, R. 1968. Bias in multinomial classification. *J. Am. Stat. Assoc.* 63:298–303
44. Ku, H. H., Kullback, S. 1974. Log-linear models in contingency table analysis. *Am. Stat.* 28:115–25
45. Ku, H. H., Varner, R. N., Kullback, S. 1971. On the analysis of multidimensional contingency tables. *J. Am. Stat. Assoc.* 66:55–64
46. Kullback, S. 1968. *Information Theory and Statistics.* New York: Dover. 399 pp.
47. Leonard, T. 1972. Bayesian methods for binomial data. *Biometrika* 59:581–90
48. Light, R. J., Margolin, B. H. 1971. An analysis of variance for categorical data. *J. Am. Stat. Assoc.* 66:534–44
49. Lindley, D. V. 1964. The Bayesian analysis of contingency tables *Ann. Math. Stat.* 35:1622–43
50. Luce, R. D. 1959. *Individual Choice Behavior.* New York: Wiley
51. Margolin, B. H., Light, R. J. 1974. An analysis of variance for categorical data, II: Small sample comparisons with chi square and other competitors. *J. Am. Stat. Assoc.* 69:755–64
52. McCarthy, P. J. 1972. The effects of discarding inliars when binomial data are subject to classification errors. *J. Am. Stat. Assoc.* 67:575–29
53. Meredith, W. M., Fredricksen, C. H., McLaughlin, D. H. 1974. Statistics and data analysis. *Ann. Rev. Psychol.* 25:453–505
54. Miettinen, O. S. 1969. Individual matching with multiple controls in the case of all-or-none responses. *Biometrics* 25:339–55
55. Moore, D. H. II 1973. Evaluation of five discrimination procedures for binary variables. *J. Am. Stat. Assoc.* 68:399–404
56. Morrison, D. G. 1972. Upper bounds for correlations between binary outcomes and probabilistic predictions. *J. Am. Stat. Assoc.* 67:68–70

57. Mosteller, F. 1968. Association and estimation in contingency tables. *J. Am. Stat. Assoc.* 63:1–28
58. Neter, J., Maynes, E. S. 1970. On the appropriateness of the correlation coefficient with a (0,1) variable. *J. Am. Stat. Assoc.* 65:501–9
59. Ogilvie, J. C., Creelman, C. D. 1968. Maximum likelihood estimation of ROC curve parameters. *J. Math. Psychol.* 5:377–91
60. Patil, K. D. 1975. Cochran's Q-test: exact distribution. *J. Am. Stat. Assoc.* 70:186–89
61. Peacock, P. B. 1971. The non-comparability of relative risks from different studies. *Biometrics* 27:903–7
62. Pirie, W. R., Hamdan, M. A. 1972. Some revised continuity corrections for discrete distributions. *Biometrics* 28:693–701
63. Shaffer, J. P. 1973. Defining and testing hypotheses in multi-dimensional contingency tables. *Psychol. Bull.* 79:127–41
64. Simpson, E. H. 1951. The interpretation of interaction in contingency tables. *J. R. Stat. Soc. Ser. B* 13:238–41
65. Sitgreaves, R. 1966. Statistical theory. *Ann. Rev. Psychol.* 17:423–34
66. Smith, J. E. K. 1973. On tests of quasi-independence in psychological research. *Psychol. Bull.* 80:329–33
67. Tate, M. W., Hyer, L. A. 1973. Inaccuracy of the X^2 test of goodness of fit when expected frequencies are small. *J. Am. Stat. Assoc.* 68:836–41
68. Williams, O. D., Grizzle, J. E. 1972. Analysis of contingency tables having ordered response categories. *J. Am. Stat. Assoc.* 67:55–63
69. Winer, B. J. 1962. *Statistical Principles in Experimental Design.* New York: McGraw-Hill. 672 pp.
70. Yarnold, J. K. 1970. The minimum expectation in X^2 goodness of fit tests and the accuracy of approximations for the null distribution. *J. Am. Stat. Assoc.* 65:864–86
71. Zahn, D. A., Roberts, G. C. 1971. Exact X^2 criterion tables with cell expectations one: an application to Coleman's measure of consensus. *J. Am. Stat. Assoc.* 66:145–48

THE SOCIAL PSYCHOLOGY OF   ❖262
SMALL GROUPS: COOPERATIVE
AND MIXED-MOTIVE INTERACTION

James H. Davis, Patrick R. Laughlin, and Samuel S. Komorita[1]

Department of Psychology, University of Illinois, Champaign, Illinois 61820

Social psychology may be defined as the study of human interaction. However, many of the phenomena of social interaction gradually have been removed from their natural habitat, the small group, to situations permitting greater experimental control and convenience in observation and measurement. For example, conformity, attraction, attitude change, and social influence are typically studied with a single individual as the unit of analysis. Accordingly, small group behavior has come to mean, largely by exclusion, the relatively free interaction of two or more actual persons. They may be cooperating to achieve a mutual goal such as solving a problem or making a decision, or they may be bargaining in outright competition.

Thus the following review is limited to theory and research involving the actual interaction of two or more people in a cooperative, mixed-motive, or competitive relationship. As Kelley & Thibaut (228) emphasize in their classic review of group problem solving, the extremes of pure cooperation and pure competition are rare. Virtually all social interaction as studied in an experimental setting is mixed-motive. However, different emphases are clear in current research, where the instructions and payoff structure define the situation as primarily cooperative or primarily mixed-motive, and studies of pure competition are indeed virtually nonexistent. We divide cooperative interaction into group problem solving and group decision making (46, 444) since most research emphasizes either the social processing of information to formulate responses (problem solving) or the collective selection among

[1]The preparation for this report was partially supported by research grant NSF SOC-7305697 from the National Science Foundation (James H. Davis, Principal Investigator), NIE NE-G-00-3-0140 from the National Institutes of Education (Patrick R. Laughlin, Principal Investigator), and NSF SOC 74-13399 from the National Science Foundation (Samuel S. Komorita, Principal Investigator). The authors wish to thank Craig Spitzer for his assistance.

response alternatives as defined by the task or goal (decision making). Accordingly, our organization into cooperative and mixed-motive interaction is not theoretical but functional, an emphasis upon the situation as defined by instructions, task, and the reward structure for the interacting subjects.

Our decision to consider primarily studies involving the interaction of two or more actual persons eliminates many of the traditional and currently active areas of small group psychology, where the other person is "present" either as an abstract stimulus on paper, videotape, etc (e.g. much work in attraction), or as a stimulus or setting for the behavior of the individual of interest, with whom the stimulus person does not actually interact (e.g. much work in conformity or social facilitation). This decision obviously reflects an emphasis rather than a value judgment on the importance of these other areas. Fortunately, a comprehensive bibliography of small group research with over 2000 indexed entries has been published recently by Hare (186). The third edition of Cartwright & Zander's book (70) and a recent collection of readings by Ofshe (353) are useful and comprehensive, and Shaw (405) has published a thoroughly eclectic textbook. Together with the earlier comprehensive reviews of group problem solving by Kelley & Thibaut (228), group structure (attraction, coalitions, communication, and power) by Collins & Raven (87), and leadership by Gibb (146), and the previous annual reviews by Gerard & Miller (145), Helmreich, Bakeman & Scherwitz (191), and Steiner (426), these sources give us the luxury of somewhat selective coverage concentrating on the years 1970–1974 inclusive.

COOPERATIVE INTERACTION: GROUP PROBLEM SOLVING

In a book entitled *Group Process and Productivity,* Steiner (428) extends his earlier theoretical analyses of potential group productivity on various types of group tasks (427, 430). He proposes the basic relationship: Actual Productivity = Potential Productivity minus Loss due to Faulty Process (motivation and coordination loss). Potential Productivity is determined by the relationship between group task demands and member resources, and thus sets the baseline against which actual group performance is assessed. The basic task distinction is between divisible tasks, which allow a division of labor over group members, and unitary tasks, which do not. Unitary tasks include: (*a*) additive tasks, where the group output is the sum of individual performances; (*b*) disjunctive tasks, where the group succeeds if any individual member succeeds, as in the Lorge-Solomon model (270); and (*c*) conjunctive tasks, where the group succeeds only if all individual members succeed. The disjunctive-conjunctive distinction defines a continuum rather than a dichotomy (256). The basic parameters for group performance on unitary tasks are thus member ability and group size. Divisible or complementary tasks allow a physical or conceptual division into subtasks, so that the group may coordinate the "division-of-ability" potentials of the group members to the "division-of-labor" potentials of the group task (257). Steiner's analysis of the sampling considerations underlying potential performance on unitary tasks is important (for example, the probability of a single solver on a disjunctive task is an increasing function of group size), and the unitary-divisible distinction indicates that divisible tasks are more interesting theoretically since potential group performance can exceed the performance of the same individuals working independently for reasons beyond statistical sampling considerations.

Hackman & Morris (170) present an analysis and review of group performance similar to Steiner (428), building on their earlier work on task and process variables (166–169, 171, 321, 322). Group interaction processes are seen as acting upon three classes of focal variables (group composition, group norms, and task design), with three associated classes of summary variables (level and utilization of member knowledge and skill, nature and utilization of task performance strategies, level and coordination of member effort) to determine group performance.

These related theoretical analyses provide a useful organization for recent research on group problem solving. By definition all empirical studies of cooperative group performance involve a dependent measure of actual group productivity. However, most studies tend to emphasize either group composition (ability relative to the task, personality variables, leadership), situational factors (reinforcement contingencies, group organization), or group process. The ideal study would of course explicitly consider composition, situation, and process.

Group Composition

ABILITY Three studies (257, 258, 260) composed dyads, triads, or tetrads respectively on the basis of ability on a difficult divisible task, the Terman Concept Mastery Test (460). After taking the test as individuals, college students were trichotomized as high (H), medium (M), or low (L) ability and then retook the same test in one of the 6 possible cooperative dyads (HH, HM, . . ., LL), 10 possible triads, or 15 tetrads, or as control H, M, or L individuals. In general, group performance was directly proportional to the number of high-ability members of the group, and as the ability level of the group increased, the group performed progressively better than the same individuals working independently [e.g. (HHH-H) > (MMM-M) > (LLL-L)]. A further comparison of homogeneous high-ability and low-ability groups of sizes one through five indicated linear improvement with increasing group size for high-ability groups and no effect of group size for low-ability groups (262). Together with related work (e.g. 136, 149–151, 155, 214, 256), recent research thus indicates that group performance is a joint function of ability and group size relative to task demands, and that overall group performance can often be predicted from a knowledge of the ability composition of the group apart from process considerations.

Jones (215) regressed athletic performance of professional tennis, baseball, football, and basketball teams on subgroup effectiveness, finding strong linear relationships for all sports. Although team performance was not regressed on individual performance (e.g. games won on batting averages), but rather addressed questions such as the co-occurrence of the best offensive and best defensive units on the same football teams, the methodology is highly suggestive for analyses of the relationship between member ability composition and group performance in naturally occurring groups outside the laboratory.

OTHER PERSONALITY CHARACTERISTICS   A number of studies have composed groups of different levels on various personality characteristics other than directly task-relevant ability, such as dominance, need achievement, anxiety, affiliation, or internal-external control (e.g. 6, 192, 201, 230, 251, 301, 399, 420, 422, 423, 464, 480). For examples, Watson (480) varied both dominance, as assessed by the Jackson Dominance Scale, and position power, finding that high-dominant individuals sent more messages and were more directive, particularly in a high-power position, and Sorrentino (423) found that emergent leadership was a joint function of achievement and affiliation motives. There is a trend to studies of the interaction of personality variables and the task situation in group performance, best exemplified in the large amount of research on leadership.

LEADERSHIP   Most recent research in leadership is dominated by the proposition that group productivity is a joint function of a personality characteristic of the leader and the situation. Fiedler's contingency model (125, 126) proposes an interaction between a personality trait of the leader which is assessed by asking him to rate the co-worker he least prefers to work with on semantic differential scales (Least Preferred Co-worker or LPC Scales) and a dimension of situational favorability jointly defined by the three variables: (a) leader-member relations (good-poor), (b) task (structured-unstructured), (c) leader position power (strong-weak). Fiedler plotted correlations from various experiments between leader LPC and group performance against the eight octants defined by the three binary dimensions, finding a curvilinear relationship in which low LPC leaders were associated with better group performance at the favorable and unfavorable ends, and high LPC leaders were associated with better group performance in the intermediate range. As such, the contingency theory is an empirical induction. A large number of further experiments have assessed the hypothesized relationships for various octants (e.g. 76, 116, 129, 185, 202, 205, 305, 336, 386, 395, 409).

This contingency theory has been severely criticized concerning the methodological adequacy of the underlying research, the statistical strength of the evidence, and the conceptual meaning of the three variables defining situational favorability and the construct assessed by the LPC scales (7, 8, 153, 154). Fiedler (127, 128, 130) has both replied to the criticisms and summarized further evidence. He acknowledges the cogency of some of the criticisms, and correctly points out that he anticipated many of them (318). His current position is that the relationship between leader LPC and group performance for both interacting and coacting task groups conforms to his model, while training groups require a predominantly relationship-oriented leadership style regardless of the situation (128).

One empirical study stands out both methodologically and for clear results. Chemers & Skrzypek (76) assessed all eight octants by independently manipulating each of the three variables defining situational favorability. Leader-member relations were assessed before the group interaction sociometrically, rather than by the post-performance judgment of the leader, and there was a strong manipulation of position power. The curve of the plotted correlations between leader LPC and group performance against the dimension of situational favorability closely fitted Fiedler's expectations.

Several comments on this controversy seem warranted. First, all agree that many of the methodological criticisms are valid, so future research hopefully will be improved despite the occasionally negative tone of the controversy. Second, if the basic problem is to assess the validity of the hypothesized curvilinear relationship, all eight octants must be assessed in a given study. Third, despite the difficulty of obtaining sufficient subjects when the group rather than the individual is the unit of analysis, future research in leadership as in all areas of small group performance must have adequate sample sizes and resulting statistical power. Fourth, further conceptual work is necessary on the basic dimension of situational favorability (for example, is the proposed ordering of the eight octants theoretically unique or optimal?) and perhaps on the meaning of the LPC construct and its correlates (317).

A recent symposium series includes two books with chapters on various aspects of leadership theory and research (135, 203), and Hollander & Julian (193, 194) present two comprehensive reviews including their studies in leader legitimacy, influence, and motivation. Kerr and co-workers (232) propose a contingency model based on the literature on consideration and initiating structure within the Ohio State Leadership Study framework, and Yukl (495) proposes a behavioral theory of leadership. Stein, Geis & Damarin (425) demonstrated that observing subjects accurately perceived the ratings on task and socioemotional leadership made by the interacting group members. Doyle (110) gives an interesting process analysis of the productivity of groups of school teachers composed on the basis of their leaders' (principals) achieved status. A study by Swinth & Tuggle (444) demonstrated that a dyadic interaction model predicted nearly 70% of the interactions of cooperative dyads on an assembly task.

A book by Vroom & Yetton on *Leadership and Decision Making* (475) is helpful for extending leadership results to organizational settings. Finally, both theoretical interest and research on leadership are shifting from experimental social psychology to organizational and administrative science.

Situational Factors

REINFORCEMENT CONTINGENCIES.   Several well-designed and comprehensive studies have indicated the importance of individual or group reinforcement contingencies in group performance. A series of seven experiments (118, 148, 233) trained individuals and then composed them in a group performance situation where two "monitors" made independent responses and an "operator" made a team response on the basis of the monitors' responses. Various patterns of individual and team feedback were given for series and parallel team arrangements and prior training levels. Among other results: (*a*) feedback after each team response improved performance while practice without feedback reduced team performance; (*b*) redundant members resulted in immediate gains but long-term losses in team performance; (c) team training was most efficient when the individuals had first mastered their own assignments. This final result may be considered another demonstration of the basic importance of member ability relative to the demands of the group task.

Smith (418) extended the classic demonstration of Bavelas et al (18) of the effects of positive and negative feedback on individual participation rates to a factorial comparison of feedback to individuals or the group which applied to individuals or the group. Feedback was more effective in altering participation rates when it was given to individuals and applied to individuals, but more change in the perception of the other group members resulted from feedback applying to the group. Scott & Cherrington (402) compared performance and intragroup attraction under competitive, cooperative, and individualistic reinforcement contingencies. Arousal was higher, performance better, and attraction to other group members lower for competitive than either cooperative or individualistic conditions, which did not differ significantly.

GROUP ORGANIZATION   Miller (313) discusses numerous aspects of the group as a "living system." Hewett, O'Brien & Hornik (192) defined four group organizations by the factorial combination of coordination (requiring or not requiring assembly of parts in sequential order on a model-building task) and collaboration (requiring or not requiring all three members to work on the same part of the model simultaneously). A significant interaction indicated higher group productivity without collaboration when coordination was required, and with collaboration when coordination was not required. Shiflett (407, 408) compared individuals and dyads who were required to use a divided labor, shared labor, or free choice work organization on easy or difficult crossword puzzles. Over two studies free choice and divided labor required less time, suggesting that the free choice procedure (no imposed organization) was best to maximize both criteria. However, in one study this was qualified by an interaction with task difficulty. A similar conclusion emerges from Howell et al (200), who found that freely interacting pairs in a decentralized arrangement solved a code-breaking task involving redundancy as well as individuals, while centralized and concocted (no communication) organizations resulted in poorer performance. An interesting theoretical analysis of an individual's "capacity for interaction in a problem solving group" or span of control (275) is relevant for both group organization and leadership. Finally, a suggestive study (316) indicated that interacting groups are more likely to intervene in an emergency than co-acting groups, which could have implications for the currently active area of bystander intervention.

There is considerable recent interest in the optimal distribution of power over the members of a cooperative group for maximal group performance and in the effects of the exercise of power (particular expert power) on the subsequent distribution of power over members (17, 172, 266, 332–335, 369, 387, 489).

Weick & Gilfillan (481) extended the classic study of Jacobs & Campbell (207) on the perpetuation of an arbitrary tradition over generations. Triads were instructed to use an easy or difficult strategy on the common target game. Subjects given the arbitrary easy strategy perpetuated it for eleven generations, while those given the arbitrary difficult strategy abandoned it after four generations and developed new strategies better adapted to the task.

Group Process

INDIVIDUAL VERSUS GROUP PERFORMANCE A series of studies has demonstrated the superiority of cooperative pairs over individuals in concept attainment for a variety of conceptual rules, task difficulty conditions, and interaction formats (253, 254, 259, 261, 263, 264, 294, 295). The basic reason seems to be that the discussion process enables the cooperative groups to evolve and use the systematic strategy of focusing, which may be shown theoretically to be the most efficient strategy on this task (255). A comparable conclusion on the fundamental importance of group discussion for group decision emerges from research on the risky shift (68), and a basic question for future research is to isolate the relevant factors in the discussion process.

However, such clear superiority of interacting groups over individuals has not been demonstrated on production tasks such as those used in brainstorming. Lamm & Trommsdorf (250), in an excellent analysis and review of the brainstorming literature, conclude: "The empirical evidence clearly indicates that subjects brainstorming in small groups produce fewer ideas than the same number of subjects brainstorming individually. Less clear evidence is available on measures of quality, uniqueness, and variety" (250, p. 361). Recent programmatic research on brainstorming is due to Bouchard and his associates (41–45).

Gustafson et al (161) compared individuals and three group process conditions (talk—estimate; estimate—feedback—estimate; estimate—talk—estimate) on judgments of subjective likelihood estimates. The estimate—talk—estimate condition resulted in the best performance. Rowse, Gustafson & Ludke (390) extended the analysis to a comparison of behavioral (four group members must agree to use a single estimate) and five mathematical aggregation rules (equal weights, peer-assigned weights, etc) for combining likelihood ratio estimates given by a group of experts. The mathematical aggregation rules were superior to the behavioral except for very small or large likelihood ratios.

COGNITIVE CONFLICT AND INTERPERSONAL LEARNING Hammond and his associates have extended the Brunswikian (56) lens model to a paradigm for the study of cognitive conflict and interpersonal learning. Individuals with systematically varied previous cognitive experiences are brought together to resolve the resulting conflict through interpersonal learning (117, 175, 177, 178, 180, 181). Rappoport & Summers (385) have edited a comprehensive collection of articles on various aspects of the paradigm for interacting groups as well as individual judgment (see also 179, 204, 463). The basic idea is that much human conflict is cognitive, involving different conceptions of the relationship between cues and criteria for different individuals and inability to understand the cognitive systems of others, rather than motivational, such as due to aggressive needs. Accordingly, the basic paradigm involves training individuals to rely on different cues in judgments and then bringing the differently trained individuals together for a common group judgment involving new cue validities. Hence each individual must learn both the new cue validities and the basis of his partner's judgment. Hammond (176) has developed computer graphics techniques to assist such learning.

Systematic research on such variables as linear versus curvilinear function forms, distribution of cue validities, and correlated cues includes work by Balke, Hammond & Meyer (12), Brehmer (50–53), Mumpower & Hammond (337), Rappoport & Cvetkovich (384), Summers, Taliaferro & Fletcher (440), as well as the chapters in Rappoport & Summers (385). An especially comprehensive and interesting study by Brehmer & Hammond (54) composed the ten possible dyads based on previous individual experience with negative or positive, linear or U-shaped, function forms. They found that the rate of acquisition of the other's cue (which the subject had learned to ignore in the individual phase) in the group phase was faster for similar than for different function forms. Hammond & Brehmer (178) present the implications of research in the paradigm for international conflict.

MOTIVATION   Ingham et al (206) tested the finding of Ringelmann (see 427, 428) that the addition of co-workers on an additive rope-pulling task resulted in a decrement in performance roughly proportional to the number of coordination links between pairs of members. In two well-controlled experiments performance decreased significantly as group size increased from one to two or three, with no further decrement for group sizes four, five, and six. In terms of Steiner's analysis (428), the loss was due to motivation rather than coordination, as demonstrated by having confederates only pretend to pull during the performance of a single naive subject. Stogdill (432) reviewed the literature on group productivity, drive, and cohesiveness, concluding that productivity and cohesiveness tend to be positively related under high group drive and negatively related under low group drive and normal operating conditions.

MINORITY INFLUENCE ON THE MAJORITY   An interesting and potentially influential theoretical analysis of social influence by Moscovici & Faucheux (325) argues that theory and research on conformity have over-emphasized the influence of the majority on the minority since the classic Asch and Sherif demonstrations, and consequently underemphasized the influence of an active committed minority on the majority. They see the influence process as one of transformation from a natural state of violence (something of a Hobbesian view) to a social state of consensus governed by norms. Consensus is obtained in different ways when the majority has a norm and the minority does not, when equal partners each have their own norms (cf our later discussion of mixed-motive interaction), and when an active minority opposes its norm to the norm of the majority. Relevant research includes Moscovici, Lage & Naffrechoux (326, 327) and Nemeth, Swedlund & Kanki (351). The latter authors found that a minority can be influential without merely repeating the same position if the minority responses are patterned and perceived as representing a consistent position held with confidence. A theoretical analysis of "social differentiation and social originality" by Lemaine (265) presents somewhat similar and provocative notions.

MODELS FORMALIZING PROCESS ASSUMPTIONS A recent trend emerging from work of various investigators in several areas of group performance is to construct mathematical models which formalize any set of assumptions about the group process and to test the predictions of the models against actual group performance. If the predictions of a given model do not depart significantly from the actual group performance, the model may be considered a sufficient and perhaps plausible explanation of the underlying group process. Thus this approach is an indirect assessment of group process rather than direct. Since most recent theory and research in this approach has tended to use group tasks emphasizing decision making rather than problem solving, we discuss it in the following section on cooperative interaction in group decision making.

COOPERATIVE INTERACTION: GROUP DECISION MAKING

The study of small group decision making continues, as it has for nearly a decade and a half, to focus heavily upon "risk-taking" by individuals and groups. A second, related research trend has gained increasing prominence, especially among European psychologists: Group polarization. The remaining research topics are generally scattered without dominant conceptual themes in evidence. One exception is the rising interest in jury decision making that grows out of a more general inclination to study courtroom phenomena. [Research on juries has recently been reviewed elsewhere by Davis, Bray & Holt (96), and Tapp will address the general issue of psychology and the law elsewhere in this volume.]

Choice Shifts

Relatively few books or monographs (e.g. 85, 133, 350, 352, 405, 419) have appeared within the last 5 years which have dealt with small group decision making in a major way. However, research on group choice shifts (nee risky shift) has benefited in the same period from an unusual number of literature reviews, critical summaries, and various integrative pieces (22, 23, 68, 69, 72, 75, 82, 84, 95, 105, 274, 371–373, 471). Integrative statements in the past have often signaled the high water mark of a trend, especially when critical or crucial aspects of the phenomenon were at issue. Research on choice shifts has lacked neither summaries nor criticisms, and the effects of the 1970–71 period of "summarizing" may finally have taken its toll; there was a marked decline in the frequency of choice shift studies during 1974. However, a number of other research trends may be growing concurrently with this demise, but which nonetheless owe a substantial intellectual debt to the choice shift era. Many studies of group decision making not involving risk (477) seem to reflect something of the choice shift research style, such as the manner of contrasting individual with group responses.

GROUP COMPOSITION Fewer recent studies have used experimental groups composed by selecting members on personality traits (e.g. 162, 249, 314, 346, 465), demographic or cultural characteristics (e.g. 66, 347, 414), and task-related behaviors such as risk-preferences (e.g. 74, 173, 486). Part of this decline in popularity may be due to the continuing inadequacies of personality trait measurement. A more troubling reason has to do with problems associated with the "patterning" hypothesis proposed by McGrath & Altman (296). Those authors argued that one should not expect a simple monotonic relationship between members' total amount of an attribute and group performance; rather, the crux of the composition-performance relation is in the patterning of different individuals with differing amounts of the attribute. The untangling of appropriate pattern-performance relationships is a formidable conceptual and experimental task, yet to be addressed seriously.

Willems & Clark (486) composed groups to be heterogeneous or homogeneous on initial risk proclivities, making their assignment contingent on pregroup individual responses to a subset of items from the choice dilemma questionnaire. They observed a significant average increase in risk-taking of members from heterogeneous but not homogeneous groups; they interpreted this as support for one of two interpretations of the "risk-as-value" hypothesis but evidence against the diffusion of responsibility hypothesis. Perhaps more importantly, they uncovered procedural problems along the way. Summing risk scores across (variable) items can obscure details of risk-taking; and composing groups on such vague grounds as heterogeneity-homogeneity violates the ideal of treatment constancy, not to mention the problem of regression to the mean.

In general, problems of measurement and control and conceptual inadequacies have continued to prevent unambiguous group composition studies of choice shifts as they have studies of other group performance variables.

SITUATIONAL/TASK FACTORS   One of the most persistent concerns of choice shift researchers continues to be the generalizability, "realness," or degree of situational dependence of the phenomenon. Most studies addressing the issue employed a mixture of task and/or physical setting variations.

The bulk of the evidence seems to favor increased caution, if not an outright cautious shift, when subjects use their own (271) or the experimenter's money (277, 288), or are faced with possible negative consequences of decisions about commercial products (213, 366), or pledge relief fund donations (16). These results seem to confirm the reservations expressed by Dion, Baron & Miller (105) about the generality of the *risky* direction of the shift in the face of negative consequences to the decision maker.

The advisory nature of the decision maker's role in the choice dilemmas items has also continued to receive attention (156, 394, 401). Most studies have suggested that one takes at least as much risk for oneself as when advising others (484, 502).

A large number of studies have abandoned to some degree not only the choice dilemma items, but by implication have reduced their intellectual debt to the original choice shift tradition. This line of research has often used outright gambling tasks (35, 36, 101, 152) or "structured choice" tasks (94)—so called because their focus is less upon the choice shift and risk taking per se than the manipulation of basic decision-making parameters through the task itself (98, 99, 210, 286, 498, 499). For example, Zajonc and his associates (498, 499) have shown that the risky or cautious shifts they observed depended upon the relative frequency of occurrence of the two events in a sequential, two-alternative choice task. Not only were they able to demonstrate that a number of common social decision processes could *not* account for the shift, but they concluded that a rather unusual social decision scheme provided the best description of the relative frequency of group choices over a number of trials. The resulting probability model was labeled a "proportionality" process by Johnson & Davis (210), who replicated portions of the Zajonc et al results and showed that another social decision model (equiprobability) was also in accord both with their data and the earlier results.

The above findings not only attest to the importance of theories yielding point predictions (an issue to which we return later), but also emphasize the role of the task itself. While alternatives and outcomes of choice dilemma items are difficult to specify and so have rarely been logically analyzed (285), structured choice tasks are easily analyzed and relevant task parameters conveniently manipulated. Davis et al (99) asked individuals and groups to decide on the attractiveness of duplex bets (cf 286, 417), which varied systematically according to bet expected value. They found high product-moment correlations between the expected value and rated attractiveness of the bet for both individuals and groups. The frequency distributions of subjects' judgments of attractiveness of bets with positive expected values were skewed toward high attractiveness; those with negative expected values were skewed in the opposite direction, and those with zero expected values were more or less symmetrically distributed. Assuming a majority rule, but a proportionality rule when lacking a majority, Davis et al predicted accurately the distribution of group decisions for the various bets, while a number of other models gave poor fits and were rejected.

Bennett, Lindskold & Bennett (24) observed choice shifts in four, but not eight person groups, whereas Myers & Arenson (340) did not find a significant relationship between group size (two, three, five, or seven members) and "shift scores." As these few studies show, group size continues to be a relatively unpopular topic, as it is throughout small group research, perhaps because of a general lack of theory which defines size as an important parameter. Moreover, the great cost of group research has resulted in much research with insufficient sample sizes as it is, and the increase in subjects required for studies of larger group sizes can only increase those costs.

SOCIAL PROCESS FACTORS   A number of choice shift studies have concentrated on the relation of individual members to the group or task (37, 60, 63, 64, 73, 106), while others have followed a slightly different line in emphasizing the decision procedure or social process that produces the decision (14, 15, 21, 34, 62, 83, 89, 196, 282, 342, 388, 413, 433, 501).

One reason for the popularity of this area may be that almost all explanations of choice shift effects stress the role of *individual change* preceeding group decision, rather than the possibility that the process of aggregating individual preferences can produce the shift. The widely held view on the role of individual change may in fact favor certain kinds of experimental procedures such as repeated-measures designs. For example, Dion, Miller & Magnan (106) argued that the diffusion-of-responsibility hypothesis of choice shifts would predict that the higher the group cohesiveness, the greater the willingness to take a risk. Four-person, high-cohesive groups were defined as those composed of subjects informed that they had been selected to get along well together; similarly low-cohesive groups were told that smooth social relations were doubtful. The original prediction was contradicted in that cohesiveness was observed to depress, not enhance, group risk taking, but Dion et al subsequently concluded that such a result was perhaps after all in accord with a diffusion-of-responsibility explanation. These results well illustrate a continuing problem that plagues choice shift research, and indeed much of social psychology in general: the use of informal theories that do not give precise, disconfirmable predictions.

CHOICE SHIFT EXPLANATIONS   Few other areas of social research have displayed to such a high degree a set of alternative theoretical explanations dating virtually from the initial work. There are four general classes of choice shift explanations: (*a*) Risk takers are especially *persuasive* and move companions to a riskier position through discussion. (*b*) Group members *familiarize* each other with the compelling arguments, perhaps not previously encountered, associated with risk taking, with a resulting increase in members' willingness to take a risk. (*c*) Responsibility for decision can be *diffused* across members in the group, with a consequent enhancement of members' risk taking proclivities, whereas the individual is more cautious since he must bear the (usually symbolic) consequences alone. (*d*) The social content of a decision item (usually the ubiquitous choice dilemma) engages a prevailing *social norm* or *cultural value* such that when discussion revals a member not as far in advance of his peers as he would prefer he revises his response to advance in the socially approved (risky) direction. The discovery of cautious shifts, where groups on the average are less likely than individuals to take a risk, created some difficulties for the first three explanations, but the fourth could be revised readily by simply positing that some items engaged a social value for caution rather than risk, etc.

Most researchers, especially within the last 5 years, seem to have concluded that the cultural value explanation is best "supported" by their data (See further summaries and reviews: 82, 105, 371–373, 471, 472). Yet Davis (99) and Zajonc (498, 499) and their associates have observed systematic choice shifts in risky and cautious directions for tasks that are devoid of obvious social content. As described earlier, neither the Zajonc nor Davis notions require that subjects *necessarily* change their personal positions prior to group decision, although they *may* do so (either before or after group decision). Thus hypotheses about the social aggregation of preferences constitute a fifth general category of theory, but one that takes no stand on "personal change."

In summary, choice shift research seems to have been poorly served by the wealth of conceptual notions so long available. Such theories have proved difficult to reject at least partly because their predictions lack sufficient explicitness. Moreover, closer scrutiny might very well show some theories to be special cases of others (61, 105, 472).

The general rhetoric of the literature implies that a single theory will be found sovereign. But the choice shift is after all a group-individual difference, a comparison already honored by 75 years of experimentation and periodic rediscovery. It seems unlikely that all "differences" on all tasks under all social conditions would be due to the same social processes (95, 99, 105, 400, 501). Different social processes can underlie shifts in different contexts. For example, a strong cultural value might exist alongside a majority social decision scheme. The former could produce the item's characteristic, individual distribution (often skewed in the direction of shift) while the latter acts to translate the former into the group distribution.

CONCEPTUAL AND PROCEDURAL CRITICISMS   Choice shift research has not lacked for critics whether on issues associated with statistical analyses (1, 2, 287, 288), the definition and use of "risk" measurement scales (22, 23, 245, 376), the nature of "risk" per se (272, 273), or the heavy devotion to within-subjects designs (71, 99, 500). [See Payne (363) for a discussion of the risk concept.] For example, familiarization hypotheses would probably not have arisen if a before-after individual condition (with no discussion) would have been compared with the individual-group condition by means of a between-subject analysis. Perhaps the most serious kind of methodological issue is that which also affects conceptual progress; the heavy and exclusive dependence on the analysis of variance technology has deflected attention from other features of the data distributions that might have refocused attention to the internal workings of the groups (68, 69, 95). Arithmetic averages contain much but not all of the information in a sample data set, a caution that is applicable beyond the choice shift research tradition.

Group Polarization

The group polarization phenomenon (331) is similar in several respects to choice shifts, but the research has tended to emphasize (*a*) "attitudinal" decisions, and (*b*) the postdiscussion responses of individual members. After some initial uncertainty as to the focus of the comparison, Myers & Lamm (345) have clearly formulated the ". . . *group polarization hypothesis:* The average post-group response will tend to be more extreme in the same direction as the average of the pre-group responses." Here, "direction" is established by the initial mean falling above or below the midpoint of the response scale. Otherwise they define a pre- post-group average difference as an "extremization." Since "polarization" has the traditional connotation of opposing subgroups, the phenomenon might more reasonably have been called group "exaggeration." Taken literally, the Myers-Lamm definition seems to lock the polarization phenomenon to within-subjects experimental designs, and is further unusual by being stated in terms of arithmetic averages rather than as abstract relations.

Groups composed of members homogeneously sampled from one end of the individual distribution have sometimes forcefully shown the polarization effect (343). On other occasions (92, 341), polarization has been observed for one extreme but not the other of homogeneously composed groups. Myers and his associates

(341, 345) have interpreted this result as evidence for informational influence as the causal mechanism on the grounds that critical information was exchanged during discussion and the asymmetry of polarization revealed the direction of the dominant individual tendencies.

Polarization research has not yet been much concerned with the composition of groups on personality or with demographic or other variables not associated with the decision task per se.

There has been a tendency, however, to study polarization in connection with several different kinds of response tasks (330, 344, 360), including a move back to choice dilemma items (324, 328), and the use of both risk and attitude items in the same study (284). Taken together, these studies have established the generality of polarization but constitute a bewildering array of approaches, tasks, etc which are perhaps even more diverse in conception and technique than is to be found in the parental tradition, choice shifts. There seems to be an inclination to regard choice shifts as somehow a special case of polarization, but the four basic explanatory mechanisms associated with the former seem also to arise in connection with the latter (345). Whereas the norm-value hypothesis has been the most popular explanation for choice shifts, the familiarization hypothesis seems to play the dominant conceptual role for those focusing on polarization.

Kerr et al (231), however, have suggested a model particularly applicable to the attitudinal decisions typically featured in polarization research, though the study was focused more on group decisions than postdiscussion members' responses. They proposed that individual members of a population have an intuitive (and perhaps relatively accurate) notion of how their parent population would distribute itself over the alternatives of an evaluative scale pertaining to some attitude object. The extra-group popularity of a position (its relative frequency) is further assumed to determine the influence the advocates of that position exert within the group. The resulting theory (called a norm-weighted average model) accurately predicted the distribution of group decisions associated with several familiar attitude objects.

Perhaps the most attractive feature of the polarization development is the fact that this trend represents a broadening of group research aims. The preoccupation with risk via the choice dilemma items seems at last to be waning, and conceptual notions appear increasingly to reflect a more sophisticated concern with individuals within groups and the processes that produce the decision, solution, etc. There seems to be a new interest in social influence (323, 325, 329), conceived more generally than in the recent past, and placed firmly within a group context where subgroup relations (especially between majorities and minorities) play an important conceptual role. Perhaps even attitude change research may move, at least part-time, from its currently minimal social context back to a group setting where powerful (267) but lightly researched effects have long been known.

Problems of design (overemphasis upon repeated measures) and data analysis (overconcentration on arithmetic means, analysis of variance, etc) plague polarization research in much the same way as observed in choice shift studies. With the emergence of polarization, the strong interest among European social psychologists in small group performance and collective action is even more evident than before, and constitutes a major difference between them and their North America counterparts who have concentrated upon social cognition within individuals.

Group Decision—Other Trends

Group decision research apart from the preceding categories has been sparse but broad, ranging from a concern with the structural complexity of the task and concommitant informational requirements (90, 434–438) to moral judgments in youthful peer groups (276). Somewhat more applied research has also appeared. Janis & Hoffman (209) found that dyads in more frequent contact developed more unfavorable attitudes toward smoking and less anxiety after cutting down, and these effects persisted longer than for lower contact and noncontact controls. Davis et al (97) observed that dyad members who had been summarily obligated to different political constituencies while role-playing in a mock election compromised through equal distances to a consensus midway between their initial positions. Their constituency's preferences on each of several issues had been given to them as opinion poll results in the form of frequency distributions.

Ready applicability was surely an important ingredient contributing to the popularity of choice shift/polarization research. After all, the reputed biasing effect (cautious/risky) of group discussion was counterintuitive and contrary to conventional wisdom which held that collective action was moderate action (69). These occasionally extreme-fostering consequences of group decision provided much of the background for Janis' (208) important popular book, *Groupthink*. A similar interest in social applications may be seen in the currently heavy concentration of attention on jury and mock jury research. [See Davis, Bray & Holt (96) and the chapter by Tapp in this volume.]

Group Decision Theory

The criticisms of theoretical explanations of choice shifts, polarization, etc, implied by preceding discussions, have been given more explicit form by Harris (189), who has condemned much social psychological theory for logical inconsistencies and formal inadequacies. On the other hand, some theorists (unfortunately) consider formal decision models as limited by assumptions of "rational man" or serving primarily to illuminate statistical artifacts (cf the discussions: 345, 364). The latter fears appear generally groundless; even those group decision models using ideas such as expected value and utility (471, 472) have relied upon neither "rationality" nor "artifacts" as explanatory concepts.

However, there exists a highly sophisticated body of theory in an area roughly described as "social choice" that currently is primarily normative in character, but has considerable potential for the description (prediction) of empirical data as well. Niemi & Weisberg (352) have edited a collection of recent theoretical papers quite likely to be applicable to empirical results, and Fishburn (132) should be consulted for a most elegant formal statement of social choice theory (social decision functions, etc). Seminal books by Black (32) and Murakami (338) discuss classic problems largely ignored by social psychologists. Perhaps due to the concentration upon normative theory, social choice theorists have been concerned with collective decision in a general way. Overall questions addressed are: What are the logical consequences of a social system that operates in such and such a fashion given the preferences that mark the individuals concerned? What social decision process could or should be required to achieve a particular result? Applicable settings range from political processes and voting to the market place, perhaps explaining the high concentration of political scientists, sociologists, and economists active in the area, and comprising the membership of the Public Choice Society. The Society journal (*Public Choice*) was established within the period of this review, but relevant papers appear in a number of other publications as well (131, 362, 449).

Social psychologists often assert that a particular group decision outcome was the result of a particular social process which itself was difficult or impossible to observe directly. Using social choice theory, it might be possible to exclude some interaction explanations by showing that the alleged social processes were improbable or could not result in the observed outcome.

Davis (95) has proposed a general model of how individual decision preferences, perhaps quite disparate initially, may be translated by social interaction into a group decision. Starting with the probability distribution for individuals across the alternatives defined by the decision task, the model permits various assumptions about the decision-related effects of social interaction to be formalized precisely and thereby used to predict the probability distribution for groups. Independent individual response data may be used to estimate the individual distribution, and observed group results may be compared directly with predicted distributions. A number of applications (e.g. 99, 231, 256, 262, 299) have demonstrated the ease whereby special cases, fitting particular groups or social settings, may be accommodated within the framework of the model. Arising from empirical work with small groups, the model would benefit in the future from theoretical efforts to include the time-dependent social dynamics and to address individual preference orders beyond the single choice —the latter being of special concern to social choice theorists as discussed above.

INTERPERSONAL CONFLICT AND MIXED-MOTIVE INTERACTION

The previous reviews of the literature have been restricted to situations in which the consequences of group action are shared by all members of the group. A group must solve a problem or make a decision and everyone must share in the responsibility for the "group product." We now turn to a more competitive situation in which the acts of the individual members are not combined in some way to yield a "group product," and the outcomes are not necessarily shared equally. The obvious consequence is that the competitive tendencies of the parties are heightened, and in many cases this consequence is highly detrimental to the group in maximizing mutual gain. This type of situation is quite pervasive, occurring at all levels of social interaction, and consequently the study of behavior in such situations is an important research problem.

The most striking change in the direction of research in mixed-motive situations, especially in the last 2 years, is the decline in research dealing with two-person prisoner's dilemma game (PDG). Considering the number of published studies on the PDG, there has been surprisingly little theoretical progress on the processes underlying cooperative behavior in this situation. Perhaps this is one of the reasons for the disillusionment with the PDG as an experimental paradigm for the study of trust and cooperation. Another reason is that some critics of PDG research have argued that the situation is so artificial and ambiguous that behavior in the situation has little relevance for behavior in real-life, mixed-motive situations. Such critics, however, fail to realize that the PDG paradigm represents an intermediate stage between a "minimal social situation" (229, 411) and more realistic real-life situations. This research strategy is based on the assumption that insights into the nature of behavior in complex social situations depends, partly at least, on the discovery of principles underlying behavior in simple (artificial, idealized) social situations. This approach is consistent with the arguments made by Guyer & Rapoport (165) when they state that ". . . the fundamental laws of physics were developed in terms of the behavior of ideal objects moving through frictionless space" (p. 410).

Despite the decline in PDG research during the past 2 years, there has been an increase in the number of general reviews of theory and research in mixed-motive situations (102, 111, 113, 224, 361, 371, 374, 441, 456), and on PDG research in particular (5, 188, 348, 349, 358, 381, 490). Hence, research interest in mixed-motive behavior does not seem to have declined.

Two-Person, Two-Choice Situations

In contrast to earlier studies, recent research seems to emphasize the effects of the individual's definition of the situation and of his perceptions of the other person. In a series of studies by Kelley & Stahelski (225–227), several hypotheses derived from Kelley's attribution theory (220b, 220c) were tested. According to attribution theory, the process of perceiving the intentions of the other in the PDG is analogous to inferring the cause of his behavior. Though some of these hypotheses received only partial support, their results showed that consistent behavior by a person yields more information and greater consensus about his intentions than inconsistent behavior; the most common error of perceiving intent occurred when a competitive person was paired with a cooperative person. The competitive person was likely to perceive that his partner was also competitive because his partner behaved competitively in reaction to his own competitive behavior; and the competitive person was relatively unaware of the effects of his own behavior on the other's behavior. Hence, competitive and cooperative persons are likely to develop different beliefs about others. Competitive persons are likely to believe that others are also uniformly competitive, whereas cooperative persons are likely to have a more heterogeneous outlook—that some are cooperative while others are competitive. Partial support for this hypothesis is reported by Eiser & Tajfel (120).

An individual's perceived intent of the other should be correlated with his attitude toward the other; hence, cooperative behavior also should be correlated with such attitudes. Based on this hypothesis, the following variables were shown to be related to behavior in the PDG: perceived intent of the other (49, 143); attitudes toward the other and the situation (119, 121); perception of the payoff structure and the response alternatives (13, 410); attitude toward the act and expectations of the other (4); and subjects who thought they were playing against a computer program were more competitive than those who thought they were playing with another person (3).

EFFECTS OF RESPONSES OF THE OTHER   Oskamp (358), in reviewing the literature on the effects of feedback programs, concludes that the matching (tit-for-tat) strategy is the most effective means of inducing cooperation, and Wilson (487) also reaches the same conclusion. One of the reasons for the effectiveness of this strategy is that it always reciprocates cooperation; it never defects unless the subject defects; and it cannot be exploited. Another reason it is effective is that it is a contingent program, and, in contrast to a noncontingent (random) program, it is responsive to changes in the subject's behavior. A subject may try to signal his intention to the other, but a noncontingent program will not react to nor reciprocate such overtures.

Several studies showed that a "pacifist" strategy is likely to lead to exploitation, and is not an effective means of inducing cooperation (470, 487). This is consistent with earlier findings. However, there were two studies which showed that a pacifist strategy, under certain conditions, may be effective (109, 160, 280). With regard to the effects of competitive strategies, Teger (457) showed that a hostile act—after a period of cooperation—may be perceived as more hostile because it is unexpected; and Komorita (239) found that for competitive subjects, a long initial sequence of competitive acts was more effective in inducing cooperation than a short sequence; however, the opposite effect was obtained for cooperative subjects.

INCENTIVES, UTILITY, AND MOTIVATIONAL ORIENTATION   Several models and indices of cooperation based on the payoff values were proposed (38, 47, 55, 122, 491), and several studies showed that the nature of the reward structure of the game affected behavior in the game (406, 493).

There were several studies on the effects of magnitude of incentives on the level of cooperation in the PDG (140, 237, 359). As in earlier research, the results are inconsistent. The results of a study by Friedland, Arnold & Thibaut (138) provide some insights into the effects of incentives. They found that the absolute magnitude of reward did not influence the level of cooperation, but the magnitude of reward —relative to Thibaut and Kelley's concept of "comparison level" (CL)—was significantly related to cooperation. Outcomes greater than CL yielded a higher level of cooperation.

McClintock & Messick and their associates (289, 290, 292, 297) use game playing behavior as an assessment device to determine the motivational orientation of subjects. In some of these studies "decomposed prisoner's dilemma games" (DPD) have been used, and Pruitt (370) has shown that alternative DPD games based on the same PDG elicit different motives in the game. Hence, Pruitt argues that different DPD games (based on the same PDG) cannot be used interchangeably to measure a single motive. But this is tacitly assumed in the approach used by McClintock & Messick. An alternative approach to the measurement of motivational orientation is to use a questionnaire (491) and then predict behavior in the PDG. Based on this approach, Griesinger & Livingston (157) have proposed a geometric model which appears promising.

CULTURE, PERSONALITY, AND SEX DIFFERENCES   During the past 5 years, a large number of studies attempted to show sex differences in cooperation. Though the results are inconsistent, the data seem to show that female pairs are generally more competitive than male pairs, but in mixed-sex pairs, the sexes do not differ significantly as to cooperativeness (20, 33, 67, 88, 199, 219, 298, 312, 415, 469, 483, 492). Also, females seem to be more sensitive to the sex of the other person as well as the sex of the experimenter (219, 415).

The relationship between personality and cooperation also seems to be inconsistent; where significant results have been obtained, the correlations are discouragingly low (48, 147, 398, 416, 459, 488). These conclusions are consistent with the conclusions of earlier reviews of personality variables and cooperative behavior (188, 458). Finally, there were several cross-cultural and subcultural comparisons of competitive-cooperative behavior (19, 216, 291, 367, 383); and there was a criticism (with a rejoinder and reply) directed at generalizations about racial differences without considering class differences or individual differences in personality (28, 58, 59, 452).

SITUATIONAL FACTORS   Several studies demonstrated that: giving subjects the opportunity to communicate in the PDG increased cooperation (443, 474, 483); format of the game evoked different levels of cooperation (163, 370); visual presence (eye contact) increased cooperation (142, 234, 482), though one study showed visual presence did not affect cooperation (293); and cooperative behavior in three different types of dilemma-type situations (using a within-subject design) did not correlate very highly, suggesting that it would be hazardous to generalize results from one situation to another (404).

COMPLIANCE TO THREATS, PROMISES, AND RULES   Many investigators have modified the two-person, two-choice paradigm for specific purposes. For example, Thibaut and his associates (461) have used variations of the two-person paradigm with the provision that one or both persons (usually the weaker) can withdraw from the relationship to seek an alternative source of reward (his comparison level for alternatives). When both members of a dyad have high external alternatives, norms are more likely to develop (339); norms may also serve the function of limiting the "threat capability" of the parties (308, 311); and an individual is more likely to observe rules (comply) when the rule-maker and the individual both benefit from compliance (462). Similarly, Marwell & Schmitt (279, 281, 282) employ a special apparatus in which cooperation can be disrupted by "risk." Their results show that the larger the "risk," the more likely ongoing cooperation will be disrupted.

One of the problems of evaluating the effects of threat is that various investigators have used the term to refer to different sets of operations. As a consequence of an earlier critique by Kelley (222), many investigators now agree that a threat may be operationally defined as an "if-then" statement of the form: "If you do (do not do) X, I will (will not) do Y." If Y has negative consequences for the target, the statement is defined as a threat; if Y has positive consequences, it is defined as a promise. Assuming Y is negative (threat), according to Deutsch (102), if X specifies an act to be performed (do X), then the statement defines a *deterrence* situation. However, if the source specifies, "If you do not do X, . . ." the statement defines a *compellence* situation. In compellence, the source wants the target to perform X, while in deterrence, the source wants the target to *avoid* performing X.

In evaluating the costs of making threats and promises, Baldwin (10, 11) makes the interesting observation that threats are cheap—only if they are successful. If the target does not comply, it may be costly to implement the threat, and if not implemented, one loses credibility. Promises, on the other hand, are costly if successful, but cheap if they are not. These are not just interesting observations but are important variables in the effectiveness of inducing compliance from the target: The more costly it is to implement a threat, the less credible the threat, and the less likely the target is to comply (319).

Empirical studies suggest that the likelihood of compliance to threats increases when the source: is accommodative (cooperative) and makes equitable demands (39, 306, 397); has high status and credibility (124); has greater power to punish the target (29, 124, 307). Moreover, if the source has the power to use threats or promises, the source is more credible if promises are used rather than threats (190, 268, 393).

With regard to the use of threats and promises, if given the opportunity to use both threats and promises, subjects prefer to make promises rather than threats (77); but males seem to have a stronger tendency to use reward power than females (20). The frequency of using promises increases if promises are reciprocated (40). The frequency of using threats seems to increase when the target complies (320, 453), and when the target can also threaten and retaliate (454). But the use of threat is inhibited when it is costly (455).

It is reasonable to ask if the use of threats is effective. The answer is yes (164, 421). Indeed, two studies showed that if a cooperative source has the power to punish the other and does not use his power, the weaker party will try to exploit him (33, 442). These results are consistent with earlier findings on the use of power (242). Finally, a review of earlier research on the effects of threat may be found in Tedeschi (450), and a recent perspective on power and social influence may be found in Tedeschi (451).

THE N-PERSON PRISONER'S DILEMMA   Though most social psychologists are familiar with the two-person PDG, few are acquainted with the N-person case ($N \geq 3$). This is unfortunate because the N-person case (NPD) has greater generality and applicability to real-life situations. In addition to the problems of energy conservation, ecology, and overpopulation, many other real-life problems can be represented by the NPD paradigm, e.g. behavior in panic situations (158, 222, 315) or "prosocial" behavior such as bystander intervention in emergencies (93, 252). It is reasonable to assume that empirical studies of the NPD may yield valuable insights into the nature of cooperative behavior in such situations.

Except for the fact that there are varying numbers of persons who may cooperate or defect, the nature of the dilemma in the NPD is almost identical to the dilemma in the two-person case: the motivational conflict between maximizing personal gain (individual interests) vs maximizing collective gain (social welfare). Hence, some of the results derived from the two-person PDG may be applicable to the NPD, and research is needed to determine the validity of such generalizations.

There were two early studies of the NPD (31, 382), but these studies did not seem to have an immediate impact on theory and research. It was only after the publication of Hardin's paper on the "Tragedy of the Commons" (183), and the emerging problems of environmental pollution, overpopulation, and resource conservation, that social scientists became aware of the implications of the NPD as a research paradigm. Since that time, three additional empirical studies have appeared (223, 278, 304), and several models which attempt to define and classify various types of N-person "dilemma-type" situations have been proposed (100, 174, 184, 303, 396). It seems reasonably safe to predict that we will see an increasing number of studies based on the NPD.

Bargaining and Negotiation

In bargaining and negotiation, in contrast to the two-choice paradigm, communication is permitted (usually by written offers), and neither party receives any outcomes until the bargaining is terminated. Hence, in the early trials, if one party is cooperative (yielding) while the other is competitive (unyielding), the cooperative person does not suffer and the competitive person cannot be said to have exploited the other. There is only a single outcome based on whether an agreement is reached, and if there is an agreement, the important factor is the terms of the agreement. In addition, a distinction is sometimes made between bargaining and negotiation (431): Bargaining consists of communicating offers and counteroffers between the parties, while negotiation includes other forms of communication (threats, promises, appeals to equity, etc), as well as the interchange of offers.

EFFECTS OF STRATEGY OF THE OTHER   A critical problem in bargaining is the effects of concessions. If a compromise settlement is to be reached, both parties must make concessions; hence, both bargainers must resolve the conflict between maximizing the probabilities of reaching agreement and achieving an advantageous bargain. Paradoxically, two theories dealing with the effects of concession-making reach opposing conclusions. Siegel & Fouraker's level of aspiration model (412) assumes that concessions by one party raises the aspiration level of the other and will evoke a tough stance. Hence, their theory implies that, "It pays to be tough." Osgood's GRIT model (356, 357), on the other hand, assumes that if negotiations are deadlocked, one side must initiate a small concession and wait for the other to reciprocate the small concession. In subsequent encounters it is assumed that these reciprocated concessions gradually become larger until an agreement is reached.

Since there is some support for both theories, the problem is to determine the conditions under which each theory is valid (239). Recent research seems to be directed toward this problem. Although there were several studies which supported the Siegel-Fouraker hypothesis (80, 115, 187, 195, 392, 424), support for their theory does not necessarily imply the rejection of Osgood's proposal. Osgood's GRIT strategy assumes that negotiations are deadlocked, and almost all of the studies supporting the Siegel-Fouraker hypothesis did not simulate such a stalemate.

In one of the few studies which did simulate such a stalemate, Hamner (182) found that a tough strategy was not effective. The tougher the strategy, the fewer who reached agreement, and a yielding strategy produced the highest level of mean payoffs. Similarly, Yukl (496, 497) found that a tough strategy lowered the aspiration level of the subject and induced greater concessions, as hypothesized by Siegel and Fouraker; however, this occurred only when there was time pressure and only when the subject did not have information about the other's payoff schedule. These results suggest that a firm strategy which is perceived to be unfair and exploitative is likely to be met with resistance, and they are consistent with the finding that an extremely tough strategy is less effective than a moderately tough strategy (27). Moreover, this interpretation is consistent with studies of the effects of inequity and bargaining: subjects compete or cooperate so as to restore equity in the relationship (25, 300, 302, 364, 389).

In a comparative study of bargaining (221) the same experiment was conducted at eight different laboratory sites, three in Europe and eight in the United States. The results of this study showed that monetary incentives (vs bargaining for points) facilitated reaching agreement, and as problem difficulty (restriction of bargaining range) increased, the number of agreements decreased. Also, the meaning of cooperation vs competition differed across the eight sites. At some sites this factor loaded heavily on the evaluative dimension (to be competitive is bad), while at other sites it loaded on the "dynamism" dimension (to be cooperative is weak). These different meanings of cooperation-competition were found to be related to the outcomes and process of negotiation. The finding that problem difficulty inhibits cooperative agreements also has been found in other studies (103, 503).

REPRESENTATIVE NEGOTIATIONS   The term "representative bargaining" refers to a situation in which a negotiator bargains not only for himself but represents a partner or group so that the consequences of his success or failure is shared by his constituents. When bargainers have role obligations and are accountable to their constituency, studies show that they are: more competitive and make smaller concessions (26, 114, 159); less likely to accept offers which deviate from the reference group position (247); and less likely to reach agreement (236, 466, 467).

If representative negotiators discuss the issue and form a prior commitment, they are found to take a more extreme position and are more competitive in the negotiations (220, 238). One explanation of this result is a "group-induced shift" in the bargaining position adopted by the bargainer (238, 246, 248). A related explanation is that "social categorization" (30, 104, 108, 380, 445–448) produces a "pro-ingroup, anti-outgroup" bias, resulting in competitive attitudes toward the outgroup. Moreover, this discrimination against the outgroup occurs even when interaction with the outgroup is not anticipated (107, 144); is enhanced when competitive interaction is anticipated (107, 378, 379); and increases with decreasing size of the group (144).

Representative bargainers were also found to be more competitive when: they were led to believe they were distrusted by their constituents, despite the belief that the opposing bargainers were cooperative (137); they were subordinates observed by a leader, or if they were leaders elected by their group (246); they discussed and formed a prior commitment on the issue (220, 238; but see 112); they were observed or evaluated by their constituents (235, 355); and when their constituents were competitively oriented rather than cooperative (391). Finally, subjects as constituents trusted and positively evaluated representative bargainers if they were effective and obedient (478).

EFFECTS OF THIRD PARTIES   In many real-world situations, mediation and arbitration are frequently effective in resolving conflict. Based on the work of Peters (365), Stevens (431), and Walton & McKersie (479), Pruitt (371), Fisher (134), and Young (494) have outlined the functions of a third party. One of the main functions is to provide a mechanism of making mutual concessions so that concessions are not likely to be perceived as a sign of weakness and raise the other's aspiration level. This function of the mediator not only has some empirical support (368), but the negotiator himself is less likely to feel weakness or to have lost face if concessions are made through a mediator (375).

Empirical studies suggest that: negotiators who anticipate arbitration (binding decisions by a third party) are more likely to concede and reach agreement than those who anticipate mediation (nonbinding suggestions by a third party) (211); mediators are more effective with negotiators who have role obligations to their constituents (466), and when the negotiations have been deadlocked (212, 375). Studies also indicate that the need to save face interacts with the effects of third-party intervention (212), and if there are multiple issues to be settled, agreement is more likely if the issues are negotiated as a set (log-rolling), rather than negotiating one issue at a time (123, 139). Finally, when subjects are placed in the role of a third party, they behave so as to restore equity between two other negotiators, even when such "justice behavior" is detrimental to their own self-interest (9).

Coalition Formation

In contrast with theoretical developments on the two-person PDG, theoretical progress in coalition formation is more advanced, at least in terms of the number of theories. Yet there are far more empirical studies of the PDG than studies of coalition formation. The main reason for this is probably convenience. It is much easier to schedule two subjects than three, three subjects than four, etc. Hence, there are many more tests of coalition theories based on the triad than on larger groups (78, 439). This is unfortunate because the most sensitive (critical) tests of theories are likely to be derived from groups larger than the triad (241).

A review of the literature in coalition formation certainly presents a confusing picture. One of the reasons for this state of affairs is that most investigators have been concerned primarily with the outcomes rather than the processes of coalition formation (241, 439). Some investigators, recognizing this limitation, have attempted to examine such processes (81, 377, 473), and two recently proposed theories (241, 243) make assumptions about the processes of coalition formation. In addition, some investigators have employed other types of paradigms which may lead to insights regarding the processes underlying coalition behavior (86, 309–311).

Another reason for the confusing state of affairs is that many studies have been based on the Vinacke-Arkoff paradigm (468), a procedure involving face-to-face interaction in a pachisi-board game. As a test of coalition theories, this paradigm has serious limitations (439). Though some investigators continue to use this paradigm (with confusing and indeterminate results), other investigators have devised alternative procedures to test coalition theories (79, 198, 217, 218, 241, 244).

One of the predominant theories of coalition formation is Gamson's Minimum Resource theory (141). The main support for the theory is based on the triad, especially with a resource distribution of 4–3–2. Gamson's theory predicts that the 3–2 coalition (the "cheapest winning") should be most frequent, and a vast majority of earlier studies, as well as recent studies, support this prediction (79, 81, 91). However, the division of rewards between the weak members (3–2) is consistently between parity (60–40 split) and equality (50–50 split). Since Gamson's theory predicts a division based on parity, some investigators claim this result is inconsistent with the theory (485), while others claim this same result supports his theory (91). Moreover, recent research based on the triad (65, 476, 485) and with groups larger than the triad (79, 240, 241) have shown that his theory has serious deficiencies.

Several new theories were proposed during the past 5 years (57, 197, 240, 241, 243, 354). Some of these are descriptive theories and make predictions about both the frequency of various coalitions and division of rewards. Other theories are normative and only address the division of rewards given particular conditions. While there is some support for each of these theories, there are insufficient data to determine whether they are promising or not. The Horowitz (197) and Komorita (240) theories make remarkably similar predictions regarding the division of rewards, yet make contrasting psychological assumptions. For example, in an "Apex" game (a class of games for which there is a single "strong" person with many weaker persons, and the union of the weaker persons is a winning coalition), the two theories make identical predictions for the division of rewards. This is an encouraging sign since one is a descriptive theory and the other normative, and there have been few attempts to bridge the gap between the contributions of game theorists and social scientists. Another encouraging sign is that some economists and mathematicians have adopted a behavioral approach and have begun to conduct experiments to test their theories (283, 403).

CONCLUSIONS

Interest in actual social interaction is increasing. As many have noted, the Lewinian emphasis on the dynamics of interacting groups which dominated the social psychology of the forties and fifties was replaced by an emphasis on the social cognition of individuals in the late fifties and sixties. Much of the renewed interest in small group interaction derives from the discovery of the "risky shift," the larger question of choice shifts in group decision making (372, 373), and the increasing realization that the fundamental question is the effect of group discussion on group decision (68). Zeitgeist considerations are also relevant. As Steiner (429) has indicated, social psychologists *are* responsive to the needs of their times. The great needs of our times are the three E's—energy, economy, and environment—in a world of suddenly limited resources relative to increased populations. This renews research interest in the collective behavior of interacting individuals and fundamental questions about the individual's relationship to the collective. Thus we predict that the experimental study of social interaction will increasingly address the basic questions of classical political economy: how are resources distributed, what are the processes of group decision making, how do the motives and objectives of individuals relate to the collective welfare?

Literature Cited

1. Abelson, R. P. 1973. Comment on "group shift to caution at the race track." *J. Exp. Soc. Psychol.* 9:517–21
2. Ibid. The statistician as viper: Reply to McCauley and Stitt, 526–27
3. Abric, J. C., Kahan, J. P. 1972. The effects of representations and behavior in experimental games. *Eur. J. Soc. Psychol.* 2:129–44
4. Ajzen, I., Fishbein, M. 1970. The prediction of behavior from attitudinal and normative variables. *J. Exp. Soc. Psychol.* 6:466–87
5. Apfelbaum, E. 1974. On conflicts and bargaining. *Ad. Exp. Soc. Psychol.,* 7:103–56
6. Aronoff, J., Messe, L. A. 1971. Motivational determinants of small group structure. *J. Pers. Soc. Psychol.* 17:319–24
7. Ashour, A. S. 1973. The contingency model of leadership effectiveness: An evaluation. *Organ. Behav. Hum. Perform.* 9:339–55
8. Ibid. Further discussion of Fiedler's contingency model of leadership effectiveness, 369–76
9. Baker, K. 1974. Experimental analysis at third-party justice behavior. *J. Pers. Soc. Psychol.* 30:307–16
10. Baldwin, D. A. 1971. Thinking about threats. *J. Confl. Resolut.* 15:71–78
11. Ibid. The costs of power, 145–55
12. Balke, W. M., Hammond, K. R., Meyer, G. D. 1973. Application of judgment theory and interactive computer graphics technology to labor-management negotiations: An example. *Admin. Sci. Q.* 18:311–27
13. Baranowski, T. A., Summers, D. A. 1972. Perception of response alternatives in a prisoner's dilemma game. *J. Pers. Soc. Psychol.* 21:35–40
14. Baron, R. S., Dion, K. L., Baron, P. H., Miller, N. 1971. Group concensus and cultural values as determinants of risk

taking. *J. Pers. Soc. Psychol.* 20:446–55
15. Baron, R. S., Monson, T. C., Baron, P. H. 1973. Conformity pressure as a determinant of risk taking: Replication and extension. *J. Pers. Soc. Psychol.* 28:406–13
16. Baron, R. S., Roper, G., Baron, P. H. 1974. Group discussion and the stingy shift. *J. Pers. Soc. Psychol.* 30:538–45
17. Baum, B. H., Sorenson, P. F., Place, W. S. 1970. The effect of managerial training on organizational control: An experimental study. *Organ. Behav. Hum. Perform.* 5:170–82
18. Bavelas, A., Hastorf, A. H., Gross, A. E., Kite, W. R. 1965. Experiments on the alteration of group structure. *J. Exp. Soc. Psychol.* 1:55–70
19. Baxter, G. W. 1973. Prejudiced liberal? Race and information effects in a two-person game. *J. Confl. Resolut.* 17:131–61
20. Bedell, J., Sistrunk, F. 1973. Power, opportunity costs, and sex in mixed-motives games. *J. Pers. Soc. Psychol.* 25:219–26
21. Bell, P. R., Jamieson, B. D. 1970. Publicity of initial decisions and the risky shift phenomenon. *J. Exp. Soc. Psychol.* 6:329–45
22. Belovicz, M. W., Finch, F. E. 1971. Comments on "the risky shift in group betting." *J. Exp. Soc. Psychol.* 7:81–83
23. Belovicz, M. W., Finch, F. E. 1971. A critical analysis of the "risky shift" phenomena. *Organ. Behav. Hum. Perform.* 6:150–68
24. Bennett, C., Lindskold, S., Bennett, R. 1973. The effects of group size and discussion time on the risky shift. *J. Soc. Psychol.* 91:137–47
25. Benton, A. A. 1971. Productivity, distributive justice, and bargaining among children. *J. Pers. Soc. Psychol.* 18:68–78
26. Benton, A. A., Druckman, D. 1974. Constituent's bargaining dentation and

intergroup negotiation. *J. Appl. Soc. Psychol.* 2:141–50

27. Benton, A. A., Kelley, H. H., Liebling, B. 1972. Effects of extremity of offers and concession rate. *J. Pers. Soc. Psychol.* 24:73–83

28. Berger, S. E., Tedeschi, J. T. 1969. Aggressive behavior of delinquent, dependent, and "normal" white and black boys in social conflicts. *J. Exp. Soc. Psychol.* 5:325–70

29. Berkowitz, N. H., Hylander, L., Bakaitis, R. 1973. Defense, vulnerability, and cooperation. *J. Pers. Soc. Psychol.* 25:401–7

30. Billig, M. G., Tajfel, H. 1973. Social categorization and similarity in intergroup behavior. *Eur. J. Soc. Psychol.* 3:27–52

31. Bixenstine, V. E., Levitt, C. A., Wilson, K. V. 1966. Collaboration among six persons in a prisoner's dilemma game. *J. Confl. Resolut.* 10:488–96

32. Black, D. 1958. *The Theory of Committees and Elections.* Cambridge, England: Cambridge Univ. Press

33. Black, T. E., Higbee, K. L. 1973. Effects of power, threat, and sex on exploitation. *J. Pers. Soc. Psychol.* 27:382–88

34. Blascovich, J. 1972. Sequence effects on choice shifts involving risk. *J. Exp. Soc. Psychol.* 8:260–65

35. Blascovich, J., Ginsburg, G. P. 1974. Emergent norms and choice shifts involving risk. *Sociometry* 37:205–18

36. Blascovich, J., Veach, T. L., Ginsburg, G. P. 1973. Blackjack and the risky shift. *Sociometry* 36:42–55

37. Blitz, R., Dansereau, D. F. 1972. The effect of underlying situational characteristics on the risky shift phenomenon. *J. Soc. Psychol.* 87:251–58

38. Bonacich, P. 1972. Norms and cohesion as adaptive responses to potential conflict: An experimental study. *Sociometry* 35:357–75

39. Bonoma, T. V., Tedeschi, J. T. 1973. Some effects of source behavior on target's compliance to threats. *Behav. Sci.* 18:34–41

40. Bonoma, T. V., Tedeschi, J. T., Helm, B. 1974. Some effects of target cooperation. *Sociometry* 37:251–61

41. Bouchard, T. J. Jr. 1971. Training, motivation, and personality as determinants of the effectiveness of brainstorming groups and individuals. *J. Appl. Psychol.* 55:324–31

42. Ibid 1972. A comparison of two group brainstorming procedures. 56:418–21

43. Bouchard, T. J. Jr., Barsaloux, J., Drauden, G. 1974. Brainstorming procedure, group size, and sex as determinants of the problem-solving effectiveness of groups and individuals. *J. Appl. Psychol.* 59:135–38

44. Bouchard, T. J. Jr., Drauden, G., Barsaloux, J. 1974. A comparison of individual, subgroup, and total group methods of problem solving. *J. Appl. Psychol.* 59:226–27

45. Bouchard, T. J. Jr., Hare, M. 1970. Size, performance, and potential in brainstorming groups. *J. Appl. Psychol.* 54:51–55

46. Bourne, L. E. Jr., Battig, W. F. 1966. Complex processes. In *Experimental Methods and Instrumentation in Psychology,* ed. J. B. Sidowski, 541–76. New York: McGraw-Hill

47. Boyle, R., Bonacich, P. 1970. The development of trust and mistrust in mixed-motive games. *Sociometry* 33:123–39

48. Braginsky, D. D. 1970. Machiavellianism and manipulative interpersonal behavior in children. *J. Exp. Soc. Psychol.* 6:77–99

49. Braver, S., Barnett, B. 1974. Perception of opponents' motives and cooperation in a mixed-motive game. *J. Confl. Resolut.* 18:686–99

50. Brehmer, B. 1973. Effects of cue validity upon interpersonal learning of inference tasks involving both linear and nonlinear relations. *Am. J. Psychol.* 86:29–48

51. Brehmer, B. 1973. Effects of task predictability and cue validity on interpersonal learning of inference tasks involving both linear and nonlinear relations. *Organ. Behav. Hum. Perform.* 10:24–46

52. Ibid 1974. Effects of cue validity and task predictability on interpersonal learning of linear inference tasks. 12:17–29

53. Ibid. The effect of cue intercorrelation on interpersonal learning of probabilistic tasks, 397–412

54. Brehmer, B., Hammond, K. R. 1973. Cognitive sources of interpersonal conflict: Analysis of interaction between linear and nonlinear cognitive systems. *Organ. Behav. Hum. Perform.* 10:290–313

55. Brew, J. S. 1973. An altruism parameter for prisoner's dilemma. *J. Confl. Resolut.* 17:351–67

56. Brunswik, E. 1956. *Perception and the Representative Design of Experiments.* Berkeley: Univ. California Press

57. Buckley, J. J., Weston, T. E. 1973. Symmetric solution to a five-person constant-sum game as a description of experimental game outcomes. *J. Confl. Resolut.* 17:703–18
58. Burgess, P. K. 1971. Critical note: Aggressive behavior of delinquent, dependent, and "normal" white and black boys in social conflicts. *J. Exp. Soc. Psychol.* 7:545–50
59. Ibid. A reply to Tedeschi and Berger, 558–59
60. Burnstein, E., Katz, S. 1971. Individual commitment to risky and conservative choices as a determinant of shifts in group decisions. *J. Pers.* 39:564–79
61. Burnstein, E., Miller, H., Vinokur, A., Katz, S., Crowley, J. 1971. Risky shift is eminently rational. *J. Pers. Soc. Psychol.* 20:462–71
62. Burnstein, E., Vinokur, A. 1973. Testing two classes of theories about group induced shifts in individual choice. *J. Exp. Soc. Psychol.* 9:123–37
63. Burnstein, E., Vinokur, A., Pichevin, M. F. 1974. What do differences between own, admired, and attributed choices have to do with group induced shifts in choice? *J. Exp. Soc. Psychol.* 10:428–43
64. Burnstein, E., Vinokur, A., Trope, Y. 1973. Interpersonal comparison versus persuasive argumentation: A more direct test of alternative explanations for group-induced shifts in individual choice. *J. Exp. Soc. Psychol.* 9:236–45
65. Caldwell, M. 1971. Coalitions in the triad: Introducing the element of change into the game structure. *J. Pers. Soc. Psychol.* 20:271–80
66. Carlson, J. A., Davis, C. M. 1971. Cultural values and the risky shift: A cross-cultural test in Uganda and the United States. *J. Pers. Soc. Psychol.* 20:392–99
67. Carment, D. W. 1974. Effects of sex role in a maximizing difference game. *J. Confl. Resolut.* 18:461–72
68. Cartwright, D. 1971. Risk taking by individuals and groups: An assessment of research employing choice dilemmas. *J. Pers. Soc. Psychol.* 20:361–78
69. Cartwright, D. 1973. Determinants of scientific progress: The case of the risky shift. *Am. Psychol.* 28:222–31
70. Cartwright, D., Zander, A. 1968. *Group Dynamics: Research and Theory.* New York: Harper & Row
71. Castore, C. H. 1972. Group discussion and prediscussion assessment of preferences in the risky shift. *J. Exp. Soc. Psychol.* 8:161–67
72. Castore, C. H., Peterson, K., Goodrich, T. A. 1971. Risky shift: Social value or social choice? An alternative model. *J. Pers. Soc. Psychol.* 20:487–94
73. Castore, C. H., Roberts, J. C. 1972. Subjective estimates of own relative riskiness and risk taking following a group discussion. *Organ. Behav. Hum. Perform.* 7:107–20
74. Cecil, E. A., Chertkoff, J. M., Cummings, L. L. 1970. Risk taking in groups as a function of group pressure. *J. Soc. Psychol.* 81:273–74
75. Cecil, E. A., Cummings, L. L., Chertkoff, J. M. 1973. Group composition and choice shift: Implications for management. *Acad. Manage. J.* 16:412–22
76. Chemers, M., Skrzypek, G. J. 1972. Experimental test of the contingency model of leadership effectiveness. *J. Pers. Soc. Psychol.* 24:172–77
77. Cheney, J., Harford, T., Solomon, L. 1972. Effects of communicating threats and promises upon the bargaining process. *J. Confl. Resolut.* 16:99–107
78. Chertkoff, J. M. 1970. Sociopsychological theories and research on coalition formation. In *The Study of Coalition Behavior* ed. S. Groennings, E. W. Kelly, M. Leisersow, 297–322. New York: Holt, Rinehart & Winston
79. Chertkoff, J. M. 1971. Coalition formation as a function of differences in resources. *J. Confl. Resolut.* 15:371–83
80. Chertkoff, J. M., Baird, S. L. 1971. Applicability of the big lie technique and the last clear chance doctrine to bargaining. *J. Pers. Soc. Psychol.* 20:298–303
81. Chertkoff, J. M., Braden, J. L. 1974. Effects of experience and bargaining restrictions on coalition formation. *J. Pers. Soc. Psychol.* 30:169–77
82. Clark, R. D. III 1971. Group induced shift towards risk: A critical appraisal. *Psychol. Bull.* 76:251–70
83. Clark, R. D. III, Crockett, W. H., Archer, R. 1971. Risk-as-value hypothesis: The relationship between perception of self, others, and the risky shift. *J. Pers. Soc. Psychol.* 20:425–29
84. Clark, R. D. III, Willems, E. P. 1972. Two interpretations of Brown's hypothesis for the risky shift. *Psychol. Bull.* 78:62–63
85. Cohen, J. E. 1971. *Casual Groups of Monkeys and Men: Stochastic Models of Elementary Social Systems.* Cambridge, Mass: Harvard Univ. Press
86. Cole, S. G. 1972. Conflict and cooperation in potentially intense conflict situ-

ations. *J. Pers. Soc. Psychol.* 22:31–50

87. Collins, B. E., Raven, B. H. 1969. Group structure: Attraction, coalitions, communication, and power. In *Handbook of Social Psychology*, ed. G. Lindzey, E. Aronson, 4:102–204. Reading, Mass: Addison-Wesley

88. Conrath, D. W. 1972. Sex role and cooperation in chickens. *J. Confl. Resolut.* 16:433–43

89. Cooper, M. R., Wood, M. T. 1974. Effects of member participation and commitment in group decision making on influence, satisfaction, and decision riskiness. *J. Appl. Psychol.* 59:127–34

90. Crawford, J. L. 1974. Task uncertainty, decision importance, and group reinforcement as determinants of communication processes in groups. *J. Pers. Soc. Psychol.* 29:619–27

91. Crosbie, P. V., Kullberg, V. K. 1973. Minimum resource or balance in coalition formation. *Sociometry* 36:476–93

92. Cvetkovich, G., Baumgardner, S. R. 1973. Attitude polarization: The relative influence of discussion group structure and reference group norms. *J. Pers. Soc. Psychol.* 26:159–65

93. Darley, J. M., Latane, B. 1968. Bystander intervention in emergencies: Diffusion of responsibility. *J. Pers. Soc. Psychol.* 8:377–83

94. Davis, J. H. 1969. *Group Performance.* Reading Mass.: Addison-Wesley

95. Davis, J. H. 1973. Group decision and social interaction: A theory of social decision schemes. *Psychol. Rev.* 80:97–125

96. Davis, J. H., Bray, R. M., Holt, R. W. 1975. The empirical study of decision processes in juries: A critical review. In *Law, Justice, and the Individual in Society: Psychological and Legal Perspectives*, ed. J. Tapp, F. Levine. New York: Holt, Rinehart & Winston. In press

97. Davis, J. H., Cohen, J. L., Hornik, J. A., Rissman, A. K. 1973. Dyadic decision as a function of the frequency distributions describing the preferences of members' constituencies. *J. Pers. Soc. Psychol.* 26:178–95

98. Davis, J. H., Hornik, J. A., Hornseth, J. P. 1970. Group decision schemes and strategy preferences in a sequential response task. *J. Pers. Soc. Psychol.* 15:397–408

99. Davis, J. H., Kerr, N. L., Sussmann, M., Rissman, A. K. 1974. Social decision schemes under risk. *J. Pers. Soc. Psychol.* 30:248–71

100. Dawes, R. M. 1973. The commons dilemma game: An N-person mixed-motive game with a dominating strategy for detection. *Oregon Res. Bull. 13, No. 2*

101. Deets, M. K., Hoyt, G. C. 1970. Variance preferences and variance shifts in group investment decision. *Organ. Behav. Hum. Perform.* 5:378–86

102. Deutsch, M. 1973. *The Resolution of Conflict.* New Haven: Yale Univ. Press

103. Deutsch, M., Canavan, D., Rubin, J. 1971. The effects of size of conflict and sex of experimenter on interpersonal bargaining. *J. Exp. Soc. Psychol.* 7:258–67

104. Dion, K. L. 1973. Cohesiveness as a determinant of ingroup-outgroup bias. *J. Pers. Soc. Psychol.* 28:163–71

105. Dion, K. L., Baron, R. S., Miller, N. 1970. Why do groups make riskier decisions than individuals? *Adv. Exp. Soc. Psychol.* 5:306–72

106. Dion, K. L., Miller, N., Magnan, J. A. 1971. Cohesiveness and social responsibility as determinants of group risk taking. *J. Pers. Soc. Psychol.* 20:400–6

107. Doise, W. et al 1972. An experimental investigation into the formation of intergroup representation. *Eur. J. Soc. Psychol.* 2:202–4

108. Doise, W., Sinclair, A. 1973. The categorization process in intergroup relations. *Eur. J. Soc. Psychol.* 3:145–58

109. Dorris, J. W. 1972. Reactions to unconditional cooperation: A field study emphasizing variables neglected in laboratory research. *J. Pers. Soc. Psychol.* 22:387–97

110. Doyle, W. J. 1971. Effects of achiever status of leader on productivity of groups. *Admin. Sci. Q.* 16:40–50

111. Druckman, D. 1971. The influence of the situation in interpart conflict. *J. Confl. Resolut.* 15:523–54

112. Druckman, D. 1971. On the effects of group representation. *J. Pers. Soc. Psychol.* 18:273–74

113. Druckman, D. 1974. Human factors in international negotiations: Social psychological aspects of international conflict. *Sage Prof. Pap. Int. Stud. No. 02–020*

114. Druckman, D., Solomon, D., Zechmeister, K. 1972. Effects of representational role obligations on the process of children's distribution of resources. *Sociometry* 35:387–410

115. Druckman, D., Zechmeister, K., Solomon, D. 1972. Determinants of bargaining behavior in a bilateral monopoly situation: Opponents' concession rate and

relative defensibility. *Behav. Sci.* 17: 514–31

116. Eagly, A. H. 1970. Leadership and role differentiation as determinants of group effectiveness. *J. Pers.* 38:509–24

117. Earle, T. C. 1973. Interpersonal learning. See Ref. 385, 240–66

118. Egerman, K. 1966. Effects of team arrangement on team performance. *J. Pers. Soc. Psychol.* 3:541–50

119. Eiser, J. R., Bhavnani, K. 1974. The effect of situational meaning on the behavior of subjects in the prisoner's dilemma game. *Eur. J. Soc. Psychol.* 4:93–97

120. Eiser, J. R., Tajfel, H. 1972. Acquisition of information in dyadic interaction. *J. Pers. Soc. Psychol.* 23:340–45

121. Emshoff, J. R., Ackoff, R. L. 1970. Explanatory models of interactive choice behavior. *J. Confl. Resolut.* 14:77–89

122. England, J. L. 1973. Mathematical models of two-party negotiations. *Behav. Sci.* 18:189–97

123. Erickson, B., Holmes, J. G., Grey, R., Walker, L., Thibaut, J. 1974. Functions of a third party in the resolution of conflict: The role of a judge in pretrial conferences. *J. Pers. Soc. Psychol.* 30: 293–306

124. Faley, T., Tedeschi, J. T. 1971. Status and reactions to threats. *J. Pers. Soc. Psychol.* 17:192–99

125. Fiedler, F. E. 1964. A contingency model of leadership effectiveness. *Adv. Exp. Soc. Psychol.* 1:149–90

126. Fiedler, F. E. 1967. *A Theory of Leadership Effectiveness.* New York: McGraw-Hill

127. Fiedler, F. E. 1971. Note on the methodology of the Graen, Orris, and Alvares studies testing the contingency model. *J. Appl. Psychol.* 55:202–4

128. Fiedler, F. E. 1971. Validation and extension of the contingency model of leadership effectiveness: A review of empirical findings. *Psychol. Bull.* 76: 128–48

129. Fiedler, F. E. 1972. Personality, motivational systems, and behavior of high and low LPC persons. *Hum. Relat.* 25:391–412

130. Fiedler, F. E. 1973. The contingency model—a reply to Ashour. *Organ. Behav. Hum. Perform.* 9:356–68

131. Fishburn, P. C. 1971. A comparative analysis of group decision methods. *Behav. Sci.* 16:538–44

132. Fishburn, P. C. 1973. *The Theory of Social Choice.* Princeton Univ. Press

133. Fisher, B. A. 1974. *Small Group Decision Making: Communication and the Group Process.* New York: McGraw-Hill

134. Fisher, R. J. 1972. Third party consultation: A method for the study and resolution of conflict. *J. Confl. Resolut.* 16:67–94

135. Fleishman, E. A., Hunt, J. G., Eds. 1973. *Current Developments in the Study of Leadership.* Carbondale, Ill: Southern Illinois Univ. Press

136. Frank, F., Anderson, L. R. 1971. Effects of task and group size upon group productivity and member satisfaction. *Sociometry* 34:135–45

137. Frey, R. L. Jr., Adams, J. S. 1972. The negotiator's dilemma: Simultaneous ingroup and out-group conflict. *J. Exp. Soc. Psychol.* 8:331–46

138. Friedland, N., Arnold, S. E., Thibaut, J. 1974. Motivational bases in mixed-motive interaction: The effects of comparison levels. *J. Exp. Soc. Psychol.* 10:188–99

139. Froman, L. A. Jr., Cohen, M. D. 1970. Compromise and logroll: Comparing the efficiency of two bargaining processes. *Behav. Sci.* 15:180–83

140. Gallo, P. S., Sheposh, J. P. 1971. Effects of incentive magnitude on cooperation in the prisoner's dilemma game: A reply to Gumpert, Deutsch, and Epstein. *J. Pers. Soc. Psychol.* 19:42–46

141. Gamson, W. A. 1961. A theory of coalition formation. *Am. Sociol. Rev.* 26: 373–82

142. Gardin, H., Kaplan, K., Firestone, I., Cowan, G. 1973. Proxemic effects on cooperation, attitude, and approach-avoidance in a prisoner's dilemma game. *J. Pers. Soc. Psychol.* 27:13–18

143. Garner, K., Deutsch, M. 1974. Cooperative behavior in dyads: Effects of dissimilar goal orientations and differing expectations about the partner. *J. Confl. Resolut.* 18:634–45

144. Gerard, H., Hoyt, M. 1974. Distinctiveness of social categorization and attitude toward ingroup members. *J. Pers. Soc. Psychol.* 29:836–42

145. Gerard, H. B., Miller, N. 1967. Group dynamics. *Ann. Rev. Psychol.* 18:287–332

146. Gibb, C. A. 1969. Leadership. See Ref. 269, 4:205–82

147. Gillis, J. S., Woods, G. T. 1971. The 16 PF as an indicator of performance in the prisoner's dilemma. *J. Confl. Resolut.* 15:393–402

148. Glaser, R., Klaus, D. J. 1966. A reinforcement analysis of group performance. *Psychol. Monogr.* 80:13 (Whole No. 621)
149. Goldman, M. 1966. A comparison of group and individual performance where subjects have varying tendencies to solve problems. *J. Pers. Soc. Psychol.* 3:604–7
150. Goldman, M. 1971. Group performance related to size and initial ability of group members. *Psychol. Rep.* 38:551–57
151. Goldman, M., McGlynn, A., Toledo, A. 1967. Comparison of individual and group performance of size three and five with various initially right and wrong tendencies. *J. Pers. Soc. Psychol.* 7:222–26
152. Goodman, B. C. 1972. Action selection and likelihood ratio estimation by individuals and groups. *Organ. Behav. Hum. Perform.* 7:121–41
153. Graen, G., Alvares, K., Orris, J., Martella, J. 1970. Contingency model of leadership effectiveness. *Psychol. Bull.* 74:285–96
154. Graen, G., Orris, J., Alvares, K. 1971. The contingency model of leadership effectiveness: Some experimental results. *J. Appl. Psychol.* 55:196–201
155. Graham, W. K., Dillon, P. C. 1974. Creative supergroups: Group performance as a function of individual performance in brainstorming tasks. *J. Soc. Psychol.* 93:101–5
156. Graham, W. K., Harris, S. G. 1970. Effects of group discussion on accepting risk and on advising others to be risky. *Psychol. Rec.* 20:219–24
157. Griesinger, D. W., Livingston, J. W. 1973. Toward a model of interpersonal motivation in experimental games. *Behav. Sci.* 18:173–88
158. Gross, D. E., Kelley, H. H., Kruglanski, A. W., Patch, M. E. 1972. Contingency of consequences and type of incentive in interdependent escape. *J. Exp. Soc. Psychol.* 8:360–77
159. Gruder, C. L. 1971. Relations with opponent and partner in mixed-motive bargaining. *J. Confl. Resolut.* 3:403–16
160. Gruder, C. L., Daslak, R. J. 1973. Elicitation of cooperation by retaliatory and non-retaliatory strategies in a mixed-motive game. *J. Confl. Resolut.* 17:162–74
161. Gustafson, D. H., Shukla, R. K., Delbecq, A., Walster, G. W. 1973. A comparative study of differences in subjective likelihood estimates made by individuals, interacting groups, delphi groups, and nominal groups. *Organ. Behav. Hum. Perform.* 9:280–91
162. Guttentag, M., Freed, R. 1971. The effect on risk-taking of group members, group homogeneity, and problem content. *J. Soc. Psychol.* 83:305–6
163. Guyer, M. J., Fox, J., Hamburger, H. 1973. Format effects in the prisoner's dilemma game. *J. Confl. Resolut.* 17:719–44
164. Guyer, M. J., Rapoport, A. 1970. Threat in a two-person game. *J. Exp. Soc. Psychol.* 6:11–25
165. Guyer, M. J., Rapoport, A. 1972. 2 X 2 games played once. *J. Confl. Resolut.* 16:409–32
166. Hackman, J. R. 1968. Effects of task characteristics on group products. *J. Exp. Soc. Psychol.* 4:162–87
167. Hackman, J. R. 1969. Toward understanding the role of tasks in behavioral research. *Acta Psychol.* 39:97–127
168. Hackman, J. R., Jones, L. E., McGrath, J. E. 1967. A set of dimensions for describing the general properties of group-generated written passages. *Psychol. Bull.* 67:379–90
169. Hackman, J. R., Kaplan, R. E. 1974. Interventions into group process: An approach to improving the effectiveness of groups. *Decis. Sci.* 5:459–80
170. Hackman, J. R., Morris, C. G. 1976. Group tasks, group interaction process, and group performance effectiveness. *Adv. Exp. Soc. Psychol.* In press
171. Hackman, J. R., Vidmar, N. 1970. Effects of size and task type of group performance and member reactions. *Sociometry* 33:37–54
172. Hadley, T. R., Jacob, T. 1973. Relationship among measures of family power. *J. Pers. Soc. Psychol.* 27:6–12
173. Haley, H. J., Rule, B. G. 1971. Group composition effects on risk taking. *J. Pers.* 39:150–61
174. Hamburger, H. 1973. N-person prisoner's dilemma. *J. Math. Sociol.* 3:27–48
175. Hammond, K. R. 1965. New directions in research on conflict resolution. *J. Soc. Issues* 2:44–66
176. Hammond, K. R. 1971. Computer graphics as an aid to learning. *Science* 172:903–8
177. Hammond, K. R. 1973. The cognitive conflict paradigm. See Ref. 385, 188–205
178. Hammond, K. R., Brehmer, B. 1973. Quasi-rationality and distrust: Implica-

tions for international conflict. See Ref. 385, 338–91

179. Hammond, K. R., Hursch, C. J., Todd, F. J. 1964. Analyzing the components of clinical inference. *Psychol. Rev.* 71:438–56

180. Hammond, K. R., Summers, D. A. 1972. Cognitive control. *Psychol. Rev.* 79:58–67

181. Hammond, K. R., Wilkins, M. M., Todd, F. J. 1966. A research paradigm for the study of interpersonal learning. *Psychol. Bull.* 65:221–32

182. Hamner, W. C. 1974. Effects of bargaining strategy and pressure to reach agreement in a stalemated negotiation. *J. Pers. Soc. Psychol.* 30:458–67

183. Hardin, G. 1968. The tragedy of the commons. *Science* 162:1243–48

184. Hardin, R. 1971. Collective action as an agreeable N-prisoner's dilemma. *Behav. Sci.* 16:472–81

185. Hardy, R. C. 1971. Effect of leadership style on the performance of small classroom groups: A test of the contingency model. *J. Pers. Soc. Psychol.* 19:367–74

186. Hare, A. P. 1972. Bibliography of small group research, 1959–1969. *Sociometry* 35:1–150

187. Harnett, D. L., Cummings, L. L., Hamner, W. C. 1973. Personality, bargaining style, and payoff in bilateral monopoly bargaining among European managers. *Sociometry* 36:325–45

188. Harris, R. J. 1971. Experimental games as a tool for personality research. In *Advances in Psychological Assessment,* ed. P. McReynolds, 2:236–59. Palo Alto: Science & Behavior Books

189. Harris, R. J. 1974. *This is a science? Social psychologists' aversion to knowing what their theories say.* Presented at Am. Psychol. Assoc. Conv., New Orleans

190. Heilman, M. E. 1974. Threats and promises: Reputational consequences and transfer of credibility. *J. Exp. Soc. Psychol.* 10:310–24

191. Helmreich, R., Bakeman, R., Scherwitz, L. 1973. The study of small groups. *Ann. Rev. Psychol.* 24:337–54

192. Hewett, T. T., O'Brien, G. E., Hornik, J. 1974. The effects of work organization, leadership style, and member compatibility on the productivity of small groups working on a manipulative task. *Organ. Behav. Hum. Perform.* 11:283–301

193. Hollander, E. P., Julian, J. W. 1969. Contemporary trends in the analysis of leadership processes. *Psychol. Bull.* 71:387–97

194. Hollander, E. P., Julian, J. W. 1970. Studies in leader legitimacy, influence, and innovation. *Adv. Exp. Soc. Psychol.* 5:34–69

195. Holmes, J. G., Throop, W. F., Strickland, L. H. 1971. The effects of prenegotiation expectations on the distributive bargaining process. *J. Exp. Soc. Psychol.* 7:582–99

196. Horne, W. C., Long, G. 1972. Effect of group discussion on universalistic-particularistic orientation. *J. Exp. Soc. Psychol.* 8:236–46

197. Horowitz, A. D. 1973. The competitive bargaining set for cooperative N-person games. *J. Math. Psychol.* 10:265–89

198. Horowitz, A. D., Rapoport, A. 1974. Test of the kernel and two bargaining set models in four- and five-person games. See Ref. 381, 160–92

199. Hottes, J., Kahn, A. 1974. Sex differences in a mixed-motive conflict situation. *J. Pers.* 42:260–75

200. Howell, W. C., Gettys, C. F., Martin, D. W., Nawrocki, L. H., Johnston, W. A. 1970. Evaluation of diagnostic tests by individuals and small groups. *Organ. Behav. Hum. Perform.* 5:211–37

201. Hrycenko, I., Minton, H. L. 1974. Internal-external control, power position, and satisfaction in task-oriented groups. *J. Pers. Soc. Psychol.* 30:871–78

202. Hunt, J. G. 1971. Leadership-style effects at two managerial levels in a simulated organization. *Admin. Sci. Quart.* 16:476–85

203. Hunt, J. G., Larson, L. L., Eds. 1974. *Contingency Approaches to Leadership.* Carbondale, Ill: Southern Illinois Univ. Press

204. Hursch, C., Hammond, K. R., Hursch, J. 1964. Some methodological considerations in multiple-cue probability studies. *Psychol. Rev.* 71:42–60

205. Ilgen, D. R., O'Brien, G. 1974. Leader-member relations in small groups. *Organ. Behav. Hum. Perform.* 12:335–50

206. Ingham, A. G., Levinger, G., Graves, J., Peckham, V. 1974. The Ringelmann effect: Studies of group size and group performance. *J. Exp. Soc. Psychol.* 10:371–84

207. Jacobs, R. C., Campbell, D. T. 1961. The perpetuation of an arbitrary tradition through several generations of a laboratory microculture. *J. Abnorm. Soc. Psychol.* 62:649–58

208. Janis, I. L. 1972. *Victims of Groupthink.* Boston: Houghton Mifflin

209. Janis, I. L., Hoffman, D. 1971. Facilitating effects of daily contact between partners who make a decision to cut down on smoking. *J. Pers. Soc. Psychol.* 17:25–35
210. Johnson, C., Davis, J. H. 1972. An equiprobability model of risk taking. *Organ. Behav. Hum. Perform.* 8:159–75
211. Johnson, D. F., Pruitt, D. G. 1972. Preintervention effects of mediation vs. arbitration. *J. Appl. Psychol.* 56:1–10
212. Johnson, D. F., Tullar, W. L. 1972. Style of third party intervention, face-saving, and bargaining behavior. *J. Exp. Soc. Psychol.* 8:319–30
213. Johnson, D. L., Andrews, I. R. 1971. Risky-shift phenomenon tested with consumer products as stimuli. *J. Pers. Soc. Psychol.* 20:382–85
214. Johnson, H. H., Torcivia, J. M. 1967. Group and individual performance on a single-stage task as a function of distribution of individual performance. *J. Pers. Soc. Psychol.* 3:266–73
215. Jones, M. B. 1974. Regressing group on individual effectiveness. *Organ. Behav. Hum. Perform.* 11:426–51
216. Kagan, S., Madsden, M. C. 1972. Rivalry in Anglo-American and Mexican children of two ages. *J. Pers. Soc. Psychol.* 24:214–20
217. Kahan, J. P., Helwig, R. A. 1971. A system of programs for computer-controlled bargaining games. *Gen. Syst.* 16:31–41
218. Kahan, J. P., Rapoport, A. 1974. Test of the bargaining set and kernal models in three-person games. See Ref. 381, 119–60
219. Kahn, A., Hottes, J., Davis, W. L. 1971. Cooperation and optional responding in the prisoner's dilemma game: Effects of sex and physical attractiveness. *J. Pers. Soc. Psychol.* 17:267–79
220a. Kahn, A. S., Kohls, J. W. 1972. Determinants of toughness in dyadic bargaining. *Sociometry* 35:305–15
220b. Kelley, H. H. 1967. Attribution theory in social psychology. *Nebr. Symp. Motiv.* 15:192–238
220c. Kelley, H. H. 1971. *Attribution in Social Interaction.* New York: Gen. Learn. Press
221. Kelley, H. H. et al 1970. A comparative experimental study of negotiation behavior. *J. Pers. Soc. Psychol.* 16:411–38
222. Kelley, H. H., Condry, J. C., Dahlke, A. E., Hille, A. H. 1965. Collective behavior in a simulated panic situation. *J. Exp. Soc. Psychol.* 1:20–54
223. Kelley, H. H., Gryzelak, J. 1972. Conflict between individual and common interest in an N-person relationship. *J. Pers. Soc. Psychol.* 21:190–97
224. Kelley, H. H., Schenitzki, D. P. 1972. Bargaining. See Ref. 289, 298–337
225. Kelley, H. H., Stahelski, A. J. 1970. Errors of perception of intentions in a mixed-motive game. *J. Exp. Soc. Psychol.* 6:379–400
226. Ibid. The inference of intentions from moves in the prisoner's dilemma game, 401–19
227. Kelley, H. H., Stahelski, A. J. 1970. Social interaction basis of cooperators' and competitors' beliefs about others. *J. Pers. Soc. Psychol.* 16:66–91
228. Kelley, H. H., Thibaut, J. W. 1969. Group problem solving. See Ref. 269, 1–101
229. Kelley, H. H., Thibaut, J. W., Radloff, R., Mundy, D. 1962. The development of cooperation in the "minimal social situation." *Psychol. Monogr.* 76 (19, Whole No. 538)
230. Kelly, R. T., Rawson, H. E., Terry, R. L. 1973. Interaction effects of achievement need and situational press on performance. *J. Soc. Psychol.* 89:141–45
231. Kerr, N. L., Davis, J. H., Meek, D., Rissman, A. K. 1975. Group position as a function of member attitudes: Choice shift effects from the perspective of social decision scheme theory. *J. Pers. Soc. Psychol.* 31:574–93
232. Kerr, S., Schriesheim, C. A., Murphy, C. J., Stogdill, R. M. 1974. Toward a contingency theory of leadership based upon the consideration and initiating structure literature. *Organ. Behav. Hum. Perform.* 12:62–82
233. Klaus, D. J., Glaser, R. 1970. Reinforcement determinants of team proficiency. *Organ. Behav. Hum. Perform.* 5:33–67
234. Kleinke, C. L., Pohlen, P. D. 1971. Affective and emotional responses as a function of other person's gaze and cooperativeness in a two-person game. *J. Pers. Soc. Psychol.* 17:308–13
235. Klimoski, R. J. 1972. The effects of intergroup forces on intergroup conflict resolution. *Organ. Behav. Hum. Perform.* 8:363–83
236. Klimoski, R. J., Ash, R. A. 1974. Accountability and negotiator behavior. *Organ. Behav. Hum. Perform.* 11:409–25
237. Knox, R. E., Douglas, R. 1971. Trivial incentives, marginal comprehension, and dubious generalizations from pris-

oner's dilemma studies. *J. Pers. Soc. Psychol.* 20:160–65

238. Kogan, N., Lamm, H., Trommsdorff, G. 1972. Negotiation constraints in the risky taking domain: Effects of being observed by partners of higher or lower status. *J. Pers. Soc. Psychol.* 23:142–56

239. Komorita, S. S. 1973. Concession-making and conflict resolution. *J. Confl. Resolut.* 17:745–62

240. Komorita, S. S. 1974. A weighted probability model of coalition formation. *Psychol. Rev.* 81:242–56

241. Komorita, S. S., Chertkoff, J. M. 1973. A bargaining theory of coalition formation. *Psychol. Rev.* 80:149–62

242. Komorita, S. S., Sheposh, J. P., Braver, S. L. 1968. Power, the use of power, and cooperative choice in a two-person game. *J. Pers. Soc. Psychol.* 8:134–42

243. Laing, J. D., Morrison, R. J. 1973. Coalitions and payoffs in three-person sequential games. *J. Math. Sociol.* 3:3–25

244. Laing, J. D., Morrison, R. J. 1974. Sequential games of status. *Behav. Sci.* 19:177–96

245. Lambert, R. 1972. Risky shift in relation to choice of metric. *J. Exp. Soc. Psychol.* 8:315–18

246. Lamm, H. 1973. Intragroup effects on intergroup negotiation. *Eur. J. Soc. Psychol.* 3:179–92

247. Lamm, H., Kogan, N. 1970. Risk taking in the context of intergroup negotiations. *J. Exp. Soc. Psychol.* 6:351–63

248. Lamm, H., Sauer, C. 1974. Discussion-induced shift toward higher demands in negotiation. *Eur. J. Soc. Psychol.* 4:85–88

249. Lamm, H., Schaude, E., Trommsdorff, G. 1971. Risky shift as a function of group members' value of risk and need for approval. *J. Pers. Soc. Psychol.* 20:430–35

250. Lamm, H., Trommsdorff, G. 1973. Group versus individual performance on tasks requiring ideational proficiency (brainstorming): A review. *Eur. J. Soc. Psychol.* 3:361–88

251. Lampkin, E. C. 1972. Effects of n-dominance and group composition on task efficiency in laboratory triads. *Organ. Behav. Hum. Perform.* 7:189–202

252. Latane, B., Darley, J. M. 1968. Group intervention of bystander intervention in emergencies. *J. Pers. Soc. Psychol.* 10:215–21

253. Laughlin, P. R. 1965. Selection strategies in concept attainment as a function of number of persons and stimulus display. *J. Exp. Psychol.* 70: 323–27

254. Laughlin, P. R. 1972. Selection versus reception concept-attainment paradigms for individuals and cooperative pairs. *J. Educ. Psychol.* 63:116–22

255. Laughlin, P. R. 1973. Selection strategies in concept attainment. In *Contemporary Issues in Cognitive Psychology,* ed. R. Solso, 277–311. Washington DC: Winston/Wiley

256. Laughlin, P. R., Bitz, D. S. 1975. Individual versus dyadic performance on a disjunctive task as a function of initial ability level. *J. Pers. Soc. Psychol.* 31:487–96

257. Laughlin, P. R., Branch, L. G. 1972. Individual versus tetradic performance on a complementary task as a function of initial ability level. *Organ. Behav. Hum. Perform.* 8:201–16

258. Laughlin, P. R., Branch, L. G., Johnson, H. H. 1969. Individual versus triadic performance on a unidimensional complementary task as a function of initial ability level. *J. Pers. Soc. Psychol.* 12:144–50

259. Laughlin, P. R., Doherty, M. A. 1967. Discussion versus memory in cooperative group concept attainment. *J. Educ. Psychol.* 58:123–28

260. Laughlin, P. R., Johnson, H. H. 1966. Group and individual performance on a complementary task as a function of initial ability level. *J. Exp. Soc. Psychol.* 2:407–14

261. Laughlin, P. R., Kalowski, C. A., Metzler, M. E., Ostap, K. M., Venclovas, S. 1968. Concept identification as a function of sensory modality, information, and number of persons. *J. Exp. Psychol.* 77:335–40

262. Laughlin, P. R., Kerr, N. L., Davis, J. H., Halff, H. M., Marciniak, K. A. 1975. Group size, member ability, and social decision schemes on an intellective task. *J. Pers. Soc. Psychol.* 31: 522–35

263. Laughlin, P. R., McGlynn, R. P. 1967. Cooperative versus competitive concept attainment as a function of sex and stimulus display. *J. Pers. Soc. Psychol.* 7:398–402

264. Laughlin, P. R., McGlynn, R. P., Anderson, J. A., Jacobson, E. S. 1968. Concept attainment by individuals versus cooperative pairs as a function of memory, sex, and concept rule. *J. Pers. Soc. Psychol.* 8:410–47

265. Lemaine, G. 1974. Social differentiation and social originality. *Eur. J. Soc. Psychol.* 4:17–52

266. Levine, E. L. 1973. Problems of organizational control in microcosm: Group performance and group member satisfaction as a function of difference in control structure. *J. Appl. Psychol.* 58:186–96
267. Lewin, K. 1958. Group decision and social change. In *Readings in Social Psychology,* ed. E. E. Maccoby, T. M. Newcomb, R. L. Hartley. New York: Holt, Rinehart & Winston
268. Lindskold, S., Bennett, R. 1973. Attributing trust and conciliatory intent from coercive power capability. *J. Pers. Soc. Psychol.* 28:180–86
269. Lindzey, G., Aronson, E., Eds. 1968–69. *Handbook of Social Psychology.* Reading, Mass: Addison-Wesley
270. Lorge, I., Solomon, H. 1955. Two models of group behavior in the solution of Eureka-type problems. *Psychometrika* 20:139–48
271. Lupfer, M. 1970. The effects of risk taking tendencies and incentive conditions on the performance of investment groups. *J. Soc. Psychol.* 82:135–36
272. Mackenzie, K. D. 1970. Risk as a value and risky shift. *Organ. Behav. Hum. Perform.* 5:125–34
273. Ibid. The effects of status upon group risk taking, 517–41
274. Ibid 1971. An analysis of risky shift experiments. 6:283–303
275. Ibid 1974. Measuring a person's capacity for interaction in a problem solving group. 12:149–69
276. Maitland, K. A., Goldman, J. R. 1974. Moral judgment as a function of peer group interaction. *J. Pers. Soc. Psychol.* 30:699–704
277. Malamuth, N. M., Feshbach, S. 1972. Risky shift in a naturalistic setting. *J. Pers.* 40:38–49
278. Marwell, G., Schmitt, D. R. 1972. Cooperation in a three-person prisoner's dilemma. *J. Pers. Soc. Psychol.* 21:376–83
279. Marwell, G., Schmitt, D. R. 1972. Cooperation and interpersonal risk: Cross-cultural and cross-procedural generalizations. *J. Exp. Soc. Psychol.* 8:594–99
280. Marwell, G., Schmitt, D. R., Boyesen, B. 1973. Pacifist strategy and cooperation under interpersonal risk. *J. Pers. Soc. Psychol.* 28:12–20
281. Marwell, G., Schmitt, D. R., Shotola, R. 1970. Sex differences in a cooperative task. *Behav. Sci.* 15:184–86
282. Marwell, G., Schmitt, D. R., Shotola, R. 1971. Cooperation and interpersonal risk. *J. Pers. Soc. Psychol.* 18:9–32

283. Maschler, M. 1962. An experiment on n-person games. *Recent Advances of Game Theory.* Princeton Univ. Conf.
284. McCauley, C. R. 1972. Extremity shifts, risk shifts and attitude shifts after group discussion. *Eur. J. Soc. Psychol.* 2:417–36
285. McCauley, C., Graham, N. 1971. Influences of values in risky decision making: A formalization. *Represent. Res. Soc. Psychol.* 2:3–11
286. McCauley, C., Kramer, L. 1972. Strategy differences between group and individual gambling. *J. Exp. Soc. Psychol.* 8:518–27
287. McCauley, C., Stitt, C. L. 1973. Reply to Abelson's comment on "group shift to caution at the race track." *J. Exp. Soc. Psychol.* 9:522–25
288. McCauley, C., Stitt, C. L., Woods, K., Lipton, D. 1973. Group shift to caution at the race track. *J. Exp. Soc. Psychol.* 9:80–86
289. McClintock, C. G. 1972. Game behavior and social motivation in interpersonal settings. In *Experimental Social Psychology* ed. C. G. McClintock. New York: Holt, Rinehart, and Winston
290. McClintock, C. G. 1972. Social motivation—a set of propositions. *Behav. Sci.* 17:438–54
291. McClintock, C. G. 1974. Development of social motives in Anglo-American children and Mexican-American children. *J. Pers. Soc. Psychol.* 29:348–54
292. McClintock, C. G., Messick, D. M., Kuhlman, D. H., Campos, F. T. 1973. Motivational bases of choice in three-choice decomposed games. *J. Exp. Soc. Psychol.* 9:572–90
293. McClintock, C. G., Nuttin, J. M. Jr., McNeel, S. P. 1970. Sociometric choice, visual presence, and game playing behavior. *Behav. Sci.* 15:124–31
294. McGlynn, R. P. 1972. Four-person group concept attainment as a function of interaction format. *J. Soc. Psychol.* 86:89–94
295. McGlynn, R. P., Schick, C. 1973. Dyadic concept attainment as a function of interaction format, memory requirements, and sex. *J. Educ. Psychol.* 65:335–40
296. McGrath, J. E., Altman, I. 1966. *Small Group Research.* New York: Holt, Rinehart & Winston
297. McNeel, S. P. 1973. Training cooperation in the prisoner's dilemma. *J. Exp. Soc. Psychol.* 9:335–48
298. McNeel, S. P., McClintock, C. G., Nuttin, J. M. Jr. 1972. Effects of sex role in

a two-person mixed-motive game. *J. Pers. Soc. Psychol.* 24:372–80

299. Mednick, S. A., Mednick, M. T. 1967. *Examiners Manual; Remote Associater Test.* Boston: Houghton-Mifflin

300. Messé, L. A. 1971. Equity in bilateral bargaining. *J. Pers. Soc. Psychol.* 17:287–91

301. Messé, L. A., Aronoff, J., Wilson, J. P. 1972. Motivation as a mediator of the mechanisms underlying role assignments in small groups. *J. Pers. Soc. Psychol.* 24:84–90

302. Messé, L. A., Dawson, J. E., Lane, I. M. 1973. Equity as mediator of the effect of reward level on behavior in the prisoner's dilemma game. *J. Pers. Soc. Psychol.* 26:60–65

303. Messick, D. M. 1973. To join or not to join: An approach to the unionization decision. *Organ. Behav. Hum. Perform.* 10:145–56

304. Meux, E. P. 1973. Concern for the common good in an N-person game. *J. Pers. Soc. Psychol.* 28:414–18

305. Michaelson, L. K. 1973. Leader orientation, leader behavior, group effectiveness, and situational favorability: An empirical extension of the contingency model. *Organ. Behav. Hum. Perform.* 9:226–45

306. Michelini, R. L., Messé, L. A. 1974. Reactions to threat as a function of equity. *Sociometry* 37:432–39

307. Michener, H. A., Cohen, E. D. 1973. Effects of punishment magnitude in the bilateral threat situation: Evidence for the deterrence hypothesis. *J. Pers. Soc. Psychol.* 26:427–38

308. Michener, H. A., Griffith, J., Palmer, R. L. 1971. Threat potential and rule enforceability as sources of normative emergence in a bargaining situation. *J. Pers. Soc. Psychol.* 20:230–39

309. Michener, H. A., Lawler, E. J. 1971. Revolutionary coalition strength and collective failure as determinants of status reallocation. *J. Exp. Soc. Psychol.* 7:448–60

310. Michener, H. A., Lyons, M. 1972. Perceived support and upward mobility as determinants of revolutionary coalition behavior. *J. Exp. Soc. Psychol.* 8:180–95

311. Michener, H. A., Zeller, R. A. 1972. The effects of coalition strength on the formation of contractual norms. *Sociometry* 35:290–304

312. Miller, G. H., Pyke, S. W. 1973. Sex, matrix variations, and perceived personality effects in mixed-motive games. *J. Confl. Resolut.* 17:335–49

313. Miller, J. G. 1971. Living systems: The group. *Behav. Sci.* 16:302–98

314. Minton, H. L., Miller, A. G. 1970. Group risk taking and internal-external control of group members. *Psychol. Rep.* 26:431–36

315. Mintz, A. 1951. Non-adaptive group behavior. *J. Abnorm. Soc. Psychol.* 46:150–59

316. Misavage, R., Richardson, J. T. 1974. The focusing of responsibility: An alternative hypothesis in help-demanding situations. *Eur. J. Soc. Psychol.* 4:5–15

317. Mitchell, T. R. 1972. Cognitive complexity and group performance. *J. Soc. Psychol.* 86:35–43

318. Mitchell, T. R., Biglan, A., Oncken, G. R., Fiedler, F. E. 1970. The contingency model: Criticisms and suggestions. *Acad. Manage. J.* 13:253–67

319. Mogy, R. B., Pruitt, D. G. 1974. Effects of a threatener's enforcement costs on threat credibility and compliance. *J. Pers. Soc. Psychol.* 29:173–80

320. Monteverde, F., Paschke, R., Tedeschi, J. T. 1974. The effectiveness of honesty and deceit as influence tactics. *Sociometry* 37:583–91

321. Morris, C. G. 1966. Task effects on group interaction. *J. Pers. Soc. Psychol.* 5:545–54

322. Morris, C. G. 1970. Changes in group interaction during problem solving. *J. Soc. Psychol.* 81:157–65

323. Moscovici, S., Doise, W. 1974. Decision making in groups. See Ref. 350, 250–88

324. Moscovici, S., Doise, W., Dulong, R. 1972. Studies in group decision II: Differences of positions, differences of opinion and group polarization. *Eur. J. Soc. Psychol.* 2:385–400

325. Moscovici, S., Faucheux, C. 1972. Social influence, conformity, bias, and the study of active minorities. *Adv. Exp. Soc. Psychol.* 6:150–202

326. Moscovici, S., Lage, E., Naffrechoux, M. 1969. Influence of a consistent minority on the responses of a majority in a color perception task. *Sociometry* 32:365–79

327. Moscovici, S., Lage, E., Naffrechoux, M. 1973. Conflict in three-person groups: The relationship between social influence and cognitive style. See Ref. 385, 304–14

328. Moscovici, S., Lecuyer, R. 1972. Studies in group decision I: Social space, patterns of communication and group consensus. *Eur. J. Soc. Psychol.* 2:221–44

329. Moscovici, S., Nemeth, C. 1974. Social

influence II: Minority influence. See Ref. 350, 217–49

330. Moscovici, S., Neve, P. 1973. Studies on polarization of judgments III: Majorities, minorities, and social judgments. *Eur. J. Soc. Psychol.* 3:479–84

331. Moscovici, S., Zavalloni, M. 1969. The group as a polarizer of attitudes. *J. Pers. Soc. Psychol.* 12:125–35

332. Mulder, M. 1971. Power equalization through participation? *Admin. Sci. Q.* 16:31–38

333. Mulder, M., Veen, P., Hijzen, T., Jansen, P. 1973. On power equalization: A behavioral example of power-distance reduction. *J. Pers. Soc. Psychol.* 26: 151–58

334. Mulder, M., Veen, P., Rodenburg, C., Frenken, J., Tielens, H. 1973. The power distance reduction hypothesis on a level of reality. *J. Exp. Soc. Psychol.* 9:87–96

335. Mulder, M., Wilke, H. 1970. Participation and power equalization. *Organ. Behav. Hum. Perform.* 5:430–48

336. Muller, H. P. 1970. Relationship between time-span of discretion, leadership behavior, and Fiedler's LPC scores. *J. Appl. Psychol.* 54:140–44

337. Mumpower, J. L., Hammond, K. R. 1974. Entangled task dimensions: An impediment to interpersonal learning. *Organ. Behav. Hum. Perform.* 11: 377–89

338. Murakami, Y. 1968. *Logic and Social Choice.* London: Routledge & Kegan Paul

339. Murdoch, P., Rosen, P. 1970. Norm formation in an interdependent dyad. *Sociometry* 33:264–75

340. Myers, D. G., Arenson, S. J. 1972. Enhancement of dominant risk tendencies in group discussion. *Psychol. Rep.* 30:615–23

341. Myers, D. G., Bach, P. J. 1974. Discussion effects on militarism-pacifism: A test of the group polarization hypothesis. *J. Pers. Soc. Psychol.* 30:741–47

342. Myers, D. G., Bach, P. J., Schreiber, F. B. 1974. Normative and informational effects of group interaction. *Sociometry* 37:275–86

343. Myers, D. G., Bishop, G. D. 1970. Discussion effects on racial attitudes. *Science* 169:778–89

344. Myers, D. G., Bishop, G. D. 1971. Enhancement of dominant attitudes in group discussion. *J. Pers. Soc. Psychol.* 20:386–91

345. Myers, D. G., Lamm, H. 1975. The group polarization phenomenon. *Psychol. Bull.* In press

346. Myers, D. G., Murdoch, P., Smith, G. F. 1970. Responsibility diffusion and drive enhancement effects on risky shift. *J. Pers.* 38:418–25

347. Myers, D. G., Schreiber, F. B., Viel, D. J. 1974. Effects of discussion on opinions concerning illegal behavior. *J. Soc. Psychol.* 92:77–84

348. Nemeth, C. 1970. Bargaining and reciprocity. *Psychol. Bull.* 74:297–308

349. Nemeth, C. 1972. A critical analysis of research utilizing the prisoner's dilemma paradigm for the study of bargaining. *Adv. Exp. Soc. Psychol.* 6:203–34

350. Nemeth, C., Ed. 1974. *Social Psychology: Classic and Contemporary Integrations.* Chicago: Rand McNally

351. Nemeth, C., Swedlund, M., Kanki, B. 1974. Patterning of the minority's responses and their influence on the majority. *Eur. J. Soc. Psychol.* 4:53–64

352. Niemi, R. G., Weisberg, H. 1972. *Probability Models of Collective Decision Making.* Columbus, Ohio: Merrill

353. Ofshe, R. J. 1973. *Interpersonal Behavior in Small Groups.* Englewood Cliffs, NJ: Prentice-Hall

354. Ofshe, R. J., Ofshe, S. L. 1970. Choice behavior in coalition games. *Behav. Sci.* 16:337–48

355. Organ, D. W. 1971. Some variables affecting boundary role behavior. *Sociometry* 34:524–37

356. Osgood, C. E. 1959. Suggestions for winning the real war with Communism. *J. Confl. Resolut.* 3:295–326

357. Osgood, C. E. 1962. *An Alternative to War or Surrender.* Urbana: Univ. Illinois Press

358. Oskamp, S. 1971. Effects of programmed strategies in the prisoner's dilemma game. *J. Confl. Resolut.* 15:225–59

359. Oskamp, S., Kleinke, C. 1970. Amount of reward as a variable in the prisoner's dilemma game. *J. Pers. Soc. Psychol.* 16:133–40

360. Paicheler, G., Bouchet, J. 1973. Attitude polarization, familiarization, and group process. *Eur. J. Soc. Psychol.* 3:83–90

361. Patchen, M. 1970. Models of cooperation and conflict: A critical review. *J. Confl. Resolut.* 14:389–408

362. Pattanaik, P. K. 1973. Group choice with lexicographic individual orderings. *Behav. Sci.* 18:118–23

363. Payne, J. W. 1973. Alternative approaches to decision making under risk: Moments versus risk dimensions. *Psychol. Bull.* 80:439–53
364. Pepitone, A. 1971. The role of justice in interdependent decision making. *J. Exp. Soc. Psychol.* 7:144–56
365. Peters, E. 1952. *Conciliation in Action.* New London: Nat. Foremen's Inst.
366. Peterson, R. A., Fulcher, D. G. 1971. Risky shift in marketing decision making: A nonconfirmation. *Psychol. Rep.* 29:1135–38
367. Pilisuk, M., Kiritz, S., Clampitt, S. 1971. Undoing deadlocks of distrust: Hip Berkeley students and the ROTC. *J. Confl. Resolut.* 15:81–95
368. Podell, J. E., Knapp, W. M. 1969. The effect of mediation on the perceived firmness of the opponent. *J. Confl. Resolut.* 13:511–20
369. Pollard, W. E., Mitchell, T. R. 1972. Decision theory analysis of social power. *Psychol. Bull.* 78:433–46
370. Pruitt, D. G. 1970. Motivational processes in the decomposed prisoner's dilemma game. *J. Pers. Soc. Psychol.* 14:227–38
371. Pruitt, D. G. 1971. Indirect communication and the search for agreement in negotiation. *J. Appl. Soc. Psychol.* 1:205–39
372. Pruitt, D. G. 1971. Choice shifts in group discussion: An introductory review. *J. Pers. Soc. Psychol.* 20:339–60
373. Ibid. Conclusions: Toward an understanding of choice shifts in group discussion, 495–510
374. Pruitt, D. G. 1972. Methods for resolving differences of interest: A theoretical analysis. *J. Soc. Issues* 28:133–54
375. Pruitt, D. G., Johnson, D. F. 1970. Mediation as an aid to face saving in negotiation. *J. Pers. Soc. Psychol.* 14:239–46
376. Pruitt, D. G., Teger, A. I. 1971. Reply to Belovicz and Finch's comments on "the risky shift in group betting." *J. Exp. Soc. Psychol.* 7:84–86
377. Psathas, G., Stryker, S. 1965. Bargaining behavior and orientations in coalition formation. *Sociometry* 28:124–44
378. Rabbie, J. M., Benoist, F., Oosterbaan, H., Visser, L. 1974. Differential power and effects of expected competitive and cooperative intergroup interaction on intragroup and outgroup attitudes. *J. Pers. Soc. Psychol.* 30:46–56
379. Rabbie, J. M., Visser, L. 1972. Bargaining strength and group polarization in intergroup polarization. *Eur. J. Soc. Psychol.* 2:401–16
380. Rabbie, J. M., Wilkins, G. 1971. Intergroup competition and its effect on intragroup and intergroup relations. *Eur. J. Soc. Psychol.* 1:215–34
381. Rapoport, A. 1974. Prisoner's dilemma —recollections and observations. In *Game Theory as a Theory of Conflict Resolution,* ed. A. Rapoport. Dordrecht, Holland: Reidel
382. Rapoport, A., Chammah, A., Dwyer, J., Gyr, J. 1962. Three person non-zero-sum negotiable games. *Behav. Sci.* 7:38–58
383. Rapoport, A., Guyer, M., Gordon, D. 1971. A comparison of performances of Danish and American students in a "threat game." *Behav. Sci.* 16:456–66
384. Rapoport, L., Cvetkovich, G. 1970. Effects of reward structure and cognitive difference in a mixed-motive two-person conflict situation. *Am. J. Psychol.* 83:119–25
385. Rapoport, L., Summers, D. A., Eds. 1973. *Human Judgment and Social Interaction.* New York: Holt, Rinehart & Winston
386. Rice, R. W., Chemers, M. M. 1973. Predicting the emergence of leaders using Fiedler's contingency model of leadership effectiveness. *J. Appl. Psychol.* 57:281–87
387. Richardson, J. T., Dugan, J. R., Gray, L. N., Mayhew, B. H. Jr. 1973. Expert Power: A behavioral interpretation. *Sociometry* 36:302–24
388. Roberts, J. C., Castore, C. H. 1972. The effects of conformity, information, and confidence upon subjects' willingness to take risk following a group discussion. *Organ. Behav. Hum. Perform.* 8:384–94
389. Ross, M., Thibaut, J., Evenbeck, S. 1971. Some determinants of the intensity of social protest. *J. Exp. Soc. Psychol.* 7:401–18
390. Rowse, G. L., Gustafson, D. H., Ludke, R. L. 1974. Comparison of rules for aggregating subjective likelihood ratios. *Organ. Behav. Hum. Perform.* 12:274–85
391. Rubin, J. Z. 1971. The nature and success of influence attempts in a four-party bargaining relationship. *J. Exp. Soc. Psychol.* 1:17–35
392. Rubin, J. Z., DiMatteo, M. R. 1972. Factors affecting the magnitude of subjective utility parameters in a tacit bargaining game. *J. Exp. Soc. Psychol.* 8:412–26
393. Rubin, J. Z., Lewicki, R. J. 1973. A three-factor experimental analysis of

538   DAVIS, LAUGHLIN & KOMORITA

promises and threats. *J. Appl. Soc. Psychol.* 3:240–57

394. Runyon, D. L. 1974. The group risky-shift effect as a function of emotional bonds, actual consequences, and extent of responsibility. *J. Pers. Soc. Psychol.* 29:670–76

395. Sashkin, M. 1972. Leadership style and group decision effectiveness: Correlational and behavioral tests of Fiedler's contingency model. *Organ. Behav. Hum. Perform.* 8:347–62

396. Schelling, T. C. 1973. Hockey helmets, concealed weapons, and daylight saving: Binary choices with externalities. *J. Confl. Resolut.* 17:379–80

397. Schlenker, B. R., Bonoma, T., Tedeschi, J. T., Pivnick, W. P. 1970. Compliance to threats as a function of the wording of the threat and the exploitativeness of the threatener. *Sociometry* 33:394–408

398. Schlenker, B. R., Helm, B., Tedeschi, J. T. 1973. The effects of personality and situational variables on behavioral trust. *J. Pers. Soc. Psychol.* 25:419–27

399. Schneider, F. W., Delaney, J. G. 1972. The effect of individual achievement motivation on group problem-solving efficiency. *J. Soc. Psychol.* 86:291–98

400. Schroeder, H. E. 1973. The risky shift as a general choice shift. *J. Pers. Soc. Psychol.* 27:297–300

401. Schulman, M. 1973. The prediction vs. the admiration of unethical risk. *J. Soc. Psychol.* 89:307–8

402. Scott, W. E. Jr., Cherrington, D. J. 1974. Effects of competitive, cooperative, and individualistic reinforcement contingencies. *J. Pers. Soc. Psychol.* 30:748–58

403. Selton, R., Schuster, K. G. 1968. Psychological variables and coalition-forming behavior. In *Risk and Uncertainty,* ed. K. Borch, J. Mossin, 221–40. London: Macmillan

404. Sermat, V. 1970. Is game behavior related to behavior in other interpersonal situations? *J. Pers. Soc. Psychol.* 16:92–109

405. Shaw, M. E. 1971. *Group Dynamics: The Psychology of Small Groups.* New York: McGraw-Hill

406. Sheposh, J. P., Gallo, P. S. 1973. Asymmetry of payoff structure in the prisoner's dilemma game. *J. Confl. Resolut.* 17:321–33

407. Shiflett, S. C. 1972. Group performance as a function of task difficulty and organizational interdependence. *Organ. Behav. Hum. Perform.* 7:442–56

408. Shiflett, S. C. 1973. Performance effectiveness and efficiency under different dyadic work strategies. *J. Appl. Psychol.* 57:257–63

409. Shiflett, S. C., Nealey, S. M. 1972. The effect of changing leader power: A test of situational engineering. *Organ. Behav. Hum. Perform.* 7:371–82

410. Shubick, M., Wolf, G., Poon, B. 1974. Perception of payoff structure and opponent's behavior in related matrix games. *J. Confl. Resolut.* 18:646–55

411. Sidowski, J. B., Wyckoff, L. B., Tabory, L. 1956. The influence of reinforcement and punishment in a minimal social situation. *J. Abnorm. Soc. Psychol.* 52:115–19

412. Siegel, S., Fouraker, L. E. 1960. *Bargaining and Group Decision Making.* New York: McGraw-Hill

413. Silverthorne, C. P. 1971. Information input and the group shift phenomenon in risk taking. *J. Pers. Soc. Psychol.* 20:456–61

414. Sinha, J. B. P., Yusuf, S. M. A. 1972. Effects of locus of control on choice shift in a cross-cultural perspective. *J. Soc. Psychol.* 88:177–83

415. Skotko, V., Langmeyer, D., Lundgren, D. 1974. Sex differences as artifacts in the prisoner's dilemma game. *J. Confl. Resolut.* 18:707–13

416. Slack, B. D., Cook, J. O. 1973. Authoritarian behavior in a conflict situation. *J. Pers. Soc. Psychol.* 25:130–36

417. Slovic, P., Lichtenstein, S. 1968. Relative importance of probabilities and payoffs in risk taking. *J. Exp. Psychol. Monogr.* 78, No. 3, part 2

418. Smith, K. H. 1972. Changes in group structure through individual and group feedback. *J. Pers. Soc. Psychol.* 24:425–28

419. Smith, P. B. 1973. *Groups within Organizations.* New York: Harper & Row

420. Smith, R. J., Cook, P. E. 1973. Leadership in dyadic groups as a function of dominance and incentives. *Sociometry* 36:561–68

421. Smith, W. P., Leginski, W. A. 1970. Magnitude and precision of punitive power in bargaining strategy. *J. Exp. Soc. Psychol.* 6:57–76

422. Sorenson, J. R. 1973. Group member traits, group process, and group performance. *Hum. Relat.* 26:639–55

423. Sorrentino, R. M. 1973. An extension of theory of achievement motivation to the study of emergent leadership. *J. Pers. Soc. Psychol.* 26:356–68

424. Starbuck, W. H., Grant, D. F. 1971. Bargaining strategies with asymmetric initiation and termination. *J. Appl. Soc. Psychol.* 1:344–63
425. Stein, R. T., Geis, F. L., Damarin, F. 1973. Perception of emergent leadership hierarchies in task groups. *J. Pers. Soc. Psychol.* 28:77–87
426. Steiner, I. D. 1964. Group dynamics. *Ann. Rev. Psychol.* 15:421–46
427. Steiner, I. D. 1966. Models for inferring relationships between group size and potential group productivity. *Behav. Sci.* 11:273–83
428. Steiner, I. D. 1972. *Group Process and Productivity.* New York: Academic
429. Steiner, I. D. 1974. Whatever happened to the group in social psychology? *J. Exp. Soc. Psychol.* 10:93–108
430. Steiner, I. D., Rajaratnam, N. 1961. A model for the comparison of individual and group performance scores. *Behav. Sci.* 6:142–47
431. Stevens, C. M. 1963. *Strategy and Collective Bargaining Negotiation.* New York: McGraw-Hill
432. Stogdill, R. M. 1972. Group productivity, drive, and cohesiveness. *Organ. Behav. Hum. Perform.* 8:26–43
433. Stokes, J. P. 1971. Effects of familiarization and knowledge of others' odds choices on shifts to risk and caution. *J. Pers. Soc. Psychol.* 20:407–12
434. Streufert, S. 1970. Complexity and complex decision making: Convergences between differentiation and integration approaches to the prediction of task performance. *J. Exp. Soc. Psychol.* 6:494–509
435. Ibid. 1972. Success and response rate in complex decision making. 8:389–403
436. Streufert, S., Castore, C. 1971. Information search and the effects of failure: A test of complexity theory. *J. Exp. Soc. Psychol.* 7:125–43
437. Streufert, S., Sandler, S. I. 1973. Perceived success and competence of the opponent, or the laboratory dien bien phu. *J. Appl. Soc. Psychol.* 3:84–93
438. Streufert, S., Streufert, S. C. 1970. Effects of failure in a complex decision making task on perceptions of cost, profit, and certainty. *Organ. Behav. Hum. Perform.* 5:15–32
439. Stryker, S. 1972. Coalition behavior. See Ref. 289, 338–80
440. Summers, D. A., Taliaferro, J. D., Fletcher, D. 1970. Judgment policy and interpersonal learning. *Behav. Sci.* 15:514–21
441. Swingle, P. G., Ed. 1970. *The Structure of Conflict.* New York: Academic
442. Swingle, P. G. 1970. Exploitative behavior in non-zero-sum games. *J. Pers. Soc. Psychol.* 16:121–32
443. Swingle, P. G., Santi, A. 1972. Communication in non-zero-sum games. *J. Pers. Soc. Psychol.* 23:54–63
444. Swinth, R. L., Tuggle, F. D. 1971. A complete dyadic process model of four man group problem solving. *Organ. Behav. Hum. Perform.* 6:517–49
445. Tajfel, H. 1970. Experiments in intergroup discrimination. *Sci. Am.* 223:96–102
446. Tajfel, H. 1972. La categorisatim sociale. In *Introduction a la Psychologie Sociale,* ed. S. Moscovici, 1:272–302. Paris: Larousse
447. Tajfel, H., Billig, M. G. 1974. Familiarity and categorization in intergroup behavior. *J. Exp. Soc. Psychol.* 10:159–70
448. Tajfel, H., Flament, C., Billig, M. G., Bundy, R. 1971. Social categorization and intergroup behavior. *Eur. J. Soc. Psychol.* 1:149–78
449. Taylor, M. 1970. The problem of salience in the theory of collective decision making. *Behav. Sci.* 15:415–30
450. Tedeschi, J. T. 1970. Threats and promises. See Ref. 441, 155–91
451. Tedeschi, J. T. Ed. 1974. *Perspectives on Social Power.* Chicago: Aldine
452. Tedeschi, J. T., Berger, S. E. 1971. Rejoinder to Burgess. *J. Exp. Soc. Psychol.* 7:551–57
453. Tedeschi, J. T., Bonoma, T. V., Lindskold, S. 1970. Threateners' reactions to prior announcement of behavioral compliance. *Behav. Sci.* 15:171–79
454. Tedeschi, J. T., Bonoma, T. V., Novinson, N. 1970. Behavior of a threatener: Retaliation vs. fixed opportunity costs. *J. Confl. Resolut.* 14:69–76
455. Tedeschi, J. T., Horai, J., Lindskold, S., Faley, T. 1970. The effects of opportunity costs and target compliance on the behavior of a threatening source. *J. Exp. Soc. Psychol.* 6:205–9
456. Tedeschi, J. T., Schlenker, B. R., Bonoma, T. V. 1973. *Conflict, Power, and Games.* Chicago: Aldine
457. Teger, A. I. 1970. The effect of early cooperation on the escalation of conflict. *J. Exp. Soc. Psychol.* 6:187–204
458. Terhune, K. W. 1970. The effects of personality in cooperation and conflict. See Ref. 441, 193–234
459. Terhune, K. W. 1974. "Wash-in, wash-out," and systemic effects in extended

prisoner's dilemma. *J. Confl. Resolut.* 18:656–85

460. Terman, L. M. 1956. *Manual for Concept Mastery Test.* New York: Psychol. Corp.

461. Thibaut, J. 1968. The development of contractual norms in bargaining: Replication and variation. *J. Confl. Resolut.* 12:102–12

462. Thibaut, J., Friedland, N., Walker, L. 1974. Compliance with rules: Some social determinants. *J. Pers. Soc. Psychol.* 30:792–801

463. Tucker, L. R. 1964. A suggested alternative formulation in the developments by Hursch, Hammond & Hursch, and by Hammond, Hursch & Todd. *Psychol. Rev.* 71:528–30

464. Vertreace, W. C., Simmons, C. H. 1971. Attempted leadership in the leaderless group discussion as a function of motivation and ego involvement. *J. Pers. Soc. Psychol.* 19:285–89

465. Vidmar, N. 1970. Group composition and the risky shift. *J. Exp. Soc. Psychol.* 6:153–66

466. Vidmar, N. 1970. Effects of representational roles and mediators on negotiation effectiveness. *J. Pers. Soc. Psychol.* 17:48–58

467. Vidmar, N., McGrath, J. E. 1970. Forces affecting success in negotiation groups. *Behav. Sci.* 15:154–63

468. Vinacke, W. E., Arkoff, A. 1957. An experimental study of coalitions in the triad. *Am. Sociol. Rev.* 22:406–14

469. Vinacke, W. E. et al 1974. Accommodative strategy and communication in a three-person matrix game. *J. Pers. Soc. Psychol.* 29:509–25

470. Vincent, J. E., Schwerin, E. W. 1971. Ratios of force and escalation in a game situation. *J. Confl. Resolut.* 15:489–511

471. Vinokur, A. 1971. Review and theoretical analysis of the effects of group processes upon individual and group decisions involving risk. *Psychol. Bull.* 76:231–50

472. Vinokur, A. 1971. Cognitive and affective processes influencing risk taking in groups. An expected utility approach. *J. Pers. Soc. Psychol.* 20:472–86

473. Vitz, P. C., Kite, W. R. 1970. Factors affecting conflict and negotiation within an alliance. *J. Exp. Soc. Psychol.* 6:233–47

474. Voissem, N. H., Sistrunk, F. 1971. Communication schedule and cooperative game behavior. *J. Pers. Soc. Psychol.* 19:160–67

475. Vroom, V. H., Yetton, P. W. 1973. *Leadership and Decision Making.* Univ. Pittsburgh Press

476. Walker, M. B. 1973. Caplow's theory of coalitions in the triad reconsidered. *J. Pers. Soc. Psychol.* 27:409–12

477. Walker, T. G., Main, E. C. 1973. Choice shifts in political decision making: Federal judges and civil liberties cases. *J. Appl. Soc. Psychol.* 3:39–48

478. Wall, J. A., Adams, J. S. 1974. Some variables affecting a constituent's evaluations of and behavior toward a boundary role occupant. *Organ. Behav. Hum. Perform.* 11:390–408

479. Walton, R. E., McKersie, R. B. 1965. *A Behavioral Theory of Labor Negotiations.* New York: McGraw-Hill

480. Watson, D. 1971. Reinforcement theory of personality and social system: Dominance and position in a group power structure. *J. Pers. Soc. Psychol.* 20:180–85

481. Weick, K. L., Gilfillan, D. P. 1971. Fate of arbitrary traditions in a laboratory microculture. *J. Pers. Soc. Psychol.* 2:179–91

482. Wichman, H. 1970. Effects of isolation and communication on cooperation in a two-person game. *J. Pers. Soc. Psychol.* 16:114–20

483. Wiley, M. G. 1973. Sex roles in games. *Sociometry* 36:526–41

484. Wilke, H., Meertens, R. 1973. Individual risk taking for self and others. *Eur. J. Soc. Psychol.* 3:403–14

485. Wilke, H., Mulder, M. 1971. Coalition formation on the gameboard. *Eur. J. Soc. Psychol.* 1:339–56

486. Willems, E. P., Clark, R. D. III. 1971. Shift toward risk and heterogeneity of groups. *J. Exp. Soc. Psychol.* 7:304–12

487. Wilson, W. 1971. Reciprocation and other techniques for inducing cooperation in the prisoner's dilemma game. *J. Confl. Resolut.* 15:167–96

488. Wood, D., Pilisuk, M., Uren, E. 1973. The martyr's personality: An experimental investigation. *J. Pers. Soc. Psychol.* 25:177–84

489. Wood, M. T. 1973. Power relationships and groups decision making in organizations. *Psychol. Bull.* 79:280–93

490. Wrightsman, L. S., O'Connor, J., Baker, N. J. 1972. *Cooperation and Competition: Readings on Mixed-Motive Games.* Belmont, Calif.: Brooks-Cole

491. Wyer, R. S. Jr. 1971. Effects of outcome matrix and partner's behavior in two-person games. *J. Exp. Soc. Psychol.* 7:190–210

492. Wyer, R. S. Jr., Malinowski, C. 1972. Effects of sex and achievement level upon individualism and competitiveness in social interaction. *J. Exp. Soc. Psychol.* 8:303–14
493. Wyer, R. S. Jr., Pohlen, S. J. 1971. Some effects of fate control upon the tendency to benefit an exploitative other. *J. Pers. Soc. Psychol.* 20:44–54
494. Young, O. R. 1972. Intermediaries: Additional thoughts on third parties. *J. Confl. Resolut.* 16:51–66
495. Yukl, G. 1971. Toward a behavioral theory of leadership. *Organ. Behav. Hum. Perform.* 6:414–40
496. Yukl, G. 1974. Effects of the situational variables and opponent concessions on a bargainer's perception, aspirations, and concessions. *J. Pers. Soc. Psychol.* 29:227–36
497. Ibid. Effects of the opponent's initial offer, concession magnitude, and concession frequency on bargaining behavior. 30:323–35

498. Zajonc, R. B., Wolosin, R. J., Wolosin, M. A. 1972. Group risk-taking under various group decision schemes. *J. Exp. Soc. Psychol.* 8:16–30
499. Zajonc, R. B., Wolosin, R. J., Wolosin, M. A., Loh, W. D. 1970. Social facilitation and imitation in group risk-taking. *J. Exp. Soc. Psychol.* 6:26–46
500. Zajonc, R. B., Wolosin, R. J., Wolosin, M. A., Sherman, J. 1978. Individual and group risk taking in a two-choice situation. *J. Exp. Soc. Psychol.* 4:89–106
501. Zaleska, M. 1974. The effects of discussion on group and individual choices among bets. *Eur. J. Soc. Psychol.* 4:229–50
502. Zaleska, M., Kogan, N. 1971. Level of risk selected by individuals and groups when deciding for self and others. *Sociometry* 34:198–213
503. Zechmeister, K., Druckman, D. 1973. Determinants of resolving conflict of interest. *J. Confl. Resolut.* 17:63–88

PROJECTIVE TESTS   ❖263

Walter G. Klopfer

Department of Psychology, Portland State University, Portland, Oregon 97207

Earl S. Taulbee

Psychology Service, Veterans Administration Center, Bay Pines, Florida 33504

INTRODUCTION

Will this be the last time that a chapter on projective tests appears in the *Annual Review of Psychology?* Will the Rorschach be a blot on the history of clinical psychology? If projective techniques are dead, some people don't seem to have gotten the message. There were more than 500 journal articles pertaining to projective techniques during the current review period (1971 through 1974), not including a number of books that have been published as new volumes or revised editions.

Comparing three national surveys (82, 83, 131) of psychological test utilization reported during the period 1947 to 1971, only minor changes are in evidence for the top ranking tests. In terms of the number of respondents mentioning use of a particular test, during the decade between the last two surveys the Rorschach dropped in rank from first to second place, replaced by the Wechsler Adult Intelligence Scale (WAIS) in the top spot; the Thematic Apperception Test (TAT) moved from fourth place to tie with the Bender-Gestalt for third; and the Machover Draw-a-Person test (DAP) dropped from second to fifth place. This stability of test preference is very significant in view of the fact that during the period covered by the surveys there was a very high turnover rate in the top 20 tests. In contrast with the clinical use of these tests indicated by the above, a greater decline in research use of the tests is implied by data in the recently published *Seventh Mental Measurements Yearbook* (17). Although the percentage of projective test references of all personality test references has dropped significantly during the past few years, the Rorschach is surpassed only by the Minnesota Multiphasic Personality Inventory (MMPI) in yearly average references (130 vs 240). The TAT has dropped to seventh place with an annual average of 74. In terms of the cumulative total references, the Rorschach, MMPI, and TAT are in the three top spots, accounting for 4202, 3306, and 1534 references, respectively (17).

Even if one were to consider research on projective tests as the beating of a dead horse, a lot of people seem eager to get in on the flogging, so much so that the voluminous nature of the current literature makes an exhaustive review impossible. The reviewers have chosen to emphasize the three most widely used projective tests —the Rorschach, TAT, and Human Figure Drawings. These tests account for more than 70% of all the current projective technique literature references. Many of the studies used new or tailor-made approaches which are difficult to review in light of the scarcity of normative data or lack of cross-validation. Some examples are the Family Story Technique, the Group Personality Projective Test, the Draw-a-Dog Scale, Draw-a-Person in the Rain Test, Draw-a-Member of a Minority test, and the Manikin Construction Task. Such exercises contribute little to producing the acceptable body of knowledge needed for establishing the reliability and validity of projective instruments.

The greatest difficulty in measuring the validity of projective instruments is the lack of acceptable criteria against which to validate them. The traditional psychiatric nomenclature has fallen into deserved disrepute because of its inconsistent, unreliable, and theoretically muddled basis. Frequently a sophisticated psychological instrument was correlated with the off-the-wall opinion of a first-year psychiatric resident. The approach of concurrent validity, or correlating one test with another, provides information about the relationship between the two tests but little else. Using as a criterion the ratings by sophisticated or naive observers and judges is constructing an experiment on a rather shaky foundation. Until research on projective tests takes into account whether the variable being investigated is behavioral, conscious, or symbolic, it will often be like comparing walnuts with peaches and coming up with little other than fruit salad. Rather than making an all-or-none judgment on the value of a projective test, it has been more productive to evaluate specific indices and configurational scores. For example, as will be made evident later in the chapter, research results on measures such as the human movement responses (M) and Klopfer's Rorschach Prognostic Rating Scale (RPRS) are encouraging.

It is perhaps unfortunate that much research effort is being expended upon the DAP in view of the generally discouraging results. In connection with the Szondi test, the 1953 review (14) had a definite effect upon the literature. Between 1951 and 1955 there were 118 studies in the American literature dealing with the Szondi test, between 1961 and 1965 there were only 6, and between 1971 and 1974 none was found.

Perhaps what we ought to be attending to is distinguishing between interpretation of the state and trait phenomena, between acute and chronic phenomena, and between behavioral and symbolic characteristics. Instead of providing a psychiatric label, we should intensify our search for the precise meaning of behavior at all levels.

THE RORSCHACH TEST

Introduction

The projective nature of the Rorschach test is best illustrated by the fact that various reviewers, in looking at the same body of evidence, arrive at such idiosyncratic conclusions. In the *Seventh MMY* Rorschach reviews, Knutson states "The Rorschach has continued to be characterized by numerous systems and an overwhelming amount of negative research. The current prediction is that Rorschach use will follow a gradual but accelerating decline in the next decade" (69, p. 440). McArthur's reaction to the inkblots is, "The rich sample of patterned interactions among a man's perceptual, cognitive, emotional, and social sides that appears in even one Rorschach response is neither matched nor approximated by any other psychological tool" (88, p. 443). There are also people in the middle. Rabin says, "It is also a field of study and research which permits workers to investigate such diverse concepts as body image, primary process thinking, hypnotizability, orality, and ego-strength. Not unlike a good deal of the general psychological literature, many Rorschach studies deal with trivialities, are inconsistent, are not replicated, and are inconclusive" (120, pp. 445–46). Reznikoff says, "Thus, while the Rorschach may be psychometrically moribund, there is convincing evidence that it is gaining new vigor as a very novel interview situation that has meaningful applications in exploring a broad spectrum of personality dimensions" (123, p. 449).

In a review of Rorschach research by Klopfer (68), it was concluded that the present status of the Rorschach test is quite different than 30 years ago when it was first introduced to the American scene. It is no longer considered a magical instrument with mysterious capacity for probing beyond the immediate and mystically revealing the inner essence of the individual. The change in attitude towards the Rorschach is due partly to the fact that most personality assessors these days refuse to recognize the presence of any such inner essence. Rather, they are interested in predicting behavior under various specified conditions. Thus the fact that the Rorschach can be so easily influenced by transient and situational variables can be considered hopeful rather than discouraging if specific sampling of behavior under specified conditions is of interest.

During the current review period there have been some encouraging developments. Potkay (114), in *The Rorschach Clinician,* has finally suggested an appropriate way of determining how clinicians actually do make judgments on the basis of Rorschach information. McCully (90) has provided new theoretical linkages in his *Rorschach Theory and Symbolism.* Exner (29), after reviewing the Rorschach systems and culling the valuable essence of each, has brought them together in a comprehensive Rorschach system which hopefully will induce more uniformity in the administration, scoring, and research use of the test. It appears that those people interested in projective methods who have ceased the fratricidal warfare that they were able to indulge in their youth are now coordinating their efforts more effectively. The results will be evident in the section to follow.

Effect of the Examiner

According to Exner & Exner (31), who surveyed 750 members of the Society for Personality Assessment and of Division 12 of the American Psychological Association, there is tremendous diversity among Rorschachers in training, in preferred system, and in general approach to administration, scoring, and interpretation. Approximately one out of five do not score at all and of the remainder, four out of five personalize their scoring. This kind of situation creates great difficulties in comparing the work of various clinicians and researchers and has led Exner to his comprehensive system (30).

Greenberg (43) found that male interns obtained significantly more responses to the Rorschach from female subjects than from male subjects. However, no cross-sex differences were found for either female interns or experienced male clinicians. An attempt by Milner & Moses (92) to cross-validate this finding failed to support Greenberg's finding that male examiners obtain more responses from female subjects than from male subjects. They found no differences due to examiner-subject gender pairing for total responses. However, they did report that male examiner-male subject pairing produced significantly more sexual content than any other gender combination.

Interpretation of Rorschach response as a function of ascribed social class was studied by Koscherak & Masling (72). Using a large number of clinical psychology students and psychologists, they found that neither the clinician's sex nor experience affected the rating, but the ascribed social class of the subject did. The lower-class protocol was rated less severely, was more frequently classified as "normal" or as a "character disorder" than the middle-class protocol, which was called "neurotic" or "psychotic". In comparison with other studies, there are contradictory findings as to whether lower class membership produces negative or positive responses in clinicians. Perhaps psychologists have become more aware of their cultural bias and are attempting to compensate, sometimes to excess.

Still another example of how the examiner can influence the subject is reported by Hersen & Greaves (54). They studied the effects of verbal reinforcement (responding with the word "good") on the total number of responses, the number of human responses, and the number of animal responses. They found that verbal reinforcement applied after each response significantly increased total R for subjects both aware and unaware of the response-reinforcement contingency. In the H and A reinforcement groups, verbal reinforcement led to increased responses, but only for subjects aware of the contingency. It seems that anyone experienced with the administration of the Rorschach test must surely concede, on the basis of these data and his own experience, that the subject can be greatly influenced by the examiner. Manifesting great interest in responses, such as in a demonstration, can certainly increase their number and their "richness." On the other hand, an examiner in a hurry certainly can reduce the length of the protocol and the number of details provided. The Rorschach is an interpersonal situation, and all that can be hoped for is that the variance contributed by the examiner can be extracted so as not to confuse the evaluation of the subject.

Age Norms

All three of the books on Rorschach responses by Ames and her colleagues have been revised and updated. *Child Rorschach Responses* (4), which was published originally in 1952, has been completely updated and enlarged to include much valuable normative, longitudinal, and developmental data. Of the three books, *Adolescent Rorschach Responses* (5) has received the most extensive revision and updating. Included is a new scoring format, more research findings, and longitudinal information concerning phasic development and sex differences for 65 children tested annually from 10 to 16 years. The revision of *Rorschach Responses in Old Age* (3) is not as complete, current, or expansive as the *Adolescent* volume. No attempt was made to summarize the general literature on gerontology, although references to some published reviews were made. The authors point out that the first mention of Rorschach responses in old age was made by Rorschach himself, and that Klopfer (68) may have been the first investigator to use the Rorschach in studying the aged. They quote him at considerable length and conclude that subsequent studies bear out the initial findings of Klopfer and Rorschach and in some instances do not go too far beyond these initial contributions. Data presented by the authors were based on the Rorschach responses of 200 men and women between the ages of 70 and 100. They concluded that the Rorschach test is apparently an extremely sensitive instrument in determining the extent to which people over 70 resemble younger adults in their intellectual and emotional functioning and the extent to which their responses show changes related to aging. Socioeconomic level discriminated better than age among the groups. In a later study, Ames (2) classified a group of aged individuals as normal adults, intact presenile, medium presenile, or deteriorated on the basis of their Rorschach records. She then tested the subjects on four other psychological tests, and found that the differences at these four levels of intactness on the scores obtained turned out to be statistically significant. Thus the findings confirmed the results reported previously.

A useful book by Levitt & Truumaa (77) presents norms for quantifiable Rorschach factors for children and adults. The approach is to aggregate already existing data and to subject this information to an appropriate summing procedure to form a basis for an interpretation.

Special Scores

THE HUMAN MOVEMENT RESPONSE Rorschach hypothesized that seeing M in the inkblots is related to kinesthetic imagery, and therefore might bear a relationship to intelligence, creative ability, "inner life," stable motility, etc. For the most part, research findings tend to support this interpretation of M. The relationship between creativity and M is supported by the findings of Raychaudhuri (122). He studied six groups of subjects as follows: male-creative and female-creative groups drawn on the basis of expert rating and recognition representing various art fields, "nonmasculine" male and "non-feminine" female groups drawn from the general population on the basis of their scores on two tests of masculinity-femininity, and male-normal and female-normal groups. He found that high M was associated with creativity, femininity in males, and with the female sex; sex differences in the creative subjects, as well as masculinity in females, was not associated with significant differences in M productivity. Findings were accounted for in terms of differential sex-role demands and the female sex's effort to overcome indirectly the sociocultural restrictions. Cultural differences between his subjects (Indian) and other subjects were not discussed. Wagner & Hoover (141, 142) tested Piotrowski's assertion that M responses denote a prototypal life role which is apt to be expressed in overt behavior. They found that groups of student drama majors, cheerleaders, and drum majorettes gave significantly more exhibitionistic M than did controls. These findings were considered to be supportive of Piotrowski's hypothesis.

SHADING DETERMINANT   Campo & de Santos (18), in a review of the scoring problems with shading responses, conclude that such responses seem to be scored in a chaotic and often inconsistent manner. They feel that this is due to the different meanings assigned to the term "shading," the use of aprioristic theoretical frames of reference, the attribution of aprioristic symbolic meanings to the content of such responses, and the various meanings of anxiety. Although Klopfer has the most complex system for scoring shading, Campo & de Santos seem to prefer it as being more sensitive and differentiated. In terms of the alleged relationship between shading and anxiety, it is encouraging to note that Auerbach & Spielberger (6) in their review concluded that the relationship demonstrated between measures of shading and state anxiety (A-State) is impressive. They reported that higher shading scores were found under stressful conditions in 9 of 13 studies, even though a number of different shading measures were employed, and these were scored by several different systems.

BODY-IMAGE SCORES   The Penetration and Barrier scores developed by Fisher & Cleveland (34) continue to be the subject of some investigation, although the rate seems to have slowed.

Carlson et al (19) factor analyzed the figure-drawing scores of a group of hospitalized psychiatric patients and derived two scales—Body Disturbance and Sexual Elaboration. The SE scale showed some correlation with Rorschach Penetration score, but not with other body-image related variables. Interpretation was in terms of sexual concerns that are emphasized in dealing with vague and diffuse boundaries. Liebetrau & Pienaar (79) studied adjustment and body image, not just with adults but at various age levels. The subjects were English-speaking South African children representative of high and low adjusted boys and girls in four age groups ranging from 6 to 12. The authors found, in conformity with earlier results, that low adjusted children compared with high adjusted children have significantly lower body boundary awareness and heightened body penetration scores. Lester & Perdue (76) predicted that murderers would differ in their body-image boundary from attempted suicides. To their surprise, the murderers obtained lower Barrier scores, which was in opposition to the prediction, and lower Penetration scores, which was in agreement with the prediction. It appears that the brain-child of Fisher and Cleveland continues to demonstrate some utility in distinguishing groups from one another.

Rorschach Prognostic Rating Scale

In a review of the RPRS by Goldfried, Stricker & Weiner (40), there are encouraging signs that the RPRS may be useful in predicting change as a function of the more traditional insight oriented therapies, but that it may turn out to be too global a measure to use for predicting success in the application of behavioral techniques. Newmark, Finklestein & Frerking (102) studied the predictive validity of the RPRS with a group of neurotics receiving behavior modification and a group receiving rational-emotive psychotherapy. The prediction turned out to be efficient for both groups, based on three outcome criteria. In another study (105) in which neurotics were treated with behavior modification techniques, similar results were reported. This seems to be a more optimistic outcome than could have been predicted from the views of Goldfried and his colleagues. The RPRS scores of a group of process schizophrenics and a group of college students were compared with Jastak's Altitude Quotient (AQ) score (28). The results were significant and positive for the total group, but did not hold for the college group alone, probably as a result of the greater homogeneity of the latter group. Berman (10) tested the hypothesis that videotaped self-confrontation is effective in the strengthening of ego processes in nonparanoid, process schizophrenics. Pre and post self-confrontation RPRS scores were not significantly different. Two studies (59, 102) reported nonsignificant relationships between the MMPI Ego-strength (Es) scale and the RPRS. These findings support the view of those who maintain that the Es scale is primarily a measure of the absence of psychopathology and not basic and inner ego-strength as may be reflected in the movement and shading scores of the RPRS.

All in all, it appears that the early encouraging results with the RPRS seem to be confirmed by more recent research, and that this particular score has continued to be of value in determining and predicting psychotherapeutic outcome of various kinds.

The Comparison of Groups

This traditional way of doing research with the Rorschach test has not been very productive in the past, but opportunistic sampling continues to bring forth more studies of this kind.

SUICIDAL PATIENTS   Neuringer (101), in a 10-year follow-up on a previous review of the use of the Rorschach in predicting suicide, concluded that the results are not very encouraging. He stated, "The current review suggests that suicide is in essence a basically labile and generalized transient-reactive-to-stress response which is a consequence of any number of enduring personality organizations and constellations rather than associated with a single specific motivational system." He also concluded that the replicative research has not supported previously promising Rorschach suicide indicators, and discouraged future investigators from using the Rorschach for this purpose. Farberow (32), after reviewing the "Single Signs," "Multiple Signs," and "Configurational" approaches to the study of suicide, concluded that to date the results have been almost uniformly negative. Another well-summarized review of the current status of the Rorschach for identifying or predicting suicidal ideation and behavior is that of Goldfried, Stricker & Weiner (40). They conclude, ". . . most of the suicide indicators have failed to receive empirical support" (p. 250). They add, "Because of the above-mentioned methodological problems associated with suicide prediction, rather than any inherent weakness in the diagnostic sensitivity of the Rorschach, we are not too optimistic about the validation of Rorschach indicators for the clinical prediction of suicide" (p. 251).

Suicidal "signs" currently receiving some attention in the literature are responses combining color and shading, and representation of transparency and cross-sections on the Rorschach (11, 22, 74, 101). Obviously, further cross-validation of these signs is necessary if they are to be used in clinical practice.

GROUPS WITH COMMON MEDICAL DIAGNOSES   The personality characteristics of a group of school-aged hemophiliacs were compared with published normative data for children. Although the hemophiliacs showed some differences in personality from normals and resembled other chronically ill persons, no single hemophiliac personality was evidenced (108). Geist (39) studied the emotional aspects of five subgroups of dermatitis patients (acne vulgaris, atopic dermatitis, hand eczema, psoriasis, and cellulitis) and found the most severe psychopathology in the psoriasis group. Unexpressed rage and psychosexual deviation were the primary psychopathological characteristics found. The hypotheses that subjects with duodenal ulcers have a greater internal organ reaction to stress situations and that the development and duration of duodenal ulcers involve factors in the social environment were investigated using children with duodenal ulcers, their healthy siblings, and children with bronchial asthma (78). Both hypotheses were supported. A general similarity of Rorschach protocols of subjects with a history of psychogenic headaches and those of other psychosomatic patients was found (134). Welman (145) administered the Rorschach, among other tests, to patients with Parkinson's disease before and after thalamotomy. A reexamination was made after 4 to 7 months and several subjects were examined again 2, 3, and 5 years later. The author concluded that thalamotomy had only a slight effect on intellectual functioning but is gravely detrimental to psychic emotional functioning.

OTHER GROUP DISCRIMINATION   Some other Rorschach studies reported positive findings for group discrimination and prediction. These included predicting marital choice (96), success in counselor training (1), and failure in medical rehabilitation programs (20). Groups discriminated included male sex offenders vs male non-sex offenders (115), hospitalized schizophrenics vs nonschizophrenic psychiatric patients (119), males who had murdered kin vs males who had murdered unrelated victims (113), successful missionary candidates for overseas and home service (111), and persons having reading deficits (130). Some groups not significantly different on the Rorschach were murderers and other felons (75), convicted rapists and males convicted of aggressive nonsexual crimes (112), and schizophrenics and nonpsychotic psychiatric patients (73). It appears that the comparison of groups continues to be rather a hit or a miss proposition. This is attributed to the fact that some groups are defined on the basis of characteristics relevant to projective test performance, whereas others are defined on the basis of symptoms that have little to do with basic personality traits.

Miscellaneous Studies

Several rather interesting studies were reported in which the Rorschach was administered to pairs of identical and fraternal twins in an effort to shed some light on the nature-nurture controversy (8, 46, 94). This type of Rorschach study has seldom appeared in this country although the European literature reports on several investigations dating back many years. In general, the findings have revealed a much greater similarity between the personalities of identical twins than of fraternal twins. The current findings are consistent with those reported earlier. Hamilton, Blewett & Sydiaha (46) studied 26 pairs of identical and 26 pairs of fraternal twins between the ages of 12 and 15, with IQs ranging from 77 to 158, and the two groups equally divided as to sex. The similarity in Rorschach scores for the identical twins was marked, with 6 out of 10 correlations being statistically significant and all but one of the others being 0.44 or greater. In contrast, none of the correlations for the fraternal twins was significant, and except for one, all were below the lowest for the identical twins. Similar findings were reported by Basit (8), who studied 7 pairs of identical and 8 pairs of fraternal twins ranging in age from 8 to 13. He found 6 out of 11 correlations significant for the identical twins but only one for the fraternal twins. Such significant relationships were not obtained by Murawski (94), who studied 20 pairs of identical and 10 pairs of fraternal twins, all college students. Of the 15 correlations computed on the identical twins, 5 reached statistical significance, whereas only 1 of the 15 was significant for the fraternal twin group. Those that did not reach statistical significance were extremely low in both groups but even more so in the fraternal twin group. These studies aren't directly comparable as all did not report on the same Rorschach variables, there were many examiner-subject situational differences, and different statistical analyses were performed. However, results of these twin studies are impressive, and it certainly appears that this is a fruitful area for future research. Additional data obtained on twins reared apart should help to nail down further the genetic as opposed to the experiential factors involved.

Some attention has been given to the effects of the Rorschach of hypnotically induced states. Howell & Carlisle (60) studied the effects of hypnotic and nonhypnotic mood changes by administering the Rorschach to subjects under conditions of posthypnotic happy and depressed and nonhypnotized happy and sad. There were virtually no differences in the quantitative scores, but two judges correctly distinguished the nonhypnotized protocols from the hypnotized protocols in every instance and detected at a significant level the "depressed" protocols from the "happy" protocols under both conditions. How they did this is not made clear. Solomon & Goodson (129) assessed the accuracy of reproduction of childhood or adolescent Rorschach performance in two groups of six young adult males from four different administration conditions, and the results were considered to be consistent with the role-playing view of hypnotic age regression. Also, Wiseman & Reyher (146) studied hypnotically induced dreams. The drive and primary process variables showed a significant increase in comparison to a waking group when a standard administration of the Rorschach was preceded by one hypnotically induced dream to each inkblot one week earlier. Thus it would appear that manipulating someone's set or state of consciousness by hypnotic means does influence Rorschach test performance. Hopefully, the next step will be to use the Rorschach results as a means of trying to clarify the theoretical meaning of hypnosis and hypnotic states.

Behavioral Measures

It is interesting that the Rorschach, which was not developed as a means of predicting behavior, sometimes succeeds in doing so. For example, Davids (26) used the Rorschach to study aggressive thoughts in a group of preadolescent boys institutionalized for emotional disturbances having to do with aggression. A list of Rorschach signs believed to be related to aggression were correlated with ratings of overt aggression by a social worker. Seven signs differentiated significantly between high and low aggressive groups. These signs correlated at a highly significant level with behavioral measures.

In a study by Ryan et al (126), Cards II and III of the Rorschach were shown to impulsive and inhibited undergraduates while eye-movement variables were measured. Inhibited subjects, in contrast to impulsive subjects, spent more total time looking at chromatic elements. Inhibited subjects tended to look at chromatic areas more frequently during the recorded period. In contrast, impulsive subjects mentioned color more often in verbal reports. It appears that eye-movement may serve as a measure of the difficulty a subject has in handling a particular stimulus element.

Rice & Gaylin (124) studied the relationships between voice quality ratings in the first and second sessions of patients being seen in time-limited, client-centered psychotherapy and their pretherapy Rorschach scores. Significant relationships were found between three vocal styles and Rorschach function scores—scores previously designed to assess an immediate level of functioning and found to be associated with qualities commonly observed in creative individuals. They view the findings as having implications for differential prognosis.

Getting it Together

It may well be that the most important event of the present review period is the publication of Exner's *The Rorschach: A Comprehensive System* (30). Exner describes it as a method which can be easily taught, manifests a high interclinician reliability, and one which will stand well against the various tests of reliability. He presents good documentation for the decisions he makes as to what to plagiarize from the various standard systems. In his sections on interpretation, it appears that the comprehensive system is as useful and expedient as might be hoped for. If Exner has convinced the researchers in the Rorschach field that they should use his system, studies will be comparable, all protocols can be used for the same research sample, and greater clarity certainly will be the result.

HOLTZMAN INKBLOT TEST

Literature on the HIT appears to be on the wax. In addition to the book by Hill (56), a good critical review has been provided by Gamble (38) and a comprehensive bibliography by Van Dyke (140).

Gamble presents a brief description of the rationale, construction, and structure of the test, and then critically reviews the research literature from 1959 to 1969, concluding that an impressive body of positive findings are in evidence, but that many more studies are needed in most areas covered by the review. Technical refinements include administration and computer scoring (now there is Piotrowski's Automated Rorschach, the first computerized application of a projective test), and a short form group administered HIT. There is evidence that "examiner" variables influence HIT protocols, although Molish (93) in his review stated, "The HIT, unlike the Rorschach, is minimally affected by situational factors and the examiner is not considered a major factor in the test's variance." This is in contrast to Gamble's conclusion that "Experimental evidence from several sources agrees that 'examiner' variables have a marked effect on certain HIT variables."

A major difference between the Rorschach and the HIT is that on the latter, responses are limited to one per card. Hayslip & Darbes (52) report a study in which they had the subjects produce five responses per card and evaluated the relationship of the remaining four responses with the first. The correlations among all possible pairs of responses failed to reach the accepted standards of high intrasubject reliability. They concluded that one response per card is misleading. Gamble's discussion indicated strong support for the view that certain HIT variables provide reliable indices of developmental changes in cognitive organization. The review further concluded that intercultural validity of certain processes involved in inkblot perception exists, that the findings reinforce the significance of the body-boundary construct in personality research, and that very little is known about the diagnostic validity of the HIT.

One study by Swartz et al (132) on mental retardates and normals revealed consistent monotonic changes with IQ level for six HIT variables providing support for these variables as indices of perceptual development. Another perceptual development study by Witzke et al (147), using male and female subjects ranging in age from 20 to 61, investigated age level and sex differences on 10 variables. One age level difference and five sex differences were found, suggesting that there is a reversal of perceptual development, as outlined by Werner's organismic-developmental theory, for women in the middle ages but not for men. A study by Hanssen & Teigen (48) investigated sex differences on the group version of the HIT. This was necessary because Holtzman had reported negligible sex differences on 22 variables, justifying the establishment of common norms for men and women. They studied several groups of male and female subjects matched by sex, age, education, and at the same time forming a continuum from a professional training sought exclusively by men, to a training sought by both sexes, to a career sought almost exclusively by women. Significant sex differences were found on several HIT variables, interpreted by the investigators as pointing to a higher degree of well-organized ideational activity, imaginative capacity, and awareness of conventional concepts in the women than in the men. It was also found that women saw more female figures than men, but that male figures were seen with the same frequency by both sexes. Possible explanations included the stimulus properties of the test, the traditional masculine orientation in the Norwegian culture, and the masculine orientation in the women seeking professional work who were among the subjects. Obviously, this study calls for replication with local subjects and with a more random sampling of the population. However, Iacino & Cook (61) found support for one of the findings reported by

Hanssen & Teigen (48) that females give significantly more M responses than males. They stated that the results seem to justify a reexamination of sex differences for each of the HIT variables with the possibility of obtaining separate norms for males and females.

Similar kinds of studies traditionally done with the Rorschach have begun to appear in the HIT literature. For instance, a group of Indian alcoholics and a group of white alcoholics were compared with no differences found (118). Overall & Gorham (110) reported a study designed to test one increasingly specific theory of age decrement, that is, the theory that increasingly poor performance is due to a developing organic brain syndrome. Over 300 VA Domiciliary members, ranging in age from 45 to 84, were administered the HIT and WAIS. It was concluded that the results reveal that the pattern of changes associated with old age is clearly different from the pattern of changes associated with chronic brain syndrome.

Several studies were reported relating HIT indices of anxiety to other measures. Cook et al (23) investigated the relationship between HIT Anxiety (Ax) and Shading (Sh) scores and trait-anxiety (A-Trait) and state-anxiety (A-State) measures. No significant relationships were found between A-Trait and the HIT indices. However, the Ax score correlated with A-State both before and during the administration of the HIT, which is consistent with the findings by others that projective testing increases a subject's anxiety level (104, 106). In another study, Iacino & Cook (61) explored the relationship between A-Trait and A-State and Ax and Sh. A-State was manipulated experimentally via threat of electric shock. None of the HIT scores reflected changes in A-State although Ax correlated significantly with A-Trait. They concluded that at this point the HIT does not appear to be a particularly valid instrument for assessing anxiety. Hartlage (50) correlated the Ax scale and a self-report anxiety questionnaire and found no significant relationship. An experimenter-designed measure of perceptual rigidity resulted in a significant negative correlation with HIT color and movement scales (66).

The questions as to whether the Holtzman is better than the Rorschach and whether it will become popular in clinical practice, as the Rorschach has been for many years, remain unanswered. So far, the results have been encouraging.

THEMATIC APPERCEPTION TEST

As has been evidenced for some time, the objective scoring systems that have been developed for the TAT are almost totally absent in routine clinical use. In addition, the entire set of 20 cards intended for each age group is hardly ever used. In practice, the productions are evaluated qualitatively and norms are personal to the examiner. We seem to be approaching the conclusion that the TAT is not a psychometric instrument at all, but rather a multidimensional method for studying complex personality and for evaluating needs, values, motivations, and attitudes. Dana (25) reviewed over a hundred studies on the TAT and concluded that they do not form a cohesive body of knowledge about the test or its application to personality evaluation. A similar conclusion can be drawn from the present review.

Contextual Factors

Uleman (137, 138) investigated the degree to which TAT responses could be manipulated through verbal conditioning. One hundred male undergraduates were given a written TAT (four cards) and the Marlowe-Crowne Social Desirability Scale. Subjects in a raffle-type verbal operant conditioning task were reinforced by signals. The results reveal that only those subjects aware of the reinforcement were conditioned. TAT motives n-Influence and n-Power were only weakly related to the reinforcement's subjective value. Results further suggest that the subject's postconditioning report of his intentions in the reinforcement value was biased in the direction of justifying or describing his own performance. Thus it appears that behavioral manifestations depend upon verbalized awareness of other aspects of the situation. The hypothesis that the quantity and thematic quality of TAT responses would decrease when the stories were taped was investigated by Cavalcanti et al (21). The hypothesis was not supported. It was also found by Martinez et al (86) that a benevolent or autocratic style of presentation made no difference on the results obtained on the TAT for a group of girls 8 to 11 years old. However, performance was influenced by instructional set, the time of day, and the application of time pressure.

How to Choose the TAT Cards to Administer

Siskind (128) found that male interns administered more sexual-romantic cards to females than to male patients but that male staff psychologists did not. Although the sample was very small, the findings are quite suggestive and fit in with an earlier report by Masling & Harris (87) that male interns administer more sexually romantic cards with female subjects. One study (44) of the differential effects of music on performance reported that subjects listening to exciting music more frequently told hostile stories and stories with female power themes. In an earlier study, Hartman (51) proposed a short "basic TAT set." Irvin & Vander Woude (62) administered the entire TAT set to male subjects and asked judges to determine the most frequent theme elicited by each card. The highest ranking cards in terms of thematic productivity were essentially the same as Hartman's basic TAT set. Highly similar results obtained on hospitalized psychiatric patients were reported in another study (103).

Normative Studies

A significant contribution was made by Murstein (95), who obtained written responses to projected TAT slides from a large group of college subjects. Stories were scored for who (in age, sex, and relationship), what, why, and end, and a reliable categorization system developed. His results indicated generally that stories were mostly negative but positive for ending, with large variations between cards. Sex differences were found for 45 of 182 chi-squares computed, with female responses more positive than males. Another study by Nawas (99) analyzed the TAT stories of 64 male and 61 female subjects who were studied as adolescents in 1952 and as young adults 8 years later. The author concluded that the evidence from long range longitudinal studies is mounting, that the assumption of continuity in human development is too simplistic, and that behavior is subject to greater change than current theories lead one to believe.

Some studies on the use of the TAT and CAT with children have been reported. Included among the findings are that card rejection is very complex and may be a result of many factors (109), that older children produce longer stories than younger ones (36), that the CAT and CAT-H are more useful for younger children than the TAT (97), and that for preschool children a puzzle form of the CAT results in greater involvement than the regular form (57).

On the other end of the spectrum, elderly people have been attended to by the development of two variations of the TAT, namely the Gerontological Apperception Test (GAT) by Wolk & Wolk (148) and the Senior Apperception Technique (SAT) developed by Bellak & Bellak (9). These test developers did not have much in the way of norms to present at the time their tests entered the marketplace. Since that time, Traxler et al (136) have studied the usefulness of the GAT in assessing personality dynamics and specific areas of functioning relevant to the lives and experiences of normal community-dwelling and senile and normal nursing home occupants. They concluded that the portraying of older people in the scenes is not sufficient to get the aged to respond readily and that in general the stories revealed only superficial aspects of personality. In another study (35) the efficacy of the GAT and TAT was compared for eliciting themes depicting loss of sexuality, loss of attractiveness, family difficulties, physical limitations, and dependency. Only in the area of physical limitations was the GAT more successful. No SAT studies appeared in the literature reviewed. An important question raised at this point is whether these stimuli, depicting older figures and portraying situations more directly relevant to problems of the aged, are superior to the TAT in the psychological assessment of the aged.

Needs

Achievement motivation in lower class high school negro females as a function of the race and sex of the figures was studied by Cowan (24), who had the figures in the pictures variously portrayed as black and white males and black and white females. The subjects attributed more achievement motivation to male than to female figures, wrote longer stories to black than to white figures and to female than to male figures. There was no effect of race of figure on need achievement. In another study, Greene & Winter (45) studied motives, involvements, and leadership among black college students. They found that n-Power was related to holding office, being rated as influential, and participating in the Black Repertory Theatre. Among Northern-reared blacks, n-Power related to ratings of activity in the extramural black community and distrust of the system. Among Southern-reared blacks, n-Power and n-Ach related to ratings of pragmatism. Honor & Vane (58) studied achievement attitudes of high school boys by comparing selected TAT cards and the California Study Methods Survey. The TAT was more effective than the CSMS in differentiating between high and low academic achievement. Uleman (139) aroused the need for influence by giving college males the power of the examiner's role. The resulting TAT content analysis reflects significant arousal within subjects, and each scoring category differentiated aroused from nonaroused subjects. n-Infl correlated with degree of influence, with feelings of confidence in the examiner's role, and with peer ratings of dominance. This suggests that n-Power relates more to argumentation and derives from feelings of powerlessness and defensiveness about power. In a series of 8 experiments using 582 subjects, Klinger (67) studied models portraying Ach, Aff, or Neu activity, context, and achievement fantasy. The results were ordered to three theoretical propositions: (a) models elicit fantasy thematically similar to their activity unless the subject is incompatibly preoccupied; in which case (b) models cause suppression of similar fantasy; but (c) in fantasy both elicitation and suppression are short lived. Thus it appears that the need scoring system continues to be an interesting and rather fruitful subject for research which is meaningful in terms of psychological and sociological theory.

Behavioral Measures

The Hostile Press TAT slides were administered to subjects not members of any protest group and to a group whose members were active in protest against US involvement in Viet Nam. As predicted, the protest group members had significantly higher Hostile Press scores (133). The hypothesis that aggressive and sexual imagery would appear only under conditions of sexual arousal was tested by Barclay (7). Male and female college students were assigned to three different arousal conditions (sex, anxiety, and laughter) and a nonarousal control. Sexually aroused subjects wrote stories higher in sexual and aggressive imagery than those in the other two arousal conditions. The scores of those in the anxiety and laughter conditions were not significantly different from the controls.

McClelland (89) administered the TAT to college students before, during, and near the end of parties. Alcoholic drinking increased power themes in the stories. Moderate drinking increased socialized power thoughts, while heavy drinking increased personal dominance thoughts. Schulman & Shontz (127) studied eight groups of college students, 10 men and 10 women per group, while in a standing, sitting-erect, sitting-bent, or supine posture. Enclosed Box problems and the uses of a Brick task were administered to four groups, with one group in each body posture. The other four groups were administered an abbreviated TAT, a task requiring the subject to talk about himself, and a test of memory for posture-related words. It was found that number of problems solved, pace of talking, number of self-referent statements, and proportions of posture-related words remembered were significantly affected by posture. It was concluded that body posture influences several types of thinking and that the study of the influence of posture on behavior has theoretical value as well as implications for personality assessment. London et al (81) studied 20 female undergraduates and 44 US Army enlisted men, and found that the TAT correlated positively with rated boredom on an experimental task (autonomic arousal).

Other Variations of the TAT

The Blacky test received very little study during this review period. Fisher & Keen (33) examined verbal recall in anal retentive, anal neutral, and anal expulsive subjects and failed to confirm previous findings that anal retentives are superior in verbal recall. Galinsky (37) reported significant differences on 7 of 30 Blacky factors, and on the Defense Preference Inventory between groups of undergraduate academic failures and successes.

The MAPS (Make-A-Picture-Story) test was used in only two of the studies reviewed. Neuringer (100) compared the protocols of suicidal, schizophrenic, and normal individuals for the presence and extent of social isolation. He concluded that the social isolation of suicidal individuals manifests itself in the MAPS by increased compensatory fantasied interpersonal contacts. Ward (143) administered the MAPS test to a group of educable mentally retarded boys and a group of nonretarded boys of similar age and socioeconomic class. Results suggest a significantly greater use of self-identification in the nonretarded group.

The above illustrates the short-lived popularity of tests that are excessively theory-bound (Blacky) or clumsy to administer in practical situations (MAPS). It appears likely that these tests will fade into oblivion.

DRAW-A-PERSON TEST

This test continues to enjoy widespread use. From the original purpose of estimating intelligence, it has become popular as a method of inferring personality characteristics. The section below will examine the justification for this procedure.

Harris (49), in his review of the DAP, states his personal conviction that the drawings must tell something about the individual's interests, preoccupations, and perhaps unconscious dynamics, although readily admitting his own biases, the all too easily made assumption of isomorphy by clinicians, and recognizing the generally negative research findings. He states that research must be initiated along different psychological dimensions of drawings than those used to date, and suggests that the evaluation of drawings according to more comprehensive, abstract principles might be more promising than the sign approach.

Contextual Factors

Dmitruk (27) investigated the influence of recent experience and situational variables by comparing the drawings of students in introductory anthropology and psychology courses. The former drew significantly more "novel" figures than the latter. The anthropology students were influenced by course content in a variety of "primitive" studies. This suggests that the clinician should be slow to attribute pathology without considering situational factors. Other studies demonstrated that stress induced by anxiety-provoking film increased the tendency to draw the opposite sex first (41), and that female subjects listening to exciting music drew taller figures (44). Melikian (91) found that a group of Saudi Arabian college males who had lived and attended school outside the country for at least a year, drew the opposite sex first and drew more figures in Western dress significantly more often than a comparable group which had never traveled or lived outside Arabia. All of the above studies clearly indicate that the concept of drawings as representing basic personality traits independently of situational and transient factors is not justified.

Graphic Signs

The hypotheses that upper left placement, shading, erasures, and line reinforcement are valid indicators of anxiety were not supported by their correlations with the IPAT (Institute for Personality and Ability Testing) Anxiety Scale (64, 65); nor is the hypothesis that the size of drawings reflects the level of self-concept supported (116).

In a study of fifth and sixth graders by Tolor & Tolor (135), it was shown that girls are more likely to draw the opposite sex first. Heinrich & Triebe (53) pooled relevant data on sex of the first figure drawn from 19 previous studies using 5- to 18-year-old subjects. Analysis of the data revealed that 83% of the nearly 5000 males and 78% of the almost 4500 females showed self-sex preference. However, the self-sex proportion of males significantly exceeded females only from the eleventh year on. Results are explained in terms of the culturally determined learning of sex-role identification.

Apparently the choice of figure drawn first seems to have more to do with cultural learning than with any innate self-concept. It would be interesting to study adult women with a feminist orientation to see whether their choice of figure drawn first would be significantly different than adult females with a more traditional orientation towards their gender role.

Another drawing characteristic that has been frequently mentioned is that of clothing vs nudity. In line with their effort to attach pejorative labels, the DAP experts have labeled these two tendencies clothes-narcissism vs body-narcissism. This matter was investigated by Gravitz (42), who obtained frequencies of fully-clothed, partially clothed, nude, and outline-only drawings made by 1000 normal adults, half of each sex. He found that (a) both groups of subjects produced essentially similar numbers of fully clothed same-sex figures, but more male-opposite drawings were fully clothed; (b) fewer male same-sex drawings were partly clothed, but this was not observed in the opposite-sex figures; (c) the frequencies of nude same-sex and opposite-sex figures were similar, although there was a nonsignificant tendency for males to make more nude drawings of both sexes; and (d) same-sex outlines only were common in males with the reverse occurring in opposite-sex drawings. These results shed little light on the matter, and it seems possible that the artistic training may have played a part in the choice of how the figures should be executed rather than a choice of whether to be narcissistic about clothes or body.

Body Image

DAP studies of body image have tended to focus on the literal representation of bodily defects or physique of the subject, both of which may well be irrelevant to the psychological nature of the body image. In a study referred to earlier (19), it was found that the Body Disturbance scores correlated highly with artistic skill and sophistication, but not with other measures. The Sexual Elaboration scores bore no relationship with body image disturbances. Kokonis (70), on the other hand, found that hospitalized schizophrenics omitted extremities more often than normals did, which he interpreted as indicating body image disturbances. In another study by

Prytula & Thompson (117), the DAP and Self-Esteem Inventory were administered to a group of male and female fifth and sixth graders. Indicators measured were body height and width, area, erasures, transparencies, and omissions, but the results offer no consistent support for the body-image hypothesis as related to self-esteem. Subjects did not differ in terms of drawing size of self-figure, nor did subjects high in self-esteem draw significantly larger figures. Studies on African paraplegics by Manganyi (84, 85) failed to support the hypothesis that they would demonstrate a body image characterized by significant pathology. Nathan (98), however, did find that the drawings of obese children were more global and less differentiated than those of a matched control group. Thus one can only conclude that using the DAP as a measure of body image is a very risky undertaking. The criteria are not clear, and some of the thecretical underpinnings seem to be rather off the mark.

Sex Role

Perhaps because of their psychoanalytic orientation, DAP theoreticians have been particularly prolific in the hypotheses concerning sex-role, sexual pathology, etc, as culled from the DAP. However, the results are not encouraging.

Jensen et al (63) found no significant differences between sex offenders and non-sexual offenders on either overall quality of the drawings as rated on a special scale for the presence and absence of specific signs considered as indicative of sexual disturbance. Another study (71) reported no significant relationship between choice of gender and sex-role identification scores in a group of schizophrenics and a group of normally functioning males. Roback (125) reported findings from studies investigating the relationship between sex of free choice figure drawings and sexual inversion, and between sex of free choice figure drawings and gender identity. Four groups of subjects, both male and female homosexual and heterosexuals, were studied. The males' erotic orientations were indicated by a phallometric test and the Kinsey scale, and that of the females by the Kinsey scale. The two groups did not differ significantly in the sex of their two "free" figure drawings. Subsequently, the DAP and Feminine Gender Identity Scale were administered to another group of male homosexual subjects. Point biserial correlations between their gender identity scores and both free choice drawings of a female were nonsignificant. Thus one is forced to conclude that gender identity and sex choice of figure drawn bear no clear relationship, and that the sex of the first figure drawn is not a useful measure of either sexual inversion or gender identity.

Miscellaneous Studies

To illustrate some of the different kinds of research being carried on with the DAP, a few other studies will be described. O'Brian & Patton succeeded in establishing a reliable objective scoring method for family drawings (107). Bolton et al (13) failed to validate an objective scoring procedure for the DAP with deaf rehabilitation clients. They correlated six composite scoring variables with a large set of criterion variables. In another study, Bolton (12) quantified the DAP protocols of deaf adults. Ratings on 16 scales were intercorrelated and the matrix factor analyzed. The personality factor proved to be independent of communication skills, IQ achievement, and manual dexterity. Handler & McIntosh (47) compared the DAP with behavioral observation and self rating in the prediction of withdrawal and aggression in third grade males. The criterion was combined teacher and peer behavior ratings for each child. The DAP was not found useful for differentiating among control, aggressive, and withdrawal subjects. Lingren (80), using Koppitz's list of 30 emotional indicators to compare matched pairs of "shy" and "aggressive" 5- to 12-year-olds, found no significant differences. Watson et al (144) studied the relationship between DAP facial expression ratings and symptom ratings to test the diagnostic utility of DAP facial expression. The results were negative. Interjudge agreement on the ratings of facial expression was inadequate.

It appears from the above review of work on the DAP that drawings can only be regarded as a suggestive kind of graphic behavior that will take on meaning as it is discussed with the subject and viewed in the context of other information. Many of the hypotheses formed by authors like Machover are at a level not clearly related to either conscious self-concept or behavior. Thus many of the studies cited above seem doomed to failure.

OTHER PROJECTIVE TESTS

As stated in the Introduction, it was not possible to review all the projective tests that have appeared in the literature during the current review period. In addition to the tests reviewed above, Wagner's Hand Test (HT) has received a fair amount of attention. One of the scores from the HT is the Acting Out Ratio (AOR), purportedly a predictor of aggressive acting-out behavior. However, the results have not been encouraging. Breidenbaugh et al (15) concluded, "The AOR lacks stability as a measurement construct, does not correlate with another projective measure of aggressive potential and is not a useful predictor of acting-out behavior as rated by teachers of emotionally disturbed pre-adolescents." In another study by Higdon & Brodsky (55) on the validity of the AOR for predicting overt and experimentally induced aggression, it was found that the score did not reflect the effects of the experimentally induced stress, nor did it correlate significantly with the content-derived hostility scale. On the other hand, significant correlations were obtained between combined supervisory rankings of satisfactory work performance of the entire police force of a small city and 6 of 21 variables on the HT (121). Research on the test was brought up to date in a book by Bricklin et al (16).

The Szondi test seems essentially moribund in this country. No studies were found in the American literature and fewer than 10 in the foreign literature. Those reviewed used small numbers of subjects, and the results generally failed to differentiate diagnostic groups or to find significant profile difference between patients and nonpatients. It appears that no real evidence for the validity or usefulness of this test has been demonstrated.

Other projective tests that have received some attention during the review period are the Kahn Symbol Arrangement Test (KSAT), the Blacky, and the Bender Visual Motor Gestalt Test. This does not include the many variations of the TAT or the Human Figure Drawing test.

CONCLUSIONS

These reviewers, after a quarter century of clinical experience and following the literature, have seen fads come and go. While they were graduate students in the late 1940s, psychoanalysis was the theoretical orthodoxy, and projective testing seemed to fit in with the kinds of questions being asked about people's intrapersonal experiences. Since that time there have been many therapeutic dogmas enunciated, and the whole question of whether assessment is necessary or not has been debated, oftentimes with great acrimony.

Psychologists with various theoretical bases have contended that their formulations are so universalistic, their treatment methods so effective with anyone, that the question of personality assessment becomes moot. Clinical psychologists recently trained in a narrowly focused way emphasizing behavioral techniques are not used to investigating the intrapsychic aspects of personality because they are unfamiliar with the value of having this kind of information.

It seems, however, that no single therapeutic dogma, no matter how promising at the beginning, has escaped the Hawthorne effect. There just isn't any panacea that is going to make everyone happy, competent, and free of stress. Therefore, the question of tailor-making treatment plans for individuals returns as a necessity. Adequate personality assessment includes attention to behavior, since this is often the major reason for the client/patient being referred. Children are referred because they annoy adults; adults are hospitalized not because of their emotional disturbance, but because of their unacceptable social behavior. Therefore, behavior cannot be ignored as part of the assessment procedure. Self-concept also needs to be evaluated since someone's opinion of himself is his or her conscious guide for making decisions and taking action. Private or symbolic aspects of personality also need to be evaluated, since it can still be safely assumed that most people are motivated in part by factors of which they are unaware.

What Role Do Projective Techniques Play in this Process?

It appears from this review and those preceding it that tests of a thematic sort often reveal much more about a person's conscious preoccupations and goals than they do about the unconscious. This is also true of the Sentence Completion Test, once considered a projective test but now widely regarded as a structured interview. However, it must be granted that the more common and effective procedures for getting conscious data are probably objective inventories and diagnostic interviews. Behavior probably can be measured best by observing it directly, although it appears that certain Rorschach indices are rather effective in predicting behaviors that as yet have not occurred, such as success from psychotherapy. The most attractive use of projective tests for measuring behavior directly is probably a form of interaction testing or consensus administration of the Rorschach (68) and other projective techniques. This has been used in groups, with couples, with families, and with teams of co-workers. It enables the examiner to get simultaneously intrapsychic information based upon the content and style of the projective responses, and at the same time have a direct view of the interaction between people who have real-life relationships.

The most distinct contribution that projective tests continue to make, however, probably is in revealing aspects of motivation and personality that do not fit neatly into either the self-concept or behavioral category. Creative capacities, hidden resources, potentialities that currently are not in use are variables that sometimes emerge better in projective test performance than through other sources of information. Until clinical psychologists give up an interest in the inner person and abandon their search for probing the depths of the psyche, they probably will continue to use, improve, and rely upon the data derived from projective techniques.

Literature Cited

1. Allen, T. W. 1972. Psychological openness and counselor effectiveness: A further investigation. *J. Pers. Assess.* 36:13–18
2. Ames, L. B. 1974. Calibration of aging. *J. Pers. Assess.* 38:507–29
3. Ames, L. B., Metraux, R. W., Rodell, J. L., Walker, R. N. 1973. *Rorschach Responses in Old Age.* New York: Brunner/Mazel. 219 pp.
4. Ames, L. B., Metraux, R. W., Rodell, J. L., Walker, R. N. 1974. *Child Rorschach Responses.* New York: Brunner/Mazel. 321 pp.
5. Ames, L. B., Metraux, R. W., Walker, R. N. 1971. *Adolescent Rorschach Responses.* New York: Brunner/Mazel. 319 pp.
6. Auerbach, S. M., Spielberger, C. D. 1972. The assessment of state and trait anxiety with the Rorschach test. *J. Pers. Assess.* 36:314–35
7. Barclay, A. M. 1971. Linking sexual and aggressive motives: Contributions of "irrelevant" arousals. *J. Pers.* 39:481–92
8. Basit, A. 1972. A Rorschach study of personality development in identical and fraternal twins. *J. Pers. Assess.* 36:23–27
9. Bellak, L., Bellak, S. S. 1973. *Senior Apperception Technique.* Larchmont, NY: C.P.S.
10. Berman, A. L. 1972. Videotape self-confrontation of schizophrenic ego and thought processes. *J. Consult. Clin. Psychol.* 39:78–85
11. Blatt, S. J., Ritzler, B. A. 1974. Suicide and the representation of transparency and cross-sections on the Rorschach. *J. Consult. Clin. Psychol.* 42:280–87
12. Bolton, B. 1972. Quantification of two projective tests for deaf clients. *J. Clin. Psychol.* 28:554–56
13. Bolton, B., Donoghue, R., Langbauer, W. 1973. Quantification of two projective tests for deaf clients: A large sample

validation study. *J. Clin. Psychol.* 29:249–50
14. Borstelmann, L. J., Klopfer, W. G. 1953. The Szondi Test: A review and critical evaluation. *Psychol. Bull.* 50:112–32
15. Breidenbaugh, B., Brozovich, R., Matheson, L. 1974. The Hand Test and other aggression indicators in emotionally disturbed children. *J. Pers. Assess.* 38:332–34
16. Bricklin, B., Piotrowski, Z. A., Wagner, E. E. 1973. *The Hand Test: A New Projective Test with Special Reference to the Prediction of Overt Aggressive Behavior.* Springfield, Ill: Thomas. 112 pp.
17. Buros, O. K., Ed. 1972. *Seventh Mental Measurements Yearbook,* Vol. 1. Highland Park, NJ: Gryphon. 935 pp.
18. Campo, V., de Santos, D. R. 1971. A critical review of the shading responses in the Rorschach: I. Scoring problems. *J. Pers. Assess.* 35:3–21
19. Carlson, K., Quinlan, D., Tucker, G., Harrow, M. 1973. Body disturbance and sexual elaboration factors in figure drawings of schizophrenic patients. *J. Pers. Assess.* 37:56–63
20. Carnes, G. D., Bates, R. E. 1971. Rorschach anatomy response correlates in rehabilitation failure subjects. *J. Pers. Assess.* 35:527–37
21. Cavalcanti, P., Garcia, V. L., Etz, I., Veiga, M. C. 1971. The influence of a tape recorder on verbal responses to a thematic test. *Arq. Bras. Psicol. Apl.* 23:137–45
22. Colson, D. B., Hurwitz, A. 1973. A new experimental approach to the relationship between color-shading and suicide attempts. *J. Pers. Assess.* 37:237–41
23. Cook, P. E., Iacino, L. W., Murray, J., Auerbach, S. M. 1973. Holtzman inkblot anxiety and shading scores related to state and trait anxiety. *J. Pers. Assess.* 37:337–39

24. Cowan, G. 1971. Achievement motivation in lower class Negro females as a function of the race and sex of the figure. *Repr. Res. Soc. Psychol.* 2:43-46
25. Dana, R. H. 1972. Thematic Apperception Test. See Ref. 17, 457-60
26. Davids, A. 1973. Aggression in thought and action of emotionally disturbed boys. *J. Consult. Clin. Psychol.* 40:322-27
27. Dmitruk, V. M. 1972. Situational variables and performance on Machover's figure-drawing test. *Percept. Mot. Skills* 35:489-90
28. Edinger, J. D., Weiss, W. U. 1974. The relation between the altitude quotient and adjustment potential. *J. Clin. Psychol.* 30:510-13
29. Exner, J. E. Jr. 1969. *The Rorschach Systems.* New York: Grune & Stratton. 381 pp.
30. Exner, J. E. Jr. 1974. *The Rorschach: A Comprehensive System.* New York: Wiley-Interscience. 488 pp.
31. Exner, J. E. Jr., Exner, D. E. 1972. How clinicians use the Rorschach. *J. Pers. Assess.* 36:403-8
32. Farberow, N. L. 1974. Use of the Rorschach in predicting and understanding suicide. *J. Pers. Assess.* 38:411-19
33. Fisher, D. F., Keen, S. L. 1972. Verbal recall as a function of personality characteristics. *J. Genet. Psychol.* 120:83-92
34. Fisher, S., Cleveland, S. E. 1958. *Body Image and Personality.* Princeton, NJ: Van Nostrand
35. Fitzgerald, B. J., Pasewark, R. A., Fleisher, S. 1974. Responses of an aged population on the Gerontological and Thematic Apperception Tests. *J. Pers. Assess.* 38:234-35
36. Friedman, R. J. 1972. TAT story length in children. *Psychol. Sch.* 9:411-12
37. Galinsky, M. D. 1971. Relationships among personality, defense, and academic failure. *J. Pers. Assess.* 35:359-63
38. Gamble, K. R. 1972. The Holtzman Inkblot Technique. *Psychol. Bull.* 77:172-94
39. Geist, H. 1971. Emotional aspects of dermatitis. *Proc. Ann. Conv. APA.* 6 (Pt 2):627-28
40. Goldfried, M. R., Stricker, G., Weiner, I. B. 1971. *Rorschach Handbook of Clinical and Research Applications.* Englewood Cliffs, NJ: Prentice-Hall. 436 pp.
41. Goldstein, H. S. 1972. Gender identity, stress and psychological differentiation in figure-drawing choice. *Percept. Mot. Skills* 35:127-32
42. Gravitz, M. A. 1971. Nudity and amount of clothing on the figure drawings of normal adults. *J. Genet. Psychol.* 118:141-45
43. Greenberg, R. P. 1972. Sexual bias on Rorschach administration. *J. Pers. Assess.* 36:336-39
44. Greenberg, R. P., Fisher, S. 1971. Some differential effects of music on projective and structured psychological tests. *Psychol. Rep.* 28:817-18
45. Greene, D. L., Winter, D. G. 1971. Motives, involvements, and leadership among black college students. *J. Pers.* 39:319-32
46. Hamilton, J., Blewett, D., Sydiaha, D. 1971. Ink-blot responses of identical and fraternal twins. *J. Genet. Psychol.* 119:37-41
47. Handler, L., McIntosh, J. 1971. Predicting aggression and withdrawal in children with the DAP and Bender-Gestalt. *J. Pers. Assess.* 35:331-35
48. Hanssen, S. V. Teigen, K. H. 1971. Sex differences on the group version of the HIT. *J. Clin. Psychol.* 27:378-82
49. Harris, D. B. 1972. The Draw-A-Person. See Ref. 17, 401-4
50. Hartlage, L. C. 1972. Common approaches to the measurement of anxiety. *Am. J. Psychiatry.* 128:1145-47
51. Hartman, A. A. 1970. A basic TAT set. *J. Proj. Tech. Pers. Assess.* 34:391-96
52. Hayslip, B. Jr., Darbes, A. 1974. Intrasubject response consistency of the Holtzman Inkblot Technique. *J. Pers. Assess.* 38:149-53
53. Heinrich, P., Triebe, J. K. 1972. Sex preferences in children's human figure drawings. *J. Pers. Assess.* 36:263-67
54. Hersen, M., Greaves, S. T. 1971. Rorschach productivity as related to verbal reinforcement. *J. Pers. Assess.* 35:436-41
55. Higdon, J. F., Brodsky, S. L. 1973. Validating hand test acting out ratios for overt and experimentally induced aggression. *J. Pers. Assess.* 37:363-68
56. Hill, E. F. 1972. *The Holtzman Inkblot Technique.* San Francisco: Jossey-Bass. 313 pp.
57. Hoar, M. W., Faust, W. L. 1973. The Children's Apperception Test: Puzzle and regular form. *J. Pers. Assess.* 37:244-47
58. Honor, S. H., Vane, J. R. 1972. Comparison of Thematic Apperception Test and questionnaire methods to obtain achievement attitudes of high-school boys. *J. Clin. Psychol.* 28:81-83

59. Horio, H. 1973. (A study of ego strength: Relationship between Barron's Es scale and RPRS.) *Jpn. J. Psychol.* 44:233–40
60. Howell, R. J., Carlisle, A. L. 1971. The effect of hypnotically induced and nonhypnotic mood changes on the Rorschach test. *Int. J. Clin. Exp. Hypn.* 19:28–36
61. Iacino, L. W., Cook, P. E. 1974. Threat of shock, state anxiety, and the Holtzman Inkblot Technique. *J. Pers. Assess.* 38:450–58
62. Irvin, F. S., Vander Woude, K. 1971. Empirical support for a basic TAT set. *J. Clin. Psychol.* 27:514–16
63. Jensen, D. E., Prandoni, J. R., Abudabbeh, N. N. 1971. Figure drawings by sex offenders and a random sample of offenders. *Percept. Mot. Skills* 32:295–300
64. Johnson, J. H. 1971. Upper left hand placement of human figure drawings as an indicator of anxiety. *J. Pers. Assess.* 35:336–37
65. Johnson, J. H. 1971. Note on the validity of Machover's indicators of anxiety. *Percept. Mot. Skills* 33:126
66. Kidd, A. H., Kidd, R. M. 1971. Relation of Holtzman scores to rigidity. *Percept. Mot. Skills* 32:1003–10
67. Klinger, E. 1973. Models, context, and achievement fantasy: Parametric studies and theoretical propositions. *J. Pers. Assess.* 37:25–47
68. Klopfer, W. G. 1968. Current status of the Rorschach Test. In *Advances in Psychological Assessment*, ed. P. McReynolds, 1:131–49. Palo Alto, Ca: Science and Behavior Books. 336 pp.
69. Knutson, J. F. 1972. Rorschach. See Ref. 17, 435–40
70. Kokonis, N. D. 1972. Body image disturbance in schizophrenia: A study of arms and feet. *J. Pers. Assess.* 36:573–75
71. Kokonis, N. D. 1972. Choice of gender on the DAP and measures of sex-role identification. *Percept. Mot. Skills* 35:727–30
72. Koscherak, S., Masling, J. 1972. Noblesse oblige effect: The interpretation of Rorschach responses as a function of ascribed social class. *J. Consult. Clin. Psychol.* 39:415–19
73. Lambley, P. 1973. Rorschach scores and schizophrenia: An evaluation of Weiner's signs in clinical practice. *J. Pers. Assess.* 37:420–23
74. Lester, D., Perdue, W. C. 1972. Suicide, homicide, and color-shading response on the Rorschach. *Percept. Mot. Skills* 35:562
75. Lester, D., Perdue, W. C. 1973. Movement responses of murderers to Rorschach stimuli. *Percept. Mot. Skills* 37:668
76. Lester, D., Perdue, W. C. 1974. Body image of murderers. *J. Gen. Psychol.* 90:187–89
77. Levitt, E. E., Truumaa, A. 1972. *The Rorschach Technique with Children and Adolescents.* New York: Grune & Stratton
78. Licko, L. 1971. (Some results of the Rorschach technique in children with the diagnosis of ulcus bulbi duoleni.) (Slok) *Psychol. Patopsychol. Dieata* 6:311–22
79. Liebetrau, C. E., Pienaar, W. D. 1974. The relation between adjustment and body image at various age levels. *J. Pers. Assess.* 38:230–33
80. Lingren, R. H. 1971. An attempted replication of emotional indicators in human drawings by shy and aggressive children. *Psychol. Rep.* 29:35–38
81. London, H., Schubert, D. S., Washburn, D. 1972. Increase of autonomic arousal by boredom. *J. Abnorm. Psychol.* 80:29–36
82. Louttit, C. M., Browne, C. G. 1947. The use of psychometric instruments in psychological clinics. *J. Consult. Psychol.* 11:49–54
83. Lubin, B., Wallis, R. R., Paine, C. 1971. Patterns of psychological test usage in United States: 1935–1969. *Prof. Psychol.* 2:70–74
84. Manganyi, N. C. 1972. Body image boundary differentiation and self-steering behavior in African paraplegics. *J. Pers. Assess.* 36:45–49
85. Manganyi, N. C. 1972. Projective stimulus ambiguity: Some theoretical and empirical considerations. *J. Pers. Assess.* 36:5–7
86. Martinez, M., Martinez, J., Malvarez, P., Gonnalex, J. 1972. (Influence on the TAT and CAT-A). (Span) *Rev. Psicol. Gen. Apl.* 27:501–7
87. Masling, J., Harris, S. 1969. Sexual aspects of TAT administration. *J. Consult. Clin. Psychol.* 33:166–69
88. McArthur, C. C. 1972. Rorschach. See Ref. 17, 440–43
89. McClelland, D. C. 1971. The power of positive drinking. *Psychol. Today* 4:40–41
90. McCully, R. S. 1971. *Rorschach Theory and Symbolism: A Jungian Approach to*

Clinical Material. Baltimore: Williams & Wilkins. 251 pp.

91. Melikian, L. H. 1972. First drawn picture and modernization. *J. Pers. Assess.* 36:576–80

92. Milner, J. S., Moses, T. H. 1974. Effects of administrator's gender on sexual content and productivity in the Rorschach. *J. Clin. Psychol.* 30:159–61

93. Molish, B. 1972. Projective methodologies. *Ann. Rev. Psychol.* 23:577–614

94. Murawski, B. J. 1971. Genetic factors in tests of perception and the Rorschach. *J. Genet. Psychol.* 119:43–52

95. Murstein, B. I. 1972. Normative written TAT responses for a college sample. *J. Pers. Assess.* 36:109–47

96. Murstein, B. I. 1972. A thematic test and the Rorschach in predicting marital choice. *J. Pers. Assess.* 36:213–17

97. Myler, B., Rosenkrantz, A., Holmes, G. 1972. A comparison of the TAT, CAT, and CAT-H among second grade girls. *J. Pers. Assess.* 36:440–44

98. Nathan, S. 1973. Body image in chronically obese children as reflected in figure drawings. *J. Pers. Assess.* 37:456–63

99. Nawas, M. M. 1971. Change in efficiency of ego functioning and complexity from adolescence to young adulthood. *Dev. Psychol.* 4:412–15

100. Neuringer, C. 1972. Suicide attempt and social isolation on the MAPS Test. *Life-Threatening Behavior.* 2:139–44

101. Neuringer, C. 1974. Suicide and the Rorschach: A rueful postscript. *J. Pers. Assess.* 38:535–39

102. Newmark, C. S., Finkelstein, M., Frerking, R. A. 1974. Comparison of the predictive validity of two measures of psychotherapy prognosis. *J. Pers. Assess.* 38:144–48

103. Newmark, C. S., Flournzano, R. 1973. Replication of an empirically derived TAT set with hospitalized psychiatric patients. *J. Pers. Assess.* 37:340–41

104. Newmark, C. S., Hetzel, W., Frerking, R. 1974. The effects of personality tests on state and trait anxiety. *J. Pers. Assess.* 38:17–20

105. Newmark, C. S., Hetzel, W., Walker, L., Holstein, S., Finkelstein, M. 1973. Predictive validity of the Rorschach Prognostic Rating Scale with behavior modification techniques. *J. Clin. Psychol.* 29:246–48

106. Newmark, C. S., Ray, J., Lyman, R. A. F., Paine, R. D. 1974. Test-induced anxiety as a function of psychopathology. *J. Clin. Psychol.* 30:261–64

107. O'Brien, R. P., Patton, W. F. 1974. Development of an objective scoring method for the Kinetic Family Drawing. *J. Pers. Assess.* 38:156–64

108. Olch, D. 1971. Personality characteristics of hemophiliacs. *J. Pers. Assess.* 35:72–79

109. Orloff, H. 1973. Thematic Apperception Test card rejection in a large sample of normal children. *Multivar. Behav. Res.* 8:63–70

110. Overall, J. E., Gorham, D. R. 1972. Organicity versus old age in objective and projective test performance. *J. Consult. Clin. Psychol.* 39:98–105

111. Paluszny, M., Zrull, J. P. 1971. The new missionary: A review of 50 candidates. *Arch. Gen. Psychiatry* 24:363–66

112. Perdue, W. C., Lester, D. 1972. Personality characteristics of rapists. *Percept. Mot. Skills* 35:514

113. Perdue, W. C., Lester, D. 1973. Those who murder kin: A Rorschach study. *Percept. Mot. Skills* 36:606

114. Potkay, C. R. 1971. *The Rorschach Clinician: A new Research Approach and Its Application.* New York: Grune & Stratton. 223 pp.

115. Prandoni, J. R., Jensen, D. E., Matranga, J. T., Waison, M. O. 1973. Selected Rorschach response characteristics of sex offenders. *J. Pers. Assess.* 37:334–36

116. Prytula, R. E., Leigh, G. G. 1972. Absolute and relative figure drawing size in institutionalized orphans. *J. Clin. Psychol.* 28:277–79

117. Prytula, R. E., Thompson, N. D. 1973. Analysis of emotional indicators in human figure drawings as related to self-esteem. *Percept. Mot. Skills* 37:795–802

118. Query, W. T., Query, J. M. 1972. Aggressive responses to the HIT by Indian and White alcoholics. *J. Cross-Cult. Psychol.* 3:413–16

119. Quinlan, D. M., Harrow, M., Tucker, G., Carlson, K. 1972. Varieties of "disordered" thinking on the Rorschach: Findings in schizophrenic and non-schizophrenic patients. *J. Abnorm. Psychol.* 79:47–53

120. Rabin, A. I. 1972. Rorschach. See Ref. 17, 443–46

121. Rand, T. M., Wagner, E. E. 1973. Correlations between Hand Test variables and patrolman performance. *Percept. Mot. Skills* 37:477–78

122. Raychaudhuri, M. 1971. Relation of creativity and sex to Rorschach M responses. *J. Pers. Assess.* 35:27–31

123. Reznikoff, M. 1972. Rorschach. See Ref. 17, 446–49
124. Rice, L. N., Gaylin, N. L. 1973. Personality processes reflected in client vocal style and Rorschach performance. *J. Consult. Clin. Psychol.* 40:133–38
125. Roback, H. B. 1974. Sex of free choice figure drawings by homosexual and heterosexual subjects. *J. Pers. Assess.* 38:154–55
126. Ryan, B. A., Boersma, F. J., Mills, D. H. 1971. A note on eye movements as a measure of emotional reactivity to chromatic elements in Rorschach stimuli. *J. Abnorm. Psychol.* 78:245–46
127. Schulman, D., Shontz, F. C. 1971. Body posture and thinking. *Percept. Mot. Skills* 32:27–33
128. Siskind, G. 1973. Sexual aspects of Thematic Apperception Test administration: A note on "mature clinicians." *J. Consult. Clin. Psychol.* 40:20–21
129. Solomon, D., Goodson, D. F. 1971. Hypnotic age regression evaluated against a criterion of prior performance. *Int. J. Clin. Exp. Hypn.* 19:243–59
130. Stavrianos, B. K. 1971. Can projective test measures aid in the detection and differential diagnosis of reading deficit? *J. Pers. Assess.* 35:80–91
131. Sundberg, N. D. 1961. The practice of psychological testing in clinical services in the United States. *Am. Psychol.* 16:79–83
132. Swartz, J. D., Cleland, C. C., Drew, C. J., Witzke, D. B. 1971. The Holtzman Inkblot Technique as a measure of perceptual development in mental retardation. *J. Pers. Assess.* 35:320–25
133. Teevan, R. C., Stamps, L. W. 1973. A motivational correlate of Viet Nam protest group members. *Psychol. Rep.* 33:777–78
134. Timsit, M. 1972. (Rorschach test and headaches.) (Fren) *Acta Psychiatr. Belg.* 72:96–116
135. Tolor, A., Tolor, B. 1974. Children's figure drawings and changing attitudes toward sex roles. *Psychol. Rep.* 34:343–49
136. Traxler, A., Swiener, R., Rogers, B. 1974. Use of the Gerontological Apperception Test (GAT) with community-dwelling and institutional aged. *Gerontologist* 14, Part II:52
137. Uleman, J. S. 1971. Awareness and motivation in generalized verbal conditioning. *J. Exp. Res. Pers.* 5:257–67
138. Uleman, J. S. 1971. Generalized verbal conditioning: Some motivational and retrospective awareness effects. *J. Exp. Res. Pers.* 5:268–77
139. Uleman, J. S. 1972. The need for influence: Development and validation of a measure, and comparison with the need for power. *Genet. Psychol. Monogr.* 85:157–214
140. Van Dyke, P. S. 1972. The Holtzman Inkblot Technique: A bibliography, 1956–1970. *Percept. Mot. Skills* 35:647–58
141. Wagner, E. E., Hoover, T. O. 1971. Exhibitionistic M in drama majors: A validation. *Percept. Mot. Skills* 32:125–26
142. Wagner, E. E., Hoover, T. O. 1972. Behavioral implications of Rorschach's human movement response: Further validation based on exhibitionistic Ms. *Percept. Mot. Skills* 35:27–30
143. Ward, J. 1973. Self identification in the Make-A-Picture Story protocols of a group of retarded boys. *Am. J. Ment. Defic.* 77:469–71
144. Watson, C. G., LaLiberte, M., Sellers, H. 1971. Personality correlates of DAP facial expression. *J. Clin. Psychol.* 27:115–17
145. Welman, A. J. 1971. (Neuropsychological examination of Parkison's disease patients—before and after thalomotomy.) (Germ) *Schweiz. Arch. Neurol. Neurochir. Psychiatr.* 108:175–88
146. Wiseman, R. J., Reyher, J. 1973. Hypnotically induced dreams using the Rorschach inkblots as stimuli: A test of Freud's theory of dreams. *J. Pers. Soc. Psychol.* 27:329–36
147. Witzke, D. B., Swartz, J. D., Drew, C. J. 1971. Level of perceptual development of normal adults as measured by the Holtzman Inkblot Technique. *Proc. Ann. Conv. APA* 6 (Part 2): 609–10
148. Wolk, R. L., Wolk, R. B. 1971. *The Gerontological Apperception Test.* New York: Behavioral Publ.

PROGRAM EVALUATION[1]   ❖264

Robert Perloff,[2] Evelyn Perloff,[3] and Edward Sussna[2]
University of Pittsburgh, Pittsburgh, Pennsylvania 15260

INTRODUCTORY PERSPECTIVES

Although this is the inaugural appearance of a chapter on program evaluation in the *Annual Review of Psychology,* our search as lay historians reveals that the first recorded instance of evaluation occurred when man, woman, and serpent were punished for having engaged in acts which apparently had not been among the objectives defined by the Program circumscribing their existence. Since that time an infinite spectrum of evaluation characterizes the relationships among individuals, groups, and institutions. Aside from the more traditional hard-nosed considerations characterizing accountability, the allocation of scarce resources, the construction of tough decisions that need to be made in order to choose among apparently equally attractive alternatives, and the esoteric challenges or caveats inherent in experimental design, it should be noted at the outset that a favorite pastime of all of us is in the overt (but more frequently covert) evaluation of each other and ourselves. Scarcely an hour goes by, let alone a day, for most of us when we do not engage in such evaluative activities as a determination of what or who is good or bad, valuable or worthless, nice or awful, fair or unfair, pleasant or unpleasant, happy or sad, or healthy or sick. Indeed, such bipolar descriptive scales as the foregoing, among others, constitute around 34% of the total variance of the semantic space and 69% of the common variance comprising the semantic differential scales developed by Osgood & Suci (86).

The ubiquity of evaluation is stressed here not frivolously, but rather to suggest that the idea of evaluation, of being evaluated, of evaluating someone or something, is so interwoven into our fundamental experience that it is scarcely surprising that we are so frequently vague in the language we use to describe program goals and at the same time so cocksure that we (think we) know what we mean by this loose language. Surely this must be one of the reasons why we have problems in being evaluated, in designing evaluation studies, and interpreting the outcomes of evalu-

[1]The authors gratefully acknowledge the assistance they received from Michael A. Belch, Bruce K. Gouldey, and Margaret L. Jonnet.
[2]Graduate School of Business, University of Pittsburgh.
[3]School of Nursing, University of Pittsburgh.

ation research. Therefore, while conventionally the role that is attributed to the psychologist in program evaluation is in the methodology for conducting evaluation research, we believe that perhaps a more significant role for the psychologist in program evaluation would be in providing those insights and remediation procedures necessary, we think, to disentangle the individual's personal involvement with evaluation from the organizational evaluations that he conducts or with an evaluation in which he himself is being evaluated.

Definitions

While illustrations of specific programs and of evaluation research methodologies will be presented later in this review, suffice it to say that by a *program* we mean a sponsored activity, more often than not from public funds, aimed at mitigating a social or economic problem in education, mental health, or the social and economic welfare of the individual. By *evaluation* conceived liberally we mean the determination of the extent to which a program achieved one or more of its objectives, the reasons it may not have achieved them, and the relationships among program effects and a variety of input variables and program characteristics.

There are many ways to evaluate a program, including judgment on the part of program management, satisfaction by the beneficiaries or consumers of the program, relating costs of a program to the benefits attributed to it where such benefit-cost analyses range from an anecdotal approach to a highly sophisticated amalgamation of econometrics and experimentation, and evaluation research. These routes toward evaluation are not necessarily mutually exclusive. For example, a benefit-cost analysis might well include a highly sophisticated experimental procedure for determining gains, benefits, or improvements. It is in this context that we view evaluation research, as one means—albeit a highly favored one among persons accustomed to making decisions rooted in analytical procedures—for evaluating programs.

By *evaluation research* we include a variety of empirically oriented research technologies, spanning the gamut from impressionistic procedures, clinical and observational procedures, field or survey methods, and an armamentarium of sophisticated research and quantitative procedures. While equal credence should not be placed on each one of these procedures, we include them in our definition descriptively, not normatively, because in this review we seek to encompass the variety of activities which at least some people designate as evaluation research, regardless of the robustness of a technique or the generalizability of its findings.

Organization of this Review

This review is organized into these sections: (*a*) the evolving multidiscipline of program evaluation; (*b*) approaches to and methodology in evaluation research; (*c*) selected issues in and examples of program evaluation; (*d*) the evaluability of programs; and (*e*) concluding observations.

Because of constraints of space and of audience definition we have chosen to cover selectively, not exhaustively, that literature and those orientations which are essentially psychological in nature, recognizing that there are many fields—health, for example—in which useful work is being done in program evaluation.

THE EVOLVING MULTIDISCIPLINE
OF PROGRAM EVALUATION

A review of the literature of and the individuals involved in program evaluation and evaluation research suggests that program evaluation as a multidiscipline flows from many fields and disciplines, including accounting, economics, education, industrial engineering, the management sciences, political science, psychology, sociology, statistics, urban affairs, and perhaps one or two others.

Recent History

Depending upon one's definition of history, program evaluation in a more or less formal manner originated in the mid-nineteenth century with the creation of what was to later become the US Office of Education (2), or in the development of social legislation predicted by Lester Ward in 1906 (28). Anderson et al (2) in their section on "evaluation history" and Caro (28) in his overview of evaluation research trace the variety of programs and problems to which evaluation efforts have been applied. Program evaluation approximating its present form really began with the development of programs started during the New Deal era of Franklin D. Roosevelt. While these programs over the years might be viewed in a shorthand fashion as involving schools and communities, the more specific range of problems for which programs have been funded and whose evaluation, primitively or comprehensively, have been conducted include alcoholism, drug addiction, education, health, housing, income maintenance, jobs, justice, juvenile delinquency, mental retardation, obesity, poverty, rehabilitation, and transportation. Most of these programs have been and are being funded by federal agencies, although some have been supported by private foundations and by the larger businesses and industries in the country. An instructive review of federal evaluation efforts is given by Buchanan & Wholey (21).

The Literature

Although the literature we cite reflects a wide array of journals in which articles on program evaluation and evaluation research appear, the one journal that stands out as being entirely and cohesively devoted to the area is *Evaluation*.

Among the representative and relatively recent books in program evaluation, one which we found to be invaluable in preparing this review is *Encyclopedia of Educational Evaluation* by Anderson et al (2). Important books dealing with theoretical and methodological issues concentrating for the main upon social experimentation or social action programs are those edited by Riecken & Boruch (100), Rossi & Williams (103), and by Suchman (117). Among the books in educational evaluation are those edited by Apple et al (3), Popham (97), Rippey (101), and Walberg (124). Covering topics in both education and social action is the book of readings edited by Weiss (128). Although Schulberg et al (107) are concerned in their book with evaluating health programs, there are a number of chapters which would be of interest to others as well, for example, those on research design and those dealing with evaluation techniques. Finally, Caro's (28) book of readings will quite likely find a wide audience because it is of general interest in much the same way as that by Anderson et al (2). Caro has aggregated chapters on scientific issues, evaluation technologies, measurement and design, pedagogies, and case materials, ranging from the implementation of evaluation research to case histories in the United States and abroad.

Incidentally, even though bits and pieces of programs have been developed and evaluated for more than 100 years, one earmark of the fledgling status of this area is that it was not until a scant 3 years ago, in the January 1973 issue of *Psychological Abstracts,* that "Program Evaluation" first appeared as an index term.

Organizations Concerned with Program Evaluation

Most of the programs that are cited in this chapter have been supported directly or indirectly by agencies in the federal government. An organization actively involved in conducting and evaluating program evaluations is the Urban Institute, a nonprofit research corporation in Washington DC. The Urban Institute has a series of publications covering impressively a multitude of topics in program evaluation. One of the Institute's recent publications (104) codifies the heterogeneity of uses or markets for program evaluation services and research, identifying an individual Consumer Market, including federal agencies carrying out their missions in developing and evaluating programs; the Program Management Market, focusing upon management's responsibility for program implementation; and a Policy Market, characterized as that set of managers engaged in debating policy issues and weighing what courses of action the government might take following an explication of program results.

Professional and scientific associations are becoming involved in program evaluation in many ways. For example, recognizing that professional and scientific associations must exercise leadership in helping to standardize procedures and provide guidelines for program evaluators, three professional societies are now planning what may develop into a joint committee on guidelines for evaluating educational programs. These societies are the American Educational Research Association, the American Psychological Association, and the National Council on Measurement and Education. Willo White (personal communication), of the Office of Scientific Affairs of the American Psychological Association, believes that a sufficiently strong ground swell of concern is present among these three associations to provide the support needed for the consummation of this joint committee's effort. This effort will take the form of a publication that will be the first of its kind in containing guidelines, caveats, and perhaps appraisals of specific procedures that will be of value to and welcomed by practitioners and researchers in program evaluation.

In December 1974, the Educational Testing Service sponsored, under contract with the Office of Naval Research, a three-day conference on the Evaluation of Education and Training Programs (9), bringing together a number of leaders in the field to hash out questions concerning evaluation as science and profession, the roles and requirements for evaluators, and consumer concerns and evaluation.

Selected Educational and Training Programs

Many program evaluation workshops and symposia have been sponsored by scientific and professional associations (16, 66, 93, 94, 110). Training institutes are also emerging. For example, a two-month annual summer institute in evaluation research was held in 1975 at the University of Massachusetts (113).

The recognition of the essentiality of rational guides for Congress in the passage of bills and the administration of public laws is evidenced by a number of special programs and publications (65). In May 1975, the Congressional Research Service of the Library of Congress sponsored a "Seminar Series on Legislative Oversight and Program Evaluation," to acquaint legislative staffs with the different requirements, processes, and resources in program evaluation.[4] There is also the "Evaluation Seminar,"[4] a once-a-month luncheon meeting conducted by Harrison Fox, a member of Senator William Brock's staff, to acquaint the legislative staffs of congress with ongoing work in program evaluation.

One characteristic differentiating a loose approach from a more disciplined approach to the solution of a problem is in the tightness of definitions used in specifying objectives, or in designating outcomes in programs, studies, or research. Hence, Horst et al (57) justifiably decry the use of vague and inadequate language in specifying the features of program intervention. What is meant, for example, by the "alienation," the "dependency," or the "community tensions" which some programs seek to mitigate? What do we mean by "good quality of life," by "improved mental health," or by "revitalized institutions"? In the same vein, Guttentag (47) admonishes program managers for their specification of such objectives as a desire "to live the good life," to "transport everyone as fast as possible from here to there," and to "minimize total transportation costs."

Two factors are militating to encourage the development of *formal* educational training programs. The first is the disenchantment with vague objectives spawning programs whose results are well nigh impossible to replicate. The second is the development of principles and methodologies which many feel are helping to shape the emerging multidiscipline of program evaluation. One such program is under the aegis of the department of psychology at Northwestern University (personal communication, Donald T. Campbell). There the doctorally oriented curriculum, while in psychology, has ties with other fields and disciplines, including industrial engineering, organizational behavior, sociology, and urban affairs. Additionally, Northwestern University has a postdoctoral program in program evaluation.

At this juncture it might be worthwhile to ask what are the unique features or the strengths indigenous to psychology that pose a challenge for psychology in making its contribution to program evaluation and evaluation research education. This issue is posed by Campbell (23) and by Campbell & Boneau (24). After suggesting that program evaluation is the embodiment of an interdisciplinary methodology which may spawn a new autonomous applied science, they suggest that psychology may be particularly equipped to contribute to program evaluation in that of all fields involved in program evaluation, psychology is the only one with a strong tradition in laboratory experimental training. While experimental design per se is no panacea, it does offer a procedure for linking causal inferences with program effectiveness interpretations. Furthermore, the psychophysical and psycho-

[4]Personal communication from Willo White, American Psychological Association.

metric traditions in psychology offer statistical procedures for estimating reliability, validity, and bias.

PROGRAM EVALUATION APPROACHES AND METHODOLOGIES

Five approaches or methodologies are presented in this section. The first concerns the values, preferences, or goals which must be explicated in order for the consumers of an evaluation to accept the results of an evaluation as being congruent with the values they impute to a program. Similarly, unless these values are operationally specified, no evaluation or research methodology can be expected to produce results that make sense. The second approach is more clearly identifiable as embracing procedures and schema identified with management needs and controls, including systems analysis and PERT. The third and fourth approaches, clinical and quasi-experimental, respectively, concern direct and specific involvement in gathering data and in determining ways in which this data collection and interpretation might produce minimally equivocal and optimally generalizable results. The final approach, benefit-cost analysis, in effect is the broadest of all and seeks to embrace in one overarching conceptual scheme the benefits (identified and measured, for example, through some clinical or quasi-experimental approach) of a program as moderated by the program's costs.

Values-Linked Approaches

GOAL-FREE VS GOAL-BASED EVALUATIONS   Scriven (109) distinguishes between goal-free evaluation and goal-based evaluation by pointing out that goal-free evaluation helps the evaluator observe and record a program's *actual* effects as opposed to its intended effects. Intended effects are relevant in evaluating a program proposal, while actual effects, including side effects or unintended effects, are more relevant in evaluating a program process or product.

FORMATIVE AND SUMMATIVE EVALUATIONS   Two kinds of program assessment are identified by Scriven (108): formative and summative evaluation. Formative evaluation is addressed to the evaluation of the process and products of a program being developed, while the summative approach speaks to the evaluation of the program's overall performance. One important operational distinction between formative and summative evaluation is that in the former approach program personnel and evaluation personnel must work together to achieve certain goals during the developmental stages of the program, while the individual engaged in summative evaluation needs to assume a more objectively Olympian posture in assaying a program's effectiveness, lest his involvement in the program itself co-opt his impartiality.

THE DECISION-THEORETIC APPROACH   A relatively new approach to program evaluation is the application of the decision-theoretic methodology for quantifying subjective expressions of values, preferences, or program outputs (36, 37, 46, 48, 49).

The principal advocate of the decision-theoretic approach to evaluation research is Marcia Guttentag, who proposes that because evaluation research does not appear to her and her cohorts as being congruent with the classical research paradigm, a procedure for systematically aggregating (via Bayesian statistics and utility theory) the value judgments of decision-makers is called for. Essentially the decision-theoretic approach that she recommends is that which has been proposed by Edwards (35). One might be encouraged to infer from the foregoing decision-theoretic articles that this approach is a substitute for the classical experimental designs which Guttentag finds wanting as a framework for conducting evaluation research. It is our judgment, however, that when a set of values or preferences is developed using the decision-theoretic approach, then some kind of design—nonexperimental, quasi-experimental, experimental, or what have you—is still required in order to link program effects (value criteria) with program treatments and other program charac-teristics, e.g. program environmental factors and client, patient, or student charac-teristics. It is our view, in a word, that the contribution of the decision-theoretic approach to evaluation research is its capability for helping in the development of criterion variables.

Some illustrations of where the decision-theoretic approach might be used, but which are not currently interpreted as being facilitated through the decision-theo-retic conceptualization, might be characterized as being consumer-linked. For ex-ample, Lebow's (69) suggestion that the patient's evaluations of medical care ought to be considered becomes all the more workable if the decision-theoretic methodol-ogy is utilized for aggregating patient assessments. Similarly, this approach might facilitate the quantification of needs assessments (59) eliciting the needs expressed by the consumers and users of programs.

There is still one other application of the decision-theoretic approach. Noble (84) suggests that peers be used not only in reviewing project proposals, but also for evaluating completed research. Similarly, in discussing evaluation approaches taken by the Ford Foundation, Goldmann (44) relates how outside consultants have helped them evaluate Foundation grants, suggesting to us that the decision-theoretic approach could help foundations consolidate consultant appraisals of the outcomes of foundation grants.

Management Oriented Approaches

Although enlightened management values analytical procedures, including re-search, as inputs for decision-making, there exist broader administrative blueprints, controls, and information systems which transcend evaluation research per se. Sometimes, for want of resources or sophistication, program evaluation manage-ment may not avail itself of evaluation research.

Among a variety of general management oriented approaches, one is selected for review (131) in which is proposed "three relatively inexpensive evaluation pro-cesses": *evaluability assessment,* providing a formal program definition, suggesting possible evaluation studies, and specifying management's perceived need for those studies; *rapid feedback assessment,* providing management with a preliminary as-sessment of the program and "with a set of options for future information purchases if the current knowledge base is judged inadequate"; and *performance monitoring,* providing the manager with "routine information showing how the program's measurable objectives are being achieved." A possibly attractive feature of this latter approach is that it permits the "program manager to purchase sequentially increasing amounts of reliable information on program intent, promise, expectations and performance."

THE SYSTEMS APPROACH   A variety of methods are extant using the paradigm of systems analysis (a procedure to aid the decision-maker in selecting an optimal course among many alternatives). One study (85), involving a university counseling center, used systems analysis for providing analyses on management and information flow, time and cost, and performance. Another (72), reports on a systems oriented procedure for evaluating mental health care programs' service delivery, yielding data concerning intake, individual case loads, and for any given patient data on his weekly progress. An application of systems analysis to special education programs (70) outlines five types of systems and discusses also feedback mechanisms, flow diagrams, logical operations, and conversion rules. The authors of a paper examining the systems approach to alcoholism programming (56) suggest that this approach is applicable to other mental health programs transcending alcoholism.

PROGRAM EVALUATION AND REVIEW TECHNIQUE   PERT is comprehensively described by Cook (30) with respect to its applications for evaluating educational programs. In his discussion of PERT (a technique for achieving program control over a diversity of program activities), Cook describes PERT's basic characteristics, shows how PERT is applicable to educational research and development projects, and describes a number of PERT implementation features. The strengths of PERT lie in its structured guidelines for helping to tie together a variety of program components, in giving overall program management the big picture so far as program progress is concerned, and in helping program personnel see how their tasks are related to the total program.

Clinical Approaches

Clinical approaches to program evaluation may be useful themselves in providing information as to a program's worth. Clinical approaches are also useful for ferreting out variables which in turn are utilized as part of another approach, for example, the decision-theoretic procedure described above or as part of the quasi-experimental methods referred to below.

A general treatment of the clinical approach to program evaluation is provided by Glaser & Backer (42), including subjective measurement methods, consultation, feedback, debriefing, and participant-observation. Because of the problems involved in evaluating treatments in the clinical setting where large groups are compared, the single-case experimental design (12) may be an appropriate procedure for examining complex behavioral disorders.

A number of other studies, proposals, and reasoned admonitions interface with clinical variables and with the involvement of or the effects upon the individual in the evaluation milieu. Johnson (60) proposes that the client may be involved in evaluating himself, and "in planning his own experiences, in receiving and giving feedback, and in socialization." Another individualistic approach asserts that "since there are few if any stimulus-response relationships in nature, psychologists must develop criteria for evaluating program success based on the experiences of the people in the setting rather than looking at such experiences as instrumental to some remote productivity criterion such as mental health, school progress, or income" (114).

DISTRUST, ANXIETY, AND FEAR OF BEING EVALUATED   Rogers & Roethlisberger (102) remind us that an impediment in interpersonal communication is the "tendency to evaluate." Relatedly, Weinstein (125) argues that the major "barrier to implementing program evaluation systems is not the lack of an adequate evaluation technology but rather lack of an adequate foundation of trust." He suggests also that psychological research in experimental games, source credibility, and interpersonal trust might generate guidelines for replacing distrust with trust.

Psychologists might apply to themselves ways for overcoming or at least reducing distrust to ameliorate, for example, the situation described by Page & Yates (88), who speak of the clinician's fear of evaluation and of his reluctance to participate in research. Perhaps another methodology for coping with the reluctance to be evaluated is one which, like unobtrusive measures (89), opts not to help build more trust but rather to avoid the issue by using procedures minimizing the evaluatee's awareness that he is the object of an evaluation. This may be akin to the engineering psychologist's philosophy in accepting man for what he is and working at changing environments and machines rather than changing individuals.

The Quasi-Experimental Design Approach

In order to have confidence that treatments of students in the classrooms, therapies for patients in clinics or hospitals, training programs for employees in industries, or intervention schemes for individuals in communities or social settings, are interpretable causally with the effects of these treatments, therapies, training, and interventions, an adequate design using appropriate control and randomization procedures needs to be developed. Because the classical experimental design is founded on assumptions which are generally viewed as inappropriate to most programs with whose evaluations we are here concerned, less demanding or quasi-experimental designs are championed by experimentally minded evaluation researchers.

The classical treatment examining experimental and quasi-experimental designs is the one developed by Campbell & Stanley (26). Other discussions (22, 25, 31, 100) of quasi-experimental evaluations extend the earlier Campbell & Stanley designs and design elements. In addition, Anderson et al (2) provide a valuable digest of quasi-experimental designs, in which three particular designs are discussed: time-series designs, pretest-postest nonequivalent group designs, and the regression-discontinuity design. Anderson et al (2) summarize well the position of the quasi-experimental camp:

> the weaker the evaluator's design control, the more important it is for him to collect *a broad range of data* by *multiple methods* from *multiple sources.* For example, if he suspects that home conditions may have as much to do with student achievement as the instructional program, he should attempt to measure home influence directly and take account of it as best he can in interpreting the evaluation results; and, if he must use subjective ratings about program effectiveness, he should try to obtain these ratings from several different groups involved in the program (instructors, students, and administrators, say) and supplement them with additional (and ideally nonreactive) kinds of measures that would appear to bear on the same question.

Since the literature in quasi-experimental designs is comparatively well known and has been discussed in different contexts in earlier volumes of the *Annual Review of Psychology,* and applications of the quasi-experimental design philosophy to educational and social programs are proliferating so rapidly, there is scarcely a need to rehash this material here, except to reiterate the fact that it is generally acknowledged by most of the individuals active in evaluation research that wherever possible and appropriate the quasi-experimental design route is the one to take in designing evaluation research studies. Among discussions concerning the applicability of quasi-experimental designs for evaluating service programs, the one by Deniston & Rosenstock (33) is of interest.

Benefit-Cost Analysis

One of the most widely used evaluation techniques in public programs in the United States and abroad is benefit-cost analysis. Within the United States, benefit-cost analysis is an integral part of many educational and health programs (34, 40, 54, 76, 120).

THE TECHNICAL CHARACTERISTICS OF BENEFIT-COST ANALYSIS   Ideally, benefit-cost analysis should be performed at a point where alternative public programs are being considered to meet specified objectives. Each program alternative may then be evaluated, with relevant costs and benefits specified on a program-by-program basis. The programs might very well be mutually exclusive alternatives; the one that offered the highest benefit-to-cost ratio, given a ratio of greater than one, would be implemented. Clearly, later evaluation of an ongoing program would make sense only to the extent that some modification in the program was contemplated.

THE CALCULATION OF PROGRAM COSTS   A program "costs" the community to the extent that an alternative expenditure is thereby foreclosed. Cost analysis is deeply rooted in the proposition that the resources available typically are limited, in relation to the number of potentially desirable public programs. Expressing the costs of proposed programs in some easily understood and common measurement, such as dollars, facilitates difficult choices. At the outset, all program costs are relevant. For an ongoing program, however, certain costs ought not to be reckoned, concerning which the definition and relevance of various cost categories are of great importance (54, 116).

Cost effectiveness is a considerably more comprehensive term than such specific ones, for example, as capital costs and operating costs. Cost effectiveness is concerned with achieving a set of program objectives, stated in both quantitative and qualitative terms, at *least cost.* Such analysis is undertaken when program output cannot be reasonably stated in monetary terms (76, 116). As a practical matter, most public services are provided at zero price or at a less-than-cost price to users; placing a monetary value on such services is at best judgmental and at worst inane (8, 52).

THE ANALYSIS OF PROGRAM BENEFITS Program benefits represent the value of the output of a given set of services to the community. Such output might be the configuration of national defense activities and its value to the public. Or it might be the value of a mental health facility to the community which it serves (18). It is no trivial task to identify the output of a complex public institution, be it a university, hospital, or criminal justice system (7, 64, 80). It is even more complicated to place a monetary value on these outputs. The argument for placing a monetary value on public services is not ideological; in fact, any measure which facilitates comparison with corresponding program costs is satisfactory. But costs are typically stated in dollars, and there are no simple alternatives to such a widely used gauge of the costs and benefits of public programs.

Externalities The primary reason that the government provides certain services in an otherwise private market society is that these services will not be forthcoming on the usual profit-oriented basis. A typical characteristic of a public service is that there are externalities, or "spillover" effects (78). These are effects which are incurred by third parties, i.e. persons not directly involved in a private transaction. These effects may be positive, as is frequently claimed for education, or negative, as in pollution. Externality benefits to the total community have been cited frequently as the basis for public support of education at all levels, including (*a*) increased income to persons other than students, (*b*) increased income to subsequent generations, (*c*) more efficient discovery and cultivation of human talents, (*d*) increased occupational mobility within the labor force, (*e*) an environment which stimulates scientific research, (*f*) reduction in antisocial behavior, (*g*) fostering of political and social stability, and (*h*) widening of personal interests, esthetic and otherwise, and the personal growth and satisfaction which that implies (126).

It is fair to say that some or all of these spillover effects exist as benefits to society, but the total value of these externalities may be overstated, particularly at higher educational or very specialized institutions (17).

In the health field, one can appreciate externalities in many public health activities, e.g. immunization of some part of the community reduces the probability of being diseased for other members (76).

Community welfare function If in fact there are positive externalities, the benefits of a given public program will be distributed extensively across society. In a strict sense, the benefits of a *private* service are designated in monetary terms as a normal procedure. However, neither the direct nor the indirect beneficiary of a *public* service is likely to pay anything like the full cost of that service. Some public services involve a user charge, e.g. tuition at a state university, the fare on an Amtrak train, or the fee at a clinic, but these charges are invariably less than the cost of service. And the indirect beneficiary of such a service pays no user charge at all (although he may be paying taxes to support that service). The problem then is to determine what value to place on a public service, such that the outputs of alternative services may be measured against each other.

A vexing issue is the aggregation of individual consumer preference functions to arrive at a community welfare function, i.e. the value that the community places on a given type and level of service. Kenneth Arrow's (4) work (since called the "Arrow Paradox") illustrates the problem of aggregating individual choices, where, for example, when considering the preferences of three individuals among three objectives, we seemingly cannot reach an unambiguous majority decision.

Although there appears to be no simple way in which the rather logically and unequivocally stated preferences of individual citizens may be translated into an acceptable collective agreement, literature is now appearing suggesting ways in which "Arrow's Paradox" can be overcome. The basic issues relate to voting rules, i.e. who shall vote on a collective decision and how many votes should each voter have (36, 37, 46, 48, 49, 99). These schemes will be recognized, of course, as the decision-theoretic approach discussed earlier in this section.

COMPARISON OF BENEFITS AND COSTS   Formulas exist (52, 121) for ascertaining the rate of return, over years, for a given program whose annual benefits and costs are specified. Hence the final evaluation of a program is a function of its rate of return compared to rates of return for alternative programs.

Where benefits are not available, at least where they cannot be stated in monetary terms, the emphasis falls on costs. Cost effectiveness then is used as the evaluative technique, and various configurations of resource allocation (implied by alternative programs) to achieve a given set of program objectives are examined. That program which achieves objectives at least cost is the preferred program.

SELECTED ISSUES AND EXAMPLES

Issues inherent in specific programs and of evaluated programs are categorized as *service, educational and training,* and *miscellaneous programs.*

Service Programs

MENTAL HEALTH AND PSYCHIATRIC SERVICES   Not unexpectedly, an enormous number of studies involve mental health centers and other facilities, including hospitals, which deal with a variety of psychological and psychiatric problems. *Guidelines for Evaluation of Continuing Education Programs in Mental Health* (81), developed under the aegis of the National Clearinghouse for Mental Health Information of the National Institute of Health, presents material on the background and meaning of evaluation and guideline charts for evaluation. A number of other general expositions are of interest, including a criticism (20) of the Nader report of mental health centers because it bases its conclusions on an inadequately small number of visits to operating centers, and a review of selected services of a county Mental Health/Mental Retardation program (15).

Complementing these foregoing more or less overall evaluative activities, there is a torrent of studies dealing with specific problem areas. We will refer to four of these.

One study examines a number of programs designed to provide behavioral treatment of obesity and reviews these programs in terms of design adequacy and outcomes (50). Recommendations for organizing and evaluating day care services (53) include a number of day care evaluative criteria. A short-term follow-up evaluation of a mental health program (98), emphasizing "family and community involvement in treatment, discharge planning, and aftercare," showed for the treatment group a 19% return rate within one year after termination of treatment, as opposed to a 61% incidence of recidivism for the control group receiving regular hospital treatment rather than the aforementioned family and community involvement treatment. The fourth example of special mental health evaluation programs suggests an interesting independent variable that might well be of value in a number of evaluation research studies (14). This variable is labeled "effort expended" in seeking treatment and is operationalized in terms of two distance measures, the actual mileage involved in traveling to the treatment center and "psychological distance," showing that "length of hospitalization was related to both distance measures curvilinearly, whereas only psychological distance had an effect on ratings improvement."

An influential source of information about a psychiatric treatment program, both for prospective patients and staff, is the published program description. One procedure for evaluating the accuracy of such descriptions is COPES, the Community-Oriented Programs Environment Scale, reported by Otto & Moos (87), containing subscales for measuring program involvement, support, spontaneity, autonomy, practical orientation, personal problem orientation, anger and aggression, order and organization, program clarity, and staff control.

EXPEDITIOUS INTERVENTION ACCESSES   A spate of facilities for treating expeditiously a variety of problems in a short-term manner, either because of the emergency nature of the situation or the scarcity of facilities in proportion to the number of potential clients, has developed in the past few years. An effort to evaluate psychiatric emergency services over a decade (136) showed a threefold admissions increase in the decade studied. Several categories for evaluating a telephone counseling service are suggested (71) in order to determine the efficiency and effectiveness of telephone counseling. A critique for evaluating crisis intervention programs (75) highlights a variety of crisis intervention parameters. Two studies (73, 79) are directed at suicide prevention accesses.

REHABILITATION PROGRAMS   A number of general discussions (51) appear in the rehabilitation literature. Examining data for 697,407 clients in 54 rehabilitation programs in 1968–69, Kunce, Miller & Cope (68) concluded that "agencies have a higher rehabilitation rate if they serve a large number of cases, have sufficient financial resources, spend more money on workshops than on training, and keep clients a shorter time in active service," and admonish rehabilitation agency evaluators against the use of a single output criterion of agency performance, since this may result in an injudicious appraisal of agency effectiveness. Perloff (90) describes a vocational rehabilitation center follow-up study describing that center's client population and assessing the outcomes of recommendations made for clients in the center's vocational rehabilitation program, concluding that while no demographic factors were found relating to outcomes, there were certain differences among clients on the basis of specific disability classifications.

Alcoholic programs   Guidelines and literature reviews for evaluating alcoholic treatment programs are available (32, 83, 105, 106). More specifically, there are studies addressed to particular programs and populations, one (132) comparing behavior therapy with a traditional approach, and another (112) examining three alcoholism rehabilitation programs for American Indians.

Drug programs   Brown (19), proposing a research model for evaluating narcotics treatment programs, ponders the validity of three measures of treatment effects: absence of drug use, degrees of arrests, or evidence of legitimate employment activities. Three methadone oriented drug withdrawal programs are selected for review. Einstein & Garitano (38), evaluating the methadone treatment process, differentiate between treatment and therapy. Sells & Watson (111) compare programs oriented toward prolonged maintenance with those disposed toward narcotic-free rehabilitation. A large-scale empirical study reported by Goldstein (45) examines the outcomes of a methadone program in California. Patients were assigned randomly and concurrently to comparison groups and evaluated by such comparison criteria as urine tests, clinical attendance, time in jail, survivors in the program, employment, and physical and mental symptoms. Little effect was observed with respect to level of dosage; at higher dosage levels, however, most subjects across all comparison groups tended to stop using heroin faster and reported more drowsiness, constipation, and impotence. From these results Goldstein draws inferences concerning (*a*) the planning and administration of methadone programs and (*b*) procedures for methadone withdrawal.

Ex-offenders   Just for illustrative purposes we cite one evaluation effort involving ex-offenders. This concerns halfway houses for inmates, suggesting that one "major shortcoming of halfway houses has been their failure to discriminate systematically for treatment purposes between the types of offenders in the programs (e.g. the inclusion of drug addicts in houses for general offenders)." Several issues relevant to the evaluation of the halfway house have been overlooked, including the nature of population served, administrative complications, staff training, and program design. These issues bear upon or may have contributed to the high rates of recidivism noted for halfway house residents (118).

Educational and Training Programs

Astin's possibly classic treatment of methodological issues bearing upon college impact studies (5, 6) should not be overlooked for its relevance to other evaluation research applications. Among other contributions, Astin suggests, as Kaiser (63) proposed earlier, that Type III (supplementing the traditional Types I & II) errors occur because a null hypothesis which is true is rejected at the same time that (implicitly) a null hypothesis which is false is accepted. Of general interest also is Stake's (115) contribution to curriculum evaluation.

HIGHER EDUCATION   The Center for Research and Development in Higher Education (55) describes a study in which institutions of higher learning seek to evaluate how they fare in their own evaluation and evaluation research efforts. Among the evaluation problem areas the respondents feel need the most work and attention are evaluating the effectiveness of new programs and developing cost effectiveness measures. Although most of the institutions reporting their experiences in this study have some form of evaluation mechanism, a question arises as to "whether the political 'clout' of the office doing the evaluation is such that people will listen to the recommendations of the evaluation specialist." *Déjà vu*?

The benefits of higher education   Student benefits are immediate (the consumption value to a consumer) and delayed, e.g. investment in increased lifetime earnings (13, 17, 52, 62, 121). The basic approach for determining the value of education is to estimate the economic return, as expressed in differences in lifetime earnings, of alternative levels of education, *ceteris paribus*. How much more is a college degree worth than a high-school diploma? A (prestigious) law degree than a (garden-variety) baccalaureate degree? While acknowledged is the spectrum of benefits to both the student and the community subsidizing his education, we focus on one benefit, perhaps in the belief that if the evaluation shows that the outlays on education are justified narrowly, all other benefits may represent a bonus. A critical issue from an evaluation standpoint is to isolate the value of education from many other factors (e.g. genetic, environmental, demographic) which are likely to influence lifetime earnings (77, 122, 127). This so-called "human capital" approach to evaluation of higher education treats expenditures on schooling as an investment, where a rate of return is calculated as in the case of a private business investment in any long-termed object, e.g. a new plant or piece of durable equipment. It may take many years for an educational investment to provide a stream of increased lifetime earnings large enough to justify the costs of incremental schooling. There is also growing concern with the issue of whether a demonstrated high rate of return for past or current students is likely to continue into the indefinite future for indefinite numbers of students.

We have no simple way of measuring the value of nonearnings benefits of education (95). How can we determine the value that a student places on the consumption of education, i.e. the satisfactions he receives from college attendance were there to be no increase in his expected lifetime earnings? Indeed, for some students the consumption value might well be negative. The point is that probably we cannot now make an empirical determination of the consumption value of college, because students pay far less than the cost of that education. In short, the preoccupation with establishing the benefits of education as increased lifetime earnings almost certainly understates the full benefits of college attendance.

Evaluating teachers and courses   The robustness over time of student evaluations is suggested by French-Lazovik (41), reporting on two similarly designed studies conducted 15 years apart (1956–57 and 1971–72) at two different universities. Described also (91) is a 5-year evaluation of the impact of a large summer institute program for high school teachers.

Zelanak & Snider (135), using an instrument similar to the semantic differential, report (not surprisingly) that "those teachers who believe the intent of evaluation is for administrative purposes have negative feelings toward the evaluation process," while (again predictably) evaluation is viewed positively by those teachers interpreting nonpejoratively the evaluation process as an instructional handmaiden. This creates a frequently observed dilemma in evaluation research. If the results of evaluation studies are not to be used administratively in improving or modifying the performance of institutional personnel, then a legitimate question is raised as to why they should be done in the first place. On the other hand, knowledge that sanctions will be applied is bound to affect the way individuals respond to evaluation inquiries, raising serious questions about the validity of the data gathered and a variety of other contaminating factors which may not be easily accounted for using even the best experimental designs, given the constraints of nonlaboratory, field studies. Perhaps some compromise solution is in order, for example, allowing a reasonably comfortable time for teachers to "shape up" before sanctions are applied. Those who are not able to "correct" their behavior quickly could be given more adequate remedial time, while those who preferred not to change or who were unable to do so might be given different assignments within the same institution or appropriate counseling to look for other employment where the demands of the job are more compatible with their values, styles, and/or capabilities.

EARLY CHILDHOOD   According to Tomlinson (123), the psychological services in a large metropolitan school district seem to pay off, judging from the report that 85% of the psychological recommendations made were in fact implemented, and that of that number a significant behavioral change occurred in 80% of the cases. Peters (96) contemplates "ethical considerations in the evaluation and dissemination of early childhood education program information, including professional standards and the credibility of evaluation research," while guidelines for evaluating early childhood education programs are advanced by Elliott (39).

Miscellaneous Programs

Now we should like to consider program evaluation methodologies and conceptualizing for programs transcending the traditional human services and educational settings we have surveyed thus far.

MANPOWER UTILIZATION   Traditional personnel selection programs (74) are evaluated against the yardstick of effective manpower utilization. Wilson & Tatge (133) scrutinize the relationship between the "assessment center" and more traditional methods for selecting and utilizing managerial personnel. Sultan & Virgo (119) present an equity model for evaluating a public employment service program.

RESEARCH PROGRAMS   Psychologists pride themselves in their devotion to research and their methodological skills in conducting field and laboratory research. Why not apply program evaluation methodology to the assessment of our research outputs? For example, Cartwright (29) reviews the considerable literature on the risky shift phenomenon, while Jones (61) compares two social psychological theories for relating self- and interpersonal evaluations. While it may be stretching the capabilities of program evaluation methodology somewhat to seek to make applications to the evaluation of *research programs,* if program evaluation is good for the goose (others) why should it not be good for the gander (ourselves)? Specifically, the various methodologies for achieving evaluations referred to under our section on program evaluation approaches and methodologies should apply to the evaluation of our own research programs.

THE EVALUABILITY OF PROGRAMS

Before the evaluation process is set in motion it must first be established that the structure or the management of a program will permit a judicious evaluation in the first place. Some observers opine, moreover, that human service programs are too difficult and expensive to evaluate (137). Less pessimistically, but still cognizant of the "between the cup and the lip" phenomenon, Weiss (129) probes a number of organizational constraints which make evaluation research frustrating at best and uninterpretable at worst.

While the literature in this area is sparse, this section will depict provisionally (*a*) program characteristics alleged to facilitate or inhibit evaluability, that is, the degree to (or ways in) which a program is capable of being evaluated; and (*b*) characteristics of successful in contrast to less or (un)successful programs.

Facilitators and Inhibitors

Time considerations are crucial. When shall an evaluation be made? At what point temporally shall measurements of change or progress be made? If the managerial or statutory requirements of a program mandate that data be gathered too early, then the effects will not have had an opportunity to become manifest, yielding (according to the investigator's decision rule) a Type II error or quite possibly a Type I error if changes are in fact noted early but become quickly extinguished. On the other hand, if observations are made later than at an optimally earlier (but not too early) point in time, Type I or Type II errors might be similarly the price the evaluator pays for an unwise temporal decision. Goldmann (44), reviewing Ford Foundation evaluation activities, observes:

it takes a great deal of time and frustration before it can be determined whether a project has a chance to succeed in a volatile community. Despite the most auspicious array of prestige and resources, for example, the Bedford-Stuyvesant Restoration Corp. had a disastrous start. But some experienced heads prevailed, it got a second chance, and it took hold.

Kubie (67) confronts "the difficulties of estimating the outcome of any slow process of maturation in education and in all psychiatric therapies," exhorting evaluators that "any process of change which may be initiated during a period of active therapy or education may not become active until the period of direct intervention has terminated."

Horst et al (57) designate essentially two structural impediments to program evaluation: (*a*) problems or desired outcomes too inadequately or illogically defined to be measurable; and (*b*) the absence of management motivation, ability, or authority to implement evaluation measurements. The foregoing impediments are extended and amplified in considerable detail in a later report (58).

In his account of Ford Foundation evaluation activities, Goldmann (44) notes that (*a*) "it usually takes special people who blend charisma, managerial skills, and a talent for the politics of social change to get a project underway"; and (*b*) "grants to individual scholars or to institutions where the individual scholar is substantively involved and committed to the project tend to be more successful than awards to big institutions that are administered impersonally."

Characteristics of Successful and Less Successful Projects

The material in this section stems from the study by Glaser & Taylor (43), analyzing 10 NIMH studies, five of which were rated as very high and five as low by NIMH's Applied Research Branch. This study was an intensive follow-up program of these 10 projects, with the view of ascertaining the "more subtle and complex reasons underlying success or failure."

The highlights of this study are aligned with six project life cycle stages distinguished by Glaser & Taylor: (*a*) the *idea* spearheading the project, (*b*) project *design*, (*c*) *funding*, (*d*) *research*, (*e*) research *findings* and *dissemination*, and (*f*) *use* of the findings.

IDEA Successful projects were more openly and energetically active in soliciting genuine criticisms of, and involvement by others with, their original conceptualizations than was the case with less successful projects. Successful projects related more frequently and cooperatively with community agency and host agency personnel than the less successful projects.

DESIGN Generally, successful project designs and proposals were prepared by a principal investigator sufficiently involved and motivated to engage in two-way communication at the risk of inviting conflict or confrontation, as opposed to relatively calm and passive design involvements and environments encouraged by the less successful projects, concerning which the authors hypothesize that "An untroubled and superficially harmonious beginning may be a poor augury rather than a good one. It may be that people do not know nor care enough to raise issues during the early stages."

FUNDING   Successful projects more often than less successful ones had their NIMH grants augmented from other sources. Successful projects were more apt than the less successful ones to acquire the "consultative services of their respective NIMH regional offices before or during the process" of fund application.

RESEARCH   Successful projects were more eager to seek and use consultation concerning the research process itself as the investigation was in process than did the less successful projects. The principal investigator of the more successful projects "negotiated differences and attempted to clear up misunderstandings with persons who were hostile or uncooperative" as opposed to the less successful projects whose researchers perceived only their own "involvement in vital research and failed to see the other person's situation or consider possible alternative courses of action."

RESEARCH FINDINGS AND DISSEMINATION   Successful projects disseminated their findings more widely in terms of publications and workshops than the less successful projects. The less successful projects, failing to interact broadly beyond their own project turfs, were therefore unable to attract a sufficiently informed and committed constituency, as opposed to the more successful project, for encouraging the dissemination of research findings.

UTILIZATION   There were more instances in which the more successful projects had their findings utilized by practitioners and researchers than was observed for the less successful projects.

CONCLUDING OBSERVATIONS

Since program evaluation is still clearly in its infancy as a field of study and is yet to achieve the cohesion and the tautness expected in a multidiscipline field, let alone a unitary discipline, it would be presumptuous, prodigal, and even disruptive to wrap up the field in a neat package, pontificating upon its past and prescribing its future. Rather, we will confine our observations in this final section to (a) an ethical caveat, (b) policy and politics, and (c) selected implications for psychology.

An Ethical Caveat

While negative or ambivalent results are troublesome, disappointing, or frustrating in any research area, the failure to show effects stemming from the investment of massive resources has especially serious consequences in programmatic efforts to introduce social or educational interventions intended to minimize inequality, diminish recidivism, reduce squalor, or in other ways improve the human condition by replacing illness, misery, and ignorance with health, happiness, and knowledge. Pedestrian as this sounds, still it is goals like these, operationally and measurably defined to be sure, to which the mammoth programs originating during the New Deal and continued by the Great Society and War Against Poverty administrations were addressed.

The problem is this. What happens if evaluation research—quite possibly inadequately designed—shows no results? All hell breaks loose when the public infers that expensive treatments (purportedly) make no difference. If housing programs do not appear to work as judged against specified criteria, do we conclude that the intended beneficiaries are unable to cope with the indoor toilets, bathtubs, and other trappings constituting genteel residential decor? Suppose huge infusions of the latest teaching methods and curricular innovations do not produce higher achievement or reading scores for a group of disadvantaged pupils when compared with a control group consisting of pupils drawn (but maybe not randomly or to account for the Hawthorne effect—ah, there's the rub?) from the same population. Do we then conclude that nothing can be done for these disadvantaged pupils, that they were "born" that way, that it is their fault that they cannot learn and profit from the marvels of educational research, psychology, and fancy hardware and gadgetry? Or consider the case where epileptics or the mentally retarded (or individuals afflicted with both maladies—sometimes nature is callous and cruel) do not seem to profit from a rehabilitation program. To this do we react by declaring that this is the nature of the epileptic and the mentally retarded, which only goes to prove the futility of throwing good money after bad?

The point is this: Balanced against the scientist's responsibility to search for and disseminate truth, and the importance of publishing results—negative, positive, or ambivalent—are the *consequences* (27, 134) of such dissemination. One consequence is the cessation of program funds—not a bad decision *if* the results are solid and replicable, but it still could be an *unwise* decision. Another is the attribution of blame to the intended beneficiary of the intervention, that in fact the program failed because the individual was incapable of being helped.

What is the answer? We do not know, except to suggest that if this is not an ethical issue—and it may not be—it certainly is a humanitarian one. Caveat researcher.

Policy and Politics

The political and policy interfaces, or more correctly the determiners, of program evaluation and hence of evaluation research have been variously documented and discussed (10, 11, 130). One political dimension braided with the politics of program evaluation concerns the importance of recognizing and doing something about individual and organizational entrenchments, and hence of engaging in those activities which promise to overcome resistance to—and hence facilitate—change (82).

There is one item, however, deserving special attention in the program evaluation policy ball park (some might dub it a bullring), a matter which does not seem to have been addressed with sufficient vigor to make an impact. We refer to the proportion of program evaluation funds allocated for evaluation and evaluation research.

THE "1% FOR EVALUATION" CANON   Achieving the status of gospel in the program evaluation community is the allocation of around 1% of a program's funds for the evaluation of that program. A multitude of pronouncements of this gospel is available, but only two are cited here, one for a private foundation (44) and the other for a federal agency (58). In this context, even recalling that beggars cannot be choosers or that the evaluation researcher should not look a bureaucratic gift horse in the mouth, we wish to stress our belief that while 1% may not be an inadequate amount—nor do we aver that it is adequate—for large-scale *programmatic* research, it is our fear that program policymakers may begin to view 1% as an adequate amount for *all* projects or programs, regardless of size. For example, considering Head Start, a $100 million national program, 1%, or $1 million, may be fine for evaluation. But consider a more "modest" program, funded at the "penurious" level of but $1 million; for this program 1% for evaluation, let alone evaluation *research,* comes to the munificent sum of $10,000. How far will $10,000 go in evaluating a $1 million program? More discouragingly, $5,000 for evaluating a $500,000 program would neither pay for a good secretary nor for data processing.

It is our judgment that while 1% for evaluation may be adequate for programs whose magnitude are congruent say, with Head Start, for the rest of us toiling in the provinces and evaluating financially less auspicious programs, perhaps a more judicious guideline might be offered. A larger percentage (e.g. 10% for a $100,000 program yields $10,000 which, while not much, is certainly preferable to the measly $1,000 the 1% "rule" would allow) would seem to be in order, but better still an amount negotiated between the program administration and the evaluation researcher on the basis of how much money is reasonably needed to implement a respectable research design capable of rendering at least minimally acceptable evaluation research.

Implications for Psychology

EVALUATING PSYCHOLOGY'S TRAINING MODELS   If psychologists look outward to apply their skills in evaluating programs and other domains, it would seem reasonable to look to program evaluation methodology for evaluating their own programs. For example, data doubtlessly exist for following up a large number of psychologists trained in a variety of academic settings. This follow-up might well reinforce or dispute the contention of Albee & Loeffler (1) that "separate professional training schools for psychology must be established, following the historically evolving model provided by other professions, to eliminate role conflicts and make clear the essential division of labor" between the psychologist as a scientist and the psychologist as a professional.

OPPORTUNITIES FOR PSYCHOLOGISTS   No one in the sciences and professions needs to be sledgehammered by the fact that in many fields declining birth rates and shrinking resources sought by aggressive importuners from all quarters have contributed to a grievous excess of the supply of scientists and professionals over the demand for this highly trained manpower pool. Therefore it behooves say, the psychologist, to sharpen his alertness to opportunities for helping public agencies and others to interpret wherever appropriate agency requirements so that they begin to appreciate the fact that more of their needs than they had previously envisioned might be satisfied through the utilization of psychologists (92). A cogent and perhaps even a striking example of such utilization is, we believe, the contribution that psychologists can make to, not to mention others like economists who have been more traditionally viewed as resources for, program evaluation and evaluation research.

Psychologists, arise! Reach for more of program evaluation's shiny brass rings. In so doing you may not only help to create more jobs for your younger cohorts now receiving their doctoral degrees and facing bleak job prospects, but also, as Wortman (134) points out, awaiting you are opportunities in program evaluation for useful and exciting research horizons in clinical, educational, experimental, industrial, measurement, and social psychology.

Literature Cited

1. Albee, G. W., Loeffler, E. 1971. Role conflicts in psychology and their implications for a reevaluation of training models. *Can. Psychol.* 12:465–81
2. Anderson, S. B., Ball, S., Murphy, R. T., Associates 1975. *Encyclopedia of Educational Evaluation.* San Francisco: Jossey-Bass. 515 pp.
3. Apple, M. W., Subkoviak, M. J., Lufler, H. S., Eds. 1974. *Educational Evaluation: Analysis and Responsibility.* Berkeley, Calif.: McCutchan. 330 pp.
4. Arrow, K. 1963. *Social Choice and Individual Values.* New York: Wiley. 124 pp.
5. Astin, A. W. 1970. The methodology of research on college impact, I. *Sociol. Educ.* 43:223–54
6. Ibid. The methodology of research on college impact, II, 437–50
7. Astin, A. W. 1974. Measuring the outcomes of higher education. *New Dir. Inst. Res.* 1:23–46
8. Azzi, C. F., Cox, J. C. 1974. Shadow prices in public program evaluation models. *Q. J. Econ.* 88:158–65
9. Ball, S., Anderson, S. B. 1975. *Professional Issues in the Evaluation of Educational/Training Programs.* Office Nav. Res. Rep. Contract No. N 0014-72-C-0433, NR154-359. In press
10. Banner, D. K. 1974. The politics of evaluation research. *Omega* 2:763–74
11. Banner, D. K., Doctors, S. I., Gordon, A. C. 1975. *The Politics of Social Evaluation.* Cambridge, Mass.: Ballinger. 170 pp.
12. Barlow, D. H., Hersen, M. 1973. Single-case experimental designs: Uses in applied clinical research. *Arch. Gen. Psychiatry* 29:319–25
13. Becker, G. 1964. *Human Capital: A Theoretical and Empirical Analysis, with Special Reference to Education.* New York: Natl. Bur. Econ. Res. 187 pp.
14. Beutler, L. E., Johnson, D. T., Neville, C. W., Workmann, S. N. 1972. Effort expended in seeking treatment as a determiner of treatment evaluation and outcome: The honor of a prophet in his own country. *J. Consult. Clin. Psychol.* 39:495–500
15. Birnberg, J. G., Perloff, R., Sussna, E. 1974. *1974 Utilization Review of Selected Services of the County of Butler MH/MR Program.* Butler County, Pa., Public Doc. 43 pp.
16. Birnberg, J. G., Perloff, R., Sussna, E. 1975. *An interdisciplinary approach to periodic program evaluation of public services.* Presented at Inst. Manage. Sci., Chicago
17. Blaug, M. 1970. *An Introduction to the Economics of Education.* Baltimore: Penguin. 363 pp.
18. Bolin, D. C., Kivens, L. 1974. Evaluation in a community mental health center: Huntsville, Ala. *Evaluation* 2:26–35
19. Brown, B. S. 1974. The role of the research in a narcotics treatment program. *Drug Forum* 3:173–82
20. Brown, B. S. 1972. A look at the overlook. *Ment. Health* 56:7,9,11
21. Buchanan, G. N., Wholey, J. S. 1972. Federal level evaluation. *Evaluation* 1:17–22

22. Campbell, D. T. 1969. Reforms as experiments. *Am. Psychol.* 24:409–29
23. Campbell, D. T. 1975. Assessing the impact of planned social change. In *Social Research and Public Policy.* ed. G. Lyons. Hanover, NH: Univ. Press New Engl. In press
24. Campbell, D. T., Boneau, C. A. 1975. *Perspectives on Research in Psychology.* Presented at Meet. Soc. Behav. Assoc. Officers, Washington DC
25. Campbell, D. T., Erlebacher, A. 1970. How regression artifacts in quasi-experimental evaluation can mistakenly make compensatory education look harmful. In *The Disadvantaged Child,* Vol. 3. *Compensatory Education: A National Debate,* ed. J. Hellmuth. New York: Bruner/Mazel. 466 pp.
26. Campbell, D. T., Stanley, J. C. 1966. Experimental and quasi-experimental designs for research in teaching. In *Handbook of Research on Teaching,* ed. N. L. Gage. Chicago: Rand McNally. 1218 pp.
27. Caplan, N., Nelson, S. D. 1973. On being useful: The nature and consequences of psychological research on social problems. *Am. Psychol.* 28:199–211
28. Caro, F. G., Ed. 1971. *Readings in Evaluation Research.* New York: Russell Sage Found. 418 pp.
29. Cartwright, D. 1973. Determinants of scientific progress: The case of research on the risky shift. *Am. Psychol.* 28:222–31
30. Cook, D. L. 1966. *Program Evaluation and Review Technique.* Coop. Res. Monogr. No. 17. Washington DC:GPO. 100 pp.
31. Cook, T. D., Campbell, D. T. 1976. The design and conduct of quasi-experiments and true experiments in field settings. In *Handbook of Industrial and Organizational Research,* ed. T. D. Cook, D. T. Campbell. Chicago: Rand McNally. In press
32. Crawford, J. J., Chalupsky, A. B. 1973. Evaluation strategies used in current alcoholism rehabilitation programs: Problems and specifications for improvement. *Proc. 81st Ann. Conv. APA* 8:791–92
33. Deniston, D. L., Rosenstock, I. M. 1973. The validity of nonexperimental design for evaluating health services. *Health Serv. Rep.* 88:153–64
34. Dorfman, R., Ed. 1965. *Measuring Benefits of Government Investments.* Washington DC: Brookings Inst. 429 pp.
35. Edwards, W. 1971. Social utilities. *Eng. Econ.* Summer Ser. 6. For more current version, see Ref. 36
36. Edwards, W., Guttentag, M. 1975. Experiments and evaluations: a re-examination. In *Experiments and Evaluations,* ed. C. Bennett, A. Lumsdaine. New York: Academic. In press
37. Edwards, W., Guttentag, M., Snapper, K. 1975. A decision-theoretic approach to evaluation research. In *Handbook of Evaluation Research,* Vol. I, E. Struening, M. Guttentag. Beverly Hills, Calif.: Sage. 704 pp.
38. Einstein, S., Garitano, W. 1973. Behind the methadone treatment drug scene. *Drug Forum* 2:325–33
39. Elliott, D. L. 1973. Planning, analyzing, and evaluating early childhood programs. In *Revisiting Early Childhood Education: Readings,* J. L. Frost. New York: Holt, Rinehart & Winston. 548 pp.
40. Foreyt, J. P., Rockwood, C. E., Davis, J. C., Desvousges, W. H., Hollingsworth, R. 1975. Benefit-cost analysis of a token economy program. *Prof. Psychol.* 6:26–33
41. French-Lazovik, G. 1974. Predictability of students' evaluations of college teachers from component ratings. *J. Educ. Psychol.* 66:373–85
42. Glaser, E. M., Backer, T. E. 1972. A clinical approach to program evaluation. *Evaluation* 1:54–55, 57–59
43. Glaser, E. M., Taylor, S. H. 1973. Factors influencing the success of applied research. *Am. Psychol.* 28:140–46
44. Goldmann, R. 1975. *Foundations and Evaluation: One Approach to Measuring Performance.* New York: Ford Found. Publ.
45. Goldstein, A. 1971. Blind dosage comparisons and other studies in a large methadone program. *J. Psychedelic Drugs* 4:177–81
46. Guttentag, M. 1972. *Evaluation of social intervention programs.* Presented at NY Acad. Sci., New York
47. Guttentag, M. 1973. Evaluation of social intervention programs. *Ann. NY Acad. Sci.* 218:3–13
48. Guttentag, M. 1973. Subjectivity and its use in evaluation research. *Evaluation* 1:60–65
49. Guttentag, M., Snapper, K. 1974. Plans, evaluations, and decisions. *Evaluation* 2:58–64, 73–74
50. Hall, S. M., Hall, R. G. 1974. Outcome and methodological considerations in

behavioral treatment of obesity. *Behav. Ther.* 5:352–64

51. Hefferen, E. A., Katz, A. H. 1971. Issues and orientations in the evaluation of rehabilitation programs. *Rehabil. Lit.* 32:98–107

52. Heinemann, H. N., Sussna, E. 1971. Criteria for public investment in the two-year college: A program budgeting approach. *J. Hum. Res.* 6:171–84

53. Heinicke, C. M., et al 1973. The organization of day care: Considerations relating to the mental health of child and family. *Am. J. Orthopsychiatry* 43:8–22

54. Herfindahl, O. C., Allen, V. K. 1974. *Economic Theory of Natural Resources.* Columbus, O.: Merrill. 404 pp.

55. Hodgkinson, H. L., Hurst, J., Levine, H. 1975. Current evaluation practices in "innovative" colleges and universities. Univ. Calif., Berkeley, *Res. Rep.* 9:1–13

56. Holder, H. D., Stratas, N. E. 1972. A systems approach to alcoholism programming. *Am. J. Psychiatry* 129:32–37

57. Horst, P., Nay, J. N., Scanlon, J. W., Wholey, J. S. 1974. Program management and the federal evaluator. *Public Admin. Rev.* 33:301–8

58. Horst, P., Scanlon, J. W., Schmidt, R. E., Wholey, J. S. 1974. *Evaluation Planning at the National Institute of Mental Health: A Case History.* Washington DC: Urban Inst. 166 pp.

59. Hunter, C. P., Lambert, N. M. 1974. Needs assessment activities in school psychology program development. *J. Sch. Psychol.* 12:130–37

60. Johnson, A. E. 1973. Client involvement in vocational evaluation: some specifics. *Vocat. Eval. Work Adjust. Bull.* 6:19–21

61. Jones, S. C. 1973. Self and interpersonal evaluations: Esteem theories versus consistency theories. *Psychol. Bull.* 79:185–99

62. Juster, T. F., Ed. 1975. *Education, Income, and Human Behavior.* Carnegie Comm. Higher Educ. & Natl. Bur. Econ. Res. Rep. New York: McGraw-Hill. 438 pp.

63. Kaiser, H. F. 1960. Directional statistical hypotheses. *Psychol. Rev.* 67:160–67

64. Klarman, H. 1965. Syphillis control programs. See Ref. 34

65. Knezo, G. J. 1974. *Program Evaluation: Emerging Issues of Possible Legislative Concern Relating to the Conduct and Use of Evaluation in the Congress and the Executive Branch.* Congr. Res. Serv. Rep. Washington DC: Libr. Congr. 79 pp.

66. Kraft, I. A., Ed. 1973. Critical human behavioral research issues in social intervention programs. *Ann. NY Acad. Sci.* 218 (whole issue)

67. Kubie, L. S. 1973. The process of evaluation of therapy in psychiatry: Critical influence of the timing of the assessment on its outcome. *Arch. Gen. Psychiatry* 28:880–84

68. Kunce, J. T., Miller, D. E., Cope, C. S. 1974. Macro data analysis and rehabilitation program evaluation. *Rehabil. Couns.* 17:132–40

69. Lebow, J. L. 1974. Consumer assessments of the quality of medical care. *Med. Care* 12:328–37

70. Lerner, J. W. 1973. Systems analysis and special education. *J. Spec. Educ.* 7:15–26

71. Lester, D. 1972. The evaluation of telephone counseling services. *Crisis Intervention* 4:53–60

72. Levin, S., Bishop, D. 1972. An evaluation tool for feedback and leverage of mental health delivery systems. *Can. Psychiatry Assoc. J.* 17:437–42

73. Litman, R. E. 1971. Suicide prevention: Evaluating effectiveness. *Life-Threatening Behav.* 1:155–62

74. Maier, M. H., Fuchs, E. F. 1973. *Effectiveness of Selection and Classification Testing.* TR No. 1179. Arlington, Va.: US Army Res. Inst. Behav. Soc. Sci. 61 pp.

75. McGee, R. K. et al 1972. Evaluation of crisis intervention programs and personnel: A summary and critique. *Life-Threatening Behav.* 2:168–82

76. Merewitz, L., Sosnick, S. H. 1971. *The Budget's New Clothes: A Critique of Planning-Programming-Budgeting and Benefit-Cost Analysis.* Chicago: Markham. 318 pp.

77. Mincer, J. 1975. Education, experience, and the distribution of earnings and employment: An overview. See Ref. 62, 71–94

78. Mishan, E. J. 1971. The postwar literature on externalities: An interpretive essay. *J. Econ. Lit.* 9:1–28

79. Motto, J. A. 1971. Evaluation of a suicide prevention cente.' by sampling the population at risk. *Life-Threatening Behav.* 1:18–22

80. Mushkin, S., Ed. 1972. *Public Prices for Public Products.* Washington DC: Urban Inst. 460 pp.

81. National Clearinghouse for Mental Health Information, NIH, 1971. *Guidelines for Evaluating of Continuing Edu-*

cation Programs in Mental Health. Washington DC: GPO. 16 pp.

82. National Institute of Mental Health 1972. *Planning for Creative Change in Mental Health Services: A Distillation of Principles on Research Utilization,* Vol. 1. Washington DC: GPO. 266 pp.

83. Newman, J. 1974. *Alcoholism Treatment Networks and Ideologies.* Grant No. AA00497-20. Washington DC: DHEW, Natl. Inst. Alcohol Abuse & Alcoholism. 258 pp.

84. Noble, J. H. Jr. 1974. Peer review: Quality control of applied social research. *Science* 185:916–21

85. O'Neil, H. F. Jr., Richardson, F. C., Carver, D., Iscoe, I. 1973. A systems analysis of a campus community mental health facility: A preliminary investigation. *Am. J. Community Psychol.* 1:362–76

86. Osgood, C. E., Suci, G. J. 1969. Factor analysis of meaning. In *Semantic Differential Technique,* ed. J. G. Snider, E. C. Osgood. Chicago: Aldine. 681 pp.

87. Otto, J. A., Moos, R. H. 1973. Evaluating descriptions of psychiatric treatment programs. *Am. J. Orthopsychiatry* 43:401–10

88. Page, S., Yates, E. 1974. Fear of evaluation and reluctance to participate in research. *Prof. Psychol.* 5:400–8

89. Palmer, J., McGuire, F. L. 1973. The use of unobtrusive measures in mental health research. *J. Consult. Clin. Psychol.* 40:431–36

90. Perloff, E. 1974. *Evaluation of health programs in the area of vocational rehabilitation.* Presented at 18th Int. Congr. Appl. Psychol., Montreal

91. Perloff, E., Kohn, C. F., Gatewood, R. D. 1970. *Project Impact: A Pilot Study Evaluating the NDEA Summer Institute Program.* Washington DC: DHEW, Off. Educ. 82 pp.

92. Perloff, R. 1972. Enhancing psychology by assessing its manpower. *Am. Psychol.* 27:355–61

93. Perloff, R. 1973. *Considerations in the evaluation of agency and instructional programs.* Presented at 81st Ann. Meet. APA, Montreal

94. Perloff, R. 1974. *Perspectives on program evaluation.* Presented at 18th Int. Congr. Appl. Psychol., Montreal

95. Perloff, R., Sussna, E. 1972. Measuring the full benefits of higher education. Univ. Pittsburgh, *Pittsburgh Bus. Rev.* 42:1–7, 10–12

96. Peters, D. L. 1974. Dissemination. In *Preschool Education: A Handbook for the Training of Early Childhood Educators,* ed. R. W. Colvin, E. M. Zaffiro. New York: Springer. 362 pp.

97. Popham, W. J., Ed. *Evaluation in Education: Current Applications.* Berkeley, Calif.: McCutchan. 585 pp.

98. Pryer, M. W., Distefano, M. K. 1973. Short-term follow-up evaluation of a rehabilitation program for multiple readmission psychiatric patients. *J. Community Psychol.* 1:180–81

99. Raiffa, H. 1968. *Decision Analysis: Introductory Lectures on Choices Under Certainty.* Reading, Mass: Addison-Wesley. 309 pp.

100. Riecken, H. W., Boruch, R. F., Eds. 1974. *Social Experimentation: A Method for Planning and Evaluating Social Intervention.* New York: Academic. 339 pp.

101. Rippey, R. M., Ed. 1973. *Studies in Transactional Evaluation.* Berkeley, Calif.: McCutchan. 327 pp.

102. Rogers, C. R., Roethlisberger, F. J. 1974. Barriers and gateways to communication. In *Organizational Psychology: A Book of Readings,* ed. D. A. Kolb, I. M. Rubin, J. M. McIntyre. Englewood Cliffs, NJ: Prentice-Hall. 437 pp.

103. Rossi, P. H., Williams, W., Eds. 1972. *Evaluating Social Programs.* New York: Seminar. 326 pp.

104. Schmidt, R. E., Horst, P., Scanlon, J. W., Wholey, J. S. 1975. *The Market for Evaluation Services in the Department of Health, Education and Welfare.* Rep. No. 962–21. Washington DC: Urban Inst. 94 pp.

105. Schuckit, M. A. 1974. *Alcoholism Treatment as a Means of Prevention.* Dep. Navy Rep. No. 75–5. Washington DC: Bur. Med. Surg. 21 pp.

106. Schuckit, M. A., Cahalan, D. 1974. *Evaluation of Alcohol Treatment Programs.* Dep. Navy Rep. No. 74–53. Washington DC: Bur. Med. Surg. 33 pp.

107. Schulberg, C., Sheldon, A., Baker, F., Eds. 1969. *Program Evaluation in the Health Fields.* New York: Behav. Publ. 582 pp.

108. Scriven, M. 1967. The methodology of evaluation. In *Perspectives of Curriculum Evaluation,* R. W. Tyler, R. M. Gagné, M. Scriven. Chicago: Rand McNally. 102 pp.

109. Scriven, M. 1972. Pros and cons about goal-free evaluation. *Eval. Comment.* 3:1–4

110. Sechrest, L. 1973. *Training in evaluation research: development of a pro-*

gram. Presented at 81st Ann. Meet. APA, Montreal

111. Sells, S. B., Watson, D. D. 1971. A spectrum of approaches in methadone treatment: Relation to program evaluation. *J. Psychedelic Drugs* 4:198–204

112. Shore, J. H., Von Fumetti, B. 1972. Three alcohol programs for American Indians. *Am. J. Psychiatry* 128:1450–54

113. Social and Demographic Research Institute 1975. *Annual Summer Institute in Evaluation Research.* Program Description Announcement. Amherst, Mass: Soc. Demogr. Res. Inst. 2 pp.

114. Sommer, R. 1973. Evaluation, yes; research maybe. *Rep. Res. Soc. Psychol.* 4:127–33

115. Stake, R. E. 1967. Toward a technology for the evaluation of educational programs. In *Perspectives of Curriculum Education,* ed. R. W. Tyler et al. Chicago: Rand McNally. 102 pp.

116. Steiss, A. W. 1972. *Public Budgeting and Management.* Lexington, Mass: Heath. 349 pp.

117. Suchman, E. A. 1967. *Evaluative Research: Principles and Practice in Public Service and Social Action Programs.* New York: Russell Sage Found. 186 pp.

118. Sullivan, D. C., Siegel, L. J., Clear, T. 1974. The halfway house, ten years later: Reappraisal of correctional innovation. *Can. J. Criminol. Correct.* 16: 188–97

119. Sultan, P. E., Virgo, J. M. 1974. Program evaluation in public employment service. *J. Econ. Bus.* 26:128–33

120. Sussna, E. 1974. *The evaluation of health programs: An economist's view.* Presented at 18th Int. Congr. Appl. Psychol., Montreal

121. Sussna, E., Heinemann, H. N. 1972. The education of health manpower in a two-year college: An evaluation model. *Socio-Econ. Plan. Sci.* 6:21–30

122. Taubman, P., Wales, T. 1975. Mental ability and higher educational attainment in the twentieth century. See Ref. 62, 95–122

123. Tomlinson, J. R. 1973. Accountability procedures for psychological services. *Psychol. Sch.* 10:42–47

124. Walberg, H. J., Ed. 1974. *Evaluating Educational Performance: A Sourcebook of Methods, Instruments, and Examples.* Berkeley, Calif.: McCutchan. 395 pp.

125. Weinstein, M. S. 1972. The role of trust in program evaluation: some guidelines for the perplexed administrator. *Can. Psychol.* 13:239–51

126. Weisbrod, B. A. 1964. *External Benefits of Public Education: An Economic Analysis.* Princeton Univ. Press. 143 pp.

127. Weisbrod, B. A., Karpoff, R. 1968. Monetary returns to college education, student ability and college quality. *Rev. Econ. Stat.* 50:491–97

128. Weiss, C. H., Ed. 1972. *Evaluating Action Programs: Readings in Social Action and Education.* Boston: Allyn-Bacon. 365 pp.

129. Weiss, C. H. 1973. Between the cup and the lip...*Evaluation* 1:49–55

130. Weiss, C. H. 1973. Where politics and evaluation research meet. *Evaluation* 1:37–45

131. Wholey, J. S., Nay, J. N., Scanlon, J. W., Schmidt, R. E. 1975. Does anyone need program evaluation...? Why not find out! *Evaluation.* In press

132. Williams, B., Gallen, M., O'Connell, W. E., Sands, P. M. 1972. The comparative effectiveness of two contrasting alcoholic treatment programs. *Newslett. Res. Psychol.* 14:21–23

133. Wilson, J. E., Tatge, W. A. 1973. Assessment centers: Further assessment needed? *Pers. J.* 52:172–79

134. Wortman, P. M. 1975. Evaluation research: A psychological perspective. *Am. Psychol.* 30:562–75

135. Zelanak, M. J., Snider, B. C. 1974. Teacher perceptions of the teacher evaluation process. *Calif. J. Educ. Res.* 25:116–20

136. Zonana, H., Henisz, J. E., Levine, M. 1973. Psychiatric emergency services a decade later. *Int. J. Psychiatry Med.* 4:273–90

137. Zusman, J., Bissonette, R. 1973. The case against evaluation: With some suggestions for improvement. *Int. J. Ment. Health* 2:111–25

AUTHOR INDEX

595

602   AUTHOR INDEX

604   AUTHOR INDEX

SUBJECT INDEX

CUMULATIVE INDEXES

CONTRIBUTING AUTHORS VOLUMES 23-27

Molish, H. B., 23:577-614
Moody, M., 24:1-52
Moot, S. A., 23:51-72
Morgan, B. B. Jr., 27:305-30
Moses, J. L., 23:545-76
Munson, P. A., 26:415-56

N

Neimark, E. D., 26:173-205

O

Orlinsky, D. E., 23:615-68

P

Patterson, M. M., 23:73-104
Pepinsky, H. B., 24:117-50
Perloff, E., 27:569-94
Perloff, R., 27:569-94
Plomp, R., 26:207-32
Postman, L., 26:291-335

R

Rapoport, A., 23:131-76

Rebec, G. V., 27:91-127
Reitan, R. M., 27:189-216
Resnick, L. B., 23:207-76
Rusak, B., 26:137-71

S

Salzinger, K., 26:621-71
Santa, J. L., 26:173-205
Schaie, K. W., 26:65-96
Scherwitz, L., 24:337-54
Sechrest, L., 27:1-27
Sekuler, R., 25:195-232
Singer, D. G., 23:375-412
Singer, J. L., 23:375-412
Smith, J. E. K., 27:487-99
Spitzer, R. L., 26:621-71
Suinn, R. M., 26:509-56
Sussna, E., 27:569-94
Sutton, S., 26:621-71

T

Tanaka, Y., 23:695-732
Tapp, J. L., 27:359-404
Taulbee, E. S., 27:543-67
Teyler, T. J., 23:73-104

Thompson, R. F., 23:73-104
Triandis, H. C., 24:355-78
Tyler, L. E., 23:177-206

W

Wallsten, T. S., 23:131-76
Walraven, P. L., 23:347-74
Wayner, M. J., 24:53-80
Weintraub, D. J., 26:263-89
Weissman, H. J., 26:1-18
Whiteley, J. M., 26:337-66
Whiteley, R. M., 26:337-66
Wilcock, J., 25:389-415
Williams, H. L., 24:279-316
Wright, J. C., 25:1-82

Z

Zangwill, O. L., 23:413-56
Zubin, J., 26:621-71
Zucker, I., 26:137-71

CHAPTER TITLES VOLUMES 23-27

638